*Less managing. More teaching. Greater learning.*

## INSTRUCTORS...

Would you like your **students** to show up for class **more prepared**?
*(Let's face it, class is much more fun if everyone is engaged and prepared...)*

Want an **easy way to assign** homework online and track student **progress**?
*(Less time grading means more time teaching...)*

Want an **instant view** of student or class performance relative to learning objectives? *(No more wondering if students understand...)*

Need to **collect data and generate reports** required for administration or accreditation? *(Say goodbye to manually tracking student learning outcomes...)*

Want to **record and post your lectures** for students to view online?

## With **McGraw-Hill's** *Connect™* **Plus Accounting,**

### INSTRUCTORS GET:

- Simple **assignment management**, allowing you to spend more time teaching.
- **Auto-graded** assignments, quizzes, and tests.
- **Detailed Visual Reporting** where student and section results can be viewed and analyzed.
- Sophisticated **online testing** capability.
- A **filtering and reporting** function that allows you to easily assign and report on materials that are correlated to accreditation standards, learning outcomes, and Bloom's taxonomy.
- An easy-to-use **lecture capture** tool.
- The option to **upload course documents** for student access.

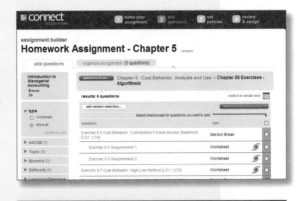

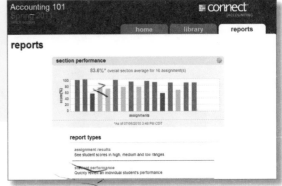

Want an online, **searchable version** of your textbook?

Wish your textbook could be **available online** while you're doing your assignments?

 ### *Connect™ Plus Accounting* eBook

If you choose to use *Connect™ Plus Accounting*, you have an affordable and searchable online version of your book integrated with your other online tools.

### *Connect™ Plus Accounting* eBook offers features like:

- Topic search
- Direct links from assignments
- Adjustable text size
- Jump to page number
- Print by section

 Want to get more **value** from your textbook purchase?

Think learning accounting should be a bit more **interesting**?

 ### Check out the STUDENT RESOURCES section under the *Connect™* Library tab.

Here you'll find a wealth of resources designed to help you achieve your goals in the course. You'll find things like **quizzes, PowerPoints, and Internet activities** to help you study. Every student has different needs, so explore the STUDENT RESOURCES to find the materials best suited to you.

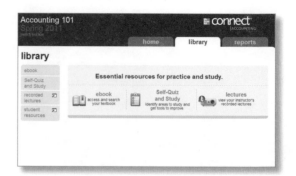

# About the Authors

## O. Ray Whittington

O. Ray Whittington, CIA, CMA, CPA, serves as the dean of the College of Commerce at DePaul University. He received his B.B.A., M.S., and Ph.D. degrees from Sam Houston State University, Texas Tech University, and the University of Houston, respectively. Professor Whittington is an active textbook author on the subjects of auditing and audit sampling. He has also published in a variety of journals, including *The Accounting Review, The Journal of Accounting Research,* and *Auditing: A Journal of Practice and Theory.* He has served as a member of the Board of Regents of The Institute of Internal Auditors and has served as Chairman on the Auditing Standards Committee of the Auditing Section and the Bylaws Committee, both of the American Accounting Association. Professor Whittington has served as a member of the AICPA Auditing Standards Board and as the president of the Auditing Section of the American Accounting Association.

## Kurt Pany

Kurt Pany, CFE, CPA, is a Professor of Accounting at Arizona State University. He received his B.S., M.B.A., and Ph.D. degrees from the University of Arizona, the University of Minnesota, and the University of Illinois, respectively. He has also served as a staff accountant with Arthur Andersen and Touche Ross, as a member of the Auditing Standards Board, and as an academic fellow with the American Institute of Certified Public Accountants. Professor Pany has published articles on auditing in such journals as *The Journal of Accounting Research, The Accounting Review, Auditing: A Journal of Practice and Theory, The Journal of Accountancy,* and *The CPA Journal.* He is a member of and has served on various committees of the American Accounting Association and the American Institute of Certified Public Accountants.

# Preface

The 18th edition of *Principles of Auditing & Other Assurance Services* provides a carefully balanced presentation of auditing theory and practice. Written in a clear and understandable manner, it is particularly appropriate for students who have had limited or no audit experience. The approach is to integrate auditing material with that of previous accounting financial, managerial, and systems courses.

The text's first nine chapters emphasize the philosophy and environment of the auditing profession, with special attention paid to the nature and economic purpose of auditing, auditing standards, professional conduct, legal liability, audit evidence, audit planning, consideration of internal control, and audit sampling. Chapters 10 through 16 (the "procedural chapters") deal with internal control and obtaining evidence about the various financial statement accounts, emphasizing a risk-based approach to selecting appropriate auditing procedures. Chapter 17 presents the auditors' reporting responsibilities when performing financial statement audits. Chapter 18 provides detailed guidance on integrated audits of public companies performed in accordance with the Sarbanes-Oxley Act of 2002 and SEC requirements. Chapters 19 and 20 present the auditors' reporting responsibilities and other attestation and accounting services, such as reviews and compilations of financial statements and reports on prospective financial statements. Chapter 21 presents coverage of internal compliance and operational auditing.

The text is well suited for an introductory one-semester or one-quarter auditing course. Alternatively, it is appropriate for a two-course auditing sequence that covers the material in greater detail. For example, an introductory course might emphasize Chapters 1 through 10, 16, and 17. A second course may include coverage of the other procedural chapters (Chapters 11 through 15); integrated audits (18); other attestation and accounting services; and internal, operational, and compliance auditing (Chapters 19, 20, and 21). The instructor might also wish to consider covering portions of Chapter 9 on sampling in the second course, with or without ACL software. Overall, the text and supporting materials provide:

1. **A balanced presentation.** The text provides a carefully balanced presentation of auditing and assurance theory and practice. The concepts are written in a clear, concise, and understandable manner. Real company examples are integrated throughout the text to bring this material to life. Finally, Keystone Computers & Networks, Inc., the text's illustrative audit case, is integrated into selected chapters, providing students with hands-on audit experience.

2. **Organization around balance sheet accounts emphasized in previous accounting courses.** Organizing the text around balance sheet accounts is a particularly straightforward and user-friendly way to address the risk assessment–based approach to auditing required by both U.S. and international auditing standards. These standards require an in-depth understanding of the audited company and its environment, a rigorous assessment of the risks of where and how the financial statements could be materially misstated, and an improved linkage between the auditors' assessed risks and the particulars of audit procedures performed in response to those risks. Chapters 5 through 7 of the text describe the risk assessment approach in detail. Chapters 10 through 16 are aligned with the risk assessment approach presented in the professional standards. Accordingly, the suggested audit approach and procedures of the professional standards flow smoothly from the approach suggested in earlier chapters of the text. In short, our organization of the book facilitates student learning of the risk assessment process in a very straightforward manner. Also, although the text chapters are structured around balance sheet accounts, they include a significant amount of material on transaction cycles. For example, Chapters 10 through 13 include detailed coverage of revenue, cash receipts, acquisitions, and disbursements cycles.

3. **CPA examination support.** Both the text's emphasis on current auditing standards and its many objective questions (both multiple choice and other objective format) are aimed at helping students pass the CPA exam. Details on these objective questions are discussed in further detail in the following section of this preface.

4. **Strong student and instructor support.** The Online Learning Center provides instructors and students with a wealth of material to help keep students up-to-date. The Center also contains quizzes and other resources to help students in this course. The address of the Center (and the text Web site) is www.mhhe.com/whittington18e.

We are confident that the 18th edition of *Principles of Auditing & Other Assurance Services* will provide students with a clear perspective of today's auditing environment.

*O. Ray Whittington*
*Kurt Pany*

# New to This Edition

The 18th edition has been thoroughly revised to reflect two very major changes in auditing:

- The AICPA's "Clarity Project," which has resulted in a complete revision and recodification of the Auditing Standards Board's standards (1) to make standards easier to read, understand, and apply, and (2) to converge those standards with the *International Standards on Auditing* to the extent considered desirable. Almost all outstanding *Statements on Auditing Standards* were revised, with an effective date for audits of financial statements for periods ending after December 15, 2012.
- Modification of the CPA exam's Auditing and Attestation section content, including the elimination of two "long" simulations on each exam and replacement with 6–7 shorter, completely objective form simulations.

# MODIFICATIONS TO REFLECT CHANGES IN THE AUDITING STANDARDS

The broad scope of the Clarity Project has resulted in changes to each chapter—some relatively minor, but others very major. Among the most major Clarity Project changes are:

- *Chapter 2: Professional Standards.* This chapter is rewritten to reflect the Auditing Standards Board's elimination of the longstanding "10 generally accepted auditing standards"—that is, the three general standards, three fieldwork standards, and four reporting standards. For purposes of AICPA professional standard coverage, this chapter now discusses in detail the new *Principles Underlying an Audit Conducted in Accordance with Generally Accepted Auditing Standards* that replaced the 10 standards. Yet, because the PCAOB standards continue to be structured around the 10 standards, those standards remain in place for public company audits and are also discussed in the chapter. In addition, coverage includes a presentation of the new "standard" audit report and modified reports. An appendix has been added to this chapter to compare major differences between international and U.S. standards.
- *Chapter 17: Auditors' Reports.* Changes in AICPA terminology reflected here better align U.S. GAAS with international standards. For example, an *unqualified* opinion is now an *unmodified* opinion; an *explanatory* paragraph is now an *emphasis of matter,* an *other matter* paragraph or a *basis for modification paragraph;* and an audit involving *other auditors* is now a *group audit.* But there have also been many other changes, including changes in the standard audit report's wording and changes in requirements in a number of areas in which a report other than "standard" is issued.
- *Chapter 19: Additional Assurance Services: Historical Financial Information.* The clarity standards, following the international standard approach, use the term "financial reporting framework" to represent the standards used to prepare historical financial information. In essence, the "financial reporting framework" becomes the "suitable criteria" for historical financial information. This results in a number of changes relating to this chapter, including the elimination of "special reports" and replacement with "special-purpose financial reporting frameworks."

In addition, two other key changes include:

- *Chapter 19: Additional Assurance Services: Historical Financial Information.* In addition to the Chapter 19 clarity changes, modification of compilation and review standards are reflected in the chapter. This area is of particular importance to students who plan to take the CPA exam because the new content specification outline shows that the degree of coverage of this area is significant.
- *Chapter 20: Additional Assurance Services: Other Information.* This chapter is rewritten to reflect the fact that the nature of these other services is evolving and, at this point, some services seem to have gained a degree of market acceptance (e.g., *SysTrust, PrimePlus/ElderCare*), while others have not (e.g., *WebTrust*). Additional new products, such as providing assurance relating to XBRL, are discussed.

# MODIFICATIONS THAT REFLECT CPA EXAM QUESTION FORMAT CHANGES

We've included many new Objective Questions because we believe they will help students both learn the material presented in the text and prepare them for such questions on the CPA exam. A number of these are labeled as "Simulation" questions in that we tried to design them to be similar to the 6–7 that one might expect on the CPA exam. Others are more brief and yet consistent with the new simulation approach. In addition, every chapter of the instructor's test bank now includes one or more other objective format questions.

The clarity modifications presented force the CPA exam to update its questions to reflect new terminology and requirements. We have revised the text and instructor's test bank questions to reflect these changes.

# McGRAW-HILL'S *CONNECT*™ *ACCOUNTING*

The new edition of Whittington/Pany will have McGraw-Hill's *Connect*™ *Accounting* available for use for the first time. All applicable multiple choice questions, problems, and simulations from the text, study guide, and test bank will be available in static form within *Connect*™ *Accounting*. See pages xvi–xviii for more details.

# Key Features of the Book

The first nine chapters of the text emphasize the philosophy and environment of the profession, with special attention paid to the nature and economic purpose of auditing and assurance services, professional standards, professional conduct, legal liability, audit evidence, audit planning, consideration of internal control, audit sampling, audit documentation, and general records.

**Chapter 1:** Emphasizes the role of the public accountant, structure of CPA firms, and various types of audits and auditors.

**Chapter 2:** Includes detailed coverage of the new *Principles Underlying an Audit Conducted in Accordance with Generally Accepted Auditing Standards,* which replace the 10 generally accepted auditing standards for audits of nonpublic companies. An appendix highlights a number of differences between international and U.S. standards.

**Chapter 3:** Updated to reflect the most recent AICPA and PCAOB requirements.

**Chapter 4:** Clear, concise coverage of CPA legal liability based on suggestions by legal scholar Professor Marianne Jennings of Arizona State University.

**Chapters 5 through 7:** Material from the risk assessment standards is thoroughly integrated throughout.

**Chapter 5:** Includes current documentation requirements.

**Chapter 6:** The risk assessment approach to an audit is concisely summarized in a summary of the audit process.

**Chapter 7:** Includes a brief overview of audits of internal control over financial reporting required for large public companies under PCAOB *Standard No. 5,* with more detailed coverage provided in Chapter 18. This chapter also presents the auditors' internal control communication responsibilities.

The **AICPA Auditing Standards Board's "Clarity Project,"** intended to both (1) make standards easier to read, understand, and apply, and (2) converge standards with the **International Standards on Auditing,** are integrated throughout as appropriate. In addition, the International Standards are described in the text.

The **Sarbanes-Oxley Act of 2002** and the resulting **Public Company Accounting Oversight Board** profoundly affect public accountants, CPA firms, and their clients. Most notably, the public accounting profession is no longer largely self-regulating. CPAs now must issue a publicly available report on the internal control of large publicly traded clients, and top management must certify the company's financial statements and provide an assessment of internal control over financial reporting. The text carefully integrates coverage of the act's nature and its effects on the profession in selected chapters. Also included is coverage of financial frauds, such as those involving Enron and WorldCom, which led to passage of the act.

1. The Role of the Public Accountant in the American Economy
2. Professional Standards
3. Professional Ethics
4. Legal Liability of CPAs
5. Audit Evidence and Documentation
6. Audit Planning, Understanding the Client, Assessing Risks, and Responding
7. Internal Control
8. Consideration of Internal Control in an Information Technology Environment
9. Audit Sampling

**Keystone Computers & Networks, Inc.,** is the text's **Illustrative Audit Case.** This feature has been updated in this edition and illustrates audit methods and provides realistic, thought-provoking case exercises. Although each portion of the case is designed to stand alone, if used in combination, the case will help the student develop problem-solving skills in planning (Chapter 6), in considering internal control and testing account balances (Chapters 11 and 14), and in completing the audit (Chapter 16). The case incorporates the use of computerized accounting applications and also integrates the fundamentals of audit sampling from Chapter 9.

**Chapters 10 through 16:** These "procedural chapters" deal with internal control and obtaining audit evidence about the various financial statement accounts; the chapters emphasize the risk-based approach to selecting appropriate audit procedures.

**Chapter 17:** Thoroughly updated to reflect new reporting requirements of the AICPA clarity standards. This chapter also includes coverage of PCAOB and international audit reports.

**Chapter 18:** Reflects PCAOB *Standard No. 5* on the audit of internal control over financial reporting required for public companies.

**Chapter 19:** Updated to include current coverage of compilation and review engagements, auditor reporting on financial statements prepared using a special-purpose framework, and other changes due to the AICPA clarity standards.

**Chapter 20:** Discusses a variety of attestation and other assurance services. The material on attestation services describes the current professional standards. Other assurance services are included at both a conceptual and practical level.

**Chapter 21:** Includes a discussion of compliance auditing based on the suggestions of Mr. Norwood J. Jackson, former Deputy Controller, Office of Federal Management, U.S. Office of Management and Budget. It is updated for the 2007 revision to the "Yellow Book."

# Features of This Edition

## Illustrative Cases

Actual business and accounting examples are used to illustrate key chapter concepts. The cases are boxed and appear throughout the text. New cases have been added for recent alleged audit failures. They are now subtitled for easy reference.

**Illustrative Case** — *Employment with Clients*

The situation in which audit clients hire audit firm personnel is difficult. On the one hand, it provides great professional opportunities for individuals who enter the public accounting profession. On the other, independence concerns have led to the restrictions presented in this section.

Questions were raised about the number of ex–Arthur Andersen employees hired by Enron Corporation prior to its collapse (see Chapter 1). Although both firms refused to disclose details, the positions and numbers of ex–Ar...

The *Washington Post* indicated that, over the years Arthur Andersen served as auditor, 86 employees left the firm and accepted positions at Enron.

In addition, questions arose as to the nature of the relationship between continuing Arthur Andersen employees and those of Enron. Again, *The Wall Street Journal* reported that Arthur Andersen auditors and consultants "shared in office birthdays, frequented lunch-time parties in a nearby park and participated in weekend fundraisers for charities. They even went on Enron employees' ski trips to Beaver Creek, Colorado." One Enron employee suggested that...

## Industry Focus Cases

These cases use examples from specific industries to provide students with a detailed, "real world" illustration of points being emphasized in the text. These cases show the importance of having a thorough knowledge of the audit client's business and industry. Like the Illustrative Cases, these cases are boxed and appear throughout the text.

**Focus on the Airline Industry**

Electronic ticketing has become basic to the airline industry. Under these systems a passenger may book a flight over the telephone or by computer and be assigned a reservation number rather than being issued a physical ticket. Since no ticket is created until the passenger checks in for the flight, the auditor is limited in the extent to which he or she can examine "paper" support for transactions. Accordingly, audit procedures must be developed relating to the associated revenues and receivables. Auditors often choose to test the computer controls in such situations.

## Auditing Fair Value Information

As the accounting profession continues to value more assets and liabilities at their fair values, difficult audit issues often arise. The text includes integrated coverage of fair value accounting in Chapters 5, 10, 11, 13, and 16.

# Illustrative Documents

Documents included in the various procedural chapters (Chapters 10 through 16) provide concise, realistic examples of the documents associated with the various transaction cycles.

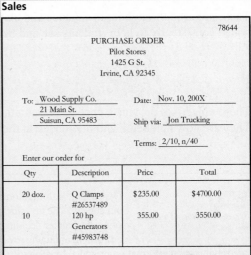

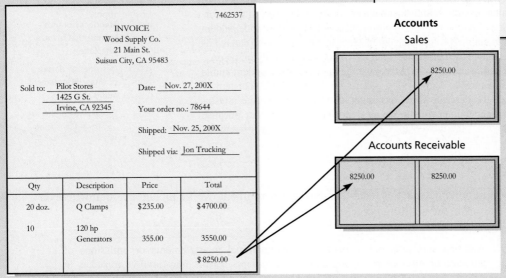

# Audit Objectives

The use of Audit Objectives is a basic tool in audit program design. These help the auditor focus on the *reason* a procedure is being done and provide a check to assure that all management assertions in the financial statements are audited.

| Primary Audit Objectives: | **1. Obtain Analyses of Cash Balances and Reconcile Them to the General Ledger.** |
|---|---|
| Existence ☑<br>Accuracy ☑<br>Cutoff ☑ | The auditors will prepare or obtain a schedule that lists all of the client's cash accounts. For cash in bank accounts, this schedule will typically list the bank, the account number, the account type, and the year-end balance per books. The auditors will trace and reconcile all accounts to the general ledger. |
| Primary Audit Objectives: | **2. Confirm Cash Balances with Financial Institutions.** |
| Existence ☑<br>Occurrence ☑<br>Accuracy ☑<br>Cutoff ☑ | One of the objectives of the auditors' work on cash is to substantiate the existence of the amount of cash shown on the balance sheet. A direct approach to this objective is to confirm amounts on deposit and obtain or prepare reconciliations between bank statements and the accounting records. |

# Illustrations, Tables, and Flowcharts

These are used throughout to enhance and clarify the presentation. In this edition, flowcharts have been color-coded consistently to help students see and better understand the concepts.

# Chapter Learning Objectives

These objectives provide a concise presentation of each chapter's most important concepts. They are now numbered and referenced in the chapter.

**LO1**

Describe the nature of assurance services.

Dependable information is essential to the very existence of our society. The investor making a decision to buy or sell securities, the banker deciding whether to approve a loan, the government in obtaining revenue based on income tax returns—all are relying upon information provided by others. In many of these situations, the goals of the providers of information may run somewhat counter to those of the users of the information. Implicit in this line of reasoning is recognition of the social need for independent public accountants—individuals of professional competence and integrity who can tell us whether the information that we use constitutes a fair picture of what is really going on.

Our primary purpose in this chapter is to make clear the nature of independent audits and the accounting profession. We begin with a discussion of the broader concept of assurance services. Next, we describe those assurance services that involve attestation, of which audits of financial statements are an important type. Another purpose of this chapter is to summarize the influence exerted by the public accounting profes-

**Learning objectives**

After studying this chapter, you should be able to:

LO1  Describe the nature of assurance services.

LO2  Identify assurance services that involve attestation.

LO3  Describe the nature of financial statement audits.

LO4  Explain why audits are needed by society.

# Fraud

Because fraud is such an important aspect of today's auditing environment, we've included a logo wherever we talk about its implications in the auditing process.

**Errors and Fraud**

Auditing standards define **errors** as unintentional misstatements or omissions of amounts or disclosures in the financial statements. Errors may involve mistakes in gathering or processing data, unreasonable accounting estimates arising from oversight or misinterpretation of facts, or mistakes in the application of applicable accounting principles.

   **Fraud,** as the term is used in AICPA AU 240 (PCAOB 316), relates to intentional acts that cause a misstatement of the financial statements. Misstatements due to fraud may occur due to either (1) fraudulent financial reporting or (2) misappropriation of assets (also referred to as "defalcation").

# ACL Software and Related Materials

CPAs in public practice and internal auditors are increasingly using ACL to perform audit procedures, including fraud detection. Accordingly, we have integrated ACL software and related materials with the text at no extra cost. The text's Web site (www.mhhe.com/whittington18e) includes two stand-alone modules: (1) audit sampling and (2) overall ACL coverage that integrates ACL into the text. Either or both of these modules may be incorporated into the course to supplement traditional coverage.

# END-OF-CHAPTER MATERIAL

The material at the end of each chapter includes a combination of: Review Questions, Questions Requiring Analysis, Objective Questions, Problems, In-Class Team Cases, Research and Discussion Cases, and/or Ethics Cases. Appendixes to Chapters 6, 11, and 14 include the case material and exercises for the Keystone Computers & Networks, Inc., the illustrative audit case. Also included with certain end-of-chapter materials are Spreadsheet Templates, Internet Assignments, and ACL Assignments.

## Review Questions

The Review Questions are closely related to the material in the chapter and provide a convenient means of determining whether students have grasped the major concepts and details contained in that chapter.

## Questions Requiring Analysis

The Questions Requiring Analysis require thoughtful consideration of a realistic auditing situation and the application of professional standards. A number of these questions are taken from CPA and CIA examinations, and others describe actual practice situations. These questions, which are generally shorter than the problems, tend to stress value judgments and conflicting opinions.

## Objective Questions

The Objective Questions are similiar in format to the CPA exam. The first Objective Question in each chapter is composed of at least 12 multiple choice questions. As indicated earlier in the preface, a number of the following Objective Questions are similar or identical to the new simulations that one might expect on the CPA exam, and each are labeled as a "Simulation." Others address basic concepts and information covered by simulations but may not in and of themselves represent an example of a complete simulation. All applicable Objective Questions/Problems are available with McGraw-Hill's *Connect Accounting*.

## Problems

Many of the Problems are drawn from CPA and CIA examinations. These problems are retained because they require a relatively detailed analysis of audit situations. Problems are keyed to the chapter's Learning Objectives. All applicable Objective Questions/Problems are available with McGraw-Hill's *Connect Accounting*.

## In-Class Team Cases

These cases are meant to be solved in class either by teams of students or, if the instructor prefers, by individuals. They help provide the student with an active learning environment in which to apply key concepts included in each chapter.

In-Class Team Case    LO 3    2–38.   Hide-It (HI), a family-owned business based in Tombstone, Arizona, builds custom homes with special features, such as hidden rooms and hidden wall safes. Hide-It has been an audit client for three years.

You are about to sign off on a "clean" opinion on HI's current annual financial statements when Art Hyde, the VP-Finance, calls to tell you that the Arizona Department of Revenue has seized control of a Hide-It bank account that includes about $450,000 of company funds; the account is not currently recorded in the accounting system and you had been unaware of it. In response to your questions about the origin of the funds, Art assures you that the funds, though not recorded as revenue, had been obtained legitimately. He explains that all of the

# Research and Discussion Cases

These cases involve controversial situations that do not lend themselves clear-cut answers. Students are required to research appropriate professional literature and then apply critical thinking skills to logically formulate and justify their personal positions on the issues involved in each case. The cases acquaint students with the professional literature, develop research and communication skills required on the new CPA exam, and demonstrate that several diverse, yet defensible, positions may be argued persuasively in a given situation.

**Research and Discussion Case**

**LO 3**  **2–39.** Enormo Corporation is a large multinational audit client of your CPA firm. One of Enormo's subsidiaries, Ultro, Ltd., is a successful electronics assembly company that operates in a small Caribbean country. The country in which Ultro operates has very strict laws governing the transfer of funds to other countries. Violations of these laws may result in fines or the expropriation of the assets of the company.

During the current year, you discover that $50,000 worth of foreign currency was smuggled out of the Caribbean country by one of Ultro's employees and deposited in one of Enormo's bank accounts. Ultro's management generated the funds by selling company automobiles, ~~were fully~~ ~~ed on Ultro~~

# Ethics Cases

Ethics Cases allow the instructor to discuss ethical issues in an integrated manner throughout the course. The cases present a series of situations that result in ethical dilemmas of the type that beginning accountants may expect to encounter in practice. These cases are included in selected chapters.

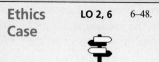

**Ethics Case**

**LO 2, 6**  **6–48.** Tammy Potter, a new partner with the regional CPA firm of Tower & Tower, was recently appointed to the board of directors of a local civic organization. The chairman of the board of the civic organization is Lewis Edmond, who is also the owner of a real estate development firm, Tierra Corporation.

Potter was quite excited when Edmond indicated that his corporation needed an audit and he wished to discuss the matter with her. During the discussion, Potter was told that Tierra Corporation needed the audit to obtain a substantial amount of additional financing to acquire another company. Presently, Tierra Corporation is successful, profitable, and committed to

# Illustrative Audit Case Exercises

These exercises all pertain to the text's updated continuing integrated case, **Keystone Computers & Networks, Inc.** While each exercise may "stand alone," when used in combination, these case exercises take the student from the original planning of an audit through the testing of controls, substantive testing, and accumulation and analysis of uncorrected misstatements. Exercises are included in Chapters 6, 11, 14, and 16.

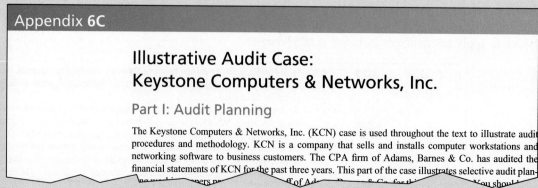

## Appendix 6C

### Illustrative Audit Case: Keystone Computers & Networks, Inc.

#### Part I: Audit Planning

The Keystone Computers & Networks, Inc. (KCN) case is used throughout the text to illustrate audit procedures and methodology. KCN is a company that sells and installs computer workstations and networking software to business customers. The CPA firm of Adams, Barnes & Co. has audited the financial statements of KCN for the past three years. This part of the case illustrates selective audit plan-

## Spreadsheet Templates

Spreadsheet templates are available on the text's Web site to be used in conjunction with selected audit case exercises. The exercises with templates are identified by a logo in the margin.

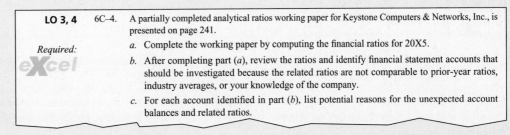

| **LO 3, 4** | 6C–4. | A partially completed analytical ratios working paper for Keystone Computers & Networks, Inc., is presented on page 241. |
| --- | --- | --- |

*Required:*
eXcel

a. Complete the working paper by computing the financial ratios for 20X5.

b. After completing part (*a*), review the ratios and identify financial statement accounts that should be investigated because the related ratios are not comparable to prior-year ratios, industry averages, or your knowledge of the company.

c. For each account identified in part (*b*), list potential reasons for the unexpected account balances and related ratios.

## Internet Assignments

Internet assignments are included among the end-of-chapter problem material for selected chapters. These assignments require students to use the **Internet** to do audit research and are identified with a logo in the margin.

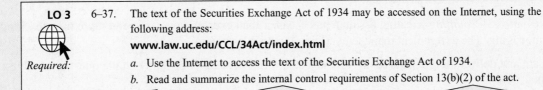

**LO 3**   6–37.   The text of the Securities Exchange Act of 1934 may be accessed on the Internet, using the following address:

**www.law.uc.edu/CCL/34Act/index.html**

*Required:*

a. Use the Internet to access the text of the Securities Exchange Act of 1934.

b. Read and summarize the internal control requirements of Section 13(b)(2) of the act.

## ACL Assignments

The text's ACL materials are included on the text's Web site (www.mhhe.com/whittington18e). Those materials are composed of two stand-alone modules—(1) audit sampling and (2) overall ACL skills coverage—that integrate ACL into text and course coverage. Either or both of these modules may be incorporated into the course to supplement traditional coverage. Also, Chapter 9 identifies with the ACL Logo problems, which the Web site supplements with ACL requirements.

# Technology New to This Edition

## McGraw-Hill's Connect™ Accounting

### Less Managing. More Teaching. Greater Learning.

McGraw-Hill's *Connect Accounting* is an online assignment and assessment solution that connects students with the tools and resources necessary to achieve success through faster learning, more efficient studying, and higher retention of knowledge.

### Online Assignments

*Connect Accounting* helps students learn more efficiently by providing feedback and practice material when and where they need it. *Connect Accounting* grades homework automatically and gives immediate feedback on any questions students may have missed.

### Simple Assignment Management

With *Connect Accounting,* creating assignments is easier than ever, so you can spend more time teaching and less time managing. The assignment management function enables you to:

- Create and deliver assignments easily with selectable end-of-chapter or Study Guide questions and test bank items.
- Streamline lesson planning, student progress reporting, and assignment grading to make classroom management more efficient than ever.
- Go paperless with the eBook and online submission and grading of student assignments.
- Have assignments scored automatically, giving students immediate feedback on their work and comparisons with correct answers.
- Access and review each response; manually change grades or leave comments for students to review.
- Reinforce classroom concepts with practice tests and instant quizzes.

### Instructor Library

The *Connect Accounting* Instructor Library is your repository for additional resources to improve student engagement in and out of class. You can select and use any asset that enhances your lecture. The *Connect Accounting* Instructor Library includes:

- Instructor's Lecture Guide
- Keystone Case and Solutions
- Solutions Manual
- Test Bank
- eBook Version of the Text

### Student Library

- The *Connect Accounting* Student Library is the place for students to access additional resources, such as lectures, practice materials, an eBook, and more.

## Student Progress Tracking

*Connect Accounting* keeps instructors informed about how each student, section, and class is performing, allowing for more productive use of lecture and office hours. The progress-tracking function enables you to:

- View scored work immediately and track individual or group performance with assignment and grade reports.
- Access an instant view of student or class performance relative to learning objectives.
- Collect data and generate reports required by many accreditation organizations, such as AACSB and AICPA.

## McGraw-Hill's *Connect*<sup>TM</sup> *Plus Accounting*

McGraw-Hill reinvents the textbook learning experience for the modern student with *Connect Plus Accounting,* which provides seamless integration of the eBook and *Connect Accounting. Connect Plus Accounting* provides all of the *Connect Accounting* features plus the following:

- An integrated eBook, allowing for anytime, anywhere access to the textbook.
- Dynamic links between the problems or questions you assign to your students and the location in the eBook where that problem or question is covered.
- A powerful search function to pinpoint and connect key concepts in a snap.

In short, *Connect Accounting* offers you and your students powerful tools and features that optimize your time and energies, enabling you to focus on course content, teaching, and student learning. *Connect Accounting* also offers a wealth of content resources for both instructors and students. This state-of-the-art, thoroughly tested system supports you in preparing students for the world that awaits.

For more information about Connect, go to www.mcgrawhillconnect.com or contact your local McGraw-Hill sales representative.

## Tegrity Campus: Lectures 24/7

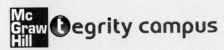 Tegrity Campus, a new McGraw-Hill company, is a service that makes class time available 24/7 by automatically capturing every lecture. With a simple one-click start-and-stop process, you capture all computer screens and corresponding audio in a format that is easily searchable, frame by frame. Students can replay any part of any class with easy-to-use browser-based viewing on a PC or Mac, an iPod, or other mobile device.

Educators know that the more students can see, hear, and experience class resources, the better they learn. In fact, studies prove it. Tegrity Campus's unique search feature helps students efficiently find what they need, when they need it, across an entire semester of class recordings. Help turn your students' study time into learning moments immediately supported by your lecture. With Tegrity Campus, you also increase intent listening and class participation by easing students' concerns about note-taking. Lecture Capture will make it more likely for you to see students' faces, not the tops of their heads.

To learn more about Tegrity, watch a two-minute Flash demo at http://tegritycampus.mhhe.com.

## Online Course Management

McGraw-Hill Higher Education and Blackboard have teamed up. What does this mean for you?

Do More

1. **Your life, simplified.** Now you and your students can access McGraw-Hill's *Connect*<sup>TM</sup> and *Create*<sup>TM</sup> right from within your Blackboard course—all with one single sign-on. Say goodbye to the days of logging in to multiple applications.
2. **Deep integration of content and tools.** Not only do you get single sign-on with *Connect*<sup>TM</sup> and *Create*<sup>TM</sup>, but you also get deep integration of McGraw-Hill content and content engines right in Blackboard. Whether you're choosing a book for your

course or building *Connect*<sup>TM</sup> assignments, all the tools you need are right where you want them—inside of Blackboard.

3. **Seamless gradebooks.** Are you tired of keeping multiple gradebooks and manually synchronizing grades into Blackboard? We thought so. When a student completes an integrated *Connect*<sup>TM</sup> assignment, the grade for that assignment automatically (and instantly) feeds your Blackboard grade center.

4. **A solution for everyone.** Whether your institution is already using Blackboard or you just want to try Blackboard on your own, we have a solution for you. McGraw-Hill and Blackboard can now offer you easy access to industry-leading technology and content, whether your campus hosts it or we do. Be sure to ask your local McGraw-Hill representative for details.

 In addition to Blackboard integration, course cartridges for whichever online course management system you use (e.g., WebCT or eCollege) are available for Whittington 18e. Our cartridges are specifically designed to make it easy to navigate and access content online. They are easier than ever to install on the latest version of the course management system available today.

## McGraw-Hill/Irwin CARES

At McGraw-Hill/Irwin, we understand that getting the most from new technology can be challenging. That's why our services don't stop after you purchase our book. You can contact our Technical Support Analysts 24 hours a day, get product training online, or search our knowledge bank of Frequently Asked Questions on our support Web site. For Customer Support, call 800-331-5094 or visit www.mhhe.com/support. One of our Technical Support Analysts will assist you in a timely fashion.

# Instructor Supplements

## Assurance of Learning Ready

Many educational institutions today are focused on the notion of assurance of learning, an important element of some accreditation standards. *Principles of Auditing & Other Assurance Services, 18e,* is designed specifically to support your assurance of learning initiatives with a simple, yet powerful solution. Each test bank question for *Principles of Auditing & Other Assurance Services, 18e,* maps to a specific chapter learning outcome/objective listed in the text. You can use our test bank software, EZ Test, to easily query for learning outcomes/objectives that directly relate to the learning objectives for your course. You can then use the reporting features of EZ Test to aggregate student results in similar fashion, making the collection and presentation of assurance of learning data simple and easy.

## AACSB Statement

The McGraw-Hill Companies is a proud corporate member of AACSB International. Recognizing the importance and value of AACSB accreditation, we have sought to recognize the curricula guidelines detailed in AACSB standards for business accreditation by connecting selected questions in *Principles of Auditing & Other Assurance Services, 18e,* to the general knowledge and skill guidelines found in the AACSB standards. The statements contained in *Principles of Auditing & Other Assurance Services, 18e,* are provided only as a guide for the users of this text. The AACSB leaves content coverage and assessment clearly within the realm and control of individual schools, the mission of the school, and the faculty. The AACSB does also charge schools with the obligation of doing assessment against their own content and learning goals. While *Principles of Auditing & Other Assurance Services, 18e,* and its teaching package make no claim of any specific AACSB qualification or evaluation, we have, within the Test Bank, labeled selected questions according to the six general knowledge and skills areas.

## McGraw-Hill's *Connect*™ *Accounting*

*Connect Accounting* offers a number of powerful tools and features to make managing your classroom easier. *Connect Accounting* with Whittington 18e offers enhanced features and technology to help both you and your students make the most of your time inside and outside the classroom. See page xvi for more details.

## Online Learning Center (www.mhhe.com/whittington18e)

The password-protected instructor side of the book's Online Learning Center (OLC) houses all of the instructor resources you need to administer your course, including:

- Instructor's Lecture Guide
- Solutions Manual
- Keystone Case and Solutions
- ACL Instructor Materials
- Test Bank
- EOC Conversion Guide
- Text Updates

If you choose to use *Connect Accounting* with Whittington, you will have access to these same resources via the Instructor Library.

## Instructor's Resource CD-ROM

The Instructor's Resource CD-ROM (ISBN-13 9780077328481; ISBN-10 0077328485) allows you to access the text's ancillary materials in one convenient CD. This includes the Instructor's Lecture Guide, Solutions Manual, Test Bank, Computerized Test Bank, Spreadsheets, all text figures, and PowerPoint presentations.

## Instructor's Lecture Guide and Solutions Manual

Our Instructor's Lecture Guide includes topical outlines of each chapter, the authors' comments on each chapter, and numerous instructional aids. A Solutions Manual includes thorough and up-to-date solutions to the text's questions, problems, and exercises. These are included on the Instructor's Resource CD and on the Online Learning Center.

## EZ Test

Available on the Instructor's Resource CD, Instructor's OLC, and within the *Connect* Instructor Library. McGraw-Hill's EZ Test is a flexible electronic testing program. The program allows instructors to create tests from book-specific items. It accommodates a wide range of question types, plus instructors may add their own questions and sort questions by format. EZ Test can also scramble questions and answers for multiple versions of the same test.

# Student Supplements

## McGraw-Hill's Connect™ Accounting

McGraw-Hill's *Connect Accounting* helps prepare students for their future by enabling faster learning, more efficient studying, and higher retention of knowledge. See page xvi for more details.

## Online Learning Center (www.mhhe.com/whittington18e)

The Online Learning Center (OLC) follows Whittington 18e chapter by chapter, offering all kinds of supplementary help for students as they read. The OLC includes the following resources to help students study more efficiently:

- Online Quizzes
- Student PowerPoint® Slides
- Keystone Case
- ACL Materials
- Auditing weblinks

If *Connect Accounting* is used in this course, students will have access to these same resources via the Student Library.

## Study Guide

A Study Guide (ISBN-13 9780077328504; ISBN-10 0077328507), written by the text's authors, enables students to review text material and test their understanding. The guide includes a summary of each chapter's highlights and an abundance of objective questions and exercises. Since the guide includes answers to the questions and exercises, it provides immediate feedback to students. The Study Guide questions are also available within *Connect Accounting*.

# REFERENCES TO AUTHORITATIVE SOURCES

Numerous references are made to the pronouncements of the American Institute of Certified Public Accountants (AICPA), The Institute of Internal Auditors (IIA), the Financial Accounting Standards Board (FASB), the Governmental Accounting Standards Board (GASB), the Public Company Accounting Oversight Board (PCAOB), the Securities and Exchange Commission (SEC), and the International Federation of Accountants (IFAC). Special attention is given to the AICPA *Code of Professional Conduct, Statements on Standards for Accounting and Review Services, Statements on Standards for Attestation Engagements, Statements on Auditing Standards,* and guidelines developed for other types of assurance services. The cooperation of the AICPA and the IIA in permitting the use of their published materials and of questions from the CPA and CIA examinations brings to the text an element of authority not otherwise available.

# Acknowledgments

The work of Donald A. Schwartz, JD, CPA, of National University, in developing the software supplement for the illustrative audit case exercises is especially appreciated. We thank Norwood Jackson (formerly of the U.S. Office of Management and Budget) for his guidance on compliance auditing.

We express our sincere thanks to the following professors who provided extensive reviews for the eighteenth edition:

Jack Armitage
*University of Nebraska at Omaha*

David Blum
*Moraine Park Technical College*

Rich Brody
*University of New Mexico*

Douglas Carmichael
*Baruch College*

Ruth Epps
*Virginia Commonwealth University*

Magdy Farag
*Cal Poly, Pomona*

Aretha Hill
*North Carolina A&T State University*

David Jenkins
*University of Delaware*

Ralph Licastro
*The Pennsylvania State University*

Heidi Meier
*Cleveland State University*

Roselyn Morris
*Texas State University, San Marcos*

Michael Pearson
*Kent State University*

Thomas Weirich
*Central Michigan University*

Jian Zhang
*San Jose State University*

We also express our appreciation to the many people who reviewed the preceding editions and offered helpful suggestions. They include:

John T. Ahern, Jr.
*DePaul University*

Jeffrey J. Archambault
*Marshall University*

Barbara Arel
*University of Vermont*

Joseph Aubert
*Bemidji State University*

Dan Baglia
*Grove City College*

Anthony T. Barbera
*SUNY College at Old Westbury*

Gary Bridges
*University of Texas at San Antonio*

Rich Brody
*University of New Mexico*

Michael Broihahn
*Barry University*

Ann Brooks
*University of New Mexico*

Thane Butt
*Champlain College*

Al Case
*Southern Oregon University*

Paul Caster
*Fairfield University*

Fred Christensen
*Boise State University*

Laurel Cobb
*Saint Leo University*

John Corless
*California State University at Sacramento*

Martha Doran
*San Diego State University*

Phil Drake
*Arizona State University*

Hans Dykxhoorn
*Western Michigan University*

Thomas English
*Boise State University*

Ruth Epps
*Virginia Commonwealth University*

Gary Frank
*University of Akron*

Diana Franz
*University of Toledo*

Lori R. Fuller
*University of Delaware*

Earl H. Godfrey, Jr.
*Gardner-Webb University*

Mary Beth Goodrich
*University of Texas at Dallas*

Jongsoo Han
*Rutgers University at Camden*

James Hansen
*University of Illinois at Chicago*

Theresa Hrncir
*Southeastern Oklahoma State University*

William Huffman
*Missouri Southern State University*

Russell Jacques
*Saint Leo University*

Bonita Kramer
*Montana State University*

Ellen Landgraf
*Loyola University, Chicago*

Pamela Legner
*College of DuPage*

Philip Levine
*Berkeley College*

D. Jordan Lowe
*Arizona State University*

Michael Milliren
*Milwaukee Area Technical College*

Perry Moore
*Lipscomb University*

Barbara Muller
*Arizona State University*

Perseus Munshi
*Arizona State University*

Albert Nagy
*John Carroll University*

Bernard Newman
*Pace University*

Kathy O'Donnell
*SUNY Buffalo*

Peggy O'Kelly
*Northeastern University*

Marshall Pitman
*University of Texas at San Antonio*

Margaret P. Pollard
*American River College*

Bruce Prager
*Hunter College*

Lynn Pringle
*Arizona State University*

Abe Qastin
*Lakeland College*

Alan Reinstein
*Wayne State University*

Raymond Reisig
*Pace University*

Shirley Rockel
*Iowa Wesleyan College*

Iris Stuart
*California State University at Fullerton*

Michael Trebesh
*Alma College*

Julie Ann Gardner-Treloar
*UCLA*

Valerie Trott
*Duquesne University*

Daniel Tschopp
*Daemen College*

Jerry Turner
*University of Memphis*

Allan Unseth
*Norfolk State University*

Patricia Villafana
*College of St. Catherine*

Judith C. Walo
*Central Connecticut State University*

Donna Whitten
*Purdue University North Central*

Jian Zhang
*San Jose State University*

Finally, we would like to thank the staff at McGraw-Hill/Irwin: Stewart Mattson, Editorial Director; Tim Vertovec, Publisher; Donna Dillon, Sponsoring Editor; Katie Jones, Development Editor; Michelle Heaster, Marketing Manager; Diane Nowaczyk, Senior Project Manager; Michael McCormick, Senior Buyer; Matt Diamond, Designer; Brian Nacik, Lead Media Project Manager; and Joyce Chappetto, Media Project Manager.

*O. Ray Whittington*
*Kurt Pany*

# Brief Contents

# Contents

## Chapter 7
## Internal Control 245

# The Role of the Public Accountant in the American Economy

**LO1**

Describe the nature of assurance services.

Dependable information is essential to the very existence of our society. The investor making a decision to buy or sell securities, the banker deciding whether to approve a loan, the government in obtaining revenue based on income tax returns—all are relying upon information provided by others. In many of these situations, the goals of the providers of information may run somewhat counter to those of the users of the information. Implicit in this line of reasoning is recognition of the social need for independent public accountants—individuals of professional competence and integrity who can tell us whether the information that we use constitutes a fair picture of what is really going on.

Our primary purpose in this chapter is to make clear the nature of independent audits and the accounting profession. We begin with a discussion of the broader concept of assurance services. Next, we describe those assurance services that involve attestation, of which audits of financial statements are an important type. Another purpose of this chapter is to summarize the influence exerted on the public accounting profession by the American Institute of Certified Public Accountants (AICPA), the Financial Accounting Standards Board (FASB), the Governmental Accounting Standards Board (GASB), the Federal Accounting Standards Advisory Board (FASAB), the Public Company Accounting Oversight Board (PCAOB), the Securities and Exchange Commission (SEC), and the International Federation of Accountants (IFAC). We will also explore various types of audits and note the impact of The Institute of Internal Auditors (IIA) and the Government Accountability Office (GAO). Finally, we will examine other types of professional services and the nature and organization of public accounting firms.

## What Are Assurance Services?

The name **assurance services** is used to describe the broad range of information enhancement services that are provided by certified public accountants (CPAs). The accountant must be "independent" to perform these services. In general, assurance services consist of two types: those that increase the reliability of information and those that involve putting information in a form or context that facilitates decision making. In this chapter, we will focus on the first type—audit and assurance services that involve reliability enhancement.

## The Attest Function

**LO2**

Identify assurance services that involve attestation.

A major subset of assurance services is called *attestation services*. To attest to information means to provide assurance as to its reliability. The profession's attestation standards define an **attest engagement** as one in which:

a practitioner is engaged to issue or does issue an examination, a review, or an agreed-upon procedures report on subject matter or an assertion about subject matter that is the responsibility of another party (e.g., management).

**FIGURE 1.1**
**The Attest Function**

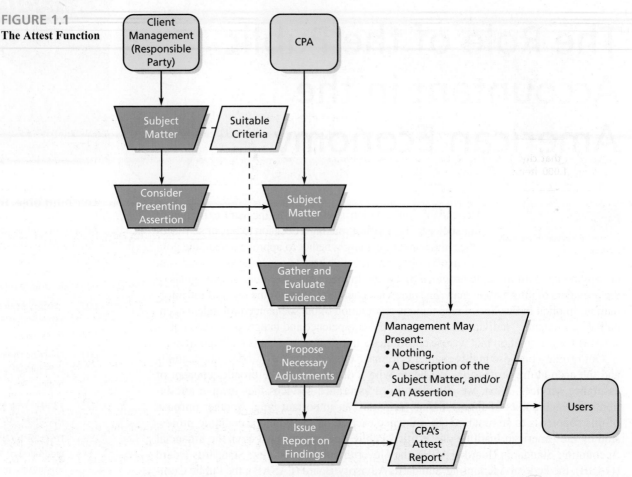

*If the criteria are not generally available to the users, they should be presented in the CPA's report or management's presentation.

CPAs attest to many types of subject matter (or assertions about subject matter), including financial forecasts, internal control, compliance with laws and regulations, and advertising claims.

Figure 1.1 describes the attest function, which begins with the subject matter that is the responsibility of another party, usually management. As an example, consider the situation in which the CPAs attest to a company's internal control over financial reporting. The subject matter of this engagement is internal control over financial reporting—internal control is the responsibility of management. The CPAs may be engaged to report directly on the internal control and express an opinion on whether a company's internal control over financial reporting follows certain *standards* (benchmarks). Alternatively, they may report on an assertion made by management that the company's internal control follows certain standards. In this second case, the audit report would include an opinion on whether management's **assertion** is accurate. Managements of public companies are now required to include in their annual reports an assertion about the effectiveness of internal control over financial reporting and to engage their auditors to attest to the effectiveness of internal control. This form of reporting is described in detail in Chapters 7 and 18.

What standards must the subject matter follow? The standards are those established or developed by groups composed of experts and are referred to as **suitable criteria.** In an internal control engagement, the standards may be those that have been established by a committee of experts on internal control. In a financial statement audit, another term arises—**financial reporting framework.** The suitable criteria in a financial statement audit are set forth in the financial reporting framework selected by management, often **generally accepted accounting principles (GAAP).** The CPAs perform a financial

**Illustrative Case**    *The Value of Attest Services*

CPAs have attested that a supermarket chain in Phoenix has the lowest overall prices in that city. The CPAs selected a sample of approximately 1,000 items and compared the prices to those of the various other major supermarkets. Representatives of the supermarket chain stated that the credibility added by the CPAs has helped to convince consumers that the chain's prices are indeed the lowest.

statement audit to gather sufficient evidence to issue an audit report with their opinion on whether the financial statements (the subject matter) follow the **applicable financial reporting framework** (that is, the financial reporting framework chosen by management, often GAAP).

The definition of an attest engagement refers to reports arising from three forms of engagements—examinations, reviews, and the performance of agreed-upon procedures. An **examination,** referred to as an *audit* when it involves historical financial statements, provides the highest form of assurance that CPAs can offer. In an examination, the CPAs select from all available evidence a combination that limits to a *low level* the risk of undetected misstatement and provides *reasonable assurance* that the subject matter (or assertion) is materially correct. A **review** is substantially lesser in scope of procedures than an examination and is designed to lend only a limited degree of assurance. If an examination or review does not meet the client's needs, the CPAs and specified user or users of the information may mutually decide on specific agreed-upon procedures that the CPAs will perform. An **agreed-upon procedures engagement** results in a report by the CPAs that describes those procedures and their findings. Figure 1.2 summarizes the three forms of attestation engagements.

## Assurance and Nonassurance Services

It is important to understand the relationships among the range of services that are offered by CPAs, because different professional standards apply to each type of service. Figure 1.3 illustrates the universe of services that may be offered by CPAs and the relationships among these services. As shown, CPAs provide both assurance and nonassurance services but a few, specifically of the management consulting type, overlap.

**FIGURE 1.2    Forms of Attestation**

| Type of Engagement | Level of Assurance Provided | Risk of Material Misstatement | Nature of Assurance in Report | Procedures |
|---|---|---|---|---|
| **Examination\*** | High ("reasonable") | Low | "In our opinion . . ." | Select from all available procedures any combination that can limit attestation risk to a low level |
| **Review** | Limited | Not defined in standards | "We are not aware of any material modifications that should be made . . ." | Generally limited to inquiry and analytical procedures |
| **Agreed-Upon Procedures** | Summary of findings | Varies by specific engagement | Includes a summary of procedures followed and findings | Procedures agreed upon with the specified user or users |

\*Referred to as an *audit* when the subject matter is historical financial statements.

FIGURE 1.3
**Relationships among
Assurance Services,
Attestation Services, and
Nonassurance Services**

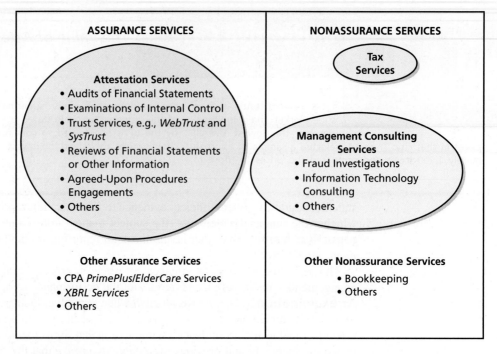

Certain management consulting services have assurance aspects. Later in this chapter, we will provide a brief description of the prevalent types of nonassurance services offered by CPA firms.

Figure 1.3 also illustrates that attestation services are only a portion of the assurance services that are offered by CPAs. A few examples of assurance services that do not involve attestation include:

- CPA *PrimePlus/ElderCare* services—providing assurance to individuals that their elderly family members' needs are being met by institutions and other professionals.
- *XBRL Services*—providing assurance on XBRL-related documents.

Throughout the first 17 chapters of this textbook, we will focus primarily on the attest function as it relates to the audit of financial statements. Other types of attestation and assurance services are discussed in Chapters 18 through 21.

## Financial Statement Audits

**LO3**

Describe the nature of financial statement audits.

In a financial statement audit, the auditors undertake to gather evidence and provide a high level of assurance that the financial statements follow generally accepted accounting principles, or some other appropriate basis of accounting. An audit involves searching and verifying the accounting records and examining other evidence supporting the financial statements. By gathering information about the company and its environment, including internal control; inspecting documents; observing assets; making inquiries within and outside the company; and performing other auditing procedures, the auditors will gather the evidence necessary to issue an audit report. That audit report states that it is the auditors' opinion that the financial statements follow generally accepted accounting principles. The flowchart in Figure 1.4 illustrates an audit of financial statements.

The evidence obtained and evaluated by the auditors focuses on whether the financial statements are presented in accordance with the applicable financial reporting framework, usually generally accepted accounting principles. More specifically, an audit addresses management's assertions that the assets listed in the balance sheet really exist, that the company has title (rights) to the assets, and that the valuations assigned to the assets have been established in conformity with generally accepted accounting principles. Evidence is gathered to show that the balance sheet contains *all the liabilities* of the company;

**FIGURE 1.4**
**Audit of Financial Statements**

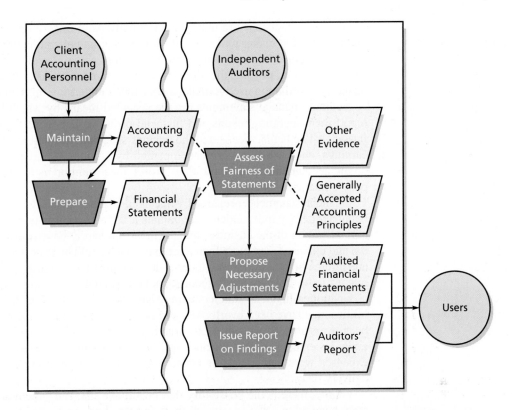

otherwise the balance sheet might be grossly misleading because certain important liabilities have been accidentally or deliberately omitted. Similarly, the auditors gather evidence about the transactions recorded in the income statement. They demand evidence that the reported sales really occurred, that sales have been recorded at appropriate amounts, and that the recorded costs and expenses are applicable to the current period and all expenses have been recognized. Finally, the auditors consider whether the financial statement amounts are accurate, properly classified, and summarized and whether the notes are informative and complete. Only if sufficient evidence is gathered in support of all these significant assertions can the auditors provide an opinion on whether the financial statements are presented in accordance with generally accepted accounting principles.

The procedures included in an audit vary considerably from one engagement to the next. Many of the procedures appropriate to the audit of a small retail store would not be appropriate for the audit of a giant corporation such as General Motors. Auditors perform audits of all types of businesses, and of governmental and nonprofit organizations as well. Banks and breweries, factories and stores, colleges and churches, school districts and labor unions—all are regularly visited by auditors. The selection of the procedures best suited to each audit requires the exercise of professional skill and judgment.

## What Creates the Demand for Audits?

Reliable accounting and financial reporting aid society in allocating resources in an efficient manner. A primary goal is to allocate limited capital resources to the production of those goods and services for which demand is great. Economic resources are attracted to the industries, the geographic areas, and the organizational entities that are shown by financial measurements to be capable of using the resources to the best advantage. Inadequate accounting and reporting, on the other hand, conceal waste and inefficiency, thereby preventing an efficient allocation of economic resources.

The contribution of the independent auditor is to provide *credibility* to information. Credibility, in this usage, means that the information can be believed; that is, it can be relied upon by outsiders, such as stockholders, creditors, government regulators, customers, and other interested third parties. These third parties use the information to make various economic decisions, such as decisions about whether to invest in the organization.

**LO4**

Explain why audits are demanded by society.

Economic decisions are made under conditions of uncertainty; there is always a risk that the decision maker will select the wrong alternative and incur a significant loss. The credibility added to the information by auditors actually reduces the decision maker's risk. To be more precise, the auditors reduce information risk, which is the risk that the financial information used to make a decision is materially misstated.

Audited financial statements are the accepted means by which business corporations report their operating results and financial position. The word *audited,* when applied to financial statements, means that the balance sheet and the statements of income, retained earnings, and cash flows are accompanied by an audit report prepared by independent public accountants, expressing their professional opinion as to the fairness of the company's financial statements.

Financial statements prepared by management and transmitted to outsiders without first being audited by independent accountants leave a credibility gap. In reporting on its own administration of the business, management can hardly be expected to be entirely impartial and unbiased, any more than a football coach could be expected to serve as both coach and referee in the same game. Independent auditors have no material personal or financial interest in the business; their reports can be expected to be impartial and free from bias.

Unaudited financial statements may have been honestly, but carelessly, prepared. Liabilities may have been overlooked and omitted from the balance sheet. Assets may have been overstated as a result of arithmetical errors or due to a lack of knowledge of generally accepted accounting principles. Net income may have been exaggerated because expenses were capitalized or because sales transactions were recorded in advance of delivery dates.

Finally, there is the possibility that unaudited financial statements have been deliberately falsified in order to conceal theft and fraud or as a means of inducing the reader to invest in the business or to extend credit. Although deliberate falsification of financial statements is not common, it does occur and can cause devastating losses to persons who make decisions based upon such misleading statements.

For all these reasons (accidental errors, lack of knowledge of accounting principles, unintentional bias, and deliberate falsification), financial statements may depart from generally accepted accounting principles. Audits provide organizations with more credible financial statements to allow users to have more assurance that those statements do not materially depart from generally accepted accounting principles.

*Illustrating the Demand for Auditing*

A decision by a bank loan officer about whether to make a loan to a business can be used to illustrate the demand for auditing. Since the bank's objective in making the loan is to earn an appropriate rate of interest and to collect the principal of the loan at maturity, the loan officer is making two related decisions: (1) whether to make the loan at all, and (2) what rate of interest adequately compensates the bank for the level of risk assumed. The loan officer will make these decisions based on a careful study of the company's financial statements along with other information. The risk assumed by the bank related to this customer has two aspects:[1]

1. **Business risk**—the risk associated with a company's survival and profitability. This includes, for example, the risk that the company will not be able to make the interest payments and repay the principal of the loan because of economic conditions or poor management decisions. Business risk is assessed by considering factors such as the financial position of the company, the nature of its operations, the characteristics of the industry in which it operates, and the quality and integrity of its management.

2. **Information risk**—the risk that the information used to assess business risk is not accurate. Information risk includes the possibility that the financial statements might contain material departures from generally accepted accounting principles.

[1] For all loans, the banker also assumes *interest rate risk,* which varies depending on the terms of the loan. Interest rate risk reflects the risk due to potential changes in the "risk-free" interest rate.

While auditing normally has only a limited effect on a company's business risk,[2] it can significantly affect the level of information risk. If the loan officer has assurance from the auditors that the company's financial statements are prepared in accordance with generally accepted accounting principles, he or she will have more confidence in his or her assessment of business risk. In addition, periodic audits performed after the loan has been made provide the loan officer with a way of monitoring management performance and compliance with the various loan provisions. By reducing information risk, the auditors reduce the overall risk to the bank; the loan officer is more likely to make the loan to the company and at a lower rate of interest. Therefore, management of the company has an incentive to provide audited financial statements to the loan officer to obtain the loan and to get the best possible interest rate.

A major portion of our economy is characterized by large corporate organizations that have gathered capital from millions of investors and that control economic resources spread throughout the country or even throughout the world. Top management in the corporate headquarters is often remote from the operations of company plants and branches and must rely on financial statements and other reports to control the corporation's resources. In brief, the decision makers in a large corporation cannot obtain much information on a firsthand basis. They must rely on information provided by lower-level management, and this fact creates a risk of receiving unreliable information. As in the case of the loan officer, auditing can reduce the risk of poor management decisions by reducing information risk and by monitoring the performance of management at every level within the organization.

The millions of individuals who have entrusted their savings to corporations by investing in securities rely upon annual and quarterly financial statements for investment decisions and for assurance that their invested funds are being used honestly and efficiently. Even greater numbers of people entrust their savings to banks, insurance companies, and pension funds, which in turn invest the money in corporate securities. Thus, directly or indirectly, almost everyone has a financial stake in corporate enterprises, and the public interest demands prompt, *reliable* financial reporting on the operations and the financial health of publicly owned corporations.

Various regulatory agencies also demand audit services. As an example, consider the income tax reporting system in our country. The information provided on tax returns is provided by taxpayers and may be biased because of the self-interest of the providers. The government attempts to compensate for this inherent weakness through verification by audits carried out by agents of the Internal Revenue Service.

## Major Auditing Developments of the 20th Century

Although the objectives and concepts that guide present-day audits were almost unknown in the early years of the 20th century, audits of one type or another have been performed throughout the recorded history of commerce and government finance. The original meaning of the word *auditor* was "one who hears" and was appropriate to the era during which governmental accounting records were approved only after a public reading in which the accounts were read aloud. From medieval times on through the Industrial Revolution, audits were performed to determine whether persons in positions of official responsibility in government and commerce were acting and reporting in an honest manner.

During the Industrial Revolution, as manufacturing concerns grew in size, their owners began to use the services of hired managers. With this separation of the ownership and management groups, the absentee owners turned increasingly to auditors to protect themselves against the danger of unintentional errors as well as fraud committed by managers and employees. Bankers were the primary outside users of financial reports (usually only

---

[2] Possible effects of an audit on business risk include modifications of management's operating decisions either due to knowledge that an audit will be performed or due to operating recommendations made by auditors. Accordingly, an audit *may* reduce business risk.

balance sheets), and they were also concerned with whether the reports were distorted by errors or fraud. Before 1900, consistent with this primary objective to detect errors and fraud, audits often included a study of all, or almost all, recorded transactions.

In the first half of the 20th century, the direction of audit work tended to move away from fraud detection toward a new goal of determining whether financial statements gave a full and fair picture of financial position, operating results, and changes in financial position. This shift in emphasis was a response to the increasing number of shareholders and the corresponding increased size of corporate entities. In addition to the new shareholders, auditors became more responsible to governmental agencies, the stock exchanges representing these new investors, and other parties who might rely upon the financial information. No longer were bankers the only important outside users of audited financial data. The fairness of reported earnings became of prime importance.

As large-scale corporate entities developed rapidly in both Great Britain and the United States, auditors began to sample selected transactions, rather than study all transactions. Auditors and business managers gradually came to accept the proposition that careful examination of relatively few selected transactions would give a cost-effective, reliable indication of the accuracy of other similar transactions.

In addition to sampling, auditors became aware of the importance of effective internal control. A company's internal control consists of the policies and procedures established to provide reasonable assurance that the objectives of the company will be achieved, including the objective of preparing accurate financial statements. Auditors found that by studying the client's internal control they could identify areas of strength as well as of weakness. *The stronger the internal control, the less testing of financial statement account balances required by the auditors.* For any significant account or any phase of financial operations in which controls were weak, the auditors expanded the nature and extent of their tests of the account balance.

With the increased reliance upon sampling and internal control, professional standards began to emphasize limitations on auditors' ability to detect **fraud.** The profession recognized that audits designed to discover fraud would be too costly. Good internal control and surety bonds were recognized as better fraud protection techniques than audits.

Beginning in the 1960s, the detection of large-scale fraud assumed a larger role in the audit process. Professional standards, which used the term *irregularities* in place of fraud, described fraudulent financial reporting and misappropriation of assets. This shift in emphasis to taking a greater responsibility for the detection of fraud resulted from (1) a dramatic increase in congressional pressure to assume more responsibility for large-scale frauds, (2) a number of successful lawsuits claiming that fraudulent financial reporting (management fraud) had improperly gone undetected by the independent auditors, and (3) a belief by public accountants that audits should be expected to detect *material* fraud.

As a result of a number of instances of fraudulent financial reporting, the major accounting organizations[3] sponsored the *National Commission on Fraudulent Financial Reporting* (the Treadway Commission) to study the causes of fraudulent reporting and make recommendations to reduce its incidence. The commission's final report, which was issued in 1987, made a number of recommendations for auditors, public companies, regulators, and educators. Many of the recommendations for auditors were enacted by the AICPA in a group of *Statements on Auditing Standards* known as the *expectation gap* standards. The commission's recommendations about internal control led to the development of an internal control framework, titled *Internal Control—Integrated Framework*, to be used to evaluate the internal control of an organization. The development of these internal control criteria increased the demand for attestation by auditors to the effectiveness of internal control. As an example, the Federal Deposit Insurance Corporation

---

[3] The sponsoring organizations included the American Institute of Certified Public Accountants, the American Accounting Association, the Financial Executives Institute, The Institute of Internal Auditors, and the Institute of Management Accountants.

(FDIC) Improvement Act of 1991 was passed requiring management of large financial institutions to engage CPAs to attest to the effectiveness of assertions by management about the effectiveness of the institution's controls over financial reporting.

In the late 1980s and early 1990s, the billions of dollars in federal funds that were required to "bail out" the savings and loan industry caused a movement toward increased regulation of federally insured financial institutions. Congress and regulatory agencies believed that the key to preventing such problems was enacting effective laws and regulations and requiring reports by auditors on compliance with provisions of these laws and regulations. An important example of this type of legislation is the FDIC Improvement Act of 1991. In addition to requiring reporting on internal control, the law also requires management of large financial institutions to engage its CPAs to attest to management's assertion about the institution's compliance with laws and regulations related to the safety and soundness of the institution.

In 1996, in response to a continuing expectation gap between user demands and auditor performance, the AICPA issued guidance to auditors requiring an explicit assessment of the risk of material misstatement in financial statements due to fraud on all audits. This auditing standard was replaced in 2002 with an even more stringent standard that requires auditors to definitively design procedures to address the risk of fraudulent financial reporting.

A factor overlaying a number of changes has been fast-paced changes in information technology. From small computer accounting systems to large mainframe computers to networked enterprise-wide information systems to the use of the Internet to initiate and process transactions, auditing methods have had to adapt. While technology has not changed the basic objective of the financial statement audit, it has resulted in the need to develop innovative computer testing techniques and tools to assure audit effectiveness.

Many of the ideas mentioned in this brief historical sketch of the development of auditing will be analyzed in detail in later sections of this book. Our purpose at this point is merely to orient you with a quick overall look at some of the major auditing developments of the 20th century. These many developments, while significant, may be overshadowed by what has and will occur in the 21st century as the accounting profession faces significant challenges to its viability.

## The Accounting Profession's Credibility Crisis

**LO5**

Describe how the credibility of the accounting profession was affected by the large number of companies reporting accounting irregularities in the beginning of this century.

In 2000, at the request of the Securities and Exchange Commission, the accounting profession established the Panel on Audit Effectiveness. The panel was charged with the responsibility of reviewing and evaluating how independent audits of financial statements are performed and assessing whether recent trends in audit practices serve the public interest. Recommendations from the panel resulted in changes in auditing standards related to the detection of fraud, documentation of audit evidence and judgments, risk assessments, and the linkage of audit procedures to audit risks. However, even before these changes in audit requirements could be implemented, a series of events in the capital markets produced a chain reaction that caused unprecedented reforms in the accounting profession.

In December 2001, Enron Corporation filed for bankruptcy shortly after acknowledging that accounting irregularities had been used to significantly inflate earnings in the current and preceding years. Shortly thereafter, it was disclosed that WorldCom had used accounting fraud to significantly overstate its reported income. In addition to these two very visible cases, a record number of public companies restated prior-period financial statements, and almost weekly the Securities and Exchange Commission announced a new investigation into another company's accounting practices. Investor uncertainty about the reliability of financial statements rocked an already weak financial market during the latter part of 2001 and the first half of 2002. It brought into question the effectiveness of financial statement audits and created a crisis of credibility for the accounting profession. More significantly, the highly publicized conviction of Andersen LLP, one of the then "Big 5" accounting firms, on charges of destruction of documents related

**Illustrative Case**    *Massive Fraud at WorldCom*

WorldCom reported over $11 billion in accounting irregularities, completely eliminating the company's previously reported profits for all of 2000 and 2001 and causing the company to declare bankruptcy.

At one time WorldCom had reported total assets in excess of $100 billion and a market value in excess of $150 billion, making it then the largest bankruptcy in U.S. history.[4]

to the Enron case brought into question the ethical principles of the public accounting profession.[5]

These events drew quick responses from a number of congressional committees, the SEC, and the U.S. Justice Department, as they began investigating corporate management and the accounting profession. By the summer of 2002, Congress had passed the **Sarbanes-Oxley Act of 2002,** which included a set of reforms that toughened penalties for corporate fraud, restricted the types of consulting CPAs may perform for public company audit clients, and created the Public Company Accounting Oversight Board (PCAOB) to oversee the accounting profession. The PCAOB, which has broad powers to develop and enforce standards for public accounting firms that audit companies that issue securities registered with the SEC, will be described in more detail later in this chapter.

Establishment of the PCAOB eliminated a significant portion of the accounting profession's system of self-regulation. It is clear that regulation of the profession, at least with respect to the audit of public (issuer) companies,[6] is no longer primarily in the hands of the accounting profession.

## Types of Audits

Audits are often viewed as falling into three major categories: (1) financial audits, (2) compliance audits, and (3) operational audits. In addition, the Sarbanes-Oxley Act requires an integrated audit for public companies.

### Financial Audits

LO6

Contrast the various types of audits and types of auditors.

A **financial audit** is an audit of the financial accounting information of an entity. An **audit of financial statements** ordinarily covers the balance sheet and the related statements of income, retained earnings, and cash flows. The goal is to determine whether these statements have been prepared in conformity with generally accepted accounting principles. Financial statement audits are normally performed by firms of certified public accountants; however, internal auditors often perform financial audits of departments or business segments. Users of auditors' reports include management, investors, bankers, creditors, financial analysts, and government agencies.

### Compliance Audits

The performance of a **compliance audit** is dependent upon the existence of verifiable data and of recognized criteria or standards, such as established laws and regulations, or an organization's policies and procedures. A familiar example is the audit of an income tax return by an auditor of the Internal Revenue Service (IRS). Such audits address whether

---

[4] The bankruptcy of Lehman Brothers Holding, Inc., in 2008 is now the largest bankruptcy in U.S. history.

[5] Ironically, the conviction of Andersen was overturned by the Supreme Court, but not before the firm had been dissolved.

[6] The AICPA and the PCAOB often use the terms *issuer* and *nonissuer* to refer to public and nonpublic companies, respectively. An issuer is a company that has securities registered with the SEC. We will use the terms public/issuer and nonpublic/nonissuer synonymously throughout this textbook.

a tax return is in compliance with tax laws and IRS regulations. The findings of the IRS auditors are transmitted to the taxpayer by means of the IRS auditor's report.

Another example of a compliance audit is the periodic bank examination by bank examiners employed by the Federal Deposit Insurance Corporation and the state banking departments. These audits measure compliance with banking laws and regulations and with traditional standards of sound banking practice.

Internal auditors perform audits of compliance with internal controls, other company policies and procedures, and applicable laws and regulations. Internal audit departments often are involved with documenting and testing internal control for management's reports required by the Sarbanes-Oxley Act.

Finally, many state and local governmental entities and nonprofit organizations that receive financial assistance from the federal government must arrange for compliance audits under the Single Audit Act or *OMB Circular A-133*. Such audits are designed to determine whether the financial assistance is spent in accordance with applicable laws and regulations. Compliance audits are described in greater detail in Chapter 21.

### Operational Audits

An **operational audit** is a study of a specific unit of an organization for the purpose of measuring its performance. The operations of the receiving department of a manufacturing company, for example, may be evaluated in terms of its *effectiveness,* that is, its success in meeting its stated goals and responsibilities. Performance is also judged in terms of *efficiency,* that is, success in using to its best advantage the resources available to the department. Because the criteria for effectiveness and efficiency are not as clearly established as are generally accepted accounting principles and many laws and regulations, an operational audit tends to require more subjective judgment than do audits of financial statements or compliance. For example, quantifiable criteria often must be developed by the auditors to be used to measure the effectiveness or efficiency of the department. Operational auditing is also discussed in detail in Chapter 21.

### Integrated Audits

The Sarbanes-Oxley Act requires that auditors of publicly traded companies in the United States perform an **integrated audit** that includes providing assurance on both the financial statements and the effectiveness of internal control over financial reporting. Specifically, the Sarbanes-Oxley Act and PCAOB *Standard No. 5*—which implements the integrated audit—require company management to assess and report on the company's internal control. The auditors, in addition to providing an opinion on the company's financial statements, report on both management's assessment and internal control effectiveness.

## Types of Auditors

In addition to the audit of financial statements by certified public accountants, other professional groups carry on large-scale auditing programs. Among these other well-known types of auditors are internal auditors, auditors of the Government Accountability Office, and internal revenue agents.

### Internal Auditors

Nearly every large corporation maintains an internal auditing staff. Internal auditors are also employed extensively by governmental and nonprofit organizations. A principal goal of internal auditors is to investigate and appraise the effectiveness with which the various organizational units of the company are carrying out their assigned functions. Much attention is given by internal auditors to the study and appraisal of internal control.

A large part of the work of internal auditors consists of operational audits; in addition, they may conduct numerous compliance audits. The number and kind of investigative projects vary from year to year. Unlike CPAs, who are committed to verify each significant item in the annual financial statements, internal auditors are not obligated to repeat their audits on an annual basis.

The internal auditing staff often reports to the audit committee of the board of directors and also to the president or another high-level executive. This strategic placement high in the organizational structure helps ensure that the internal auditors will have ready access to all units of the organization, and that their recommendations will be given prompt attention by department heads. It is imperative that the internal auditors be independent of the department heads and other line executives whose work they review. Thus, it would generally not be desirable for the internal auditing staff to be under the authority of the chief accountant. Regardless of their reporting level, however, the internal auditors are not independent in the same sense as the independent auditors. The internal auditors are employees of the organization in which they work, subject to the restraints inherent in the employer–employee relationship.

The Institute of Internal Auditors (IIA) is the international organization of internal auditors. It has developed various standards relating to internal auditing, and it administers the certified internal auditor (CIA) examination. Chapter 21 provides further discussion of the internal auditing profession and the CIA designation.

### Government Accountability Office Auditors

Congress has long had its own auditing staff, headed by the comptroller general and known as the Government Accountability Office, or GAO.[7] The work of GAO auditors includes compliance, operational, and financial audits. These assignments include audits of government agencies to determine that spending programs follow the intent of Congress and operational audits to evaluate the effectiveness and efficiency of selected government programs. GAO auditors conduct examinations of corporations holding government contracts to verify that contract payments by the government have been proper. In addition, the financial statements of a number of federal agencies and the consolidated financial statements of the federal government are audited by the GAO.

The enormous size of many of the federal agencies has caused the GAO to stress the development of computer auditing techniques and statistical sampling plans. Its pioneering in these areas has led to the recognition of the GAO as a sophisticated professional auditing staff.

### Internal Revenue Agents

The Internal Revenue Service is responsible for enforcement of the federal tax laws. Its agents conduct compliance audits of the income tax returns of individuals and corporations to determine that income has been computed and taxes paid as required by federal law. Although IRS audits include some simple individual tax returns that can be completed in an hour or so in an IRS office, they also include field audits of the nation's largest corporations and often involve highly complex tax issues.

## The Public Accounting Profession

**LO7**

Explain the regulatory process for auditors of public companies and auditors of nonpublic companies.

In recognition of the public trust afforded to public accountants, each state recognizes public accountancy as a profession and issues the certificate of **certified public accountant.** The CPA certificate is a symbol of technical competence. This official recognition by the state is comparable to that accorded to the legal, medical, and other professions.

The licensing of CPAs by the states reflects a belief that the public interest will be protected by an official identification of competent professional accountants who offer their services to the public. Although CPAs provide various types of tax, consulting, and accounting services which are also provided by non-CPAs, the various states generally

---

[7] The GAO changed its name from the General Accounting Office to the Government Accountability Office in 2004.

restrict the performance of audits of financial statements to CPAs. It is this performance of the attest function on financial statements that is most unique to CPAs.

## American Institute of Certified Public Accountants

The **American Institute of Certified Public Accountants (AICPA)** is a voluntary national organization of more than 330,000 members. The following four major areas of the AICPA's work are of particular interest to students of auditing:

1. Establishing standards and rules to guide CPAs in their conduct of professional services.
2. Carrying on a program of research and publication.
3. Promoting continuing professional education.
4. Contributing to the profession's self-regulation.

### Establishing Standards

The AICPA has assigned to its Auditing Standards Board (ASB) responsibility for issuing official pronouncements on auditing matters. A most important series of pronouncements on auditing by the Auditing Standards Board is entitled **Statements on Auditing Standards (SASs).** The ASB currently has the authority to issue auditing standards only for audits of nonpublic companies. As indicated previously, the Public Company Accounting Oversight Board (PCAOB) issues standards for audits of public companies. The PCAOB has adopted the Auditing Standards Board's *Statements on Auditing Standards* that were in effect as of April 16, 2003, as interim standards for audits of publicly traded companies. The standards are "interim" in that they serve as a starting point as the PCAOB develops its own set of standards.

The AICPA also issues *Statements on Standards for Attestation Engagements (SSAEs)*. These statements provide CPAs with guidance for attesting to information other than financial statements, such as financial forecasts. Chapter 2 also provides a description of the SSAEs.

The Accounting and Review Services Committee of the AICPA establishes standards for reporting on financial statements when the CPAs' role is to compile or review the financial statements rather than to perform an audit. The series of pronouncements by this committee is called *Statements on Standards for Accounting and Review Services (SSARS)*. The SSARSs provide guidance for the many sensitive situations in which a public accounting firm is in some way associated with the financial statements of a nonpublic company and, therefore, needs to make clear the extent of the responsibility that the public accounting firm assumes for the fairness of the statements. SSARSs are discussed more fully in Chapter 19.

### Research and Publication

In addition to the professional standards indicated above, the AICPA issues additional technical guidance. Many accounting students are familiar with the *Journal of Accountancy,* published monthly. Another AICPA monthly journal is *The Tax Advisor.* Publications bearing directly on auditing include:

- *Industry Audit and Accounting Guides.* These guides cover various industries, including, for example, *Audits of Casinos.*
- *Audit Risk Alerts.* These annual publications update auditors on practice issues and recently issued professional pronouncements that affect the audits of entities in various industries.
- *Auditing Practice Releases.* This series is intended to keep auditors informed of new developments and advances in auditing procedures.

A number of other AICPA publications bear directly on accounting issues, including:

- *Accounting Research Studies.* The results of studies of accounting methods are described in these publications.

- *Statements of Position* of the Accounting Standards Division. These statements express the AICPA's position on the appropriate method of accounting for particular events or transactions.
- *Accounting Trends & Techniques.* This is an annual study of current reporting practices of 600 large corporations.

### Continuing Professional Education

Another important activity of the AICPA is the development of a continuing professional education program. Continuing education is a necessity for CPAs to remain knowledgeable about the unending stream of changes in accounting principles, tax law, auditing, computers, and consulting services. Continuing education programs are offered by the AICPA, state societies, and other professional organizations. State laws require CPAs to participate in continuing education programs as a condition for license renewal.

### Professional Regulation

Historically, most of the regulation of accounting firms has been performed by the accounting profession itself through the AICPA. While the SEC has provided oversight and some regulation, prior to 2002 Congress had enacted limited legislation to regulate the profession. This situation changed significantly in 2002 with the passage of the Sarbanes-Oxley Act. As indicated previously, this legislation created the PCAOB, which now regulates all accounting firms that audit public (issuer) companies. The AICPA now provides very limited regulation for auditors of public companies but continues to regulate the accounting firms that do not audit public companies.

*Regulation of Individual CPAs*   The membership of the AICPA has adopted ethical rules for CPAs in the form of its goal-oriented *Code of Professional Conduct*. This ethical code sets forth positively stated principles on which CPAs can make decisions about appropriate conduct. The AICPA *Code of Professional Conduct* is described in detail in Chapter 3.

Self-regulation also is apparent in the requirements for regular membership in the AICPA, which include the following:

1. Members in public practice must practice with a firm enrolled in an approved practice-monitoring (peer review) program.
2. Members must obtain continuing education: 120 hours every three years for members in public practice and 90 hours every three years for other members.

*Regulation of Public Accounting Firms*   An AICPA member can meet the practice-monitoring membership requirement if his or her firm is enrolled in the AICPA Peer Review Program. When a CPA firm enrolls in the AICPA Peer Review Program, it agrees to comply with the AICPA's Quality Control Standards and to have a peer review of its accounting and auditing practice every three years. Firms that are required to be registered with and inspected by the Public Company Accounting Oversight Board (PCAOB) are required to have their AICPA peer review administered by the National Peer Review Committee. For these firms, the AICPA peer review focuses on the engagements that are not inspected by the PCAOB staff.

Many firms that are registered with the PCAOB become members of the AICPA *Center for Audit Quality (CAQ)*. The CAQ is dedicated to enhancing investor confidence and public trust in the global capital markets by fostering high-quality performance by public company auditors; convening and collaborating with other stakeholders to advance the discussion of critical issues requiring action and intervention; and advocating policies and standards that promote public company auditors' objectivity, effectiveness, and responsiveness to dynamic market conditions.

A *peer review* involves a critical review of one public accounting firm's practices by another public accounting firm. Such an external review clearly offers a more objective evaluation of the quality of performance than could be made by self-review. The purpose of this concept is to encourage rigorous adherence to the AICPA's quality control standards. Quality control standards and the peer review process are discussed in detail in Chapter 2.

*The AICPA—In Perspective*

Throughout its existence, the AICPA has contributed enormously to the evolution of generally accepted accounting principles as well as to the development of professional standards. The many technical divisions and committees of the institute (such as the Auditing Standards Board) provide a means of focusing the collective experience and ability of the profession on current problems. However, with the passage of the Sarbanes-Oxley Act, the AICPA's influence and responsibility have been significantly diminished.

## The CPA Examination

The **CPA examination** is a uniform national examination prepared and graded by the American Institute of Certified Public Accountants. The exam is computerized and given on demand at computer centers throughout most of the year.

Although the preparation and grading of the examination are in the hands of the AICPA, the issuance of CPA certificates is a function of each state or territory. Passing the CPA examination does not, in itself, entitle the candidate to a CPA certificate; states have experience and education requirements that must be met before the CPA certificate is awarded.

The CPA examination is essentially an academic one; in most states, candidates are not required to have any work experience to sit for the examination. In the opinion of the authors, the ideal time to take the examination is immediately after the completion of a comprehensive program of accounting courses in a college or university. The format of the CPA examination includes the following four parts:

1. Auditing & Attestation.
2. Financial Accounting & Reporting (business enterprises, not-for-profit organizations, and governmental entities).
3. Regulation (professional and legal responsibilities, business law, and taxation).
4. Business Environment & Concepts.

The exam consists of multiple choice questions and simulations, which are designed to replicate "real world" practice cases. The compilation of the questions and problems included in this textbook involved a review of CPA questions used in prior years and the selection of representative questions and problems. Use of this material is with the consent of the AICPA. Many other problems and questions (not from CPA examinations) are also included with each chapter.

## State Boards of Accountancy

Permits to practice as a CPA are granted by the state boards of accountancy in the various states. These boards also regulate the profession and may suspend or revoke an accountant's certificate. While all state boards require successful completion of the CPA examination, the requirements for education and experience vary. A few states require only a baccalaureate degree, while most require 150 semester hours of education or a master's degree to sit for the CPA examination. The experience required generally ranges from none to two years. The AICPA currently is attempting to get states to adopt the revised Uniform Accounting Act to facilitate CPA practice across state lines. The state boards are organized through the National Association of State Boards of Accounting (NASBA).

## Financial Accounting Standards Board

Auditors must determine whether financial statements are prepared in conformity with generally accepted accounting principles. The AICPA has designated the Financial Accounting Standards Board as the body with power to set forth these principles for entities other than federal, state, and local governments. Thus, *FASB Statements,* exposure drafts, public hearings, and research projects are all of major concern to the public accounting profession.

The structure, history, and pronouncements of the FASB (and its predecessor, the Accounting Principles Board) are appropriately covered in introductory, intermediate, and advanced accounting courses.

## Governmental Accounting Standards Board

The Governmental Accounting Standards Board (GASB) was formed in 1984 to establish and improve standards of financial accounting for state and local government entities. The operational structure of the GASB is similar to that of the FASB. Auditors of state and local government entities, such as cities and school districts, look to the GASB pronouncements for the appropriate accounting principles.

## Federal Accounting Standards Advisory Board

In 1990, the federal Office of Management and Budget, the U.S. Treasury, and the General Accounting Office (since renamed the Government Accountability Office) established the Federal Accounting Standards Advisory Board (FASAB) to develop accounting standards for the U.S. government. This body issues standards that are used to audit a number of major federal agencies and the U.S. government as a whole as required by the Government Management Reform Act of 1994.

## The Public Company Accounting Oversight Board

As indicated previously, the **Public Company Accounting Oversight Board (PCAOB)** was created in 2002 to oversee and discipline CPAs and public accounting firms that audit public (issuer) companies. This five-member board, under the authority of the SEC, has the responsibility to establish or adopt "auditing, attestation, quality control, ethics, and independence standards relating to the preparation of audit reports" for SEC registrants (almost all publicly traded companies in the United States). In addition, the PCAOB has the responsibility to:

- Register public accounting firms that audit public companies.
- Perform inspections of the practices of registered firms.
- Conduct investigations and disciplinary proceedings of registered firms.
- Sanction registered firms.

As indicated previously, the inspection program of the PCAOB covers only the public company audit practice of CPA firms. The results of the inspections are posted on the PCAOB's Web site at www.pcaobus.org.

## Securities and Exchange Commission

The **Securities and Exchange Commission (SEC)** is an agency of the U.S. government. It administers the Securities Act of 1933, the Securities Exchange Act of 1934, and other legislation concerning securities and financial matters. In addition, the SEC has oversight responsibility for the PCAOB. The primary function of the SEC is to protect investors and the public by requiring full disclosure of financial information by companies offering securities for sale to the public. A second objective is to prevent misrepresentation, deceit, or other fraud in the sale of securities.

The term *registration statement* is an important one in any discussion of the impact of the SEC on accounting practice. To *register* securities means to qualify them for sale to the public by filing with the SEC financial statements and other data in a form acceptable to the commission. A registration statement contains *audited financial statements,* including balance sheets for a two-year period and income statements, statements of retained earnings, and statements of cash flows for a three-year period.

The legislation creating the SEC made the commission responsible for determining whether the financial statements presented to it reflect proper application of accounting principles. To aid the commission in discharging this responsibility, the securities acts provide for an examination and report by a public accounting firm registered with the Public Company Accounting Oversight Board. From its beginning, the SEC has been

**Illustrative Case** | *Exiting the Consulting Business*

Most of the large CPA firms sold or spun off their consulting practices. As examples, IBM bought the consulting practice of PricewaterhouseCoopers LLP, KPMG LLP spun off its consulting practice and took it public, and Ernst & Young LLP sold its consulting practice to Cap Gemini. The firms now provide a limited set of consulting services.

a major user of audited financial statements and has exercised great influence upon the development of accounting principles, the strengthening of auditing standards, and the concept of auditor independence.

Protection of investors, of course, requires that the public have available the information contained in a registration statement concerning a proposed issue of securities. The issuing company is therefore required to deliver to prospective buyers of securities a *prospectus,* or selling circular, from the registration statement. The registration of securities does not insure investors against loss; the SEC does not pass on the merit of securities. There is, in fact, only one purpose of registration: to provide disclosure of the important facts so that the investor has available all pertinent information on which to base an intelligent decision as to whether to buy a given security. If the SEC believes that a given registration statement does not meet its standards of disclosure, it may require amendment of the statement or may issue a stop order preventing sale of the securities.

To improve the quality of the financial statements filed with it and the professional standards of the independent accountants who report on these statements, the SEC has adopted a basic accounting regulation known as *Regulation S-X* and entitled *Form and Content of Financial Statements.* Between 1937 and 1982, the SEC issued 307 *Accounting Series Releases (ASRs)* addressing various accounting and auditing issues. In 1982, the series was replaced by two series—*Financial Reporting Releases* and *Accounting and Auditing Enforcement Releases. Financial Reporting Releases* present the SEC's current views on financial reporting and auditing issues. *Accounting and Auditing Enforcement Releases* summarize enforcement activities against auditors when the SEC has found deficiencies in the auditors' work. In addition, the standards of the PCAOB must be adopted through the SEC's regulation process.

## The International Federation of Accountants

The **International Federation of Accountants (IFAC)** is the global organization of accounting professional bodies. Members of IFAC are not individuals. Instead, membership consists of approximately 160 professional accountancy bodies (e.g., the AICPA) from approximately 125 countries and jurisdictions. IFAC was established to help foster a coordinated worldwide accounting profession with harmonized standards. Boards established by IFAC have the following responsibilities:

- The **International Auditing and Assurance Standards Board (IAASB)** establishes *International Standards on Auditing (ISAs), International Standards on Quality Control (ISQC),* and standards for other assurance and related services.
- The **International Ethics Standards Board for Accountants (IESBA)** establishes ethical standards and guidance for professional accountants.
- The **International Accounting Education Standards Board (IAESB)** develops guidance to improve accounting education around the world.

The pronouncements of these boards do not override the national auditing standards of its members. Rather they are meant to foster the development of consistent worldwide professional standards. Members from countries that do not have their own standards are encouraged to adopt IFAC standards. Members from countries that already have standards are encouraged to compare them to IAASB standards and seek to eliminate any material inconsistencies. The AICPA's Auditing Standards Board has worked to harmonize its standards with those of the IAASB such that there are only minor differences between them. These differences are summarized in Chapter 2.

## Other Types of Professional Services

In addition to auditing and other assurance services, public accounting firms offer other types of services to their clients, including tax services, consulting services, accounting and review services, fraud investigation services, and personal financial planning. Public accounting firms tend to specialize in particular types of services depending on their size and the expertise of their personnel.

### Tax Services

Tax services that are performed by public accounting firms fall into two broad categories: compliance work and tax planning. Compliance work involves preparing the federal, state, and local tax returns of corporations, partnerships, individuals, and estates and trusts. Tax planning, on the other hand, involves consulting with clients on how to structure their business affairs to legally minimize the amount and postpone the payment of their taxes.

### Consulting Services

Public accounting firms offer a variety of services that are designed to improve the effectiveness and efficiency of their clients' operations. Initially, these services developed as a natural extension of the audit and primarily involved consulting on accounting and internal control systems. In recent years, public accounting firms have expanded by offering a host of services that tend to be more operational in nature. Examples are developing strategic planning models and management information systems and performing executive search services.

Performance of consulting services for audit clients has been a significant issue with respect to the independence of auditors, so much so that a number of restrictions have been placed on the types and extent of consulting services that may be performed for public company audit clients. This issue will be discussed in more detail in Chapter 3.

### Accounting and Review Services

Audits are expensive. For a small business, the cost of an audit will run into the thousands of dollars; for large corporations, the cost may exceed a million dollars. The most common reason for a small business to incur the cost of an audit is the influence exerted by a bank that insists upon audited financial statements as a condition for granting a bank loan. If a small business is not in need of a significant amount of bank credit, the cost of an audit may exceed its benefits.

An alternative is to retain a public accounting firm to perform other services for nonpublic (nonissuer) companies, such as the compilation or review of financial statements. To compile financial statements means to prepare them; this service is often rendered when the client does not have accounting personnel capable of preparing statements. The public accounting firm issues a compilation report on the financial statements that provides *no assurance* that the statements are presented fairly in accordance with generally accepted accounting principles.

A review of financial statements by a public accounting firm is an attestation service that is substantially less in scope than an audit. It is designed to provide *limited assurance* on the credibility of the statements. A review stresses inquiries by the CPA and the comparison of amounts in the statements to comparable financial and nonfinancial data. These comparisons, which are referred to as analytical procedures, are useful in bringing to light possible misstatements of financial statement amounts. Compilations and reviews are discussed in Chapter 19.

### Litigation Support Services

The level of litigation in the United States has created a fast-growing area of practice. CPAs are often used in business litigation cases as expert witnesses to calculate damages or explain complex business and accounting concepts to judges and juries. As a result, many public accounting firms have developed departments that specialize in litigation support services.

### Fraud Investigation Services

Fraud investigation services generally involve engaging professionals to investigate suspected or known fraud. These types of services are also referred to as *forensic accounting services,* but forensic accounting is somewhat broader and includes litigation support services. Because of increased identified incidences of defalcation and theft, fraud investigation has become a significant part of the work performed by many internal audit departments. These types of services are also a practice specialty for many public accounting firms. To demonstrate expertise in the area of fraud investigation, the designation "Certified Fraud Examiner" has been developed by the Association of Certified Fraud Examiners.

### Personal Financial Planning

Public accounting firms also may advise individuals on their personal financial affairs. For example, a public accounting firm may review a client's investment portfolio and evaluate whether the nature of the investments meets the client's financial objectives. The public accounting firm might also advise the client on the nature and amount of insurance coverage that is appropriate. The AICPA offers the designation "Personal Financial Specialist" to CPAs who satisfy certain experience requirements and pass a one-day examination on personal financial planning topics, such as income tax planning, risk management planning, investment planning, retirement planning, and estate planning.

## Organization of the Public Accounting Profession

**LO8**

Describe how public accounting firms are typically organized and the responsibilities of auditors at the various levels in the organization.

Many public accounting firms are organized as either sole practitioners or partnerships. A CPA may also practice as a member of a professional corporation or, in many states, as a *limited liability partnership (LLP)* or a *limited liability company (LLC)*.

*Professional corporations* differ from traditional corporations in a number of respects. For example, all shareholders and directors of a professional corporation must be engaged in the practice of public accounting. In addition, shareholders and directors of the professional corporation may be held personally liable for the corporation's actions, although they may choose to carry liability insurance to cover damages caused by negligent actions. *Limited liability partnerships (companies)* are similar to professional corporations, but they provide for the protection of the personal assets of any shareholders or partners not directly involved in providing services on engagements resulting in litigation.

In comparison with a sole proprietorship, partnerships and professional corporations with multiple owners have several advantages. When two or more CPAs join forces, the opportunity for specialization is increased, and the scope of services offered to clients may be expanded. Also, qualified members of the staff may be rewarded by admission to the partnership or issuance of stock. Providing an opportunity to become part owner of the business is an important factor in the public accounting firm's ability to attract and retain competent personnel.

Public accounting firms range in size from one person to over 100,000 on the professional staff. In terms of size, public accounting firms are often grouped into the following four categories: local firms, regional firms, national firms, and Big 4 firms.

### Local Firms

Local firms typically have one or two offices, include only one CPA or a few CPAs as partners, and serve clients in a single city or area. These firms often emphasize income tax, consulting, and accounting services. Auditing is usually only a small part of the practice and tends to involve small business concerns that find a need for audited financial statements to support applications for bank loans.

### Regional Firms

Many local firms have become regional firms by opening additional offices in neighboring cities or states and increasing the number of professional staff. Merging with other local firms is often a route to regional status. This growth is often accompanied by an increase in the amount of auditing as compared to other services.

### National Firms

Public accounting firms with offices in most major cities in the United States are called national firms. These firms may operate internationally as well, either with their own offices or through affiliations with firms in other countries.

### Big 4 Firms

Often in the news are the large international public accounting firms. Until 1989, there were eight of these firms. However, mergers and the dissolution of (Arthur) Andersen LLP have reduced them to the Big 4. Since only a very large public accounting firm has sufficient staff and resources to audit a giant corporation, these firms audit nearly all of the largest American corporations. Although these firms offer a wide range of professional services, auditing represents a large, if not the largest, share of their work. Annual revenue of an international firm is in the billions of dollars. In alphabetical order, the four firms are Deloitte & Touche LLP, Ernst & Young LLP, KPMG LLP, and PricewaterhouseCoopers LLP.

### Alternative Practice Structure Firms

Beginning in the late 1990s, a number of publicly traded companies—including American Express, CBIZ, Inc., and H&R Block—began purchasing public accounting firms. These companies are often referred to as "consolidators" because they purchase public accounting firms in various cities and consolidate them into the overall corporation. In essence, the approach is to purchase the nonattest portion of the practice, hire public accounting firm partners and other personnel as employees of the publicly traded company, and perform those services. The attest and auditing partners retain that status in the public accounting firm, but ordinarily they are also employees of the publicly traded company. The public accounting firm then provides attestation services, using partners and other staff members leased from the public company. This trend is having a significant effect on the public accounting profession, as we will indicate in several places throughout the text. For example, ethical complications of these structures are discussed in Chapter 3.

## Industry Specialization

Public accounting firms have long recognized the value of industry specialization. When they possess a detailed knowledge and understanding of a client's industry, the auditors can be more effective at collecting and evaluating audit evidence. Also, they are in a better position to make valuable suggestions that will improve the client's operations and to provide the client consulting services.

A number of large public accounting firms have organized their firms along industry lines. Each industry group is made up of personnel involved in providing audit, tax, and consulting services for a specialized industry. The firms believe that such an organizational structure leads to the performance of higher-quality, integrated services to firms in specialized industries.

## Responsibilities of the Professional Staff

Human resources—the competence, judgment, and integrity of personnel—represent the greatest asset of any public accounting firm. The professional staff of a typical public accounting firm includes partners, managers, senior accountants, and staff assistants.

### Partners

The lead partner on an engagement is responsible for assuring that the audit is performed in accordance with applicable professional standards. Accordingly, this individual is ultimately responsible for adequate planning, supervision, and execution of the audit. Partners are also responsible for maintaining primary contacts with clients. These contacts include discussing with clients the objectives and scope of the audit work, resolving controversies that may arise as to how items are to be presented in the financial statements, and attending the client's stockholders' meetings to answer any questions regarding the financial statements or the auditors' report. Other responsibilities of the partner include recruiting new staff members, general supervision of the professional staff, reviewing audit working papers, and signing the audit reports.

Specialization by each partner in a different area of the firm's practice is often advantageous. One partner, for example, may have expertise in tax matters and head the firm's tax department; another may specialize in SEC registrations; and a third may devote full time to design and installation of computer information systems.

The partnership level in a public accounting firm is comparable to that of top management in an industrial organization. Executives at this level are concerned with the long-run well-being of the organization and of the community it serves. They should and do contribute important amounts of time to civic, professional, and educational activities in the community. Participation in the state society of certified public accountants and in the AICPA is, of course, important if the partners are to do their share in building the profession. Contribution of their specialized skills and professional judgment to leadership of civic organizations is equally important to developing the economic and social environment in which business and professional accomplishment is possible.

An important aspect of partners' active participation in various business and civic organizations is the prestige and recognition that may come to their firms. Many clients select a particular public accounting firm because they have come to know and respect one of the firm's partners. Thus, partners who are widely known and highly regarded within the community may be a significant factor in attracting business to the firm.

## Managers

In large public accounting firms, managers or supervisors perform many of the duties that would be discharged by partners in smaller firms. A manager may be responsible for supervising two or more concurrent audit engagements. This supervisory work includes reviewing the audit working papers and discussing with the audit staff and with the client any accounting or auditing problems that may arise during the engagement. The manager is responsible for determining the audit procedures applicable to specific audits and for maintaining uniform standards of fieldwork. Often, managers have the administrative duties of compiling and collecting the firm's billings to clients.

Familiarity with tax laws, as well as a broad and current knowledge of accounting theory and practice, is an essential qualification for a successful manager. Like the partner, the audit manager may specialize in specific industries or other areas of the firm's practice.

## Senior Auditors

The responsibility assumed by the senior "in-charge" auditor varies based on the size of the engagement. On a smaller engagement, the senior auditor may assume responsibility for planning and conducting the audit and drafting the audit report, subject to review and approval by the manager and partner. On larger engagements a senior auditor may assume responsibility for supervising some aspect of the audit, such as the audit of accounts receivable. In conducting the audit, the senior will delegate most audit tasks to assistants based on an appraisal of each assistant's ability to perform particular phases of the work. A well-qualified university graduate with a formal education in accounting may progress from staff assistant to senior auditor within two or three years, or even less.

One of the major responsibilities of the senior is on-the-job staff training. In assigning work to staff assistants, the senior should make clear the end objectives of the particular audit operation. By assigning assistants a wide variety of audit tasks and by providing constructive criticism of the assistants' work, the senior should try to make each audit a significant learning experience for the staff assistants.

Reviewing working papers shortly after they are completed is another duty of the senior in charge of an audit. This enables the senior to control the progress of the work and to ascertain that each phase of the engagement is adequately covered. At the conclusion of the fieldwork, the senior will make a final review, including tracing items from individual working papers to the financial statements.

The senior will also maintain a continuous record of the hours devoted by all members of the staff to the various phases of the audit. In addition to maintaining uniform professional standards of fieldwork, the senior is responsible for preventing the accumulation of excessive staff hours on inconsequential matters and for completing the entire engagement within the budgeted time, if possible.

### Staff Assistants

The first position of a college graduate entering the public accounting profession is that of staff assistant. Staff assistants usually encounter a variety of assignments that fully utilize their capacity for analysis and growth. Of course, some routine work must be done in every audit engagement, but college graduates with thorough training in accounting need have little fear of being assigned for long to extensive routine procedures when they enter the field of public accounting. Most firms are anxious to increase the assigned responsibility to younger staff members as rapidly as they are able to assume it. Ordinarily, the demand for accounting services is so high as to create a situation in which every incentive exists for the rapid development of promising assistants.

The audit staff members of all public accounting firms attend training programs that are either developed "in house" or sponsored by professional organizations. One of the most attractive features of the public accounting profession is the richness and variety of experience acquired even by the beginning staff member. Because of the high quality of the experience gained by certified public accountants as they move from one audit engagement to another, many business concerns select individuals from the public accounting field to fill such executive positions as controller or treasurer.

## Professional Development for Public Accounting Firm Personnel

A major challenge in public accounting is keeping abreast of current developments within the profession. New business practices; new pronouncements by the Auditing Standards Board, the PCAOB, the SEC, the FASB, and the GASB; and changes in the tax laws are only a few of the factors that require members of the profession continually to update their technical knowledge.

A public accounting firm must make certain that the professional staff remains continuously up-to-date on technical issues. To assist in this updating process, most large public accounting firms maintain a separate professional development section.

Professional development sections offer a wide range of seminars and educational programs to personnel of the firm. The curriculum of each program is especially designed to suit the needs and responsibilities of participants. Partners may attend programs focusing on the firm's policies on audit quality control or current developments in a specialized industry; on the other hand, programs designed for staff assistants may cover audit procedures or use of the firm's audit software. In addition to offering educational programs, the professional development section usually publishes a monthly newsletter or journal for distribution to personnel of the public accounting firm and other interested persons.

Many public accounting firms that are too small to maintain their own professional development departments have banded together into associations of public accounting firms. These associations organize educational programs, distribute information on technical issues, and engage in other professional activities that are designed to meet the needs of their members. Since the costs of the association's professional activities are shared by all members, the firms are provided with many of the benefits of having their own professional development department at a fraction of the cost.

## Seasonal Fluctuations in Public Accounting Work

One of the traditional disadvantages of the public accounting profession has been the concentration of work during the "busy season" from December through April, followed by a period of slack demand during the summer months. This seasonal trend is caused by the fact that many companies keep their records on a calendar-year basis and require auditing services immediately after the December 31 closing of the accounts. Another important factor is the spring deadline for filing of federal income tax returns.

Auditors often work a considerable number of hours of overtime during the busy season. Some public accounting firms pay their staff for overtime hours. Other firms allow their staff to accumulate the overtime in an "overtime bank" and to "withdraw" these hours in the form of additional vacation time during the less busy times of the year.

## Relationships with Clients

The wide-ranging scope of public accountants' activities today demands that CPAs be interested in and well informed on economic trends, political developments, and other topics that play a significant part in business and social contacts. Although an in-depth knowledge of accounting is the most important qualification of the CPA, an ability to meet people easily and to gain their confidence and goodwill may be no less important in achieving success in the profession of public accounting. The ability to work effectively with clients will be enhanced by a sincere interest in their problems and by a relaxed and cordial manner.

The question of the auditor's independence inevitably arises in considering the advisability of social activities with clients. The partner in today's public accounting firm may play golf or tennis with the executives of client companies and other business associates. These relationships actually may make it easier to resolve differences of opinions that arise during an audit, if management comes to know and respect the partner. This mutual understanding need not prevent the CPA from standing firm on matters of accounting principle. Alternatively, such relationships have the potential for impairing auditor independence. Auditor response to differences of opinions when such relationships exist is perhaps the "moment of truth" for the practitioners of a profession.

The CPA must always remember that the concept of independence embodies an *appearance* of independence. This appearance of independence may be impaired if an auditor becomes excessively involved in social activities with clients. For example, if a CPA frequently attends lavish parties held by a client or dates an officer or employee of a client corporation, the question might be raised as to whether the CPA will appear independent to outsiders. This dilemma is but one illustration of the continual need for judgment and perspective on the part of the auditor.

## Chapter Summary

This chapter explored the nature of assurance services, the attest function, independent audits, and the auditing profession. To summarize:

1. CPAs provide a wide array of information enhancement services referred to as assurance services. Currently, the primary type of assurance service provided by CPAs involves attestation. When performing attestation services, CPAs enhance the reliability of information by issuing an examination, review, or agreed-upon procedures report on subject matter or an assertion that is the responsibility of another party. In the case of financial statement audits, the report most frequently includes an opinion about whether management's financial statements conform to generally accepted accounting principles.

2. Since audits involve examinations of financial information by independent experts, they increase the credibility of the information contained in the statements. Decision makers both within and outside the organization can use audited financial information with confidence that it is not likely to be materially misstated. Audits reduce information risk and, therefore, they reduce the overall risk of making various types of economic decisions.

3. The nature and emphasis of auditing has changed over the years. Auditing began with the objective of detecting fraud by examination of all, or most, business transactions. Today the objective of an audit is to attest to the fairness of the financial statements. Because of the large size of business organizations, audits necessarily

involve the use of sampling techniques based on the auditors' consideration of the organization's controls. CPAs also are being asked to assume more responsibility for attesting to compliance with laws and regulations and the effectiveness of controls.

4. Due to a number of very visible instances of fraudulent financial reporting, Congress passed the Sarbanes-Oxley Act of 2002. This act significantly changed the nature of audits of public (issuer) companies, as well as the regulation of auditors that perform such audits. The act created the Public Company Accounting Oversight Board (PCAOB) to regulate audits and auditors of public companies.

5. The auditing profession is much broader than auditors involved in public accounting; it also includes internal auditors and various governmental auditors, such as auditors of the Government Accountability Office and the Internal Revenue Service.

6. Various professional and regulatory organizations have a significant influence on the auditing profession, including the American Institute of Certified Public Accountants, the Financial Accounting Standards Board, the Governmental Accounting Standards Board, the Federal Accounting Standards Advisory Board, the Public Company Accounting Oversight Board, the Securities and Exchange Commission, and the International Federation of Accountants.

7. In addition to performing attestation engagements, public accounting firms offer tax services, consulting services, and accounting and review services. Public accounting firms range in size from sole practitioners to the large international firms referred to as the Big 4 firms. The professional staff of a typical medium-to-large public accounting firm includes partners, managers, senior accountants, and staff assistants.

## Key Terms Introduced or Emphasized in Chapter 1

**Agreed-upon procedures engagement (3)**   An attest engagement in which the CPAs agree to perform procedures for a specified party and issue a report that is restricted to use by that party.

**American Institute of Certified Public Accountants (AICPA) (13)**   The national professional organization of CPAs engaged in promoting high professional standards to ensure that CPAs serve the public interest.

**Applicable financial reporting framework (3)**   The financial reporting framework adopted by management and, where appropriate, those charged with governance in the preparation of the financial statements that is acceptable in view of the nature of the entity and the objectives of the financial statements, or that is required by law or regulation.

**Assertion (2)**   A representation or declaration made by the responsible party, typically management of the entity.

**Assurance services (1)**   Professional services that enhance the quality of information, or its context, for decision makers. Many assurance services involve some form of attestation.

**Attest engagement (1)**   An engagement in which the CPAs issue an examination, a review, or an agreed-upon procedures report on subject matter or an assertion about subject matter that is the responsibility of another party (e.g., management).

**Audit of financial statements (10)**   An examination designed to provide an opinion, the CPA's highest level of assurance that the financial statements follow generally accepted accounting principles, or another acceptable basis of accounting.

**Business risk (of the client) (6)**   The risk assumed by investors or creditors that is associated with the company's survival and profitability.

**Certified public accountant (12)**   A person licensed by the state to practice public accounting as a profession, based on having passed the Uniform CPA Examination and having met certain educational and experience requirements.

**Compliance audit (10)**   An audit to measure the compliance of the organization with some established criteria (e.g., laws and regulations, or internal control policies and procedures).

**CPA examination (15)**   A uniform examination administered by the American Institute of Certified Public Accountants for state boards of accountancy to enable them to issue CPA licenses. The examination covers the topics of accounting and reporting, auditing, business environment, regulation, and professional responsibilities.

**Examination (3)**   An attest engagement designed to provide the highest level of assurance that CPAs provide on an assertion. An examination of financial statements is referred to as an *audit*.

**Financial audit (10)**   An audit of the financial accounting information of an organization or segment of the organization. This may involve a complete set of financial statements or a portion of a statement.

**Financial reporting framework (2)**   A set of criteria used to determine measurement, recognition, presentation, and disclosure of all material items appearing in the financial statements: For example, accounting principles generally accepted in the United States of America, or *International Financial Reporting Standards (IFRS)* issued by the International Accounting Standards Board (IASB).

**Fraud (8)**   Intentional misstatement of financial statements by management (fraudulent financial reporting), or theft of assets by employees (employee fraud). Fraud also is referred to as *irregularities*.

**Generally accepted accounting principles (GAAP) (2)**   Concepts or standards established by such authoritative bodies as the FASB and the GASB and accepted by the accounting profession as essential to proper financial reporting.

**Information risk (6)**   The risk that the information used by investors, creditors, and others to assess business risk is not accurate.

**Integrated audit (11)**   As required by the Sarbanes-Oxley Act and the Public Company Accounting Oversight Board, an audit that includes providing assurance on both the financial statements and internal control over financial reporting. Integrated audits are required of publicly traded companies in the United States.

**International Accounting Education Standards Board (IAESB) (17)**   A committee of the International Federation of Accountants, established to develop guidance to improve the standards of accountancy education around the world. The organization focuses on (1) the essential elements of accreditation, which are education, practical experience, and tests of professional competence, and (2) the nature and extent of continuing professional education needed by accountants.

**International Auditing and Assurance Standards Board (IAASB) (17)**   A committee of the International Federation of Accountants, established to issue standards on auditing and reporting practices to improve the degree of uniformity of auditing practices and related services throughout the world.

**International Ethics Standards Board for Accountants (IESBA) (17)**   A committee of the International Federation of Accountants, established to develop ethical standards and guidance for use by professional accountants. It encourages member bodies to adopt high standards of ethics for their members and promotes good ethical practices globally. The IESBA also fosters international debate on ethical issues faced by accountants.

**International Federation of Accountants (IFAC) (17)**   A worldwide organization of national accounting bodies established to help foster a coordinated worldwide accounting profession with harmonized standards.

**Operational audit (11)**   An analysis of a department or other unit of a business or governmental organization to measure the effectiveness and efficiency of operations.

**Public Company Accounting Oversight Board (PCAOB) (16)**   The five-member board established in 2002 to oversee the audit of public (issuer) companies that are subject to the securities laws. The board has authority to establish or adopt, or both, rules for auditing, quality control, ethics, independence, and other standards relating to the preparation of audit reports.

**Review (3)**   An engagement designed to express limited assurance relating to subject matter or an assertion. As discussed in further detail in Chapter 19, the procedures performed are generally limited to inquiries and analytical procedures.

**Sarbanes-Oxley Act of 2002 (10)**   A set of reforms that toughened penalties for corporate fraud, restricted the kinds of consulting CPAs can perform for audit clients, and created the Public Company Accounting Oversight Board to oversee CPAs and public accounting firms.

**Securities and Exchange Commission (SEC) (16)**   A government agency authorized to regulate companies seeking approval to issue securities for sale to the public.

***Statements on Auditing Standards (SASs) (13)***   A series of statements issued by the Auditing Standards Board of the AICPA. Generally accepted auditing standards are developed and issued in the form of SASs in the context of an audit of financial statements performed by an auditor.

**Suitable criteria (2)**   The standards or benchmarks used to measure and present the subject matter and against which the CPA evaluates the subject matter. Suitable criteria are criteria that are established or developed by groups composed of experts that follow due process procedures, including exposure of the proposed criteria for public comment. Suitable criteria must have each of the following attributes: objectivity, measurability, completeness, and relevance.

## Review Questions

1–1. In late 2001 through 2002, the accounting profession faced a "crisis of credibility." Describe the events that led up to this crisis.

1–2. Define assurance services. What are the two distinct types?

1–3. What is the most common type of attest engagement? What is most frequently being "asserted" by management on this type of engagement?

1–4. What is the principal use and significance of an audit report to a large corporation with securities listed on a stock exchange? To a small family-owned enterprise?

1–5. Describe several business situations that would create a need for a report by an independent public accountant concerning the fairness of a company's financial statements.

1–6. Explain the following statement: One contribution of the independent auditor is to lend *credibility* to financial statements.

1–7. The overall risk of the investment in a business includes both business risk and information risk. Contrast these two types of risk. Which one is most directly affected by the auditors?

1–8. Contrast the objectives of auditing at the beginning of this century with the objectives of auditing today.

1–9. What does an operational audit attempt to measure? Does an operational audit involve more or fewer subjective judgments than a compliance audit or an audit of financial statements? Explain. To whom is the report usually directed after completion of an operational audit?

1–10. Distinguish between a compliance audit and an operational audit.

1–11. Is an *independent status* possible or desirable for internal auditors as compared with the independence of a public accounting firm? Explain.

1–12. Spacecraft, Inc., is a large corporation that is audited regularly by a public accounting firm but also maintains an internal auditing staff. Explain briefly how the relationship of the public accounting firm to Spacecraft differs from the relationship of the internal auditing staff to Spacecraft.

1–13. Describe briefly the function of the GAO.

1–14. List two of the important contributions to auditing literature by the AICPA.

1–15. What is meant by a *peer review* in public accounting?

1–16. How does the role of the SEC differ from that of the AICPA?

1–17. Apart from auditing, what other professional services are offered by public accounting firms?

1–18. What are the advantages of organizing a public accounting firm as a partnership rather than a sole proprietorship?

1–19. How does a professional corporation differ from a traditional corporation?

1–20. Public accounting firms are sometimes grouped into categories of local firms, regional firms, national firms, and international firms. Explain briefly the characteristics of each. Include in your answer the types of services stressed in each group.

1–21. Describe the various levels or positions of accounting personnel in a large public accounting firm.

1–22. List three of the more important responsibilities of a partner in a public accounting firm.

1–23. What is the International Auditing and Assurance Standards Board? What is the purpose of its pronouncements? Do these pronouncements establish standards that override a member nation's auditing standards?

## Questions Requiring Analysis

**LO 5, 7**

1–24. As a result of a number of events that caused Congress to doubt the ability of the accounting profession to regulate itself, a number of reforms were made to the accounting profession's system of self-regulation.

*Required:*

a. Provide a brief overview of the legislation that altered the self-regulation process of the accounting profession.

b. Explain the regulation process for accounting firms that audit public companies.

c. Explain the regulation process for accounting firms that do not audit public companies.

**LO 4**

1–25. A corporation is contemplating issuing debenture bonds to a group of investors.

*Required:*

a. Explain how independent audits of the corporation's financial statements facilitate this transaction.

b. Describe the likely effects on the transaction if the corporation decides not to obtain independent audits of its financial statements.

**LO 5, 7**

1–26. The Sarbanes-Oxley Act of 2002 created the Public Company Accounting Oversight Board. Explain the major responsibilities of this board.

**LO 4**    1–27.   The self-interest of the provider of financial information (whether an individual or a business entity) often runs directly counter to the interests of the user of the information.

*Required:*      a.   Give an example of such opposing interests.

                  b.   What may be done to compensate for the possible bias existing because of the self-interest of the individual or business entity providing the financial information?

# Objective Questions

**All applicable questions are available with McGraw-Hill's *Connect*<sup>TM</sup> *Accounting.***

**LO 1, 2**    1–28.   **Multiple Choice Questions**

Select the best answer for each of the following items and give reasons for your choice.

a.   Which of the following best describes the relationship between assurance services and attest services?

    (1)   While attest services involve financial data, assurance services involve nonfinancial data.

    (2)   While attest services require objectivity, assurance services do not require objectivity.

    (3)   Both attest and assurance services require independence.

    (4)   Attest and assurance services are different terms referring to the same types of services.

**LO 3**      b.   Which of the following has primary responsibility for the fairness of the representations made in financial statements?

    (1)   Client's management.

    (2)   Independent auditor.

    (3)   Audit committee.

    (4)   AICPA.

**LO 3**      c.   The most important benefit of having an annual audit by a public accounting firm is to:

    (1)   Provide assurance to investors and other outsiders that the financial statements are reliable.

    (2)   Enable officers and directors to avoid personal responsibility for any misstatements in the financial statements.

    (3)   Meet the requirements of government agencies.

    (4)   Provide assurance that illegal acts, if any exist, will be brought to light.

**LO 7**      d.   The Sarbanes-Oxley Act created the Public Company Accounting Oversight Board a (PCAOB). Which of the following is *not* one of the responsibilities of that board?

    (1)   Establish independence standards for auditors of public companies.

    (2)   Review financial reports filed with the SEC.

    (3)   Establish auditing standards for audits of public companies.

    (4)   Sanction registered audit firms.

**LO 7**      e.   Which of these organizations has the responsibility to perform inspections of auditors of public companies?

    (1)   American Institute of Certified Public Accountants.

    (2)   Securities and Exchange Commission.

    (3)   Financial Accounting Standards Board.

    (4)   Public Company Accounting Oversight Board.

**LO 6**      f.   Governmental auditing, in addition to including audits of financial statements, often includes audits of efficiency, effectiveness, and:

    (1)   Adequacy.

    (2)   Evaluation.

    (3)   Accuracy.

    (4)   Compliance.

**LO 6**      g.   In general, internal auditors' independence will be greatest when they report directly to the:

    (1)   Financial vice president.

    (2)   Corporate controller.

    (3)   Audit committee of the board of directors.

    (4)   Chief executive officer.

**LO 5**      h.   Which of the following did *not* precipitate the passage of the Sarbanes-Oxley Act of 2002 to regulate public accounting firms:

    (1)   Disclosures related to accounting irregularities at Enron and WorldCom.

    (2)   Restatements of financial statements by a number of public companies.

(3) Conviction of the accounting firm of Arthur Andersen LLP.

(4) Ethical scandals at the AICPA.

**LO 6**

*i.* Which of the following organizations establishes accounting standards for U.S. government agencies?

(1) The Financial Accounting Standards Board.

(2) The Governmental Accounting Standards Board.

(3) The Federal Accounting Standards Advisory Board.

(4) The Public Company Accounting Oversight Board.

**LO 6**

*j.* Which of the following is correct about forensic audits?

(1) All audit engagements are forensic in nature.

(2) Forensic audits are performed by law firms; they are not performed by CPA firms.

(3) Forensic audits are equivalent to compliance audits.

(4) Forensic audits are usually performed in situations in which fraud has been found or is suspected.

**LO 3**

*k.* What best describes the purpose of the auditors' consideration of internal control in a financial statement audit for a nonpublic company?

(1) To determine the nature, timing, and extent of audit testing.

(2) To make recommendations to the client regarding improvements in internal control.

(3) To train new auditors on accounting and control systems.

(4) To identify opportunities for fraud within the client's operations.

**LO 6**

*l.* Which of the following is an example of a compliance audit?

(1) An audit of financial statements.

(2) An audit of a company's policies and procedures for adhering to environmental laws and regulations.

(3) An audit of a company's internal control over financial reporting.

(4) An audit of the efficiency and effectiveness of a company's legal department.

(AICPA, adapted)

**LO 3**    **1–29.** The role of the auditor in the American economy has changed over the years in response to changes in our economic and political institutions. Consequently, the nature of an audit today is quite different from that of an audit performed in the year 1900. Classify the following phrases into two groups: (1) phrases more applicable to an audit performed in 1900 and (2) phrases more applicable to an audit performed today.

*a.* Complete review of all transactions.

*b.* Assessment of internal control.

*c.* Auditors' attention concentrated on balance sheet.

*d.* Emphasis upon use of sampling techniques.

*e.* Determination of fairness of financial statements.

*f.* Audit procedures to prevent or detect fraud on the part of all employees and managers.

*g.* Registration statement.

*h.* Fairness of reported earnings per share.

*i.* Influence of stock exchanges and the investing public upon use of independent auditors.

*j.* Concern about fraudulent financial reporting.

*k.* Generally accepted auditing standards.

*l.* Bankers and short-term creditors as principal users of audit reports.

*m.* Pressure for more disclosure.

*n.* Auditing for compliance with laws and regulations.

**LO 7**    **1–30.** Auditors must be familiar with available professional literature from a variety of sources. Listed below are 10 publications in the fields of auditing and accounting.

1. *Statements on Auditing Standards (SASs).*

2. *The Journal of Accountancy.*

3. *Regulation S-X, Form and Content of Financial Statements.*

4. *Statements on Standards for Accounting and Review Services (SSARSs).*

5. *Financial Reporting Releases (FRRs).*

6. *Accounting and Reporting Standards for Corporate Financial Statements.*

7. *Accounting and Reporting Standards for Governmental Entities.*

8. *Industry Audit and Accounting Guides.*

9. *Auditing Practice Releases.*

10. *The Tax Advisor.*

The list of organizations shown below includes the sponsors or publishers of the preceding 10 publications.

*a.* Accounting Principles Board (APB).

*b.* Securities and Exchange Commission (SEC).

*c.* American Institute of Certified Public Accountants (AICPA).

*d.* Financial Accounting Standards Board (FASB).

*e.* Internal Revenue Service (IRS).

*f.* Government Accountability Office (GAO).

*g.* Governmental Accounting Standards Board (GASB).

*Required:*

Identify the sponsoring organization for each of the 10 publications. (Some of the organizations may not have a publication in this list.) Organize your answer in a two-column format. In the left-hand column, list the number and name of each publication in the order shown above. In the right-hand column, list the identifying letter and the abbreviation of the sponsoring organization. For example, on line 1, list (1) *Statements on Auditing Standards* in the left column and (*c*) AICPA in the right column.

**LO 3, 7**  1–31. Each auditing term (or organizational name) in Column 1 below bears a close relationship to a term in Column 2.

| Column 1 | Column 2 |
|---|---|
| 1. Quality control | a. Regulation of auditors of public companies |
| 2. Operational audit | b. Opinion |
| 3. Internal control | c. Material information |
| 4. Government Accountability Office | d. Credibility |
| 5. Disclosure | e. Peer review |
| 6. Critical characteristic that must be maintained by the accounting profession | f. Registration statement |
| 7. Public Company Accounting Oversight Board | g. Accounting service |
| 8. Securities and Exchange Commission | h. Measurement of effectiveness and efficiency of a unit of an organization |
| 9. Audited financial statements | i. Basis for sampling and testing |
| 10. Compilation of financial statements | j. Auditing staff reporting to Congress |

*Required:*

Identify the most closely related terms in Columns 1 and 2. Organize your answer in a two-column format by copying the numbers and terms in Column 1 as given. Then, rearrange the sequence of terms in Column 2 so that each line of your schedule will contain two closely related terms.

**LO 6**  1–32. CPAs become involved in a variety of types of engagements. For each of the following statements, indicate whether it relates to an examination (E), review (R), or agreed-upon procedures (A) engagement. If the statement does not relate to examinations, reviews, or agreed-upon procedures, reply N.

| Statement | Type of Engagement |
|---|---|
| *a.* When financial statements are involved, this is referred to as an audit. | |
| *b.* The term "We are not aware of any material modifications that should be made" is often included in the report. | |
| *c.* The report issued provides a summary of procedures followed and findings. | |
| *d.* The report issued provides "reasonable assurance." | |
| *e.* The procedures involved are generally limited to inquiry and analytical procedures. | |
| *f.* The report issued provides "absolute assurance." | |
| *g.* The report issued provides "limited assurance." | |
| *h.* The procedures followed are agreed upon with the specified user or users. | |
| *i.* This type of engagement provides more assurance than a review. | |
| *j.* The CPA need not be independent to perform this service. | |

**LO 1, 2, 6**   1–33.   Match the following definitions (or partial definitions) of the various types of services to the appropriate service. Each service may be used once or not at all.

| Definition (or Partial Definition) | Service |
|---|---|
| *a.* An attest engagement in which the CPAs agree to perform procedures for a specified party and issue a report that is restricted to use by that party. | 1. Agreed-upon procedures engagement |
| *b.* An engagement designed to express limited assurance relating to subject matter or an assertion. | 2. Assurance services |
| *c.* An engagement in which the CPAs issue an examination, a review, or an agreed-upon procedures report on subject matter or an assertion about subject matter that is the responsibility of another party (e.g., management). | 3. Attest engagement<br>4. Audit of financial statements<br>5. Compliance audit |
| *d.* An examination designed to provide an opinion that is the CPA's highest level of assurance that the financial statements follow generally accepted accounting principles, or another acceptable basis of accounting. | 6. Examination<br>7. Integrated audit<br>8. Operational audit<br>9. Review |
| *e.* As required by the Sarbanes-Oxley Act and the Public Company Accounting Oversight Board, an audit that includes providing assurance on both the financial statements and internal control over financial reporting. | |
| *f.* Professional services that enhance the quality of information, or its context, for decision makers. | |
| *g.* An attest engagement designed to provide the highest level of assurance that CPAs provide on an assertion. | |

**LO Various**   1–34.   Match the following definitions (or partial definitions) of the various types of services to the appropriate term. Each term may be used once or not at all.

| Definition (or Partial Definition) | Service |
|---|---|
| *a.* A government agency authorized to regulate companies seeking approval to issue securities for sale to the public. | 1. American Institute of Certified Public Accountants |
| *b.* A representation or declaration made by the responsible party, typically management of the entity. | 2. Assertion |
| *c.* A series of statements issued by the Auditing Standards Board of the AICPA. Generally accepted auditing standards are developed and issued in the form of these statements. | 3. Financial Accounting Standards Board<br>4. Financial reporting framework |
| *d.* A set of criteria used to determine measurement, recognition, presentation, and disclosure of all material items appearing in the financial statements. | 5. Integrated audit<br>6. Public Company Accounting Oversight Board |
| *e.* A set of reforms that toughened penalties for corporate fraud, restricted the kinds of consulting CPAs can perform for audit clients, and created the Public Company Accounting Oversight Board to oversee CPAs and public accounting firms. | 7. Sarbanes-Oxley Act of 2002<br>8. Securities and Exchange Commission |
| *f.* The five-member board established in 2002 to oversee the audit of public (issuer) companies that are subject to the securities laws. The board has authority to establish or adopt (or both) rules for auditing, quality control, ethics, independence, and other standards relating to the preparation of audit reports. | 9. *Statements on Auditing Standards*<br>10. Subject matter<br>11. Suitable criteria |
| *g.* The national professional organization of CPAs engaged in promoting high professional standards to ensure that CPAs serve the public interest. | |
| *h.* The standards or benchmarks used to measure and present the subject matter and against which the CPA evaluates the subject matter. They are criteria that are established or developed by groups composed of experts that follow due process procedures, including exposure of the proposed criteria for public comment. | |

**LO 3, 6**    1–35.    For the purposes of this problem, assume the existence of five types of auditors: CPA, GAO, IRS, bank examiner, and internal auditor. Also assume that the work of these various auditors can be grouped into five classifications: audits of financial statements, compliance audits, operational audits, accounting services, and consulting services.

For each of the following topics, you are to state the type of auditor most probably involved. Also identify the topic with one of the above classes of work.

You should organize your answer in a three-column format as follows: Column 1, the number of the topic; Column 2, the type of auditor involved; and Column 3, the class of work.

1. Financial statements of a small business to be submitted to a bank in support of a loan application.

2. Financial statements of a large bank listed on the New York Stock Exchange to be distributed to stockholders.

3. Review of the management directive stating the goals and responsibilities of a corporation's mail-handling department.

4. Review of costs and accomplishments of a military research program carried on within the air force to determine whether the program was cost effective.

5. Examination on a surprise basis of Midtown State Bank. Emphasis placed on verification of cash, marketable securities, and loans receivable and on consistent observation of the banking code.

6. Analysis of the accounting system of a small business with the objective of making recommendations concerning installation of a computer-based system.

7. Determination of fairness of financial statements for public distribution by a corporation that has a professional-level internal auditing staff.

8. Review of the activities of the receiving department of a large manufacturing company, with special attention to efficiency of materials inspection and promptness of reports issued.

9. Review of the tax return of the corporate president to determine whether charitable contributions are adequately substantiated.

10. Review of daily attendance during spring term at Blue Ridge Consolidated School District to ascertain whether payments received from the state were substantiated by pupil-day data and whether disbursements by the district were within authorized limits.

11. Review of transactions of a government agency to determine whether disbursements under the Payment-In-Kind program of the U.S. Department of Agriculture followed the intent of Congress.

12. Compilation of quarterly financial statements for a small business that does not have any accounting personnel capable of preparing financial statements.

## Problems

**All applicable problems are available with McGraw-Hill's *Connect*™ *Accounting*.** ▓ **connect** |ACCOUNTING

**LO 3, 4**    1–36.    Feller, the sole owner of a small hardware business, has been told that the business should have its financial statements audited by an independent CPA. Feller, having some bookkeeping experience, has personally prepared the company's financial statements and does not understand why such statements should be audited by a CPA. Feller discussed the matter with Farber, a CPA, and asked Farber to explain why an audit is considered important.

*Required:*    *a.* Describe the objectives of an independent audit.

*b.* Identify five ways in which an independent audit may be beneficial to Feller.

**LO 3**    1–37.    In a discussion between Peters and Ferrel, two auditing students, Peters made the following statement: "A CPA is a professional person who is licensed by the state for the purpose of providing an independent expert opinion on the fairness of financial statements. To maintain an attitude of mental independence and objectivity in all phases of audit work, it is advisable that the CPA not fraternize with client personnel. The CPA should be courteous but reserved and dignified at all times. Indulging in social contacts with clients outside business hours will make it more difficult to be firm and objective if the CPA finds evidence of fraud or of unsound accounting practices."

Ferrel replied as follows: "You are 50 years behind the times, Peters. An auditor and a client are both human beings. The auditor needs the cooperation of the client to do a good job; you're much more likely to get cooperation if you're relaxed and friendly rather than being cold and impersonal. Having a few beers or going to a football game with a client won't keep the CPA from being independent. It will make the working relationship a lot more comfortable, and will probably cause the client to recommend the CPA to other business people who need auditing services. In other words, the approach you're recommending should be called 'How to Avoid Friends and Alienate Clients.' I will admit, though, that with so many women entering public accounting and other women holding executive positions in business, a few complications may arise when auditor–client relations get pretty relaxed."

Evaluate the opposing views expressed by Peters and Ferrel.

## In-Class Team Case

**LO 6, 8**

*Required:*

1–38.   Will Williams, a college senior, has begun the interviewing process. He has discovered a great variety of organizations in search of "accounting majors." He finds that various public accounting firms, corporations, the GAO, and the IRS are all interviewing candidates at his school.

Will has come to you for advice. He has suggested that although he has had only one class session of auditing, he already realizes that it is going to be a great course; however, he also especially enjoyed his tax and accounting systems courses.

Compare and contrast his possibilities with public accounting firms, corporations, the GAO, and the IRS if he wishes to emphasize the following areas of expertise:

a.   Taxation.

b.   Auditing.

c.   Systems design.

For example, first compare and contrast his likely responsibilities with each of the above organizations if he chooses to emphasize taxation.

## Research and Discussion Case

**LO 3, 8**

1–39.   Smith & Co., a local Dallas public accounting firm, is incorporated as a professional corporation, with three shareholders, all CPAs. The shareholders have developed a combination of marketing, software, and professional expertise that has allowed them to perform the accounting service of compiling individuals' personal financial statements in an extremely efficient manner.

The three shareholders are interested in "going national" with their accounting service but lack the capital necessary to expand to other cities. They are currently considering the possibility of obtaining outside capital as a way to expand their business by offering their firm's services to individuals in other markets. They estimate that if they raised $4 million of capital they could open and staff 15 offices within the next 12 months.

In a recent meeting of the three shareholders, the possibility of raising the capital through incorporation as a traditional corporation and thereby selling stock to the public was discussed. The original three shareholders would retain 51 percent of the total stock, which would be traded over the counter. The only work performed through the new corporation would be the compilation of individuals' financial statements.

Subsequently, the shareholders were dismayed to learn that states do not generally allow CPAs to practice as a traditional corporation. Also, those states that do allow "limited liability companies" generally require that shareholders be involved in public accounting. Only by establishing a separate organization not held out as a public accounting firm will the current three shareholders be allowed to follow their expansion plan.

a.   Summarize the arguments for allowing public accounting firms to sell ownership interests to individuals not in public accounting through incorporation as a traditional corporation.

b.   Summarize the arguments in favor of restricting public accounting firm ownership to those involved in public accounting.

c.   Express your personal opinion as to whether ownership of public accounting firms should be restricted to individuals involved in public accounting.

## Suggested References

AICPA, *Professional Standards,* Volume 2, Commerce Clearing House, Section ET 505 (*Code of Professional Conduct,* Rule 505).

Appropriate chapters from other accounting and business textbooks that discuss the advantages of the corporate form of business.

# Professional Standards

Standards are established to guide performance and to provide criteria to measure performance of individuals and organizations. Public accounting standards that we deal with in this text address (1) engagement performance requirements (auditing, attestation, and other engagement standards), (2) CPA firm requirements (**quality control standards**), and (3) CPA individual personal standards that go beyond the requirements of laws and regulations (ethical standards).

Our purpose in this chapter is to make clear the general nature of these standards. This includes discussions of auditing standards, attestation standards, quality control standards and, to a limited extent, ethical standards (discussed in detail in Chapter 3). In our discussion of the auditing standards, we also consider in detail the nature of the independent **auditors' report**—that brief but important document that emerges as the end product of an audit.

## Auditing Standards for Public and Nonpublic Companies

**LO1**

Describe the authority of the two types of auditing standards in effect in the United States—AICPA generally accepted auditing standards and PCAOB standards.

Implementation of the Sarbanes-Oxley Act of 2002 divided audit standards setting responsibility in the United States between (1) the AICPA for nonpublic companies ("non-issuers" of public securities) and (2) the Public Company Accounting Oversight Board for public companies ("issuers" of public securities). Previously, the AICPA's standards, based on their general acceptance, applied to audits of both public and nonpublic companies. The Sarbanes-Oxley Act created the **Public Company Accounting Oversight Board (PCAOB)** and charged that body with the responsibility for adopting and enforcing professional standards for integrated audits of public (issuers) companies. Recall from Chapter 1 that the integrated audit involves auditing both the company's financial statements and its internal control over financial reporting. The PCAOB also is charged with the responsibility of regulating the public company audit practices of registered CPA firms. To complicate matters further, the state boards of accountancy have the authority to regulate CPAs and CPA firms that practice within their state or jurisdiction. Figure 2.1 on page 34 summarizes the regulatory authority of the PCAOB, the AICPA, and the state boards of accountancy.

In the majority of this textbook we will focus on the generally accepted auditing standards established by the AICPA. While the current AICPA standards differ in form from those of the PCAOB, in many areas overall auditor responsibility does not differ significantly. In areas in which there are significant differences, we will discuss them. In addition, Chapter 18 specifically focuses on the integrated audit required for a public company, which involves the audit of the company's financial statements and attestation to its internal control over financial reporting.

## Learning objectives

After studying this chapter, you should be able to:

**LO1** Describe the authority of the two types of auditing standards in effect in the United States—AICPA generally accepted auditing standards and PCAOB standards.

**LO2** Identify the nature and underlying principles of generally accepted auditing standards.

**LO3** Discuss the auditors' responsibility for detecting errors, fraud, and noncompliance with laws and regulations.

**LO4** Explain the key elements of the auditors' standard report.

**LO5** Discuss the other types of reports that are issued by auditors.

**LO6** Describe the attestation standards.

**LO7** Describe the quality control standards and their purposes.

**LO8** Explain the status of international accounting and auditing standards and the content of the international audit report.

**FIGURE 2.1** Regulation of the Profession

| Regulatory Bodies | Authority of Regulatory Bodies | |
|---|---|---|
| | Integrated Audits* for Public Companies | Audits for Nonpublic Companies |
| **Public Company Accounting Oversight Board (PCAOB)** | 1. Establishes standards* for the audits of public companies: <br> • Auditing <br> • Quality control <br> • Independence <br> • Ethical behavior <br> 2. PCAOB standards have authority based on federal legislation. <br> 3. Registers CPA firms to audit public companies and may revoke a firm's registration or bar an individual CPA from participating in public company audits. <br> 4. Performs inspections of the public company audit practices of registered CPA firms. | No standard-setting or regulatory responsibilities regarding CPA services for nonpublic companies. |
| **American Institute of Certified Public Accountants (AICPA)** | No standard-setting or regulatory responsibilities regarding public company audits.** | 1. Establishes standards for: <br> • Auditing <br> • Attestation <br> • Accounting and review <br> • Quality control <br> • Independence <br> • Ethical behavior <br> 2. AICPA standards have authority based on their general acceptance by state boards of accountancy, other legislative organizations, and the courts. <br> 3. Firms may subject themselves to AICPA regulation by voluntarily joining one or both of the AICPA sections: (1) the Private Companies Practice Section (PCPS), or (2) the Center for Public Company Audit Firms. Both sections have voluntary peer review programs. <br> 4. The AICPA Center for Public Company Audit Firms' peer review program covers the nonpublic practices of firms whose public company practices are inspected by the PCAOB. <br> 5. The individual membership requirements of the AICPA require members to practice in a firm that participates in a practice review program. |
| **State Boards of Accountancy** | 1. License CPAs and CPA firms to practice public accountancy in their states or jurisdictions and can revoke the right to practice in those jurisdictions. <br> 2. In their jurisdictions, state boards have regulatory responsibility for both public and nonpublic practice. <br> 3. State boards adopt AICPA and PCAOB standards but may supplement them with their own requirements. | |

*The PCAOB adopted AICPA professional standards issued through April 16, 2003, as its interim standards. In addition, the SEC has oversight responsibility for the PCAOB and all standards must be approved and issued by the SEC.

**Technically, the AICPA general ethics requirements also would apply to **an AICPA member** performing services for public companies.

## AICPA Generally Accepted Auditing Standards

**LO2**

Identify the nature and underlying principles of generally accepted auditing standards.

The AICPA's Auditing Standards Board (ASB) issues auditing standards in the form of *Statements on Auditing Standards (SASs)* following a process that includes deliberations in meetings open to the public, public exposure of proposed SASs, and a formal vote. In 2010–2011, all existing standards were rewritten to enhance their clarity and to converge them to the extent considered desirable with those of the International Auditing and Assurance Standards Board (described later in this chapter).

*Statements on Auditing Standards* are identified under two numbering systems: the original SAS number and an AU number. The SAS numbering system organizes SASs by date of issue, whereas the AU numbering system organizes them by topic. Throughout this textbook, we will make reference to the AICPA Auditing Standards Board's section (e.g., AICPA AU 230). Because the PCAOB standards have different references, we will also provide the PCAOB section (e.g., PCAOB 312).

### Underlying Principles

Until 2011, the generally accepted auditing standards included 10 standards organized as general, field work, and reporting standards around which the various *Statements on Auditing Standards* provided detailed guidance. Thus, in a broad sense, the combination of the 10 standards and the other portions of the codified *Statements on Auditing Standards* were considered **generally accepted auditing standards (GAAS).** The 10 standards have been eliminated from AICPA standards, but not PCAOB standards. Therefore, we present them under our discussion of *PCAOB Auditing Standards.*

The Auditing Standards Board replaced the 10 standards with the set of principles presented in Figure 2.2.

These principles provide a summary of the information discussed throughout the *Professional Standards* and this text. They make clear that the purpose of an audit is to provide an opinion on the financial statements, with an underlying premise that management is responsible both for preparing financial statements in accordance with the **applicable financial reporting framework** and for providing the auditors with access to necessary information. As discussed in Chapter 1, a **financial reporting framework** is a set of criteria used to prepare the financial statements; in the United States the financial reporting framework most frequently used is generally accepted accounting principles.[1] Such a framework is necessary in an audit because the auditors' report provides assurance on whether the financial statements follow that framework.

The auditors have a personal responsibility to have appropriate competence, comply with ethical requirements, and maintain professional skepticism and professional judgment. *Professional skepticism* includes a questioning mind, being alert to conditions that may indicate possible misstatement due to fraud or error, and a critical

---

[1] Financial reporting frameworks may differ on several dimensions. First, a financial reporting framework may be viewed as being either a *fair presentation framework* or a *compliance framework.* A fair presentation framework includes compliance with its requirements and acknowledges explicitly or implicitly that management may need to provide disclosures beyond those specifically required by the framework, or (2) explicitly states that it may be necessary for management to depart from a requirement of the framework to achieve fair presentation in rare circumstances. A compliance framework only requires that the preparer comply with specific disclosure requirements. While the International Auditing Standards provide both types, GAAS only address fair presentation frameworks because they are believed to be the only frameworks used in the United States.

Financial reporting frameworks also differ in that a framework may be either a **general-purpose financial reporting framework** (most frequently, generally accepted accounting principles, but also International Accounting Standards), or a **special-purpose financial reporting framework** (e.g., cash or tax basis financial statements—discussed further in Chapter 19).

**FIGURE 2.2**　Principles Underlying an Audit Conducted in Accordance with Generally Accepted Auditing Standards

| | |
|---|---|
| **Purpose of an Audit** | The purpose of an audit is to provide financial statement users with an opinion by the auditor on whether the financial statements are presented fairly, in all material respects, in accordance with the applicable financial reporting framework. An auditor's opinion enhances the degree of confidence that intended users can place in the financial statements. |
| **Premise of an Audit** | An audit in accordance with generally accepted auditing standards is conducted on the premise that management and, where appropriate, those charged with governance, have responsibility:<br>a. For the preparation and fair presentation of the financial statements in accordance with the applicable financial reporting framework; this includes the design, implementation, and maintenance of internal control relevant to the preparation and fair presentation of financial statements that are free from material misstatement, whether due to fraud or error.<br>b. To provide the auditor with:<br>• All information, such as records, documentation, and other matters that are relevant to the preparation and fair presentation of the financial statements.<br>• Any additional information that the auditor may request from management and, where appropriate, those charged with governance.<br>• Unrestricted access to those within the entity from whom the auditor determines it necessary to obtain audit evidence. |
| **Personal Responsibilities of the Auditor** | Auditors are responsible for having *appropriate competence and capabilities* to perform the audit; complying with relevant ethical requirements; and maintaining professional skepticism and exercising professional judgment throughout the planning and performance of the audit. |
| **Auditor Actions in Performing the Audit** | To *express an opinion,* the auditor obtains reasonable assurance about whether the financial statements as a whole are free from material misstatement, whether due to fraud or error.<br><br>To *obtain reasonable assurance,* which is a high, but not absolute, level of assurance, the auditor:<br>• Plans the work and properly supervises any assistants.<br>• Determines and applies appropriate materiality level or levels throughout the audit.<br>• Identifies and assesses risks of material misstatement, whether due to fraud or error, based on an understanding of the entity and its environment, including the entity's internal control.<br>• Obtains sufficient appropriate audit evidence about whether material misstatements exist, through designing and implementing appropriate responses to the assessed risks.<br><br>The auditor is *unable to obtain absolute assurance* that the financial statements are free from material misstatement because of inherent limitations, which arise from:<br>• The nature of financial reporting;<br>• The nature of audit procedures; and<br>• The need for the audit to be conducted within a reasonable period of time and so as to achieve a balance between benefit and cost. |
| **Reporting Results of an Audit** | Based on an evaluation of the audit evidence obtained, the auditor expresses, in the form of a written report, *an opinion in accordance with the auditor's findings, or states that an opinion cannot be expressed.* The opinion states whether the financial statements are presented fairly, in all material respects, in accordance with the applicable financial reporting framework. |

assessment of audit evidence. It requires that throughout the audit the auditors be alert for:

- Audit evidence that contradicts other audit evidence.
- Information that raises a question about the reliability of documents and responses to inquiries.
- Conditions indicating possible fraud.
- Circumstances suggesting the need for additional audit procedures beyond those ordinarily required.

Finally, auditors' work when performing an audit result in their being able to obtain *reasonable, not absolute, assurance* that the financial statements follow the applicable financial reporting framework. **Reasonable assurance** implies that there is a low level of risk remaining that the auditors express an opinion that the financial statements are properly stated when they are not. Obtaining absolute assurance is not possible due to (1) the nature of financial reporting (e.g., the necessary use of judgment), (2) the nature of audit procedures (e.g., they often do not provide absolutely conclusive evidence) and (3) the need to conduct an audit within a reasonable period of time at a reasonable cost. Accordingly, the auditors express an opinion on the financial statements, not a statement of fact.

Critical to the profession is the need for **independence** when performing audits (and other assurance services). An opinion by CPAs as to the fairness of a company's financial statements (or other information) is of questionable value unless they are truly independent. Indeed, if auditors own shares of stock in a company that they audit, or if they serve as members of the board of directors, they might subconsciously be biased in the performance of auditing duties. The auditors should therefore avoid any relationship with a client that would cause an outsider who had knowledge of all the facts to doubt their independence. It is not enough that auditors *be* independent; they must conduct themselves in such a manner that informed members of the public will have no reason to doubt their independence. The public accounting profession's ethical standards include independence requirements; these requirements are discussed in detail in Chapter 3.

### Details Related to AICPA Guidance

The *Statements on Auditing Standards (SASs)* provide a variety of specific auditing requirements and guidance to be considered by auditors. SASs ordinarily include the following sections:

- Introduction, including scope.
- Objective(s).
- Definitions of important terms.
- Requirements.
- Application and other explanatory material.

While the purposes of each of the above first four sections of the SASs are obvious, one should realize that the application and other explanatory information provide further explanation of a particular AU section and guidance (often including examples) for carrying them out. The auditors are required to understand the application and other explanatory material, although how they apply the guidance depends on the exercise of professional judgment in the circumstances consistent with the objective of the AU section.

More detailed, but less authoritative, guidelines for addressing specific audit problems are provided in *interpretive publications,* which include appendixes to the SASs, *AICPA Audit and Accounting Guides,* and AICPA auditing *Statements of Position.* The auditors should be aware of and consider the interpretive publications applicable to their audits. If they fail to apply the auditing guidance in such publications, they should be prepared to explain how they complied with the related SAS.

When describing auditor responsibility, the exact wording of a SAS is extremely important. In some cases, the standard establishes an unconditional requirement that auditors must follow in all circumstances, while in others it provides matters to be considered, but not necessarily performed. Figure 2.3 provides a summary of the meanings of the most relevant wording. Thus, for example, if a pronouncement states that an auditor "must" perform a particular procedure and it is relevant to the audit, it *must* be performed. If a pronouncement says a procedure "should" be performed, there might be circumstances in which alternate procedures may be performed instead. When a standard uses words such as "may," "might," or "could," the auditors should consider using the guidance; the application and other explanatory material in the AUs often include these terms.

**FIGURE 2.3**

Professional
Responsibilities:
Terminology Used in
Auditing Standards:
PCAOB and Auditing
Standard Board
Combined

| Responsibility Level | Meaning | Words Used to Indicate Responsibility |
|---|---|---|
| **Unconditional Responsibility** | Auditor must fulfill responsibilities in all cases where such requirements are relevant.* | "Must" "Shall" (PCAOB only) "Is required" (PCAOB only) |
| **Presumptively Mandatory Responsibility** | Auditor must comply with requirements unless auditor demonstrates and documents that alternative actions were sufficient to achieve the objectives of the standards. | "Should" |
| **Responsibility to Consider (this third level of responsibility is only established in PCAOB documents)** | Auditor should consider, whether auditor follows depends on exercise of professional judgment in the circumstances. | "May" "Might" "Could" Other phrases indicating a responsibility to consider |

*Example of when a requirement is not relevant: If the client does not have an internal audit function, the standard titled "Using the Work of Internal Auditors" would not apply.

The various terms, illustrated in Figure 2.3, are used in essentially an equivalent manner in the auditing standards of the PCAOB.

Other auditing publications include such publications as AICPA *Auditing Practice Releases;* various technical studies published by the AICPA; auditing textbooks; and articles in professional journals, such as the *Journal of Accountancy* and *The CPA Journal.* Other auditing publications have no authoritative status but may be helpful *to* the auditors in understanding and applying the SASs. The role and authority of various auditing publications are summarized in Figure 2.4. Keep in mind, however, that compliance with auditing standards does not represent an ideal level of audit performance, but rather a *minimum standard* for all engagements.

## PCAOB Auditing Standards

The PCAOB adopted the AICPA auditing standards in existence April 16, 2003, as its interim standards. Subsequently, the PCAOB began issuing its own series of *Auditing Standards.* These adopted and issued standards are required to be followed when auditors audit the financial statements (and internal control) of issuers of securities (public companies). Throughout the text, while we will emphasize AICPA standards, we will include discussions of PCAOB standards where they differ significantly from those of the AICPA. As a starting point, the *PCAOB Auditing Standards* are structured around the following standards that the AICPA standards previously referred to as the 10 generally accepted auditing standards.

**General Standards**

1. The audit is to be performed by a person or persons having adequate technical training and proficiency as an auditor.
2. In all matters relating to the assignment, an independence in mental attitude is to be maintained by the auditor or auditors.
3. Due professional care is to be exercised in the performance of the audit and the preparation of the report.

## Standards of Fieldwork

1. The work is to be adequately planned and assistants, if any, are to be properly supervised.
2. A sufficient understanding of internal control is to be obtained to plan the audit and to determine the nature, timing, and extent of tests to be performed.
3. Sufficient competent evidential matter is to be obtained through inspection, observation, inquiries, and confirmations to afford a reasonable basis for an opinion regarding the financial statements under audit.

## Standards of Reporting

1. The report shall state whether the financial statements are presented in accordance with generally accepted accounting principles (GAAP).
2. The report shall identify those circumstances in which such principles have not been consistently observed in the current period in relation to the preceding period.
3. Informative disclosures in the financial statements are to be regarded as reasonably adequate unless otherwise stated in the report.
4. The report shall contain either an expression of opinion regarding the financial statements, taken as a whole, or an assertion to the effect that an opinion cannot be expressed. When an overall opinion cannot be expressed, the reasons therefor should be stated. In all cases where an auditor's name is associated with financial statements, the report should contain a clear-cut indication of the character of the auditor's work, if any, and the degree of responsibility the auditor is taking.

The general standards are personal in nature in that they deal with auditor training and proficiency, auditor independence, and the need for due professional care. These standards apply to all parts of a PCAOB audit, including fieldwork and reporting.

The three standards of fieldwork relate to planning the audit and accumulating evidence sufficient for the auditors to obtain an opinion on the financial statements. Audit planning involves developing an overall strategy relating to collecting and evaluating

**FIGURE 2.4**
**GAAS Hierarchy**

| Category | Status | Audit Guidance |
|---|---|---|
| 1. Standards | Basically must be applied, but also consider the Figure 2.3 responsibility levels (e.g., unconditional v. presumptively mandatory). | *Statements on Auditing Standards (SASs)* Other standards that apply for PCAOB and government audits, etc. |
| 2. Interpretive Publications* | Recommendations on the application of SASs; the auditor should consider them. | Auditing interpretations of GAAS Audit guidance in *AICPA Audit and Accounting Guides* AICPA *Statements of Position— Auditing and Attestation* |
| 3. Other Auditing Publications | No authoritative status, but may help the auditor understand and apply the standards. | Various AICPA publications, including *Auditing Practice Releases, Technical Practice Aids, Audit Risk Alerts, Professional Issues Task Force Practice Alerts,* and other publications Auditing articles in *Journal of Accountancy* and other professional journals Others (e.g., continuing education program materials, textbooks, guidebooks, audit programs) |

*These are documents issued under authority of ASB after all ASB members have been provided an opportunity to comment.

the evidence to be obtained. By understanding and testing **internal control,** the auditors can assess whether it offers assurance that the financial statements will be free from material errors and fraud. These assessments enable the auditors to evaluate the risks of material misstatement of the financial statements. To address these risks, the auditors perform procedures to substantiate the amounts in the financial statements being audited. Examples of such evidence include written confirmations from outsiders and the first-hand observation of assets by the auditors. Assessing risks of misstatement and gathering and evaluating evidence lies at the very heart of the audit process and is a continuing theme throughout this textbook.

The four reporting standards establish some specific directives for preparation of the auditors' report. The report must specifically state whether the financial statements are in conformity with generally accepted accounting principles. That is, it must contain an opinion on the financial statements as a whole, or must disclaim an opinion. **Consistency** in the application of generally accepted accounting principles and adequate informative disclosure in the financial statements is to be assumed unless the audit report states otherwise.

Since the 10 standards in essence summarize auditor responsibilities detailed further in the various professional standards of both the AICPA and the PCAOB, their elimination from the AICPA standards does not result in differing audit requirements for public versus nonpublic companies.

# THE AUDITORS' RESPONSIBILITY FOR DETECTING MISSTATEMENTS

**LO3**

Discuss the auditors' responsibility for detecting errors, fraud, and noncompliance with laws and regulations.

As indicated earlier in this chapter, the auditors have a responsibility to plan and perform the audit to obtain reasonable assurance about whether the financial statements are free of material misstatement.[2] Reasonable assurance is achieved when **audit risk,** the risk that the auditors may unknowingly fail to appropriately modify the opinion on financial statements that are materially misstated, is at an acceptably low level. Financial statements may be misstated due to various causes, including errors, fraud, and noncompliance with certain laws and regulations.

## Errors and Fraud

Auditing standards define **errors** as unintentional misstatements or omissions of amounts or disclosures in the financial statements. Errors may involve mistakes in gathering or processing data, unreasonable accounting estimates arising from oversight or misinterpretation of facts, or mistakes in the application of applicable accounting principles.

**Fraud,** as the term is used in AICPA AU 240 (PCAOB 316), relates to intentional acts that cause a misstatement of the financial statements. Misstatements due to fraud may occur due to either (1) fraudulent financial reporting or (2) misappropriation of assets (also referred to as "defalcation").

During the planning of an audit, the auditors are required to assess the risk of material misstatements—whether caused by error or fraud. Based on that assessment, they plan and perform their audit to obtain reasonable assurance of detecting such misstatements. To obtain reasonable assurance, the auditors must exercise due care in planning, performing, and evaluating the results of their audit procedures. This requires auditors to exercise professional skepticism. As indicated earlier in this chapter, professional skepticism involves having a questioning mind and a critical assessment of audit evidence throughout the audit process.

The area of fraud provides a good illustration of why an audit can provide reasonable, but not absolute, assurance of detecting material misstatement of the financial statements.

---

[2] The professional standards on these responsibilities are presented in AICPA AU 315, "Understanding the Entity and Its Environment and Assessing the Risks of Material Misstatement," and AICPA AU 240 (PCAOB 316), "Consideration of Fraud in a Financial Statement Audit."

Fraud is difficult to detect because it often involves concealment schemes such as forgery, deliberate failure to record transactions, or intentional misrepresentations made to the auditors. When accompanied by collusion among several employees, the concealment may make the fraud very difficult to detect. Also, when management fraud is involved, it may be more difficult to detect than employee fraud because management is often in a position to manipulate accounting records and to override control procedures. Indeed, the risk of not detecting a material misstatement resulting from fraud is ordinarily higher than the risk of not detecting one resulting from error.

## Compliance with Laws and Regulations

The auditors' responsibility for identifying client noncompliance with laws and regulations (hereafter, laws) depends upon their nature. The *Professional Standards* identify two types of laws—those with a direct effect on the financial statement amounts and others.

Certain laws have a *direct effect* on the financial statements in that they determine the reported amounts and disclosures in those statements. Noncompliance with these laws results in the need for accounting journal entries. Examples include laws that affect the accounting for transactions under government contracts and the accrual of income tax and pension costs. Other laws do not have a direct effect in the determination of amounts and related disclosures, but compliance with them is required to stay in business, or to avoid financial penalties. Examples of these laws include corporate business laws, environmental laws and regulations, and antitrust laws. In this text, we will refer to the former as *laws with a direct effect* and the latter as *other laws*. The difference between them is important because auditors have a higher level of responsibility for detecting violations of laws with a direct effect.

As explained in AICPA AU 250 (PCAOB 317), the auditors should obtain an understanding of the legal and regulatory framework applicable to the entity and how the organization complies with that framework. Concerning laws with a direct effect, the auditors must gather sufficient appropriate audit evidence to obtain reasonable assurance of detecting material misstatements resulting from noncompliance—this is the same responsibility the auditors have for material errors and fraud.

Other laws often deal with operating aspects of the business, such as environmental standards and workplace conditions. The auditors are not required to design procedures to obtain reasonable assurance of detecting violations of these other laws. Instead, they are required to perform specified audit procedures that may identify instances of noncompliance with other laws that may have a material effect (other than the amounts) on the financial statements, including:

- Inquiring of management and those charged with governance as to whether the entity is in compliance with such laws.
- Inspecting correspondence, if any, with relevant licensing or regulatory authorities.

Also, throughout the audit the auditors should remain alert for indications of noncompliance or suspected noncompliance with any laws that may arise from performing other audit procedures.

Additional audit procedures are required for all illegal acts when noncompliance is identified or suspected. In such situations, the auditors should (1) obtain an understanding of the act and the circumstances in which it has occurred, and (2) obtain further information to evaluate the possible effect on the financial statements. Unless they are all involved in management and are aware of the matters identified, the auditors should communicate to those charged with governance any identified or suspected noncompliance with laws identified, other than matters that are clearly inconsequential. When the violations are considered intentional and material, the auditors should communicate the matter to those charged with governance as soon as practicable.

If the auditors suspect that management or those charged with governance are involved in noncompliance, they should communicate the matter to the next higher level of authority in the organization, if it exists, such as the audit committee. Where no higher authority exists that is uninvolved, or if the auditors believe that the communication may not be acted upon or do not know whom to report to, they should consider the need to obtain legal advice.[3]

# AUDITORS' REPORTS

**LO4**

Explain the key elements of the auditors' standard report.

The end product of an audit of a business entity is a report expressing the auditors' opinion on the client's financial statements. The form of auditors' report discussed in detail in the following two sections is generally referred to as a **standard report**. It includes an unmodified (unqualified) opinion indicating that the audit was adequate in scope and that the financial statements present fairly the financial position, results of operations, and cash flows in conformity with generally accepted accounting principles.[4] Under these circumstances, the auditors are taking *no exceptions* and inserting *no modifications or qualifications* in the report.

The content of the auditors' report varies somewhat depending on whether it results from the audit of a nonpublic or public company. We first present the standard audit report for a nonpublic company, followed by the report for a public company and a brief discussion of how the two reports differ from one another.

## Nonpublic Company Audit Reports—Standard

The auditors' report for a nonpublic company begins with a title that includes the word "independent" and is addressed to the person or persons who retained the auditors. In the case of corporations, the selection of an auditing firm is usually made by the audit committee of the board of directors and ratified by the stockholders.

The auditors' *standard report* (as illustrated on the next page) consists of an introductory sentence indicating the financial statements audited, followed by sections outlining management's and the auditors' responsibility and the auditors' opinion.

*Management's Responsibility*

Management is responsible for the financial statements. It has the responsibility of maintaining adequate accounting records and of preparing proper financial statements for the use of stockholders and creditors. Even though the financial statements are sometimes constructed and printed in the auditors' office, primary responsibility for the statements remains with management.

Once we recognize that the financial statements are the statements of the company and not of the auditors, we realize that the auditors have no right to make changes in the financial statements. What action then should the auditors take if they do not agree with the presentation of a material item in the balance sheet or income statement?[5] Assume,

---

[3] Private Securities Reform Act of 1995 places additional requirements upon public companies registered with the Securities and Exchange Commission and their auditors when (1) the illegal act has a material effect on the financial statements, (2) senior management and the board of directors have not taken appropriate remedial actions, and (3) the failure to take remedial action is reasonably expected to warrant departure from a standard audit report (or to warrant resignation). In such circumstances, the auditors "shall, as soon as practicable," communicate their conclusions directly to the board of directors. Within one day, the company must notify the Securities and Exchange Commission of having received such a communication and must send a copy of that notification to the auditor. If the auditors do not receive such notice within the one-day period, they must furnish the report to the SEC within one business day after the failure of the company to give the required notice.

[4] The term "unmodified" is included in the current standards; historically, the term "unqualified" has been used. The term "unqualified" is still used in PCAOB standards. We will consider the two terms as synonymous, but will ordinarily use the term "unmodified" when discussing nonpublic company audits. Also, because the standards present multiple year reports as examples, we also present them—if only one year is audited, the report should be modified accordingly.

---

**Independent Auditors' Report**

To the Audit Committee of ABC Company:

We have audited the accompanying financial statements of ABC Company, which comprise the balance sheets as of December 31, 20X1 and 20X0, and the related statements of income, changes in stockholders' equity and cash flows for the years then ended, and the related notes to the financial statements.

*Management's Responsibility for the Financial Statements*

Management is responsible for the preparation and fair presentation of these financial statements in accordance with accounting principles generally accepted in the United States of America; this includes the design, implementation, and maintenance of internal control relevant to the preparation and fair presentation of financial statements that are free from material misstatement, whether due to fraud or error.

*Auditor's Responsibility*

Our responsibility is to express an opinion on these financial statements based on our audits. We conducted our audits in accordance with auditing standards generally accepted in the United States of America. Those standards require that we plan and perform the audit to obtain reasonable assurance about whether the financial statements are free of material misstatement.

An audit involves performing procedures to obtain audit evidence about the amounts and disclosures in the financial statements. The procedures selected depend on the auditor's judgment, including the assessment of the risks of material misstatement of the financial statements, whether due to fraud or error. In making those risk assessments, the auditor considers internal control relevant to the entity's preparation and fair presentation of the financial statements in order to design audit procedures that are appropriate in the circumstances, but not for the purpose of expressing an opinion on the effectiveness of the entity's internal control. An audit also includes evaluating the appropriateness of accounting policies used and the reasonableness of significant accounting estimates made by management, as well as evaluating the overall presentation of the financial statements.

We believe that the audit evidence we have obtained is sufficient and appropriate to provide a basis for our audit opinion.

*Opinion*

In our opinion, the financial statements referred to above present fairly, in all material respects, the financial position of ABC Company as of December 31, 20X1 and 20X0, and the results of its operations and its cash flows for the years then ended in accordance with accounting principles generally accepted in the United States of America.

*Williams & Co. LLP*

Phoenix, Arizona
February 5, 20X2

---

for example, that the auditors believe that the balance in the allowance for uncollectible accounts is not sufficient to cover the probable collection losses in the accounts receivable.

The auditors will first discuss the problem with management and point out why they believe that the valuation allowance is inadequate. If management agrees to increase the balance, an adjusting entry will be made for that purpose, and the problem is solved. If management is not convinced by the auditors' arguments and declines to increase the allowance, the auditors will probably *qualify* their opinion by stating in the report that the financial statements reflect fairly the company's financial position and operating results, *except for the effects of not providing an adequate provision for uncollectible accounts.* Usually such issues are satisfactorily disposed of in discussions between the auditors and management, and a qualification of the auditors' opinion is avoided. A full consideration of the use of qualifications in the auditors' report is presented in Chapter 17.

---

[5] The income statement is sometimes titled the statement of operations.

*The Auditors' Responsibility*

The auditors' responsibility is to express an opinion on the financial statements based on having conducted an audit following generally accepted auditing standards of the United States of America.[6] Underlying this opinion is the auditors' belief that they have obtained reasonable assurance that the financial statements are free of material misstatement. To obtain reasonable assurance, they obtain audit evidence by performing various audit procedures. Examples of audit evidence obtained include analysis of the client's accounting records, observation of tangible assets, inspection of such documents as purchase orders and contracts, and the gathering of evidence from outsiders (such as banks, customers, and suppliers). Because of the variety of types of evidence obtained, it is appropriate that the auditors state in their report that they have audited *the financial statements* rather than to say that they have audited the accounting records. In the illustration, the auditors' report covers the years for which financial statements were presented by the company. Reporting on such comparative financial statements is discussed in detail in Chapter 17.

*Opinion*

The opinion paragraph consists of only one sentence, which is restated here with certain significant phrases shown in italics:

> *In our opinion,* the financial statements referred to above present fairly, in all material respects, the financial position of XYZ Company as of December 31, 20X1 and 20X0, and the results of its operations and its cash flows for the year then ended in *conformity with accounting principles generally accepted in the United States of America.*

Each of the italicized phrases has a special significance. The first phrase, "in our opinion," makes clear that the auditors are expressing nothing more than an informed opinion; they are not guaranteeing or certifying that the statements are accurate, correct, or true. In an earlier period of public accounting, the wording of the audit report contained the phrase "we certify that," but this expression was discontinued on the grounds that it was misleading. To "certify" implies absolute assurance of accuracy, which an audit does not provide.

The auditors cannot guarantee the correctness of the financial statements because the statements include many estimates, not absolute facts. Furthermore, the auditors do not make a complete and detailed examination of all transactions. Their audit is limited to a program of tests that leaves the possibility of some misstatements going undetected. Because of limitations inherent in the accounting process and because of practical limitations of time and cost in performing an audit, the auditors' work culminates in the expression of an opinion and not in the issuance of a guarantee of accuracy.

*What Is "Material"?*    Auditors cannot issue an unmodified opinion on financial statements that contain material deficiencies. The term *material* may be defined as "sufficiently important to influence decisions made by reasonable users of financial statements." Materiality is influenced by the size of the organization that is being audited. In the audit of a small client—such as a condominium property owners' association—$1,000 might be considered material. On the other hand, in the audit of a company such as IBM or Microsoft, an amount of $10 million might be considered immaterial.

In practice, one of the most significant elements of professional judgment is the ability to draw the line between material and immaterial departures from generally accepted

---

[6] Historically, *audit reports* referred simply to generally accepted auditing standards and generally accepted accounting principles. The globalization of business resulted in a modification of the standard report that identifies the source of the standards followed (e.g., International, United States [of America], or some other country's standards). In this text, we will use the new terminology in report illustrations, but, like the standards, we will refer to generally accepted auditing standards (GAAS) and generally accepted accounting principles (GAAP) in other contexts.

accounting principles. The auditor who raises objections over immaterial items will soon lose the respect of both clients and associates. On the other hand, the auditor who fails to identify and disclose material deficiencies in financial statements may be liable for the losses of those who rely upon the audited statements. In short, applying the concept of materiality is one of the most complex problems faced by auditors.

Materiality depends upon both the *dollar amount* and the *nature of the item.* For example, a $500,000 error in the balance of the Cash account is ordinarily far more significant than a $500,000 error in the balance of Accumulated Depreciation. If a corporation sells assets to a member of top management and then buys the assets back at a higher price, this *related party transaction* warrants disclosure even though the dollar amounts are not large in relation to the financial statements as a whole. The reason for requiring disclosure of such a transaction is based more on the nature of the transaction than upon the dollar amount. Materiality is discussed in more detail in Chapter 6.

*Adequate Informative Disclosure*   If financial statements are to present fairly, in all material respects, the financial position and operating results of a company, there must be **adequate disclosure** of all essential information. A financial statement may be misleading if it does not give a complete picture. For example, if an extraordinary item arising from an uninsured flood loss of plant and equipment were combined with operating income and not clearly identified, the reader might be misled as to the earning power of the company. Adequate disclosure means the information is accurate and complete and has been clearly conveyed to the financial statement user.

*Generally Accepted Accounting Principles (GAAP)*   The next key phrase refers to the applicable financial reporting framework—in the United States, most frequently "accounting principles generally accepted in the United States of America." In evaluating whether a particular accounting principle used by a client is generally accepted, the auditors may refer to the Financial Accounting Standards Board (for public and nonpublic nongovernmental companies), the Government Accounting Standards Board (for state and local government entities), and the Federal Accounting Standards Advisory Board (for federal government audits), as well as a variety of other sources.

Effective in 2009, the accounting guidance for public and nonpublic entities has only two levels: (1) authoritative GAAP, and (2) nonauthoritative accounting guidance and literature. The *FASB Codification* is the source of authoritative GAAP to be applied by nongovernmental entities (businesses and not-for-profit entities). The codification is updated through *Accounting Standards Updates.* The rules and interpretive releases of the Securities and Exchange Commission under the federal securities laws are also sources of authoritative GAAP for public companies. If the guidance for a transaction or event is not specified within the authoritative GAAP or SEC guidance, the company should first consider accounting principles for similar transactions or events in authoritative GAAP. Finally, when no other guidance can be found, nonauthoritative accounting guidance should be consulted. Sources of nonauthoritative accounting guidance and literature include:

- Practices that are widely recognized and prevalent either generally or in the industry.
- FASB Concepts Statements.
- AICPA Issues Papers.
- International Financial Reporting Standards.
- Pronouncements of professional associations or regulatory agencies.
- Technical Information Service Inquiries and Replies included in AICPA.
- Technical Practice Aids.
- Accounting textbooks, handbooks, and articles.

The appropriateness of the above nonauthoritative accounting guidance and literature depends on its relevance to particular circumstances, how specific it is, the general recognition of the issuer or author as a authority, and the extent of its use in practice.

Figure 2.5 illustrates the hierarchy of guidance for state and local governmental entities and federal government audits. When there is a conflict between the accounting treatment suggested by pronouncements from two different categories, the pronouncement from the higher category should be followed. For example, authoritative body pronouncements prevail over pronouncements of other experts and widely recognized practices and pronouncements. When there is a conflict within a category, logic dictates that the auditors should select the accounting principle that most clearly reflects the *economic substance* of the particular transaction.

## Public Company Audit Reports—Unmodified (Unqualified)

As discussed in Chapter I, the Sarbanes-Oxley Act requires that auditors of publicly traded (issuer) companies in the United States perform an integrated audit that includes providing assurance on both the financial statements and the effectiveness of internal control over financial reporting. In these audits, the auditors may either issue separate reports on the financial statements and internal control, or issue a combined report. The following separate report on the financial statements of a publicly traded company

**FIGURE 2.5  The GAAP Hierarchy for Governmental Entities**

| Category | State and Local Governments* | Federal Government** |
|---|---|---|
| a. Authoritative Body Pronouncements | • GASB *Statements* and *Interpretations*<br>• FASB and AICPA pronouncements made applicable by a GASB *Statement* or *Interpretation* | • FASB *Statements* and *Interpretations*<br>• AICPA, FASB, and GASB pronouncements made applicable by an FASAB *Statement* or *Interpretation* |
| b. Pronouncements of Bodies Composed of Expert Accountants, Exposed for Public Comment | • GASB *Technical Bulletins*<br>• AICPA *Industry Audit* and *Accounting Guides* and *Statements of Position* (cleared by GASB) | • FASAB *Technical Bulletins*<br>• AICPA *Industry Audit* and *Accounting Guides* and *Statements of Position* (cleared by FASAB) |
| c. Pronouncements of Bodies Composed of Expert Accountants, Not Exposed for Public Comment | • *Consensus Positions of the GASB Emerging Issues Task Force*<br>• AICPA *Practice Bulletins* (cleared by GASB) | • *Technical Releases* of the Accounting and Auditing Policy Committee of the FASAB<br>• AICPA *Practice Bulletins* (cleared by the FASAB) |
| d. Widely Recognized Practices and Pronouncements | • GASB staff "Questions and Answers"<br>• Widely accepted industry practices | • FASAB staff *Implementation Guides*<br>• Widely accepted federal government practices |
| e. Other Accounting Literature | • GASB *Concepts Statements*<br>• Pronouncements in (a) through (d) of nongovernmental hierarchy not specifically made applicable<br>• APB *Statements*<br>• FASB *Concepts Statements*<br>• AICPA *Issues Papers* and *Technical Practice Aids*<br>• International Accounting Standards Committee *Statements*<br>• Pronouncements of other professional associations or regulatory agencies<br>• Accounting textbooks, handbooks, and articles | • FASAB *Concepts Statements*<br>• Pronouncements in (a) through (d) of GASB and FASB not specifically made applicable<br>• FASB and GASB *Concepts Statements*<br>• AICPA *Issues Papers* and *Technical Practice Aids*<br>• International Accounting Standards Committee *Statements*<br>• Pronouncements of other professional associations or regulatory agencies<br>• Accounting textbooks, handbooks, and articles |

*Government Accounting Standards Board Statement No. 55,* "The Hierarchy of Generally Accepted Accounting Principles for State and Local Governments."
**Statement of Federal Financial Accounting Standards 34,* "The Hierarchy of Generally Accepted Accounting Principles. Including the Application of Standards Issued by the Financial Accounting Standards Board."

illustrates the differences as compared to the standard audit report for the audit of a non-public company.[7]

---

### Report of Independent Registered Public Accounting Firm

To the Board of Directors and Stockholders of XYZ Company:

We have audited the accompanying balance sheets of XYZ Company as of December 31, 20X1 and 20X0, and the related statements of income, retained earnings, and cash flows for each of the three years ended December 31, 20X1. These financial statements are the responsibility of the Company's management. Our responsibility is to express an opinion on these financial statements based on our audit.

We conducted our audit in accordance with standards of the Public Company Accounting Oversight Board (United States). Those standards require that we plan and perform the audit to obtain reasonable assurance about whether the financial statements are free of material misstatement. An audit includes examining, on a test basis, evidence supporting the amounts and disclosures in the financial statements. An audit also includes assessing the accounting principles used and significant estimates made by management, as well as evaluating the overall financial statement presentation. We believe that our audit provides a reasonable basis for our opinion.

In our opinion, the financial statements referred to above present fairly, in all material respects, the financial position of XYZ Company as of December 31, 20X1 and 20X0, and the results of its operations and its cash flows for each of the three years ended December 31, 20X1, in conformity with accounting principles generally accepted in the United States of America.

We also have audited, in accordance with the standards of the Public Company Accounting Oversight Board (United States), the effectiveness of XYZ Company's internal control over financial reporting as of December 31, 20X1, based on *Internal Control-Integrated Framework* issued by the Committee of Sponsoring Organizations of the Treadway Commission (COSO) and our report dated February 26, 20X2, expressed unqualified opinions.

Los Angeles, Calif.　　　　　　　　　　　*Blue, Gray & Company*
February 26, 20X2　　　　　　　　　　　Certified Public Accountants

---

Notice that "auditing standards generally accepted in the United States of America" is replaced by the standards of the "Public Company Accounting Oversight Board (United States)" and a final paragraph is added referring to the auditors' report on internal control. The report on internal control is illustrated in Chapter 18. The description of management and the auditors' responsibilities are more brief than for the nonpublic company report.

## Other Types of Auditors' Reports

LO5

Discuss the other types of reports that are issued by auditors.

A report with an *unmodified* ("unqualified" per PCAOB standards) opinion is the type of report the client ordinarily wants. In some audits, however, the circumstances do not permit the auditors to provide an unmodified opinion on the financial statements. As alternatives to a report with an unmodified opinion, auditors may issue a report with a *qualified opinion.* an *adverse opinion,* or a *disclaimer of opinion.* In some situations, auditors also include additional information in a report with an unmodified opinion.

Auditors issue a **qualified opinion** on financial statements when there is some limitation on the scope of their audit, or when one or more items in the financial statements are not presented in accordance with applicable accounting principles. The limitation or exception must be significant but not so significant as to overshadow an overall opinion on the financial statements.

An **adverse opinion** states that the financial statements *are not fairly presented.* In practice, an adverse opinion is rare, because it would be of little use to the client. If the financial statements contain such material departures from applicable accounting

---

[7] Because public companies are ordinarily required to provide balance sheets for the two most recent years, and statements of income, retained earnings, and cash flows for three years, we present an audit report on such comparative financial statements.

principles as to warrant an adverse opinion, this situation is discussed among the auditors and the client's management. Management probably would agree to make the changes necessary to avoid an adverse opinion or will decide to terminate the audit engagement and thus avoid paying additional audit fees.

Auditors will issue a **disclaimer of opinion** if they are unable to determine the overall fairness of the financial statements. This type of report results from very significant limitations in the scope of the auditors' examination.

When a qualified, adverse, or disclaimer of opinion is issued on the financial statements, the report is modified to describe the matter of concern. In certain other circumstances, information may be added to what remains a report with an unmodified opinion. For example, audit reports are modified to inform users of financial statements of changes in accounting principles in relation to the prior year, or the fact that another audit firm is responsible for a significant portion of the audit.

## The Attestation Standards

Describe the attestation standards.

The generally accepted auditing standards were adopted by the AICPA to provide guidance for the performance of audits of historical financial statements. The expansion of the attestation function has led the accounting profession to develop more general attestation standards, which are contained in *Statement on Standards for Attestation Services No. 1 (SSAE 1)*. These attestation standards, presented in Figure 2.6, are meant to serve as a general framework and set boundaries for the attest function. Since the issuance of SSAE 1, the Auditing Standards Board has issued a number of SSAEs that provide guidance

**FIGURE 2.6**
**AICPA Attestation Standards**

**General Standards**

1. The engagement shall be performed by a practitioner having *adequate technical training* and *proficiency in the attest function.*
2. The engagement shall be performed by a practitioner having *adequate knowledge in the subject matter.*
3. The practitioner shall perform the engagement only if he or she has reason to believe that the *subject matter is capable of evaluation or measurement* against criteria (standards or benchmarks) that are suitable and available to users.
4. In all matters relating to the engagement, an *independence* in mental attitude shall be maintained by the practitioner.
5. *Due professional care* shall be exercised in the planning and the performance of the engagement.

**Standards of Fieldwork**

1. The work shall be *adequately planned* and assistants, if any, shall be properly *supervised.*
2. *Sufficient evidence* shall be obtained to provide a reasonable basis for the conclusion that is expressed in the report.

**Standards of Reporting**

1. The report shall *identify the subject matter* or the assertion being reported on and state the *character of the engagement.*
2. The report shall state the *practitioner's conclusion* about the subject matter or the assertion based on the criteria against which the subject matter was measured.
3. The report shall state all of the practitioner's *significant reservations* about the engagement.
4. The report on an engagement to evaluate subject matter that has been prepared based on *agreed-upon criteria* or an assertion related thereto, or on an engagement to apply *agreed-upon procedures,* should contain a statement *restricting its use* to the parties who have agreed upon such criteria or procedures.

**FIGURE 2.7** **Applicability of *Statements on Standards for Attestation Services (SSAEs)***

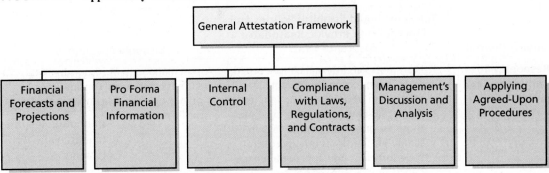

for attesting to specific types of information, such as prospective financial statements and internal control over financial reporting. The relationship of these attestation standards is shown in Figure 2.7. The PCAOB adopted the AICPA attestation standards as interim standards for attestation engagements related to the financial reporting of public companies.

## Quality Control in CPA Firms

**LO7**

Describe the quality control standards and their purposes.

A CPA firm should establish adequate quality control policies and procedures to provide reasonable assurance that it follows professional standards on every engagement. To provide CPA firms with guidance in establishing quality control policies, the AICPA has issued *Statements on Quality Control Standards* which identify six "elements" of quality control. The elements of quality control may be regarded as the areas in which the AICPA considers it desirable for a CPA firm to establish quality control procedures.

The AICPA does not require specific quality control procedures. In fact, it states that the specific procedures should depend upon the size of the firm, the number of offices, and the nature of the firm's practice. Thus, the quality control procedures employed by a 200-office international firm will differ considerably from those employed by a single-office firm that audits only small businesses. Technically, the *Statements on Quality Control* apply only to auditing, other attestation, and accounting services for which professional standards have been established by the AICPA. As a practical matter, however, every CPA firm should have quality control procedures applicable to *every aspect of its practice.* In the broad sense, the concept of "quality control" means that CPA firms should establish controls to provide assurance that they meet their responsibilities to their clients and to the public.

Figure 2.8 indicates the six areas in which the AICPA has indicated that quality control procedures are appropriate. In addition, the table explains the basic objective to be achieved in each area and provides an example procedure that a CPA firm might implement as a step toward achieving the objective. The PCAOB also has adopted the AICPA quality control standards as its interim quality control standards, making them applicable to public company practice.

## Regulation of Accounting Firms

In the United States, public accounting firms are regulated by a number of organizations, including the Public Company Accounting Oversight Board, the American Institute of Certified Public Accountants, the Securities and Exchange Commission, the various courts, and the state boards of accountancy.

## FIGURE 2.8 Elements of Quality Control

| Element of Quality Control | The Firm Should Establish Policies and Procedures to Provide Reasonable Assurance That: | Example Procedures |
|---|---|---|
| **Leadership Responsibilities for Quality within the Firm ("Tone at the Top")** | 1. It promotes an internal culture based on the recognition that quality is essential in performing engagements.<br>2. It provides reasonable assurance that those assigned operational responsibility for the firm's quality control have sufficient and appropriate experience, ability, and authority. | Assign management responsibilities so that commercial considerations do not override the quality of work performed. |
| **Relevant Ethical Requirements** | The firm and its personnel comply with relevant ethical requirements. (Policies relating to independence are particularly emphasized.) | At least annually, the firm should obtain written confirmation of compliance with its independence policies and procedures from all firm personnel who are required to be independent. |
| **Acceptance and Continuance of Client Relationships and Specific Engagements** | It will undertake and continue relationships and engagements only where the firm:<br>1. Is competent to perform the engagement.<br>2. Can comply with legal and ethical requirements.<br>3. Has considered client integrity. | Deciding whether to continue a client relationship by considering significant issues that have arisen during the current and previous engagements. |
| **Human Resources** | It has sufficient personnel with needed competence, capabilities, and commitment. | Design effective recruitment processes and procedures to help the firm select individuals of integrity who have the capacity to develop the necessary competence and capabilities. |
| **Engagement Performance** | The firm's engagements are consistently performed in accordance with professional standards and regulatory and legal requirements with policies and procedures addressing:<br>1. Engagement performance.<br>2. Supervision responsibilities.<br>3. Review responsibilities. | Design policies and procedures that address the tracking of progress of each engagement. |
| **Monitoring** | The policies and procedures relating to quality control are relevant, adequate, and operating effectively. | Communicate, at least annually, the results of the monitoring to engagement partners and other appropriate individuals within the firm. |

## Public Company Accounting Oversight Board

As described in Chapter 1, the Public Company Accounting Oversight Board (PCAOB) was established in 2002[8] with the following functions:

* Register public accounting firms that prepare audit reports for financial statement issuers.
* Establish or adopt auditing, quality control, ethics, independence, and other standards relating to audit reports for issuers.

[8] Until 2002, the *Public Oversight Board (POB)* served as a part of the profession's system of self-regulation. It was an autonomous board made up of five prominent individuals with a broad spectrum of business, professional, regulatory, and legislative experience. The POB oversaw the activities of the AICPA's SEC Practice Section (including its peer review activities), made inquiries into alleged audit failures, and periodically reported to the SEC and Congress. The POB was disbanded in 2002, with its responsibilities subsequently taken over by the Public Company Accounting Oversight Board.

- Conduct inspections of registered public accounting firms.
- Perform other duties or functions to promote high professional standards for audits, and enforce compliance with the Sarbanes-Oxley Act of 2002 (discussed in Chapter 1).

The PCAOB is composed of five members—only two of which are CPAs—selected from among prominent individuals who have demonstrated a commitment to the interests of investors and the public and an understanding of the issues faced by the PCAOB. Members are appointed by the Securities and Exchange Commission and may serve no more than two five-year terms.

All accounting firms that audit SEC registrants must register with the PCAOB. As part of that registration process, each firm pledges to cooperate with any inquiry made by the PCAOB. The PCAOB may impose monetary damages and may suspend firms and accountants from working on engagements for publicly traded companies. It may also make referrals to the Justice Department to consider criminal cases.

As discussed below, PCAOB staff performs inspections of the public audit practices of **registered public accounting firms** for compliance with the Sarbanes-Oxley Act, PCAOB and SEC requirements, and professional standards. CPA firms that audit more than 100 public companies are inspected annually, and firms that audit 100 or fewer public companies are audited at least every three years.

## Peer Review and Inspections

Members of the AICPA who are in public practice and have financial reporting responsibilities must have a sample of their work reviewed by an independent party. To meet this requirement, CPA firms undergo a **peer review** performed directly by a CPA, a CPA firm, or a team of CPAs. There are two types of peer reviews: *system review* and *engagement review*.

A *system review* involves peer reviewers' study and appraisal of a CPA firm's system of quality control to perform accounting and auditing work. The approach of the peer reviewers includes obtaining an understanding of the CPA firm's accounting and auditing practice and the design of the firm's system through inquiry of CPA firm personnel and review of documentation about the system, such as firm manuals. The peer reviewers also select a sample of the CPA firm's engagements (emphasizing the higher risk ones) and examine related working paper files and reports, interview selected CPA firm personnel, and examine various administrative and personnel files. The peer review report issued includes a rating of pass, pass with deficiencies, or fail. A pass rating provides reasonable assurance in that it includes the peer reviewers' opinion that the system is appropriately designed and is being complied with by the CPA firm in all material respects. A pass with deficiencies rating differs in that it indicates that in certain situations (outlined in the report) the system is not appropriately designed or complied with. A fail rating indicates that the peer reviewer has determined that the CPA firm's system is not suitably designed or being complied with.

An *engagement review,* the second type of peer review, is one in which the peer reviewers select a sample of a CPA firm's actual accounting work, including accounting reports issued and CPA firm documentation to evaluate whether the reports and procedures are appropriate. This type of peer review is of lesser scope since it does not emphasize the overall system of quality control. It is only available for CPA firms that do not perform audits, but do perform reviews and/or compilations. The report issued may be pass, pass with deficiencies, or fail, as is the case with a system review, but the restricted nature of an engagement review results in a report in which the pass and pass with deficiencies reports provide only limited assurance. Thus, a pass report indicates that nothing came to the peer reviewers' attention indicating a material departure from the professional standards as contrasted to a statement that in the peer reviewers' opinion no material departure exists.

In addition to peer reviews, CPA firms with SEC registrants as clients are required to have an inspection performed by the PCAOB staff. Inspections are performed annually for CPA firms with numerous public clients and less frequently for those with fewer public clients. The Sarbanes-Oxley Act provides that an **inspection** shall include at least the following three general components:

1. An inspection and review of selected audit and review engagements.
2. An evaluation of the sufficiency of the quality control system of the firm and the manner of the documentation and communication of the system.
3. Tests of the audit, supervisory, and quality control procedures considered necessary.

Inspections by the PCAOB staff differ from peer reviews conducted by CPA firms. Generally, the PCAOB staff focuses on selected quality control issues only and may also consider other aspects of practice management, such as the determinates of partner compensation. In addition, while peer reviews focus on evaluating and testing compliance with the firm's quality control system, a PCAOB inspection focuses primarily on evaluating the performance of a sample of individual audit and review engagements. In selecting the engagements for inspection, the PCAOB staff uses a risk assessment process to identify engagements that have a higher risk of lack of compliance with professional standards. As an example, an engagement may be selected primarily because it is in a high-risk industry. Once an audit is selected, the inspection focuses on the high-risk aspects of that engagement, such as the audit work on revenue recognition and accounting estimates. When a lack of compliance with professional standards is found, the PCAOB staff attempts to determine the cause of the lack of compliance, which may lead to the identification of a defect in the firm's quality control system.

Each inspection results in a written report transmitted to the SEC and appropriate regulatory authorities. Also included is the letter of comments by the PCAOB inspectors and any responses by the CPA firm. While the content of most portions of the reports is made available to the public, discussions of potential defects in a firm's quality control system are not made public unless the firm does not address the issue within 12 months.

## International Accounting and Auditing Standards

**LO8**

Explain the status of international accounting and auditing standards and the content of the international audit report.

*International Financial Reporting Standards (IFRS)* are developed by the **International Accounting Standards Board (IASB),** which has the objective of developing, in the public interest, a single set of high-quality, understandable and enforceable global accounting standards. Historically, the SEC has required foreign companies that issue their securities in U.S. markets to present their financial statements in accordance with U.S. generally accepted accounting principles (GAAP), or reconcile their financial statements to U.S. GAAP. Effective March 4, 2008, the SEC eliminated the requirement when the financial statements have been prepared using IFRS. This is generally viewed as the first step in moving towards the acceptance of IFRS for all companies filing with the SEC.

Acceptance of IFRS by the SEC does not alter the requirements for audits of the financial statements by a registered CPA firm under the auditing standards established by the PCAOB. However, it does have some impact on the audit process because of the differences between IFRS and U.S. GAAP. Apart from some specific differences in rules, IFRS are considered to be more principle based than U.S. GAAP. Therefore, IFRS generally require the application of more judgment. Many professionals believe that the judgment involved in the application of IFRS makes audits of financial statements prepared in accordance with IFRS somewhat more challenging than audits of financial statements in accordance with U.S. GAAP.

### The International Audit Report

As discussed previously, international auditing standards are developed by the **International Auditing and Assurance Standards Board (IAASB)** of the **International Federation of Accountants (IFAC)**. In 2011, the Auditing Standards Board aligned the format and content of its standards with the international standards. In addition, future Auditing Standards Board projects will ordinarily be developed concurrently with the development of *International Standards on Auditing.*

Exceptions to international standards exist when they are considered necessary as a result of national circumstances. The differences between the international audit report and the audit reports issued in accordance with AICPA auditing standards are summarized in the section below. Other differences between international auditing standards and AICPA auditing standards are summarized in Appendix 2A.

The reporting guidance and the audit report of the IAASB are very similar to that required under U.S. standards for non-issuer companies issued by the AICPA Auditing Standards Board.

---

### Independent Auditors' Report

To the Shareholders of ABC Company:

We have audited the accompanying financial statements of ABC Company, which comprise the balance sheet as of December 31, 20X1, the income statement, the statement of changes in equity, the cash flow statement for the year then ended, and a summary of significant accounting policies and other explanatory notes.

*Management's Responsibility for the Financial Statements*
Management is responsible for the preparation and fair presentation of these financial statements in accordance with International Financial Reporting Standards. This responsibility includes: designing, implementing, and maintaining internal control relevant to the preparation and fair presentation of financial statements that are free from material misstatement, whether due to fraud or error; selecting and applying appropriate accounting policies; and making accounting estimates that are reasonable in the circumstances.

*Auditor's Responsibility*
Our responsibility is to express an opinion on these financial statements based on our audit. We conducted our audit in accordance with *International Standards on Auditing*. Those standards require that we comply with ethical requirements and plan and perform the audit to obtain reasonable assurance that the financial statements are free from material misstatement.

An audit involves performing procedures to obtain audit evidence about the amounts and disclosures in the financial statements. The procedures selected depend on the auditor's judgment, including the assessment of the risks of material misstatement of the financial statements, whether due to fraud or error. In making those risk assessments, the auditor considers internal control relevant to the entity's preparation and fair presentation of the financial statements in order to design audit procedures that are appropriate in the circumstances, but not for the purpose of expressing an opinion on the effectiveness of the entity's internal control. An audit also includes evaluating the appropriateness of accounting policies used and the reasonableness of accounting estimates made by management, as well as evaluating the overall presentation of the financial statements.

We believe that the audit evidence we have obtained is sufficient and appropriate to provide a basis for our audit opinion.

*Opinion*
In our opinion, the financial statements present fairly, in all material respects, the financial position of ABC Company as of December 31, 20X1, and its financial performance and its cash flows for the year then ended in accordance with *International Financial Reporting Standards*.

February 17, 20X2         *Robert Blue*
Los Angeles, California, USA       Blue, Gray & Company

---

The international reporting model allows the auditors certain reporting options. As an example, instead of indicating that the financial statements "present fairly, in all material respects," the auditors may substitute the phrase "give a true and fair view," as required of auditors in the United Kingdom. Also, the report may indicate that the financial statements comply with the provisions of the country's relevant statutes or laws. The report may be signed using the personal name of the auditor, the firm, or both—as is done in the above illustration. Inclusion of the city of the CPA firm office that performed the audit is a required part of the international report.

In some countries, auditors have other reporting responsibilities, such as a responsibility to report certain matters that come to the auditors' attention. If those matters are addressed in the international audit report on the financial statements, they should be included in a separate section of the report after the opinion paragraph.

**Chapter Summary**

This chapter described the nature of generally accepted auditing standards, attestation standards, and quality control standards. To summarize:

1. The passage of the Sarbanes-Oxley Act of 2002 has significantly altered the regulatory environment of auditors and audit firms. Previously, the AICPA played a primary role in the development of auditing, attestation, and quality control standards and in the self-regulation of individual auditors and CPA firms. Now, the AICPA issues standards applicable only to nonpublic accounting and auditing engagements. The PCAOB issues standards for public company audits and regulates the public company practices of auditors and registered audit firms.

2. The AICPA issues *Statements on Auditing Standards,* which represent generally accepted auditing standards relevant to the audits of nonpublic (nonissuer) companies. The PCAOB adopted AICPA standards in existence at April 16, 2003, and has supplemented them with its own pronouncements.

3. An audit provides reasonable assurance of detecting material misstatements of the financial statements (both errors and fraud) and noncompliance with laws that have a direct and material effect on the determination of financial statement amounts. Although an audit does not obtain reasonable assurance of detecting noncompliance with laws that have only an indirect effect on the financial statements, the auditors remain alert for such acts. If instances of noncompliance are discovered, regardless of type, the auditors must carefully evaluate their effects on the financial statements.

4. The auditors' standard unmodified report for a nonpublic (nonissuer) company consists of an introductory sentence identifying the financial statements that were audited, followed by sections outlining management's responsibility, the auditors' responsibility, and the auditors' opinion. The audit report for a public (issuer) company, while more brief, provides similar information and a final paragraph referring to the auditors' report on internal control. Concerning the auditing standards followed, the nonissuer refers to "auditing standards generally accepted in the United States of America," while the issuer report refers to "standards of the Public Company Oversight Board (United States)."

5. Alternatives to unmodified opinions are qualified opinions, adverse opinions, and disclaimers of opinion. Qualified opinions are issued when there is a limitation on the scope of an audit or when financial statements are not presented in accordance with generally accepted accounting principles. Adverse opinions are issued when financial statements are so misstated as to not be fairly presented on an overall basis. Disclaimers of opinion are issued when the auditors are unable to conclude on the overall fairness of the financial statements.

6. The AICPA's attestation standards were adopted to provide a general framework for the attest function and to set boundaries for these types of engagements. The 11 attestation standards are structured as general standards, standards of fieldwork, and standards of reporting.

7. CPA firms establish quality control systems to ensure that all professional engagements are performed in accordance with applicable professional standards. The AICPA's quality control standards provide guidance in developing these systems. CPA firms with SEC reporting clients undergo inspections of their public company audit practice by the Public Company Accounting Oversight Board. In addition, CPA firms arrange to have their practices peer reviewed by other CPAs. Obtaining such practice reviews is a requirement for membership in the AICPA.

8. International financial markets would be facilitated if auditing and accounting standards were more uniform. Currently, the International Auditing and Assurance Standards Board issues pronouncements designed to foster the development of consistent worldwide auditing standards.

## Key Terms Introduced or Emphasized in Chapter 2

**Adequate disclosure (45)** All essential information as required by generally accepted accounting principles (or some other appropriate basis of accounting) is included in the financial statements.

**Adverse opinion (47)** An opinion issued by the auditors that the financial statements they have audited *do not present fairly* the financial position, results of operation, or cash flows in conformity with accounting principles generally accepted in the United States of America.

**Applicable financial reporting framework (35)** The financial reporting framework adopted by management and, where appropriate, those charged with governance in the preparation of the financial statements that are acceptable in view of the nature of the entity and the objective of the financial statements, or that is required by law or regulation.

**Audit risk (40)** The risk that the auditors may unknowingly fail to appropriately modify their opinion on financial statements that are materially misstated.

**Auditors' report (33)** A very precise document designed to communicate exactly the character and limitations of the responsibility being assumed by the auditors.

**Consistency (40)** The concept of using the same accounting principles from year to year so that the successive financial statements issued by a business entity will be comparable.

**Disclaimer of opinion (48)** A form of report in which the auditors state that they do not express an opinion on the financial statements; it should include a separate paragraph stating the auditors' reasons for disclaiming an opinion and also disclosing any reservations they may have concerning the financial statements.

**Error (40)** An unintentional misstatement of financial statements or omission of an amount or a disclosure.

**Financial reporting framework (35)** A set of criteria used to determine measurement recognition, representation, and disclosure of all material items appearing in the financial statements: for example, accounting principles generally accepted in the United States of America, and *International Financial Reporting Standards (IFRS)*.

**Fraud (40)** For financial statement audits, "fraud" includes two types of intentional misstatements of financial statements—misstatements arising from fraudulent financial reporting and misstatements arising from misappropriation of assets. Legally, fraud is the misrepresentation by a person of a material fact, known by that person to be untrue or made with reckless indifference as to whether the fact is true, with intent to deceive and with the result that another party is injured.

**General purpose financial reporting framework (35)** A financial reporting framework designed to meet the common financial needs of a wide range of users.

**Generally accepted auditing standards (GAAS) (35)** Auditing standards issued by the AICPA's Auditing Standards Board (ASB). GAAS are the standards for the auditors' work in fulfilling the overall objectives of a financial statement audit. GAAS address the general responsibilities of the auditors as well as the auditors' further considerations relevant to the application of those responsibilities.

**Independence (37)** A most important auditing standard, which prohibits CPAs from expressing an opinion on financial statements of an enterprise unless they are independent with respect to such enterprise; independence is impaired by a direct financial interest, service as an officer or trustee, certain loans to or from the enterprise, and various other relationships.

**Inspection (52)** (conducted by the Public Company Accounting Oversight Board) A process that leads to an assessment of the degree of compliance of each registered public accounting firm and associated persons of that firm with the Sarbanes-Oxley Act of 2002 and the board's requirements in connection with its performance of audits, issuance of audit reports, and related matters.

**Internal control (40)** A process, effected by the entity's board of directors, management, and other personnel, designed to provide reasonable assurance regarding the achievement of objectives in the following categories: (1) reliability of financial reporting; (2) effectiveness and efficiency of operations; and (3) compliance with applicable laws and regulations.

**International Accounting Standards Board (IASB) (52)** An independent, privately funded accounting standard-setter that is committed to developing a single set of high-quality, understandable, and enforceable global accounting standards.

**International Auditing and Assurance Standards Board (IAASB) (52)** A committee of the International Federation of Accountants, established to issue standards on auditing and reporting practices to improve the degree of uniformity of auditing practices and related services throughout the world.

**International Federation of Accountants (IFAC) (52)** A worldwide organization of national accounting bodies established to help foster a coordinated worldwide accounting profession with harmonized standards.

**Peer review (51)** A study and appraisal by an independent evaluator ("peer reviewer") of a CPA firm's work. In a *system review,* the evaluator considers the CPA firm's system of quality control to perform accounting and auditing work. In an *engagement review,* the evaluator studies and evaluates a sample of a CPA firm's actual accounting work, including accounting reports issued and documentation prepared by the CPA firm as well as other procedures that the firm performed. Engagement reviews are only available for CPA firms that do not perform audits or other similar engagements.

**Public Company Accounting Oversight Board (PCAOB) (33)** A board established by the Sarbanes-Oxley Act of 2002 to provide oversight of accounting firms that audit public companies by (1) establishing or adopting professional and ethical standards, (2) conducting inspections of CPA firms, and (3) enforcing compliance with professional and ethical standards. The board is composed of five individuals appointed by the SEC.

**Qualified opinion (47)** The appropriate form of audit report when there is a limitation in the scope of the audit or when the financial statements depart from GAAP significantly enough to require mention in the auditors' report, but not so significantly as to necessitate disclaiming an opinion or expressing an adverse opinion.

**Quality control standards (33)** AICPA standards for establishing quality control policies and procedures that provide reasonable assurance that all of a CPA firm's engagements are conducted in accordance with applicable professional standards.

**Reasonable assurance (37)** In the context of an audit of financial statements, a high, but not absolute, level of assurance that the financial statements do not contain material misstatements due to errors or fraud. A level of reasonable assurance implies a low level of audit risk, the risk that the auditors express an inappropriate audit opinion when the financial statements are materially misstated.

**Registered public accounting firm (51)** A public accounting firm registered with the Public Company Accounting Oversight Board in accordance with the Sarbanes-Oxley Act of 2002. Any CPA firm auditing SEC reporting companies must be registered.

**Special-purpose financial reporting framework (35)** A financial reporting framework other than GAAP, which is one of the following bases of accounting; cash basis, tax basis, regulatory basis, or contractual basis.

**Standard report (42)** An audit report with (1) an unmodified (unqualified) opinion and (2) no additional matters emphasized (e.g., a change in accounting principles) beyond the information required in all audit reports. Note that while this term is frequently used in practice, the AICPA no longer formally uses it in its standards.

## Review Questions

2–1. Contrast the roles of the AICPA and the PCAOB in the development of auditing standards.

2–2. What is the difference between generally accepted accounting principles (GAAP) and AICPA generally accepted auditing standards (GAAS)?

2–3. What is a financial reporting framework? Why is a financial reporting framework important to a financial statement audit?

2–4. What relationship exists between AICPA generally accepted auditing standards (GAAS) and the *Statements on Auditing Standards (SASs)*?

2–5. In the context of an audit of financial statements, explain what is meant by professional skepticism.

2–6. Explain briefly the auditors' responsibility for detecting noncompliance with laws by clients.

2–7. Evaluate the following quotation: "If a CPA firm completes a nonpublic company audit of Adam Company's financial statements following AICPA generally accepted auditing standards and is satisfied with the results of the audit, an unmodified audit report may be issued. On the other hand, if no audit is performed of the current year's financial statements, but the CPA firm has performed satisfactory audits in prior years, has confidence in the management of the company, and makes a quick review of the current year's financial statements, a qualified report may be issued."

Do you agree? Give reasons to support your answer.

2–8. Pike Company has had an annual audit performed by the same firm of certified public accountants for many years. The financial statements and copies of the audit report are distributed to stockholders each year shortly after completion of the audit. Who is primarily responsible for the fairness of these financial statements? Explain.

2–9. Draft the standard form of audit report commonly issued after a satisfactory audit of a nonpublic client's financial statements.

2–10. Davis & Co., Certified Public Accountants, after completing an audit of Samson Company, decided that it would be unable to issue an unmodified opinion. What circumstances might explain this decision?

2–11. State the principal assertions made by the auditors in the opinion paragraph of the AICPA auditors' standard report.

2–12. Alan Weston, CPA, completed an audit of Kirsten Manufacturing Company and issued a standard audit report. What does this tell us about the extent of the auditing procedures included in the audit?

2–13. When a CPA firm completes an audit of a nonpublic business and issues a report, does it express an opinion on the client's accounting records, financial statements, or both? Give reasons.

2–14. A CPA firm does not guarantee the financial soundness of a client when it renders an opinion on financial statements, nor does the CPA firm guarantee the absolute accuracy of the statements. Yet the CPA firm's opinion is respected and accepted. What is expected of the CPA firm in order to merit such confidence?

2–15. If a CPA firm has performed a thorough professional audit of a client's financial statements, should it not be able to issue a report dealing with facts rather than the mere expression of an opinion? Explain.

2–16. What is a "material" amount from the perspective of auditors? Give an example of how that amount may differ based on the nature of the item.

2–17. Explain how the auditors determine whether a client's accounting is appropriate when the *FASB Codification* includes no specific guidance with respect to accounting for a particular type of transaction.

2–18. Do the AICPA attestation standards supersede any of the AICPA generally accepted auditing standards? Explain.

2–19. What is the meaning of *quality control* and *peer review* as these terms relate to the operation of a CPA firm? Is peer review mandatory? Explain.

2–20. Explain the basic objective of establishing quality control procedures in the following areas.

   *a.* Engagement performance.

   *b.* Human resources.

   *c.* Monitoring.

2–21. Do the AICPA's *Statements on Quality Control Standards* require every CPA firm to implement similar quality control procedures? Explain.

2–22. What are the duties and responsibilities of the Public Company Accounting Oversight Board?

2–23. Distinguish between the system review and the engagement review types of peer reviews.

2–24. Briefly describe four differences between an international audit report and one based on the PCAOB reporting standards.

## Questions Requiring Analysis

*Required:*

**LO 1, 7**  2–25. Various organizations develop standards for audits and regulate CPA firms. Compare and contrast the roles of the AICPA, the PCAOB, and the state boards of accountancy along the following dimensions:

   *a.* Standard setting.

   *b.* Regulation of CPA firms.

   *c.* Source of authority.

**LO 1**  2–26. An attitude of independence is a most essential element of an audit by a firm of certified public accountants. Describe several situations in which the CPA firm might find it somewhat difficult to maintain this independent point of view.

**LO 1, 3**  2–27. Jane Lee, a director of a nonpublic corporation with a number of stockholders and lines of credit with several banks, suggested that the corporation appoint as controller John Madison, a certified public accountant on the staff of the auditing firm that had made annual audits of the corporation for many years. Lee expressed the opinion that this move would effect a considerable savings in professional fees because annual audits would no longer be needed.

She proposed to give the controller, if appointed, an internal auditing staff to carry on such continuing investigations of accounting data as appeared necessary. Evaluate this proposal.

**LO 3**  2–28.   Reed, CPA, accepted an engagement to audit the financial statements of Smith Company. Reed's discussions with Smith's new management and the predecessor auditor indicated the possibility that Smith's financial statements may be misstated due to the possible occurrence of errors, fraud, and illegal acts.

*Required:*

a. Identify and describe Reed's responsibilities to detect Smith's errors and fraud. Do *not* identify specific audit procedures.

b. Describe Reed's responsibilities to detect Smith's material noncompliance with laws. Do *not* identify specific audit procedures.

c. Identify and describe Reed's responsibilities to report Smith's noncompliance with laws.

(AICPA, adapted)

**LO 7**  2–29.   While the AICPA administers a peer review program for CPA firms, the PCAOB staff performs practice inspections.

*Required:*

a. Identify the two basic types of peer review.

b. On what part of a firm's practice does the PCAOB staff focus its inspections?

c. Describe a PCAOB inspection.

d. Describe how the PCAOB staff selects an audit engagement for inspection.

## Objective Questions

**All applicable questions are available with McGraw-Hill's *Connect™ Accounting*.**

2–30.   **Multiple Choice Questions**

Select the best answer for each of the following items and give reasons for your choice.

**LO 1**

a. Which of the following organizations can revoke the right of an individual to practice as a CPA?

(1) The Public Company Accounting Oversight Board.

(2) The American Institute of Certified Public Accountants.

(3) The Securities and Exchange Commission.

(4) The applicable state board of accountancy.

**LO 2**

b. The AICPA over time has played an important role in standards setting. Which of the following standards are currently established by the AICPA?

(1) Accounting standards applicable to nonpublic companies.

(2) Auditing standards applicable to audits of nonpublic companies.

(3) Quality control standards applicable to audits of public companies.

(4) Standards for reviews of the interim financial information issued by public companies.

**LO 2**

c. Which of the following does the FASB consider a source of nonauthoritative guidance for use when there is no authoritative guidance available?

(1) The *FASB Codification.*

(2) *FASB Concepts Statements.*

(3) *SEC Rules.*

(4) *SEC Interpretive Releases*

**LO 1**

d. Financial statement audits performed under PCAOB requirements are designed to provide which type(s) of assurance with respect to the detection of material misstatements due to errors or fraud?

|     | Reasonable | Absolute |
| --- | --- | --- |
| (1) | Yes | Yes |
| (2) | Yes | No |
| (3) | No | Yes |
| (4) | No | No |

**LO 7**

e. A basic objective of a CPA firm is to provide professional services that conform with professional standards. Reasonable assurance of achieving this basic objective is provided through:

(1) Compliance with generally accepted reporting standards.

(2) A system of quality control.

(3) A system of peer review.

(4) Continuing professional education.

**LO 4**    *f.* Which of the following is *not* explicitly included in a standard report for a nonpublic company?

(1) The CPA's opinion that the financial statements comply with generally accepted accounting principles.

(2) That generally accepted auditing standards were followed during the audit.

(3) That internal control of the client was satisfactory.

(4) An identification of the financial statements audited.

**LO 1**    *g.* The general group of the 10 *PCAOB Auditing Standards* requires that:

(1) The auditors maintain an independent mental attitude.

(2) The audit be conducted in conformity with generally accepted accounting principles.

(3) Assistants, if any, be properly supervised.

(4) The auditors obtain an understanding of internal control.

**LO 7**    *h.* Which AICPA quality control standard would *most* likely be satisfied when a CPA firm maintains records indicating which partners or employees of the firm were previously employed by the CPA firm's clients?

(1) Professional relationship.

(2) Engagement performance.

(3) Relevant ethical requirements.

(4) Monitoring.

**LO 3**    *i.* An audit provides reasonable assurance of detecting material:

|  | **Fraudulent Financial Reporting** | **Misappropriation of Assets** |
|---|---|---|
| (1) | Yes | Yes |
| (2) | Yes | No |
| (3) | No | Yes |
| (4) | No | No |

**LO 5**    *j.* Which of the following is *not* included in an integrated audit report on the financial statements of a public company?

(1) The report states that the audit was performed in accordance with AICPA standards.

(2) The report indicates that the financial statements are the responsibility of management.

(3) The report indicates that the auditors have also audited the effectiveness of the company's internal control.

(4) The report is signed in the name of the CPA firm.

**LO 1**    *k.* Audit firms that are subject to inspections by the PCAOB staff include:

(1) All audit firms.

(2) Audit firms that are registered with the SEC.

(3) Audit firms that are registered with the PCAOB.

(4) Audit firms that are registered with a state board of accountancy.

**LO 8**    *l.* Which of the following is *not* a difference noted when comparing the AICPA audit report to the international audit report?

(1) The international audit report may use the phrase "true and fair view."

(2) The international audit report may be signed using the personal name of the audit partner, the audit firm, or both.

(3) The international audit report requires inclusion of the city of the CPA firm office that performed the audit.

(4) The international audit report includes an opinion on internal control.

(AICPA, adapted)

**LO 4**  2–31.  **Simulation**

Casa Royale, Inc., a nonpublic company, retained Ying and Company CPA to perform an audit of the financial statements for the current year. Howard Smythe, the partner in charge of the audit, drafted the following unmodified report:

---

### Independent Auditor's Report

To the Management of Casa Royale, Inc.:

We have examined the accompanying consolidated balance sheet of Casa Royale, Inc., and its subsidiaries, as of December 31, 20X1, and the related consolidated statements of income, retained earnings, and cash flows for the years then ended.

*Management's Responsibility for the Financial Statements*
Management is responsible for the preparation and fair presentation of these consolidated financial statements in accordance with accounting principles generally accepted in the United States of America; this includes the design, implementation, and maintenance of internal control relevant to the preparation and fair presentation of consolidated financial statements that are free from material misstatement, whether due to fraud or error.

*Auditor's Responsibility*
Our responsibility is to express an opinion on these financial statements based on our audit. We conducted our audit in accordance with auditing standards generally accepted in the United States of America. Those standards require that we plan and perform the audit to obtain reasonable assurance about whether the consolidated financial statements are free of material misstatement.

An audit involves performing procedures to obtain audit evidence about the amounts and disclosures in the consolidated financial statements. The procedures selected depend on the auditor's judgment, including the assessment of the risks of material misstatement of the consolidated financial statements, whether due to fraud or illegal acts. In making those risk assessments, the auditor considers internal control relevant to the entity's preparation and fair presentation of the consolidated financial statements in order to design audit procedures that are appropriate in the circumstances, but not for the purpose of expressing an opinion on the effectiveness of the entity's internal control. An audit also includes evaluating the appropriateness of accounting policies used and the reasonableness of significant accounting estimates made by management, as well as evaluating the overall presentation of the consolidated financial statements.

We believe that the audit evidence we have obtained is adequate to provide a basis for our audit opinion.

*Opinion*
In our opinion, the consolidated financial statements referred to above present fairly, in all material respects, the financial position of Casa Royale, Inc., and its subsidiaries as of December 31, 20X1, and the results of their operations and their cash flows for the years then ended in accordance with auditing standards generally accepted in the United States of America.

*Howard Smythe, Partner*
Phoenix, Arizona
February 12, 20X2

---

Respond as to the accuracy of the following comments made by a reviewer of the report:

| Reviewer's Comments | Comment Is Correct (yes or no) |
|---|---|
| a. The report should not be addressed to management. | |
| b. The report should indicate that we have "audited," rather than "examined," the financial statements (first paragraph after introduction). | |
| c. The report should not indicate anything concerning management's responsibility for internal control. | |
| d. The report should state that the auditors' responsibility is to express "reasonable assurance," not an opinion (first paragraph under "auditor's" responsibility). | |
| e. The audit is designed to assess risks of material misstatements due to errors or fraud; the term "illegal acts" is incorrect (second paragraph under auditor's responsibility). | |
| f. The report should not refer to the auditors "evaluating the appropriateness of accounting policies," since those are the responsibility of management. | |
| g. The evidence should be sufficient and appropriate rather than "adequate" (third paragraph under auditor's responsibility). | |

| Reviewer's Comments | Comment Is Correct (yes or no) |
|---|---|
| *h.* The opinion should not include "in all material respects" since the auditors are providing an opinion on the accuracy of the financial statements (opinion paragraph). | |
| *i.* The opinion should be on "accounting principles generally accepted in the United States of America," not on auditing standards (opinion paragraph). | |
| *j.* The signature on the report should be that of the CPA firm, not that of the partner. | |

LO 4    2–32.    State whether you agree (A) or disagree (D) with each of the following statements concerning the auditors' standard report of a nonpublic company.

| Statement | Agree (A) or Disagree (D) |
|---|---|
| *a.* The report must begin with "CPA's Report" at the top. | |
| *b.* The report is ordinarily addressed "to whom it may concern." | |
| *c.* The report indicates that management is responsible for the preparation of the financial statements. | |
| *d.* The report indicates that the auditors' responsibility is to obtain particular assurance about whether the financial statements are free of material misstatements. | |
| *e.* The report ordinarily concludes on whether the financial statements are in conformity with generally accepted auditing standards. | |
| *f.* The report indicates that the audit procedures selected depend on the auditors' judgment. | |
| *g.* The report indicates that the audit evidence obtained is sufficient and appropriate to provide a basis for the audit opinion. | |
| *h.* The report indicates that the auditors consider and provide an opinion on internal control. | |

LO 5    2–33.    Match each the following statements with the appropriate type of auditors' report (each auditors' report may be used once, more than once, or not at all):

     A. Adverse.

     D. Disclaimer.

     Q. Qualified.

     S. Standard unmodified.

| Statement | Type of Audit Report |
|---|---|
| *a.* The auditors are unable to determine the overall fairness of the financial statements. | |
| *b.* This is the report most clients prefer. | |
| *c.* A limitation on the scope of the audit is significant, but not so as to overshadow an overall opinion. | |
| *d.* The financial statements are not fairly presented. | |
| *e.* A material departure from GAAP exists, but not so material as to overshadow an overall opinion. | |

LO 2    2–34.    State whether each of the following is or is not a principle (or a portion of a principle) underlying an audit conducted in accordance with Generally Accepted Auditing Standards.

| Principles | Yes (Y) or No (N) |
|---|---|
| 1. The purpose of an audit is to provide financial statement users with an opinion by the auditors on whether the financial statements are presented fairly, in all material and immaterial respects, in accordance with the applicable financial reporting framework. | |
| 2. The auditors are responsible for having appropriate competence and capabilities to perform the audit. | |

| Principles | Yes (Y) or No (N) |
|---|---|
| 3. The auditors are unable to obtain absolute assurance that the financial statements are free from material misstatement. | |
| 4. The opinion states whether the financial statements are presented fairly, in all material respects, in accordance with the applicable financial reporting framework. | |
| 5. Inherent limitations of an audit include the need to conduct an audit to achieve a balance between the benefit to management and the benefit to the auditors. | |

**LO 1, 2, 3, 4**    2–35.    For each term in the first column select the partial (or complete) definition or illustration. Each partial (or complete) definition or illustration may be used only once.

| Term | Partial (or Complete) Definition or Illustration |
|---|---|
| a. A report providing a summary of findings | 1. A CPA firm that may conduct only audits of public companies |
| b. A report providing reasonable assurance | 2. A CPA firm that may conduct audits of public or non-public companies |
| c. An error | 3. Agreed-upon procedures report |
| d. Financial reporting framework | 4. A review of a CPA firm conducted by PCAOB |
| e. Fraud | 5. An independent peer review |
| f. Inspection | 6. An unintentional misstatement |
| g. Quality control elements | 7. Audit report |
| h. Registered public accounting firm | 8. Generally accepted accounting principles |
| | 9. Generally accepted auditing standards |
| | 10. Human resources and monitoring |
| | 11. Independence and reasonable assurance |
| | 12. Misappropriation of assets |
| | 13. Review report |

## Problems

**All applicable problems are available with McGraw-Hill's *Connect*™ *Accounting*.**  connect |ACCOUNTING

**LO 1, 2, 3**    2–36.    Joe Rezzo, a college student majoring in accounting, helped finance his education with a part-time job maintaining all accounting records for a small business, White Company, located near the campus. Upon graduation, Rezzo passed the CPA examination and joined the audit staff of a national CPA firm. However, he continued to perform all accounting work for White Company during his "leisure time." Two years later, Rezzo received his CPA certificate and decided to give up his part-time work with White Company. He notified White that he would no longer be available after preparing the year-end financial statements.

On January 7, Rezzo delivered the annual financial statements as his final act for White Company. The owner then made the following request: "Joe, I am applying for a substantial bank loan, and the bank loan officer insists upon getting audited financial statements to support my loan application. You are now a CPA, and you know everything that's happened in this company and everything that's included in these financial statements, and you know they give a fair picture. I would appreciate it if you would write out the standard audit report and attach it to the financial statements. Then I'll be able to get some fast action on my loan application."

*Required:*

a. Would Rezzo be justified in complying with White's request for an auditor's opinion? Explain.

b. If you think Rezzo should issue the audit report, do you think he should first perform an audit of the company despite his detailed knowledge of the company's affairs? Explain.

c. If White had requested an audit by the national CPA firm for which Rezzo worked, would it have been reasonable for that firm to accept and to assign Rezzo to perform the audit? Explain.

**LO 6**    2–37.    Bart James, a partner in the CPA firm of James and Day, received the following memorandum from John Gray, president of Gray Manufacturing Corporation, an audit client of many years.

Dear Bart:

I have a new type of engagement for you. You are familiar with how much time and money we have been spending in installing equipment to eliminate the air and water pollution caused by our manufacturing plant. We have changed our production process to reduce discharge of gases; we have changed to more expensive fuel sources with less pollution potential; and we have discontinued some products because we couldn't produce them without causing considerable pollution.

I don't think the stockholders and the public are aware of the efforts we have made, and I want to inform them of our accomplishments in avoiding danger to the environment. We will devote a major part of our annual report to this topic, stressing that our company is the leader of the entire industry in combating pollution. To make this publicity more convincing, I would like to retain your firm to study what we have done and to attest as independent accountants that our operations are the best in the industry as far as preventing pollution is concerned.

To justify your statement, you are welcome to investigate every aspect of our operations as fully as you wish. We will pay for your services at your regular audit rates and will publish your "pollution opinion" in our annual report to stockholders immediately following some pictures and discussion of our special equipment and processes for preventing industrial pollution. We may put this section of the annual report in a separate cover and distribute it free to the public. Please let me know at once if this engagement is acceptable to you.

*Required:*   Put yourself in Bart James's position and write a reply to this client's request. Indicate clearly whether you are willing to accept the engagement and explain your attitude toward this proposed extension of the auditor's attest function.

**In-Class Team Case**   **LO 3**   2–38.

Hide-It (HI), a family-owned business based in Tombstone, Arizona, builds custom homes with special features, such as hidden rooms and hidden wall safes. Hide-It has been an audit client for three years.

You are about to sign off on a "clean" opinion on HI's current annual financial statements when Art Hyde, the VP-Finance, calls to tell you that the Arizona Department of Revenue has seized control of a Hide-It bank account that includes about $450,000 of company funds; the account is not currently recorded in the accounting system and you had been unaware of it. In response to your questions about the origin of the funds, Art assures you that the funds, though not recorded as revenue, had been obtained legitimately. He explains that all of the money came from separately billed but unrecorded change orders to items in contracts completed before you became HI's auditor, and before he or any members of current management became involved with the company. You subsequently determine that there is insufficient evidence to allow you to reconstruct the nature of these cash transactions, although the following analysis is available from the Arizona Department of Revenue:

| | |
|---|---|
| Deposits 1/17/X2–12/3/X4 | $455,000 |
| Interest earned 1/2/X2–12/31/X8 | 95,000 |
| Withdrawals 2/12/X3–4/7/X7 | (100,000) |
| Balance 12/31/X8 | $450,000 |

Art also informs you that HI has agreed to pay a combined tax and penalty of 12 percent on the total funds deposited within 120 days as required by a recently enacted rule that provides amnesty for tax evaders. Furthermore, he states that negotiations with the Internal Revenue Service are in process.

*Required:*   a. The professional standards define errors as unintentional misstatements or omissions of amounts or disclosures in the financial statements. Is the situation described an error?

b. The professional standards state that fraud relates to intentional misstatements or omissions of amounts or disclosures in the financial statements. Misstatements due to fraud may occur due to either (*a*) fraudulent financial reporting or (*b*) misappropriation of assets. Does the situation appear to be fraud? If so, is it fraudulent financial reporting, misappropriation of assets, or both?

c. The professional standards outline certain auditor responsibilities relating to identifying client noncompliance with laws and distinguish between laws with a "direct effect" on the financial statements and other laws. Does the situation herein relate to noncompliance with laws as discussed within the auditing standards? If so, is the noncompliance related to a law with a direct effect on the financial statements or another law.

d. Should the CPA firm resign in this situation? If the decision is not clear-cut, what additional information would you desire before deciding?

**Research and Discussion Case**

LO 3

2–39.    Enormo Corporation is a large multinational audit client of your CPA firm. One of Enormo's subsidiaries, Ultro, Ltd., is a successful electronics assembly company that operates in a small Caribbean country. The country in which Ultro operates has very strict laws governing the transfer of funds to other countries. Violations of these laws may result in fines or the expropriation of the assets of the company.

During the current year, you discover that $50,000 worth of foreign currency was smuggled out of the Caribbean country by one of Ultro's employees and deposited in one of Enormo's bank accounts. Ultro's management generated the funds by selling company automobiles, which were fully depreciated on Ultro's books, to company employees.

You are concerned about this illegal act committed by Ultro's management and decide to discuss the matter with Enormo's management and the company's legal counsel. However, Enormo's management and board of directors seem to be unconcerned with the matter and express the opinion that you are making far too much of a situation involving an immaterial dollar amount. They also believe that it is unnecessary to take any steps to prevent Ultro's management from engaging in illegal activities in the future. Enormo's legal counsel indicates that the probability is remote that such an illegal act would ever be discovered, and that if discovery were to occur, it would probably result in a fine that would not be material to the client's consolidated financial statements.

Your CPA firm is ready to issue the integrated audit report on Enormo's financial statements and internal control for the current year, and you are trying to decide on the appropriate course of action regarding the illegal act.

*Required:*

a.    Discuss the implications of this illegal act by Ultro's management.

b.    Describe the courses of action that are available to your CPA firm regarding this matter.

c.    State your opinion as to the course of action that is appropriate. Explain.

**Suggested References**

AICPA, *Professional Standards,* Volume 2, Commerce Clearing House, *Statements on Quality Control Standards,* Section QC 10.

"Consideration of Fraud in a Financial Statement Audit" (New York, 1996), AICPA AU 240 (PCAOB 316).

"Consideration of Laws and Regulations in an Audit of Financial Statements," AICPA AU 250 (PCAOB 319).

*FASB Accounting Standards Codification,* section 450–20.

---

## Appendix 2A

# Comparison of International Standards on Auditing with AICPA Auditing Standards

Although AICPA *Statements on Auditing Standards (SASs)* and *International Standards on Auditing (ISAs)* are similar in most areas, they do differ in some. This appendix identifies a number of those differences and indicates the chapter in the text that includes coverage of the related topic. Both the SASs and ISAs differ from *PCAOB Auditing Standards* in that they do not require an audit of internal control over financial reporting.

| Topic | AICPA SASs | International ISAs |
|-------|-----------|-------------------|
| **Professional Requirements (Chapter 2)** | Two categories: Unconditional requirements and presumptively mandatory requirements. | One category: Auditor required to comply, except in "exceptional" circumstances. |
| **Terms of Engagement (Chapter 6)** | Auditor must remind client of the existing terms of the engagement. Before accepting engagement, auditor should request management to authorize contact with predecessor and auditor should evaluate responses obtained from predecessor in determining whether to accept engagement. | Requires considering whether there is a need to remind client. No similar requirement. |

| | | |
|---|---|---|
| **Documentation (Chapter 5)** | Throughout the standards, documentation requirements are often more detailed. | Requirements often less detailed. |
| **Initial Audit Engagements (Chapter 6)** | When predecessor has audited prior period financial statements, successor should request management to authorize review of audit documentation. Requires procedures beyond reviewing predecessor's documentation on opening balances. | Not required.<br><br>Not required. |
| **Confirmation of Accounts Receivable (Chapter 11)** | Presumptively required unless accounts receivable are immaterial, the use of confirmations requests would be ineffective, or the risk of misstatement is low. | Not required. |
| **Fraud (Chapter 2)** | Requires a brainstorming session focused on fraud factors and the possibility of management override of controls. | Includes a more general requirement for a discussion of the susceptibility of the financial statements to material misstatements. |
| **Inquiry to Lawyers (Chapter 16)** | Required unless no litigation, claims, or assessments that may give rise to a risk of material misstatement exist. Documentation for basis of a decision not to inquire of lawyer is required. | Only required when an auditor "assumes a risk of material misstatement." |
| **Audit Reports Opinion (Chapters 2, 17)**<br><br>**Changes in Accounting Principles (Chapter 17)**<br>**Going Concern (Chapter 17)**<br><br><br><br><br>**Group Audits (Chapter 17)**<br><br><br><br>**Audit Report Signed (Chapters 2, 17)** | Audit opinion is on whether financial statements "present fairly" in all material respects.<br>An emphasis of matter paragraph is added when a client has changed accounting principles.<br>Time horizon on judgment of whether a company is a going concern is not to exceed a year. It is not necessary to design procedures solely to identify whether there is a going concern question—the results of procedures performed for other purposes are sufficient.<br>Auditors of group financial statements may make reference in their report to reliance on component auditors for a portion of the audit.<br>With CPA firm name. | Audit opinion either on "present fairly" or "give a true and fair view."<br>Not required.<br><br>Time horizon is at least, but not limited to, one year. Must obtain sufficient appropriate audit evidence to evaluate management's assessment of the entity's ability to continue as a going concern.<br>Not allowed<br><br><br>CPA firm name and/or engagement partner. |
| **Communicating with Those Charged with Governance**<br>**Internal Control Deficiencies (Chapter 7)**<br><br>**Other Matters (Chapter 16)** | Distinguishes between significant deficiencies in internal control and material weaknesses. The auditor must identify each in the communication.<br>When the board of directors includes non-management directors, it should be informed of (1) material corrected misstatements identified by the auditor and (2) the auditor's views about significant matters that management has consulted with other accountants on. | Only considers significant deficiencies, with no consideration of material weaknesses.<br>Not required |
| **Attest and Assurance Engagements Other than Financial Statements\* (Chapters 2, 19, 20)** | Attest engagements are those in which a practitioner is engaged to issue or does issue an examination, a review, or an agreed-upon procedures report on subject matter or an assertion about the subject matter that is the responsibility of another party. Assurance engagements are broader in that they are professional services that enhance the quality of information, or its context, for decision makers. Most assurance engagements are also structured as attest engagements. | The term *attest engagement* is not used in the international standards. Assurance engagements include examinations and reviews and are therefore similar to AICPA attest engagements for those two services. Agreed-upon procedures are considered a *related service* and not an assurance service. |

\*The relevant standards for attest and assurance engagements are not the AICPA *SASs* or the *ISAs*, but rather *Statements on Standards for Attestation Engagements* and *International Standards on Assurance Engagements*, respectively.

# Professional Ethics

All recognized professions have acknowledged the importance of ethical behavior and have developed codes of professional ethics. Our purpose in this chapter is to discuss the nature of professional ethics as well as to present and discuss the AICPA *Code of Professional Conduct,* the additional requirements for auditors of public companies, and The Institute of Internal Auditors *Code of Ethics.*

## The Nature of Ethics

**LO1**

Describe the nature of ethics and ethical dilemmas.

Ethics has been defined as the study of moral principles and values that govern the actions and decisions of an individual or group. While personal ethics vary from individual to individual at any point in time, most people within a society are able to agree about what is considered ethical and unethical behavior. In fact, a society passes laws that define what its citizens consider to be the more extreme forms of unethical behavior.

Much of what is considered unethical in a particular society is not specifically prohibited. So how do we know whether we are acting ethically? Who decides what standards of conduct are appropriate? Is any type of behavior "ethical" as long as it does not violate a law or a rule of one's profession?

A good starting point for considering ethics is to examine the context in which most ethical questions arise—relationships among people. Any relationship between two or more individuals carries with it sets of expectations by each of the individuals involved. Certainly, the relationship between a certified public accountant (CPA) and a client offers a number of interesting challenges. For example: Is it ethical for a senior auditor to underreport the number of hours worked on an audit engagement? Is it ethical to accept tickets to a baseball game from an audit client? May a CPA ethically allow a client to pay for a business lunch and still maintain independence? Are there ethical issues involved in a situation in which a staff auditor wishes to date the controller of one of his firm's audit clients? Does it matter whether the staff auditor works on that engagement?

### What Are Ethical Dilemmas?

An ethical dilemma is a situation that an individual faces involving a decision about appropriate behavior. A simple example of an ethical dilemma is presented below.

Assume that a student at your college finds an expensive wristwatch in one of the restrooms. What actions, if any, does the student take to find the original owner?

An ethical dilemma generally involves a situation in which the welfare of one or more other individuals is affected by the results of the decision. In the dilemma presented above, the welfare of the wristwatch's original owner is affected by the student's decision.

Ethical dilemmas faced by auditors often have an effect on the welfare of a large number of individuals or groups. As an example, if an auditor makes an unethical decision about the content of an audit report, the wealth of thousands of investors and creditors may be affected.

## A Framework for Ethical Decisions

How do we make decisions about an appropriate course of action when faced with an ethical dilemma? As a starting point, let's consider how people make decisions in general. Certainly, many decisions require little conscious thought. The untied shoelace is quickly retied. The disposable pen that skips is quickly discarded and replaced. However, when the results of the decision have more significant consequences, a formal decision process is generally used. The steps involved in making any decision generally include:

1. Identify the problem.
2. Identify possible courses of action.
3. Identify any constraints relating to the decision.
4. Analyze the likely effects of the possible courses of action.
5. Select the best course of action.

Various frameworks have been proposed for addressing ethical dilemmas.[1] However, since almost every decision faced by a CPA has an ethical dimension, it would appear to be appropriate to analyze ethical dilemmas using the general decision-making framework presented above. Let's illustrate the use of this framework in the following situation.

## Making Ethical Decisions—A Professional Example

Assume that you have worked for a public accounting firm for approximately six months, and you were recently assigned to the audit of a small manufacturing company. The senior auditor on the job assigned you the task of extracting financial information about comparable companies from several financial databases on the Internet. She indicated that the work must be completed by Monday morning. While you had hoped to complete the assignment on Friday, things didn't work out and you had to come to work on Saturday.

On Saturday, your expectation that it would take only a couple hours to complete the task faded and you didn't finish until 4 p.m., after eight hours of work. You believe that part of the problem was that you were out late Friday night at a Kings of Leon concert and you just weren't all that efficient. Although you completed the task, you exceeded the budgeted hours for the task by six hours. Because of the circumstances (inefficient work and the blown budget), you are tempted to underreport the number of hours that you actually worked. While your firm has an informal policy that encourages employees to report all hours worked, you are aware that the policy is often ignored by other staff auditors. In addition, you are aware that your evaluation on this audit will be based not only on the quality of your work, but also on your ability to meet time budgets. You have been criticized on your evaluations on previous engagements for taking too long to perform certain tasks.

Since you are paid a straight monthly salary and a year-end bonus based on performance, your pay will not be directly affected by underreporting the hours worked. You could even argue that not reporting the hours might improve your evaluation and lead to a bigger bonus.

Now let's analyze this ethical dilemma using the decision-making framework previously presented.

1. *Identify the problem.* The problem in this case is that you have exceeded the time budget for your assigned task.
2. *Identify possible courses of action.* Although there are any number of options for reporting the number of hours worked, for simplicity's sake let's assume that you are considering only two: (1) reporting only two of the eight hours worked on Saturday to exactly meet the budget, or (2) reporting all eight hours.

---

[1] For a description of models that have been suggested for use to resolve ethical dilemmas faced by professionals, see *Ethical Decisions in Medicine* by Howard Brody (Boston: Little, Brown and Company, 1981), second edition.

3. *Identify any constraints relating to the decision.* Ethical dilemmas such as this one frequently involve both internal and external standards that serve as constraints. Internal standards may be the result of your religious or other beliefs about the manner in which you should behave and make decisions. These standards involve such concepts as truthfulness, fairness, loyalty, and caring for others. Perhaps you believe that one must be absolutely truthful in every situation; alternatively, you might believe that in certain circumstances absolute truthfulness is not necessary. As an example, some people might believe that caring for others is sometimes more important than telling the truth. They might decide that it is not proper to tell a patient with heart failure that he is unlikely to survive the night, even if he asks. Some people's concepts of loyalty and fairness might also prevent them from being completely truthful in all cases.

   External standards are those that are imposed upon an individual by society, peers, organizations, employers, or his or her profession. In this circumstance, the relevant external standards include the informal firm policy about reporting time and the AICPA *Code of Professional Conduct,* which requires "integrity" on the part of CPAs.

4. *Analyze the likely effects of the possible courses of action.* Because ethical dilemmas ordinarily affect individuals who are not involved in the decision-making process, this step involves considering the implications of the various courses of action on both the individual involved and anyone else who is affected by the decision. Also, it is important to consider both the short-term and the long-term effects. The following table presents these considerations as they apply to the two alternative courses of action in this situation.

5. *Select the best course of action.* You are the only one who can determine how to respond in situations such as this. The individual whose utmost consideration is career advancement may believe that underreporting the time is the solution. However, that individual should realize that in the long run he or she may be "caught" and the negative reaction by the firm could be extreme. Alternatively, the individual with the simple rule "tell the truth" has the obvious solution of reporting all the hours.

| Alternative 1: Report Only Two Hours | | |
|---|---|---|
| **Effect on:** | **Positive Effects:** | **Negative Effects:** |
| You | • Performance evaluation may be improved<br>• Bonus may be positively affected | • Is inconsistent with AICPA *Code of Professional Conduct*<br>• Is not consistent with informal firm policy<br>• Action is dishonest |
| The CPA firm | | • Informal policy is violated<br>• Possible underbilling of the client<br>• May encourage the development of unrealistic budgets in the future that may affect the morale of employees and could lead to substandard performance of audits<br>• Underreporting of time on a large scale may adversely affect the firm's ability to attract and retain employees |
| Other staff | • The senior auditor may be positively evaluated by completing the job on budget | • May lead to the development of unrealistic budgets that adversely affect morale and lead to improper performance evaluations or force staff to underreport time |
| The client | • May lead to a lower total audit fee (particularly if combined with other underreporting of time) | • May cause substandard audits in the future if staff members struggle to meet unrealistic budgets |

### Alternative 2: Report All Eight Hours

| Effect on: | Positive Effects: | Negative Effects: |
|---|---|---|
| You | • Action is truthful<br>• Consistent with informal firm policy<br>• Consistent with AICPA *Code of Professional Conduct* | • Performance evaluation may be negatively affected<br>• Bonus may be negatively affected |
| The CPA firm | • Results in proper billing of client<br>• More realistic budgets may be developed in the future | |
| Other staff | • More realistic budgets may lead to higher morale | • Senior auditor may be negatively evaluated due to budget overrun |
| The client | • May lead to better audits as staff auditors will be given more realistic budgets in the future | • May lead to a higher (though more accurate) audit fee |

*Discussion*

This ethical dilemma is constructed to illustrate the steps involved in making a professional decision. It is simplified in that the CPA could realistically decide to report any number of hours between zero and eight. Notice that one might attempt to "rationalize" underreporting some time by focusing on the inefficiency of the work and the inappropriateness of charging the client for this inefficiency. Another solution to this dilemma would be to charge the hours, but make it clear in a note to the senior auditor that you do not believe it fair to charge the client for some of the hours because of your inefficiency.

While this dilemma had a "correct" answer of eight hours, many other decisions involve "gray areas," where there are no obvious answers. For example, consider the case in which the auditors are engaged by management of a company to evaluate the appropriateness of an accounting method that is being used to account for certain transactions. Presumably, if the auditors agree with management's accounting method, they will be engaged to audit the company. In researching the issue, the auditors find that no accounting standards specifically apply. While the auditors believe that there is some justification for management's method of accounting, they believe that another method is more acceptable. This is clearly an ethical dilemma in which there is no definitive answer. Nonetheless, auditors who do not carefully consider whether management's method can be justified, or who sacrifice their principles to obtain the audit engagement, are not playing a very valuable role in society.

The above examples show that an individual's self-interest may be inconsistent with acting in accordance with his or her ethical beliefs. This is often the case in many of the ethical dilemmas that are faced by individuals as well as professional accountants.

The purpose of the remainder of this chapter is to discuss the requirements of the AICPA *Code of Professional Conduct* and The Institute of Internal Auditors *Code of Ethics*. In addition, we will describe the additional requirements for auditors of public companies. These requirements attempt to provide auditors with a minimum set of standards for making ethical decisions. They cannot, however, address all situations, and the auditors often are called on to use professional judgment to make decisions in ethically perplexing situations.

## The Need for Professional Ethics

To understand the importance of a code of ethics to public accountants and other professionals, one must understand the nature of a profession as opposed to other vocations. There is no universally accepted definition of what constitutes a profession; yet, for generations, certain types of activities have been recognized as professions while others have

**LO2**

Describe a profession's reasons for establishing professional ethics.

not. Medicine, law, engineering, architecture, and theology are examples of disciplines long accorded professional status. Public accounting is a relative newcomer to the ranks of the professions, but it has achieved widespread recognition in recent decades.

All the recognized **professions** have several common characteristics. The most important of these characteristics are (1) a responsibility to serve the public, (2) a complex body of knowledge, (3) standards of admission to the profession, and (4) a need for public confidence. Let us briefly discuss these characteristics as they apply to public accounting.

### Responsibility to Serve the Public

The certified public accountant is a representative of the public—creditors, stockholders, consumers, employees, and others—in the financial reporting process. The role of the independent auditor is to ensure that information is *fair to all parties* and not biased to benefit one group at the expense of another. This responsibility to serve the public interest must be a basic motivation for the professional. Public accountants must maintain a high degree of independence from their clients if they are to be of service to the larger community. Independence is perhaps the most important concept embodied in public accounting's *Code of Professional Conduct.*

### Complex Body of Knowledge

Any practitioner or student of accounting has only to look at the abundance of authoritative pronouncements governing financial reports to realize that accounting is a complex body of knowledge. One reason such pronouncements continue to proliferate is that accounting must reflect what is taking place in an increasingly complex environment. As the environment changes—such as the trend toward business reorganizations beginning in the 1980s through today—accounting principles and auditing practices must adapt. The continual growth in the "common body of knowledge" for practicing accountants has led the AICPA and other professional and regulatory bodies to enact continuing education requirements for CPAs. The need for technical competence and familiarity with current standards of practice is embodied in the *Code of Professional Conduct.*

### Standards of Admission to the Profession

Attaining a license to practice as a certified public accountant requires an individual to meet minimum standards for education and experience. The individual must also pass the uniform CPA examination showing mastery of the body of knowledge described above. Once licensed, certified public accountants must adhere to the ethics of the profession or risk disciplinary action.

### Need for Public Confidence

Physicians, lawyers, certified public accountants, and all other professionals must have the confidence of the public to be successful. To the CPA, however, public confidence is of special significance. The CPA's product is credibility. Without public confidence in the attestor, the attest function serves no useful purpose.

Professional ethics in public accounting as in other professions have developed gradually and are still in a process of change as the practice of public accounting itself changes. Often new concepts are added as a result of unfortunate incidents which, though they reflect unfavorably upon the profession, may not specifically violate existing standards.

## Professional Ethics in Public Accounting

Careless work or lack of integrity on the part of any CPA may lead the public to a negative view toward the entire profession. Consequently, the members of the public accounting profession acted in unison through the AICPA to develop a code of conduct. This code provides practical guidance to the individual member in maintaining a professional attitude. In addition, this code is designed to provide assurance to clients and to the public that the profession intends to maintain high standards and to enforce compliance by individual members.

Concerns about the credibility of audits, as discussed in Chapter 1, caused Congress to question the AICPA's ethical rules and enforcement processes. As a result, the Public Company Accounting Oversight Board (PCAOB) was given the authority to develop and enforce ethical rules for audits of public companies. As with other professional standards, the PCAOB adopted the AICPA ethical standards existing at April 16, 2003, as interim standards until it could develop its own. The ethical standards of the PCAOB do not currently differ significantly from those of the AICPA, with the exception of the rules relating to the types of nonattest services that may be performed for audit clients. In this chapter, we will focus on the AICPA standards, pointing out where ethical rules for audits of public companies differ.

# The AICPA *Code of Professional Conduct*

**LO3**

Discuss the Principles section of the American Institute of Certified Public Accountants (AICPA) *Code of Professional Conduct.*

The AICPA *Code of Professional Conduct* is designed to provide a framework for expanding professional services and responding to other changes in the profession, such as the increasingly competitive environment. It consists of two sections. The first section, the **Principles,** is a goal-oriented, positively stated discussion of the profession's responsibilities to the public, clients, and fellow practitioners. The Principles provide the framework for the Rules, the second section of the Code. The **Rules** are enforceable applications of the Principles. They define acceptable behavior and identify sources of authority for performance standards.

To provide guidelines for the scope and application of the Rules, the AICPA issues **Interpretations.** Senior Technical Committees of the AICPA, such as the Auditing Standards Board, interpret the Rules applying to their area of responsibility; the Professional Ethics Executive Committee issues interpretations that apply to all professional activities. The AICPA also issues **Ethics Rulings** that explain the application of the Rules and Interpretations to specific factual circumstances involving professional ethics. Figure 3.1 summarizes the relationships among the Principles, Rules, Interpretations, and Ethics Rulings.

A portion of the Principles section of the *Code of Professional Conduct* is quoted on the following page, followed by a presentation and analysis of the section of the Code that includes the Rules.

**FIGURE 3.1**
**AICPA Professional Ethics**

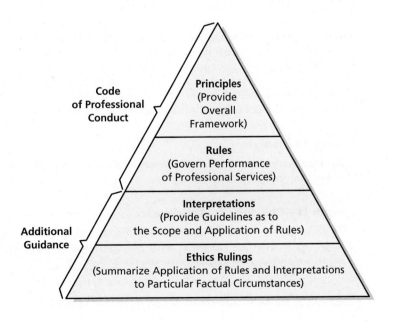

**Section I—Principles**[2]

**Preamble**

Membership in the American Institute of Certified Public Accountants is voluntary. By accepting membership, a certified public accountant assumes an obligation of self-discipline above and beyond the requirements of laws and regulations.

These Principles of the *Code of Professional Conduct* of the American Institute of Certified Public Accountants express the profession's recognition of its responsibilities to the public, to clients, and to colleagues. They guide members in the performance of their professional responsibilities and express the basic tenets of ethical and professional conduct. The Principles call for an unswerving commitment to honorable behavior, even at the sacrifice of personal advantage.

**Article I—Responsibilities**

*In carrying out their responsibilities as professionals, members should exercise sensitive professional and moral judgments in all their activities.*

As professionals, certified public accountants perform an essential role in society. Consistent with that role, members of the American Institute of Certified Public Accountants have responsibilities to all those who use their professional services. Members also have a continuing responsibility to cooperate with each other to improve the art of accounting, maintain the public's confidence, and carry out the profession's special responsibilities for self-governance. The collective efforts of all members are required to maintain and enhance the traditions of the profession.

**Article II—The Public Interest**

*Members should accept the obligation to act in a way that will serve the public interest, honor the public trust, and demonstrate commitment to professionalism.*

A distinguishing mark of a profession is acceptance of its responsibility to the public. The accounting profession's public consists of clients, credit grantors, governments, employers, investors, the business and financial community, and others who rely on the objectivity and integrity of certified public accountants to maintain the orderly functioning of commerce. This reliance imposes a public interest responsibility on certified public accountants. The public interest is defined as the collective well-being of the community of people and institutions the profession serves.

In discharging their professional responsibilities, members may encounter conflicting pressures from among each of those groups. In resolving those conflicts, members should act with integrity, guided by the precept that when members fulfill their responsibility to the public, clients' and employers' interests are best served.

Those who rely on certified public accountants expect them to discharge their responsibilities with integrity, objectivity, due professional care, and a genuine interest in serving the public. They are expected to provide quality services, enter into fee arrangements, and offer a range of services—all in a manner that demonstrates a level of professionalism consistent with these Principles of the *Code of Professional Conduct*.

All who accept membership in the American Institute of Certified Public Accountants commit themselves to honor the public trust. In return for the faith that the public reposes in them, members should seek continually to demonstrate their dedication to professional excellence.

**Article III—Integrity**

*To maintain and broaden public confidence, members should perform all professional responsibilities with the highest sense of integrity.*

**Article IV—Objectivity and Independence**

*A member should maintain objectivity and be free of conflicts of interest in discharging professional responsibilities. A member in public practice should be independent in fact and appearance when providing auditing and other attestation services.*

---

[2] Copyright by the American Institute of Certified Public Accountants, Inc.

### Article V—Due Care

*A member should observe the profession's technical and ethical standards, strive continually to improve competence and the quality of services, and discharge professional responsibility to the best of the member's ability.*

### Article VI—Scope and Nature of Services

*A member in public practice should observe the Principles of the* Code of Professional Conduct *in determining the scope and nature of services to be provided.*
Each of these Principles should be considered by members in determining whether or not to provide specific services in individual circumstances. In some instances, they may represent an overall constraint on the nonattest services that might be offered to a specific client. No hard-and-fast rules can be developed to help members reach these judgments, but they must be satisfied that they are meeting the spirit of the Principles in this regard.

In order to accomplish this, members should—

* Practice in firms that have in place internal quality-control procedures to ensure that services are competently delivered and adequately supervised.

* Determine, in their individual judgments, whether the scope and nature of other services provided to an audit client would create a conflict of interest in the performance of the audit function for that client.

* Assess, in their individual judgments, whether an activity is consistent with their role as professionals.

### Section II—Rules

**LO4**

Describe each of the Rules contained in the AICPA *Code of Professional Conduct.*

#### Applicability

*The bylaws of the American Institute of Certified Public Accountants require that members adhere to the Rules of the* Code of Professional Conduct. *Members must be prepared to justify departures from these Rules.*

Figure 3.2 is a complete listing of the Rules, which are presented and analyzed.

**Background on Independence and the AICPA Conceptual Framework for Independence Standards**

The public accounting profession acknowledges the critical importance of **independence,** both independence of mind (i.e., actual independence) and independence in appearance. **Independence of mind** is a state of mind that permits the CPA to perform an attest service without being affected by influences that might compromise professional judgment, thereby allowing that individual to act with integrity and to exercise objectivity and professional skepticism. **Independence in appearance** requires the avoidance of circumstances that might cause a reasonable and informed third party, aware of all relevant information, including safeguards applied, to reasonably conclude that the integrity,

**FIGURE 3.2**
**The Rules of the AICPA** *Code of Professional Conduct*

| Rule | Title |
|---|---|
| 101 | Independence |
| 102 | Integrity and Objectivity |
| 201 | General Standards |
| 202 | Compliance with Standards |
| 203 | Accounting Principles |
| 301 | Confidential Client Information |
| 302 | Contingent Fees |
| 501 | Acts Discreditable |
| 502 | Advertising and Other Forms of Solicitation |
| 503 | Commissions and Referral Fees |
| 504 | (Deleted) |
| 505 | Form of Organization and Name |

LO5

Explain the concept of independence and identify circumstances in which independence is impaired.

objectivity, or professional skepticism of an audit firm or member of the attest engagement team has been compromised.

Independence in appearance is a particularly difficult area. Acknowledging that it is impossible to enumerate all of the circumstances in which the appearance of independence might be questioned, the AICPA *Conceptual Framework for Independence Standards* suggests that CPAs should evaluate whether a particular **threat** would lead a reasonable person, aware of all the relevant facts, to conclude that an unacceptable risk of nonindependence exists. Figures 3.3 and 3.4 summarize threats to CPA independence and the CPA's approach to dealing with those threats.

As presented in Figure 3.4, if the *Code of Professional Conduct* directly sets forth requirements for a particular threat to independence, that resolves the issue—the rule must be followed. For example, the *Code of Professional Conduct* prohibits a member of the audit team for a client company from holding any common stock in that company.

**FIGURE 3.3**   **Broad Categories of Threats to Independence**

| Threat | Definition | Examples |
|---|---|---|
| Self-review | As a part of an attest engagement, using evidence that results from the firm's non-attest work | 1. The CPA firm has provided nonaudit services relating to the information system and the accountant is now considering results obtained from that information system in the audit |
| Advocacy | Actions promoting an attest client's interest or position | 1. Promoting client securities as part of an initial public offering<br>2. Representing a client in U.S. tax court |
| Adverse interest | Actions between the public accountant and the client that are in opposition | 1. Threatened or actual litigation between the public accountant and the client |
| Familiarity | Accountants having a close or long-standing relationship with client personnel or with individuals who performed nonattest services | 1. A spouse or close friend holds a key position with the client (e.g., chief executive officer)<br>2. A partner has provided attest services for a prolonged period<br>3. An accountant performs insufficient audit procedures when considering the results of a nonattest service performed by the accountant's firm<br>4. An accountant for the CPA firm recently was a director or officer at the client firm |
| Undue influence | An attest client's management coerces the public accountant or exercises excessive influence over the accountant | 1. Threat to replace firm over a disagreement on the application of an accounting principle<br>2. Pressure to reduce audit procedures for the purpose of reducing audit fees<br>3. A gift from the client that is other than clearly insignificant |
| Financial self-interest | A potential benefit to the accountant from a financial interest in, or some other financial relationship with, an attest client | 1. Having a direct financial interest or a material indirect financial interest in the client<br>2. Having a loan from the client<br>3. Excessive reliance on revenue from a single attest client<br>4. Having a material joint venture with the client |
| Management participation | The accountant taking on the role of client management or otherwise performing management functions | 1. Serving as an officer or director of the client<br>2. Establishing and maintaining internal controls for the client<br>3. Hiring, supervising, or terminating the client's employees |

**FIGURE 3.4**
**Evaluating Threats to Independence**

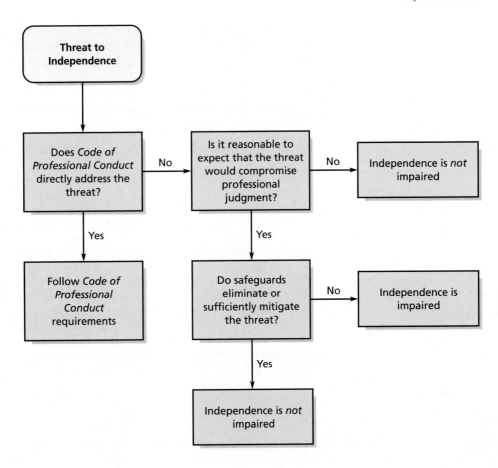

In such circumstances, no further consideration is required—that individual is not independent.

If the Code does *not* directly address a threat, the CPA must consider it from the perspective of a reasonable and informed third party who has knowledge of all the relevant information. If it is *not* reasonable to expect that a reasonably informed third party would consider the threat serious enough to compromise independence, no further consideration is necessary. However, if the identified threat *is* considered potentially serious, the CPA should consider whether adequate safeguards exist to eliminate or sufficiently mitigate it.

**Safeguards** are controls that mitigate or eliminate threats to independence. There are three broad categories of safeguards:

- Safeguards created by the profession, legislation, or regulation (e.g., education requirements, competency requirements for professional licensure).
- Safeguards implemented by the attest client (e.g., management with suitable skills and experience to make managerial decisions, or effective oversight by an independent board of directors).
- Safeguards put in place by the CPA firm, including policies and procedures for implementing professional and regulatory requirements (e.g., firm leadership that stresses the importance of independence, training that emphasizes independence, or strong policies and procedures).

After considering the facts and circumstances, including any safeguards, the CPAs make a final decision about whether or not independence is impaired.

**Rule 101—Independence**

*A member in public practice shall be independent in the performance of professional services as required by standards promulgated by bodies designated by Council.*

Interpretation 101–1 of the Code contains examples of transactions, interests, and relationships that impair independence. Specifically, the interpretation indicates that public accounting firm independence will be considered to be impaired if:

A. During the period of a professional engagement a covered member:
1. Had or was committed to acquire any direct or material indirect financial interest in the client.
2. Was a trustee of any trust or executor or administrator of any estate if such trust or estate had or was committed to acquire any direct or material indirect financial interest in the client and
   (i)  The covered member had the authority to make investment decisions for the trust or estate; or
   (ii) The trust or estate owned more than 10 percent of the client's outstanding equity securities or other ownership interests or the value of the trust's or estate's holdings in the client exceeded 10 percent of the total assets of the trust or estate.
3. Had a **joint closely held investment** that was material to the covered member.
4. Except as specifically permitted in Interpretation 101–5, had any loan to or from the client, any officer or director of the client, or any individual owning 10 percent or more of the client's outstanding equity securities or other ownership interests.[3]
B. During the period of the professional engagement, a partner or professional employee of the firm, his or her immediate family, or any group of such persons acting together owned more than 5 percent of a client's outstanding equity securities or other ownership interests.
C. During the period covered by the financial statements or during the period of the professional engagement, a partner or professional employee of the firm was simultaneously associated with the client as a:
1. Director, officer, or employee, or in any capacity equivalent to that of a member of management;
2. Promoter, underwriter, or voting trustee; or
3. Trustee for any pension or profit-sharing trust of the enterprise.

## Analysis of Independence

The independence rule does not apply to all services performed by public accountants. CPAs perform a host of services in which the client is the major beneficiary and which do not require independence, such as management consulting, tax, and accounting services. In performing these services, the CPAs are not providing assurance on information for third parties, and *observance of the independence rule is not required* as long as no attestation services are also being provided to the client.

The independence rule applies to auditing, but it also applies to all other attestation services, such as reviews of financial statements, examinations of financial forecasts, and the application of agreed-upon procedures to information. Our comments below regarding independence apply to CPAs when they perform any attestation service for a client.

*Independence Terminology*

It is important to recognize that independence concerns exist both at the individual CPA level and at the public accounting firm level; one, both, or neither may be considered independent with respect to a client or potential client. A public accounting firm does not necessarily lose independence with respect to an engagement when one (or more) of its employees or partners are not independent. For example, if a professional employee of a public accounting firm owns stock in a company, he or she is not independent. The public accounting firm may or may not be considered independent based on a consideration of

---

[3] Interpretation 101–5 allows certain loans from financial institution clients, including (1) automobile loans and leases collateralized by the automobile, (2) loans of the surrender value under the terms of an insurance policy, (3) borrowings fully collateralized by cash deposits at the same financial institution (e.g., "passbook loans"), and (4) credit cards and cash advances on checking accounts up to $5,000. In addition, certain "grandfathered loans," outstanding when the interpretation was issued, are allowed (e.g., a home mortgage with a financial institution that subsequently becomes an audit client); however, these loans must be current as to all terms and may not be renegotiated.

## Illustrative Case — *Indirect Financial Interests*

John Bates, a partner and covered member in the public accounting firm of Reynolds and Co., owns shares in a regulated mutual investment fund, which in turn holds shares of stock in audit clients of Reynolds and Co. The public accounting firm inquired of the AICPA Professional Ethics Division whether this financial interest by Bates affected his independence with respect to the clients.

The response was that this indirect interest would not normally impair the independence of the CPA, because investment decisions are made only by the mutual fund's management. However, if the portfolio of the mutual fund were heavily invested in securities of a client of Reynolds and Co., the indirect interest could become material to Bates and thereby impair his independence. Since Bates was found to be independent, his firm is independent.

additional factors. Interpretation 101–1, presented earlier, sets forth the general rules in this area.

Of primary importance to understanding Section A of Interpretation 101–1 is an understanding of the terms (1) "covered member," (2) "direct and indirect financial interests," and (3) "office in which the lead attest engagement partner primarily practices."

The first phrase, **covered member,** refers to an individual, firm, or entity that is capable of influencing an attest engagement and includes:

- An individual on the **attest engagement team.**
- An **individual in a position to influence the attest engagement** (e.g., a partner who directly supervises the partner who is in charge of the attest engagement).
- A partner in the office in which the partner in charge of the attest engagement primarily practices in connection with the attest engagement.
- Certain partners or **managers** who provide nonattest services to the client.
- The public accounting firm, including its employee benefit plan.
- Any entity controlled by one or more of the above.

A covered member must comply with the highest level of independence restrictions on financial, business, and other relationships with a client. A careful reading of Interpretation 101–1 reveals that the individuals within the firm affected under the three sections differ as follows:

Section A—Applies only to *covered members.*
Sections B and C—Apply to all *partners* and all *professional employees.*

Second, Section A of Interpretation 101–1 uses the terms "direct" and "indirect" financial interests. These terms are important because for an individual CPA *any* **direct financial interest** in an attest client impairs independence, while only a *material* **indirect financial interest** impairs independence. A direct financial interest includes an investment in the client, such as owning capital stock or providing loans to the client. An indirect financial interest generally involves an intermediary of some sort; for example, a CPA may invest in companies or in mutual funds, which in turn may hold financial interests in attest clients.

Finally, the *office in which the lead attest engagement partner primarily practices* in connection with the attest engagement is important because other partners in that office are treated as covered members under the requirements of Section A of Interpretation 101–1. Rather than use this rather bulky phrase in subsequent discussion, we will refer to the office as the "engagement office." Figure 3.5 summarizes public accounting firm independence as it is affected by a lack of independence by various individuals in the firm.

FIGURE 3.5 **The Effects of Partner and Professional Staff Relationships on Firm Independence***

| Section of Interpretation 101–1 | Serving on the Attest Engagement | In the Engagement Office | In Other Offices |
|---|---|---|---|
| A. Has direct or material indirect financial interest, loan, or joint business investment; or served as trustee or administrator of estate or trust that has direct or material indirect interest | Firm not independent | ***Professional Employee*** Firm independent (*unless the individual is a covered member*) ***Partner:*** Firm not independent | Firm independent (*unless the individual is a covered member*) |
| B. Owns 5 percent or more of client's outstanding equity or other ownership interest, or | Firm not independent | Firm not independent | Firm not independent |
| C. Simultaneously associated with client as director, officer, employees, promoter, trustee, etc. | | | |

*In all cases, the employee (or partner) is not independent.

One way to consider situations that may impair independence is to consider them as being related to (1) CPA financial and other personal matters, (2) interests of relatives and friends, or (3) CPA performance of nonattest services.

*Financial and Other Personal Interests in Attest Clients*

The restrictions on financial interests included in Section A of Interpretation 101–1 apply only to covered members. When a public accounting firm acquires a new attest client,[4] those who will become covered members must free themselves from any financial or other interest described in Section A of Interpretation 101–1. By disposing of such interests, the CPAs avoid a challenge to their independence in dealing with the new client. To illustrate, assume that a professional employee who is not a partner (e.g., a senior) has a direct financial interest in a prospective client and is going to be placed on the engagement team. That individual is not independent because of the financial interest. Figure 3.5 shows that the public accounting firm also is not independent if that employee retains the investment and serves on the attest engagement—lack of independence by a covered member results in a lack of firm independence. The solution here is to make certain that the employee either disposes of the investment or does not become a covered member (i.e., does not work on the engagement). Thus, the independence of a large public accounting firm is not necessarily impaired merely because one employee has a financial interest in the client. Many problems may be resolved easily by assigning a nonindependent professional employee to other engagements.

Part B of the interpretation sets forth the general provision that the CPA firm is not independent if any firm partners or professional employees, or their immediate families, own more than 5 percent of the equity of the client.

*Past Employment with the Client*   A lack of independence arising from a financial interest described in Sections A or B of Interpretation 101–1 can be remedied simply by disposing of the financial interest before the engagement commences. This is not true of employment relationships considered in Section C of Interpretation 101–1. CPAs who

---

[4] The period for which independence is required is the **period of the professional engagement,** which begins when a CPA either signs an initial engagement letter (or other agreement) or begins to perform an attest engagement, whichever is earlier. It ends with the termination of the professional relationship. The period *does not* end with the issuance of a report and recommence with the beginning of the following year's attest engagement.

## Illustrative Case — *Employment with Clients*

The situation in which audit clients hire audit firm personnel is difficult. On the one hand, it provides great professional opportunities for individuals who enter the public accounting profession. On the other, independence concerns have led to the restrictions presented in this section.

Questions were raised about the number of ex–Arthur Andersen employees hired by Enron Corporation prior to its collapse (see Chapter 1). Although both firms refused to disclose details, the positions and numbers of ex–Arthur Andersen employees hired by Enron seem significant. *The Wall Street Journal* reported that Enron executives who had previously worked with Arthur Andersen in auditing included its chief accounting officer, its chief financial officer, and the vice president of corporate development.

The *Washington Post* indicated that, over the years Arthur Andersen served as auditor, 86 employees left the firm and accepted positions at Enron.

In addition, questions arose as to the nature of the relationship between continuing Arthur Andersen employees and those of Enron. Again, *The Wall Street Journal* reported that Arthur Andersen auditors and consultants "shared in office birthdays, frequented lunch-time parties in a nearby park and participated in weekend fundraisers for charities. They even went on Enron employees' ski trips to Beaver Creek, Colorado." One Enron employee suggested that "people just thought they were Enron employees . . . they walked and talked the same way." Consistently, the *Washington Post* reported that the chief accounting officer was the Arthur Andersen partner's "regular golfing buddy," and that people at Enron referred to Andersen as "Enron Prep."

previously were employed by the client in a management capacity must disassociate themselves from that client and must not participate in audits of any periods during which they were employed by the client. The firm remains independent of the client (even if the individual is a partner), but the individual CPA is not independent.

*Future Employment with a Client*  Partners and covered members must report to the public accounting firm any specific offer or the intention to seek employment with an audit client. After such communication, the public accounting firm should remove that CPA from all engagements for that client until the offer has been rejected or employment is no longer being sought. The firm should also consider whether additional procedures are necessary to provide reasonable assurance that all work of that CPA was performed with objectivity and integrity.

When a public accounting firm professional accepts employment with the audit client, the engagement team should consider the need to modify future engagement procedures to adjust for the risk that audit effectiveness could be reduced due to the professional's knowledge of the audit plan. When the professional will have significant interaction with the engagement team, the firm should assess whether the existing team members have the appropriate experience and status to deal effectively with the former firm professional. Particular care should be taken in reviewing the audit when the former firm professional joins an attest client in a **key position**—one in which he or she has primary responsibility for, or influence over, accounting or financial statement reporting decisions.

For auditors of public companies, the restrictions are more stringent. The Sarbanes-Oxley Act of 2002 requires that one year pass before a member of the audit team may accept employment with an SEC registrant in certain designated positions (e.g., chief executive officer, controller, chief financial or accounting officer).

*Past Due Professional Fees*  If fees owed by a client to a public accounting firm become long overdue, it may appear that the firm's prospects for collection depend upon the nature of the CPAs' report on the current financial statements. Thus, the public accounting firm's independence is considered impaired if fees for professional services rendered in prior years have not been collected before issuance of the CPAs' report for the current year.

*Gifts*   An outsider may question the independence and objectivity of a public accounting firm in a situation in which a partner or employee receives an expensive gift from a client or gives an expensive gift to a client. Therefore, the value of any gifts received by a CPA should be clearly insignificant to the recipient and reasonable in the circumstances.

*Litigation*   Litigation involving the public accounting firm and the client may also affect the independence of CPAs. The relationship between the CPAs and client management must be characterized by complete candor and full disclosure. A relationship with these characteristics may not exist when litigation places the CPAs and client management in an adversarial position. CPAs in litigation, or potential litigation, with a client must evaluate the situation to determine whether the significance of the litigation affects the client's confidence in the CPAs or the CPAs' objectivity.

### Interests of a CPA's Relatives and Friends

How is independence affected by a financial interest or business position held by a relative of a CPA? The answer depends on the *closeness* of the family relationship and on whether the CPA works in the engagement office.

*Immediate Family Interests*   The independence rules generally assume that the interests of CPAs and their immediate families are indistinguishable from each other. Thus, as a general rule, a covered member's **immediate family members** (spouses, spousal equivalents, or dependents) are subject to the independence requirements. Accordingly, for example, under Section A of Interpretation 101–1, if a covered member's spouse owns even one share of a client's stock, the situation is evaluated as if the covered member held the stock and independence is impaired. A public accounting firm may retain its independence with respect to the engagement only by making certain that the CPA is not a covered member for that particular client.

There are two exceptions to the general rule that the interests of CPAs and their immediate families are considered indistinguishable from one another. A family member may be employed with the attest client if the family member is not in a position to influence the client's financial statements. More specifically, the family member must not be employed in a key position. Because such an employment situation is covered under Section C of Interpretation 101–1, this requirement applies to all partners and professional employees. The second exception allows, in certain instances, an immediate family member of a covered member to hold a financial interest through an employer's benefit plan. This exception does not, however, apply to the immediate family of partners or professionals on the attest engagement team or of those who can influence the engagement team.

An effective approach for considering an immediate family member's financial or business interest is to first assume it is that of the CPA. If the CPA is not independent under that assumption, he or she is not independent unless one of the two exceptions in the above paragraph applies. Concerning CPA firm independence, an independence judgment may be made using Figure 3.5.

*Interests of Close Relatives*   Independence may also be impaired by financial interests or business relationships of close relatives (e.g., parents, siblings, or nondependent children). The independence standard for **close relatives** applies to (1) members of the attest engagement team, (2) individuals in a position to influence the attest engagement, and (3) any partner in the engagement office. For these three groups, public accounting firm independence is impaired if a close relative has:

- A key position with the client, or
- A financial investment in the client that
  - Is material to the close relative and *of which the accountant has knowledge;* or
  - Enables the close relative to exercise **significant influence** over the client.

**FIGURE 3.6    Effect on Independence of Family Members, Relatives, and Friends\***

| Relative | Effect on Accountant and Firm Independence |
|---|---|
| **Immediate Family** (spouse, spousal equivalent, or dependent) | **General Rule:** Immediate family members are under the same restrictions as is the accountant. Accordingly, if a family member violates a rule, interpretation, or ruling that applies to the accountant, the accountant is not independent. For matters under section A of Rule 101, firm independence is impaired only if the accountant is a covered member. For matters under section B and C, firm independence is always impaired. <br><br> **Exceptions to the General Rule:** The accountant and firm are independent: <br> 1. When a family member is employed by a client in *other than* a key position, and <br> 2. In certain circumstances in which the immediate family member participates in a benefit plan related to a client. |
| **Close Relatives** (parent, sibling, or nondependent child) | Accountant and firm independence is impaired if an individual on the audit team has a close relative who has: <br> 1. A key position with the client, or <br> 2. A material financial interest of which the accountant has knowledge. |
| **Other Relatives and Friends** | Independence is only impaired when a reasonable person aware of all relevant facts relating to a situation would conclude that there is an unacceptable threat to independence; this evaluation (at both the accountant and the firm level) is made based on the AICPA *Conceptual Framework for Independence Standards*. |

\*Summary omits consideration of certain detailed factors that may affect independence. Consult Rule 101 and Interpretation 101–1 for a detailed consideration of the effect on independence of family members and relatives.

*Other Considerations for All Relatives and Friends*    The ethics standards do not attempt to enumerate every circumstance in which the appearance of independence might be questioned. In addition to the above guidance, a CPA should consider whether personal or business relationships would lead a reasonable person, aware of all the relevant factors, to conclude that there is an unacceptable threat to independence. This evaluation (at both the accountant and the firm level) is made using the AICPA *Conceptual Framework for Independence Standards*. Figure 3.6 provides a brief summary of the complex independence requirements that apply to a CPA's relatives. Professional employees with potential problems should consult their firm's policies, as well as Interpretation 101–1 on family relationships.

*Issues Arising from Providing Nonattest Services*

An ethical issue that has been at the forefront of the profession in recent years is the possible threat to the CPAs' independence when they perform attest services and nonattest services for the same client. What restrictions exist on providing nonattest services for a client?

The AICPA's Interpretation 101–3 requires that while the CPAs should not perform management functions or make management decisions for the attest client, they may provide advice, research materials, and recommendations to assist the client. In such circumstances, the client must agree to:

- Make all management decisions and perform all management functions.
- Designate a competent employee, preferably within senior management, to oversee the services.
- Evaluate the adequacy and results of the services performed.
- Accept responsibility for the results of the services.
- Establish and maintain internal control, including monitoring ongoing activities.

Before performing nonattest services, the CPAs must establish and document in writing the understanding with the client, including objectives of the engagement, services to be

## Illustrative Case

### Independence and Nonattest Work

A number of highly publicized cases were highlighted by the SEC and Congress as examples of situations in which performing nonattest services for a client may have affected auditor independence.

As an example, Global Crossing Ltd. reported it paid Arthur Andersen $2.3 million in audit fees in 2000, but the company paid Arthur Andersen more than $12 million in fees for nonattest work.

performed, the client's acceptance of its responsibilities, the CPAs' responsibilities, and any limitations of the engagement. Interpretation 101–3 provides the following examples of general activities that would impair a CPA's independence:

- Authorizing, executing, or consummating a transaction.
- Preparing source documents (e.g., purchase orders, payroll time records, and customer orders).
- Having custody of client assets.
- Supervising client employees in their normal recurring activities.
- Determining which recommendations should be implemented.
- Reporting to the board of directors on behalf of management.
- Serving as a client's stock transfer or escrow agent, registrar, or general counsel.

The above examples make it clear that a CPA who becomes a part-time controller for a client and assumes a *decision-making role* in the client's affairs is not in a position to make an independent audit of the financial statements. However, a CPA who provides bookkeeping or accounting services for the client can maintain independence under the AICPA rules. As long as the client takes responsibility for the financial statements and the auditors perform their engagement in accordance with generally accepted auditing standards, independence is not impaired. Of course, the accounting services provided cannot include executing transactions or performing other management functions. If the AICPA ruled that independence is impaired whenever the auditors perform accounting services, such a ruling would adversely affect many small public accounting firms with practices including considerable financial statement write-up work and occasional audits for small nonpublic clients. As we will describe in the next section, the rules for auditors of public companies prohibit them from performing any accounting or bookkeeping services for the client, along with a host of other services.

The AICPA maintains that public accounting firms have long been rendering consulting services to management while continuing to perform audits in an independent manner that serves the public interest. The AICPA and public accounting firms believe that the additional knowledge of the client that comes from performing these services actually enhances the audit. It also allows public accounting firms to have associates with more expertise, especially in the area of information technology. However, this is not the view of many critics of the profession, including some individuals from the Securities and Exchange Commission (SEC) and Congress. These concerns led to the provisions of the Sarbanes-Oxley Act of 2002 that prohibit the performance of a wide range of nonattest services for public company audit clients.

### Independence—Requirements for Audits of Public Companies

Independence standards for public companies are currently a combination of pronouncements by the AICPA and the SEC and the legal requirements of the Sarbanes-Oxley Act of 2002, as enforced and interpreted by the PCAOB. Historically, the AICPA has issued,

**LO6**

Contrast the independence rules for audits of public companies with those for audits of nonpublic companies.

and continues to issue, independence standards which apply to its members. The SEC also has established independence standards for audits of public companies that supplement those of the AICPA.

With passage of the Sarbanes-Oxley Act of 2002, the PCAOB is now responsible for adopting or establishing the ethical and independence standards for audits of public companies, with the authority and oversight of the SEC. The Sarbanes-Oxley Act of 2002 makes it unlawful for a registered public accounting firm that audits a public company to provide a variety of nonattest services to that client. Figure 3.7 summarizes those services as well as the AICPA's guidance. Bear in mind that the AICPA's guidance is relevant for nonpublic clients only. In addition, CPAs generally may provide allowed nonattest services only if they are approved in advance by the audit committee of the client's board

**FIGURE 3.7**   **Comparison of Sarbanes-Oxley and AICPA Requirements Regarding Providing Nonattest Services to Audit Clients**

| Service Not Allowed by Sarbanes-Oxley | AICPA *Code of Professional Conduct* Requirements |
|---|---|
| Bookkeeping or other services related to the accounting records or financial statements | Allowed, providing the auditors *do not:*<br>• Determine or change journal entries without client approval.<br>• Authorize or approve transactions.<br>• Prepare source documents.<br>• Make changes to source documents without client approval. |
| Financial information systems design and implementation | Auditors are allowed to:<br>• Implement a system not developed by auditor (e.g., off-the-shelf accounting packages).<br>• Assist in setting up a chart of accounts and financial statement format.<br>• Design, develop, install, or integrate an information system unrelated to the financial statements or accounting records.<br>• Provide training to client employees on the information and control system. |
| Appraisal, valuation, and actuarial services | Allowed, providing services *do not:*<br>• Relate to a material portion of the financial statements, *and*<br>• Involve a significant degree of subjectivity. |
| Internal audit outsourcing services | Allowed, providing the client understands its responsibility for internal control and:<br>• Designates competent individual(s) within the company to be responsible for the internal audit.<br>• Determines scope, risk, and frequency of internal audit activities.<br>• Evaluates findings and results.<br>• Evaluates adequacy of audit procedures performed. |
| Management functions or human resources | Auditors may provide various types of advice but may not perform management functions. |
| Various investment services | Certain services are allowed, including:<br>• Assisting in developing corporate finance strategies.<br>• Recommending allocation of funds to investments. |
| Legal services and expert services unrelated to auditing | Legal services are not directly addressed; various other services are allowed if auditors do not make management decisions. |
| Certain tax services, such as tax planning for potentially abusive tax transactions and providing individual tax services to client officers who play a significant role in financial reporting | No specific restrictions. |

**Illustrative Case** — *Tax Services and Independence*

The issue of independence and tax services was vividly illustrated in the Sprint Corp. case. Sprint had a policy of allowing its audit firm, Ernst & Young LLP, to perform tax planning services for its top executives. The chief executive officer and the president of Sprint adopted a tax shelter strategy recommended by Ernst & Young. When the shelter was determined to be ineffective, the executives were faced with potential liabilities of millions of dollars in back taxes, which created a conflict of interest between them and Ernst & Young. Rather than discharge the auditors, the board of directors of Sprint elected to force out the two executives. The Sprint case and similar cases resulted in the PCAOB standards restricting the performance of tax services for the executives of audit clients.

of directors. Also, clients must disclose in their annual report fees paid for (1) audit services, (2) audit-related services, (3) tax services, and (4) other services.

*Independence Requirements of Government Auditing Standards* The Government Accountability Office (GAO)—formerly called the General Accounting Office—develops additional requirements for audits of entities that receive federal financial assistance. These requirements are included in *Government Auditing Standards,* which are discussed in Chapter 21. With regard to auditor independence, *Government Auditing Standards* also are more restrictive than those of the AICPA. As an example, a public accounting firm cannot allow personnel working on nonattest engagements to also work on the audit. In addition, *Government Auditing Standards* place restrictions on the nature of the nonattest services that may be provided to an audit client. Nonattest services must be deemed not to be significant or material to the subject matter of the audit. Under the GAO's interpretation of this requirement, restrictions are placed on the nature of bookkeeping, payroll, valuation, information technology, human resources, and internal audit services.

*Independence—Reality*

It is certainly naïve to believe that all CPAs are able to maintain complete independence when performing attest services in an environment in which they work closely with client management and are paid fees by their clients. Yet, as we have emphasized, independence is essential to performance of the attest function. While performing attest services, it is essential that CPAs bear in mind the stakeholders other than management that rely upon the information with which they are associated.

Recent regulations by the SEC and stock exchanges have served to increase the CPAs' independence in dealings with management and to improve the quality of financial reporting by public companies. The New York Stock Exchange, the American Stock Exchange, and NASDAQ have established requirements for independent **audit committees** by all listed companies. According to these requirements, audit committees must consist of at least three independent and financially literate individuals, and the chairman must have accounting or financial management expertise. In addition, the Sarbanes-Oxley Act of 2002 makes the audit committee directly responsible for appointing, compensating, and overseeing the public accounting firm. The SEC regulations require public companies to file a copy of the audit committee's charter every three years and disclose whether its members are independent of management. All of these requirements increase the auditors' ability to deal independently with management.

**Analysis of Integrity and Objectivity**

**Rule 102—Integrity and Objectivity**

*In the performance of any professional service, a member shall maintain objectivity and integrity, shall be free of conflicts of interest, and shall not knowingly misrepresent facts or subordinate his or her judgment to others.*

Rule 102 applies to all members of the AICPA and all services provided by CPAs. It recognizes that clients, employers, or others may at times attempt to influence the judgment of CPAs on professional matters. To maintain the confidence and respect of the public, CPAs must never subordinate their professional judgments to others. Interpretation 102–1 states that a CPA will be found to have knowingly misrepresented facts in violation of Rule 102 when he or she knowingly:

- Makes, or permits or directs another to make, materially incorrect entries in a client's financial statements or records.
- Fails to correct financial statements that are materially false or misleading when the member has such authority.
- Signs, or permits or directs another to sign, a document containing materially false and misleading information.

It is often difficult to determine if an individual has "knowingly misrepresented facts." Thus, in evaluating whether a CPA has violated that Section of Rule 102, we must look to whether, based on the circumstances, the CPA *should have* known of the misrepresentation. A ruling that a CPA violated Rule 102 is most commonly based upon evidence that the CPAs should have been knowledgeable about the facts.

## Analysis of General Standards

### Rule 201—General Standards

*A member shall comply with the following standards and with any interpretations thereof by bodies designated by Council.*

> *A. Professional Competence. Undertake only those professional services that the member or the member's firm can reasonably expect to be completed with professional competence.*
> *B. Due Professional Care. Exercise due professional care in the performance of professional services.*
> *C. Planning and Supervision. Adequately plan and supervise the performance of professional services.*
> *D. Sufficient Relevant Data. Obtain sufficient relevant data to afford a reasonable basis for conclusions or recommendations in relation to any professional services performed.*

In addition to performing audits and other attestation services, CPAs also provide accounting, review, tax, and consulting services. Clients and the general public expect these services to be performed with competence and professional care. Therefore, the general standards of Rule 201 apply to *all CPA services.*

## Analysis of Compliance with Standards

### Rule 202—Compliance with Standards

*A member who performs auditing, review, compilation, management consulting, tax, or other professional services shall comply with standards promulgated by bodies designated by Council.*

Rule 202 requires CPAs to adhere to professional standards issued by other technical bodies. To date, the Council of the AICPA has recognized six bodies and given them authority for the performance standards summarized in Figure 3.8. CPAs must become familiar with such statements and apply them to their engagements. To violate standards prescribed by these bodies is to violate Rule 202 of the Code.

*Professional Standards for Consulting Services*

As indicated in Figure 3.8, the AICPA's Management Consulting Services Executive Committee is authorized to issue *Statements on Standards for Consulting Services* to provide practitioners with authoritative guidance on providing consulting services to their clients. Consulting services are broadly defined by these standards to include virtually all services other than auditing and attestation services, accounting and review services,

FIGURE 3.8   Technical Bodies and Their Authority

| Technical Body | Authority | Performance Standards[†] |
|---|---|---|
| Auditing Standards Board (ASB) | Prescribes auditing standards for audits of nonpublic companies and responsibilities with respect to supplementary information outside the financial statements | *Statements on Auditing Standards* |
| Management Consulting Services Executive Committee (MCSEC) | Prescribes standards for management advisory services | *Statements on Standards for Consulting Services* |
| Accounting and Review Services Committee (ARSC) | Prescribes standards for unaudited financial information services for nonpublic companies | *Statements on Standards for Accounting and Review Services* |
| ASB, MCSEC, and ARSC | Prescribe attestation standards in their areas | *Statements on Standards for Attestation Engagements* |
| Financial Accounting Standards Board, Governmental Accounting Standards Board, and Federal Accounting Standards Advisory Board* | Prescribe disclosure standards for supplementary information outside the financial statements | *Statements of Financial Accounting Standards, Statements of Governmental Accounting Standards, Statements of Federal Financial Accounting Standards,* and related *Interpretations* |

*Rule 203 gives these bodies authority for accounting standards.
[†]The list includes only the highest-level standards. The bodies also issue various forms of interpretive guidance.

and tax services. To the general standards contained in Rule 201, these standards add the following additional requirements for these types of engagements:

1. *Client interest.* The practitioner should strive to meet the objectives of the client while maintaining integrity and objectivity.
2. *Understanding with client.* The practitioner should establish a written or oral understanding with the client about the nature, scope, and limitations of the consulting engagement.
3. *Communication with client.* The practitioner should inform the client of (*a*) any conflicts of interest that may occur with respect to the engagement, (*b*) any significant reservations about the scope or benefits of the engagement, and (*c*) all significant findings or events.

## Analysis of Accounting Principles

### Rule 203—Accounting Principles

*A member shall not (1) express an opinion or state affirmatively that the financial statements or other financial data of any entity are presented in conformity with generally accepted accounting principles or (2) state that he or she is not aware of any material modifications that should be made to such statements or data in order for them to be in conformity with generally accepted accounting principles, if such statements or data contain any departure from an accounting principle promulgated by bodies designated by Council to establish such principles that has a material effect on the statements or data taken as a whole. If, however, the statements or data contain such a departure and the member can demonstrate that due to unusual circumstances the financial statements or data would otherwise have been misleading, the member can comply with the rule by describing the departure, its approximate effects, if practicable, and the reasons why compliance with the principle would result in a misleading statement.*

Rule 203 recognizes the authority of certain designated bodies to issue accounting principles. Under this rule, the AICPA has designated the *Accounting Standards*

*Codification* of the Financial Accounting Standards Board (FASB), the Governmental Accounting Standards Board (GASB), and the Federal Accounting Standards Advisory Board (FASAB) as primary sources of generally accepted accounting principles. CPAs should not issue an unqualified opinion on a set of financial statements that materially depart from one of these pronouncements, except in the situation in which application of the pronouncement would result in misleading financial statements.

## Analysis of Confidential Client Information

### Rule 301—Confidential Client Information

*A member in public practice shall not disclose any confidential client information without the specific consent of the client.*

*This rule shall not be construed (1) to relieve a member of the member's professional obligations under rules 202 and 203, (2) to affect in any way the member's obligation to comply with a validly issued and enforceable subpoena or summons, (3) to prohibit review of a member's professional practice under AICPA or state CPA society authorization, or (4) to preclude a member from initiating a complaint with or responding to any inquiry made by a recognized investigative or disciplinary body.*

*Members of a recognized investigative or disciplinary body and professional practice reviewers shall not use to their own advantage or disclose any member's confidential client information that comes to their attention in carrying out their official responsibilities. However, this prohibition shall not restrict the exchange of information with a recognized investigative or disciplinary body or affect, in any way, compliance with a validly issued and enforceable subpoena or summons.*

Rule 301 stresses the confidential nature of information obtained by CPAs from their clients. The nature of accountants' work makes it necessary for them to have access to their clients' most confidential financial affairs. Independent accountants may thus gain insider knowledge of impending business combinations, proposed financing, prospective stock splits or dividend changes, contracts being negotiated, and other confidential information that, if disclosed or otherwise improperly used, could bring the accountants quick monetary profits. Of course, the client could be financially injured, as well as embarrassed, if the CPAs were to "leak" such information. Any loose talk by independent public accountants concerning the affairs of their clients would immediately brand them as lacking in professional ethics. On the other hand, the confidential relationship between the CPA and the client is not a justification for the CPA to cooperate in any deceitful act. The personal integrity of the CPA is essential to the performance of the attest function.

### *Reporting Illegal Acts*

Should auditors be required to report illegal acts by clients to regulatory agencies? Rule 301 of the Code of Conduct prohibits CPAs from directly disclosing such information to outside parties, unless the auditors have a legal duty to do so. An amendment of the Securities Exchange Act of 1934, the *Private Securities Reform Act of 1995,* includes a requirement for fraud reporting, or *whistleblowing,* by the auditors. The requirements of this law apply when the client has committed an illegal act and (a) it has a material effect on the financial statements, (b) senior management and the board of directors have not taken appropriate remedial action, and (c) the failure to take remedial action is reasonably expected to warrant a departure from a standard audit report, or resignation by the auditors. In these circumstances, the auditors must, *as soon as practicable,* communicate their conclusions directly to the client's board of directors. Within one day, the management of the client must send a notification to the Securities and Exchange Commission of having received such a communication from the auditors, and a copy of the notification should be sent to the auditors. If the auditors do not receive the copy within the one-day period, they have one day to *directly communicate* the matter to the SEC.

Auditors also are required to communicate illegal acts in other situations. When illegal activities cause the auditors of a public company to lose faith in the integrity of senior management, they will resign and a Form 8-K, which discloses the reasons for the auditors' resignation, will be filed with the SEC by management. The auditors must file a response to the filing indicating whether or not they agree with management's reasons, and providing the details when they disagree. In addition, when the auditors are performing an audit in accordance with the Single Audit Act, they may be required to disclose illegal acts by the client to an agency that provides federal financial assistance to the client. Single audits are described in detail in Chapter 21.

### Confidentiality versus Privileged Communications

The communications between CPAs and their clients are confidential, but they are not *privileged* under common law, as are communications with attorneys, clergymen, or physicians. The difference is that disclosure of legally privileged communications cannot be required by a subpoena or court order. Thus, CPAs may be compelled to disclose their communications with clients in certain types of court proceedings. Some individual states, however, have adopted statutes providing that public accountants cannot be required by the state courts to give evidence gained in confidence from clients. But state laws do not apply to federal courts where there are not privileged communications.

## Analysis of Contingent Fees

**Rule 302—Contingent Fees**

*A member in public practice shall not:*
1. *Perform for a contingent fee any professional services for, or receive such a fee from a client for whom the member or the member's firm performs:*
   a. *An audit or review of a financial statement; or*
   b. *A compilation of a financial statement when the member expects, or reasonably might expect, that a third party will use the financial statement and the member's compilation report does not disclose a lack of independence; or*
   c. *An examination of prospective financial information; or*
2. *Prepare an original or amended tax return or claim for a tax refund for a contingent fee for any client.*

   *The prohibition in (1) above applies during the period in which the member or the member's firm is engaged to perform any of the services listed above and the period covered by any historical financial statements involved in any such listed services.*

   *Except as stated in the next sentence, a contingent fee is a fee established for the performance of any service pursuant to an arrangement in which no fee will be charged unless a specified finding or result is attained, or in which the amount of the fee is otherwise dependent upon the finding or result of such service. Solely for purposes of this rule, fees are not regarded as being contingent if fixed by courts or other public authorities, or, in tax matters, if determined based on the results of judicial proceedings or the findings of governmental agencies.*

   *A member's fees may vary depending, for example, on the complexity of services rendered.*

An accountant is prohibited by Rule 302 from providing services on a contingent fee basis in certain circumstances. A CPA may not receive a contingent fee for the preparation of original or amended tax returns or claims for tax refunds. Preparation of a tax return includes giving advice on how particular items should be handled on the return. Also, no contingent fee engagements are allowed for services performed for a client that also engages that public accounting firm to perform audits, reviews, certain compilations of financial statements, or examinations of **prospective financial information.** For example, consulting services may not be performed for a contingent fee for an audit client of the public accounting firm.

The CPAs may perform services for contingent fees for other clients. Consider a public accounting firm with a prospective new client whose management requests assistance in redesigning its cash disbursements system. In such circumstances, if none of the services described in part 1 of the rule are provided for that client, the CPAs may perform the service for a contingent fee. For example, the CPAs may redesign the disbursements system and receive a fee that is contingent on the amount of cost savings realized by the client in processing future cash disbursements. The CPAs' fee might be, for example, 25 percent of the next four years' cost savings.

The PCAOB rules contain an additional restriction with respect to contingent fees. The auditors of public companies are prohibited from accepting engagements for tax services that are determined based on the results of judicial proceedings or the findings of government agencies.

## Analysis of Acts Discreditable

### Rule 501—Acts Discreditable

*A member shall not commit an act discreditable to the profession.*

Rule 501 gives the AICPA the authority to discipline those members who act in a manner damaging to the reputation of the profession. The three circumstances outlined in Interpretation 102–1 (page 85) related to misleading entries and financial statements are considered discreditable. Beyond these illustrations, the rule is not specific as to what constitutes a discreditable act; it is subject to interpretation. In the past, such acts as signing a false or misleading opinion or statement, committing a felony, and engaging in discrimination or harassment in employment practices have been interpreted to be violations of Rule 501.

Is it discreditable to refuse to return records relating to a client's accounting system? The answer here depends upon the facts and circumstances and the records involved. For example:

- *Client-provided records* always should be returned to the client.
- *Client records prepared by the CPA* (e.g., tax returns, general ledger, subsidiary journals, payroll records) should be provided to the client, unless they are incomplete or fees are due to the CPA for preparing those records.
- *Supporting records not reflected in the client's books and records* (e.g., adjusting entries, closing entries, consolidating entries) should be provided to the client, but may be withheld if there are fees due to the CPA for preparing those records.
- *CPA working papers* (audit programs, analytical procedure schedules, analyses) are the CPA's property and need not be provided to the client, unless so required by state or federal laws.

An exception to the second and third points listed above exists in cases in which a client experiences a loss of records due to a natural disaster or an act of war. In those situations, the CPA should comply with a request to provide such records.

## Analysis of Advertising and Other Forms of Solicitation

### Rule 502—Advertising and Other Forms of Solicitation

*A member in public practice shall not seek to obtain clients by advertising or other forms of solicitations in a manner that is false, misleading, or deceptive. Solicitation by the use of coercion, overreaching, or harassing conduct is prohibited.*

For many years advertising by CPAs was strictly forbidden by the AICPA Rules. Most certified public accountants considered advertising in any form to be unprofessional. However, this prohibition was dropped because it was deemed a possible violation of federal antitrust laws. Members of the public accounting profession may advertise their services so long as the advertising is not false, misleading, or deceptive. Unethical advertising includes that which creates unjustified expectations of favorable results or indicates an ability to influence a court or other official body.

Acceptable advertising is that which is informative and based upon verifiable fact. Indications of the types of services offered, certificates and degrees of members of the firm, and fees charged for services are all acceptable forms of advertising.

## Analysis of Commissions and Referral Fees

### Rule 503—Commissions and Referral Fees

1. *Prohibited commissions. A member in public practice shall not for a commission recommend or refer to a client any product or service, or for a commission recommend or refer any product or service to be supplied by a client, or receive a commission, when the member or the member's firm also performs for that client:*
   a. *An audit or review of a financial statement.*
   b. *A compilation of a financial statement when the member expects, or reasonably might expect, that a third party will use the financial statement and the member's compilation report does not disclose a lack of independence.*
   c. *An examination of prospective financial information.*
   *This prohibition applies during the period in which the member is engaged to perform any of the services listed above and the period covered by any historical financial statements involved in such listed services.*
2. *Disclosure of permitted commissions. A member in public practice who is not prohibited by this rule from performing services for or receiving a commission and who is paid or expects to be paid a commission shall disclose that fact to any person or entity to whom the member recommends or refers a product or service to which the commission relates.*
3. *Referral fees. Any member who accepts a referral fee for recommending or referring any service of a CPA to any person or entity or who pays a referral fee to obtain a client shall disclose such acceptance or payment to the client.*

Clients look to their CPAs for objective advice on the purchase of products and services, including services from other CPAs. Historically, CPAs have been prohibited from accepting a commission from the providers of such products and services. The consent agreement between the AICPA and the Federal Trade Commission, mentioned under Rule 302, also caused a change in this rule to allow the collection of commissions as described in sections (2) and (3) of Rule 503. As an example, CPAs that do not perform financial statement audits, reviews, certain compilations, or examinations of prospective information for a client may receive commissions for purchasing and selling securities for that client, provided they disclose the existence of the commissions to the client.

## Analysis of Form of Organization and Name

### Rule 505—Form of Organization and Name

*A member may practice public accounting only in a form of organization permitted by state law or regulation, whose characteristics conform to resolutions of Council.*

*A member shall not practice public accounting under a firm name that is misleading. Names of one or more past owners may be included in the firm name of a successor organization.*

*A firm may not designate itself as "Members of the American Institute of Certified Public Accountants" unless all of its owners are members of the Institute.*

The *Code of Professional Conduct* allows CPAs to practice in any legal business form. This includes the ability to practice as professional corporations, limited liability partnerships (companies), partnerships, or sole practitioners.

Many state laws, as well as the *Code of Professional Conduct,* allow CPAs to form professional corporations. Professional corporations have certain tax advantages not available to partnerships, such as tax deductibility of pension and profit-sharing plans. The shareholders of professional corporations retain liability for acts of the corporation, regardless of whether they participated in the engagement resulting in the liability. Besides providing for financial liability, the organization must be established such that two-thirds ownership, voting rights, and control over professional matters must rest with individuals authorized to practice public accounting.

Currently, most states allow CPAs to practice in the form of a limited liability partnership (company). Although similar to professional corporations in many ways, limited liability forms of organization protect the personal assets of any partner or shareholder not directly involved in providing services on engagements resulting in liability.

Previous versions of Rule 505 prohibited public accountants from practicing under a name that was fictitious or indicated a specialization. Because this prohibition was sensitive to antitrust attack, the revised Rule 505 allows fictitious names so long as they are not false, misleading, or deceptive.

## Alternative Practice Structures

As indicated in Chapter 1, public accounting firms are entering into what is referred to as "alternative practice structures" in which publicly traded companies (e.g., CBIZ, Inc., and H&R Block) purchase public accounting firms. A typical alternative practice arrangement may be as follows:

- Public Company buys the nonattest portion of a public accounting firm's practice from the public accounting firm's partners for cash, stock, or a combination of both.
- Public Company has subsidiaries such as a bank, an insurance company, a broker-dealer, and a professional services subsidiary that offer clients the nonattest public accounting services.
- Public accounting firm partners and employees become employees of Public Company, performing nonattest public accounting work under the Public Company name.
- The attest practice of the public accounting firm remains intact with the "shell" of the public accounting firm and continues to be owned by the original partners of the public accounting firm (who are now also employees of Public Company).
- The public accounting firm leases staff from Public Company to perform the attest services.

Figure 3.9 summarizes the typical structures of these types of firms.

Alternative practice structures present a number of questions and potential threats to independence. For example, because the partners of the attest firm are employees of Public Company, these partners may have a difficult time maintaining independence when auditing a client that is important to Public Company. To illustrate, pressure may be exerted by Public Company management to issue a standard unqualified report when there is substantial doubt concerning going-concern status relating to a client that has a significant debt to Public Company. Or perhaps Public Company may provide attest clients with services that place personnel in a position equivalent to that of client management.

## The CPA as Tax Advisor—Ethical Problems

What is the responsibility of the CPA in serving as tax advisor? The CPA has a primary responsibility to the client: that is, to see that the client pays the proper amount of tax and no more. In the role of tax advisor, the certified public accountant may properly resolve questionable issues in favor of the client; the CPA is not obliged to maintain the posture of independence required in attestation work. However, CPAs must adhere to the same standards of objectivity and integrity in tax work as in all other professional activities.

**FIGURE 3.9  Illustration of an Alternative Practice Structure**

| | **Public Company** | **CPA Firm** |
|---|---|---|
| Structure | Publicly traded corporation owned by stockholders | Partnership or other form of organization authorized to perform audit and attest services owned by the partners |
| Services performed | Nonattest services | Audit and attest services |
| Staffing of engagements | Partners and staff who are now employees of the public company | Partners and staff time are leased from the public company |
| Management of the practice | Practice is managed by officers of the public company | Practice is managed by partners of the CPA firm |

**Illustrative Case**    *The Impact of Liability*

Large malpractice lawsuits and economic conditions resulted in the 1990 bankruptcy of Leventhol & Horwath, the seventh largest public accounting firm in the United States. Not only did the partners lose their investment in the firm, but they found themselves personally liable for a portion of the partnership liabilities.

In 2002, Arthur Andersen, a limited liability partnership (LLP), suffered serious financial losses and dissolution due to legal liability. Partners not involved with engagements resulting in legal liability have to this point been able to limit their liability to the loss of their capital accounts in accord with the provisions of an LLP.

A second responsibility of CPAs on tax engagements is to the public, whose interests are represented by the government—more specifically by the Internal Revenue Service (IRS). To meet this responsibility, CPAs must observe the preparer's declaration on the tax returns they prepare. The declaration requires the preparer to state that the return is "true, correct, and complete . . . based on all information of which the preparer has any knowledge." To comply with this declaration, what steps must the public accounting firm take to acquire knowledge relating to the tax return? The firm is not required to perform an audit; knowledge of the return may be limited to information supplied to the firm by the client. However, if this information appears unreasonable or contradictory, the CPAs are obligated to make sufficient investigation to resolve these issues. Information that appears plausible to a layperson might appear unreasonable to CPAs, since they are experts in evaluating financial data. CPAs are not obligated to investigate any and all information provided by the taxpayer, but they cannot ignore clues that cast doubt on the accuracy of these data.

In addition to being guided by the declaration on the tax return, CPAs should look to a series of pronouncements issued by the AICPA, entitled *Statements on Responsibilities in Tax Practice.* These statements address such questions as: Under what circumstances should a CPA sign the preparer's declaration on a tax return? What is the CPA's responsibility for errors in previously filed returns? Should CPAs disclose the taking of positions that differ from IRS interpretations of the tax code? Note that the purpose of this series is to provide guidance to CPAs, and the statements are not directly enforceable under the *Code of Professional Conduct.*

## Enforcement of Professional Ethics

The AICPA and the state societies of CPAs have established a joint ethics enforcement plan. Under the plan, complaints about a CPA's conduct are first referred to the Professional Ethics Division of the AICPA for investigation. If the Professional Ethics Division finds the complaint to be valid, it may take several courses of action. For minor violations, the Division may take direct remedial action, such as requiring the member to get additional continuing education. More serious violations are turned over to the joint trial board for a hearing. If found guilty, the offending member may be censured, suspended from membership for up to two years, or expelled permanently from the AICPA. Although expulsion from the AICPA would not in itself cause the loss of a CPA's license, the damage to the CPA's professional reputation would be substantial.

The provisions of the AICPA Rules have been used as a model by the boards of accountancy throughout the country to develop the ethical standards in their states. Thus, revocation of the CPA's license to practice also is a possible consequence of violation of the AICPA ethical standards.

Finally, ethical violations by auditors of public companies also are investigated and enforced by the SEC and the Public Company Accounting Oversight Board. Severe violations may result in suspension of the CPA's or the public accounting firm's right to practice as an auditor of public companies. Lesser penalties may involve monetary fines or remedial measures, such as the required implementation of new quality control procedures.

*The International Code of Ethics for Professional Accountants*

As indicated in Chapter 1, the International Federation of Accountants (IFAC) has established the International Ethics Standards Board for Accountants to establish international ethical standards, titled the *Code of Ethics for Professional Accountants*. In general, the provisions of the international *Code of Ethics for Professional Accountants* is quite similar to the provisions of the AICPA *Code of Professional Conduct*.

The international ethics rules regarding independence in audit and review engagements are similar to the AICPA rules. Both require the concepts of independence in mind and in appearance. However, the international ethics rules have fewer definitive prohibitions. Like the AICPA Code, when there is no definitive prohibition, the following conceptual approach is used:

1. Identify threats to independence;
2. Evaluate the significance of the threats identified; and
3. Apply safeguards, when necessary, to eliminate the threats or reduce them to an acceptable level. If safeguards do not reduce the risk to an acceptable level, the firm should not accept or continue the engagement, or assign the particular individual to the engagement team. The firm should document these considerations and the conclusion. Threats to independence arise from self-interest, self-review, advocacy, familiarity, or intimidation.

International rules regarding confidentiality and fee arrangements are also not as specific as AICPA rules because laws and regulations regarding such matters vary from country to country.

# Ethics for Internal Auditors

Internal auditors, acting through their national organization, The Institute of Internal Auditors, have developed their own code of professional ethics. The Institute of Internal Auditors *Code of Ethics* is organized with an Introduction, Fundamental Principles, and a Code of Conduct. The Code of Conduct primarily addresses internal auditors' obligations to their employers, but it also includes provisions that prescribe integrity, objectivity, and competency in the practice of the internal auditing profession. Violation of the articles of the Code could result in revocation of the auditor's membership in The Institute of Internal Auditors or forfeiture of the auditor's "Certified Internal Auditor" designation. The Institute of Internal Auditors *Code of Ethics* is reproduced below.

**LO7**

Discuss The Institute of Internal Auditors Code of Ethics.

**The Institute of Internal Auditors**
*Code of Ethics*

**Introduction**

The purpose of The Institute's *Code of Ethics* is to promote an ethical culture in the profession of internal auditing.

> *Internal auditing is an independent, objective assurance and consulting activity designed to add value and improve an organization's operations. It helps an organization accomplish its objectives by bringing a systematic, disciplined approach to evaluate and improve the effectiveness of risk management, control, and governance processes.*

A code of ethics is necessary and appropriate for the profession of internal auditing, founded as it is on the trust placed in its objective assurance about risk management, control, and governance. The Institute's *Code of Ethics* extends beyond the definition of internal auditing to include two essential components:

1. Principles that are relevant to the profession and practice of internal auditing;
2. Rules of Conduct that describe behavior norms expected of internal auditors. These rules are an aid to interpreting the Principles into practical applications and are intended to guide the ethical conduct of internal auditors.

The *Code of Ethics* together with The Institute's *Professional Practices Framework* and other relevant Institute pronouncements provide guidance to internal auditors serving others. "Internal auditors" refers to Institute members, recipients of or candidates for IIA professional certifications, and those who provide internal auditing services within the definition of internal auditing.

## Applicability and Enforcement

This *Code of Ethics* applies to both individuals and entities that provide internal auditing services. For Institute members and recipients of or candidates for IIA professional certifications, breaches of the *Code of Ethics* will be evaluated and administered according to The Institute's Bylaws and Administrative Guidelines. The fact that a particular conduct is not mentioned in the Rules of Conduct does not prevent it from being unacceptable or discreditable, and therefore, the member, certification holder, or candidate can be liable for disciplinary action.

## Principles

Internal auditors are expected to apply and uphold the following principles:

### Integrity

The integrity of internal auditors establishes trust and thus provides the basis for reliance on their judgment.

### Objectivity

Internal auditors exhibit the highest level of professional objectivity in gathering, evaluating, and communicating information about the activity or process being examined. Internal auditors make a balanced assessment of all the relevant circumstances and are not unduly influenced by their own interests or by others in forming judgments.

### Confidentiality

Internal auditors respect the value and ownership of information they receive and do not disclose information without appropriate authority unless there is a legal or professional obligation to do so.

### Competency

Internal auditors apply the knowledge, skills, and experience needed in the performance of internal auditing services.

## Rules of Conduct

### 1. Integrity

Internal auditors:

1.1.    Shall perform their work with honesty, diligence, and responsibility.
1.2.    Shall observe the law and make disclosures expected by the law and the profession.
1.3.    Shall not knowingly be a party to any illegal activity, or engage in acts that are discreditable to the profession of internal auditing or to the organization.
1.4.    Shall respect and contribute to the legitimate and ethical objectives of the organization.

### 2. Objectivity

Internal auditors:

2.1.    Shall not participate in any activity or relationship that may impair or be presumed to impair their unbiased assessment. This participation includes those activities or relationships that may be in conflict with the interests of the organization.
2.2.    Shall not accept anything that may impair or be presumed to impair their professional judgment.
2.3.    Shall disclose all material facts known to them that, if not disclosed, may distort the reporting of activities under review.

### 3. Confidentiality

Internal auditors:

3.1.    Shall be prudent in the use and protection of information acquired in the course of their duties.
3.2.    Shall not use information for any personal gain or in any manner that would be contrary to the law or detrimental to the legitimate and ethical objectives of the organization.

**4. Competency**

Internal auditors:

4.1.   Shall engage only in those services for which they have the necessary knowledge, skills, and experience.

4.2.   Shall perform internal auditing services in accordance with the *Standards for the Professional Practice of Internal Auditing.*

4.3.   Shall continually improve their proficiency and the effectiveness and quality of their services.

---

**Chapter Summary**

This chapter explained the need for professionals to adhere to high standards of professional conduct and described the details of the codes of ethics that apply to both external and internal auditors. To summarize:

1. Ethics are the moral principles and values that govern the behavior of individuals and groups. An *ethical dilemma* is a situation that involves a decision about appropriate behavior. A key aspect of an ethical dilemma is that it generally affects parties that are not involved in the decision. For example, if management of a corporation decides to pollute the environment, it affects all of the members of society. Professional accountants are faced with difficult personal and professional ethical dilemmas on a daily basis.

2. Among the characteristics common to recognized professions are (a) acknowledgment of a responsibility to serve the public, (b) existence of a complex body of knowledge, (c) standards of admission to the profession, and (d) a need for public confidence.

3. The membership of the AICPA has adopted the *Code of Professional Conduct,* consisting of two sections—Principles and Rules. In addition, the AICPA issues Interpretations and Ethics Rulings to provide further guidance on appropriate ethical conduct.

4. Independence is required when CPAs perform audits and other types of attest engagements. The AICPA *Conceptual Framework for Independence Standards* provides a risk-based approach for considering threats and safeguards related to independence. Interpretation 101–1 provides guidance on various financial and business relationships that may impair a CPA's independence. That standard prohibits all direct financial interests in a client, as well as material indirect financial interests. Certain independence rules apply only to covered members and others apply to all partners and professional employees. In the audit of a public company, the auditors must also adhere to the ethics and independence requirements of the SEC, the Sarbanes-Oxley Act of 2002, and the Public Company Accounting Oversight Board.

5. The Rules of the AICPA *Code of Professional Conduct* set forth the professional standards that must be followed by CPAs when performing various types of professional services. For example, Rule 202 requires auditors to adhere to *Statements on Auditing Standards.* Accounting standards of the FASB, the GASB, and the FASAB are enforced by Rule 203.

6. In performing an audit, the auditors have access to the details of the client's most confidential information. If the auditors disclosed this information, they might damage their clients' businesses. Therefore, CPAs are required to maintain a confidential relationship with their clients.

7. CPAs generally may accept engagements for contingent fees and receive commissions for referrals, but only if they do not also provide certain attestation or compilation services for the client.

8. A public accounting firm may practice public accounting in any form of organization permitted by law or regulation, including as a sole practitioner, partnership, professional corporation, or limited liability partnership (company).

9. The *Code of Ethics* of The Institute of Internal Auditors primarily addresses internal auditors' obligations to their employers, but it also includes provisions requiring integrity, objectivity, and competency in the practice of internal auditing.

**Key Terms Introduced or Emphasized in Chapter 3**

**Attest engagement team (77)**    Consists of individuals participating in the attest engagement, including those who perform concurring and second partner reviews. The attest engagement team includes all employees and contractors retained by the firm who participate in the attest engagement, irrespective of their functional classification (for example, audit, tax, or management consulting services), except specialists as discussed in the professional standards and individuals who perform only routine clerical functions, such as word processing and photocopying.

**Audit committee (84)**    A committee of a corporation's board of directors that engages, compensates, and oversees the work of the independent auditors, monitors activities of the internal auditing staff, and intervenes in any disputes between management and the independent auditors. Members of the audit committee must be independent directors, that is, members of the board of directors who do not also serve as corporate officers or have other relationships that might impair independence.

**Close relative (80)**    A parent, sibling, or nondependent child.

**Covered member (77)**    A covered member may be (*a*) an individual on the attest engagement team; (*b*) an individual in a position to influence the attest engagement; (*c*) a partner or manager who provides nonattest services to the attest client beginning once he or she provides 10 hours of nonattest services to the client within any fiscal year and ending on the latter of the date (1) the firm signs the report on the financial statements for the fiscal year during which those services were provided, or (2) he or she no longer expects to provide 10 or more hours of nonattest services to the attest client on a recurring basis; (*d*) a partner in the office in which the lead attest engagement partner primarily practices in connection with the attest engagement; (*e*) the firm, including the firm's employee benefit plans; or (*f*) an entity whose operating, financial, or accounting policies can be controlled by any of the individuals or entities described in (*a*) through (*e*) or by two or more such individuals or entities if they act together.

**Direct financial interest (77)**    A personal investment under the direct control of the investor. The *Code of Professional Conduct* prohibits CPAs from having any direct financial interests in their attest clients. Investments made by a CPA's spouse or dependents also are regarded as direct financial interests of the CPA.

**Ethics Rulings (71)**    Pronouncements of the AICPA that explain the application of Rules and Interpretations of the *Code of Professional Conduct* to specific factual circumstances involving professional ethics.

**Immediate family member (80)**    A spouse, spousal equivalent, or dependent (whether or not related).

**Independence (73)**    Independence includes two concepts—independence of mind and independence in appearance.

**Independence in appearance (73)**    The avoidance of circumstances that would cause a reasonable and informed third party, having knowledge of all relevant information, including safeguards applied, to reasonably conclude that the integrity, objectivity, or professional skepticism of a firm or a member of the attest engagement team has been compromised.

**Independence of mind (73)**    The state of mind that permits the performance of an attest service without being affected by influences that compromise professional judgment, thereby allowing an individual to act with integrity and exercise objectivity and professional skepticism.

**Indirect financial interest (77)**    An investment in which the specific investment decisions are not under the direct control of the investor. An example is an investment in a professionally managed mutual fund. The *Code of Professional Conduct* allows CPAs to have indirect financial interests in attest clients, as long as the investment is not material in relation to the CPA's net worth.

**Individual in a position to influence the attest engagement (77)**    An individual who (*a*) evaluates the performance or recommends the compensation of the attest engagement partner; (*b*) directly supervises or manages the attest engagement partner, including all successively senior levels above that individual through the firm's chief executive; (*c*) consults with the attest engagement team regarding technical or industry-specific issues related to the attest engagement; or (*d*) participates in or oversees at all successively senior levels quality control activities, including internal monitoring, with respect to the specific attest engagement.

**Interpretations (71)**    Guidelines issued by the AICPA for the scope and application of the Rules of Conduct.

**Joint closely held investment (76)**    An investment in an entity or property by the member and the client (or the client's officers or directors, or any owner who has the ability to exercise significant influence over the client) that enables them to control (as defined by GAAP for consolidation purposes) the entity or property.

**Key position (79)**   A position in which an individual has (*a*) primary responsibility for significant accounting functions that support material components of the financial statements; (*b*) primary responsibility for the preparation of the financial statements; or (*c*) the ability to exercise influence over the contents of the financial statements, including when the individual is a member of the board of directors, or similar governing body, chief executive officer, president, chief financial officer, chief operating officer, general counsel, chief accounting officer, controller, director of internal audit, director of financial reporting, treasurer, or any equivalent position.

**Manager (77)**   A professional employee of the public accounting firm who either has continuing responsibility for the overall planning and supervision of engagements or has the authority to determine that an engagement is complete subject to final partner approval, if required.

**Period of the professional engagement (78)**   A period that begins when a member either signs an initial engagement letter or other agreement to perform attest services or begins to perform an attest engagement for a client, whichever is earlier. The period lasts for the entire duration of the professional relationship (which could cover many periods) and ends with the formal or informal notification, by either the member or the client, of the termination of the professional relationship or by the issuance of a report, whichever is later. Accordingly, the period does not end with the issuance of a report and recommence with the beginning of the following year's attest engagement.

**Principles (71)**   The part of the AICPA *Code of Professional Conduct* that expresses the profession's responsibilities to the public, clients, and colleagues and provides a framework for the Rules.

**Profession (70)**   An activity that involves a responsibility to serve the public, has a complex body of knowledge, has standards for admission, and has a need for public confidence.

**Prospective financial information (88)**   Presentations of future financial position, results of operations, or cash flows. Such presentations are often referred to as financial forecasts or projections.

**Rules (71)**   A group of enforceable ethical standards included in the AICPA *Code of Professional Conduct*.

**Safeguards (to independence) (75)**   Controls that mitigate or eliminate threats to independence. Safeguards range from partial to complete prohibitions of the threatening circumstance to procedures that counteract the potential influence of a threat.

**Significant influence (80)**   The criteria established in accounting standards to determine the ability of an investor to exercise significant influence over another entity. In general, these criteria include an ownership interest of 20 percent or more of the entity.

**Threats (to independence) (74)**   Circumstances that could impair independence. The AICPA categorizes seven types of threats—self-review, advocacy, adverse interest, familiarity, undue influence, financial self-interest, and management participation.

## Review Questions

3–1.   What is meant by the term *ethical dilemma?* Describe an ethical dilemma that you have faced.

3–2.   What are the two major types of constraints on decisions that involve ethical issues? Provide examples of each type.

3–3.   What is the basic purpose of a code of ethics for a profession?

3–4.   Briefly describe the two parts of the AICPA *Code of Professional Conduct*.

3–5.   According to the AICPA *Conceptual Framework for Independence Standards*, list and describe three categories of threats to accountant independence.

3–6.   In Chapter 2, the 10 generally accepted auditing standards were discussed. How does the AICPA *Code of Professional Conduct* relate, if at all, to these 10 generally accepted auditing standards?

3–7.   Explain how a CPA might have an indirect financial interest in an audit client. Does the AICPA *Code of Professional Conduct* prohibit such interests?

3–8.   Bill Scott works as a manager in the Phoenix office of an international public accounting firm. His father has just taken a position as a purchasing agent for one of the public accounting firm's Phoenix clients. Has Bill's independence been impaired with respect to this audit client? Has the public accounting firm's independence been impaired if Bill does not work on the audit?

3–9.   Three months ago, a national public accounting firm hired Greg Scott to work as a staff auditor in its New York office. Yesterday, Scott's father was hired to be the chief financial officer of one of the public accounting firm's New York office clients. Has the independence of the public accounting firm with respect to this client been impaired?

3–10.  Sara Kole, CPA, has been requested by the president of Noyes Company, a closely held corporation and audit client, to cosign Noyes Company checks with the Noyes treasurer when the president is away on business trips. Would Kole violate the AICPA *Code of Professional Conduct* if she accepted this request? Explain.

3–11.  With respect to ethics, what are the responsibilities of the Public Company Accounting Oversight Board? What is the source of the Board's authority?

3–12.  Describe what is meant by the term "covered member." Which part (or parts) of AICPA *Code of Professional Conduct* Standard 101 on independence relies on the concept of a covered member?

3–13.  How do the rules for the audit of public versus nonpublic companies differ with respect to the independence of a CPA who performs routine accounting services for a client?

3–14.  What bodies are given authority to issue performance standards under Rule 202 of the AICPA *Code of Professional Conduct?* What authoritative standards does each body issue?

3–15.  Comment on the following: In performing a consulting engagement for a client, a CPA may perform any services that the client requests.

3–16.  Identify the circumstances under which a CPA may *not* perform professional services on a contingent fee basis.

3–17.  Jian Zhang is a CPA who often serves as an expert witness in court cases. Is it proper for Zhang to receive compensation in a damage suit based on the amount awarded to the plaintiff? Discuss.

3–18.  Sandy Schultz, CPA, has performed a consulting services job in which she made recommendations which ultimately resulted in one of her audit clients purchasing a computer manufactured by the AMZ Computer Corporation. Shortly thereafter, Ms. Schultz was surprised when she received a $1,000 unsolicited commission from AMZ Computer Corporation. Would acceptance of this commission violate the AICPA *Code of Professional Conduct?* Explain.

3–19.  Laura Clark, wife of Jon Clark, CPA, is a life insurance agent. May Jon Clark refer audit clients needing officer life insurance to Laura Clark or to another life insurance agent who will share a commission with Laura Clark? Explain.

3–20.  In what organizational forms may CPAs practice public accounting?

3–21.  Must a CPA maintain independence and an impartial mental attitude when preparing a client's income tax return? Explain.

3–22.  In preparing a client's income tax return, a CPA feels that certain expenses are unreasonably high and probably are overstated. Explain the CPA's responsibilities in this situation.

3–23.  What board establishes international ethical standards for accountants? How do these standards compare to the AICPA *Code of Professional Conduct?*

3–24.  "Since internal auditors are employees, they have no ethical responsibilities to others beyond their employers." Comment on this statement.

**Questions Requiring Analysis**   **LO 5, 6**

*Required:*

3–25.  Sally Adams is an audit manager for the firm of Jones & Smith, CPAs, and is assigned to the audit of Libra Fashions, Inc. Near the middle of the audit, Sally was offered the job of Libra's chief financial officer.

   *a.* Discuss the implications of this offer assuming Libra is a nonpublic corporation.

   *b.* Discuss the implications of this offer assuming Libra is a public company.

**LO 5**  3–26.  Roger Royce, CPA, has encountered a situation that he thinks may pose a threat to his independence with respect to Watson, Inc., an audit client. The situation is not addressed by an independence rule or regulation. Using the AICPA *Conceptual Framework for Independence Standards,* describe how Royce can determine whether the threat truly impairs his independence.

**LO 5**    3–27.  Jenko Corp. is an audit client of the Phoenix office of Williams and Co., CPAs. Williams and Co. has offices in Arizona, including ones in Phoenix, Tucson, and Tombstone. For purposes of independence, the AICPA requires that no "covered member" may have a direct or a material indirect financial interest in an audit client such as Jenko. Determine whether each of the following individuals is a covered member.

   *a.* Bill Jones is a partner in the Tucson office of Williams. He does not work on the Jenko audit.

b. Mary Adams is a first-year staff assistant who works on the Jenko audit.

c. Mary Anderson is a partner in the Phoenix office of Williams. She does not work on the Jenko audit.

d. Bill Jepson, a staff auditor who does not work on the audit, owns an immaterial amount of stock of Jenko Corp.

e. Ken Sanders, a Tombstone office partner, provides no services for the Jenko audit other than serving as a consultant to the attest team regarding industry-related issues specific to Jenko.

**LO 5** 3–28. The firm of Williams, Kline & Chow, CPAs, is the auditor of Yuker Corporation, a nonpublic company. The president of Yuker, Karen Lester, has been putting pressure on Chee Chow, the audit partner, to accept a questionable accounting principle. She has even threatened to take steps to replace the CPA firm if he does not acquiesce. Does this situation impair the CPA firm's independence? Explain your answer.

**LO 5** 3–29. Tracy Smith, CPA, is in charge of the audit of Olympic Fashions, Inc. Seven young members of the public accounting firm's professional staff are working with Smith on this engagement, and several of the young auditors are avid skiers. Olympic Fashions owns two condominiums in Aspen, Colorado, which it uses primarily to entertain clients. The controller of Olympic Fashions has told Smith that she and any of her audit staff are welcome to use the condominiums at no charge any time that they are not already in use. How should Smith respond to this offer? Explain.

**LO 4, 5** 3–30. Harris Fell, CPA and member of the AICPA, was engaged to audit the financial statements of Wilson Corporation. Fell had half-completed the audit when he had a dispute with the management of Wilson Corporation and was discharged. Hal Compton, CPA, was promptly engaged to replace Fell. Wilson Corporation did not compensate Fell for his work to date; therefore, Fell refused to allow Wilson Corporation's management to examine his working papers. Some of the working papers consisted of adjusting journal entries and supporting analysis. Wilson Corporation's management had no other source for this information. Did Fell violate the AICPA *Code of Professional Conduct?* Explain fully.

**LO 4** 3–31. Ron Barber, CPA, is auditing the financial statements of DGF, Inc., a publicly held company. During the course of the audit, Barber discovered that DGF has been making illegal bribes to foreign government officials to obtain business, and he reported the matter to senior management and the board of directors of DGF.

*Required:*

a. If management and the board of directors take appropriate remedial action, should Barber be required to report the matter outside the company?

b. Describe Barber's appropriate response if management and the board of directors fail to take appropriate remedial action.

## Objective Questions

**All applicable questions are available with McGraw-Hill's *Connect*<sup>TM</sup> *Accounting*.** ▓ **connect** |ACCOUNTING

3–32. **Multiple Choice Questions**

Select the best answer for each of the following. Explain the reasons for your selection.

**LO 5** a. Which of the following is not a covered member for an attest engagement under Rule 101 of the AICPA *Code of Professional Conduct?*

(1) An individual assigned to the attest engagement.

(2) A partner in the office of the partner in charge of the attest engagement.

(3) A manager who is in charge of providing tax services to the attest client.

(4) A partner in the national office of the firm that performs marketing services.

**LO 4** b. Which of the following is not prohibited by the AICPA *Code of Professional Conduct?*

(1) Advertising in newspapers.

(2) Payment of commission to obtain an audit client.

(3) Acceptance of a contingent fee for a review of financial statements.

(4) Engaging in discriminatory employment practices.

**LO 4** c. In which of the following situations would a public accounting firm have violated the AICPA *Code of Professional Conduct* in determining its fee?

(1) A fee is based on whether or not the public accounting firm's audit report leads to the approval of the client's application for bank financing.

(2) A fee is to be established at a later date by the Bankruptcy Court.

(3) A fee is based upon the nature of the engagement rather than upon the actual time spent on the engagement.

(4) A fee is based on the fee charged by the client's former auditors.

**LO 5**   d. A public accounting firm would *least* likely be considered in violation of the AICPA independence rules in which of the following instances?

(1) A partner's checking account, which is fully insured by the Federal Deposit Insurance Corporation, is held at a financial institution for which the public accounting firm performs attest services.

(2) A manager of the firm donates services as vice president of a charitable organization that is an audit client of the firm.

(3) An attest client owes the firm fees for this and last year's annual engagements.

(4) A covered member's dependent son owns stock in an attest client.

**LO 4**   e. Which of the following is implied when a CPA signs the preparer's declaration on a federal income tax return?

(1) The return is not misleading based on all information of which the CPA has knowledge.

(2) The return is prepared in accordance with generally accepted accounting principles.

(3) The CPA has audited the return.

(4) The CPA maintained an impartial mental attitude while preparing the return.

**LO 4**   f. The AICPA *Code of Professional Conduct* states that a CPA shall not disclose any confidential information obtained in the course of a professional engagement except with the consent of the client. This rule may preclude a CPA from responding to an inquiry made by:

(1) An investigative body of a state CPA society.

(2) The trial board of the AICPA.

(3) A CPA-shareholder of the client corporation.

(4) An AICPA quality review body.

**LO 4**   g. Which of the following is most likely to be a violation of the AICPA rules of conduct by Bill Jones, a sole practitioner with no other employees?

(1) Jones performs consulting services for a percentage of the client's savings; these are the only services provided for the client.

(2) Jones names his firm Jones and Smith, CPAs.

(3) Jones advertises the services he provides in an Internet set of telephone "yellow pages."

(4) Jones, without client consent, makes available working papers for purposes of a peer review of his practice.

**LO 4**   h. Bill Adams, CPA, accepted the audit engagement of Kelly Company. During the audit, Adams became aware of his lack of competence required for the engagement. What should Adams do?

(1) Disclaim an opinion.

(2) Issue an adverse opinion.

(3) Suggest that Kelly Company engage another CPA to perform the audit.

(4) Rely on the competence of client personnel.

**LO 6**   i. Which of the following nonattest services may be performed by the auditors of a public company?

(1) Internal audit outsourcing.

(2) Tax planning for all company officers.

(3) Bookkeeping services.

(4) Preparation of the company's tax return.

**LO 5**   j. In providing nonattest services to an attest client, a CPA is allowed to perform which of the following functions?

(1) Maintaining custody of the client's securities.

(2) Training client employees.

(3) Supervising client employees.

(4) Acting as the third approver of large client expenditures.

**LO 4**

k. Rule 202—Compliance with Standards, requires CPAs to adhere to all of the following applicable standards, except:

(1) Statements on Standards for Consulting Services.

(2) Statements on Auditing Standards.

(3) Statements on Standards for Attestation Engagements.

(4) Statements on Responsibilities in Tax Practice.

**LO 7**

l. Which of the following provisions is *not* included in The Institute of Internal Auditors *Code of Ethics?*

(1) Performance of work with honesty, diligence, and responsibility.

(2) Prudence in the use and protection of information acquired in the course of their duties.

(3) Use of appropriate sampling methods to select areas for audit.

(4) Continual improvement in proficiency and effectiveness and the quality of services provided.

(AICPA, adapted)

**LO 4, 6**

**3–33. Simulation**

The firm of Wilson and Wiener (WW), CPAs, has had requests from a number of clients and prospective clients to perform various types of services. Please reply as to whether the appropriate independence rules (AICPA and/or PCAOB) allow the following engagements using the following key:

*A—Allowable, given these facts.*

*N—Not allowable, given these facts.*

(If both AICPA and PCAOB rules apply and one of them does not allow the services, answer N.)

| Case | Request | Public or Nonpublic Client | Allowable (A) or Not Allowable (N)? |
|------|---------|----------------------------|-------------------------------------|
| a. | Provide internal audit outsourcing, as well as perform the audit | Public | |
| b. | Prepare the corporate tax return, as well as perform the audit | Public | |
| c. | Prepare the corporate tax return, as well as perform the audit | Nonpublic | |
| d. | Provide bookkeeping services, as well as perform the audit; WW will not determine journal entries, authorize transactions, or prepare or modify source documents | Nonpublic | |
| e. | Provide financial information systems design and implementation assistance; WW provides no attest services for that company | Public | |
| f. | Serve on the board of directors of the company; WW provides no attest services for the company | Public | |
| g. | Implement an off-the-shelf accounting package, as well as perform the audit | Nonpublic | |
| h. | Provide actuarial services related to certain liabilities, as well as perform the audit; the subjectively determined liabilities relate to a material portion of the financial statements | Nonpublic | |
| i. | Provide actuarial services related to certain liabilities, as well as perform the audit; the subjectively determined liabilities relate to a material portion of the financial statements | Public | |
| j. | Provide tax planning services for corporate executives of an audit client (not for the company) | Public | |

**LO 4**  3–34.  Donald Westerman is president of Westerman Corporation, a nonpublic manufacturer of kitchen cabinets. He has been approached by Darlene Zabish, a partner with Zabish and Co., CPAs, who suggests that her firm can design a payroll system for Westerman that will either save his corporation money or be free. More specifically, Ms. Zabish proposes to design a payroll system for Westerman on a contingent fee basis. She suggests that her firm's fee will be 25 percent of the savings in payroll for each of the next four years. After four years Westerman will be able to keep all future savings. Westerman Corporation's payroll system costs currently are approximately $200,000 annually, and the corporation has not previously been a client of Zabish.

Westerman discussed this offer with his current CPA, Bill Zabrinski, whose firm annually audits Westerman Corporation's financial statements. Zabrinski states that this is a relatively simple task, and that he would be willing to provide the service for $30,000.

*Required:*

a. Would Zabish violate the AICPA *Code of Professional Conduct* by performing the engagement?

b. Would Zabrinski violate the AICPA *Code of Professional Conduct* by performing the engagement?

c. Now assume that Westerman has indicated to Zabrinski that he is leaning toward accepting Zabish's offer. Zabrinski then offers to provide the service for 15 percent of Westerman's savings for the next three years. Would performing the engagement in accordance with the terms of this offer violate the AICPA *Code of Professional Conduct?*

d. Now go back to the original information (do not consider Zabrinski's 15 percent offer in part c). If Westerman Corporation was a public company ("an issuer"), would Zabish violate PCAOB standards by performing the engagement?

e. Now go back to the original information (do not consider Zabrinski's 15 percent offer in part c). If Westerman Corporation was a public company ("an issuer"), would Zabrinski violate PCAOB standards by performing the engagment?

**LO 5**  3–35.  The firm of McGraw and West, CPAs, has two offices, one in Phoenix and one in San Diego. The firm has audited the Cameron Corporation out of its Phoenix office for the past five years. For each of the following independent cases, which occurred during the year under audit, indicate whether the independence of either (*a*) the CPA involved or (*b*) the firm would be impaired.

a. Mary McGraw, a partner in the San Diego office, fell wildly in love with Bill Smith, the treasurer for Cameron Corporation. They were married in Las Vegas. During the week, McGraw still lives in San Diego and works in that office, while Bill Smith lives in Phoenix, working for Cameron. On weekends they commute to their home in Yuma. Mary does not participate in the engagement.

b. Jim West is the father of Will West, a Phoenix partner. Jim West has a material investment in Cameron. Will West is unaware of his father's investment, but does participate in the engagement.

c. Bill Johnson, a senior in the San Diego office, has a material investment in the capital stock of Cameron. He does not participate in the engagement.

d. Sandra Steversen, a staff assistant in the Phoenix office, works on the Cameron audit. Her uncle works as the chief accounting officer for Cameron.

e. Bill Adams, a senior in the Phoenix office, does not work on the Cameron audit, but owns 9 percent of Cameron's outstanding equity (common stock).

**LO 4**  3–36.  The firm of Harwood & Toole, CPAs, has been the auditor and tax return preparer for Tucker, Inc., a nonpublic company, for several years. In the current year, the management of Tucker discharged Harwood & Toole from the audit and tax engagement because of a disagreement over a tax matter. Management of Tucker has not paid Harwood & Toole any of the current year's audit and tax fees. Another CPA firm has been hired and management of Tucker has requested that Harwood & Toole provide the following items:

a. Accounting records of Tucker, Inc., in the possession of Harwood & Toole.

b. Copies of adjusting entries prepared by the staff of Harwood & Toole.

c. A copy of Tucker's partially completed tax return prepared by the staff of Harwood & Toole.

d. Copies of Harwood & Toole's audit working papers from prior engagements.

*Required:*

e. Several consolidating entries prepared by Tucker, Inc, and reviewed by Harwood & Toole.

Indicate which of the items must be provided to management of Tucker by Harwood & Toole.

**LO 4**  3–37.  James Daleiden, CPA, is interested in expanding his practice through acquisition of new clients. For each of the following independent cases, indicate whether Daleiden would violate the AICPA *Code of Professional Conduct* by engaging in the suggested practice and explain why. If more information is needed to arrive at a final determination, indicate the nature of such information.

  a.  Daleiden wishes to form a professional corporation and use the name "AAAAAAAA the CPAs," to obtain the first ad in the yellow pages of the telephone book.

  b.  Daleiden wishes to prepare a one-page flyer which he will have his son stuff on the windshields of each car at the Pleasant Valley shopping mall. The flyer will outline the services provided by Daleiden's firm and will include a $50-off coupon for services provided on the first visit.

  c.  Daleiden has a thorough knowledge of the tax law. He has a number of acquaintances who prepare their own tax returns. He proposes to offer to review these returns before they are filed with the Internal Revenue Service. For this review, he will charge no fee unless he is able to identify legal tax savings opportunities. He proposes to charge each individual one-third of the tax savings he is able to identify.

  d.  Daleiden and his associates audit a number of municipalities. He proposes to contact other CPAs and inform them of his interest in obtaining more of these types of audits. He offers a $500 "finder's fee" to CPAs who forward business to him.

  e.  Daleiden wishes to advertise that if he is hired to perform the audit, he will discount his fees on tax services (he does intend to grant a discount).

**LO 5**  3–38.  The firm of Bell & Greer, CPAs, has been asked to perform attest services for Trek Corporation (a nonpublic company) for the year ended December 31, Year 5. Bell & Greer has two offices: one in Los Angeles and the other in Newport Beach. Trek Corporation would be audited by the Los Angeles office. For each of the following cases, indicate whether Bell and Greer's independence is definitely impaired. If it is not definitely impaired, but might be under some circumstances, discuss those circumstances.

  a.  A partner in the Los Angeles office of Bell & Greer has been a long-time personal friend of the chief executive officer of Trek Corporation.

  b.  The former controller of Trek Corporation became a partner in the Newport Beach office of Bell & Greer on March 15, Year 5, resigning from Trek Corporation on that date.

  c.  A manager in the Newport Beach office of Bell & Greer is the son of the treasurer of Trek Corporation.

  d.  A partner in the Los Angeles office of Bell & Greer jointly owns a cattle ranch in Montana with one of the directors of Trek Corporation. The value of the investment is material to both parties.

  e.  Trek Corporation has not yet paid Bell & Greer for professional services rendered in Year 4. This fee is substantial in amount and is now 15 months past due.

**LO 5**  3–39.  The firm of Schilling & Co., CPAs, has offices in Chicago and Green Bay, Wisconsin. Gillington Company, which has 1 million shares of outstanding stock, is audited by the Chicago office of Schilling; Welco of the Chicago office is the partner in charge of the audit. For each of the following circumstances, indicate whether the public accounting firm's independence is impaired with respect to Gillington Company.

  a.  Johnson, a partner in the Chicago office, owns 100 shares of the stock of Gillington. He has no responsibilities with respect to the Gillington audit.

  b.  Gizmo, a partner in the Green Bay office, owns 600 shares of the stock of Gillington. He has no responsibilities with respect to the Gillington audit.

  c.  Masterson is a staff assistant in the Green Bay office and owns 10 percent of Gillington's outstanding common stock. Masterson provides no services to Gillington and is not able to influence the engagement.

  d.  Schilling, the partner in charge of the entire firm, works in the Green Bay office. He owns 100 shares of Gillington stock (market value $2 per share), but provides no services on the engagement.

  e.  Gorman is a staff assistant on the audit. Gorman's mother owns shares of Gillington that are material to her net worth and of which Gorman has knowledge.

**LO 5**  3–40.  **Simulation**

Gloria and Deloria, CPAs, have recently started their public accounting firm and intend to provide attestation and a variety of consulting services for their clients, which are all nonpublic. Both Ms. Gloria and Mr. Deloria have particular expertise in designing payroll and other disbursement systems. Ms. Gloria is concerned about whether any of the following services would impair their audit independence.

a. For each of the services in the accompanying table provide a judgment as to whether providing the service would impair attest independence. In all 12 situations, assume that management has designated a management-level individual to be responsible for overseeing the CPA's services and has established appropriate internal control. Also assume that the client is privately held and does not report to the SEC.

b. Now assume that the 12 services are being contemplated for nonattest clients. Which of the services does the AICPA *Code of Professional Conduct* prohibit under this assumption?

| Situation Number | Service Description | Independence Impaired (Yes, No, Indeterminate) | Additional Information Needed for "Indeterminate" Replies |
|---|---|---|---|
| 1 | Customize and implement a prepackaged payroll system. | | |
| 2 | Manage the portion of a client's local area network system related to payroll. | | |
| 3 | Using payroll time records approved by management, generate unsigned payroll checks on a continuing basis for the client; the client signs the checks. | | |
| 4 | Prepare the payroll tax return form and sign it on behalf of management. | | |
| 5 | Approve employee time cards. | | |
| 6 | Accept responsibility to sign checks, but only in emergency situations. | | |
| 7 | Monitor employee time cards and make changes when errors are detected. | | |
| 8 | Post client-approved entries to client's trial balance. | | |
| 9 | Provide all the initial training and instruction to client employees on a newly implemented payroll information and control system. | | |
| 10 | Screen candidates and recommend the most highly qualified candidate to serve as treasurer for the client. | | |
| 11 | Supervise client personnel in the daily operation of the payroll system. | | |
| 12 | Present payroll business risk considerations to the board of directors on behalf of management. | | |

## Problems

All applicable problems are available with McGraw-Hill's *Connect*™ *Accounting.* ▓ connect
|ACCOUNTING

**LO 1**  3–41.  Gary Watson, a graduating business student at a small college, is currently interviewing for

a job. Gary was invited by both Tilly Manufacturing Co. and Watson Supply Company to travel to a nearby city for an interview. Both companies have offered to pay Gary's expenses. His total expenses for the trip were $96 for mileage on his car and $45 for meals. As he prepares the letters requesting reimbursement, he is considering asking for the total amount of the expenses from both employers. His rationale is that if he had taken separate trips, each employer would have had to pay that amount.

a. Who are the parties that are directly affected by this ethical dilemma?

b. Are the other students at the college potentially affected by Gary's decision? Explain.

    *c.* Are the professors at the college potentially affected by Gary's decision? Explain.

    *d.* What would you do in this situation?

    *e.* What would you do if both companies mailed you $141 for your expenses with no action on your part?

**LO 4**    3–42.    Roland Company, a retail store, has utilized your services as independent auditor for several years. During the current year, the company opened a new store, and in the course of your annual audit, you verify the cost of the fixtures installed in the new store by examining purchase orders, invoices, and other documents. This audit brings to light an understated invoice nearly a year old in which a clerical error by the supplier, Western Showcase, Inc., caused the total of the invoice to read $28,893.62 when it should have read $82,893.62. The invoice was paid immediately upon receipt without any notice of the error, and subsequent statements and correspondence from Western Showcase, Inc., showed that the account with Roland Company had been paid in full. Assume that the amount in question is material in relation to the financial position of both companies.

*Required:*

    *a.* What action should you take in this situation?

    *b.* If the client should decline to take any action in the matter, would you insist that the unpaid amount of $54,000 be included in the liabilities shown on the balance sheet as a condition necessary to your issuance of an unqualified audit report?

    *c.* Assuming that you were later retained to make an audit of Western Showcase, Inc., would you utilize the information gained in your audit of Roland Company to initiate a reopening of the account with that company?

**LO 4**    3–43.    Thomas Gilbert and Susan Bradley formed a professional corporation called "Financial Services Inc.—A Professional Corporation," each taking 50 percent of the authorized common stock. Gilbert is a CPA and a member of the AICPA. Bradley is a CPCU (Chartered Property Casualty Underwriter). The corporation performs auditing and tax services under Gilbert's direction and insurance services under Bradley's supervision.

    One of the corporation's first audit clients was Grandtime Company. Grandtime had total assets of $600,000 and total liabilities of $270,000. In the course of his examination, Gilbert found that Grandtime's building with a carrying value of $240,000 was pledged as collateral for a 10-year term note in the amount of $200,000. The client's financial statements did not mention that the building was pledged as collateral for the 10-year term note. However, as the failure to disclose the lien did not affect either the value of the assets or the amount of the liabilities, and his examination was satisfactory in all other respects, Gilbert rendered an unqualified opinion on Grandtime's financial statements. About two months after the date of his opinion, Gilbert learned that an insurance company was planning to loan Grandtime $150,000 in the form of a first-mortgage note on the building. Realizing that the insurance company was unaware of the existing lien on the building, Gilbert had Bradley notify the insurance company of the fact that Grandtime's building was pledged as collateral for a term note.

    Shortly after the events described above, Gilbert was charged with several violations of professional ethics.

*Required:*

Identify and discuss at least four ethical implications of those acts by Gilbert that were in violation of the AICPA *Code of Professional Conduct*.

**In-Class Team Cases**

**LO 6**    3–44.    The issue of whether the performance of nonattest (consulting) services for audit clients impairs independence of the auditors has been widely debated within the public accounting profession. Restrictions on the performance of consulting are a major aspect of the Sarbanes-Oxley Act of 2002.

*Required:*

    *a.* Describe the restrictions that are placed on the performance of nonattest services for audit clients by the Sarbanes-Oxley Act of 2002.

    *b.* List arguments for restricting nonattest services for audit clients.

    *c.* List arguments against restricting nonattest services for audit clients.

    *d.* Present your opinion and support it with one or more of the arguments listed above.

**LO 5**    3–45.    You are the Partner-in-Charge of a large metropolitan office of a regional public accounting firm. Two members of your professional staff have come to you to discuss problems that may affect the firm's independence. Neither of these situations has been specifically answered by the AICPA Professional Ethics Division. Therefore, you must reach your own conclusions as to what to advise your staff members, and what actions, if any, are to be taken by the firm.

*Case 1:* Don Moore, a partner in the firm, has recently moved into a condominium which he shares with his girlfriend, Joan Scott. Moore owns the condominium and pays all the expenses relating to its maintenance. Otherwise, the two are self-supporting. Scott is a stockbroker, and recently she has started acquiring shares in one of the audit clients of this office of the public accounting firm. The shares are held in Scott's name. At present, the shares are not material in relation to her net worth.

*Case 2:* Mary Reed, a new staff auditor with the firm, has recently separated from her husband. Mary has filed for divorce, but the divorce cannot become final for at least five months. The property settlement is being bitterly contested. Mary's husband has always resented her professional career and has just used community property to acquire one share of common stock in each of the publicly owned companies audited by the office in which Mary works.

*Required:*

For each case, you are to:

a.  Set forth arguments indicating that the firm's independence has *not* been impaired.

b.  Set forth arguments indicating that the firm's independence *has* been impaired.

c.  Express your personal opinion. Identify those arguments from part (*a*) or part (*b*) that you found most persuasive. If you believe that the firm's independence has been impaired, make suggestions about how the problem might be resolved.

## Research and Discussion Case

**LO 4**

3–46.  The International Bank of Commerce (IBC) is an audit client of your public accounting firm. IBC is a multinational financial institution that operates in 23 countries. During the current year's audit, you have discovered the following problems:

a.  Improper loans were made to stockholders and other related parties.

b.  Loans were recorded on the books that appear to be either false or deceitful.

You are especially concerned about these findings because it appears that members of senior management were aware of, and participated in, these illegal activities. In accordance with professional standards, you have communicated these illegal acts to IBC's audit committee of the board of directors. However, you are not satisfied with the committee's reaction to the situation. The chairman of the audit committee thanked you cordially, but the committee took no action to investigate the activities or prevent their occurrence in the future.

*Required:*

a.  Describe the consequences if you immediately communicated these matters directly to the SEC.

b.  Describe your appropriate course of action in this situation.

c.  Present arguments for and against requiring auditors to report illegal acts directly to regulatory agencies.

## Suggested References

AICPA, *Professional Standards,* Volume 2, Commerce Clearing House, Section ET 101. (*Code of Professional Conduct,* Rule 101).

AICPA, *Professional Standards,* Volume 2, Commerce Clearing House, Section ET 301. (*Code of Professional Conduct,* Rule 301).

AICPA AU 250, *Consideration of Laws and Regulations in an Audit of Financial Statements,* PCAOB 317.

# Legal Liability of CPAs

In this era of litigation, investors and creditors who suffer financial losses and experience market downturns are likely to find certified public accountants (CPAs), as well as attorneys and corporate directors, tempting targets for recovery through suits that allege professional "malpractice." Because of this situation, CPAs should approach every engagement with the prospect that they may be required to defend their work in court. Even if the court finds in favor of the CPAs, the costs of defending a legal action can be astronomical. As a result of the number of lawsuits and the cost of defending them, the price of professional liability insurance is high.

Costs are not the only concern in this area; lawsuits damage a professional's reputation. In extreme cases, the CPAs may even be tried criminally for certain types of conduct or omissions during an audit. Everyone who is considering a career in public accounting should be aware of the potential legal liability inherent in the practice of accounting.

## The Scope of CPA Liability

**LO1**

Describe the types of CPA liability.

The sheer number of parties suffering significant losses due at least partially to the use of information on which CPAs have reported creates a situation in which potential liability may exceed that of other professionals such as physicians. If a physician or an attorney is negligent, the injured party is usually limited to the professional's patient or client. If CPAs are negligent in expressing an opinion on financial statements, millions of investors as well as firm creditors may sustain losses.

Amounts in excess of $300 million have been awarded to parties as a result of litigation against public accounting firms. Although public accounting firms often maintain professional liability insurance for such losses, the amounts awarded to plaintiffs have sometimes exceeded the limits of the public accounting firms' professional liability insurance. Such awards potentially may require further payments by the firm itself, personnel who worked on the engagement, and certain other partners.

### Litigation Placed in Perspective

Any large public accounting firm that performs thousands of audits will, at one time or another, find that it has issued an unmodified report on financial statements that, in hindsight, appear to be misleading in some respect. In some circumstances, CPA liability may be relatively obvious. In others, it may not be obvious whether the situation is due to inadequate performance or other factors. To illustrate, consider the audit of the financial statements of a computer manufacturer and, more specifically, the allowance for estimated warranty costs included therein. The estimate made in February, when the financial statements are issued, may seriously understate the subsequent actual costs incurred if a large number of computers are returned because of a manufacturing defect. Investors who have sustained large losses may attempt to recover those losses, regardless of whether they believe the CPAs are at fault. Thus, if the cost of bringing suit against a company's CPAs is relatively low and offers even a chance of recovery, the injured parties may initiate legal action.

**Illustrative Case** | *Litigation*

Sources at the Accountants' Coalition, a Washington lobbying group, have confirmed that during some recent years CPAs have spent approximately 20 percent of their revenues from audit and accounting services on litigation costs and settlements. A vice president of a major insurance company stated in *The Wall Street Journal* that his company is no longer willing to insure accounting firms for liability. The company continues to insure engineers, architects, attorneys, physicians, and surgeons. "The risks aren't as great," the vice president observed. Even when a claim is litigated successfully, the costs can be high. The chair of an international public accounting firm described a lawsuit against his firm for an audit with fees of approximately $20,000. Although the firm successfully defended itself in the case that went to trial, the cost of the firm's defense was approximately $6 million.

CPAs must recognize occasional allegations of misconduct as a fact of life. Some of the lawsuits brought against CPAs will be frivolous—often simple attempts by **plaintiffs** to recover their losses. Others will have a basis in fact—perhaps judgmental errors were made by the CPAs during the engagement. No matter how careful CPAs are, any public accounting firm may find itself a **defendant** in litigation.

## Sources of CPA Liability

**LO2**

Distinguish between CPAs' liability under common law and under statutory law.

In the United States, CPAs have both **common law** liability and **statutory law** liability. Common law liability develops through case decisions generally arising due to breach of contract, negligence, and fraud. Statutory liability develops when a governmental unit (e.g., a state or the federal government) passes laws and regulations that either implicitly or explicitly impose potential liability upon CPAs.

The standards for recovery as well as individuals afforded remedies vary by source or "theory" of liability. These theories are explained briefly in the following overview and then discussed in detail in the remaining sections of the chapter.

1. *Contract.* CPAs enter into a contract with their client (ordinarily through the engagement letter) and agree to provide services. The potential for liability occurs when there is a **breach of contract** and when damages result due to a failure of one or both parties to a contract to perform in accordance with the contract's provisions.[1] A public accounting firm might be sued by the client for breach of contract, for example, if the firm has failed to perform the engagement in accordance with the engagement letter and the client has suffered resulting damages.

2. *Negligence.* Both clients and third parties sue CPAs for the **tort**[2] of negligence. **Negligence,** also referred to as ordinary or simple negligence, is a violation of a legal duty to exercise a degree of care that an ordinary prudent person would exercise under similar circumstances. For the CPA, negligence is failure to perform a duty in accordance with applicable standards. For practical purposes, negligence may be viewed as "failure to exercise due professional care."

   **Gross negligence** is the lack of even slight care, indicative of a *reckless disregard* for one's professional responsibilities. Substantial failures on the part of an auditor to comply with generally accepted auditing standards might be interpreted as gross negligence. As discussed in detail later in this chapter, the question of whether third parties must prove a CPA guilty of gross negligence (rather than ordinary negligence) to recover losses revolves in part around jurisdictional differences in interpretation of the common law.

[1] Breach of contract liability is based on failure to carry out a duty created in the contract.

[2] Legally, a tort is a wrongful act, injury, or damage (not involving breach of contract) for which a civil action can be brought.

3. *Fraud.* **Fraud** is defined as misrepresentation by a person of a material fact, known by that person to be untrue or made with reckless indifference as to whether the fact is true, with the intention of deceiving the other party and with the result that the other party is injured. Rule 102 of the AICPA *Code of Professional Conduct* (discussed in Chapter 3) states that a member of the AICPA shall not knowingly misrepresent facts. The CPAs found to have violated this provision of Rule 102 might be sued for fraud by the client or another injured party.

   **Constructive fraud** differs from fraud as defined above in that constructive fraud does not involve a misrepresentation with intent to deceive. Gross negligence on the part of an auditor has been interpreted by the courts as constructive fraud.

4. *Statutory liability.* CPAs have statutory liability under both the federal securities laws and state securities laws, often called "blue sky" laws. The Securities Act of 1933, which applies to initial stock offerings, imposes liability on CPAs for their audit work relating to financial statements used to register the securities for sale. The Securities Exchange Act of 1934 imposes liability on CPAs for their work on the financial statements included with a company's ongoing reports to the Securities and Exchange Commission. The standards for liability differ under these statutes, but each provides a means for recovery against the CPAs by investors.

Sources of liability for CPAs also include criminal statutes and the Racketeer Influenced Corrupt Organizations (RICO) Act (discussed later in the chapter).

An injured party, the plaintiff, may elect to bring suit against CPAs under common law, any applicable statute law, or both. As one might expect, plaintiffs usually select the theory or theories that have the best prospects for success. Since the federal securities acts allow class action lawsuits, in which an entire class of investors becomes the plaintiff in a single legal action, and hold CPAs auditing financial statements to very strict standards, most lawsuits against auditors by stockholders or bondholders of publicly owned corporations allege violations of these federal statutes.

CPA liability may arise from improper performance on any type of engagement—audit, other attest, tax, accounting services, or consulting services. However, CPAs are not liable to any party if they can prove that they performed their services with *due professional care.* Exercising due professional care is a *complete defense* against any charge of improper conduct. However, CPAs do face the disadvantage that investors, juries, and judges view their conduct knowing the outcome of the investment and the company's fate. Such hindsight may work against the CPAs. Often the issue comes down to the simple question of whether the CPAs should have known or seen the problems that were evolving.

## CPAs' Liability to Their Clients under Common Law

**LO3**

Explain the proof requirements for clients and third parties seeking recovery from CPAs under common law and the defenses available to CPAs.

When CPAs take on any type of engagement, they are obliged by their contract with the client—generally the engagement letter—to exercise due professional care. This obligation exists whether or not it is specifically set forth in the contract with the client. The "client" is ordinarily the company itself,[3] as contrasted to the shareholders. But the contract obligations are important because they may provide the client and third parties additional recovery rights. If the CPAs fail to perform according to the terms of the contract, the CPAs have liability to clients through the common law theory of breach of contract.

[3] The client's rights in some circumstances may be assigned to others. The *right of subrogation* allows insurers who pay the insured for a loss any right of action that the insured had. For example, if a fidelity bonding company pays the CPAs' client for a loss due to employee theft, the fidelity bonding company would have the same recovery rights against the CPAs as did the client. Also, a bankruptcy trustee or receiver of a company that has failed will ordinarily have the client's rights.

If, however, the work is completed according to the terms of the contract, but the work has errors or falls short of professional standards, the CPAs' client would have tort action for negligence against the CPAs. In many cases, the client would have both types of recovery theories available for use against the CPAs.

Although legal differences exist between breach of contract and tort actions, in general, to establish CPA liability, a client must prove the following elements:

1. *Duty.* The CPAs accepted a duty of due professional care to exercise skill, prudence, and diligence.[4]
2. *Breach of duty.* The CPAs breached their duty of due professional care through negligent performance.
3. *Losses (damages).* The client suffered losses.
4. *Causation (proximate cause).* The damages were caused by the CPAs' negligent performance.

## The Elements of Duty and Breach of Duty

The auditors' duty is defined by generally accepted auditing standards, the engagement letter, and legal considerations. In a breach of contract action, the client establishes that the CPAs' duty was breached by showing either that the auditors did not perform the obligations listed in the engagement letter or that the performance did not meet professional standards. For example, the CPAs may be sued for not performing the contractual obligations when, through no fault of the client, the audit was not completed by some agreed-upon time. Alternatively, a lawsuit arguing that the audit did not meet professional standards may be based upon the CPAs' failure to detect a fraud perpetrated by a client employee. In this second example, the key factor in determining whether the CPAs are liable is not just whether the CPAs failed to uncover fraud, but whether this failure stems from the CPAs' negligence.

Regardless of the type of engagement involved, the CPAs must perform the contract according to its terms and the performance of the work under the contract must meet applicable professional standards.

In Chapter 2, we discussed the auditors' responsibility for detecting misstatements due to **errors** and fraud. Auditors must design their audits to obtain *reasonable assurance* of detecting misstatements due to errors and fraud that are material to the financial statements. In doing so, they must exercise due care and professional skepticism in planning, performing, and evaluating the results of audit procedures.

These requirements *do not imply* that auditors were negligent whenever misstatements due to errors or fraud are later found to exist in audited financial statements. An audit has certain limitations; it does not involve a complete and detailed examination of all records and transactions. To do so would entail a prohibitive cost, which would certainly not be

---

[4] This element is often relatively easy to prove since by accepting an engagement the CPAs assume a responsibility to exercise due care.

| **Illustrative Case** | *Contributory Negligence* |

In *Cenco, Inc. v. Seidman & Seidman* (1982) the court clarified the auditors' liability to the corporation when prior management has been engaged in improper activities.

Several former top managers of Cenco had engaged in a massive fraudulent scheme to inflate the corporation's inventories. However, seven of nine members of the board of directors were not involved in the fraud, although there was evidence that they were negligent in allowing the fraud to go undetected.

When the fraud was discovered, the stockholders sued the corporation, its corrupt managers, and Seidman &

Seidman, the corporation's auditors. The corporation then filed a cross-complaint against Seidman, and Seidman responded with a contributory negligence defense. Seidman settled the class action suit by the stockholders before it went to the jury. In the cross-complaint by the corporation, the jury found that Seidman was not liable for breach of contract, negligence, or fraud. In upholding the decision, the U.S. Court of Appeals for the Seventh Circuit indicated it was appropriate to impute the actions of corrupt management to the corporation. Thus, the corporation was a party to the fraud and not entitled to recover losses from the auditors.

warranted under ordinary business conditions. There can never be absolute assurance that errors or fraud do not exist among the transactions not included in the CPAs' tests. Also, the possibility exists that the documents have been so skillfully forged, or some other fraud has been so expertly concealed, that the application of normal auditing techniques would not reveal the fraud. When a public accounting firm's audit *has been performed in accordance with generally accepted auditing standards,* the firm has not breached its duty and *should not be held liable* for failure to detect the existence of errors or fraud.

## The Element of Losses (Damages)

A plaintiff's losses, or damages, are dependent upon the nature of the engagement performed by the CPAs. On a financial statement audit, they may include losses by the client from embezzlement. On a tax engagement, they may include tax penalties or extra taxes paid.

## The Element of Causation (Proximate Cause)

*Causation* exists when damage to another is directly attributable to a wrongdoer's act. Even though a public accounting firm might have been negligent in rendering services, it will not be liable for the *plaintiff's* loss if its negligence was not the cause of the loss. The auditors' primary defense to litigation brought for breach of contract or negligence is ordinarily to show that the audit was performed with due professional care and that there was no negligence in the performance of the contract and professional duties.

An additional possible defense for the auditors is that the loss is due to other causes. The auditors might be able to show that, regardless of whether negligence was involved, the negligence alleged by the client was not the **proximate cause** of the client's loss. Demonstrating the client's **contributory negligence** is one means of showing that the auditors' negligence was not the cause (or sole cause) of the client's loss. In jurisdictions (e.g., states) that follow pure contributory negligence doctrines, the auditors may entirely eliminate their liability to the client by establishing the defense of contributory negligence by the client. However, very few states follow the doctrine of contributory negligence.

Many states rely on the concept of **comparative negligence.** Comparative negligence permits juries to examine the issue of causation and assess a percentage figure of fault to the CPAs, any other defendants, and the client. This system permits the allocation of damages among the parties based on the extent to which each is at fault. For example, a jury might determine that the CPAs were 50 percent at fault for the losses resulting from a failure to detect an employee embezzlement scheme, that management consultants were 30 percent responsible, and that client management was 20 percent responsible. The client will be able to recover from the CPAs and the management consultants 50 percent and 30 percent, respectively, of the losses. This allocation of damages is also referred to as **proportionate liability.**

**Joint and several liability** represents another approach to liability that in general benefits a plaintiff's litigation against multiple defendants. Under joint and several liability, the defendants are liable for their pro rata share of any damages awarded (as is the case with proportionate liability), but they also may be held liable for damages of other defendants who prove to be unable to pay their share of the damages. Using our earlier example in which the CPAs were found to be 50 percent responsible for losses, if the management consultants did not have the ability to pay all of the losses attributed to them, the auditors as joint defendants would be required to make up the difference.

## Auditors' Common Law Liability to Third Parties

Clients have recourse against auditors for damages caused by an improper audit through both breach of contract and tort actions against the auditors. But what about the many third parties who rely upon audited financial statements? How may these parties recover their losses from auditors who have performed an improper audit?

As is the case for clients, third parties must establish that losses resulted from the CPAs' performance and that the CPAs breached a duty of due professional care. In a typical case, a third party seeking damages from a public accounting firm seeks to establish that it sustained a loss caused by relying upon misleading financial statements which included an audit report that was the product of an inadequate audit. The auditors named as defendants in a common law action are in the position of having to refute the charges brought by the plaintiffs.

A plaintiff who can establish gross negligence or fraud on the part of the auditors (as well as breach of duty and losses) will be able to establish liability against the auditors. Also, in certain situations, the plaintiff need only establish ordinary negligence to establish liability against the auditors. Auditors' liability to third parties for ordinary negligence under common law varies from one jurisdiction to another. Three general approaches may be used to summarize auditors' liability to third-party financial statement users under common law in the various state courts—the *Ultramares (Known User) Approach,* the *Restatement (Foreseen User) Approach,* and the *Rosenblum (Foreseeable User) Approach.*

**Ultramares (Known User) Approach[5]**

The most widely cited common law **precedent** stems from the landmark case ***Ultramares v. Touche & Co.*** (1931). In this case, the defendant CPAs issued an unqualified opinion on the balance sheet of a company engaged in the importation and sale of rubber. On the basis of the CPAs' opinion, Ultramares, a factor, made several loans to the company. Shortly thereafter, the company was declared bankrupt, and Ultramares sued the CPAs for ordinary negligence. The New York Court of Appeals (the state's highest court) ruled that the CPAs should be held liable for *ordinary negligence* only to their client and any third party (beneficiary) specifically identified as a user of the CPAs' report. The court went on to indicate that the auditors should be held liable to *unidentified* third-party users of the audit report for *gross negligence or fraud.* In the *Ultramares* case, the audit was performed "primarily for the benefit" of the client; Ultramares was not specifically identified as a user of the audit report. Therefore, to recover its losses, Ultramares would have been required to prove that the CPAs were grossly negligent in performing their audit. The case eventually was settled out of court, with no determination of whether the auditors had been grossly negligent.

[5] This approach is referred to by numerous other titles, including the *third-party beneficiary approach,* the *primary benefit approach,* and the *privity (or near privity)* approach.

The *Ultramares* precedent has been reaffirmed and interpreted in many subsequent cases. These cases have clarified the conditions necessary for parties to be considered to be **third-party beneficiaries** of the audit. For example, the New York Court of Appeals upheld and interpreted the *Ultramares* precedent in the case of **Credit Alliance Corp. v. Arthur Andersen & Co.** (1985). The court stated that before auditors may be held liable for ordinary negligence to a third party, they must have *been aware* that the financial statements were to be used for a particular purpose by a *known party or parties,* and must have taken *some action* to indicate that knowledge.

**Restatement of Torts (Foreseen User) Approach**

The principle of auditor liability for ordinary negligence to third parties is expanded by the American Law Institute's (ALI's) **Second Restatement of the Law of Torts** (*Restatement*). *Restatements of law* are compilations of the majority view of the common law of the states on various topics such as contracts and torts and are meant to serve as guides for judges when they are issuing opinions in which there are common law issues. The *Restatement* approach to third-party liability, also referred to as the foreseen third-party approach, expands the auditors' liability for ordinary negligence to include third parties who are foreseen users of the audited financial statements. *The specific identity of foreseen users need not be known to the CPAs.*

The courts in many states have followed the *Restatement* principle, including a court in Rhode Island in the leading case of *Rusch Factors, Inc. v. Levin* (1968). In that case, the CPAs were found liable for ordinary negligence to a third party that subsequently provided financing to the audit client. The third party had *not* been specifically identified to the CPAs, although they were aware that the financial statements were to be used to help obtain the financing. In *Williams Controls v. Parente, Randolph, Orlando & Associates,* 39 F. Supp. 2d 517 (1999), a more recent example, the court held the auditors liable to a purchaser of a client's business even though that purchaser was not the one originally identified when the audit began. The court noted that when the audit engagement letter was signed the auditors knew that their work would be used for purposes of completing a sale of one of the client's divisions. Who the buyer would be was irrelevant for purposes of auditor liability under the *Restatement* principle. The courts of many states follow this principle of liability to third parties.[6]

**Rosenblum (Foreseeable User) Approach**

This approach was based originally on the 1983 New Jersey **Rosenblum v. Adler** Supreme Court case, which rejected the approaches arising out of *Ultramares* and the *Second Restatement of Torts* and established a very different standard. In this case, the defendant CPAs issued an unqualified report on the financial statements of Giant Stores Corporation, which showed the corporation to be profitable. In reliance upon these statements, Rosenblum sold a catalog showroom business to Giant in exchange for shares of Giant's stock. Shortly afterward, Giant filed for bankruptcy and the stock became worthless. Rosenblum sued Giant's CPAs, alleging ordinary negligence. The case was dismissed by the trial court, on the premise that the CPAs were not liable to unidentified third parties for ordinary negligence. However, the New Jersey Supreme Court reversed the lower court, finding that CPAs *can be held liable for ordinary negligence* to any third party the auditors could "reasonably foresee" as recipients of the statements for routine business purposes. This approach has the potential effect of expanding CPA liability to third parties whose purposes are totally unknown to the CPAs. At this point, however, few states have elected to follow the *Rosenblum* approach.

[6] Some courts have applied a type of modified rule in which they have limited the liability of the auditors to the intended user and not any subsequent users who are substituted, such as a second bank or another buyer. One of the reasons for this limitation to the primary intended party is that circumstances change with each departing user of the financial statements and the auditors should have the benefit of full information before liability is imposed.

## Illustrative Case

### Liability to Third Parties under the Restatement of the Law of Torts

Dianne Holiday, CPA, performed the audit of Lyman Corporation for the year ended December 31. Holiday was aware that Lyman intended to use the audit report to obtain a bank loan. However, no specific bank was identified to Holiday. After the report was issued, Lyman obtained loans from the First National Bank and Dime Box State Bank. Also, Wallace Manufacturing Co. relied on Holiday's opinion in providing trade credit to Lyman. If the court applied the known user principles of the *Restatement* (foreseen user) approach, Holiday could be held liable to First National and Dime Box if she was found guilty of ordinary negligence in the performance of her audit. The banks form a limited class of third parties who could be foreseen to rely on the audit report. Wallace Manufacturing Co., on the other hand, would have to prove *gross negligence* on the part of Holiday to recover its losses. The audit was not performed for the use of trade creditors; therefore, Wallace would not be considered a part of a limited class of foreseen users.

## Summary of Third-Party Liability Approaches

Common law cases are decided, in large part, by reference to established precedents—that is, past decisions. The *Ultramares* (known user), *Restatement* (foreseen user), and *Rosenblum* (foreseeable user) approaches create conflicting precedents as to which third parties can hold the auditors liable for ordinary negligence. Variants of each of these approaches exist in the various states. Figure 4.1 summarizes differences in third-party ability to recover damages for CPAs' ordinary negligence liability under the three basic approaches.

# Liability to Third Parties under Statutory Law

**LO4**

Explain the proof requirements for plaintiffs under statutory law and the defenses available to the auditors.

Statutory law is written law, created by state or federal legislative bodies. Most states have "blue sky" laws, which regulate the issuance and trading of securities within the state. The two most important federal laws relating to auditors' liability are the **Securities Act of 1933** (the 1933 Act) and the **Securities Exchange Act of 1934** (the 1934 Act). CPAs also must be concerned with the application of the Racketeer Influenced and Corrupt Organizations Act (RICO). Even though our discussion of statutory law will be limited to these three federal acts, CPAs should be familiar with other federal laws along with the blue sky laws in those states in which their clients sell securities.

Litigation against auditors that is based on statutory provisions does not enjoy the latitude available under common law. While common law can vary from state to state

**FIGURE 4.1**
**Summary of Third-Party Common Law Liability for Ordinary Negligence**

| Approach | Requirements for a Third Party to Recover Losses Due to CPAs' Ordinary Negligence |
|---|---|
| *Ultramares* approach (known user approach) | The auditors knew that the audited financial statements were for use for a *particular purpose by a known user* (third-party beneficiary). |
| *Restatement* approach (foreseen user approach) | The auditors knew the audited financial statements were for use for a *particular purpose*, but the auditors *did not necessarily know the specific user* (e.g., the financial statements were known to be for use in helping to sell the business to an unidentified purchaser). |
| *Rosenblum* approach (foreseeable user approach) | The auditors should have realized that it was *reasonably foreseeable* that the financial statements would be used by this user. |

and can evolve with differing factual circumstances and changing conditions, statutorily based litigation is constrained to a greater extent by the underlying law.

## Securities Act of 1933

The 1933 Act requires a company intending to offer its securities for sale to the public to first file a **registration statement** with the SEC.[7] This registration statement includes audited financial statements and numerous other disclosures. Under the 1933 Act, both the company filing the registration statement and its auditors may be held liable to purchasers of the securities in the event that the registration statement is found to contain material misstatements or omissions.[8] The wording of Section 11(a) of the act provides as follows:

> In case any part of the registration statement, when such part became effective, contained an untrue statement of a material fact or omitted to state a material fact required to be stated therein or necessary to make the statements therein not misleading, any person acquiring such security (unless it is proved that at the time of such acquisition he knew of such untruth or omission) may . . . sue.

### Plaintiffs' Rights under the 1933 Act

The 1933 Act offers protection to only a limited group of investors—those who initially purchase a security offered for sale under the registration statement.[9] For those investors, however, the 1933 Act shifts much of the burden of proof from the plaintiff to the defendant. The plaintiffs (security purchasers) need only prove that (1) they sustained a loss and (2) the registration statement was misleading. They *need not prove*[10] that they relied upon the registration or that the auditors were negligent.

### Auditors' Defenses under the 1933 Act

If auditors are to avoid liability for the plaintiffs' losses, they generally must affirmatively prove that (1) they conducted the audit with **due diligence,** (2) the plaintiffs' losses were not caused by misstated financial statements, (3) the plaintiffs knew of the financial statement misstatement when the securities were purchased, or (4) the statute of limitations—one year after the discovery of the misstatement, but no more than three years after the security was first offered to the public—had expired.

As a practical matter, it is the due diligence defense that auditors often raise. Section 11 of the act states that the auditors are not liable if they:

> had, after reasonable investigation, reasonable ground to believe and did believe, at the time . . . the registration statement became effective, that the statements therein were true and that there was no omission to state a material fact.

---

[7] The 1933 Act requires registration statements to be filed by any company that will offer securities for sale to the public through the mails or interstate commerce. There are certain exceptions, for example, for charitable institutions and other not-for-profit organizations, and for offerings of small dollar amounts.

[8] The auditors are liable for misstatements or omissions only in those portions of the registration statement covered by their audit and report.

[9] Secondary purchasers who bought securities within the first year of the registration statement also may bring suit against the company and the auditors under the Securities Act of 1933.

[10] An exception exists in that Section 11 requires reliance when the plaintiff purchases the security after the issuance of an earnings statement covering a period of at least 12 months following the effective date of the registration statement.

The due diligence standard of the 1933 Act establishes a high level of auditors' responsibility for justifying their performance. Not only are auditors liable for losses caused by acts of ordinary negligence, but they must *prove their innocence* rather than merely refute the accusations of the plaintiffs. Establishing the due diligence defense has proved difficult for auditors, and the standing precedent on interpretation of due diligence is *Escott v. BarChris Construction Corporation,* 283 F. Supp. 643 (1968). The case was an action under Section 11 of the Securities Act of 1933 by purchasers of BarChris's registered debentures against the directors, underwriters, and independent auditors of BarChris. Subsequent to issuance of the debentures, BarChris, a builder of bowling alleys, went bankrupt. The plaintiffs claimed that the registration statement for the debentures contained materially false statements and material omissions; the defendants all countered with the due diligence defense. The court found that the registration statement (Form S-1) was false and misleading and that with a few exceptions none of the defendants had established their due diligence defense. The court also found that the public accounting firm had failed to comply with generally accepted auditing standards. The court was especially critical of the public accounting firm's conduct of the S-1 review, so called because it is an investigation carried out by the public accounting firm some time after completion of the audit, but just prior to the effective date of the registration statement filed with the SEC. In an S-1 review, the CPAs look for any evidence arising since their audit that indicates that the registration statement is misleading as filed. The court criticized the public accounting firm for performing too limited a review and for being "too easily satisfied with glib answers by management" to inquiries.

While the *BarChris* case was decided over 40 years ago, it remains the standing precedent for auditor liability. In fact, its interpretation of Section 11, in terms of the auditors' defenses, was so stringent that there are relatively few additional cases related to Section 11 liability because of defendants' unwillingness to litigate cases fully when there is such a strict standard of auditor liability.

## Securities Exchange Act of 1934

The Securities Exchange Act of 1934 requires all companies under SEC jurisdiction to file annual audited and quarterly reviewed financial statements with the SEC.[11] The act also creates potential liability for the filing company and its auditors to anyone who buys or sells the company's securities in the event that these annual statements are found to be misleading. While the 1933 Act creates liability only to those investors involved in the initial distribution of a public offering, the 1934 Act expands that liability to subsequent purchasers and sellers of the stock. The two primary liability sections of the act are Sections 10 and 18.

Section 10, with Rule 10b-5 promulgated by the SEC under Section 10(b) of the act, reads as follows:

It shall be unlawful for any person, directly or indirectly, by the use of any means or instrumentality of interstate commerce or of the mails, or of any national securities exchange . . .

(1) to employ any device, scheme, or artifice to defraud,

(2) to make any untrue statement of a material fact or to omit to state a material fact necessary in order to make the statements . . . not misleading, or

(3) to engage in any act, practice, or course of business which operates or would operate as a fraud or deceit upon any person, in connection with the purchase or sale of any security.

[11] Companies under SEC jurisdiction include those (1) whose securities are listed on a national stock exchange or (2) with equity securities traded on the over-the-counter market, and total assets exceeding $5 million and 500 or more stockholders.

Section 18(a) of the 1934 Act, which relates to misstated financial statements, provides for liability to [emphasis added]:

> any person (not knowing that such statement was false or misleading) who, in reliance upon such statement, shall have purchased or sold a security at a price which was affected by such statement, for damages by such reliance, *unless the person sued shall prove that he acted in good faith* and had no knowledge that such statement was false or misleading.

### Plaintiffs' Rights under the 1934 Act

The 1934 Act offers protection to both original and subsequent purchasers and sellers of securities. Under both Section 10 and Section 18, the plaintiffs (security purchasers and sellers) must prove that (1) they sustained losses, (2) the financial statements were misleading, and (3) they relied upon the financial statements. Section 10(b) and Rule 10b-5, as interpreted by the landmark **Ernst & Ernst v. Hochfelder** case, require that the plaintiffs prove **scienter** (intent to deceive, manipulate, or defraud) on the part of the auditors.

*Ernst & Ernst v. Hochfelder* was brought by a group of investors against the public accounting firm that for 21 years had audited the financial statements of First Securities Company of Chicago, a small brokerage firm. The president of First Securities, who was also its majority stockholder, committed suicide, leaving a note stating that the firm was insolvent and disclosing a fraud that he had perpetrated upon several investors. The president had persuaded the investors to mail him their personal checks, the funds from which he was to invest in escrow accounts yielding high returns to the investors. There were no such escrow accounts in the accounting records of First Securities Company; instead, the president was engaged in a **Ponzi scheme** in which he diverted the investors' checks to his own use immediately upon receipt.

The investors filed suit under SEC Rule 10b-5 (and the related Securities Exchange Act of 1934 Section 10[b]) against the public accounting firm, charging it with *ordinary negligence,* and thus with responsibility for the investors' losses in the fraud. The plaintiffs *did not accuse the public accounting firm of fraud or intentional misconduct.* That is, they did not attempt to prove scienter.

The basis for the plaintiffs' charge of negligence was that the public accounting firm failed to discover a weakness in First Securities Company's control that enabled the company's president to carry on the fraud. The control weakness, called the "mail rule," was the president's policy that *only he* could open mail addressed to him at First Securities, or addressed to First Securities to his attention. It is common practice at financial institutions for *all* incoming mail to be opened in the mailroom, in part to avoid the possibility of employees' perpetrating some type of fraud.

The case was ultimately resolved by the U.S. Supreme Court, which ruled that an action for damages under Section 10(b) of the 1934 Act and the related SEC Rule 10b-5 was not warranted in the absence of scienter on the auditors' part. The court held that auditors are liable under Section 10(b) only upon proof of intent to deceive, manipulate, or defraud.[12] In summary, the auditors' primary defense under Section 10 is that there is no scienter. That is, auditors show that they did not perform the audit with the intent to deceive, manipulate, or defraud.

### Auditors' Defenses under the 1934 Act

Under Section 18, the auditors may avoid liability by proving "good faith," which they will normally be able to establish unless they have been guilty of gross negligence or fraud. In addition, to avoid liability for the plaintiffs' losses under either Section 10 or 18, the auditors may rely on causation—that the losses experienced by the plaintiffs were caused by factors other than the auditors' behavior.

[12] The Court did not rule on whether the existence of reckless behavior would be sufficient to establish scienter and thereby impose liability.

## Illustrative Case — Proportionate vs. Joint and Several Liability

Assume that $50 million of damages is awarded to a plaintiff and the auditors' percentage of responsibility is established at 10 percent. The following summarizes three possible liability approaches:

*Strictly proportionate liability:*    The auditors' share will be $5 million (10% × $50 million).

*Proportionate liability as per the 1934 Act:*    Liability is the strictly proportionate liability amount of $5 million plus, if some defendants are unable to pay their share:

1. Joint and several liability to small investors with a net worth of less than $200,000 and recoverable damages that exceed 10 percent of their net worth, and

2. Additional liability to other investors of a maximum of 50 percent of the proportionate share; in this situation, an additional $2,500,000 (50% × $5,000,000).

Thus, the maximum liability to the auditors is $7,500,000 plus (1).

*Joint and proportionate liability:*    If some other defendants are unable to pay their share, the auditors' share increases proportionately. In the extreme, if no other defendants are able to pay any amount, the auditors are liable for the entire $50 million.

### Proportionate Liability under the 1934 Act

Historically, defendants in actions under the 1934 Act were jointly and severally liable for all the plaintiffs' losses. However, the Private Securities Litigation Reform Act of 1995 amended the 1934 Act to place limits on the amount of the auditors' liability. In general, the amendment establishes proportionate liability. If one or more of the defendants are not able to pay their share of the losses, the auditors will have unlimited joint and several liability only to certain small investors. To other investors, the auditors' liability for losses caused by other parties is limited to an amount not to exceed 50 percent of the auditors' proportionate share of the losses. If the auditors were knowingly involved in violations of the law, complete joint and several liability may be imposed.

In addition to the 1995 reforms, Congress passed the Securities Litigation Uniform Standards Act in 1998 to establish uniform standards for bringing class action securities suits in both state and federal courts. Under these standards, plaintiffs and their lawyers must follow certain certification procedures and there are consolidation rules with regard to the trial of these cases.

## Comparison of the 1933 and 1934 Acts

**LO5**

Compare the requirements for CPA liability under the Securities Act of 1933 with those under the Securities Exchange Act of 1934.

The 1933 and 1934 Acts differ in investors protected and the burden of proof required. The 1933 Act offers recourse only to individuals acquiring the initial distribution of securities, whereas the 1934 Act offers recourse to *any* person buying or selling the securities at a later date.

In comparison to common law, both of the federal securities acts shift significant burdens of proof from the plaintiffs to the defendants. However, some differences exist between the defendant's burden under the 1933 Act and the 1934 Act. Under the 1933 Act, plaintiffs *need not prove reliance* upon the audited financial statements. The 1934 Act, however, generally requires plaintiffs to prove that they relied upon the misleading statements.

Next, both acts place the burden of proving adequate performance on the defendants. The 1933 Act requires the auditors to prove "due diligence"; if they were ordinarily negligent, they will not be able to establish this defense. The 1934 Act is more lenient in that Section 10 requires the existence of scienter, while Section 18 requires auditors to prove that they acted in good faith. Because it requires the existence of gross negligence or fraud, the "good faith" defense is considerably easier to establish than is "due diligence." Figure 4.2 summarizes important similarities and differences between the two acts.

FIGURE 4.2 **Summary of Auditor Civil Liability under the 1933 Securities Act (Section 11) and the 1934 Securities Exchange Act (Sections 10 and 18)**

| Act | What Must Be Proved by the Third Party? | | | Basic Standard of Liability |
|---|---|---|---|---|
| | A Loss? | Misleading Financial Statements? | Reliance on Financial Statements? | |
| 1933 Securities Act— Section 11 | Yes | Yes | No | Auditor must prove due diligence |
| 1934 Securities Exchange Act—Section 10 | Yes | Yes | Yes | Third party must prove existence of scienter (auditors' intent to deceive, manipulate, or defraud) |
| 1934 Securities Exchange Act—Section 18 | Yes | Yes | Yes | Auditor must prove good faith |

## Racketeer Influenced and Corrupt Organizations Act

In 1970, Congress enacted the Racketeer Influenced and Corrupt Organizations Act (RICO) as a weapon against mobsters and racketeers who were influencing legitimate business. A discussion of RICO would appear to be out of place in a discussion of legal liability of auditors. However, the act broadly defines the term *racketeering activities* to include crimes such as mail fraud and fraud in the sale of securities. Prior to 1993, these provisions were used successfully in a small number of cases against CPAs in which it could be shown that the CPAs knew, or perhaps should have known, of material misstatements of financial statements when the problems were indicative of a pattern of improper activity. A primary concern with the RICO Act is the provision that allows triple damages in civil cases brought under the act.

In 1993, a favorable ruling by the U.S. Supreme Court, in the case of *Reves v. Ernst & Young,* relieved much of the concern about auditors' liability under the RICO Act. The court decided that the accountants cannot be held liable under the RICO Act unless they actually participated in the operation or management of the organization. Subsequently, the Private Securities Litigation Reform Act of 1995 eliminated securities fraud as an offense in a civil RICO action unless there is a prior conviction. However, a number of states continue to have their own versions of RICO.

## Auditors' Criminal Liability under the Securities Acts

Both the Securities Act of 1933 and the Securities Exchange Act of 1934 include provisions for *criminal charges* against CPAs who willfully (knowingly) allow misstatements in SEC filings, as do other statutes. Most directly relevant are Section 24 of the Securities Act of 1933 and Section 32(a) of the Securities Exchange Act of 1934. In addition, in extreme cases, CPAs can be prosecuted under the criminal provisions of RICO, where it can be shown that the CPAs actually participated in the management or operation of a company that is indicted under RICO.

The *Continental Vending Machine Corporation* case was accompanied by a celebrated criminal case involving three members of the public accounting firm that audited Continental's financial statements. The criminal charges rocked the profession, because there was no intent to defraud on the part of the CPAs; they were convicted of criminal fraud on the basis of gross negligence. The verdict of guilty was affirmed by a U.S. Court of Appeals, and the U.S. Supreme Court refused to review the case. The three CPAs were later pardoned by the president of the United States.

In the *Continental Vending* case (*United States v. Simon,* 425 F.2d 796 [1969]), the U.S. government brought charges of fraud against three CPAs. The charges hinged upon a note to Continental's audited financial statements, which read:

> The amount receivable from Valley Commercial Corp. (an affiliated company of which . . . [Continental's president] is an officer, director, and stockholder) bears interest at 12 percent a year. Such amount, less the balance of the notes payable to that company, is secured by the assignment to the Company of Valley's equity in certain marketable securities. As of . . . [the date of the auditors' report] . . . the amount of such equity at current market quotations exceeded the net amount receivable.

The note did not disclose—and the auditors were aware—that the affiliated company had loaned approximately that same amount to Continental's president. The president was unable to repay the affiliate, which was unable to repay Continental. In addition, most of the collateral furnished by the president was stock and convertible debentures of Continental itself.

The auditors' defense in this case was that the note complied with existing generally accepted accounting principles. Eight "leaders of the profession" testified as expert witnesses that the note was consistent with generally accepted accounting principles and the audit was performed in accordance with generally accepted auditing standards. However, the judge rejected this argument and instructed the jury to evaluate whether the financial statements were "fairly presented" without reference to generally accepted accounting principles. The finding by the jury that the balance sheet did not present fairly Continental's financial position led to conviction of the three CPAs.

Because the *Continental Vending* case involved both criminal and civil proceedings, it has significant implications for the public accounting profession. Not only is civil liability an ever-present hazard for CPAs, but criminal charges also may be involved.

## Criminal Liability under Other Statutes

In addition to the securities laws, CPAs and public accounting firms may be subject to prosecution under a host of other criminal statutes. This fact became all too apparent to the profession when, in June 2002, Arthur Andersen became the first major accounting firm ever convicted of a felony. The indictment, which named only the firm and not any employees or partners, accused Arthur Andersen of the "wholesale destruction of documents" relating to the Enron Corporation collapse. Representatives of Arthur Andersen stated that the firm was merely applying its document retention policy in destroying the documents. While prosecutors emphasized the great volume of documents destroyed, the jury, in finding Arthur Andersen guilty, based its verdict primarily on an e-mail message written by an Arthur Andersen attorney. In that e-mail message, the attorney advised an Arthur Andersen partner to revise a memo to omit certain information, including a comment that an Enron press release included an earnings announcement that was misleading. Arthur Andersen representatives acknowledged that the conviction effectively put the firm out of business. The case is particularly relevant to the profession in that it illustrates how the actions of a relatively small number of employees can lead to disastrous results for the firm. Ultimately, the conviction was overturned by the U.S. Supreme Court based on the fact that the jury was given inappropriate instructions.

## SEC and Public Company Accounting Oversight Board Regulation

The SEC has issued rules for the appearance and practice of CPAs, attorneys, and others before the commission under the statutes it administers. Rule of Practice 2(e), giving the SEC the power of suspension and disbarment, has the following wording:

> The Commission may deny, temporarily or permanently, the privilege of appearing or practicing before it in any way to any person who is found by the Commission . . . (1) not to possess the requisite qualifications to represent others, or (2) to be lacking in character or integrity or to have engaged in unethical or improper professional conduct.

On occasion, the SEC has taken punitive action against public accounting firms when it has found the audit work deficient with regard to financial statements filed with the commission. These actions against public accounting firms usually arise when a listed corporation encounters financial difficulties and it later appears that misleading financial statements had served to conceal for a time the losses being incurred by the company. In recent years, the SEC has taken action against public accounting firms by the use of consent decrees in which the CPAs have agreed to certain penalties or restrictions. For example, a public accounting firm may settle charges brought by the SEC through a consent decree in which it agrees not to accept new SEC clients during a specified period and to permit a review of its practice.

The Private Securities Litigation Reform Act of 1995 (discussed earlier in this chapter) requires auditors to play a more active disclosure role with respect to their clients. Under these changes to the 1934 Act, auditors who discover illegal acts by a client are required to report them to the board of directors of their clients, and, in some cases, the auditors are required to report those activities to the SEC. Auditors are relieved of any SEC sanctions if they timely report required information about clients to the SEC. The failure to take the necessary statutory steps for disclosure and reporting can result in additional liability for the auditor, including the possibility that such failure rises to the level of fraud or collusion with the client.

As discussed in Chapter 2, the Public Company Accounting Oversight Board also may conduct investigations and disciplinary proceedings on both registered public accounting firms and professional employees (including owners). Board sanctions may include monetary damages, suspension of firms and accountants from working on engagements for publicly traded companies, and referral of criminal cases to the Justice Department.

## CPAs' Liability for Accounting and Review Services

LO6

Describe CPA legal liability for accounting and review services.

Up to this point, we have emphasized the liability of public accounting firms when they are associated with audited financial statements. In addition, CPAs are subject to legal liability when they perform accounting services, such as write-up work and *compilations* of unaudited financial statements. These services differ from audits in that the CPAs neither perform the verification procedures involved in an audit nor issue an auditors' opinion as to the fairness of the financial information.

The term **compilation of financial statements** refers to the *preparation* of financial statements based upon information provided to the CPAs by the client (or the client's representatives). A compilation is *not intended to lend any assurance* to any party that the CPAs have determined the information to be reliable. A **review of financial statements** consists of *limited* verification procedures, *substantially less in scope than an audit,* designed to provide users of the unaudited financial statements with a *limited* degree of assurance as to the statements' reliability. Compilations and reviews are described in Chapter 19.

Do CPAs associated with unaudited financial statements have any potential legal liability? The answer is *yes.* The CPAs, acting as *accountants* rather than as *auditors,* still have a liability to their client to exercise due professional care. In addition, they still may be liable for losses to third parties.

When CPAs are associated with unaudited financial statements, a possibility exists that the client or third parties may misinterpret the extent of their services and believe that the accountants are acting as auditors. The risks to public accounting firms engaged in the preparation of unaudited financial statements were brought sharply into focus by the *1136 Tenants' Corporation v. Rothenberg* case. In this case, an incorporated apartment cooperative, which was owned by its shareholder-tenants and managed by a separate realty agent, orally retained a public accounting firm for a period of 17 months to perform certain services, including the preparation of financial statements for the cooperative. The public accounting firm's fee was to be only $600 per year.

The public accounting firm submitted financial statements of the corporation for one full year and the first six months of the following year. The financial statements bore the notation "subject to comments in letter of transmittal." The referenced letter of transmittal read in part:

> Pursuant to our engagement, we have reviewed and summarized the statements of your managing agent and other data submitted to us by . . . [the agent], pertaining to 1136 Tenants' Corporation. . . .
>
> The following statements were prepared from the books and records of the Corporation. No independent verifications were undertaken thereon.

The client corporation later sued the public accounting firm for damages totaling $174,000 for the CPAs' alleged failure to discover defalcations of the corporation's funds committed by the managing agent. The client contended that the CPAs had been retained to render all necessary accounting and *auditing* services for it. The CPAs maintained they had been engaged to do write-up work only, although a working paper they had prepared supporting accrued expenses payable in the balance sheet included an entry for "audit expense."

The New York state trial court ruled in favor of the plaintiff on a decision affirmed by the Appellate Court of New York. The latter found that the CPAs' working papers indicated that the CPAs had examined the client's bank statements, invoices, and bills, and had made notations in their working papers concerning "missing invoices."

In summary, the court held the CPAs liable because it found that they had led their client to believe that they were performing an audit. Consequently, the courts held the CPAs responsible for performing their work in accordance with generally accepted auditing standards, which they clearly had not done. More important, however, the court also concluded that the CPAs had a duty to follow up on significant problems (the missing invoices) uncovered during their engagement. Thus, it is probable that the public accounting firm would have been held liable to its client *even if the court had recognized that the firm was not performing an audit.* Whenever CPAs encounter evidence that their client may be sustaining a loss through embezzlement or other fraud, they should warn the client immediately.

There are several lessons for public accounting firms in the *1136 Tenants' Corporation* case:

1. CPAs who prepare unaudited financial statements should adhere closely to Rules of Conduct 102 and 202 of the AICPA *Code of Professional Conduct.* Rule 102 states that a CPA shall not knowingly misrepresent facts, and Rule 202 requires a public accounting firm to comply with professional standards, including standards for accounting and review services. The actions of the public accounting firm described in the preceding paragraph might be construed as violating both rules.

2. **Engagement letters** are as essential for accounting and review services as they are for independent audits. Oral arrangements for accounting and review services are of scant assistance when there is a dispute as to the nature of the services to be rendered by the public accounting firm to the client.

3. The CPAs engaged to perform *accounting or review* services should be alert for, and follow up on, such unusual items as missing invoices. As professionals, CPAs are bound to exercise *due professional care,* even though their engagements do not include independent audits of the client's financial statements.

4. CPAs should report on financial statements clearly and concisely, using, to the extent possible, the standardized language set forth in *Statements on Auditing Standards* and

*Statements on Standards for Accounting and Review Services.* Reports should indicate the nature of the services rendered and the degree of responsibility being assumed by the public accounting firm.

## CPAs' Posture in the Age of Litigation

In addition to the preceding court cases, numerous other actions against CPAs, under both common law and the 1933 and 1934 Securities Acts, are pending trial. It is apparent that lawsuits will continue to plague the public accounting profession, as they have the legal and medical professions. The question thus is: What should be CPAs' reaction to this age of litigation?

In the opinion of the authors, positive actions helpful to CPAs in withstanding threats of possible lawsuits include the following:

1. Greater emphasis upon compliance with the public accounting profession's generally accepted auditing standards and ethical requirements. Close analysis of the court cases and other actions described in this chapter discloses numerous instances in which the auditors appear not to have complied fully with one or more of the auditing and ethical standards.

2. Retaining legal counsel that is familiar with CPAs' legal liability. The CPAs should thoroughly discuss all potentially dangerous situations with their legal counsel and should carefully consider their counsel's advice.

3. Maintenance of adequate liability insurance coverage. Although liability insurance coverage should not be considered a substitute for the CPAs' compliance with the preceding recommendations, public accountants must protect themselves against possible financial losses from lawsuits. Adequate liability insurance is essential.

4. Thorough investigation of prospective clients. As indicated in preceding sections of this chapter, many court cases involving CPAs have been accompanied by criminal charges against top management of the CPAs' clients. CPAs should use great care in screening prospective clients to avoid the risks involved in professional relationships with the criminally inclined.

5. Obtaining a thorough knowledge of the client's business. One of the major causes of audit failures has been a lack of understanding by auditors of the client's business and of industry practices.

6. Use of engagement letters for all professional services. Controversies over what services were performed by the CPAs can be minimized by a clearly written contract describing the agreed-upon services. CPAs also may insert various types of clauses to limit liability in engagement letters. For example, a clause may be included in the letter that indemnifies and holds harmless the CPAs from all liability and costs resulting from knowing misrepresentations by management. Engagement letters are discussed in Chapter 6.

7. In planning engagements, carefully assessing the risk of errors and fraud in the client's financial statements. The CPAs should exercise special care when the client has material weaknesses in internal control.

8. Exercising extreme care in audits of clients in financial difficulties or with a high degree of business risk. Creditors and shareholders of companies that are insolvent or in bankruptcy are likely to seek recovery of their losses. As the court cases described in this chapter demonstrate, litigation involving CPAs tends to center around the auditing of clients who later become bankrupt. Other litigation-sensitive audit engagements include rapid-growth entities, entities that have recently completed or are contemplating initial public offerings, and entities with material-related party transactions.

9. Making certain that working papers have been professionally and completely assembled. Chapter 5 provides details on working paper preparation and assembly.

# Chapter Summary

This chapter described the legal environment of auditors, emphasizing legal liability under both common law and statutory law. To summarize:

1. Under common law, CPAs are liable to their clients for failure to exercise due professional care. Accordingly, ordinary negligence is a sufficient degree of misconduct to hold CPAs liable for damages caused to their clients.

2. Auditors' liability to third parties under common law varies from state to state. One way to summarize these differences is to consider three general approaches: (*a*) *Ultramares* (known user) approach, (*b*) *Restatement* (foreseen user) approach, and (*c*) *Rosenblum* (foreseeable user) approach. Under the *Ultramares* (known user) approach, CPAs are held liable for ordinary negligence only to third-party beneficiaries for whose benefit the audit was performed. Other third parties must prove gross negligence on the part of the auditors. Under the *Restatement* (foreseen user) approach, liability for ordinary negligence to third parties is extended to include any limited class of parties that could be foreseen to rely upon the financial statements. The *Rosenblum* (foreseeable user) approach extends the auditors' liability for ordinary negligence even further to include any third party the auditors could reasonably foresee as recipients of the financial statements.

3. Auditors may also be held liable to third parties under the federal securities laws, which allow class action lawsuits by purchasers or sellers of a company's securities. The Securities Act of 1933 is unique in that most of the burden of proof in litigation is shifted to the auditors, with the primary defenses available to the auditor consisting of (1) knowledge of the plaintiffs of the errors or omissions or (2) due diligence by the auditors. Due diligence is a difficult defense to establish.

4. CPAs are also subject to criminal prosecution for violation of various statutes, including criminal fraud in which their conduct was intentional or involved collusion with the client.

5. To protect themselves from the liability crisis of today, auditors strive to adhere to a high level of professional performance. They also attempt to avoid engagements that have a very high risk of litigation.

# Key Terms Introduced or Emphasized in Chapter 4

**Breach of contract (108)**    Failure of one or both parties to a contract to perform in accordance with the contract's provisions. A public accounting firm might be sued for breach of contract, for example, if the firm failed to perform the engagement in accordance with the engagement letter. Negligence on the part of the CPAs also constitutes breach of contract.

**Common law (108)**    Unwritten law that has developed through court decisions; it represents judicial interpretation of a society's concept of fairness. For example, the right to sue a person for fraud is a common law right.

**Comparative negligence (111)**    A concept used by certain courts to allocate damages between negligent parties based on the degree to which each party is at fault. The allocation of damages is referred to as *proportionate liability.*

**Compilation of financial statements (121)**    The preparation of financial statements by CPAs based on representations of management, with the expression of no assurance concerning the statements' compliance with generally accepted accounting principles.

**Constructive fraud (109)**    Performing duties with such recklessness that persons believing the duties to have been completed carefully are being misled. It differs from fraud in that constructive fraud does not involve knowledge of misrepresentations within the financial statements.

**Contributory negligence (111)**    Negligence on the part of the plaintiff that has contributed to his or her having incurred a loss. Contributory negligence may be used as a defense, because the court may limit or bar recovery by a plaintiff whose own negligence contributed to the loss.

***Credit Alliance Corp. v. Arthur Andersen & Co.* (113)**    A common law decision by the New York Court of Appeals (New York's highest court) stating that auditors must demonstrate knowledge of reliance on the financial statements by a third party for a particular purpose to be held liable for ordinary negligence to that party. Basically, this case upheld the *Ultramares v. Touche & Co.* rule.

**Defendant (108)**   The party against which damages and suit are brought by the plaintiff.

**Due diligence (115)**   A public accounting firm's contention that its audit work was adequate to support its opinion on financial statements included in a registration statement filed with the SEC under the Securities Act of 1933.

**Engagement letter (122)**   A written contract summarizing the contractual relationship between the CPAs and the client. The engagement letter typically specifies the scope of professional services to be rendered, expected completion dates, and the basis for determination of the CPAs' fee. Engagement letters are discussed more fully in Chapter 6.

***Ernst & Ernst v. Hochfelder* (117)**   A landmark case in which the U.S. Supreme Court decided that auditors could not be held liable under the Securities Exchange Act of 1934 for ordinary negligence.

**Error (110)**   An unintentional misstatement of financial statements or omission of an amount or a disclosure.

**Fraud (109)**   Misrepresentation by a person of a material fact, known by that person to be untrue or made with reckless indifference as to whether the fact is true, with intent to deceive and with the result that another party is injured.

**Gross negligence (108)**   Lack of even slight care, indicative of a reckless disregard for one's professional responsibilities. Substantial failures on the part of an auditor to comply with generally accepted auditing standards might be interpreted as gross negligence.

**Joint and several liability (112)**   A legal concept that holds a class of defendants jointly responsible for losses attributed to the class as well as liable for any share of losses that cannot be collected from those unable to pay their share. Thus, a financially responsible defendant may be required to pay losses attributed to defendants that do not have the ability to pay.

**Negligence (108)**   Violation of a legal duty to exercise a degree of care that an ordinarily prudent person would exercise under similar circumstances. Also referred to as ordinary or simple negligence.

**Plaintiff (108)**   The party claiming damages and bringing suit against the defendant.

**Ponzi scheme (117)**   A swindle in which a quick return on an initial investment is paid out of funds of new investors to lure the victims into bigger risks. This is named for Charles Ponzi, who in 1919 convinced people he could make them a 50 percent profit in 45 days by an international trading scam. Old investors were paid off with cash from new investors. Ultimately such schemes collapse and the newest investors lose their investment because there is no actual appreciation of assets involved.

**Precedent (112)**   A legal principle that evolves from a common law court decision and then serves as a standard for future decisions in similar cases.

**Proportionate liability (112)**   A method of allocating damages to each group that is liable according to that group's pro rata share of any damages recovered by the plaintiff. For example, if the plaintiff was awarded a total of $1,000,000 and the CPAs were found to bear 40 percent of the responsibility for the damages, the CPAs would be assessed $400,000.

**Proximate cause (111)**   Damage to another is directly attributable to a wrongdoer's act. The issue of proximate cause may be raised as a defense in litigation. Even though a public accounting firm might have been negligent in rendering services, it will not be liable for the plaintiff's loss if its negligence was not the proximate cause of the loss.

**Registration statement (115)**   A document including audited financial statements that must be filed with the SEC by any company in order to sell its securities to the public through the mails or interstate commerce. The Securities Act of 1933 provides liability to security purchasers for material misrepresentations in registration statements.

**Review of financial statements (121)**   The performance of limited investigative procedures that are substantially less in scope than an audit made in accordance with generally accepted auditing standards. The procedures provide the CPAs with a basis to provide *limited assurance* that the financial statements are in accordance with generally accepted accounting principles.

***Rosenblum v. Adler* (113)**   A common law decision by the New Jersey Supreme Court that holds CPAs liable for acts of ordinary negligence to "reasonably foreseeable third parties" not in privity of contract. Conflicts with the precedents established in both the *Ultramares* and the *Restatement of Law of Torts* approaches to liability.

**Scienter (117)**   Intent to deceive, manipulate, or defraud. The U.S. Supreme Court held in the *Hochfelder* case that scienter must be proved for the auditors to be held liable under the Securities Exchange Act of 1934.

**Second Restatement of the Law of Torts (113)**    A summary of tort liability, which when applied to auditor common law liability, expands auditors' liability for ordinary negligence to include third parties of a limited class of known or intended users of the audited financial statements. Conflicts with the precedents established by the *Ultramares* and the *Rosenblum* approaches to liability.

**Securities Act of 1933 (114)**    A federal securities statute covering registration statements for securities to be sold to the public. The act requires auditors to exercise "due diligence" and creates both civil and criminal penalties for misrepresentation.

**Securities Exchange Act of 1934 (114)**    A federal securities statute requiring public companies to file annual audited financial statements with the SEC. The act requires auditors to "act in good faith" and creates civil and criminal penalties for misrepresentation.

**Statutory law (108)**    Written law created by state or federal legislative bodies. CPAs must concern themselves particularly with the federal securities acts and state blue sky laws. These laws regulate the issuance and trading of securities.

**Third-party beneficiary (113)**    A person, not the auditors or their client, who is named in a contract (or known to the contracting parties) with the intention that such person should have definite rights and benefits under the contract.

**Tort (108)**    A civil wrong. For financial statements audits, the primary tort involved is that of performing the engagement negligently.

***Ultramares v. Touche & Co.* (112)**    A common law decision by the New York Court of Appeals (New York's highest court) stating that auditors are liable to third parties not in privity of contract for acts of fraud or gross negligence, but not for ordinary negligence. Conflicts with precedents established by the *Restatement of Torts* and *Rosenblum* approaches to liability.

## Review Questions

4–1.    Explain why the potential liability of auditors for professional "malpractice" exceeds that of physicians or other professionals.

4–2.    Distinguish between ordinary negligence and gross negligence within the context of the CPAs' work.

4–3.    What is meant by the term *privity?* How does privity affect the auditor's liability under common law?

4–4.    Define the term *third-party beneficiary.*

4–5.    Distinguish between common law and statutory law.

4–6.    Briefly describe the differences in liability to third parties under the known user, foreseen user, and foreseeable user approaches to CPA liability.

4–7.    Briefly describe the different common law precedents set by the *Ultramares v. Touche & Co.* case and the *Rosenblum v. Adler* case.

4–8.    What landmark case was embraced by the court in the case of *Credit Alliance Corp. v. Arthur Andersen & Co.?* Identify the two factors that the court stated must be proved for the auditors to be held liable for ordinary negligence to a third party.

4–9.    Compare auditors' common law liability to clients and third-party beneficiaries with their common law liability to other third parties.

4–10.    Contrast *joint and several liability* with *proportionate liability.*

4–11.    Compare the rights of plaintiffs under common law with the rights of persons who purchase securities registered under the Securities Act of 1933 and sustain losses. In your answer, emphasize the issue of who must bear the burden of proof.

4–12.    State briefly a major distinction between the Securities Act of 1933 and the Securities Exchange Act of 1934 with respect to the type of transactions regulated.

4–13.    Why was the *Ernst & Ernst v. Hochfelder* decision considered a "victory" for the accounting profession?

4–14.    How was the *Continental Vending* case unusual with respect to penalties levied against auditors?

4–15.    Why did Congress enact the Racketeer Influenced and Corrupt Organizations Act? Why has it been of concern to auditors? What subsequent developments have reduced this concern?

4–16.    How does the SEC regulate auditors who appear and practice before the commission?

4–17. In the *1136 Tenants' Corporation* case, what was the essential difference in the way the client and the CPAs viewed the work to be done in the engagement?

4–18. Comment on the following statement: While engagement letters are useful for audit engagements, they are not necessary for compilation and review engagements.

4–19. Rogers and Green, CPAs, admit they failed substantially to follow generally accepted auditing standards in their audit of Martin Corporation. "We were overworked and understaffed and never should have accepted the engagement," said Rogers. Does this situation constitute fraud on the part of the public accounting firm? Explain.

## Questions Requiring Analysis

**LO 3** 4–20. Glover, Inc., engaged Herd & Irwin, CPAs, to assist in the installation of a new computerized production system. Because the firm did not have experienced staff available for the engagement, Herd & Irwin assigned several newly hired staff assistants without sufficient supervision. As a result, Glover, Inc., incurred significant losses when the production system crashed, causing significant backlogs and lost product sales.

*Required:* Describe the possible legal implications of this situation for Herd & Irwin.

**LO 3** 4–21. Jensen, Inc., filed suit against a public accounting firm, alleging that the auditors' negligence was responsible for failure to disclose a large defalcation that had been in process for several years. The public accounting firm responded that it may have been negligent, but that Jensen, Inc., was really to blame because it had completely ignored the public accounting firm's repeated recommendations for improvements in internal control.

*Required:* If the public accounting firm was negligent, is it responsible for the loss sustained by the client? Does the failure by Jensen, Inc., to follow the auditors' recommendation for better internal control have any bearing on the question of liability? Explain.

**LO 3** 4–22. The public accounting firm of Hanson and Brown was expanding very rapidly. Consequently, it hired several staff assistants, including James Small. Subsequently, the partners of the firm became dissatisfied with Small's production and warned him that they would be forced to discharge him unless his output increased significantly.

At that time, Small was engaged in audits of several clients. He decided that to avoid being fired, he would reduce or omit entirely some of the required auditing procedures listed in audit programs prepared by the partners. One of the public accounting firm's non-SEC clients, Newell Corporation, was in serious financial difficulty and had adjusted several of its accounts being examined by Small to appear financially sound. Small prepared fictitious working papers in his home at night to support purported completion of auditing procedures assigned to him, although he in fact did not examine the Newell adjusting entries. The public accounting firm rendered an unqualified opinion on Newell's financial statements, which were grossly misstated. Several creditors, relying upon the audited financial statements, subsequently extended large sums of money to Newell Corporation.

*Required:* Would the public accounting firm be liable to the creditors who extended the money in reliance on the erroneous financial statements if Newell Corporation should fail to pay its creditors? Explain.

**LO 3** 4–23. Wanda Young, doing business as Wanda Young Fashions, engaged the CPA partnership of Scott & Green to audit her financial statements. During the audit, Scott & Green discovered certain irregularities that would have indicated to a reasonably prudent auditor that James Smith, the chief accountant, might be engaged in a fraud. However, Scott & Green, not having been engaged to discover defalcations, submitted an unqualified opinion in its report and did not mention the potential defalcation problem.

*Required:* What are the legal implications of the above facts as they relate to the relationship between Scott & Green and Wanda Young? Explain.

**LO 3** 4–24. Susan Harris is a new assistant auditor with the public accounting firm of Sparks, Watts, and Wilcox, CPAs. On her third audit assignment, Harris examined the documentation underlying 60 disbursements as a test of controls over purchasing, receiving, vouchers payable, and cash disbursement procedures. In the process, she found five disbursements for the purchase of materials with no receiving reports in the documentation. She noted the exceptions in her working papers and called them to the attention of the senior auditor. Relying on prior experience with the client, the senior auditor disregarded Harris's comments, and nothing further was done about the exceptions.

Subsequently, it was learned that one of the client's purchasing agents and a member of its accounting department were engaged in a fraudulent scheme whereby they diverted the receipt of materials to a public warehouse while sending the invoices to the client. When the client discovered the fraud, the conspirators had obtained approximately $700,000—$500,000 of which was obtained after the completion of the audit.

*Required:*

Discuss the legal implications and liabilities to Sparks, Watts, and Wilcox as a result of the above facts.

(AICPA, adapted)

**LO 4, 5**    4–25.    Sawyer and Sawyer, CPAs, audited the financial statements of Rattler Corporation that were included in Rattler's Form 10-K, which was filed with the SEC. Subsequently, Rattler Corporation went bankrupt and the stockholders of the corporation brought a class-action lawsuit against management, Sawyer and Sawyer, and the corporation's board of directors and attorneys for misstatements of the financial statements.

Assume that the jury in the case decides that responsibility for $5 million in losses should be allocated as follows:

| | |
|---|---|
| Management | 70% |
| Board of directors | 20 |
| Auditors | 5 |
| Attorneys | 5 |
| | 100% |

*Required:*

a. Under what securities act would the stockholders initiate this lawsuit?

b. Assuming that all the defendants in the case are financially able to pay their share of the losses, calculate the amount of losses that would be allocated to Sawyer and Sawyer.

c. Assuming that the attorneys had no financial resources, describe how Sawyer and Sawyer's share of the losses might be increased.

**LO 3, 4, 5**    4–26.    The international CPA firm of Arthur Andersen faced significant liability in conjunction with its audits of Enron Corporation.

*Required:*

a. From a legal liability perspective, describe the unique features of this audit case.

b. Describe the important implications of this audit case for a firm of public accountants.

**LO 4**    4–27.    Gordon & Moore, CPAs, were the auditors of Fox & Company, a brokerage firm. Gordon & Moore examined and reported on the financial statements of Fox, which were filed with the Securities and Exchange Commission.

Several of Fox's customers were swindled by a fraudulent scheme perpetrated by two key officers of the company. The facts establish that Gordon & Moore were negligent, but not reckless or grossly negligent, in the conduct of the audit, and neither participated in the fraudulent scheme nor knew of its existence.

The customers are suing Gordon & Moore under the antifraud provisions of Section 10(b) and Rule 10b-5 of the Securities Exchange Act of 1934 for aiding and abetting the fraudulent scheme of the officers. The customers' suit for fraud is predicated exclusively on the negligence of the auditors in failing to conduct a proper audit, thereby failing to discover the fraudulent scheme.

*Required:*

Answer the following, setting forth reasons for any conclusions stated.

a. What is the probable outcome of the lawsuit? Explain.

b. What other theory of liability might the customers have asserted?

(AICPA, adapted)

## Objective Questions

**All applicable questions are available with McGraw-Hill's** *Connect*™ **Accounting.** ▓ connect |ACCOUNTING

4–28.    **Multiple Choice Questions**

Select the best answer for each of the following questions and explain the reasons for your choice.

**LO 3**    a. If a CPA performs an audit recklessly, the CPA will be liable to third parties who were unknown and not foreseeable to the CPA for:

(1) Strict liability for all damages incurred.

(2) Gross negligence.

   (3)  Either ordinary or gross negligence.

   (4)  Breach of contract.

**LO 3**   b.  Which of the following approaches to auditors' liability is least desirable from the CPA's perspective?

   (1)  The *Ultramares* approach.

   (2)  The *Rosenblum* approach.

   (3)  The *Restatement of Torts* approach.

   (4)  The Foreseen User approach.

**LO 3**   c.  In cases of breach of contract, plaintiffs generally have to prove all of the following, except:

   (1)  The CPAs had a duty.

   (2)  The CPAs made a false statement.

   (3)  The client incurred losses related to the CPAs' performance.

   (4)  The CPAs breached their duty.

**LO 2, 3**   d.  If the CPAs provided negligent tax advice to a public company, the client would bring suit under:

   (1)  The Securities Act of 1933.

   (2)  The Securities Exchange Act of 1934.

   (3)  The federal income tax law.

   (4)  Common law.

**LO 3**   e.  Which of the following cases reaffirmed the principles in the *Ultramares* case?

   (1)  *Credit Alliance Corp. v. Arthur Andersen & Co.*

   (2)  *Rosenblum v. Adler.*

   (3)  *Ernst & Ernst v. Hochfelder.*

   (4)  *Escott v. BarChris Construction Corporation.*

**LO 3**   f.  Under common law, the CPAs who were negligent may mitigate some damages to a client by proving:

   (1)  Contributory negligence.

   (2)  The CPAs' fee was not material.

   (3)  The CPAs were not competent to accept the engagement.

   (4)  The CPAs' negligence was caused by the fact that they had too much work.

**LO 4**   g.  Under the Securities and Exchange Act of 1934, auditors and other defendants are faced with:

   (1)  Joint liability.

   (2)  Joint and several liability.

   (3)  Proportionate liability.

   (4)  Limited liability.

**LO 4**   h.  A CPA issued an unqualified opinion on the financial statements of a company that sold common stock in a public offering subject to the Securities Act of 1933. Based on a misstatement in the financial statements, the CPA is being sued by an investor who purchased shares of this public offering. Which of the following represents a viable defense?

   (1)  The investor has *not* proved fraud or negligence by the CPA.

   (2)  The investor did *not* actually rely upon the false statement.

   (3)  The CPA detected the false statement after the audit date.

   (4)  The false statement is immaterial in the overall context of the financial statements.

**LO 3**   i.  Which of the following elements is most frequently necessary to hold a CPA liable to a client?

   (1)  Acted with scienter or guilty knowledge.

   (2)  Was not independent of the client.

   (3)  Failed to exercise due care.

   (4)  Did not use an engagement letter.

**LO 4**

j. Which statement best expresses the factors that purchasers of securities registered under the Securities Act of 1933 need to prove to recover losses from the auditors?

(1) The purchasers of securities must prove ordinary negligence by the auditors and reliance on the audited financial statements.

(2) The purchasers of securities must prove that the financial statements were misleading and that they relied on them to purchase the securities.

(3) The purchasers of securities must prove that the financial statements were misleading; then, the burden of proof is shifted to the auditors to show that the audit was performed with "due diligence."

(4) The purchasers of securities must prove that the financial statements were misleading and the auditors were negligent.

**LO 4**

k. The most significant result of the *Continental Vending* case was that it:

(1) Created a more general awareness of the possibility of auditor criminal prosecution.

(2) Extended the auditor's responsibility to all information included in registration statements.

(3) Defined the CPA's responsibilities for unaudited financial statements.

(4) Established a precedent for auditors being held liable to third parties under common law for ordinary negligence.

**LO 6**

l. The *1136 Tenants'* case was important because of its emphasis upon the legal liability of the CPA when associated with:

(1) A review of annual statements.

(2) Unaudited financial statements.

(3) An audit resulting in a disclaimer of opinion.

(4) Letters for underwriters.

(AICPA, adapted)

**LO 4, 5**

4–29. Dandy Container Corporation engaged the accounting firm of Adams and Adams to audit financial statements to be used in connection with an interstate public offering of securities. The audit was completed, and an unqualified opinion was expressed on the financial statements that were submitted to the Securities and Exchange Commission along with the registration statement. Two hundred thousand shares of Dandy Container common stock were offered to the public at $11 a share. Eight months later the stock fell to $2 a share when it was disclosed that several large loans to two "paper" corporations owned by one of the directors were worthless. The loans were secured by the stock of the borrowing corporations, which was owned by the director. These facts were not disclosed in the financial statements. The director involved and the two corporations are insolvent.

*Required:*

State whether each of the following statements is true or false, and explain why.

a. The Securities Act of 1933 applies to the above-described public offering of securities.

b. The accounting firm has potential liability to any person who acquired the stock.

c. An insider who had knowledge of all the facts regarding the loans to the two paper corporations could nevertheless recover from the accounting firm.

d. In court, investors who bought shares in Dandy Container need only show that they sustained a loss and that failure to explain the nature of the loans in question constituted a false statement or misleading omission in the financial statements.

e. The accountants could avoid liability if they could show they were not negligent.

f. The accountants could avoid or reduce the damages asserted against them if they could establish that the drop in the stock's market price was due in whole or in part to other causes.

g. The Securities and Exchange Commission would defend any action brought against the accountants in that the SEC examined and approved the registration statement.

4–30. Assume that in a particular audit the CPAs were negligent but not grossly negligent. Indicate whether they would be "liable" or "not liable" for the following losses proximately caused by their negligence and determine that liability under the various theories discussed and followed by different states:

a. Loss sustained by client; suit brought under common law.

b. Loss sustained by trade creditor, not in privity of contract; suit brought in a state court that adheres to the *Ultramares v. Touche Co.* precedent.

c. Loss sustained by a bank known to the auditors to be relying on the financial statements for a loan; suit brought in a state court that adheres to the *Credit Alliance v. Arthur Andersen* precedent.

d. Losses to stockholders purchasing shares at a public offering; suit brought under the Securities Act of 1933.

e. Loss sustained by a bank named as a third-party beneficiary in the engagement letter; suit brought under common law.

f. Loss sustained by a lender not in privity of contract; suit brought in a state court that adheres to the *Rosenblum v. Adler* precedent.

g. Losses sustained by stockholders; suit brought under Sections 18(a) and 10(b) of the Securities Exchange Act of 1934.

**LO 2, 3, 4, 5**   4–31.   Match the important cases listed below with the appropriate legal precedent or implication.

*Case:*

a. *Hochfelder v. Ernst*

b. *Escott v. BarChris Construction Corp.*

c. *Credit Alliance v. Arthur Andersen & Co.*

d. *Ultramares v. Touche & Co.*

e. *Rosenblum v. Adler*

f. *Rusch Factors, Inc. v. Levin*

g. *United States v. Simon (Continental Vending)*

*Legal precedent or implication:*

1. A landmark case establishing that auditors should be held liable to third parties not in privity of contract for gross negligence, but not for ordinary negligence.

2. A case in which the court used the guidance of the *Second Restatement of the Law of Torts* to decide the auditors' liability to third parties under common law.

3. A landmark case in which the auditors were held liable under Section 11 of the Securities Act of 1933.

4. A case in which auditors were held liable for criminal negligence.

5. A case that established that auditors should not be held liable under the Securities Exchange Act of 1934 unless there was intent to deceive.

6. A case that established the precedent that auditors should be held liable under common law for ordinary negligence to all foreseeable third parties.

7. A common law case in which the court held that auditors should be held liable for ordinary negligence only to third parties they know will use the financial statements for a particular purpose.

**LO 4, 5**   4–32.   Items (*a*) through (*f*) relate to what a plaintiff who purchased securities must prove in a civil liability suit against a CPA. For each item, determine whether it must be proved assuming application of the following acts:

1. Only applies to Section 11 of the 1933 Securities Act.

2. Only applies to Section 10(b) of the Securities Exchange Act.

3. Applies to both acts.

4. Applies to neither of the acts.

The plaintiff security purchaser must allege or prove:

a. Material misstatements were included in a filed document.

b. A monetary loss occurred.

c. Lack of due diligence by the CPA.

d. Privity with the CPA.

e. Reliance on the document.

f. The CPA had scienter.

(AICPA, adapted)

**LO 1, 2, 3, 4, 5**    4–33    For each definition (or portion of a definition) in the first column, select the term that most closely applies. Each term may be used only once or not at all.

| Partial (or Complete) Definition | Term |
|---|---|
| a. A federal securities statute covering registration statements for securities to be sold to the public. | 1. Breach of contract |
| b. A method of allocating damages to each group that is liable according to that group's pro-rata share of any damages recovered by the plaintiff. For example, if the plaintiff was awarded a total of $500,000 and the CPAs were found to bear 30 percent of the responsibility for the damages, the CPAs would be assessed $150,000. | 2. Common law<br>3. Constructive fraud<br>4. Defendant<br>5. Fraud<br>6. Joint and several liability<br>7. Negligence |
| c. Damage to another is directly attributable to a wrongdoer's act. This issue may be raised as a defense in litigation—that is, the defense may argue that some other factor caused the loss. | 8. Ponzi scheme<br>9. Proximate cause<br>10. Proportionate liability<br>11. Scienter |
| d. Failure of one or both parties to a contract to perform in accordance with the contract's provisions. | 12. Securities Act of 1933<br>13. Securities Exchange Act of 1934 |
| e. Intent to deceive, manipulate, or defraud. This concept is used in the 1934 Securities Exchange Act to establish auditor liability. | 14. Statutory law |
| f. Misrepresentation by a person of a material fact, known by that person to be untrue or made with reckless indifference as to whether the fact is true, with intent to deceive and with the result that another party is injured. | |
| g. Performing duties with such recklessness that persons believing the duties to have been completed carefully are being misled. The person performing the duties does not have knowledge of misrepresentations within the financial statements. | |
| h. Unwritten law that has developed through court decisions; it represents judicial interpretation of a society's concept of fairness. | |
| i. Violation of a legal duty to exercise a degree of care that an ordinarily prudent person would exercise under similar circumstances. | |
| j. Written law created by state or federal legislative bodies. | |

## Problems

**All applicable problems are available with McGraw-Hill's *Connect™ Accounting*.** ▦ connect
ǀACCOUNTING

**LO 4, 5**    4–34.    Risk Capital Limited, a publicly held Delaware corporation, was considering the purchase of a substantial amount of the treasury stock held by Florida Sunshine Corporation, a closely held corporation. Initial discussions with the Florida Sunshine Corporation began late in 20X0.

Wilson and Wyatt, CPAs, Florida Sunshine's public accountants, regularly prepared quarterly and annual unaudited financial statements. The most recently prepared unaudited financial statements were for the fiscal year ended September 30, 20X0.

On November 15, 20X0, after protracted negotiations, Risk Capital agreed to purchase 100,000 shares of no-par Class A treasury stock of Florida Sunshine at $12.50 per share. However, Risk Capital insisted upon audited statements for the calendar year 20X0. The contract specifically provided: "Risk Capital shall have the right to rescind the purchase of said stock if the audited financial statements of Florida Sunshine for calendar year 20X0 show a material adverse change in the financial position of the Corporation."

At the request of Florida Sunshine, Wilson and Wyatt audited the company's financial statements for the year ended December 31, 20X0. The December 31, 20X0, audited financial statements furnished to Florida Sunshine by Wilson and Wyatt showed no material adverse change from the September 30, 20X0, unaudited statements. Risk Capital relied upon the audited statements and purchased the treasury stock of Florida Sunshine. It was subsequently discovered that, as of the balance sheet date, the audited statements contained several misstatements and that in fact there had been a material adverse change in the financial position of the corporation. Florida Sunshine has become insolvent, and Risk Capital will lose virtually its entire investment.

Risk Capital seeks recovery against Wilson and Wyatt.

*Required:*

a. Discuss each of the theories of liability that Risk Capital will probably assert as its basis for recovery.

b. Assuming that only ordinary negligence by Wilson and Wyatt is proved, will Risk Capital prevail? State yes or no and explain.

**LO 3** 4–35. Meglow Corporation, a closely held manufacturer of dresses and blouses, sought a loan from Busch Factors. Busch had previously extended $50,000 credit to Meglow but refused to lend any additional money without obtaining copies of Meglow's audited financial statements.

Meglow contacted the public accounting firm of Seavers & Dean to perform the audit. In arranging for the audit, Meglow clearly indicated that its purpose was to satisfy Busch Factors as to the corporation's sound financial condition and to obtain an additional loan of $100,000. Seavers & Dean accepted the engagement, performed the audit in a negligent manner, and rendered an unqualified opinion. If an adequate audit had been performed, the financial statements would have been found to be misleading.

Meglow submitted the audited financial statements to Busch Factors and obtained an additional loan of $70,000. Busch refused to lend more than that amount. After several other factors also refused, Meglow finally was able to persuade Maxwell Department Stores, one of its customers, to lend the additional $30,000. Maxwell relied upon the financial statements audited by Seavers & Dean.

Meglow is now in bankruptcy, and Busch seeks to collect from Seavers & Dean the $120,000 it loaned Meglow. Maxwell seeks to recover from Seavers & Dean the $30,000 it loaned Meglow.

*Required:*

a. Will Busch recover? Explain.

b. Will Maxwell recover? Explain.

**LO 2, 3, 4, 5** 4–36. After Commuter Airlines was forced into bankruptcy, the company's stockholders brought suit against Thomas & Ross, the company's independent auditors. Three independent assumptions concerning this litigation are listed below:

a. Commuter Airlines is not under SEC jurisdiction. The plaintiff's suit is brought under common law in a state court that adheres to the *Ultramares* doctrine of auditors' liability.

b. Commuter Airlines had recently issued its publicly held securities. The stockholders' suit is brought in federal court under the Securities Act of 1933.

c. Commuter Airlines is under SEC jurisdiction. The stockholders' suit is brought in federal court alleging violations of Sections 18(a) and 10(b) of the Securities Exchange Act of 1934.

*Required:*

Under each of the independent assumptions, separately explain (1) the allegations that must be proved in court by the plaintiffs, and (2) any defenses for which the auditors must bear the burden of proof if they are to avoid or reduce their liability.

**LO 6** 4–37. Charles Worthington, the founding and senior partner of a successful and respected public accounting firm, was a highly competent practitioner who always emphasized high professional standards. One of the policies of the firm was that all reports by members or staff be submitted to Worthington for review.

Recently, Arthur Craft, a junior partner in the firm, received a phone call from Herbert Flack, a close personal friend. Flack informed Craft that he, his family, and some friends were planning to create a corporation to engage in various land development ventures; that various members of the family are presently in a partnership (Flack Ventures), which holds some land and other assets; and that the partnership would contribute all its assets to the new corporation and the corporation would assume the liabilities of the partnership.

Flack asked Craft to prepare a balance sheet of the partnership that he could show to members of his family, who were in the partnership, and to friends, to determine whether they might have an interest in joining in the formation and financing of the new corporation. Flack said he had the partnership general ledger in front of him and proceeded to read to Craft the names of the accounts and their balances at the end of the latest month. Craft took the notes he made during the telephone conversation with Flack, classified and organized the data into a conventional balance sheet, and had his secretary type the balance sheet and an accompanying letter on firm stationery. He did not consult Worthington on this matter or submit this work to him for review.

The transmittal letter stated: "We have reviewed the books and records of Flack Ventures, a partnership, and have prepared the attached balance sheet at March 31, 20X0. We did not perform an audit in conformity with generally accepted auditing standards, and therefore do not express an opinion on the accompanying balance sheet." The balance sheet was prominently marked "unaudited." Craft signed the letter and instructed his secretary to send it to Flack.

*Required:*

What legal problems are suggested by these facts? Explain.

**LO 6**   4–38.   The limitations on professional responsibilities of CPAs when they are associated with unaudited financial statements are often misunderstood. These misunderstandings can be reduced substantially if CPAs carefully follow professional pronouncements in the course of their work and take other appropriate measures.

*Required:*

The following list describes four situations CPAs may encounter in their association with and preparation of unaudited financial statements. Briefly discuss the extent of the CPAs' responsibilities and, if appropriate, the actions to be taken to minimize misunderstandings. Identify your answers to correspond with the letters in the following list.

a. A CPA was engaged by telephone to perform accounting work, including the compilation of financial statements. His client believes that the CPA has been engaged to audit the financial statements and examine the records accordingly.

b. A group of business executives who own a farm managed by an independent agent engage Linda Lopez, a CPA, to compile quarterly unaudited financial statements for them. Ms. Lopez compiles the financial statements from information given to her by the independent agent. Subsequently, the business executives find the statements were inaccurate because their independent agent was embezzling funds. The executives refuse to pay Ms. Lopez's fee and blame her for allowing the situation to go undetected, contending that she should not have relied on representations from the independent agent.

c. In comparing the trial balance with the general ledger, a CPA finds an account labeled "Audit Fees" in which the client has accumulated the CPA's quarterly billings for accounting services, including the compilation of quarterly unaudited financial statements.

d. To determine appropriate account classification, John Day, CPA, reviewed a number of the client's invoices. He noted in his working papers that some invoices were missing but did nothing further because he thought they did not affect the unaudited financial statements he was compiling. When the client subsequently discovered that invoices were missing, he contended that the CPA should not have ignored the missing invoices when compiling the financial statements and had a responsibility to at least inform him that they were missing.

**LO 3**   4–39.   Mark Williams, CPA, was engaged by Jackson Financial Development Company to audit the financial statements of Apex Construction Company, a small closely held corporation. Williams was told when he was engaged that Jackson Financial needed reliable financial statements that would be used to determine whether to purchase a substantial amount of Apex Construction's convertible debentures at the price asked by the estate of one of Apex's former directors.

Williams performed his audit in a negligent manner. As a result of his negligence, he failed to discover substantial defalcations by Carl Brown, the Apex controller. Jackson Financial purchased the debentures, but it would not have done so if the defalcations had been discovered. After discovery of the fraud, Jackson Financial promptly sold them for the highest price offered in the market at a $70,000 loss.

*Required:*

a. What liability does Williams have to Jackson Financial? Explain.

b. If Apex Construction also sues Williams for negligence, what are the probable legal defenses Williams's attorney would raise? Explain.

c. Will the negligence of Mark Williams, CPA, prevent him from recovering on a liability insurance policy covering the practice of his profession? Explain.

**LO 3**   4–40.   Cragsmore & Company, a medium-sized partnership of CPAs, was engaged by Marlowe Manufacturing, Inc., a closely held corporation, to audit its financial statements for the year ended December 31, 20X3.

Before preparing the audit report, William Cragsmore, a partner, and Joan Willmore, a staff senior, reviewed the disclosures necessary in the notes to the financial statements. One note involved the terms, costs, and obligations of a lease between Marlowe and Acme Leasing Company.

Willmore suggested that the note disclose the following: "Acme Leasing Company is owned by persons who have a 35 percent interest in the capital stock and who are officers of Marlowe Manufacturing, Inc."

On Cragsmore's recommendation, this was revised by substituting "minority shareholders" for "persons who have a 35 percent interest in the capital stock and who are officers."

The audit report and financial statements were forwarded to Marlowe Manufacturing for review. The officer-shareholders of Marlowe who also owned Acme Leasing objected to the revised wording and insisted that the note be changed to describe the relationship between Acme and Marlowe as merely one of affiliation. Cragsmore acceded to this request.

The audit report was issued on this basis with an unqualified opinion. But the working papers included the drafts that showed the changes in the wording of the note.

Subsequent to delivery of the audit report, Marlowe suffered a substantial uninsured fire loss and was forced into bankruptcy. The failure of Marlowe to carry any fire insurance coverage was not noted in the financial statements.

*Required:* What legal problems for Cragsmore & Company are suggested by these facts? Discuss.

(AICPA, adapted)

---

**In-Class Team Case** **LO 2, 3, 4, 5**

4–41. The following appeared in a brief article in a major business newspaper: A local court is in the process of ruling on whether the public accounting firm of James Willis and Co., CPAs, PC, should be required to pay all or part of $16 million in damages relating to Geiger Co. for failing to detect a scheme to defraud the company, a former audit client.

Geiger Co., an SEC registrant, charges that Willis was negligent in failing to discover fraud committed by the company's controller and wants Willis to foot the bill for all $16 million in claims by and against the company. The company claims that if it had known about the fraud, it could have stopped it and recovered financially. The bank involved claims that it granted the loan based on misstated financial statements. The shareholders involved claim that they purchased the stock on the American Stock Exchange at an inflated price due to the misstated financial statements. They acknowledged that while stock had been outstanding and traded for many years (10) prior to the fraud, they made their investment decisions relying upon the misstated financial statements.

Willis's general counsel said, "We anxiously await a decision that will show that CPAs are not guarantors for everything that goes on in the company." Geiger Co.'s lawyer said that she anxiously awaited a decision because it will "clearly show that CPAs are liable for finding fraud."

Assume that Willis performed that audit with ordinary negligence and this ordinary negligence is the reason that the defalcation was not discovered and recovered. Further, assume that the $16,000,000 of loss is properly allocated as follows:

| | |
|---|---|
| Company itself | $8,000,000 |
| Bank that gave a commercial loan | 5,000,000 |
| Shareholders | 3,000,000 |

Reply from the perspective that the only issues involved here are whether the plaintiffs involved may recover from a CPA that has performed the engagement with this degree of negligence. Assume the situation described above, and assume that other elements of proof (e.g., loss, proximate cause) are not at issue.

*Required:*

a. Assume that the case is brought under common law, and that the state in which Geiger Co. is headquartered follows the *known user* approach for third-party legal liability.

1. Should Willis be found liable to the company, Geiger Co., itself? Explain.

2. Should Willis be found liable if sued by a bank that used the financial statements as a basis for providing a loan and, due to the misstatement, lost $5 million on the loan? Explain.

3. Should Willis be found liable if sued by shareholders who invested in the stock of the company? Assume these investors invested relying upon the misstated financial statements and as a result thereof lost $3 million. Explain.

4. Which of answers 1, 2, and 3 might change if the jurisdiction involved followed the *Restatement of Torts* approach? Explain.

b. Assume that the case is brought under the Securities Act of 1933. Answer the following from the perspective of CPA liability under that act.

1. Should Willis be found liable to the company, Geiger Co., itself? Explain.

2. Should Willis be found liable if sued by a bank that used the financial statements as a basis for providing a loan and, due to the misstatement, lost $5 million on the loan? Explain.

3. Should Willis be found liable if sued by shareholders who invested in the stock of the company? Assume these investors invested relying upon the misstated financial statements and as a result thereof lost $3 million. Explain.

4. Which, if any, of answers 1, 2, and 3 might change if the stock involved had been issued to the public for the first time and the financial statements involved had been included in a registration statement for the securities? Explain.

c. Assume that the case is brought under the Securities Exchange Act of 1934. Answer the following from the perspective of CPA liability under that act.

1. Should Willis be found liable to the company, Geiger Co., itself? Explain.

2. Should Willis be found liable if sued by a bank that used the financial statements as a basis for providing a loan and, due to the misstatement, lost $5 million on the loan? Explain.

3. Should Willis be found liable if sued by shareholders who invested in the stock of the company? Assume these investors invested relying upon the misstated financial statements and as a result thereof lost $3 million. Explain.

## Research and Discussion Case

4–42. You are a partner in the Denver office of a national public accounting firm. During the audit of Mountain Resources, you learn that this audit client is negotiating to sell some of its unproved oil and gas properties to SuperFund, a large investment company. SuperFund is an audit client of your New York office.

Mountain Resources acquired these properties several years ago at a cost of $15 million. The company drilled several exploratory wells but found no developable resources. Last year, you and Mountain Resources agreed that the value of these unproved properties had been "impaired" as defined in *Accounting Standards Codification*, section 932-360-35-11. The company wrote the carrying value of the properties down to an estimated realizable value of $9 million and recognized a $6 million loss. You concurred with this treatment and issued an unqualified auditors' report on the company's financial statements.

You are now amazed to learn that the sales price for these properties being discussed by Mountain Resources and SuperFund is $42 million. You cannot understand why Super-Fund would pay such a high price and you wonder what representations Mountain Resources may have made to SuperFund concerning these properties. The management of Mountain Resources declines to discuss the details of the negotiations with you, calling them "quite delicate" and correctly pointing out that the future sale of these properties will not affect the financial statements currently under audit.

*Required:*

a. Summarize the arguments for advising SuperFund (through your New York office) that you consider the properties grossly overpriced at $42 million.

b. Summarize the arguments for remaining silent and not offering any advice to SuperFund on this matter.

c. Express your personal opinion as to the course of action you should take. Indicate which arguments from part (a) or part (b) most influenced your decision.

## Suggested References

AICPA, *Professional Standards,* Volume 2, Commerce Clearing House, Section ET 301 (*Code of Professional Conduct,* Rule 301).

AICPA, "Consideration of Fraud in a Financial Statement Audit" (AICPA AU 240; PCAOB 316).

AICPA, "Consideration of Laws and Regulations in an Audit of Financial Statements" (AICPA AU 250; PCAOB 317).

*FASB Accounting Standards Codification,* section 932-360-35-11, "Extraction Activities—Oil and Gas."

# Audit Evidence and Documentation

In performing financial statement audits, the auditors gather and evaluate *audit evidence* to form an opinion about whether the financial statements follow the appropriate criteria, usually generally accepted accounting principles. The auditors must gather sufficient appropriate audit evidence to provide a reasonable basis for their opinion on the financial statements.

## The Relationships among Audit Risk, Audit Evidence, and Financial Statement Assertions

**LO1**

Explain the relationship between audit risk, audit evidence, and financial statement assertions.

As discussed in Chapter 2, the term **audit risk** refers to the possibility that the auditors may unknowingly fail to appropriately modify their opinion on financial statements that are materially misstated. In other words, it is the risk that the auditors will issue an unqualified opinion on financial statements that contain a material departure from generally accepted accounting principles. The quantity of audit evidence needed is affected both by the risk of misstatement (the greater the risk, the more audit evidence required) and also by the quality of the audit evidence (the lower the quality, the more evidence required).

Auditors must obtain sufficient appropriate audit evidence to reduce audit risk to a low level in every audit. When auditors have less than that level of audit evidence, an obvious solution is to increase the extent of the audit procedures: that is, obtain more evidence. However, another approach that is often possible is to perform more effective audit procedures. For example, externally generated evidence may in some circumstances be obtained instead of internally generated evidence, or evidence may be obtained by performing procedures closer to (or after) the balance sheet date rather than at an earlier date.

### Financial Statement Assertions

Management is responsible for the fair presentation of financial statements in conformity with generally accepted accounting principles. One way to view this responsibility is that management is responsible for presenting financial statements that have proper *amounts in the various accounts,* including properly recorded *transactions,* and properly presented *disclosures* (e.g., the notes to the financial statements). For each of the major financial statement components—(1) account balances, (2) classes of transactions and events occurring during the period under audit (transactions), and (3) presentations and disclosures (disclosures)—management may be viewed as implicitly or explicitly making assertions regarding the propriety of the information. The assertions, as presented in AICPA AU 500 (PCAOB 326), are summarized in Figure 5.1.

## Learning objectives

After studying this chapter, you should be able to:

LO1 Explain the relationship between audit risk, audit evidence, and financial statement assertions.

LO2 Identify and explain the components of audit risk.

LO3 Distinguish between the concepts of *sufficient* and *appropriate* as they apply to audit evidence.

LO4 List and describe types of audit evidence.

LO5 Describe the considerations involved in auditing subjective areas, such as certain financial statement items valued at fair value.

LO6 Describe the purposes of audit documentation.

LO7 Discuss the factors that affect the auditors' judgment as to the nature and extent of audit documentation.

LO8 Identify matters that must be included in audit working papers.

LO9 Describe the types of working papers and the way they are organized.

FIGURE 5.1   **Financial Statement Assertions**

| Assertions about Account Balances (Accounts) | Assertions about Classes of Transactions and Events | Assertions about Presentation and Disclosure (Disclosures) |
|---|---|---|
| *Existence*—Assets, liabilities, and equity interests exist. | *Occurrence*—Transactions and events that have been recorded have occurred and pertain to the entity. | *Occurrence*—Disclosed events and transactions have occurred. |
| *Rights and obligations*—The entity holds or controls the rights to assets, and liabilities are the obligations of the entity. | | *Rights and obligations*—Disclosed events pertain to the entity. |
| *Completeness*—All assets, liabilities, and equity interests have been recorded. | *Completeness*—All transactions and events have been recorded. | *Completeness*—All disclosures that should have been included have been included. |
| *Valuation and allocation*—Assets, liabilities, and equity interests are included at appropriate amounts. | *Accuracy*—Amounts and other data relating to recorded transactions have been recorded appropriately. | *Accuracy and valuation*—Information is disclosed fairly and at appropriate amounts. |
| | *Cutoff*—Transactions and events have been recorded in the correct accounting period. | |
| | *Classification*—Transactions and events have been recorded in the proper accounts. | *Classification and understandability*—Information is presented and described clearly. |

All assertions do not apply to all financial statement items. **Relevant assertions** are those that, without regard to the effect of controls, have a reasonable possibility of containing a misstatement that could cause the financial statements to be materially misstated. For example, the existence and completeness assertions may always be relevant to the cash account; however, valuation is not unless currency translation is involved.

In designing audit procedures, the auditors may use the assertions considered relevant in Figure 5.1, or a condensed set, provided that all financial statement aspects of generally accepted accounting principles are covered. In other words, auditors may combine or summarize the assertions, as long as all material and relevant assertions are covered by the auditors' procedures. Consistent with this approach, in this text we combine the assertions presented in Figure 5.1 as follows:

1. *Existence and occurrence.* Assets, liabilities, and equity interests exist and recorded transactions and events have occurred.
2. *Rights and obligations.* The company holds rights to the assets, and liabilities are the obligations of the company.
3. *Completeness.* All assets, liabilities, equity interests, and transactions that should have been recorded have been recorded.
4. *Cutoff.* Transactions and events have been recorded in the correct accounting period.
5. *Valuation, allocation, and accuracy.* All transactions, assets, liabilities, and equity interests are included in the financial statements at proper amounts.
6. *Presentation and disclosure.* Accounts are described and classified in accordance with generally accepted accounting principles, and financial statement disclosures are complete, appropriate, and clearly expressed.

Chapter 6 presents more information on the nature of these assertions, which are emphasized throughout the text.

## Audit Risk at the Account Balance, Class of Transaction, or Disclosure Level

**LO2**

Identify and explain the components of audit risk.

Financial statement assertions are important to auditors because they must consider audit risk at the assertion level for all significant account balances, transaction classes, and disclosures. Audit risk consists of (1) the risk of material misstatement of a relevant assertion related to an account balance, class of transaction, or disclosure and (2) the risk that the auditors will not detect such misstatement.

### The Risk of Material Misstatement (Inherent Risk and Control Risk)

The risk of material misstatement may be separated into two components—inherent risk and control risk.

**Inherent risk** is the possibility of material misstatement of an assertion before considering the client's internal control. Factors that affect inherent risk relate to either the nature of the client and its environment or the nature of the particular financial statement element.

Business characteristics of the client and its environment affect the inherent risk of the audit as a whole. Therefore, these characteristics affect the assertions about a number of financial statement accounts. For example, business characteristics such as the following are indicative of high inherent risk:

- Inconsistent profitability of the client relative to other firms in the industry.
- Operating results that are highly sensitive to economic factors.
- Going concern problems.
- Large known and likely misstatements detected in prior audits.
- Substantial turnover, questionable reputation, or inadequate accounting skills of management.

Since these factors increase the overall risk of the audit, they are important to the auditors' decisions about whether to accept the engagement.

Inherent risk also varies by the nature of the account. Assume that in a given business the balance of the Inventory account amounts to only one-fifth that of the Property and Equipment account. Does this relationship indicate that the auditors should spend only one-fifth as much time in the audit of inventory as in the audit of plant and equipment? The answer to this question is no. Inventory is much more susceptible to error or theft than are plant and equipment, and the great number of inventory transactions affords an opportunity for misstatements to be well hidden. Inherent risk also varies by the assertion about a particular account. As an example, valuation of assets is often a more difficult assertion to audit than is existence of the assets. In general, assertions with high inherent risk involve:

- Difficult-to-audit transactions or balances.
- Complex calculations.
- Difficult accounting issues.
- Significant judgment by management.
- Valuations that vary significantly based on economic factors.

In assessing inherent risk, it is often useful to segregate transactions into three types—routine, nonroutine, and estimation. **Routine transactions** involve recurring financial statement activities recorded in the accounting records in the normal course of business. Examples of routine transactions are sales, purchases, cash disbursements, cash receipts, and payroll transactions. The routine nature of these transactions restricts inherent risk, although controls certainly must be implemented to assure proper recording.

**Nonroutine transactions** involve activities that occur only periodically, such as the taking of physical inventories, calculating depreciation expense, and adjusting financial statements for foreign currency gains and losses. Inherent risk may be high for nonroutine transactions because they are not part of the normal flow of transactions and specialized skills may be needed to perform the activity.

Generally, the transactions with the highest level of inherent risk are **estimation transactions,** which are the activities that create accounting estimates. These activities have high inherent risk because they involve management judgments or assumptions. Examples of estimation transactions include estimating the allowance for uncollectible accounts, establishing warranty reserves, and assessing assets for impairment.

The auditors use their knowledge of the client's industry and the nature of its operations, including information obtained in prior year audits, to assess inherent risk for the financial statement assertions.

**Control risk** is the risk that a material misstatement could occur in a relevant assertion and not be prevented or detected on a timely basis by the client's internal control. It is a function of the effectiveness of both the design and operation of internal control in achieving the client's objectives relevant to the preparation of its financial statements.

Both inherent risk and control risk exist independently of the audit of financial statements. That is, the risk of misstatement exists regardless of whether an audit is performed. The auditor may make separate assessments of the two risks or an overall assessment of the risk of material misstatement for the relevant assertions.

**Detection risk** is the risk that the auditors will fail to detect a material misstatement that exists in a relevant assertion. Detection risk is a function of the effectiveness of the audit procedures and their application by the auditors. Accordingly, unlike inherent risk and control risk, it does not exist when no audit is performed. Rather than "assessing" detection risk, auditors seek to restrict it through performance of substantive procedures.

Detection risk results because the auditors' substantive procedures are not 100 percent effective, due to both sampling and other factors. As discussed later in this chapter, substantive procedures of two general types are performed: (1) tests of details of balances, transactions, and disclosures, and (2) substantive analytical procedures. For a given level of audit risk, detection risk varies inversely with the risk of material misstatement; for example, the greater the risk of material misstatement, the less the detection risk that can be accepted by the auditors.

## Audit Risk Illustrated

Figure 5.2 describes the interrelationships between the three components of audit risk. The bag of sand in the figure represents *inherent risk,* the susceptibility of an account balance to material misstatements. The sieves represent the ways by which the client and the auditors attempt to remove the misstatements from the financial statements. The first sieve represents the client's internal control, and the risk that it will fail to detect or prevent a misstatement is *control risk.* The auditors' audit procedures are represented by the second sieve, and the risk that it will fail to detect a misstatement is *detection risk.* The risk that the misstatements will get through both sieves is *audit risk.*

## Measuring Audit Risk

Auditors may either consider the risk of material misstatement directly, or separately consider its components of inherent risk and control risk. For purposes of considering the relationships among the risks, we provide a separate assessment approach. Auditing standards allow either a quantified or nonquantitative approach, but they also include the following formula to illustrate the relationships among audit risk, inherent risk, control risk, and detection risk:

$$AR = \underbrace{IR \times CR}_{RMM} \times DR$$

where

$\quad AR = $ Audit risk
$\quad\ IR = $ Inherent risk
$\quad CR = $ Control risk
$\quad DR = $ Detection risk
$RMM = $ Risk of material misstatement

**FIGURE 5.2**
**An Illustration of Audit Risk**

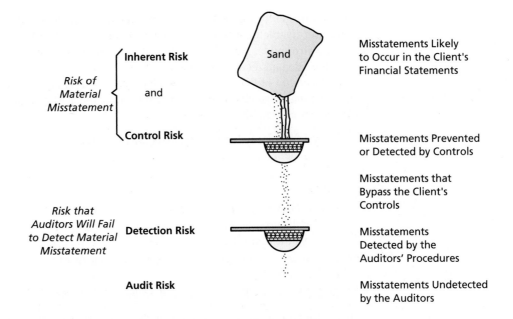

To illustrate how audit risk may be quantified, assume that the auditors have assessed inherent risk for a particular assertion at 50 percent and control risk at 40 percent. In addition, they have performed audit procedures that they believe have a 20 percent risk of failing to detect a material misstatement in the assertion. The audit risk for the assertion may be computed as follows:

$$AR = IR \times CR \times DR$$
$$= .50 \times .40 \times .20 = .04$$

Thus, the auditors face a 4 percent audit risk that material misstatement has occurred and evaded both the client's controls and the auditors' procedures. Realize, however, that the model expresses general relationships and is not necessarily intended to be a mathematical model to precisely consider the factors that influence audit risk in actual audit situations.

As indicated previously, it is important to realize that while auditors gather evidence to *assess* inherent risk and control risk, they gather evidence to *restrict* detection risk to the appropriate level. Inherent risk and control risk are a function of the client and its operating environment. Regardless of how much evidence the auditors gather, they cannot change these risks. Therefore, evidence gathered by the auditors is used to assess the levels of inherent and control risk.

Detection risk,[1] on the other hand, is a function of the effectiveness of the audit procedures performed. If the auditors wish to reduce the level of detection risk, they simply obtain additional appropriate evidence. As a result, detection risk is the only risk that is completely a function of the sufficiency of the procedures performed by the auditors.

## Audit Evidence

**LO3**

Distinguish between the concepts of *sufficient* and *appropriate* as they apply to audit evidence.

**Audit evidence** is all the information used by the auditor in arriving at the conclusions on which the audit opinion is based. It includes the information contained in the accounting records underlying the financial statements and other information.

What constitutes **sufficient** and **appropriate** audit evidence? Sufficiency is the measure of the quantity of audit evidence that must be obtained. Appropriateness is the measure of the quality of that audit evidence—both its relevance and its reliability in providing support for, or detecting misstatements in, financial statement assertions.

[1] Detection risk may be disaggregated into (1) risks related to tests of details of transactions and balances (TD) and (2) risks related to substantive analytical procedures (AP).

*Relevance* relates to the assertion being addressed. For example, confirming a client's accounts receivable with customers may provide evidence on the existence of the receivables, but it provides very limited information relating to whether the client has completely recorded all receivable accounts.

The *reliability* of evidence is dependent on the circumstances in which it is obtained. While this makes generalizations difficult and subject to exceptions, audit evidence is *ordinarily* more reliable when it is:

1. Obtained from knowledgeable independent sources *outside the client company* rather than nonindependent sources.
2. Generated internally through a system of *effective controls* rather than ineffective controls.
3. Obtained *directly* by the auditor rather than indirectly or by inference (e.g., observation of application of a control is more reliable than the client's response to an inquiry concerning the control).
4. *Documentary* in form (paper, electronic media, or other media) rather than an oral representation.
5. Provided by *original documents* rather than photocopies or facsimiles.

In addition to the above, audit evidence that arises from two or more different sources provides auditors more total assurance than the items would provide if considered individually. For example, an auditor may observe an employee opening the mail and processing cash receipts to evaluate the operating effectiveness of controls over cash receipts. But, because that observation is only at the point in time it is made, the auditor also may make inquiries of client personnel and inspect documentation of the operation of such controls to obtain a combination of audit evidence that is considered very reliable. Conversely, if inconsistencies arise between the sources of audit evidence, the auditor may derive little assurance with respect to the effective operation of the control.

The term *sufficient* relates to the quantity of evidence that the auditors should obtain. The quantity of audit evidence needed is affected by the risk of misstatements (the greater the risk, the more audit evidence required) and also the reliability of the evidence. In the great majority of cases the auditor finds it necessary to rely on evidence that is persuasive rather than conclusive. Auditors are seldom convinced beyond *all* doubt that all aspects of the statements are properly stated.

## Types of Audit Evidence

LO4

List and describe types of audit evidence.

The auditors gather a combination of many types of audit evidence to adequately restrict audit risk. The *major types* of audit evidence may be summarized as follows:

1. Accounting information system
2. Documentary evidence
3. Third-party representations
4. Physical evidence
5. Computations
6. Data interrelationships
7. Client representations

### 1. Accounting Information System

An accounting information system consists of the methods and records established to record, process, summarize, and report the company's transactions and to maintain accountability over related assets, liability, and equity. This includes the initial entries that are often a part of integrated information systems. Ordinarily included here are the ledgers and journals (or equivalent electronic tables that capture those data).

Since the financial statements are prepared based upon the accounting records, auditors are required to document in their working papers how the accounting records agree or reconcile with the financial statements. They are also required to understand the financial reporting process, including how:

- Transactions are entered into the general ledger (or equivalent record).
- Journal entries (including adjustments) are initiated, recorded, and processed in the general ledger.

The records themselves and their support provide the auditors with some evidence when they test record accuracy through procedures such as analysis, the reperformance of procedures followed in the financial reporting process, and the reconciliation of related types of information. As an example, consider the procedure of verifying an amount in the financial statements by following it back through the accounting records. The auditors will ordinarily carry this process through the ledgers to the journals and compare the item to such basic documentary evidence as a paid check, invoice, or other source documents. The consistency of processing among the various records in and of itself provides a certain amount of audit evidence.

The dependability of ledgers and journals as evidence is indicated by the extent of internal control over their preparation. Whenever possible, subsidiary ledgers for receivables, payables, and plant equipment should be maintained by persons not responsible for the general ledger. All general journal entries should be approved in writing by the controller or other official. If ledgers and journals are produced by a computer system, various computer controls should be in effect. When controls of this type exist and the records appear to be well maintained, the auditors may regard the ledgers and journals as affording some support for the financial statements.

### 2. Documentary Evidence

Documentary evidence includes a variety of records in support of the company's business and accounting information system, including checks, invoices, contracts, and minutes of meetings. The competence of documentary evidence depends in part on whether it was created within the company (e.g., a sales invoice) or outside the company (e.g., a vendor's invoice). Some documents created within the company (e.g., checks) are sent outside the organization for endorsement and processing; because of this critical review by outsiders, these documents are regarded as more reliable than other documents created by client personnel.

In appraising the reliability of documentary evidence, the auditors should consider whether the document is of a type that could easily be forged or created in its entirety by a dishonest employee. A stock certificate evidencing an investment in marketable securities is usually elaborately engraved and would be difficult to falsify. On the other hand, a note receivable may be created by anyone in a moment either by filling in the blank spaces in one of the standard note forms available at any office supply store or by filling data into a template included in computer software.

*Documentary Evidence Created outside the Client Organization and Transmitted Directly to the Auditors* A few documents are prepared outside the client organization and transmitted directly to the auditors. An example is the *cutoff bank statement,* which is a bank statement covering a specified number of business days (usually 7 to 10) after the client's balance sheet date. Auditors use this statement to determine that reconciling items shown on the year-end bank statement are complete and have cleared the bank within a reasonable time. Cutoff bank statements are discussed in more detail in Chapter 10.

On some audits, the auditors may be provided with access to electronic client records maintained by a third party (e.g., electronic bank statements and copies of checks maintained by the client's bank). In these circumstances, the auditors must be assured of the security of the records and their access to them.

*Documentary Evidence Created outside the Client Organization and Held by the Client* Many externally created documents examined by the auditors will be in the client's possession. Examples include bank statements, vendors' invoices and statements, property tax bills, notes payable, contracts, customers' purchase orders, and stock and bond certificates. In deciding how much reliance to place upon this type of evidence, the auditors should consider whether the document is of a type that could be easily created or altered by someone in the client's employ. The auditors should be particularly cautious in accepting as audit evidence photo or fax copies of documents, or documents that appear to have been altered in any way. Both photo and fax copies may be easily altered in a manner that makes detection difficult. Alterations to a document may have been made deliberately to misstate the facts and to mislead auditors or others who rely upon the document.

Pointing out the possibility that externally created documents in the client's possession might have been forged or altered is not intended to discredit this type of evidence. Externally created documents in the possession of the client are used extensively by auditors and are considered, in general, as a stronger type of evidence than documents created by the client.

*Documentary Evidence Created and Held within the Client Organization*    When available, the most dependable single piece of *documentary evidence* created within the client's organization ordinarily is a paid check. The check bears the endorsement of the payee and a perforation or stamp indicating payment by the bank. Because of this review and processing of a check by outsiders, the auditors will usually look upon a paid check as a strong type of evidence. The paid check may be viewed as evidence that an asset was acquired at a given cost, or as proof that a liability was paid or an expense incurred.

Most documents created within the client organization represent a lower quality of evidence than a paid check because they circulate only within the company and do not receive the critical review of an outsider. Examples of internally created documents that do not leave the client's possession are sales invoices, shipping notices, purchase orders, receiving reports, and credit memoranda. Of course, the original copy of a sales invoice or purchase order is sent to the customer or supplier, but the copy available for the auditor's inspection has not left the client's possession.

The degree of reliance to be placed on documents created and used only within the organization depends on the effectiveness of the internal control. If the control procedures are so designed that a document prepared by one person must be critically reviewed by another, and if all documents are serially numbered and all numbers in the series accounted for, these documents may represent reasonably good evidence. Adequate internal control will also provide for extensive segregation of duties so that no one employee handles a transaction from beginning to end. An employee who maintains records or creates documents, such as credit memoranda, should not have access to cash. Under these conditions there is no incentive for an employee to falsify a document, since the employee creating documents does not have custody of assets.

On the other hand, if internal control is weak, the auditors cannot place as much reliance on documentary evidence created within the organization and not reviewed by outsiders. If an employee is authorized to create documents such as sales invoices and credit memoranda and also has access to cash, an incentive exists to falsify documents to conceal a theft. If documents are not controlled by serial numbers, the possibility arises that the auditors are not being given access to all documents or that duplicates are being used to support fictitious transactions. Not only is there the danger of fictitious documents being created to cover theft by an employee, but also there is the possibility that management is purposely presenting misleading financial statements and has prepared false supporting documents for the purpose of deceiving the auditors.

*Electronic Documents*    Much of the "hard-copy" documentation described above is not maintained when the client has a sophisticated computerized accounting system. When an **electronic data interchange (EDI)** system is used, source documents such as invoices, purchase orders, checks, and bills of lading are replaced with "electronic documents."

A purchase transaction may be automatically initiated by a client's computer by sending an electronic message directly to a supplier's computer system. This electronic message replaces the traditional purchase order. The other documentation of the purchase transaction may consist of an invoice and a bill of lading generated in electronic form by the supplier's computer system. To determine the degree of reliance that may be placed upon such electronic documents, the auditors will test the controls over the computer system. Chapter 8 describes the controls that are used in computerized information systems in detail, and Chapters 10 through 16 include illustrations of such systems.

### 3. Third-Party Representations

Auditors obtain a variety of representations from a number of outside parties, such as the client's customers, vendors, financial institutions, and attorneys. In addition, evidence may be obtained from specialists in some audits.

*Confirmations*   Confirmation requests are used in the audit of a number of accounts, including cash, accounts and notes receivable, debt accounts, and capital stock accounts. As an example, in the audit of accounts receivable, customers are requested by the client to send a reply directly to the auditors that confirms the amount owed to the client.

As indicated in AICPA AU 505 (PCAOB 330), confirmation requests to third parties (e.g., customers, vendors, financial institutions) can be used to address any of the assertions about a particular financial statement amount. However, they do not address all assertions equally well. Confirmations generally are effective at providing evidence about the assertion of *existence* of accounts, but they are less effective at addressing *completeness* and the appropriate *valuation.* For example, while a returned account receivable confirmation provides reliable evidence about the existence of an obligation, it does not address whether the debtor can actually pay the obligation. The account actually may be worthless.

To ensure the reliability of the confirmation process, the auditors should carefully design the confirmation requests to seek the appropriate information and make it easy for the recipient to respond. The auditors also should consider whether it is necessary to specifically address the confirmation request to an individual in the outside organization who is authorized to confirm the information. As an example, information about the terms of a debt agreement at a financial institution might best be sent to the client's loan officer.

To make sure that the confirmation reply comes directly to the auditors and not to the client, the auditors will enclose with the confirmation request a return envelope addressed to the auditors' office. If the replies were addressed to the auditors at the client's place of business, an opportunity would exist for someone in the client's organization to intercept a returned confirmation and alter the information reported, or even destroy the document. The envelope containing the confirmation should bear the auditors' return address. In that way, if the address is fictitious, the confirmation may be returned by the post office directly to the auditors. As discussed in more detail in Chapter 11, when information is confirmed electronically, procedures must be followed to ensure that the process is secure.

*Lawyers' Letters*   The primary source of information about litigation that is pending against the client is obtained from *lawyers' letters.* To obtain these letters, the auditors ask the client to request their attorneys to furnish directly to the auditors their agreement with management's assessment of any litigation being handled for the client. Lawyers' letters are discussed in Chapter 16.

*Consulting with Specialists*   Auditors may not be experts in performing such technical tasks as judging the value of highly specialized inventory or making actuarial computations to verify liabilities for postretirement benefits. Audit evidence about such matters is best obtained from qualified specialists. Other examples of audit tasks that may require the use of a specialist include valuations of works of art of restricted securities and legal interpretations of regulations or contracts.

## Illustrative Case — *Need for a Specialist*

During the observation of the physical inventory of a company manufacturing semiconductors—small chips of photographically etched silicon that channel electricity along microscopic pathways—one of the auditors counted semiconductors purportedly worth several hundred thousand dollars. He then asked why apparently identical appearing semiconductors on another wall were not being counted. The client informed him that those semiconductors were defective and could not be sold. To the auditor, the defective semiconductors were identical in appearance with those included in the count. Shortly thereafter, the auditor, Pany, entered academia.

In AICPA AU 620 (PCAOB 336), the Auditing Standards Board recognized the necessity for auditors to consult with experts, when appropriate, as a means of gathering sufficient appropriate audit evidence. A **specialist** is an individual or organization possessing expertise in a field other than accounting and auditing, such as expertise in valuation of complex financial instruments and other assets, actuarial calculations, estimation of oil and gas reserves, and valuation of environmental liabilities. The specialist may be hired by the client (the "client's specialist") or by the auditors (the "auditors' specialist").

The auditors are responsible for performing procedures to evaluate the adequacy of the professional qualifications and reputation of the specialist. This usually involves making inquiries about the specialist's credentials and experience. While auditors engage specialists because they seek assistance in specialized areas, they cannot accept a specialist's findings blindly. They must obtain an adequate understanding of the methods or assumptions used by the specialist and evaluate their relevance and reasonableness in relation to the auditor's other findings and conclusions. Also, if the specialist's work involves the use of source data that are significant, the auditors should evaluate that data's relevance, completeness, and accuracy. The auditors should not refer to the specialist in their audit report unless the specialist's findings do not support the representations in the financial statements, thus causing the auditors to modify their opinion.

Although the auditors would ordinarily prefer to employ their own specialist, a client's specialist may be acceptable, even one that is an employee of the client. However, the auditors should assess the risk that the specialist's objectivity might be impaired because of this relationship. If the auditors believe that the specialist's objectivity might be impaired, they should perform additional procedures or hire another specialist.

### 4. Physical Evidence

Audit evidence that the auditors can obtain by examining an asset that physically exists is referred to as **physical evidence.** The best evidence of the existence of certain assets is the auditors' examination of the assets themselves. The existence of property and equipment, such as automobiles, buildings, office equipment, and factory machinery, may be conclusively established by physical examination. Similarly, evidence about the existence of cash may be obtained by counting, and the client's inventory may be observed as it is counted by client personnel. The auditors also can determine whether a control procedure is being performed by observing the employees performing the procedure.

At first thought, it might seem that physical examination of an asset would conclusively verify all assertions relating to the account, but this is often not true. As an example, the observation of the client's count of inventory may leave some important questions unanswered. The quality and condition of merchandise or of goods in process are vital in determining their salability. If the goods counted by the auditors contain hidden defects or are obsolete, a mere counting of units does not substantiate their

## Illustrative Case

### Reliance on Management Representations

The income statement of the National Student Marketing Corporation (NSMC) included total gains of $370,000 from the sale of two subsidiary companies to employees of the subsidiaries. Consideration for the sale was notes receivable collateralized by 7,700 shares of NSMC stock. Because both subsidiaries had been operating at substantial losses, NSMC's independent auditors obtained written representations from three officers of NSMC that there were no indemnification or repurchase commitments given to the purchasers.

The SEC criticized the auditors for relying too heavily on management representations regarding the sales. The SEC considered the sales to be sham transactions that would have been brought to light had the auditors sufficiently extended their audit procedures. NSMC had executed various side agreements to assume all risks of ownership after the "sale" of one subsidiary and had agreed to make cash contributions and guarantee a bank line of credit for the other subsidiary after the "sale." Further, the NSMC stock collateralizing the notes receivable had been given to the subsidiaries' "purchasers" by officers of NSMC.

balance sheet valuation. Therefore, CPAs are alert to any clues that raise doubt as to the quality or condition of inventories. Occasionally, the auditors may need to arrange for specialists, such as engineers and chemists, to provide information about the quality or condition of inventories.

The auditors' physical examination also does not provide proof of ownership of assets. A fleet of automobiles used by salespeople and company executives, for example, might be leased rather than owned. In addition, physical examination does not substantiate the cost of the assets.

In summary, physical examination or observation provides high-quality evidence as to the *existence* of certain assets, but generally it needs to be supplemented by other types of evidence to determine the ownership, proper valuation, and condition of those assets. For some types of assets, such as accounts receivable or intangible assets, even the existence of the assets cannot be verified through physical evidence.

### 5. Computations

Another type of audit evidence consists of the results of computations made independently by the auditors to prove the arithmetical accuracy of the client's analyses and records. In its simplest form, an auditor's computation might consist of footing a column of figures in a sales journal or in a ledger account to provide that column total. Independent computations may be used to prove the accuracy of such client calculations as earnings per share, depreciation expense, allowance for uncollectible accounts, revenue recognized on a percentage-of-completion basis, and provisions for federal and state income taxes. Specialists may become involved in certain computations. For example, because the computation of a client's liability for postretirement benefits involves actuarial assumptions and computations beyond the auditor's area of expertise, auditors usually rely on the services of an actuary to compute this liability.

### 6. Data Interrelationships

Data interrelationships involve the comparison of relationships among financial and, sometimes, nonfinancial data. Data interrelationships differ from computations. As indicated in the preceding section, computations verify mathematical processes. Data interrelationships rely upon plausible relationships among both financial and nonfinancial data. For example, a plausible relationship may exist in an industry between annual square footage of sales space and retail sales. Analytical procedures, the primary means used by auditors to analyze data interrelationships, are described later in this chapter.

### 7. Oral and Written Client Representations

Throughout an audit the auditors ask a great many questions of the officers and employees of the client's organization. Oral inquiries are made on an endless range of topics—the location of records and documents, the reasons underlying an unusual accounting procedure, the probabilities of collecting a long past-due account receivable. In making inquiries, auditors should consider the knowledge, objectivity, experience, responsibility, and qualifications of the individual being questioned and should use carefully structured questions to address relevant issues. Client replies should be carefully evaluated and, as appropriate, followed up with additional questions.

Generally, oral client representations are not sufficient in themselves, but they may be useful in disclosing situations that require investigation or in corroborating other forms of evidence. For example, after making a careful analysis of all past-due accounts receivable, an auditor will normally discuss with the credit manager the prospects of collecting specific accounts. If the opinions of the credit manager are in accordance with the estimates of uncollectible accounts that have been made independently by the auditor, this oral evidence will constitute support for the conclusions reached. In repeat audits of a business, the auditor will be in a better position to evaluate the opinions of the credit manager based on the manager's estimates in prior years.

Auditors also obtain written representations from clients. At the conclusion of the audit, the CPAs obtain from the client a written **representation letter** summarizing the most important oral representations made by management during the engagement. Many specific items are included in this representation letter. For example, management usually represents that all liabilities known to exist are reflected in the financial statements. The representations generally fall into the following broad categories:

1. All accounting records, financial data, and minutes of directors' meetings have been made available to the auditors.
2. The financial statements are complete and were prepared in conformity with generally accepted accounting principles.
3. Management believes that the adjusting entries brought to its attention by the auditors and not recorded are not material, individually or in the aggregate.
4. Management acknowledges its responsibility to design and implement programs and controls to prevent and detect fraud and to disclose information to the auditors on alleged or suspected fraud.
5. All items requiring disclosure (such as loss contingencies, noncompliance with laws and regulations, and related party transactions) have been properly disclosed.

AICPA AU 580 (PCAOB 333) requires auditors to obtain a representation letter on every engagement and provides suggestions as to its form and content. These letters are dated as of the **date of the auditors' report** and usually are signed by both the client's chief executive officer and chief financial officer.

A client representation letter *should never be used as a substitute for performing other audit procedures.* The financial statements already constitute written representation by the client; hence, a representation letter does little more than assert that the original representations were correct.

Although representation letters are not a substitute for other necessary audit procedures, they do serve several important audit purposes. One purpose is to remind the client officers of their primary and personal responsibility for the financial statements. Another purpose is to document in the audit working papers the client's responses to the significant questions asked by the auditors during the engagement. Also, a representation by management may be the only evidence available with respect to management's *future intentions.* For example, whether maturing debt is classified as a current or a long-term liability may depend upon whether management has both the ability and the *intent* to refinance the debt.

## Audit Procedures

Auditors perform audit procedures to obtain audit evidence that will allow them to draw reasonable conclusions as to whether the client's financial statements follow generally accepted accounting principles. More specifically, auditors perform the following types of audit procedures:

1. **Risk assessment procedures** are designed to obtain an understanding of the client and its environment, including its internal control, to assess the risks of material misstatement.
2. **Tests of controls** are designed to test the operating effectiveness of controls in preventing or detecting material misstatements.
3. **Substantive procedures** are designed to detect material misstatements of relevant assertions. Substantive procedures include (*a*) analytical procedures and (*b*) tests of details of account balances, transactions, and disclosures.

Chapters 6 and 7 provide basic guidance on risk assessment procedures and on tests of controls. The following section addresses substantive procedures. In thinking about substantive procedures, it is helpful to consider their *nature* (type and form), *timing* (when performed), and *extent* (quantity of evidence obtained).

**Nature of Substantive Procedures**

Substantive procedures include analytical procedures (discussed in detail later in this chapter) and tests of details. These tests are part of the auditors' **further audit procedures**[2] because their nature, timing, and extent are based on the results of the risk assessment procedures. Tests of details may be divided into three types: (1) tests of account balances, (2) tests of classes of transactions, and (3) tests of disclosures. Recall that this is the manner in which the assertions are presented in Figure 5.1. Tests of details of balances directly address whether there are misstatements in the ending balance of an account (e.g., confirmation of ending accounts receivable balances). Tests of details of transactions (also referred to as direct tests of transactions) address whether particular types of transactions (e.g., purchases and retirements of equipment) have been properly accounted for during the period. Tests of details of disclosures address whether financial statement disclosures are properly presented.

The nature of the substantive procedures used on an audit will be responsive to the assessed risks of misstatement, with the objective of efficiently obtaining sufficient appropriate audit evidence to achieve the planned level of assurance for each audit area.

One way for the auditors to address a high risk area is to select a more effective audit procedure. For example, if the auditors want to increase the assurance obtained relating to the existence of accounts receivable, they could decide to directly test the ending balance by confirming the accounts rather than relying upon the inspection of internal documents. While the details of audit procedures for various accounts and transaction cycles will be discussed in Chapters 10 through 16, Figure 5.3 summarizes the most common types of audit procedures that the auditors may decide to use and provides examples of each.

**Timing of Substantive Audit Procedures**

Audit procedures may be performed before the client's year-end (i.e., at interim dates) or subsequent to year-end. The auditors may obtain more assurance by shifting audit procedures from an interim date to after year-end. Performing procedures at an interim date increases audit risk, because material misstatements may arise in the remaining period, between the date of the tests and year-end. This incremental audit risk must be controlled by performing additional audit procedures that cover the remaining period, or by the fact that

[2] Further audit procedures include the tests of controls and substantive procedures that are performed based on the results of the auditors' risk assessments.

**FIGURE 5.3    Audit Procedures**

| Audit Procedure | Examples |
|---|---|
| *Inquiry*—Seeking information of knowledgeable persons within or outside the organization; inquiry may be oral or written | • Inquiry of plant manager as to a sequence of operations<br>• Inquiry of attorney relating to litigation |
| *Inspection of records or documents*—Examining a record or document | • A test of controls to inspect records for evidence of proper authorization<br>• Inspect certain records as evidence of ownership (e.g., land) |
| *Inspection of tangible assets*—Physically examining an asset | • Inspect the condition of inventory items |
| *Observation*—Watching a process or procedure being performed by the entity's personnel or the performance of control activities | • Observe client personnel performing manufacturing functions<br>• Observe the client counting its inventory |
| *External confirmation*—Obtaining a written response about a particular item from a third party (e.g., debtor, creditor) | • Confirmation of accounts receivable |
| *Recalculation*—Testing the mathematical accuracy of documents or records | • Recalculating a total, such as using computer assisted audit techniques to determine whether a file has been summarized properly by the client |
| *Reperformance*—An independent execution of procedures or controls that were originally performed by the client (often as a part of the client's internal control) | • Reperforming the aging of accounts receivable manually or by using computer assisted audit techniques |
| *Analytical procedures*—Evaluations of financial information through analysis of plausible relationships among both financial and nonfinancial data; *scanning* is an analytical procedure involving the auditor's use of professional judgment to review accounting data to identify significant or unusual items and then to test those items | • Calculating days sales in ending accounts receivable and comparing to the prior year<br>• Scanning all ending income statement account balances and comparing them with the preceding year and/or this year's budget |

the auditors are confident that the client's controls are operating effectively to prevent material misstatements. The timing of audit procedures is discussed in more detail in Chapter 6.

## Extent of Substantive Procedures

Holding other factors such as the nature and timing of procedures constant, the greater the risk of material misstatement, the greater the needed extent of substantive procedures. The main way in which the auditors increase the extent of substantive tests of transactions and balances is to examine more items. To be cost effective, audits must involve the use of samples, but the sample sizes must be sufficient to restrict audit risk to a low level. The considerations used in determining appropriate sample sizes are described in Chapter 9.

## Cost of Audit Procedures

CPAs can no more disregard the cost of alternative audit procedures than a store manager can disregard a difference in the cost of competing brands of merchandise. While cost is not the primary factor influencing auditors in deciding what evidence should be obtained, it is always an important consideration. Also, the greater the risk of material misstatement of the item to be verified, the stronger the evidence required by the auditors, and the greater the cost they are willing to incur in obtaining it. As we have indicated, sufficient appropriate audit evidence is obtained when audit risk is reduced to an acceptable level. Therefore, the most efficient set of audit procedures is that which achieves the required low level of audit risk at the minimum audit cost.

# Analytical Procedures

Analytical procedures involve evaluations of financial statement information by a study of relationships among financial and nonfinancial data. A basic premise underlying the application of analytical procedures is that plausible relationships among data may reasonably be expected to exist and continue in the absence of known conditions to the contrary. Therefore, the auditors can use these relationships to obtain evidence about the reasonableness of financial statement amounts. AICPA AU 520 (PCAOB 329) provides guidance on the nature of these procedures and examples of how they are applied.

## Nature of Analytical Procedures

Techniques used in performing analytical procedures range in sophistication from straightforward analysis of trends and ratios to complex mathematical models involving many relationships and data from many previous years. A simple analytical procedure is to compare revenue and expense amounts for the current year to those of prior periods, noting significant differences. A more sophisticated analytical procedure might involve the development of a multiple regression model to estimate the amount of sales for the year using economic and industry data. Analytical procedures also may involve computations of percentage relationships of various items in the financial statements, such as gross profit percentages. In all these approaches, the auditors attempt to identify unexpected differences or the absence of expected differences. Such differences may indicate misstatements in the financial statements that should be investigated fully by the auditors.

Essentially, the process of performing analytical procedures consists of four steps:

1. Develop an expectation of an account (or ratio) balance.
2. Determine the amount of difference from the expectation that can be accepted without investigation.
3. Compare the company's account (ratio) balance with the expectation.
4. Investigate and evaluate significant differences from the expectation.

*Developing an Expectation*

A variety of types of information are available to the auditors to develop expectations for analytical procedures, including:

1. Financial information for comparable prior periods.
2. Anticipated results, such as budgets and forecasts.
3. Relationships among elements of financial information within a period.
4. Information derived from similar firms in the same industry, such as industry averages.
5. Relationships between financial information and relevant nonfinancial data.

Every audit client generates internal financial information that may be used in performing analytical procedures. Financial reports of prior years, forecasts, production reports, and monthly performance reports are but a few data sources that may be expected to bear predictable relationships to financial statement amounts. In establishing these relationships, auditors may use dollar amounts, physical quantities, ratios, or percentages. To increase the precision of the procedures, separate relationships may be computed for each division or product line.

Industry averages are available through such sources as Dun & Bradstreet's *Key Business Ratios* and Robert Morris Associates's *Annual Statement Studies.* These averages provide a potentially rich source of information for developing expectations for analytical procedures. Comparisons with industry statistics may alert auditors to classification errors, improper applications of accounting principles, or other misstatements in specific items in the client's financial statements. In addition, these comparisons may highlight the client's strengths and weaknesses relative to similar companies, thus providing the auditors with a basis for making constructive recommendations to the client.

Certain problems may be encountered in using industry averages for analytical procedures because of a lack of comparability among companies and the inability to obtain current industry data. In comparison to the auditors' client, other companies in the same industry may be larger or smaller, engage in other lines of business that affect their ratios, or use different accounting methods. In addition, the time required to assemble industry averages creates a situation in which the most recent averages are always a year or so old. Thus, auditors should carefully consider the comparability and timeliness of the data before drawing conclusions based upon comparisons with industry averages.

*Types of Expectations*    Auditors develop expectations using a number of different techniques, including trend analysis, ratio analysis, regression analysis, and reasonableness tests. *Trend analysis* involves the review of changes in an account balance over time. For example, a review of the client's sales for the past three years might reveal a consistent growth rate of about 7 percent. This information would assist the auditors in developing an expectation about what sales should be for the current year.

*Ratio analysis* involves comparisons of relationships between two or more financial statement accounts, or comparisons of account balances to nonfinancial data (e.g., revenue per sales order). Traditional financial ratios typically are classified into four categories:

1. Liquidity ratios, such as the current ratio and the quick ratio.
2. Leverage ratios, such as the debt to equity ratio and the long-term debt to equity ratio.
3. Profitability ratios, such as gross profit percentage and return on total assets.
4. Activity ratios, such as inventory turnover and accounts receivable turnover.

Because ratio analysis involves examination of the relationships between two or more variables and may involve industry data, it is often a richer form of analysis than is trend analysis.

There are two basic approaches to ratio analysis, horizontal analysis and cross-sectional analysis. While **horizontal analysis** involves a review of the client's ratios and trends over time, **cross-sectional analysis** involves comparisons of the ratios of similar firms at a point in time—that is, cross-sectional analysis involves comparing the client's ratios to industry averages.

Figure 5.4 provides an illustration of horizontal (trend) and cross-sectional analysis of a client's income statement. The figure also illustrates a *common-size* income statement, in which all revenues and expenses are presented as a percentage of net sales. A common-size income statement is particularly useful because many expenses, such as cost of goods sold, would be expected to bear a predictable relationship to net sales. A common-size balance sheet presents all assets, liabilities, and owners' equity amounts as a percentage of total assets. The development of **common-size financial statements** is also known as **vertical analysis.**

If the auditors decide to use a more sophisticated analysis, it will often take the form of regression analysis. *Regression analysis* involves the use of statistical models to quantify the auditors' expectation about a financial statement amount or ratio. As an example, the auditors could develop an expectation about the client's sales for this year with a model that uses the amount spent on advertising, the square footage of selling space, and personal disposable income. Regression analysis has advantages over other forms of analysis in that more variables may be used to predict the financial statement balance, and the reliability and precision of the expectation may be precisely measured.

Another method that is used to develop a more precise expectation of a financial statement balance is a reasonableness test. A *reasonableness test* is similar to regression analysis in that an explicit expectation is computed for the financial statement amount using financial or nonfinancial data. As an example, the auditors might use the average occupancy rate and the average room rates of a hotel to develop an estimate of the hotel's revenues for the period.

A reasonableness test differs from regression analysis in that it is less formal and is not based on a statistical model.

**FIGURE 5.4** Techniques for Analytical Procedures

**Brody Corporation Income Statement**

| | Dollars (000s Omitted) | | | | | Common-Size Statements | | | 20X7 |
|---|---|---|---|---|---|---|---|---|---|
| | 20X6 (Audited) | 20X7 (Audited) | Percent Change | 20X8 (Unaudited) | Percent Change | 20X6 (Audited) | 20X7 (Audited) | 20X8 (Unaudited) | Industry Averages |
| Gross sales | 78,428 | 82,212 | 4.8 | 88,236 | 7.3 | 103% | 105% | 103% | 104% |
| Less: Returns and allowances | 2,284 | 4,235 | 85.4 | 2,644 | −37.6 | 3% | 5% | 3% | 4% |
| Net sales | 76,144 | 77,977 | 2.4 | 85,592 | 9.8 | 100% | 100% | 100% | 100% |
| Cost of goods sold | 46,213 | 46,478 | 0.6 | 51,234 | 10.2 | 61% | 60% | 60% | 58% |
| Gross profit | 29,931 | 31,499 | 5.2 | 34,358 | 9.1 | 39% | 40% | 40% | 42% |
| Selling & administrative expenses | 20,105 | 22,487 | 11.8 | 21,834 | −2.9 | 26% | 29% | 26% | 28% |
| Income from operations | 9,826 | 9,012 | −8.3 | 12,524 | 39.0 | 13% | 12% | 15% | 14% |
| Interest expense | 1,930 | 1,584 | −17.9 | 3,189 | 101.3 | 3% | 2% | 4% | 3% |
| Net income before taxes | 7,896 | 7,428 | −5.9 | 9,335 | 25.7 | 10% | 10% | 11% | 11% |
| Income taxes | 3,807 | 6,189 | 62.6 | 7,761 | 25.4 | 5% | 8% | 9% | 4% |
| Net income | 4,089 | 1,239 | −69.7 | 1,574 | 27.0 | 5% | 2% | 2% | 7% |
| EPS | 0.78 | 0.24 | −69.2 | 0.30 | 25.0 | | | | |
| **Ratios** | | | | | | | | | |
| Current | 1.7 | 1.9 | | 1.9 | | | | | 2.1 |
| Quick | 1.0 | 1.1 | | 1.1 | | | | | 1.3 |
| Receivables turnover | 5.3 | 5.6 | | 4.7 | | | | | 5.1 |
| Days' sales in ending receivables | 68.1 | 64.3 | | 76.6 | | | | | 65.6 |
| Inventory turnover | 4.7 | 3.2 | | 1.7 | | | | | 3.5 |
| Days' sales in ending inventory | 76.0 | 75.0 | | 112.5 | | | | | 74.4 |
| Interest expense/ outstanding debt | 0.11 | 0.08 | | 0.08 | | | | | 0.09 |

Horizontal (Trend) Analysis

Vertical Analysis

Cross-Sectional Analysis

153

*Determine Amount of Difference that Can Be Accepted*

The amount of difference between the expectation and the financial statement balance or ratio that can be accepted without investigation is determined primarily by the amount that is considered to be a material misstatement. However, this amount must be consistent with the degree of assurance desired from the procedure. If regression analysis is used, the items that should be investigated will be specifically identified by the statistical model based on the degree of precision and reliability specified by the auditors. When trend or ratio analysis is used, the auditors typically use professional judgment to specify an absolute amount of difference or a percentage difference that will result in investigation.

*Compare the Account (Ratio) Balance with the Expected Balance*

Once the auditors have determined the expectation and the amount of difference that can be accepted, they can make the actual comparisons to determine where the significant differences lie.

*Investigate and Evaluate Significant Differences*

The auditors must investigate any significant differences between their expectations and the client's financial statement amounts or ratios to determine whether they represent misstatements. This may involve reconsidering the methods and factors used in developing the expectation. Inquiry of management may be of assistance in this regard. Management's explanations, however, must ordinarily be corroborated with other audit evidence. If the auditors are unable to corroborate management's explanation or management has no explanation, they will often be required to expand their tests of the related financial statement amounts to determine whether or not they are materially misstated. Figure 5.5 provides some of the misstatements or problems that may be discovered when the auditors investigate significant differences uncovered by various analytical procedures.

## Timing of Analytical Procedures

Auditing standards require the application of analytical procedures at the *risk assessment* stage and near the end of the audit. The auditors also may decide to use them during the audit as *substantive procedures* to provide evidence as to the reasonableness of the specific account balances.

Analytical procedures performed as risk assessment procedures are used to assist the auditors in determining the nature, timing, and extent of further audit procedures that will be used to obtain evidence about specific accounts. At the risk assessment stage, the objective of analytical procedures is to help the auditors identify unusual transactions, events, or amounts that indicate a heightened risk of material misstatement of the

**FIGURE 5.5**   **Potential Misstatements Disclosed by Analytical Procedures**

| Analytical Procedure | Potential Misstatements |
| --- | --- |
| 1. Comparison of inventory levels for the current year to those of prior years | Misstatement of inventory; inventory obsolescence problem |
| 2. Comparison of research and development expense to the budgeted amount | Misclassification of research and development expenses |
| 3. Comparison of accounts receivable turnover for the current year to that of prior years | Misstatement of sales or accounts receivable; misstatement of the allowance for uncollectible accounts |
| 4. Comparison of the client's gross profit percentage to published industry averages | Misstatement of sales and accounts receivable; misstatement of cost of goods sold and inventory |
| 5. Comparison of production records in units to sales | Misstatement of sales; misstatement of inventory |
| 6. Comparison of interest expense to the average outstanding balance of interest-bearing debt | Understatement of liabilities; misstatement of interest expense |

financial statements. Risk assessment analytical procedures also are used to increase the auditors' understanding of the client's business. During the risk assessment stage, auditors are required to perform analytical procedures relating to revenue to identify any unusual or unexpected relationships involving revenue accounts that may be indicative of fraud. For example, one procedure might be to compare revenue recorded by month during the current year with comparable prior years' revenue.

Analytical procedures may be used as substantive procedures to provide evidence about one or more financial statement assertions. While the auditors are not required to use substantive analytical procedures, they are usually the most efficient test of certain assertions. For example, performing analytical procedures often is the most efficient way to evaluate the completeness of various revenue and expense accounts. Chapters 10 through 16 illustrate the use of analytical procedures as substantive procedures for various types of financial statement accounts.

Finally, analytical procedures must be used near the end of the audit, to assist the auditor in forming an overall conclusion on financial statements and in assessing the adequacy of the evidence that has been collected and the validity of the conclusions reached. At this stage, analytical procedures generally include reviewing the financial statements and notes and recomputing ratios (if necessary) to identify any unusual or unexpected balances or relationships that have not been previously identified and explained.

| **Extent of Analytical Procedures** | Auditors must consider the cost and likely effectiveness of analytical procedures in determining the extent to which they will be used for a particular audit. While the cost is often low due to the availability of computers to perform computations and the simplicity of many procedures performed manually, the effectiveness of analytical procedures will vary from one audit to the next. |
|---|---|

A primary measure of the effectiveness of an analytical procedure is its *precision.* Precision depends on a number of factors, including the predictability of the relationships, the technique used to develop the expectation, and the reliability of the underlying data used. If much "noise" exists in relationships between variables (e.g., sales and cost of goods sold), material differences might exist and not be identified by analytical procedures. Generally, precision can be improved by performing a more detailed analysis. For example, precision may be improved by performing analytical procedures with monthly rather than annual data.

The reliability of the underlying data that are used for analytical procedures may be evaluated by considering the source of the data. If the client generated the data, the auditors will consider the controls applied to their development. In some cases, the auditor may have to apply audit procedures to the data to test their reliability before they are used in the analytical procedure.

# Audit Evidence for Subjective Areas

**LO5**

Describe the considerations involved in auditing subjective areas, such as certain financial statement items valued at fair value.

Gathering evidence in the areas of accounting estimates, fair values, and related party transactions merits special attention due to the required judgments that need to be made by both management and the auditors.

**Evidence Regarding Accounting Estimates**

The auditors must be especially careful in considering financial statement accounts that are affected by estimates made by management (often referred to as accounting estimates), particularly those for which a wide range of accounting methods are considered acceptable. As discussed previously, accounting estimates are usually created by *estimation transactions.* Examples of accounting estimates include allowances for loan losses and obsolete inventory and estimates of warranty liabilities. Making accounting estimates is management's responsibility, and such estimates are generally more susceptible to material misstatement than other financial statement amounts that are more certain in amount. AICPA AU 540 (PCAOB 342) requires the auditors to determine that (*a*) all necessary estimates have been developed, (*b*) accounting estimates are reasonable, and (*c*) accounting estimates are properly accounted for and disclosed.

Determining whether all necessary estimates have been developed and accounted for properly (steps [*a*] and [*c*]) requires knowledge of the client's business and the applicable generally accepted accounting principles. When evaluating the reasonableness of accounting estimates (step [*b*]), the auditors obtain an understanding of how management developed the estimates and then use one or more of these three basic approaches:

1. Review and test management's process of developing the estimates, which often involves evaluating the reasonableness of the steps performed by management.
2. Independently develop an estimate of the amount to compare to management's estimate.
3. Review subsequent events or transactions bearing on the estimate, such as actual payments of an estimated amount made subsequent to year-end.

As discussed in Chapter 2, the auditors should perform a retrospective analysis of significant accounting estimates for evidence of bias on the part of management. If the auditors find that prior estimates appear biased, they will consider this factor in evaluating management estimates for the current year audit.

The wide range of potential accounting methods complicates the auditing of transactions involving accounting estimates. Pensions, leases, and long-term construction contracts are just a few examples of transactions with complex accounting methods that vary depending on the nature of the agreements and the specific circumstances. It is the auditors' responsibility to evaluate whether the accounting rules followed are appropriate in the given circumstances.

## Evidence Regarding Fair Values

In recent years, changes in accounting standards have required companies to significantly increase the use of fair values for measuring, presenting, and disclosing various assets, liabilities, and components of equity. For example, fair values are used for various investments, intangible assets, impaired assets, and derivatives. In addition, financial accounting standards allow companies to voluntarily select fair value valuation for a number of items.[3]

Fair value is defined to be the price that would be received to sell an asset, or the amount that must be paid to transfer a liability in an orderly transaction between market participants at the measurement date. In auditing their clients' fair values, auditors must keep in mind that the goal is to achieve a fair value as defined earlier in this paragraph and to determine that valuation techniques[4] are consistently applied, or, if revisions are needed, they are accounted for as a change in accounting estimate.

---

[3] Those items include loans receivable and payable, investments in equity securities, including those using the equity method, rights and obligations under insurance contracts and warranty agreements, host financial instruments from embedded derivative instruments, firm commitments involving financial instruments, and written loan commitments.

[4] The FASB presents three basic valuation techniques to establish fair value: market, income, and cost. The market approach uses prices and other relevant information generated by market transactions involving identical or comparable assets or liabilities (for example, in the case of marketable securities, market value). The income approach uses valuation techniques to convert future amounts (for example, cash flows or earnings) to a single discounted present value amount. The cost approach is based on the amount that would be required to replace the service capacity of an asset (this is a "replacement cost"). In some circumstances, a single valuation approach may be appropriate, while in others multiple techniques will be appropriate.

The client must select inputs (assumptions) to use in applying valuation techniques. *FASB ASC* 820-10, "Fair Value Measurements and Disclosures," provides the following three-level hierarchy:

- Level 1: Inputs of observable quoted prices in active markets for identical assets or liabilities (e.g., a closing stock price listed in *The Wall Street Journal* for an investment).
- Level 2: Inputs of other observable quoted prices, generally for similar assets or liabilities in active markets (e.g., a company may discount the future cash flows of its not publicly traded debt securities at the rate used by the market for its publicly traded debt securities).
- Level 3: Inputs that are unobservable for the assets or liability (e.g., a private company uses judgment to determine a proper rate to discount the future cash flows of its not publicly traded securities).

The hierarchy gives the highest priority to quoted prices in active markets (level 1) and lowest priority to unobservable inputs (level 3). The auditors must be alert for circumstances in which management may have an incentive to inappropriately characterize fair value measurements within the hierarchy. For example, a situation in which level 2 inputs are used may inappropriately be disclosed by management in the notes to the financial statements as level 1 inputs. In addition, the auditors must determine that all required disclosures relating to fair value are presented.

In planning and performing audit procedures related to fair value measurements, the auditors should obtain an understanding of the company's process for determining fair value measurements and disclosures, including relevant controls. In addition, the auditors should:

- Evaluate whether management's assumptions related to inputs are reasonable and reflect, or are not inconsistent with, market information.
- If management relies on historical financial information in the development of an input, consider the extent to which such reliance is justified.
- Evaluate whether the company's method for determining fair value measurements is applied consistently and, if so, whether the consistent application is appropriate given the current situation.

Fair value determination is easiest when there are published price quotations in an active market (e.g., a stock exchange). Determining fair value becomes more difficult when an active market does not exist: for example, in cases involving certain real estate investment properties and complex derivative financial instruments. In valuing assets that do not have active markets, fair value may be determined by analogizing to another existing market, or through the use of a valuation model (e.g., a model based on forecasts and discounting of future cash flows). The approach to auditing fair values is similar to that of other estimates in that one or more of three approaches are used: (1) review and test management's process, (2) independently develop an estimate, or (3) review subsequent events.

When using the audit approach of reviewing management's process, the auditors consider whether the assumptions used by management are reasonable, whether the valuation model seems appropriate, and whether management has used all relevant information that is reasonably available. The second approach, which involves developing the auditors' own estimate, offers the advantage of allowing the auditors to compare that estimate with the estimate developed by management. Often auditors will use a combination of these two approaches and also may decide to employ the assistance of a valuation specialist.

The third audit approach involves the use of information obtained subsequent to year-end to help evaluate the reasonableness of management's estimate. For example, the sale of an investment property shortly after the year-end may provide evidence on its value as of year-end. Yet, even in this situation, auditors must carefully consider the audit evidence since the sale might be impacted by circumstances that changed subsequent to year-end. For example, the prices of actively traded marketable securities that change

| Illustrative Case | *Risks Related to Accounting Estimates* |
|---|---|

The financial difficulty of the savings and loan industry during the late 1980s and early 1990s provides a good example of the potential risks to CPAs posed by accounting estimates. A number of savings and loan institutions ran into financial difficulties due in large part to making loans that subsequently proved to be uncollectible.

One savings and loan institution that made over $1 billion in real estate loans during the late 1980s originally estimated its required loan loss reserve to be $11 million. Subsequently, the Federal Deposit Insurance Corporation (FDIC) alleged that those loans resulted in losses of $450 million. Shortly thereafter, the FDIC filed a lawsuit against the CPA firm that had audited the institution.

after the year-end may not constitute appropriate evidence of values that existed at year-end. Regardless of the approach or approaches followed, the auditors should evaluate whether the required disclosures related to fair values have been properly presented.

**Evidence Regarding Related Party Transactions**

How should auditors react if a corporation buys a parcel of real estate from one of its executive officers at an obviously excessive price? This situation illustrates the type of problem that may arise for auditors when the client company enters into **related party transactions.** The term *related parties* refers to individuals or entities who may have dealings with the client in which one party is significantly influenced by the other such that it may not pursue its separate interests. Examples of related parties include officers, directors, principal owners, and members of their immediate families; and affiliated companies, such as subsidiaries. A related party transaction is any transaction between the company and these parties, other than normal compensation arrangements, expense allowances, and similar transactions arising in the ordinary course of business. Since transactions with related parties are not conducted at "arm's length," the auditors should be aware that the *economic substance* of these transactions might differ from their form. Related party transactions have often been used to facilitate fraudulent financial reporting. Accordingly, auditors should determine the business purpose of any significant and unusual related party transactions that they encounter.

Even if the transactions are recorded appropriately, the auditors also must be concerned that material related party transactions are *adequately disclosed* in the client's financial statements or the related notes.[5]

Disclosure of related party transactions should include the nature of the relationship; a description of the transactions, including dollar amounts; and amounts due to and from related parties, together with the terms and manner of settlement.

The primary challenge for the auditors is identifying any related party transactions that management has not disclosed, because they may be recorded in the accounting records with all other transactions. Common methods of determining related parties include making inquiries of management and reviewing SEC filings, stockholders' listings, and *conflict-of-interest statements* obtained by the client from its executives. A list of all known related parties should be prepared at the beginning of the audit so that the audit staff may be alert for related party transactions throughout the engagement. This list is retained in the auditors' permanent file for reference and updating in successive engagements. As they perform the audit, the auditors will be alert for transactions with

---

[5] *FASB Accounting Standards Codification* section 850-10, "Related Party Disclosures," contains requirements for disclosure of related party transactions.

these parties and for any transactions with unusual terms that might be indicative of related party negotiations.

## Audit Documentation

**LO6**

Describe the purposes of audit documentation.

Audit documentation, also known as **working papers** or workpapers, is the record of the audit procedures performed, relevant audit evidence obtained, and the conclusions the auditors reach. AICPA AU 230 (PCAOB 339) requires that audit documentation provide (1) evidence of the auditors' basis for concluding on the achievement of the audit's overall objectives, and (2) evidence that the audit was planned and performed in accordance with GAAS. In addition to these primary objectives, audit documentation also serves the following functions:

- Assists both continuing audit team members and auditors new to the engagement in planning and performing the audit; as such it also serves as a record of matters of continuing significance for future audits.
- Assists audit team members responsible for supervision in reviewing the quality of the work performed.
- Demonstrates the accountability of the various audit team members for the work performed.
- Assists (1) internal firm quality control reviewers, (2) inspection or peer review individuals, and (3) successor auditors in performing their respective roles.

Audit working papers take the form of bank reconciliations or analyses of ledger accounts; others may consist of photocopies of **minutes** of directors' meetings; still others might be organization charts or flowcharts of the client's internal control. Working trial balances, audit programs, correspondence (including e-mail) concerning significant matters, internal control questionnaires, letters or representations obtained from the client and from the client's legal counsel, and returned confirmation forms—all of these schedules, lists, notes, and documents—are part of the auditors' audit documentation.

**LO7**

Discuss the factors that affect the auditors' judgment as to the nature and extent of audit documentation.

How detailed must documentation be? This depends on several factors, such as the nature of the auditing procedure being performed, the risk of misstatement involved in the area being tested, the significance of the evidence to the overall audit, the extent of judgment involved in performing the work, and the nature of the findings or results. The auditors must document all audit findings that they believe to be significant. In addition, audit documentation should be sufficient to allow an **experienced auditor** to understand the audit work performed, the evidence obtained, and the significant conclusions reached. In this context, an experienced auditor is one who possesses the competencies and skills to perform an audit of the client, but who has had no previous experience with the client. The working papers also should demonstrate that the accounting records agree or reconcile to the financial statements being audited.

**LO8**

Identify matters that must be included in audit working papers.

It is very important for the auditors to document audit findings or issues that are significant and the actions taken to address them. Such matters include the selection of appropriate accounting principles, accounting for complex and unusual transactions, and issues related to accounting estimates. Auditors also should document test results that indicate that the financial statements may be materially misstated, any significant difficulties encountered in applying auditing procedures, proposed audit adjustments, and findings that could result in a modification of the audit report. Finally, audit documentation should identify those who performed and reviewed the work and the related dates of performance.

## Confidential Nature of Working Papers

To conduct a satisfactory audit, the auditors must be given unrestricted access to all information about the client's business. Much of this information is confidential, such as the profit margins on individual products, tentative plans for business combinations with other companies, and the salaries of officers and key employees. Officers of the client company would not be willing to make available to the auditors information that is restricted from competitors, employees, and others unless they could rely on the auditors' maintaining a professional silence on these matters.

Much of the information gained in confidence by the auditors is recorded in their working papers; consequently, the working papers are confidential in nature. The AICPA *Code of Professional Conduct* includes a rule that generally prohibits a member in public practice from disclosing confidential information.

Under normal circumstances, auditors think of confidential information as being information that must not be divulged *outside* the client organization. But the confidential nature of information in the auditors' working papers has another dimension: Often it must not be divulged *within* the client organization. If, for example, the client does not want certain employees to know the levels of executive salaries, the auditors obviously should not defeat this policy by exposing their working papers to unauthorized client personnel. Also, the working papers may identify particular accounts, branches, or time periods to be tested by the auditors; to permit the client's employees to learn of these in advance would weaken the significance of the tests.

Since audit working papers are highly confidential, they must be safeguarded at all times. Safeguarding working papers usually includes keeping them locked in a file cabinet or an audit case during lunch and after working hours.

## Ownership of Audit Working Papers

Audit working papers are the *property of the auditors,* not of the client. At no time does the client have the right to demand access to the auditors' working papers. After the audit, the working papers are retained by the auditors.

Clients may sometimes find it helpful to refer to information from the auditors' working papers from prior years. Auditors usually are willing to provide this information, but their working papers should not be regarded as a substitute for the client's own accounting records. Rule *501-Acts Discreditable* of the AICPA Code of Professional Conduct explains the ethical requirements related to auditor working papers and client records.

## Working Papers and Auditors' Liability

The **audit file** includes the working papers for a particular engagement and is the principal record of the work performed during the audit. If the auditors are subsequently charged with negligence, the working papers included in the audit file will be a major factor in refuting or substantiating the charge. Although properly prepared audit documentation will help the auditors should litigation follow, improperly prepared documentation will work against them.

If a lawsuit is brought against the auditors, the plaintiffs will subpoena the audit documentation and analyze it in great detail, looking for contradictions, omissions, or any evidence of carelessness or fraud. This possibility suggests the need for public accounting firms to make their own critical review of the documentation at the end of each engagement. During this review, the auditors should bear in mind that any unexplained contradictory statements may be used at a later date to support a charge of improper auditing.

How long should audit documentation be retained? The professional standards require a period of not less than five years, while the Sarbanes-Oxley Act of 2002 requires that auditors maintain documentation for seven years. Thus, for public clients, auditors must retain working papers for seven years, but they may destroy them after five years if the client is a nonpublic company.

*Changing Audit Documentation after the Date of the Audit Report*

Auditors are given 60 days after the audit **report release date** (the date the client is granted permission to use the report) to complete the audit file by assembling a complete and final set of audit documentation.[6] During this period, they are able to perform routine

---

[6] Public Company Accounting Oversight Board *Standard No. 3*, "Audit Documentation," allows only a 45-day period for publicly traded clients.

file-assembling procedures such as deleting or discarding superseded documentation and sorting, collating, and cross-referencing final working papers. In addition, they may sign off on various checklists and add information received subsequent to the date of the auditors' report (e.g., an original confirmation that was previously faxed). The updated or revised audit documentation should contain all of the information, evidence, and conclusions that were in any superseded documentation. However, if certain information is no longer relevant or valid, it may be discarded during this 60-day period.[7] After the close of this 60-day period, referred to as the **documentation completion date,** no information may be discarded from audit working papers.

If new information is added to the working papers after the issuance of the audit report—either before or after the documentation completion date—documentation should include (1) when and by whom changes were made and reviewed, (2) specific reasons for the changes, and (3) the effect, if any, of the changes on the auditors' conclusions.

### Differences of Opinion

On occasion, inconsistencies will arise in the working papers because different members of the audit staff—say, a senior and the engagement partner—reach different conclusions on some complex auditing or accounting issue. In such cases, the disagreeing auditors should discuss the matter to see if they can reach agreement. If they are able to do so, the working papers should be revised to reflect their common opinion. If they are not able to reach agreement, the opinion of the partner-in-charge of the engagement will prevail with respect to the content of the auditors' report. However, all other members of the audit team have the right to document in the working papers *their disagreement* with the ultimate decision. In the event that a staff person elects to document his or her disagreement, the partner-in-charge obviously should be extremely thorough in documenting the rationale underlying the firm's ultimate decision in a carefully written memorandum. The SEC interprets the Sarbanes-Oxley Act of 2002 as requiring that working papers be retained regardless of whether they support or are inconsistent with the auditors' final conclusion relating to significant matters. However, the act does not require retention of preliminary views when those preliminary views are based on incomplete information or data.

## Types of Working Papers

Describe the types of working papers and the way they are organized.

Since the audit working papers document a variety of information gathered by the auditors, there are numerous types of papers. However, there are certain general categories into which most working papers may be grouped. These are (1) audit administrative working papers; (2) working trial balance and lead schedules; (3) adjusting journal entries and reclassification entries; (4) supporting schedules, analyses, reconciliations, and computational working papers; and (5) corroborating documents.

### Audit Administrative Working Papers

Auditing is a sophisticated activity requiring planning, supervision, control, and coordination. Certain working papers are specifically designed to aid the auditors in the planning and administration of engagements. These working papers include audit plans and programs, internal control questionnaires and flowcharts, engagement letters, and time budgets. Memoranda of the planning process and significant discussions with client management are also considered **administrative working papers.**

### Working Trial Balance

The **working trial balance** is a schedule listing the balances of the accounts in the general ledger for the current and previous year and also providing columns for the auditors' proposed adjustments and reclassifications and for the final amounts that will appear in the financial statements. A working trial balance is the "backbone" of the entire set of audit working papers; it is the key schedule that controls and summarizes all supporting papers. A portion of a working trial balance is shown in Figure 5.6.

[7] See Chapter 16's section on "Post-Audit Responsibilities" for additional auditor responsibilities when it is discovered that an important audit procedure was omitted or that facts existing at the date of the balance sheet were not appropriately considered.

FIGURE 5.6   **Working Trial Balance Abstract**

| | | | Unadjusted Trial | | | |
|---|---|---|---|---|---|---|
| | | Prior Period Balance | Balance | | Adjustments | Balance Sheet |
| Account # | Account Name | 12/31/X4 | DR (CR) | Ref # | DR (CR) | DR (CR) |
| 1001.01 | Cash | 398,743 | 481,413.00 | | | 481,413 |
| 1010.01 | Short-Term Investments | | 167,890.00 | | | 167,890 |
| 1040.01 | Accounts Receivable | 2,053,914 | 2,298,722.00 | | | 2,298,722 |
| 1045.01 | Allowance for Doubtful Accounts | (45,325) | (56,984.00) | AJE-11 | (10,456.00) | (67,440) |
| 1050.01 | Inventories | 2,567,665 | 2,701,814.00 | AJE-12 | (129,799.00) | 2,572,015 |

Process Company, Inc.
Working Trial Balance
For the Period Ended December 31, 20X5

Prepared by ATT

Reviewed by RBS
Page 1

In many audits, the client furnishes the auditors with a working trial balance after all normal end-of-period journal entries have been posted. Before accepting the trial balance for their working papers, the auditors should compare the amounts to the general ledger to determine that the trial balance is prepared accurately.

*Lead Schedules*

Separate **lead schedules** (also called *grouping sheets* or *summary schedules*) are set up to combine similar general ledger accounts, the total of which appears on the working trial balance as a single amount. For example, a lead schedule for Cash might combine the following general ledger accounts: Petty Cash, $500; General bank account, $196,240; Factory Payroll bank account, $500; and Dividend bank account, $1,000. Similar lead schedules would be set up for Accounts Receivable, Inventories, Stockholders' Equity, Net Sales, and other balance sheet or income statement captions.

*Adjusting Journal Entries and Reclassification Entries*

During the course of an audit engagement, the auditors may discover various types of misstatements in the client's financial statements and accounting records. These misstatements may be large or small in amount; they may arise from the omission of transactions or from the use of incorrect amounts; or they may result from improper classification or **cutoff,** or from misinterpretation of transactions. Generally, these misstatements are accidental errors; however, the auditors may find them to be the result of fraud.

To correct **material** errors or fraud discovered in the financial statements and accounting records, the auditors draft **adjusting journal entries (AJEs),** which they recommend for entry in the client's accounting records. In addition, the auditors develop **reclassification journal entries (RJEs)** for items that, although correctly recorded in the accounting records, must be reclassified for fair presentation in the client's financial statements. For example, accounts receivable with large credit balances should be *reclassified* as a liability in the balance sheet. Reclassification entries affect only the financial statement presentation; therefore, they are *not recorded* in the client's accounting records. Reclassification entries appear only on accounting worksheets.

*Supporting Schedules*

Although all types of working papers may loosely be called schedules, auditors prefer to use this term to describe a listing of the elements or details comprising the balance in an asset or liability account at a specific date. Thus, a list of amounts owed to vendors making up the balance of the Trade Accounts Payable account is properly described as a *schedule.*

*Analysis of a Ledger Account*

An analysis of a ledger account is another common type of audit working paper. The purpose of an analysis is to show *the changes* in an asset, liability, equity, revenue, or expense account during the period covered by the audit. If a number of the changes are individually immaterial, they may be recorded as a single item in the analysis working paper. Account analyses are most useful in substantiating those accounts affected by relatively few transactions during the year. Examples include plant asset accounts, long-term debt accounts, capital stock accounts, and retained earnings.

To analyze a ledger account, the auditors first list the beginning balance and indicate the nature of the items comprising this balance. Next, the auditors list and investigate the nature of all debits and credits to the account during the period. These entries, when combined with the beginning balance, produce a figure representing the balance in the account as of the audit date. If any misstatements or omissions of importance are detected during this analysis of the account, the necessary adjusting journal entry approved by the client is entered on the working paper to produce the adjusted balance required for the financial statements.

*Reconciliations*

Frequently, auditors wish to prove the relationship between amounts obtained from different sources. When they do so, they obtain or prepare working papers known as reconciliations. These reconciliations provide evidence as to the accuracy of one or both of the amounts and are important to the audit of many accounts, including cash, accounts receivable, and inventories.

*Computational Working Papers*

Another type of supporting working paper is the computational working paper. The auditors' approach to verifying certain types of accounts and other figures is to make an independent computation and compare their results with the amounts shown by the client's records. Examples of amounts that might be verified by computation are interest expense, depreciation, payroll taxes, income taxes, pension liabilities, and earnings per share.

*Corroborating Documents*

Auditing is not limited to the examination of financial records, and working papers are not confined to schedules and analyses. During the course of an audit, the auditors may gather much purely expository material to substantiate their report. One common example is copies of minutes of directors' and stockholders' meetings. Other examples of **corroborating documents** include copies of articles of incorporation and bylaws; copies of important contracts, bond indentures, and mortgages; memoranda pertaining to examination of records; audit confirmations; and representation letters from the client and from the client's legal counsel.

## Organization of Working Papers

The auditors usually maintain two files of working papers for each client: (1) current files for every completed audit and (2) a permanent file of relatively unchanging data. The current file (as for the *200X* audit) pertains solely to that year's audit; the permanent file contains such things as copies of the articles of incorporation, which are of continuing audit interest.

*The Current Files*

The auditors' report for a particular year is supported by the working papers contained in the current files. Many CPA firms have found it useful to organize the current files around the arrangement of the accounts in the client's financial statements. The administrative working papers usually begin the current files, including a draft of the financial statements and the auditors' report. These working papers are followed by the working trial balance and the adjusting and reclassification entries. The remaining portion of the current files consists of working papers supporting the balances and other representations in the client's

FIGURE 5.7    **Organization of the Current Files**

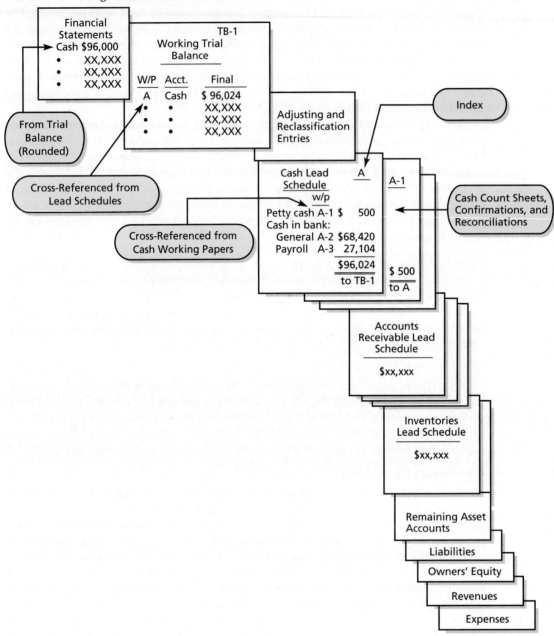

financial statements. It begins with working papers for each asset account and continues with papers for liabilities, owners' equity accounts, and revenue and expense accounts.

Each working paper in a file is assigned an index number, and information is tied together through a system of cross-referencing. In this way, a reviewer may trace back amounts on the working trial balance to the supporting working papers. Figure 5.7 illustrates a system of cross-referencing and a typical arrangement of the current files after the administrative working papers.

*The Permanent File*

The **permanent file** serves three purposes: (1) to refresh the auditors' memories on items applicable over a period of many years; (2) to provide new staff members with a quick summary of the policies and organization of the client; and (3) to preserve working papers on items that show relatively few or no changes, thus eliminating the necessity for their preparation year after year.

Much of the information contained in the permanent file is gathered during the course of the first audit of a client's records. A considerable portion of the time spent on a first audit is devoted to gathering and appraising background information, such as copies of articles of incorporation and bylaws, leases, patent agreements, pension plans, labor contracts, long-term construction contracts, known related parties, charts of accounts, and prior years' tax returns.

Analyses of accounts that show few changes over a period of years are also included in the permanent file. These accounts may include land, buildings, accumulated depreciation, long-term investments, long-term liabilities, capital stock, and other owners' equity accounts. The initial investigation of these accounts must often include the transactions of many years. Once these historical analyses have been brought up to date, the work required in subsequent examinations will be limited to a review of the current year's transactions in these accounts. In this respect, the permanent file is a timesaving device because current changes in such accounts need only be added to the permanent papers without reappearing in the current working papers. Adequate cross-referencing in the working papers, of course, should be provided to show where in the permanent file such information can be found.

## Guidelines for Preparation of Working Papers

We will now summarize in a few short paragraphs our basic guidelines for preparing working papers that will meet current professional standards.

A separate, properly identified working paper should be prepared for each topic. Proper identification of a working paper is accomplished by a heading that includes the name of the client company, a clear description of the information presented, and the applicable date or the period covered. If the working paper was prepared by the client's staff, it should be labeled "PBC" (prepared by client) and appropriately tested.

Complete and specific identification of documents examined, employees interviewed, and sites visited is essential for good working paper practice. The preparer of a working paper should date and sign or initial the working paper; the signatures or initials of the senior, manager, or partner who reviewed the working paper should also appear on the paper.

Working papers should be appropriately referenced and cross-referenced to the working trial balance or relevant lead schedule. Where reference is necessary between working papers, there must be adequate cross-referencing.

The nature of verification work performed by the auditors should be clearly indicated on each working paper. A review of paid purchase invoices, for example, might be supplemented by inspection of the related purchase orders and receiving documents to substantiate the authenticity of the invoices examined; a description of this verification procedure should be included on the working paper. As audit working papers are prepared, the auditors will use several different symbols to identify specific steps in the work performed. These symbols, or **tick marks,** provide a very concise means of indicating the audit procedures applied to particular amounts. Whenever tick marks are employed, they must be accompanied by a legend explaining their meaning.

The working papers should include comments by the auditors indicating their conclusions on each aspect of the work. In other words, the auditors should clearly express the opinion they have formed as a result of having performed the audit procedures summarized in the working paper. Figure 5.8 illustrates such a conclusion related to the audit of the allowance for uncollectible accounts, along with other aspects of a properly prepared working paper.

## Computer-Generated Working Papers

Traditionally, working papers have been prepared in pencil on columnar paper. Today, many working papers are prepared on laptop computers carried by the auditors to the work site. When an adjustment is entered on computer-based working papers, it appears instantly on the appropriate lead schedules, the adjustments schedule, and

FIGURE 5.8   **Preparation of a Working Paper**

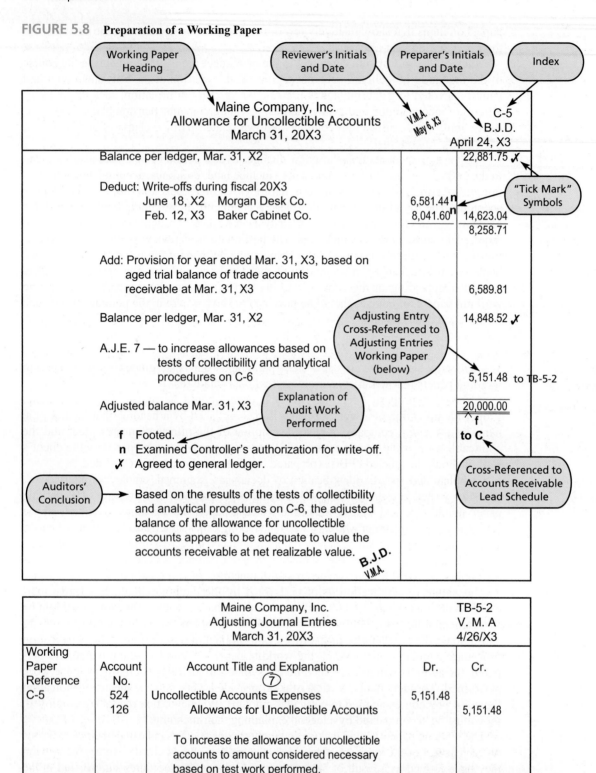

the working trial balance. The necessary cross-references are automatically entered on each schedule. If the adjustment affects taxable income, the income tax expense account and the tax liability are automatically adjusted using the client's marginal tax rate. In addition, all the subtotals, column totals, and cross-footings in the working papers are instantly adjusted.

## Illustrative Case — *Audit Documentation Issues*

Lack of documentation is a continuing issue in peer review findings. Recent AICPA reports indicate the following recurring deficiencies regarding audit documentation:

- Failure to adequately document key audit areas
- Failure to adequately document key elements of the understanding obtained regarding each of the aspects of the client and its environment, including each of the components of internal control and the sources of information from which the understanding was obtained

- Failure to document the assessment of the risks of material misstatement
- Failure to document the overall responses to the assessed risks of material misstatement
- Failure to adequately document the performance of analytical procedures, especially the expectations developed
- Failure to adequately document the audit procedures performed

Automated audit working papers tend to decrease these deficiencies by forcing consistency of performance and review by the audit team.

When working papers are maintained manually, all of these entries and changes must be made by hand with a pencil, an eraser, and a calculator. With a computer, an adjustment that might take a half hour or more to "push through" manual working papers can be entered in a few seconds. Thus, computers have taken much of the "pencil pushing" and the "number crunching" out of working paper preparation.

Many CPA firms are making full use of the document scanning, data linking, networking, and telecommunications capabilities of personal computers. These firms can produce numerous electronic working papers, creating a nearly "paperless audit."

## Review of Audit Working Papers

Working papers are reviewed at every supervisory level of a CPA firm. Senior auditors review the working papers of staff assistants; managers review all working papers prepared by staff assistants and by senior auditors; the partner in charge of the engagement reviews the entire set of working papers. Many CPA firms also require a review by a second partner.

### What Do Reviewers Look For?

All reviewers look to see that the working papers properly document the audit. However, there are differences in the nature of the reviews. The senior's review is the most technical, and it generally is performed promptly after the completion of the individual working paper. Seniors look primarily to see that the staff assistant has performed the audit procedures properly and that the assistant's findings and conclusions are clearly expressed.

The reviews by managers and partners are often performed near the *end* of the engagement, when the reviewer may examine at one time the entire set of working papers. These reviewers are primarily interested in determining that the audit was performed in accordance with generally accepted auditing standards and that the working papers properly support the auditors' report that will be issued on the financial statements. There are several advantages to reviewing all of the working papers at once. The reviewer can determine that the working papers "tie together"—that is, that amounts are properly carried forward from one working paper to another. As we mentioned earlier in the chapter, these reviewers should look critically for any inconsistencies, omissions, or "loose ends" that might later support a plaintiff's allegations of improper auditing. In addition, the reviewer should consider whether the various immaterial discrepancies that were passed without adjustment might *cumulatively* have a material effect upon the financial statements.

The purposes of a *second partner review* are to provide assurance that all the CPA firm's in-house *quality control policies* have been complied with, as well as to provide a "second opinion" that the audit was performed in accordance with generally accepted auditing standards. The second partner review, sometimes called a *quality review* or a *cold review,* usually is performed by a partner with no personal or professional ties to the audit client. Multioffice CPA firms sometimes bring in a partner from another office to perform the second partner review. Not until all these reviewers have "signed off" on the audit working papers is the CPA firm's name signed to the auditors' report.

## Chapter Summary

This chapter focused on the concept of sufficient appropriate audit evidence and the manner in which this evidence is documented in the audit working papers. To summarize:

1. Auditing standards require the auditors to obtain sufficient appropriate audit evidence to support their audit opinion. Sufficiency is the measure of the quantity of the evidence. Appropriateness of evidence relates to its relevance and its reliability in providing support for or detecting misstatements in account balances, transactions, and disclosures. Sufficiency and appropriateness are interrelated and lead to audit decisions on the *nature* of audit evidence that is collected, its *timing,* and its *extent.*

2. Audit evidence is gathered by the auditors to reduce audit risk—the risk that the auditors may fail to modify their opinion on financial statements that are materially misstated. Since financial statements consist of a series of assertions by management, the auditors must obtain sufficient appropriate audit evidence about each significant financial statement assertion.

3. At the account balance, class of transaction, and disclosure levels, audit risk consists of (*a*) the risk that a material misstatement in an assertion has occurred (composed of inherent risk and control risk) and (*b*) the risk that the auditors will not detect the misstatement (detection risk). Audit evidence is gathered by the auditors to *assess* the risk of material misstatement and to *restrict* detection risk.

4. Auditors perform audit procedures to obtain audit evidence that will allow them to draw reasonable conclusions as to whether the client's financial statements follow generally accepted accounting principles. An audit consists of (*a*) risk assessment procedures (to obtain an understanding of the client and its environment), (*b*) tests of controls (to test the operating effectiveness of controls), and (*c*) substantive procedures (to detect material misstatements in relevant assertions). Tests performed in response to the auditors' risk assessments are referred to as *further audit procedures.*

5. Substantive procedures include tests of details and analytical procedures. Tests of details ordinarily involve testing recorded support for account balances, transactions, and disclosures. Substantive analytical procedures often provide evidence about account balances, transactions, and disclosures through analyzing relationships among data. Analytical procedures are also performed to assist the auditor in risk assessment and as an overall review of the financial information near completion of the audit.

6. Auditors must be especially careful in considering financial statement accounts that are affected by estimates made by management, such as the allowance for doubtful accounts. The inherent risk of these types of accounts is generally much greater than for other financial statement accounts.

7. Audit documentation is the connecting link between the client's accounting records and the auditors' report. Such documentation is the property of the auditors and is primarily used to illustrate the auditors' compliance with professional standards and to support the auditors' opinion. Other functions of audit documentation include providing assistance in planning and performing the audit; facilitating supervision and review of audit work; providing a record of matters relevant to future audits; enabling other auditors to conduct peer reviews and inspections; and assisting successor auditors.

## Key Terms Introduced or Emphasized in Chapter 5*

**Adjusting journal entries (AJEs) (162)**   Journal entries designed to correct misstatements found in a client's records.

**Administrative working papers (161)**   Working papers specifically designed to help the auditors in the planning and administration of the engagement, such as audit programs, internal control questionnaires and flowcharts, time budgets, and engagement memoranda.

**Appropriate (141)**   A measure of the quality of the evidence obtained.

**Audit evidence (141)**   Any information that corroborates or refutes the auditors' premise that the financial statements present fairly the client's financial position and operating results.

**Audit file (160)**   The unit of storage for a specific audit engagement. The audit documentation for each year's audit of a company is included in its audit file.

**Audit risk (137)**   The risk that the auditors may unknowingly fail to appropriately modify their opinion on financial statements that are materially misstated.

**Common-size financial statements (152)**   Financial statements that present each amount as a percentage of some financial statement base. As an example, a common-size income statement presents all revenues and expenses as a percentage of net sales. See *vertical analysis*.

**Control risk (140)**   The risk that a material misstatement that could occur in an account will not be prevented or detected on a timely basis by internal control.

**Corroborating documents (163)**   Documents and memoranda included in the working papers that substantiate representations contained in the client's financial statements. These working papers include audit confirmations, lawyers' letters, copies of contracts, copies of minutes of directors' and stockholders' meetings, and representation letters from the client's management.

**Cross-sectional analysis (152)**   A technique that involves comparing the client's ratios for the current year with those of similar firms in the same industry.

**Cutoff (162)**   The process of determining that transactions occurring near the balance sheet date are assigned to the proper accounting period.

**Date of the auditor's report (148)**   The date on which the auditor has obtained sufficient appropriate audit evidence to support the opinion on the financial statements or other financial information being reported upon. The audit report is ordinarily dated as of this date.

**Detection risk (140)**   The risk that the auditors' procedures will lead them to conclude that a financial statement assertion is not materially misstated when in fact such misstatement does exist.

**Documentation completion date (161)**   The date on which documentation should be completed. This is within 60 days of the delivery date.

**Electronic data interchange (EDI) (144)**   A system in which data are exchanged electronically between the computers of different companies. In an EDI system, source documents are replaced with electronic transactions created in a standard format.

**Estimation transaction (140)**   A transaction involving management's judgments or assumptions, such as determining the allowance for doubtful accounts, establishing warranty reserves, and assessing assets for impairment.

**Experienced auditor (159)**   For purposes of audit documentation, an individual who has *practical audit experience* and a reasonable understanding of (1) audit processes; (2) *Statements on Auditing Standards* and applicable legal and regulatory requirements; (3) the business environment in which the entity operates; and (4) auditing and financial reporting issues relevant to the entity's industry. Having *practical audit experience* is equivalent to possessing the competencies and skills that would have enabled the experienced auditor to perform the audit.

**Further audit procedures (149)**   The additional procedures that are performed based on the results of the auditors' risk assessment procedures. Such procedures include additional tests of controls (if needed) and substantive tests of account balances, classes of transactions, and disclosures.

**Horizontal analysis (152)**   A technique that involves comparing financial statement amounts and ratios for a particular company from year to year.

**Inherent risk (139)**   The risk of material misstatement of a financial statement assertion, assuming there were no related controls.

**Lead schedule (162)**   A working paper with columnar headings similar to those in a working trial balance, set up to combine similar ledger accounts, the total of which appears in the working trial balance as a single amount.

\* Note: Figure 5.3 defines a number of audit procedures. Those terms are not repeated in this glossary.

**Material (162)**   Of substantial importance. Significant enough to affect evaluations or decisions by users of financial statements. Information that should be disclosed so that financial statements constitute a fair presentation. Involves both qualitative and quantitative considerations.

**Minutes (159)**   A formal record of the issues discussed and actions taken in meetings of stockholders or the board of directors.

**Nonroutine transaction (139)**   A transaction that occurs only periodically, such as counting and pricing inventory, calculating depreciation expense, or determining prepaid expenses.

**Permanent file (164)**   A file of working papers containing relatively unchanging data, such as copies of articles of incorporation and bylaws; copies of minutes of directors', stockholders', and committee meetings; and analyses of such ledger accounts as land and retained earnings.

**Physical evidence (146)**   Evidence derived by the auditors from physical examination.

**Reclassification journal entry (RJE) (162)**   A working paper entry drafted by the auditors to assure fair presentation of the client's financial statements, such as an entry to transfer accounts receivable credit balances to the current liabilities section of the client's balance sheet. Since reclassification entries do not correct misstatements in the client company's accounting records, they are not posted to the client's ledger accounts.

**Related party transaction (158)**   A transaction in which one party has the ability to influence significantly the management or operating policies of the other party, to the extent that one of the transacting parties might be prevented from pursuing fully its own separate interests.

**Relevant assertion (138)**   A financial statement assertion that has a reasonable possibility of containing a misstatement or misstatements that would cause the financial statements to be materially misstated. The determination of whether an assertion is a relevant assertion is made without regard to the effect of controls.

**Report release date (160)**   The date the auditor grants the client permission to use the auditor's report. This date is ordinarily close to the audit report date.

**Representation letter (148)**   A single letter or separate letters prepared by officers of the client company at the auditors' request setting forth certain representations about the company's financial position or operations.

**Risk assessment procedures (149)**   Procedures performed by the auditor to obtain an understanding of the entity and its environment, including its internal control. Risk assessment procedures ordinarily include inquiries of management and others within the entity, analytical procedures, and observation and inspection. Risk assessment procedures often provide the auditors with a limited amount of evidence about the operating effectiveness of the client's internal control.

**Routine transaction (139)**   A transaction for a recurring financial activity recorded in the accounting records in the normal course of business, such as sales, purchases, cash receipts, cash disbursements, and payroll.

**Specialist (146)**   A person or firm possessing special skill or knowledge in a field other than accounting or auditing, such as an actuary.

**Substantive procedures (tests) (149)**   Procedures performed by the auditor to detect material misstatements in account balances, classes of transactions, and disclosures.

**Sufficient (141)**   A measure of the quantity of the audit evidence required.

**Tests of controls (149)**   Procedures performed by the auditor to test the operating effectiveness of controls in preventing or detecting material misstatements at the relevant assertion level.

**Tick mark (165)**   A symbol used in working papers by the auditor to indicate a specific step in the work performed. Whenever tick marks are used, they must be accompanied by a legend explaining their meaning.

**Vertical analysis (152)**   A form of analysis that presents financial statement amounts for a period as a percentage of some financial statement base. This analysis involves the preparation of *common-size financial statements.*

**Working papers (159)**   Papers that document the evidence gathered by auditors to show the work they have done, the methods and procedures they have followed, and the conclusions they have developed in an audit of financial statements or other type of engagement.

**Working trial balance (161)**   A working paper that lists the balances of accounts in the general ledger for the current and the previous year and also provides columns for the auditors' adjustments and reclassifications and for the final amounts that will appear in the financial statements.

## Review Questions

5–1. Describe the relationship between detection risk and audit risk.

5–2. Identify and describe the two components of the risk of material misstatement.

5–3. Define inherent risk. Can the auditors reduce inherent risk by performing audit procedures?

5–4. Distinguish among routine, nonroutine, and estimation transactions. Include an example of each.

5–5. Distinguish between the component of audit risk that the auditors gather evidence to assess versus the component of audit risk that they collect evidence to restrict.

5–6. In a conversation with you, Mark Rogers, CPA, claims that both the *sufficiency* and the *appropriateness* of audit evidence are a matter of judgment in every audit. Do you agree? Explain.

5–7. "The best means of verification of cash, inventory, office equipment, and nearly all other assets is a physical count of the units; only a physical count gives the auditors complete assurance as to the accuracy of the amounts listed on the balance sheet." Evaluate this statement.

5–8. As part of the verification of accounts receivable as of the balance sheet date, the auditors might inspect copies of sales invoices. Similarly, as part of the verification of accounts payable, the auditors might inspect purchase invoices. Which of these two types of invoices do you think represents the stronger type of evidence? Why?

5–9. In verifying the asset accounts Notes Receivable and Marketable Securities, the auditors examined notes receivable and stock certificates. Which of these documents represents the stronger type of evidence? Why?

5–10. When in the course of an audit might the auditor find it useful to apply analytical procedures?

5–11. Give at least four examples of *specialists* whose findings might provide appropriate evidence for the independent auditors.

5–12. What are the major purposes of obtaining representation letters from audit clients?

5–13. The cost of an audit might be significantly reduced if the auditors relied upon a representation letter from the client instead of observing the physical counting of inventory. Would this use of a representation letter be an acceptable means of reducing the cost of an audit?

5–14. List and briefly describe the three approaches to auditing accounting estimates that are included in a client's financial statements.

5–15. "In deciding upon the type of evidence to be gathered in support of a given item on the financial statements, the auditors should not be influenced by the differences in cost of obtaining alternative forms of evidence." Do you agree? Explain.

5–16. When auditing a client's asset that is valued at fair value, would the auditors expect that asset to be valued at the price to purchase the asset as of the measurement date, or the price that would be received to sell it? Explain.

5–17. What are *related party transactions?*

5–18. What disclosures should be made in the financial statements regarding material related party transactions?

5–19. Evaluate the following statement: "Identifying related parties and obtaining a client representation letter are two required audit procedures normally performed on the last day of fieldwork."

5–20. What are the major functions of audit working papers?

5–21. Why are the prior year's audit working papers a useful reference to staff assistants during the current audit?

5–22. List the major types of audit working papers and give a brief explanation of each. For example: One type of audit working paper is an account analysis. This working paper shows the changes that occurred in a given account during the period under audit. By analyzing an account, the auditors determine its nature and content.

5–23. "Audit working papers are the property of the auditors, who may destroy the papers, sell them, or give them away." Criticize this quotation.

5–24. Describe a situation in which a set of audit working papers might be used by third parties to support a charge of gross negligence against the auditors.

5–25. Should the working trial balance prepared by the auditors include revenue and expense accounts if the balances of these accounts for the audit year have been closed into retained earnings prior to the auditors' arrival? Explain.

5–26. Why are the final figures from the prior year's audit included in a working trial balance or lead schedule?

5–27. Should the auditors prepare adjusting journal entries to correct all errors they discover in the accounting records for the year under audit? Explain.

5–28. Explain the meaning of the term *permanent file* as used in connection with audit working papers. What kinds of information are usually included in the permanent file?

5–29. List several rules to be observed in the preparation of working papers that reflect current professional practice.

5–30. "I have finished my testing of footings of the cash journals," said the assistant auditor to the senior auditor. "Shall I state in the working papers the periods for which I verified footings, or should I just list the totals of the receipts and disbursements I have proved to be correct?" Prepare an answer to the assistant's question, stressing the reasoning involved.

5–31. What is the purpose of a "second partner review"? What should be the extent of the second partner's association with the engagement being reviewed?

5–32. In their review of audit working papers, what do managers and partners look for?

## Questions Requiring Analysis

**LO 1** 5–33. Financial statements contain a number of assertions about account balances, classes of transactions, and disclosures.

    *a.* Identify who makes these assertions.

    *b.* List and describe each of the assertions regarding each financial statement component.

**LO 1** 5–34. Marion Watson & Co., CPAs, is planning its audit procedures for its tests of the valuation of inventories of East Coast Manufacturing Co. The auditors on the engagement have assessed inherent risk and control risk for valuation of inventories at 100 percent and 50 percent, respectively.

*Required:*

    *a.* Calculate the appropriate level of detection risk for the audit of this assertion, given that the auditors wish to restrict audit risk for the assertion to 3 percent.

    *b.* Calculate the appropriate level of detection risk for the audit of this assertion, given that the auditors wish to restrict audit risk for the assertion to 5 percent.

**LO 4** 5–35. In an audit of financial statements, the auditors gather various types of audit evidence. List seven major types of evidence and provide a procedural example of each.

**LO 3, 4** 5–36. Comment on the reliability of each of the following examples of audit evidence. Arrange your answer in the form of a separate paragraph for each item. Explain fully the reasoning employed in judging the reliability of each item.

    *a.* Copies of client's sales invoices.

    *b.* Auditors' independent computation of earnings per share.

    *c.* Paid checks returned with a bank statement.

    *d.* Response from customer of client addressed to auditors' office confirming amount owed to client at balance sheet date.

    *e.* Representation letter signed by controller of client company stating that all liabilities of which she has knowledge are reflected in the company's accounts.

**LO 4** 5–37. Analytical procedures are extremely useful throughout the audit.

*Required:*

    *a.* Explain how analytical procedures are useful in:

        (1) The risk assessment stage of the audit.

        (2) The substantive procedures stage of the audit.

        (3) Near the end of the audit.

    *b.* List the five sources of information that are available to the auditors in developing expectations for analytical procedures.

    *c.* List and describe four techniques that may be used by the auditors in developing expectations for analytical procedures.

**LO 4** 5–38. When analytical procedures disclose unexpected changes in financial relationships relative to prior years, the auditors consider the possible reasons for the changes. Give several possible reasons for the following significant changes in relationships:

    *a.* The rate of inventory turnover (ratio of cost of goods sold to average inventory) has declined from the prior year's rate.

    *b.* The number of days' sales in accounts receivable has increased over the prior year.

**LO 4** 5–39. Auditors are required on every engagement to obtain a representation letter from the client.

*Required:*
    *a.* What are the objectives of the client's representation letter?
    *b.* Who should prepare and sign the client's representation letter?
    *c.* When should the client's representation letter be obtained?

**LO 4** 5–40. What would you accept as satisfactory documentary evidence in support of entries in the following?

    *a.* Sales journal.
    *b.* Sales returns journal.
    *c.* Voucher or invoice register.
    *d.* Payroll journal.
    *e.* Check register.

**LO 6, 7, 8** 5–41. You are instructing an inexperienced staff assistant on her first auditing assignment. She is to examine an account. An analysis of the account has been prepared by the client for inclusion in the audit working papers. Prepare a list of the comments, commentaries, and notations that the staff assistant should make or have made on the account analysis to provide an adequate working paper as evidence of her examination. (Do not include a description of audit procedures applicable to the account.)

(AICPA, adapted)

**LO 6, 8** 5–42. The partnership of Smith, Frank & Clark, a CPA firm, has been the auditor of Greenleaf, Inc., for many years. During the annual audit of the financial statements for the year ended December 31, 20X2, a dispute developed over whether certain disclosures should be made in the financial statements. The dispute resulted in Smith, Frank & Clark's being dismissed and Greenleaf's engaging another CPA firm. Greenleaf demanded that Smith, Frank & Clark turn over all working papers applicable to the Greenleaf audits or face a lawsuit. Smith, Frank & Clark refused. Greenleaf has instituted a suit against Smith, Frank & Clark to obtain the working papers.

*Required:*
    *a.* Will Greenleaf succeed in its suit? Explain.
    *b.* Discuss the rationale underlying the rule of law applicable to the ownership of audit working papers.

(AICPA, adapted)

**LO 7, 8** 5–43. "Working papers should contain facts and nothing but facts," said student A. "Not at all," replied student B. "The audit working papers may also include expressions of opinion. Facts are not always available to settle all issues." "In my opinion," said student C, "a mixture of facts and opinions in the audit working papers would be most confusing if the papers were produced as a means of supporting the auditors' position when their report has been challenged." Evaluate the issues underlying these arguments.

**LO 6** 5–44. At 12 o'clock, when the plant whistle sounded, George Green, an assistant auditor, had his desk completely covered with various types of working papers. Green stopped work immediately, but not wanting to leave the desk with such a disorderly appearance, he took a few minutes to sort the papers into proper order, place them in a neat pile, and weight them down with a heavy paperweight. He then departed for lunch. The auditor-in-charge, who had been observing what was going on, was critical of the assistant's actions. What do you think was the basis for criticism by the auditor-in-charge?

## Objective Questions

All applicable questions are available with McGraw-Hill's *Connect*<sup>TM</sup> *Accounting.* ▓**connect** |ACCOUNTING

5–45. **Multiple Choice Questions**

Select the best answer for each of the following questions. Explain the reasons for your selection.

**LO 1**
    *a.* Which of the following is *not* a financial statement assertion made by management?
        (1) Existence of recorded assets and liabilities.
        (2) Completeness of recorded assets and liabilities.
        (3) Valuation of assets and liabilities.
        (4) Effectiveness of internal control.

LO 2  b. Which of the following business characteristics is *not* indicative of high inherent risk?

(1) Operating results that are highly sensitive to economic factors.

(2) Large likely misstatements detected in prior audits.

(3) Substantial turnover of management.

(4) A large amount of assets.

LO 4  c. As part of their audit, auditors obtain a representation letter from their client. Which of the following is *not* a valid purpose of such a letter?

(1) To increase the efficiency of the audit by eliminating the need for other audit procedures.

(2) To remind the client's management of its primary responsibility for the financial statements.

(3) To document in the audit working papers the client's responses to certain verbal inquiries made by the auditors during the engagement.

(4) To provide evidence in those areas dependent upon management's future intentions.

LO 4  d. Which of the following statements best describes why auditors investigate related party transactions?

(1) Related party transactions generally are illegal acts.

(2) The substance of related party transactions may differ from their form.

(3) All related party transactions must be eliminated as a step in preparing consolidated financial statements.

(4) Related party transactions are a form of management fraud.

LO 3  e. Of the following, which is the *least* reliable type of audit evidence?

(1) Confirmations mailed by outsiders to the auditors.

(2) Correspondence between the auditors and suppliers.

(3) Copies of sales invoices inspected by the auditors.

(4) Canceled checks returned in the year-end bank statement directly to the client.

LO 4  f. Analytical procedures are most likely to detect:

(1) Weaknesses of a material nature in internal control.

(2) Unusual transactions.

(3) Noncompliance with prescribed control activities.

(4) Improper separation of accounting and other financial duties.

LO 4  g. Which of the following is *not* a primary approach to auditing an accounting estimate?

(1) Review and test management's process for developing the estimate.

(2) Review subsequent transactions.

(3) Confirm the amounts.

(4) Develop an independent estimate.

LO 6  h. A primary purpose of the audit working papers is to:

(1) Aid the auditors by providing a list of required procedures.

(2) Provide a point of reference for future audit engagements.

(3) Support the underlying concepts included in the preparation of the basic financial statements.

(4) Support the auditors' opinion.

LO 9  i. In what section of the audit working papers would a long-term lease agreement be filed?

(1) Current working paper file.

(2) Permanent working paper file.

(3) Lead schedule file.

(4) Corroborating documents file.

LO 6  j. Which of the following is *not* a function of audit working papers?

(1) Assist management in illustrating that the financial statements are in accordance with generally accepted accounting principles.

(2) Assist audit team members responsible for supervision in reviewing the work.

(3) Assist auditors in planning future engagements.

(4) Assist peer reviewers and inspectors in performing their roles.

**LO 4**    *k.* In using the work of a specialist, the auditors referred to the specialist's findings in their report. This would be an appropriate reporting practice if the:

(1) Client is not familiar with the professional certification, personal reputation, or particular competence of the specialist.

(2) Auditors, as a result of the specialist's findings, give a qualified opinion on the financial statements.

(3) Client understands the auditors' corroborative use of the specialist's findings in relation to the representations in the financial statements.

(4) Auditors, as a result of the specialist's findings, decide to indicate a division of responsibility with the specialist.

**LO 8**    *l.* A difference of opinion concerning accounting and auditing matters relative to a particular phase of the audit arises between an assistant auditor and the auditor responsible for the engagement. After appropriate consultation, the assistant auditor asks to be disassociated from the resolution of the matter. The working papers would probably:

(1) Remain silent on the matter since it is an internal matter of the auditing firm.

(2) Note that the assistant auditor is completely dissociated from responsibility for the auditors' opinion.

(3) Document the additional work required, since all disagreements of this type will require expanded substantive procedures.

(4) Document the assistant auditor's position and how the difference of opinion was resolved.

**LO 1, 2, 4**    5–46.    **Simulation**

Auditors consider financial statement assertions to identify appropriate audit procedures. For items *a* through *f,* match each assertion with the statement that most closely approximates its meaning. Each statement may be used only once.

| Assertion | Statement |
|---|---|
| *a.* Completeness | 1. There is such an asset. |
| *b.* Cutoff | 2. The company legally owns the assets. |
| *c.* Existence and occurrence | 3. All assets have been recorded. |
| *d.* Presentation and disclosure | 4. Transactions are recorded in the correct accounting period. |
| *e.* Rights and obligations | 5. Assets are recorded at proper amounts. |
| *f.* Valuation | 6. Assets are properly classified. |

Auditors perform audit procedures to obtain audit evidence that will allow them to draw reasonable conclusions as to whether the client's financial statements follow generally accepted accounting principles. Match each audit procedure with its type. Each type of audit procedure is used; one is used twice.

| Audit Procedures | Type of Audit Procedure |
|---|---|
| *g.* Prepare a flowchart of internal control over sales | 7. Analytical procedures. |
| *h.* Calculate the ratio of bad debt expense to credit sales | 8. Tests of controls. |
| *i.* Determine whether disbursements are properly approved | 9. Risk assessment procedures (other than analytical procedures). |
| *j.* Confirm accounts receivable | 10. Test of details of account balances, transactions, or disclosures. |
| *k.* Compare current financial information with comparable prior periods | |

**LO 1, 2, 3**   5-47. State whether each of the following statements is correct or incorrect concerning audit risk and its components—inherent risk, control risk, and detection risk.

a. The risk of material misstatement is composed of the three components of audit risk.

b. Inherent risk is the possibility of material misstatement before considering the client's internal control.

c. Less control risk means an increase in the risk of material misstatement.

d. Detection risk does not exist when no audit is performed.

e. Rather than restrict detection risk through the performance of more substantive procedures, auditors assess it.

f. Absent any other changes, an increase in the risk of material misstatement results in an increase in audit risk.

g. Audit risk refers to the possibility that the auditors may unknowingly fail to appropriately modify their opinion on financial statements that are materially or immaterially misstated.

h. Both inherent risk and control risk exist independently of the audit of financial statements.

**LO 4**   5-48. Reply to the following questions relating to analytical procedures.

a. Performing analytical procedures may help an auditor to:

(1) Achieve audit objectives related to a particular assertion.

(2) Develop an effective system of quality control.

(3) Meet PCAOB requirements that analytical procedures be performed relating to every major account.

(4) Increase the level of detection risk.

b. Analytical procedures performed near the end of the audit to assist the auditor in forming an overall conclusion on the financial statements are aimed primarily at:

(1) Gathering evidence concerning account balances that have not changed from the prior year.

(2) Retesting internal control procedures.

(3) Considering unusual or unexpected account balances that were not previously identified.

(4) Performing a test of transactions to corroborate management's financial statement assertions.

c. What type of analytical procedure would an auditor most likely use in developing relationships among balance sheet accounts?

(1) Trend analysis.

(2) A detailed test of balance analysis.

(3) Ratio analysis.

(4) Risk analysis.

d. The cost of analytical procedures in terms of time needed to perform, when compared to other tests, is ordinarily considered:

(1) Low.

(2) High.

(3) Identical.

(4) Indeterminate.

e. In developing an expectation for analytical procedures, the auditors are least likely to consider:

(1) Financial information for comparable prior periods.

(2) Relationships between financial information and relevant nonfinancial data.

(3) Anticipated costs of audit completion.

(4) Relationships among elements of financial information within a period.

# Problems

**All applicable problems are available with McGraw-Hill's *Connect™ Accounting*. ■ connect |ACCOUNTING**

**LO 1** 5–49. Audit risk should be considered when planning and performing an audit of financial statements in accordance with generally accepted auditing standards.

*Required:*
   *a.* Define audit risk.
   *b.* Describe its components of inherent risk, control risk, and detection risk.
   *c.* Explain the interrelationship among these components.
   *d.* Which (if any) of these components is completely a function of the sufficiency of the evidence gathered by the auditors' procedures? Explain your answer.
   *e.* Comment on the following: "Since cash is often less than 1 percent of total assets, inherent and control risk for that account must be low. Accordingly, detection risk should be established at a high level."

(AICPA, adapted)

**LO 3, 4** 5–50. Assume that the auditors find serious weaknesses in the internal control of Oak Canyon, Inc., a producer and distributor of fine wines. Would these internal control weaknesses cause the auditors to rely more or less upon each of the following types of evidence during their audit of Oak Canyon?

   *a.* Documents created and used only within the organization.
   *b.* Physical evidence.
   *c.* Evidence provided by specialists.
   *d.* Analytical procedures.
   *e.* Accounting records.

*Required:* For each of the above five items, state your conclusion and explain fully the underlying reasoning.

**LO 3, 4** 5–51. During your examination of the accounts receivable of Hope Ranch, a new client, you notice that one account is much larger than the rest, and you therefore decide to examine the evidence supporting this customer's account. Comment on the relative reliability and adequacy of the following types of evidence:

   *a.* Computer printout from accounts receivable subsidiary ledger.
   *b.* Copies of sales invoices in amount of the receivable.
   *c.* Purchase orders received from customer.
   *d.* Shipping documents describing the articles sold.
   *e.* Letter received by client from customer acknowledging the correctness of the receivable in the amount shown on client's accounting records.
   *f.* Letter received by auditors directly from customer acknowledging the correctness of the amount shown as receivable on client's accounting records.

**LO 4** 5–52. Trend analysis, common-size financial statements, and ratios are presented for the Brody Corporation in Figure 5.4. Assume that you are auditing Brody's financial statements for the year ended 12/31/X8. You have performed tests of controls over the recording of gross sales and believe that the system is operating effectively and that 7 percent represents an accurate estimate of the increase in gross sales for 20X8 over the amount for 20X7. You should also assume that the financial statements for 20X6 and 20X7 are not misstated.

*Required:*
   *a.* Analyze Figure 5.4 and identify any accounts that appear to represent significant variations from what one might expect. For each of the accounts, identify another account that might also be out of line due to the manner in which the double-entry bookkeeping system records transactions.
   *b.* Identify any ratios that appear to represent significant variations from what one might expect. For each ratio, identify the financial statement account or accounts that may be misstated.

**LO 5** 5–53. Included in the financial statements are a variety of accounting estimates (e.g., allowance for doubtful accounts, obsolete inventory, warranty liability). Audit procedures must be designed to obtain evidence about the assertions of management related to all accounts, including those based on accounting estimates.

*Required:*

    *a.* List three approaches to auditing accounting estimates. Provide an example of how an auditor might apply each of the three approaches in auditing the allowance for doubtful accounts, which management has established at 1 percent of credit sales.

    *b.* Discuss the meaning of the valuation or allocation assertion as it relates to the allowance for doubtful accounts.

    *c.* Discuss factors that bear on whether the allowance for doubtful accounts is likely to be an account with high inherent risk.

**LO 4, 8**    5–54.    Criticize the following working paper that you are reviewing as senior auditor on the December 31 audit of Pratt Company.

---

### Pratt Company
### Cash

| | | |
|---|---|---|
| Per bank | $44,874.50√ | |
| Deposit in transit | 5,843.10① | |
| Bank charges | (2.80)② | |
| Outstanding checks | | |
|     1,246.40√ | | |
|     3,412.72√ | | |
|     840.00√ | | |
|     1,013.60③ | | |
|     1,200.00③ | | |
|     967.50Y | | 8,680.22 |
| Per ledger | *f* | $42,034.58√ |

*f* Footed column

√ Verified

①The client saved a copy of the deposit slip that is filled out. Per discussion with client, this represents cash sales on 12/31/X0. I agreed totals to the Cash Receipts Journal on 12/31/X0. Properly posted on bank statement as having been received by bank on 1/9/X1.

②Represents December bank service charge. Agreed charge to December bank statement in which bank charged client $2.80. Recorded as cash disbursement in January of 20X1.

③Per client, check written (to pay account receivable) before year-end, but not mailed until 1/2/X1 because on 12/31/X0 the last office mail was picked up at 3 p.m. due to year-end party of mail room employees.

*J.M.W.*

*1-15-X1*

---

**LO 4**    5–55.    Marilyn Terrill is the senior auditor for the audit of Uden Supply Company for the year ended December 31, 20X4. In planning the audit, Marilyn is attempting to develop expectations for planning analytical procedures based on the financial information for prior years and her knowledge of the business and the industry, including:

1. Based on economic conditions, she believes that the increase in sales for the current year should approximate the historical trend.

2. Based on her knowledge of industry trends, she believes that the gross profit for 20X4 should be about 2 percent less than the percentage for 20X3.

3. Based on her knowledge of regulations, she is aware that the effective tax rate for the company for 20X4 has been reduced by 5 percent from that in 20X3.

4. Based on a review of the general ledger, she determined that average depreciable assets have increased by 10 percent.

5. Based on her knowledge of economic conditions, she is aware that the effective interest rate on the company's line of credit for 20X4 was approximately 12 percent. The average outstanding balance of the line of credit is $2,300,000. This line of credit is the company's only interest-bearing debt.

6. Based on her discussions with management and her knowledge of the industry, she believes that the amount of other expenses should be consistent with the trends from prior years.

Comparative income statement information for Uden Supply Company is presented in the accompanying table.

| | 20X1 Audited | 20X2 Audited | 20X3 Audited | 20X4 Expected |
|---|---|---|---|---|
| **UDEN SUPPLY COMPANY** Comparative Income Statements Years Ended December 20X1, 20X2, and 20X3 (Thousands) | | | | |
| Sales | 8,700 | 9,400 | 10,100 | _____ |
| Cost of goods sold | 6,000 | 6,500 | 7,000 | _____ |
| Gross profit | 2,700 | 2,900 | 3,100 | _____ |
| Sales commissions | 610 | 660 | 710 | _____ |
| Advertising | 175 | 190 | 202 | _____ |
| Salaries | 1,061 | 1,082 | 1,103 | _____ |
| Payroll taxes | 184 | 192 | 199 | _____ |
| Employee benefits | 167 | 174 | 181 | _____ |
| Rent | 60 | 61 | 62 | _____ |
| Depreciation | 60 | 63 | 66 | _____ |
| Supplies | 26 | 28 | 30 | _____ |
| Utilities | 21 | 22 | 23 | _____ |
| Legal and accounting | 34 | 37 | 40 | _____ |
| Miscellaneous | 12 | 13 | 14 | _____ |
| Interest expense | 210 | 228 | 240 | _____ |
| Net income before taxes | 80 | 150 | 230 | _____ |
| Income taxes | 18 | 33 | 50 | _____ |
| Net income | 62 | 117 | 180 | _____ |

**Required:**

a. Describe the purpose of analytical procedures performed in the risk assessment stage of the audit.

b. Develop the expected amounts for 20X4 for each of the income statement items.

c. Uden's unaudited financial statements for the current year show a 31 percent gross profit rate. Assuming that this represents a misstatement from the amount that you developed as an expectation, calculate the estimated effect of this misstatement on net income before taxes for 20X4.

d. Indicate whether you believe that the difference calculated in part (c) is material. Explain your answer.

**In-Class Team Case**    **LO 4**    5–56. Houseco, an audit client of Jones, CPA, for the past five years, is a manufacturer of various household products. Approximately four years ago, Houseco developed a better toaster than had been available and sales took off, especially during the most recent two years, 20X7 and 20X8. Currently, the company controls approximately 25 percent of the toaster market in the United States. In addition, the company manufactures other products, including vacuum cleaners, floor polishers, and electric fondue pots.

Much of the increased sales performance is due to Donald Skaldon, who became the chief executive officer in 20X4. Donald and several other officers were able to accomplish a leveraged stock buyout in 20X6. This seems to have worked out very well since Donald suggests that his net worth grew from less than $300,000 to well over $5 million due to increases in the value of the common stock he holds in the company. He is also excited since the company's unaudited results show earnings per share of $1.21, one cent more than the most optimistic analysts had projected. He points out to Jones that sales are up over 38 percent compared to the previous year and net income has increased by 54 percent. All is well.

**Houseco Balance Sheet**

| | Dollars (000s Omitted) | | | Vertical Analysis | | | Horizontal Analysis | |
|---|---|---|---|---|---|---|---|---|
| | 12/31/X6 (Audited) | 12/31/X7 (Audited) | 12/31/X8 (Unaudited) | 12/31/X6 (Audited) | 12/31/X7 (Audited) | 12/31/X8 (Unaudited) | (X7–X6)/X6 (Audited) | (X8–X7)/X7 (Unaudited) |
| **Assets** | | | | | | | | |
| Cash | 63 | 514 | 885 | 0% | 1% | 1% | 716% | 72% |
| Accounts receivable | 14,402 | 27,801 | 51,076 | 33% | 43% | 43% | 93% | 84% |
| Inventories—RM | 2,682 | 9,182 | 18,049 | 6% | 14% | 15% | 242% | 97% |
| Inventories—WIP | 491 | 638 | 4,151 | 1% | 1% | 4% | 30% | 551% |
| Inventories—FG | 6,589 | 9,757 | 16,935 | 15% | 15% | 14% | 48% | 74% |
| Total inventories | 9,762 | 19,577 | 39,153 | 23% | 30% | 33% | 101% | 100% |
| Other current assets | 708 | 1,449 | 3,015 | 2% | 2% | 3% | 105% | 108% |
| Total current assets | 24,935 | 49,341 | 94,111 | 58% | 76% | 80% | 98% | 91% |
| Fixed assets (net) | 18,267 | 15,900 | 24,029 | 42% | 24% | 20% | (13%) | 51% |
| Total assets | 43,202 | 65,241 | 118,140 | 100% | 100% | 100% | 51% | 81% |
| **Liability and Equity** | | | | | | | | |
| Accounts payable | 7,344 | 15,072 | 13,288 | 17% | 23% | 11% | 105% | (12%) |
| Accrued liabilities | 3,127 | 5,468 | 4,710 | 7% | 8% | 4% | 75% | (14%) |
| Current portion L/T debt | 2,707 | 900 | 1,250 | 6% | 1% | 1% | (67%) | 39% |
| Income taxes payable | 1,554 | 2,619 | 3,782 | 4% | 4% | 3% | 69% | 44% |
| Total current liabilities | 14,732 | 24,059 | 23,030 | 34% | 37% | 19% | 63% | (4%) |
| Bank debt | 14,800 | 19,841 | 62,057 | 34% | 30% | 53% | 34% | 213% |
| Deferred income taxes | 685 | 1,254 | 1,881 | 2% | 2% | 2% | 83% | 50% |
| Total liabilities | 30,217 | 45,154 | 86,968 | 70% | 69% | 74% | 49% | 93% |
| Common stock | 7,775 | 7,775 | 7,903 | 18% | 12% | 7% | 0% | 2% |
| Retained earnings | 5,210 | 12,312 | 23,269 | 12% | 19% | 20% | 136% | 89% |
| Total liabilities and equity | 43,202 | 65,241 | 118,140 | 100% | 100% | 100% | 51% | 81% |

**Houseco Income Statement**

| | Dollars (000s Omitted) | | | Vertical Analysis | | | Horizontal Analysis | |
|---|---|---|---|---|---|---|---|---|
| | 12/31/X6 (Audited) | 12/31/X7 (Audited) | 12/31/X8 (Unaudited) | 12/31/X6 (Audited) | 12/31/X7 (Audited) | 12/31/X8 (Unaudited) | (X7–X6)/X6 (Audited) | (X8–X7)/X7 (Unaudited) |
| Gross sales | 78,428 | 133,504 | 183,767 | 103% | 104% | 101% | 70% | 38% |
| Less: Returns and allowances | 2,284 | 5,270 | 2,644 | 3% | 4% | 1% | 131% | (50%) |
| Net sales | 76,144 | 128,234 | 181,123 | 100% | 100% | 100% | 68% | 41% |
| Cost of goods sold | 46,213 | 70,756 | 94,934 | 61% | 55% | 52% | 53% | 34% |
| Gross margin | 29,931 | 57,478 | 86,189 | 39% | 45% | 48% | 92% | 50% |
| Sell, advertising, R&D expenses | 20,105 | 42,600 | 64,285 | 26% | 33% | 35% | 112% | 51% |
| Income from operations | 9,826 | 14,878 | 21,904 | 13% | 12% | 12% | 51% | 47% |
| Interest expense | 1,930 | 1,584 | 3,189 | 3% | 1% | 2% | (18%) | 101% |
| Income before taxes | 7,896 | 13,294 | 18,715 | 10% | 10% | 10% | 68% | 41% |
| Income taxes | 3,807 | 6,189 | 7,761 | 5% | 5% | 4% | 63% | 25% |
| Net income | 4,089 | 7,105 | 10,954 | 5% | 6% | 6% | 74% | 54% |
| EPS | .46 | .78 | 1.21 | | | | | |
| **Ratios** | | | | | | | | |
| Current | 1.7 | 2.1 | 4.1 | | | | | |
| Quick | 1.0 | 1.2 | 2.3 | | | | | |
| Receivable turnover | 5.3 | 6.3 | 4.7 | | | | | |
| Days' sales in ending receivables | 68.1 | 57.1 | 76.6 | | | | | |
| Inventory turnover | 4.7 | 4.8 | 3.2 | | | | | |
| Days' sales in ending inventory | 76.0 | 75.0 | 112.5 | | | | | |
| Interest expense/Debt | 0.11 | 0.08 | 0.05 | | | | | |

Jones is beginning the risk assessment analytical procedures for the 20X8 audit to obtain information to help plan the nature, timing, and extent of other audit procedures. More specifically, he wants to identify areas that may represent specific risks relevant to this year's audit.

*Required:*

Use the balance sheet on page 180 and the income statement on page 181 to identify accounts that may represent specific risks relevant to this year's audit. For each area, briefly note why you think it represents a risk.

## Research and Discussion Cases

**LO 1, 3, 4**   5–57.   You are the partner on the audit of Datasave, Inc., a small publicly held corporation that manufactures high-speed disk drives for the computer industry. The audit of Datasave had been progressing satisfactorily until you were about a month away from issuing your opinion. Suddenly, and quite mysteriously, Carl Wagner, the financial vice president, resigned. John Ross, who had been a manager with a large CPA firm, was quickly hired to replace Wagner. Although the change in Datasave's chief financial officer caused some disruption, the audit was completed on a timely basis.

As the last step in the audit process, you have prepared the representation letter for signing. You wanted the letter to be signed by William Cox, the president; Robert Star, the controller; and Wagner, who occasionally came to the company's offices to resolve matters regarding his past compensation. The signatures of Cox and Star were obtained, and you approached Wagner for his signature. In response to your request, Wagner replied, "I no longer am employed with this crazy company. Why should I take any responsibility for the financial statements?" Despite your attempts to persuade him, Wagner refused to sign the letter. Wagner also refused to discuss the reasons for his resignation, other than to say the reasons were personal.

When you discussed the problem of Wagner's refusal to sign with Cox, he indicated that there was no problem because Ross would sign the letter. You see this as a possible solution, but you are aware that Ross knows very little about the financial statements for the year under audit. Also, you are still somewhat concerned about the reasons for Wagner's resignation.

*Required:*

a. Describe fully the alternatives that are available to you in this situation.

b. Express your personal opinion as to the appropriate course of action and provide reasoning to support your opinion.

**LO 6, 8**   5–58.   Marshall and Wyatt, CPAs, has been the independent auditor of Interstate Land Development Corporation for several years. During these years, Interstate prepared and filed its own annual income tax returns.

During 20X6, Interstate requested Marshall and Wyatt to audit all the necessary financial statements of the corporation to be submitted to the Securities and Exchange Commission (SEC) in connection with a multistate public offering of 1 million shares of Interstate common stock. This public offering came under the provisions of the Securities Act of 1933. The audit was performed carefully and the financial statements were fairly presented for the respective periods. These financial statements were included in the registration statement filed with the SEC.

While the registration statement was being processed by the SEC, but before the effective date, the Internal Revenue Service (IRS) obtained a federal court subpoena directing Marshall and Wyatt to turn over all its working papers relating to Interstate for the years 20X2–20X5. Marshall and Wyatt initially refused to comply for two reasons. First, Marshall and Wyatt did not prepare Interstate's tax returns. Second, Marshall and Wyatt claimed that the working papers were confidential matters subject to the privileged communications rule. Subsequently, however, Marshall and Wyatt did relinquish the subpoenaed working papers.

Upon receiving the subpoena, Wyatt called Dunkirk, the chair of Interstate's board of directors, and asked him about the IRS investigation. Dunkirk responded, "I'm sure that the IRS people are on a fishing expedition and that they will not find any material deficiencies."

A few days later, Dunkirk received a written memorandum from the IRS stating that it was contending Interstate had underpaid its taxes during the period under review. The memorandum revealed that Interstate was being assessed $800,000, including penalties and interest for the three years. Dunkirk forwarded a copy of this memorandum to Marshall and Wyatt.

This $800,000 assessment was material relative to the financial statements as of December 31, 20X6. The amount for each year individually, exclusive of penalty and interest, was not material relative to each respective year.

*Required:*

    a. In general terms, discuss the extent to which a CPA firm's potential liability to third parties is increased in an audit of financial statements that is included in an SEC registration.

    b. Discuss the implications of the IRS investigation, if any, relative to Marshall and Wyatt's examination of Interstate's 20X6 financial statements. Discuss any additional investigative procedures that the auditors should undertake or any audit judgments that should be made as a result of this investigation.

    c. Could Marshall and Wyatt have validly refused to surrender the subpoenaed working papers to the IRS? Explain.

(AICPA, adapted)

**Suggested
References**

Part a:
This textbook, pages 116–120.

Part b:
An intermediate accounting text.
PCAOB 333. PCAOB 560.
*FASB Accounting Standards Codification* section 450-20, "Loss Contingencies."

Part c:
This textbook, pages 160–161.

# Audit Planning, Understanding the Client, Assessing Risks, and Responding

## Learning objectives

After studying this chapter, you should be able to:

LO1    Describe the major steps in the audit process.

LO2    Identify the factors that auditors consider in accepting new clients.

LO3    Explain the auditors' responsibilities when planning an audit.

LO4    Describe the nature of the risk assessment procedures that auditors use to obtain an understanding of the client and its environment.

LO5    Describe the manner in which an audit is affected by the auditors' assessment of audit risk and materiality.

LO6    Describe how the auditors address fraud risk.

LO7    Discuss how the auditors design further audit procedures in response to the assessed risks of material misstatement.

LO8    Distinguish between the systems and the substantive procedures portions of the audit program.

In this chapter, we first provide an overview of the entire audit process. Then we discuss obtaining a client, planning an audit, obtaining an understanding of the client and its industry, assessing risks related to the client, and responding to those risks. After describing the audit process, we address questions such as: How do auditors determine whether a prospective client should be accepted as a client? After accepting an audit client, how do auditors go about planning the engagement and identifying the areas with a "high risk" of material misstatement? When one considers the potential legal liability involved, it becomes obvious that auditors do not merely accept a new audit client and then arrive at the premises to "start auditing."

## The Audit Process

 **LO1**

Describe the major steps in the audit process.

Although specific audit procedures vary from one engagement to the next, the following stages are involved with every engagement.

1. Plan the audit.
2. Obtain an understanding of the client and its environment, including internal control.
3. Assess the risks of misstatement and design further audit procedures.
4. Perform further audit procedures.
5. Complete the audit.
6. Form an opinion and issue the audit report.

1. *Plan the audit.* Audit planning begins with determining the requirements for the engagement, including the financial statements to be audited, any other requirements (e.g., regulatory filings), and the timing of the engagement. During this stage auditors establish an understanding with their client as to the nature of services to be provided and the responsibilities of each party. In addition, they develop an overall audit strategy, an audit plan, and an audit program.

While we describe the audit planning process as the first step in an audit, it should be recognized that significant portions of the planning process cannot be completed until the auditors have a sufficient understanding of the client and its environment, including internal control. Therefore, in the first audit of a new client, much of the planning process will be performed after the auditors have obtained this understanding, as described as stage two. In the audit of a continuing client, the auditors will have gained the required understanding and, therefore, may do most of the planning at the beginning of the audit.

It should be recognized that in audit planning auditors use a risk-based approach in which they are continually considering the possibility of material financial statement misstatements. As a result, the plan may need to be revised as a result of information on risks as well as audit findings that are gathered throughout the audit. As an example, if the auditors' procedures discover misstatements of an account, their finding may cause them to plan additional procedures for a particular account.

2. *Obtain an understanding of the client and its environment.* Auditors must gather sufficient background information to assess the risks of material misstatement of the financial statements and to design the nature, timing, and extent of further audit procedures. **Risk assessment procedures** are used to gather this information and include inquiries of management, analytical procedures, observation and inspection, and other procedures. At this stage of the audit, the auditors are attempting to obtain an overall understanding of the client and its environment, including its objectives and strategies and related business risks, the manner in which management measures and reviews financial performance, and the client's internal control. This understanding helps the auditors identify account balances, transactions, and disclosures with a high risk of material misstatement.

Obtaining an understanding of the nature of internal control is an essential part of this process because it allows auditors to identify accounts and classes of transactions that may be misstated and to tailor audit procedures to the existing internal control system. Information on internal control comes from interviewing client personnel, observing the application of specific controls, inspecting documents and reports, and tracing transactions through the information system, as well as reviewing prior years' audit working papers.

3. *Assess the risks of misstatement and design further audit procedures.* Auditors use their understanding of the client and its environment to identify account balances, transactions, and disclosures that might be materially misstated. At the assertion level, the auditors consider:

- What could go wrong?
- How likely is it that it will go wrong?
- What are the likely amounts involved?

Information gathering procedures provide the auditors with evidence on inherent and control risks for significant assertions. Remember that **inherent risk** is the risk of material misstatement of an **assertion** without considering internal control. Many inherent risks arise because of **business risks** faced by management, including the possibility of material misstatement due to fraud.

The auditors' consideration of **control risk** involves analyzing the design and implementation of internal control to decide whether the internal control system appears adequate to prevent or detect and correct material misstatements. For example, if the auditors believe that inherent risk is higher for an important area and internal control is weak (i.e., control risk is high), they will assess the risk of material misstatement as high. On the other hand, if inherent risk is assessed as low and controls seem capable of preventing or detecting and correcting misstatements, the auditors may decide to perform tests of controls to support an assessment that control risk is low. If those tests indicate that the controls are operating effectively, the auditors may conclude that the risk of material misstatement is low.

Based on the assessed risk of misstatement for various account balances, classes of transactions, and disclosures, the auditors will design and perform further audit procedures.

4. *Perform further audit procedures.* Further audit procedures include a combination of additional **tests of controls** and **substantive procedures** relating to account balances, transactions, and disclosures. Tests of controls are performed to determine whether key controls are properly designed and *operating effectively*. To illustrate a test of a control, consider the control activity in which the accounting department accounts for the serial sequence of all shipping documents before preparing the related journal entries. The purpose of this control is to ensure that all shipments of merchandise are recorded in the accounting records (i.e., to ensure the completeness of recorded sales and accounts receivable). To test the operating effectiveness of the control, the auditors might review

evidence of the client's accounting for the sequence of shipping documents and select a sample of shipping documents prepared at various times throughout the year to inspect the related journal entries.

Notice that a test of a control measures the effectiveness of a particular control in preventing or detecting a misstatement; it *does not* substantiate the dollar amount of an account balance. Also, a particular control may affect several financial statement accounts. If, for example, the tests described in the preceding paragraph indicate that the accounting department does not effectively account for the serial sequence of shipping documents, the auditors should be alert for the possibility of misstatements of sales revenue, accounts receivable, cost of goods sold, and inventories. Internal control is discussed further in Chapter 7.

Substantive procedures are performed to restrict detection risk, the risk that auditors will not detect a material misstatement. These procedures, described in detail in Chapter 5, include direct tests of account balances, transactions, and disclosures, as well as substantive analytical procedures. Chapters 10 through 16 provide detailed examples and discussions of these further audit tests for the various financial statement accounts.

5. *Complete the audit.* The auditors perform a number of procedures near the time of completion of the audit. These procedures, discussed in detail in Chapter 16, include completing the search for unrecorded liabilities, completing the review of minutes of meetings, performing final analytical procedures, completing the search to identify loss contingencies and subsequent events, and obtaining a representation letter from management. Finally, overall audit findings are evaluated to arrive at a conclusion as to whether the financial statements follow generally accepted accounting principles.

6. *Issue the audit report.* The final step in the process is issuance of the audit report based on the conclusions reached in the preceding steps. Details on audit reports are presented in Chapter 17.

These six stages in the audit process are summarized in Figure 6.1. In addition to presenting information on obtaining clients, the remainder of this chapter emphasizes the first four steps of the audit process: (1) plan the audit, (2) obtain an understanding of the client and its environment, (3) assess the risk of misstatement, and (4) perform further audit procedures. Because of the complexity of internal control issues, Chapters 7 and 8 provide detailed information on that topic. Chapters 16 and 17 discuss completing the audit and the types of audit reports issued. The remaining chapters discuss audit sampling (Chapter 9); details on audit evidence relating to various account balances, classes of transactions, and disclosures (Chapters 10 through 16); and various other reporting issues (Chapters 18 through 21).

## Obtaining Clients

**LO2**

Identify the factors that auditors consider in accepting new clients.

Public accounting is a competitive profession, and most CPA firms are anxious to obtain new clients. Some new engagements are easily obtained through business transactions, such as the acquisition of a company by an existing client and the client's desire to have the entire audit performed by one CPA firm. Others are obtained competitively through a partner's business or social contacts, which lead to a request that the CPA firm submit a proposal for performing the company's annual audit. Such prospective clients may range from start-up companies seeking a first audit to long-established companies considering replacing their current auditor. What risks are involved with a prospective new client? How does a CPA firm evaluate the risk associated with a prospective new client? What other professional responsibilities exist relating to acquiring a new client?

As a starting point, it is essential for a CPA firm to maintain its integrity, objectivity, and reputation for providing high-quality services. No auditor can afford to be regularly associated with clients who are engaging in management fraud or other misleading practices. The continuing wave of litigation involving auditors underscores the need for CPA firms to develop quality control policies for thoroughly investigating prospective clients *before accepting an engagement.* The CPAs should investigate the history of the prospective client, including such matters as the identities and reputations of the directors, officers, and major stockholders.

**FIGURE 6.1**

**Stages of an Audit**

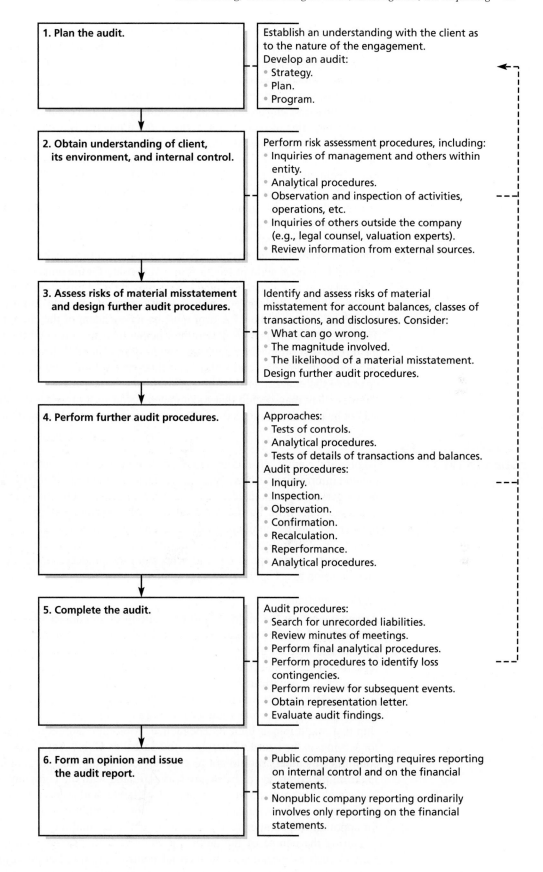

Even if the auditors perform an audit in accordance with generally accepted auditing standards, they may be sued by stockholders or creditors that sustain a loss. Therefore, auditors will consider the reputation of management and the financial strength and credit rating of a prospective client to help assess the overall risk of association with the particular business. This overall risk is often referred to as **engagement risk**.

To help assess engagement risk, the auditors generally obtain management's permission to make inquiries of other third parties about a prospective audit client. For example, the client's banker can provide information regarding the client's financial history and credit rating. The client's legal counsel can provide information about the client's legal environment, including such matters as pending litigation and disputes with regulatory agencies.

Engagement risk is increased when the client company is in a weak financial position or is greatly in need of additional capital. When an audit client goes bankrupt, the auditors often are named as defendants in lengthy and costly lawsuits, with possible damage to their professional reputation. For that reason, some CPAs choose to avoid engagements entailing a relatively high engagement risk; others may accept such engagements, recognizing the need to expand audit procedures to compensate for the unusually high levels of risk.

In addition to evaluating engagement risk, the auditors should consider whether they can complete the audit in accordance with generally accepted auditing standards. As discussed in Chapter 3, the CPA firm must be independent of the client to perform an audit. Therefore, the auditors must determine whether there are any conditions that would prevent them from performing an *independent* audit of the client. Consideration also will be given to whether the partners and staff have appropriate training and experience to competently complete the engagement. If the auditors have no experience in a particularly complex industry, they may decide that a competent audit of a prospective client in that industry cannot be performed unless the CPA firm hires appropriately experienced personnel.

## Submitting a Proposal

To obtain the audit, the auditors may be asked to submit a competitive proposal that will include information on the nature of services that the firm offers, the qualifications of the firm's personnel, anticipated fees, and other information to convince the prospective client to select the firm. The CPA firm also may be asked to make an oral presentation to the prospective client's audit committee and management to provide a basis for the selection. As discussed in further detail later in this chapter, when the auditors replace other auditors, they must attempt to communicate with the predecessor auditors before making a final decision to accept the new engagement.

### Audit Committees

Arrangements for the audit should be made through contact with the company's **audit committee**. Public companies must establish such a committee within the board of directors to take an active role in overseeing the company's accounting and financial reporting policies and practices. Audit committees are required by the New York Stock Exchange, the American Stock Exchange, and NASDAQ.

An audit committee must be composed of at least three *independent directors*— that is, those *outside directors* (neither officers nor employees) who have no other relationship that might impair their independence. Although audit committee members are paid for serving on the board of directors, the Sarbanes-Oxley Act of 2002 provides that audit committee members should not receive any consulting, advisory, or other compensatory fee from the company, or be in any way affiliated with the company. Also, the members of the audit committee must be financially literate, and at least one member (usually the chairman) must be a financial expert. Finally, the audit committee must be responsible for appointment, compensation, and oversight of the auditors.

During the course of the audit, the auditors will discuss with the audit committee matters such as weaknesses in internal control, proposed audit adjustments, disagreements with management as to accounting principles, the quality of accounting principles used by the company, and indications of management fraud or other illegal acts by

## Illustrative Case    *Fraud at ZZZZ Best Co.*

ZZZZ Best Co. was a carpet cleaning company started in 1981 by Barry Minkow, a 16-year-old high school student. Although the company experienced significant growth during the mid-1980s, it was not fast enough for Minkow. He hired several officers with criminal records and conceived a plan to restore damaged buildings for insurance companies. A number of multi-million-dollar restoration contracts were supposedly undertaken that later were found to be completely fictitious. Minkow attempted to cover up the scheme by spending several million dollars to lease a building and make it appear to be a legitimate restoration project when the CPAs insisted upon visiting the site. Prior to the time the fraud was uncovered, the company's stock had a market value in excess of $211 million. Shortly thereafter, the stock was worthless. This case clearly illustrates the risks involved in accepting young companies with rapid growth, the need to investigate the background of key officers of a company, and the need to have a thorough understanding of the client's operations and industry.

corporate officers. Since these communications assist the audit committee in its oversight of the financial reporting process of the company, they are required by generally accepted auditing standards. Chapters 7 and 16 present a detailed discussion of the required communications to audit committees.

Not all entities have audit committees. For example, the concept of an audit committee does not apply to businesses organized as sole proprietorships, partnerships, and small, closely held corporations. Arrangements for an audit of these businesses often are made with the owners, a partner, or an executive, such as the president or the controller.

### Fee Arrangements

When the business engages the services of independent public accountants, it will usually ask for an estimate of the cost of the audit. Staff time is the basic unit of measurement for audit fees. Each public accounting firm develops a per hour or per diem fee schedule for each category of audit staff, based on direct salaries and such related costs as payroll taxes and benefits. The direct rate is then increased for overhead costs and a profit element. In addition to standard per diem or per hour fees, clients are charged for direct costs incurred by the public accounting firm for staff travel, report processing, and other out-of-pocket expenditures.

Estimating a fee for an audit involves the application of the CPA firm's daily or hourly rates to the estimated time required. Since the exact number of hours cannot be determined in advance, the auditors may merely give a rough estimate of the fee. Or they may multiply the rates by the estimated time and quote a range or bracket of amounts within which the total fee will fall. In a competitive situation, a fixed fee may be quoted that is "discounted" from the standard to meet the competition.

## Communication with Predecessor Auditors

AICPA AU 210 (PCAOB 315) requires the successor auditors to attempt to communicate with the predecessor *before accepting the engagement.* Because the **predecessor auditors** are an excellent source of information about a prospective client, in many circumstances this communication will occur before a formal proposal is presented to a prospective client. In other situations (e.g., the prospective client's request or other reasons), the communication will occur subsequent to presentation of a formal proposal.

Because auditors are ethically prohibited from disclosing confidential client information without the client's consent, the **successor auditors** must ask management of the prospective client to authorize the predecessor auditors to respond fully to the successor's inquiries. If a prospective client is reluctant to authorize communications with the predecessor auditors, the successor auditors should seriously consider the implications in deciding whether to accept the engagement.

When permission has been granted, the successor auditors' inquiries (which may be written or oral) are aimed at matters that will assist the auditors in determining whether to accept the engagement. Accordingly, the auditors may include inquiries aimed at obtaining information about:

- The integrity of management.
- Disagreements with management over accounting, auditing, or similarly significant matters.
- Predecessor auditors' communications to those charged with governance regarding fraud and noncompliance with laws or regulations.
- Predecessor auditors' communications to management and those charged with governance regarding internal control significant deficiencies and material weaknesses.
- The predecessor auditors' understanding about the reasons for the change of auditors.

This communication is extremely important since it aids the successor auditors in evaluating the *integrity of management* and other issues related to the risk of the audit. A review of cases involving management fraud reveals that in a significant number of the cases management had recently changed the company's auditors, often because of disagreements over accounting principles.

For public companies, there is another source of information available for investigating a change in auditors. Regulations of the SEC require companies subject to its jurisdiction to file a Form 8-K reporting changes in independent auditors and the reasons therefore. The companies also must report the details of any significant disagreements between management and the auditors occurring over the prior three years. The auditors that have resigned or been discharged must provide a response, indicating whether they agree with the company's form and providing any necessary details. This requirement discourages management from the practice of **shopping for accounting principles,** in which management changes auditors to a CPA firm that is more likely to sanction a disputed accounting principle. A company's management might, for example, search for auditors who would accept a questionable revenue recognition method as being in accordance with generally accepted accounting principles. Concern about shopping also led to the issuance of AICPA AU 915 (PCAOB 625), which provides guidance to public accountants when they get a request for a *written or oral* report on the accounting treatment of a prospective or completed transaction from a company that is audited by another CPA firm.

Before providing a report on accounting principles, accountants should take steps to make sure they have a complete understanding of the form and substance of the transaction, including consulting with the company's current auditors. They also should review existing accounting principles and consult appropriate references and experts to provide an adequate basis for their conclusions. Although cases in which management actually shops for accounting principles are not common, it is clear that if management is allowed to change auditors casually, undue pressure is placed on auditors' independence.

Shopping for accounting principles is also discouraged by the provision of the Sarbanes-Oxley Act of 2002 requiring that the audit committee of a public company be responsible for the appointment, compensation, and oversight of the auditors.

## Planning the Audit

Explain the auditors' responsibilities when planning an audit.

Audit planning involves developing an overall audit strategy for the conduct, organization, and staffing of the audit. The nature, timing, and extent of planning vary by characteristics of the company being audited and the auditors' experience with that company. Certainly the planning of the audit of a new client is ordinarily more difficult. But, for all audits, planning begins very early in the process and is iterative in that it continues throughout the audit as the auditors modify planned procedures in response to circumstances identified throughout the audit.

**Establishing an Understanding with the Client**

The auditors should establish an understanding with the client regarding the services to be performed. This understanding should include (1) the objective and scope of the audit, (2) auditor and management responsibilities, (3) inherent limitations of an audit, (4) the applicable financial reporting framework (e.g., GAAP), and (5) the expected form and content of reports to be issued by the auditors. This understanding should be in the form of a written **engagement letter** (or other suitable written agreement). When the engagement letter is accepted by the authorized client official, it presents an *executor contract* between the auditor and the client. While engagement letters do not follow a standard format, a sample engagement letter is presented in Figure 6.2.

**FIGURE 6.2**
**Engagement Letter for Financial Statement Audit**

---

### Letterhead

September 1, 20X5

Mr. Terry Keystone, Chairman of Board of Directors
Keystone Computers & Networks, Inc.
14645 40<sup>th</sup> Street
Phoenix, AZ 84280

Dear Mr. Keystone:

*[The objective and scope of the audit]*
You have requested that we audit the financial statements of Keystone Computers & Networks, Inc., which comprise the balance sheet at December 31, 20X5, and the related statements of income, changes in stockholders' equity, and cash flows for the year then ended and the related notes to the financial statements. We are pleased to confirm our acceptance and our understanding of this audit engagement by means of this letter. Our audit will be conducted with the objective of our expressing an opinion on the financial statements.

*[The responsibilities of the auditor]*
We will conduct our audit in accordance with auditing standards generally accepted in the United States (GAAS). Those standards require that we plan and perform the audit to obtain reasonable assurance about whether the financial statements are free of material misstatement. An audit involves performing procedures to obtain audit evidence about the amounts and disclosures in the financial statements. The procedures selected depend on the auditor's judgment, including the assessment of the risks of material misstatement of the financial statements, whether due to fraud or error. An audit also includes evaluating the appropriateness of accounting policies used and the reasonableness of accounting estimates made by management, as well as evaluating the overall presentation of the financial statements. Because of the inherent limitations of an audit, together with the inherent limitations of internal control, there is an unavoidable risk that some material misstatements may not be detected, even though the audit is properly planned and performed in accordance with GAAS. In making our risk assessments, we consider internal control relevant to the entity's preparation of the financial statements in order to design audit procedures that are appropriate in the circumstances, but not for the purpose of expressing an opinion on the effectiveness of the entity's internal control. However, we will communicate to you in writing concerning any significant deficiencies in internal control relevant to the audit of the financial statements that we have identified during the audit.

*[The responsibilities of management and identification of the applicable financial reporting framework]*
Management is responsible for the preparation and fair presentation of these financial statements in accordance with accounting principles generally accepted in the United States of America; this includes the design, implementation, and maintenance of internal control relevant to the preparation and fair presentation of consolidated financial statements that are free from material misstatement, whether due to fraud or error.

Our audit will be conducted on the basis that management [*and, where appropriate, those charged with governance*] acknowledge and understand that they have responsibility:

(a) For the preparation and fair presentation of the financial statements in accordance with accounting principles generally accepted in the United States.

(b) For such internal control as management determines is necessary to enable the preparation of financial statements that are free from material misstatement, whether due to fraud or error; and

(c) To provide us with:

    (i) Access to all information that management is aware is relevant to the preparation of the financial statements, such as records, documentation, and other matters;

    (ii) Additional information that we may request from management for the purpose of the audit; and

    (iii) Unrestricted access to persons within the entity from whom we determine it necessary to obtain audit evidence.

As part of our audit process, we will request from management [and, where appropriate, those charged with governance] written confirmation concerning representations made to us in connection with the audit.

We look forward to full cooperation from your staff during our audit.

[*Insert other information, such as fee arrangements, billings, timing, and other specific terms, as appropriate.*]

[*Reporting*]
The form and content of our report may need to be amended in the light of our audit findings. We will issue a written report upon completion of our audit of Keystone Computers & Networks, Inc.'s financial statements. Our report will be addressed to the board of directors. We cannot provide assurance that an unmodified opinion will be expressed. Circumstances may arise in which it is necessary for us to modify our opinion, add an emphasis of matter or other matter paragraph(s), or withdraw from the engagement.

Please sign and return the attached copy of this letter to indicate your acknowledgement of, and agreement with, the arrangements for our audit of the financial statements including our respective responsibilities.

Very truly yours,

*Charles Adams*

Charles Adams, CPA
Acknowledged and agreed on behalf of Keystone Computers & Networks, Inc. by:
[*Signed, dated, and returned by client*]

In addition to obtaining an understanding with the client, the auditors will perform procedures to determine that:

- The firm meets professional independence requirements.
- There are no issues relating to management integrity that may affect the auditors' willingness to continue the engagements.
- There is no misunderstanding with the client as to the terms of the engagement.
- For recurring audits, assess whether circumstances require the terms of the audit to be revised. If not, remind the client of the terms of the engagement either in writing or orally.

## Develop an Overall Audit Strategy and Audit Plan

When the auditors have obtained a sufficient understanding of the client, they establish an **overall audit strategy** that considers those characteristics of the audit which determine its scope, such as industry reporting requirements, client locations, and the basis of reporting followed by the client. Issues such as timing of the audit, deadlines for reporting, and key dates that information will be received from management will be determined. Also, the auditors will make preliminary judgments on areas of high risk of material misstatement, material locations, and accounts; determine the expected approach to considering internal control; and consider recent significant client and industry factors.

When the overall audit strategy has been established, the auditors are able to start developing the **audit plan**. The audit plan is more detailed than the audit strategy and includes the nature, timing, and extent of audit procedures to be performed by the audit team members in order to obtain sufficient audit evidence. Although audit plans differ in form and content among public accounting firms, a typical plan includes a description of the nature, timing, and extent of:

1. Planned risk assessment procedures sufficient to assess the risks of material misstatement.
2. Planned further audit procedures for each material class of transactions, account balance, and disclosure. This includes tests of controls and substantive procedures.
3. Other audit procedures in order to comply with generally accepted auditing standards.

The audit plan is documented with an **audit program,** which is a detailed list of the audit procedures to be performed in the course of the audit. A tentative audit program is developed based on the auditors' initial risk assessments. This tentative program, however, may require frequent modification as the audit progresses. For example, the nature, timing, and extent of substantive procedures are influenced by the auditors' final assessment of the risk of material misstatement. Thus, not until tests of controls have been completed can a final version of the audit program be completed. Even this version may require modification if the auditors revise their preliminary estimates of materiality or risk for the engagement, or if substantive procedures disclose unexpected problems such as an additional fraud risk factor. Audit programs are discussed in detail in the final section of this chapter.

Public accounting firms usually charge clients on a time basis, and detailed time budgets can assist the auditor in estimating the audit fee. A **time budget** for an audit is constructed by estimating the time required for each step in the audit program for each of the various levels of auditors and totaling those estimated amounts. Time budgets serve other functions in addition to providing a basis for estimating fees. The time budget communicates to the audit staff those areas the manager or partner believes are of high risk and require more time. It also is an important tool of the audit senior, who uses it to measure the efficiency of the staff and to determine at each stage of the engagement whether the work is progressing at a satisfactory rate.

There is always pressure to complete an audit within the estimated time. The staff assistant who takes more time than normal to complete a task is not likely to be popular with supervisors or to win rapid advancement. Ability to do satisfactory work when given abundant time is not a sufficient qualification, *for time is never abundant in public accounting.*

The development of time budgets is facilitated in repeat engagements by reference to the preceding year's detailed time records. Sometimes time budgets prove quite unattainable because the client's records are not in satisfactory condition or because of other special circumstances that arise. Even when time estimates are exceeded, there can be no compromise with qualitative standards in the performance of the fieldwork. The CPA firm's professional reputation and its legal liability to clients and third parties do not permit any shortcuts or the omission of audit procedures to meet a predetermined time estimate.

## Use of the Client's Staff

The auditors should obtain an understanding with the client as to the extent to which the client's staff, including the internal auditors, can help prepare for the audit. The client's staff may prepare many audit working papers for the auditors, thus reducing the cost of the audit. Among the tasks that may be assigned to the client's employees are preparation of a trial balance of the general ledger, preparation of an aged trial balance of accounts receivable, analyses of accounts receivable written off, lists of property additions and retirements during the year, and analyses of various revenue and expense accounts. Most of these "working papers" will ordinarily be in the form of computer spreadsheets and other computerized data files.

## Involvement of More than One CPA Firm

When a portion of the client (e.g., a subsidiary in a distant city) is audited by another CPA firm, efforts must be coordinated. For example, if the accounts of the subsidiary are to be consolidated with the overall enterprise, and if that subsidiary is audited by another

CPA firm, the auditors must coordinate the timing of necessary reports and procedures to be performed. This situation is discussed in Chapter 17.

## Use of Specialists

CPAs may lack the qualifications necessary to perform certain technical tasks relating to the audit. For example, judging the valuation of a diamond inventory may require employing a specialist in gem appraisal, or evaluating the reasonableness of the fair value of a complex financial derivative instrument may require the use of a securities valuation expert. Effective planning involves arranging the appropriate use of specialists both inside and outside of the client organization. This should include consideration of the need for specialized skills in assessing the effects on the audit of the client's use of information technology. Using the work of specialists was discussed in detail in Chapter 5.

## Additional First-Year Considerations

In the first audit of the client, the auditors should obtain sufficient appropriate evidence about whether the **opening balances** for the various accounts contain misstatements that materially affect the current period's financial statements. For example, consider accounts such as plant and equipment and inventories. To determine the propriety of depreciation expense for the current year and the proper balances in plant and equipment accounts at the balance sheet date, the auditors must plan to investigate the validity of the property accounts at the beginning of the current period. Similarly, if the auditors arc unable to obtain satisfactory evidence as to the balance of *beginning inventories,* they may not have sufficient evidence about cost of goods sold, and it may be necessary to disclaim an opinion on the income statement.

AICPA AU 510 (PCAOB 315) requires that the auditors determine whether the prior period's closing balances were properly brought forward to the current period, and whether those balances reflect the application of appropriate accounting policies. When satisfactory prior year audits of the business have been performed by a predecessor auditor, as discussed earlier, the successor auditors will ordinarily have communicated with the predecessor about matters such as management integrity, disagreements that the predecessor may have had with management, communications with the audit committee, and the predecessor's understanding of the reason for the change of auditors. Auditors also ordinarily initiate a second communication with the predecessor auditors subsequent to acceptance of the new client. This second communication relates primarily to the contents of the predecessor auditors' working papers related to opening balances and the consistency of application of accounting principles. In addition to reviewing the predecessor auditors' working papers relating to opening balances, the successor auditors will evaluate whether audit procedures planned for the current audit will provide evidence about the opening balances. Based on this evaluation, the successor auditors will decide whether it is necessary to perform additional procedures specifically designed to obtain evidence regarding the opening balances.

In cases in which no satisfactory recent audit has been performed, an extensive analysis of transactions of prior years will be necessary to establish account balances as of the beginning of the current year.

## Obtaining an Understanding of the Client and Its Environment

**LO4**

Describe the nature of the risk assessment procedures that auditors use to obtain an understanding of the client and its environment.

The required understanding of the client is used by the auditors to help plan the audit and to assess the risks of material misstatement at the financial statement and **relevant assertion** levels. Guidance on obtaining this required understanding of the client is contained in AICPA AU 315 (PCAOB 314).

## Risk Assessment Procedures

To obtain the understanding of the entity and its environment, auditors perform risk assessment procedures, which include:

- Inquiries of management and others within the entity.
- Analytical procedures.
- Observation and inspection relating to client activities, operations, documents, reports, and premises.
- Other procedures, such as inquiries of others outside the company (e.g., legal counsel, valuation experts) and reviewing information from external sources (e.g., analysts, banks, rating organizations, and business and industry journals).

These risk assessment procedures are supplemented by further audit procedures in the form of tests of controls and substantive procedures to obtain sufficient audit evidence to express an opinion on the financial statements.

### *Information on the Client's Business and Its Environment*

When should a health club recognize its revenue from the sale of lifetime memberships? Is a company organized to produce a single motion picture a going concern? What basis should be used to record a barter of goods over the **Internet?** What is a reasonable depreciable life for today's most advanced information systems? We will not attempt to answer these questions in this textbook; we raise them simply to demonstrate that the auditors must obtain a good working knowledge of an audit client's business and its environment if they are to design effective audit procedures. An understanding of the client and its environment encompasses:

- The nature of the client, including the client's application of accounting policies.
- The industry, regulatory, and other external factors affecting the client.
- The client's objectives and strategies and related business risks.
- Methods used by the client to measure and review performance.
- The client's internal control.

Performing procedures to obtain an understanding of the entity and its environment is an essential part of planning and performing an audit. Specifically, the understanding establishes a frame of reference for the auditors to use in (1) considering the appropriateness of the accounting policies applied by the client, (2) identifying areas where special audit consideration may be necessary (specialized risks), (3) establishing appropriate materiality, (4) developing expectations for analytical procedures, (5) designing and performing audit procedures, and (6) evaluating audit evidence.

### *The Nature of the Client*

What is the client's business model? Who are its major customers and suppliers? What types of transactions does the client engage in? How are they accounted for? These are the types of questions that the auditors attempt to answer to obtain an understanding of the nature of the client. The auditors' understanding of the nature of the client will include the client's competitive position, organizational structure, governance processes, accounting policies and procedures, ownership, capital structure, and product lines. Then the auditors turn their attention to the client's critical business processes and obtain an understanding of how these processes create value for the client's customers. Using a manufacturing company as an example, the auditors will obtain an understanding of:

- The processes used to procure, store, and manage raw materials.
- The processes used to machine, assemble, package, and test products.
- The processes used to create demand for products and services and to manage relations with customers.
- The processes used to establish contract terms and to bill and collect receivables.
- The processes used to take orders and deliver goods.

- The activities performed after the goods and services have been delivered (e.g., installation, training, warranty, and customer service).
- The processes used to acquire and maintain human resources and technology, including research and development.

### Industry, Regulatory, and Other External Factors

The factors envisioned here include industry conditions, such as the competitive environment, supplier and customer relationships, and technological developments. They also include the regulatory, legal, and political environment and general economic conditions. These factors may subject the client to specialized risks that may in turn affect the audit. Many firms—including the Big 4 firms to varying degrees—have adopted a financial model to evaluate the client's industry that considers the attractiveness and other characteristics of the industry. Concerning the *overall attractiveness of the industry,* auditors consider such factors as:

- Barriers to entry.
- Strength of competitors.
- Bargaining power of suppliers of raw materials and labor.
- Bargaining power of customers.

The other *characteristics of the client's industry* that auditors consider include factors such as economic conditions and financial trends, governmental regulations, changes in technology, and widely used accounting methods.

### Objectives and Strategies and Related Business Risks

The client's objectives are the overall plans of the entity as defined by management. Management attempts to achieve these objectives by developing strategies, or operational actions. However, achieving management's objectives is always subject to business risks. As described in the previous section, these are the conditions that threaten management's ability to execute strategies and achieve objectives. The auditors obtain an understanding of the client's operating and financing strategies and attempt to identify significant business risks faced by the client. Significant risks that may be identified for a particular client might include risks related to competition, changes in government regulations, changes in technology, volatility of raw materials prices, interruption of supplies of critical raw materials, changes in major markets, or increases in interest rates. In obtaining their understanding of these matters, the auditors are particularly interested in management's risk assessment process. Well-operated companies use formal processes for identifying business risks and devising ways to mitigate them. An understanding of this process can assist the auditors in identifying significant business risks and evaluating their audit significance. Many of these business risks may create risks of material misstatement of the financial statements.

### Methods of Measuring and Reviewing Performance

Management may use a variety of techniques to measure and review performance, such as budgets, key performance indicators, variance analysis, and segment performance reports. Many firms have developed a *balanced scorecard* that uses a combination of financial and nonfinancial performance measures to assess the financial, customer, internal business process, and learning and growth perspectives of the organization. These measurement systems assist management in gauging progress toward meeting its objectives. External parties also may measure and review the client's performance. Examples include bond rating agencies, credit agencies, and financial analysts. The methods of measuring and reviewing performance are important to the auditors in determining the incentives of management and other employees because their compensation is often tied to the measures. These incentives may create pressure on management or employees to misstate the financial statements or otherwise engage in fraud. In addition, the auditors may use these measures in designing analytical procedures to provide evidence about the fairness of the financial statements.

*Internal Control*

Internal control is designed to provide reasonable assurance of achieving objectives related to reliable financial reporting, efficiency and effectiveness of operations, and compliance with applicable laws and regulations. The nature and extent of the audit work to be performed on a particular engagement depend largely upon the effectiveness of the client's internal control in preventing or detecting material misstatements in the financial statements. Before auditors can evaluate the effectiveness of internal control, they need a knowledge and understanding of how it works: what controls exist and who performs them, how various types of transactions are processed and recorded, and what accounting records and supporting documentation exist. The auditors must have a sufficient understanding of the design and implementation of internal control to plan the audit. Chapter 7 focuses on the auditors' consideration of internal control.

## Sources of Information

Much information about the nature of the client may be obtained through inquiries of management and other personnel. For example, the auditors may use inquiry to determine the major types of sales transactions and the nature of the client's customers. The auditors may combine inquiry and inspection to determine the content of sales contracts and the accounting policies used for recognizing revenues under the contracts. They also make inquiries of other personnel within the organization. As an example, production personnel can provide the auditors with a more detailed understanding of production processes. In addition, informal discussions between the auditors and key officers of the client can provide information about the history, size, operations, accounting records, and internal control of the enterprise. Finally, the auditors may make numerous inquiries to identify and assess fraud risks as described later in this chapter.

Many other sources of information on clients are available to the auditors. AICPA *Audit and Accounting Guides* and *Industry Risk Alerts,* trade publications, and governmental agency publications are useful in obtaining an orientation to the client's industry. Previous audit reports, annual reports to stockholders, SEC filings, and prior years' tax returns are excellent sources of financial background information.

*Electronic Research*

A number of *computerized research tools* are available to allow the auditors to efficiently obtain information for use in their audits. Some examples include:

1. Accounting and auditing professional standards may be searched and retrieved on the FASB's *Financial Accounting Research System* and the AICPA's *reSOURCE ONLINE Accounting and Auditing Literature.* In addition, the FASB provides its standards on its Web site, www.fasb.org. The *Financial Accounting Research System* provides, on a CD-ROM, *Statements on Financial Accounting Standards,* Emerging Issues Task Force Abstracts, and FASB Implementation Guides. The AICPA's *reSOURCE ONLINE Accounting and Auditing Literature* provides access to all AICPA professional standards, audit and accounting guides, and technical practice aids over the Internet.

2. Financial information about companies in the client's industry may be obtained from a number of sources, including *Compustat* and *Disclosure SEC Database (Disclosure).* Subscribers to *Disclosure* may search and retrieve financial data that have been extracted from SEC filings and annual reports of public companies. Auditors also may obtain the SEC filings of certain public companies, including their financial statements, on *EDGAR* (Electronic Data Gathering, Analysis, and Retrieval system), which may be accessed on the Internet.

3. Current developments for companies and their industries may be obtained from the Internet. The Internet provides online access to newspaper and journal articles. In addition, many companies and industry associations have *home pages* that describe current developments and statistics. Appendix 6A includes several Internet addresses that may be useful in performing accounting and auditing research.

## Illustrative Case · Understanding the Client's Business

The importance of an understanding of the client's business was dramatically illustrated by the Volkswagen AG case. In this case, the company reported that "criminal manipulation" of its foreign-exchange positions had cost the firm as much as $259 million.

The fraud prompted the resignation of the company's chief financial officer and the firing of its foreign-exchange manager. The auditors did not detect the fraud until fraudulent contracts came due and were rejected by banks. An insider suggested that auditors often don't know enough about complicated currency instruments to detect such problems.

### Tour of Plant and Offices

Another useful preliminary step for the auditors is to arrange an inspection tour of the plant and offices of a prospective client. This tour will give the auditors some understanding of the plant layout, manufacturing process, principal products, and physical safeguards surrounding inventories. During the tour, the auditors should be alert for signs of potential problems. Rust on equipment may indicate that plant assets have been idle; excessive dust on raw materials or finished goods may indicate a problem of obsolescence. A knowledge of the physical facilities will assist the auditors in planning how many audit staff members will be needed to participate in observing the physical inventory.

The tour affords the auditors an opportunity to observe firsthand what types of information technology and internal documentation are used to record such activities as receiving raw materials, transferring materials into production, and shipping finished goods to customers. An understanding of these computer applications and documentation is essential to the auditors' consideration of internal control. Inquiries of personnel in various departments may provide the auditors with critical information about the client's operations and may serve to confirm information obtained from financial management.

In visiting the offices, the auditors will learn the location of various facilities and accounting records. The auditors can ascertain the practical extent of segregation of duties within the client organization by observing the number of office employees. In addition, the tour will afford an opportunity to meet the key personnel whose names appear on the organization chart. The auditors will record the background information about the client in a *permanent file* available for reference in future engagements.

### Analytical Procedures

As described in Chapter 5, **analytical procedures** involve comparisons of financial statement balances and ratios for the period under audit with auditor expectations developed from sources such as the client's prior years' financial statements, published industry statistics, and budgets. When used for risk assessment purposes, analytical procedures assist the auditors in *planning* the nature, timing, and extent of audit procedures that will be used for the specific accounts. The approach used is one of obtaining an understanding of the client's business and transactions and identifying areas that may represent higher risks. The auditors will then plan a more thorough investigation of these potential problem areas. Auditors perform analytical procedures as a part of the risk assessment process for *every* audit.

An example of the use of an analytical procedure for risk assessment purposes is the comparison of the client's inventory turnover for the current year with comparable statistics from prior years. A significant decrease in inventory turnover might lead the auditors to consider the possibility that the client has excessive amounts of inventory. As a result, the auditors would plan more extensive procedures to search for inventory items that may be obsolete.

### The Statement of Cash Flow and Obtaining an Understanding of the Client

The auditors may use the statement of cash flows to analyze cash flows while obtaining an understanding of the client, particularly as a part of risk assessment analytical procedures. For a profitable, growing company, one ordinarily expects positive operating cash flows, perhaps slightly higher than net income due to the addition of depreciation and amortization items back to income. Cash flows from investing are often negative for such a company as it makes capital expenditures and investments. The direction of cash flows from financing is expected to vary among years depending upon issuance and redemption of stock and debt.

Continuing with the example of a profitable, growing company, when the auditors find that cash from operations is significantly less than net income, investigation of the reason or reasons is appropriate. Possible reasons include large increases in current assets (e.g., accounts receivable and inventory) and decreases in liabilities (e.g., accounts payable), and recognition of large amounts of revenues for which no cash has been received. While such conditions may or may not indicate a misstatement, they are worthy of follow-up and explanation.

## Determining Materiality

The concept of materiality recognizes that some matters are important to the fair presentation of financial statements, while others are not. The materiality concept is basic to the audit, because the audit report states that an audit is performed to obtain reasonable assurance about whether the financial statements are free of *material* misstatement.

Materiality judgments depend both upon the financial reporting framework being used and on the auditors' professional judgment. U.S. generally accepted accounting principles refer to *FASB Statement of Financial Accounting Concepts No. 2,* "Qualitative Characteristics of Accounting Information," which defines *materiality* as

> . . . the magnitude of an omission or misstatement of financial information that, in the light of surrounding circumstances, makes it probable that the judgment of a reasonable person relying on the information would have been changed or influenced by the omission or misstatements.

Alternatively, PCAOB *Auditing Standard No. 11,* "Consideration of Materiality in Planning and Performing an Audit," points out that in interpreting the federal securities laws the Supreme Court of the United States has held that a fact is material if there is:

> a substantial likelihood that the . . . fact would have been viewed by the reasonable investor as having significantly altered the "total mix" of information made available.

Although one may question whether these two descriptions differ significantly from one another, it is important to realize that they both involve a consideration of quantitative and qualitative factors—particularly when evaluating a misstatement that has been identified. Under certain circumstances, a misstatement that would ordinarily be considered immaterial in quantitative terms may be material because of its nature. As an example, an illegal payment of an otherwise immaterial amount could be material if there is a reasonable possibility that it could lead to a material contingent liability or a material loss of revenue.

Auditors consider materiality both in planning the audit and in evaluating audit findings. In *planning* the audit, auditors use materiality in determining the proper scope of audit procedures. The audit must be planned to obtain reasonable assurance of detecting material misstatements of the financial statements. In *evaluating* audit findings, the auditors use materiality to evaluate whether actual or likely misstatements that have been found are material to the financial statements. This is a critical decision because a material misstatement should result in audit opinion modification, while an immaterial misstatement should not. Because this chapter emphasizes planning, we will emphasize the planning concept of materiality, but we also will provide a brief discussion of materiality for evaluation purposes. Materiality for evaluation purposes is also addressed in Chapter 16.

### Planning Materiality

The auditors' purpose in considering materiality at the planning stage of the audit is to determine the appropriate scope of their audit procedures. Audit procedures should be designed to detect material misstatements, so that the auditors do not waste time searching for immaterial misstatements that cannot affect the auditors' report. As described in Chapter 5, the scope of the auditors' procedures for an account is directly related to the risk of material misstatement of that account. The auditors will perform extensive procedures on an account with a high risk of material misstatement. No audit procedures will be performed on an account that is quantitatively immaterial unless, based on qualitative considerations, the account is significant. For example, an Accounts Receivable from Officers account might be considered material regardless of its size.

While planning the audit, the auditors also may become aware of a number of accounting expediencies followed by the client that may result in immaterial misstatements. The concept of materiality often allows auditors to "pass over" certain conceptual accounting errors, such as charging low-cost items like small tools or business machines directly to expense accounts. But even in these situations, the auditors need to carefully consider the possibility that the effect of such accounting expediencies may differ materially from results obtained following generally accepted accounting principles. Accounting expediencies are not acceptable simply because the client's management says the amounts involved are immaterial or because the amounts involved were considered immaterial in the past.

*Quantifying Planning Materiality at the Overall Financial Statement Level*   Auditing standards require that auditors determine materiality levels for the overall financial statements. As an example, the auditors may conclude that a $100,000 misstatement of net income before taxes is material for purposes of the income statement, and $200,000 for the balance sheet. Many possible misstatements affect both the balance sheet and the income statement; for example, an overstatement of ending inventory both overstates assets on the balance sheet and net income on the income statement. Because of such possible misstatements, the auditors will design their audit to detect the smallest misstatement that would be material to any one of the financial statements, in this case $100,000.

Auditors may use *rules of thumb* related to a financial statement base, such as net income, total revenues, or total assets, to develop these estimates of overall materiality. Rules of thumb that are commonly used in practice include:

- 5 percent to 10 percent of net income before taxes.
- ½ percent to 1 percent of total assets.
- ½ percent to 1 percent of total revenues.
- 1 percent of total equity.

The appropriate financial statement base for computing materiality will vary based on the nature of the client's business. For example, total revenues for a financial institution are often too small to use as the base in conjunction with the percentages presented above. In addition, if a company is in a near break-even position, net income for the year will be much too small to be used as the financial statement base. In that situation, the auditors will often choose another financial statement base or use an average of net income over a number of prior years.

Auditors often use a "sliding scale" for calculating overall materiality. For example, they might use 1 percent of total sales for materiality on the audit of a small business and ½ percent of total sales on the audit of a large corporation. This is because the absolute amount of materiality is also important. Consider a small business with $2,000,000 in revenue. If ½ percent of total revenue was used as a rule of thumb, $10,000 would be calculated as overall materiality. However, it is unlikely that $10,000 would affect a user's decision about the financial position and results of operations of any such company. In addition, it would be impractical to audit the company to that level of precision.

*Allocating Overall Materiality to Individual Accounts*   Once the auditors have determined planning materiality for the overall financial statements, they may allocate materiality to individual financial statement accounts. Such an allocation is most frequently made to help establish the scope of substantive procedures when audit sampling is being

## Illustrative Case — *Materiality Guidelines*

One of the Big 4 CPA firms developed the following table to assist its audit staff in determining planning materiality based on the greater of total assets or total sales.

| If the Greater of Total Assets or Total Revenues Is: | | Materiality Is: | |
|---|---|---|---|
| Over | But Not Over | Times | The Excess Over |
| $ 0 | $ 30,000 | 0 + .05900 | $ 0 |
| 30,000 | 100,000 | 1,780 + .03100 | 30,000 |
| 100,000 | 300,000 | 3,970 + .02140 | 100,000 |
| 300,000 | 1,000,000 | 8,300 + .01450 | 300,000 |
| 1,000,000 | 3,000,000 | 18,400 + .01000 | 1,000,000 |
| 3,000,000 | 10,000,000 | 38,300 + .00670 | 3,000,000 |
| 10,000,000 | 30,000,000 | 85,500 + .00460 | 10,000,000 |
| 30,000,000 | 100,000,000 | 178,000 + .00313 | 30,000,000 |
| 100,000,000 | 300,000,000 | 397,000 + .00214 | 100,000,000 |
| 300,000,000 | 1,000,000,000 | 826,000 + .00145 | 300,000,000 |
| 1,000,000,000 | 3,000,000,000 | 1,840,000 + .00100 | 1,000,000,000 |
| 3,000,000,000 | 10,000,000,000 | 3,830,000 + .00067 | 3,000,000,000 |
| 10,000,000,000 | 30,000,000,000 | 8,550,000 + .00046 | 10,000,000,000 |
| 30,000,000,000 | 100,000,000,000 | 17,800,000 + .00031 | 30,000,000,000 |
| 100,000,000,000 | 300,000,000,000 | 39,700,000 + .00021 | 100,000,000,000 |
| 300,000,000,000 | — | 82,600,000 + .00015 | 300,000,000,000 |

To illustrate application of the table, assume that a company has $12,670,000 of total assets and $20,520,000 of total revenue. Planning materiality would be calculated as described below:

$$\$85,500 + .00460\ (\$20,520,000 - \$10,000,000) = \$133,892$$

used for one or more accounts. When materiality is allocated to a particular account, *Statements on Auditing Standards* and the *International Auditing Standards* refer to this amount as **performance materiality** for the account. At the individual audit test level, the amount may be further adjusted to arrive at tolerable misstatement. For example, assume that auditors are using statistical sampling for several tests relating to the accounts receivable account. Also assume that planning materiality is set at $1,000,000 for the overall financial statements. To facilitate audit testing, the auditors may decide that $750,000 is the appropriate amount for performance materiality for accounts receivable, and $600,000 is the appropriate amount for tolerable misstatement for the individual tests of accounts receivable.[1]

When considering the allocation of materiality to individual accounts, it is important to understand that simply allocating planning materiality to all accounts dollar for dollar, so that the total amount of all the performance materiality or tolerable misstatement disaggregation is equal to overall planning materiality, is far too conservative. The reason is that misstatements of various accounts often counterbalance each other. That is, the overstatement of one asset may be offset by the understatement of another. Another reason that materiality should not be allocated dollar for dollar is the double-entry bookkeeping system, which allows detection of misstatements in an account by auditing a related

---

[1] *PCAOB Auditing Standards* do not include the performance materiality concept, but use tolerable misstatement to include both the disaggregated planning materiality amount for accounts and for individual audit tests.

account. For example, if at year-end a purchase of inventory on credit is recorded at an improper amount, the misstatement may be detected by the tests of inventories, accounts payable, or cost of goods sold.

A number of techniques are used to allocate materiality to individual accounts in practice—we will describe two. In using the first technique, the auditors multiply the amount of overall planning materiality by some factor, usually from 1.5 to 2. This amount is then allocated to the various balance sheet accounts.

The second technique involves allocating materiality only to those accounts that are to be tested with audit sampling. In using this approach, the auditors typically determine performance materiality by reducing overall planning materiality by an estimate of the aggregate amount of misstatement that will go undetected. Some amount of undetected misstatement is expected in every audit because the auditors design their tests to detect only material misstatement—smaller amounts often go undetected. Finally, the auditors determine tolerable misstatement for the particular audit test based on the amount of performance materiality for the account. Tolerable misstatement may be the same amount or lower than performance materiality for the account depending on the audit sampling technique being used. Chapter 9 illustrates how tolerable misstatement is used in conjunction with substantive procedures using various audit sampling techniques.

### Evaluation Materiality

As indicated previously, the use of evaluation materiality typically involves circumstances in which one or more misstatements have been identified and the auditors must evaluate whether the amounts involved are material. The auditors' approach is to first consider whether the misstatements identified are quantitatively material. Here the auditors must consider not only the known amount of misstatement but also any likely or projected misstatement. As an example, if the auditors test 10 percent of a population and find a $10,000 misstatement, they would estimate that the entire population is misstated by about $100,000 ($10,000 ÷ 10%).[2] Rules-of-thumb materiality amounts applied for planning purposes are often used in this quantitative analysis. If the auditors believe that the estimated amount of misstatement is not quantitatively material, they must still consider whether qualitative factors make the item material.

*Qualitative Considerations of Materiality*    Qualitative factors are particularly significant to evaluation materiality. As an example, related party transactions of relatively small amounts might be considered material to the company's financial statements. Examples of other factors that may make an item qualitatively material include the following:

- A misstatement of the financial statements that would affect a company's compliance with a contractual agreement might be material regardless of its amount. As an illustration, assume that a company's long-term debt agreement requires the company to maintain working capital of at least $500,000; otherwise, the total debt becomes payable upon demand. If the company's working capital on the balance sheet is only slightly more than $500,000, a small misstatement might disguise a violation of the debt agreement. Since the violation would mean that the company's long-term debt should be reclassified as a current liability, the small misstatement becomes material to the financial statements.

- A misstatement that would cause a company not to make the consensus earnings-per-share estimate of financial analysts might be considered material even though it is somewhat less than what would normally be considered material.

Evaluation materiality and the overall process of evaluating audit procedures are described in greater detail in Chapter 16.

---

[2] The topics of projection of misstatements and evaluating overall audit findings are discussed in Chapters 9 and 16.

# Assessing the Risks of Material Misstatement and Designing Further Audit Procedures

**LO5**

Describe the manner in which an audit is affected by the auditors' assessment of audit risk and materiality.

As discussed in Chapter 5, the term **audit risk** refers to the possibility that the auditors may unknowingly fail to appropriately modify their opinion on financial statements that are materially misstated. At the overall financial statement level, audit risk is the chance that a material misstatement exists in the financial statements and the auditors do not detect it with their audit procedures. Auditors are aware that few audits involve material misstatements of financial statements, but when such misstatements do exist, they can result in millions of dollars of potential liability to the auditors. Experience has shown that many undetected misstatements of financial statements are intentional fraud, rather than unintentional errors.

## Assessing Risks of Material Misstatement

The auditors must plan and perform the audit to obtain reasonable assurance that material misstatements, whether caused by errors or fraud, are detected. Accordingly, in designing an audit, the auditors must identify and assess the risks of material misstatement of the financial statements. Remember that this risk is a combination of inherent and control risk.

The general approach followed during risk assessment is to use all the evidence obtained about the client and its environment to:

- Identify risks.
- Relate the identified risks to what can go wrong at the relevant assertion level.
- Consider whether the risks are of a magnitude that could result in a material misstatement.
- Consider the likelihood that the risks could result in a material misstatement.

In other words, the auditors try to relate each identified risk to "what can go wrong" at the assertion level. As an example, if the auditors identify a risk of inventory obsolescence, this means that there is a risk that the inventory may be misstated with respect to the valuation assertion. In assessing this risk, the auditors will consider any controls established by management to mitigate this risk. Then, the auditors consider whether this risk could result in a material misstatement of inventory and cost of goods sold, and the likelihood that the material misstatement could actually occur. Finally, they use all of these risk assessments to plan and perform the audit.

In performing risk assessment, it is important for the auditors to recognize that risks of material misstatement occur at both the financial statement level and the relevant assertion level for account balances, transaction classes, and disclosures. These two types of risks may affect the audit in different ways.

### Financial Statement Level Risks

Risks at the financial statement level are those that relate to the overall financial statements and potentially affect many individual assertions. The following examples help to illustrate financial statement level risks:

- Risks related to an ineffective control environment and weaknesses in general information technology controls (discussed in Chapters 7 and 8).
- A lack of sufficient capital to continue operations.
- A declining industry.
- Risks related to the selection and application of significant accounting policies.

Financial statement level risks potentially affect relevant assertions about many accounts and disclosures. As a result, assessing their audit impact often requires considerable judgment. For example, poor controls over access to the IT system may allow unauthorized personnel to inappropriately change data affecting many different transaction classes and account balances. Questions about the integrity of management may raise a variety of questions relating to numerous financial statement amounts and disclosures. Because of the characteristics of financial statement level risks, an overall response by the auditor is often appropriate, such as:

- Assigning to the audit more experienced staff or individuals with specialized skills.
- Providing more supervision for the audit staff and emphasizing the need for them to maintain professional skepticism.
- Incorporating additional elements of unpredictability in the selection of further audit procedures to be performed.
- Increasing the overall scope of audit procedures.

*Relevant Assertion Level Risks*

Most risks of misstatement relate to one or a few relevant assertions that relate to one or more significant accounts or disclosures. Recall from Chapter 5 that a relevant assertion is one that has a reasonable possibility of containing a material misstatement (without regard to controls over it). Similarly, the PCAOB defines a significant account or disclosure as one that has a reasonable possibility of containing a material misstatement. Recall that we have summarized these assertions as:

1. Existence or occurrence.
2. Rights and obligations.
3. Completeness.
4. Cutoff.
5. Valuation or allocation.
6. Presentation and disclosure.

As an example, a risk related to inaccurate counting of inventory at year-end affects the valuation of inventory and the accuracy of cost of goods sold. For this type of risk, the auditors consider the risk and the related controls and assess the magnitude and likelihood of the risk for each of the relevant assertions. Finally, they will adjust the nature, timing, or extent of the audit procedures designed to detect the misstatement. In this case, if the auditors conclude there is an increased risk of material misstatement of the financial statements due to inaccurate inventory counting, they may decide to assign more audit staff members to observe the inventory count by client personnel.

*Significant Risks that Require Special Audit Consideration*

While assessing risks, the auditors should determine which of the identified risks require special audit consideration. Such risks are referred to as **significant risks**, and it is expected that one or more will be identified on every audit. In Chapter 5, we distinguished among routine, nonroutine, and estimation transactions (see pages 139–140). Significant risks often relate to nonroutine transactions and estimation transactions. For example, estimates of the value of a significant inventory of precious metals or gems might represent a significant risk in an audit of a chain of jewelry stores. In other businesses, such risks may arise due to transactions such as unusual revenue transactions or critical accruals that must be subjectively determined by management. In addition, a significant risk for a particular audit may arise from a fraud risk. In responding to significant risks, the auditors must:

- Carefully consider the design and implementation of the related controls.
- Not rely on evidence about the operating effectiveness of the related controls that has been gathered in prior periods.[3]
- Not rely solely on analytical procedures to obtain audit evidence about the related financial statement assertions.

---

[3] Details on tests of controls are presented in Chapter 7. As discussed in that chapter, reliance upon prior period tests of controls may be justified for other controls under certain circumstances.

As indicated on the previous page, significant risks often involve risks related to fraud. Because of the importance and unique nature of fraud, the Auditing Standards Board issued AICPA AU 240 (PCAOB 316) to provide more specific guidance for the auditors in assessing the risks of material misstatement of the financial statements due to *fraud.*

## Addressing the Risks of Material Misstatement Due to Fraud

The auditors' consideration of risks of material misstatement from fraud recognizes that there are two distinct types: (1) misstatements arising from **fraudulent financial reporting (management fraud),** and (2) misstatements arising from **misappropriation of assets (defalcations).** The auditors' fraud risk assessment involves identifying risks of material misstatement of the financial statements due to fraud and determining the appropriate audit response. To identify fraud risks, the auditors perform a number of procedures, including having discussions with engagement personnel, making inquiries of management and others within the organization, performing analytical procedures, and considering fraud risk factors.

**LO6**

Describe how the auditors address fraud risk.

### Discussions with Engagement Personnel

AICPA AU 315 (PCAOB 314) requires that auditors have a discussion with the audit team members about the susceptibility of the client's financial statements to material misstatements, while AICPA AU 240 (PCAOB 316) requires a discussion on susceptibility to fraud. For efficiency, the two discussions are often held concurrently. These discussions allow the more experienced team members to share insights and exchange ideas about how and where the entity's financial statements might be susceptible to material misstatement—due to either error or fraud—and to emphasize the importance of maintaining the proper degree of professional skepticism regarding the possibility of such misstatements. The discussion also will review errors that are expected to occur based on the results of prior audits. The discussion should involve the auditor with final responsibility for the audit (the engagement partner) and key members of the audit team. Although having all team members present may often be possible and desirable, this is not required. Professional judgment is also used in determining how and when it should occur and the extent of the discussion. Related, the PCAOB standards emphasize that communication among the team members about significant matters affecting the risks of material misstatement should continue throughout the audit.

### Making Inquiries Related to Fraud

Inquiries of management and other personnel assist the auditors in identifying fraud risks. Therefore, the auditors are required to inquire of members of management as to their knowledge of fraud and alleged fraud, their understanding of the risks of fraud, and

| **Illustrative Case** | *Litigation and Management Fraud* |

A recent analysis of SEC enforcement cases involving fraud reported that in 89 percent of cases the CEO and/or the CFO in the company were named in the fraud. Misappropriation of assets was indicated in only 14 percent of the cases. In a vast majority of the cases, management engaged in fraudulent financial reporting motivated by such factors as meeting analysts' earnings expectations, concealing deteriorating financial conditions, and preparing for debt or equity offerings. Finally, revenue frauds accounted for over 60 percent of the cases.[4]

---

[4] Mark Beasley; Joseph Carcello; Dana Hermanson; and Terry Neal, "Fraudulent Financial Reporting: 1998–2007—An Analysis of U.S. Public Companies (2010)," the Committee of Sponsoring Organizations of the Treadway Commission (COSO).

## Illustrative Case

## *Fraud at WorldCom*

At the time, WorldCom, Inc., became the largest company to file for bankruptcy in corporate history. The bankruptcy was precipitated by the discovery of one of the largest accounting frauds, with profits fraudulently inflated by more than $11 billion. Company internal memos indicate that senior WorldCom executives overrode internal control and ordered subordinates to alter the company's books.

programs or controls that have been implemented to mitigate those risks. The auditors also inquire about how management monitors operating units or business segments in other locations, and how management communicates its views about ethical behavior to employees. The auditors should obtain management's perspective regarding the effectiveness of internal control in detecting fraud and whether this perspective has been reported to the audit committee.

Inquiries are directed to internal auditors and members of the audit committee to get their views about fraud risks and determine whether these individuals have knowledge of fraud or suspected fraud. To get a more complete perspective and corroborate management's responses, auditors should also make inquiries of other employees, such as operating personnel not directly involved in financial reporting; employees involved in initiating, recording, or processing complex or unusual transactions; and in-house legal counsel. These inquiries are important because fraud often is uncovered through information received in response to inquiries.

### Performing Risk Assessment Analytical Procedures to Identify Fraud Risks

Risk assessment analytical procedures also may provide the auditors with indications of fraud risks. When the results of analytical procedures reveal an unusual or unexpected relationship, this may provide an indication that the financial statements may be misstated due to fraud. Because revenue manipulation is one of the most common techniques used in fraudulent financial reporting, the professional standards require the auditor to perform risk assessment analytical procedures related to revenue. For example, the auditors might compare monthly revenue for the current year with comparable prior years for an indication that revenue may be misstated.

### Considering Fraud Risk Factors

In identifying fraud risks, the auditors also consider various fraud risk factors. Fraud risk factors do not necessarily indicate fraud; however, they often are present where fraud exists. AICPA AU 240 (PCAOB 316) provides lists of such factors organized around the three fundamental conditions necessary for the commission of fraud: (1) some type of incentive or pressure, (2) an opportunity to commit the fraud, and (3) an attitude that allows the individual to rationalize the act. As an illustration, an accounts receivable clerk who is having financial difficulty may feel pressured to commit fraud, and a weakness in internal control may provide that individual with the opportunity to steal cash receipts. Finally, the employee may be able to rationalize the theft based on a belief that he or she is underpaid. Appendix 6B provides listings of fraud risk factors for misstatements arising from both fraudulent financial reporting and misappropriation of assets.

### Identifying Fraud Risks

After holding the engagement team discussion, performing the inquiries and planning analytical procedures, and considering the presence of fraud risk factors and other information that might be relevant, the auditors are ready to identify fraud risks that may require an audit response. In identifying the risks that require an audit response, the auditors consider a number of factors, including the type and significance of the risk, the likelihood that the risk will result in a material misstatement, and its pervasiveness. Since material misstatements due to fraudulent financial reporting often involve management override of internal control, resulting in overstatement of revenue, auditors ordinarily should presume that there is a fraud risk related to revenue recognition. For all fraud risks identified by the auditors, they should obtain an understanding of the programs and controls enacted by management to mitigate the risks. This information about controls will assist the auditors in determining the significance of the risk and in designing an effective audit approach to address the risks.

Even if specific risks of material misstatement due to fraud are not identified by the auditors, there is always a possibility of management override of internal control. Therefore, the professional standards require the auditors to address this risk apart from whether they identify other fraud risks. Figure 6.3 provides conditions that may indicate fraud.

*Responding to Fraud Risks*

How do the auditors respond to fraud risks? They respond in the following three ways: (1) a modification in approach having an overall effect on how the audit is conducted; (2) an alteration in the nature, timing, and extent of the procedures performed; and (3) performance of procedures to further address the risk of management override of internal control.

*Overall Response*   In response to fraud risks, the auditors may modify their overall approach to the audit in one or more of the following ways:

• *Professional skepticism and audit evidence.* The auditors may respond by designing procedures to obtain more reliable evidence in support of specific financial statement

**FIGURE 6.3**   **Conditions Indicative of Fraud**

| Discrepancies in the Accounting Records | Conflicting or Missing Evidential Matter | Problematic or Unusual Relationships between the Auditors and Client |
|---|---|---|
| • Transactions that are not recorded in a complete or timely manner or are improperly recorded as to amount, accounting period, classification, or entity policy<br>• Unsupported or unauthorized balances or transactions<br>• Last-minute adjustments that significantly affect financial results<br>• Evidence of employees' access to systems and records inconsistent with that necessary to perform their authorized duties | • Missing documents<br>• Unavailability of other than photocopied or electronically transmitted documents when documents in original form are expected to exist<br>• Significant unexplained items on reconciliations<br>• Inconsistent, vague, or implausible responses from management or employees arising from inquiries or analytical procedures<br>• Unusual discrepancies between the entity's records and confirmation replies<br>• Missing inventory or physical assets of significant magnitude<br>• Unavailable or missing electronic evidence, inconsistent with the entity's record-retention practices or policies<br>• Inability to produce evidence of key systems development and program-change testing and implementation activities for current-year system changes and deployments | • Denial of access to records, facilities, certain employees, customers, vendors, or others from whom audit evidence might be sought<br>• Undue time pressures imposed by management to resolve complex or contentious issues<br>• Complaints by management about the conduct of the audit or management intimidation of audit team members, particularly in connection with the auditors' critical assessment of audit evidence or in the resolution of potential disagreements with management<br>• Unusual delays by the entity in providing requested information<br>• Tips or complaints to the auditors about fraud<br>• Unwillingness to facilitate auditor access to key electronic files for testing through the use of computer-assisted audit techniques<br>• Denial of access to key information technology operations staff and facilities including security, operations, and systems development personnel |

items or by obtaining additional corroboration of management's explanations or representations concerning material matters, such as through third-party confirmation, the use of a specialist, or examination of documentation from independent sources.

- *Assigning personnel and supervision.* The auditors may respond by assigning additional staff with specialized skill and knowledge or by assigning more experienced staff to the engagement. In addition, the extent of the supervision of the audit staff should be adjusted to reflect the fraud risks identified.
- *Accounting principles.* The auditors may decide to further consider management's selection and application of significant accounting principles, particularly those related to subjective measurements and complex transactions.
- *Predictability of auditing procedures.* The auditors may incorporate an added element of unpredictability in the selection of auditing procedures. As examples, they may use differing sampling techniques, adjust the timing of testing from what otherwise would be expected, or perform procedures at locations on an unannounced basis.

*Alterations in Audit Procedures*   Alterations of the nature, timing, or extent of audit procedures to address a fraud risk may involve applying procedures that provide more reliable evidence, shifting tests from the interim period to near year-end, or increasing the sample size for a particular substantive procedure. As an example, the auditors might decide to interview personnel involved in activities in areas where a fraud risk has been identified to obtain their insights about the risk and how controls address that risk. Linking audit procedures to risks is described in more detail later in this chapter.

*Response to the Possibility of Management Override*   As indicated previously, on every audit, the auditors are required to design procedures to further address the risk of management override of controls. Specifically, these procedures include:

- *Examining journal entries and other adjustments for evidence of material misstatement due to fraud.* Material misstatements of financial statements due to fraud often involve the manipulation of the financial reporting process by recording inappropriate journal entries or adjustments. Therefore, the auditors should review such entries and adjustments for suspicious characteristics, such as entries made to unrelated, unusual, or seldom-used accounts; entries recorded at the end of the period or as post-closing entries that have little or no explanation or description; or entries made either before or during the preparation of the financial statements that do not have account numbers.
- *Reviewing accounting estimates for biases.* Fraudulent financial reporting often is accomplished through intentional misstatement of accounting estimates, such as the allowance for uncollectible accounts. Thus, auditors should perform a retrospective review of significant accounting estimates reflected in the financial statements of the prior year to determine whether management judgments and assumptions relating to the estimates indicate a possible bias on the part of management. For example, in performing a retrospective review of the allowance for uncollectible accounts, the auditors might compare management's estimate used in the prior financial statements with the amounts eventually determined to be uncollectible. Evidence of bias in the prior year should be considered in auditing the current year accounting estimates.
- *Evaluating the business rationale for significant unusual transactions.* During the course of the audit, if the auditors encounter significant transactions that are outside the normal course of business for the client or otherwise appear unusual, they should gain an understanding of their business rationale. The auditors should be especially alert for significant unusual transactions with related parties.

*Evaluating the Results of Audit Tests*   The auditors' concern about fraud does not stop at the planning phase of the audit. Throughout the engagement, the auditors should be alert for conditions that may indicate that a fraud was committed, such as those presented in Figure 6.3. In addition, analytical procedures performed during the course of the audit may reveal unusual or unexpected relationships that may indicate the occurrence of fraud.

As an example, an unexpected relationship between sales volume as determined from the accounting records and sales volume determined from production statistics maintained by operations personnel may indicate a fraudulent misstatement of sales.

At or near completion of the audit, the auditors should evaluate whether the accumulated results of audit procedures and other observations affect the assessment of the risks of material misstatement due to fraud made earlier in the audit.

*Discovery of Fraud*   What do the auditors do if they obtain evidence of fraud? They should evaluate the implications for the audit and communicate their suspicions to an appropriate level of management, at least one level above the level involved. If the fraud involves senior management or material misstatement of the financial statements, the matter should be reported to the audit committee of the board of directors. In very serious situations, the auditors may decide to withdraw from the engagement.

## Designing Further Audit Procedures in Response to Assessed Risks

### LO7

Discuss how the auditors design further audit procedures in response to the assessed risks of material misstatement.

The auditors' selection of **further audit procedures** is based on the materiality of the account balances, transactions, and disclosures being audited and the assessed risks of material misstatement. These further audit procedures include substantive procedures for all relevant assertions and, if needed, tests of controls. Tests of controls are needed when the auditors' risk assessment includes an expectation that controls are operating effectively, or when substantive procedures alone do not provide sufficient appropriate audit evidence. Chapters 10 through 16 include detailed illustrations of tests of controls and substantive procedures. Here we simply provide an overview of factors that may affect the nature of further audit procedures.

Designing further audit procedures is a critical process that involves complex judgment to *link* specific audit procedures with the assessed risks at the relevant assertion level. When designing further audit procedures, auditors consider the *nature, timing,* and *extent* of appropriate procedures. As discussed in Chapter 5, the higher the risk, the more reliable and relevant is the *nature* of the audit evidence sought by the auditor. For example, to improve reliability it may be possible to increase the use of externally generated evidence in a risky area. When considering the *timing* of audit procedures, auditors may perform tests of controls or substantive procedures at an interim date or at period end. The higher the risk of material misstatement, the more likely it is that the auditors may decide to perform audit procedures nearer to, or at, the period end. In addition, a high risk of material misstatement for a particular assertion may result in an increase in the *extent* of audit procedures performed. To respond to higher risk on an overall basis, auditors may incorporate additional elements of unpredictability in the selection of audit procedures (e.g., modify the timing and approach related to inventory observations and receivable confirmations).

What other responses are appropriate when assessed risks of material misstatement are high? First, all auditors on the engagement, but particularly those working in high-risk areas, should apply a heightened degree of skepticism. In staffing the high-risk audit, the firm should consider:

- Assigning more experienced staff to the engagement.
- Assigning individuals with specialized skills to the engagement.
- Increasing the extent of supervision for the engagement.

Thus, further audit procedures in response to high assessed levels of risk may lead both to changes in the nature, timing, and extent of audit procedures and to changes in the staffing and supervision of the engagement. As indicated, substantive audit procedures are determined based on the auditors' assessment of the risks of material misstatement (inherent and control risks) of various assertions about account balances, transactions, and disclosures. It is important for the auditors to design substantive procedures that are clearly focused on and linked to the risks. As an example, assume that a software company sells expensive software systems and maintenance using standard contracts.

Also assume that the auditors have identified as a significant business risk and inherent risk that sales personnel, informally or through written side agreements, may be modifying the terms of contracts with customers, which may affect the amount of revenue that should be recognized. The auditors must design tests that are focused on determining whether such modifications of terms have been made, perhaps by using tailored confirmations from customers about the existence of such side agreements. In addition, to the extent considered necessary, staff with experience with this sort of transaction might be assigned to the audit, and supervision of staff in this area may be increased. Details of audit procedures for account balances, transactions, and disclosures are emphasized in Chapters 10 through 16.

*Audit Documentation*

For the risk assessment, the auditors should document (1) the discussion of the audit team concerning the risk of material misstatements due to error or fraud, (2) the key elements of the understanding of the entity and its environment, (3) the assessment of the risk of material misstatement at both the financial statement level and the relevant assertion level, and (4) the risks identified. After the procedures have been performed, the auditors should document:

- The auditors' overall responses to address the assessed risk of misstatement at the financial statement level.
- The nature, timing, and extent of further audit procedures performed.
- The linkage of those procedures with the assessed risks at the relevant assertion level.
- The results of the audit procedures.
- With regard to the use of audit evidence, the conclusions reached about the operating effectiveness of controls obtained in a prior audit (this is discussed in Chapter 7).
- Significant risks identified and related controls.
- Those circumstances in which substantive procedures alone will not provide sufficient evidence.

With respect to the auditors' consideration of fraud, the requirements are similar in that auditors must document (1) the discussion among engagement team personnel about fraud risks; (2) the procedures performed to identify fraud risks; (3) the fraud risks identified and the response to those risks; (4) any other conditions that caused the auditors to perform additional fraud-related procedures; and (5) the nature of any communications made to management, the audit committee, or others about fraud.

## The Audit Trail and Directional Testing

In developing audit procedures, the auditors are assisted by the organized manner in which accounting systems record, classify, and summarize data. The flow of accounting data begins with the recording of thousands of individual transactions on such documents as invoices and checks. The information recorded on these original "source" documents is summarized in journals and the amounts in the journals are posted to ledger accounts. At the end of the year, the balances in the ledger accounts are arranged in the form of financial statements.

In thinking of the accounting records as a whole, we may say that a continuous trail of evidence exists—a trail of evidence that links the thousands of individual transactions composing a year's business activity with the summary figures in the financial statements. In a manual accounting system, this *audit trail* consists of source documents, journal entries, and ledger entries. An audit trail also exists within a computer-based accounting system, although it may have a substantially different form; this is discussed in Chapter 8.

Just as a hiker may walk in either direction along a mountain path, an auditor may follow the audit trail in either of two directions. Figure 6.4 illustrates these concepts relating to the *direction of testing*. For example, the auditor may follow specific transactions from

**FIGURE 6.4**
**Direction of Tests**

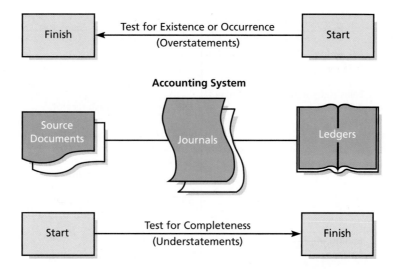

their origin (the source documents) forward to their inclusion in the financial statement summary figures. This approach provides the auditor with assurance that all transactions have been properly interpreted and processed; it is a test of the *completeness assertion.* If a transaction was never recorded, the omission can be detected only by tracing in the direction from the source documents to the journals and ledgers. Note, however, that transactions that are not supported *can never* be found by tracing forward from source documents to the journal entries (left to right).

If the auditors' objective is to detect unsupported financial statement amounts, they should follow the stream of evidence back to its source. This type of test involves tracing back amounts recorded in the financial statements for the period to ledgers and journals and, finally, *vouching* them to the original source documents, such as invoices and receiving reports. By vouching from right to left in Figure 6.4, the auditors may identify journal entries that are not supported and, possibly, not valid. This process of vouching, working backward from the financial statement figures to the detailed documents, provides evidence that financial statement figures are based upon valid transactions; it tests the *existence or occurrence assertion.*

Although the technique of working along the audit trail is a useful one, bear in mind that the auditors also must acquire evidence from sources other than the client's accounting records.

## Transaction Cycles (Classes of Transactions)

A **transaction cycle**, or class of transactions, is the sequence of procedures applied by the client in processing a particular type of recurring transaction. The term *cycle* conveys the idea that the same sequence of procedures is applied to each included transaction. Because of their importance to financial reporting, the auditors' consideration of internal control often is organized around the client's major transaction cycles. While they differ from company to company, typical cycles include (1) the revenue (sales and collections) cycle, (2) the acquisition (purchases and disbursements) cycle, (3) the conversion (production) cycle, (4) the payroll cycle, (5) the investing cycle, and (6) the financing cycle.

To illustrate a specific transaction cycle, consider a company's processes for sales and collections of receivables. The activities performed to process sales transactions might include receiving a customer's purchase order, approving credit, shipping merchandise, preparing the sales invoice, recording the sale, recording the accounts receivable, billing the customer, and handling and recording the cash remitted by the customer. Ultimately, both a sales entry (recorded in the sales journal) and a cash receipts entry (recorded in the cash receipts journal) capture the essential information for financial reporting purposes. That information is then recorded in the appropriate ledger accounts (e.g., accounts receivable, sales, and cash). Figure 6.5 shows the accounts receivable general ledger

**FIGURE 6.5**
**Transactions Affecting Accounts Receivable**

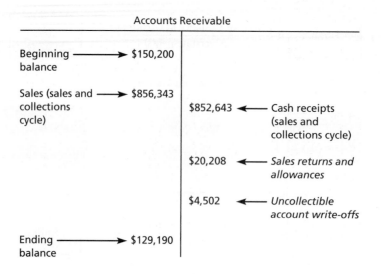

## The Audit Program

account and how the sales and collections cycle affects that account. The figure also illustrates how sales returns and allowances and write-offs of uncollectible accounts affect the Accounts Receivable account.

The audit program may be viewed as including two major sections. The first section deals with the procedures to assess the effectiveness of the client's internal control (the "systems portion"), and the second section deals with financial statement account balances (the "substantive test portion").

### The Systems (Internal Control) Portion of the Program

As indicated above, the systems portion of the audit program is generally organized around the major transaction cycles of the client's accounting system. Audit procedures in the systems portion of the program typically include obtaining an understanding of the controls for each transaction cycle, preparing a flowchart for each cycle, testing the significant controls, and assessing control risk for the related financial statement assertions.

Figure 6.5 is helpful in illustrating the relationship between tests of controls over transactions and substantive procedures. Note that while the auditors' overall objective is to determine whether the ending financial statement balance is correct, two approaches are possible: (1) testing controls over transactions that occurred during the year, or (2) testing the ending account balance directly. That is, if the controls over the transactions that are recorded into the account are effective, assurance is obtained regarding the ending balance. Alternatively, auditors may directly test the ending balance of the account. As a practical matter, auditors use a combination of these two approaches. Indeed, even if controls are considered extremely strong, some substantive procedures must be performed for all significant financial statement accounts.

The systems portion of the audit program includes tests of controls over transactions. The evidence obtained from these tests may be of two types: evidence about the effectiveness of controls and evidence that substantiates the recorded amount of the transactions. For example, a test of a control may involve selecting a sample of sales transactions to test whether recorded transactions were properly approved. This procedure provides evidence to help assess control risk (or the combination of inherent risk and control risk). It does *not* provide evidence to restrict detection risk, since no evidence substantiating the transactions and related balances has been collected (for example, a sale may be approved but may be recorded at an erroneous amount). However, if the auditors simply extend the test to include a determination of whether the transactions were properly recorded, evidence is collected to substantiate sales transactions and the accounts receivable balance.

Accordingly, some tests of controls provide substantive evidence about an account or class of transactions. These procedures are referred to as **dual-purpose procedures (tests)** since they serve as both a test of controls and a substantive test of the details of the transactions that occurred during the year. It should be emphasized, however, that the systems portion of the audit program primarily addresses tests of internal control and assessing control risk.

As a result of their consideration of internal control, the auditors will make appropriate modifications in the substantive procedures portion of the audit program. For example, because of weaknesses in internal control over the proper recording of sales, the auditors may assess control risk (or combined inherent and control risk) for the assertion of existence of accounts receivable as high and decide to send additional accounts receivable confirmations. Alternatively, strong controls may lead the auditors to decide to perform less extensive substantive procedures than would be the case if controls did not function effectively.

## The Substantive Procedures Portion of the Program

The portion of the audit program aimed at substantiating financial statement amounts is organized in terms of major financial statement accounts and classes of transactions, such as cash, accounts receivable, sales, inventories, and plant and equipment. Substantive procedures are used to restrict detection risk for these accounts. As an example, consider the financial statement account, accounts receivable. Examples of audit procedures for accounts receivable include: Confirm with debtors their balance due, review the year-end cutoff of sales transactions, and analyze subsequent collections of year-end receivables. These procedures all help substantiate the year-end accounts receivable balance.

Most audit firms organize much of the substantive portion of their audit programs around the balance sheet accounts. Then, they complete the programs with any additional procedures needed to substantiate income statement accounts and information in financial statement notes. An advantage of this balance sheet approach is that highly reliable evidence generally is available to substantiate assets and liabilities. For example, the ending balance of accounts receivable as presented in Figure 6.6 is usually subject to direct verification by such procedures as inspection of externally created documentary evidence, confirmation, and review of subsequent cash collections. Other assets such as inventory may be physically examined. Liabilities can be verified by examination of externally created documents, confirmation, and inspection of canceled checks after the liability has been paid.

In contrast, consider the nature of revenues and expenses in double-entry accounting. The entry to record revenues or expenses has two parts: (1) the recognition of the revenue or expense, and (2) the corresponding change in an asset or liability account. Revenues and expenses have no tangible form; they exist only as entries in the client's accounting records, representing changes in owners' equity. Consequently, the best evidence supporting the existence of revenues or expenses is often the verifiable change in the related asset or liability account. As a result, many income statement accounts may be verified indirectly by auditing the related balance sheet accounts.

### Indirect Verification of Income Statement Accounts

Figure 6.6 shows the relationship between income statement accounts and the related changes in cash or other balance sheet items. By substantiating the changes in the asset and liability accounts, the auditors indirectly verify revenue, cost of goods sold, and expenses. As an example, most revenue transactions involve a debit to either Cash or Accounts Receivable. If the auditors are able to satisfy themselves that all cash receipts and all changes in accounts receivable during the year have been properly recorded, they have indirect evidence that revenue transactions have been accounted for properly.

**FIGURE 6.6**  The Auditors' Approach to Auditing Financial Statement Accounts

| | Income Statement Items | | Cash Transactions | | Balance Sheet Items |
|---|---|---|---|---|---|
| **Financial Statement Relationships** | Revenue | = | Cash receipts from customers | − | Beginning balance of Accounts Receivable |
| | | | | + | Ending balance of Accounts Receivable |
| | Cost of goods sold | = | Cash payments for merchandise | − | Beginning balance of Accounts Payable |
| | | | | + | Ending balance of Accounts Payable |
| | | | | + | Beginning balance of Inventory |
| | | | | − | Ending balance of Inventory |
| | Expenses | = | Cash payments for expenses | − | Beginning balance of Accrued Expenses |
| | | | | + | Ending balance of Accrued Expenses |
| | | | | + | Beginning balance of Prepaid Expenses |
| | | | | − | Ending balance of Prepaid Expenses |
| | ↑ | | ↑ | | ↑ |
| **Auditors' Approach to Substantiation** | Verify indirectly by substantiating right-hand side of equation; also use analytical procedures, direct computations, and tests of transactions | | Substantiate by testing transactions; also perform reconciliations of cash accounts | | Substantiate by reference to last year's audit working papers |
| | | | | | Substantiate by substantive tests in current year |

### Direct Verification of Income Statement Accounts

Not all of the audit evidence pertaining to income statement accounts is indirect. The verification of a major balance sheet item often involves several closely related income statement accounts that can be verified through computation or other direct evidence. For example, in substantiating the marketable securities owned by the client, it is a simple matter to compute the related interest revenue, dividends revenue, and gains or losses on sales of securities. In substantiating the balance sheet items of plant assets and accumulated depreciation, the auditors make computations that also substantiate depreciation expense. Uncollectible accounts expense is substantiated in conjunction with the balance sheet item Allowance for Doubtful Accounts. In addition to these computations, the auditors' *analytical procedures* provide direct evidence as to the reasonableness of various revenues and expenses.

Certain income statement accounts, such as revenues, are of such significance that the auditors virtually always obtain direct evidence about the fairness of the amounts, typically by performing tests of details of a sample of transactions or substantive analytical procedures.

## Summary of the Relationship between Tests of Controls and Substantive Procedures

Tests of controls provide auditors with evidence as to whether prescribed controls are in use and operating effectively. The results of these tests assist the auditors in evaluating the *likelihood* that material misstatements have occurred. Substantive procedures, on the other hand, are designed to *detect* material misstatements if they exist in the financial statements. The amount of substantive testing done by the auditors is greatly influenced by their assessment of the likelihood that material misstatements exist.

To illustrate, assume that a client's procedures manual indicates that the finished goods warehouse is to be locked at all times and accessible only to authorized personnel. Through tests of controls consisting of inquiry and observation, the auditors learn that the warehouse often is unlocked and that several employees who are not authorized to be in the warehouse regularly eat lunch there. Because the client's internal control procedure is not operating properly, the auditors should recognize that the *risk* of inventory shortages is increased. However, the tests of controls have *not* determined that an inventory shortage does, in fact, exist.

The principal substantive procedure to detect shortages of inventories is the auditors' observation of a physical inventory taken by the client. As part of this observation, the auditors make test counts of various items. In the case of the unlocked warehouse, the auditors' test has shown that internal control cannot be relied upon to prevent shortages. Therefore, the auditors should increase the number of test counts in an effort to verify the existence of inventory.

## Objectives of Audit Programs

The audit procedures contained in the audit program are designed to be responsive to potential material misstatements of the financial statements. To make sure that the program addresses all potential misstatements, auditors often develop audit objectives for each significant account balance and class of transactions. These objectives follow directly from management assertions that are contained in the client's financial statements. From these assertions, general objectives may be developed for each major type of balance sheet account, including assets, liabilities, and owners' equity, and the related income statement accounts. Figure 6.7 presents the relationships between financial statements, management's account balance assertions (discussed in Chapter 5), and audit objectives.

## General Objectives of Audit Programs for Assets

The audit program for each financial statement account must be tailored to address potential misstatements of that account. The potential misstatements for cash are not identical to the potential misstatements for accounts receivable. For example, questions about proper net realizable value cause valuation to be a bigger risk for accounts receivable. However, it is useful to realize that each audit program follows basically the same general approach to

**FIGURE 6.7**
**Relationship of Financial Statement Assertions to the Audit**

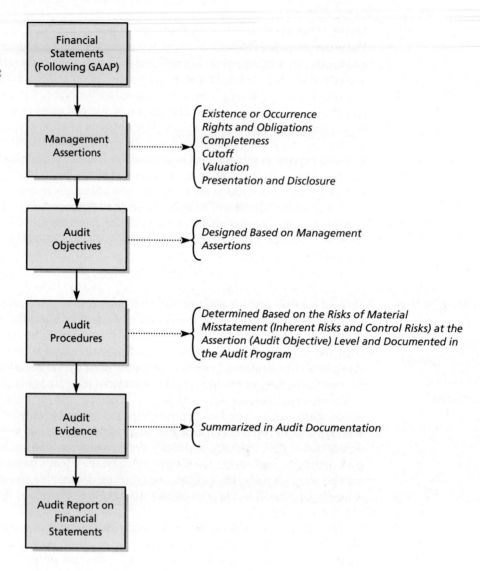

verify the balance sheet items and related income statement amounts. To varying degrees based on the auditors' assessments of risk, the substantive audit program for each asset account will need to include procedures to address the following general objectives:

---

**Substantive Audit Program for Asset Accounts Stated in Terms of General Objectives**

A. Establish the *existence* of assets.

B. Establish that the company has *rights* to the assets.

C. Establish *completeness* of recorded assets.

D. Verify the *cutoff* of transactions.

E. Determine the appropriate *valuation* of the assets.

F. Determine the appropriate financial statement *presentation and disclosure* of the assets.

---

Changes in these audit objectives, with respect to audit programs for liability and owners' equity accounts, will be discussed in later chapters.

# Substantiation of Account Balances

The central purpose of the auditors' risk assessment process, including their assessment of control risk, is to determine the nature, timing, and extent of the audit work necessary to substantiate the account. In subsequent chapters, considerable attention will be given to the auditors' inherent and control risk assessments; let us now discuss the objectives of the auditors' substantive procedures.

**Existence of Assets**

The first step in substantiating an asset is to verify the existence of the item. For assets such as cash on hand, marketable securities, and inventories, existence of the asset usually may be verified by physical observation or inspection, and by *vouching* from the recorded entry to the documents created when the assets were acquired.

When assets are in the custody of others, such as cash in banks and inventory on consignment, the appropriate audit procedure may be direct confirmation with the outside party. The existence of accounts receivable normally is verified by confirming with customers the amounts receivable. To verify the existence of intangibles, the auditors must gather evidence that costs have been incurred and that these costs represent probable future economic benefits.

**Rights to the Assets**

Usually, the same procedures that verify existence also establish the company's rights to the asset. For example, confirming cash balances in bank accounts establishes existence of the cash and the company's ownership rights to that cash. Similarly, inspecting marketable securities verifies both existence and ownership because the registered owner's name usually appears on the face of the security certificate.

With other assets, such as plant and equipment, physical examination establishes existence *but not ownership*. Plant and equipment may be rented or leased rather than owned. To verify the client's rights to plant assets, the auditors must inspect documentary evidence such as property tax bills, purchase documents, and deeds.

The client may not hold legal title to all assets that are appropriately included in the financial statements. Instead, the client may own *rights* to use the assets conveyed by contracts, such as leases. The ownership of these rights may be established by reviewing the underlying contracts.

**Establishing Completeness**

Effective internal control provides assurance that acquisitions are recorded and helps the auditors to establish the completeness of recorded assets. When such controls are found to be ineffective, the scope of substantive procedures must be increased, but this is often a difficult task. When the auditors are testing the completeness of assets, they are looking for assets that have been acquired but not recorded in the accounting records. Therefore, analyzing recorded entries in the asset accounts will not be effective for this purpose; the auditors must take a different approach.

Many tests for unrecorded assets involve *tracing* from the "source documents" created when the assets were acquired to entries in the accounting records. To test for unrecorded accounts receivable, for example, the auditors might select a sample of shipping documents related to sales made during the year and determine that accounts receivable were properly recorded.

Observation and physical examination are important to testing the completeness of recorded physical assets. To illustrate, during the observation of the client's physical inventory, the auditors are alert for inventory items that are not counted or included in the inventory summary. Physically examining equipment may reveal purchases that have not been properly capitalized.

Analytical procedures also may be used to bring conditions to light that indicate that all assets may not be recorded. For example, a low gross profit percentage for the current year in comparison to prior years may indicate that the client has a substantial amount of unrecorded inventory.

## Verifying the Cutoff

As a part of the auditors' procedures for establishing completeness as well as existence of recorded assets, the auditors will verify the client's *cutoff* of transactions included in the period. The financial statements should reflect all transactions occurring through the end of the period and none that occur subsequently. The term *cutoff* refers to the process of determining that transactions occurring near the balance sheet date are assigned to the proper accounting period.

The impact of cutoff errors upon the financial statements varies with the nature of the error. For example, a cutoff error in recording acquisitions of plant assets affects the balance sheet but probably does not affect the income statement, since depreciation usually is not recorded on assets acquired within a few days of year-end. On the other hand, a cutoff error in recording shipments of merchandise to customers affects both inventory and the cost of sales. In order to improve their financial picture, some clients may "hold their records open" to include in the current year cash receipts and revenue from the first part of the next period.

To verify the client's cutoff of transactions, the auditors should review transactions recorded shortly before and after the balance sheet date to ascertain that these transactions are assigned to the proper period. Since such documents as checks, receiving reports, and shipping documents are usually serially numbered, noting the last serial number issued during the period will assist the auditors in determining that a proper cutoff has been made in recording transactions.

## Valuation of Assets

Determining the proper valuation of assets requires a thorough knowledge of generally accepted accounting principles. The auditors must not only establish that the accounting method used to value a particular asset is generally accepted, but also determine that the method of valuation is appropriate and properly applied in the circumstances. Once the auditors are satisfied as to the appropriateness of the method, the auditors will perform procedures to test the accuracy of the client's application of the method of valuation to the asset.

A number of assets are valued at cost. Therefore, a common audit procedure is to vouch the acquisition cost of assets to paid checks and other documentary evidence. If the acquisition cost is subject to depreciation or amortization, the auditors must evaluate the reasonableness of the cost allocation program and verify the computation of the remaining unallocated cost. Increasingly, generally accepted accounting principles require assets to be valued at fair values. Assets valued at fair value, or the lower of cost or market, and those whose carrying value must be compared to fair value to determine whether their values are impaired necessitate an examination of their fair values. Fair values are audited by comparison to prices on existing markets or by examination of valuation models used to develop the values.

Finally, the amount appearing as an asset on a financial statement is almost always the accumulation of many smaller items. For example, the amount of inventory on a financial statement might consist of the cost of thousands or, perhaps, hundreds of thousands of individual products. The auditors must test the clerical accuracy of the underlying records to determine that they accumulate to the total appearing in the general ledger and, therefore, the amount in the financial statements. The auditors often use their audit software to perform these tests of clerical accuracy of the records.

## Financial Statement Presentation and Disclosure

Even after all dollar amounts have been substantiated, the auditors must perform procedures to ensure that the financial statement presentation conforms to the requirements of authoritative accounting pronouncements and the general principle of adequate disclosure. Procedures falling into this category include the review of subsequent events; search for related party transactions; investigation of loss contingencies; review of disclosure of such items as accounting policies, leases, compensating balances, and pledged assets; and consideration of the classification and description of items in the financial statements.

# An Illustration of Audit Program Design

The preceding general objectives apply to all types of assets. Audit procedures for a particular asset account must be designed to address the *specific audit objectives and risks* related to that asset. These specific objectives and risks vary with the nature of the asset and the generally accepted accounting principles that govern its valuation and presentation.

In designing an audit program for a specific account, the auditors start by listing the specific objectives related to the account. Then, they identify the inherent risks related to each of these specific audit objectives. You can think of these risks as declarations of "what could go wrong and thereby result in a material misstatement of the account." Figure 6.8 provides a description of the relationships among audit objectives, risks of material misstatement, and audit procedures.

Figure 6.8 includes examples of identified risks related to each audit objective and only one procedure to address each risk. Usually, a greater number of risks are related to each objective and several procedures may have to be performed to address a particular risk. For example, the audit objective of determining that receivables are properly presented in the balance sheet is not achieved solely by performing procedures focusing on the risk of inadequate disclosure of related party transactions. The audit program must include procedures that focus on other risks related to presentation and disclosure, such as procedures that focus on the risk that the financial statements fail to disclose that receivables have been pledged as collateral for debt. In addition, the complete audit program will include tests of the client's internal control that provide support for the auditors' assessments of control risk.

Chapters 10 through 16 consider the manner in which auditors design tests of controls and substantive procedures for various financial statement accounts. Specific audit objectives and sample audit procedures are presented for various accounts to provide a framework for our discussion. It is important to remember that the audit programs presented in the textbook merely illustrate *typical* procedures. In actual practice, audit programs must be tailored to each client's risks and internal control. The audit procedures comprising audit programs may vary substantially from one engagement to the next.

## Timing of Audit Work

The value of audited financial statements is enhanced if the statements are available on a timely basis after the year-end. To facilitate an early release of the audit report, auditors normally begin the audit well before the balance sheet date. The period before the balance sheet date is termed the **interim period**. Audit work that can always be started during the interim period includes the consideration of internal control, and substantive tests of transactions that have occurred to the interim date.

As discussed in Chapter 5, interim tests of certain financial statement balances, such as accounts receivable, may also be performed, but this results in additional risk that must be controlled by the auditors. Significant misstatements due to error or fraud could arise in these accounts during the *remaining period* between the time that the interim test was performed and the balance sheet date. Thus, to rely on the interim test of a significant account balance, the auditors must perform additional tests of the account during the remaining period.

Performing audit work during the interim period has numerous advantages, in addition to facilitating the timely release of the audited financial statements. The independent auditors may be able to assess internal control more effectively by observing and testing

**FIGURE 6.8**  **Relationships among Audit Objectives, Risks of Material Misstatement, and Audit Procedures**

| General Audit Objectives for Assets | Specific Audit Objectives for Accounts Receivable | Risks of Material Misstatement: "What Can Go Wrong" | Example Audit Procedures |
|---|---|---|---|
| Existence of assets | All recorded receivables exist. | Receivables may have been recorded that do not exist. | Confirm a sample of receivables by direct communication with debtors. |
| | | Management may have fraudulently overstated revenue and receivables by making inappropriate adjusting journal entries. | Review monthly adjusting entries for suspicious items. |
| Rights to assets | The client has rights to the receivables. | Accounting personnel may erroneously be treating a sale of receivables as a liability. | Review confirmations of liabilities to determine if receivables have been sold or factored. |
| Completeness of assets | All receivables are recorded. | Management may have shipped items before the end of the period but not recorded the sales and related receivables until the subsequent period. | Select a sample of sales invoices in the subsequent period and examine the related shipping document for date of shipment. |
| Cutoff of transactions | Sales and cash receipt transactions are recorded in the proper period. | Sales and receivables for the next period may be recorded in the current period. | Vouch sales and cash receipt transactions occurring near period end. |
| Valuation of assets | Receivables are presented at net realizable value. | Allowance for uncollectible accounts may be misestimated by management. | Investigate the credit ratings for delinquent and large receivables. |
| | | Allowance for sales returns and allowances may be misestimated by management. | Compare the amount of credits given to customers in the subsequent period to the amount estimated by management. |
| | | Software routine to develop aged trial balance of receivables may have been erroneously programmed. | Obtain an aged trial balance of receivables, test its clerical accuracy, and reconcile to the ledgers. |
| Financial statement presentation of assets | Receivables are properly presented in the balance sheet, with appropriate disclosures. | Accounting personnel may have failed to identify related party transactions. | Provide a list of related parties to all members of the audit team to assist in identification of the transactions. |

controls at various times throughout the year. Also, they can give early consideration to accounting problems. Another advantage is that interim auditing creates a more uniform workload for CPA firms. With a large client, such as General Motors, the auditors may have office space within the client's buildings and perform audit procedures throughout the entire year.

## Chapter Summary

This chapter explained the manner in which auditors plan an audit, obtain an understanding of the client, assess risks of misstatements, and respond to those risks. To summarize:

1. The audit process may be viewed as including the following six stages: (*a*) plan the audit; (*b*) obtain an understanding of the client and its environment, including internal control; (*c*) assess the risks of misstatement and design further audit procedures; (*d*) perform further audit procedures; (*e*) complete the audit; and (*f*) form an opinion and issue the audit report.

2. Investigating a potential audit client is essential because auditors want to avoid accepting clients that have unscrupulous management. As part of their investigation, the auditors are required to attempt communication with the predecessor auditors.

3. In planning the audit, the auditors establish an understanding with the client, ordinarily in writing through use of an engagement letter that makes clear the nature of the engagement, any limitations on the work, and the responsibilities of the client. During planning, auditors develop an overall audit strategy and audit plan, including an audit program. The audit procedures that are contained in the audit program are designed around the assertions of management, which are embodied in the financial statements and the auditors' assessments of risks and controls.

4. The auditors perform risk assessment procedures (including inquiries, analytical procedures, observation and inspection, and other procedures) to obtain an understanding of the client and its environment. They plan their audit to provide reasonable assurance that the financial statements are free from material misstatement, whether caused by error or fraud.

5. Auditors are particularly concerned about fraud—both fraudulent financial reporting and misappropriation of assets. To identify fraud risks, the auditors have an audit team discussion of potential fraud (as well as errors), make inquiries, perform analytical procedures, and consider the presence of fraud risk factors. The auditors react to fraud risks as they do to other risks of material misstatements, with an overall response or a modification of the nature, timing, and extent of audit procedures. Additionally, the auditors are required in all audits to perform procedures to address the risk of management override of internal control.

6. The auditors must apply the materiality concept, which recognizes that some matters are important to the fair presentation of financial statements, while others are not. Auditors arrive at a measure of materiality for planning purposes and disaggregate it into tolerable misstatements for the various accounts. In evaluating findings, auditors also use materiality. While the materiality measures for both planning and evaluation include quantitative and qualitative considerations, the planning measure emphasizes quantitative considerations, while the evaluation measure emphasizes both quantitative and qualitative considerations.

7. Auditors assess the risks of misstatement they have identified to design further audit procedures. Further audit procedures include both tests of controls and substantive procedures.

## Key Terms Introduced or Emphasized in Chapter 6

**Analytical procedures (198)**   Tests that involve comparisons of financial data for the current year to that of prior years, budgets, nonfinancial data, or industry averages. From a planning standpoint, analytical procedures help the auditors obtain an understanding of the client's business, identify financial statement amounts that appear to be affected by errors or fraud, or identify other potential problems.

**Assertions (185)**   Representations of management that are communicated, explicitly or implicitly, by the financial statements.

**Audit committee (188)**   A committee composed of outside directors (members of the board of directors who are neither officers nor employees) charged with responsibility for appointing, compensating, and overseeing the auditors.

**Audit plan (192)**   A description of the nature, timing, and extent of the audit procedures to be performed. It is often documented with an audit program.

**Audit program (193)**   A detailed listing of the specific audit procedures to be performed in the course of an audit engagement. Audit programs provide a basis for assigning and scheduling audit work and for determining what work remains to be done. Audit programs are specially tailored to the risks and internal controls of each engagement.

**Audit risk (203)**   At the overall engagement level, this is the risk that the auditors may unknowingly fail to appropriately modify their opinion on financial statements that are materially misstated. At the financial statement assertion level, it is the risk that a particular assertion about an account balance is materially misstated.

**Business risks (185)**   Risks that threaten management's ability to achieve the organization's objectives.

**Control risk (185)**   The risk that a material misstatement that could occur in an account will not be prevented or detected on a timely basis by internal control.

**Dual-purpose procedure (test) (213)**   An audit procedure that serves as a test of controls and a substantive test of the details of the transactions that occurred during the year. For example, a test of controls over equipment acquisitions may address authorization (providing evidence on control effectiveness) and whether the transaction tested has been properly recorded in the year's acquisitions (providing substantive evidence on the dollar amounts). As another example, a substantive procedure may reveal a misstatement and be extended to determine the nature of the control that did not operate effectively, thereby providing evidence on operating effectiveness.

**Engagement letter (191)**   A formal letter sent by the auditors to the client at the beginning of an engagement summarizing such matters as the nature of the engagement, any limitations on the scope of audit work, work to be done by the client's staff, and the basis for the audit fee. The purpose of engagement letters is to avoid misunderstandings; they are essential on nonaudit engagements as well as audits.

**Engagement risk (188)**   The risk of loss or injury to the auditors' reputation by association with a client that goes bankrupt or one whose management lacks integrity.

**Fraudulent financial reporting (management fraud) (205)**   Material misstatement of financial statements by management with the intent to mislead financial statement users.

**Further audit procedures (209)**   Substantive procedures for all relevant assertions and tests of controls when the auditors' risk assessment includes an expectation that controls are operating effectively, or when substantive procedures alone do not provide sufficient appropriate audit evidence. The auditors perform risk assessment procedures to obtain an understanding of the client and its environment, including internal control. They then conduct a risk assessment and determine the appropriate further audit procedures.

**Inherent risk (185)**   The risk of material misstatement of an assertion about an account without considering internal control.

**Interim period (219)**   The time interval from the beginning of audit work to the balance sheet date. Many audit procedures can be performed during the interim period to facilitate early issuance of the audit report.

**Internet (195)**   An international network of independently owned computers that operates as a giant computing network. Data on the Internet are stored on "Web servers," which are computers scattered throughout the world.

**Misappropriation of assets (defalcations) (205)**   Theft of client assets by an employee or officer of the organization.

**Opening balances (194)**   Those account balances that exist at the beginning of the period. Opening balances are based upon the closing balances of the prior period and reflect the effects of transactions and events of prior periods and accounting policies applied in the prior period. Opening balances also include matters requiring disclosure that existed at the beginning of the period, such as contingencies and commitments.

**Overall audit strategy (192)**   This strategy involves determining overall characteristics of the engagement that define its scope, determining the engagement's reporting objectives to plan the timing of procedures, and considering important factors that will determine the focus of the audit team's efforts. When the overall audit strategy has been established, the auditors start the development of a more detailed audit plan to address the various matters identified in the audit strategy.

**Performance materiality (201)**   The amount set by the auditors at less than materiality for accounts (or individual financial statements) to reduce to an appropriately low level the probability that the aggregate of uncorrected and undetected misstatements exceeds materiality for the financial statements as a whole.

**Predecessor auditors (189)**   A CPA firm that formerly served as auditor but has resigned from the engagement or has been notified that its services have been terminated.

**Relevant assertion (194)**   A financial statement assertion that has a reasonable possibility of containing a misstatement or misstatements that would cause the financial statements to be materially misstated. The determination of whether an assertion is a relevant assertion is based on inherent risk, without regard to the effect of controls.

**Risk assessment procedures (185)**   The audit procedures performed to obtain an understanding of the entity and its environment, including the entity's internal control. They are designed to identify and assess the risks of material misstatement, whether due to fraud or error, at the financial statement and assertion levels. Risk assessment procedures include (a) inquiries of management and others within the entity; (b) analytical procedures; and (c) observation and other procedures, including inquiries of others outside the entity.

**Shopping for accounting principles (190)**   Conduct by some enterprises that discharge one independent auditing firm after seeking out another firm that will sanction a disputed accounting principle or financial statement presentation.

**Significant risks (204)**   Identified and assessed risks of material misstatement that, in the auditor's judgment, require special audit consideration.

**Substantive procedures (185)**   Tests of account balances and transactions designed to detect any material misstatements in the financial statements. The nature, timing, and extent of substantive procedures are determined by the auditors' assessment of risks and their consideration of the client's internal control.

**Successor auditors (189)**   The auditors who have accepted an engagement or who have been invited to make a proposal for an engagement to replace the CPA firm that formerly served as auditor.

**Tests of controls (185)**   Tests directed toward the design or operation of a control to assess its effectiveness in preventing or detecting material misstatements of financial statement assertions.

**Time budget (193)**   An estimate of the time required to perform each step in the audit.

**Transaction cycle (211)**   The sequence of procedures applied by the client in processing a particular type of recurring transaction. The term *cycle* reflects the idea that the same sequence of procedures is applied to each similar transaction. The auditors' consideration of internal control often is organized around the client's major transaction cycles.

## Review Questions

6–1.   What information should a CPA firm seek in its investigation of a prospective client?

6–2.   In a public company, what requirements must members of the board of directors satisfy in order to serve on the audit committee?

6–3.   State the purpose and nature of an engagement letter.

6–4.   Discuss what is meant by the phrase "shopping for accounting principles." What mechanisms have served to prevent this practice by management?

6–5.   Criticize the following statement: "Throughout this audit, for all purposes, we will define a 'material amount' as $500,000."

6–6.   Describe the two types of misstatements due to fraud. Which one generally is of more concern to the auditors?

6–7.   Many CPA firms are taking a business risk approach to audits. Define what is meant by business risk. Provide an example of a business risk that could result in a risk of material misstatement of the financial statements.

6–8.   Should a separate audit program be prepared for each audit engagement, or can a standard program be used for most engagements?

6–9.   "An audit program is desirable when new staff members are assigned to an engagement, but an experienced auditor should be able to conduct an audit without reference to an audit program." Do you agree? Discuss.

6–10.   Describe the risk of material misstatement of an assertion. List the two components that make up this risk.

6–11.   Certain audit risks are significant in that they require special audit consideration. Describe the typical characteristics of these significant risks.

6–12.   Suggest some factors that might cause an audit engagement to exceed the original time estimate. Would the extra time be charged to the client?

6–13. What problems are created for a CPA firm when audit staff members underreport the amount of time spent in performing specific audit procedures?

6–14. Why is audit work usually organized around balance sheet accounts rather than income statement accounts?

6–15. Identify the general objectives of the auditors' substantive procedures with respect to any major asset category.

6–16. What is meant by making a proper year-end *cutoff?* Explain the effects of errors in the cutoff of sales transactions in both the income statement and the balance sheet.

6–17. What are the purposes of the audit procedures of (*a*) tracing a sample of journal entries forward to the ledgers and (*b*) vouching a sample of ledger entries back to the journals?

6–18. Charles Halstead, CPA, has a number of clients who desire audits at the end of the calendar year. In an effort to spread his workload more uniformly throughout the year, he is preparing a list of audit procedures that could be performed satisfactorily before the year-end balance sheet date. What audit work, if any, might be done in advance of the balance sheet date?

6–19. Define and differentiate between a test of controls and a substantive procedure.

6–20. The audit plan, the audit program, and the time budget are three important working papers prepared early in an audit. What functions do these working papers serve in the auditors' compliance with generally accepted auditing standards? Discuss.

6–21. Auditing standards require the auditors to have a team meeting regarding the risk of fraud for the engagement. What is the purpose of this meeting?

6–22. How can a CPA make use of the preceding year's audit working papers in a recurring audit?

6–23. When planning an audit, the auditors must assess the levels of risk and materiality for the engagement. Explain how the auditors' judgments about these two factors affect the auditors' planned audit procedures.

## Questions Requiring Analysis

**LO 2** 6–24. Morgan, CPA, is approached by a prospective audit client who wants to engage Morgan to perform an audit for the current year. In prior years, this prospective client was audited by another CPA. Identify the specific procedures that Morgan should follow in deciding whether to accept this client.

**LO 2, 3** 6–25. Mary Deming has been asked to accept an engagement to audit a small financial institution. Deming has not previously audited a financial institution.

*Required:*

    *a.* Describe the types of knowledge about the prospective client and its environment that Deming must obtain to plan the engagement.

    *b.* Explain how Deming may obtain this knowledge.

    *c.* Discuss how this knowledge of the client and its environment will help Deming in planning and performing an audit in accordance with generally accepted auditing standards.

**LO 1, 3, 4, 7** 6–26. Assume that you have been assigned to the audit of Lockyer Manufacturing Company. You have completed the procedures for gathering information about the company and its environment, including internal control.

    *a.* Describe the next stage of the audit process.

    *b.* Explain how the auditors may respond to high risk audit engagements and high risk audit assertions.

    *c.* Describe the nature of *further audit procedures,* including when the procedures must include tests of controls.

**LO 3** 6–27. A CPA has been asked to audit the financial statements of a nonpublic company for the first time. All preliminary discussions have been completed between the CPA, the company, the predecessor auditors, and all other necessary parties. The CPA is now preparing an engagement letter. List the items that should be included in the engagement letter.

**LO 6** 6–28. Auditors must plan and perform their audits to provide reasonable assurance of detecting material misstatements in financial statements, including those resulting from fraud.

*Required:*

    *a.* Distinguish between fraudulent financial reporting and misappropriation of assets.

    *b.* Describe the three fundamental conditions necessary for the commission of fraud. Provide an illustration of these three conditions for a case of fraudulent financial reporting.

    *c.* Describe the three ways in which the auditors may respond to fraud risks in an audit.

**LO 5** 6–29. In planning every audit, the auditors are required to consider materiality for audit purposes. Described below are financial statement data from two separate companies:

|  | Franklin Co. | Tyler Co. |
|---|---|---|
| Total assets | $34,900,000 | $2,700,000 |
| Total revenue | 29,600,000 | 4,500,000 |
| Equity | 13,800,000 | 1,000,000 |
| Net income before taxes | 1,600,000 | 90,000 |

*Required:*

a. Develop an estimate of the appropriate amount of planning materiality for Franklin Co., and describe how you arrived at the estimate.

b. Develop an estimate of the appropriate amount of planning materiality for Tyler Co., and describe how you arrived at the estimate.

c. Describe five characteristics of a small misstatement that might render it qualitatively material.

**LO 5** 6–30. The auditors sometimes decide to allocate the amount of planning materiality to various financial statement accounts.

*Required:*

a. Explain why auditors typically decide to allocate planning materiality to individual financial statement accounts.

b. Describe why the total amount of planning materiality allocated to individual accounts may exceed overall materiality.

**LO 6** 6–31. John Wells, CPA, is planning the audit of CVG Services, Inc. As a result of his risk assessment procedures, Wells has identified several fraud risks.

*Required:*

a. Explain in detail how Wells might respond to risks of material misstatement of the financial statements due to fraud.

b. Describe the auditors' communication responsibilities in situations in which the auditors believe fraud has occurred.

**LO 3, 4** 6–32. Listed below are several of the auditors' general objectives in performing substantive procedures on an asset account:

1. Establish the existence of assets.
2. Establish that the company has rights to the assets.
3. Establish the completeness of recorded assets.
4. Verify the cutoff of transactions.
5. Determine the appropriate valuation of the assets.
6. Establish the clerical accuracy of the underlying records.
7. Determine the appropriate financial statement presentation and disclosure of the assets.

*Required:*

Indicate the general objective (or objectives) of each of the following audit procedures:

a. Observe the client's physical inventory.

b. Locate on the client's premises a sample of the equipment items listed in the subsidiary plant and equipment ledger.

c. Obtain a listing of inventory and reconcile the total to the general ledger.

d. Trace a sample of shipping documents to recorded sales transactions.

e. Identify related parties.

f. Vouch selected purchases of securities to brokers' advices.

**LO 4, 5** 6–33. In designing further audit procedures, the auditors must assess the risks of material misstatement of the financial statements.

*Required:*

a. Describe the auditors' general approach to such risk assessment.

b. Identify potential responses to financial statement level risks.

c. Explain what is meant by a significant risk.

d. Describe how a significant risk must be treated in an audit.

**LO 7** 6–34. Richard Foster, an assistant auditor, was assigned to the year-end audit work of Sipher Corporation. Sipher is a small manufacturer of language translation equipment. As his first assignment, Foster was instructed to test the cutoff of year-end sales transactions. Since Sipher uses a calendar year-end for its financial statements, Foster began by obtaining the computer-generated sales ledgers and journals for December and January. He then traced ledger postings for a few days before and after December 31 to the sales journals, noting the dates of the journal entries. Foster noted no journal entries that were posted to the ledger in the wrong accounting period. Thus, he concluded that the client's cutoff of sales transactions was effective.

*Required:* Comment on the validity of Foster's conclusion. Explain fully.

**LO 2, 3, 4, 5** 6–35. SEC filings of certain public companies can be accessed from EDGAR (Electronic Data Gathering, Analysis, and Retrieval system), which has the following Internet address:

**www.sec.gov/edgar.shtml**

*Required:*

a.  Use EDGAR to locate a company in the software industry.

b.  Access the latest Form 10-K for the company and read the "Management's Discussion and Analysis" section.

c.  Describe four significant business risks of the company as described in its "Management's Discussion and Analysis."

**LO 6** 6–36. In every audit engagement, the auditors must identify fraud risks that may require an audit response. Described below are four circumstances or factors that may create an increased risk of material misstatement of the financial statements due to fraud.

1.  The compensation of management of a subsidiary of the client is heavily dependent on the net income of the subsidiary and controls over subsidiary management are weak.

2.  The compensation of management of a telecommunications firm is significantly tied to revenue, and analytical procedures indicate that revenue may be overstated. The company engages in complex sales agreements.

3.  Futures traders in an energy company are compensated based on the performance of their purchases and sales of energy futures contracts. The markets for these contracts have few participants, resulting in the need to value contracts on hand at year-end based on complex valuation models applied by the traders.

4.  A chain of discount markets has inconsistent profit margins across stores as indicated by analytical procedures.

*Required:*

a.  For each of the four circumstances, indicate the fraud risk that the auditors should consider.

b.  For each of the four circumstances, indicate a possible appropriate response by the auditors.

**LO 3** 6–37. The text of the Securities Exchange Act of 1934 may be accessed on the Internet, using the following address:

**www.law.uc.edu/CCL/34Act/index.html**

*Required:*

a.  Use the Internet to access the text of the Securities Exchange Act of 1934.

b.  Read and summarize the internal control requirements of Section 13(b)(2) of the act.

## Objective Questions

**All applicable questions are available with McGraw-Hill's *Connect*<sup>TM</sup> *Accounting*.** ▦ connect
|ACCOUNTING

**LO 6** 6–38. **Multiple Choice Questions**

Select the best answer for each of the following. Explain the reasons for your selection.

a.  In planning and performing an audit, auditors are concerned about risk factors for two distinct types of fraud: fraudulent financial reporting and misappropriation of assets. Which of the following is a risk factor for misappropriation of assets?

(1) Generous performance-based compensation systems.

(2) Management preoccupation with increased financial performance.

(3) An unreliable accounting system.

(4) Strained relationships between management and the auditors.

**LO 2** b.  The audit committee of a company must be made up of:

(1) Representatives from the client's management, investors, suppliers, and customers.

(2) The audit partner, the chief financial officer, the legal counsel, and at least one outsider.

(3) Representatives of the major equity interests, such as preferred and common stockholders.

(4) Members of the board of directors who are not officers or employees.

**LO 2, 3**

   *c.* Which of the following should not normally be included in the engagement letter for an audit?

     (1) A description of the responsibilities of client personnel to provide assistance.

     (2) An indication of the amount of the audit fee.

     (3) A description of the limitations of an audit.

     (4) A listing of the client's branch offices selected for testing.

**LO 7**

   *d.* Which portion of an audit is least likely to be completed before the balance sheet date?

     (1) Tests of controls.

     (2) Issuance of an engagement letter.

     (3) Substantive procedures.

     (4) Assessment of control risk.

**LO 2**

   *e.* Which of the following should the auditors obtain from the predecessor auditors before accepting an audit engagement?

     (1) Analysis of balance sheet accounts.

     (2) Analysis of income statement accounts.

     (3) All matters of continuing accounting significance.

     (4) Facts that might bear on the integrity of management.

**LO 4**

   *f.* As one step in testing sales transactions, a CPA traces a random sample of sales journal entries to debits in the accounts receivable subsidiary ledger. This test provides evidence as to whether:

     (1) Each recorded sale represents a bona fide transaction.

     (2) All sales have been recorded in the sales journal.

     (3) All debit entries in the accounts receivable subsidiary ledger are properly supported by sales journal entries.

     (4) Recorded sales have been properly posted to customer accounts.

**LO 1, 7**

   *g.* The primary objective of tests of details of transactions performed as substantive procedures is to:

     (1) Comply with generally accepted auditing standards.

     (2) Attain assurance about the reliability of the accounting system.

     (3) Detect material misstatements in the financial statements.

     (4) Evaluate whether management's policies and procedures are operating effectively.

**LO 5**

   *h.* The risk that the auditors will conclude, based on substantive procedures, that a material misstatement does not exist in an account balance when, in fact, such misstatement *does* exist is referred to as

     (1) Business risk.

     (2) Engagement risk.

     (3) Control risk.

     (4) Detection risk.

**LO 5**

   *i.* Which of the following elements underlies the application of generally accepted auditing standards, particularly the standards of fieldwork and reporting?

     (1) Adequate disclosure.

     (2) Quality control.

     (3) Materiality and audit risk.

     (4) Client acceptance.

**LO 6**

   *j.* Which of the following best describes what is meant by the term "fraud risk factor"?

     (1) Factors that, when present, indicate that risk exists.

     (2) Factors often observed in circumstances where frauds have occurred.

     (3) Factors that, when present, require modification of planned audit procedures.

     (4) Weaknesses in internal control identified during an audit.

**LO 6**    *k.* Three conditions generally are present when fraud occurs. Select the one below that is *not* one of those conditions.

  (1) Incentive or pressure.

  (2) Opportunity.

  (3) Supervisory position.

  (4) Attitude.

**LO 6, 7**    *l.* Which of the following is most likely to be an overall response to fraud risks identified in an audit?

  (1) Supervise members of the audit team less closely and rely more upon judgment.

  (2) Use less predictable audit procedures.

  (3) Use only certified public accountants on the engagement.

  (4) Place increased emphasis on the audit of objective transactions rather than subjective transactions.

(AICPA, adapted)

**LO 3, 4, 6**    **6–39.   Simulation**

Michael Green, CPA, is considering audit risk at the financial statement level in planning the audit of National Federal Bank (NFB) Company's financial statements for the year ended December 31, 20X1. Audit risk at the financial statement level is influenced by the risks of material misstatements (including fraud risks), which may be indicated by a combination of factors related to management, the environment, and the entity. For each of the following factors, indicate whether they increase or decrease the risk of material misstatement and (2) whether they create a risk of fraud.

| Factor | Effect on Risks of Material Misstatement (Increase or Decrease) | Create a Risk of Fraud? (Yes or No) |
|---|---|---|
| a.  NFB is a continuing audit client. | | |
| b.  The banking industry has been significantly impacted by the downturn in the economy in recent years. | | |
| c.  NFB operates in a growing, prosperous area and has remained profitable over the years. | | |
| d.  Government regulation and overview of the banking industry is extensive and effective. | | |
| e.  NFB's board of directors is controlled by Smith, the majority stockholder, who also acts as the chief executive officer. | | |
| f.  Interest rates have been very volatile recently. | | |
| g.  Management at the bank's branch offices has authority for directing and controlling NFB's operations and is compensated based on branch profitability. | | |
| h.  The internal auditor reports directly to Harris, a minority shareholder, who also acts as chairman of the board's audit committee. | | |
| i.  The accounting department has experienced little turnover in personnel during the five years Green has audited NFB. | | |
| j.  During 20X1, NFB increased the efficiency of its accounting operations by installing a new, sophisticated computer system. | | |
| k.  NFB's formula has consistently underestimated the allowance for loan losses in current years. | | |
| l.  Management has been receptive to Green's suggestions relating to accounting adjustments. | | |

**LO 4, 5**  6–40.  **Simulation**

You are working with William Bond, CPA, and you are considering the risk of material misstatement in planning the audit of Toxic Waste Disposal (TWD) Company's financial statements for the year ended December 31, 20X0. TWD is a privately owned entity that contracts with municipal governments to remove environmental waste.

Based only on the information below, indicate whether each of the following factors would most likely increase (I), decrease (D), or have no effect (NE) on the risk of material misstatement.

| Information | Effect on Risk of Material Misstatement |
|---|---|
| a. Because municipalities have received increased federal and state funding for environmental purposes, TWD returned to profitability for the first year following three years with losses. | |
| b. TWD's Board of Directors is controlled by Mead, the majority stockholder, who also acts as the chief executive officer. | |
| c. The internal auditor reports to the controller and the controller reports to Mead. | |
| d. The accounting department has experienced a high rate of turnover of key personnel. | |
| e. TWD's bank has a loan officer who meets regularly with TWD's CEO and controller to monitor TWD's financial performance. | |
| f. TWD's employees are paid biweekly. | |
| g. TWD has such a strong financial presence in its industry to allow it often to dictate the terms or conditions of transactions with its suppliers. | |
| h. During 20X1, TWD changed its method of preparing its financial statements from the cash basis to generally accepted accounting principles. | |
| i. During 20X1, TWD sold one-half of its controlling interest in United Equipment Leasing (UEL) Co. TWD retained significant influence over UEL. | |
| j. During 20X1, litigation filed against TWD from an action 10 years ago that alleged that TWD discharged pollutants into state waterways was dropped by the state. Loss contingency disclosures that TWD included in prior years' financial statements are being removed from the 20X1 financial statements. | |
| k. During December 20X1, TWD signed a contract to lease disposal equipment from an entity owned by Mead's parents. This related-party transaction is not disclosed in TWD's notes to the 20X1 financial statements. | |
| l. During December 20X1, TWD completed a barter transaction with a municipality. TWD removed waste from the municipally owned site and acquired title to another contaminated site at below market price. TWD intends to service this new site in 20X2. | |
| m. During December 20X1, TWD increased its casualty insurance coverage on several pieces of sophisticated machinery from historical cost to replacement cost. | |
| n. Inquiries about the substantial increase in revenue TWD recorded in the fourth quarter of 20X1 disclosed a new operating policy. TWD guaranteed to several municipalities that it would refund the federal and state funding paid to TWD if any municipality fails a federal or state site clean-up inspection in 20X2. | |
| o. An initial public offering of TWD's stock is planned for late 20X2. | |

**LO 2, 3, 4, 5, 6, 7**  6–41.  **Simulation**

You have been hired to perform the audit of Hanmei, Inc.'s financial statements. When planning such an audit, you often may need to access the profession's auditing standards to perform research. For each of the following circumstances, select the topic most closely related in the Professional Standards topics on the following page. A topic may be selected once, more than once, or not at all.

*Transactions*

*a.* Possible risk factors related to misappropriation of assets

*b.* The relationship between materiality used for planning versus evaluation purposes

    *c.* Hanmei, Inc., has transactions with the corporation president's brother

    *d.* Comparing a client's unaudited results for the year with last year's audited results

    *e.* Requirements relating to identifying violations of occupational safety and health regulations

    *f.* The need to "brainstorm" among audit team members about how accounts could be intentionally misstated

    *g.* Details on considering design effectiveness of controls

    *h.* The importance of considering the possibility of overstated revenues (e.g., through premature revenue recognition)

*Professional Standards Topics*

1. Analytical procedures
2. Materiality in planning and performing an audit
3. Consideration of fraud in a financial statement audit
4. Understanding the entity and its environment and assessing the risks of material misstatement
5. Consideration of laws and regulations
6. Management representations
7. Related parties

**LO 4, 5**    **6–42.** Assume the following general flow of documents in an accounting system. Reply to the following questions:

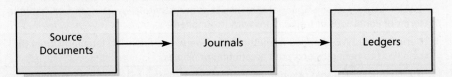

    *a.* The auditors are concerned about source documents that reflect valid transactions that have not been recorded in the journals. Which procedure would be most effective?

        (1) Trace *from* source documents *to* journals.

        (2) Vouch *from* journals *to* source documents.

        (3) Either (1) or (2).

    *b.* The auditors are concerned about transactions that have been recorded in the journals (and subsequently in the ledgers) that are not valid—that is, a transaction is recorded, but it did not actually occur (e.g., a fraudulent overstatement of sales). Which procedure would be most effective?

        (1) Trace *from* source documents *to* journals.

        (2) Vouch *from* journals *to* source documents.

        (3) Either (1) or (2).

    *c.* The auditors are concerned about transactions that have been recorded for improper amounts. Which procedure would be most effective?

        (1) Trace *from* source documents *to* journals.

        (2) Vouch *from* journals *to* source documents.

        (3) Either (1) or (2).

    *d.* Tracing from source documents to journals most directly tests:

        (1) Completeness (understatements).

        (2) Existence (overstatements).

    *e.* Vouching from journals (or ledgers) to source documents most directly tests:

        (1) Completeness (understatements).

        (2) Existence (overstatements).

**LO All**   6–43.   For each definition (or portion of a definition) in the first column, select the term that most closely applies. Each term may be used only once or not at all.

| Definition (or Portion) | Term |
|---|---|
| a. A detailed listing of the specific audit procedures to be performed in the course of an audit engagement. | 1. Audit plan |
| b. A description of the nature, timing, and extent of the audit procedures to be performed. It is often documented with an audit program. | 2. Audit program |
| | 3. Audit risk |
| | 4. Representation letter |
| c. An estimate of the time required to perform each step in the audit. | 5. Business risk |
| d. The purpose of this document is to avoid misunderstandings between the auditors and the client. | 6. Control risk |
| | 7. Engagement letter |
| e. The risk of material misstatement of an assertion about an account without considering internal control. | 8. Inherent risk |
| f. At the overall engagement level, this is the risk that the auditors may unknowingly fail to appropriately modify their opinion on financial statements that are materially misstated. | 9. Significant risk |
| | 10. Survival risk |
| | 11. Time budget |
| g. An identified risk that requires special audit consideration. | |
| h. A risk that threatens management's ability to achieve the organization's objectives. | |

## Problems

**All applicable problems are available with McGraw-Hill's *Connect*™ *Accounting*.** 🔲 connect |ACCOUNTING

**LO 1, 2, 3**   6–44.   You are invited by John Bray, the president of Cheviot Corporation, to discuss with him the possibility of your conducting an audit of the company. The corporation is a small, closely held manufacturing organization that appears to be expanding. No previous audit has been performed by independent certified public accountants. Your discussions with Bray include an analysis of the recent monthly financial statements, inspection of the accounting records, and discussion of policies with the chief accountant. You also are taken on a guided tour of the plant by the president. He then makes the following statement:

> Before making definite arrangements for an audit, I would like to know about how long it will take and about how much it will cost. I want quality work and expect to pay a fair price, but since this is our first experience with independent auditors, I would like a full explanation as to how the cost of the audit is determined. Will you please send me a memorandum covering these points?

Write the memorandum requested by John Bray.

**LO 3, 6**   6–45.   Valley Finance Company opened four personal loan offices in neighboring cities on January 2. Small cash loans are made to borrowers who repay the principal with interest in monthly installments over a period not exceeding two years. Ralph Norris, president of the company, uses one of the offices as a central office and visits the other offices periodically for supervision and internal auditing purposes.

*Required:*   Assume that you agreed to audit Valley Finance Company's financial statements for the year ended December 31. No scope limitations were imposed.

*a.* How would you determine the scope necessary to complete your audit satisfactorily? Discuss.

*b.* Would you be responsible for the discovery of fraud in this audit? Discuss.

**LO 3**   6–46.   You are a new staff assistant with the Houston office of a national public accounting firm. Yesterday you read an article in *The Wall Street Journal* in which the managing partner of your firm's New York office discussed the problems caused for the public accounting profession by auditors underreporting the number of hours worked on audits.

You found this article interesting because of the experience you are having on the audit of Regal Industries, one of your office's largest clients. The fieldwork at Regal is being run by Mark Thomas, a very hard-working senior who is highly regarded within your office. Thomas made senior in record time and has established a reputation for bringing jobs in on schedule. Four staff assistants, including yourself, are working under Thomas.

At the end of the engagement, Thomas will write a performance report on each assistant, which will be placed in the assistant's personnel file. The manager on the engagement also writes a performance evaluation on each assistant and on Thomas. You have heard, however, that managers usually agree with whatever the senior has said about an assistant's performance.

The budgeted time estimates for almost every audit procedure being performed at Regal seem too short. No one is able to finish anything on schedule. Last week, Thomas approached all the staff assistants about working Saturday to "catch up." He said that he was going to work a short day on Saturday and would not report the hours on his time sheet. He said that if you would do the same, he would buy lunch after you finished up on Saturday. You and two other assistants agreed. The fourth assistant, Dave Scott, declined, saying that he was going to a baseball game on Saturday.

The work on Saturday ran smoothly, and it was nice to wear jeans instead of dress clothes. You did quit a little early, although it was about 3:30, not noon. Afterward, Thomas bought everyone lunch at a popular restaurant.

During the following workweek, you noticed that Thomas seemed quite friendly toward you and the other two assistants who had worked on Saturday. He also was complimentary of your work. He was not complimentary of Scott's work; in fact, you heard him comment to the engagement manager that he thought Scott would be a "short-timer," a phrase used to describe staff assistants who do not last long in public accounting. You were not too sympathetic to Scott's plight, however, as you and the other staff assistants also feel that Scott's work on the engagement has been substandard.

It is now Thursday afternoon, and Thomas has just asked the three of you who worked last Saturday if you will do the same thing again this week. He did not ask Scott. Again, Thomas offered to buy lunch if you would leave the hours off your time sheets. You suspect that Thomas has read the article in *The Wall Street Journal*, because he seemed a little defensive about asking you to underreport your time. He pointed out that you are not paid by the hour anyway, so leaving the extra hours off your time sheet "doesn't really cost you anything."

*Required:*

a. Briefly explain why the managing partner of an office would probably oppose the practice of underreporting hours worked by the audit staff.

b. Briefly explain why a senior might *not* oppose the practice.

c. Explain how you think the other two staff assistants asked to work Saturday will probably respond. If you would respond differently, explain.

d. Suggest quality control procedures that you think could be implemented by a CPA firm to discourage the underreporting of time by audit staff members.

**LO 3, 4, 7**   6–47.   Precision Industries, Inc., is a manufacturer of electronic components. When a purchase order is received from a customer, a sales clerk prepares a serially numbered sales order and sends copies to the shipping and accounting departments. When the merchandise is shipped to the customer, the shipping department prepares a serially numbered shipping advice and sends a copy to the accounting department. Upon receipt of the appropriate documents, the accounting department records the sale in the accounting records. All shipments are *FOB shipping point.*

*Required:*

a. How can the auditors determine whether Precision Industries, Inc., has made a proper year-end cutoff of sales transactions?

b. Assume that all shipments for the first five days of the following year were recorded as occurring in the current year. If not corrected, what effect will this cutoff error have upon the financial statements for the current year?

**Ethics Case**   **LO 2, 6**   6–48.   Tammy Potter, a new partner with the regional CPA firm of Tower & Tower, was recently appointed to the board of directors of a local civic organization. The chairman of the board of the civic organization is Lewis Edmond, who is also the owner of a real estate development firm, Tierra Corporation.

Potter was quite excited when Edmond indicated that his corporation needed an audit and he wished to discuss the matter with her. During the discussion, Potter was told that Tierra Corporation needed the audit to obtain a substantial amount of additional financing to acquire another company. Presently, Tierra Corporation is successful, profitable, and committed to growth. The audit fee for the engagement should be substantial.

Since Tierra Corporation appeared to be a good client prospect, Potter tentatively indicated that Tower & Tower wanted to do the work. Potter then mentioned that Tower & Tower's quality control policies require an investigation of new clients and approval by the managing partner, Lee Tower.

Potter obtained the authorization of Edmond to make the necessary inquiries for the new client investigation. Edmond was found to be a highly respected member of the community. Also, Tierra Corporation was highly regarded by its banker and its attorney, and the Dun & Bradstreet report on the corporation reflected nothing negative.

As a final part of the investigation process, Potter contacted Edmond's former tax accountant, Bill Turner. Potter was surprised to discover that Turner did not share the others' high opinion of Edmond. Turner related that on an IRS audit 10 years ago, Edmond was questioned about the details of a large capital loss reported on the sale of a tract of land to a trust. Edmond told the IRS agent that he had lost all the supporting documentation for the transaction, and that he had no way of finding out the names of the principals of the trust. A search by an IRS auditor revealed that the land was recorded in the name of Edmond's married daughter and that Edmond himself was listed as the trustee. The IRS disallowed the loss and Edmond was assessed a civil fraud penalty. Potter was concerned about these findings, but eventually concluded that Edmond had probably matured to a point where he would not engage in such activities.

*Required:*

a. Present arguments supporting a decision to accept Tierra Corporation as an audit client.

b. Present arguments supporting a decision *not* to accept Tierra Corporation as an audit client.

c. Assuming that you are Lee Tower, set forth your decision regarding acceptance of the client, identifying those arguments from part (*a*) or part (*b*) that you found most persuasive.

## Appendix 6A

# Selected Internet Addresses

### Accounting and Auditing Web Sites

American Institute of CPAs—www.aicpa.org

Association of Certified Fraud Examiners—www.acfe.com

The Committee of Sponsoring Organizations of the Treadway Commission (COSO)—www.coso.org

The Institute of Internal Auditors—www.theiia.org

The International Federation of Accountants—www.ifac.org

### Large Accounting Firms

BDO USA LLP—www.bdo.com/

Deloitte LLP—www.deloitte.com/

Ernst & Young LLP—www.ey.com/

Grant Thornton LLP—www.gt.com/

KPMG LLP—www.us.kpmg.com/

McGladrey LLP—www.mcgladrey.com/

PricewaterhouseCoopers LLP—www.pwcglobal.com/

### Securities and Exchange Commission

Home page—www.sec.gov/

EDGAR page—www.sec.gov/edgar.shtml

Securities Act of 1933—www.law.uc.edu/CCL/33Act/index.html

Securities Exchange Act of 1934—www.law.uc.edu/CCL/34Act/index.html

### Public Company Accounting Oversight Board

PCAOB—www.pcaob.org

# Examples of Fraud Risk Factors

## Risk Factors Relating to Misstatements Arising from Fraudulent Financial Reporting

### INCENTIVES AND PRESSURES

1. Financial stability or profitability is threatened by economic, industry, or entity operating conditions, such as (or as indicated by):
   a. High degree of competition or market saturation, accompanied by declining margins.
   b. High vulnerability to rapid changes, such as changes in technology, product obsolescence, or interest rates.
   c. Significant declines in customer demand and increasing business failures in either the industry or overall economy.
   d. Operating losses making the threat of bankruptcy, foreclosure, or hostile takeover imminent.
   e. Recurring negative cash flows from operations or an inability to generate cash flows from operations while reporting earnings and earnings growth.
   f. Rapid growth or unusual profitability, especially compared to that of other companies in the same industry.
   g. New accounting, statutory, or regulatory requirements.

2. Excessive pressure exists for management to meet the requirements or expectations of third parties due to the following:
   a. Profitability or trend level expectations of investment analysts, institutional investors, significant creditors, or other external parties (particularly expectations that are unduly aggressive or unrealistic), including expectations created by management in, for example, overly optimistic press releases or annual report messages.
   b. Need to obtain additional debt or equity financing to stay competitive—including financing of major research and development or capital expenditures.
   c. Marginal ability to meet exchange listing requirements or debt repayment or other debt covenant requirements.
   d. Perceived or real adverse effects of reporting poor financial results on significant pending transactions, such as business combinations or contract awards.

3. Information available indicates that management or the board of directors' personal financial situation is threatened by the entity's financial performance arising from the following:
   a. Significant financial interests in the entity.
   b. Significant portions of their compensation (for example, bonuses, stock options, and earn-out arrangements) being contingent upon achieving aggressive targets for stock price, operating results, financial position, or cash flow.
   c. Personal guarantees of debts of the entity.

4. There is excessive pressure on management or operating personnel to meet financial targets set up by the board of directors or management, including sales or profitability incentive goals.

### OPPORTUNITIES

1. The nature of the industry or the entity's operations provides opportunities to engage in fraudulent financial reporting that can arise from the following:
   a. Significant related party transactions not in the ordinary course of business or with related entities not audited or audited by another firm.
   b. A strong financial presence or ability to dominate a certain industry sector that allows the entity to dictate terms or conditions to suppliers or customers that may result in inappropriate or non-arm's-length transactions.
   c. Assets, liabilities, revenues, or expenses based on significant estimates that involve subjective judgments or uncertainties that are difficult to corroborate.
   d. Significant, unusual, or highly complex transactions, especially those close to period end that pose difficult "substance over form" questions.

   *e.* Significant operations located or conducted across international borders in jurisdictions where differing business environments and cultures exist.

   *f.* Significant bank accounts or subsidiary or branch operations in tax-haven jurisdictions for which there appears to be no clear business justification.

2. There is ineffective monitoring of management as a result of the following:

   *a.* Domination of management by a single person or small group (in a non-owner-managed business) without compensating controls.

   *b.* Ineffective board of directors or audit committee oversight over the financial reporting process and internal control.

3. There is a complex or unstable organizational structure, as evidenced by the following:

   *a.* Difficulty in determining the organization or individuals that have controlling interest in the entity.

   *b.* Overly complex organizational structure involving unusual legal entities or managerial lines of authority.

   *c.* High turnover of senior management, counsel, or board members.

4. Internal control components are deficient as a result of the following:

   *a.* Inadequate monitoring of controls, including automated controls and controls over interim financial reporting (where external reporting is required).

   *b.* High turnover rates or employment of ineffective accounting, internal audit, or information technology staff.

   *c.* Ineffective accounting and information systems, including situations involving reportable conditions.

## ATTITUDES AND RATIONALIZATIONS

Risk factors reflective of attitudes and/or rationalizations by board members, management, or employees that allow them to engage in and/or justify fraudulent financial reporting may not be susceptible to observation by the auditor. Nevertheless, the auditor who becomes aware of the existence of such information should consider it in identifying the risks of material misstatement arising from fraudulent financial reporting. For example, auditors may become aware of the following information that may indicate a risk factor:

1. Ineffective communication, implementation, support, or enforcement of the entity's values or ethical standards by management or the communication of inappropriate values or ethical standards.

2. Nonfinancial management's excessive participation in or preoccupation with the selection of accounting principles or the determination of significant estimates.

3. Known history of violations of securities laws or other laws and regulations, or claims against the entity, its senior management, or board members alleging fraud or violations of laws and regulations.

4. Excessive interest by management in maintaining or increasing the entity's stock price or earnings trend.

5. A practice by management of committing to analysts, creditors, and other third parties to achieve aggressive or unrealistic forecasts.

6. Management failing to correct known significant deficiencies on a timely basis.

7. An interest by management in employing inappropriate means to minimize reported earnings for tax-motivated reasons.

8. Recurring attempts by management to justify marginal or inappropriate accounting on the basis of materiality.

9. A strained relationship between management and the current or predecessor auditor, as exhibited by the following:

   *a.* Frequent disputes with the current or predecessor auditor on accounting, auditing, or reporting matters.

   *b.* Unreasonable demands on the auditor, such as unreasonable time constraints regarding the completion of the audit or the issuance of the auditor's report.

   *c.* Formal or informal restrictions on the auditor that inappropriately limit access to people or information or the ability to communicate effectively with the board of directors or audit committee.

   *d.* Domineering management behavior in dealing with the auditor, especially involving attempts to influence the scope of the auditor's work or the selection or continuance of personnel assigned to or consulted on the audit engagement.

# Risk Factors Relating to Misstatements Arising from Misappropriation of Assets

## INCENTIVES AND PRESSURES

1. Personal financial obligations may create pressure on management or employees with access to cash or other assets susceptible to theft to misappropriate those assets.

2. Adverse relationships between the entity and employees with access to cash or other assets susceptible to theft may motivate those employees to misappropriate those assets. For example, adverse relationships may be created by the following:
   a. Known or anticipated future employee layoffs.
   b. Recent or anticipated changes to employee compensation or benefit plans.
   c. Promotions, compensation, or other rewards inconsistent with expectations.

## OPPORTUNITIES

1. Certain characteristics or circumstances may increase the susceptibility of assets to misappropriation. For example, opportunities to misappropriate assets increase when there are the following:
   a. Large amounts of cash on hand or processed.
   b. Inventory items that are small in size, of high value, or in high demand.
   c. Easily convertible assets, such as bearer bonds, diamonds, or computer chips.
   d. Fixed assets that are small in size, marketable, or lacking observable identification of ownership.

2. Inadequate internal control over assets may increase the susceptibility of misappropriation of those assets. For example, misappropriation of assets may occur because there is the following:
   a. Inadequate segregation of duties or independent checks.
   b. Inadequate management oversight of employees responsible for assets (for example, inadequate supervision or monitoring of remote locations).
   c. Inadequate job applicant screening of employees with access to assets.
   d. Inadequate record keeping with respect to assets.
   e. Inadequate system of authorization and approval of transactions (for example, in purchasing).
   f. Inadequate physical safeguards over cash, investments, inventory, or fixed assets.
   g. Lack of complete and timely reconciliations of assets.
   h. Lack of timely and appropriate documentation of transactions (for example, credits for merchandise returns).
   i. Lack of mandatory vacations for employees performing key control functions.
   j. Inadequate management understanding of information technology, which enables information technology employees to perpetrate a misappropriation.
   k. Inadequate access controls over automated records, including controls over and review of computer systems event logs.

## ATTITUDES AND RATIONALIZATIONS

Risk factors reflective of employee attitudes and/or rationalizations that allow them to justify misappropriations of assets are generally not susceptible to observation by the auditor. Nevertheless, the auditor who becomes aware of the existence of such information should consider it in identifying the risks of material misstatement arising from misappropriation of assets. For example, auditors may become aware of the following attitudes or behavior of employees who have access to assets susceptible to misappropriation:

1. Disregard for the need for monitoring or reducing risks related to misappropriation of assets.

2. Disregard for internal control over misappropriation of assets by overriding existing controls or by failing to correct known internal control deficiencies.

3. Behavior indicating displeasure or dissatisfaction with the company or its treatment of the employee.

4. Changes in behavior or lifestyle that may indicate assets have been misappropriated.

# Illustrative Audit Case: Keystone Computers & Networks, Inc.

## Part I: Audit Planning

The Keystone Computers & Networks, Inc. (KCN) case is used throughout the text to illustrate audit procedures and methodology. KCN is a company that sells and installs computer workstations and networking software to business customers. The CPA firm of Adams, Barnes & Co. has audited the financial statements of KCN for the past three years. This part of the case illustrates selective audit planning working papers prepared by the staff of Adams, Barnes & Co. for this year's audit. You should read through the information to obtain an understanding of the nature of the information that is important to planning an audit engagement. The working papers include:

- The balance sheet and income statement for the company for the prior year, 20X4.
- A trial balance for 12/31/X5, with comparative amounts for 12/31/X4.

**KEYSTONE COMPUTERS & NETWORKS, INC.**
Balance Sheet
December 31, 20X4

**Assets**

| | |
|---|---:|
| Current Assets | |
| Cash | $ 53,964 |
| Trade receivables, less allowance for doubtful accounts of $96,000 | 8,438,524 |
| Accounts receivable—officers | 57,643 |
| Inventory | 1,234,589 |
| Prepaid expenses | 156,900 |
| Total current assets | $ 9,941,620 |
| Equipment and leasehold improvements, at cost | |
| Equipment and furniture | $ 1,090,634 |
| Leasehold improvements | 98,900 |
| | $ 1,189,534 |
| Less accumulated depreciation | (250,987) |
| | $ 938,547 |
| Intangible assets net of amortization | $ 1,000,000 |
| | $11,880,167 |

**Liabilities and Stockholders' Equity**

| | |
|---|---:|
| Current Liabilities | |
| Line of credit | $ 6,612,550 |
| Accounts payable | 1,349,839 |
| Current maturities of capital lease obligations | 43,200 |
| Accrued expenses | 178,900 |
| Total current liabilities | $ 8,184,489 |
| Capital lease obligations, less current maturities | $ 456,700 |
| Total liabilities | $ 8,641,189 |
| Stockholders' equity | |
| Common stock, $1 par value; 1,000,000 shares authorized; 200,000 shares issued and outstanding | $ 200,000 |
| Additional paid-in capital | 423,500 |
| Retained earnings | 2,615,478 |
| | $11,880,167 |

## KEYSTONE COMPUTERS & NETWORKS, INC.
### Statements of Income and Retained Earnings
### Year Ended December 31, 20X4

| | | | |
|---|---:|---:|---:|
| Net sales | | | $96,459,566 |
| Cost of goods sold | | | 74,122,435 |
| Gross profit | | | $22,337,131 |
| **Selling expenses:** | | | |
| Salaries | $3,167,889 | | |
| Payroll benefits and taxes | 913,456 | | |
| Advertising and promotion | 1,200,786 | | |
| Travel and entertainment | 609,788 | | |
| Miscellaneous | 334,890 | | |
| | | $ 6,226,809 | |
| **Operating and administration expenses:** | | | |
| Operating salaries | $4,878,900 | | |
| Administrative salaries | 4,234,234 | | |
| Payroll benefits and taxes | 1,812,344 | | |
| Rent | 797,800 | | |
| Utilities | 210,495 | | |
| Insurance | 356,890 | | |
| Legal and accounting | 457,577 | | |
| Bad debt | 234,500 | | |
| Supplies | 556,345 | | |
| Depreciation and amortization | 334,565 | | |
| Software development | 289,100 | | |
| Miscellaneous | 234,556 | | |
| | | $14,397,306 | |
| Total selling, operating, and administrative expenses | | | $20,624,115 |
| Operating income | | | $ 1,713,016 |
| Interest expense | | | 421,344 |
| Income before income taxes | | | $ 1,291,672 |
| **Income taxes:** | | | |
| Current | | $ 256,765 | |
| Deferred | | 45,632 | |
| | | | 302,397 |
| Net income | | | $ 989,275 |
| Retained earnings, January 1, 20X4 | | | $ 1,626,203 |
| Retained earnings, December 31, 20X4 | | | $ 2,615,478 |

- The analytical ratios working paper, partially completed. (The ratios for 20X5 have been left off.)
- The audit plan for the audit of the financial statements for the year ended 12/31/X5.
- A fraud risk assessment.
- The engagement letter for the audit, presented in Figure 6.2 (pages 191–192) of this chapter.

## KEYSTONE COMPUTERS & NETWORKS, INC.
### Working Trial Balance
For the Period Ended December 31, 20X5

| Account # | Account Name | Prior Period Balance 12/31/X4 | Unadjusted Trial Balance Dr (Cr) | Ref # | Adjustments Dr (Cr) | Adjusted Balance Dr (Cr) |
|---|---|---|---|---|---|---|
| 1000.10 | Cash—First Natl. Bank | 52,764 | 76,234 | | | |
| 1000.30 | Cash in register | 1,200 | 1,200 | | | |
| 1050.10 | Accounts receivable—trade | 8,534,524 | 10,235,457 | | | |
| 1050.40 | Accounts receivable—officers | 57,643 | 84,670 | | | |
| 1050.90 | Allowance for bad debts | (96,000) | (104,000) | | | |
| 1100.10 | Inventories | 1,234,589 | 1,375,835 | | | |
| 1300.10 | Prepaid expenses | 156,900 | 176,456 | | | |
| 2050.10 | Furniture & fixtures | 300,980 | 344,900 | | | |
| 2050.30 | Office equipment | 789,654 | 974,676 | | | |
| 2050.80 | Leasehold improvements | 98,900 | 91,230 | | | |
| 2050.90 | Accumulated depreciation | (250,987) | (404,560) | | | |
| 2100.00 | Software development cost | | 178,000 | | | |
| 2200.00 | Intangible assets | 1,000,000 | 800,000 | | | |
| 3050.10 | Accounts payable—trade | (1,349,839) | (1,429,033) | | | |
| 3100.00 | Capital lease obligations—current | (43,200) | (45,675) | | | |
| 3200.10 | Accrued liabilities | (178,900) | (203,450) | | | |
| 3300.30 | Unearned service revenue | | (42,300) | | | |
| 3400.50 | Line of credit | (6,612,550) | (8,632,105) | | | |
| 4400.30 | Capital lease obligations—noncurrent | (456,700) | (423,680) | | | |
| 5050.10 | Capital stock | (200,000) | (200,000) | | | |
| 5100.10 | Paid-in capital | (423,500) | (423,500) | | | |
| 5700.10 | Retained earnings | (1,626,203) | (2,615,478) | | | |
| 5900.00 | Dividends | | 415,000 | | | |
| | | 989,275 | 229,877 | | | |
| | | (989,275) | (229,877) | | | |
| | | 0 | 0 | | | |

239

## KEYSTONE COMPUTERS & NETWORKS, INC.
### Working Trial Balance
### For the Period Ended December 31, 20X5

| Account # | Account Name | Prior Period Balance 12/31/X4 | Unadjusted Trial Balance Dr (Cr) | Ref # | Adjustments Dr (Cr) | Adjusted Balance Dr (Cr) |
|---|---|---|---|---|---|---|
| 6000.10 | Sales of computers | (44,890,788) | (42,345,675) | | | |
| 6010.10 | Software licenses | (248,900) | (236,700) | | | |
| 6020.10 | Service revenue | (4,567,888) | (4,325,777) | | | |
| 6030.10 | Consulting revenue | (46,751,990) | (45,677,899) | | | |
| 7020.10 | Cost of sales | 74,122,435 | 72,134,566 | | | |
| 7070.10 | Salaries—sales | 3,167,889 | 2,765,677 | | | |
| 7070.50 | Payroll benefits—sales | 913,456 | 857,368 | | | |
| 7075.10 | Advertising & promotion | 1,200,786 | 1,567,889 | | | |
| 7080.10 | Travel & entertainment | 609,788 | 445,600 | | | |
| 7080.30 | Miscellaneous exp.—sales | 334,890 | 278,656 | | | |
| 7090.10 | Salaries—operations | 4,878,900 | 4,544,860 | | | |
| 7090.30 | Salaries—administrative | 4,234,234 | 3,945,670 | | | |
| 7090.50 | Payroll benefits—admin. | 1,812,344 | 1,734,565 | | | |
| 7100.10 | Rent | 797,800 | 721,345 | | | |
| 7140.10 | Utilities | 210,495 | 234,839 | | | |
| 7200.10 | Insurance | 356,890 | 378,677 | | | |
| 7260.30 | Legal & accounting | 457,577 | 485,767 | | | |
| 7320.10 | Bad debt expense | 234,500 | 256,678 | | | |
| 7410.10 | Supplies | 556,345 | 478,900 | | | |
| 7600.10 | Depreciation and amort. | 334,565 | 367,867 | | | |
| 7650.10 | Software development | 289,100 | 345,645 | | | |
| 7700.10 | Miscellaneous exp.—administrative | 234,556 | 245,456 | | | |
| 7800.10 | Interest expense | 421,344 | 476,899 | | | |
| 7900.10 | Current income taxes | 256,765 | 80,100 | | | |
| 7900.70 | Deferred income taxes | 45,632 | 9,150 | | | |
| 9000.00 | P & L Summary | 989,275 | (229,877) | | | |
| | | 0 | 229,877 | | | |
| | | 0 | 0 | | | |

240

KEYSTONE COMPUTERS & NETWORKS, INC.

Analytical Review Ratios

For the Period Ended December 31, 20X5

Prepared by _____ *WL* _____

Reviewed by _____

| Ratio | Ending 12/31/X5 | Ending 12/31/X4 | Industry |
|---|---|---|---|
| Current ratio | | 1.2 | 1.3 |
| Days' sales in accounts receivable, computed with average accounts receivable | | 33.2 | 37.0 |
| Allowance for doubtful accounts/accounts receivable | | 1.1% | — |
| Bad debt expense/net sales | | 0.2% | — |
| Total liabilities/net worth | | 2.7 | 2.9 |
| Return on total assets | | 8.3% | 9.0% |
| Return on net worth | | 30.5% | 29.0% |
| Return on net sales | | 1.0% | 2.3% |
| Gross profit/net sales | | 23.2% | 24.0% |
| Selling, operating, and administrative expense/net sales | | 21.4% | 23.9% |
| Times interest earned | | 4.1 | 5.5 |

KEYSTONE COMPUTERS & NETWORKS, INC.

Audit Strategy

December 31, 20X5

| | | Date |
|---|---|---|
| Prepared by: | Warren Love (Senior) | August 14, 20X5 |
| Reviewed by: | Karen West (Manager) | August 28, 20X5 |
| Reviewed by: | Charles Adams (Partner) | September 5, 20X5 |

## OBJECTIVES OF THE ENGAGEMENT

Audit of the financial statements of Keystone Computers & Networks, Inc. (KCN), for the year ended December 31, 20X5. Also, the company's debt agreement with Western Financial Services requires the company to furnish the lender a report by our firm on KCN's compliance with various restrictive debt covenants.

## BUSINESS AND INDUSTRY CONDITIONS

KCN sells and installs computers and networking hardware and software to business customers and provides other information technology consulting services. KCN also has begun developing its own computer networking software to be sold as a product to its customers. The company's primary competitive strategy is to maintain a high level of technical expertise and a broad range of services.

KCN's long-term success is contingent on its ability to attract and retain qualified information technology personnel. The market for such individuals is very competitive. However, the company has a competitive advantage because of its desirable geographic location (Phoenix), which has a large number of colleges with technology programs.

The market for computers and related products is extremely competitive. KCN competes with large retailers of computers, such as Dell, Hewlett Packard, and Apple. The company also competes with other value-added resellers who provide computers and software products and consulting services directly to customers. To effectively compete, the company must be able to obtain inventories of state-of-the-art equipment on a timely basis. Because the company does not have the buying power of some of its other competitors, it generally must charge a higher price for its products. Its customers are willing to pay the higher price because of the high level of expertise and service that the company provides.

The market for computer products and technology services is also very sensitive to economic conditions. Recent reports indicate that the U.S. economy will be challenged for the next few years. The annual growth in spending for information technology products and services is expected to be 3 percent per year for the next three years. In the past year, the company has decided to increase sales by extending credit to clients with slightly higher credit risk.

## PLANNING MEETINGS

On July 20, Karen West and I met with Loren Steele, controller, and Sam Best, president, of KCN to discuss the planning of the audit for the current year. On August 2, a planning meeting was held in our office with all members of the engagement team assigned to the audit.

## OWNERSHIP AND MANAGEMENT

KCN is a closely held company owned by five stockholders: Terry Keystone, Mark Keystone, John Keystone, Keith Young, and Rita Young. Terry and Mark Keystone are active members of the company's board of directors. None of the other owners take an active part in the management of the business.

## OBJECTIVES, STRATEGIES, AND BUSINESS RISKS

KCN's primary business objectives are to increase revenues by 6 percent and increase net income by 8 percent each year for the next three years. Major strategies to achieve those objectives include:

- Aggressive marketing of products and services through increased advertising.
- Sales to customers with a higher credit risk profile.
- New software development.

The primary business risks associated with the company's strategies include:

- The U.S. economy may suffer on additional significant downturn.
- Competitors may engage in predatory pricing to gain market share.
- Increased advertising expenditures may not produce desired results.
- Credit losses may exceed the benefits of increased sales.
- Software development activities may not generate viable products.

The company has developed the following responses to these risks:

- Careful monitoring of economy and industry conditions.
- Careful monitoring of competitor actions.
- Hiring of marketing consulting firm to evaluate the performance of advertising methods.
- Daily review of aging of accounts receivable by Loren Steele, controller.
- Use of carefully controlled software development budget.

## MEASUREMENT AND REVIEW OF FINANCIAL PERFORMANCE

Management uses the following measures to monitor the company's performance:

- Inventory and receivables turnover.
- Aging of accounts receivable.
- Sales and gross margins by type of revenue.
- Net income.
- Total inventory balance.

## PROCEDURES TO OBTAIN AN UNDERSTANDING OF THE CLIENT AND ITS ENVIRONMENT

The following procedures were performed to update our understanding of the client and its environment:

- Roll forward of information from the prior year's audit.
- Inquiries of management:

    Loren Steele       7/20, 8/15

    Sam Best       7/20, 8/16
- Reading of quarterly board of directors' meetings held on 4/05 and 7/12.
- Review of monthly performance reports for January through July.
- Industry reports—IT and consulting services.
- Review of KCN's Web site.
- Review of selected articles in *The Wall Street Journal.*

## SIGNIFICANT RISKS

Several significant risks were noted as a result of obtaining information about KCN and its environment, including:

| Risk | Implications and Response |
|---|---|
| 1. KCN has engaged in a strategy to sell to customers with higher credit risk. | |
| 2. The officers of the company receive significant bonuses based on quarterly results. | |

## SIGNIFICANT ACCOUNTING AND AUDITING MATTERS

The company began offering for sale extended warranties on computers during the current year. We need to review the method of revenue recognition to determine whether it complies with the requirements of *FASB ASC* 605-20-25.

In the prior year, KCN began developing networking software products for sale. This year the company has started capitalizing certain costs of development. We need to review the method of accounting for the cost of software development to determine whether it complies with the requirements of *FASB ASC* 985-20-25.

In 20X3, KCN acquired for $1,200,000 a small business accounting system (Plumbtree Systems) that it licenses to its customers. Recently, sales of the licenses for the software have begun to decline. In addition, a recent article in a trade journal ranked the system poor in relation to its competitors. This may indicate that an impairment in the value of the software may have occurred.

## PLANNING MATERIALITY

Because the firm has experienced steady growth in sales and earnings over the last three years, we believe that operating results are the most appropriate basis for estimating planning materiality as described below:

| **Comparison of Bases** | | | **Computation of Planning Materiality** | | | |
|---|---|---|---|---|---|---|
| **Financial Statement Base** | **Annualized for 12/31/X5** | | **Base** | **Amount** | **Percentage** | **Materiality Estimate** |
| Sales | $92,000,000 | | Sales | $92,000,000 | 1% | $920,000 |
| Total assets | 13,000,000 | | Total assets | 13,000,000 | 1 | 130,000 |
| Pretax net income | 320,000 | | Pretax net income | 320,000 | 10 | 32,000 |

The range for planning materiality is from $32,000 to $920,000. Based on the company's steady growth in sales and earnings and the fact that the company is not a public company, we have selected $300,000 as a reasonable materiality amount for planning purposes.

## SCHEDULING AND STAFFING PLAN

Based on discussions with Ms. Steele, the following are tentative dates of importance for the audit:

| | |
|---|---|
| Begin interim audit work | October 15, 20X5 |
| Complete interim audit work | by November 15, 20X5 |
| Issue management letter on interim work | by November 30, 20X5 |
| Observe physical inventory | December 31, 20X5 |
| Begin year-end audit work | February 1, 20X6 |
| Complete fieldwork | by February 20, 20X6 |
| Closing conference | February 25, 20X6 |
| Issue audit report | by March 5, 20X6 |
| Issue letter required by financing agreement | by March 5, 20X6 |
| Issue updated management letter | by March 10, 20X6 |

Staffing time requirements for the engagement are described below:

| | Assistant | Senior | Manager | Partner | Total |
|---|---|---|---|---|---|
| Interim | 40 | 40 | 10 | 8 | 98 |
| Final | 40 | 30 | 15 | 12 | 97 |
| | 80 | 70 | 25 | 20 | 195 |

---

| Fraud Risk Assessment | | |
|---|---|---|
| | | **G-10** |
| | | **CA** |
| **Client:** *Keystone Computers & Networks, Inc.* | | **CA 8/14/X5** |

**Financial Statement Date:** *12/31/X5*

| Procedure | Performed by | Comments |
|---|---|---|
| 1. Consider the results of the discussion among engagement personnel about the risk of material misstatement due to fraud. | _CA_ | *See G-21 for a description of the discussion.* |
| 2. Consider results of inquiries of management about the risks of fraud and how they are addressed. | _CA_ | |
| 3. Consider the results of risk assessment analytical procedures. | _CA_ | |
| 4. Consider the existence of fraud risk factors listed on G-30 through G-35. | _CA_ | |
| 5. Consider any other information that might be relevant to the risk of material misstatement due to fraud. | _CA_ | |

**Risks of Material Misstatement Due to Fraud**

*Management may be motivated to misstate financial results due to impending sale of the company.*

**Responses**

**Overall Responses**

*Risks were considered in staffing the engagement and determining the appropriate level of supervision.*

**Alterations of the Nature, Timing, and Extent of Further Audit Procedures**

*Risks were considered in designing audit procedures for sales and accounts receivable and inventories. (See R-6 and R-9.)*

*Procedures were performed to address the risk of management override of internal controls. (See G-23–G-24.)*

---

## Appendix 6C Problems

**LO 3**

**6C–1.** The audit plan for the audit of Keystone Computers & Networks, Inc., appears on pages 237–244. Review each major section of the audit plan and briefly describe the purpose and content of the section. Organize your solution in the following manner:

| Section | Purpose | Content |
|---|---|---|
| Objectives of the engagement | To describe the services that are to be rendered to the client. | The objectives are (1) audit of KCN's financial statements for the year ended 12/31/X5, and (2) issuance of a letter on compliance with covenants of the client's letter of credit agreement. |

**LO 3, 4**

**6C–2.** In the audit plan for the audit of Keystone Computers & Networks, Inc., on page 243 there is a section on significant risks. For each of the risks, identify the implications and potential responses.

**LO 7**

**6C–3.** In the audit plan for the audit of Keystone Computers & Networks, Inc., on page 243 there is a section on significant accounting and auditing matters. The second matter described involves capitalizing the costs of developing a software program for sale.

*Required:*

a. Research this issue and write a brief memorandum for the working papers describing the issue and summarizing the appropriate method of accounting for the development costs.

b. Based on your research, describe the major audit issue that you believe will be involved in auditing the software development costs.

**LO 3, 4**

**6C–4.** A partially completed analytical ratios working paper for Keystone Computers & Networks, Inc., is presented on page 241.

*Required:*

*eXcel*

a. Complete the working paper by computing the financial ratios for 20X5.

b. After completing part (*a*), review the ratios and identify financial statement accounts that should be investigated because the related ratios are not comparable to prior-year ratios, industry averages, or your knowledge of the company.

c. For each account identified in part (*b*), list potential reasons for the unexpected account balances and related ratios.

# Internal Control

Our discussion of internal control in this chapter has four major objectives: first, to explain the meaning and significance of internal control; second, to discuss the major components of a client's internal control; third, to show how auditors go about considering internal control to meet the requirements of the second standard of fieldwork; and fourth, to provide an overview of audits of internal control performed under Section 404(b) of the Sarbanes-Oxley Act. No attempt is made in this chapter to present in detail the controls applicable to particular account balances and classes of transactions. Detailed information along those lines will be found in succeeding chapters as each phase of the audit is presented.

As discussed in Chapter 1, internal control has attained greatest significance in large-scale business organizations. Accordingly, the major part of the discussion in this chapter is presented in terms of the large corporation. A separate section is presented at the end of the chapter, however, dealing with the problem of achieving internal control in a small business.

## The Meaning of Internal Control

**LO1**

Define what is meant by internal control.

Differences of opinion have long existed about the meaning and objectives of internal control. Until the early 1990s, many people interpreted the term **internal control** as the steps taken by a business to prevent fraud—both misappropriation of assets and fraudulent financial reporting. Others, while acknowledging the importance of internal control for fraud prevention, believed that internal control has an equal role in assuring control over manufacturing and other processes. Such differences in interpretation also existed in the professional publications issued by the American Institute of Certified Public Accountants; The Institute of Internal Auditors, Inc.; and the Research Foundation of the Financial Executives Institute. It was not until the early 1990s that the various professional organizations worked together to develop a consensus on the nature and scope of internal control.

As a result of a number of instances of fraudulent financial reporting in the 1970s and early 1980s, the major accounting organizations[1] sponsored the National Commission on Fraudulent Financial Reporting (the Treadway Commission) to study the causal factors that are associated with fraudulent reporting and make recommendations to reduce the incidence of fraudulent reporting. The commission made a number of recommendations that directly addressed internal control. For example, it emphasized the importance of a competent and involved audit committee and an active and objective internal audit function in preventing fraudulent practices. It also called on the sponsoring organizations to work together to integrate the various internal control concepts and definitions in order to develop common criteria to evaluate internal control. Accordingly, the Committee of Sponsoring Organizations (COSO) commissioned a study to:

- Establish a common definition of internal control to serve the needs of different parties.
- Provide a standard against which businesses and other entities can assess their control systems and determine how to improve them.

[1] The sponsoring organizations included the American Institute of Certified Public Accountants; the American Accounting Association; the Financial Executives Institute; The Institute of Internal Auditors, Inc.; and the Institute of Management Accountants.

## Learning objectives

After studying this chapter, you should be able to:

LO1   Define what is meant by internal control.

LO2   Distinguish among the major components of a client's internal control: the control environment, risk assessment, control activities, the accounting information system, and monitoring of controls.

LO3   Describe the auditors' consideration of internal control.

LO4   Discuss the techniques used by auditors to obtain an understanding of internal control.

LO5   Explain how internal control relates to a financial statement audit.

LO6   Describe the major types of tests of controls.

LO7   Describe the auditors' responsibility for communicating control-related matters.

LO8   Describe the nature of the audits performed under Section 404(b) of the Sarbanes-Oxley Act of 2002.

The study, titled *Internal Control—Integrated Framework*,[2] defines internal control as [emphasis added]:

> A *process,* effected by the entity's board of directors, management, and other personnel, designed to provide *reasonable assurance* regarding the achievement of *objectives* in the following categories:
>
> - Reliability of financial reporting.
> - Effectiveness and efficiency of operations.
> - Compliance with applicable laws and regulations.

COSO's definition of internal control emphasizes that internal control is a *process,* or a means to an end, and not an end in and of itself. The process is effected by individuals, not merely policy manuals, documents, and forms. By including the concept of *reasonable assurance,* the definition recognizes that internal control cannot realistically provide absolute assurance that an organization's objectives will be achieved. Reasonable assurance recognizes that the cost of an organization's internal control should not exceed the benefits expected to be obtained.

Finally, the definition of internal control is comprehensive in that it addresses the achievement of *objectives* in the areas of financial reporting, operations, and compliance with laws and regulations. It encompasses the methods by which top management delegates authority and assigns responsibility for such functions as selling, purchasing, accounting, and production. Internal control also includes the program for preparing, verifying, and distributing to various levels of management those current reports and analyses that enable executives to maintain control over the variety of activities and functions that are performed in a large organization. The use of budgetary techniques, production standards, inspection laboratories, time and motion studies, and employee training programs involves engineers and many others far removed from accounting and financial activities; yet all of these programs and activities are a part of internal control.

In the three areas of internal control—financial reporting, operations, and compliance—COSO states that a series of control objectives and subobjectives exists. To illustrate this concept, consider internal control over financial reporting. At the top level, the overall objective is to prepare and issue reliable financial information. At the very detailed level, as applied to accounts receivable, COSO illustrates the following control objectives (sub-objectives):

1. All goods shipped are accurately billed in the proper period.
2. Invoices are accurately recorded for all authorized shipments and only for such shipments.
3. Authorized and only authorized sales returns and allowances are accurately recorded.
4. The continued completeness and accuracy of accounts receivable is ensured.
5. Accounts receivable records are safeguarded.

These control objectives are similar to the management assertions that were discussed in the preceding two chapters (see, for example, Figure 5.1). This is obviously the case because the overall objective of internal control over financial reporting is to prepare financial statements in accordance with generally accepted accounting principles. Specifically, COSO says that supporting the control objectives is a series of assertions that underlie the financial statements. However, there is one major difference between control objectives and assertions; the control objectives are broader in that they relate not only to financial reporting, but also to operations and compliance.

Which controls are most relevant to the audit of financial statements? Generally, the controls that are relevant to an audit are those that pertain to the reliability of financial reporting—that is, those that affect the preparation of financial information for external

---

[2] COSO has recently issued guidance for smaller companies titled *Internal Control over Financial Reporting—Guidance for Smaller Public Companies.*

reporting purposes. However, other controls may be relevant if they affect the reliability of data that the auditors use to perform auditing procedures. For example, controls applicable to nonfinancial data (e.g., production statistics) that the auditors use in performing analytical procedures may be relevant to an audit.

Controls designed to safeguard the organization's assets are relevant to an audit if they affect the reliability of financial reporting. For example, controls that limit access to the company's inventories may be relevant to a financial statement audit, while controls to prevent the excess use of materials in production generally are not. As long as the financial statements reflect the cost of the materials used, the auditors are not directly concerned with the inefficiencies of production.

## The Relationship of Internal Control and Corporate Governance

Internal control overlaps with the broader concept of *corporate governance.* Effective corporate governance involves establishing incentives and monitoring devices to prevent inappropriate behavior on the part of management of an organization. With respect to incentives, it is important for the board of directors of the organization to establish an executive compensation system that aligns management's behavior with the objectives of the shareholders of the firm. Internal control is a primary internal corporate governance monitoring device, but effective corporate governance also relies on external monitoring devices such as external auditors, the SEC, stock exchanges, creditors, rating agencies, investment bankers, and security analysts.

## The Foreign Corrupt Practices Act of 1977

The importance of establishing and maintaining effective internal control is also illustrated by the passage of the **Foreign Corrupt Practices Act**. In the mid-1970s, hundreds of American corporations acknowledged having made payments (bribes and kick-backs) to officials in foreign countries to obtain business. In most cases, the payments were legal under the laws of the countries in which they were made, but they were not in accordance with American standards of business ethics. In some instances, these questionable payments were made without the authorization or knowledge of the top executives of the corporations involved. By passing the Foreign Corrupt Practices Act of 1977, Congress ordered an end to this practice. Payments to foreign officials for the purpose of securing business are specifically prohibited for *all American businesses* by the anti-bribery provisions of the act. To prevent top management from asserting that they were not aware of the payments, internal control provisions also were included in the act. These provisions require *all corporations under the jurisdiction of the SEC* (regardless of whether the corporation has international operations) to maintain a system of internal control that will provide reasonable assurance that:

1. Transactions are executed with the knowledge and authorization of management.
2. Transactions are recorded as necessary to permit the preparation of reliable financial statements and maintain accountability for assets.
3. Access to assets is limited to authorized individuals.
4. Accounting records of assets are compared to existing assets at reasonable intervals and appropriate action is taken with respect to any differences.

Violations of the Foreign Corrupt Practices Act can result in fines up to $1 million and imprisonment of the members of management who are responsible. Thus, an effective system of internal control, long viewed as essential to the operation of a large organization, is required by federal law.

## Means of Achieving Internal Control

Internal control varies significantly from one organization to the next, depending on such factors as organization size, nature of operations, and objectives. Yet certain features are essential to satisfactory internal control in almost any organization. In all systems, a variety of controls must be designed to accomplish the control objectives. Controls over financial reporting are often classified as preventive, detective, or corrective.

**LO2**

Distinguish among the major components of a client's internal control: the control environment, risk assessment, control activities, the accounting information system, and monitoring of controls.

**Preventive controls** are aimed at avoiding the occurrence of misstatements in the financial statements. Examples of preventive controls include segregation of duties and requiring approval of period-ending journal entries. **Detective controls** are designed to discover misstatements after they have occurred. A policy requiring the preparation of monthly bank reconciliations is an example of a control that could detect misstatements of cash receipts or disbursements. When detective controls discover a misstatement, a **corrective control** is ordinarily needed to remedy the situation. Maintaining backup copies of key transactions and master files to allow the correction of data entry errors is a common example of a corrective control. It is important to realize that preventive controls often operate at the individual transaction level, while detective controls may operate at the transaction level or at a higher level.

The various controls designed to achieve a control objective often overlap. That is, the controls are **complementary** in that they function together to achieve the same control objective. To illustrate, consider the control that requires all cash disbursements to be authorized and the complementary control of requiring reconciliations of bank statements. These controls work together to help ensure that unauthorized transactions are prevented or detected. Controls are referred to as **redundant** if they address the same financial statement assertion or control objective. Finally, a **compensating control** reduces the risk that an existing or potential control weakness will result in a misstatement. As an example, a small business may not have enough personnel to allow for the adequate segregation of duties, but the owner–manager of the business may carefully review accounting records and reports to compensate for the weakness.

Internal control of an organization may be viewed as including five components: (1) the control environment, (2) the risk assessment process, (3) control activities, (4) the information system relevant to financial reporting and communication (hereafter, the accounting information system), and (5) the monitoring of controls.

## The Control Environment

The control environment sets the tone of an organization by influencing the control consciousness of people. It may be viewed as the foundation for the other components of internal control. Control environment factors include integrity and ethical values; commitment to competence, board of directors, or audit committee; management's philosophy and operating style; organizational structure; assignment of authority and responsibility; and human resource policies and practices.

### Integrity and Ethical Values

The effectiveness of internal control depends directly upon the communication and enforcement of the integrity and ethical values of the personnel who are responsible for creating, administering, and monitoring controls. Top management should develop a clearly articulated statement of ethical values. Also, management should establish behavioral, ethical, and antifraud programs that discourage employees from engaging in inappropriate acts and should provide proper recourse when they become aware of such acts.

A client's antifraud programs and controls include both broad programs designed to prevent, deter, and detect fraud (e.g., programs to promote a culture of honesty and ethical behavior) and specific controls designed to mitigate specific risks of fraud (e.g., controls over access to inventory). Appendix 7A provides examples of fraud programs and controls.

### Commitment to Competence

Employees should possess the skills and knowledge essential to the performance of their job. If employees lack skills or knowledge, they may be ineffective in performing their assigned duties. This is especially critical when the employees are involved in performing controls. Ideally, management should be committed to hiring employees with appropriate levels of education and experience and providing them with adequate supervision and

## Illustrative Case

### Importance of Organizational Structure

During an audit of a non-public company, the auditors' study of organizational lines of authority and their use of an internal control questionnaire disclosed that the receiving department personnel were under the direction of the purchasing agent. Accounts payable department employees had also been instructed to accept informal memoranda from the purchasing agent as evidence of receipt of merchandise and propriety of invoices.

Because of this deficiency in internal control, the auditors made a very thorough examination of purchase invoices and came across a number of large December invoices from one supplier bearing the notation: "Subject to adjustment at time of delivery of merchandise." Investigation of these transactions disclosed that the merchandise had not yet been delivered, but the invoices had been paid. The purchasing agent explained that he had requested the advance billing in an effort to reduce taxable income for the year under audit, during which profits had been higher than usual. Further investigation revealed that the purchasing agent held a substantial personal interest in the supplier's making the advance billings, and that top management of the client company was not aware of this conflict of interest.

training. It is especially important for individuals involved in financial reporting to be competent in the selection and evaluation of accounting principles.

## Board of Directors or Audit Committee

The control environment of an organization is significantly influenced by the effectiveness of its board of directors or its audit committee. The board of directors and audit committee are responsible for overseeing the actions of management. Factors that bear on the effectiveness of the board or audit committee include the extent of its independence from management, the experience and stature of its members, the extent to which it raises and pursues difficult questions with management, and its interaction with the internal and external auditors. In audits of SEC registrants, the Sarbanes-Oxley Act of 2002 requires that the audit committee be directly responsible for the appointment, compensation, and oversight of the work of the CPA firm (including resolution of any disagreements between management and the CPA firm).

As described in Chapter 6, the audit committee of the board of directors should be composed of independent directors who are not officers or employees of the organization and who do not have other relationships that impair independence. This enables the audit committee to be effective at overseeing the quality of the organization's financial reports and internal control and acting as a deterrent to management override of controls and management fraud. In addition, the audit committee should have one or more members who have financial reporting expertise.

## Management Philosophy and Operating Style

Managements differ in both their philosophies toward financial reporting and their attitudes toward taking business risks. Some managements are extremely aggressive in financial reporting and place great emphasis on meeting or exceeding earnings projections. They may be willing to undertake activities of high risk with the prospect of high return. Other management teams are extremely conservative and risk averse. These differing philosophies and operating styles may have an impact on the overall reliability of the financial statements.

Management's philosophy and operating style also are reflected in the way the organization is managed. Controls in an informal organization are often implemented by face-to-face contact between employees and management. A more formal organization will establish written policies, performance reports, and exception reports to control its various activities.

## Organizational Structure

Another control environment factor is the entity's **organizational structure**. A well-designed organizational structure provides a basis for planning, directing, and controlling operations. It divides authority, responsibilities, and duties among members of an organization by dealing with such issues as centralized versus decentralized decision making and appropriate segregation of duties among the various departments. When management decision making is centralized and dominated by one individual, that individual's abilities and moral character are extremely important to the auditors. When a decentralized style is used, procedures to monitor the decision making of the many managers involved become equally important.

The organizational structure of an entity should separate responsibilities for (1) *authorization* of transactions, (2) *record keeping* for transactions, and (3) *custody* of assets. In addition, to the extent practical, execution of the transaction should be segregated from these other responsibilities. The effectiveness of such structure is usually obtained by having designated department heads who are evaluated on the basis of the performance of their respective departments. The top executives of the major departments should be of equal rank and should report directly to the president or to an executive vice president. The partial organization chart in Figure 7.1 illustrates such an

**FIGURE 7.1**
**Partial Organization Chart**

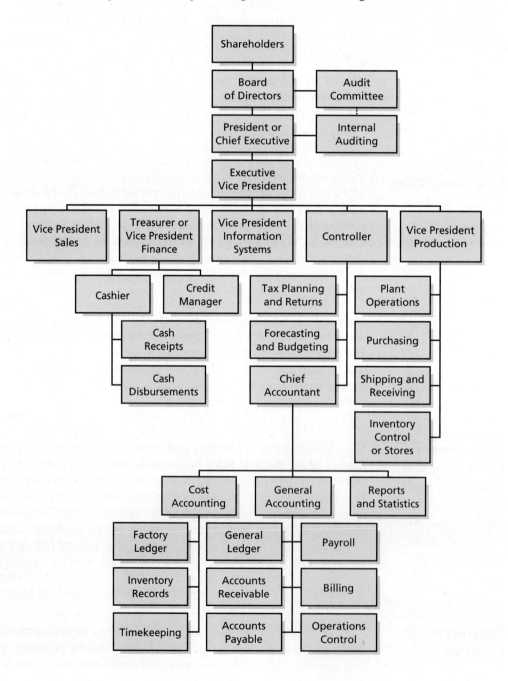

arrangement. If, for example, the controller were a line subordinate to the vice president of production, the organizational independence of the accounting department would be greatly impaired.

*Responsibilities of Finance and Accounting Departments*

Finance and accounting are the two departments most directly involved in the financial affairs of a business enterprise. The division of responsibilities between these departments illustrates the separation of the accounting function from operations and also from the custody of assets. Under the direction of the *treasurer,* the finance department is responsible for financial operations and custody of liquid assets. Activities of this department include planning future cash requirements, establishing customer credit policies, and arranging to meet the short- and long-term financing needs of the business. In addition, the finance department has custody of bank accounts and other liquid assets, invests idle cash, handles cash receipts, and makes cash disbursements. In short, it is the finance department that conducts financial activities.

The accounting department, under the authority of the *controller,* is responsible for all accounting functions and, often, the design and implementation of internal control. With respect to financial activity, the accounting department records financial transactions but does not handle financial assets. Accounting records establish accountability over assets and provide the information necessary for financial reports, tax returns, and daily operating decisions. With respect to internal control, the accounting department maintains the independent records with which quantities of assets and operating results are compared. Often, this reconciliation function is performed by the *operations control group* or some other subdepartment within accounting.

Many of the subdepartments often found within accounting are illustrated in Figure 7.1. It is important for many of these subdepartments to be relatively independent of one another. For example, if the operations control group reconciles assets on hand to the accounting records, it is essential that the operations control personnel not maintain those records.

## Assignment of Authority and Responsibility

Personnel within an organization need to have a clear understanding of their responsibilities and the rules and regulations that govern their actions. Therefore, to enhance the control environment, management develops employee job descriptions and clearly defines authority and responsibility within the organization. Policies also may be established describing appropriate business practices, knowledge and experience of key personnel, and the use of resources.

## Human Resource Policies and Procedures

Ultimately, the effectiveness of internal control is affected by the characteristics of the organization's personnel. Thus, management's policies and practices for hiring, providing orientation for, training, evaluating, counseling, promoting, and compensating employees have a significant effect on the effectiveness of the control environment. As an example, standards for hiring the most qualified individuals with an emphasis on education, experience, and evidence of integrity and ethical behavior illustrate the organization's commitment to hiring competent and trustworthy people. Effective human resource policies often can mitigate other weaknesses in the control environment.

*Fidelity Bonds*

Effective human resource management is not a guarantee against losses from dishonest employees. It is often the most trusted employees who engineer large embezzlements. That they are so highly trusted explains why they have access to cash, securities, and company records and are in a position that makes embezzlement possible.

Many organizations purchase fidelity bonds to cover employees handling cash or other negotiable assets. **Fidelity bonds** are a form of insurance in which a bonding company agrees to reimburse an employer, within limits, for losses attributable to theft or embezzlement by bonded employees. Companies with only a few employees at risk may obtain individual fidelity bonds; larger concerns may prefer to obtain a blanket fidelity bond covering a number of employees. Before issuing fidelity bonds, underwriters investigate thoroughly the past records of the employees to be bonded. This service offers added protection by preventing the employment of persons with dubious records in positions of trust. Bonding companies are much more likely to prosecute fraud cases vigorously than are employers; general awareness of this fact is another deterrent against dishonesty on the part of bonded employees.

## Risk Assessment

Organizations ordinarily face a variety of risks from external and internal sources that threaten their ability to meet their objectives in the areas of operations, financial reporting, and compliance with laws. Risk assessment is management's process for identifying, analyzing, and responding to such risks.

In Chapters 5 and 6, we described the auditor's risk assessment in a financial statement audit. How is the auditors' risk assessment related to the organization's risk assessment? Although there are similarities, the auditors' risk assessment is primarily concerned with evaluating the likelihood of material misstatements in the financial statements. While this can encompass both operations and compliance with laws, the scope of management risk analysis in the areas of operations and compliance with laws is broader.

## Control Activities

Control activities are policies and procedures that help ensure that management's directives are carried out. These policies and procedures promote actions that address the risks that face the organization. While there are many different types of control activities performed in an organization, only the following types are generally relevant to an audit of the organization's financial statements:

- Performance reviews.
- Information processing controls.
- Physical controls.
- Segregation of duties.

**Performance Reviews**

These controls include reviews of actual performance as compared to budgets, forecasts, and prior period performance; relating different sets of data to one another; and performing overall reviews of performance. Performance reviews provide management with an overall indication of whether personnel at various levels are effectively pursuing the objectives of the organization. By investigating the reasons for unexpected performance, management may make timely changes in strategies and plans or take other appropriate corrective action.

**Information Processing Controls**

A variety of control activities are performed to check the accuracy, completeness, and authorization of transactions. The two broad categories of information processing controls include *general control activities,* which apply to all information processing procedures, and *application control activities,* which apply only to one particular activity. Examples of general control activities would include those that help ensure the reliability of all information processing activities.

To understand the nature of application control activities, consider the controls over payroll that help to ensure that (1) only authorized payroll transactions are processed, and (2) authorized payroll transactions are processed completely and accurately. These

## Illustrative Case

### *Importance of Segregation of Custody and Record Keeping*

A manufacturer of golf clubs operated a large storeroom containing thousands of sets of golf clubs ready for shipment. Detailed perpetual inventory records were maintained by the employee in charge of the storeroom. A shortage of several sets of clubs developed as a result of theft by another employee who had acquired an unauthorized key to the storeroom. The employee responsible for the storeroom discovered the discrepancy between the clubs in stock and the quantities of clubs as shown by the records. Fearing criticism of his record keeping, he changed the inventory records to agree with the quantities on hand. The thefts continued, and large losses were sustained before the shortages were discovered. If the inventory records had been maintained by someone not responsible for physical custody of the merchandise, there would have been no incentive to conceal a shortage by falsifying the records.

application control activities would only affect the reliability of payroll processing. Chapter 8 provides a description of general and application control activities in a computer environment.

An important aspect of information processing controls is the proper authorization of all types of transactions. Authorization of transactions may be either general or specific. *General authorization* occurs when management establishes criteria for acceptance of a certain type of transaction. For example, top management may establish general price lists and credit policies for new customers. Transactions with customers that meet these criteria can then be approved by the credit department. *Specific authorization* occurs when transactions are authorized on an individual basis. For example, top management may consider individually and authorize specifically any sales transaction in excess of a specified amount, say $100,000.

Another control over information processing is a system of well-designed forms and documents. To illustrate, consider the processing of a credit sales transaction. The accounting department receives copies of internal documents prepared by the sales, credit, and shipping departments to properly record the transaction. The documents inform the accounting department that the sale was authorized and approved and goods were shipped to the customer.

A control of wide applicability is the use of serial numbers on documents. Serial numbers provide control over the number of documents issued. Checks, tickets, sales invoices, purchase orders, stock certificates, and many other business papers can be controlled in this manner. For some documents, such as checks, it may be desirable to account for the sequence used by a monthly or weekly inspection of the documents issued. For other documents, as in the case of serially numbered admission tickets, control may be achieved by noting the last serial number issued each day, and thereby computing the total value of tickets issued during the day. In computerized accounting systems, the computer may assign numbers to the transactions and documents.

## Physical Controls

These controls include those that provide physical security over both records and other assets. Activities that safeguard records may include maintaining control at all times over unissued prenumbered documents, as well as other journals and ledgers, and restricting access to computer programs and data files.

Only authorized individuals should be allowed access to the company's valuable assets. Direct physical access to assets may be controlled through the use of safes, locks, fences, and guards. Improper indirect access to assets, generally accomplished by falsifying financial records, must also be prevented. This may be accomplished by safeguarding the financial records, as described above.

FIGURE 7.2
**Establishing
Accountability
for Assets**

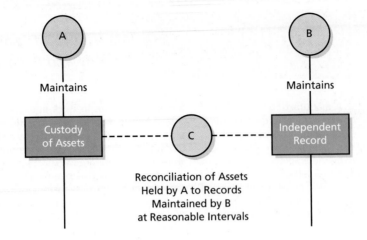

Periodic comparisons should be made between accounting records and the physical assets on hand. Investigation as to the cause of any discrepancies will uncover weaknesses either in procedures for safeguarding assets or in maintaining the related accounting records. Without these comparisons, waste, loss, or theft of the related assets may go undetected.

Figure 7.2 illustrates the use of an independently maintained record to establish accountability for assets. It is *not* essential that all three parties in the diagram (A, B, and C) be employees of the company; one or more may be an outside party or an electronic device. For example, if A is a bank with custody of cash on deposit, B would be the company employees maintaining records of cash receipts and disbursements, and C might be a computer program that performs periodic bank reconciliations. Or, if A is a salesclerk with custody of cash receipts from sales, B could be a cash register with a locked-in tape, and C could be the departmental supervisor. Regardless of the nature of the parties involved, the principle remains the same: Accounting records should be maintained independently of custody of the related assets and should be compared at reasonable intervals to asset quantities on hand.

## Segregation of Duties

A fundamental concept of internal control is that no one department or person should handle all aspects of a transaction from beginning to end. We have already discussed the segregation of responsibilities among departments. In a similar manner, no one individual should perform more than one of the functions of *authorizing* transactions, *recording* transactions, and *maintaining custody* over assets. Also, to the extent possible, individuals executing the specific transaction should be segregated from these functions. The goal is to not allow an individual to have **incompatible duties** that would allow him or her to both perpetrate and conceal errors or fraud in the normal course of his or her duties.

A credit sales transaction may be used to illustrate appropriate authorization and segregation procedures. Top management may have generally authorized the sale of merchandise at specified credit terms to customers who meet certain requirements. The credit department may approve the sales transactions by ascertaining that the extension of credit and the terms of sale are in compliance with company policies. Once the sale is approved, the shipping department executes the transaction by obtaining custody of the merchandise from the inventory stores department and shipping it to the customer. The accounting department uses copies of the documentation created by the sales, credit, and shipping departments as a basis for recording the transaction and billing the customer. With this segregation of duties, no one department or individual can initiate and execute an unauthorized transaction.

# The Accounting Information System[3]

Information is needed at all levels of an organization to assist management in meeting the organization's objectives. Of major concern to the auditors is the accounting information system and the way in which responsibilities for internal control over financial reporting are communicated throughout the organization.

An organization's accounting information system consists of the methods and records established to record, process, summarize, and report an entity's transactions and to maintain accountability for the related assets, liabilities, and equity. Accordingly, an accounting information system should:

1. Identify and record all valid transactions.
2. Describe on a timely basis the transactions in sufficient detail to permit proper classification of transactions for financial reporting.
3. Measure the value of transactions in a manner that permits recording their proper monetary value in the financial statements.
4. Determine the time period in which transactions occurred to permit recording of transactions in the proper accounting period.
5. Present properly the transactions and related disclosures in the financial statements.

In addition to the typical system of journals, ledgers, and other record keeping devices, an *accounting information system* should include a chart of accounts and a manual of accounting policies and procedures as aids for communicating policies. A *chart of accounts* is a classified listing of all accounts in use, accompanied by a detailed description of the purpose and content of each. A *manual of accounting policies and procedures* states clearly in writing the methods of treating transactions. In combination, the chart of accounts and manual of accounting policies and procedures should provide clear guidance that will allow proper and uniform handling of transactions.

Proper communication involves providing employees with an understanding of their individual roles and responsibilities relating to financial reporting. Open communication channels are essential to proper functioning of an information system. Personnel that process information should understand how their activities relate to the work of others and the importance of reporting exceptions and other unusual items to an appropriate level of management.

# Monitoring of Controls

Monitoring of controls, the last component of internal control, is a process to assess the quality of internal control performance over time. It is important to monitor internal control to determine whether it is operating as intended and whether any modifications are necessary. Monitoring can be achieved by performing ongoing activities or by separate evaluations. *Ongoing monitoring activities* include regularly performed supervisory and management activities, such as continuous monitoring of customer complaints, or reviewing the reasonableness of management reports. *Separate evaluations* are monitoring activities that are performed on a nonroutine basis, such as periodic audits by the internal auditors.

### The Internal Audit Function

An important aspect of the organization's monitoring system is the internal audit function. Internal auditors investigate and appraise internal control and the efficiency with which the various units of the organization are performing their assigned functions, and

---

[3] *Internal Control–Integrated Framework* refers to this component as the information system and communication. However, the accounting information system is of primary importance to an audit of financial statements.

## Illustrative Case — *Management Override*

Management override is often as simple as posting improper adjusting journal entries to modify financial results. In a complaint filed by the Securities and Exchange Commission against WorldCom, Inc., the SEC accused senior management of disguising the true performance of the company by using undisclosed and improper accounting that overstated income by capitalizing various costs that should have been treated as expenses. *The New York Times* reported that the company's ex-controller admitted to investigators that he was aware of the expense shifts, but that financial pressures being faced by the company left him with little choice. The ability of management to override internal control is difficult to prevent. Companies must rely upon active participation by the audit committee and an effective internal audit department.

they report their findings and recommendations to management and the audit committee. As representatives of top management, internal auditors are interested in determining whether each branch or department has a clear understanding of its assignment; is adequately staffed; maintains good records; properly safeguards cash, inventories, and other assets; and cooperates harmoniously with other departments. In addition, internal auditors monitor management and help prevent management override of internal control. The manner in which the CPAs use the work of internal auditors is discussed later in this chapter; the internal auditing profession is discussed in detail in Chapter 21.

## Limitations of Internal Control

Internal control can do much to protect against both errors and fraud and to ensure the reliability of accounting data. Still, it is important to recognize the existence of inherent limitations of internal control. Mistakes may be made in the performance of controls as a result of a misunderstanding of instructions, mistakes of judgment, carelessness, distraction, or fatigue. Errors may also occur in designing, maintaining, or monitoring automated controls. Control activities—whether manual or automated—dependent upon separation of duties may be circumvented by collusion among two or more people or inappropriate management override of internal control. Management, for example, may enter into side agreements with customers that alter the terms and conditions of the company's standard contract in ways that would preclude revenue recognition, or management may improperly modify the accounting records.

The extent of the controls adopted by a business also is limited by cost considerations. It is not feasible from a cost standpoint to establish controls that provide absolute protection from fraud and waste; reasonable assurance in this regard is generally the best that can be achieved.

## Enterprise Risk Management

In 2004, the Committee of Sponsoring Organizations (COSO) issued *Enterprise Risk Management–Integrated Framework*. This framework goes beyond internal control to focus on how organizations can maximize value for their stakeholders by effectively managing risks and opportunities. Advantages of an enterprise risk management framework include:

- Aligning the organization's risk appetite and its strategy.
- Enhancing risk response decisions by focusing on the best techniques for managing risk—risk avoidance, reduction, sharing, and acceptance.

- Reducing operational surprises and losses.
- Identifying and managing multiple and cross-enterprise risks.
- Seizing opportunities.
- Improving the deployment of capital.

Similar to COSO's internal control framework, the enterprise risk management framework has the following eight components.

1. *Internal environment.* The internal environment is the basis for all other components of ERM, providing discipline and structure. It encompasses the tone of the organization, and sets the basis for how risk is viewed and addressed by an organization's people, including risk management philosophy and risk appetite, and integrity and ethical values.

2. *Objective setting.* The organization's mission sets forth in broad terms what the organization aspires to achieve. Strategic objectives are high-level goals aligned with the organization's mission. These high-level objectives are linked and integrated with the specific objectives established for various activities. By setting objectives, the organization can identify critical risk factors, which are the key things that must go right for the objectives to be met.

3. *Event identification.* An event is an incident that occurs or might occur that affects implementation of strategy or achievement of objectives. Events may be negative (risks), positive (opportunities), or both. Risks require a response while opportunities should be channeled back to management's strategy or objective-setting processes. Some events may be external in nature, such as those resulting from economic, natural environment, political, social, or technological factors. Other events result from internal factors such as the organization's infrastructure, personnel, processes, or technology.

4. *Risk assessment.* Risks must be analyzed, considering likelihood and impact, as a basis for determining how they should be managed.

5. *Risk response.* In this aspect of ERM, management selects risk responses that are consistent with the risk appetite of the organization including:
   - *Avoidance.* This response involves exiting the activity that gives rise to the risk.
   - *Reduction.* This response involves taking action to reduce risk likelihood or impact, or both. For example, risk reduction might involve managing the risk or adding additional controls to processes.
   - *Sharing.* This response involves reducing risk likelihood or impact by transferring or sharing a portion of the risk. Techniques for sharing include insurance, hedging, and outsourcing.
   - *Acceptance.* This response involves taking no action because the risk is consistent with the risk appetite of the organization.

6. *Control activities.* Policies and procedures should be established and implemented to help ensure that the risk responses are effectively carried out.

7. *Information and communication.* Relevant information must be identified, captured, and communicated to enable people to carry out their responsibilities regarding risk management.

8. *Monitoring.* The entire ERM process should be monitored to make needed modifications. Monitoring is accomplished by ongoing management activities and separate evaluations, such as those performed by internal auditors.

It is not necessary for a company to implement an enterprise risk management system that meets these criteria in order to have effective internal control. However, management of firms that implement these systems should do a much better job of managing business risks.

# Financial Statement Audits: The Role of Internal Control

**LO3**

Describe the auditors' consideration of internal control.

Recall from Chapter 6 that the overall approach that auditors use in a financial statement audit includes:

1. Plan the audit.
2. Obtain an understanding of the client and its environment, including internal control.
3. Assess the risks of misstatement and design further audit procedures.
4. Perform further audit procedures.
5. Complete the audit.
6. Form an opinion and issue the audit report.

Internal control is most directly related to stages 2 through 4.

The auditors use **risk assessment procedures** to obtain an understanding of internal control. The understanding obtained, combined with the auditors' other evidence, allows them to assess the risk of material misstatement. Recall that the risk of misstatement is composed of **inherent risk** and **control risk** as:

Results of the risk assessment are used *to design the nature, timing, and extent of further audit procedures.* Recall from Chapters 5 and 6 that the possible **further audit procedures** include **tests of controls** and **substantive procedures**. The design of further audit procedures depends upon the results obtained while obtaining an understanding of internal control and assessing the risks of material misstatement. The auditors make decisions about the proper combination of tests of controls (which allow a lower assessment of control risk) and substantive procedures (which restrict detection risk). The following three sections provide details on how auditors obtain an understanding of internal control, how they assess the risks of material misstatement, and how they design and perform tests of controls.

## Obtain an Understanding of the Client and Its Environment, Including Internal Control

As discussed in Chapter 6, the auditors perform risk assessment procedures to obtain an understanding of the client and its environment, including internal control. This understanding provides auditors with information to assess the risks of material misstatement and with information on the types of further audit procedures that should be performed. For example, to perform substantive procedures to verify the existence of accounts receivable, the auditors need to know and understand the nature of the underlying source documents.

In making a judgment about the extent of the understanding of internal control that is necessary, the auditors should realize that the information will subsequently be used to:

- Identify types of potential misstatements.
- Consider factors that affect the risks of material misstatement.
- Design tests of controls (when applicable) and substantive procedures.

As we have discussed in Chapter 6, in addition to audit evidence on internal control, audit evidence is collected on the industry in which the client operates and on its overall environment. Previous year audit results may also provide relevant information relating to the current audit. Also, while performing risk assessment procedures, auditors may realize the need to obtain additional staff support with specialized skills, such as someone with a specialized understanding of information technology. As an example, a professional with information technology skills may be needed on the audit team due to the complexity of the client's systems.

While obtaining an understanding of internal control, the auditors consider its design and determine that it has been implemented (placed in operation). It is helpful to realize that considering the design of a control and determining that it is implemented represent two different operations. For example, the client may provide a detailed flowchart of the *design* of controls over the payroll function. To determine whether it has been implemented, the auditors ordinarily observe the process and make certain that it seems as described. Yet, at this point, no detailed testing of that function (i.e., tests of controls) will ordinarily have been performed.

The auditors also consider inherent risks, judgments about materiality, and the nature of the client's operations.

## Required Auditor Understanding of Internal Control Components

In all audits, the auditors' understanding of internal control must encompass each of the internal control components—the control environment, risk assessment, control activities, the accounting information and communication system, and monitoring.

### The Control Environment

The auditors must obtain sufficient knowledge to understand management's attitudes, awareness, and actions concerning the control environment. It is important that the auditors concentrate on the substance of controls, rather than their form. For example, an organization may have, but not enforce, a *code of conduct* prohibiting unethical activities.

The company's antifraud programs are of particular importance to the auditors because the professional standards require that the auditor evaluate whether such programs are suitably designed and implemented. This includes broad programs designed to prevent, deter, and detect fraud, as well as more specific controls. As indicated earlier in this chapter, Appendix 7A provides examples of fraud programs and controls.

### Risk Assessment

The auditors must obtain an understanding of the client's process for identifying and responding to business risks. This understanding includes how management identifies these risks, estimates their significance, and decides upon actions to manage them. If the client has implemented an enterprise risk management system, the auditors will obtain an understanding of the processes and controls that are implemented in the system. An understanding of the risk assessment process assists the auditors in identifying risks of material misstatement, since many such risks arise as a result of business risks faced by the client.

Factors such as the following might be indicative of increased financial reporting risk for a client:

- Changes in the organization's regulatory or operating environment.
- Changes in personnel.
- New or revamped information systems.
- Rapid growth of the organization.
- Changes in technology affecting production processes or information systems.
- New business models, products, or activities.
- Corporate restructurings.
- Expansion or acquisition of foreign operations.
- Adoption of new accounting principles or changing accounting principles.

*Control Activities*

While obtaining an understanding of the other internal control components (the control environment, risk assessment, the accounting information system, and monitoring), auditors generally obtain some knowledge about the client's control activities. For example, while obtaining an understanding of documents relating to cash transactions, it is likely that the auditors will discover whether the bank accounts are reconciled. Whether it is necessary for the auditors to devote additional attention to obtaining an understanding of the other control activities depends on the circumstances of the engagement.

The auditors may find it necessary to understand and test certain control activities to audit a particular assertion. For example, when auditing a charitable organization that receives significant cash donations, the auditors may be unable to effectively plan the audit for the completeness assertion for cash contributions without understanding and testing controls related to cash receipts. In other circumstances, the auditors may conclude that it would be too costly to audit a particular assertion using only substantive procedures; the most efficient course of action is to increase their understanding and testing of the client's internal control.

*The Accounting Information System*

To understand the accounting information system, the auditors must become familiar with:

- The classes of transactions that are significant to the financial statements.
- How the incorrect processing of transactions is resolved.
- How the information captures significant nonroutine transactions and accounting estimates.
- The procedures used to prepare financial statements and related disclosures, and how misstatements may occur.
- How financial reporting roles and responsibilities and significant matters relating to financial reporting are communicated.

In obtaining an understanding of the client's accounting information system and the related control activities, auditors generally find it useful to divide the overall system into its major transaction cycles. The term **transaction cycle** refers to the policies and the sequence of procedures for processing a particular type of transaction. For example, the accounting system in a manufacturing business might be subdivided into the following major transaction cycles:

1. *Revenue (or sales and collections) cycle*—including processes, procedures, and policies for obtaining orders from customers, approving credit, shipping merchandise, preparing sales invoices (billing), recording revenue and accounts receivable, and handling and recording cash receipts.

2. *Acquisition (or purchases and disbursements) cycle*—including processes, procedures, and policies for initiating purchases of inventory, other assets, and services; placing purchase orders, inspecting goods upon receipt, and preparing receiving reports; recording liabilities to vendors; authorizing payment; and making and recording cash disbursements.

3. *Conversion (production) cycle*—including processes, procedures, and policies for storing materials, placing materials into production, assigning production costs to inventories, and accounting for the cost of goods sold.

4. *Payroll cycle*—including processes, procedures, and policies for hiring, terminating, and determining pay rates; timekeeping; computing gross payroll, payroll taxes, and amounts withheld from gross pay; maintaining payroll records; and preparing and distributing paychecks.

5. *Financing cycle*—including processes, procedures, and policies for authorizing, executing, and recording transactions involving bank loans, leases, bonds payable, and capital stock.

6. *Investing cycle*—including processes, procedures, and policies for authorizing, executing, and recording transactions involving investments in fixed assets and securities.

The transaction cycles for a particular company depend upon the nature of the company's business activities. A bank, for example, has no production cycle, but has both a lending cycle and a demand deposits cycle. Also, different auditors may elect to define a given company's transaction cycles in different ways. For example, the sales and collections cycle may alternatively be defined as two separate transaction cycles for (1) the processing and recording of credit sales, and (2) the handling and recording of cash receipts. The important point to recognize is that dividing internal control into transaction cycles enables the auditor to focus upon the controls that affect the reliability of assertions about specific accounts in the financial statements.

*Monitoring of Controls*

Finally, the auditors should obtain a sufficient understanding of the entity's monitoring methods relating to financial reporting to understand how those procedures are used to initiate actions to address inadequate performance. The auditors will also consider how the work of the internal auditors contributes to internal control. The auditors' consideration of the work of internal auditors is described later in this chapter.

## Areas Difficult to Control

Certain areas are particularly difficult for management to control. If potentially significant, those areas require special audit consideration. In terms of the audit risk model, the risk of material misstatement is very high for certain assertions in these areas. These assertions requiring special audit consideration often involve nonroutine transactions or accounting estimates.

*Nonroutine* transactions are those that are unusual, due to either size or nature, and occur relatively infrequently. A variety of risks relating to significant nonroutine transactions arise due to factors such as management or other employee intervention—often manual—to specify accounting treatment of complex calculations. In addition, these transactions may be with related parties. Similarly, many accounting *estimates* are of high risk due to their subjective or complex nature, or the need to make assumptions about the effects of future events. Examples include accounts valued at fair value and revenue accounts that may require estimates subject to differing interpretation (e.g., sales in which the amount of actual realization is difficult to measure).

When determining whether an identified risk of misstatement requires special audit consideration, the auditors consider factors such as the following:

- Complexity of calculations involved.
- Risk of fraud.
- Selection and application of accounting policies.
- Internal and external circumstances giving rise to business risks (e.g., technological change in the industry).
- Recent developments in the industry and economy.

## Risk Assessment Procedures for Internal Control

How do auditors obtain an understanding of a client's internal control? Procedures to obtain audit evidence about the design and implementation of relevant controls may include *inquiring* of entity personnel, *observing* the application of specific controls, *inspecting* documents and reports, and *tracing* transactions through the information

LO4

Discuss the techniques used by auditors to obtain an understanding of internal control.

system relevant to financial reporting. Auditors ordinarily use one or a combination of these approaches to obtain the needed understanding of internal control. One restriction exists, however, in that inquiry alone is not sufficient to evaluate the design of a control and to determine whether it has been implemented.

In repeat engagements, the auditors will stress areas shown as having questionable controls in prior years. It is imperative, however, that auditors recognize that the pattern of operations is an ever-changing one—controls that were adequate last year may now be ineffective.

Auditors may determine the duties and responsibilities of client personnel by inspecting organization charts and job descriptions and interviewing client personnel. Many clients have procedures manuals and flowcharts describing the approved practices to be followed in all phases of operations. Another excellent source of information is in the reports, working papers, and audit programs of the client's internal auditing staff.

The auditors' understanding of internal control encompasses not only the design of controls, but also whether they have been implemented (placed in operation). Implemented means that the control actually exists and is in use; that is, it does not just exist in theory or on paper.

While obtaining an understanding of internal control, the auditors may also obtain evidence about the *operating effectiveness* of various controls. The distinction between knowing that a control has been implemented and obtaining evidence on its *operating effectiveness* is important. To properly perform an audit, auditors are required to determine that the major controls have been implemented; they are *not* required to evaluate their operating effectiveness. However, if the auditors wish to assess control risk at a level below maximum, they must obtain evidence of the operating effectiveness of those controls. This evidence is obtained by performing tests of controls, which are discussed later in this chapter.

## Documenting the Understanding of Internal Control

As the independent auditors obtain a working knowledge of internal control, they must document the information in their working papers. The form and extent of this documentation is affected by the size and complexity of the client, as well as the nature of the client's internal control. The documentation usually takes the form of internal control questionnaires, written narratives, or flowcharts.

*Internal Control Questionnaire*

The traditional method of describing internal control is to fill in a standardized **internal control questionnaire**. Many public accounting firms have developed their own questionnaires for this purpose. The questionnaire usually contains a separate section for each major transaction cycle, enabling the work of completing the questionnaire to be divided conveniently among several audit staff members.

Most internal control questionnaires are designed so that a "no" answer to a question indicates a weakness in internal control, and requires the auditors to identify types of potential misstatements arising therefrom. In addition, questionnaires may provide for a distinction between major and minor control weaknesses, an indication of the sources of information used in answering questions, and explanatory comments regarding control deficiencies. A disadvantage of standardized internal control questionnaires is their lack of flexibility. They often contain many questions that are "not applicable" to specific systems, particularly systems for small companies. Also, the situation in which an internal control strength compensates for a weakness may not be obvious from examining a completed questionnaire. An internal control questionnaire relating to cash receipts is illustrated in Figure 7.3.

An internal control questionnaire is intended as a means for the auditors to document their understanding of internal control. If completion of the questionnaire is regarded as an end in itself, there may be a tendency for the auditors to fill in the "yes" and "no" answers in a mechanical manner, without any real understanding or study of the

**FIGURE 7.3**
**Internal Control**
**Questionnaire**

**Internal Control Questionnaire**
**Cash Receipts—Sales Cycle**

Client _Bennington Co., Inc._     Audit Date _December 31, 200X_

Names and Positions of Client Personnel Interviewed:
_Lorraine Martin—Cashier;  Helen Ellis—Head Bookkeeper;  Wm. Dale—Manager_

| Question | Answer | | | | | |
|---|---|---|---|---|---|---|
| | Not Appl. | Yes | No | Weakness Major | Weakness Minor | Remarks |
| 1. Are all persons receiving or disbursing cash bonded? | | ✓ | | | | |
| 2. Is all incoming mail opened by a responsible employee who does not have access to accounting records? | | | ✓ | ✓ | | *H. Ellis is head bookkeeper* |
| 3. Does the employee assigned to the opening of incoming mail prepare a list of all checks and money received? | | | ✓ | | ✓ | *See mitigating control in #13* |
| 4. a) Is a copy of the listing of mail receipts forwarded to the accounts receivable department for comparison with the credits to customers' accounts? | ✓ | | | | | |
| b) Is a copy of this list turned over to an employee other than the cashier for comparison with the cash receipts records? | ✓ | | | | | |
| 5. Are receipts from cash sales and other over-the-counter collections recorded by sales registers or point-of-sale terminals? | ✓ | | | | | |
| 6. Are the daily totals of cash registers or other mechanical devices verified by an employee not having access to cash? | ✓ | | | | | |
| 7. Are physical facilities and mechanical equipment for receiving and recording cash adequate and conducive to good control? | | ✓ | | | | |
| 8. Is revenue from investments, rent, concessions, and similar sources scheduled in advance so that nonreceipt on due date would be promptly investigated? | ✓ | | | | | |
| 9. Do procedures for sale of scrap materials provide for direct reporting to accounting department concurrently with transfer of receipts to cashier? | ✓ | | | | | |
| 10. Are securities and other negotiable assets in the custody of someone other than the cashier? | ✓ | | | | | |
| 11. Are collections by branch offices deposited daily in a bank account subject to withdrawal only by home office executives? | ✓ | | | | | |
| 12. Are each day's receipts deposited intact and without delay by an employee other than the accounts receivable bookkeeper? | | ✓ | | | | |
| 13. Are the duplicate deposit tickets returned by the bank and compared with the cash receipts record and mailroom list of receipts by an employee other than the cashier or accounts receivable bookkeeper? | | ✓ | | | | *W. Dale Manager* |
| 14. Are the duplicate deposit tickets properly filed and available for inspection by auditors? | | ✓ | | | | *Chronological sequence* |
| 15. Are NSF checks or other items returned by the bank delivered directly to an employee other than the cashier and promptly investigated? | | ✓ | | | | *W. Dale Manager* |
| 16. Is the physical arrangement of offices and accounting records designed to prevent employees who handle cash from having access to accounting records? | | | ✓ | | ✓ | *Small company doesn't permit this* |

Prepared by _V.M. Harris_     Date _Sept. 6, 0X_     Manager Review _____  Date _____
Senior Review _____     Date _____     Partner Review _____  Date _____

transaction cycle. For this reason, some public accounting firms prefer to use written narratives or flowcharts in lieu of, or in conjunction with, questionnaires.

### Written Narratives of Internal Control

**Written narratives of internal control** are memoranda that describe the flow of transaction cycles, identifying the employees performing various tasks, the documents prepared, the records maintained, and the division of duties. Figure 7.4 is a written narrative, describing internal control over cash receipts received in the form of checks.

### Flowcharts of Internal Control

Many CPA firms consider systems flowcharts to be more effective than questionnaires or narrative descriptions in documenting their understanding of a client's accounting information system and the related control activities. A **systems flowchart** is a diagram—a

**FIGURE 7.4**
Written Narrative on
Internal Control

---

**Bennington Co., Inc.**
**Cash Receipts Procedures**
**December 31, 200X**

All checks are received by mail. Lorraine Martin, cashier, picks up the mail every morning at the post office and delivers it unopened to Helen Ellis, the head bookkeeper.

Ellis opens and distributes the mail. Customers' checks are given to Martin, who inputs them as a batch into the cash receipts application program, which prepares duplicate deposit slips, records the cash, and posts the accounts receivable subsidiary ledger. Martin deposits the checks intact at the First National Bank and returns with a validated duplicate deposit slip, which Ellis files chronologically.

Any customers' checks charged back by the bank are given by Ellis to the manager, William Dale, who follows up and redeposits the checks. Ellis also forwards monthly bank statements unopened to Dale. Dale reconciles the monthly bank statement, compares the dates and amounts of deposits with the entries in the cash receipts journal, and reviews the propriety of sales discounts recorded in the cash receipts journal.

Martin, Ellis, and Dale are all bonded.

Val Martin Harris
September 6, 200X

---

symbolic representation of a system or a series of procedures with each procedure shown in sequence. To the experienced reader, a flowchart conveys a clear image of the system, showing the nature and sequence of procedures, division of responsibilities, sources and distribution of documents, and types and location of accounting records and files. The standard symbols used in systems flowcharting are illustrated in Figure 7.5; however, the symbols used and the flowcharting technique vary somewhat among different public accounting firms.

Separate systems flowcharts are prepared for each major transaction cycle. Each flowchart is divided into vertical columns representing the various departments (or employees) involved in processing the transactions. Departmental responsibility for procedures, documents, and records is shown by reviewing the related flowcharting symbol beneath the appropriate departmental heading. Flowcharts usually begin in the upper left-hand corner; directional flowlines then indicate the sequence of activity. The normal flow of activity is from top to bottom and from left to right. These basic concepts of systems flowcharting are illustrated in Figure 7.6.

The advantage of a flowchart over a questionnaire or a narrative is that a flowchart provides a clearer, more specific portrayal of the client's system. There is less opportunity for misunderstanding, omitted areas, or ambiguous statements when one uses lines and symbols rather than words to describe internal control. Furthermore, in each successive annual audit, updating a flowchart is a simple process requiring only that the auditor add or change a few lines and symbols.

A possible disadvantage of flowcharts is that internal control weaknesses are not identified as prominently as in questionnaires. A "no" answer in an internal control questionnaire is a conspicuous red flag calling attention to a dangerous situation. A flowchart may not provide so clear a signal that a particular control is absent or is not being properly enforced. For that reason, some CPA firms use both flowcharts and questionnaires to describe internal control. The flowchart clearly depicts internal control, while the questionnaire serves to remind the auditors of controls that should be present.

### The Walk-Through

After describing internal control in their working papers, the auditors often will verify that it has been implemented by performing a walk-through of each transaction cycle. The term **walk-through** refers to tracing one or two transactions through each step in the cycle. To perform a walk-through of the sales and collections cycle, for example, the auditors might begin by selecting several sales orders and following the related transactions through the client's sequence of procedures. The auditors would determine whether such procedures as credit approval, shipment of merchandise, preparation of sales invoices, recording of the accounts receivable, and processing of the customers' remittances were performed by appropriate client personnel and in the sequence indicated in the audit working papers. If the auditors find that internal control functions differently from the working paper description, they will modify the working papers to describe the actual process.

**FIGURE 7.5**
**Widely Used**
**Flowcharting Symbols**

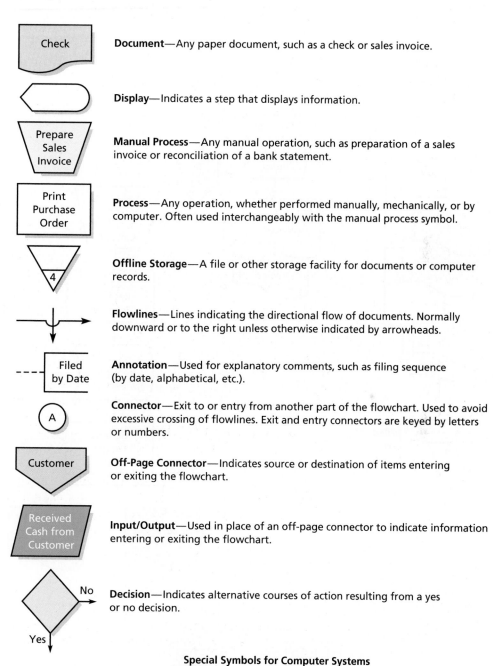

**Document**—Any paper document, such as a check or sales invoice.

**Display**—Indicates a step that displays information.

**Manual Process**—Any manual operation, such as preparation of a sales invoice or reconciliation of a bank statement.

**Process**—Any operation, whether performed manually, mechanically, or by computer. Often used interchangeably with the manual process symbol.

**Offline Storage**—A file or other storage facility for documents or computer records.

**Flowlines**—Lines indicating the directional flow of documents. Normally downward or to the right unless otherwise indicated by arrowheads.

**Annotation**—Used for explanatory comments, such as filing sequence (by date, alphabetical, etc.).

**Connector**—Exit to or entry from another part of the flowchart. Used to avoid excessive crossing of flowlines. Exit and entry connectors are keyed by letters or numbers.

**Off-Page Connector**—Indicates source or destination of items entering or exiting the flowchart.

**Input/Output**—Used in place of an off-page connector to indicate information entering or exiting the flowchart.

**Decision**—Indicates alternative courses of action resulting from a yes or no decision.

**Special Symbols for Computer Systems**

Magnetic Disk    Online Storage    Magnetic Tape

**FIGURE 7.6  Cash Receipts Flowchart**

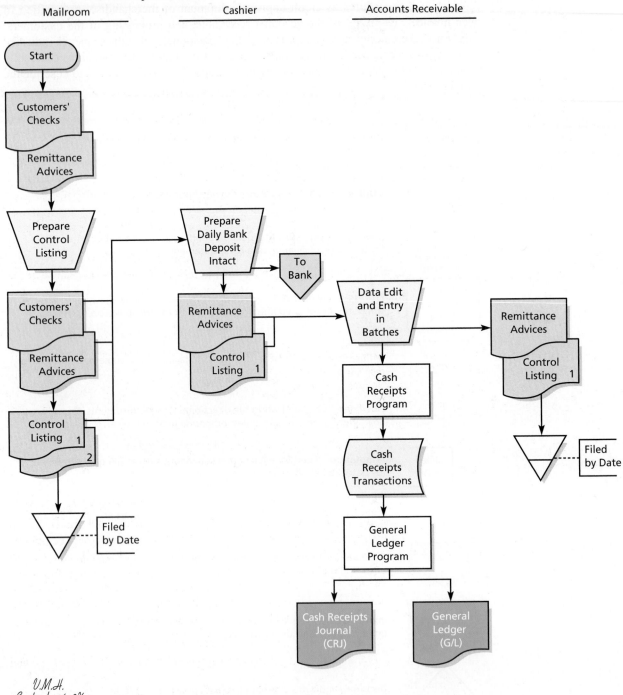

## Assess the Risks of Material Misstatement

**LO5**

Explain how internal control relates to a financial statement audit.

The auditors should identify and assess the risks of material misstatement at both the financial statement level and the relevant assertion level for account balances, transaction classes, and disclosures. The general approach followed during risk assessment is to use all the audit evidence obtained on the client and its environment, including internal control, to:

- Identify risks.
- Relate the identified risks to what can go wrong at the relevant assertion level.

• Consider whether the risks are of a magnitude that could result in a material misstatement.

• Consider the likelihood that the risks could result in a material misstatement.

The auditors' understanding of the entity's internal control is a key input in identifying the risks of material misstatement. For example, the auditors use their understanding of the client's information system to identify risks of material misstatement that relate directly to the recording of transactions such as the following:

• Routine transactions (e.g., revenue, purchases, and cash receipts and disbursements).

• Nonroutine transactions (e.g., taking of inventory, calculating depreciation expense).

• Estimation transactions (e.g., determining the allowance for doubtful accounts).

Since strong controls over an area are likely to result in the proper recording of transactions, the expected effectiveness of internal control is often a key factor in assessing the risks of material misstatement. Yet when the auditors assess the risks of material misstatement at this stage of the audit, they have little information on the actual effectiveness of controls. Ordinarily they know the system as it has been described to them, and they have determined that it has been implemented. This allows them to assess only the effectiveness of the design of the system. If they wish to rely on the controls with respect to particular assertions, they must perform tests of controls to obtain audit evidence about their actual effectiveness.[4]

**Assess Risks at the Financial Statement Level**

Risks at the financial statement level are those that relate to the overall financial statements and potentially affect many individual assertions. The following are examples of risks at the financial statement level:

• Preparing the period end financial statements, including the development of significant accounting estimates and the preparation of the notes.

• The selection and application of significant accounting policies.

• IT general controls (these controls are discussed in further detail in Chapter 8).

• The control environment.

Risks such as these potentially affect many relevant assertions in that they cannot effectively be isolated. In addition to the various accounts they may affect, these risks are difficult for the auditors because assessing the associated risks often requires considerable judgment. For example, poorly controlled access to the IT system may allow unauthorized personnel to access and inappropriately change data of many types. Questions about the integrity of management also may raise a variety of questions relating to the financial statements. Because of these characteristics of financial statement level risks, an overall response by the auditor is often required. This response might include:

• Assigning more experienced staff or those with specialized skills.

• Providing more supervision and emphasizing the need to maintain professional skepticism.

• Incorporating additional elements of unpredictability in the selection of further audit procedures to be performed.

• Increasing the overall scope of audit procedures, including their nature, timing, or extent.

---

[4] As we have indicated in Chapter 5, the process is not as sequential as implied. Auditors will at some points have performed tests of controls while obtaining an understanding of internal control. The point we make here is that simply obtaining an understanding of the system and its implementation is not ordinarily sufficient to evaluate its operating effectiveness. As indicated later in this chapter, however, an exception to this general rule sometimes exists for certain automated controls whose very implementation implies operating effectiveness.

## Assess Risks at the Relevant Assertion Level

Some risks of misstatement relate to one or a few **relevant assertions.** For example, risks associated with the failure to recognize an impairment loss on a long-lived asset affect only the valuation assertion and related impairment loss associated with that asset. Risks related to inaccurate counting of inventory at year-end affect the valuation of inventory and the accuracy of cost of goods sold.

When auditors assess risks at the relevant assertion level, they consider both the design of the control and its implementation. When the design itself is deficient, the issue of whether the control has been implemented loses importance since it is unlikely that the control will be effective. Ordinarily, the auditors will then consider whether the situation results in a risk of material misstatement and the need for substantive procedures to determine whether such a material misstatement exists.

When the design seems strong, auditors must determine that it has been implemented and that it exists more than simply "on paper." Determining whether it has been implemented ordinarily involves observing the procedure. The auditors may also decide to perform further audit procedures to determine whether the controls operate effectively— these procedures are tests of controls.

A decision to perform tests of controls is based on both the auditors' consideration of whether controls are likely to be operating effectively and whether testing those controls is likely to be cost effective. In other words, the auditors must ask themselves, "Is the time required to perform tests of controls to justify a lower assessment of control risk justified in terms of its resulting decrease in the scope of substantive procedures?" The lower **assessed level of control risk** (or risk of material misstatement) is appropriate only when the auditors have evidence on the operating effectiveness obtained by performing tests of controls.

The auditors' approach also may be dictated by other audit evidence that is available and by the nature of the client's information system. For example, when the client uses a sophisticated information technology system, the auditors may conclude that substantive procedures cannot, in and of themselves, provide sufficient audit evidence. When this is the case, there may be no other option than relying upon a combination of tests of controls and substantive procedures.

## Design and Perform Further Audit Procedures

After assessing the risks of material misstatement, the auditors consider what can go wrong and design further audit procedures. Further audit procedures ordinarily consist of substantive procedures and, when the assessed level of risk presumes that controls operate effectively, tests of controls. At this point, the risk assessments are preliminary because the auditors may be assuming that controls that have not been tested are operating effectively. The preliminary assessments of control risk are often referred to as the **planned assessed level of control risk.**

Tests of controls can focus on either financial statement or assertion level controls. Ordinarily, controls that operate at the financial statement level, such as the control environment or IT general controls, are only indirectly related to particular assertions. The emphasis for tests of controls must ordinarily be upon the operating effectiveness of controls that are directly related to relevant assertions. In addition, the auditors will consider the need to obtain audit evidence on the effective operation of financial statement level controls for which the effectiveness of direct controls depends.

## Tests of Controls

**LO6**

Describe the major types of tests of controls.

The auditors perform tests of controls to obtain evidence about the operating effectiveness of controls. The approach is to (1) identify the controls likely to prevent or detect material misstatements and (2) perform tests of controls to determine whether they are operating effectively. Tests of controls address the following:

- How controls were applied.
- The consistency with which controls were applied.
- By whom or by what means (e.g., electronically) the controls were applied.

As indicated previously, the auditors may have gathered some evidence about the effectiveness of certain controls while they performed procedures to obtain an understanding of internal control and determined that the controls were implemented. For example, in evaluating the design of the control environment, the auditors may have made inquiries about management's use of budgets, observed management's comparison of monthly budgeted and actual expenses, and inspected reports pertaining to the investigation of variances. For efficiency purposes, the auditors may have decided to perform virtually all of the tests of controls during the process of obtaining an understanding of internal control. However, for many audits the auditors will design additional tests of controls at this point to support their planned assessed level of control risk. The auditors will use their understanding of the client's internal control to design these additional tests of controls.

### Nature of Tests of Controls

The audit procedures used to test the effectiveness of internal control include:

- *Inquiries* of appropriate client personnel.
- *Inspection* of documents and reports.
- *Observation* of the application of controls.
- *Reperformance* of the controls.

Tests of controls focus on the operation of controls rather than on the accuracy of financial statement amounts. To illustrate this distinction, assume that the client has implemented the control of requiring a second person to review the quantities, prices, extensions, and footing of each sales invoice. The purpose of this control is to prevent material errors in the billing of customers and the recording of sales transactions.

To test the operating effectiveness of this control of requiring a second person review, the auditors may make inquiries of client personnel and observe application of the procedure. They might also select a sample of, say, 20 sales invoices prepared throughout the year. They would inspect the invoice copy for the initials of the reviewer, and reperform the procedure by comparing the quantities to those listed on the related shipping documents, comparing unit prices to the client's price lists and verifying the extensions and footings. The results of this test provide the auditors with evidence as to the existence and valuation of the recorded sales and accounts receivable. If numerous deviations from the control are found, the auditors will expand their substantive procedures with respect to existence and valuation of accounts receivable and sales transactions. For example, a substantive test of financial statement amounts might involve selecting a sample of recorded sales transactions to determine that they have been properly recorded and included in the year's total sales.

The control described above leaves documentary evidence of performance, the reviewer's initials, that allows it to be tested by sampling. Controls that do not leave documentary evidence of performance must be tested entirely through observation by the auditors and inquiry of client personnel. Segregation of duties, for example, is tested by observing the client's employees as they perform their duties, and inquiring as to who performed those duties throughout the period under audit. The auditors also should determine whether employees performed *incompatible duties* when other employees were absent from work on sick leave or vacation.

### Timing of Tests of Controls

Timing of the performance of tests of controls depends upon the auditors' objectives. If the auditors test the operation of controls at a particular time, their audit evidence generally relates only to that time (e.g., tests of counting procedures performed during the annual physical inventory counting at period end). However, tests of certain controls provide evidence about operating effectiveness throughout the period (e.g., tests of general controls pertaining to modifying and using a computer program). For many controls, the auditors will want evidence on operating effectiveness by sampling from throughout the period.

### Extent of Tests of Controls

The general approach to increasing the evidence from a test of control is to increase the extent of the test (e.g., increase the number of items tested). However, automated controls provide an exception to this approach. Because of the inherent consistency of operation of automated controls, the auditors often use an audit approach of determining that the control is working at a point in time and that no inappropriate changes were made to the program during the period. In such cases, determining that a control has been implemented may be sufficient to serve as audit evidence on operating effectiveness. Chapter 9 discusses determining sample sizes for tests of controls.

*Evidence from Tests of Controls Performed in Prior Audits*

When the client has been audited in prior years, the auditors may have obtained evidence about the operating effectiveness of controls from tests performed in those audits. If the auditors plan to use this evidence, they should obtain evidence about whether changes in specific controls have occurred subsequent to the prior year's audit. If there have been changes, the new controls must be tested in the current audit to provide a basis for reducing control risk. However, if the auditors determine that the controls have not changed, they may rely on evidence of operating effectiveness obtained from prior years' audits. But to what extent may they rely upon them? Both AICPA and *International Auditing Standards* require that tests of control be performed at least every third audit. PCAOB standards do not allow testing controls every third audit—PCAOB standards provide that annually some evidence regarding operating effectiveness must be obtained when controls are relied upon.

## Revise the Risk of Material Misstatement Based on the Results of Tests of Controls

After the auditors have completed the tests of controls, they must determine if it is necessary to revise their assessed levels of control risk (or risks of material misstatement) based on the results of those tests. If the results indicate that controls operated as effectively as had been assumed, no revision is necessary. The original audit plan is still appropriate. However, if the results reveal that controls are less effective than had been originally thought (i.e., control risk is higher than originally assessed), the auditors will revise their planned assessments and carefully consider the possible misstatements that may exist in the financial statements. Then, they will design additional substantive audit procedures to address the additional risk of misstatement.

Although unlikely, a final possibility is that controls are found to operate more effectively than expected. In this case, modifications may include a decrease in the extent of substantive audit procedures.

## Design and Perform Substantive Procedures

The auditors' assessment of the risk of material misstatement (or separate assessments of inherent and control risks) determines the nature, timing, and extent of substantive audit procedures for the various assertions in the financial statements. For assertions with a high risk of material misstatement, the auditors will plan substantial substantive procedures. On the other hand, when the assessments of the risk of material misstatement of an assertion are low, the substantive procedures will be restricted or in some circumstances eliminated for that assertion. Chapters 10 through 16 provide details of the way in which auditors design substantive procedures for various accounts and assertions.

The auditors' consideration of internal control is complex. Figure 7.7 is a flowchart that highlights the major steps in the auditors' consideration of internal control.

## Documentation

The auditors' consideration of internal control is documented as a part of the overall risk assessment and evidence accumulation process. In addition to documenting their overall understanding of internal control, the auditors must document:

- The overall responses to address the assessed risks of material misstatement at the financial statement level.
- The nature, timing, and extent of the further audit procedures.
- The linkage of those procedures with the assessed risks at the relevant assertion level.

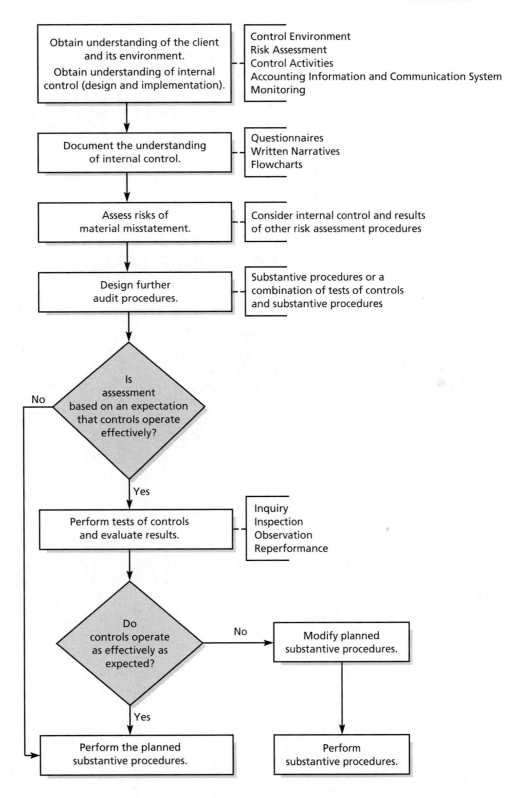

**FIGURE 7.7**
**The Auditors' Consideration of Internal Control**

- The results of the audit procedures.
- The conclusions reached with regard to the use of the current audit evidence about the operating effectiveness of controls that was obtained in a prior audit.

Figure 7.8 provides an illustration of a working paper summarizing the auditors' assessment of inherent risk, control risk, and the combined risk of material misstatement.

**FIGURE 7.8** Working Paper for Summarizing Assessment of Risk

Client: _Arntco, Inc._      Date: _9/16/X3_         Balance Sheet Date: _12/31/X3_

Completed by: _R.W._         Reviewed by: _K.J._         Date: _10/28/X3_

| Ref | | Description of Risk | Significant Risk? | Relevant Assertion(s) | Assessed Risk of Material Misstatement (see A-6 explaining the basis for these determinations) | | | Summary of Audit Approach |
|---|---|---|---|---|---|---|---|---|
| W/P | Item No. | | | | Inherent Risk | Control Risk | Combined Risk of Material Misstatement | |
| B-6 | | Gross Receivables and Gross Sales | Yes | Existence / Occurrence | Moderate | High | Moderate | • _Confirm a sample at 12/3. Ask about any disputes over invoices and compare to internal files to confirm accuracy of company records provided._ |
| B-9 | | | No | Completeness | Moderate | High | Moderate | • _Perform limited sales cutoff tests._ |
| B-6 | | | No | Accuracy | Moderate | High | Moderate | • _Be alert to sales existence issues related to sales from 1st 9 months._ |
| B-11 | | | No | Cutoff | Low | High | Low* | • _Use computer data extraction to perform detailed substantive analytical procedures._ |
| B-11 | | | No | Completeness | Low | High | Moderate | |

* The low exposure at year-end due to closing the business for an extended holiday was considered in reaching this conclusion and was documented. See Brainstorming Session documentation at A-23.

Source: Adapted AICPA *Audit Guide: Assessing and Responding to Risk in a Financial Statement Audit, 2007.*

## Decision Aids for Audit Program Modification

Modifying audit programs for various levels of control risk while considering other factors such as levels of materiality and inherent risk involves complex judgments. How many additional items should the auditors test to compensate for high control risk? Is the risk of material misstatement for a particular assertion low enough to make it feasible to test the assertion at an interim date rather than at year-end? Without guidance from the CPA firm, different auditors within that firm might arrive at different answers to these questions. In fact, research on these types of audit judgments has revealed just that; there is a good deal of variance in auditors' program decisions.

CPA firms initially reacted to this problem by developing policies that place limits on individual auditors' decisions. The establishment of minimum audit sample sizes for particular types of tests is an example of such a policy. More recently, CPA firms have attempted to add even more structure to auditors' program decisions through the use of decision aids or guides. An **audit decision aid** is a checklist, standard form, or computer program that helps the auditors make a particular decision by ensuring that they consider all relevant information or by assisting them in combining the information to make the decision. By reducing the variance in auditors' program judgments, decision aids promote the performance of audits that meet firm and professional requirements.

## Consideration of the Work of Internal Auditors

Many of the audit procedures performed by **internal auditors** are similar in nature to those employed by independent auditors. This raises the question of how the work of the internal auditors affects the independent auditors' work. This issue is addressed in AICPA AU 610 (PCAOB 322).

Because the internal audit function is an important aspect of the client's monitoring component of internal control, the independent auditors consider the existence and quality of the function in their assessment of control risk. Through its contribution to internal control, the work of the internal auditors may reduce the amount of audit testing performed by the independent auditors.

The independent auditors begin by obtaining an understanding of the work of the internal auditors to determine its relevance to the audit. They make inquiries about such matters as the internal auditors' activities and audit plans. If the independent auditors conclude that the internal auditors' work is relevant and that it would be efficient to consider it, they assess the *competence* and *objectivity* of the internal audit staff and evaluate the quality of their work.

In evaluating the competence of the internal auditors, the independent auditors consider the educational level, professional experience, and professional certifications of the internal audit staff. They also investigate the internal auditors' policies, programs, procedures, working papers, and reports and the extent to which the internal auditors' activities are supervised and reviewed. Objectivity is evaluated by considering the organizational status of the director of internal audit, including whether the director reports to an officer of sufficient status to ensure broad audit coverage, and whether he or she has direct access to the audit committee of the board of directors. The internal auditors' policies for assigning independent staff to audit areas are also reviewed.

If, after assessing competence and objectivity, the independent auditors intend to use the internal auditors' work, they will evaluate and test their work. The evaluation includes a review of the scope of the internal auditors' work and the quality of their programs and reports. This investigation and evaluation provides the independent auditors with a sound basis for determining the extent to which the work of the internal auditors allows them to limit their own audit procedures.

In addition to reducing the extent of the independent auditors' substantive procedures, the internal auditors' work may affect the independent auditors' procedures in obtaining an understanding of internal control and assessing risk. For example, the independent auditors may use the internal auditors' documentation of internal control. The internal auditors also may provide direct assistance to the independent auditors in preparing working papers and performing certain audit procedures. However, the independent auditors should not over-rely on the internal auditors' work; they must obtain sufficient appropriate evidence to support their opinion on the financial statements. Regardless of the extent of the internal auditors' work, the independent auditors must perform direct testing of those financial statement assertions with a high risk of material misstatement. Judgments about assessments of inherent and control risks, the materiality of misstatements, the sufficiency of tests performed, and other matters affecting the opinion must be those of the independent auditors. Also, the independent auditors should be directly involved in evaluating audit evidence that requires significant subjective judgment.

## Communication of Control-Related Matters

**LO7**

Describe the auditors' responsibility for communicating control-related matters.

While establishing and maintaining effective internal control is an important responsibility of management, providing independent oversight over internal control and the company's financial reporting process is the responsibility of the audit committee or a similar body charged with governance. The auditors may provide assistance to both management and the audit committee by communicating internal control deficiencies and material weaknesses (and an explanation of their potential effects) that they have identified during the audit process, often along with recommendations for corrective action. This is a service in addition to issuance of the audit report. In fulfilling this responsibility, the auditors must understand the concepts of a deficiency in internal control, a significant deficiency, and a material weakness. Auditing standards require communication of the latter two.

A **deficiency in internal control** over financial reporting exists when the design or operation of a control does not allow management or employees, in the normal course of performing their assigned functions, to prevent or detect material misstatements on a timely basis. A **significant deficiency** is a deficiency in internal control over financial reporting (or combination of deficiencies) that is less severe than a material weakness, yet important enough to merit attention by those responsible for oversight of the company's financial reporting.

A **material weakness** is a deficiency in internal control over financial reporting (or a combination of deficiencies) such that there is a reasonable possibility that a material misstatement of the company's financial statements will not be prevented or detected on a timely basis. Figures 7.9 and 7.10 illustrate the relationships among control deficiencies, significant deficiencies, and material weaknesses.

As indicated previously, the auditors are required to communicate both significant deficiencies and material weaknesses to management and those charged with governance. This communication must be in writing. Figure 7.11 presents an example of a letter to an audit committee. Notice that the last paragraph of the letter limits its use to the audit committee, management, and others in the organization.

Because timely communication is particularly important to management, the auditors ordinarily report significant deficiencies and material weaknesses as they are discovered during the course of the audit. The exact timing is influenced by the urgency of needed

**FIGURE 7.9**

**Comparison of Control Deficiencies in Internal Control**

| Deficiency | Severity | Required Communication to Management and Those Charged with Governance? |
|---|---|---|
| Less than Significant Deficiency | Not directly considered | No |
| Significant Deficiency | Less severe than a material weakness | Yes |
| Material Weakness | Reasonable possibility of a material misstatement | Yes |

## FIGURE 7.10
**Relationships among Control Deficiencies**

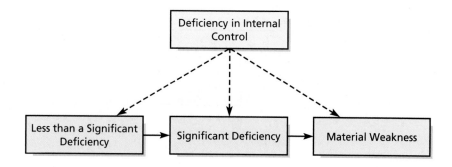

corrective follow-up action, but such communication should be no later than 60 days following the report release date.

Auditors also may agree with management and the board of directors to communicate internal control deficiencies that are not significant deficiencies, as well as other deficiencies (e.g., matters dealing with operational efficiencies). These matters are typically communicated to management in a **management letter**. This letter serves as a valuable reference document for management and also may serve to minimize the auditors' legal liability in the event of a defalcation or other loss resulting from a weakness in internal control. Many auditing firms place great emphasis upon providing clients with a thorough and carefully considered management letter. These firms recognize that such a report can be a valuable and constructive contribution to the efficiency and effectiveness of the client's operations. The quality of the auditors' recommendations reflects their professional expertise and creative ability and the thoroughness of their investigation.

# Internal Control Reporting by Public Companies and Their Auditors

**LO8**

Describe the nature of the audits performed under Section 404(b) of the Sarbanes-Oxley Act of 2002.

The Sarbanes-Oxley Act of 2002 requires public (issuer) companies to provide reports on internal control by both management and the auditors. The requirements for the report by the auditors go well beyond those of the reports to management and those charged with governance described in the preceding section; it must be based on an audit of internal control. In Chapter 18, we present detailed information on audits of internal control, but in this section we provide a brief overview of the audit and reporting requirements of the Sarbanes-Oxley Act.

Section 404 of the Sarbanes-Oxley Act is composed of two subsections. Section 404(a) requires each annual report (e.g., Form 10-K) filed with the Securities and Exchange Commission to include a report in which management (1) acknowledges its responsibility for establishing and maintaining adequate internal control over financial reporting (hereafter, internal control), and (2) provides an assessment of internal control effectiveness *as of the end of the most recent fiscal year* (the "**as of date**"). To have an adequate basis to issue this report, management must:

- Accept responsibility for the effectiveness of internal control.
- Evaluate the effectiveness of internal control using suitable control criteria.
- Support the evaluation with sufficient evidence.

Section 404(b) of the act requires the company's auditors to attest to, and report on, internal control over financial reporting. As implemented, section 404(b) applies to public companies with a market capitalization of $75,000,000 or more. Public Company Accounting Oversight Board (PCAOB) standards provide guidance to the auditors for meeting Section 404(b)'s requirements. PCAOB standards (1) describe an **integrated audit** that addresses both the financial statements and internal control and (2) provide specific requirements for the audit of internal control.

FIGURE 7.11    **Report to Audit Committee**

---

*Wilson & Quinn*
Certified Public Accountants
1134 California Street
San Diego, California 92110

March 12, 20X2

Audit Committee of the Board of Directors
Fleet Feet Shoe Stores, Inc.
2567 University Blvd.
San Diego, California 92105

Committee members:
In planning and performing our audit of the financial statements of Fleet Feet Shoe Stores, Inc., for the year ended December 31, 20X1, we considered its internal control over financial reporting in order to determine our auditing procedures for the purpose of expressing our opinion on the financial statements and not to provide assurance on internal control. Our consideration of internal control would not necessarily disclose all deficiencies in internal control that might be significant deficiencies or material weaknesses. However, as discussed below, we noted certain deficiencies involving internal control that we consider to be significant deficiencies and material weaknesses under auditing standards established by the American Institute of Certified Public Accountants. A *significant deficiency* is a deficiency in internal control over financial reporting (or combination of deficiencies) that is less severe than a material weakness, yet important enough to merit attention by those responsible for oversight of the company's financial reporting.

A *material weakness* is a deficiency in internal control over financial reporting (or a combination of deficiencies) such that there is a reasonable possibility that a material misstatement of the company's financial statements will not be prevented or detected on a timely basis. We believe that the following deficiency constitutes a material weakness:

Capitalization of certain repairs and maintenance expense items.  A material amount of certain of these expense items was improperly recorded into the property and plant asset accounts. The company's controls related both to the original recording and to the review of that recording were ineffective in preventing or detecting the misstatements. We recommend that a competent accounting clerk be given the responsibility for reviewing items capitalized in property and plant asset accounts.

We consider the following deficiency to be a significant deficiency in internal control:

Failure to prepare certain receiving reports.  Personnel at individual stores failed to prepare receiving reports for shipments of goods directly from wholesalers. This significant deficiency increases the chance that the company will pay for merchandise that has not been received. We recommend that a policy be established requiring the preparation of receiving reports for all shipments received from suppliers.

This report is intended solely for the information and use of the audit committee (board of directors, board of trustees, or owners in owner-managed enterprises), management, and others within the organization (and specified regulatory agency) and is not intended to be and should not be used by anyone other than these specified parties.

Sincerely,

*James Wilson*

Wilson & Quinn, CPAs

Recall from Chapter 1 that essential to performing an attest engagement is the existence of **suitable criteria** that serve as the standards or benchmarks to measure and present the subject matter. The Committee of Sponsoring Organizations (COSO) internal control framework provides "suitable control criteria" for management's internal control report and the auditors' audit of internal control. Therefore, for an integrated audit, there are two sets of suitable criteria involved: COSO for the internal control audit and the applicable financial reporting framework for the financial statement audit.

As you would expect, the requirements to perform an integrated audit result in an increase in audit procedures directed toward testing the effectiveness of internal control. As we have discussed throughout this chapter, evidence to support the auditors' opinion on financial statements comes from a combination of tests of controls and substantive procedures. For financial statement audits, the auditors have a choice about the mix of the evidence obtained from testing controls versus the evidence obtained from substantive procedures. Auditors may decide not to test particular controls in financial statement audits, frequently because it is more efficient to perform substantive procedures.

When the auditors perform an integrated audit, the option of not testing controls for a significant account is not available, because controls over all significant accounts must be tested to provide a basis for the opinion on internal control. The auditors must have sufficient evidence to provide an opinion on internal control at the as of date, ordinarily the last day of the reporting period.

## Overall Approach for an Audit of Internal Control

To integrate the internal control audit and the financial statement audit, most auditors plan the internal control audit and then determine the additional testing that is necessary to support an opinion on the financial statements. The internal control audit may be viewed as having the following five stages:

1. Plan the engagement.
2. Use a top-down approach to identify controls to test.
3. Test and evaluate design effectiveness of internal control.
4. Test and evaluate operating effectiveness of internal control.
5. Form an opinion on the effectiveness of internal control over financial reporting.

### 1. Plan the Engagement

In an integrated audit, the planning of the internal control audit is coordinated with the planning of the financial statement audit. For both audits, the auditors consider matters related to the client's industry, business, and regulatory environment and its internal control, as discussed in Chapter 6. The auditors' procedures to obtain the required knowledge of the client's internal control at the planning stage of the engagement will differ significantly depending upon the nature of the client and the auditors' previous experience with that client. For example, when the auditors have previously performed audits for the client, the auditors begin the integrated audit with more information than in a circumstance in which the client is new.

The auditors must determine whether management has addressed controls over all relevant assertions related to all significant accounts and disclosures in the financial statements. Those controls are of various types and include controls over:

- Initiating, authorizing, recording, processing, and reporting significant accounts and disclosures.
- Selecting and applying appropriate accounting principles.
- Fraud, through antifraud programs.
- Various types of significant transactions, including overall company-level controls and information technology general controls, and transactions related to the period end financial reporting process (e.g., consolidating adjustments, reclassifications, and final adjustments).

### 2. Use a Top-Down Approach to Identify Controls to Test

As described previously, in an audit of financial statements, the auditors must obtain an understanding of the design of controls in each of the major internal control components—control environment, risk assessment, control activities, information and communication, and monitoring. In an integrated audit, the auditors have this information available through performance of the financial statement audit. The approach used in the internal control audit is "top-down" in the sense that it starts at the top—the financial statements and entity-level controls—and links the financial statement elements and entity-level controls to significant accounts, relevant assertions, and to the major classes of transactions. The goal is to focus on testing those controls that are most important to the auditor's conclusion on internal control, while avoiding those that are less important. The procedures used to obtain an understanding of the relevant controls are the same procedures used to gain this understanding in a financial statement audit. As is the case with financial statement audits, documentation of the understanding is accomplished with flowcharts, checklists, questionnaires, and memos.

### 3. Test and Evaluate Design Effectiveness

Auditors next evaluate the design of controls—if the design is not effective, then it makes no sense to test whether the controls operate effectively. To test design effectiveness, the auditors identify the company's control objectives and risks in each financial reporting area and then identify relevant controls that satisfy each control objective. Once they have identified the relevant controls, the auditors evaluate the likelihood of control failure, the magnitude of any related misstatement due to such failure, and the degree to which other compensating controls achieve the same control objectives. Then they assess whether the controls, if operating properly, can effectively prevent or detect misstatements that could be material. Procedures performed by the auditors to evaluate design effectiveness include inquiry, observation, additional walk-throughs, inspection of relevant documentation, and specific evaluation of whether the controls are likely to prevent or detect misstatements.

### 4. Test and Evaluate Operating Effectiveness

Tests of the operating effectiveness of controls are used to determine whether the controls function as designed and whether the individuals performing the controls possess the necessary authority and qualifications. An integrated audit requires the auditors to test controls for all relevant assertions about major accounts. These tests must be designed to provide a high level of assurance that these controls are operating effectively. Generally, the more frequently a control operates, the more often it should be tested, and controls that are more critical should be tested more extensively.

### 5. Form an Opinion on the Effectiveness of Internal Control

The auditors' report on internal control under PCAOB standards expresses an opinion on whether the company maintained, in all material respects, effective internal control over financial reporting.

An unqualified audit opinion may be issued when no material weaknesses in internal control have been identified as existing at year-end and when there have been no restrictions on the scope of the auditors' work. If one or more material weaknesses in internal control are found, an adverse opinion should be issued. Scope limitations may result in either a qualified opinion or a disclaimer of opinion, depending on the significance of the limitation.

## Internal Control in the Small Company

The preceding discussion of internal control and its consideration by the independent auditors has been presented in terms of large corporations. In the large concern, excellent internal control may be achieved by extensive segregation of duties so that no one person handles a transaction completely from beginning to end. In the very small concern, with only one or two office employees, there is little or no opportunity for division of duties and responsibilities. Consequently, internal control tends to be weak, if not completely absent, unless the owner/manager recognizes its importance and participates in key activities.

Because of the absence of strong internal control in small concerns, the independent auditors must rely much more on substantive procedures of account balances and transactions than is required in larger organizations. Although it is well to recognize that internal control can seldom be strong in a small business, this limitation is no justification for ignoring available forms of control. Auditors can make a valuable contribution to small client companies by encouraging the installation of such controls as are practicable in the circumstances. The following specific practices are almost always capable of use in even the smallest business:

1. Record all cash receipts immediately.
   a. For over-the-counter collections, use cash registers easily visible to customers. Record register readings daily.
   b. Prepare a list of all mail remittances immediately upon opening the mail and retain this list for subsequent comparison with bank deposit tickets and entries in the cash receipts journal.
2. Deposit all cash receipts intact daily.
3. Make all payments by serially numbered checks, with the exception of small disbursements from petty cash.
4. Reconcile bank accounts monthly and retain copies of the reconciliations in the files.
5. Use serially numbered sales invoices, purchase orders, and receiving reports.
6. Issue checks to vendors only in payment of approved invoices that have been matched with purchase orders and receiving reports.
7. Balance subsidiary ledger with control accounts at regular intervals and prepare and mail customers' statements monthly.
8. Prepare comparative financial statements monthly in sufficient detail to disclose significant variations in any category of revenue or expense.

Adherence to these basic control practices significantly reduces the risk of material error or fraud going undetected. If the size of the business permits a segregation of the duties of cash handling and record keeping, a fair degree of control can be achieved. If it is necessary that one employee serve as both accounting clerk and cashier, then active participation by the owner in certain key functions is necessary to prevent or detect the concealment of fraud or errors. In a few minutes each day, the owner, even though not trained in accounting, can create a significant amount of internal control by personally (1) reading daily cash register totals, (2) reconciling the bank account monthly, (3) signing all checks and canceling the supporting documents, (4) approving all general journal entries, and (5) critically reviewing comparative monthly statements of revenue and expense.

## Chapter Summary

This chapter explained the meaning and significance of internal control, the major components of the client's internal control, and the manner in which auditors consider internal control. To summarize:

1. Internal control is a process, effected by the entity's board of directors, management, and other personnel, designed to provide reasonable assurance regarding the achievement of objectives in the categories of (a) effectiveness and efficiency of operations, (b) reliability of financial reporting, and (c) compliance with applicable laws and regulations.
2. The five components of internal control include the control environment, risk assessment, control activities, the accounting information and communication system, and monitoring. The portion of internal control relevant to auditors is that which pertains to the entity's ability to prepare reliable financial statements.

3. Auditor responsibility with respect to internal control includes obtaining an understanding of internal control, assessing the risks of misstatement, and designing further audit procedures (tests of controls). The understanding of internal control should include knowledge about the design of relevant controls and whether they have been implemented by the client.

4. In assessing the risks of material misstatement (the "risk assessment"), the auditors consider (*a*) what can go wrong at the relevant assertion level, (*b*) whether the risks are of a magnitude that could result in a material misstatement, and (*c*) the likelihood that the risk could result in a material misstatement. Risks ordinarily exist at the overall financial statement level as well as at the account balance, class of transaction, and disclosure levels.

5. Auditors perform tests of controls when the risk assessment includes an expectation of the operating effectiveness of controls. The risk assessment includes such an expectation when (1) substantive procedures alone do not provide sufficient appropriate audit evidence, or (2) auditors wish to reduce the scope of substantive procedures through performance of tests of controls. Auditors will ordinarily wish to reduce the scope of substantive procedures and perform tests of controls in circumstances in which they believe such an approach is cost justified. However, in all circumstances for relevant assertions some substantive procedures must be performed.

6. Tests of controls address (*a*) how controls were applied, (*b*) the consistency with which controls were applied, and (*c*) by whom or by what means the controls were applied. Tests of controls include inquiries of appropriate client personnel, inspection of documents and reports, observation of the application of controls, and reperformance of controls.

7. Auditors are required to communicate all significant deficiencies and material weaknesses to management and those charged with governance.

8. Large public companies are required to have an integrated audit in accordance with the Sarbanes-Oxley Act of 2002 and Public Company Accounting Oversight Board *Standard No. 5*. Integrated audits consist of both an audit of internal control and an audit of the financial statements. The audit report on internal control includes both an opinion on management's assessment of internal control and the auditors' own assessment of internal control.

## Key Terms Introduced or Emphasized in Chapter 7

**As of date (275)**    A concept applied to internal control reporting by the Sarbanes-Oxley Act of 2002 and PCAOB *Standard No. 5*. The internal control reports of both management and the auditors are as of the final day of the reporting period—the "as of date."

**Assessed level of control risk (268)**    The level of control risk used by the auditors in determining the acceptable detection risk for a financial statement assertion and, accordingly, in deciding on the nature, timing, and extent of substantive procedures.

**Audit decision aid (273)**    A standard checklist, form, or computer program that assists auditors in making audit decisions by ensuring that they consider all relevant information or that aids them in weighting and combining the information to make a decision.

**Compensating control (248)**    A control that reduces the risk that an existing or potential control weakness will result in a failure to meet a control objective (e.g., avoiding misstatements). Compensating controls are ordinarily controls performed to detect, rather than prevent, the original misstatement from occurring.

**Complementary controls (248)**    Controls that function together to achieve the same control objective.

**Control risk (258)**    The possibility that a material misstatement due to error or fraud in a financial statement assertion will not be prevented or detected by the client's internal control.

**Corrective control (248)**    A control established to remedy control problems (e.g., misstatements) that are discovered through detective controls.

**Deficiency in internal control (274)**    A situation in which the design or operation of a control does not allow management or employees, in the normal course of performing their functions, to prevent or detect misstatements on a timely basis. A *deficiency in design* exists when either a control necessary to meet a control objective is missing or the existing control is not designed to operate effectively. A *deficiency in operation* exists when a properly designed control does not operate as designed, or when the person performing the control does not possess the necessary authority or qualifications to perform the control effectively.

**Detective controls (248)** Controls designed to discover control problems soon after they occur.

**Fidelity bonds (251)** A form of insurance in which a bonding company agrees to reimburse an employer for losses attributable to theft or embezzlement by bonded employees.

**Foreign Corrupt Practices Act (247)** Federal legislation prohibiting payments to foreign officials for the purpose of securing business. The act also requires all companies under SEC jurisdiction to maintain a system of internal control providing reasonable assurance that transactions are executed only with the knowledge and authorization of management.

**Further audit procedures (258)** Substantive procedures for all relevant assertions and tests of controls when the auditors' risk assessment includes an expectation that controls are operating effectively. The auditors perform risk assessment procedures to obtain an understanding of the client and its environment, including internal control. They then conduct a risk assessment and determine the appropriate further audit procedures.

**Incompatible duties (254)** Assigned duties that place an individual in a position to both perpetrate and conceal errors or fraud in the normal course of job performance.

**Inherent risk (258)** The risk of material misstatement of a financial statement assertion, assuming there are no related controls.

**Integrated audit (275)** An audit where auditors, in addition to an opinion on the financial statements, express an opinion on the effectiveness of a company's internal control over financial reporting, in accordance with PCAOB *Auditing Standard No. 5*. Public companies with a market capitalization of $75,000,000 or more are required to undergo integrated audits.

**Internal auditors (273)** Corporation employees who design and execute audit programs to test the effectiveness and efficiency of all aspects of internal control. The primary objective of internal auditors is to evaluate and improve the effectiveness and efficiency of the various operating units of an organization rather than to express an opinion as to the fairness of financial statements.

**Internal control (245)** A process, effected by the entity's board of directors, management, and other personnel, designed to provide reasonable assurance regarding the achievement of objectives in the categories of (1) effectiveness and efficiency of operations, (2) reliability of financial reporting, and (3) compliance with applicable laws and regulations. Prior to 1996, the AICPA's *Professional Standards* referred to an entity's internal control as its internal control structure.

**Internal control questionnaire (262)** One of several methods of describing internal control in audit working papers. Questionnaires are usually designed so that "no" answers prominently identify weaknesses in internal control.

**Management letter (275)** A report to management containing the auditors' recommendations for correcting any deficiencies disclosed by the auditors' consideration of internal control. In addition to providing management with useful information, a management letter may also help limit the auditors' liability in the event a control weakness subsequently results in a loss by the client.

**Material weakness (274)** A deficiency in internal control over financial reporting (or a combination of deficiencies) such that there is a reasonable possibility that a material misstatement of the company's financial statements will not be prevented or detected on a timely basis.

**Organizational structure (249)** The division of authority, responsibility, and duties among members of an organization.

**Planned assessed level of control risk (268)** The level of control risk the auditors assume in designing further audit procedures, which include an appropriate combination of tests of controls and substantive procedures.

**Preventive controls (248)** Controls that deter control problems before they occur.

**Redundant controls (248)** Duplicate controls that achieve a control objective.

**Relevant assertions (268)** Assertions that have a meaningful bearing on whether an account balance, class of transaction, or disclosure is fairly stated. For example, valuation may not be relevant to the cash account unless currency translation is involved; however, existence and completeness are always relevant.

**Risk assessment procedures (258)** Audit procedures performed to obtain an understanding of the client and its environment, including its internal control. Some of the information obtained by performing these procedures may be used by the auditor as audit evidence to support assessments of the risks of material misstatement. Risk assessment procedures include (*a*) inquiries of management and others within the entity, (*b*) analytical procedures, and (*c*) observation and other procedures, including inquiries of others outside the entity.

**Significant deficiency (274)**   A deficiency in internal control over financial reporting (or combination of deficiencies) that is less severe than a material weakness, yet important enough to merit attention by those responsible for oversight of the company's financial reporting.

**Substantive procedures (tests) (258)**   Procedures performed by the auditor to detect material misstatements in account balances, classes of transactions, and disclosures.

**Suitable criteria (277)**   Criteria are the standards or benchmarks used to measure and present the subject matter and against which the CPA evaluates the subject matter. Suitable criteria are established or developed by groups composed of experts that follow due process procedures, including exposure of the proposed criteria for public comment. Suitable criteria must have each of the following attributes: objectivity, measurability, completeness, and relevance.

**Systems flowchart (263)**   A symbolic representation of a system or series of procedures with each procedure shown in sequence. Systems flowcharts are a widely used method of describing internal control in audit working papers.

**Tests of controls (258)**   Procedures performed by the auditor to test the operating effectiveness of controls in preventing or detecting material misstatements at the relevant assertion level. These tests are performed when the auditor's risk assessment includes an expectation of the operating effectiveness of controls, including circumstances in which planned substantive procedures alone do not provide sufficient appropriate audit evidence.

**Transaction cycle (260)**   The sequence of procedures applied by the client in processing a particular type of recurring transaction. The auditors' working paper description of internal control often is organized around the client's major transaction cycles.

**Walk-through (264)**   A procedure in which an auditor follows a transaction from origination through the company's processes, including information systems, until it is reflected in the company's financial records, using the same documents and information technology that company personnel use. Walk-through procedures usually include a combination of inquiry, observation, inspection of relevant documentation, and reperformance of controls.

**Written narrative of internal control (263)**   A written summary of internal control for inclusion in audit working papers. Written narratives are more flexible than questionnaires, but by themselves are practical only for describing relatively small, simple systems.

## Review Questions

7–1.   What is internal control?

7–2.   Identify the five components of an organization's internal control.

7–3.   List the factors that make up an organization's *control environment.*

7–4.   How does separation of the record keeping function from custody of assets contribute to internal control?

7–5.   Name three factors you consider of greatest importance in protecting a business against losses through embezzlement.

7–6.   Describe what is meant by the *risk assessment* component of internal control and how it contributes to internal control.

7–7.   Describe the two types of *monitoring* and provide an example of each.

7–8.   Identify the four types of *control activities* and describe how each type contributes to effective internal control.

7–9.   One basic concept of internal control is that no one employee should handle all aspects of a transaction. Assuming that a general category of transactions has been authorized by top management, how many employees (or departments) should participate in each transaction, as a minimum, to achieve strong internal control? Explain in general terms the function of each of these employees.

7–10.   Compare the objectives of the internal auditors with those of the independent auditors.

7–11.   What consideration, if any, may independent auditors give to the work of a client's internal audit staff?

7–12.   What are the purposes of the consideration of internal control required by generally accepted auditing standards?

7–13.  A prospective client informs you that all officers and employees of the company are bonded, and he requests that under these circumstances you forgo a consideration of internal control in order to reduce the cost of an audit. Construct a logical reply to this request.

7–14.  Suggest a number of sources from which you might obtain the information needed to prepare a description of internal control in the audit working papers.

7–15.  "All experienced auditors would design exactly the same audit program for a particular audit engagement." Do you agree? Explain.

7–16.  Under what circumstances are tests of controls *efficient* audit procedures?

7–17.  How is the auditors' understanding of the client's internal control documented in the audit working papers?

7–18.  What is a management letter? What is the letter's significance?

7–19.  List and describe the eight components of the COSO Enterprise Risk Management Framework.

7–20.  You have discussed with the president of Vista Corporation several material weaknesses in internal control that have come to your attention during your audit. At the conclusion of this discussion, the president states that he will personally take steps to remedy these problems and that there is no reason for you to bring these matters to the attention of the board of directors. He explains that he believes the board should deal with major policy decisions and not be burdened with day-to-day management problems. How would you respond to this suggestion? Explain fully.

7–21.  Distinguish between the two subsections of Section 404 of the Sarbanes-Oxley Act of 2002.

7–22.  List the five stages of the auditors' overall approach in an audit of internal control performed in accordance with PCAOB requirements.

**Questions Requiring Analysis**

**LO 2**   7–23.  Management is responsible for designing and maintaining its organization's internal control. In designing internal control, management must consider controls related to each of the five major internal control components: the control environment, risk assessment, the accounting information system, control activities, and monitoring.

*Required:*

a.  Management is considering controls for the following three *control environment* factors. For each, describe how the factor contributes to effective internal control.

(1)  Integrity and ethical values.

(2)  Commitment to competence.

(3)  Board of directors or audit committee.

b.  Explain how *risk assessment* contributes to effective internal control, and identify four factors that result in increased financial reporting risk.

c.  Identify the five major objectives of an *accounting information system*.

d.  Describe the purpose of the following two types of *control activities*.

(1)  Performance reviews.

(2)  Information processing.

e.  Explain the two types of *monitoring* and provide an example of each.

**LO 1, 2**   7–24.  The definition of internal control as contained in COSO's *Internal Control–Integrated Framework* and the professional standards is quite broad and comprehensive.

*Required:*

a.  Define *internal control* and its purpose.

b.  Explain the major concepts that are included in the definition of internal control.

c.  List and describe the five components of internal control.

d.  Identify the major limitations of internal control.

**LO 3**   7–25.  Auditors may restrict substantive procedures based on the results of tests of controls.

*Required:*

a.  Discuss and contrast the concepts of the planned assessment of control risk and the revised assessment of the risk after tests of controls have been performed.

b.  Using internal control for the existence assertion for accounts receivable, provide an example that distinguishes among the concepts discussed in part (*a*) above.

**LO 3**   7–26.  The auditors' consideration of internal control begins with obtaining an understanding of the client's internal control.

*Required:*

a.  Describe the remaining stages of the auditors' consideration.

b.  Provide examples of audit procedures that are performed at each stage (including the stage of obtaining an understanding).

**LO 3, 5**  7–27. Henry Bailey, CPA, is planning the audit of The Neighborhood Store, a local grocery cooperative. Because The Neighborhood Store is a small business operated entirely by part-time volunteer personnel, internal control is weak. Bailey has decided that he will assess control risk at the highest level for all assertions and not restrict audit procedures in any area. Under these circumstances, may Bailey omit the consideration of internal control in this engagement? Explain.

**LO 3, 4, 5**  7–28. Adherence to generally accepted auditing standards requires, among other things, a proper understanding of the existing internal control. The most common approaches to documenting the understanding of internal control include the use of a questionnaire, preparation of a written narrative, preparation of a flowchart, or a combination of these methods.

*Required:*

a. Discuss the advantages to CPAs of documenting internal control by using:

   (1) An internal control questionnaire.

   (2) A written narrative.

   (3) A flowchart.

b. If they are satisfied that no material weaknesses in internal control exist after completing their description of internal control, is it necessary for the CPAs to conduct tests of controls? Explain.

**LO 1**  7–29. Management is responsible for establishing effective internal control for its organization, including measures to prevent, deter, and detect fraud. Appendix 7A on pages 293–295 describes antifraud programs and measures.

*Required:*

a. What are the three major categories of antifraud measures and the measures that should be established under each category?

b. Under the measure of "create a positive workplace environment" provide:

   (1) Two examples of antifraud controls.

   (2) Two examples of factors that detract from a positive workplace environment.

(AICPA, adapted)

**LO 3, 4**  7–30. Assume that you are auditing the financial statements of Wexler, Inc. As you are reviewing the work on internal control, you become concerned about the adequacy of documentation. Describe the required documentation of internal control matters.

**LO 1**  7–31. During your first audit of a medium-size manufacturing company, the owner, John Bell, explains that in order to establish clear-cut lines of responsibility for various aspects of the business, he has made one employee responsible for the purchasing, receiving, and storing of merchandise. A second employee has full responsibility for maintenance of accounts receivable records and collections from customers. A third employee is responsible for personnel records, timekeeping, preparation of payrolls, and distribution of payroll checks. Bell asks your opinion concerning this plan of organization. Explain fully the reasons supporting your opinion.

**LO 4**  7–32. Internal auditing is a staff function found in virtually every large corporation. The internal audit function is also performed in many smaller companies as a part-time activity of individuals who may or may not be called "internal auditors." The differences between the audits by independent auditors and the work of internal auditors are more basic than is generally recognized.

*Required:*

a. Briefly discuss the auditing work performed by the independent public accountant and the internal auditor with regard to:

   (1) Auditing objectives.

   (2) General nature of auditing work.

b. In conducting their audit, the independent auditors may consider the work of the internal auditors. Discuss briefly the reason for this consideration.

**LO 3, 4**  7–33. Randall, Inc., is a private company that manufactures heavy machinery. The company has an active audit committee and board of directors. The audit committee consists of two outside directors and Howard Kress, the company chief financial officer. The audit committee meets quarterly to provide oversight of financial reporting, including reviewing new accounting policies and unusual transactions. Howard Kress personally reviews and approves any related party transactions. Internal audits of operating units are performed by the internal auditor, who reports directly to Laura Howe, the chief operating officer.

The company has a written code of conduct, and employees agree to adhere to the code when they are hired. The company also has a hotline for confidential reporting of unethical behavior that is staffed by the corporate controller. The audit committee reviews summaries of all incidents and investigations performed.

*Required:* Identify the weaknesses in Randall's system of corporate governance and provide suggestions for improvement in the system. Organize your answer as follows:

| Weakness | Recommended Improvement |
| --- | --- |
| | |

## Objective Questions

**All applicable questions are available with McGraw-Hill's *Connect*<sup>TM</sup> *Accounting*.** connect ACCOUNTING

7–34. **Multiple Choice Questions**

Select the best answer for each of the following questions. Explain the reason for your selection.

**LO 1**

*a.* Which of the following would be *least likely* to be considered an objective of internal control?

(1) Checking the accuracy and reliability of accounting data.

(2) Detecting management fraud.

(3) Encouraging adherence to managerial policies.

(4) Safeguarding assets.

**LO 2**

*b.* An entity's ongoing monitoring activities often include:

(1) Periodic audits by internal auditors.

(2) The audit of the annual financial statements.

(3) Approval of cash disbursements.

(4) Management review of weekly performance reports.

**LO 3**

*c.* A primary objective of procedures performed to obtain an understanding of internal control is to provide the auditors with:

(1) Knowledge necessary to determine the nature, timing, and extent of further audit procedures.

(2) Audit evidence to use in reducing detection risk.

(3) A basis for modifying tests of controls.

(4) An evaluation of the consistency of application of management policies.

**LO 3**

*d.* An auditor may compensate for a weakness in internal control by increasing the extent of:

(1) Tests of controls.

(2) Detection risk.

(3) Substantive tests of details.

(4) Inherent risk.

**LO 2**

*e.* Controls over financial reporting are often classified as preventative, detective, or corrective. Which of the following is an example of a detective control?

(1) Segregation of duties over cash disbursements.

(2) Requiring approval of purchase transactions.

(3) Preparing bank reconciliations.

(4) Maintaining backup copies of key transactions.

**LO 4**

*f.* Which of the following symbols indicate that a file has been consulted?

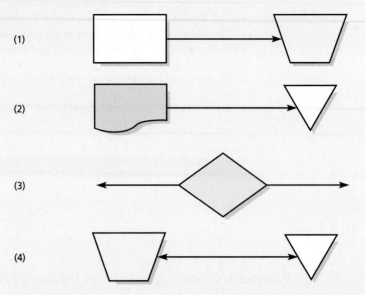

(1)

(2)

(3)

(4)

**LO 4, 6**

*g.* When a CPA decides that the work performed by internal auditors may have an effect on the nature, timing, and extent of the CPA's procedures, the CPA should consider the competence and objectivity of the internal auditors. Relative to objectivity, the CPA should:

(1) Consider the organizational level to which the internal auditors report the results of their work.

(2) Review the internal auditors' work.

(3) Consider the qualifications of the internal audit staff.

(4) Review the training program in effect for the internal audit staff.

**LO 2**

*h.* Effective internal control in a small company that has an insufficient number of employees to permit proper separation of responsibilities can be improved by:

(1) Employment of temporary personnel to aid in the separation of duties.

(2) Direct participation by the owner in key record keeping and control activities of the business.

(3) Engaging a CPA to perform monthly write-up work.

(4) Delegation of full, clear-cut responsibility for a separate major transaction cycle to each employee.

**LO 2**

*i.* Which of the following is not an advantage of establishing an enterprise risk management system within an organization?

(1) Reduces operational surprises.

(2) Provides integrated responses to multiple risks.

(3) Eliminates all risks.

(4) Identifies opportunities.

**LO 2**

*j.* Management of Warren Company has decided to respond to a particular risk by hedging the risk with futures contracts. This is an example of:

(1) Avoidance.

(2) Acceptance.

(3) Reduction.

(4) Sharing.

**LO 8**

*k.* To have an adequate basis to issue a management report on internal control under Section 404(a) of the Sarbanes-Oxley Act, management must do all of the following, *except:*

(1) Establish internal control with no material weakness.

(2) Accept responsibility for the effectiveness of internal control.

(3) Evaluate the effectiveness of internal control using suitable control criteria.

(4) Support the evaluation with sufficient evidence.

**LO 8**     *l.* When the auditors are performing a first-time internal control audit in accordance with the Sarbanes-Oxley Act and PCAOB standards, they must:

(1) Modify their report for any significant deficiencies identified.

(2) Use a "bottom-up" approach to identify controls to test.

(3) Test controls for all significant accounts.

(4) Perform a separate assessment of controls over operations.

**LO 1**     7–35. You are performing an audit of Systex Corporation and evaluating various controls. Classify the following controls as being primarily preventive (P), detective (D), or corrective (C). Explain your answers.

*a.* Annual physical inventory.

*b.* Monthly reconciliation of bank accounts.

*c.* Segregation of duties over purchasing.

*d.* Supervisory approval of time cards.

*e.* Dual signatures for checks.

*f.* Adjustment of perpetual inventory records to physical counts.

*g.* Management review of budget/actual information.

*h.* Internal audits of payroll.

**LO 2**     7–36. Listed below are controls that have been developed by the management of Cirus Manufacturing Co.

1. Management surveys customers about their satisfaction with the company's service.

2. The human resources department investigates the educational background of prospective employees.

3. Invoices are reviewed for accuracy before they are mailed to customers.

4. Management periodically evaluates the threats to preparing reliable financial statements.

5. The internal auditors periodically evaluate the controls in the various departments of the company.

6. Management has developed and distributed a *code of conduct*.

7. Budgets and forecasts are used by the production departments to control expenses.

8. The accounting department uses a manual of accounting policies and procedures.

9. Entry into the warehouse is strictly controlled by security personnel.

10. Management has prepared and distributed an organizational chart.

*Required:*     For each of the controls, identify the internal control component and, if applicable, the subcomponent or factor to which it relates.

**LO 1, 2, 3, 4, 6**     7–37. Auditors must have an understanding of the various terms that relate to their consideration of internal control of an organization.

*Required:*     For each term presented below, select the category that most clearly defines or includes the term. The categories may be selected once, more than once, or not at all.

| Term | Category |
|------|----------|
| 1. Accounting information system | *a.* Generally of no concern to auditors |
| 2. Control environment | *b.* Control condition |
| 3. Flowchart | *c.* Component of internal control |
| 4. Controls over operating effectiveness | *d.* Documentation |
| 5. Less severe than a material weakness | *e.* Implemented |
| 6. Monitoring | *f.* Material weakness |
| 7. Questionnaire | *g.* Test of control |
| 8. Walk-through | *h.* Significant deficiency |
| 9. Allows a reasonable possibility of a material misstatement | *i.* Relationship of costs and benefits |
| 10. Reasonable assurance | |

**LO 2, 6**     7–38. For each term in the first column, find the closest definition (or portion of a definition) in the second column. Each definition may be used only once or not at all.

| Term | Definition (or Portion) |
|------|------------------------|
| a. Compensating control | 1. A control established to remedy misstatements that are discovered |
| b. Complementary control | 2. A control that functions together with another control to achieve the same control objective |
| c. Corrective control | 3. A control that reduces the risk that an existing or potential control weakness will result in a failure to meet a control objective |
| d. Deficiency in internal control | |
| e. Material weakness in internal control | 4. A control that reduces the risk of misstatement by remediating control deficiencies through automated means |
| f. Walk-through | 5. A deficiency in internal control such that there is a reasonable possibility that a material misstatement will not be prevented or detected on a timely basis |
| g. Transaction cycle | 6. A deficiency in internal control that is less severe than a material weakness, but more severe than a significant deficiency |
| | 7. A situation in which a control does not allow management or employees, in the normal course of performing their functions, to prevent or detect misstatements on a timely basis |
| | 8. Duplicate controls that achieve a control objective |
| | 9. Procedures cycled periodically through the auditors' internal control deviation analysis |
| | 10. The sequence of procedures applied by the client in processing a particular type of recurring transaction |
| | 11. A procedure in which an auditor follows a transaction from origination through the company's processes, including information systems, until it is reflected in the company's financial records |

**LO 3**    7–39.    Answer the following questions relating to tests of controls and control risk.

    *a.* Tests of controls do not address:

        (1) How controls were applied.

        (2) How controls were originated.

        (3) The consistency with which controls were applied.

        (4) By what means the controls were applied.

    *b.* Which of the following is least likely to be a test of controls?

        (1) Inquiries of client personnel.

        (2) Inspection of documents.

        (3) Observation of confirmations.

        (4) Reperformance of controls.

    *c.* Tests of controls ordinarily are designed to provide evidence of:

        (1) Balance correctness.

        (2) Control implementation.

        (3) Disclosure adequacy.

        (4) Operating effectiveness.

    *d.* The preliminary assessments of control risk are often referred to as:

        (1) The assessed level of control risk.

        (2) The planned assessed level of control risk.

        (3) Control risk.

        (4) Internal control objectives risk.

  *e.* At the completion of the audit, the auditors are least likely to know:

   (1) The assessed level of control risk.

   (2) The planned assessed level of control risk.

   (3) Actual control risk.

   (4) The scope of tests of controls.

## Problems

**All applicable problems are available with McGraw-Hill's *Connect*™ *Accounting*.** ▨ connect |ACCOUNTING

**LO 3**   7–40.   Orange Corp., a high-technology company, utilizes the following procedures for recording materials and transferring them to work in process.

  (1) Upon receipt of raw materials by stores, the storekeeper prepares a stock-in report with part number and quantities, files the original by date, and sends a copy to accounting.

  (2) The inventory accounting clerk uses the stock-in report to post the perpetual inventory records using standard costs and files the stock-in report by date.

  (3) Raw materials requisitions, which show part number and quantity, are prepared by the manufacturing clerk and approved by the supervisor of manufacturing. A copy of the requisition is sent to accounting, and the original is filed by job order.

  (4) The inventory accounting clerk reviews the requisitions for completeness, transfers the cost from raw materials to work in process, and files the requisitions by date.

*Required:*   Prepare a flowchart that describes the client's system of recording raw materials and transferring them to work in process.

**LO 1, 3**   7–41.   Island Trading Co., a client of your CPA firm, has requested your advice on the following problem. It has three clerical employees who must perform the following functions:

  (1) Maintain general ledger.

  (2) Maintain accounts payable ledger.

  (3) Maintain accounts receivable ledger.

  (4) Maintain cash disbursements journal and prepare checks for signature.

  (5) Issue credit memos on sales returns and allowances.

  (6) Reconcile the bank account.

  (7) Handle and deposit cash receipts.

*Required:*   Assuming that there is no problem as to the ability of any of the employees, the company requests your advice on assigning the above functions to the three employees in such a manner as to achieve the highest degree of internal control. It may be assumed that these employees will perform no other accounting functions than the ones listed and that any accounting functions not listed will be performed by persons other than these three employees.

  *a.* List four possible unsatisfactory combinations of the above-listed functions.

  *b.* State how you would recommend distributing the above functions among the three employees. Assume that, with the exception of the nominal jobs of the bank reconciliation and the issuance of credits on returns and allowances, all functions require an equal amount of time.

**LO 4**   7–42.   Prospect Corporation, your new audit client, processes its sales and cash receipts in the following manner:

  (1) *Sales.* Salesclerks prepare sales invoices in triplicate. The original and second copy are presented to the cashier, and the third copy is retained by the sales clerk in the sales book. When the sale is for cash, the customer pays the sales clerk, who presents the money to the cashier with the invoice copies.

   A credit sale is approved by the cashier from an approved credit list. After receiving the cash or approving the invoice, the cashier validates the original copy of the sales invoice and gives it to the customer. At the end of each day, the cashier recaps the sales and cash received, files the recap by date, and forwards the cash and the second copy of all sales invoices to the accounts receivable clerk.

   The accounts receivable clerk balances the cash received with cash sales invoices and prepares a daily sales summary. Cash sales are posted by the accounts receivable clerk to the cash receipts journal, and the daily sales summary is filed by date. Cash from cash sales is included in the daily bank deposit (preparation of the bank deposit is described with cash receipts in the following section). The accounts receivable clerk posts credit sales invoices to the accounts receivable ledger and then sends all invoices to the inventory control clerk in the sales department.

The inventory clerk posts to the inventory control cards and files the sales invoices numerically.

(2) *Cash receipts.* The mail is opened each morning by a mail clerk in the sales department. The mail clerk prepares a remittance advice (showing customer and amount paid) for each check and forwards the checks and remittance advices to the sales department supervisor. The supervisor reviews the remittance advices and forwards the checks and advices to the accounting department supervisor.

The accounting department supervisor, who also functions as credit manager in approving new credit and all credit limits, reviews all checks for payments on past-due accounts and then gives the checks and remittance advices to the accounts receivable clerk, who arranges the advices in alphabetical order. The remittance advices are posted directly to the accounts receivable ledger cards. The checks are endorsed by stamp and totaled. The total is posted to the cash receipts journal. The remittance advices are filed chronologically.

After receiving the cash from the previous day's cash sales from the cashier, the accounts receivable clerk prepares the daily deposit slip in triplicate. The original and second copy of the deposit slip accompany the bank deposit, and the third copy is filed by date. The bank deposit is sent directly to National Bank.

*Required:*

a. Prepare a systems flowchart of internal control over sales transactions as described in part (1) above.

b. Prepare a systems flowchart of internal control over cash receipts as described in part (2) above.

**LO 4** 7–43. You have been asked by the board of trustees of a local church to review its accounting procedures. As part of this review you have prepared the following comments relating to the collections made at weekly services and record keeping for members' pledges and contributions:

(1) The church's board of trustees has delegated responsibility for financial management and the financial records to the finance committee. This group prepares the annual forecast and approves major disbursements, but is not involved in collections or record keeping. No internal or independent audit has been considered necessary in recent years because the same trusted employee has kept church records and served as financial secretary for 15 years.

(2) The offering at the weekly service is taken by a team of ushers. The head usher counts the offering in the church office following each service. He then places the offering and a notation of the amount counted in the church safe. The next morning the financial secretary opens the safe and recounts the offering. He withholds about $100 to meet cash expenditures during the coming week and deposits the remainder of the offering intact. In order to facilitate the deposit, members who contribute by check are asked to draw their checks to cash.

(3) At their request, a few members are furnished prenumbered, predated envelopes in which to insert their weekly contributions. The head usher removes the cash from the envelopes to be counted with the loose cash included in the offering and discards the envelopes. No record is maintained of issuance or return of the envelopes, and the envelope system is not encouraged.

(4) Each member is asked to prepare a contribution pledge card annually. The pledge is regarded as a moral commitment by the member to contribute a stated weekly amount. Based upon the amounts shown on the pledge cards, the financial secretary furnishes a letter requesting members to support the tax deductibility of their contributions.

*Required:* Describe the weaknesses and recommend improvements in procedures for:

a. Offerings given at weekly services.

b. Record keeping for members' pledges and contributions.

Organize your answer sheets as follows:

| Weakness | Recommended Improvement |
|---|---|
|  |  |

(AICPA, adapted)

**In-Class Team Case**   **LO 3, 4, 5**   7–44.

Assume that you have been hired by Willington, CPA, as a new staff assistant. He informs you that his approach to audits has always been to assess control risk at the maximum and perform all the substantive procedures he considers necessary. However, he has recently read an article in *The Journal of Accountancy* that indicates that a more efficient audit may sometimes be achieved by performing some tests of controls and thereby assessing control risk at a lower level. Willington shows you the following table that came from the article:

| Inherent Risk | Assessed Level of Control Risk | | |
|---|---|---|---|
|  | **Low** | **Moderate** | **Maximum** |
| **Low** | Highest allowable detection risk (*lowest allowable scope of substantive procedures*) | High detection risk (*low scope of substantive procedures*) | Moderate detection risk (*moderate scope of substantive procedures*) |
| **Moderate** | High detection risk (*low scope of substantive procedures*) | Moderate detection risk (*moderate scope of substantive procedures*) | Low detection risk (*very high scope of substantive procedures*) |
| **Maximum** | Moderate detection risk (*moderate scope of substantive procedures*) | Low detection risk (*very high scope of substantive procedures*) | Lowest detection risk (*highest scope of substantive procedures*) |

Willington understands that the table is only for illustrative purposes and that other "in between" levels of the various risks are possible, but he wants you to use the ones in the table to help him understand the trade-offs between tests of controls and substantive procedures. He understands that these risks would be assessed at the assertion level for the various accounts, but he wants to better understand how the various tests performed in an audit "tie together." To keep things simple, he says to assume that inherent risk is at the maximum level in all cases.

He has roughed out a table that he wants you to complete for the following three cases:

*Case A:*     Controls, as described by management, appear strong, and Willington wishes to test them to the extent possible. In this case, he realizes that the results of the tests of controls may reveal that the controls are not operating effectively. Accordingly, Case A has three subcases:

A(1) Controls are found to be strong and operate effectively.

A(2) Controls are found to operate moderately effectively.

A(3) Controls, despite management's description, are found to be ineffective.

*Case B:*     Controls, as described by management, appear strong, but Willington wishes to use his old approach of not testing them.

*Case C:*     Controls, as described by management, appear weak.

*Required:*    Fill out the chart on the following page using the following reply options.

| Question | Reply Options | |
|---|---|---|
| 1. At what level is the planned assessed level of control risk? | *Low*<br>*Moderate*<br>*Maximum* | |
| 2. Describe the scope of tests of control that will be performed. | *None*<br>*Tests performed* | |
| 3. At what level is the assessed level of control risk? | *Low*<br>*Moderate*<br>*Maximum* | |
| | **a. Acceptable Level of Detection Risk** | **b. Scope of Substantive Procedures** |
| 4. What are the (a) acceptable level of detection risk and (b) the resulting scope of substantive procedures? | *Lowest*<br><br>*Low*<br><br>*Moderate*<br><br><br><br>*High*<br><br><br>*Highest* | *Highest scope*—Heavy emphasis on externally generated evidence, performed at year-end, and/or using larger samples<br>*High scope*—Emphasis on externally generated evidence, performed at year-end, and/or using larger samples<br>*Moderate*—Balance between externally generated evidence and internally generated evidence performed at year-end or interim period, and/or with moderate sample sizes<br>*Low scope*—Emphasis on internally generated evidence, performed at interim dates, and/or using smaller samples<br>*Lowest scope*—Heavy emphasis on internally generated evidence, performed at interim dates, and/or using smaller samples |

| | Case A—Controls Appear Strong; Auditor Decides to Test Controls to Extent Possible | | | Case B—Controls Appear Strong but Auditor Does Not Test | Case C—Controls Appear Weak |
|---|---|---|---|---|---|
| 1. At what level is the planned assessed level of control risk?* (*low; moderate; maximum*) | | | | | |
| 2. Describe the scope of tests of controls that will be performed. (*none; tests performed*) | | | | | |
| **Results of Tests of Controls** | **A(1)—Controls Strong (Operating Effectively)** | **A(2)—Controls Operating Moderately Effectively** | **A(3)—Controls Operating Ineffectively** | | |
| 3. At what level is the assessed level of control risk? (*low; moderate; maximum*) | | | | | |
| 4. (a) What is the acceptable level of detection risk? (*lowest; low; moderate; high; highest*) | | | | | |
| 5. (b) Describe the scope (nature, timing, and extent) of substantive procedures. (*highest; high; moderate; low; lowest*) | | | | | |

\* Inherent risk is assessed at the maximum level; evaluation of controls is based on management's description.

## Appendix 7A

 # Antifraud Programs and Control Measures

The AICPA, with a number of other organizations, prepared a document—*Management Antifraud Programs and Controls: Guidance to Help Prevent, Deter, and Detect Fraud.* That document suggests three categories of measures:

1. Create and maintain a culture of honesty and high ethics.
2. Evaluate the risks of fraud and implement processes, procedures, and controls to mitigate those risks.
3. Develop an appropriate oversight process.

Figure 7.12 summarizes the measures and provides examples.

FIGURE 7.12  **Antifraud Measures**

### 1. Create and Maintain a Culture of Honesty and High Ethics

| Measure | Examples of Measure |
|---|---|
| Set tone at the top | • Establish, communicate, and enforce a corporate code of conduct with employee involvement.<br>• Management's activities should show employees that dishonest or unethical behavior will not be tolerated.<br>• Examples of factors that *detract* from a positive tone:<br>  ▪ Statement by management of an absolute need to meet operating and financial targets.<br>  ▪ Establishment of unachievable goals. |
| Create a positive workplace environment | • Encourage and empower employees to help create a positive workplace.<br>• Allow employees to participate in developing and updating the code of conduct.<br>• Encourage employees and give them the means to communicate concerns about potential violations of the code of conduct without fear of retribution.<br>• Examples of factors that *detract* from a positive workplace environment:<br>  ▪ Top management that does not seem to care about or reward appropriate behavior.<br>  ▪ Negative feedback and lack of recognition for job performance.<br>  ▪ Perceived inequities in the organization.<br>  ▪ Autocratic rather than participative management.<br>  ▪ Low organizational loyalty or feelings of ownership.<br>  ▪ Unreasonable budget expectations or other financial targets.<br>  ▪ Fear of delivering "bad news" to supervisors and/or management.<br>  ▪ Less than competitive compensation.<br>  ▪ Poor training and promotion opportunities.<br>  ▪ Lack of clear organizational responsibilities.<br>  ▪ Poor communication practices or methods within the organization. |
| Hire and promote appropriate employees | • Conduct background investigations on individuals being considered for employment or for promotion to a position of trust.<br>• Thoroughly check a candidate's education, employment history, and personal references.<br>• Train new employees about the entity's values and code of conduct.<br>• Incorporate into regular performance reviews an evaluation of how each individual has contributed to creating an appropriate workplace environment in line with the entity's values and code of conduct.<br>• Periodically objectively evaluate compliance with the entity's values and code of conduct. |
| Properly train employees | • Training should include information on the company's values and its code of conduct.<br>• Training should include information on the need to communicate certain matters and the manner in which it should be done.<br>• Conduct refresher training.<br>• Require periodic confirmation by employees of their responsibilities. |
| Discipline | • Expectations about the consequences of committing fraud should be clearly communicated throughout the company.<br>• Appropriate actions should be taken in response to alleged fraud, including:<br>  ▪ A thorough investigation of the incident.<br>  ▪ Appropriate and consistent actions against violators.<br>  ▪ Relevant controls should be assessed and improved.<br>  ▪ Communications and training should reinforce the entity's values, code of conduct, and expectations. |

**FIGURE 7.12** *Continued*

### 2. Evaluate the Risks of Fraud and Implement Processes, Procedures, and Controls to Mitigate Those Risks

| Measure | Examples of Measure |
|---|---|
| Identify and measure fraud risks | • Consider vulnerability of company to fraudulent financial reporting, misappropriation of assets, and corruption (bribery and other such illegal acts).<br>• Consider organizational, industry, and country-specific characteristics that influence the risk of fraud. |
| Mitigate fraud risks | • Change certain activities (e.g., cease doing business in certain locations).<br>• Change certain processes (e.g., implement lockbox system at a bank instead of receiving payments at the company's various locations). |
| Implement and monitor controls and other measures | • Evaluate whether controls have been implemented in areas of high risk of fraud.<br>• Implement appropriate oversight measure by board of directors or audit committee to control for risk of management override of controls. |

### 3. Develop an Appropriate Oversight Process

| Measure | Examples of Measure |
|---|---|
| Management | • Oversee activities of employees by implementing and monitoring processes and controls. |
| Audit committee (or board of directors where no audit committee exists) | • Evaluate management's identification of fraud risks, implementation of antifraud measures, and creation of an appropriate "tone at the top."<br>• Consider likelihood of management override.<br>• Consider communicating with management one or two levels below senior management.<br>• Have an open and candid dialogue with independent auditors on management's risk assessment process and internal control. |
| Internal auditors | • Determine whether fraud has been committed.<br>• Evaluate fraud risks.<br>• Deter fraud. |
| Independent auditors | • Assist management and audit committee in assessment of company's process for identifying, assessing, and responding to fraud risks. |

# Chapter 8

# Consideration of Internal Control in an Information Technology Environment

## Learning objectives

After studying this chapter, you should be able to:

**LO1** Contrast the characteristics of an information technology–based system with those of a less sophisticated system.

**LO2** Describe the nature of various types of information technology–based systems.

**LO3** Describe the appropriate organizational structure in an information technology environment.

**LO4** Distinguish among general control activities, application control activities, and user control activities in an information technology–based system.

**LO5** Explain the manner in which the auditors obtain an understanding of internal control in an information technology environment.

**LO6** Discuss the ways in which the auditors may test controls in an information technology environment.

**LO7** Describe the nature of generalized audit software programs and the ways that they are used by the auditors.

In a traditional IT environment, information is processed on a large mainframe computer by a separate information systems department, often using software developed or modified by employees of that department. The other departments of the company, referred to as *user departments,* send their data to the information systems department and receive computer-generated reports when processing is complete. However, in recent years, commercially available software packages are replacing client-developed software and many information processing activities have been decentralized.

Commercially available computer software varies from applications costing less than $100 that are in essence electronic checkbooks (e.g., *Quicken, Money*) or basic general ledger systems (e.g., *Quickbooks*) to ERP systems costing into the tens, and even hundreds, of millions of dollars (e.g., systems by J.D. Edwards, BAAN, Oracle, Peoplesoft, and SAP).

Computer applications are frequently implemented by personnel within user departments, using **off-the-shelf software** packages. This eliminates the need for the client to employ computer programmers for those applications. A typical small business uses a relatively small computer[1] to run an off-the-shelf general ledger package that provides the basis for its accounting system. Indeed, the computing power of such a computer often is sufficient to meet all the accounting needs of a small business.

A typical large business has a **client/server** IT architecture in which a number of "client" computers are connected either to the corporate mainframe system or to another "server" computer. Data are entered and reports are generated at the various locations by user department personnel; the nature of the application determines the combination of processing performed on the client and server computers.

Although IT has created some challenging problems for professional accountants, it has also broadened the horizons of these professionals and expanded the range and value of the services they offer. Technology is more than a tool for performing routine accounting tasks with unprecedented speed and accuracy. It makes possible the development of information that could not have been gathered in the past because of time and cost limitations. When a client maintains accounting records with a complex and sophisticated IT-based system, auditors often find it helpful, and even necessary, to utilize technology in performing many auditing procedures.

This chapter will consider some of the most significant ways in which auditing work is affected by IT, but it cannot impart extensive technical knowledge. Independent auditors will find additional familiarity with IT to be of ever-increasing value in the accounting profession.

---

[1] A number of terms have evolved to describe a relatively small computer, including *microcomputer, desktop computer, personal computer, workstation, user operated computer,* and, simply, *computer.* Also, portable versions of these computers include *laptops* and *notebooks.* While some continue to distinguish among these terms, increases in computing power and versatility have blurred many original distinctions.

# Nature of IT-Based Systems

Before considering the impact of IT on the work of the certified public accountant, some understanding of the nature of IT and its capabilities is needed. An IT-based system usually consists of a digital computer and peripheral equipment known as *hardware* and equally essential *software,* consisting of various programs and routines for operating the system.

## Hardware

The principal hardware component of a digital computer is the *central processing unit* (CPU). The CPU processes programs of instructions for manipulating (moving and changing) data. The data may be numbers, characters, images (in digital form), sound (in digital form), or anything else that can be represented by a set of on/off characters (bits).

Digital computer circuitry has two states in that any given circuit may be *on* or *off.* Using an internal code, or machine language, capable of representing with two symbols any kind of data, all data may be expressed internally by the computer by a combination of on and off circuits. An example of a machine language is the *binary* number system.

Peripheral to the central processing unit are devices for recording input and devices for secondary storage, output, and communications. Peripheral devices in direct communication with the CPU are said to be **online,** in contrast to **offline** equipment not in direct communication with the CPU.

A first step in IT processing is to convert the data to machine-readable form. This is the role of recording and input devices, such as optical scanners, electronic cash registers, and bar code readers.

Secondary storage devices are used to augment the capacity of the storage unit of the CPU. Examples of secondary storage devices are magnetic tape, magnetic disk, and optical compact disk drives. Magnetic and optical compact disk drives have the advantage of **direct (random) access,** which allows for faster location and retrieval of data. Magnetic tapes and magnetic cartridges allow for only **sequential access;** data are retrieved by a linear search.

Machines also must be used to translate the output of the computer back into a recognizable code or language. Output equipment includes printers and display terminals.

## Software

Information technology–based systems use two major types of software: system software and application software. **System software** consists of programs that control and coordinate hardware components and provide other support to application software. The system software known as the **operating system** is important to the control of IT operations because it may be used to control access to programs and stored data and to maintain a log of all system activities. Common operating systems include Unix, Linux, Mac OS, and Windows. Other system software includes *utility programs,* for recurring tasks such as sorting, sequencing, and merging of data, and *specialized security (access control) software.*

Programs designed to perform a specific data processing task, such as payroll processing, are known as **application software.** Early application programs were laboriously written in machine language, but today programming languages such as *COBOL* (common business-oriented language), **C++,** and **JAVA** are much like English. Programming in C++ and other *source languages* is made possible by another type of software, the *compiler,* which is a computer program used to translate a *source-language program* into machine language. The machine-language version of a program is called an *object program.*

## Characteristics of Various Types of IT-Based Systems

In some ways, IT-based systems enhance the reliability of financial information. Information technology processes transactions uniformly and eliminates the human errors that may occur in a manual system. On the other hand, defects in programs can result in processing all transactions incorrectly. Also, errors or fraudulent items that do occur in IT processing may not be detected by the client's personnel because few people are involved with information processing. Thus, IT precision does not ensure that the output will be reliable.

Information technology–based systems differ as to their characteristics. A system, regardless of its size, may possess one or more of the following elements:

**LO2**

Describe the nature of various types of information technology–based systems.

1. Batch processing.
2. Online capabilities.
3. Database storage.
4. IT networks.
5. End user computing.

### Batch Processing

When **batch processing** is used, input data are gathered and processed periodically in discrete groups. An example of batch processing is accumulating all of a day's sales transactions and processing them as a "batch" at the end of that day. While batch IT-based systems do not provide up-to-the-minute information, they are often more efficient than other types of systems.

### Online Capabilities

*Online systems* allow users to have direct (online) access to the data stored in the system. Online systems may be divided into two types: (1) online transaction processing (OLTP) and (2) online analytical processing (OLAP) systems.

**Online transaction processing (OLTP)** systems are used to process various types of accounting and other transactions. When an online system is in use, individual transactions may be entered directly from the originators at remote locations. The transactions may be held in a transaction file and later posted to the records as a batch, or real-time processing may be used. In *online real-time* (OLRT) systems, transactions are processed immediately and all accounting records are updated instantaneously. These systems are frequently found in banks and other financial institutions. Online real-time systems allow a teller at any branch to update a customer's account immediately by recording deposits or withdrawals on a computer terminal. Similarly, customers are able to transact business directly with the system by inserting an identification card in an automatic teller machine (ATM).

The use of an online real-time system results in significant changes in internal control. Original source documents may not be available to support input into the system, and the overall amount of the hard copy (printed) audit trail may be substantially reduced. In these systems, essential controls should be programmed into the software. For example, the validity of data should be checked by the computer as transactions and data are entered into the system.

**Online analytical processing (OLAP)** involves the use of software technology that enables a user to query the system and conduct various analyses, ordinarily directly from the user's desktop computer. For example, management of an airline may download its online transaction processing reservation database into a **data warehouse**—another database that allows more efficient detailed statistical and graphical analysis of the reservation information. Management may then use the statistical reports and analyses generated by the OLAP system to make various operating decisions. The data also may be used in conjunction with decision support systems or expert systems. **Decision support systems** combine models and data in an attempt to solve unstructured problems with extensive user involvement. Alternatively, an **expert system** guides decision processes in a well-defined area and allows decisions comparable to those of an expert. As an example, banks may use expert systems to assess the credit risk of potential loan customers.

### Database Storage

In a traditional IT-based system, each computer application has its own *application data files*. For example, the **master file** of accounts receivable is an application data file, maintained by the accounts receivable department, that contains customer account activity for a period of time and information about each customer. Much of the information in this file is also included in the customer master file maintained by the sales department. While this data redundancy has a storage cost, a bigger issue is data inconsistencies that may arise because the information may not be up-to-date in all files.

In a **database system,** separate application files are replaced with integrated database files that are shared by many users and application programs. A database system eliminates much data redundancy, and since the database is normally stored on a direct access device, the system responds quickly to users' requests for information. Both batch or online real-time systems can use database storage.

From a control standpoint, it is essential that the database be secured against improper access or alteration. Organizations that use database systems often create a **database administrator** function, with responsibility for implementing and maintaining central databases and controlling access to the data.

### IT Networks

The advent of **telecommunications**—the electronic transmission of information by radio, wire, **fiber optics, microwave,** laser, and other electromagnetic systems—has made it possible to transfer information between computers. **Networks** of computers linked together through telecommunication links enable companies to communicate information back and forth between geographically dispersed business locations. Indeed, this has led to the creation and development of electronic commerce.

Networks that span a large geographical area are called **wide area networks (WANs).** In contrast, a **local area network (LAN)** is a communications network that allows resources, data, and program sharing within a limited geographical area. An example is a network that connects computers and printers within a single building.

Networking enables companies to implement **distributed data processing,** in which information and programs are shared by a large number of users. The network may provide company executives with online access to the vast amount of data stored in a number of the company's computers. Users may selectively retrieve data and process it to their personal specifications with microcomputers located in their departments.

Because data in an IT network may potentially be altered at any location that can access the system, weak controls at a single location can jeopardize the reliability of the entire networked system. Accordingly, security controls should be established at each location to ensure that data can be changed and accessed only by authorized personnel.

Many companies take advantage of **Internet** technology in establishing their networks. Some companies use the Internet to facilitate the exchange of information through remote locations or for electronic commerce involving buying or selling products over the Internet. Other companies have adopted Internet software for use in their closed networks, which are referred to as **intranets.** When these intranets include external business partners, they are often referred to as **extranets.**

### Electronic Commerce

The development of **electronic commerce** (e-commerce) continues to have a profound effect on accounting information systems. Electronic commerce involves the electronic processing and transmission of data between customer and client. A variety of activities may be involved, including electronic trading of goods and services, online delivery of digital products, and electronic funds transfer. **Electronic data interchange (EDI)** systems enable a company and its customers or suppliers to use telecommunication links to exchange business data electronically over a private line of communication, as contrasted to the Internet. Source documents, such as invoices, purchase orders, checks, and bills of lading, are replaced with electronic transactions.

Controls over electronic commerce systems include the use of private communication lines, firewalls, terminal controls, data encryption, and antivirus software.

*End User Computing*

When a company implements **end user computing,** the user departments are responsible for the development and execution of certain IT applications. This involves a decentralized processing system, in which a user department both generates and uses its own information. For these applications, the information systems department is generally not involved, although certain files may be kept for user departments in mainframe storage. End user computing is possible because of the processing power now available with microcomputers. The end user IT system is the opposite of the traditional data processing environment, in which all information needed by users is provided by programs that are purchased or written and tested by the information systems department.

Controls over end user computing are only as good as those instituted by the user departments. For example, if user departments do not adequately test new programs, the reliability of all information in a system may be compromised. As is the case with IT networks, security controls must be established at each location to prevent unauthorized access to the company's data.

## Impact of IT on the Audit Trail

Information technology may affect the fundamental manner in which transactions are initiated, recorded, processed, and reported. In a manual or mechanical data processing system, an audit trail (transaction trail) of hard-copy paper documentation links individual transactions with the summary figures in the financial statements. For example, individuals may manually record sales orders on paper forms, authorize credit, prepare shipping reports and invoices, record sales in a sales journal, and maintain accounts receivable records. The controls an auditor may test in such a system are also manual, and may include such procedures as approvals and reviews of activities and reconciliations and follow-up on reconciling items. Alternatively, in an electronic commerce environment, the information systems may use automated procedures to initiate, record, process, and report transactions. Records in electronic format may replace such paper documents as sales orders, invoices, shipping documents, and related accounting records. Two areas of high risk in such systems are unauthorized access and equipment failure. Control in such systems consists of a combination of automated controls and manual controls. In many applications, IT is able to electronically create, update, and delete data in computer-based records without any visible evidence of a change being made. In addition, the development of telecommunications has created an environment in which data may be altered not only within a specific computer, but by various computers both within and outside the client's organization.

During the early development of IT-based systems, the electronic transfer of information led to some concern among accountants that computerized processing would obscure or even eliminate the audit trail. Although it is technically possible to design an information system that would leave no audit trail, such a system would be neither practical nor desirable. An adequate audit trail is necessary to enable management to direct and control the operations of the business, to permit file reconstruction in the event of transmission and processing errors or computer failure, and to accommodate the needs of independent auditors and governmental agencies.

An audit difficulty with advanced IT-based systems is that while an audit trail may exist, it may not exist in printed form; it may be available only in machine-readable form. Because it can be quite voluminous, audit trail information may be kept online for only a short period of time and then transferred to a low-cost storage medium, such as magnetic tape. Electronic commerce conducted over the Internet provides a good example because often no printed output may exist related to initiating and processing transactions. After processing, the details of the transactions are often stored on a long-term basis on magnetic tape.

When electronic commerce is being used, the auditors should consider client data retention and processing policies in planning the nature and timing of their audit procedures. For example, the auditors might identify transactions to be tested at the time they are processed so that information about the transactions can be obtained before it is purged from the IT-based system. Also, emphasis should be placed on coordinating the efforts of external and internal auditors to ensure adequate audit coverage.

The client's methods of processing transactions and policies for retaining audit trail information may even affect the auditors' overall approach to auditing certain assertions. To illustrate, when EDI transaction data are retained for a limited period, the auditors may find that the lack of hard-copy records makes performance of a primarily substantive audit for certain assertions difficult or impossible. Accordingly, for those assertions, the auditors may switch to a systems approach that includes tests of controls performed throughout the period to reflect the client's record retention policies. Thus, when significant information is initiated, recorded, processed, or reported electronically, the auditor may determine that it is not possible to design effective substantive procedures that by themselves would provide sufficient competent audit evidence.

During the design of an IT-based system, management will normally consult with both its internal and its external auditors to ensure that an adequate audit trail is built into the system and retained. In an IT-based system, of course, the audit trail may consist of computer printouts, computer logs, and documents stored in machine-readable form, rather than the more traditional handwritten source documents, journals, and ledgers. Portions of the audit trail, such as the date and time of the last change in a record, and the person making the change, are often stored as part of the online records.

# Internal Control in an IT Environment

The discussion of internal control in Chapter 7 stressed the need for a proper division of duties. In a manual information system, no one employee should have complete responsibility for a transaction, and the work of one person should be verified by the work of another handling other aspects of the same transaction. The division of duties in such a manner ensures accurate records and reports and protects the company against losses from fraud or carelessness.

In an IT-based system, work normally divided among many employees may be performed electronically. Consolidation of activities and integration of functions are to be expected, since technology can conveniently handle many related aspects of a transaction. For example, a computerized payroll system could maintain personnel files with information on seniority, insurance, and the like; calculate employee pay; distribute labor costs; and prepare payroll checks and payroll records.

Despite the integration of several functions in an IT-based system, the importance of internal control is not in the least diminished. The essential factors described in Chapter 7 for satisfactory internal control remain relevant. Separation of duties and clearly defined responsibilities continue to be key factors. These traditional control concepts are augmented, however, by controls written into the computer programs and controls built into the computer hardware. Our discussion of controls in an IT-based environment will include a description of the organizational structure of the information system function, internal auditing of an IT-based system, and control activities.

## Organizational Structure of the Information System Function

**LO3**

Describe the appropriate organizational structure in an information technology environment.

In an IT-based system, there is a tendency to combine the performance of many data processing functions. In a manual or mechanical system, these combinations of functions may be considered incompatible from the standpoint of achieving strong internal control. For example, in a manual system, the function of recording cash receipts is generally segregated from responsibility for posting entries to the subsidiary accounts receivable. Because one of these procedures serves as a check upon the other, assigning both functions to one employee would enable the employee to conceal his or her own errors. A properly programmed computer, however, has no tendency or motivation to conceal its errors and may record these transactions simultaneously. Therefore, what appears to be an

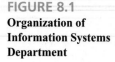

**FIGURE 8.1**
**Organization of Information Systems Department**

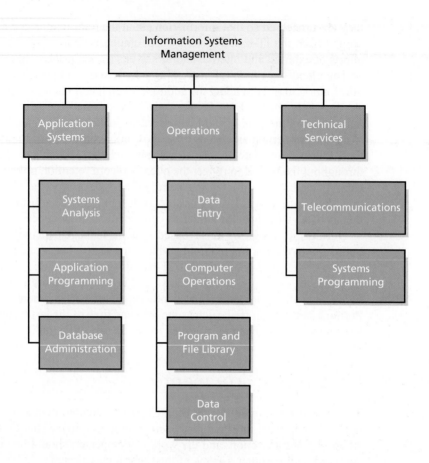

incompatible combination of functions may be combined in an IT-based system without weakening internal control.

When apparently incompatible functions are combined in the IT-based system, compensating controls are necessary to prevent improper human intervention with processing. A person with the opportunity to make unauthorized changes in programs or data files is in a position to exploit the concentration of data processing functions in an IT-based system. For example, an IT-based system used to process accounts payable may be designed to approve a vendor's invoice for payment only when that invoice is supported by a purchase order and receiving report. An employee able to make unauthorized changes to data or programs in that system could cause unsubstantiated payments to be made to specific vendors.

Computer programs and data files cannot be changed without the use of IT equipment. When changes are made, however, there may be no visible evidence of the alteration. Thus, the organization of the information systems department should prevent its personnel from having inappropriate access to equipment, programs, or data files. This is accomplished by providing definite lines of authority and responsibility, segregation of functions, and clear definition of duties for each employee in the department. The organization of the information systems department varies from one company to another in terms of reporting responsibility, relationships with other departments, and responsibilities within the department. As illustrated by Figure 8.1, the organizational structure of a well-staffed information systems department should include the separation of responsibilities discussed next.

*Information Systems Management*

The information systems manager (director) should supervise the operation of the department and may report to the vice president of finance or administrative services or to the controller. When the head of information systems reports to the controller, the controller should not have direct involvement with IT operations. Alternatively, the position may be elevated to the vice president level, with reporting responsibility directly to the president. In many companies this high-level person is called the *chief information officer* (CIO).

### Systems Analysis

Systems analysts are responsible for designing the information system. After considering the objectives of the business and the IT processing needs of the various user departments, they determine the goals of the system and the means of achieving them. Using system flowcharts and other tools, they outline the IT-based system.

### Application Programming

Guided by the specifications provided by the systems analysts, *the application programmers* design flowcharts of the computer programs required by the system. They then code the required programs in computer language, generally making use of specialized programming languages, such as C++, and software tools, such as assemblers, compilers, and utility programs. They test the programs with *test data* composed of genuine or dummy records and transactions and perform the necessary debugging. Finally, the application programmers prepare the necessary application documentation, such as the computer operator instructions.

### Database Administration

The database administrator has the responsibility for planning and administering the company's database. The primary objectives of this individual are to design the database and to control its use.

### Data Entry

Personnel involved with this function prepare and verify input data for processing. Central data entry operators have largely been replaced with new technology. Today, data may be input via terminals or desktop computers in user departments, scanned directly from source documents or via EDI. Data changes for online real-time systems are normally entered directly into the system by users through telecommunication links so that computer files can be updated immediately.

### IT Operations

IT operators run and monitor central computers in accordance with standard instructions. On occasion, the IT operators may need to intervene through the console during a run in order to correct an indicated error. The IT's operating system should be programmed to maintain a detailed log of all operator intervention. The separation of IT operations from programming is an important one from the standpoint of achieving effective internal control. An employee performing both functions has more opportunity to make unauthorized changes in programs.

### Program and File Library

The purpose of the file library is to protect computer programs, master files, transaction (detail) tapes, and other records from loss, damage, and unauthorized use or alteration. To ensure adequate control, the librarian maintains a formal checkout system for making files and programs available to authorized users.

In many systems, a portion of the library function is performed by the computers. The computer operators or the users enter special code numbers or passwords to gain access to programs and files stored within the system. The system automatically maintains a log showing when these programs and files are used and by whom.

### Data Control

The data control group of an information systems department reviews and tests all input procedures, monitors processing, reviews exception reports, handles the reprocessing of exceptions detected by the system, and reviews and distributes all IT output. This group also reviews the log of operator interventions and the library log of program usage.

## Illustrative Case — Fraud by Programmers

A programmer for a large bank wrote a program for identifying and listing all overdrawn accounts. Later, he was able to insert a **patch** in the program to cause the computer to ignore overdrafts in his own account. The programmer was then able to over-draw his bank account at will, without the overdraft coming to management's attention. The fraud was not discovered until there were computer problems and the listing of over-drawn accounts had to be prepared manually.

### Telecommunications

*Telecommunications specialists* are responsible for maintaining and enhancing IT networks and network connections in a company. They monitor the network for indications of problems, including attempts to improperly access IT-based systems via the network.

### Systems Programming

*Systems programmers* are responsible for troubleshooting the operating system or systems in use, upgrading it when new software releases are provided by the vendor, and working with application system programs when the applications interact with the operating system in a nonstandard or problematical way. Systems programmers are normally responsible for the proper functioning of the security features built into or added to operating systems.

### Other Organizational Controls

Besides segregating functions, the information systems department should cross-train programmers, rotate operator assignments, require mandatory vacations, and obtain adequate fidelity bonds for information systems employees. At least two information systems employees should be present whenever the IT facility is in use. Careful screening policies in hiring information systems personnel are also important to achieve effective internal control.

## Computer-Based Fraud

The history of computer-based fraud shows that the person responsible for frauds in many situations set up the system and controlled its modifications.

The number of personnel and the organizational structure will of course determine the extent to which segregation of duties is possible. At a minimum, the function of programming should be separated from the function of controlling data entry, and the function of the computer operator should be segregated from those functions having detailed knowledge or custody of the programs. If one person is permitted to perform duties in several of these functions, internal control is weakened, and the opportunity exists for fraudulent data to be inserted in the system.

Whenever the responsibilities for record keeping and custody of the related assets are combined, the opportunities for an employee to conceal the abstraction of assets are increased. Since record keeping is an essential part of the information system's function, it is highly desirable to limit the access of information systems personnel to company assets. These employees can be considered to have direct access to cash if the information systems department prepares signed checks. They also have indirect access to assets if, for example, the computer is used to generate shipping orders authorizing the release of inventory.

This combination of record keeping with access to assets seriously weakens internal control unless adequate *compensating controls* are present. One type of compensating control is the use of predetermined *batch totals,* such as document counts and totals of significant data fields, prepared in departments independent of information systems. For

| Illustrative Case | *Fraud at Equity Funding* |
|---|---|

Equity Funding Corporation of America went into bankruptcy after it was discovered that the company's financial statements had been grossly and fraudulently misleading for a period of years. A subsidiary of the company had been manufacturing bogus insurance policies on fictitious persons and then selling these policies to other insurance companies. When the fraud was discovered, Equity Funding's balance sheet included more than $120 million in fictitious assets, far exceeding the $75 million net income reported over the 13-year life of the company.

Perhaps the most startling revelation of the Equity Funding scandal was that numerous officers and employees of the company had worked together for years to perpetrate and conceal the fraud. The fictitious transactions had been carefully integrated into the company's computer-based accounting system. A wide variety of fraudulent supporting documents had been prepared for the sole purpose of deceiving auditors and governmental regulatory agencies. Upon disclosure of the activities, several members of top management were convicted of criminal charges.

The Equity Funding scandal is often described as a computer-based fraud. It was not the use of computers, however, that enabled the company to deceive auditors and government investigators. Rather, the fraudulent activities were successfully concealed for a number of years because of the unprecedented willingness of a large number of company officers and employees to participate in the scheme. Collusion of the magnitude existing at Equity Funding renders internal control ineffective.

example, if the information systems department performs the function of printing checks, another department should be responsible for authorizing the preparation of the checks. The authorizing department should maintain a record of the total number and dollar amount of checks authorized. These independently prepared batch totals should then be compared with the IT output before the checks are released.

Organizational controls are reasonably effective in preventing an individual employee from perpetrating a fraud, but they do not work as well at preventing fraud involving collusion. If key employees or company officers conspire in an effort to commit fraud, controls that rely upon separation of duties can be rendered inoperative.

## Internal Auditing in an IT Environment

While the information systems department is primarily responsible for day-to-day maintenance of the controls for IT processing, the internal auditors are interested in evaluating the overall efficiency and effectiveness of information systems operations and the related controls throughout the company.

The internal auditors should participate in the design of the IT-based system to ensure that the system provides a proper audit trail and includes adequate controls. Once the system becomes operative, internal auditors review all aspects of the system on a test basis to determine whether prescribed controls are operating as planned. Among other things, the internal auditors perform tests to determine that no changes are being made in the system without proper authorization, programming personnel are functionally separate from IT operating personnel, adequate documentation is being maintained, control activities are functioning effectively, and the data control group is performing its assigned functions.

## Control Activities in an IT System

**LO4**

Distinguish among general control activities, application control activities, and user control activities in an information technology–based system.

Information technology control activities often are classified as general control activities, application control activities, and user control activities. Whereas **general control activities** apply to a number of or to all IT applications, application control activities and user control activities relate to only a specific application, such as the preparation of payroll. **Application control activities** include both *programmed control activities,* which are written into the computer programs, and *manual follow-up activities* performed on the exception reports that are generated by the system. **User control activities** are those performed by users to test the accuracy and completeness of IT reports. Figure 8.2 illustrates the relationship among these three types of IT control activities.

**FIGURE 8.2**
**IT Control Activities**

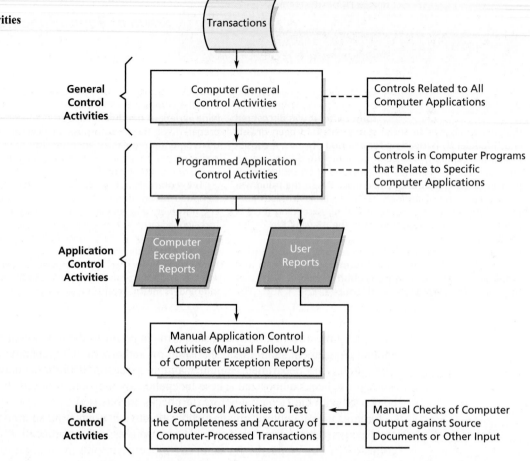

# General Control Activities

General control activities support many applications. General control activities include activities to control (*a*) developing and customizing new programs and systems, (*b*) changing existing programs and systems, (*c*) access to programs and data, and (*d*) IT operations.

*Developing and Customizing New Programs and Systems*

These controls ensure that the systems and programs that are developed or customized by the information systems department meet users' needs, are free from errors, and include adequate controls and documentation. Examples include policies requiring user involvement in purchase and development processes and appropriate testing of systems and programs before they are implemented. By requiring the information systems department to obtain technical assistance from personnel in other departments, such as the internal auditors, assurance is provided that the hardware and system software being purchased or developed will include appropriate controls.

Another important consideration in developing or customizing new IT-based systems and applications is the preparation of adequate *system documentation*. The purpose of system documentation is to provide an overall description of the IT-based system in the form of system flowcharts and descriptions of the nature of input, operations, and output. It also establishes responsibilities for entering data, performing control tasks, and correcting and reprocessing erroneous data. Documentation describing each application program, as a minimum, should include:

1. A description of the purpose of the program.
2. Program approval and change sheets showing authorization for the initial program and subsequent changes.

are *input validation (edit) checks* that are performed on the data being entered. Examples of these controls include:

- *Limit test.* A test of the reasonableness of a field of data, using a predetermined upper and/or lower limit.
- *Validity test.* A comparison of data (for example, employee, vendor, and other codes) against a master file or table for accuracy.
- *Self-checking number.* A self-checking number contains redundant information, such as the last two digits being a mathematical combination of the others, thus permitting a check for accuracy.

Input validation checks increase the accuracy of input data by rejecting any data that fail to meet an edit check and by informing the user that revised information is needed. The data can also be tested for completeness. For example, the program can determine whether all required fields in an on-screen form have been completed.

Input controls in batch IT systems are used to determine that no data are lost or added to the batch. The sequence of serial numbers or source documents composing each batch should be accounted for. In addition, the following controls help ensure the accuracy and completeness of batch processing:

- *Item (or record) count.* An item count is a count of the number of items or transactions being input in a given batch.
- *Control total.* A control total is the total of one field of information for all items in a batch. An example would be total sales for a batch of sales orders.
- *Hash total.* A hash total is a total of one field of information for all items in a batch, used in the same manner as a control total. The difference between a hash total and a control total is that a hash total has no intrinsic meaning. An example of a hash total would be the sum of the employee Social Security numbers being input for payroll processing.

A comparison of totals may be performed either by the hardware or manually by the control group.

*Processing controls* are designed to ensure the reliability and accuracy of IT processing activities. A number of the input controls described above are programmed as processing controls, including limit tests, validity tests, self-checking numbers, item counts, and control and hash totals. In addition, *file labels,* such as **header labels,** may be used to ensure that the proper transaction file or master file is being used on a specific run. For magnetic tapes, *internal labels* that are machine-readable are used in conjunction with gummed-paper external labels to prevent operators from accidentally processing the wrong file.

### Manual Follow-Up Activities

Most manual follow-up activities consist of review and analysis of outputs that have been generated in the form of *exception reports.* For example, a report might be produced that lists transactions where information is missing or inconsistent with other information or appears to be invalid for some other reason.

The effectiveness of manual follow-up activities depends upon the effectiveness of the programmed control activities that produce the exception reports. Thus, if a program does not generate an exception for an improper transaction, no manual follow-up is likely since the transaction is not included on the exception report. In addition, problems will persist if user departments do not take actions to correct transactions listed on exception reports, or if they fail to analyze the underlying causes for the exceptions.

## User Control Activities

User control activities are designed to test the completeness and accuracy of IT-processed transactions. These controls are generally designed to ensure the reliability of IT output (summary reports and transaction data). Reconciliation of control totals generated by the system to the totals developed at the input phase is an important aspect of user control activities. In some systems, user departments may appraise the reliability of output from the information systems department by extensive review and testing. For example, sales invoices generated by the IT-based system may be tested for clerical accuracy and pricing by an accounting clerk. Although these user control activities can be very effective, it is generally more efficient to implement effective application control activities and have users merely test the overall reasonableness of the output.

## Control in Decentralized and Single Workstation Environments

**Decentralized processing systems** generally involve the use of one or more user operated workstations to process data. Similarly, a single workstation may be used by a relatively small company to process data. While decentralized and single **workstation** systems have a smaller capacity and are slower at processing data than mainframe computers, they have the advantage of giving company employees direct access to a computer system without the constraints of **centralized processing systems.** For that reason, even audit clients with sophisticated centralized computer systems are likely to use workstations for a variety of on-site record keeping functions.

In decentralized environments, computers are located in users' departments and operated by user personnel who have little or no computer training. Processing usually is performed with commercial off-the-shelf packages. For secondary storage when the computer is operating, workstations use hard-disk drives where programs are stored. High-volume disks are used as backup for the hard disks.

Internal control over **user operated computers** is enhanced when computer processing procedures are documented and users are well trained. To ensure that the client can reconstruct financial records, backup disks or tapes of files should be made frequently and stored away from the originals in a secure location. Since the computers are located in user departments, there is a greater risk of use by unauthorized personnel. Therefore, the computers should be programmed to require the user to enter an authorization code to gain access to application menus that control specific programs and files. In addition, management should consider installing hardware controls, such as a locking on/off switch on the computer to prevent unauthorized use of the machine after business hours, or keeping critical programs on removable hard drives that can be locked up when not in use. The auditors are concerned with these and other controls over user operated computers when the information processed by them may affect the reliability of the information in the client's financial statements.

A significant risk in the use of user operated (decentralized) computers is the possibility of software viruses. A **software virus** is a program that has the ability to attach itself to a legitimate program and modify other programs and systems. Viruses can cause loss of data and programs. Controls that help to prevent computer viruses include:

- Obtain software only from reputable sources.
- Prohibit the use of unauthorized programs.
- Prohibit the downloading of programs from sources such as computer bulletin boards.
- Use antivirus software.

# The Auditors' Consideration of Internal Control in an IT Environment

LO5

Explain the manner in which the auditors obtain an understanding of internal control in an information technology environment.

Recall from Chapter 6 that the overall approach that auditors use in a financial statement audit includes:

1. Plan the audit.
2. Obtain an understanding of the client and its environment, including internal control.
3. Assess the risks of material misstatement and design further audit procedures.

4. Perform further audit procedures.
5. Complete the audit.
6. Form an opinion and issue the audit report.

As is the case for all types of internal control, the auditors' consideration of IT controls relates most directly to stages 2 through 4. Recall from Chapters 5 through 7 that the auditors first obtain an understanding of the client and its environment (stage 2) and then use this understanding to assess risk and design further audit procedures (stage 3). Further audit procedures, consisting of tests of controls (as appropriate) and substantive procedures, are then performed (stage 4).

## Obtaining an Understanding of IT-Based System Controls

Specialized skills may be needed to understand internal control or to design effective audit tests for clients with IT-based systems. Therefore, training and education about IT systems and controls are an important part of the professional development programs of many CPA firms. Some CPA firms have trained *IT specialists* who act as consultants to the firm's other auditors on audits that involve particularly complex IT systems. Other CPA firms rely on outside consultants to provide this assistance on complex engagements. In either case, the auditor in charge of the engagement should have sufficient IT-related knowledge to review the adequacy of the procedures performed by the specialist. The results of the specialist's procedures must be considered when planning the nature, timing, and extent of other audit procedures.

### Documenting IT-Based System Controls

The auditors' documentation of the client's IT-based system varies depending on the complexity of the system. For a client with simple internal control, a *written narrative* might be adequate. However, IT-based systems are usually documented by the use of systems flowcharts or specially designed internal control questionnaires.

*Systems Flowcharts*   As explained in Chapter 7, *systems flowcharts* are a commonly used technique for documenting internal control in audit working papers. An advantage of using systems flowcharts is that the information systems department should have them available as part of the standard documentation.

An illustration of a systems flowchart for sales, accounts receivable, and cash receipts appears in Figure 8.3. The following description of the illustrated procedures and IT systems should be helpful in studying the illustrated flowchart.

1. Orders are received from sales representatives, and sales invoices are printed. A computer file of sales transactions is generated as a by-product of order processing and sales invoice preparation. Two copies of the invoices are mailed to the customer, one copy is sent to the shipping department, and one copy is filed offline.
2. Individual cash remittances from customers are received from the mailroom and verified to a batch total, which is also received from the mailroom. These remittances are entered via terminals to a computer file of cash receipts transactions, with the total input being compared to the batch total. After comparison of batch totals, any necessary corrections are made to the transactions file.
3. The accounts receivable master file is updated by processing both the sales transactions file and the cash receipts transactions file. A by-product of the updating of the accounts receivable master file is an exception report for the run and a printout (on an online terminal) of any job messages.

The client's documentation of IT processing activities usually includes program flowcharts as well as systems flowcharts. Program flowcharts illustrate the detailed logic of specific computer programs. In some circumstances, auditors may use program flowcharts to obtain an understanding of the program controls contained in specific IT applications. This, however, involves careful consideration of the detailed logic of the program, is

**FIGURE 8.3**
**Systems Flowchart**

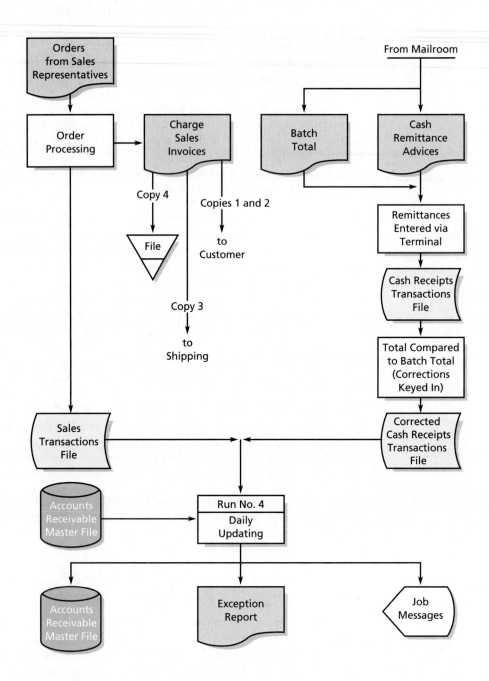

extremely time-consuming, and generally exceeds the level of knowledge required to plan the audit.

*Internal Control Questionnaires for IT-Based Systems*   As an alternative or supplement to systems flowcharts, the auditor may decide to document an IT-based system with specialized questionnaires. A specialized IT internal control questionnaire for the general control activities over access to the IT-based system is illustrated in Figure 8.4.

**Assessing the Risks of Material Misstatement**

Recall from Chapter 7 that during the risk assessment stage of an audit the auditors assess the risks of material misstatement by using all the audit evidence obtained on the client and its environment, including its internal control, to:

- Identify risks.
- Relate the identified risks to what can go wrong at the relevant assertion level.

FIGURE 8.4   **Internal Control Questionnaire**

| Access to IT System Resources | Yes, No, N/A | KP 8/15/X1 Comments |
|---|---|---|
| 1. Does the company have documented policies and procedures for IT security? | No | No written policies. |
| 2. Are there adequate physical controls to restrict access to the IT facilities to authorized individuals? | Yes | Card key access. Visitors are accompanied by authorized personnel. |
| 3. Are programmers restricted from access to application programs, job control language, and live data files? | Yes | The operating system security program restricts access to other programs and data. |
| 4. Has a test library procedure been established so that programming is not performed using live data files and applicable programs? | Yes | Test data files are used for testing programs. |
| 5. Are operators restricted from access to source programs? | Yes | Source programs cannot be accessed by operators. |
| 6. Are utility programs that can alter data without any audit trail adequately controlled and their use logged for subsequent management reviews? | Yes | Access to utility programs is restricted by the security program. |
| 7. Is there terminal access control software that restricts who can access the system, what programs can be used, and what files the user and/or program can access? | Yes | Access restricted by use of passwords. |
| 8. Does terminal access control rely on passwords or other identification/validation processes to control access to the system? | Yes | Unattended terminals log off automatically after 10 minutes of inactivity. |
| 9. Are passwords controlled to ensure that they are confidential, unique, and updated to reflect needed changes on a timely basis? | Yes | Policies restrict access to passwords. |
| 10. Are all significant events (security violations, use of critical software, or system commands, etc.) logged and promptly investigated by appropriate management personnel? | Yes | Reviewed by security manager. |

Source: Adapted from the AICPA Audit Guide, *Consideration of Internal Control in a Financial Statement Audit* (New York, 1996).

- Consider whether the risks are of a magnitude that could result in a material misstatement.
- Consider the likelihood that the risks could result in a material misstatement.

The nature of the client's IT system will affect the risks that management must confront in designing controls for the system. As an example, if the client employs end user computing, management must design and implement appropriate controls for that aspect of the IT system. Figure 8.5 illustrates typical risks related to IT system areas and controls that are often implemented for those areas. In assessing the risks of material misstatement, the auditors must identify these risks and evaluate the effectiveness of the related controls in mitigating those risks.

Assessing the risks of material misstatement involves evaluating the effectiveness of a client's automated and manual controls. In this section, we focus on tests of controls over IT-based systems.

*Determining the Approach to the Audit*

**LO6**

Discuss the ways in which the auditors may test controls in an information technology environment.

After obtaining an understanding of the client's internal control, the auditors are in a position to determine an effective and efficient approach to the audit. When the client's IT-based system is relatively simple and produces hard-copy documents and records, the auditors may decide that it is efficient to bypass extensive testing of IT processing. Using

**FIGURE 8.5**    **Assessing the Risks of Various Types of IT**

| Information Technology | Typical Risks | Selected Controls |
|---|---|---|
| Computer operations | Unauthorized access; destruction of infrastructure or data | Physical controls; segregation of duties; program and user controls |
| Computer programs | Unauthorized changes | Controls over access; segregation of duties; testing of programs; backup copies |
| Data files, including databases | Unauthorized changes; destruction of data | Controls over access; segregation of duties; backup copies; program and user controls |
| IT networks and electronic commerce | Unauthorized changes to data or programs; introduction of unauthorized data or programs; unauthorized interception or viewing of data; viruses | Firewalls; physical control over terminals; password systems; data encryption; antivirus software |
| End user computing (user operated computers) | Unauthorized access to data or programs | Password systems; physical controls over terminals; testing of user programs and applications |

this approach, the auditors will test transactions manually. If the results of these tests are satisfactory, the auditors will assume that the client's system is processing data properly. This technique is called *auditing around the computer* because the auditors bypass the computer rather than performing tests of the IT controls. While auditing around the computer can be an effective approach in certain circumstances, it is unacceptable if the reason for its use is merely the auditors' lack of understanding of the client's IT processing activities. The approach of auditing around the computer often relies upon substantive procedures to reduce detection risk to an acceptable level. Such an approach is only appropriate when an auditor is satisfied that such substantive procedures will be effective in reducing detection risk to an acceptable level. When a significant amount of information supporting the financial statements is in electronic form, an auditor may determine that it is not possible to design effective substantive procedures that by themselves provide sufficient evidence that the financial statements are not materially misstated. Examples of such situations include the following:

- A client conducts business using information technology to initiate orders for goods using predetermined decision rules and pays for the related payables using system-generated information regarding the receipt of goods.
- A client provides electronic services to its customers (for example, an Internet service provider or a telephone company) and uses the computer to log services provided to users, initiate billing, process billing, and record such amounts.

In both of the above situations, an auditor will normally decide that it is necessary to test controls, in addition to performing substantive procedures.

### Tests of Controls

The purpose of tests of controls is to provide reasonable assurance that the controls described in the audit working papers are actually operating as designed. Regardless of the nature of the client's system, auditors must perform tests of those controls that—based on the auditors' risk assessment—are presumed to be operating effectively. The nature of the IT-based system may, however, affect the specific procedures employed by the auditors in testing the controls.

### Procedures to Test General Control Activities

The auditors will usually begin their consideration of IT control activities by testing general control activities. This is an efficient approach since the effectiveness of specific application control activities is dependent on the existence of effective general control activities over all IT activities. The auditors, for example, would get little audit evidence from testing programmed control activities in a payroll program in an environment where programmers can easily make unauthorized changes in any program. In the absence of controls over program modification, the auditors have no evidence that the program being tested is identical to the one used to process data during the year. Such weaknesses would limit the auditors' ability to rely on application control activities.

Tests of the effectiveness of controls for development of new programs and systems may include making inquiries of personnel, reviewing the minutes of meetings of users and the IT staff, and inspecting the documentation of the tests performed on the systems before they were implemented. The auditors may have discussions with users to determine that they understand the systems and to obtain their assessments of the operation of the system.

To test controls over program changes, the auditors may review the documentation of any changes made and compare them to the log of manager approvals. Manuals being used by users and operators may be inspected to determine that they are the most recent versions.

Controls over access to programs and data may be tested through inquiry of client personnel and observation of the segregation of duties and physical controls over equipment. The IT-generated log of access violations may be inspected for evidence of review and follow-up by control group personnel.

Operations controls may be tested through inquiry of computer operators about adherence to policies and follow-up on exceptions and other problems. The auditor may also review reports summarizing appropriate corrective actions taken on operations problems by computer operators, vendors, programmers, the database administrator, and users.

### Procedures to Test Application Control Activities

Tests of application control activities vary significantly, depending upon the nature of the system and application. For example, in a batch system, input controls may be tested by accounting for the serial sequence of source documents in selected batches, reviewing and verifying reconciliations of batch control totals, and comparing control totals to IT output. In an online real-time system, on the other hand, control totals are normally not used, and the auditors will design tests to ensure that only authorized data are accepted as input and input validation checks are applied to ensure the accuracy of the data.

A primary approach to assessing application control activities is to test the manual follow-up activities by inspecting the exception reports generated by the system and reviewing the way in which the exceptions were handled. Analysis of exception reports may be especially effective when commercial off-the-shelf software is being used, but only if the auditors are confident that the software has not been modified. The controls that were configured into the system upon installation may have been "turned off" if the client has ineffective general controls over changes to existing systems. In such circumstances, the auditor may be familiar with the nature, strengths, and limitations of these software programs and have knowledge of the original control configuration. Thus, testing the operation of the system itself may be of lesser importance than in circumstances in which the client has developed its own software.

When the auditors are unsure of the software's operation, testing using computer-assisted audit techniques (CAAT) becomes especially helpful. These techniques include the use of *test data, integrated test facilities, controlled programs, program analysis techniques, tagging and tracing,* and *generalized audit software programs.* Computer-assisted audit techniques are used by both external and internal auditors.

### Test Data

In the audit of a manual accounting system, the auditors trace sample transactions through the *records* from their inception to their final disposition. In the audit of an IT-based system, a comparable approach is the use of **test data.** The test data developed by the client's programmers may be used by the independent auditors once they have satisfied themselves by studying of flowcharts and printouts that the tests are valid. As an alternative, the auditors may develop their own test data, but this approach is often too time-consuming to be practicable.

To test programmed control activities, the test data should include significant exceptions that would affect the auditors' assessment of control risk (or the risk of material misstatement). Among these would be transactions with missing data, erroneous transactions, illogical transactions, out-of-balance batches, and out-of-sequence records. The auditors will carefully appraise the programmed control activities that relate to financial statement assertions for which they wish to conclude that controls operate effectively. Dummy transactions and records used in test data can be specially coded to avoid contamination of the client's genuine records and files. If the client's IT-based system includes an integrated test facility, the auditors may use this facility to prevent their test data from contaminating the client's files.

### Integrated Test Facility

One method used by internal and external auditors to test and monitor controls in data processing applications is an **integrated test facility.** An integrated test facility is a subsystem of dummy records and files built into the regular IT-based system. These dummy files permit test data to be processed simultaneously with regular (live) input without adversely affecting the live data files or output. The test data, which include transactions and exceptions pertaining to controls to be tested, affect only the dummy files and dummy output. For this reason, an integrated test facility is often called the *minicompany approach* to testing the system. Integrated test facilities may be built into both batch and online real-time IT systems.

The auditors monitor the processing of test data, studying the effects upon the dummy files, exception reports, and other output produced. An integrated test facility for payroll applications, for example, could be set up by including a fictitious department and records for fictitious employees in the payroll master file. Input data for the dummy department would be included with input data from actual departments. The auditors would monitor all output relating to the dummy department, including payroll records, exception reports, and payroll checks. In this situation, strict control would be necessary to prevent misuse of the dummy payroll checks.

A problem with integrated test facilities is the risk that someone may manipulate the real data files by transferring data to or from the dummy files. Controls should exist to prevent unauthorized access to the dummy files, and the auditors should monitor all activity in these files. Also, the test facility must be carefully designed to ensure that real files are not inadvertently contaminated with the fictitious test data.

### Controlled Programs

As an alternative or supplement to the test data approach, the auditors may monitor the processing of current data by using a duplicate program that is held under their control. They then compare their output to that developed by the client's copy of the program. They may also reprocess historical data with their controlled program for comparison with the original output. Reprocessing historical data may alert the auditors to undocumented changes in the client's programs.

**Controlled programs** are advantageous because the auditor may test the client's program with both genuine (live) and test data. Through controlled programs, auditors may test programmed control activities without risk of contaminating the client's files. Also, the testing may be conducted at an independent IT facility without using the client's computer or information systems personnel.

### Program Analysis Techniques

**Program analysis techniques** have been developed that can generate computer-made flowcharts of other programs. A trained auditor can examine the flowcharts to test the logic of application programs and to ensure that the client's program documentation describes the program that is actually being used.

### Tagging and Tracing Transactions

This technique involves *tagging* transactions with an indicator when they are entered into the system. The computer provides the auditors with a printout of the details of the steps in processing tagged transactions. This printout is examined for evidence of unauthorized program steps. **Tagging and tracing** is possible only when the appropriate logic has been built into the IT-based system.

### Generalized Audit Software

Many large CPA firms use **generalized audit software** (computer programs) that can be used to test the reliability of the client's programs as well as to perform many specific auditing functions. This audit software is suited for use on a wide variety of IT-based systems. ACL and IDEA are two widely used commercial products.

One application of computer audit software is to verify the reliability of the client's programs through a process termed *parallel simulation.* The generalized audit software may be set up to perform processing functions essentially equivalent to those of the client's programs. If the client's program is operating properly, the output of the client's processing of a group of transactions should be equivalent to the output from the generalized audit software package.

A significant value of generalized audit software lies in the fact that the auditors are able to conduct independent processing of live data. Often, the verification of the client's output would be too large a task to be undertaken manually, but it can be done efficiently using generalized audit software. Even when manual verification is possible, the use of generalized audit software allows the auditors to expand greatly the size of the sample of transactions to be tested. An extensive examination of the client's files may become a feasible and economic undertaking. It is not necessary, however, to duplicate all the client's IT processing. Testing should be performed only to the extent necessary to support the auditors' assessment of control risk.

### Procedures to Test User Control Activities

Tests of user control activities will vary significantly with the nature of the control. However, the primary objective is to obtain assurance that users are, at a minimum, testing IT output for reasonableness. Therefore, typical tests involve inquiries of users about test procedures performed and inspection of any documentation that exists.

## Designing Substantive Procedures with Computers

**LO7**

Describe the nature of generalized audit software programs and the ways that they are used by the auditors.

To use the computer to test the records, the auditors must first find a way to access the records. In many situations, this is not particularly difficult. As an example, if a client uses a personal computer, the auditors may obtain a copy of the client's records that can be analyzed and processed on the auditors' computer. In other situations, the auditors may decide to "download" the client's data using a computer link between the client's computer and the auditors' computer. Finally, the auditors' generalized audit software may be run on the client's IT-based system to directly access the client's computer records.

Once the auditor has accessed the client's records, substantive procedures applied to the records can be performed using generalized audit software. Audit software may be used to rearrange the data in a format more useful to the auditors, compare the data to other files, make computations, and select random samples. Applications of this nature include:

1. *Examining the client's records for overall quality, completeness, and valid conditions.* In auditing a manual system, the auditors become aware of the general quality,

accuracy, and validity of the client's records through visual observation. Since the auditors do not have the same physical contact with computer-based records, the audit software may be used to scan the client's files for various improprieties. For example, the accounts receivable file may be scanned for account balances in excess of credit limits, and the depreciation expense may be recomputed for each item in the plant assets file. The great speed of the computer often makes it possible to perform such calculations for each item in the population, rather than having to rely upon a sample-based test.

2. *Rearranging data and performing analyses.* The audit software may be used to rearrange the data in the client's files into a format more useful to the auditors. For example, the accounts receivable file may be reorganized into the format of an aged trial balance. Data from the client's files may be printed out in the format of the auditors' working papers. In addition, the audit software can make analytical computations, such as computing turnover ratios to identify slow-moving inventory.

3. *Selecting audit samples.* Audit samples may be selected from the client's files on a random basis or using any other criteria specified by the auditors. Examples include selection of the inventory items to be test counted and the accounts receivable to be confirmed. An additional time savings may result if the audit software is used to print out the actual confirmation requests.

4. *Comparing data on separate files.* When similar data are contained in two or more files, the audit software can compare the files and identify any discrepancies. For example, the changes in accounts receivable over a period of time may be compared to the details of the cash receipts and credit sales transactions files. Also, actual operating results may be compared to budgets or forecasts.

5. *Comparing the results of audit procedures with the client's records.* Data obtained by the auditors may be used (or converted to machine-readable form) and compared to the data in computer-based files. For example, as is discussed in further detail in Chapter 11, confirmation requests may be sent, and replies received, electronically. Also, the results of the auditors' inventory test counts can be compared to the perpetual inventory file.

## Using Audit Software: An Illustration

To illustrate some of the possible uses of generalized audit software, let us consider a specific example. Assume that an auditor is planning to observe a client's physical count of inventories at a specific date. All inventory is stored either in the client's distribution center or at a public warehouse. The client maintains computer-based perpetual inventory records, which are updated daily. This inventory file contains the following information:

| | |
|---|---|
| Part number. | Location. |
| Cost per unit. | Date of last sale. |
| Description of item. | Quantity on hand. |
| Date of last purchase. | Quantity sold during the year. |

The client has provided the auditor with a computerized copy of the inventory file as of the date of the physical count.

The left-hand column in Figure 8.6 indicates typical inventory audit procedures the CPA might perform. The right-hand column indicates how generalized audit software might be helpful in performing these procedures.

Auditors do not need extensive technical IT knowledge in order to make use of generalized audit software. In fact, many CPA firms have found that they can train auditors to effectively use generalized audit software within a few days. Because of the simplified procedures that have been developed, auditors can, after limited training, use generalized audit software independently—that is, without assistance from the client's information systems personnel.

**FIGURE 8.6**
**Illustration of the Uses of Generalized Audit Software**

| Basic Inventory Audit Procedure | How Generalized Audit Software Might Be Used |
|---|---|
| 1. Observe the physical count, making appropriate test counts. | Determine which items are to be test counted by selecting from the inventory file a sample of items that provides the desired dollar coverage. |
| 2. Test the mathematical accuracy of the inventory extensions and footings. | For each item in the inventory file, multiply the quantity on hand by the cost per unit and add the extended amounts. |
| 3. Compare the auditors' test counts to the inventory records. | Organize the auditors' test counts and compare them to inventory records. |
| 4. Compare the client's physical count data to the inventory records. | Compare the quantity of each item counted to the quantity on hand in the inventory file. |
| 5. Perform a lower-of-cost-or-market test by obtaining a list of current costs per item from vendors. | Compare the current costs per unit to the cost per unit in the inventory file; print out the extended value for each item, using the lower of the two unit costs, and add extended amounts. |
| 6. Test purchase and sales cutoff. | List a sample of items on the inventory file for which the date of last purchase or last sale is on, or immediately before, the date of the physical count. |
| 7. Confirm the existence of items located in public warehouses. | List items located in public warehouses and print confirmations. |
| 8. Analyze inventory for evidence of obsolescence or slow-moving items. | List items from the inventory file for which the turnover ratio (quantity sold divided by quantity on hand) is low or for which the date of last sale indicates a lack of recent transactions. |

Source: AICPA, adapted from Uniform CPA Examination.

# Computer Service Centers and Outsourced Computer Processing

*Computer service organizations* provide processing services to customers who decide not to invest in their own processing of particular data. *Outsourcing companies* run computer centers and provide a range of computer processing services to companies that have decided to concentrate much or all of their central computer processing. Often very large companies outsource much or all of their central computer processing. In addition, many companies enter arrangements with outsourcing companies to handle the electronic business that they conduct over the Internet. These situations create similar requirements for the auditors. For simplicity, the term *service organization* will be used to refer to both a computer service center and an outsourcing company.

The auditors must be concerned about controls at the service organization when the services provided are *part of the client's information system.* A service organization's services are part of the client's information system if they affect any of the following:

- Classes of transactions significant to its financial statements.
- The procedures by which the transactions are initiated, authorized, recorded, processed, corrected (as necessary), transferred to the general ledger, and reported in the financial statements.
- Related accounting records and supporting information.

- The capture of events and conditions significant to the financial statements other than transactions.
- The financial reporting process used to prepare financial statements.
- The controls surrounding journal entries.

When a service organization provides services as part of the client's information system, the service organization's controls interact with the client's internal control. Accordingly, the auditor's understanding of internal control must be based, in part, on an understanding of processing activities at the service organization. A visit to the service organization may be necessary to obtain this understanding. In addition, if the audit plan includes a presumption that certain controls operate effectively, the auditors must obtain evidence of their operating effectiveness regardless of whether those controls are applied by the client or by the service organization.

When there is a low degree of interaction between the client's controls and those at the service organization, the auditors may find that controls applied by the client are adequate to ensure that errors or fraud in transactions are detected. For example, the client's personnel may develop input control totals and compare them to the service organization's output. They may also reperform computer calculations on a test basis. When such controls are adequate, the auditors need test only client controls to test operating effectiveness; there is no need to perform tests of controls at the service organization.

In other situations, there is a high degree of interaction and the controls performed at the service organization are necessary to achieve the client's control objectives. This means that the auditors' assessment of control risk cannot be significantly reduced without evidence that controls at the service organization are operating effectively. To obtain this evidence, the auditors may have to perform tests at the service organization.

## Reports of Service Auditors

Most service organizations perform similar processing services for numerous clients. If the auditors of each client (called *user auditors*) were to visit the service organization for the purpose of reviewing controls, they would ask similar questions and perform similar tests of controls. It may be advantageous for the service organization to engage its own auditors (called *service auditors)* to study their internal control and issue a **service auditors' report.** The user auditors may then elect to rely on this report as an alternative to visiting the service organization themselves.

*Statement on Standards for Attestation Engagements No. 16,* "Reporting on Controls at a Service Organization" presents two types of reports that service auditors may provide:

- *Type 1 report*—A report on a management's description of a service organization's system and the suitability of the design of controls.
- *Type 2 report*—A report on a management's description of a service organization's system and the suitability of the design and operating effectiveness of controls (throughout the period covered by the service auditor's report).

AICPA AU 402 (PCAOB 324) provides guidance on proper use of a Type 1 or Type 2 report. Note the essential difference in the two types of reports is that Type 2 addresses operating effectiveness of controls, while Type 1 does not.

To consider the service organization's controls in their risk assessments, the user auditors must have evidence that those controls are operating effectively. For example, consider claims expense and the related liability in the financial statements of a health insurance company. When the claims processing function is outsourced, health plan customers often are instructed to submit their claims directly to a claims processer. In this situation, the claims processer represents a service organization that is relevant to the claims portion of the company's internal control. The auditors of the health insurance company may obtain the needed audit evidence from tests performed directly by themselves the user auditors, or by a Type 2 report issued by the service auditors. If the service auditors' report provides an adequate basis for the user auditors' assessment, usually there is no need for the user auditors to perform their own tests at the organization. They may decide to rely solely on the results of the service auditors' tests. However, the user auditors should take steps to satisfy themselves as to the professional reputation of the service auditors.

## Chapter Summary

This chapter describes the auditors' consideration of internal control in an IT environment. To summarize:

1. Auditors encounter IT-based record keeping in virtually every audit engagement. Even the smallest of audit clients can be expected to use a computer to process its accounting records.

2. The use of an IT system by a client does not change the need to establish effective internal control; however, it does change the nature of the controls. More advanced IT features, such as online capabilities, database storage, IT networks, and end user computing, present special control risks. Therefore, specialized controls are needed, including passwords, validity tests, and computer logs.

3. The use of information technology may significantly affect the control system of the organization. From an organizational standpoint, it is essential to segregate the function of programming from the function of controlling input to the computer programs, and the function of the computer operator from the function of those having detailed knowledge or custody of the computer programs.

4. IT controls are often classified as general control activities, application control activities, and user control activities. General control activities apply to all IT applications, and application control activities and user control activities relate only to a specific application. The auditors often consider general control activities first, because application and user control activities cannot be assumed to be effective if the general control activities are weak.

5. To test application control activities, the auditors will often use computer-assisted audit techniques, such as test data, integrated test facilities, controlled programs, program analysis techniques, and tagging and tracing transactions.

6. While generalized audit software also may be used to test application controls, it is more often used by the auditors to perform substantive procedures applied to computerized records. Generalized audit software may be used to perform such functions as testing the clerical accuracy of records, making comparisons of related data, and selecting random samples.

## Key Terms Introduced or Emphasized in Chapter 8

**Application control activities (305)**   Controls relating to a specific IT task, such as preparation of payroll.

**Application software (297)**   Software designed to perform a specific task, for example, preparation of the general ledger.

**Batch processing (298)**   A system in which like transactions are processed periodically as a group.

**C++ (297)**   A programming language that is widely used because of its portability across various types of hardware.

**Centralized processing (systems) (310)**   Computer systems in which processing is performed by one computer or by a cluster of coupled computers in a single location. Data are often input and reports printed using workstations. When the workstations themselves perform significant processing, the system becomes a client/server environment.

**Change request log (307)**   A log that consists of suggestions for changes in programs. These changes have often been initiated by users who have noted problems or possible enhancements for a program.

**Client/server (IT architecture) (296)** A network system in which several computers (clients) share the memory and other capabilities of a larger computer (the server), or that of printers, databases, and so on.

**Controlled programs (316)** Duplicate client application programs that are maintained under the auditors' control in order to test the programmed control activities.

**Data warehouse (298)** A subject-oriented, integrated collection of data used to support management decision-making processes.

**Database administrator (299)** The administrative function of maintaining and safeguarding databases.

**Database system (299)** A system that eliminates data redundancy and enforces data integrity by storing data separately from (outside) programs and that contains data for two or more IT applications.

**Decentralized processing (systems) (310)** Computer systems in different locations. Although data may be transmitted between the computers periodically, such a system involves only limited communications among systems. Contrast with distributed processing and centralized processing.

**Decision support systems (298)** IT information systems that combine models and data in an attempt to solve nonstructured problems with extensive user involvement.

**Direct (random) access (297)** A storage technique in which each piece of data is assigned an address and may be retrieved without searching through other stored data. A magnetic disk drive is a direct access device.

**Distributed data processing (299)** An IT system that uses communication links to share data and programs among various users in remote locations throughout the organization. The users may process the data in their own departments.

**Electronic commerce (299)** Involves the electronic processing and transmission of data between customer and client. A variety of activities may be included, such as electronic trading of goods and services, online delivery of digital products, and electronic funds transfer.

**Electronic data interchange (EDI) (299)** A system in which data are exchanged electronically between the computers of different companies. In an EDI system, source documents are replaced with electronic transactions created in a standard format.

**End user computing (300)** An environment in which a user department is responsible for developing or purchasing, and running, an IT system (application) with minimal or no support from the central information systems department.

**Expert system (298)** A computerized information system that guides decision processes within a well-defined area and allows the making of decisions comparable to those of an expert.

**Extranet (299)** Private corporate IT networks that use Internet software to link employees and business partners.

**Fiber optic transmission (299)** Transmission using a glass or plastic filament cable to communicate signals in the form of light waves.

**General control activities (305)** Control activities applicable to all or many IT systems in an organization. General control activities include controls over the development of programs and systems, controls over changes to programs and systems, controls over IT operations, and controls over access to programs and data.

**Generalized audit software (317)** Computer programs used by auditors to locate and process data contained in a client's IT-based records. The programs perform such functions as rearranging the data in a format more useful to the auditors, comparing records, selecting samples, and making computations. This software is compatible with a wide variety of different IT systems.

**Hard copy (308)** IT output in printed form, such as printed listings, reports, and summaries.

**Header label (309)** A machine-readable record at the beginning of a file that identifies the file.

**Integrated test facility (316)** A set of dummy records and files included in an IT system enabling test data to be processed simultaneously with live input.

**Internet (299)** An international network of independently owned computers that operates as a giant computing network. Data on the Internet are stored on "Web servers," computers scattered throughout the world.

**Intranet (299)** Internal networks to a company that allow employees to use Internet capabilities, such as browsers, search engines, and e-mail.

**JAVA (297)** An object-oriented computer language that operates on many different platforms.

**Local area network (LAN) (299)** A communications network that interconnects computers within a limited area, typically a building or a small cluster of buildings.

**Master file (298)**   A file of relatively permanent data or information that is updated periodically.

**Microwave transmission (299)**   Transmission using electromagnetic waves of certain radio frequencies.

**Networks (of computers) (299)**   A group of interconnected computers, allowing transfers of data between them.

**Offline (297)**   Pertaining to peripheral devices or equipment not in direct communication with the central processing unit of the computer.

**Off-the-shelf software (296)**   Commercially available software created for a variety of users in the same industry or with the same application.

**Online (297)**   Pertaining to peripheral devices or equipment in direct communication with the central processing unit of the computer.

**Online analytical processing (OLAP) (298)**   An information system that allows the user to query the system, conduct an analysis, etc., while the user is at a computer. The database for an OLAP system is often generated from the transactions-based database used for online transaction processing.

**Online transaction processing (OLTP) (298)**   A processing method in which the IT system processes data immediately after it is captured and provides updated information to the user on a timely basis. OLTP examples include airlines reservation systems and banking systems.

**Operating system (297)**   Software that coordinates and controls hardware components. For example, authorization procedures may be programmed into the operating system to restrict access to files and programs to authorized personnel only.

**Operations manual (307)**   A manual that contains the instructions for processing a program. The manual should include sufficient information to allow operators to effectively operate programs, but should not include detailed program documentation.

**Patch (304)**   A new section of coding added in a rough or expedient way to modify a program.

**Program analysis techniques (316)**   Techniques for testing programmed control activities that involve the examination of computer-generated flowcharts of application programs.

**Program flowchart (307)**   A graphic representation of the major steps and logic of a computer program.

**Sequential access (297)**   A storage technique in which data are read and written in linear (e.g., account number) sequence. A magnetic tape drive is a sequential storage device.

**Service auditors' report (320)**   A report issued by the auditor of a service organization to provide information about the internal control of the organization. User auditors make use of these reports in considering the internal control over data processing performed for their clients by the service organization.

**Software virus (310)**   A program that can attach itself to a legitimate program and modify other programs and systems. A virus may cause the loss of data or programs on a system.

**System software (297)**   Programs that control and coordinate hardware components and provide other support to application software.

**Tagging and tracing (317)**   A technique for testing programmed control activities in which selected transactions are tagged when they are entered for processing. A computer program provides a printout of the steps in processing the tagged transactions that may be reviewed by the auditors.

**Telecommunications (299)**   The electronic transmission of information by radio, wire, fiber optics, microwave, laser, and other electromagnetic systems.

**Test data (315)**   A set of dummy records and transactions developed to test the adequacy of a computer program or system.

**User control activities (305)**   Controls performed by users of IT information to test its accuracy and completeness.

**User operated computer (310)**   A general-purpose computer designed to be used by one person at a time. This computer is often connected to a network of computers, and the user utilizes it for a variety of business-related purposes.

**Wide area network (WAN) (299)**   A communications network that interconnects computers within a large geographical area.

**Workstation (310)**   A general-purpose computer designed to be used by one person at a time. A workstation is often connected to a network of computers. Increases in the power of personal computers have blurred the distinction between personal computers and workstations. While workstations are generally more powerful, in this text we will not distinguish between the two.

## Review Questions

8–1. An IT system uses two types of software: system software and application software. Explain the difference between these two types of software.

8–2. Distinguish between end user computing and a distributed data processing network.

8–3. What is meant by a local area network?

8–4. Distinguish between user control activities and manual application control activities.

8–5. What are internal and external file labels? Why are they used?

8–6. Distinguish general control activities from application control activities and give examples of the types of controls included in each of these broad categories.

8–7. An information systems department usually performs numerous IT processing functions that would be separated in a manual system. Does this imply that separation of duties is not a practical means of achieving internal control in a computerized system? Explain.

8–8. Explain briefly what is meant by an "online real-time system."

8–9. Explain the meaning of the term *documentation* as it pertains to computers and an information systems department. How might a client's documentation be used by the auditors?

8–10. The number of personnel in an information systems department may limit the extent to which segregation of duties is feasible. What is the minimum amount of segregation of duties that will permit satisfactory internal control?

8–11. Compare the responsibilities and objectives of the data control group in an information systems department to those of the internal auditors with respect to IT processing activities.

8–12. Define and give the purpose of each of the following controls:

   *a.* Record counts

   *b.* Limit test

   *c.* Validity test

   *d.* Hash totals

8–13. Differentiate between a system flowchart and a program flowchart.

8–14. List and define three types of *data transmission controls*.

8–15. Describe briefly the controls that should be established over the operation of a workstation to prevent use by unauthorized personnel.

8–16. What is meant by the term *telecommunications?*

8–17. Explain briefly what is meant by a *distributed data processing system*.

8–18. Explain briefly what is meant by *electronic data interchange* (EDI). How does EDI affect a company's audit trail?

8–19. Is it probable that the use of IT will eventually eliminate the audit trail, making it impossible to trace individual transactions from their origin to the summary totals in the financial statements? Explain.

8–20. Do auditors usually begin their consideration of internal control over IT activities with a review of general or application control activities? Explain.

8–21. Describe the audit technique known as *tagging and tracing*. What is the purpose of the technique?

8–22. What is a computer service center? Are the auditors of a client that uses a service center concerned about the controls applied at the organization? Explain.

## Questions Requiring Analysis

**LO 3**    8–23. A primary requirement of effective internal control is a satisfactory plan of organization. Explain the characteristics of a satisfactory plan of organization for an information systems department, including the relationship between the department and the rest of the organization.

**LO 2, 3**    8–24. Distinguish between batch processing and online real-time (OLRT) processing. In which of these systems is strong internal control over input most easily attained? Explain.

**LO 2**    8–25. Auditors encounter the use of user operated computers on almost every audit engagement.

   *a.* How do user operated computers differ from large computers?

   *b.* When are the auditors concerned with internal control over the use of user operated computers?

**LO 6** 8–26. The use of test data is one method of performing tests of processing controls in an IT-based system. Identify and discuss several other methods by which auditors may test internal processing controls over IT activity.

**LO 7** 8–27. Discuss how generalized audit software can be used to aid the auditors in examining accounts receivable in a fully IT-based system.

**LO 6** 8–28. An integrated test facility (ITF) is a method used by both internal and external auditors for testing IT-based system controls. Discuss the advantages and disadvantages of implementing an ITF.

(CIA, adapted)

**LO 4** 8–29. Many companies have part or all of their IT processing done by computer service centers.

    *a.* What controls should the company maintain to ensure the accuracy of processing done by a service center?

    *b.* How do auditors assess internal control over applications processed for an audit client by a service center?

    *c.* What is a service auditors' report on the processing of transactions by a service organization?

    *d.* What two types of reports are provided by service auditors?

    *e.* How do user auditors use each type of report?

## Objective Questions

All applicable questions are available with McGraw-Hill's *Connect*^TM *Accounting.* ▓ connect |ACCOUNTING

8–30. **Multiple Choice Questions**

Select the best answer for each of the following questions. Explain the reasons for your selection.

**LO 2**     *a.* LAN is the abbreviation for:

        (1) Large Area Network.

        (2) Local Area Network.

        (3) Longitudinal Analogue Network.

        (4) Low Analytical Nets.

**LO 1, 2**     *b.* End user computing is most likely to occur on which of the following types of computers?

        (1) Mainframe.

        (2) Decision support systems.

        (3) Personal computers.

        (4) Personal reference assistants.

**LO 4**     *c.* When erroneous data are detected by computer program controls, data may be excluded from processing and printed on an exception report. The exception report should probably be reviewed and followed up by the:

        (1) Data control group.

        (2) System analyst.

        (3) Supervisor of IT operations.

        (4) Computer programmer.

**LO 4**     *d.* An accounts payable program posted a payable to a vendor not included in the online vendor master file. A control which would prevent this error is a:

        (1) Validity check.

        (2) Range check.

        (3) Limit test.

        (4) Control total.

**LO 2**     *e.* When an online real-time (OLRT) IT processing system is in use, internal control can be strengthened by:

        (1) Providing for the separation of duties between data input and error handling operations.

        (2) Attaching plastic file protection rings to reels of magnetic tape before new data can be entered on the file.

        (3) Making a validity check of an identification number before a user can obtain access to the computer files.

        (4) Preparing batch totals to provide assurance that file updates are made for the entire input.

**LO 2, 4**

f. The auditors would most likely be concerned with which of the following controls in a distributed data processing system?

(1) Hardware controls.

(2) Systems documentation controls.

(3) Access controls.

(4) Disaster recovery controls.

**LO 7**

g. The auditors would be least likely to use software to:

(1) Access client data files.

(2) Prepare spreadsheets.

(3) Assess computer control risk.

(4) Construct parallel simulations.

**LO 7**

h. Auditors often make use of computer programs that perform routine processing functions such as sorting and merging. These programs are made available by IT companies and others and are referred to as:

(1) Compiler programs.

(2) Utility programs.

(3) User programs.

(4) Supervisory programs.

**LO 5**

i. Which of the following is least likely to be considered by the auditors considering engagement of an information technology specialist on an audit?

(1) Complexity of the client's systems and IT controls.

(2) Number of financial institutions at which the client has accounts.

(3) Client's use of emerging technologies.

(4) Extent of the client's participation in electronic commerce.

**LO 7**

j. Which of the following is an advantage of generalized audit software packages?

(1) They are all written in one identical computer language.

(2) They can be used for audits of clients that use differing computing equipment and file formats.

(3) They have reduced the need for the auditor to study input controls for computer-related procedures.

(4) Their use can be substituted for a relatively large part of the required tests of controls.

**LO 4**

k. The increased presence of user operated computers in the workplace has resulted in an increasing number of persons having access to the system. A control that is often used to prevent unauthorized access to sensitive programs is:

(1) Backup copies of data on diskettes.

(2) User identification passwords.

(3) Input validation checks.

(4) Record counts of the number of input transactions in a batch being processed.

**LO 6**

l. An auditor will use the computer test data method in order to gain assurances with respect to the:

(1) Security of data in a system.

(2) IT system capacity.

(3) Controls contained within a program.

(4) Degree of data entry accuracy for batch input data.

**LO 2**

8–31. Auditors should be familiar with the terminology employed in IT processing. The following statements contain some of the terminology so employed. Indicate whether each statement is true or false.

a. A recent improvement in computer hardware is the ability to automatically produce error listings. Previously, this was possible only when provisions for such a report were included in the program.

    *b.* The control of input and output to and from the information systems department should be performed by an independent *data control group.*

    *c.* An internal-audit computer program that continuously monitors IT processing is a feasible approach for improving internal control in *OLRT systems.*

    *d.* An *internal label* is one of the controls built into magnetic tape drive hardware by the hardware manufacturers.

    *e.* A limit test in a computer program is comparable to a decision that an individual makes in a manual system to judge a transaction's reasonableness.

    *f.* A principal advantage of using magnetic tape files is that data need not be recorded *sequentially.*

    *g.* A major advantage of disk files is the ability to gain random access to data on the disk.

    *h.* The term *grandfather-father-son* refers to a method of protecting computer records rather than to generations in the evolution of computer hardware.

    *i.* When they are not in use, tape and disk files should be stored apart from the computer room under the control of a librarian.

**LO 6, 7**    8–32.    For each of the following descriptions, select the computer audit procedure most closely related. Computer audit procedures may be used once, more than once, or not at all.

| Definition | Computer Audit Procedures |
|---|---|
| a. Auditing by manually testing the input and output of a computer system. | 1. Auditing "around" the computer |
| b. Dummy transactions developed by the auditor and processed by the client's computer programs, generally for a batch processing system. | 2. Tagging and tracing<br>3. Integrated test facility<br>4. Parallel simulation |
| c. Fictitious and real transactions are processed together without the client's operating personnel knowing the testing process. | 5. Limit test<br>6. Test data |
| d. May include a simulated division or subsidiary in the accounting system with the purpose of running fictitious transactions through it. | |
| e. The auditors use generalized audit software to perform processing functions essentially equivalent to those of the client's programs. | |

**LO 1, 2**    8–33.    For each definition (or partial definition) in the first column below, identify the most closely related term. Each term may be used once or not at all.

| Definition (or Partial Definition) | Term |
|---|---|
| a. A subject-oriented, integrated collection of data used to support management decision-making processes. | 1. Batch processing |
| b. A system in which like transactions are processed periodically as a group. | 2. Data warehouse<br>3. Database system |
| c. An environment in which a user department is responsible for developing, or purchasing and running, an IT system (application) with minimal or no support from the central information systems department. | 4. Decentralized processing system<br>5. End user computing<br>6. Extranet<br>7. Operating system |
| d. A system that eliminates data redundancy and enforces data integrity by storing data separately from (outside) programs and that contains data for two or more IT applications. | 8. System software |
| e. Computer systems in different locations. | |

## Problems

**All applicable problems are available with McGraw-Hill's *Connect*™ *Accounting*.** ▆ connect
                                                                            |ACCOUNTING

**LO 2, 4**    8–34.    The Ultimate Life Insurance Company has a database system that stores policy and payment information. The company is now planning to provide its branch offices with terminals that have online access to the central IT facility.

*Required:*    a.  Define a *database*.

b.  Give one fundamental advantage of a database.

c.  Describe three security measures to safeguard the database system from improper access through the terminals.

(CIA, adapted)

**LO 5, 6**    8–35.    CPAs may audit around or through computers in the audit of the financial statements of clients who use IT to process accounting data.

*Required:*    a.  Describe the auditing approach referred to as "auditing around the computer."

b.  Under what conditions do CPAs decide to audit through the computer instead of around the computer?

c.  In auditing through the computer, CPAs may use test data.

(1) What is test data?

(2) Why do CPAs use test data?

d.  How can the CPAs be satisfied that the computer programs presented to them for testing are actually those used by the client for processing accounting data?

(AICPA, adapted)

**LO 3, 4**    8–36.    Johnson, CPA, was engaged to audit the financial statements of Horizon Incorporated, which has its own IT installation. While obtaining an understanding of internal control, Johnson found that Horizon lacked proper segregation of the programming and operating functions. As a result, Johnson intensified the consideration of internal control surrounding the system and concluded that the existing compensating general control activities provided reasonable assurance that the objectives of internal control were being met.

*Required:*    a.  In a properly functioning IT environment, how is the separation of the programming and operating functions achieved?

b.  What are the compensating general control activities that Johnson most likely found?

(AICPA, adapted)

**LO 4, 5**    8–37.    As you are planning the annual audit of Norton Corporation, you note that the company has a number of user operated computers in use in various locations. One of the machines has been installed in the stores department, which has the responsibility for disbursing stock items and for maintaining stores records. In your audit, you find that one employee receives the requisitions for stores, disburses the stock, maintains the records, operates the computer, and authorizes adjustments to the total amounts of stock recorded by the computer.

When you discuss the applicable controls with the department manager, you are told that the user operated computer is assigned exclusively to that department. Therefore, the manager contends that it does not require the same types of controls applicable to large IT systems.

*Required:*    a.  Comment on the manager's contention.

b.  Discuss five types of control that would apply to this microcomputer application.

(CIA, adapted)

**LO 7**    8–38.    A CPA's client, The Outsider, Inc., is a medium-sized manufacturer of products for the leisure time activities market (camping equipment, scuba gear, bows and arrows, and so on). During the past year, an IT-based system was installed, and inventory records of finished goods and parts were converted to computer processing. Each record of the inventory master file contains the following information:

| | |
|---|---|
| Item or part number. | Total value of inventory on hand at cost. |
| Description. | Date of last sale or usage. |
| Size. | Quantity sold or used this year. |
| Unit of measure code. | Economic order quantity. |
| Quantity on hand. | Code number of major vendor. |
| Cost per unit. | Code number of secondary vendor. |

For the year-end inventory count, the client intends to select one of each item or part to scan into an electronic file—Outsider inventory count file. With each item or part's bar code (used as the item or part's number), the software creates individual item records with:

Item or part number.
Description.
Size.

In addition, a quantity field exists in the client count file. After the bar code is scanned, the inventory count team counts the quantity on hand of the item and enters it manually into the file.

Subsequent to the count, the count data are processed against the inventory master file. The quantity-on-hand figures in the inventory master file are adjusted to reflect the actual count. A report is generated with all quantity adjustments of more than $100 in value. These items are investigated by the client, and all required adjustments are made. When adjustments have been completed, the final year-end balances are computed and posted to the general ledger.

The CPA has available generalized audit software that can read and process the data. Also, the CPA intends to take test counts in a manner similar to the client—scan a bar code into an electronic file and physically count and input the item quantities. Her file (the "CPA inventory count file") captures the same information as the client count file (part number, description, and size).

*Required:*

a. In general and without regard to the facts above, discuss the nature of generalized audit software and list the various types of uses of such software.

b. List and describe at least five ways generalized audit software can be used to assist in the audit of inventory of The Outsider, Inc. (For example, the software can be used to read the inventory master file and list items of high unit cost or total value. Such items can be included in the CPA's test counts to increase the dollar coverage of the audit.)

(AICPA, adapted)

**LO 4** 8–39. You are auditing for the first time the financial statements of Central Savings and Loan Association for the year ending December 31, 20X3. The CPA firm that audited the association's financial statements for the prior year issued an unqualified audit report.

The association uses an online real-time IT-based system. Each teller in the association's main office and seven branch offices has an online terminal. Customers' mortgage payments and savings account deposits and withdrawals are recorded in the accounts by the computer from data input by the teller at the time of the transaction. The teller keys the proper account by account number and enters the information in the terminal to record the transaction. The IT facility is housed at the main office.

*Required:*

You would expect the association to have certain controls in effect because an online real-time IT-based system is used. List the controls that should be in effect solely because this type of system is used, classifying them as:

a. Those controls pertaining to input of information.

b. All other types of IT controls.

**LO 4, 5** 8–40. Lee Wong, CPA, is auditing the financial statements of the Alexandria Corporation, which has a batch-processing IT-based system for shipping and invoicing that it purchased from a software vendor. The following comments have been extracted from Wong's notes on IT operations and the processing and control of shipping notices and customer invoices.

Each type of computer run is assigned to a specific employee who is responsible for making program changes, running the program, and answering questions. This procedure has the advantage of eliminating the need for records of IT operations because each employee is responsible for his or her own computer runs. At least one IT department employee remains in the computer room during office hours, and only IT department employees have keys to the computer room.

System documentation consists of those materials furnished by the software vendor—a set of record formats and program listings. These and the tape library are kept in a corner of the IT department.

The corporation considered the desirability of program controls, but decided to retain the manual controls in place prior to the conversion to the software vendor's system.

Company products are shipped directly from public warehouses, which forward shipping notices to general accounting. There a billing clerk enters the price of the item and accounts for the numerical sequence of shipping notices from each warehouse. The billing clerk also prepares control tapes of the units shipped and the unit prices.

Shipping notices and control tapes are forwarded to the IT department for inputting and processing. Extensions are made on the computer. Output consists of invoices (in six copies) and a daily sales register. The daily sales register shows the aggregate totals of units shipped and unit prices, which the computer operator compares to the control tapes.

All copies of the invoice are returned to the billing clerk. The clerk mails three copies to the customer, forwards one copy to the warehouse, maintains one copy in a numerical file, and retains one copy in an open invoice file that serves as a detailed accounts receivable record.

*Required:*

Describe weaknesses in internal control over information and data flows and the procedures for processing shipping notices and customer invoices, and recommend improvements in these controls and processing procedures. Organize your answer sheets as follows:

| Weakness | Recommended Improvement |
|---|---|
|  |  |

(AICPA, adapted)

**In-Class Team Case**  **LO4, 5**  8–41.   The accompanying flowchart summarizes Jenz Corporation's processing of sales. Some of the flowchart symbols are labeled to indicate controls and records. For each symbol numbered 1 through 13, select one response from either the list of operations and controls (A through O) or the list of documents, journals, ledgers, and files (P through Z).

| **Operations and Controls** | **Documents, Journals, Ledgers, and Files** |
|---|---|
| A.  Enter shipping data | P.  Shipping document |
| B.  Verify agreement of sales order and shipping document | Q.  General ledger master file |
| C.  Write-off of accounts receivable | R.  General journal |
| D.  To warehouse and shipping department | S.  Master price file |
| E.  Authorize accounts receivable write-off | T.  Sales journal |
| F.  Prepare aged trial balance | U.  Sales invoice |
| G.  To sales department | V.  Cash receipts journal |
| H.  Release goods for shipment | W.  Uncollectible accounts file |
| I.  To accounts receivable department | X.  Shipping file |
| J.  Enter price data | Y.  Aged trial balance |
| K.  Determine that customer exists | Z.  Open order file |
| L.  Match customer purchase order with sales order | |
| M.  Perform customer credit check | |
| N.  Prepare sales journal | |
| O.  Prepare sales invoice | |

(AICPA, adapted)

**Jenz Corporation**

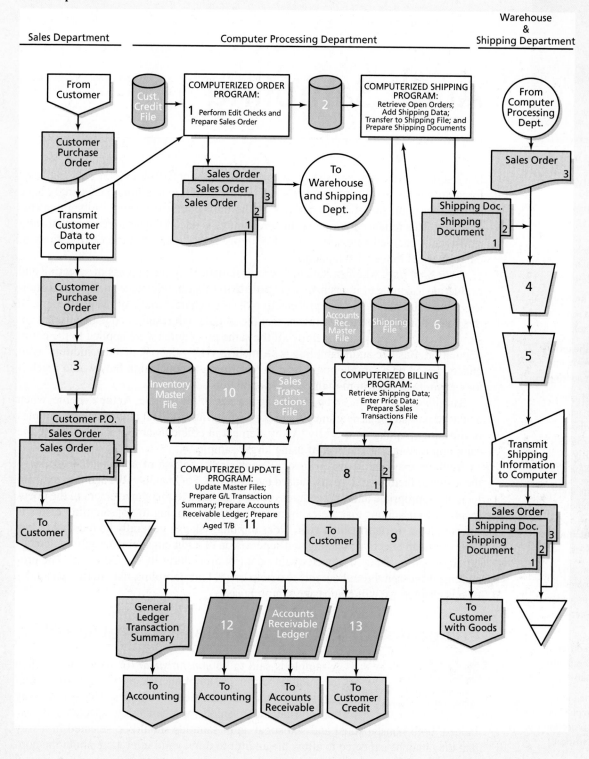

# 9

# Audit Sampling

In Chapter 5, we discussed the need for sufficient appropriate evidence as the basis for audit reports. As business entities have evolved in size, auditors increasingly have had to rely upon sampling procedures as the only practical means of obtaining this evidence. This reliance upon sampling procedures is one of the basic reasons that audit reports are regarded as expressions of opinion, rather than absolute certifications of the fairness of financial statements.

*Audit sampling,* whether statistical or nonstatistical, is the process of selecting and evaluating a sample of items from a **population** of audit relevance such that the auditors expect the sample to be representative of some characteristic of the population. In this context, **representative** means that the sample will result in conclusions that are similar to those that would be drawn if the same procedures were applied to the entire population. Basic to audit sampling is **sampling risk**—the risk that the auditors' conclusion based on a sample might be different from the conclusion they would reach if they examined every item in the entire population.

Sampling risk is *reduced* by increasing the size of the sample. At the extreme, when an entire population is examined there is no sampling risk. But auditing large samples or the entire population is costly. A key element in efficient sampling is to balance the sampling risk against the cost of using larger samples.

Auditors may also draw erroneous conclusions because of *nonsampling errors*—those due to factors not directly caused by sampling. For example, the auditors may fail to apply appropriate audit procedures, or they may fail to recognize errors in the documents or transactions that are examined. The risk pertaining to nonsampling errors is referred to as **nonsampling risk.** Nonsampling risk can generally be reduced to low levels through effective planning and supervision of audit engagements and implementation of appropriately designed quality control procedures by the CPA firm. The procedures discussed throughout this text help control nonsampling risk. In the remainder of this chapter, we will emphasize sampling risk.

## Comparison of Statistical and Nonstatistical Sampling

**LO1**

Distinguish between statistical and nonstatistical sampling.

A sample is said to be *nonstatistical* (or judgmental) when the auditors estimate sampling risk by using *professional judgment* rather than statistical techniques. This is not to say that nonstatistical samples are carelessly selected samples. Indeed, both nonstatistical and statistical audit samples should be selected in a way that they may be expected to allow the auditor to draw valid inferences about the population. In addition, the misstatements found in either a nonstatistical or a statistical sample should be used to estimate the total amount of misstatement in the population (called the **projected misstatement**). However, nonstatistical sampling provides no means of quantifying sampling risk. Thus, the auditors may find themselves taking larger and more costly samples than are necessary, or unknowingly accepting a higher than acceptable degree of sampling risk.

The use of *statistical sampling does not eliminate professional judgment* from the sampling process. It does, however, allow the auditors to measure and control sampling risk. Through *statistical sampling* techniques, the auditors may specify in advance the sampling risk that they want in their sample results and then compute a sample size that controls sampling risk at the desired level. Since statistical sampling techniques are based upon the laws of probability, the auditors are able to control the extent of the sampling risk in relying upon sample results. Thus, statistical sampling may assist auditors in (1) designing efficient samples, (2) measuring the sufficiency of the evidence obtained, and (3) objectively evaluating sample results. However, these advantages are not obtained without additional costs of training the audit staff, designing sampling plans, and selecting items for examination. For these reasons, nonstatistical samples are widely used by auditors, especially for tests of relatively small populations. Both statistical and nonstatistical sampling can provide auditors with sufficient appropriate evidence.[1]

## Selecting a Random Sample

**LO2**

Describe the methods of selecting a representative sample.

A common mistake is to equate statistical sampling with random sampling. *Random sampling* is simply a method of selecting items for inclusion in a sample; it can be used in conjunction with either statistical or nonstatistical sampling. To emphasize this distinction, we will use the term **random selection** rather than "random sampling" to refer to the procedure of selecting the items for inclusion in a sample.

The principle involved in unrestricted random selection is that every item in the population has an *equal chance* of being selected for inclusion in the sample. Although random selection results in a statistically unbiased sample, it is not necessarily a representative sample. Sampling risk still exists that purely by chance a sample will be selected that does not possess essentially the same characteristics as the population. However, since the *risk of a nonrepresentative* random sample stems from the laws of probability, this risk may be measured by statistical formulas.

The sample also may not be representative of the actual population because the population being sampled differs from the actual population. The auditors select an audit sample from a **physical representation of the population**. For example, a sample of accounts payable may be selected from a computer listing (the physical representation) of recorded accounts payable. Any conclusions based on this sample relate only to the population on the computer listing. The auditors' conclusions do not consider the possibility that certain creditors (with balances due) are completely omitted from the listing. Stated in terms of the financial statement assertions, *existence* is addressed to a greater extent than is *completeness*. Therefore, it is essential that the auditors consider whether the physical representation reflects the proper population.

The concept of a random sample requires that the person selecting the sample will *not influence or bias* the selection either consciously or unconsciously. Thus, some type of impartial selection process is necessary to obtain a truly random sample. Techniques often used for selecting random samples include *random number tables, random number generators,* and *systematic selection.*

### Random Number Tables

One of the easiest methods of selecting items at random is the use of a *random number table.* A portion of a random number table is illustrated in Figure 9.1. The random numbers appearing in Figure 9.1 are arranged into columns of five digits. Except that the columnar arrangement permits the reader of the table to select numbers easily, the columns are *purely arbitrary* and otherwise meaningless. Each digit on the table is a random digit; the table does not merely represent a listing of random five-digit numbers.

In using a random number table, the first step is to establish correspondence between the digits in the table and the items in the population. This is most easily done when the items in the population are consecutively numbered. On occasion, however, auditors may find it necessary to renumber the population to obtain correspondence. For example, if transactions are numbered A—001, B—001, and so on, the auditors may assign numbers to replace the alphabetic characters. Next, the auditors must select a starting point and a systematic route to be used in reading the random number table. Any route is permissible, as long as it is followed consistently.

---

[1] AICPA AU 530 (PCAOB 350) and the AICPA *Audit Guide, Audit Sampling,* provide auditors with guidelines for planning, performing, and evaluating both statistical and nonstatistical samples.

FIGURE 9.1
Table of Random
Numbers

| Row | Columns | | | | |
|-----|---------|---------|---------|---------|---------|
|     | **(1)** | **(2)** | **(3)** | **(4)** | **(5)** |
| 1   | 04734 | 39426 | 91035 | 54839 | 76873 |
| 2   | 10417 | 19688 | 83404 | 42038 | 48226 |
| 3   | 07514 | 48374 | 35658 | 38971 | 53779 |
| 4   | 52305 | 86925 | 16223 | 25946 | 90222 |
| 5   | 96357 | 11486 | 30102 | 82679 | 57983 |
| 6   | 92870 | 05921 | 65698 | 27993 | 86406 |
| 7   | 00500 | 75924 | 38803 | 05386 | 10072 |
| 8   | 34862 | 93784 | 52709 | 15370 | 96727 |
| 9   | 25809 | 21860 | 36790 | 76883 | 20435 |
| 10  | 77487 | 38419 | 20631 | 48694 | 12638 |

To illustrate the use of a random number table, assume that a client's accounts receivable are numbered from 1 to 5,000 and that the auditors want to select a random sample of 50 accounts for confirmation. Using the table in Figure 9.1, the auditors decide to start at the top of column 2 and to proceed from top to bottom. Reading only the first four digits of the numbers in column 2, the auditors would select 3942, 1968, and 4837 as three of the account numbers to be included in their sample. The next number, 8692, would be ignored, since there is no account with that number. The next numbers to be included in the sample would be 1148, 592, 2186, and so on.

In using a random number table, it is possible that the auditors will draw the same number more than once. If they ignore the number the second time it is selected and go on to the next number, they are *sampling without replacement.* This term means that an item once selected is not replaced in the population of eligible items, and consequently it cannot be drawn for inclusion in the sample a second time.

The alternative to sampling without replacement is sampling with replacement. *Sampling with replacement* means that once an item has been selected, it is immediately replaced into the population of eligible items and may be selected a second time. When applied to a random number table, the procedure is to include the number in the analysis as frequently as it occurs in the sample.

Statistical formulas can be used to compute sample size either with or without replacement. Most frequently auditors use sampling without replacement. This results in a *slightly smaller* required sample size and eliminates questions about the propriety of including items more than once in evaluating the sample results.

### Random Number Generators

Even when items are assigned consecutive numbers, the selection of a large sample from a random number table may be a very time-consuming process. Computer programs called *random number generators* may be used to provide any length list of random numbers applicable to a given population. Random number generators may be programmed to select random numbers with specific characteristics, so that the list of random numbers provided to the auditors includes only numbers present in the population. A random number generator is a standard program in all generalized audit software and spreadsheet packages (e.g., ACL, IDEA, and Excel).

### Systematic Selection

**Systematic selection** involves selecting *every nth item* in the population following one or more random starting points. To illustrate systematic selection, assume that auditors wish to examine 200 paid checks from a population of 10,000 checks. If only one random starting point were used, the auditors would select every 50th check (10,000 ÷ 200) in the population. As a starting point, the auditors would select at random one of the first 50 checks. If the random starting point is check No. 37, check Nos. 37, 87 (37 + 50), and 137 (87 + 50) would be included in the sample, as well as every 50th check number after 137.

If the auditors had elected to use five random starting points, 40 checks (200 ÷ 5) would have to be selected from each random start. Thus, the auditors would select every 250th check number (10,000 ÷ 40) after each of the five random starting points between 1 and 250.

Selecting every *nth* item in the population may *not* result in a random sample when positions in the population are assigned in other than a random order. For example, if expensive inventory parts are always assigned an identification number ending in 9, systematic selection could result in a *highly biased sample* that would include too many expensive items or too many inexpensive items.

To prevent drawing a nonrandom or biased sample when systematic selection is used, the auditors should first attempt to determine whether the population is arranged in random order. If the population is not in random order, the auditors should use multiple random starting points for their systematic selection process.

The systematic selection technique has the advantage of enabling the auditors to obtain a sample from a population of unnumbered documents or transactions. If the documents to be examined are unnumbered, there is no necessity under this method to number them either physically or mentally, as required under the random number table selection technique. Rather, the auditors merely count off the sampling interval to select the documents or use a ruler to measure the interval. *Generalized audit software packages* include routines for systematic selection of audit samples from computer-based files.

## Other Methods of Sample Selection

Two other selection techniques that are used by auditors include *haphazard selection* and *block selection.* Neither of these two methods applies probabilistic methods to selecting the items for the sample. For that reason, they should not generally be used in conjunction with statistical sampling plans.

### Haphazard Selection

When haphazard sample selection is used, the auditors select the items from the population on an *arbitrary basis,* but without any conscious bias. For example, a haphazard sample of **vouchers** contained in a file drawer might be selected by pulling vouchers from the drawer without regard for the voucher's size, shape, or location in the drawer. If used, a haphazard sample should not consist of items selected in a careless manner; the sample should be expected to be representative of the population.

### Block Selection

A block sample consists of all items in a selected time period, numerical sequence, or alphabetical sequence. For example, in testing internal control over cash disbursements, the auditors might decide to vouch all disbursements made during the months of April and December. In this case, the sampling unit is months rather than individual transactions. Thus, the sample consists of two blocks selected from a population of 12. Due to *the relatively large number of blocks needed to form a reasonable audit conclusion,* block sampling cannot generally be relied upon to efficiently produce a representative sample.

## Stratification

Auditors often stratify a population before computing the required sample size and selecting the sample. **Stratification** is the technique of dividing a population into relatively homogeneous subgroups called *strata.* These strata then may be sampled separately; the sample results may be evaluated separately, or combined, to provide an estimate of the characteristics of the total population. Whenever items of extremely high or low values or other unusual characteristics are segregated in this manner, each stratum becomes more homogeneous. The effect is to *require a smaller number of sample items* to evaluate the several strata separately than to evaluate the total population without the use of stratification.

Besides increasing the efficiency of sampling procedures, stratification enables auditors to relate sample selection to the materiality or other characteristics of items and, possibly, to apply different audit procedures to each stratum. For example, in selecting accounts receivable for confirmation (discussed in detail in Chapter 11), auditors might stratify and test the population as follows:

| Stratum | Composition of Stratum | Number of Accounts (Method of Selection Used) |
|---|---|---|
| 1 | Accounts of $10,000 and over | All accounts |
| 2 | Accounts of $5,000 to $9,999.99 | 50 accounts (random number generator) |
| 3 | Accounts of less than $5,000 | 30 accounts (random number generator) |

When the auditors are using audit sampling for substantive testing, stratification is almost always applied. For example, the auditors generally will not accept sampling risk for any item that by itself could materially misstate the population. For that reason, the auditors will test every item with a book balance of more than the tolerable misstatement. They will then select samples from each of the other strata.

## Types of Statistical Sampling Plans

**LO3**

Understand the different types of sampling plans used in auditing.

The sampling procedures used to accomplish specific audit objectives are called *sampling plans*. Statistical sampling plans may be used to estimate many different characteristics of a population, but every estimate is of either (1) *an occurrence rate* or (2) *a numerical quantity*. The sampling terms corresponding to occurrence rates and numerical quantities are *attributes* and *variables,* respectively. Specifically, the major types of statistical sampling plans used for audit sampling include the following:

1. *Attributes sampling.* This sampling plan enables the auditors to estimate the rate of occurrence of certain characteristics in the population (e.g., deviations from performance of a prescribed control). **Attributes sampling** frequently is used in performing tests of controls. For example, the auditor might use attributes sampling to estimate the percentage of the cash disbursements processed during the year that were not approved.

2. *Discovery sampling.* This form of attributes sampling is designed to locate at least one deviation (exception) in the population. **Discovery sampling** often is used in situations in which the auditors expect a very low rate of occurrence of some critical deviation. As an example, the auditors might use discovery sampling to attempt to locate a fraudulent cash disbursement.

3. *Classical variables sampling.* These sampling applications provide the auditors with an estimate of a numerical quantity, such as the dollar balance of an account. As would be expected, this technique is primarily used by auditors to perform substantive procedures. For example, variables sampling might be used to plan, perform, and evaluate a sample of accounts receivable selected for confirmation. Frequently used variables sampling plans include **mean-per-unit estimation, ratio estimation, and difference estimation.**

4. *Probability-proportional-to-size (PPS) sampling.* This technique, which is also referred to as *dollar-unit sampling,* applies attributes sampling theory to develop an estimate of the total dollar amount of misstatement in a population. **Probability-proportional-to-size sampling** is used as an alternative to classical variables sampling methods for performing substantive tests of transactions or balances. Unlike classical variables sampling techniques that define the sampling unit as each transaction or account balance in the population, PPS sampling defines the sampling unit as each individual dollar making up the book value of the population. A transaction or account is selected for audit if a dollar from that transaction or account is selected from the population. Therefore, each transaction or account has a probability proportional to its size of being selected for inclusion in the sample.

Sometimes one sampling plan may be used for the *dual purposes* of (1) testing a control and (2) substantiating the dollar amount of an account balance. For example, a **dual-purpose test** might be used to evaluate the effectiveness of a control over recording sales transactions and to estimate the total overstatement or understatement of the sales account.[2]

## Allowance for Sampling Risk (Precision)

**LO4**

Explain the effects of changes in various population characteristics and changes in sampling risk on required sample size.

Whether the auditors' objective is estimating attributes or variables, the sample results may lead to inaccurate inferences about the population. Some degree of **sampling error**—the difference between the actual rate or amount in the population and that indicated by the sample—is usually present. In utilizing statistical sampling techniques, auditors are able to measure and control the risk of material sampling error by deciding on the appropriate levels of sampling risk and the allowance for sampling risk.

The **allowance for sampling risk** is the amount used to create a range, set by + or − limits from the sample results, within which the true value of the population characteristic being measured is likely to lie. For example, assume a sample is taken to determine the occurrence rate of a certain type of deviation from the performance of a control. The sample indicates a deviation rate of 2.1 percent. We have little assurance that the deviation rate in the population is exactly 2.1 percent, but we know that the sample result probably approximates the population deviation rate. Therefore, using statistical sampling techniques, we may set an interval around the sample result within which we expect the population deviation rate to be. An allowance for sampling risk of ±1 percent would indicate that we expect the true population deviation rate to lie between 1.1 and 3.1 percent.

The wider the interval we allow, the more confident we may be that the true population characteristic is within it. In the preceding example, an allowance for sampling risk of ±2 percent would mean that we assume the population deviation rate to be between 0.1 percent and 4.1 percent. While being more confident that the true population characteristic falls within an interval is desirable, we realize that the increased size of the interval leads to a less precise conclusion.

The allowance for sampling risk may also be used to construct a dollar interval. For example, we may attempt to establish the total dollar value of receivables within an interval of ±$10,000. As is discussed later in this chapter, the allowance for sampling risk required by auditors usually is determined in light of the amount of tolerable misstatement. **Tolerable misstatement,** as described in Chapter 6, is materiality for the audit procedure being performed for a particular account. It is equal to or less than *performance materiality* for the account, which is an estimate of the maximum monetary misstatement that may exist in an account that, when combined with the misstatements in other accounts, will not cause the financial statements to be materially misstated.

## Sample Size

The size of the sample has a significant effect upon both the allowance for sampling risk and sampling risk. With a very small sample, we cannot have low sampling risk unless we allow a very large allowance for sampling risk (**precision**). As the sample size increases, both sampling risk and the allowance for sampling risk decrease. In other words, the smaller the allowance for sampling risk or the smaller the sampling risk desired by the auditors, the larger the required sample.

Sample size is also affected by certain characteristics of the population being tested. As the population increases in size, the sample size necessary to estimate the population with specified sampling risk and allowance for sampling risk will increase; however, if the population size is above approximately 500, an increase in its size has only a very small effect on the required sample size. In attributes sampling, sample size also increases as the **expected population deviation rate** increases. Finally, in classical variables sampling, greater variability among the item values in the population (a larger standard deviation) increases the required sample size.

[2] The size of a sample used for a dual-purpose test should be the larger of the two samples that would have been required for the two separate purposes.

# Audit Sampling for Tests of Controls

**LO5**

Plan, perform, and evaluate samples for tests of controls using statistical and nonstatistical methods.

Tests of controls are used to determine whether the client's internal control is operating in a way that would prevent or detect material misstatements in the financial statements. As discussed in Chapter 7, audit sampling cannot be used to test the operating effectiveness of all controls. In general, sampling can be used only when performance of the control leaves some *evidence of performance,* such as a completed document or the initials of the person performing the procedure. This evidence of performance allows the auditors to determine whether the control was applied to each item included in the sample. The results of tests of controls are most frequently presented in terms of the *rate of deviation* from performance of the prescribed control—also called the **deviation rate.**

A deviation from performance of a control does not necessarily indicate a misstatement of the financial statements. To illustrate the distinction between deviations and financial statement misstatements, assume that the auditors have selected a sample of 50 large cash disbursement vouchers to test for approval by the assistant controller. If the auditors find that 5 of the 50 vouchers were not properly approved, the deviation rate in the sample is 10 percent (5 deviations ÷ 50 vouchers), but the financial statements may not be misstated. All five vouchers may represent valid cash disbursements that were properly recorded. However, the auditors may conclude from the results of this test that there is a relatively high risk of invalid cash disbursements, because the sample results indicate that the assistant controller fails to approve about 10 percent of the vouchers processed. The auditors will use this evidence to increase the assessed level of control risk for the financial statement accounts that are affected by the cash disbursements cycle. Also, existence of the weakness will ordinarily be communicated to management and, if appropriate, to the audit committee. The communication of control-related matters is discussed in Chapter 7.

## Sampling Risk for Tests of Controls

When performing tests of controls, the auditors are concerned with two aspects of sampling risk:

1. *The risk of assessing control risk too high.* This risk is the possibility that the sample results will cause the auditors to assess control risk at a higher level than is warranted based on the actual operating effectiveness of the control.

2. *The risk of assessing control risk too low.* This more important risk is the possibility that the sample results will cause the auditors to assess control risk at a lower level than is warranted based on the actual operating effectiveness of the control. Figure 9.2 illustrates these two aspects of sampling risk for tests of controls.

The **risk of assessing control risk too high** relates to the *efficiency* of the audit process. When the sample results cause the auditors to assess control risk at a higher level than it actually is, the auditors will perform more substantive testing than is necessary in the circumstance. This unnecessary testing reduces the efficiency of the audit, but it does not lessen the *effectiveness* of the audit as a means of detecting material misstatements in the client's financial statements. For that reason, the auditors usually do not attempt to directly control the risk of assessing control risk too high.

**FIGURE 9.2**    **Sampling Risk for Tests of Controls**

| The Test of Controls Sample Indicates: | Actual Extent of Operating Effectiveness of the Control Procedure Is: | |
| --- | --- | --- |
| | **Adequate for Planned Assessed Level of Control Risk** | **Inadequate for Planned Assessed Level of Control Risk** |
| **Extent of Operating Effectiveness Is Adequate** | Correct decision | Incorrect decision (risk of assessing control risk too low) |
| **Extent of Operating Effectiveness Is Inadequate** | Incorrect decision (risk of assessing control risk too high) | Correct decision |

The **risk of assessing control risk too low** is of utmost concern. If the auditors assess control risk to be lower than it actually is, they will inappropriately reduce the extent of their substantive procedures. This unwarranted reduction in substantive procedures lessens the overall effectiveness of the audit as a means of detecting material misstatements in the client's financial statements. Therefore, the auditors carefully control the risk of assessing control risk too low when performing tests of controls.

In attributes sampling, the **confidence level** is the complement of the risk of assessing control risk too low. Accordingly, if the risk of assessing control risk too low is .05, the confidence level is .95. Thus, a statement that the confidence level of a control is .95 is equivalent to a statement that the risk of assessing control risk too low is .05. The professional standards currently use both of these terms to discuss sampling risk.

## Attributes Sampling

As indicated previously, attributes sampling is widely used for tests of controls when auditors are estimating the rate of deviations from prescribed controls. For example, if an attributes sample indicates a deviation rate of 5 percent with an allowance for sampling risk of ±3 percent, the auditors could infer that between 2 and 8 percent of the items in the population contain deviations. In this example, 2 percent is the *lower deviation rate* (lower precision limit) and 8 percent is the *upper deviation rate* (upper precision limit) for the sample estimate. Tests of controls are designed to provide the auditors with assurance that deviation rates do not exceed acceptable levels. Therefore, the auditors are concerned only with the upper deviation rate for the sample estimate. The relevant question from the above example is whether the auditors can accept a deviation rate as high as 8 percent, not whether they can accept a deviation rate as low as 2 percent. The lower deviation rate is not pertinent to the objective of the test. For this reason, auditors generally use one-sided tests in attributes sampling; they consider only the upper deviation rate that will permit them to assess control risk at the planned level. In tests of controls, the upper deviation rate is called the **tolerable deviation rate.**

Attributes sampling for tests of controls generally involves the following 10 steps:

1. Determine the objective of the test.
2. Define the attributes and deviation conditions.
3. Define the population to be sampled.
4. Specify the risk of assessing control risk too low and the tolerable deviation rate.
5. Estimate the expected population deviation rate.
6. Determine the sample size.
7. Select the sample.
8. Test the sample items.
9. Evaluate the sample results.
10. Document the sampling procedure.

### Determine the Objective of the Test

The objective of tests of controls is to provide evidence about the design or operating effectiveness of internal control. The auditors perform tests of controls when the audit plan includes an expectation that controls operate effectively. That is, the audit plan includes a risk of material misstatement that is affected by an assumption that controls operate effectively. Accordingly, an attributes sample will be selected and tested to provide audit evidence that a particular control is operating effectively in order to support the auditors' planned assessed level of control risk.

### Define the Attributes and Deviation Conditions

The auditors use professional judgment to define the attributes and deviation conditions for a particular test of controls. Attributes are characteristics that provide evidence that a control was actually performed. An example is the existence of the initials of the individual performing the control on the appropriate document. When a sample item does not have one or more of the attributes, it is classified as a deviation. As an example, assume that the auditors are performing a test of controls for the valuation of sales transactions. One of the controls that they decide to test is the review of sales invoices that is performed by an accounting clerk. The clerk's review includes (1) comparing quantities on each invoice to shipping documents, (2) comparing prices on each invoice to authorized price lists, (3) testing the clerical accuracy of each invoice, and (4) initialing a copy of the invoice to indicate that the procedure was performed. In performing the test of this control, the auditors will classify a transaction as a deviation if any one or more of the following deviation conditions exists.

1. The quantities on the invoice do not agree with the shipping documents.
2. The prices on the invoice do not agree with authorized price lists.
3. The invoice has a clerical inaccuracy.
4. The invoice copy is not initialed by the accounting clerk.

It is important that the attributes and deviation conditions be precisely defined before the test of control is performed; otherwise, a staff accountant may not make the appropriate decision about which sample items represent deviations.

If a document selected for testing cannot be located, the auditors generally will not be able to apply alternate procedures to determine whether the control was applied. Simply selecting another item is not appropriate. In such circumstances, at a minimum, the misplaced document should be treated as a deviation for evaluation purposes and documented. Also, because the disappearance of documents is consistent with many possible explanations, ranging from unintentional misfiling to material fraud, the auditors should carefully consider the overall implications of the situation.

## Define the Population

The auditors should determine that the population from which the sample is to be selected is appropriate for the specific audit objective. For example, if the auditors wish to test the operating effectiveness of a control designed to ensure that all shipments have been recorded as sales, they will not select a sample from the sales journal—that population is created by recorded sales and could not be expected to contain shipments that were not recorded. The appropriate population for detecting such deviations would be a population that contains all of the items shipped (e.g., the file of shipping documents).

## Specify the Risk of Assessing Control Risk Too Low and the Tolerable Deviation Rate

How do auditors determine the appropriate risk of assessing control risk too low and the tolerable deviation rate for a test of a control? The answer, in short, is professional judgment. The risk of assessing control risk too low—that is, the risk that the actual deviation rate exceeds the tolerable deviation rate—is a critical risk in tests of controls. As discussed previously, this risk impacts the effectiveness of the audit. Since the results of tests of controls play a major role in determining the nature, timing, and extent of other audit procedures, auditors usually specify a low level of risk—for example, 5 or 10 percent.

Auditors specify the tolerable deviation rate based on (1) their planned assessed level of control risk, and (2) the degree of assurance desired from the audit evidence in the sample. The lower the planned assessed level of control risk (or the more assurance desired from the sample), the lower the tolerable deviation rate.

The AICPA's *Audit Guide: Audit Sampling* includes the following overlapping ranges to illustrate the relationship between the planned assessed level of control risk and the tolerable deviation rate:

| Planned Assessed Level of Control Risk | Tolerable Deviation Rate |
| --- | --- |
| Low | 2–7% |
| Moderate | 6–12% |
| Slightly below the maximum | 11–20% |
| Maximum | Omit test |

**FIGURE 9.3**
Factors Affecting Sample Size for Tests of Controls

| Factor | Change in Factor | Effect upon Required Sample Size |
|---|---|---|
| **Auditors' Requirements:** | | |
| Risk of assessing control risk too low | Increase | Decrease |
| Tolerable deviation rate | Increase | Decrease |
| **Population Characteristics:** | | |
| Population deviation rate (expected) | Increase | Increase |
| Population size | Increase | Increase (if population is small) |

## Estimate the Expected Population Deviation Rate

In addition to the tolerable deviation rate and the risk of assessing control risk too low, the expected population deviation rate also affects the sample size in attributes sampling. This expected deviation rate is significant because it represents the rate that the auditors expect to discover in their sample from the population.

In estimating the expected population deviation rate, the auditors often use the sample results from prior years, as documented in their working papers. The auditors may also estimate the rate based on their experience with similar tests on other audit engagements or by examining a small pilot sample.

## Determine the Sample Size

As indicated earlier, the three major factors that determine the sample size for a test of a control are the *risk of assessing control risk too low, the tolerable deviation rate,* and *the expected population deviation rate.* The population size also has an effect on sample size, but only when the population is very small. Figure 9.3 summarizes the effects of these factors on the required sample size for a test of controls.

*Tables to Determine Sample Size*

To enable auditors to use attributes sampling without resorting to complex mathematical formulas, tables such as the one in Figure 9.4 have been developed.

Figure 9.4 may be used to determine required sample sizes at 5 percent risk of assessing control risk too low. Similar tables are available for other levels of risk, such as 1 percent and 10 percent. The horizontal axis of the table is the tolerable deviation rate specified by the auditors. The vertical axis is the expected deviation rate estimated by the auditors to exist within the population. The numbers in the body of the table indicate the required sample sizes. The number in parentheses shown after the required sample size is the allowable number of deviations that may be observed in the sample for the results to support the auditors' planned assessed level of control risk.[3]

To use Figure 9.4, the auditors stipulate the expected deviation rate in the population and the tolerable deviation rate.[4] Then, the auditors read the sample size from the table at the intersection of the stipulated tolerable deviation rate and the expected population deviation rate. For example, assume the auditors expect the deviation rate in the population to be 1 percent and specify a 9 percent tolerable deviation rate to justify their planned assessed level of control risk related to this control. Figure 9.4 shows that these specifications result in a sample size of 51 items, which must contain no more than 1 control deviation if the auditors' planned control risk assessment is to be supported by the test.

[3] The number of deviations allowable in a sample sometimes exceeds the expected deviation rate multiplied by the sample size. This is because the allowable number of deviations is always rounded to the nearest whole number because it is not possible to observe a partial deviation in a sample item. The sample sizes have been adjusted to reflect this rounding.

[4] Some tables require the auditors to specify population size. Figures 9.4 and 9.5 assume an infinite population. When populations are small, required sample sizes are only slightly smaller.

**FIGURE 9.4** **Statistical Sample Sizes for Tests of Controls at 5 Percent Risk of Assessing Control Risk Too Low (with Allowable Number of Deviations in Parentheses)**

| Expected Population Deviation Rate (As Percentages) | Tolerable Deviation Rate | | | | | | | | | | |
|---|---|---|---|---|---|---|---|---|---|---|---|
| | 2% | 3% | 4% | 5% | 6% | 7% | 8% | 9% | 10% | 15% | 20% |
| 0.00% | 149(0) | 99(0) | 74(0) | 59(0) | 49(0) | 42(0) | 36(0) | 32(0) | 29(0) | 19(0) | 14(0) |
| 0.25 | 236(1) | 157(1) | 117(1) | 93(1) | 78(1) | 66(1) | 58(1) | 51(1) | 46(1) | 30(1) | 22(1) |
| 0.50 | * | 157(1) | 117(1) | 93(1) | 78(1) | 66(1) | 58(1) | 51(1) | 46(1) | 30(1) | 22(1) |
| 0.75 | * | 208(2) | 117(1) | 93(1) | 78(1) | 66(1) | 58(1) | 51(1) | 46(1) | 30(1) | 22(1) |
| 1.00 | * | * | 156(2) | 93(1) | 78(1) | 66(1) | 58(1) | 51(1) | 46(1) | 30(1) | 22(1) |
| 1.25 | * | * | 156(2) | 124(2) | 78(1) | 66(1) | 58(1) | 51(1) | 46(1) | 30(1) | 22(1) |
| 1.50 | * | * | 192(3) | 124(2) | 103(2) | 66(1) | 58(1) | 51(1) | 46(1) | 30(1) | 22(1) |
| 1.75 | * | * | 227(4) | 153(3) | 103(2) | 88(2) | 77(2) | 51(1) | 46(1) | 30(1) | 22(1) |
| 2.00 | * | * | * | 181(4) | 127(3) | 88(2) | 77(2) | 68(2) | 46(1) | 30(1) | 22(1) |
| 2.25 | * | * | * | 208(5) | 127(3) | 88(2) | 77(2) | 68(2) | 61(2) | 30(1) | 22(1) |
| 2.50 | * | * | * | * | 150(4) | 109(3) | 77(2) | 68(2) | 61(2) | 30(1) | 22(1) |
| 2.75 | * | * | * | * | 173(5) | 109(3) | 95(3) | 68(2) | 61(2) | 30(1) | 22(1) |
| 3.00 | * | * | * | * | 195(6) | 129(4) | 95(3) | 84(3) | 61(2) | 30(1) | 22(1) |
| 3.25 | * | * | * | * | * | 148(5) | 112(4) | 84(3) | 61(2) | 30(1) | 22(1) |
| 3.50 | * | * | * | * | * | 167(6) | 112(4) | 84(3) | 76(3) | 40(2) | 22(1) |
| 3.75 | * | * | * | * | * | 185(7) | 129(5) | 100(4) | 76(3) | 40(2) | 22(1) |
| 4.00 | * | * | * | * | * | * | 146(6) | 100(4) | 89(4) | 40(2) | 22(1) |
| 5.00 | * | * | * | * | * | * | * | 158(8) | 116(6) | 40(2) | 30(2) |
| 6.00 | * | * | * | * | * | * | * | * | 179(11) | 50(3) | 30(2) |
| 7.00 | * | * | * | * | * | * | * | * | * | 68(5) | 37(3) |

Note: This table assumes a large population.
* Sample size is too large to be cost effective for most audit applications.
Source: AICPA, *Audit Guide, Audit Sampling* (New York, 2001).

## Select the Sample

When the auditors use attributes sampling, it is essential that the sample items be selected in a manner that achieves a random sample. Random samples may be selected using random number tables, random number generators, or systematic sampling. When selecting the sample items, the auditors often select extra items to be substituted for any voided, unused, or inapplicable items. An inapplicable item is one that would not be expected to have a particular attribute. For example, assume the auditors are testing a sample of cash disbursement transactions to determine that they are all supported with receiving reports. If a rent payment is selected, the item would be inapplicable, because it would not be expected to be supported with a receiving report.

## Test the Sample Items

When testing the sample items, an auditor examines each sample item for the attributes of interest. Each item will be classified as to whether it contains a deviation from the prescribed control. The auditor performing the test should also be alert for evidence of any unusual matters, such as evidence of fraud or related party transactions.

## Evaluate the Sample Results

After testing the sample items and summarizing the deviations from a prescribed control, the auditors evaluate the sample results. In evaluating the results, the auditors must consider not only the actual number of deviations observed, but also the nature of the deviations. The auditors' evaluation will include the following four steps:

1. *Determine the deviation rate.* Calculating the deviation rate in the sample involves dividing the number of observed deviations by the sample size.
2. *Determine the achieved upper deviation rate.* The auditors will use computer software or a table to determine the achieved upper deviation rate (also referred to as the

achieved upper precision limit). This deviation rate represents the maximum population deviation rate that the auditors can expect based on the results of the sample.

3. *Consider the qualitative aspects of the deviations.* In addition to considering the deviation rate in the sample, the auditors will consider the nature of the deviations and any implications for other phases of the audit. Deviations that result from intentional acts (fraud) are of much more concern than those that are due to a misunderstanding of instructions or carelessness.

4. *Reach an overall conclusion.* The auditors will combine the sample evidence with the results of other relevant tests of controls to determine if the combined results support the auditors' planned assessed level of control risk. If not, the auditors will increase the assessed level of control risk, which will result in an increase in the extent of the planned substantive tests.

*Tables to Evaluate Sample Results*

The tables presented in this chapter may be used to evaluate sample results in two different, but related, ways. The first approach is to use Figure 9.4. When the number of deviations found in the sample does not exceed the allowable number of deviations (the parenthetical number in Figure 9.4), the auditors conclude that the population's deviation rate does not exceed the tolerable deviation rate. Therefore, the results support the auditors' planned assessed level of control risk. On the other hand, when the number of deviations found in the sample exceeds the allowable number of deviations, the auditors conclude that the population's deviation rate exceeds the tolerable deviation rate and therefore they must generally increase their assessed level of control risk.

The second approach for evaluating sample results is to use Figure 9.5. This approach allows auditors to obtain a more precise conclusion—one which includes determining the achieved upper deviation rate. The achieved upper deviation rate is the maximum deviation rate that is supported by the sample results. When the achieved upper deviation rate is more than the tolerable deviation rate, the planned assessed level of control risk relating to the control is not supported.

**FIGURE 9.5**  **Statistical Sampling Results Evaluation Table for Tests of Controls: Achieved Upper Deviation Rate at 5 Percent Risk of Assessing Control Risk Too Low**

| Sample Size | Actual Number of Deviations Found | | | | | | | | | | |
|---|---|---|---|---|---|---|---|---|---|---|---|
| | 0 | 1 | 2 | 3 | 4 | 5 | 6 | 7 | 8 | 9 | 10 |
| 25 | 11.3 | 17.6 | * | * | * | * | * | * | * | * | * |
| 30 | 9.5 | 14.9 | 19.6 | * | * | * | * | * | * | * | * |
| 35 | 8.3 | 12.9 | 17.0 | * | * | * | * | * | * | * | * |
| 40 | 7.3 | 11.4 | 15.0 | 18.3 | * | * | * | * | * | * | * |
| 45 | 6.5 | 10.2 | 13.4 | 16.4 | 19.2 | * | * | * | * | * | * |
| 50 | 5.9 | 9.2 | 12.1 | 14.8 | 17.4 | 19.9 | * | * | * | * | * |
| 55 | 5.4 | 8.4 | 11.1 | 13.5 | 15.9 | 18.2 | * | * | * | * | * |
| 60 | 4.9 | 7.7 | 10.2 | 12.5 | 14.7 | 16.8 | 18.8 | * | * | * | * |
| 65 | 4.6 | 7.1 | 9.4 | 11.5 | 13.6 | 15.5 | 17.4 | 19.3 | * | * | * |
| 70 | 4.2 | 6.6 | 8.8 | 10.8 | 12.6 | 14.5 | 16.3 | 18.0 | 19.7 | * | * |
| 75 | 4.0 | 6.2 | 8.2 | 10.1 | 11.8 | 13.6 | 15.2 | 16.9 | 18.5 | 20.0 | * |
| 80 | 3.7 | 5.8 | 7.7 | 9.5 | 11.1 | 12.7 | 14.3 | 15.9 | 17.4 | 18.9 | * |
| 90 | 3.3 | 5.2 | 6.9 | 8.4 | 9.9 | 11.4 | 12.8 | 14.2 | 15.5 | 16.8 | 18.2 |
| 100 | 3.0 | 4.7 | 6.2 | 7.6 | 9.0 | 10.3 | 11.5 | 12.8 | 14.0 | 15.2 | 16.4 |
| 125 | 2.4 | 3.8 | 5.0 | 6.1 | 7.2 | 8.3 | 9.3 | 10.3 | 11.3 | 12.3 | 13.2 |
| 150 | 2.0 | 3.2 | 4.2 | 5.1 | 6.0 | 6.9 | 7.8 | 8.6 | 9.5 | 10.3 | 11.1 |
| 200 | 1.5 | 2.4 | 3.2 | 3.9 | 4.6 | 5.2 | 5.9 | 6.5 | 7.2 | 7.8 | 8.4 |

Note: This table presents upper limits as percentages. This table assumes a large population.
* Over 20 percent.
Source: AICPA, *Audit Guide, Audit Sampling* (New York, 2008).

To illustrate the second approach for evaluation of a sample, assume that two deviations are found in the sample of 51. As indicated previously, the auditors selected this sample with a specified risk of assessing control risk too low of 5 percent, a tolerable deviation rate of 9 percent, and an expected population deviation rate of 1 percent. A maximum of 1 deviation was allowable. Referring to Figure 9.5, we find that the exact sample size of 51 does not appear. When this happens, the auditors may interpolate; use more detailed tables, sometimes generated by a computer program; or use the largest sample size listed on the table that does not exceed the sample size actually selected. Using the latter approach, the auditors evaluate the results using a slightly smaller size of 50. Figure 9.5 indicates that when 2 deviations are found in a sample size of 50, the achieved upper deviation rate is 12.1 percent. This tells the auditors that, statistically, there is a 5 percent chance that the actual deviation rate is higher than 12.1 percent; but this exceeds the 9 percent tolerable deviation rate. The most likely effect of this sample result will be an increase in the assessed level of control risk, with a corresponding increase in the scope of substantive testing for the related financial statement assertions. Only when the upper deviation rate found in Figure 9.5 is less than or equal to the tolerable deviation rate would the sample results support the auditors' planned assessed level of control risk.

## Document the Sampling Procedure

Finally, the auditors will document the significant aspects of the prior nine steps in the working papers. This documentation should include an identification of the selected items.

## Detailed Illustration of Attributes Sampling

The following procedures for applying attributes sampling are based upon the use of the tables in Figures 9.4 and 9.5; however, only slight modifications of the approach are necessary if other tables are used.

1. *Determine the objective of the test.* Assume that the auditors wish to test the effectiveness of the client's control of matching receiving reports with purchase invoices as a step in authorizing payments for purchases of materials. They are interested in the clerical accuracy of the matching process and in determining whether the control that requires the matching of purchase invoices and receiving reports is operating effectively.

2. *Define the attributes and deviation conditions.* The auditors define the deviation conditions as any one or more of the following with respect to each invoice and the related receiving report:
   a. Any invoice not supported by a receiving document.
   b. Any invoice supported by a receiving document that is applicable to another invoice.
   c. Any difference between the invoice and the receiving document as to quantities received.

For this test, the only procedure required is inspection of the documents and matching of the receiving reports with invoices.

3. *Define the population to be sampled.* The client prepares a serially numbered voucher for every purchase of materials. The receiving report and purchase invoice are attached to each voucher. Therefore, the sampling unit for the test is an individual voucher. Since the test of controls is being performed during the interim period, the population to be tested consists of 3,653 vouchers for purchases of material during the first 10 months of the year under audit. If at any point the auditor determines that the physical representation of the population (the 3,653 vouchers) has omitted vouchers that should be included in the first 10 months, the auditors should also test those vouchers.

4. *Specify the risk of assessing control risk too low and the tolerable deviation rate.* The auditors realize that errors in matching receiving reports with purchase orders can affect the financial statements through overpayments to vendors and misstatements of purchases and accounts payable. They also plan to assess control risk at a low level for

the assertions of existence, occurrence, and valuation of purchases, inventories, and accounts payable. Based on these considerations, the auditors decide upon a tolerable deviation rate of 7 percent, with a 5 percent risk of assessing control risk too low.

5. *Estimate the expected population deviation rate.* In the audits of the previous three years, the auditors observed that exceptions for the type described above produced deviation rates of 1.2 percent, 1.3 percent, and 1.1 percent. Therefore, the auditors conservatively select an expected deviation rate of 1.5 percent.

6. *Determine the sample size.* Since the stipulated risk of assessing control risk too low is 5 percent, Figure 9.4 is applicable. At the intersection of the column for a tolerable deviation rate of 7 percent and the row for a 1.5 percent expected deviation rate, the sample size is found to be 66 items. The allowable number of deviations in the sample is 1.

7. *Select the sample.* Since the vouchers are serially numbered, the auditors decide to use a generalized audit software program to generate a list of random numbers to select the sample for testing.

8. *Test the sample items.* The auditors proceed to examine the vouchers and supporting documents for each of the types of deviations previously defined. As they perform the test, the auditors will be alert for any unusual matters, such as evidence of fraud.

9. *Evaluate the sample results.* In evaluating the sample results, the auditors consider not only the actual number of deviations observed, but also the nature of the deviations. We will discuss three possible sets of circumstances: (*a*) the actual number of deviations is equal to or less than the allowable number; (*b*) the actual number of deviations is more than the allowable number; and (*c*) one or more deviations observed contain evidence of a deliberate manipulation or circumvention of internal control.

First, assume that no deviation is identified. Recall that the allowable number of deviations from Figure 9.4 is 1. Because the number of deviations (here, none) does not exceed the allowable number, the auditors may conclude that there is less than a 5 percent risk that the population deviation rate is greater than 7 percent, the tolerable rate. In this case, the sample results support the auditors' planned assessed level of control risk. Alternatively, using the second approach and referring to Figure 9.5, for a sample size of 65 (the highest number still less than the actual sample size), the auditors find that when zero deviations are observed the achieved upper deviation rate is 4.6 percent. This rate supports the auditors' planned assessed level of control risk.

Next, assume that the number of deviations observed in the sample is 3, and none of the observed deviations indicate deliberate manipulation or circumvention of internal control. Using the first approach for evaluating results presented earlier, because this exceeds the allowable 1 deviation, the auditors simply conclude that the achieved upper deviation rate is greater than 7 percent. Or, if they wish to use the second approach for evaluating results, they may use Figure 9.5 to find that the achieved upper deviation rate is 11.5 percent. In light of these results, the auditors should increase the assessed level of control risk in this area and increase the extent of their substantive testing procedures (i.e., decrease detection risk). As a preliminary step to any modification of their audit program, the auditors should investigate the cause of the unexpectedly high deviation rate.

Finally, assume that one or more of the deviations discovered by the auditors indicates a deliberate circumvention of controls indicative of possible fraud. In such a circumstance, other auditing procedures become necessary. The auditors must evaluate the effect of the deviation on the financial statements and adopt auditing procedures that are specifically designed to detect the type of deviation observed. Indeed, the nature of the deviation may be more important than its rate of occurrence.

10. *Document the sampling procedures.* Finally, each of the nine prior steps, as well as the basis for overall conclusions, should be documented in the auditors' working papers. Figure 9.6 is an illustrative working paper that documents the results of this test of controls, as well as tests of other controls for the purchasing cycle.

FIGURE 9.6  **Documentation of the Results of Tests of Controls**

| SCANTECH, INC. | R-22 |
| Attributes Sampling Summary—Purchase Transactions | WEB |
| December 31, 20X2 | 11/23/X2 |

**Objectives of test:** (1) To test the operating effectiveness of the procedures for matching receiving reports with purchase invoices; (2) to test the operating effectiveness of the procedures for matching purchase orders with purchase invoices; (3) to test the operating effectiveness of the procedures for testing the clerical accuracy of purchase invoices.

**Population:** Voucher register entries for the first 10 months of the year.  Size: 3,653

**Sampling unit:** Individual vouchers.

**Random selection procedure:** Random number generator.

**Risk of assessing control risk too low:** 5 percent.

| | Planning Parameters: | | | Sample Results: | |
| | Tolerable Deviation Rate | Expected Deviation Rate | Sample Size | Number of Deviations | Achieved Maximum Rate |
| Attributes Tested: | | | | | |
|---|---|---|---|---|---|
| 1. Quantity and other data on receiving report agree with purchase invoice. | 7% | 1.5% | 66 | 1 | 7.1% |
| 2. Prices and other data on purchase order agree with purchase invoice. | 10% | 1% | 46 | 0 | 6.5% |
| 3. Clerical accuracy of purchase invoice has been verified. | 7% | 0% | 42 | 0 | 7.3% |

**Conclusion:** The results support the assessment of a low level of control risk for existence and valuation of purchases, inventory, and accounts payable.

## Other Statistical Attributes Sampling Approaches

*Discovery Sampling*

Discovery sampling is actually a modified case of attributes sampling. The purpose of a discovery sample is to detect at least one deviation, with a predetermined risk of assessing control risk too low if the deviation rate in the population is greater than the specified tolerable deviation rate. One important use of discovery sampling is to locate examples of a suspected fraud.

Although discovery sampling is designed to locate relatively rare items, it cannot locate a needle in a haystack. If an extremely small number of deviations exist within a population (e.g., 0.1 percent or less), no sample of reasonable size can provide adequate assurance that an example of the deviation will be encountered. Still, discovery sampling can (with a very high degree of confidence) ensure detection of deviations occurring at a rate as low as 0.3 to 1 percent.

Discovery sampling is used primarily to search for critical deviations. When a deviation is critical, such as evidence of fraud, any deviation rate may be intolerable. Consequently, if such deviation is discovered, the auditors may abandon their sampling procedures and undertake a thorough examination of the population. If no deviations are found in discovery sampling, the auditors may conclude (with the specified risk of assessing control risk too low) that the critical deviation does not occur to the extent of the tolerable deviation rate.

To use discovery sampling, the auditors must specify their desired risk of assessing control risk too low and the tolerable deviation rate for the test. The required sample size then may be determined by referring to an appropriate attributes sampling table, with the assumption that the expected deviation rate in the population is 0 percent.

To illustrate discovery sampling, assume that auditors have reason to suspect that someone has been preparing fraudulent purchase orders, receiving reports, and purchase invoices in order to generate cash disbursements for fictitious purchase transactions. In order to determine whether this has occurred, it is necessary to locate only one set of the fraudulent documents in the client's file of paid vouchers.

Assume the auditors desire a 5 percent risk that their sample will not bring to light a fraudulent voucher if the population contains 2 percent or more fraudulent items. Referring to Figure 9.4, the auditors find that a sample size of 149 is required for an expected population deviation rate of 0 percent and a tolerable deviation rate of 2 percent. Assuming that the auditors select and examine the 149 vouchers and no fraudulent vouchers are found, they may conclude that there is only a 5 percent risk that there are more than 2 percent fraudulent vouchers in the population.

*Sequential (Stop-or-Go) Sampling*

Another approach used in practice is **sequential (stop-or-go) sampling.** Under a sequential sampling plan, the audit sample is taken in several stages. The auditors start by examining a small sample. Then, based on the results of this initial sample, they decide whether to (1) assess control risk at the planned level, (2) assess control risk at a higher level than planned, or (3) examine additional sample items to get more information. If the sample results do not provide enough information to make a clear-cut decision about internal control, the auditors examine additional items and repeat the decision process until the tables being used indicate that a decision as to the assessed level of control risk can be made.

The primary advantage of a sequential approach is that for very low population deviation rates smaller sample sizes may be required as compared to the fixed-sized sample plans. Disadvantages of sequential approaches include the fact that sample sizes may be larger for populations with moderate deviation rates and the process of drawing samples at several stages may not be as efficient.

## Nonstatistical Attributes Sampling

The major differences between statistical and nonstatistical sampling in attributes sampling are the steps for determining sample size and evaluating sample results. As is the case with statistical sampling, auditors who use nonstatistical sampling need to consider the risk of assessing control risk too low and the tolerable deviation rate when determining the required sample size. But these factors need not be quantified. In evaluating results, the auditors should compare the deviation rate of the sample to the tolerable deviation rate. If the sample size was appropriate and the sample deviation rate is somewhat lower than the tolerable deviation rate, the auditors can generally conclude that the risk of assessing control risk too low is at an acceptable level. As the sample deviation rate gets closer to the tolerable deviation rate, it becomes less and less likely that the population's deviation rate is lower than the tolerable level. The auditors must use their professional judgment to determine the point at which the assessed level of control risk should be increased above the planned level.

# Audit Sampling for Substantive Procedures

**LO6**

Plan, perform, and evaluate samples for substantive procedures using mean-per-unit sampling.

Substantive procedures are designed to detect misstatements, due to both errors and fraud, that may exist in the financial statements. Accordingly, the sampling plans that are used for substantive procedures are designed to estimate the dollar amount of misstatement in a particular account balance. Based on the sample results, the auditors then conclude

FIGURE 9.7
Sampling Risk for
Substantive Procedures

| The Substantive Procedure Sample Indicates: | The Population Actually Is: | |
|---|---|---|
| | **Not Materially Misstated** | **Materially Misstated** |
| **The Population Is Not Materially Misstated** | Correct decision | Incorrect decision (risk of incorrect acceptance) |
| **The Population Is Materially Misstated** | Incorrect decision (risk of incorrect rejection) | Correct decision |

whether there is an unacceptably high risk of material misstatement in the balance. The actual steps involved may be summarized as:

1. Determine the objective of the substantive procedure.
2. Define the population and sampling unit.
3. Choose an audit sampling technique.
4. Determine the sample size.
5. Select the sample.
6. Test the sample items.
7. Evaluate the sample results.
8. Document the sampling procedure.

Statistical procedures typically used for substantive tests include classical variables and probability-proportional-to-size sampling plans. This chapter emphasizes classical variables plans, especially the mean-per-unit estimation method. Appendix 9A presents an overview of the probability-proportional-to-size method.

## Sampling Risk for Substantive Procedures

Similar to sampling risk for tests of controls, there are two aspects of sampling risk for substantive procedures, including:

1. *The risk of incorrect rejection (alpha risk) of an account.* This is the possibility that sample results will indicate that an account balance is materially misstated when, in fact, it is not misstated.
2. *The risk of incorrect acceptance (beta risk) of an account.* This is the possibility that sample results will indicate that an account balance is not materially misstated when, in fact, it is materially misstated.

The nature of these risks parallels the sampling risks of tests of controls. If the auditors make the first type of error and incorrectly reject an account balance, their audit will lack efficiency since they will perform additional audit procedures that will eventually reveal that the account is not materially misstated. Thus, the risk of incorrect rejection ordinarily does not relate to the effectiveness of the audit.[5]

If the auditors make the second type of error, incorrect acceptance, the effectiveness of the audit is compromised. Therefore, the risk of incorrect acceptance is of primary concern to auditors; failure to detect a material misstatement may lead to accusations of negligence and to extensive legal liability. Figure 9.7 illustrates both aspects of sampling risk for substantive procedures.

## Classical Variables Sampling

Classical **variables sampling** plans enable auditors to estimate a numerical quantity, such as the dollar amount of an account balance. This makes these techniques particularly useful for performing substantive procedures. Classical variables sampling methods include *mean-per-unit estimation, ratio estimation,* and *difference estimation.*

---

[5] Audit effectiveness will be negatively affected if incorrect rejection leads to client recording of an improper journal entry to adjust the account to the misstated amount suggested by the auditors' substantive procedures.

## Mean-per-Unit Estimation

Mean-per-unit estimation enables auditors to estimate the mean audited value of the items in a population, with specified sampling risk and allowance for sampling risk (precision), by determining the mean audited value of the items in a sample. An estimate of the total audited value of the population is obtained by multiplying the sample **mean** (the average audited value in the sample) times the number of items in the population. The *projected misstatement* (the most likely amount of misstatement in the population) may then be calculated as the difference between this estimated total audited value and the client's book value. The assumption underlying mean-per-unit estimation is that a sample's mean audited value will, for a certain sampling risk and allowance for sampling risk, represent the true audited mean of the population.

## Controlling Sampling Risk

The risks of incorrect acceptance and incorrect rejection may be controlled independently of one another. For example, auditors may design a sample that limits both risks to 10 percent, or they may hold the **risk of incorrect acceptance** to 5 percent while allowing the **risk of incorrect rejection** to rise to 40 percent or more. In establishing the planned level of the risk of incorrect acceptance, auditors must consider the extent of the evidence that must be obtained from the substantive procedure. This is determined by the auditors' assessments of inherent risk and control risk for the assertions being tested, and the extent of the evidence obtained from any other substantive tests of those assertions. Appendix 9B describes this process in greater detail.

The risk of incorrect rejection also must be established. In stipulating this risk the auditors should consider the time and other costs involved in performing additional audit procedures when the sample results erroneously indicate that a correct book balance is materially misstated.

In mean-per-unit estimation, as was the case with attributes sampling, the allowance for sampling risk is used to control sampling risk. The appropriate planned allowance for sampling risk may be determined from the following formula.

$$\text{Planned allowance for sampling risk} = \frac{\text{Tolerable misstatement}}{1 + \dfrac{\text{Incorrect acceptance coefficient}}{\text{Incorrect rejection coefficient}}}$$

The *tolerable misstatement*, as described in Chapter 6, is materiality for the particular audit procedure. Risk coefficients from a table such as Figure 9.8, not the risks themselves, are inserted into the formula. Notice that the risks and coefficients vary inversely—that is, a *decreased* risk is consistent with an *increased* coefficient.

## Determination of Sample Size

The factors directly included in the sample size formula for mean-per-unit estimation are (1) the population size, (2) the planned risk of incorrect rejection, (3) the estimated variability (**standard deviation**) among item values in the population, and (4) the planned

**FIGURE 9.8**
**Risk Coefficients**

| Acceptable Level of Risk | Incorrect Acceptance Coefficient | Incorrect Rejection Coefficient |
|---|---|---|
| 1.0% | 2.33 | 2.58 |
| 4.6 | 1.68 | 2.00 |
| 5.0 | 1.64 | 1.96 |
| 10.0 | 1.28 | 1.64 |
| 15.0 | 1.04 | 1.44 |
| 20.0 | 0.84 | 1.28 |
| 25.0 | 0.67 | 1.15 |
| 30.0 | 0.52 | 1.04 |
| 40.0 | 0.25 | 0.84 |
| 50.0 | 0.00 | 0.67 |

## FIGURE 9.9 Factors Affecting Sample Size for Substantive Procedures

| Factor | Change in Factor | Effect on Required Sample Size |
|---|---|---|
| **Auditors' Requirements:** | | |
| Risk of incorrect rejection | Increase | Decrease |
| Risk of incorrect acceptance | Increase | Decrease |
| Tolerable misstatement | Increase | Decrease |
| **Population Characteristics:** | | |
| Population size | Increase | Increase (if population is small) |
| Standard deviation (if classical variables sampling is used) | Increase | Increase |
| Expected misstatement (if probability-proportional-to-size sampling is used) | Increase | Increase |

allowance for sampling risk. The relationship of these factors to the required sample size is expressed by the following formula:[6]

$$\text{Sample size} = \left(\frac{\text{Population size} \times \text{Incorrect rejection coefficient} \times \text{Estimated standard deviation}}{\text{Planned allowance for sampling risk}}\right)^2$$

We have already described how most of the factors in this formula are determined. The auditors may obtain an estimate of the population's standard deviation of audited values by calculating the standard deviation of the book values of the population, or by using the standard deviation of the audited values obtained in the previous year's audit. Alternatively, auditors may obtain an estimate of the standard deviation of the audited values by taking a pilot sample of approximately 50 items.[7] Generalized audit software packages include routines designed to estimate the standard deviation of the book values of a population either from a pilot sample or from the population book values. Figure 9.9 summarizes the effect of the standard deviation as well as the other factors on the required sample size.

## Evaluation of Sample Results

Recall that the auditors determined sample size based on the planned sampling risks and on an estimate of the standard deviation of the population. When the auditors' estimate of the population's standard deviation is exactly the same as that found in the sample, the planned allowance for sampling risk may be used for evaluation purposes. However, this is seldom the case. The auditors' estimate of the population standard deviation usually differs from that of the subsequent sample. When this occurs, the sample taken does not control both risks at their planned levels because the auditors have underestimated or overestimated the variability of the population in computing the required sample size.

[6] This formula is based upon an infinite population. The effect on sample size when the population is finite but of significant size is small. Symbolically, this formula may be stated as:

$$n = \left(\frac{N \times U_r \times SD}{A}\right)^2$$

where $n$ = sample size, $N$ = population size, $U_r$ = incorrect rejection coefficient, $SD$ = estimated standard deviation, and $A$ = planned allowance for sampling risk.

[7] An estimate of the standard deviation may be made from a sample by taking the square root of the following quotient: the sum of the squares of the deviation of each sample item value from the sample mean, divided by one less than the number of items in the sample. Symbolically, the formula for estimating the standard deviation is:

$$\sqrt{\frac{\Sigma(x - \bar{x})^2}{n - 1}}$$

Although there are various ways of adjusting the allowance for sampling risk, one that maintains the risk of incorrect acceptance at its planned level is described below:

$$\begin{array}{c} \text{Adjusted} \\ \text{allowance for} \\ \text{sampling risk} \end{array} = \begin{array}{c} \text{Tolerable} \\ \text{misstatement} \end{array} - \frac{\left( \begin{array}{ccc} & \text{Incorrect} & \text{Sample} \\ \text{Population size} \times & \text{acceptance} \times & \text{standard} \\ & \text{coefficient} & \text{deviation} \end{array} \right)}{\sqrt{\text{Sample size}}}$$

Once the auditors calculate the adjusted allowance for sampling risk, the client's book value is accepted or rejected based on whether it falls within the interval constructed by the audited sample mean ± the adjusted allowance for sampling risk. If the book value falls within the interval, the sample results support the conclusion that the account balance is materially correct. On the other hand, if the client's book value does not fall within the interval, the sample results indicate that there is too great a risk that the account balance is materially misstated. In this situation, either the client or the auditors will ordinarily analyze the account further to identify more misstatements. In either case, the expansion of procedures will provide more evidence as to the need for and amount of any required adjustment.

## Illustration of Mean-per-Unit Estimation

1. *Determine the objective of the test.* Assume that the auditors wish to test the existence and gross valuation of recorded accounts receivable of a small public utility client. They wish to test the book value of accounts receivable by confirming a sample of the accounts through direct correspondence with the customers.

2. *Define the population and sampling unit.* The client's records have 100,000 accounts recorded at a total book value of $6,250,000. The auditors believe that the customers will be able to confirm the total outstanding account balance. Therefore, the account balance is used as the sampling unit instead of the individual transactions making up the balance. Figure 9.10 summarizes the accounts.

**FIGURE 9.10**
**Population of Accounts Receivable**

| ABC COMPANY<br>Accounts Receivable<br>December 31, 20X3 | | |
| --- | --- | --- |
| **Account Number** | **Account Name** | **Book Value** |
| 000,001 | Aaron, William | $        65.55 |
| 000,002 | Adams, James | 66.44 |
| 000,003 | Adams, Susan | 82.42 |
| 000,004 | Ahohn, Jennifer | 55.14 |
| 000,005 | Ahrons, Kenneth | 44.96 |
| ⋮ | ⋮ | ⋮ |
| 003,000 | Carhon, Sandra | 65.00 |
| ⋮ | ⋮ | ⋮ |
| 099,999 | Zenit, Darlene | 82.50 |
| 100,000 | Zyen, Chem | 99.20 |
| Total book value | | $6,250,000.00 |
| Mean account value* | | $        62.50 |

* $6,250,000/100,000.

3. *Choose an audit sampling technique.* The auditors have decided to use the mean-per-unit technique.

4. *Determine the sample size.* To calculate the required sample size, the auditors must determine (*a*) the tolerable misstatement for the test, (*b*) the planned levels of sampling risk (the risks of incorrect acceptance and rejection), (*c*) the estimate of the population standard deviation, and (*d*) the population size.

Based on their consideration of internal control, the auditors believe that all accounts are included in the 100,000 accounts in the client's subsidiary ledger (the physical representation of the population). In view of the amount of performance materiality for accounts receivable, the auditors assess the tolerable misstatement to be $364,000. Since internal control over existence and valuation of accounts receivable is very weak, the auditors assess control risk at the maximum level, that is, 100 percent. In addition, they assess inherent risk at 100 percent and plan to perform only very limited other substantive tests of these assertions. Therefore, the auditors decide on a 5 percent risk of incorrect acceptance. Based on a consideration of the costs of performing additional procedures when an account is improperly rejected, a 4.6 percent risk of incorrect rejection is planned by the auditors. From this information and by using risk coefficients obtained from Figure 9.8, the planned allowance for sampling risk may be calculated as follows:

$$\text{Planned allowance for sampling risk} = \frac{\text{Tolerable misstatement}}{1 + \dfrac{\text{Incorrect acceptance coefficient}}{\text{Incorrect rejection coefficient}}}$$

$$= \frac{\$364{,}000}{1 + \dfrac{1.64}{2.00}}$$

$$= \$200{,}000$$

To estimate the standard deviation of the population, the auditors use a generalized audit software program to calculate the standard deviation of the recorded book values of the individual customers' accounts. The result is $15.

Using the sample-size formula, the required sample size may now be computed as follows:

$$\text{Sample size} = \left( \frac{\text{Population size} \times \begin{array}{c}\text{Incorrect}\\ \text{rejection}\\ \text{coefficient}\end{array} \times \begin{array}{c}\text{Estimated}\\ \text{standard}\\ \text{deviation}\end{array}}{\text{Planned allowance for sampling risk}} \right)^{2}$$

$$= \left( \frac{100{,}000 \times 2.00 \times \$15}{\$200{,}000} \right)^{2} = \left( \frac{\$3{,}000{,}000}{\$200{,}000} \right)^{2}$$

$$= 225 \text{ accounts}$$

5. *Select the sample.* The client's accounts receivable are from residential customers and do not vary greatly in size. For this reason, the auditors decide to use a random number table to select an unstratified random sample.

6. *Test the sample items.* The auditors send the confirmations and perform additional procedures as appropriate.

7. *Evaluate the sample results.* Confirmation of the 225 accounts, as summarized in Figure 9.11, results in a sample with a mean audited value of $61 per account. Figure 9.11 also indicates that the mean book value of the 225 accounts in the sample was $63. Notice

**FIGURE 9.11**

**Auditors' Sample of Accounts Receivable**

ABC COMPANY
Sample of Accounts Receivable
December 31, 20X3

| Sample Item Number | Account Number | Account Name | Book Value | Audited Value | Difference |
|---|---|---|---|---|---|
| 001 | 000,002 | Adams, James | $ 66.44 | $ 66.44 | $ 0.00 |
| 002 | 000,005 | Ahrons, Kenneth | 44.96 | 43.00 | 1.96 |
| 003 | 001,100 | Banner, Jane | 92.16 | 92.16 | 0.00 |
| 004 | 002,200 | Boynton, Willis | 72.12 | 68.50 | 3.62 |
| 005 | 003,000 | Carhon, Sandra | 65.00 | 65.00 | 0.00 |
| : | : | : | : | : | : |
| : | : | : | : | : | : |
| : | : | : | : | : | : |
| 224 | 093,212 | Yelbow, Sharlene | 82.50 | 82.50 | 0.00 |
| 225 | 100,000 | Zyen, Chem | 99.20 | 92.00 | 7.20 |
| Total value (sample) | | | $14,175.00 | $13,725.00 | $450.00 |
| Mean values (total value/225) | | | $63.00 | $61.00 | $2.00 |

that this $63 mean sample book value differs somewhat from the mean book value of the entire population, $62.50, in Figure 9.10. This difference of $0.50 per account is due to chance and is not directly used in the mean-per-unit analysis.

As a first case, assume that the confirmation results also indicate a standard deviation of the sample's audited values of $15. Since the sample's standard deviation equals that used in planning, the adjusted allowance for sampling risk equals the planned allowance of $200,000. In this case, the auditors' estimate of the total value of the population is $6,100,000, and the acceptance interval for the sample result is that amount plus or minus the allowance for sampling risk of $200,000, calculated as follows:

$$\text{Estimated total audited value} = \text{Mean audited value} \times \text{Number of accounts}$$
$$= \$61 \times 100,000 \text{ accounts} = \$6,100,000$$

$$\text{Acceptance interval} = \text{Estimated total audited value} \pm \text{Allowance for sampling risk}$$
$$= \$6,100,000 \pm \$200,000$$
$$= [\$5,900,000 \text{ } to \text{ } \$6,300,000]$$

Because the client's book value of $6,250,000 falls within this acceptance interval, the sample results indicate that the client's valuation of accounts receivable is not materially misstated. However, the sample results indicate a *projected misstatement* of $150,000, calculated as follows:

$$\text{Projected misstatement} = \text{Estimated total audited value} - \text{Book value of population}$$
$$= \$6,100,000 - \$6,250,000$$
$$= \$150,000 \text{ overstatement}$$

This projected misstatement will be considered when the auditors are analyzing the total amount of potential misstatement in the financial statements. Also, the auditors may suggest that the client correct the accounts that their test revealed to be misstated, even though the misstatements are less than the tolerable misstatement amount.

How do the auditors evaluate the results if the sample's standard deviation differs from the estimate? They may use the formula presented earlier (page 351) to calculate an adjusted allowance for sampling risk. For example, if the standard deviation of the

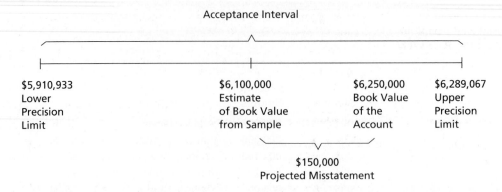

**FIGURE 9.12**
**Acceptance Interval for Substantive Procedure**

Acceptance Interval

| $5,910,933 Lower Precision Limit | $6,100,000 Estimate of Book Value from Sample | $6,250,000 Book Value of the Account | $6,289,067 Upper Precision Limit |

$150,000
Projected Misstatement

sample's audited values had instead been equal to $16, the adjusted allowance for sampling risk may be calculated as follows:

$$\begin{matrix}\text{Adjusted}\\\text{allowance for}\\\text{sampling risk}\end{matrix} = \begin{matrix}\text{Tolerable}\\\text{misstatement}\end{matrix} - \cfrac{\left(\text{Population size} \times \begin{matrix}\text{Incorrect}\\\text{acceptance}\\\text{coefficient}\end{matrix} \times \begin{matrix}\text{Sample}\\\text{standard}\\\text{deviation}\end{matrix}\right)}{\sqrt{\text{Sample size}}}$$

$$= \$364,000 - \frac{(100,000 \times 1.64 \times \$16)}{\sqrt{225}}$$

$$= \$189,067$$

Thus, the acceptance interval would be constructed as $6,100,000 ± $189,067 ($5,910,933 to $6,289,067). As illustrated by Figure 9.12, the client's book value ($6,250,000) also falls within this interval. Therefore, the sample results still indicate that the account does not contain a material misstatement.

As in other types of sampling, the auditors should consider the qualitative aspects of any misstatements found in their sample. "What caused the misstatements?" "Do any of the misstatements indicate fraud?" and "What are the implications of the misstatements for other audit areas?" are questions the auditors would attempt to answer in their qualitative evaluation of the results.

8. *Document the sampling procedures.* Each of the prior seven steps, as well as the basis for overall conclusions, should be documented in the auditors' working papers. This documentation should include an identification of the items tested.

## Difference and Ratio Estimation

Mean-per-unit estimation uses the mean audited value of the sample as the basis for estimating the projected misstatement and total audited value of a population. Two other options are difference and ratio estimation. Although closely related, difference estimation and ratio estimation are two distinct sampling plans; each is appropriate under slightly different circumstances.

In applying difference estimation, the auditors use a sample to estimate the average difference between the audited value and book value of items in a population. The average difference is estimated by dividing the net misstatement in the sample by the number of items in the sample.[8] The projected misstatement is determined by multiplying

---

[8] Symbolically, the estimated average difference is computed as follows:

$$\hat{d} = \frac{1}{n}\sum_{j=1}^{n}(a_j - b_j)$$

Where $\hat{d}$ (pronounced *d* caret) represents the estimated average difference between audited value ($a_j$) and book value ($b_j$) of each sample item.

the estimated average difference by the number of items in the population. This may be viewed as:

$$\text{Projected misstatement} = \left[\frac{\text{Sample net misstatement}}{\text{Sample items}}\right] \times \text{Population items}$$

The estimated total audited value is equal to the book value of the account plus or minus the projected misstatement, depending upon whether the misstatement is an understatement or an overstatement.

In ratio estimation, the auditors use a sample to estimate the ratio of the misstatement in a sample to its book value and project it to the entire population.[9] The ratio of misstatements is simply the sample net misstatement divided by the book value of the items in the sample. An estimate of the projected misstatement is obtained by multiplying this estimated ratio by the total population book value, as illustrated below:

$$\text{Projected misstatement} = \left[\frac{\text{Sample net misstatement}}{\text{Book value of sample}}\right] \times \text{Population book value}$$

Alternatively, identical results are obtained by using the average misstatement in the sample, divided by the average book value in the sample, and multiplying times the total population book value, as illustrated below:

$$\text{Projected misstatement} = \left[\frac{\text{Sample average misstatement}}{\text{Sample average book value}}\right] \times \text{Population book value}$$

The estimated total audited value equals the book value of the account plus or minus the projected misstatement, depending upon whether the misstatement is an understatement or an overstatement.

### Use of Difference and Ratio Estimation

The use of difference and ratio estimation techniques requires that (1) each population item has a book value, (2) an audited value may be determined for each sample item, and (3) differences between audited and book values (misstatements) are relatively frequent. If the occurrence rate of misstatements is very low, a prohibitively large sample is required to disclose a representative number of misstatements. When these requirements are met, ratio estimation or difference estimation is often more efficient than mean-per-unit estimation.

Difference estimation is most appropriate when the size of misstatements does not vary significantly in comparison to book value. This might be the case when errors are occurring randomly, independently of account size.

Ratio estimation is preferred when the size of misstatements is nearly proportional to the book values of the items. That is, it is appropriate when larger accounts have large misstatements and smaller accounts have small misstatements. For example, this might often be the case for receivables—small accounts might be expected to have small misstatements in dollar terms and large accounts to have large misstatements in dollar terms.

**Illustration of Difference and Ratio Estimation**

The information presented in Figures 9.10 and 9.11 may be used to illustrate the use of difference and ratio estimation techniques. Recall that the population consists of 100,000 accounts with an aggregate book value of $6,250,000; Figure 9.11 indicates that the total book and audited values of the sample are, respectively, $14,175 and $13,725. The

---

[9] Symbolically, this process is expressed:

$$\hat{R} = \frac{\sum (a_j - b_j)}{\sum b_j}$$

where $\hat{R}$ represents the estimated ratio of misstatement to book value, $a_j$ represents the audited value of each sample item, and $b_j$ represents the book value of each sample item.

auditors calculate the required sample size, randomly select the accounts to be sampled, and apply auditing procedures to determine the correct account balances. In actuality, differences in the sample size formulas[10] would cause the sample size to differ from that obtained using the mean-per-unit method, but in this illustration we will continue to assume a sample size of 225, as summarized in Figure 9.11.

*Difference Estimation*

If difference estimation is used, the auditors would estimate the average difference per item to be a $2 overstatement ($450 ÷ 225 items). Multiplying the $2 by the 100,000 accounts in the population indicates that the projected misstatement for accounts receivable is a $200,000 overstatement, as calculated below:

$$\text{Projected misstatement} = \left[\frac{\text{Sample net misstatement}}{\text{Sample items}}\right] \times \text{Population items}$$

$$= \frac{\$450}{225} \times 100,000$$

$$= \$2 \times 100,000$$

$$= \$200,000$$

The estimated total audited value of the account is calculated as follows:

$$\text{Estimated total audited value} = \text{Population book value} - \text{Projected overstatement}$$

$$= \$6,250,000 - \$200,000$$

$$= \$6,050,000$$

*Ratio Estimation*

For ratio estimation, the auditors would estimate the projected misstatement using the following formula:

$$\text{Projected misstatement} = \left[\frac{\text{Sample net misstatement}}{\text{Book value of sample}}\right] \times \text{Population book value}$$

$$= \left[\frac{\$450}{\$14,175}\right] \times \$6,250,000 = \$198,413$$

Alternatively, averages may be used as follows:

$$\text{Projected misstatement} = \left[\frac{\text{Sample average misstatement}}{\text{Sample average book value}}\right] \times \text{Population book value}$$

$$= \left[\frac{\$2}{\$63}\right] \times \$6,250,000 = \$198,413$$

Because the projected misstatement indicates an overstatement, this difference is subtracted from the book value to obtain the estimated total audited value as follows:

$$\text{Estimated total audited value} = \text{Population book value} - \text{Projected overstatement}$$

$$= \$6,250,000 - \$198,413$$

$$= \$6,051,587$$

If the projected misstatement had been an understatement, the amount would have been added to the population book value.

Formulas are available for both difference and ratio estimation to calculate an adjusted allowance for sampling risk to control sampling risk in a manner similar to the

[10] The major differences in the formulas are that the standard deviations used would be those for the ratios and differences.

mean-per-unit method. Since we do not present them, we do not take the analysis further than the calculation of projected misstatement and the estimated total audited value.

# Nonstatistical Sampling for Substantive Procedures

**LO8**

Plan, perform, and evaluate samples for substantive procedures using nonstatistical methods.

The major differences between statistical and nonstatistical sampling in substantive testing are in the procedures used to determine the sample size and evaluate the sample results. In using nonstatistical sampling, the auditors may decide not to quantify the factors used to arrive at the sample size, although they will consider the relationships that are summarized in Figure 9.9. In evaluating the sample results, the auditors also project the misstatements found in the sample to the population and consider sampling risk, but the level of risk is not quantified. While the auditors may use unassisted judgment for determining the sample size and for evaluating the sample results, many CPA firms have adopted structured approaches to nonstatistical sampling that are based on statistical methods. This increases the consistency of sampling judgments that are made by various auditors throughout the firm.

## Illustration of Nonstatistical Sampling

The following example illustrates the use of a structured nonstatistical sampling plan.

1. *Determine the objective of the procedures.* Assume that the auditors are performing a test of the valuation of inventory by testing the pricing of a sample of inventory items by reference to vendors' invoices. The inventory consists of 2,000 items with a book value of $3,000,000.
2. *Define the population and sampling unit.* The physical representation of the population consists of a listing of the inventory items on hand at year-end, and the auditors have determined that the sampling unit will be each individual product.
3. *Choose the audit sampling technique.* The auditors have decided to use a structured approach to nonstatistical sampling.
4. *Determine the sample size.* To determine the required sample size, the auditors will use the following formula:

$$\text{Sample size} = \left\lceil \frac{\text{Population book value} \times \text{Reliability factor}}{\text{Tolerable misstatement}} \right\rceil$$

The **reliability** factor for the formula is selected from a table such as the one that is illustrated by Figure 9.13. It is based on the auditors' combined assessment of inherent and control risk and the auditors' assessment of the risk that other substantive procedures will fail to detect a material misstatement of the assertions. Both risks are assessed on qualitative scales from maximum risk (100 percent) to low risk.

In our example, assume that the auditors have assessed the combination of inherent and control risk at slightly below the maximum. They have also performed analytical procedures on the inventory account that the auditors believe have a moderate risk

**FIGURE 9.13**
**Reliability Factors for Nonstatistical Sampling Plan**

| Combined Assessment of Inherent and Control Risk | Risk that Other Substantive Procedures (e.g., Analytical Procedures) Will Fail to Detect a Material Misstatement | | |
|---|---|---|---|
| | **Maximum** | **Moderate** | **Low** |
| Maximum | 3.0 | 2.3 | 1.9 |
| Slightly below maximum | 2.7 | 2.0 | 1.6 |
| Moderate | 2.3 | 1.6 | 1.2 |
| Low | 1.9 | 1.2 | 1.0 |

Note: This table is applicable when the auditors expect few misstatements in the population.

of not detecting a material misstatement in the valuation of the inventory account. Using these assessments of risk, the auditors obtain a reliability factor of 2.0 using Figure 9.13. If the auditors have decided that $100,000 is the amount of tolerable misstatement for the test, the sample size would be calculated as follows:

$$\text{Sample size} = \left[ \frac{\text{Population book value} \times \text{Reliability factor}}{\text{Tolerable misstatement}} \right]$$

$$= \left[ \frac{\$3,000,000 \times 2.0}{\$100,000} \right]$$

$$= 60 \text{ items}$$

5. *Select the sample.* Even though nonstatistical sampling is being used, the auditors generally select the sample on a stratified basis.

6. *Test the sample items.* The auditors examine vendors' invoices supporting the price of each product selected for testing. Assume that the auditors find two products that were priced at improper prices, resulting in a total overstatement of the account of $6,600. In addition, the total book value of the sample is calculated to be $1,100,000.

7. *Evaluate the sample results.* In evaluating the sample results, the auditors will begin by projecting the misstatements found in the sample to the population. A number of methods may be used. However, the auditors typically use the ratio or difference method illustrated on pages 354–357. In this example, the auditors decide to use the ratio method of projecting the misstatement, as illustrated below:

$$\text{Projected misstatement} = \left[ \frac{\text{Sample net misstatement}}{\text{Book value of sample}} \right] \times \text{Population book value}$$

$$= \left[ \frac{\$6,600}{\$1,100,000} \right] \times \$3,000,000$$

$$= \$18,000$$

After calculating the projected amount of misstatement in the population, the auditors will then compare that amount with the amount of tolerable misstatement. In this situation, the auditors compare $18,000 with $100,000, and use professional judgment to evaluate whether there is a sufficiently low risk of material misstatement of the account. Since the projected misstatement is only 18 percent ($18,000 ÷ $100,000) of tolerable misstatement, the auditors would likely conclude that the account balance is acceptable. As the amount of projected misstatement gets closer to the amount of tolerable misstatement for the account, the auditors are more likely to conclude that the risk of material misstatement is too high.[11] When the auditors conclude that the risk of misstatement is high, they will not accept the client's book balance as being materially correct and will either convince the client to adjust the book value or perform additional audit tests on the population.

The auditors will also perform a qualitative evaluation of the misstatements found in the population to determine if there are implications for other aspects of the audit. Intentional misstatements would generally have greater implications for the audit than clerical errors.

8. *Document the sampling procedures.* The nonstatistical sampling procedures described on pages 357–358 would be documented in a manner similar to that used for statistical sampling plans.

---

[11] Some references suggest that when the projected misstatement exceeds one-third of the tolerable misstatement, the sampling risk is becoming "too high."

## Chapter Summary

This chapter presented the concepts and techniques used by auditors to perform audit sampling. To summarize:

1. Audit sampling is defined as applying an audit procedure to less than 100 percent of the items in a population to make some conclusion about that population.

2. Auditors may use statistical or nonstatistical sampling to perform tests of controls or substantive procedures. Statistical sampling allows the auditors to measure and control sampling risk. Sampling risk is the risk that the auditors will make an incorrect conclusion from the sample results because the sample is not representative of the population.

3. The major type of statistical sampling plan for tests of controls is attributes sampling, which can provide the auditors with an estimate of the extent of the deviations from a prescribed internal control policy or procedure.

4. The two aspects of sampling risk for tests of controls include the risk of assessing control risk too high, which relates to the efficiency of the audit, and the risk of assessing control risk too low, which is critical because it relates to the effectiveness of the audit.

5. The major factors that affect the required sample size for an attributes sample are the risk of assessing control risk too low, the tolerable deviation rate, and the expected deviation rate in the population.

6. The two aspects of sampling risk for substantive procedures include the risk of incorrect rejection and the risk of incorrect acceptance. The risk of incorrect acceptance is the critical risk, because if the auditors accept a materially misstated account balance, they may issue an inappropriate audit opinion.

7. When a classical variables sampling plan is used, the required sample size is determined by the risk of incorrect acceptance, the risk of incorrect rejection, the amount of tolerable misstatement for the test, and the standard deviation of the items in the account.

8. Classical variables sampling methods include mean-per-unit estimation, difference estimation, and ratio estimation.

9. In evaluating the results of a classical variables sampling plan, the auditors compute an acceptance interval; if the client's book value falls within the interval, it is accepted as being materially correct. Otherwise, the auditors generally must perform additional testing to determine whether the client's balance is actually misstated or the sample was not representative.

10. Many CPA firms use structured approaches to nonstatistical sampling for substantive procedures. Such approaches increase the consistency of sampling decisions by various staff members within the firms.

## Key Terms Introduced or Emphasized in Chapter 9

**Allowance for sampling risk (ASR) (337)**   Also referred to as *precision,* an interval around the sample results in which the true population characteristic is expected to lie.

**Attributes sampling (336)**   A sampling plan enabling the auditors to estimate the rate of deviation (occurrence) in a population.

**Confidence level (339)**   In attributes sampling, the complement of the risk of assessing control risk too low. In variables sampling, the complement of the risk of incorrect acceptance. Thus, if the risk of assessing control risk too low (or of incorrect acceptance) is .05, the confidence level is .95.

**Deviation rate (338)**   A defined rate of departure from prescribed controls. Also referred to as *occurrence rate* or *exception rate.*

**Difference estimation (336)**   A sampling plan that uses the difference between the audited (correct) values and book values of items in a sample to calculate the estimated total audited value of the population. Difference estimation is used in lieu of ratio estimation when the differences are not nearly proportional to book values.

**Discovery sampling (336)** A sampling plan for locating at least 1 deviation, providing that the deviation occurs in the population with a specified frequency.

**Dual-purpose test (337)** A test designed to test a control and to substantiate the dollar amount of an account using the same sample.

**Expected population deviation rate (337)** An advance estimate of a deviation rate. This estimate is necessary for determining the required sample size in an attributes sampling plan.

**Mean (349)** The average item value, computed by dividing total value by the number of items composing total value.

**Mean-per-unit estimation (336)** A classical variables sampling plan enabling the auditors to estimate the average dollar value (or other variable) of items in a population by determining the average value of items in a sample.

**Nonsampling risk (332)** The aspects of audit risk not due to sampling. This risk normally relates to "human" rather than "statistical" errors.

**Physical representation of the population (333)** The population from which the auditors sample. The physical representation of the population differs from the actual population when it does not include items that exist in the actual population (e.g., the auditors sample from a trial balance of receivables which may or may not include all actual receivables).

**Population (332)** The entire field of items from which a sample might be drawn.

**Precision (337)** See *allowance for sampling risk*.

**Probability-proportional-to-size (PPS) sampling (336)** A variables estimation procedure that uses attributes theory to express a conclusion in monetary (dollar) amounts.

**Projected misstatement (332)** An estimate of the most likely amount of monetary misstatement in a population.

**Random selection (333)** Selecting items from a population in a manner in which every item has an equal chance of being included in the sample.

**Ratio estimation (336)** A sampling plan that uses the ratio of audited (correct) values to book values of items in the sample to calculate the estimated total audited value of the population. Ratio estimation is used in lieu of difference estimation when the differences are nearly proportional to book values.

**Reliability (357)** The complement of the risk of incorrect acceptance.

**Representative sample (332)** A sample possessing essentially the same characteristics as the population from which it was drawn.

**Risk of assessing control risk too high (338)** This risk is the possibility that the assessed level of control risk based on the sample is greater than the true operating effectiveness of the control.

**Risk of assessing control risk too low (339)** This most important risk is the possibility that the assessed level of control risk based on the sample is less than the true operating effectiveness of the controls.

**Risk of incorrect acceptance (349)** The risk that sample results will indicate that a population is not materially misstated when, in fact, it is materially misstated.

**Risk of incorrect rejection (349)** The risk that sample results will indicate that a population is materially misstated when, in fact, it is not.

**Sampling error (337)** The difference between the actual rate or amount in the population and that of the sample. For example, if an actual (but unknown) deviation rate of 3 percent exists in the population, and the sample's deviation rate is 2 percent, the sampling error is 1 percent.

**Sampling risk (332)** The risk that the auditors' conclusion based on a sample might be different from the conclusion they would reach if the test were applied to the entire population. For tests of controls, sampling risks include the risks of assessing control risk too high and too low; for substantive testing, sampling risks include the risks of incorrect acceptance and rejection.

**Sequential (stop-or-go) sampling (347)** A sampling plan in which the sample is selected in stages, with the need for each subsequent stage being conditional on the results of the previous stage.

**Standard deviation (349)** A measure of the variability or dispersion of item values within a population; in a normal distribution, 68.3 percent of all item values fall within ±1 standard deviation of the mean, 95.4 percent fall within ±2 standard deviations, and 99.7 percent fall within ±3 standard deviations.

**Stratification (335)** Dividing a population into two or more relatively homogeneous subgroups (strata). Stratification increases the efficiency of most sampling plans by reducing the variability of items in each stratum. The sample size necessary to evaluate the strata separately is smaller than would be needed to evaluate the total population.

**Systematic selection (334)** The technique of selecting a sample by drawing every *nth* item in the population, following one or more random starting points.

**Tolerable deviation rate (339)** The maximum population rate of deviations from a prescribed control that the auditor will tolerate without modifying the planned assessment of control risk.

**Tolerable misstatement (337)** An estimate of materiality for the particular audit test.

**Variables sampling (348)** Sampling plans designed to estimate a numerical measurement of a population, such as a dollar value.

**Voucher (335)** A document authorizing a cash disbursement. A voucher usually provides space for the initials of employees performing various approval functions. The term *voucher* may also be applied to the group of supporting documents used as a basis for recording liabilities or for making cash disbursements.

## Review Questions

9–1. Define, and differentiate between, nonstatistical (judgmental) sampling and statistical sampling.

9–2. Describe the difference between sampling risk and nonsampling risk.

9–3. Explain what is meant by the following statement: "When sampling, the auditors must determine that the physical representation of the actual population is complete."

9–4. In selecting items for examination, an auditor considered three alternatives: (*a*) random number table selection, (*b*) systematic selection, and (*c*) random number generator selection. Which, if any, of these methods would lead to a random sample if properly applied?

9–5. Explain briefly the term *systematic selection* as used in auditing and indicate the precautions to be taken if a random sample is to be obtained. Is systematic selection applicable to unnumbered documents? Explain.

9–6. Explain the meaning of sampling without replacement and sampling with replacement.

9–7. Which technique results in a smaller sample size, sampling with or without replacement?

9–8. An auditor is sampling with replacement and, by chance, a particular account has been selected twice. Should it be included two times in the sample?

9–9. What are the three major factors that determine the sample size for an attributes sampling plan?

9–10. When using attributes sampling, the auditors must estimate the expected population deviation rate. What sources are used to make this estimate?

9–11. When performing attributes sampling, may auditors include several types of attributes in their definition of a deviation? Explain.

9–12. What effects will an auditor's belief that the population's actual deviation rate exceeds the tolerable deviation rate have on the test of controls sample size?

9–13. What is a dual-purpose test?

9–14. When performing a dual-purpose test, how does the auditor arrive at the required sample size?

9–15. If a sample of 100 items indicates a deviation rate of 3 percent, should the auditors conclude that the entire population also has approximately a 3 percent deviation rate?

9–16. What relationship exists between the expected population deviation rate and sample size?

9–17. What would be the difference between an attributes sampling plan and a variables sampling plan in a test of inventory extensions?

9–18. Describe what is meant by a sequential sampling plan.

9–19. In performing a substantive test of the book value of a population, auditors must be concerned with two aspects of sampling risk. What are these two aspects of sampling risk, and which aspect is of greater importance to auditors? Explain.

9–20. Explain how the auditors may obtain an estimate of a population's standard deviation to determine an appropriate sample size.

9–21. For what purposes is the planned allowance for sampling risk used in mean-per-unit sampling?

9–22. Using the approach presented in this chapter for mean-per-unit sampling, when is it necessary to calculate an adjusted allowance for sampling risk?

9–23. The mean of the audited values in a sample is $20. The accounts in that sample have a mean book value of $21, and the entire population of 10,000 accounts has an average book value of $19. Using mean-per-unit sampling, calculate the estimated total audited value of the account.

9–24. What conditions are necessary for the auditors to use either the ratio or difference estimation techniques?

9–25. What options are available to an auditor when the client's book value falls outside the acceptance interval calculated using the estimate of the total value of the population (the adjusted allowance for sampling risk)?

9–26. Explain how, in using the mean-per-unit method to evaluate results, the auditors use the differences between the audited values and the book values of the individual items in their sample.

9–27. Is it correct to say that when using nonstatistical variables sampling, one is unable to project the misstatements identified to the entire population? Explain why this is or is not the case.

9–28. When using nonstatistical sampling, what relationship must exist between the projected misstatement and tolerable misstatement in order for the auditors to conclude that an account balance is acceptable?

**Questions Requiring Analysis**

**LO 1, 5**

9–29. CPAs may decide to apply nonstatistical or statistical techniques to audit testing.

   a. List and explain the advantages of applying statistical sampling techniques to audit testing.

   b. List and discuss the decisions involving professional judgment that must be made by the CPAs in applying statistical sampling techniques to tests of controls.

   c. You have applied attributes sampling to the client's pricing of the inventory and discovered from your sampling that the sample deviation rate exceeds your tolerable rate. Discuss the courses of action you take.

**LO 5**
**ACL**

9–30. In performing a test of controls for sales order approvals, the CPAs stipulate a tolerable deviation rate of 8 percent with a risk of assessing control risk too low of 5 percent. They anticipate a deviation rate of 2 percent.

*Required:*

   a. What type of sampling plan should the auditors use for this test?

   b. Using the appropriate table or formula from this chapter, compute the required sample size for the test.

   c. Assume that the sample indicates four deviations. May the CPAs conclude with a 5 percent risk of assessing control risk too low that the population deviation rate does not exceed the tolerable rate of 8 percent?

   d. Use ACL to compute the required sample size for the test. Assume that the population size is composed of 100,000 items.

   e. Assume that the sample indicates four deviations using the sample size determined in *d*. Use ACL to calculate the results. May the CPAs conclude with a 5 percent risk of assessing control risk too low that the population deviation rate does not exceed the tolerable rate of 8 percent?

**LO 5**

9–31. An auditor has reason to suspect that fraud has occurred through forgery of the treasurer's signature on company checks. The population under consideration consists of 3,000 checks. Can discovery sampling rule out the possibility that any forged checks exist?

**LO 8**

9–32. An auditor used a nonstatistical sampling plan to audit the inventory of an auto supply company. The auditor tested the recorded cost of a sample of inventory items by reference to vendors' invoices. In performing the test, the auditor verified all the items on two pages selected at random from the client's 257-page inventory listing. The sampling plan resulted in a test of $50,000 of the total book value of $5,000,000, and the auditor found a total of $5,000 in overstatements in the sample. Since the senior indicated that the amount of a material misstatement in the inventory account was $100,000, the auditor concluded that the recorded inventory value was materially correct.

*Required:* Evaluate the auditor's sampling plan and the manner in which the results were evaluated.

**LO 6**

9–33. Cathy Williams is auditing the financial statements of Westerman Industries. In the performance of mean-per-unit estimation of credit sales, Williams has decided to limit the risk of incorrect rejection to 25 percent and the risk of incorrect acceptance to 10 percent. Williams considers the tolerable misstatement in this revenue account to be ±$500,000. Calculate the planned allowance for sampling risk.

**LO 7**

9–34. Ratio estimation and difference estimation are two widely used variables sampling plans.

*Required:*

   a. Under what conditions are ratio estimation or difference estimation appropriate sampling plans for estimating the total dollar value of a population?

   b. What relationship determines which of these two plans will be most efficient in a particular situation?

**LO 8**    9–35.    Bill Jones wishes to use nonstatistical sampling to select a sample of his client's 3,000 accounts receivable, which total $330,000. He believes that $30,000 represents a reasonable tolerable misstatement. He also has assessed both the combination of inherent and control risk at the maximum level and the risk that other substantive procedures will fail to detect a material misstatement at the maximum. He wishes to use a structured approach. Use the formula presented in the text to calculate the required sample size.

**LO 6**    9–36.    During an audit of Potter Company, an auditor needs to estimate the total value of the 5,000 invoices processed during June. The auditor estimates the standard deviation of the population to be $30. Determine the size sample the auditor would select to achieve an allowance for sampling risk (precision) of ±$25,000 with 4.6 percent risk of incorrect rejection.

(AICPA, adapted)

## Objective Questions

**All applicable questions are available with McGraw-Hill's *Connect*^TM *Accounting*.** ▦ connect | ACCOUNTING

9–37.    **Multiple Choice Questions**

Select the best answer for each of the following questions. Explain the reasons for your selection.

**LO 1**
   *a.* Which of the following is an element of sampling risk?

     (1) Choosing an audit procedure that is inconsistent with the audit objective.

     (2) Concluding that no material misstatement exists in a materially misstated population based on taking a sample that includes no misstatement.

     (3) Failing to detect an error on a document that has been inspected by an auditor.

     (4) Failing to perform audit procedures that are required by the sampling plan.

**LO 5, 6**
   *b.* In assessing sampling risk, the risk of incorrect rejection and the risk of assessing control risk too high relate to the:

     (1) Efficiency of the audit.

     (2) Effectiveness of the audit.

     (3) Selection of the sample.

     (4) Audit quality controls.

**LO 2**
   *c.* Which of the following statistical sampling techniques is least desirable for use by the auditors?

     (1) Random number table selection.

     (2) Block selection.

     (3) Systematic selection.

     (4) Random number generator selection.

**LO 2**
   *d.* The auditors' primary objective in selecting a sample of items from an audit population is to obtain:

     (1) A random sample.

     (2) A stratified sample.

     (3) A representative sample.

     (4) A large sample.

**LO 5**
   *e.* Discovery sampling is particularly effective when:

     (1) There are a large number of errors in the population.

     (2) The auditors are looking for critical deviations that are not expected to be frequent in number.

     (3) The auditors know where deviations are likely to occur.

     (4) The population is large in size.

**LO 4**
   *f.* The auditors are using unstratified mean-per-unit sampling to audit accounts receivable as they did in the prior year. Which of the following changes in characteristics or specifications would result in a larger required sample size this year than that required in the prior year?

     (1) Larger variance in the dollar value of accounts.

     (2) Smaller population size.

     (3) Larger tolerable misstatement.

     (4) Higher risk of incorrect acceptance.

**LO 3, 5**

g. Which of the following sampling techniques is typically used for tests of controls?
    (1) Mean-per-unit sampling.
    (2) Difference sampling.
    (3) Attribute sampling.
    (4) Probability-proportional-to-size sampling.

**LO 6**

h. Which of the following is accurate regarding tolerable misstatement?
    (1) Tolerable misstatement is directly related to materiality.
    (2) Tolerable misstatement cannot be determined until the sample results are evaluated.
    (3) Tolerable misstatement does not affect sample size.
    (4) Tolerable misstatement is a measure of reliability of the sample.

**LO 5**

i. In which of the following circumstances is it least likely that tests of controls will be performed?
    (1) The expected deviation rate exceeds the tolerable deviation rate.
    (2) The planned assessed level of control risk is at a level slightly below the maximum.
    (3) The risk of assessing control risk too low is less than the expected deviation rate.
    (4) The tolerable deviation rate exceeds the risk of assessing control risk too low.

**LO 6**

j. An auditor needs to estimate the average highway weight of tractor-trailer trucks using a state's highway system. Which estimation method is most appropriate?
    (1) Mean per unit.
    (2) Difference.
    (3) Ratio.
    (4) Probability proportional to size.

**LO 6**

k. The auditors have sampled 50 accounts from a population of 1,000 accounts receivable. The sample items have a mean book value of $200 and a mean audited value of $203. The book value in the population is $198,000. What is the estimated audited value of the population using the mean-per-unit method?
    (1) $198,000.
    (2) $200,000.
    (3) $201,000.
    (4) $203,000.

**LO 7**

l. Using the same facts as in (k) above, what is the estimated total audited value of the population using the difference method?
    (1) $198,000.
    (2) $200,000.
    (3) $201,000.
    (4) $203,000.

9–38. The 10 following statements apply to unrestricted random sampling without replacement. Indicate whether each statement is true or false. Briefly discuss each false statement.

a. When sampling from the population of accounts receivable for certain objectives, the auditor might sample only active accounts with balances.

b. To be random, every item in the population must have an equal chance of being selected for inclusion in the sample.

c. In general, all items in excess of a material misstatement need to be examined and sampling of them is inappropriate.

d. It is likely that five different random samples from the same population could produce five different estimates of the true population mean.

e. A 100 percent sample would have to be taken to eliminate sampling risk.

f. The effect of the inclusion by chance of a very large or very small item in a random sample can be lessened by increasing the size of the sample.

g. The standard deviation is a measure of the variability of items in a population.

h. The larger the standard deviation of a population, the smaller the required sample size.

i. Unrestricted random sampling with replacement may result in a larger sample size than unrestricted random sampling without replacement.

j. Unrestricted random sampling normally results in a smaller sample size than does stratified sampling.

**LO 4** 9–39. The professional development department of a large CPA firm has prepared the following illustration to familiarize the audit staff with the relationships of sample size to population size and variability and the auditors' specifications in regard to the tolerable misstatement and the risk of incorrect acceptance.

| | Characteristics of Population 1 Relative to Population 2 | | Auditors' Specifications as to a Sample from Population 1 Relative to a Sample from Population 2 | |
| --- | --- | --- | --- | --- |
| | Size | Variability | Tolerable Misstatement | Planned Risk of Incorrect Acceptance |
| Case 1 | Larger | Equal | Equal | Equal |
| Case 2 | Equal | Larger | Larger | Equal |
| Case 3 | Larger | Equal | Smaller | Equal |
| Case 4 | Smaller | Smaller | Equal | Lower |
| Case 5 | Smaller | Equal | Larger | Higher |

*Required:* For each of the five cases in the above illustration, indicate the relationship of the sample size to be selected from population 1 relative to the sample from population 2. Select your answer from the following numbered responses and state the reasoning behind your choice. The required sample size from population 1 is:

(1) Larger than the required sample size from population 2.

(2) Equal to the required sample size from population 2.

(3) Smaller than the required sample size from population 2.

(4) Indeterminate relative to the required sample size from population 2.

**LO 2, 3, 5, 6, 8** 9–40. For each term in the first column below, identify its definition (or partial definition). Each definition may be used once or not at all.

| Term | Definition (or Partial Definition) |
| --- | --- |
| *a.* Allowance for sampling risk | 1. A classical variables sampling plan enabling the auditors to estimate the average dollar value (or other variable) of items in a population by determining the average value of items in a sample. |
| *b.* Deviation rate | 2. A defined rate of departure from prescribed controls. Also referred to as *occurrence rate* or *exception rate*. |
| *c.* Discovery sampling | 3. A sampling plan enabling the auditors to estimate the rate of deviation (occurrence) in a population. |
| *d.* Projected misstatement | 4. A sampling plan for locating at least 1 deviation, providing that the deviation occurs in the population with a specified frequency. |
| *e.* Reliability | 5. A sampling plan in which the sample is selected in stages, with the need for each subsequent stage being conditional on the results of the previous stage. |
| *f.* Risk of assessing control risk too low | 6. Also referred to as *precision,* an interval around the sample results in which the true population characteristic is expected to lie. |
| *g.* Risk of incorrect acceptance | 7. An estimate of the most likely amount of monetary misstatement in a population. |
| *h.* Sampling risk | 8. The complement of the risk of incorrect acceptance. |
| *i.* Tolerable deviation rate | 9. The maximum population rate of deviations from a prescribed control that the auditors will accept without modifying the planned assessment of control risk. |
| | 10. The possibility that the assessed level of control risk based on the sample is less than the true operating effectiveness of the controls. |
| | 11. The possibility that the assessed level of control risk based on the sample is greater than the true operating effectiveness of the control. |
| | 12. The risk that sample results will indicate that a population is materially misstated when, in fact, it is not. |
| | 13. The risk that sample results will indicate that a population is not materially misstated when, in fact, it is materially misstated. |
| | 14. The risk that the auditors' conclusion based on a sample might be different from the conclusion they would reach if the test were applied to the entire population. |

## Problems

**LO 5**   9–41.  The use of statistical sampling techniques in an audit of financial statements does not eliminate judgmental decisions.

*Required:*

    a. Identify and explain four areas in which judgment may be exercised by CPAs in planning a statistical test of controls.

    b. Assume that the auditors' sample shows an unacceptable deviation rate. Discuss the various actions that they may take based upon this finding.

    c. A nonstratified sample of 80 accounts payable vouchers is to be selected from a population of 3,200. The vouchers are numbered consecutively from 1 to 3,200 and are listed, 40 to a page, in the voucher register. Describe four different techniques for selecting a random sample of vouchers for inspection.

(AICPA, adapted)

**LO 5**   9–42.  As part of your audit of the Abba Company accounts payable function, your audit program
*ACL*        includes a test of controls addressing the company policy requiring that all vouchers be properly approved. You estimate the population deviation rate to be 3 percent.

*Required:*

    a. In addition to an estimate of population deviation rate, what factors affect the size of the sample needed?

    b. What bases could be used to provide an estimate of the population deviation rate?

    c. Assume that a sample of 100 has been drawn, audit tests performed, and a sample deviation rate of 4 percent computed. Furthermore, you have selected a 5 percent risk of assessing control risk too low as appropriate. Use the appropriate table to determine the achieved upper deviation rate.

    d. What actions can be taken to deal with a situation in which the achieved upper deviation rate exceeds the tolerable rate?

    e. Make the same assumptions as in part (c). Use ACL to determine the achieved upper deviation rate.

**LO 5**   9–43.  You have been asked to test the effectiveness of Ingo Corporation's control of manually
*ACL*        approving all purchases over $25,000. During the year, Ingo Corporation has made 1,000,000 purchases, of which 3,000 were over $25,000. Jian Zhang, CIA, your supervisor, has asked you to use a tolerable deviation rate of 4 percent (although she expects the rate to be only approximately 0.25 percent) and a 5 percent risk of assessing control risk too low.

    a. What is the planned assessed level of control risk (using the table on page 340 of the text)?

    b. Determine the appropriate sample size using Figure 9.4.

    c. Use Figure 9.5 to determine the achieved upper deviation rate if no deviations were included in the sample. What is the assessed level of control risk?

    d. What is the achieved upper deviation rate if 2 deviations are found in the sample? What is the assessed level of control risk?

    e. What is the achieved upper deviation rate if 8 deviations are found in the sample? What is the assessed level of control risk?

    f. Determine the appropriate sample size using ACL. Use this sample for (g), (h), and (i).

    g. Determine the achieved upper deviation rate if no deviations are included in the sample. What is the assessed level of control risk?

    h. What is the achieved upper deviation rate if 2 deviations are found in the sample? What is the assessed level of control risk?

    i. What is the achieved upper deviation rate if 8 deviations are found in the sample? What is the assessed level of control risk?

**LO 6, 7**   9–44.  Scott Duffney, CPA, has randomly selected and audited a sample of 100 of Will-Mart's accounts receivable. Will-Mart has 3,000 accounts receivable accounts with a total book value of $3,000,000. Duffney has determined that the account's tolerable misstatement is $250,000.

His sample results are as follows:

| | |
|---|---|
| Average audited value | $990 |
| Average book value | 998 |

*Required:*

Calculate the accounts receivable estimated audited value and projected misstatement using the:

(a) Mean-per-unit method.

(b) Ratio method.

(c) Difference method.

**LO 6** 9–45. The auditors wish to use mean-per-unit sampling to evaluate the reasonableness of the book value of the accounts receivable of Smith, Inc. Smith has 10,000 accounts receivable accounts with a total book value of $1,500,000. The auditors estimate the population's standard deviation to be equal to $25. After examining the overall audit plan, the auditors believe that the test's tolerable misstatement is $60,000, and that a risk of incorrect rejection of 5 percent and a risk of incorrect acceptance of 10 percent are appropriate.

*Required:*  a. Calculate the required sample size.

b. Assuming the following results:

Average audited value          $146

Standard deviation of sample      28

Use the mean-per-unit method to:

(1) Calculate the point estimate of the account's audited value.

(2) Calculate the projected misstatement for the population.

(3) Calculate the adjusted allowance for sampling risk.

(4) State the auditors' conclusion in this situation.

**LO 6** 9–46. You are the auditor of Jexel, an auto air conditioner service and repair company, and you have decided to use the mean-per-unit method to test the existence and gross valuation of recorded accounts receivable. The client's records include 10,000 accounts with a total book value of $1,250,000. You decide to use tolerable misstatement of $182,000, an incorrect acceptance risk of 5 percent, and an incorrect rejection risk of 4.6 percent. Using generalized audit software, you estimated the standard deviation of the population as $25.

a. Determine the sample size.

b. Assume you tested the sample and got the following results: The mean audited value of the 25 accounts was $122. Assuming that the standard deviation of the sample's audited value is also $25, will you accept the account as not being materially misstated? What is the projected misstatement for the population?

c. Assuming that the standard deviation of the sample's audited value is $20, will you accept the account as not being materially misstated? Show your calculations. What is the projected misstatement for the population?

**LO 6, 7** 9–47. In the audit of Potomac Mills, the auditors wish to test the costs assigned to manufactured goods. During the year, the company has produced 2,000 production lots with a total recorded cost of $5.9 million. The auditors select a sample of 200 production lots with an aggregate book value of $600,000 and vouch the assigned costs to the supporting documentation. Their audit discloses misstatements in the cost of 52 of the 200 production lots; after adjustment for these misstatements, the audited value of the sample is $582,000.

*Required:*  a. Show how the auditors would compute an estimate of the total cost of production lots manufactured during the year using each of the following sampling plans. (Do not compute the allowance for sampling risk or the risk of incorrect acceptance of the estimates.)

(1) Mean-per-unit estimation.

(2) Ratio estimation.

(3) Difference estimation.

b. Explain why mean-per-unit estimation results in a higher estimate of the population value than does ratio estimation in this particular instance.

**LO 5, 7, 8** 9–48. To test the pricing and mathematical accuracy of sales invoices, the auditors selected a sample of 200 sales invoices from a total of 41,600 invoices that were issued during the year under audit. The 200 invoices represented total recorded sales of $22,800. Total sales for the year amounted to $5 million. The test disclosed that of the 200 invoices audited, five were not properly priced or contained errors in extensions and footings. The five incorrect invoices represented $720 of the total recorded sales, and the errors found resulted in a net understatement of these invoices by $300.

*Required:*  Explain what conclusions the auditors may draw from the above information, assuming the sample was selected:

a. Using nonstatistical sampling.

b. As part of a difference estimation plan for estimating the total population value.

c. As part of an attributes sampling plan using a stipulated tolerable deviation rate of 5 percent and a risk of assessing control risk too low of 5 percent.

**LO 8** 9–49. The auditors of Landi Corporation wish to use a structured approach to nonstatistical sampling to evaluate the reasonableness of the accounts receivable. Landi has 15,000 receivable accounts with a total book value of $2,500,000. The auditors have assessed the combined level of inherent and control risk at a moderate level and believe that their other substantive procedures are so limited as to require a "maximum" risk assessment. After considering the overall audit plan, the auditors believe that the test's tolerable misstatement is $57,500.

*Required:*

a. Calculate the required sample size.

b. Assuming the following results:

| | |
|---|---|
| Number of items in sample | 100 |
| Total audited value of sample items | $16,200 |
| Total book value of sample items | $17,000 |

(1) Use the ratio estimation method to calculate the projected misstatement of the population.

(2) Use the difference estimation method to calculate the projected misstatement of the population.

c. Use the results obtained in (b) to arrive at a conclusion as to whether to "accept" or "reject" the population.

**LO 8**   9–50.   The auditors wish to test the valuation of accounts receivable in the audit of Kaplan Corporation. The client has $1,000,000 of total recorded receivables, composed of 2,000 accounts. The auditors have decided to use structured nonstatistical sampling and have determined the following:

| | |
|---|---|
| Tolerable misstatement | $50,000 |
| Assessment of inherent and control risk | Moderate |
| Risk related to other substantive procedures | Moderate |

*Required:*

a. Calculate the required sample size.

b. Assume that the auditors have tested the sample and discovered three misstatements:

| Book Value | Audited Value |
|---|---|
| $100 | $ 90 |
| 512 | 600 |
| 900 | 520 |

The remainder of the sample had an average value (book and audited) of $501.00. Use the ratio estimation method to calculate the projected misstatement of the population.

c. Use the results obtained in (b) to come to a conclusion about whether to "accept" or "reject" the population.

**In-Class Team Case**

**LO 5**   9–51.

Baker, CPA, was engaged to audit Mill Company's financial statements for the year ended December 31, 200X. After obtaining an understanding of Mill's internal control, Baker decided to obtain audit evidence about the effectiveness of both the design and operation of the controls that may support a low assessed level of control risk concerning Mill's shipping and billing functions. During the prior years' audits, Baker had used nonstatistical sampling, but for the current year Baker decided to use a statistical sample in the tests of controls to eliminate the need for judgment.

Baker wanted to assess control risk at a low level, so a tolerable rate of deviation of 20 percent was established. To estimate the population deviation rate and the achieved upper deviation rate, Baker decided to apply the discovery sampling method with an expected population deviation rate of 3 percent for the 8,000 shipping documents, and he decided to defer consideration of the risk of assessing control risk too low until the sample results had been evaluated. Baker used the tolerable rate, the population size, and the expected population deviation rate to determine that a sample size of 80 would be sufficient. When it was subsequently determined that the actual population was about 10,000 shipping documents, Baker increased the sample size to 100.

Baker's objective was to ascertain whether Mill's shipments had been properly billed. Baker took a sample of 100 invoices by selecting the first 25 invoices from the first month of each quarter. Baker then compared the invoices to the corresponding prenumbered shipping documents.

When Baker tested the sample, 8 deviations were discovered. Additionally, one shipment that should have been billed at $10,443 was actually billed at $10,434. Baker considered this $9 to be immaterial and did not count it as a deviation.

In evaluating the sample results, Baker made the initial determination that a reliability level of 95 percent (risk of assessing control risk too low of 5 percent) was desired and, using the appropriate statistical sampling table, determined that for 8 observed deviations from a sample size of 100, the achieved upper deviation rate was 14 percent. Baker then calculated the allowance for sampling risk (5 percent), the difference between the actual sample deviation rate (8 percent), and the expected deviation rate (3 percent). Baker reasoned that the actual sample deviation rate (8 percent) plus the allowance for sampling risk (5 percent) was less than the achieved upper deviation rate (14 percent); therefore, the sample supported a low level of control risk.

*Required:* Describe each incorrect assumption, statement, and inappropriate application of attributes sampling in Baker's procedures.

(AICPA, adapted)

 Problem material that can be completed using the ACL software packaged with your new text can be found on the text Web site at www.mhhe.com/whittington18e.

# Probability-Proportional-to-Size (PPS) Sampling

**Probability-proportional-to-size (PPS) sampling**[12] is a technique that applies the theory of attributes sampling to estimate the total dollar amount of misstatement in a population. It is popular because of its ease of use and because it often results in smaller samples than classical variables sampling approaches.

Whereas classical variables sampling plans define the population as a group of accounts or transactions, PPS sampling defines the population as the individual dollars comprising the population's book value. Thus, a population of 5,000 accounts receivable with a total dollar value of $2,875,000 is viewed as a population of 2,875,000 items (dollars), rather than 5,000 items (accounts).

## Determination of Sample Size

The factors affecting sample size in PPS sampling are (1) the population book value, (2) the reliability factor, (3) the tolerable misstatement, (4) the expected misstatement in the account, and (5) the expansion factor. Specifically, the sample size for PPS may be computed as follows:

$$\text{Sample size} = \frac{\text{Population book value} \times \text{Reliability factor}}{\text{Tolerable misstatement} - (\text{Expected misstatement} \times \text{Expansion factor})}$$

Several of the factors in the PPS formula need very little additional explanation. The population book value is the recorded amount of the population being audited. The tolerable misstatement is the maximum monetary misstatement that may exist in the population without causing the financial statements to be materially misstated. The expected misstatement is the auditors' estimate of the dollar amount of misstatement in the population. The auditors estimate the expected misstatement using professional judgment based on prior experience and knowledge of the client. The other factors used to calculate sample size are based on the auditors' desired risk of incorrect acceptance and are obtained from tables, such as the one in Figure 9.14. The "zero misstatements" row of Figure 9.14 is always used for obtaining the reliability factor for determining sample size. Thus, if a 10 percent risk of incorrect acceptance is desired, the auditors use a reliability factor of 2.31. The expansion factor comes directly from Figure 9.15. For a 10 percent risk of incorrect acceptance, the factor is 1.5.

[12] Variations of this sampling technique are called **_dollar-unit sampling_** and _monetary-unit sampling_.

**FIGURE 9.14** Reliability Factors for Misstatements of Overstatement

| Number of Overstatement Misstatements | Risk of Incorrect Acceptance | | | | | | | | |
|---|---|---|---|---|---|---|---|---|---|
| | 1% | 5% | 10% | 15% | 20% | 25% | 30% | 37% | 50% |
| 0* | 4.61 | 3.00 | 2.31 | 1.90 | 1.61 | 1.39 | 1.21 | 1.00 | 0.70 |
| 1 | 6.64 | 4.75 | 3.89 | 3.38 | 3.00 | 2.70 | 2.44 | 2.14 | 1.68 |
| 2 | 8.41 | 6.30 | 5.33 | 4.72 | 4.28 | 3.93 | 3.62 | 3.25 | 2.68 |
| 3 | 10.05 | 7.76 | 6.69 | 6.02 | 5.52 | 5.11 | 4.77 | 4.34 | 3.68 |
| 4 | 11.61 | 9.16 | 8.00 | 7.27 | 6.73 | 6.28 | 5.90 | 5.43 | 4.68 |
| 5 | 13.11 | 10.52 | 9.28 | 8.50 | 7.91 | 7.43 | 7.01 | 6.49 | 5.68 |
| 6 | 14.57 | 11.85 | 10.54 | 9.71 | 9.08 | 8.56 | 8.12 | 7.56 | 6.67 |
| 7 | 16.00 | 13.15 | 11.78 | 10.90 | 10.24 | 9.69 | 9.21 | 8.63 | 7.67 |
| 8 | 17.41 | 14.44 | 13.00 | 12.08 | 11.38 | 10.81 | 10.31 | 9.68 | 8.67 |
| 9 | 18.79 | 15.71 | 14.21 | 13.25 | 12.52 | 11.92 | 11.39 | 10.74 | 9.67 |
| 10 | 20.15 | 16.97 | 15.41 | 14.42 | 13.66 | 13.02 | 12.47 | 11.79 | 10.67 |

\* The 0 row is always used for the reliability factor in the sample size formula and for basic precision.
Source: AICPA, *Audit Guide: Audit Sampling* (New York, 2001).

**FIGURE 9.15**
**Expansion Factors for Expected Misstatement**

Source: AICPA, *Audit Guide: Audit Sampling* (New York, 2001).

| | Risk of Incorrect Acceptance | | | | | | | | |
|---|---|---|---|---|---|---|---|---|---|
| | 1% | 5% | 10% | 15% | 20% | 25% | 30% | 37% | 50% |
| Factor | 1.9 | 1.6 | 1.5 | 1.4 | 1.3 | 1.25 | 1.2 | 1.15 | 1.0 |

## Controlling Sampling Risk

As is the case with classical variables sampling approaches, the auditors decide on an appropriate level of risk of incorrect acceptance based on the extent of the evidence required from the sample. This level of risk is then used to obtain the appropriate factors to calculate sample size. The risk of incorrect rejection is indirectly controlled by the auditors' estimate of expected misstatement that is used to calculate the PPS sample size. To reduce the risk of incorrect rejection, the auditors increase their estimate of expected misstatement. If the auditors underestimate the expected misstatement, the sample size will not be large enough and additional testing may be necessary in order to accept the account balance as being materially correct.

## Method of Sample Selection

Auditors generally use a *systematic selection* approach when using PPS. However, since the sampling unit is based on dollars, not individual accounts, the sampling interval is also based on dollars. The sampling interval is calculated as follows:

$$\text{Sample interval} = \frac{\text{Population book value}}{\text{Sample size}}$$

To illustrate, assume that the auditors are sampling 200 items from a population of accounts receivable totaling $300,000; the sampling interval is calculated to be $1,500 ($300,000 ÷ 200). A random starting point is selected between $1 and $1,500, say, $412. The account with the 412th dollar will be the first sample item. Then, the sample will include the accounts receivable that contain every $1,500 from the starting point, as illustrated in Figure 9.16. The accounts included in Figure 9.16 are considered "logical units" because when applying PPS the auditors generally cannot audit only the dollar selected but must audit the entire account, invoice, or voucher. Consider the confirmation of accounts receivable. Sending a confirmation of a specific dollar in a selected balance is not generally feasible; the auditors must confirm the entire account balance or transaction from the account balance. Also note that, in using a systematic sampling plan, every account with a book value as large or larger than the sampling interval will be included in the sample. In our example, since every 1,500th dollar is being selected in Figure 9.16, account 0003 for $1,700 will always be included.

## Evaluation of Sample Results

After the sample has been selected and procedures applied to arrive at audited values for the individual accounts, the PPS sample is evaluated. The PPS evaluation procedure involves calculating an **upper limit on misstatement**, which is an estimate of the maximum amount of misstatement in the account.

FIGURE 9.16
**PPS Selection Process**

| Account Number | Book Value | Cumulative Total | Dollar Selected | Sample Item Book Value |
|---|---|---|---|---|
| 0001 | $1,000 | $ 1,000 | $ 412 | $1,000 |
| 0002 | 42 | 1,042 | | |
| 0003 | 1,700 | 2,742 | 1,912 | 1,700 |
| 0004 | 666 | 3,408 | | |
| 0005 | 50 | 3,458 | 3,412 | 50 |
| . | . | . | . | . |
| . | . | . | . | . |
| . | . | . | . | . |
| 4217 | 17 | 300,000 | | |

The upper limit on misstatement has two already familiar components—the **projected misstatement** and the *allowance for sampling risk.* However, in PPS sampling, the allowance for sampling risk is made up of two other components, the **basic precision** and the **incremental allowance.** Mathematically, these relationships may be described as follows:

$$\text{Upper limit on misstatement} = \text{Projected misstatement} + \text{Allowance for sampling risk, and}$$

$$\text{Allowance for sampling risk} = \text{Basic precision} + \text{Incremental allowance}$$

Therefore:

$$\text{Upper limit on misstatement} = \text{Projected misstatement} + \text{Basic precision} + \text{Incremental allowance}$$

As is the case with the classical sampling approaches, the projected misstatement may be viewed as the auditors' "best estimate" of the most likely misstatement in the population. The projected misstatement in the population is determined by summing the projected misstatement for each account, or other logical unit, in the sample. Thus, when the sample includes no misstatements, the projected misstatement is zero. If misstatements do exist in the sample, the method used to project the misstatements in a particular account depends on whether the book value of the account found to be in error is less than the sampling interval. For accounts with book values that are less than the amount of the sampling interval, the projected misstatement is calculated by multiplying the percentage of misstatement in the account, known as the **tainting,** times the sampling interval. Thus, if an account with a book value of $100 is found to have an audited value of $60, the misstatement in the account is $40 ($100 − $60) and the tainting is 40 percent ($40 ÷ $100). The tainting of 40 percent would then be multiplied by the sampling interval to get the projected misstatement for that account. Accounts with balances less than the sampling interval are used to represent other unselected items in that interval. Thus, for accounts with book values that are less than the sampling interval, *the account's tainting percentage is projected to the entire interval from which it was selected.*

For accounts with book values equal to or greater than the sampling interval, *the actual misstatement in the account is used as the projected misstatement.* The reason for the difference in the methods of calculation of the projected misstatement is that every account with a book value equal to or greater than the sampling interval will be included in the sample. These items do not represent other unselected items in that sampling interval; therefore, the actual misstatement in the account is equal to the projected misstatement.

The next step in determining the upper limit on misstatements involves calculating the two components of the allowance for sampling risk—the basic precision and the incremental allowance. The basic precision is always found by multiplying the reliability factor for zero misstatements from Figure 9.14 by the sampling interval.

When misstatements are discovered in the sample, the incremental allowance is found by (1) ranking the projected misstatements for the accounts with book values less than the sampling interval from largest projected misstatement to smallest projected misstatement, (2) multiplying each projected misstatement by an incremental factor calculated from the reliability factors in Figure 9.14, and (3) summing the resulting amounts. When no misstatements of accounts with book values less than the sampling interval are found in the sample, the incremental allowance is zero.

To complete the quantitative evaluation of the sample results, the auditors compute the upper limit on misstatements. When misstatements are found, the upper limit is computed by adding together the projected misstatement, the basic precision, and the incremental allowance. Of course, if no misstatements are found in the sample, the upper limit on misstatements consists only of the basic precision.

After the upper limit on misstatements is calculated, the auditors compare it to the tolerable misstatement for the account. If the upper limit on misstatements is less than or equal to tolerable misstatement, the sample results support the conclusion that the population is not misstated by more than tolerable misstatement at the specified level of sampling risk. On the other hand, if the upper limit on misstatements exceeds the amount of tolerable misstatement, the sample results do not provide the auditors with enough assurance that the misstatement in the population is less than the tolerable misstatement.

## Illustration of PPS Sampling

The small public utility client case used to illustrate mean-per-unit sampling on pages 351–354 is used to illustrate PPS sampling. The population, in that case, had a book value of $6,250,000 and the auditors decided on a tolerable misstatement for the test of $364,000 and a 5 percent risk of incorrect acceptance. Additionally, assume that based on prior audits, the auditors expect $50,000 of misstatement in the population.

Since the auditors are using a risk of incorrect acceptance of 5 percent, the reliability factor from Figure 9.14 is 3.00, and the expansion factor from Figure 9.15 is 1.6. Remember that for calculating sample size the zero misstatement row of Figure 9.14 is always used. Using this information, the sample size and sampling interval may be calculated as follows:

$$\text{Sample size} = \frac{\text{Population book value} \times \text{Reliability factor}}{\text{Tolerable misstatement} - (\text{Expected misstatement} \times \text{Expansion factor})}$$

$$= \frac{\$6,250,000 \times 3.00}{\$364,000 \times (\$50,000 \times 1.6)} = 66$$

$$\text{Sampling interval} = \frac{\text{Population book value}}{\text{Sample size}}$$

$$= \frac{\$6,250,000}{66} = \$95,000 \text{ (approximately)}$$

Using the PPS selection method, the auditors select the accounts, perform confirmation procedures, and find the following three misstatements:

| Book Value | Audited Value |
|---|---|
| $ 100 | $ 90 |
| 2,000 | 1,900 |
| 102,000 | 102 |

Based on the above results, the projected misstatement, basic precision, and the incremental allowance are calculated in Figure 9.17.

The calculation of projected misstatement is straightforward, and no table values are required. Note that the tainting percentages for the first two misstatements are computed by dividing the misstatement amount by the book value of the account. Then, the tainting percentages are multiplied by the sampling interval to calculate the projected misstatement. Because the book value of the account containing the third misstatement is greater than the sampling interval of $95,000, the projected misstatement for that account is equal to the amount of the misstatement.

The second element of the upper limit on misstatement, basic precision, is simply the reliability factor for zero misstatements and a risk of incorrect acceptance of 5 percent (from Figure 9.14) multiplied by the sampling interval.

The calculation of the incremental allowance uses the projected misstatements of the accounts with book values less than the sampling interval. These projected misstatements are ranked by size from largest projected misstatement to smallest and multiplied by the increment in the reliability factors, reduced by 1. These incremental reliability factors are derived from the factors in Figure 9.14. Because a 5 percent risk of incorrect acceptance was selected and two misstatements were found in accounts with balances less than the sampling interval, the factors of 3.00, 4.75, and 6.30 are taken from Figure 9.14. An incremental factor is calculated as the difference between successive factors. For example, the incremental factor for the first error is 4.75 − 3.00, or 1.75. Then 1 is subtracted from the incremental factor to arrive at the factor that is multiplied by the first projected misstatement, in this case 0.75. This process is repeated for each additional projected misstatement.

**FIGURE 9.17** **PPS Illustration of Calculation of Upper Limit on Misstatement**

**Projected Misstatement:**

| Book Value | Audited Value | Misstatement | Tainting Percentage | Sampling Interval | Projected Misstatement | Upper Limit on Misstatements |
|---|---|---|---|---|---|---|
| $ 100 | $ 90 | $ 10 | 10% | $95,000 | $ 9,500 | |
| 2,000 | 1,900 | 100 | 5 | 95,000 | 4,750 | |
| 102,000 | 102 | 101,898 | NA | NA | 101,898 | |
| $104,100 | $2,092 | $102,008 | | | | $116,148 |

Basic Precision: = Reliability factor × Sampling interval
= 3.0 × $95,000 = $285,000

**Incremental Allowance:**

| Reliability Factor | Increment | (Increment − 1) | Projected Misstatement | Incremental Allowance | |
|---|---|---|---|---|---|
| 3.00 | — | — | — | — | |
| 4.75 | 1.75 | 0.75 | $9,500 | $7,125 | |
| 6.30 | 1.55 | 0.55 | 4,750 | 2,613 | 9,738 |
| Upper Limit on Misstatement: | | | | | $410,886 |

Because the upper limit ($410,886) is in excess of the tolerable misstatement ($364,000), the auditors would not accept the population as being materially correct. Thus, adjustment of the account, expansion of the test, or audit report modification would be appropriate.[13] In this situation, the most logical approach would be to persuade the client to adjust for the $102,008 in actual misstatements found in the sample. This would reduce the upper limit on misstatements to $308,878 ($410,886 − $102,008) and enable the auditors to accept the account as being materially correct.

---

**Focus on Generalized Audit Software**

ACL Services Ltd. is a leading provider of generalized audit software. That software can, among many other things, perform probability-proportional-to-size sampling (referred to as *monetary unit sampling*). The following is a printout of results using ACL for the problem we have presented in this appendix:

**Confidence: 95%, Interval 95,000**

| Item | Error | Most Likely Error | Upper Error Limit |
|---|---|---|---|
| Basic Precision | | | 285,000.00 |
| 100.00 | 10.00 | 9,500.00 | 16,625.00 |
| 2,000.00 | 100.00 | 4,750.00 | 7,363.00 |
| 102,000.00 | 101,898.00 | 101,898.00 | 101,898.00 |
| Totals | | 116,148.00 | 410,886.00 |

Some of the terminology used differs as follows:

| ACL | Text |
|---|---|
| Confidence | 1 − Risk of incorrect acceptance |
| Most likely error | Projected misstatement |
| Upper error limit | Upper limit on misstatement |

Notice that ACL doesn't separately present the incremental allowance. To obtain the "incremental allowance" one may subtract both the basic precision and the most likely error from the total ($410,886.00 − $116,148.00 − $285,000.00 = $9,738.00).

---

## Considerations in Using PPS Sampling

Although the formulas for PPS sampling at first seem difficult, once a user becomes familiar with them, they are easier to apply in practice than the classical variables sampling methods. An estimate of the standard deviation of the population need not be made, and the PPS selection method automatically

[13] In many circumstances such as this, the client requests that the auditors expand the test either to identify the specific misstatements or to determine that the account is not materially misstated.

FIGURE 9.18

Relative Advantages
and Disadvantages of
Classical Variables
Sampling and Probability-
Proportional-to-Size
Sampling

| Classical Variables Sampling | |
|---|---|
| **Advantages** | **Disadvantages** |
| 1. When there are many misstatements in the population, variables sampling techniques will result in a smaller sample size.<br>2. Items with zero and negative balances do not require any special treatment.<br>3. Sample size may be somewhat easier to expand if that becomes necessary. | 1. To determine the sample size, the standard deviation of the population must be estimated.<br>2. To evaluate results, the sample's standard deviation must be calculated.<br>3. Variables sampling (especially mean-per-unit) usually must be stratified, requiring the use of a computer to perform the computations. |

| Probability-Proportional-to-Size (PPS) Sampling | |
|---|---|
| **Advantages** | **Disadvantages** |
| 1. The technique is generally easier to use.<br>2. No estimate of the standard deviation of the population is needed.<br>3. The technique automatically stratifies the population because items are selected based on their dollar amount.<br>4. When there are few misstatements, the technique will generally result in a smaller sample size.<br>5. Sample selection can begin before the entire population is available. | 1. Special considerations are required to handle understated accounts and negative balances.<br>2. Each item in the population must have a book value.<br>3. When misstatements are found, the technique might overstate the allowance for sampling risk.<br>4. For accounts with a moderate number of misstatements, the sample size may exceed that of the classical techniques. |

results in an efficient stratification of the sample. The method also provides smaller sample sizes when few misstatements are expected in the sample.

The advantages of PPS sampling do not come without cost. If there are a moderate number of differences between recorded and audited amounts, classical variables sampling methods will result in a smaller sample size. Also, when using PPS sampling, special consideration must be given to (1) accounts with zero balances, (2) accounts with negative balances, and (3) accounts that are understated. CPA firms use various methods to overcome these limitations. Figure 9.18 summarizes advantages and disadvantages of the classical and PPS approaches.

## Appendix 9B

# Audit Risk

What level of risk of incorrect acceptance is acceptable for a substantive procedure? Based on the discussion in Chapter 5, we know that the extent of substantive procedures is determined by the levels of inherent and control risk for the assertions being tested. This relationship was illustrated by the formula for **audit risk** that follows:

$$AR = IR \times CR \times DR$$

where

AR = The allowable audit risk that a material misstatement might remain undetected for the account balance and related assertions.

IR = **Inherent risk,** the risk of a material misstatement in an assertion, assuming there were no related controls.

CR = **Control risk,** the risk that a material misstatement that could occur in an assertion will not be prevented or detected on a timely basis by internal control.

DR = **Detection risk,** the risk that the auditors' procedures will fail to detect a material misstatement if it exists.

Since substantive procedures may consist of both tests of details using sampling and other types of substantive procedures, such as analytical procedures, one modification of this formula is necessary to calculate the risk of incorrect acceptance for a substantive procedure. Detection risk must be separated into two components:

AP = The risk that analytical procedures and any other substantive procedures not using audit sampling will fail to detect a material misstatement.

TD = The allowable risk of incorrect acceptance for the substantive test of details.

With this modification, the revised formula is presented below:

$$AR = IR \times CR \times AP \times TD$$

Mathematically, we may rearrange the terms in the formula as follows to solve for the appropriate risk of incorrect acceptance for the substantive test of details:

$$TD = \frac{AR}{IR \times CR \times AP}$$

To illustrate, assume that the auditors are willing to accept a 5 percent audit risk of material misstatement in the assertion of existence of the client's accounts receivable. They believe that the inherent risk of that assertion is 100 percent. After considering internal control over the revenue cycle, they assess control risk at a level of 50 percent, and they believe that the analytical procedures performed to test the assertion have a 40 percent risk of failing to detect a material misstatement. The appropriate level of risk of incorrect acceptance may be calculated as follows:

$$TD = \frac{AR}{IR \times CR \times AP}$$
$$= \frac{.05}{(1.00) \times (0.50) \times (0.40)}$$
$$= 0.25$$

Thus, the auditors must plan an audit sample for the substantive test of details with a risk of incorrect acceptance of 25 percent.

Implementing this formula in practice is quite difficult—it is not easy to precisely quantify the various levels of risks. For this reason, most CPA firms have implemented approaches that are less mathematical. However, the formula is useful in illustrating the relationships between the various types of risk. We know from the formula that in circumstances in which the auditors assess inherent risk and control risk as high and do not perform other effective tests of the assertion, the risk of incorrect acceptance must be set at a very low level. Decreases in inherent risk, control risk, or the risk that other procedures will fail to detect a material misstatement allow the auditors to accept a higher risk of incorrect acceptance for the substantive test of details.

## Key Terms Introduced or Emphasized in Chapter 9 Appendixes

**Audit risk (374)**   The risk that the auditors may unknowingly fail to appropriately modify their opinion on financial statements that are materially misstated.

**Basic precision (371)**   In probability-proportional-to-size sampling, the reliability factor (for zero misstatements at the planned risk of incorrect acceptance) times the sampling interval.

**Control risk (374)**   The risk of a material misstatement occurring in an assertion and not being detected on a timely basis by internal control.

**Detection risk (374)**   The risk that the auditors' procedures will lead them to conclude that an assertion is not materially misstated, when in fact such misstatement does exist.

**Dollar-unit sampling (369)**   See *probability-proportional-to-size sampling.*

**Incremental allowance (371)**   In probability-proportional-to-size sampling, an amount determined by ranking the misstatements for logical units that are less than the sampling interval and considering incremental changes in reliability factors.

**Inherent risk (374)**   The risk of material misstatement in an account, assuming there were no related controls.

**Probability-proportional-to-size (PPS) sampling (369)** A variables sampling procedure that uses attributes theory to express a conclusion in monetary (dollar) amounts.

**Projected misstatement (371)** In probability-proportional-to-size sampling, an amount calculated for logical units less than the size of the sampling interval by multiplying the percentage of misstatement (the "tainting") times the sampling interval.

**Tainting (371)** In probability-proportional-to-size sampling, the percentage of misstatement of an item (misstatement amount divided by book value).

**Upper limit on misstatement (370)** In probability-proportional-to-size sampling, the sum of projected misstatement, basic precision, and the incremental allowance. This total is used to evaluate sample results.

## Questions and Problems for Chapter 9 Appendixes

9A–1. List the factors affecting sample size in a PPS sample.

9A–2. "When using a systematic sample selection technique with PPS sampling, every account larger than the sampling interval will automatically be included in the sample." Do you agree? Explain.

9A–3. When using PPS sampling, do auditors select sample items based on individual dollars, audit individual dollars, or both?

9A–4. A company has an inventory with a book value of $4,583,231, which includes 116 product lines and a total of 326,432 units. How many items compose this population for purposes of applying a probability-proportional-to-size sampling plan? Explain.

9A–5. "When no misstatements are found in a PPS sample, the upper limit on misstatement is equal to zero." Is this statement correct? Explain.

9A–6. A PPS sample with a sampling interval of $2,000 includes an item with an audited value of $90. This value was $30 lower than the account's book value. Calculate the tainting percentage for this account.

9A–7. The reliability factor table provides factors for as many as three computations when planning and evaluating the results of a PPS sample. Describe in general terms each of these computations.

9A–8. In a probability-proportional-to-size sample with a sampling interval of $20,000, an auditor discovered that a selected account receivable with a recorded amount of $10,000 had an audit amount of $2,000. Calculate the projected misstatement for this one item.

9A–9. Chris York, CPA, is considering the use of probability-proportional-to-size sampling in examining the sales transactions and accounts receivable of Carter Wholesale Company.

*Required:*

a. How does the definition of the items in an accounts receivable population vary between probability-proportional-to-size sampling and mean-per-unit sampling?

b. Should a population of accounts receivable be stratified by dollar value before applying probability-proportional-to-size sampling procedures? Discuss.

9A–10. The auditors of Dunbar Electronics want to limit the risk of material misstatement in the valuation of inventories to 2 percent. They believe that there exists a 50 percent risk that a material misstatement could have bypassed the client's internal control and that the inherent risk of the account is 80 percent. They also believe that the analytical procedures performed to test the assertion have a 40 percent risk of failing to detect a material misstatement.

*Required:*

a. Briefly discuss what is meant by audit risk, inherent risk, control risk, and the risk that analytical procedures might fail to detect a material misstatement.

b. Calculate the maximum allowable risk of incorrect acceptance for the substantive test of details.

c. What level of detection risk is implicit in this problem?

*ACL* 9A–11. The auditors wish to test the valuation of accounts receivable in the audit of Desert Enterprises of Bullhead City. The client has $500,000 of total recorded receivables, composed of 850 accounts. The auditors have determined the following:

| | |
|---|---|
| Tolerable misstatement | $25,000 |
| Risk of incorrect acceptance | 5% |
| Expected misstatement | $ 2,000 |

The auditors have decided to use probability-proportional-to-size sampling.

*Required:*

a.  For planning the sample, calculate:
    (1) Required sample size.
    (2) Sampling interval.

b.  Assume that the auditors have tested the sample and discovered three misstatements:

| Book Value | Audited Value |
|---|---|
| $   50 | $   47 |
| 800 | 760 |
| 8,500 | 8,100 |

    (1) Projected misstatement.
    (2) Basic precision.
    (3) Incremental allowance.
    (4) Upper limit on misstatement.

c.  Explain how the auditors would consider the results calculated in (*b*).

d.  Use ACL to calculate the required sample size and sampling interval.

e.  Assume the auditors have tested the sample and discovered five misstatements:

| Book Value | Audited Value |
|---|---|
| $   50 | $   47 |
| 300 | 325 |
| 800 | 760 |
| 912 | 867 |
| 8,500 | 8,100 |

    Use ACL to calculate PPS results.

## Objective Questions

**All applicable question are available with McGraw-Hill's *Connect*™ *Accounting*.**  ▓ **connect**
|ACCOUNTING

9A–12.  **Simulation**

Reply as to whether you believe the following statements are correct (C) or incorrect (I) concerning PPS sampling.

a.  The size of a PPS sample is not based on the estimated variation of audited amounts.

b.  PPS sampling results in a stratified sample.

c.  Individually significant items are automatically identified.

d.  PPS sampling results in a smaller sample size when numerous small misstatements are expected.

e.  If few misstatements are expected, PPS sampling will usually result in a smaller sample size than classical variables sampling methods.

f.  One does not need a book value for individual items to evaluate a PPS sample.

g.  A PPS sample eliminates the need to project results to the overall population.

h.  PPS sampling is "preferred" by professional standards.

Use the following information for parts *i* and *j:*

| | |
|---|---|
| Tolerable misstatement | $  50,000 |
| Sample size | 100 |
| Expected misstatement | $   5,000 |
| Recorded amount of accounts receivable | $300,000 |

i.  The sampling interval is $500.

j.  Increasing the expected misstatement to $10,000 will increase the sample size.

9A–13.    **Simulation**

The following is a computer printout generated by audit software using probability-proportional-to-size (PPS) sampling:

**WINZ CORPORATION**
Receivable Sampling Evaluation Results
December 31, 20X2

Population book value = $2,400,000; Tolerable misstatement = $280,000

**Projected Misstatement**

| Book Value | Audited Value | Misstatement | Tainting Percentage | Sampling Interval | Projected Misstatement |
|---|---|---|---|---|---|
| $ 1,000.00 | $    987.50 | $      12.50 | 1.25% | $80,000.00 | $    1,000.00 |
| 750.00 | 600.00 | 150.00 | 20% | $80,000.00 | 16,000.00 |
| 85,000.00 | 60,000.00 | 25,000.00 | NA | NA | 25,000.00 |
| | | | | | $  42,000.00 |
| | | | | | $240,000.00 |

Basic Precision = 3.0 * $80,000

**Incremental Allowance**

| Reliability Factor | Increment | (Increment−1) | Projected Misstatement | Incremental Allowance |
|---|---|---|---|---|
| 3.00 | | | | |
| 4.75 | 1.75 | .75 | $16,000.00 | $12,000.00 |
| 6.30 | 1.55 | .55 | 1,000.00 | 550.00 |
| | | | | $12,550.00 |

The software uses factors from the following PPS sampling table:

**TABLE**
Reliability Factors for Overstatements

| Number of Overstatements | Risk of Incorrect Acceptance | | | | |
|---|---|---|---|---|---|
| | 1% | 5% | 10% | 15% | 20% |
| 0 | 4.61 | 3.00 | 2.31 | 1.90 | 1.61 |
| 1 | 6.64 | 4.75 | 3.89 | 3.38 | 3.00 |
| 2 | 8.41 | 6.30 | 5.33 | 4.72 | 4.28 |
| 3 | 10.05 | 7.76 | 6.69 | 6.02 | 5.52 |
| 4 | 11.61 | 9.16 | 8.00 | 7.27 | 6.73 |

**Analysis**

**Situation**          **Research**

Answer the following questions relating to the above worksheet:

| Questions | Answers |
|---|---|
| a. What was the planned sample size? | 1. 30 items |
| b. What is the total *misstatement* in the sample? | 2. 60 items |
| c. What is the most likely total misstatement in the population? | 3. 76 items |
| d. Calculate the upper limit on misstatement. | 4. 90 items |
| e. Calculate the allowance for sampling risk. | 5. 0 |
| f. Would one "accept" or "reject" the population as being materially correct? | 6. $ 12,550.00 |
| g. What is the risk of incorrect acceptance? | 7. $ 25,162.50 |
| | 8. $ 42,000.00 |
| | 9. $ 54,550.00 |
| | 10. $ 80,000.00 |
| | 11. $252,550.00 |
| | 12. $280,000.00 |
| | 13. $294,550.00 |
| | 14. $354,550.00 |
| | 15. Accept |
| | 16. Reject |
| | 17. 5% |
| | 18. 20% |
| | 19. 100% |

In-Class Team
Case for
Chapter 9
Appendixes

**9A–14.** Edwards has decided to use probability-proportional-to-size (PPS) sampling, sometimes called dollar-unit sampling, in the audit of a client's accounts receivable balance. Few, if any, misstatements of the account balance are expected.

Edwards plans to use the following PPS sampling table:

| Number of Overstatement Misstatements | Risk of Incorrect Acceptance | | | | |
|---|---|---|---|---|---|
| | 1% | 5% | 10% | 15% | 20% |
| 0 | 4.61 | 3.00 | 2.31 | 1.90 | 1.61 |
| 1 | 6.64 | 4.75 | 3.89 | 3.38 | 3.00 |
| 2 | 8.41 | 6.30 | 5.33 | 4.72 | 4.28 |
| 3 | 10.05 | 7.76 | 6.69 | 6.02 | 5.52 |
| 4 | 11.61 | 9.16 | 8.00 | 7.27 | 6.73 |

*Required:*

a. Identify the advantages of using PPS sampling over classical variables sampling.

b. Calculate the sampling interval and the sample size Edwards should use given the following information:

| | |
|---|---|
| Tolerable misstatement | $ 15,000 |
| Risk of incorrect acceptance | 5% |
| Estimated misstatement | $     0 |
| Recorded amount of accounts receivable | $300,000 |

Note: Requirements (c) through (f) are not related to (a) and (b).

c. Assuming a sampling interval of $5,000, calculate the total projected misstatement if the following three errors were discovered in a PPS sample:

| Misstatement | Book Value | Audited Value |
|---|---|---|
| 1 | $ 400 | $ 320 |
| 2 | 500 | 0 |
| 5 | 6,000 | 2,500 |

d. Calculate basic precision and incremental allowance.

e. Calculate the upper limit on misstatements.

f. Will you accept or reject the account as materially correct? Explain.

g. Use ACL to calculate the sampling interval and the sample size using the information in *b*.

h. Use ACL to calculate results using the errors in *c*.

(AICPA, adapted)

Integrating
Problem for
Chapter 9 and
the Appendixes

**9A–15.** Bill Pei, CPA, is about to begin his audit of the accuracy of his client's accounts receivable. Based on experience, he expects that approximately 1 percent of the client's 40,000 accounts have errors. The total book value of receivables is $5 million. Pei has established $390,000 as the amount of tolerable misstatement, 5 percent for the risk of incorrect acceptance, and 10 percent for the risk of incorrect rejection. The auditor estimates the standard deviation of the accounts to be $45.

*Required:*

a. Using mean-per-unit sampling, calculate the required sample size.

b. Now ignore part (a). Assume that as part of an attributes sampling plan using a stipulated tolerable rate of 5 percent and a risk of assessing control risk too low of 5 percent, the auditor wishes to test the receivables valuation—that is, each account will be considered as either correct or a deviation. What sample size would be required for this test?

*Additional information for parts (c) through (g):*

Now ignore your (a) and (b) answers and assume that the auditor selected a random sample of 208 accounts (square root = 14.4), representing a total book value of receivables of $40,800. He found five errors, representing a $20,300 overstatement as follows:

| Misstatement | Book Value | Audited Value |
|---|---|---|
| 1 | $26,000 | $5,950 |
| 2 | 1,000 | 900 |
| 3 | 220 | 200 |
| 4 | 180 | 120 |
| 5 | 100 | 30 |
| | $27,500 | $7,200 |

The standard deviation of the book value of the sample was $50, while the standard deviation of the audited values of the sample was $55.

c. Using mean-per-unit estimation, what is the projected misstatement for the population?

d. Using mean-per-unit sampling, calculate the adjusted allowance for sampling risk and use it to calculate the appropriate interval for use in deciding whether to "accept" or "reject" the population.

e. Using difference estimation, calculate the projected misstatement for the population.

f. Given the five misstatements presented earlier, what statistical conclusion may be made using attributes sampling (recall part [b] from the previous page)?

g. Assume a sampling interval of $24,038 ($5,000,000/208). Using PPS sampling, calculate:

(1) Projected misstatement.

(2) Basic precision.

(3) Incremental allowance for sampling risk.

# Cash and Financial Investments

This chapter describes the approach to the audit of cash and financial investments. Our discussion of these two types of assets is combined because of the interrelationship between them. Cash and many financial investments are liquid in nature, and transfers between the two accounts occur frequently.

## Cash

### Sources and Nature of Cash

**LO1**

Describe the sources and nature of cash.

Cash normally includes general, payroll, petty cash, and, less frequently, savings accounts. General accounts are checking accounts similar in nature to those maintained by individuals. Cash sales, collections of receivables, and investment of additional capital typically increase the account; business expenditures decrease it. Under the terms of a bank loan agreement, the cash in a company's general account sometimes must be maintained at a specified minimum balance, referred to as a *compensating balance.*

Payroll and petty cash accounts are "imprest" at a low balance. When payroll is paid, a transfer is made from the general account to the payroll account. Petty cash, used for very small expenditures, is replenished as necessary.

Cash equivalents are often combined with cash items to create the current asset classification called "cash and cash equivalents." *Cash equivalents* include money market funds, certificates of deposit, savings certificates, and other similar types of deposits. Any item that cannot be converted to cash on short notice should be classified as an investment, a receivable, or a prepaid expense, rather than as a cash equivalent.

Normal internal control activities (e.g., reconciliation of bank accounts) detect most errors that occur in these accounts. On the other hand, the liquid nature of cash increases the risk of fraud, which may be more difficult to detect.

### The Auditors' Objectives in the Audit of Cash

**LO2**

Identify the auditors' objectives in the audit of cash.

The auditors' *objectives* in the audit of cash and cash transactions are to:

1. Use the understanding of the client and its environment to consider *inherent risks,* including fraud risks, related to cash.
2. Obtain an understanding of *internal control* over cash.
3. Assess the risks of material misstatement of cash and design tests of controls and substantive procedures that:
   a. Substantiate the *existence* of recorded cash and the *occurrence* of cash transactions.
   b. Determine the accuracy of cash transactions.
   c. Establish the *completeness* of recorded cash.
   d. Verify the *cutoff* of cash transactions.
   e. Determine that the client has *rights* to recorded cash.
   f. Determine that the *presentation* and *disclosure* of cash, including restricted funds (such as compensating balances and bond sinking funds), are appropriate.

## Learning objectives

After studying this chapter, you should be able to:

LO1    Describe the sources and nature of cash.

LO2    Identify the auditors' objectives in the audit of cash.

LO3    Explain the nature of the cash receipts and disbursements cycles, and describe the fundamental controls over the business processes related to cash.

LO4    Use the understanding of the client and its environment to consider inherent risks, including fraud risks, related to cash.

LO5    Obtain an understanding of internal control over cash.

LO6    Assess the risks of material misstatement of cash and design further audit procedures, including tests of controls and substantive procedures, to address the risks.

LO7    Describe the risks involved in auditing financial investments, including why the auditors might need specialized skills.

LO8    Identify the auditors' objectives in the audit of financial investments.

LO9    Describe typical internal controls over the business processes related to financial investments.

LO10   Describe tests of controls and substantive procedures used to audit financial investments.

In addition to the preceding list, the auditors might add a valuation objective that relates to procedures for reconciling underlying records to the general ledger results and, if appropriate, proper valuation of foreign currency translation. We omit a separate valuation objective in the above list due to the ordinarily very limited valuation issues relating to cash (e.g., there is no need to consider valuation issues such as *net realizable value,* as with receivables, or the *lower of cost or market,* as with inventories).

## How Much Audit Time for Cash?

The consideration of materiality applies to audit work on cash as well as to other aspects of the audit. The counting of a small petty cash fund, which is inconsequential in relation to the company's overall financial position, accomplishes little in achieving the auditors' objective of expressing an opinion on the financial statements. Nevertheless, auditors do devote a larger proportion of the total audit hours to cash than might be suggested by the relatively small amount of cash shown on the balance sheet.

Several reasons exist to explain the auditors' traditional emphasis on cash transactions. Liabilities, revenue, expenses, and most other assets flow through the Cash account; that is, these items either arise from or result in cash transactions. Thus, the examination of cash transactions assists the auditors in the substantiation of many other items in the financial statements.

Another reason contributing to extensive auditing of cash is that cash is the most liquid of assets and offers the greatest temptation for theft, embezzlement, and misappropriation. Inherent risk is high for liquid assets, and auditors tend to respond to high-risk situations with more intensive investigation. However, the detection of fraud is relevant to the overall fairness of the client's financial statements only if such fraud is material in amount.

On occasion, auditors may encounter evidence of small-scale employee fraud. After determining that such fraud could *not* have a material effect upon the financial statements, the auditors should review the situation with the management and the audit committee of the board of directors before investigating the matter further. This discussion will alert the client to the situation, protect the auditors from charges of negligence, and avoid wasting audit time on matters that are not material to the financial statements and that may better be pursued by client personnel.

## Internal Control over Cash Transactions

**LO3**

Explain the nature of the cash receipts and disbursements cycles, and describe the fundamental controls over the business processes related to cash.

Most of the processes relating to cash handling are the responsibility of the finance department, under the direction of the treasurer. These processes include handling and depositing cash receipts; signing checks; investing idle cash; and maintaining custody of cash, marketable securities, and other negotiable assets. In addition, the finance department must forecast cash requirements and make both short-term and long-term financing arrangements.

Ideally, the functions of the finance department and the accounting department should be integrated in a manner that provides assurance that:

1. All cash that should have been received *was* in fact received, recorded accurately, and deposited promptly.
2. Cash disbursements have been made for authorized purposes only and have been properly recorded.
3. Cash balances are maintained at adequate, but not excessive, levels by forecasting expected cash receipts and payments related to normal operations. The need for obtaining loans or for investing excess cash is thus made known on a timely basis.

A detailed study of the business processes of the client is necessary in developing the most efficient control procedures, but there are some general guidelines to good cash-handling practices in all types of business. These guidelines for achieving internal control over cash may be summarized as follows:

1. Do not permit any one employee to handle a transaction from beginning to end.
2. Separate cash handling (custody) from record keeping.

3. Centralize receiving of cash to the extent practical.

4. Record cash receipts on a timely basis.

5. Encourage customers to obtain receipts and observe cash register totals.

6. Deposit cash receipts daily.

7. Make all disbursements by check or electronic funds transfer, with the exception of small expenditures from petty cash.

8. Have monthly bank reconciliations prepared by employees not responsible for making cash payments or custody of cash. The completed reconciliation should be reviewed promptly by an appropriate official.

9. Monitor cash receipts and disbursements by comparing recorded amounts to forecasted amounts and investigating variances from forecasted amounts.

## Internal Control over Cash Receipts

### Cash Sales

Control over cash sales is strongest when two or more employees (usually a salesclerk and a cashier) participate in each transaction with a customer. Restaurants and cafeterias often use a centrally located cashier who receives cash from the customer along with a sales ticket prepared by another employee. Theaters generally have a cashier selling prenumbered tickets, which are collected by a door attendant when the customer is admitted. If tickets or sales checks are serially numbered and all numbers accounted for, this separation of responsibility for the transaction is an effective means of preventing fraud.

In many retail establishments, the nature of the business is such that one employee must make over-the-counter sales, deliver the merchandise, receive cash, and record the transaction. In this situation, dishonesty may be discouraged by proper use of cash registers or electronic point-of-sale systems. The protective features of cash registers include (1) visual display of the amount of the sale in full view of the customer; (2) a printed receipt, which the customer is urged to take with the merchandise; and (3) accumulation of the total of the day's sales.

### Electronic Point-of-Sale Systems

Many retail stores use various types of electronic cash registers, including online computer terminals. Often, an electronic scanner reads the *universal product code* on the product. The salesperson need only scan the code for the register to record the sale at the product's price, which is stored in the computer. Thus, the risk of a salesperson recording sales at erroneous prices is substantially reduced.

Besides providing strong control over cash sales, electronic point-of-sale systems often may be programmed to perform numerous other control functions. For example, online registers may verify the credit status of charge account customers, update accounts receivable and perpetual inventory records, and provide special printouts accumulating sales data by product line, salesperson, department, and type of sale.

### Collections from Credit Customers

In many manufacturing and wholesale companies, cash receipts include checks received through the mail. This situation poses little threat of defalcation unless one employee is permitted to receive and deposit these checks and also to record the credits to the customers' accounts. Typical internal control over cash received through the mail is described below.

Incoming mail usually is opened in the mailroom, where an employee endorses the checks "for deposit only" to the company's account and prepares a *control listing* of the incoming cash receipts. This listing shows the amount received from each customer and identifies the customer by name or account number. A copy of the control listing is forwarded to the controller. Another copy of the control listing and the cash receipts are forwarded to the cashier. The remittance advices and a copy of the control listing (shown below) are forwarded to the employee responsible for the customers' accounts.

**Check (and remittance advice)**

| | |
|---|---|
| **Pilot Stores** | **987604** |
| 1425 G St. | |
| Irvine, CA 92345 | Date: Dec. 5, 20XX |
| **Pay to the** | |
| **order of**  Wood Supply Co. | **$8085.00** |
| **Eight thousand eighty-five and no/100** | |
| **First National Bank** | **Pilot Stores** |
| **California** | *Jackie Cohen* |
| **Remittance Advice** | |
| **Wood Supply Co.** | |
| **Inv. #7462537** | **$8085.00** |

| CONTROL LISTING | | |
|---|---|---|
| Payer | Cust. No. | Amount |
| Xxxxxxxxx | ##### | $$$$$.$$ |
| Xxxxxxxxx | ##### | $$$$$.$$ |
| Xxxxxxxxx | ##### | $$$$$.$$ |
| Pilot Stores | 12654 | $8085.00 |
| Xxxxxxxxx | ##### | $$$$$.$$ |
| Xxxxxxxxx | ##### | $$$$$.$$ |
| | | $$$$$.$$ |

Which controls tend to prevent the mailroom employee from abstracting the receipts from several customers, destroying the remittance advices, and omitting these receipts from the control listing? First, incoming cash receipts consist primarily of checks made payable to the company. Second, if customers' accounts are not credited for payments made, the customers will complain to the company. If these customers can produce paid checks (or electronic check copies) supporting their claims of payment and these checks do not appear on the mailroom control listings, responsibility for the abstraction is quickly focused upon the mailroom employee.

The checks are transferred to the cashier (with a copy of the control listing), who deposits the day's receipts intact in the bank. Control is exercised over the cashier by periodic reconciliation of the operations control copies of the mailroom control listings with the cash receipts journal and the details of the validated deposit slips received from the bank.

### Direct Receipt of Funds by Financial Institutions

Sales proceeds are often received directly by the clients' financial institution, which then notifies the business of the receipt through a variety of manners, including lockbox systems, credit cards, debit cards, and electronic transfer of funds by customers.

Businesses receiving a large volume of cash through the mail may use a lockbox system to strengthen internal control and hasten the depositing of cash receipts. The **lockbox** is actually a post office box controlled by the company's financial institution. Financial institution employees pick up mail at the post office box several times a day, credits the company's checking account for cash received, and sends the remittance advices to the company. Internal control is strengthened by the fact that the financial institution has no access to the company's accounting records.

Proceeds from credit card and debit card sales are handled in a similar manner by the bank(s) involved with the process. Ultimately, proceeds are deposited into the business's cash account.

### Electronic Funds Transfer

**Electronic funds transfer (EFT) systems** process funds-related transactions for customers as an alternative to paying by check. Increasingly, **electronic data interchange (EDI)** systems, which allow the interchange of data from one company's computer to another's, are electronically transferring funds between companies' bank accounts. These systems reduce paper flow and may reduce processing costs and delays. They do, however, require an extensive set of computer network controls relating to system access and data entry, as well as backup controls for situations in which a system breakdown occurs.

### Recording Cash Receipts

The employee responsible for the customers' accounts ledger enters the details of cash receipts into the computer in batches. The cash receipts program creates a file of cash receipt transactions that is used to update the general ledger and the master file of accounts receivable. This computer program creates control totals and exception reports that detail any invalid customer account numbers or unusual payment amounts. The manual follow-up procedures on exceptions reports and the reconciliations of control totals are performed by the operations control group.

The division of responsibilities, sequence of procedures, and controls over cash sales and collections from customers are illustrated in the systems flowchart in Figure 10.1.

## Internal Control over Cash Disbursements

Ideally, cash disbursements should be made by check, electronic funds transfer, or, for minor items, from petty cash funds.

### Checking Account Disbursements

A principal advantage of requiring disbursement by check is obtaining evidence of receipt from the payee in the form of an endorsement on the check. Other advantages include (1) the centralization of disbursement authority in the hands of a few designated officials—only persons authorized to sign checks; (2) a permanent record of disbursements; and (3) a reduction in the amount of cash kept on hand.

To secure in full the internal control benefits implicit in the use of checks, it is essential that all checks be prenumbered and all numbers in the series be accounted for. Unissued prenumbered checks should be adequately safeguarded against theft or misuse. Voided checks should be defaced to eliminate any possibility of further use and filed in the regular sequence of paid checks. Dollar amounts should be printed on all checks by the computer or a check-protecting machine. This practice makes it difficult for anyone to alter a check by raising its amount.

Officials authorized to sign checks should review the documents supporting the payment and perforate (deface) these documents at the time of signing the check to prevent them from being submitted a second time. The official signing checks should maintain control of the checks until they are placed in the mail. Typically, the check comes to the official complete except for signature. To make a variety of fraudulent schemes involving falsified documents less likely, the signed checks should not be returned to the accounting department, which prepared them for signature.

Most companies issuing a large volume of checks use computers or check-signing machines. The authorized signature (usually that of the treasurer) may be printed automatically on each check as it is processed. If the computer generates signed checks, item counts, control totals, and cash totals (reconciled by finance department personnel) may be used to make certain that checks are issued only for authorized cash disbursements. When a check-signing machine is used, the machine should be safeguarded with physical locks and keys and/or passwords. Additional controls may be established for large checks, such as the requirement for a second manual signature.

Reconciliation of monthly bank statements is essential to adequate internal control over cash receipts and disbursements. An employee having no part in authorizing or accounting for cash transactions or in handling cash should reconcile bank statements. Statements from the bank should come unopened to this employee. Each month the completed bank reconciliation should be reviewed by a responsible company official and approved in writing.

A voucher system is one method of achieving strong internal control over cash disbursements by providing assurance that all disbursements are properly authorized and reviewed before a check is issued. In a typical voucher system, the accounting department

**FIGURE 10.1** **Cash Receipts Cycle**

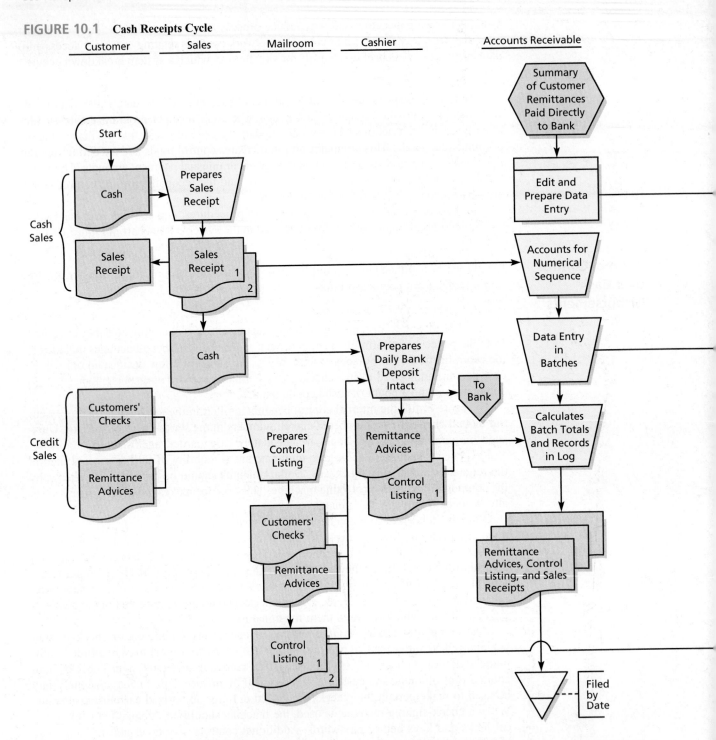

is responsible for assembling the appropriate documentation to support every cash disbursement. For example, before authorizing payment for merchandise purchased, the accounting department assembles copies of the purchase order, receiving report, and vendor's invoice and determines that these documents are in agreement. After determining that the transaction is properly supported, an accounting employee prepares a voucher, which is filed in a tickler file according to the date upon which payment will be made.

A **voucher,** in this usage, is an authorization sheet that provides space for the initials of the employees performing various authorization functions. Authorization functions include such procedures as extending and footing the vendor's invoice; determining the

| Data Processing | Operations Control | Bank |
|---|---|---|

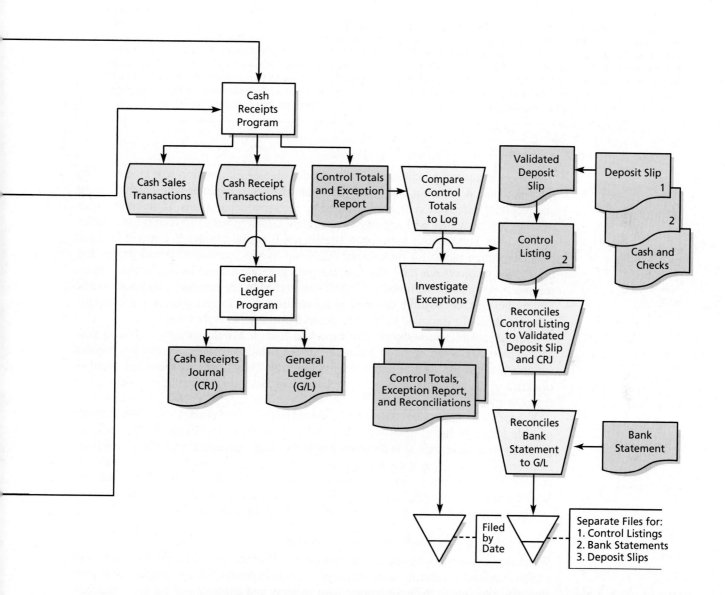

agreement of the invoice, purchase order, and receiving report; and recording the transaction in the accounts. Transactions are recorded in a **voucher register** (which normally replaces a purchases journal) by an entry debiting the appropriate asset, liability, or expense account and crediting Vouchers Payable. The separation of the function of invoice verification and approval from the function of cash disbursement is another step that tends to prevent errors and fraud. On the payment date, the voucher and supporting documents are removed from the tickler file and the check is prepared *but not signed.* The voucher, supporting papers, and the check (complete except for signature) are forwarded to the finance department for signature.

**Illustrative Case**     *Importance of Cash Controls*

One large construction company ignored basic controls over cash disbursements. Unissued checks were stored in an unlocked supply closet, along with Styrofoam coffee cups. The company check-signing machine deposited signed checks into a box that was equipped with a lock. Despite warnings from their independent auditors, company officials found it "too inconvenient" to keep the box locked or to pay attention to the check counter built into the machine. The company maintained very large bank balances and did not bother to reconcile bank statements promptly.

A three-week-old bank statement and a group of paid checks were given to an employee with instructions to prepare a bank reconciliation. The employee noticed that the group of paid checks accompanying the bank statement was not complete. No paid checks could be found to support over $700,000 in charges on the bank statement. Further investigation revealed that more than $1 million in unauthorized and unrecorded checks had been paid from various company bank accounts. The checks had been issued out of sequence and had been signed by the company check-signing machine. The company was unable to determine who was responsible for the theft, and the money was never recovered.

In a computerized purchasing system, vendor invoice information will be entered by the accounting department and it may be matched by the computer with purchase order and receiving information that was entered by the other departments. If the information matches, the computer will approve the payment and automatically record the voucher as a payable. Transactions with inconsistencies will not be processed, but will be listed on an exception report for review and follow-up by the operations control group. Just prior to the invoice's due date, the computer will generate a check or an electronic funds transfer in payment of the invoice. If checks are signed by the computer, they need not be sent to the vouchers payable department for mailing. As a further control, the computer software should be designed to identify unusual disbursements for review.

Another control the auditors may expect to find in a well-managed accounts payable department is the monthly balancing of the detailed records of accounts payable (or vouchers) to the general ledger control account. These reconciliations are saved as evidence of the performance of this procedure and as an aid in locating any subsequent errors or fraud.

*Vendors' statements,* received monthly, should be reconciled promptly with the accounts payable ledger or list of open vouchers, and any discrepancies should be fully investigated. In some industries, it is common practice to make advances to vendors, which are recovered by making percentage deductions from invoices. When advances are made, the auditors should ascertain that procedures are being followed to ensure that deductions from the invoices are being made in accordance with the terms of the agreement.

The operation of a voucher system is illustrated in the flowchart in Figure 10.2.

### Internal Control over Employee Reimbursements

When employees incur business expenses on behalf of the company, the company must establish effective controls over employee reimbursements. Many companies require employees to submit expense reports with receipts and explanations for their expenditures. The reports are typically approved by the employee's supervisor and submitted to the accounting department for processing. This documentation is used to support the reimbursement through the company's normal payment system. Employees are often reimbursed through direct deposit to their bank accounts.

Many companies issue business credit cards to employees that incur significant amounts of expenses on behalf of the company. Employees are required to document explanations for their credit card expenditures and perhaps also maintain credit card receipts to support the expenditures.

## FIGURE 10.2   Flowchart of a Cash Disbursements Cycle (Voucher System)*

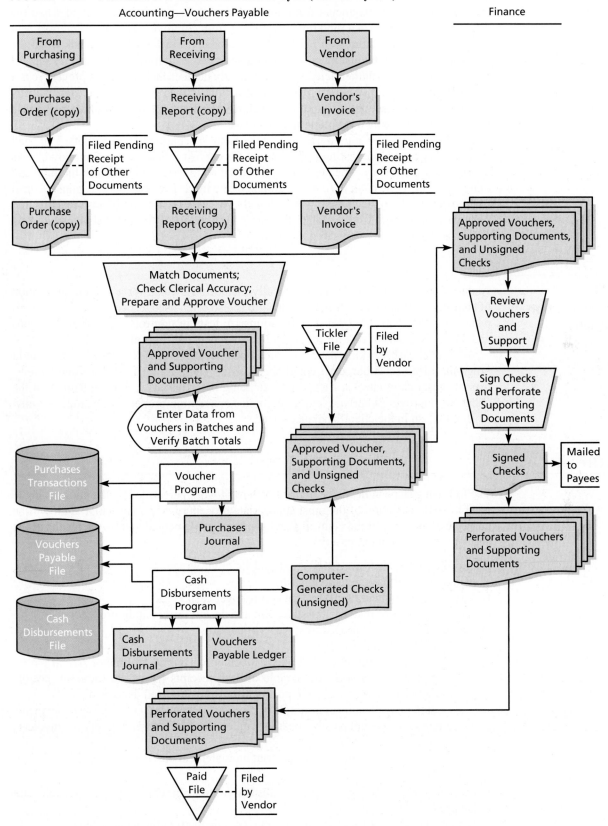

*This flowchart presents disbursements by check. Disbursements by credit card, debit card, and electronic transfer are similar, with the check being replaced by documentation relating to the particular type of disbursement. The cash receipts discussion in this chapter discusses these alternate forms of cash receipts.

*Internal Control Aspects of Petty Cash Funds*

Internal control over payments from an imprest petty cash fund is achieved when the custodian of the petty cash fund reviews support from employees seeking reimbursement for their small expenditures on behalf of the company. Further control exists when the custodian requests replenishment of the fund and another individual reviews the support for completeness and authenticity and subsequently defaces that support to prevent reuse.

Audit tests of petty cash emphasize transactions rather than the year-end balance. The auditors may test one or more replenishment transactions by examining petty cash vouchers and verifying their numerical sequence.

Petty cash funds are sometimes kept in the form of separate bank accounts. The bank should be instructed in writing not to accept for deposit in such an account any checks payable to the company. The deposits will be limited to checks to replenish the fund and drawn payable to the bank or to the custodian of the fund. The prohibition against deposit of checks payable to the company is designed to prevent the routing of cash receipts into petty cash, since this would violate the basic assumption of limited disbursements and review at the time of replenishing the fund.

## Audit Documentation for Cash

Auditors' working papers for cash typically include a flowchart or a written description of controls. An internal control questionnaire is also often used, especially in larger companies. A related working paper will summarize tests of controls for cash transactions and the assessments of risk for the financial statement assertions about cash.

Additional cash working papers include documentation of risk assessments, an audit program, a lead schedule, cash count sheets, bank confirmations, bank reconciliations, lists of outstanding checks, lists of checks being investigated, recommendations to the client for improving internal control, and notes concerning proper presentation and disclosure of cash in the client's balance sheet.

## Audit of Cash

The following steps indicate the general pattern of work performed by the auditors in the audit of cash. Selection of the most appropriate procedures for a particular audit will be guided by the nature of the controls that have been implemented and by the results of the auditors' risk assessment process.

A. Use the understanding of the client and its environment to consider inherent risks, including fraud risks, related to cash.
B. Obtain an understanding of internal control over cash.
C. Assess the risks of material misstatement and design further audit procedures.
D. Perform further audit procedures—tests of controls.
   1. Examples of tests of controls:
      *a.* Test the accounting records and reconciliations by reperformance.
      *b.* Compare the details of a sample of cash receipts listings to the cash receipts journal, accounts receivable postings, and authenticated deposit slips.
      *c.* Compare the details of a sample of recorded disbursements in the cash payments journal to account payable postings, purchase orders, receiving reports, invoices, and paid checks.
   2. If necessary, revise the risk of material misstatement based on the results of tests of controls.
E. Perform further audit procedures—substantive procedures for cash transactions and balances.
   1. Obtain analyses of cash balances and reconcile them to the general ledger.
   2. Send standard confirmation forms to financial institutions to verify amounts on deposit.

**FIGURE 10.3**
**Objectives of Major Substantive Procedures for Cash Transactions and Balances**

| Substantive Procedures | Primary Audit Objectives |
|---|---|
| Obtain analyses of cash balances and reconcile them to general ledger. | *Existence* and *accuracy* |
| Confirm cash balances with financial institutions. Obtain reconciliations of bank balances and consider reconciling bank activity. Obtain bank cutoff statement. Count cash on hand. | *Existence, occurrence, accuracy, cutoff,* and *rights* |
| Verify the client's cutoff of cash transactions. Analyze bank transfers occurring year-end. | *Cutoff, existence, occurrence, rights,* and *completeness* |
| Investigate payments to related parties. Evaluate financial statement presentation and disclosure. | *Presentation* and *disclosure* |

3. Obtain or prepare reconciliations of bank (financial institution) accounts as of the balance sheet date and consider the need to reconcile bank activity for additional months.
4. Obtain a cutoff bank statement containing transactions of at least seven business days subsequent to the balance sheet date.
5. Count and list cash on hand.
6. Verify the client's cutoff of cash receipts and cash disbursements.
7. Analyze bank transfers for the last week of the audit year and the first week of the following year.
8. Investigate any checks representing large or unusual payments to related parties.
9. Evaluate proper financial statement presentation and disclosure of cash.

Figure 10.3 relates these substantive procedures to the primary audit objectives.

**LO4**

Use the understanding of the client and its environment to consider inherent risks, including fraud risks, related to cash.

### A. Use the Understanding of the Client and Its Environment to Consider Inherent Risks, Including Fraud Risks, Related to Cash.

Risks of material misstatement arise jointly from inherent risk and control risk. Most inherent risks relate to business risks faced by the client's management. In the area of cash and financial investments, management is particularly concerned with business risks related to the possible theft of these liquid assets. This is also a significant concern of the auditors as most misstatements of assets involve overstatement.

In addition to concerns about the overstatement of cash, auditors are aware that cash may have been improperly abstracted during the period, even though the year-end cash may be properly stated. To distinguish between the situations, assume that the client's balance sheet shows "Cash $250,000." For most clients, the primary risks are that errors or fraud either (1) create a situation in which $250,000 overstates actual cash, or (2) create a situation in which the $250,000 recorded year-end balance should be higher.

Concerning the first risk (overstated cash), a shortage may have been concealed merely by the insertion of a fictitious check in the cash on hand at year-end, or by the omission of an outstanding check from the year-end bank reconciliation. Note that the omission of an outstanding check may be indicative of either an error or fraud. For example, poor internal control may result in a situation in which human error resulted in the check not being recorded in disbursements. On the other hand, although recorded in cash disbursements, the check may have been omitted from the outstanding check list to allow the individual who has embezzled that amount of cash to hide fraud.

Concerning the second risk—the year-end cash is correct, but should be higher—the auditors' problem is not misstated cash, but fraud and its effect on other accounts.

Consequently, the auditors have in mind such basic questions as: (1) Do the client's records reflect all cash transactions that took place during the year? and (2) Were all cash payments properly authorized and for a legitimate business purpose? Examples of fraud that may be disclosed in searching for answers to these questions are:

1. Interception of cash receipts before any record is made.
2. Payment for materials not received.
3. Duplicate payments.
4. Overpayments to employees or payments to fictitious employees.
5. Payments for personal expenditures of officers or related parties.

Based on their knowledge of the client and its environment, the auditors may identify other business risks that result in risks of material misstatements. In some engagements, the auditors may be particularly concerned with the risk of the completeness of recorded cash. As an example, management of a privately held company may be motivated to understate assets (including cash) to minimize income taxes. Also, for a particular client there may be a significant risk that management maintains bank accounts not recorded on the books for such purposes as making illegal bribes. Thus, in such situations, there is a heightened risk that not all cash may be recorded in the financial records. In other cases, the manner in which the client collects cash may present significant business and inherent risks. For example, a charitable organization may receive a large amount of funds from cash donations, creating a significant inherent risk that not all cash donations may be received and recorded.

The auditors also may identify fraud risks related to cash transactions. In such cases, the auditors should obtain an understanding of the programs and controls used by management to mitigate these risks and determine whether the controls have been implemented. Strengths and weaknesses in the client's internal control serve to mitigate or increase the effects of these fraud risks.

**LO5**

Obtain an understanding of internal control over cash.

## B. Obtain an Understanding of Internal Control over Cash.

In the audit of a small business, the auditors may prepare a written description of controls, based upon the questioning of owners and employees and upon firsthand observation. For larger companies, a flowchart or internal control questionnaire is usually employed to describe internal control. An internal control questionnaire for cash receipts was illustrated in Chapter 7. Among the questions included in a questionnaire for cash disbursements are whether all disbursements (except those from petty cash) are made by prenumbered checks and whether voided checks are marked "void" and saved. The existence of these controls permits the auditors to determine that all disbursements have been recorded by accounting for the sequence of checks issued or voided during the period.

Other points to be made clear by the questionnaire include (1) whether check-signing authority is restricted to selected executives not having access to accounting records or to vouchers and other documents supporting checks submitted for signature, and (2) whether checks are mailed directly to the payees after being signed. The internal control questionnaire will also cover cash disbursements for payroll and for dividends, as well as bank reconciliation procedures.

After the auditors have prepared a flowchart (or other description) of internal control, they will conduct a walk-through of the system. The term *walk-through* means to trace a transaction or a few transactions through each step of the system to determine that transactions actually are being processed in the manner indicated by the flowchart. The walk-through allows the auditors to determine that internal control as described in the working papers has actually been implemented.

As the auditors verify their understanding of the cash receipts and disbursements cycles, they will observe whether there is appropriate segregation of duties and inquire about who performed various functions throughout the year. They will also inspect the various documents and reconciliations that are important to the client's internal control over cash receipts and disbursements. Cash forecasts or budgets also will be inspected and the auditors will review the evidence of the follow-up on variances from forecasted amounts of receipts and disbursements. In some cases, the auditors will review exception reports generated by the computer and the evidence of the follow-up on them. These tests of controls provide the auditors with evidence to support their assessed level of control risk.

**LO6**

Assess the risks of material misstatement of cash and design further audit procedures, including tests of controls and substantive procedures, to address the risks.

## C. Assess the Risks of Material Misstatement and Design Further Audit Procedures.

After obtaining an understanding of the client's internal control over cash receipts and disbursements, the auditors determine their planned assessed levels of the risks of material misstatement (or the separate inherent and control risks) for the assertions about cash. If additional evidence of effectiveness of the controls is needed to support these assessed levels, the auditors will design additional tests of control. In designing these tests, the auditors must decide which ones will result in sufficient reductions in substantive procedures to justify the time spent performing them.

By considering these risk assessments, the auditors are able to identify "what could go wrong" to cause the cash accounts to be materially misstated. Figures 10.4 and 10.5 provide examples of possible material misstatements of cash that may be identified by the auditors based on the client's operations and environment, and on weaknesses in its internal control over cash receipts and cash disbursements. Once these risks of material misstatement have been identified and assessed, the auditors can plan appropriate substantive procedures that address them.

## D. Perform Further Audit Procedures—Tests of Controls.

### 1. Examples of Tests of Controls.

Tests directed toward the effectiveness of controls help to evaluate the client's internal control and determine whether the auditors' planned assessed levels of the risks of material misstatement can be supported. Certain tests of controls are performed as the auditors obtain an understanding of the client's internal control; these tests were described in our discussion of that process. The following are examples of typical further tests of controls.

### a. Test the Accounting Records and Reconciliations by Reperformance.

To determine that the client's accounting procedures are operating effectively, the auditors perform tests of the accuracy of the client's journals and ledgers. In a computer-based system, journal and ledger entries may be created simultaneously from the same source documents, and the auditors might choose to use computer assisted audit techniques (CAATs) to test the accuracy of the accounting records.

In a manual system, information on source documents is entered first in a journal; at a later date the information is summarized and posted from journals to ledgers. The auditors must manually determine that the documents are accurately entered to the journals, the journals are accurately footed, and the data are properly posted to the ledgers. The auditors also may decide to test the client's procedures for reconciling bank (financial institution) accounts. They may select a sample of the reconciliations performed during the year, noting who performed them, and *reperform* the reconciliation process by reference to accounting records, bank statements, and canceled checks.

### b. Compare the Details of a Sample of Cash Receipts Listings to the Cash Receipts Journal, Accounts Receivable Postings, and Authenticated Deposit Slips.

Satisfactory internal control over cash receipts demands that each day's collections be deposited intact no later than the next banking day. To provide assurance that cash receipts have been deposited intact, the auditors should compare the detail of

**FIGURE 10.4    Potential Misstatements—Cash Receipts**

| Description of Misstatement | Examples | Internal Control Weaknesses or Factors that Increase the Risk of the Misstatement |
|---|---|---|
| Recording fictitious cash receipts | **Fraud:**<br>• Overstating cash receipts on the books by transferring cash between bank accounts without appropriate recording of the transfer to cover up an embezzlement of cash | • Lack of segregation of duties of the functions of access to cash and record keeping; no effective review of bank reconciliations |
| Failure to record receipts from cash sales | **Fraud:**<br>• A cashier fails to ring up and record cash sales and embezzles the cash | • Inadequate supervision of cashiers; failure to encourage customers to obtain cash receipts |
|  | **Error:**<br>• A bookkeeper accidentally omits the recording of the receipts from one cash register for the day | • Inadequate controls for reconciling cash register tapes and accounting records; inadequate controls for reconciling bank accounts |
| Failure to record cash from collection of accounts receivable | **Fraud:**<br>• A cashier embezzles cash payments by customers on receivables, without recording the receipts in the customers' accounts<br>• A bookkeeper who has access to cash receipts embezzles cash collected from customers and writes off the related receivables | • Lack of segregation of duties between personnel who have access to cash receipts and those who make entries into the accounts receivable records<br>• Lack of segregation of duties between personnel who have access to cash receipts and those who make entries into the accounts receivable records |
|  | **Error:**<br>• A bookkeeper accidentally fails to record payment on a receivable | • Inadequate reconciliations of subsidiary records of accounts receivable with the general ledger control account |
| Early (late) recognition of cash receipts—"cutoff problems" | **Fraud:**<br>• Holding the cash receipts journal open to record next year's cash receipts as having occurred in this year | • Ineffective board of directors, audit committee, or internal audit function; "tone at the top" not conducive to ethical conduct; undue pressure to show improved financial position |
|  | **Error:**<br>• Recording cash receipts based on bad information about date of receipt | • Failure to list and deposit cash receipts on a timely basis |

the original cash receipts listings (mailroom listings and register tapes) to the detail of the daily deposit tickets. The *detail* of cash receipts refers to a listing of the amount of each individual check and the total amount of currency composing the day's receipts.

FIGURE 10.5    Potential Misstatements—Cash Disbursements

| Description of Misstatement | Examples | Internal Control Weaknesses/Factors that Increase the Risk of the Misstatement |
|---|---|---|
| Inaccurate recording of a purchase or disbursement | **Fraud:**<br>• A bookkeeper prepares a check to himself and records it as having been issued to a major supplier | • Inadequate segregation of duties of record keeping and preparing cash disbursements, or check signer does not review and cancel supporting documents |
|  | **Errors:**<br>• A disbursement is made to pay an invoice for goods that have not been received | • Ineffective controls for matching invoices with receiving documents before disbursements are authorized |
|  | • Disbursements for travel and entertainment are improperly included with merchandise purchases | • Ineffective accounting coding procedures may result from incompetent accounting personnel, inadequate chart of accounts, or no controls over the posting process |
| Duplicate recording and payment of purchases | **Error:**<br>• A purchase is recorded when an invoice is received from a vendor and recorded again when a duplicate invoice is sent by the vendor | • Ineffective controls for review and cancellation of supporting documents by the check signer |
| Unrecorded disbursements | **Fraud:**<br>• In conjunction with unrecorded (but deposited) cash receipts, an employee writes and cashes an unrecorded check for the identical amount | • Ineffective control over record keeping for and access to cash |

Comparison of the daily entries in the cash receipts journal with bank deposits may disclose a type of fraud known as *lapping*. Lapping is the concealment of a cash shortage by delaying the recording of cash receipts. The table on the following page provides an illustration.

If cash collected from customer A is withheld by the cashier, a subsequent collection from customer B may be entered as a credit to A's account. B's account will not be shown as paid until a collection from customer C is recorded as a credit to B. Unless the money abstracted by the cashier is replaced, the accounts receivable as a group remain overstated; but judicious shifting of the overstatement from one account receivable to another may avert protests from customers receiving monthly statements. The following schedule makes clear how a lapping activity may be carried on. In companies in which the cashier has access to the general accounting records, shortages created in this manner have sometimes been transferred to inventory accounts or elsewhere in the records for temporary concealment.

Lapping is most easily carried on when an employee who receives collections from customers is responsible for the posting of customers' accounts. Familiarity with customers' accounts makes it relatively easy to lodge a shortage in an account that will not be currently questioned.

| Date | Actually Received From | Actual Cash Receipts | Recorded as Received From | Receipts Recorded and Deposited | Receipts Withheld |
|---|---|---|---|---|---|
| Dec. 1 | Abbott | $ 750 | | | $ 750 |
| | Crane | 1,035 | Crane | $1,035 | |
| 2 | Barstow | 750 | Abbott | 750 | |
| | White | 130 | White | 130 | |
| 3 | Crawford | 1,575 | Barstow | 750 | 825 |
| | Miller | 400 | Miller | 400 | |
| | | $4,640 | | $3,065 | $1,575 |

### c. Compare the Details of a Sample of Recorded Disbursements in the Cash Disbursements Journal to Accounts Payable Postings, Purchase Orders, Receiving Reports, Invoices, and Paid Checks.

Satisfactory internal control over cash disbursements requires that controls exist to provide assurance that disbursements are properly authorized. Testing cash disbursements involves tracing selected items back through the cash disbursements journal to original source documents, including vouchers, purchase orders, receiving reports, invoices, and paid checks. While examining these documents, the auditors have an opportunity to test many of the controls over cash disbursements. For example, they will notice whether all paid vouchers and supporting documents have been perforated or canceled. Also, they will determine whether agreement exists among the supporting documents and note the presence of all required authorization signatures. The auditors also may review the file of paid checks to test the client's procedures for accounting for the numerical sequence of checks.

### 2. If Necessary, Revise the Risk of Material Misstatement Based on the Results of Tests of Controls.

When the auditors have completed the procedures described in the preceding sections, they should reassess the level of control risk for each financial statement assertion regarding cash. The auditors then decide what modifications, if any, are necessary to the planned audit program of substantive procedures for cash transactions and balances.

### E. Perform Further Audit Procedures—Substantive Procedures for Cash Transactions and Balances.

### 1. Obtain Analyses of Cash Balances and Reconcile Them to the General Ledger.

The auditors will prepare or obtain a schedule that lists all of the client's cash accounts. For cash in bank accounts, this schedule will typically list the bank, the account number, the account type, and the year-end balance per books. The auditors will trace and reconcile all accounts to the general ledger.

### 2. Confirm Cash Balances with Financial Institutions.

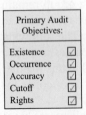

One of the objectives of the auditors' work on cash is to substantiate the existence of the amount of cash shown on the balance sheet. A direct approach to this objective is to confirm amounts on deposit and obtain or prepare reconciliations between bank statements and the accounting records.

Confirmation of amounts on deposit by direct communication with financial institution officials is obtained in most audits. Account balances are often confirmed with a standard form as illustrated by Figure 10.6. This **standard confirmation form,** agreed to by the AICPA, the American Bankers Association, and the Bank Administration Institute, addresses *only* the client's deposit and loan balances. Information identifying

**FIGURE 10.6    Confirmation Form**

## STANDARD FORM TO CONFIRM ACCOUNT
## BALANCE INFORMATION WITH FINANCIAL INSTITUTIONS

| ORIGINAL |
|---|
| To be mailed to accountant |

The Fairview Corporation
_____
CUSTOMER NAME

**Financial Institution's Name and Address**

Security National Bank
1000 Wilshire Boulevard
Los Angeles, California 90017-3562

We have provided to our accountants the following information as of

the close of business on  December 31 , 20 X3 ,
regarding our deposit and loan balances. Please confirm the accuracy
of the information, noting any exceptions to the information provided.
If the balances have been left blank, please complete this form by furnishing
the balance in the appropriate space below. *Although we do not request
or expect you to conduct a comprehensive, detailed search of your records,
if during the process of completing this confirmation additional information
about other deposit and loan accounts we may have with you comes to your
attention, please include such information below. Please use the enclosed
envelope to return the form directly to our accountants.

1. At the close of business on the date listed above, our records indicated the following deposit balance(s):

| ACCOUNT NAME | ACCOUNT NO. | INTEREST RATE | BALANCE* |
|---|---|---|---|
| General Account | 133-7825 | None | $89,548.92 |
| Payroll Account | 133-8765 | None | 8,212.05 |

2. We were directly liable to the financial institution for loans at the close of business on the date listed above as follows:

| ACCOUNT NO./ DESCRIPTION | BALANCE* | DATE DUE | INTEREST RATE | DATE THROUGH WHICH INTEREST IS PAID | DESCRIPTION OF COLLATERAL |
|---|---|---|---|---|---|
| 55-8965T Credit | $324,877 | 6/15/X7 | $12\frac{1}{2}\%$ | 12/15/X3 | Furniture & Fixtures |
| Line | $200,000 | 3/31/X4 | $13\frac{1}{4}\%$ | 12/31/X3 | Unsecured |

*Judith Fareri*
(Customer's Authorized Signature)

January 16, 20X4
(Date)

The information presented above by the customer is in agreement with our records. Although we have not conducted a comprehensive, detailed search
of our records, no other deposit or loan accounts have come to our attention except as noted below.

*Jeanne M. Mebus*
(Financial Institution Authorized Signature)

January 31, 20X4
(Date)

*Audit Inquiry Clerk*
(Title)

| EXCEPTIONS AND/OR COMMENTS |
|---|
|  |

Please return this form directly to our accountants:

Douglas & Troon, CPAs
800 Hill Street
Los Angeles, CA  90014-7865

*Ordinarily, balances are intentionally left blank if they are not
available at the time the form is prepared.

Approved 1990 by American Bankers Association, American Institute of Certified Public Accountants, and Bank Administration
Institute. Additional forms available from: AICPA – Order Department, P.O. Box 1003, NY, NY 10108 – 1003

0451 5951

accounts and loans and their balances is normally included on the form to assist the
financial institution in completing it. Thus, the form is primarily used to *corroborate* the
existence of recorded information. However, the confirmation may also lead to the *discovery* of additional accounts or loans and, therefore, it provides limited evidence about
the *completeness* of recorded amounts. Although the personnel at the financial institution
will not conduct a detailed search of the records, they will include information about
additional deposits and loans that they note while completing the confirmation.

## Illustrative Case

### Electronic Confirmation of Cash and Loans

Confirmation.com provides an electronic service for CPAs and financial institutions. This service represents the implementation of a "business plan" developed by Brian Fox, CPA, as a part of an assignment in a master's level course.

While working as a CPA, Brian Fox identified certain inefficiencies and potential for fraud inherent in the written confirmation process. His vision for a solution, which has similarities to the "Paypal" model, was to develop a secure clearinghouse in which both CPAs and financial institutions could be assured that not only was the confirmation transmission process itself secure, but also that the proper, authorized individuals were responding.

Confirmation.com offers both In-Network and Out-of-Network electronic confirmations. When an audit team begins its fieldwork, they request confirmations electronically through Confirmation.com, which then allows the appropriate individuals at the banks to respond to the requests through the network. While the paper confirmation process ordinarily takes several weeks (at a minimum), electronic confirmation replies are often received within a day. Currently, most large banks and thousands of CPAs use the In-Network services of Confirmation.com. Confirmation.com's Out-of-Network service allows electronic confirmations to be sent to banks outside of the network.

---

In more and more situations, auditors confirm balances with financial institutions electronically. As indicated in the *Illustrative Case* above, the auditors often use a clearing house approach. The personnel at the financial institution provide the auditors (with the client's authorization) access to a secure Web site that contains the requested information. Alternatively, the information may be provided on a Web site controlled and maintained by a trusted third-party service provider. When Web site location and access information is provided by the financial institution or a trusted third-party service provider, it meets the definition of a written confirmation from a third party and may be considered appropriate. However, if the Web site location and access information is obtained only from the client personnel, the information cannot be considered to be confirmed by a third party. In these situations, there is a risk that client personnel may create a fictitious Web site or account to misstate the balances being confirmed.

The details of other financial arrangements may be confirmed with financial institutions, using separate confirmation letters sent to the individual at the financial institution who is responsible for the client's financial arrangements or is knowledgeable about those arrangements. For example, the auditors may send a separate confirmation form to corroborate compensating balance arrangements or authorized check signers. These confirmation forms are described in detail in Chapter 15.

### 3. Obtain or Prepare Reconciliations of Bank (Financial Institution) Accounts as of the Balance Sheet Date and Consider the Need to Reconcile Bank Activity for Additional Months.

| Primary Audit Objectives: | |
|---|---|
| Existence | ☑ |
| Occurrence | ☑ |
| Accuracy | ☑ |
| Cutoff | ☑ |
| Rights | ☑ |

Determining a company's cash position at the close of the period requires a reconciliation of the balance per the bank statement at that date with the balance per the company's accounting records. Even though the auditors may not be able to begin their fieldwork for some time after the close of the year, they will prepare a bank reconciliation as of the balance sheet date or test the one prepared by the client.

If the client has made the year-end reconciliation, there is no need to duplicate the work. However, the auditors should examine the reconciliation in detail to satisfy themselves that it has been properly prepared. Inspection of a reconciliation prepared by the client will include verifying the arithmetical accuracy, comparing balances to the bank statement and ledger account, and investigating the reconciling items. The importance of a careful review of the client's reconciliation is indicated by the fact that a cash shortage may be concealed merely by omitting a check from the outstanding check list or by purposely making an error in addition on the reconciliation.

## Illustrative Case

### Controlling Confirmation Requests

The need to control the confirmation process is illustrated in the Parmalat fraud case. In that case, an *SEC Litigation Release* reports that the auditors received a bank confirmation confirming that a subsidiary of Parmalat held the equivalent of $4.8 billion (denominated in euros) in cash and marketable securities in a Bank of America account in New York City. The bank account and marketable securities did not exist.

It is believed that the auditors used Parmalat's internal mail to request financial information, and the confirmation was intercepted by a member of management. According to *The Wall Street Journal*, prosecutors believed that the reply information on the fraudulent confirmation was created in Parmalat's main offices by scanning Bank of America's logo into a computer, printing it out, and then passing the sheet of paper several times through a fax machine to make it look more authentic.

There are many satisfactory forms of bank reconciliations. The form most frequently used by auditors begins with balance per bank and ends with unadjusted balance per the accounting records. The format permits the auditors to post adjusting entries affecting cash directly to the bank reconciliation working paper so that the final adjusted balance can be cross-referenced to the cash lead schedule or to the working trial balance.

The mechanics of balancing the ledger account with the bank statement by no means completes the auditors' verification of cash on deposit. The authenticity of the individual items making up the reconciliation must be established by reference to their respective sources. The balance per the bank statement, for example, is not accepted at face value but is verified by direct confirmation with the bank, as described in the preceding pages. Other verification procedures associated with the reconciliation of the bank statement will now be discussed.

The auditors should investigate any checks outstanding for a long period of time (e.g., six months). If checks remain outstanding for long periods, internal control over cash disbursements is weakened. Employees who become aware that certain checks have long been outstanding and may never be presented have an opportunity to conceal a cash shortage merely by omitting the old outstanding check from the bank reconciliation. Such omissions will serve to increase the apparent balance of cash on deposit and may thus induce an employee to abstract a corresponding amount of cash on hand. It is good practice for the client to eliminate long-outstanding checks of this nature by an entry debiting the Cash account and crediting Unclaimed Wages or another special liability account. This will reduce the work required in bank reconciliations, as well as lessen the opportunity for fraud.

When internal control over the recording of cash receipts and disbursements is considered weak, the auditors may use additional reconciliation procedures. For example, a **proof of cash** may be prepared, which, in addition to reconciling the account balance, reconciles cash transactions occurring during a specified period. Specifically, the technique is used to identify:

- Cash receipts and disbursements recorded in the accounting records, but not on the bank statement.
- Cash deposits and disbursements recorded on the bank statement, but not in the accounting records.
- Cash receipts and disbursements recorded at different amounts by the bank than in the accounting records.

A proof of cash is essentially a fraud detection procedure that may be used for any months during the year.

A proof of cash for the test period of September is illustrated in Figure 10.7. Notice that this working paper is so organized that the first and last columns reconcile the cash

**FIGURE 10.7  Proof of Cash**

THE FAIRVIEW CORPORATION
Account No. 101
Proof of Cash for September 20X1
December 31, 20X1

A-6
SM
11/15/X1

| | Balance 8/31/X1 | Deposits | Checks and Charges | Balance 9/30/X1 |
|---|---|---|---|---|
| Per Bank Statement | $39,236.40 ✗ | $46,001.00 ✗ | $40,362.90 ✗ | $44,874.50 ✗ |
| Deposits in Transit | | | | |
| at 8/31/X1 | 600.00 ✗ | (600.00) | | |
| at 9/30/X1 | | 837.50 | | 837.50 |
| Outstanding Checks | | | | |
| at 8/31/X1 | (1241.00) ⑷ | | (1241.00) | |
| at 9/30/X1 | | | 3402.00 | (3402.00) ⑷ |
| Bank Service Charge | | | | |
| August | 4.60 ✓ | | 4.60 | |
| September | | | (2.80) | 2.80 ✗ |
| Check of customer A.D. Speeler charged back by Bank 9/12/X1, redeposited 9/12/X1 | | (900.00) | (900.00) | |
| Per Books | $38,600.00 | $45,338.50 | $41,625.70 | $42,312.80 |

✓  Traced to client's 8/31/X1 bank statement.

✗  Traced to client's 9/30/X1 bank statement.

⑷  Per adding machine tape at A-4-2.

⑷  Per adding machine tape at A-4-3.

Μ  Traced to general ledger.

Footed cash receipts journal and check register for 9/X1. Accounted for numerical sequence of all checks issued September 20X1 (26610-6792). No exceptions noted.

K.W. 10/16/X1

balance per bank and the balance per accounting records at the beginning of the test period (Column 1) and at the end of this period (Column 4). These outside columns are equivalent to typical monthly bank reconciliations. The two middle columns reconcile the bank's record of deposits with the client's record of cash receipts (Column 2) and the bank's record of paid checks with the client's record of cash disbursements (Column 3).

Next, consider the source of the figures used in this reconciliation. The amounts "per bank statement" are taken from the September 30 bank statement. The subsequent rows of deposits, checks, and other items are taken from the August and September bank reconciliations, and the amounts "per books" are taken from the client's Cash general ledger account and cash receipts and disbursements journals.

**4. Obtain a Cutoff Bank Statement Containing Transactions of at Least Seven Business Days Subsequent to the Balance Sheet Date.**

A **cutoff bank statement** is a statement covering a specified number of *business days* (usually 7 to 10) following the end of the client's fiscal year. The client will request the bank to prepare such a statement and mail it directly to the auditors. The auditors may also obtain cutoff information electronically from the bank's Web site. In order to accept this as appropriate evidence, the auditors must become satisfied that the Web site is valid.

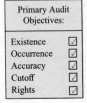

| Primary Audit Objectives: | |
|---|---|
| Existence | ☑ |
| Occurrence | ☑ |
| Accuracy | ☑ |
| Cutoff | ☑ |
| Rights | ☑ |

This information is used to test the accuracy of the year-end reconciliation of the company's bank accounts. It allows the auditors to examine firsthand the checks (ordinarily on computer media) listed as outstanding and the details of deposits in transit on the company's reconciliation.

With respect to checks that were shown as outstanding at year-end, the auditors should determine the dates on which the bank paid these checks. By noting the dates of payment of these checks, the auditors can determine whether the time intervals between the dates of the check and the time of payment by the bank were unreasonably long. Unreasonable delay in the presentation of these checks for payment constitutes a strong implication that the checks were not mailed by the client until some time after the close of the year. The appropriate adjusting entry in such cases consists of a debit to Cash and a credit to a liability account.

In examining the cutoff bank statement, the auditors will also watch for any paid checks issued on or before the balance sheet date but not listed as outstanding on the client's year-end bank reconciliation. Thus, the cutoff bank statement provides assurance that the amount of cash shown on the balance sheet was not overstated by omission of one or more checks from the list of checks outstanding.

### Check 21 Act

Historically, checks have taken days to clear in large part because they have literally been flown about the country in the clearing process. Under the **Check Clearing for the 21st Century Act ("Check 21 Act")** checks may be processed electronically. Electronic processing involves creating a "substitute check," an electronic image of the original that is processed in hours rather than days. The substitute check is the legal equivalent of the original check for all purposes. Under the Check 21 Act, any financial institution in the check clearing process may *truncate* (destroy) paper checks and create a substitute check for processing.

This new form of check processing has several audit implications. First, if the client's checks are processed electronically, the auditors who wish to see evidence of the check itself must rely upon the substitute check because the original check will no longer be available; the substitute check may be available in paper, electronic, or both forms. Second, it becomes virtually impossible for a client to kite checks (manipulate bank balances so that temporarily overstated cash balances conceal a cash shortage, as discussed later in this chapter) if its financial institutions use this form of processing. However, the auditors should realize that while processing will be much faster, they should still expect reconciliations to include outstanding checks, because some checks drawn near the end of the year may be sent through the mail, and some checks will not be promptly presented for payment by payees.

### 5. Count and List Cash on Hand.

Primary Audit Objectives:

Existence ☑
Occurrence ☑
Accuracy ☑
Cutoff ☑
Rights ☑

Cash on hand ordinarily consists of undeposited cash receipts, petty cash funds, and change funds. The petty cash funds and change funds may be counted at any time before or after the balance sheet date; many auditors prefer to make a surprise count of these funds.

The count of cash on hand is of special importance in the audit of banks and other financial institutions. Whenever auditors make a cash count, they should insist that the *custodian of the funds be present throughout the count.* At the completion of the count, the auditors should obtain from the custodian a signed and dated acknowledgment that the funds were counted in the custodian's presence and were returned intact by the auditors. Such procedures avoid the possibility of an employee trying to explain a cash shortage by claiming that the funds were intact when turned over to the auditors.

A first step in the verification of cash on hand is to establish control over all negotiable assets, such as cash funds, securities and other investments, notes receivable, and warehouse receipts. Unless all negotiable assets are verified at one time, an opportunity exists for a dishonest officer or employee to conceal a shortage by transferring it from one asset category to another.

It is not uncommon to find included in cash on hand some personal checks cashed for the convenience of officers, employees, and customers. Such checks, of course, should not be entered in the cash receipts journal because they are merely substitutes for currency previously on hand. The auditors should determine that these checks are valid and collectible, thus qualifying for inclusion in the balance sheet figure for cash. This may be accomplished by the auditors' examination of the last bank deposit for the period and determination that it includes all checks received through year-end. The auditors will retain a validated deposit slip from this deposit for comparison to any checks subsequently charged back by the bank.

### 6. Verify the Client's Cutoff of Cash Receipts and Cash Disbursements.

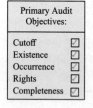

Primary Audit
Objectives:

Cutoff ☑
Existence ☑
Occurrence ☑
Rights ☑
Completeness ☑

An accurate cutoff of cash receipts (and of cash disbursements) at year-end is essential to a proper statement of cash on the balance sheet. The balance sheet figure for cash should include all cash received on the final day of the year and none received subsequently. If the auditors can arrange to be present at the client's office at the close of business on the last day of the fiscal year, they will be able to verify the cutoff by counting the undeposited cash receipts. It will then be impossible for the client to include in the records any cash received after this cutoff point without the auditor being aware of such actions.

Of course, the auditors cannot visit every client's place of business on the last day of the fiscal year, nor is their presence at this time normally essential to a satisfactory verification of cash. As an alternative to a count on the balance sheet date, auditors can verify the cutoff of cash receipts by determining that deposits in transit as shown on the year-end bank reconciliation appear as credits on the bank statement on the first business day of the new year. Results of the auditors' consideration of internal control will dictate the necessary scope of these procedures.

The auditors should be aware of possible **window dressing** related to cash transactions. For example, if the cash receipts are not deposited daily, cash received for a few days after the close of the year may be included in a deposit dated as of year-end, thus overstating the cash balance at the balance sheet date.

Other approaches to window dressing improve but do not outright misrepresent the cash position. For example, a corporate officer who has borrowed money from the corporation may repay the loan just before the end of the year and then promptly obtain the loan again after year-end; in such a situation, disclosure in the notes to the financial statements may be appropriate.

Other forms of window dressing do not require action by the auditors. Many companies make strenuous efforts at year-end to achieve an improved financial picture by rushing shipments to customers, pressing for collection of receivables, and sometimes paying liabilities down to an unusually low level. Such efforts to improve the financial picture to be reported are not improper. Before giving approval to the balance sheet presentation of cash, the auditors must exercise their professional judgment to determine whether the client has engaged in window dressing of a nature that causes the financial statements to be misleading.

### 7. Analyze Bank Transfers for the Last Week of the Audit Year and the First Week of the Following Year.

Primary Audit
Objectives:

Cutoff ☑
Existence ☑
Occurrence ☑
Rights ☑
Completeness ☑

The purpose of analyzing bank transfers is to disclose overstatements of cash balances resulting from **kiting.** Many businesses maintain checking accounts with a number of banks and often find it necessary to transfer funds from one bank to another. When a check drawn on one bank is deposited in another, several days (called the float period) usually pass before the check clears the bank on which it is drawn. During this period, the amount of the check is included in the balance on deposit at both banks. *Kiting* refers to manipulations that utilize such temporarily overstated bank balances to conceal a cash shortage or meet short-term cash needs. Note that kiting is much more difficult in an environment of ever-increasing electronic transfers between accounts (rather than using paper checks) due to the virtual disappearance of the float period.

Auditors can detect manipulations of this type by preparing a schedule of bank transfers for a few days before and after the balance sheet date. This working paper lists all bank transfers and shows the dates that the receipt and disbursement of cash were recorded in the cash journals and on the bank statements. A partial illustration of a schedule of bank transfers is shown below.

| | Bank Accounts | | | Date of Disbursement | | Date of Receipt | |
|---|---|---|---|---|---|---|---|
| Check No. | From | To | Amount | Books | Bank | Books | Bank |
| 5897 | General | Payroll | $30,620 | 12/28 | 1/3 | 12/28 | 12/28 |
| 6006 | General | Branch 4 | 24,018 | 1/2 | 1/4 | 12/30 | 12/30 |
| 6029 | Branch 2 | General | 10,000 | 1/3 | 1/5 | 1/3 | 12/31 |

### Disclosure of Kiting

By comparing the dates on the schedule of bank transfers, auditors can determine whether any manipulation of the cash balance has taken place. The increase in one bank account and decrease in the other bank account should be recorded in the cash journals in the same accounting period. Notice that Check No. 6006 in the transfer schedule was recorded in the cash journals as a receipt on December 30 and a disbursement of January 2. As a result of recording the debit and credit parts of the transaction in different accounting periods, cash is overstated on December 31. For the cash receipts journal to remain in balance, some account must have been credited on December 30 to offset the debit to Cash. If a revenue account was credited, the results of operations were overstated along with cash.

Kiting may also be used to conceal a cash shortage. Assume, for example, that a financial executive misappropriates $10,000 from a company's general checking account. To conceal the shortage on December 31, the executive draws a check transferring $10,000 from the company's branch bank account to the general account. The executive deposits the transfer check in the general account on December 31, but records the transfer in the accounting records as occurring early in January. As of December 31, the shortage in the general account has been replaced, no reduction has yet been recorded in the branch account, and no shortage is apparent. Of course, the shortage will reappear in a few days when the transfer check is paid from the branch account.

A bank transfer schedule should disclose this type of kiting because the transfer deposit appears on the general account bank statement in December, while the transaction is not recorded in the cash journals until January. Check No. 6029 in the transfer schedule illustrates this discrepancy. These illustrations suggest the following rules for determining when it is likely that a cash transfer has misstated the cash balance:

1. The dates of recording the transfer *per the books* (from the cash disbursements and cash receipts journals, respectively) are from different financial statement periods, *or*
2. The date the check was recorded *by the bank* (either the disbursement or the receipt, but not both) is from the financial statement period prior to when it is recorded on the books.

A third type of kiting uses the float period to meet short-term cash needs. For example, assume that a business does not have sufficient cash to meet the month-end payroll. The company might draw a check on its general account in one bank, deposit it in a payroll account in another bank, and rely upon subsequent deposits being made to the general account before the transfer check is presented for payment. If the transfer is properly recorded in the accounting records, this form of kiting will not cause a misstatement of the cash balance for financial reporting purposes. However, banks attempt to detect this practice and may not allow the customer to draw against the deposit until the check has cleared the other account. In some deliberate schemes to defraud banks, this type of kiting has been used to create and conceal overdrafts of millions of dollars.

**8. Investigate Any Checks Representing Large or Unusual Payments to Related Parties.**

Any large or unusual checks payable to directors, officers, employees, affiliated companies, or cash should be carefully reviewed by the auditors to determine whether the transactions (1) were properly authorized and recorded and (2) are adequately disclosed in the financial statements.

To provide assurance that cash disbursements to related parties were authorized transactions and were properly recorded, the auditors should determine that each such transaction has been charged to the proper account, is supported by adequate vouchers or other documents, and was specifically approved in advance by an officer other than the one receiving the funds.

The need for financial statement disclosure of transactions with related parties was discussed in Chapter 5. To determine that such transactions are adequately disclosed, the auditors must obtain evidence concerning the relationship between the parties, the substance of each transaction (which may differ from its form), and the effect of each transaction upon the financial statements. Disclosure of related party transactions should include the nature of the relationships, a description of the transactions, and the dollar amounts involved.

**9. Evaluate Proper Financial Statement Presentation and Disclosure of Cash.**

The balance sheet figure for cash should include only those amounts that are available for use in current operations. A bank deposit that is restricted in use (for example, cash deposited with a trustee for payments on long-term debt) should not be included in cash. Agreements to maintain *compensating balances* should be disclosed. The auditors must also make sure that the caption "Cash" or "Cash and Equivalents" on the client's balance sheet corresponds to that used in the statement of cash flows.

## Interim Audit Work on Cash

To avoid a concentration of audit work shortly after the year-end, CPA firms try to complete as many auditing procedures as possible on an interim basis during the year. The consideration of internal control over cash, for example, can be performed in advance of the client's year-end. The audit work on cash at year-end can then be limited to such substantive procedures as a review of the client's bank reconciliations, confirmation of year-end bank balances, investigation of the year-end cutoff, and a general review of cash transactions during the interval between the interim work on cash and the end of the period.

# Financial Investments

The most important group of financial investments, from the viewpoint of the auditors, consists of marketable stocks and bonds because they are found more frequently and usually are of greater dollar value than other kinds of investment holdings. Other types of investments often encountered include commercial paper issued by corporations, mortgages and trust deeds, and the cash surrender value of life insurance policies. The auditors also must be concerned with derivatives that are used to hedge various financial and operational risks or for speculation. Derivatives are financial instruments that "derive" their value from other financial instruments, underlying assets, or indexes. For example, a simple derivative would involve a commitment by a company to purchase a commodity at a certain price at some point in the future. Other derivatives are much more complex, involving, for example, relationships between fluctuations in European interest rates and the price of copper.

## The Need for Specialized Knowledge

The audit of financial investments can be very complex, requiring specialized skill or knowledge in performing audit tasks such as:

- Identifying controls at service organizations that provide financial services and are part of the client's information system.
- Obtaining an understanding of information systems for securities and derivatives that are highly dependent on computer technology.

**Illustrative Case** | *Auditing Derivative Transactions*

Enron used derivative contracts in its energy trading division as one way of significantly overstating its reported net income. The company purchased and sold long-term futures contracts for commodities, such as gas, for which there were no active markets and therefore no reliable prices to value the contracts for financial statements. Company employees, who benefited directly from the profits made from the trading activities, priced the contracts using discretionary valuation models based on their own assumptions and methods. Unrealized trading "gains" accounted for slightly more than half of the company's $1.41 billion reported pretax profit for 2000 and about one-third of its reported pretax profit for 1999.

- Applying complex accounting principles to various types of financial investments.
- Understanding the methods used to determine the fair values of financial investments, especially those that must be valued using complex valuation models.
- Assessing inherent and control risk for assertions about derivatives used in hedging activities.

Therefore, the auditors may decide that the assistance of specialists either within or outside the firm is needed to assist in the audit of complex financial investments.

## The Auditors' Objectives in Auditing Financial Investments

**LO8**

Identify the auditors' objectives in the audit of financial investments.

The auditors' *objectives* in the examination of financial investments are to:

1. Use the understanding of the client and its environment to assess *inherent risks* including fraud risks.
2. Obtain an understanding of *internal control* over investments.
3. Assess the risks of *material misstatements* of investments and design further audit procedures that:
   a. Substantiate the *existence* of recorded financial investments and the *occurrence* of investment transactions.
   b. Establish the *completeness* of financial investments and investment transactions.
   c. Verify the *cutoff* of investment transactions.
   d. Determine that the client has *rights* to recorded investments.
   e. Determine that the *valuation* of financial investments is appropriate; that is, determine that such valuation is in accordance with the cost, fair value, or equity method of accounting and that any unrealized appreciation or depreciation in value is appropriately recorded.
   f. Determine that the *presentation* and *disclosure* of financial investments and realized and unrealized gains and losses are appropriate.

In conjunction with their audit of financial investments, the auditors will also verify the related accounts of interest income and dividends, accrued interest revenue, and realized and unrealized gains and losses on investments.

The liquid nature of financial investments that are marketable makes the potential for fraud high. Auditors must coordinate their cash and marketable securities audit procedures to detect any possible fraud involving unauthorized substitution (e.g., the sale of securities to hide a cash shortage) between the accounts.

## Internal Control over Financial Investments

The major elements of adequate internal control over financial investments include the following:

- Formal investment policies that limit the nature of investments in securities and other financial instruments.

**LO9**

Describe typical internal controls over the business processes related to financial investments.

- An investment committee of the board of directors that authorizes and reviews financial investment activities for compliance with investment policies.
- Separation of duties between the executive authorizing purchases and sales of securities and derivative instruments, the custodian of the securities, and the person maintaining the records of investments.
- Complete detailed records of all securities and derivative instruments owned and the related provisions and terms.
- Registration of securities in the name of the company.
- Periodic physical inspection of securities on hand by an internal auditor or an official having no responsibility for the authorization, custody, or record keeping of investments.
- Determination of appropriate accounting for complex financial instruments by competent personnel.

In many concerns, segregation of the functions of custody and record keeping is achieved by the use of an independent safekeeping agent, such as a stockbroker, bank, or trust company. Since the independent agent has no direct contact with the employee responsible for maintaining accounting records of the investments in securities, the possibilities of concealing fraud through falsification of the accounts are greatly reduced. If securities that exist in certificate form are not placed in the custody of an independent agent, they should be kept in a bank safe-deposit box under the joint control of two or more of the company's officials. *Joint control* means that neither of the two custodians may have access to the securities except in the presence of the other. A list of securities in the box should be maintained in the box, and the deposit or withdrawal of securities should be recorded on this list along with the date and signatures of all persons present. The safe-deposit box rental should be in the name of the company, not in the name of an officer having custody of securities.

Complete detailed records of all securities and derivative instruments owned are essential to satisfactory control. These records frequently consist of a subsidiary record for each security and derivative instrument, with such identifying data as the exact name, face amount or par value, certificate number, number of shares, date of acquisition, name of broker, cost, terms, and any interest or dividend payments received. Actual interest and dividends should be compared to budgeted amounts, and significant variances should be investigated. The purchase and sale of investments often is entrusted to a responsible financial executive, subject to frequent review by an investment committee of the board of directors.

An internal auditor or other responsible employee should, at frequent intervals, inspect the securities on hand, compare the serial numbers and other identifying data of the securities examined with the accounting records, and reconcile the subsidiary record for securities with the control account. If the entity engages in derivative transactions, the individual should also review the terms of derivative instruments for compliance with investment policies and proper financial accounting and disclosure.

In some situations, the auditors may need to consider controls at a service organization because it provides services that are part of the client's information system. Such services include those that affect the initiation of transactions, accounting processing or accounting records, or financial statement reporting. As an example, the auditors must be concerned about the controls of a stockbroker that initiates purchases and sales of investments and reports the results to the client. As described in Chapter 8, the auditors may obtain information about the controls at a service organization by reviewing user manuals or other systems documentation, reviewing service contracts, obtaining the report of a service auditor, or personally visiting the service organization.

## Internal Control Questionnaire

A questionnaire used by the auditors in assessing controls relating to financial investments will include questions such as the following: Does the client have investment policies that reflect appropriate risk management? Are securities and similar instruments under the joint control of responsible officials? Are all persons having access to securities properly bonded? Is an independent safekeeping agent retained? Are competent personnel involved in reviewing and accounting for derivative instruments? Are all purchases and sales of securities and derivatives authorized by a financial executive and reviewed by an investment committee of the board of directors?

## Audit of Financial Investments

**LO10**

Describe tests of controls and substantive procedures used to audit financial investments.

The following steps indicate the general pattern of work performed by the auditors in the audit of financial investments. Selection of the most appropriate procedures for a particular audit will be guided by the nature of the controls that have been implemented and by the results of the auditors' risk assessment process.

A. Use the understanding of the client and its environment to consider inherent risks, including fraud risks related to financial investments.
B. Obtain an understanding of internal control over financial investments.
C. Assess the risks of material misstatement and design further audit procedures.
D. Perform further audit procedures—tests of controls.
　1. Examples of tests of controls:
　　*a.* Trace several transactions for purchases and sales of investments through the accounting system.
　　*b.* Review and test reports of investment activity prepared for the investment committee.
　　*c.* Inspect reports by internal auditors regarding their periodic inspection and review of securities and derivative instruments.
　　*d.* Inspect monthly reports on securities owned, purchased, and sold and amounts of revenue earned and budgeted.
　2. If necessary, revise the risk of material misstatement based on the results of tests of controls.
E. Perform further audit procedures—substantive procedures for investment transactions and year-end balances.
　1. Obtain or prepare analyses of the investment accounts and related revenue, gain, and loss accounts and reconcile them to the general ledger.
　2. Inspect securities on hand and review agreements underlying derivatives.
　3. Confirm securities and derivative instruments with holders and counterparties.
　4. Vouch selected purchases and sales of financial investments during the year and verify the client's cutoff of investment transactions.
　5. Review investment committee minutes and reports.
　6. Perform analytical procedures.
　7. Make independent computations of revenue from securities.
　8. Inspect documentation of management's intent to classify derivative transactions as hedging activities.
　9. Evaluate the method of accounting for investments.
　10. Test the valuation of financial investments.
　11. Evaluate financial statement presentation and disclosure of financial investments.

**Risks of Material Misstatement of Financial Investments**

As discussed earlier, the fact that securities are often very liquid significantly increases the risk of fraud. In addition, the accounting for financial investments can be very complex, increasing the risk that the investments will not be valued appropriately. If client personnel engage in speculation, they may be motivated to use various improper techniques to hide or delay reporting losses. The use of derivatives almost always increases

**FIGURE 10.8    Potential Misstatements—Financial Investments**

| Description of Misstatement | Examples | Internal Control Weaknesses or Factors that Increase the Risk of the Misstatement |
| --- | --- | --- |
| Misstatement of recorded value of investments | **Error:**<br>• Failure to record changes in market values of investments<br>**Fraud:**<br>• Misstatement of the value of closely held investment<br>• Recording fictitious securities | • Inadequate accounting manual; incompetent accounting personnel<br>• Ineffective board of directors, audit committee, or internal audit function; "tone at the top" not conducive to ethical conduct; undue pressure to meet earnings targets |
| Unauthorized investment transactions | **Fraud:**<br>• An employee with access to securities converts them for personal use | • Inadequate segregation of duties of record keeping for and custody of securities |
| Incomplete recording of investments | **Error:**<br>• Failure to record derivative agreements that are embedded in other agreements | • Inadequate accounting manual; incompetent accounting personnel<br>• Inadequate monitoring by internal auditors |

the risk of material misstatement of the financial statements. In assessing the risks of material misstatement, the auditors will consider these inherent risks in combination with the control risks identified by the auditors' understanding of the client and its environment and tests of controls over investments.

Some of the risks of material misstatement identified by the auditors may be considered to be significant risks that require special audit consideration. As an example, if the client uses foreign currency futures contracts to hedge its exposure to foreign investments and does not have accounting personnel with adequate knowledge of the related accounting standards, the auditors may decide to evaluate the accounting for all or most of the transactions occurring during the period.

Figure 10.8 provides illustrations of typical errors and fraud that the auditors might identify and assess in the audit of financial investments. Such misstatements may arise due to improper valuation, unauthorized transactions, or inadequate disclosure of such matters as derivative trading activities.

## Substantive Procedures for Financial Investments

Primary Audit Objectives:

Existence ☑
Rights ☑
Occurrence ☑

AICPA AU 501 (PCAOB 332) provides guidance on auditing financial investments, including the types of substantive procedures that are typically performed. Figure 10.9 presents these substantive procedures, which are described in the next section.

### 1. Obtain or Prepare Analyses of the Investment Accounts and Related Revenue, Gain, and Loss Accounts and Reconcile Them to the General Ledger.

The analysis of financial investments will show the beginning and ending balances for the year, purchases and sales of investments during the year, interest and dividends earned, and realized and unrealized gains and losses. The auditors may verify the beginning balances of investments by reference to the prior year's audit working papers. If numerous purchases and sales of investments have occurred during the year, separate schedules of those transactions may support an overall summary schedule of investments. The auditors will make certain that totals on the schedules agree with totals recorded in the general ledger.

**FIGURE 10.9**   Objectives of Major Substantive Procedures for Financial Investments

| Substantive Procedures | Primary Audit Objectives |
|---|---|
| Obtain analysis of investments and related accounts and reconcile to ledger. | *Existence* and *rights* *Occurrence* |
| Inspect securities on hand and review agreements underlying derivatives. Confirm securities and derivative instruments with holders and counterparties. Vouch selected purchases and sales of investments during the year. Verify the client's cutoff of investment transactions. | *Existence* and *rights* *Occurrence* and *accuracy* *Completeness* *Cutoff* *Valuation* |
| Review investment committee minutes and reports. | *Completeness* |
| Perform analytical procedures. Make independent computations of revenue from securities. | *Existence* *Rights* *Occurrence* *Completeness* |
| Inspect documentation of management's intent to classify derivative transactions as hedges. Evaluate the method of accounting for investments. Test the valuation of financial investments. | *Valuation* *Presentation* |
| Evaluate financial statement presentation and disclosure of financial investments. | *Presentation* |

## 2. Inspect Securities on Hand and Review Agreements Underlying Derivatives.

The auditors will count securities held by the client at year-end, verify that the securities are registered in the company's name, and record in the working papers a description of the securities, including the serial numbers. When the client's records indicate that a particular security has been held since the last audit, the auditors may compare the serial number of the certificate with that shown in the prior year's working papers. This will allow the auditors to detect securities that have been sold without authorization during the year and replaced before this year's audit.

While the count of securities ideally is made at the balance sheet date, concurrently with the count of cash and other negotiable instruments, this is not always possible. When not possible, if the securities are kept in a bank safe-deposit box, the client may instruct the bank in writing on the balance sheet date that no one is to have access to the box unless accompanied by the auditors. This arrangement makes it possible to count the securities at a more convenient time after the balance sheet date. Also, banks maintain records of access to safe-deposit boxes that can be examined by the auditors to determine who has had access to the box and at what dates. A representative of the client should be present when the auditors count the securities, and that individual should acknowledge in writing that the securities were returned intact.

The auditors will also review and analyze the **derivative** instruments and other agreements that may contain embedded derivatives. For example, a loan agreement might contain a provision to swap a fixed interest rate for a variable interest rate under certain circumstances. This analysis is designed to determine that all derivatives are properly recorded and valued in the financial statements.

## 3. Confirm Securities and Derivative Instruments with Holders and Counterparties.

Client-owned securities and other financial instruments will often be in the hands of brokers or banks for safekeeping. In such cases, the auditors send a confirmation request, signed by the client, to the holders of the investments to determine existence and ownership. If the broker or bank initiates investment transactions and maintains the related accountability for them, or records investment transactions and processes the related data, the auditors should consider obtaining a service auditor's report on the processing of transactions, as described in Chapter 8. The auditors also often confirm the terms of derivative instruments with the counterparties—the other parties obligated under the agreements.

As with cash information from financial institutions, the auditors may decide to get evidence about the client's securities electronically. This approach is appropriate providing that the auditors can be assured that the information is obtained from a valid Web site without possibility of client manipulation.

Primary Audit Objectives:

Existence ☑
Occurrence ☑
Rights ☑
Completeness ☑
Accuracy ☑
Valuation ☑
Cutoff ☑

### 4. Vouch Selected Purchases and Sales of Financial Investments during the Year and Verify the Client's Cutoff of Investment Transactions.

To determine that investments purchased and sold during the period are recorded properly, the auditors vouch a sample of transactions by reference to **brokers' advices** and cash records. In addition, they review transactions for one or two weeks after the balance sheet date to ensure a correct cutoff of transactions. Sometimes sales occur shortly before the balance sheet date but go unrecorded until the securities are delivered to the broker early in the next period. Also, inspection and confirmation procedures will help ensure a proper cutoff of securities transactions.

Primary Audit Objectives:

Completeness ☑

### 5. Review Investment Committee Minutes and Reports.

Review of investment committee minutes and reports may disclose unrecorded purchases and sales of securities or other financial instruments. This procedure is especially important if the client uses derivatives because transactions giving rise to derivatives may not involve the payment or receipt of cash. For example, if a client engages in a foreign exchange forward contract, there may be no exchange of cash at the time the contract is executed. In addition, derivatives may be embedded in other financial instruments such as a loan agreement.

Primary Audit Objectives:

Existence ☑
Rights ☑
Occurrence ☑
Completeness ☑

### 6. Perform Analytical Procedures or Make Independent Computations.

The auditors can use analytical procedures to test the reasonableness of the amounts of recorded dividend and interest income, or they can verify the amounts by independent computation. Dividends that should have been received and recorded can be computed by referring to **dividend record books** published by investment advisory services. These books show dividend declarations, amounts, and payment dates for all listed stocks. Interest earned on bonds and notes also can be computed independently by the auditors and compared with recorded amounts in the client's records. This provides evidence that investment income has not been embezzled, the client actually owns the securities recorded in the accounting records, and there are no unrecorded derivative instruments.

Primary Audit Objectives:

Valuation ☑
Presentation ☑

### 7. Inspect Documentation of Management's Intent to Classify Derivative Transactions as Hedging Activities.

To account for a derivative instrument as a hedge of an asset, liability, or future transaction, management must establish at inception the intent to hedge, the method to be used to assess its effectiveness as a hedge, and the measurement approach for determining the ineffective portion of the hedge. Therefore, review of the documentation of management's intent is essential to the audit of the client's accounting for derivative instruments.

Primary Audit Objectives:

Valuation ☑
Presentation ☑

### 8. Evaluate the Accounting Methods Used and Test the Valuation.

Organizations have an option in reporting financial investments because they may either follow the guidance in *FASB ASC* 320 (formally FASB No. 115) *or* elect the fair value option.[1] *FASB ASC* 320 divides securities into three portfolios—trading securities, available-for-sale securities, and held-to-maturity securities. Securities in both the

---

[1] Among the accounting pronouncements on fair value are *FASB ASC* 820 and *ASC* 825.

*trading* and *available-for-sale* portfolios are valued at their current market values. Any unrealized gains and losses on securities in the trading portfolio are recorded in the income statement; unrealized gains and losses on securities classified as available-for-sale are excluded from net income and reported in a separate component of stockholders' equity until they are realized. Professional standards allow companies to elect the fair value option for all securities; the fair value option results in unrealized income and losses being recorded on the income statement (as is always the case with trading securities).

Accounting for derivative instruments is guided by *FASB ASC* 815 (formally FASB No. 133) and *FASB ASC* 825 (formally FASB No. 159). Under *FASB ASC* 815, all derivative instruments are valued at their fair values, but the unrealized gains or losses are accounted for differently depending on whether or not the instruments are classified as hedges. Unrealized gains or losses on the effective portions of hedges of recorded assets or liabilities are offset by related increases and decreases in the hedged assets or liabilities. Unrealized gains or losses on the effective portions of hedges of future transactions are recorded as part of other comprehensive income in the client's financial statements. Such gains or losses become adjustments to the recording of the hedged transactions when they occur. Finally, under *FASB ASC* 815, unrealized gains or losses on the ineffective portions of hedge derivatives and nonhedge derivatives are recorded as a part of net earnings in the client's financial statements. As is the case with other securities, *FASB ASC* 825 allows an option to companies to choose to use fair value accounting rather than the approach outlined in *FASB ASC* 815.

The fair value of securities and derivatives in many situations may be obtained by reference to sales prices on organized exchanges. If there is not an active market for the securities or derivatives, fair value may be deduced from active markets for similar instruments. However, to use prices from similar markets, the auditors must consider whether adjustments are needed for differences between the instrument being traded in the market and the instrument being valued. Finally, if no active market is available to value the security or derivative, management may have to use a valuation model, such as the Black Sholes option pricing model. In these situations, the auditors must evaluate the reasonableness of the significant assumptions underlying the model. Chapter 5 provides a more detailed discussion of audits of assets valued at fair values.

To audit the fair values of marketable securities or derivatives, current market prices can be obtained by reference to quotes in financial publications, such as *The Wall Street Journal* or various sources on the Internet, or by obtaining representations from securities brokers. If a security or derivative has no active market, management may obtain an appraisal of fair value from a securities appraiser. In such cases, the auditors should refer to AICPA AU 620 (PCAOB 336), which requires that they consider the professional qualifications and reputation of the appraiser and obtain an understanding of the methods and assumptions used. When a valuation model, such as an option-pricing model, is used, the auditors should assess the reasonableness and appropriateness of the model and evaluate the reasonableness of the underlying assumptions. The auditors should determine that the model considers all aspects of risk, such as counterparty credit risk, risk of adverse changes in market factors, and risk of losses from legal or regulatory action.

For derivatives classified as hedges, the auditors must satisfy themselves as to the continued effectiveness of the derivative as a hedge and determine that the gains and losses from the effective and ineffective portions of the hedge are appropriately classified.

If the company has the positive intent and ability to hold marketable debt securities to maturity, they may be classified as *held-to-maturity* and valued at cost, net of any unamortized discount or premium. Nonmarketable securities also are usually valued at cost. When the cost method is used, the auditors determine the value by vouching the original purchase and recomputing any unamortized discount or premium. To determine that there is no permanent decline in value of the investment, the auditors will obtain information about its current market value.

| Illustrative Case | *The Mortgage Crisis* |
| --- | --- |

A large number of companies, especially financial institutions, invested in mortgage-backed securities prior to 2007. A mortgage-backed security is one that represents an undivided interest in a group of mortgages. Some of these securities were guaranteed by government and private mortgage or bond insurers, such as the Government National Mortgage Association (Ginnie Mae), the Federal Home Loan Mortgage Corporation (Freddie Mac), and MBIA, Inc. The combination of increased interest rates, resetting of teaser (low initial) interest rates, and decline in house prices that began in the latter part of 2006 and accelerated in 2007 and 2008 resulted in significant difficulties with regard to the valuation of such securities. The market for mortgage-backed securities dried up and this led to financial difficulties, including bankruptcies and restructurings of many of the entities that guaranteed these securities. With a lack of good market data, auditors were forced to look to markets for similar securities and models that estimated fair value using discounted cash flows. In an environment of deteriorating markets and increases in default rates, it is easy to see the challenges that auditors faced with evaluating management's assertions about the fair values of these mortgage-based securities.

Investments in common stock that give the investor company the ability to exercise significant influence over operating and financial policies of the investee require use of the equity method of accounting. Ownership of 20 percent of the voting stock of an investee is used as a general indication of ability to exert influence in the absence of evidence to the contrary. Such factors as investor representation on the investee's board of directors and material intercompany transactions also suggest an ability to exercise influence.

When auditing an investment accounted for by the equity method, the auditors must verify that the investment was properly recorded initially. They also must obtain evidence regarding subsequent amounts of income from the investment and other adjustments to the investment account. This evidence is usually obtained from *audited* financial statements of the investee.

If the audited financial statements of an investee are not available for the period covered by the independent auditors' report on the investor, the auditors should perform a sufficient investigation of the investee's financial statements to determine the fairness of amounts recorded by the investor. In some cases, this might involve performing audit procedures at the investee's place of business.

If the auditors find evidence of impairment of the value of any investment, it should be written down to its net realizable value.

### 9. Evaluate Financial Statement Presentation and Disclosure of Financial Investments.

Primary Audit
Objectives:

Presentation ☑

Auditing the presentation and disclosure of financial investments varies depending on whether a company has adopted the fair value option for valuation. If the company has *not* adopted the option, the auditors must determine that investments are properly separated into short-term and long-term portfolios. In addition, generally accepted accounting principles require the disclosure of the method of accounting for the securities and aggregate market values of the various portfolios. Disclosure also must be provided as to the amount of realized and unrealized gains and losses, as well as the allowance for market decline of both the current and long-term portfolios. Finally, the financial statements should disclose the details about debt and equity securities and derivative instruments held at year-end.

If the company adopts the fair value option, the auditors must determine that the disclosures are made in accordance with the appropriate accounting standards. The required disclosures are based largely on the manner in which the fair value hierarchy has been implemented (Chapter 5 presents a discussion of the fair value hierarchy).

## Chapter Summary

This chapter described the fundamental controls over cash receipts and disbursements and financial investments. It also explained how the auditors design tests of controls for cash and financial investments and substantive procedures for these accounts. To summarize:

1. Since cash generally has a high degree of inherent risk, more audit time is devoted to the audit of the account than is indicated by its dollar amount.

2. Internal control over cash receipts should provide assurance that all cash received is recorded promptly and accurately. Control over cash sales is strongest when two or more employees participate in each transaction, or when a cash register or an electronic point-of-sale system controls collections. When cash receipts consist of checks received through the mail, the receipts should be listed and controlled by personnel who do not maintain cash or accounts receivable records. The control listing should be reconciled to the entries in the cash receipts journal and deposit records from the financial institution.

3. Internal control over cash disbursements is best achieved when all payments are made by check or well-controlled electronic funds transfers, except for payment of minor items from petty cash funds. Separation of the functions of preparing the payments and signing the checks tends to prevent errors and fraud in cash disbursements.

4. The principal objectives of the substantive procedures for cash are to (*a*) substantiate the existence of recorded cash and the occurrence of cash transactions; (*b*) determine the accuracy of cash transactions; (*c*) establish the completeness of recorded cash; (*d*) verify the cutoff of cash transactions; (*e*) determine that the client has rights to recorded cash; and (*f*) evaluate the adequacy of the presentation and disclosure of the cash accounts. A primary substantive procedure for cash is confirmation of the balances of the company's accounts with financial institutions.

5. The high value and liquid nature of many financial investments makes the separation of the authorization, custody, and record keeping functions especially important. In addition, securities should be registered in the name of the company; complete, detailed records of securities should be maintained; and securities should be physically inspected periodically. Derivative instruments are financial investments that may present significant risks because of the complex accounting and valuation principles that are applicable.

6. Auditors often vouch investment transactions during the year and inspect securities on hand at year-end. The liquid nature of many investments in securities makes cutoff tests especially important. Appropriate accounting for securities and derivatives is very complex and depends on the nature of the instrument and management's intent. Therefore, in auditing the valuation of certain financial investments, the auditors may use the work of a specialist, such as a security appraiser.

## Key Terms Introduced or Emphasized in Chapter 10

**Brokers' advice (410)**   A notification sent by a stockbrokerage firm to a customer reporting the terms of a purchase or sale of securities.

**Check Clearing for the 21st Century Act ("Check 21 Act") (401)**   This act allows financial institutions to create and process electronic "substitute checks" in place of customer written hard-copy checks. The purpose of this act is to decrease the time for check clearing.

**Cutoff bank statement (400)**   A bank statement covering a specified number of business days (usually 7 to 10) after the client's balance sheet date. Auditors use this statement to determine that checks issued on or before the balance sheet date and paid during the cutoff period were listed as outstanding on the year-end bank reconciliation. Another use is to determine that reconciling items shown on the year-end bank reconciliation have cleared the bank within a reasonable amount of time.

**Derivatives (409)**   Financial instruments that "derive" their value from other financial instruments, underlying assets, or indexes. Examples are options, forward contracts, and futures contracts.

**Dividend record book (410)**   A reference book published monthly by investment advisory services reporting detailed information concerning all listed and many unlisted securities; includes dividend dates and amounts, current prices of securities, and other condensed financial data.

**Electronic data interchange (EDI) (384)**   A computer network between companies that allows the interchange of data from one company's computer to the other's (e.g., allows purchases and sales between two firms to be processed electronically).

**Electronic funds transfer (EFT) system (384)**   A computer system that transmits and processes funds-related cash disbursement and receipt transactions. Increasingly, companies are electronically transferring funds between bank accounts rather than issuing checks. See also *electronic data interchange*.

**Kiting (402)**   Manipulations causing an amount of cash to be included simultaneously in the balance of two or more bank accounts. Kiting schemes are based on the float period—the time necessary for a check deposited in one bank to clear the bank on which it was drawn.

**Lockbox (384)**   A post office box controlled by a company's bank at which cash remittances from customers are received. The bank picks up the remittances, immediately credits the cash to the company's bank account, and forwards the remittance advices to the company.

**Proof of cash (399)**   An audit procedure that reconciles the bank's record of cash activity with the client's accounting records for a test period. The working paper used for the proof of cash is a four-column bank reconciliation.

**Standard confirmation form (396)**   A confirmation form, agreed to by the AICPA, the American Bankers Association, and the Bank Administration Institute, that is designed to provide corroborating evidence about the client's account balances and outstanding loans.

**Voucher (386)**   A document authorizing a cash disbursement. A voucher usually provides space for employees to initial after they have performed approval functions. (The term *voucher* may also be applied to the group of documents supporting a cash disbursement.)

**Voucher register (387)**   A special journal used to record the liabilities for payment originating in a voucher system. The debit entries are the cost distribution of the transaction, and the credits are Vouchers Payable. Every transaction recorded in a voucher register corresponds to a voucher authorizing future payment of cash.

**Window dressing (402)**   Action taken by the client shortly before the balance sheet date to improve the financial picture presented in the financial statements.

## Review Questions

10–1.   Describe circumstances that might cause the auditors to identify understatement of assets as a significant audit risk.

10–2.   Give two reasons audit work on cash is likely to be more extensive than might appear to be justified by the relative amount of the balance sheet figure for cash.

10–3.   "If the auditors discover any evidence of employee fraud during their work on cash, they should extend their investigation as far as necessary to develop a complete set of facts, regardless of whether the amounts involved are or are not material." Do you agree with the quoted statement? Explain.

10–4.   It is sometimes said that audit work on cash is facilitated by the existence of two independent records of the client's cash transactions, which are available for comparison by the auditors. Identify these two independent records.

10–5.   Explain how a lockbox system contributes to internal control over cash receipts.

10–6.   The auditors' work on cash may include preparing a description of controls and performing tests of controls. Which of these two steps should be performed first? What is the purpose of tests of controls?

10–7.   State one broad general objective of internal control over each of the following: cash receipts, cash disbursements, and cash balances.

10–8.   Among the departments of J-R Company are a purchasing department, receiving department, accounting department, and finance department. If you were preparing a flowchart of a voucher system to be installed by the company, in which department would you show:

   *a.* The assembling of the purchase order, receiving report, and vendor's invoice to determine that these documents are in agreement?

   *b.* The preparation of a check?

   *c.* The signing of a check?

   *d.* The mailing of a check to the payee?

   *e.* The perforation of the voucher and supporting documents?

10–9. Describe the audit implications of the Check Clearing for the 21st Century Act.

10–10. During your audit of a small manufacturing firm, you find numerous checks for large amounts drawn payable to the treasurer and charged to the Miscellaneous Expense account. Does this require any action by the auditor? Explain.

10–11. Prepare an example of lapping of cash receipts, showing actual transactions and the cash receipts journal entries.

10–12. During your reconciliation of bank accounts in an audit, you find that a number of checks for small amounts have been outstanding for more than a year. Does this situation call for any action by the auditor? Explain.

10–13. What information do CPAs request from a financial institution on the standard confirmation form?

10–14. How can the auditors corroborate compensating balance arrangements?

10–15. What action should be taken by the auditors when the count of cash on hand discloses a shortage?

10–16. Explain the objectives of each of the following audit procedures for cash:

    *a.* Obtain a cutoff bank statement subsequent to the balance sheet date.

    *b.* Compare paid checks returned with the bank statement to the list of outstanding checks in the previous reconciliation.

    *c.* Trace all bank transfers during the last week of the audit year and the first week of the following year.

    *d.* Investigate any checks representing large or unusual payments to related parties.

10–17. Explain two procedures by which auditors may verify the client's cutoff of cash receipts.

10–18. What is the meaning of the term *window dressing* when used in connection with year-end financial statements? How might the term be related to the making of loans by a corporation to one or more of its executives?

10–19. An audit client that has never before invested in securities recently acquired more than a million dollars in cash from the sale of real estate no longer used in operations. The president intends to invest this money in marketable securities until such time as the opportunity arises for advantageous acquisition of a new plant site. He asks you to enumerate the principal factors you would recommend to create strong internal control over marketable securities.

10–20. A well-financed audit client of your CPA firm invests large amounts in marketable securities. As part of its internal control, the company uses a monthly report of securities transactions. The report is prepared by the controller and presented to the investment committee of the board of directors. What information should this report contain?

10–21. What information should be noted by the auditors during their inspection of securities on hand?

10–22. Salvador Corporation made an investment in Letter.com, Inc., in exchange for 100,000 options to purchase Letter.com's stock at $20 per share. Since the stock options are not marketable, Salvador's management has this derivative valued by a security appraiser. The appraiser uses an option-pricing model to determine the fair value of the derivative for the financial statements. Describe how you would audit the valuation of the stock options.

10–23. In what ways can the audit of financial investments present special risks requiring specialized skill and knowledge?

10–24. How can the auditors determine that all dividends applicable to marketable securities owned by the client have been received and recorded?

10–25. If a security or derivative is not marketable, how do the auditors typically obtain evidence about the fair value of the instrument?

## Questions Requiring Analysis

**LO 3**

10–26. Fluid Controls, Inc., a manufacturing company, has retained you to perform an audit for the year ended December 31. Prior to the year-end, you begin to obtain an understanding of the new client's controls over business processes related to the cash account.

    You find that nearly all the company's cash receipts are in the form of checks received through the mail, but there is no prelisting of cash receipts before they are recorded in the accounts. Also, the incoming mail is opened either by the cashier or by the employee maintaining the accounts receivable subsidiary ledger, depending on which employee has time available. The controller stresses the necessity of flexibility in assignment of duties to the 20 employees comprising the office staff, in order to keep all employees busy and achieve maximum economy of operation.

*Required:*    *a.* Explain how prelisting of cash receipts strengthens internal control.

*b.* List specific duties that should not be performed by an employee assigned to prelist the cash receipts in order to avoid any opportunity for that employee to conceal embezzlement of cash receipts.

(AICPA, adapted)

**LO 4, 5**    10–27.    Henry Mills is responsible for preparing checks, recording cash disbursements, and preparing bank reconciliations for Signet Corporation. While reconciling the October bank statement, Mills noticed that several checks totaling $937 had been outstanding for more than one year. Concluding that these checks would never be presented for payments, Mills prepared a check for $937 payable to himself, forged the treasurer's signature, and cashed the check. Mills made no entry in the accounts for this disbursement and attempted to conceal the theft by destroying the forged check and omitting the long-outstanding checks from subsequent bank reconciliations.

*Required:*    *a.* Identify the weaknesses in Signet Corporation's internal control.

*b.* Explain several audit procedures that might disclose the fraudulent disbursement.

**LO 4, 5, 6**    10–28.    During the first few months of the year, John Smith, the cashier in a small company, was engaged in lapping operations. However, he was able to restore the amount of cash "borrowed" by March 31, and he refrained from any fraudulent acts after that date. Will the year-end audit probably lead to the discovery of his lapping activities? Explain.

**LO 4, 5**    10–29.    An assistant auditor received the following instructions from her supervisor: "Here is a cutoff bank statement covering the first seven business days of January. Compare the paid checks returned with the statement and dated December 31 or earlier with the list of checks outstanding at December 31." What type of fraud might this audit procedure bring to light? Explain.

**LO 4, 5**    10–30.    "When auditors are verifying a client's bank reconciliation, they are particularly concerned with the possibility that the list of outstanding checks may include a nonexistent or fictitious check, and they also are concerned with the possibility of omission from the reconciliation of a deposit in transit." Criticize the above quotation and revise it into an accurate statement.

**LO 4, 5, 6**    10–31.    In the audit of a client with a fiscal year ending June 30, the CPAs obtain a July 10 bank statement directly from the bank. Explain how this cutoff bank statement will be used:

*a.* In the review of the June 30 bank reconciliation.

*b.* To obtain other audit information.

(AICPA, adapted)

**LO 3, 5, 6**    10–32.    In the audit of Wheat, Inc., for the year ended December 31, you discover that the client had been drawing checks as creditors' invoices became due but had not been mailing the checks immediately. Because of a working capital shortage, some checks have been held for two or three weeks.

The client's controller informs you that unmailed checks totaling $48,500 were on hand at December 31 of the current year. He states that these December-dated checks had been entered in the cash disbursements journal and charged to the respective creditors' accounts in December because the checks were prenumbered. However, these checks were not actually mailed until early January. The controller wants to adjust the cash balance and accounts payable at December 31 by $48,500 because the Cash account had a credit balance. He objects to submitting to his bank your audit report showing an overdraft of cash.

Discuss the propriety of adjusting the cash balance and accounts payable by the indicated amount of outstanding checks.

**LO 3**    10–33.    Explain how each of the following items would appear in a four-column proof of cash for the month of November. Assume the format of the proof of cash begins with bank balances and ends with the unadjusted balances per the accounting records.

*a.* Outstanding checks at November 30.

*b.* Deposits-in-transit at October 31.

*c.* Check issued and paid in November, drawn payable to Cash.

*d.* The bank returned $1,800 in NSF checks deposited by the client in November; the client redeposited $1,450 of these checks in November and $350 in December, making no additional entries in the accounting records.

**LO 9, 10**    10–34.    During the current year, the management of Hanover, Inc., entered into a futures contract to hedge the price of silver that will be needed for next year's production. The contract, which is held by Hanover's commodity broker, is marketable and exchanged on the Chicago Board of Trade.

*Required:*

a. Describe the types of controls that should be established by a company that engages in derivative trading.

b. List the substantive procedures that the auditors would use to audit this derivative.

**LO 6**  10–35.  During your audit of Miles Company, you prepared the following bank transfer schedule:

### MILES COMPANY
#### Bank Transfer Schedule
#### December 31, 20X1

| Check Number | Bank Accounts From | Bank Accounts To | Amount | Date Disbursed Books | Date Disbursed Bank | Date Deposited Books | Date Deposited Bank |
|---|---|---|---|---|---|---|---|
| 2020 | 1st Natl. | Suburban | $32,000 | 1/4 | 1/5 | 12/31 | 1/3 |
| 2021 | 1st Natl. | Capital | 21,000 | 12/31 | 1/4 | 12/31 | 1/3 |
| 3271 | 2nd State | Suburban | 6,700 | 1/3 | 1/5 | 1/3 | 12/30 |
| 0659 | Midtown | Suburban | 5,500 | 12/30 | 1/5 | 12/30 | 1/3 |

*Required:*

a. Describe the purpose of a bank transfer schedule.

b. Identify those transfers that should be investigated and explain the reason.

(AICPA, adapted)

**LO 8, 10**  10–36.  You are the auditor in charge of the audit of Steffens Corporation. In the audit of investments, you have just been given the following list of securities held by Steffens Corporation at December 31, 20X3.

### STEFFENS CORPORATION
#### Schedule of Marketable Securities
#### December 31, 20X3

| | Market Value December 31 |
|---|---|
| 10,000 shares of Microsoft Corp. | $521,000 |
| 6,000 shares of General Motors Corp. | 194,000 |
| 8,000 shares of Beta Corporation | (not publicly traded) |
| 400 Hilton 5% Convertible Bonds | 361,000 |

*Required:*

a. Identify the potential audit problems that may be indicated by the schedule.

b. To value the shares of Beta Corporation, management has employed a securities valuation firm. Explain the audit considerations involved in auditing the value developed by the valuation firm.

## Objective Questions

All applicable questions are available with McGraw-Hill's *Connect*™ *Accounting.* ▩ connect
|ACCOUNTING

10–37.  **Multiple Choice Questions**

Select the best answer for each of the following situations and give reasons for your choice.

**LO 3**

a. Which of the following controls would most likely reduce the risk of diversion of customer receipts by a client's employees?

(1)  A bank lockbox system.

(2)  Prenumbered remittance advices.

(3)  Monthly bank reconciliations.

(4)  Daily deposit of cash receipts.

**LO 3**

b. To provide assurance that each voucher is submitted and paid only once, the auditors most likely would examine a sample of paid vouchers and determine whether each voucher is:

(1)  Supported by a vendor's invoice.

(2)  Stamped "paid" by the check signer.

(3)  Prenumbered and accounted for.

(4)  Approved for authorized purchases.

**LO 5**   c. In testing controls over cash disbursements, the auditors most likely would determine that the person who signs checks also:

    (1) Reviews the monthly bank reconciliation.

    (2) Returns the checks to accounts payable.

    (3) Is denied access to the supporting documents.

    (4) Is responsible for mailing the checks.

**LO 6**   d. To gather evidence regarding the balance per bank in a bank reconciliation, the auditors would examine any of the following *except:*

    (1) Cutoff bank statement.

    (2) Year-end bank statement.

    (3) Bank confirmation.

    (4) General ledger.

**LO 7**   e. You have been assigned to the year-end audit of a financial institution and are planning the timing of audit procedures relating to cash. You decide that it would be preferable to:

    (1) Count the cash in advance of the balance sheet date in order to disclose any kiting operations at year-end.

    (2) Coordinate the count of cash with the cutoff of accounts payable.

    (3) Coordinate the count of cash with the count of marketable securities and other negotiable assets.

    (4) Count the cash immediately upon the return of the confirmation letters from the financial institution.

**LO 5**   f. Which of the following procedures would the auditors most likely perform to test controls relating to management's assertion about the completeness of cash receipts for cash sales at a retail outlet?

    (1) Observe the consistency of the employees' use of cash registers and tapes.

    (2) Inquire about employees' access to recorded but undeposited cash.

    (3) Trace deposits in the cash receipts journal to the cash balance in the general ledger.

    (4) Compare the cash balance in the general ledger with the bank confirmation request.

**LO 3**   g. Reconciliation of the bank account should not be performed by an individual who also:

    (1) Processes cash disbursements.

    (2) Has custody of securities.

    (3) Prepares the cash budget.

    (4) Reviews inventory reports.

**LO 4, 6**   h. The auditors suspect that a client's cashier is misappropriating cash receipts for personal use by lapping customer checks received in the mail. In attempting to uncover this embezzlement scheme, the auditors most likely would compare the:

    (1) Details of bank deposit slips with details of credits to customer accounts.

    (2) Daily cash summaries with the sums of the cash receipts journal entries.

    (3) Individual bank deposit slips with the details of the monthly bank statements.

    (4) Dates uncollectible accounts are authorized to be written off with the dates the write-offs are actually recorded.

**LO 9**   i. In order to guard against the misappropriation of company-owned marketable securities, which of the following is the *best* course of action that can be taken by a company with a large portfolio of marketable securities?

    (1) Require that one trustworthy and bonded employee be responsible for access to the safekeeping area where securities are kept.

    (2) Require that employees who enter and leave the safekeeping area sign and record in a log the exact reason for their access.

    (3) Require that employees involved in the safekeeping function maintain a subsidiary control ledger for securities on a current basis.

    (4) Require that the safekeeping function for securities be assigned to a bank or stockbroker that will act as a custodial agent.

**LO 9**   j. Hall Company had large amounts of funds to invest on a temporary basis. The board of directors decided to purchase securities and derivatives and assigned the future purchase and sale decisions to a responsible financial executive. The best person or persons to make periodic reviews of the investment activity would be:

(1) An investment committee of the board of directors.

(2) The chief operating officer.

(3) The corporate controller.

(4) The treasurer.

**LO 10**     *k.* The auditors who physically examine securities should insist that a client representative be present in order to:

(1) Detect fraudulent securities.

(2) Lend authority to the auditors' directives.

(3) Acknowledge the receipt of securities returned.

(4) Coordinate the return of securities to the proper locations.

**LO 10**     *l.* The best way to verify the amounts of dividend revenue received during the year is:

(1) Recomputation.

(2) Verification by reference to dividend record books.

(3) Confirmation with dividend-paying companies.

(4) Examination of cash disbursements records.

**LO 1, 2, 3, 4, 6**    10–38.   **Simulation**

You are working on your firm's fifth audit of SSC. The previous audits have all resulted in standard unqualified audit reports. Read the following write-up from your audit files concerning SSC and its industry, and then reply to the questions that follow.

**Company Information**

In 20X1, Gary Sherwood founded Sherwood Stone Company (SSC). In the middle of its second year of existence, the company completed development of a large extraction pit area and constructed an aggregate processing plant that is equipped to crush, screen, and wash aggregate products. By 20X4, the sand and gravel operation was profitable and growing market conditions justified modifications and expansion. Currently, SSC produces a wide range of sand and stone products from its pit near Bisbee, Arizona. The materials it develops are composed of sand and stone materials for commercial construction and highway projects.

SSC sells to a wide variety of commercial and governmental customers, with only one of its numerous customers—Wingo Corporation—accounting for more than 5 percent of total sales. In total, Wingo has represented approximately 30 percent of sales (and receivables) for the past few years. Wingo Corporation is by far Arizona's largest street and road contractor and seems solid financially. Virtually all of SSC's sales are on credit, although all but the smallest contracts require "progress" billings that result in payment being received by SSC on a pro rata basis with delivery of materials to the customer. Payments from customers are made directly to the company's lockbox system with SSC's local bank. All transactions occur in U.S. dollars, and SSC maintains both a general checking account and a payroll account.

SSC has worked closely with Wingo Corporation in developing a superior road paying product ("QuietRide"). Not only is the car ride relatively quiet on QuietRide roads, but it is also relatively cool (thus lengthening the life of automobile tires) and less likely to lead to cars sliding in rainy conditions. Although Wingo Corporation holds the overall patent, SSC has patented a critical component that is used in the product (the component is "QSand"). The product now accounts for approximately 25 percent of the company's sales (all to Wingo Corporation) and 33 percent of its profits.

The success of QSand has led SSC to start developing another product, QDeck. QDeck will be a final finishing coat over the pool deck—the concrete walking and lounging area that surrounds a swimming pool. QDeck is intended to address two problems: (1) individuals slipping and falling on pool decks while walking with wet feet, and (2) individuals burning their feet on the deck on particularly hot days. Gary indicates that the current compound seems to allow good traction and decks remain much cooler than products of other companies. The problem being addressed at this point is that the current compound seems to crack easily and has a relatively short useful life. Indeed, in one test of the product on the deck at Gary's home, Gary's wife Madonna cut her foot on one of the cracks and required several stitches to close the wound. Gary laughed and said that at least she didn't slip or burn her feet on that hot day when it happened. More seriously, he suggested that this deficiency is currently being worked on and must be solved before the product goes to market. The product is being independently developed and is intended for both residential and commercial markets.

In 20X8, the company experienced a level of profitability just slightly above that of 20X7—but this was well below the net incomes of the preceding few years. Gary suggested to you that, surprisingly, intense price competition from several smaller competitors in the Bisbee area caused the somewhat low level of profitability. But, he added, he didn't expect the problem to last for long because he doubted that those companies could continue to operate selling at those lower prices. Gary had hoped for a more profitable year in 20X8, as a significant amount of the company's long-term debt is payable in 20X9. SSC is currently involved in discussions with the bank on refinancing.

SSC added significant additional crushing and washing plant and equipment during 20X8 to increase production in the future by more than 100 percent while expanding capabilities to produce custom specification materials.

No dividends have been paid during the past two years, although previously most of the earnings were distributed through dividends to SSC's five shareholders—CEO and Chair of the Board of Directors Gary Sherwood, his wife Madonna Sherwood, CFO Jane Zhan, and two college friends of Gary's who invested in the company, Cindy Stone and Kelly Higgins. These five individuals make up the company's board of directors.

The Bank of Arizona is the financial institution with which SSC maintains its two cash accounts (a general and payroll cash account) and from which it obtains a significant portion of its financing; the inventories are pledged on the Bank of Arizona loan. This year, in reaction to pressure from the bank, SSC established an audit committee composed of Madonna Sherwood, Cindy Stone, and Kelly Higgins.

**Industry Information**

The industry activities consist of the extraction and preparation of sand and rock products. These activities include the cleaning, separating, and sorting of quarried sand and the process of crushing rocks. The products are in the form of sand used in making concrete; sand used in laying bricks (which contains little soil); sand used for fill (which contains a large amount of soil); and quartz sand. It excludes the products of gravel quarrying (sandstone, gravel stone, and iron sand).

While sales within the industry are relatively unaffected by changes in technology or obsolescence, industry sales rely heavily upon both the residential and commercial construction markets as well as government spending. During the past five years, construction has performed well and that trend is expected to continue for at least the next several years. Sand and gravel production has increased at approximately 4 percent per year during this time period, as has construction within the central Arizona area.

**Questions**

a. Which of the following represents a correct statement concerning the risk of misappropriation of cash for SSC?

   (1) This is not a major concern since sales are made on credit.

   (2) Deposit of cash into a lockbox system decreases the risk of misappropriation.

   (3) Misappropriation of cash is not a significant problem in a commercial company.

   (4) The success of QSand increases the risk that cash will be misappropriated.

b. Which of the following correctly identifies a risk facing SSC that might adversely affect cash receipts during the coming years?

   (1) Establishment of the audit committee.

   (2) Increase in the popularity of home swimming pools.

   (3) Sales to many different customers.

   (4) Sales to Wingo.

c. Which of the following correctly identifies a risk facing SSC that might adversely affect sales during the coming years?

   (1) A general slowdown in the economy.

   (2) Sales to many smaller customers other than Wingo Corporation.

   (3) Increased attention to developing new products.

   (4) A board of directors dominated by management.

d. Which of the following correctly identifies a risk facing SSC that might affect its ability to continue as a going concern over the long run?

    (1) Competition from several competitors.

    (2) Your CPA firm's decision to issue standard unmodified audit reports not mentioning the going-concern status during the past five years.

    (3) Obsolescence of all products due to rapid changes in technology in the industry.

    (4) The nature of inventory items—small in size, high in value.

e. Of the following, the most significant risk factor relating to the risk of misstatement arising from fradulent financial reporting for SSC is that:

    (1) Company officers serve on the board of directors.

    (2) The company must refinance a significant portion of its debt.

    (3) The company operates in the Bisbee, Arizona, area.

    (4) The company paid no dividend this year.

f. In addition to the risk factor identified in the preceding question, another risk factor relating to misstatements arising from fraudulent financial reporting is:

    (1) Earnings this year are lower than management had hoped.

    (2) Accounts payable are limited to commercial suppliers.

    (3) Sales are made to residential, commercial, and governmental purchasers.

    (4) The industry faces great technological changes in almost all of its products.

**LO 3, 4, 5, 6**   10–39.  **Simulation**

Items *a* through *l* represent possible errors and fraud that you suspect may be present at Rex Company. The accompanying *List of Auditing Procedures* represents procedures that the auditor would consider performing to gather evidence concerning possible errors an fraud. For each item, select one or two procedures, as indicated, that the auditor most likely would perform to gather evidence in support of that item. The procedures on the list may be selected once, more than once, or not at all.

---

### List of Auditing Procedures

A. Compare the details of the cash receipts journal entries with the details of the corresponding daily deposit slips.

B. Scan the debits to the fixed asset accounts and vouch selected amounts to vendors' invoices and management's authorization.

C. Perform analytical procedures that compare documented authorized pay rates to the entity's budget and forecast.

D. Obtain the cutoff bank statement and compare the cleared checks to the year-end bank reconciliation.

E. Prepare a bank transfer schedule.

F. Inspect the entity's deeds to its real estate.

G. Make inquiries of the entity's attorney concerning the details of real estate transactions.

H. Confirm the terms of borrowing arrangements with the lender.

I. Examine selected equipment repair orders and supporting documentation to determine the propriety of the charges.

J. Send requests to confirm the entity's accounts receivable on a surprise basis at an interim date.

K. Send a second request for confirmation of the receivable to the customer and make inquiries of a reputable credit agency concerning the customer's creditworthiness.

L. Examine the entity's shipping documents to verify that the merchandise that produced the receivable was actually sent to the customer.

M. Inspect the entity's correspondence files for indications of customer disputes for evidence that certain shipments were on consignment.

N. Perform edit checks of data on the payroll transaction tapes.

O. Inspect payroll check endorsements for similar handwriting.

P. Observe payroll check distribution on a surprise basis.

Q. Vouch data in the payroll register to documented authorized pay rates in the human resources department's files.

R. Reconcile the payroll checking account and determine if there were unusual time lags between the issuance and payment of payroll checks.

S. Inspect the file of prenumbered vouchers for consecutive numbering and proper approval by an appropriate employee.

T. Determine that the details of selected prenumbered vouchers match the related vendors' invoices.

U. Examine the supporting purchase orders and receiving reports for selected paid vouchers.

---

### Possible Misstatements Due to Errors and Fraud

a. The auditor suspects that a kiting scheme exists because an accounting department employee who can issue and record checks seems to be leading an unusually luxurious lifestyle. (**Select only 1 procedure.**)

b. An auditor suspects that the controller wrote several checks and recorded the cash disbursements just before year-end but did not mail the checks until after the first week of the subsequent year. (**Select only 1 procedure.**)

c. The entity borrowed funds from a financial institution. Although the transaction was properly recorded, the auditor suspects that the loan created a lien on the entity's real estate that is not disclosed in its financial statements. (**Select only 1 procedure.**)

d. The auditor discovered an unusually large receivable from one of the entity's new customers. The auditor suspects that the receivable may be fictitious because the auditor has never heard of the customer and because the auditor's initial attempt to confirm the receivable has been ignored by the customer. (**Select only 2 procedures.**)

e. The auditor suspects that fictitious employees have been placed on the payroll by the entity's payroll supervisor, who has access to payroll records and to the paychecks. (**Select only 1 procedure.**)

f. The auditor suspects that selected employees of the entity received unauthorized raises from the entity's payroll supervisor, who has access to payroll records. (**Select only 1 procedure.**)

g. The entity's cash receipts of the first few days of the subsequent year were properly deposited in its general operating account after the year-end. However, the auditor suspects that the entity recorded the cash receipts in its books during the last week of the year under audit. (**Select only 1 procedure.**)

h. The auditor suspects that vouchers were prepared and processed by an accounting department employee for merchandise that was neither ordered nor received by the entity. (**Select only 1 procedure.**)

i. The details of invoices for equipment repairs were not clearly identified or explained to the accounting department employees. The auditor suspects that the bookkeeper incorrectly recorded the repairs as fixed assets. (**Select only 1 procedure.**)

j. The auditor suspects that a lapping scheme exists because an accounting department employee who has access to cash receipts also maintains the accounts receivable ledger and refuses to take any vacation or sick days. (**Select only 2 procedures.**)

k. The auditor suspects that the entity is inappropriately increasing the cash reported on its balance sheet by drawing a check on one account and not recording it as an outstanding check on that account and simultaneously recording it as a deposit in a second account. (**Select only 1 procedure.**)

l. The auditor suspects that the entity's controller has overstated sales and accounts receivable by recording fictitious sales to regular customers in the entity's books. (**Select only 2 procedures.**)

**LO 6**   10–40.   **Simulation**

Items 1 through 6 represent the items that an auditor ordinarily would find on a client-prepared bank reconciliation. The accompanying **List of Auditing Procedures** represents substantive auditing procedures. For each item, select one or more procedures, as indicated, that the auditor most likely would perform to gather evidence in support of that item. The procedures on the list may be selected once, more than once, or not at all.

*Assume*

- The client prepared the bank reconciliation on 10/2/X5.
- The bank reconciliation is mathematically accurate.
- The auditor received a cutoff bank statement dated 10/7/X5 directly from the bank on 10/11/X5.
- The 9/30/X5 deposit in transit—outstanding checks #1281, #1285, #1289, and #1292—and the correction of the error regarding check #1282 appeared on the cutoff bank statement.
- The auditor assessed control risk concerning the financial statement assertions related to cash at the maximum.

---

### List of Auditing Procedures

| | |
|---|---|
| A. Trace to cash receipts journal. | H. Inspect supporting documents for reconciling |
| B. Trace to cash disbursements journal. | item not appearing on cutoff statement. |
| C. Compare to 9/30/X5 general ledger. | I. Trace items on the bank reconciliation to cutoff |
| D. Confirm directly with bank. | statement. |
| E. Inspect bank credit memo. | J. Trace items on the cutoff statement to bank |
| F. Inspect bank debit memo. | reconciliation. |
| G. Ascertain reason for unusual delay. | |

---

GENERAL COMPANY
Bank Reconciliation
1st National Bank of US Bank Account
September 30, 20X5

| | | | | |
|---|---|---|---|---|
| a. Select 2 Procedures | — | Balance per bank | | $ 28,375 |
| b. Select 5 Procedures | — | Deposits in transit | | |
| | | 9/29/X5 | $4,500 | |
| | | 9/30/X5 | 1,525 | 6,025 |
| | | | | 34,400 |
| c. Select 5 Procedures | — | Outstanding checks | | |
| | | # 988    8/31/X5 | 2,200 | |
| | | #1281   9/26/X5 | 675 | |
| | | #1285   9/27/X5 | 850 | |
| | | #1289   9/29/X5 | 2,500 | |
| | | #1292   9/30/X5 | 7,225 | (13,450) |
| | | | | 20,950 |
| d. Select 1 Procedure | — | Customer note collected by bank | | (3,000) |
| e. Select 2 Procedures | — | Error: Check #1282; written on 9/26/X5 for $270 was erroneously charged by bank as $720; bank was notified on 10/2/X5 | | 450 |
| f. Select 1 Procedure | — | Balance per books | | $ 18,400 |

**LO 4, 6**   10–41.   **Simulation**

Auditors perform a number of procedures relating to cash—some unique, some not unique. For each substantive procedure below, identify its primary objective or indicate that the procedure serves no purpose.

Substantive Procedures:

*a.*  Prepare a bank transfer schedule.

*b.*  Prepare a four-column proof of cash.

*c.*  Use a standard confirmation form to confirm account balance information.

*d.*  Obtain bank cutoff statements.

*e.*  Search for large checks to directors, officers, and employees.

Replies: A primary objective of the procedure is to:

1.  Detect kiting.
2.  Detect lapping.
3.  Determine that receivables are converted to cash in a reasonable amount of time.
4.  Establish the valuation of cash to reflect currency translation losses and gains.
5.  Reconcile cash receipt and disbursement totals between company records and bank records.
6.  Verify reconciling items on the year-end bank reconciliation.
7.  Verify year-end cash and liability balance information.
8.  Identify related party transactions.
9.  None. This procedure serves no purpose related to cash.

(AICPA, adapted)

# Problems

**All applicable problems are available with McGraw-Hill's *Connect*™ *Accounting*.**  ■**connect** |ACCOUNTING

**LO 3, 4**   10–42.   The cashier of Mission Corporation intercepted customer A's check, payable to the company in the amount of $500, and deposited it in a bank account that was part of the company petty cash fund, of which he was custodian. He then drew a $500 check on the petty cash fund bank account payable to himself, signed it, and cashed it. At the end of the month, while processing the monthly statements to customers, he was able to change the statement to customer A to show that A had received credit for the $500 check that had been intercepted. Ten days later he made an entry in the cash receipts journal that purported to record receipt of a remittance of $500 from customer A, thus restoring A's account to its proper balance but overstating cash in the bank. He covered the overstatement by omitting from the list of outstanding checks in the bank reconciliation two checks, the aggregate amount of which was $500.

*Required:*

Discuss briefly what you regard as the more important deficiencies in internal control in the above situation and, in addition, include what you consider a proper remedy for each deficiency.

(AICPA, adapted)

**LO 4, 5**    10–43.   John Harris, CPA, has been engaged to audit the financial statements of the Spartan Drug Store, Inc. Spartan is a medium-sized retail outlet that sells a wide variety of consumer goods. All sales are for cash or check. Cashiers utilize cash registers to process these transactions. There are no receipts by mail and there are no credit card or charge sales.

*Required:*

Construct the "Processing Cash Collections" segment of the internal control questionnaire on "Cash Receipts" to be used in the evaluation of internal control over the Spartan Drug Store, Inc. Each question should elicit either a yes or a no response. Do *not* discuss the controls over cash sales.

(AICPA, adapted)

**LO 3, 4, 5**    10–44.   Following are typical questions that might appear on an internal control questionnaire for investments in marketable securities.

1. Is custody of investment securities maintained by an employee who does not maintain the detailed records of the securities?

2. Are securities registered in the company name?

3. Are investment activities reviewed by an investment committee of the board of directors?

*Required:*

a. Describe the purpose of each of the above controls.

b. Describe the manner in which each of the above procedures might be tested.

c. Assuming that the operating effectiveness of each of the above procedures is found to be inadequate, describe how the auditors might alter their substantive procedures to compensate for the increased level of control risk.

**LO 6**    10–45.   You are the senior auditor-in-charge of the July 31, 20X0, audit of Reliable Auto Parts, Inc. Your newly hired staff assistant reports to you that she is unable to complete the four-column proof of cash for the month of April 20X0, which you instructed her to do as part of the consideration of internal control over cash.

Your assistant shows you the working paper that she has prepared. Your review of your assistant's work reveals that the dollar amounts of all the items in her working paper are correct. You learn that the accountant for Reliable Auto Parts, Inc., makes no journal entries for bank service charges or note collections until the month following the bank's recording of the item. In addition, Reliable's accountant makes no journal entries whatsoever for NSF checks that are redeposited and cleared. Your assistant's working paper appears on the next page.

*Required:*

Prepare a corrected four-column proof of cash in good form for Reliable Auto Parts, Inc., for the month of April 20X0.

**LO 4, 5, 6**    10–46.   During the audit of Sunset Building Supply, you are given the following year-end bank reconciliation prepared by the client:

**SUNSET BUILDING SUPPLY**
Bank Reconciliation
December 31

| | |
|---|---:|
| Balance per 12/31 bank statement | $48,734 |
| Add: Deposits in transit | 4,467 |
| | $53,201 |
| Less: Checks outstanding | 20,758 |
| Balance per ledger, 12/31 | $32,443 |

According to the client's accounting records, checks totaling $31,482 were issued between January 1 and January 14 of the following year. You have obtained a cutoff bank statement

RELIABLE AUTO PARTS, INC.
Proof of Cash for April 20X0
July 31, 20X0

| | Balance 3/31/X0 | Deposits | Checks | Balance 4/30/X0 |
|---|---|---|---|---|
| Per bank statement | $ 71,682.84 | $61,488.19 | $ 68,119.40 | $ 65,051.63 |
| Deposits in transit: | | | | |
| At 3/31/X0 | 2,118.18 | | | (2,118.18) |
| At 4/30/X0 | | 4,918.16 | | 4,918.16 |
| Outstanding checks: | | | | |
| At 3/31/X0 | (14,888.16) | | 14,888.16 | |
| At 4/30/X0 | | | (22,914.70) | 22,914.70 |
| Bank service charges: | | | | |
| March 20X0 | (22.18) | | 22.18 | |
| April 20X0 | | | (19.14) | 19.14 |
| Note receivable collected by bank 4/30/X0 | | 18,180.00 | | 18,180.00 |
| NSF check of customer L. G. Waite, charged back by bank 3/31/X0, redeposited and cleared 4/3/X0 | (418.19) | 418.19 | | |
| Balances as computed | 58,472.49 | 85,004.54 | 60,095.90 | 108,964.45 |
| Balances per book | 59,353.23 | 45,689.98 | 76,148.98 | 28,894.23 |
| Unlocated difference | $ (880.74) | $39,314.56 | $(16,053.08) | $ 80,071.22 |

dated January 14 containing paid checks amounting to $50,440. Of the checks outstanding at December 31, checks totaling $3,600 were not returned in the cutoff statement, and of those issued per the accounting records in January, checks totaling $8,200 were not returned.

*Required:*

a. Prepare a working paper comparing (1) the total of all checks returned by the bank or still outstanding with (2) the total per the client's records of checks outstanding at December 31 plus checks issued from January 1–14.

b. Suggest four possible explanations for the situation disclosed in your working paper. State what action you would take in each case, including any adjusting entry you would propose.

**LO 6** 10–47. MLG Company's auditor received confirmations and cutoff statements with related checks and deposit tickets for MLG's three general-purpose bank accounts directly from the banks. The auditor has assessed control risk for the assertions about cash as low. The proper cutoff of external cash receipts and disbursements was established. No bank accounts were opened or closed during the year.

*Required:* Prepare the audit program of substantive procedures to verify MLG's bank balances. Ignore any other cash accounts.

(AICPA, adapted)

**In-Class Team Cases**

**LO 4, 5, 6** 10–48. Listed below are eight interbank cash transfers for Steven Smith Co., indicated by the letters *a* through *h,* for late December 20X1 and early January 20X2.

| | Disbursing Bank (Month/Day) | | Receiving Bank (Month/Day) | | |
|---|---|---|---|---|---|
| | Per Bank | Per Books | Per Bank | Per Books | Amount |
| a. | 12/29 | 12/29 | 12/29 | 12/29 | $52,000 |
| b. | 1/02 | 12/30 | 12/31 | 12/30 | 16,000 |
| c. | 1/04 | 12/31 | 1/02 | 1/02 | 24,000 |
| d. | 1/04 | 12/31 | 1/02 | 12/31 | 44,000 |
| e. | 1/04 | 1/01 | 1/03 | 1/01 | 15,600 |
| f. | 1/02 | 1/01 | 12/31 | 12/31 | 76,000 |
| g. | 1/03 | 1/02 | 12/31 | 1/02 | 42,000 |
| h. | 12/31 | 1/03 | 12/30 | 1/03 | 10,000 |

For each of the transfers *a* through *h*, (1) indicate whether cash is *understated, overstated,* or *correct* as a result of the transfer; and (2) provide a brief example of what could cause the situation. Answer in a form such as the one illustrated here.

| Transfer | Understated, Overstated, or Correct | Example |
|---|---|---|
| a. | Correct | *Book entries:* The transfer was recorded in the accounting records as a check written on the disbursing bank on December 29 and a corresponding cash receipt recorded to receiving bank on that date. *Bank entries:* The check was taken to the receiving bank on December 29 and deposited. The accounts are both in the same bank, and accordingly the transaction was recorded in both accounts as of that date. |
| b. | | |
| ⋮ | | |
| h. | | |

**LO 1, 2, 4, 5, 6**  10–49. An improper cutoff of transactions around year-end occurs when journal entries are recorded in the wrong year. In this case, you are to determine the effects of various cutoff misstatements relating to recording cash receipts received on accounts receivable and the recording of credit sales. To effectively consider the effects of an improper cutoff, it is helpful to consider the underlying journal entries:

| Type of Transaction | Proper Journal Entry (Entries) | |
|---|---|---|
| *Cash receipt on an account receivable* | Cash | 3,000.00 |
| | Accounts Receivable | 3,000.00 |
| *Credit sale—periodic inventory system* | Accounts receivable | 2,000.00 |
| | Sales | 2,000.00 |
| *Credit sale—perpetual inventory system* | Accounts receivable | 2,000.00 |
| | Sales | 2,000.00 |
| | Cost of Goods Sold | 1,300.00 |
| | Inventory | 1,300.00 |

An example of a possible improper cutoff is to "close" the cash receipts journal on December 30 and include December 31 sales in the subsequent year (e.g., the entry is dated January 1 rather than December 31). As a result, cash is understated by $3,000, while accounts receivable is overstated by $3,000 for the year just ended. The effects of closing the sales journal depend upon whether a periodic inventory or perpetual inventory system is in use. The effects of "leaving open" journals past year-end and dating January entries as of December may be determined in a similar manner.

*Required:*  Assume that the client made the following actual credit sales and received cash receipts as follows after 12/29/20X8:

| | Sales | Cost of Goods Sold | Cash Receipts (Receivables Collected) |
|---|---|---|---|
| 12/30/X8 | $1,000 | $ 600 | $4,000 |
| 12/31/X8 | 2,000 | 1,300 | 3,000 |
| 1/1/X9 | 3,500 | 2,200 | 2,500 |
| 1/2/X9 | 4,000 | 2,900 | 3,200 |

Determine the overstatements and understatements that would result from the following situations. Assume that each situation is independent of one another. As an illustration, situation 1 has been solved for you. To simplify the problem, in the case of a perpetual inventory, assume that the year-end inventory count did not identify and correct the misstatement(s).

| Situation | Cash | Acct. Rec. | Inventory | CGS | Sales | Income |
|---|---|---|---|---|---|---|
| 1. Zhang Inc. left the cash receipts journal open after year-end for an extra day and included January 1 cash receipts in the December 31 totals. The company uses a periodic inventory system. What effect would this have on 20X8? | $2,500 (o) | $2,500 (u) | | | | |
| 2. Zhang Inc. closed the cash receipts journal at 12/29 and reported the last two days of cash receipts in January of 20X9. The company uses a periodic inventory system. What effect would this have on 20X8? | | | | | | |
| 3. Zhang Inc. left the sales journal open after year-end for an extra day and included January 1 sales in the December 31 totals. The company uses a periodic inventory system. What effect would this have on 20X8? | | | | | | |
| 4. Same as 3, but the company uses a perpetual inventory system. | | | | | | |
| 5. Zhang Inc. closed the sales journal at 12/29 and reported the two last days' sales in January of 20X9. The company uses a perpetual inventory system. What effect would this have on 20X8? | | | | | | |
| 6. Zhang Inc. left both the sales journal and the cash receipts journal open through January 2 and reported the first two days' transactions in December of 20X8. The company uses a periodic inventory system. What effect would this have on 20X8? | | | | | | |

**Research and Discussion Case**

**LO 4, 5**    10–50.

On October 21, Rand & Brink, a CPA firm, was retained by Suncraft Appliance Corporation to perform an audit for the year ended December 31. A month later, James Minor, president of the corporation, invited the CPA firm's partners, George Rand and Alice Brink, to attend a meeting of all officers of the corporation. Mr. Minor opened the meeting with the following statement:

"All of you know that we are not in a very liquid position, and our October 31 balance sheet shows it." We need to raise some outside capital in January, and our December 31 financial statements (both balance sheet and income statement) must look reasonably good if we're going to make a favorable impression upon lenders or investors. I want every officer of this company to do everything possible during the next month to ensure that, at December 31, our financial statements look as strong as possible, especially our current position and our earnings.

"I have invited our auditors to attend this meeting so they will understand the reason for some year-end transactions that might be a little unusual. It is essential that our financial statements carry the auditors' approval, or we'll never be able to get the financing we need. Now, what suggestions can you offer?"

The vice president for sales was first to offer suggestions: "I can talk some of our large customers into placing some orders in December that they wouldn't ordinarily place until the first part of next year. If we get those extra orders shipped, it will increase this year's earnings and also increase our current assets."

The vice president in charge of production commented: "We can ship every order we have now and every order we get during December before the close of business on December 31. We'll have to pay some overtime in our shipping department, but we'll try not to have a single unshipped order on hand at year-end. Also, we could overship some orders, and the customers wouldn't make returns until January."

The controller spoke next: "If there are late December orders from customers that we can't actually ship, we can just label the merchandise as sold and bill the customers with December 31 sales invoices. Also, there are always some checks from customers dated December 31 that don't reach us until January—some as late as January 10. We can record all those customers' checks bearing dates of late December as part of our December 31 cash balance."

The treasurer offered the following suggestions: "I owe the company $50,000 on a call note I issued to buy some of our stock." I can borrow $50,000 from my mother-in-law about Christmas time and repay my note to the company. However, I'll have to borrow the money from the company again early in January, because my mother-in-law is buying a condo and will need the $50,000 back by January 15.

"Another thing we can do to improve our current ratio is to write checks on December 31 to pay most of our current liabilities. We might even wait to mail the checks for a few days or mail them to the wrong addresses. That will give time for the January cash receipts to cover the December 31 checks."

The vice president of production made two final suggestions: "Some of our inventory, which we had tentatively identified as obsolete, does not represent an open-and-shut case of being unsalable. We could defer any write-down until next year. Another item is some machinery we have ordered for delivery in December. We could instruct the manufacturer not to ship the machines and not to bill us before January."

After listening to these suggestions, the president, James Minor, spoke directly to Rand and Brink, the auditors. "You can see I'm doing my best to give you full information and cooperation. If any of these suggested actions would prevent you from giving a clean bill of health to our year-end statements, I want to know about it now so we can avoid doing anything that would keep you from issuing an unqualified audit report. I know you'll be doing a lot of preliminary work here before December 31, but I'd like for you not to bill us before January. Will you please give us your reactions as to what has been said in this meeting?"

*Required:*

a. Put yourself in the role of Rand & Brink, CPAs, and evaluate *separately* each suggestion made in the meeting. What general term is applicable to most of the suggested actions?

b. Could you assure the client that an unqualified audit report would be issued if your recommendations were followed on all the matters discussed? Explain.

c. Would the discussion in this meeting cause you to withdraw from the engagement?

## Ethics Case

10–51. Today you had lunch with your friend Sarah Teasdale. Sarah has worked with Zaird & Associates, CPAs, for about two years. You've been with Zaird for only nine months. You discussed with her your difficulties in getting jobs done in the budgeted number of hours. Sarah said, "Yeah, that's a problem. You'll get quicker with experience, but—don't tell anyone I told you this—some of those audit programs are pretty awful and include some pretty outdated and even some stupid procedures." Sometimes I just sign the program, but skip doing the procedure. "I don't do this often, but sometimes the procedure isn't capable of detecting anything." You said little to her after this, but are now thinking about whether you need to become more "practical" about how you perform your work.

*Required:*

a. Identify your problem here.

b. Identify your possible courses of action. For each of these courses identify any constraints relating to the decision (e.g., personal standards, societal norms, professional ethical standards, other professional standards), and analyze the course of action's likely effects.

c. Select the best course of action.

# Accounts Receivable, Notes Receivable, and Revenue

This chapter describes the audit of receivables and revenue, both products of the revenue cycle. In broad terms, this cycle includes receiving orders from customers, providing and billing merchandise or services to customers, and recording and collecting accounts receivable. Receivables from customers include both accounts receivable and various types of notes receivable.

## Receivables

### Sources and Nature of Accounts Receivable

**LO1**

Describe the nature of receivables.

Accounts receivable include not only claims against customers arising from the sale of goods or services, but also a variety of miscellaneous claims such as loans to officers or employees, loans to subsidiaries, claims against various other firms, claims for tax refunds, and advances to suppliers.

Trade notes and accounts receivable usually are relatively large in amount and should appear as separate items in the current assets section of the balance sheet at their net realizable value. Auditors are especially concerned with the presentation and disclosure of loans to officers, directors, and affiliated companies. These related party transactions are commonly made for the convenience of the borrower rather than to benefit the lending company. Consequently, such loans are often collected only at the convenience of the borrower. It is a basic tenet of financial statement presentation that transactions not characterized by arm's-length bargaining should be fully disclosed.

### Sources and Nature of Notes Receivable

Notes receivable are written promises to pay certain amounts at future dates. Typically, notes receivable are used for handling transactions of substantial amount; these negotiable documents are widely used. In banks and other financial institutions, notes receivable usually constitute the single most important asset.

An installment note or contract may be used in an exchange that grants possession of goods to a purchaser but permits the seller to retain a lien on the goods until the final installment under the note has been received. Installment notes are widely used in the sale of industrial machinery, farm equipment, and automobiles. Other transactions that may lead to the acquisition of notes receivable include the disposal of items of plant and equipment; the sale of divisions of a company; the issuance of capital stock; and the making of loans to officers, employees, and affiliated companies.

## Learning objectives

After studying this chapter, you should be able to:

LO1    Describe the nature of receivables.

LO2    Describe the auditors' objectives in the audit of receivables and revenue.

LO3    Describe the documents, records, and accounts that compose the revenue (sales) transactions cycle and the fundamental controls over receivables and revenue.

LO4    Use the understanding of the client and its environment to consider inherent risks (including fraud risks) related to receivables and revenue.

LO5    Obtain an understanding of internal control over receivables and revenue.

LO6    Assess the risks of material misstatement of receivables and revenue and design further audit procedures, including tests of controls and substantive procedures, to address the risks.

## The Auditors' Objectives in Auditing Receivables and Revenue

**LO2**

Describe the auditors' objectives in the audit of receivables and revenue.

The auditors' *objectives* in the audit of receivables and revenue are to:

1. Use the understanding of the client and its environment to consider *inherent risks,* including fraud risks, related to receivables and revenue.
2. Obtain an understanding of *internal control* over receivables and revenue.
3. Assess the risks of material misstatement and design tests of controls and substantive procedures that:
   a. Substantiate the *existence* of receivables and the *occurrence* of revenue transactions.
   b. Establish the *completeness* of receivables and revenue transactions.
   c. Verify the *cutoff* of revenue transactions.
   d. Determine that the client has *rights* to recorded receivables.
   e. Establish the proper *valuation* of receivables and the *accuracy* of revenue transactions.
   f. Determine that the *presentation* and *disclosure* of information about receivables and revenue are appropriate, including the separation of receivables into appropriate categories, adequate reporting of any receivables pledged as collateral, and disclosure of related party sales and receivables.

Because of the close relationship between revenue and accounts receivable, the two can best be considered jointly. The determination of the amount of revenue to be recognized for a particular period is integrally related to a number of financial statement accounts, including sales and accounts receivable, adjustments to sales and accounts receivable, service revenue, deferred revenues, and cash. In addition, it is a major determinant of the amount of net income that the company reports for a particular period. Therefore, the audit of revenue and receivables is an area of significant risk to auditors.

## Internal Control of Accounts Receivable and Revenue

To understand internal control over accounts receivable and revenue, the auditors must consider the various components, including the control environment, risk assessment, monitoring, the (accounting) information and communication system, and control activities.

## Control Environment

Because of the risk of intentional misstatement of revenues, the control environment is very important to effective internal control over revenue and receivables. Of particular importance is an independent audit committee of the board of directors that monitors management's judgments about revenue recognition principles and estimates, as well as an effective internal audit function. Management should establish a *tone at the top* of the organization that encourages integrity and ethical financial reporting. These ethical standards should be communicated and observed throughout the organization. Also, incentives for dishonest reporting, such as undue emphasis on meeting unrealistic sales or earnings targets, should be eliminated.

Appropriate revenue recognition may involve complex accounting principles, estimates, and computations. As a result, management should make a *commitment to competence,* especially as it relates to key financial and accounting personnel. Increased control is indicated when management effectively identifies the skills and training needed to perform key functions and implements effective procedures to ensure that these functions are performed by competent personnel.

*Management's philosophy and operating style,* as indicated by its attitude toward financial reporting, are also important in the control of revenue and receivables. The relevant questions include: Is management aggressive or conservative in selecting methods of revenue recognition? Are estimates of uncollectible accounts developed in a conscientious manner?

With regard to the client's *human resource policies and practices,* management should make appropriate background checks of prospective employees and obtain fidelity bonds

## Illustrative Case

### *Fraudulent Revenue Recognition*

The National Commission of Fraudulent Financial Reporting sponsored a study of incidences of fraudulent financial reporting, as reported in SEC Accounting and Auditing Enforcement Releases from 1985 through 1997. The researchers found inappropriate revenue recognition in 50 percent of the cases.

on employees in positions of trust. Internal control is also improved when individuals who maintain accounting records or cash are required to take vacations and when their assigned duties are rotated periodically.

## Risk Assessment

As discussed in Chapter 6, risk assessment involves identification, analysis, and management of risks relevant to the preparation of financial statements. In relation to the revenue cycle, management should develop a formal process of monitoring external factors, such as changes in economic conditions, competition, customer demand, and regulations that may affect the risk of achieving the company's sales objectives. In addition, management should evaluate the effects of internal factors, such as changes in accounting principles, the introduction of new products and services, and the use of new types of sales transactions. These factors may create new risks for the company, indicating a need to implement new types of controls to prevent the misstatement of revenue.

## Revenue Cycle— Accounting System and Control Activities

**LO3**

Describe the documents, records, and accounts that compose the revenue (sales) transactions cycle and the fundamental controls over receivables and revenue.

For many companies, the primary source of revenue is from the sale of goods or services to customers on credit. Ineffective controls over credit sales and receivables can be costly to a business. When control activities over sales on account are inadequate, large credit losses are almost inevitable. For example, merchandise may be shipped to customers whose credit standing has not been approved. Shipments may be made to customers without notice being given to the billing department; consequently, no sales invoice is prepared. Sales invoices may contain errors in prices and quantities; and if sales invoices are not controlled by serial numbers, some may be lost and never recorded as accounts receivable. To avoid such difficulties, strong controls over credit sales are necessary. Usually, internal control over credit sales is strengthened by a division of duties so that different departments or individuals are responsible for (1) preparation of the sales order, (2) credit approval, (3) issuance of merchandise from stock, (4) shipment, (5) billing, (6) invoice verification, (7) maintenance of control accounts, (8) maintenance of customers' ledgers, (9) approval of sales returns and allowances, and (10) authorization of write-offs of uncollectible accounts. When this degree of subdivision of duties is feasible, accidental errors are likely to be detected quickly through the comparison of documents and amounts emerging from independent units of the company, and the opportunity for fraud is reduced to a minimum. While our discussion of the accounting system and control activities will be developed primarily in terms of the sales processes of manufacturing companies, most of the principles also apply to service organizations.

### *Controlling Customers' Orders*

The controlling and processing of orders received from customers require carefully designed operating procedures and numerous controls if costly errors are to be avoided. Important initial steps include registering the customer's *purchase order,* reviewing items and quantities to determine whether the order can be filled within a reasonable time, and preparing a *sales order* (see on the next page). The sales order is a translation of the terms of the customer's order into a set of specific instructions for the guidance

PURCHASE ORDER

78644

**PURCHASE ORDER**
Pilot Stores
1425 G St.
Irvine, CA 92345

To: Wood Supply Co.
21 Main St.
Suisun, CA 95483

Date: Nov. 10, 20X0
Ship via: Jon Trucking
Terms: 2/10, n/40

Enter our order for

| Qty. | Description | Price | Total |
|------|-------------|-------|-------|
| 20 doz. | Q Clamps #26537489 | $235.00 | $4700.00 |
| 10 | 120 hp Generators #45983748 | 355.00 | 3550.00 |
| | | | |

Wood Supply Co.
By *Bill Jones*

476538

**SALES ORDER**
Wood Supply Co.
21 Main St.
Suisun, CA 95483

To: Pilot Stores
1425 G St.
Irvine, CA 92345

Date: Nov. 23, 20X0

Credit Approval: *MS*

Cust. No.: 12654

| Description | Part No. | Quantity |
|-------------|----------|----------|
| Q Clamps | 26537489 | 20 doz. |
| 120 hp Generators | 45983748 | 10 |

of various divisions, including the credit, finished goods stores, shipping, billing, and accounts receivable units. The action to be taken by the factory upon receipt of a sales order will depend upon whether the goods are standard products carried in stock or are to be produced to specifications set by the customer.

*Credit Approval*

Before sales orders are processed, the credit department must determine whether goods may be shipped to the customer on open account. This department is supervised by a credit manager who reports to the treasurer or the vice president of finance. The credit department implements management's credit policies and uses them to evaluate prospective and continuing customers by studying the customer's financial statements and by referring to reports of credit agencies, such as Dun & Bradstreet, Inc. Once a new customer has been granted a line of credit, approval of a particular sales transaction involves a simple determination of whether the customer has sufficient unused credit. This process is often performed by the IT system. If the sales transaction will cause the customer's credit limit to be exceeded, the computer will print out the details for the credit department, which will initiate the process of determining whether to increase the customer's line of credit. When credit is not approved, the customer is notified and an effort is made to negotiate some other terms, such as cash on delivery.

*Issuing Merchandise*

Companies that carry standard products in stock maintain a finished goods storeroom supervised by a storekeeper. The storekeeper issues the goods covered by a sales order to the shipping department only after the sales order has been approved by the credit department. Perpetual inventory records of finished goods should be maintained by the accounting department, not by the storekeeper.

*The Shipping Function*

When the goods are transmitted by the finished goods storeroom to the shipping department, this group must arrange for space in railroad cars, aircraft, or motor freight carriers. Shipping documents, such as *bills of lading* (see on the next page), are created at the time of loading the goods into cars or trucks. The shipping documents are numerically controlled and are entered in a shipping register before being forwarded to the billing department. When shipments are made by truck, some type of gate control is also needed to

| | | 10026574 |
|---|---|---|
| **BILL OF LADING** | | |

Wood Supply Co.
21 Main St.
Suisun, CA 95483        Date: Nov. 25, 20X0

Shipped to:        Order No: 476538

    Pilot Stores
    1425 G St.        Shipper: *Jon Trucking*
    Irving, CA 92345

| Quantity | Description | Weight |
|---|---|---|
| 5 Boxes | 20 doz. Q Clamps #26537489 | 142 |
| 10 Crates | 10 hp Generators #45983748 | 2560 |
| | | 2702 |

**Shipper's Acceptance:** *Bill Warren*

| | | 7462537 |
|---|---|---|
| **INVOICE** | | |

Wood Supply Co.
21 Main St.
Suisun, CA 95483

Sold to: Pilot Stores        Date: Nov. 27, 20X0
    1425 G St.
    Irvine, CA 92345        Your order no. 78644

        Shipped: Nov. 25, 20X0
        Shipped via: *Jon Trucking*
        Terms: 2/10, n/40

| Qty. | Description | Price | Total |
|---|---|---|---|
| 20 doz. | Q Clamps | $235.00 | $ 4700.00 |
| 10 | 120 hp Generators | 355.00 | 3550.00 |
| | | | $ 8250.00 |

ensure that all goods leaving the plant have been recorded as shipments. This may require the surrender to the gatekeeper of copies of shipping documents.

*The Billing Function*

The term *billing* means notifying the customer of the amount due for goods or services delivered. This notification is accomplished by preparing and mailing a *sales invoice* (see above). A department not under the control of sales executives should perform billing. The function is generally assigned to a separate section within the accounting, data processing, or finance department. The billing section has the responsibility of (1) accounting for the serially numbered shipping documents, (2) comparing shipping documents with sales orders and customers' purchase orders and change notices, (3) entering pertinent data from these documents on the sales invoice, (4) applying prices and discounts from price lists to the invoice, (5) making the necessary extensions and footings, and (6) accumulating the total amounts billed. When a formal contract exists, as is often the case when dealing with governmental entities, that contract usually specifies prices, delivery procedures, inspection and acceptance routines, method of liquidating advances, and numerous other details. Accordingly, the contract is an extremely important source of information for preparation of the sales invoice.

Sales invoices are often generated by the IT system based upon information that has already been entered into the system. Shipping department personnel input information about the quantities of goods shipped, and prices to be charged either have been entered by personnel in the sales department when the sales order was generated or are contained in a master file of sales prices. As the sales invoices are printed, the IT system also creates an electronic sales transactions file that is used in conjunction with the cash receipts transactions file to update the master file of accounts receivable. Periodically, the IT system updates the general ledger and prints the sales journal and the subsidiary ledger of accounts receivable. The computer also generates monthly statements for mailing to customers.

Controls should be established to ensure the accuracy of the invoices before they are mailed to customers. When a manual accounting system is in use, these controls might consist of a second-person review of the accuracy of prices, credit terms, transportation charges, extensions, and footings. When an IT-based billing system is in use, this objective is generally achieved by implementing input validation (edit) checks and various batch processing controls.

```
                                              No. 4584
              CREDIT MEMORANDUM
                  Wood Supply Co.
                    21 Main St.
                 Suisun, CA 95483

  Customer: Howe Carpet Co.        Date: Dec. 15, 20X0
            894 Reed St.
            Orange, CA 92786

  Customer No.: 687960              Invoice No. 7598597
  Receiving Report No.: N/A
```

| Description | Amount |
|---|---|
| Allowance for substandard goods | $550.00 |
|  |  |

**Authorized by:** *Janis Morris*

*Collection of Receivables*

Most receivables held by companies are collected by receipt of customers' checks and remittance advices through the mail.[1] The cashier will control and deposit checks. The remittance advices or a listing of the receipts will then be forwarded to the accounts receivable section of the data processing department, which will record them in the appropriate accounts in the customers' ledger. The total reduction in accounts receivable will be posted periodically to the general ledger control account from the total of the accounts receivable column in the cash receipts journal. Internal control over collections from customers is shown in the cash receipt flowchart in Figure 10.1 of Chapter 10.

An *aged trial balance* of customers' accounts should be prepared at regular intervals for use by the credit department in carrying out its collection program.

*Adjustments to Sales and Receivables*

All adjustments to sales for allowances, returns, and write-offs of accounts receivable should be supported by serially numbered *credit memoranda* (see above) signed by an officer or responsible employee having no duties relating to cash handling or to the maintenance of customers' ledgers. Good internal control over credits for returned merchandise usually includes a requirement that the goods be received and examined before credit is given. The credit memoranda should then bear the serial number of the receiving report on the returned shipment.

The credit manager should initiate the process of uncollectible receivable write-off, with subsequent authorization by the treasurer. Receivables that are written off should then be either turned over to a collection agency or retained and transferred to a separate ledger and control account. The records may be of a memorandum nature rather than part of the regular accounting system. Also, when possible—generally when the debtor is still in existence—statements requesting payment should continue to be mailed. Otherwise, any subsequent collections may be embezzled by employees without the necessity of falsifying records to conceal the theft.

The division of responsibility, sequence of procedures, and basic documentation of the handling of credit sales transactions are illustrated in the systems flowchart in Figure 11.1 on pages 436–437.

---

[1] Chapter 10 provides information on cash receipts directly by financial institutions (e.g., lockbox systems, debit and credit card sales proceeds, and other electronic receipts).

## Monitoring

Ongoing monitoring activities by management primarily involve reviewing various types of performance reports, including sales by product line, by major customer, by geographic area, and by salesperson. In addition, management often will carefully review the aging of accounts receivable and may solicit feedback from customers about the accuracy of billings. When unexpected amounts or relationships are discovered, management should follow up to determine the underlying reasons.

Internal auditors also contribute to the monitoring process. As a part of their audit activities, they may periodically take over the mailing of monthly statements to customers, or send confirmations and investigate discrepancies reported. They also may perform extensive reviews of shipping reports, invoices, cash receipts, credit memoranda, and the aged trial balances of accounts receivable to determine whether prescribed control activities are being carried out consistently. (In addition, reports of regulatory agencies should be considered in making improvements in internal control.) These periodic evaluations also can be used to improve the operating effectiveness of control activities.

## Internal Control over Notes Receivable

As previously stated, a basic characteristic of effective control consists of the subdivision of duties. As applied to notes receivable, this principle requires that:

- The custodian of notes receivable not have access to cash or to the general accounting records.
- The acceptance and renewal of notes be authorized in writing by a responsible official who does not have custody of the notes.
- The write-off of defaulted notes be approved in writing by responsible officials and effective procedures adopted for subsequent follow-up of such defaulted notes.

These rules are obviously corollaries of the general proposition that the authorization, recording, and custodial functions should be separate, especially for cash and receivables.

If the acceptance of a note from a customer requires written approval of a responsible official, the likelihood of fictitious notes being created to offset a theft of cash is significantly reduced. The same review and approval should be required for renewal of a note; otherwise, an opportunity to hide the diversion of the proceeds of a paid note exists through the perpetrator's recording it as having been renewed. The protection given by this procedure for executive approval of notes will be stronger if the internal auditing department periodically confirms notes directly with the makers.

The abstraction of cash receipts is sometimes concealed by failing to make an entry to record receipt of a partial payment on a note. Satisfactory control over the recording of partial payments requires that the date and amount of the payment and the new unpaid balance should be recorded and maintained by the accounting system. Notes written off as uncollectible should be kept under accounting control because occasionally debtors may attempt to reestablish their credit in later years by paying old dishonored notes. Any credit memoranda or journal vouchers for partial payments, write-offs, or adjustment of disputed notes should be authorized by proper officials and kept under numerical control.

Adequate controls over notes receivable secured by mortgages and trust deeds must include follow-up procedures that assure prompt action on delinquent property taxes and insurance premiums, as well as nonpayment of interest and principal installments.

In many companies, internal control is strengthened by the preparation of monthly reports summarizing notes receivable transactions during the month and the details of notes owned at the end of the reporting period. These reports are often designed to focus executive attention immediately upon any delinquent notes and to require advance approval for renewals of maturing notes. In addition, a monthly report on notes receivable ordinarily will show the amounts collected during the month, the new notes accepted, notes discounted, and interest earned. The person responsible for reporting on note transactions should be someone other than the custodian of the notes.

**FIGURE 11.1**   **Dixieline Industries Ltd.: Credit Sales Systems Flowchart, December 31, 20X0**

DIXIELINE INDUSTRIES LTD.
CREDIT SALES SYSTEMS FLOWCHART
DECEMBER 31, 20X0

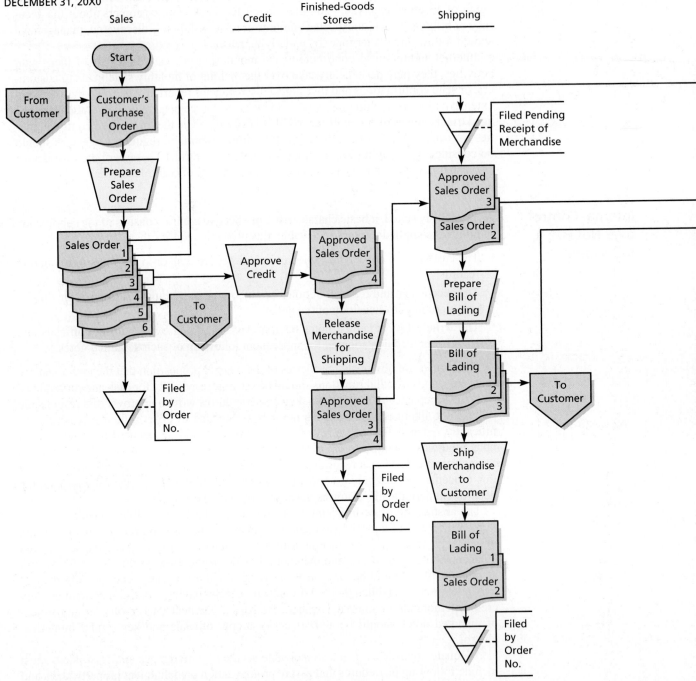

**Audit Documentation for Receivables and Revenue**

Besides preparing lead schedules for receivables and net revenue, the auditors obtain or prepare the following working papers:

1. Aged trial balance of trade accounts receivable (often a computer printout).
2. Analyses of other accounts receivable.
3. Analysis of notes receivable and related interest.
4. Analysis of allowance for uncollectible accounts and notes.

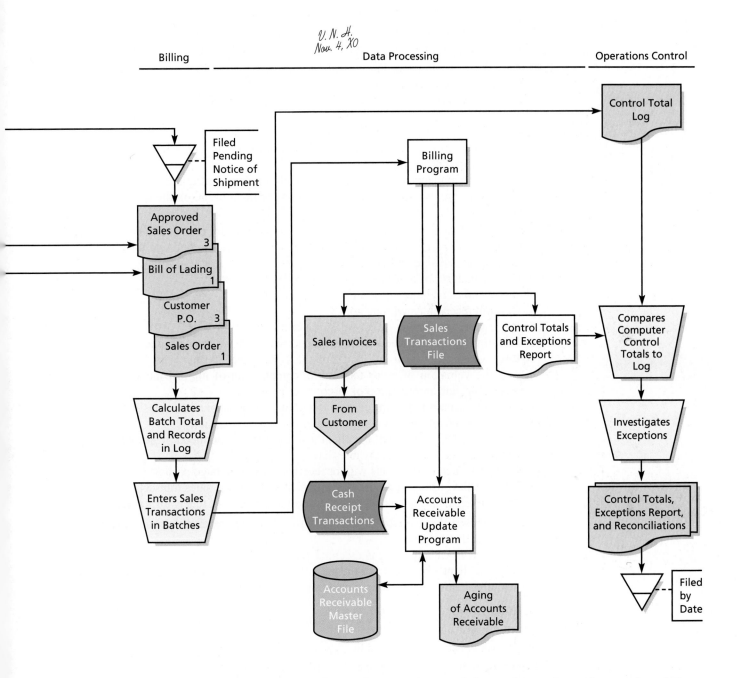

5. Comparative analyses of revenue by month, by product, or by territory, or by relating forecasted revenue to actual revenue.

6. Documentation of internal controls.

7. Risk analyses and audit programs.

## Audit of Receivables and Revenue

The following steps indicate the general pattern of work performed by the auditors in the verification of receivables and revenue. Selection of the most appropriate procedures for a particular audit will be guided by the nature of the internal controls that have been implemented and by the results of the auditors' risk assessments.

A. Use the understanding of the client and its environment to consider inherent risks, including fraud risks, related to receivables and revenue.

B. Obtain an understanding of internal control over receivables and revenue.

C. Assess the risks of material misstatement and design further audit procedures.

D. Perform further audit procedures—tests of controls.
1. Examples of tests of controls:
    a. Examine significant aspects of a sample of sales transactions.
    b. Compare a sample of shipping documents to related sales invoices.
    c. Review the use and authorization of credit memoranda.
    d. Reconcile selected cash register tapes and sales tickets with sales journals.
    e. Test IT application controls.
    f. Examine evidence of review and approval of revenue estimates.
2. If necessary, revise the risks of material misstatement based on the results of tests of controls.

E. Perform further audit procedures—substantive procedures for receivables and revenue.
1. Obtain an *aged trial balance* of trade accounts receivable and analyses of other accounts receivable and reconcile to ledgers.
2. Obtain analyses of notes receivable and related interest.
3. Inspect notes on hand and confirm those with holders.
4. Confirm receivables with debtors.
5. Review the year-end cutoff of sales transactions.
6. Perform analytical procedures for accounts receivable, notes receivable, and revenue.
7. Review significant year-end sales contracts for unusual terms.
8. Test the valuation of notes receivable, computation of interest income, interest receivable, and amortization of discount or premium.
9. Evaluate the propriety of the client's accounting methods for receivables and revenue.
10. Evaluate accounting estimates related to revenue recognition.
11. Determine the adequacy of the client's allowance for uncollectible accounts.
12. Ascertain whether any receivables have been pledged.
13. Investigate any transactions with or receivables from related parties.
14. Evaluate the business purpose of significant and unusual sales transactions.
15. Evaluate financial statement presentation and disclosure of receivables and revenue.

Figure 11.2 relates these major substantive procedures for receivables and revenue to their primary audit objectives.

As discussed in Chapter 6, it is essential for the auditors to have a thorough understanding of the client's business and the industry in which it operates. Regarding revenue and receivables, this understanding includes matters such as:

- The types of products and services sold.
- The classes and categories of the client's customers.
- Whether the business is affected by seasonal or cyclical demand.
- Typical marketing policies for the client and its industry.
- Policies regarding pricing, sales returns, discounts, extension of credit, and normal delivery and payment terms.
- Compensation arrangements that are based on recorded revenue.
- Typical revenue recognition principles used in the industry and their methods of application.

An understanding of these matters helps ensure that the auditors effectively execute the audit program for receivables and revenue.

LO4

Use the understanding of the client and its environment to consider inherent risks (including fraud risks) related to receivables and revenue.

### A. Use the Understanding of the Client and Its Environment to Consider Inherent Risks, Including Fraud Risks.

The auditors use their understanding of the client's environment to assess the inherent risks for the assertions about receivables and revenue. The auditors face a number of

**FIGURE 11.2**   **Objectives of Major Substantive Procedures for Receivables and Revenue**

| Substantive Procedures | Primary Audit Objectives |
| --- | --- |
| Obtain aged listing of receivables and reconcile to ledgers. Obtain analyses of notes receivable and related interest. | *Valuation* and *accuracy* |
| Inspect notes on hand and confirm those not on hand. | *Existence, occurrence,* and *rights* |
| Confirm receivables with debtors. | *Existence, occurrence,* and *rights* *Valuation* and *accuracy* |
| Review the year-end cutoff of sales transactions. | *Existence, occurrence,* and *rights* *Completeness* *Cutoff* |
| Perform analytical procedures. Review significant year-end sales contracts. | *Existence, occurrence,* and *rights* *Completeness* *Valuation* and *accuracy* |
| Verify interest earned on notes receivable. | *Existence, occurrence,* and *rights* *Completeness* |
| Evaluate the propriety of client's accounting for transactions. Evaluate accounting estimates related to revenues. | *Valuation* and *accuracy* |
| Determine adequacy of allowance for uncollectible accounts. | *Valuation* |
| Ascertain the existence of pledged receivables. Investigate receivables from related parties. | *Presentation* and *disclosure* |
| Evaluate the business purpose of significant and unusual sales transactions. | *Valuation* and *accuracy* *Presentation* and *disclosure* |
| Evaluate financial statement presentation and disclosure. | *Presentation* and *disclosure* |

potential inherent risks related to receivables and revenue. Most of these risks are derived from business risks that are faced by management, such as the risks of:

- A decline in sales due to economic declines, product obsolescence, increased competition, or shifts in product or service demand.
- Inability to collect receivables.
- Improper revenue recognition.
- Restrictions placed on sales by laws and regulations.

 Risks of material misstatement also arise from the possibility of fraud. Improper revenue recognition has been the most common technique used by management to engage in fraudulent financial reporting. Therefore, the audit of revenue and receivables is often an area of significant risk to auditors. This is so much so that *SAS 99,* "Consideration of Fraud in a Financial Statement Audit," indicates that the auditors should ordinarily presume that there is a risk of material misstatement due to fraud relating to revenue recognition.

If the auditors identify a fraud risk related to receivables and revenue, they will make sure that they understand the controls established by management to control the risk. They will also determine that the controls have been implemented. Finally, the auditors will design their responses to the risks. As discussed in Chapter 6, the auditors' responses may take one or more of the following forms:

1. A response that has an overall effect on how the audit is conducted. For example, the auditors might assign personnel with significant experience in the client's industry to evaluate the accounting principles used to recognize revenue.
2. A response involving the design of audit procedures. For example, the auditors might require the confirmation of accounts receivable to be performed at year-end as opposed to an interim date.

## Illustrative Case     *Typical Cases of Fraudulent Revenue Recognition*

### CASE 1

The case of California Micro Devices Corp. is typical of situations involving management misstatement of revenue. In this case, management had no revenue recognition policies and significantly overstated revenue using a number of techniques, including:

* Recording revenue on products that were not yet shipped or even ordered.
* Failing to decrease revenue for returned products.
* Paying distributors "handling fees" to accept shipments of products for which they had unlimited rights of return and booking the shipments as sales.

It was reported that, at the peak of the fraud, as much as 70 percent of total sales was in the "fake" category.

### CASE 2

According to an SEC release, civil fraud charges were filed against certain members of management of Peregrine Systems, Inc., a software development company. Peregrine's financial results were restated for its 2000, 2001, and 2002 fiscal years, reducing aggregate revenue during those years by $507 million.

According to the complaint, members of top management determined near the end of each quarter in that period how much additional revenue was needed to meet or exceed analysts' expectations. To meet the numbers, management entered into sham deals with resellers of the company's software. When the related uncollectible receivables began to build, management obtained loans collateralized by the receivables, which were treated as sales of the receivables. Eventually, some of the receivables were written off as a part of the write-off of assets acquired in an unrelated acquisition.

3. A response involving performing procedures to further address the risk of material misstatement due to management's override of internal control. For example, the auditors will evaluate particularly carefully the business purpose of any unusual and significant sales transactions that they encounter, and they will evaluate the allowance for uncollectible accounts for evidence of management bias.

### B. Obtain an Understanding of Internal Control over Receivables and Revenue.

**LO5**

Obtain an understanding of internal control over receivables and revenue.

The auditors' consideration of controls over receivables and revenue may begin with the preparation of a written description or flowchart and the completion of an internal control questionnaire. Typical of the questions comprising an internal control questionnaire for revenue and receivables are the following: Are orders from customers initiated and reviewed by the sales department? Are sales invoices prenumbered and all numbers accounted for? Are all sales approved by the credit department before shipment? Are estimates of revenue performed by competent personnel using appropriate methods?

After the auditors have prepared a description of the controls, they will determine whether the client is actually using the policies and procedures—that is, whether they have been *implemented*. As the auditors confirm their understanding of the revenue cycle, they will observe whether there is an appropriate segregation of duties and inquire as to who performed various functions throughout the year. They will also review revenue budgets and the follow-up on the variances; perform a walk-through of the cycle; inspect various documents, such as bills of lading, sales invoices, and customer statements; and review document files to determine that the client is appropriately accounting for the sequence of prenumbered documents. Figure 11.3 (on pages 442–443) illustrates these documents and the primary accounts involved in the revenue cycle.

### C. Assess the Risks of Material Misstatement and Design Further Audit Procedures.

**LO6**

Assess the risks of material misstatement of receivables and revenue and design further audit procedures, including tests of controls and substantive procedures, to address the risks.

After considering the information about the client and its environment, including internal control, the auditors assess the risks of material misstatement related to the assertions about receivables and revenue. To make these assessments, the auditors must consider the relationships between specific misstatements and internal controls. Figure 11.4 (on pages 444–445) provides examples of potential misstatements of revenue and weaknesses in internal control that make them more likely to occur.

The auditors' assessments of the risks of material misstatement (inherent and control risks) are used to design further audit procedures, including tests of controls and substantive procedures. The further audit procedures must include tests of controls when the auditors' assessments of control risk assume that controls are operating effectively but, in regard to their understanding of the client's internal control, the auditors have not obtained sufficient evidence that controls are operating effectively.

Some of the risks identified by the auditors will be considered to be *significant risks* that require special audit consideration. As an example, if the client executes complex sales contracts, there may be a significant risk of misstatement of sales revenue that requires specific audit tests. In this case, the auditors may decide to confirm the terms of contracts with the client's customers. It is important to remember that for any significant risk, the auditors:

1. Must evaluate the design of the related controls and determine that they are implemented.
2. May not rely solely on analytical procedures to address the risk.
3. May not rely on evidence obtained in prior periods regarding the operating effectiveness of the related controls.

### D. Perform Further Audit Procedures—Tests of Controls.

Tests directed toward the effectiveness of controls help to evaluate the client's internal control and determine whether the auditors' planned assessed levels of control risk can be supported. Certain tests of controls are performed as the auditors obtain an understanding of the client's internal control; these were described in our earlier discussion of that process.

### 1. Examples of Tests of Controls.

### a. Examine Significant Aspects of a Sample of Sales Transactions.

To determine that the controls portrayed in the flowchart are effectively functioning in everyday operations, the auditors will examine significant aspects of a sample of sales transactions. The size of the sample and the transactions included therein may be determined by either statistical or nonstatistical sampling techniques. The auditors often use generalized computer audit software to select the transactions to be tested.

In manufacturing companies, the audit procedure for verification of a sales transaction that has been selected for testing may begin with a comparison of the customer's purchase order, the client's sales order, and the duplicate copy of the sales invoice. The descriptions and quantities of items are compared on these three documents and traced to the duplicate copy of the related shipping document. The credit manager's signature denoting approval of the customer's credit should appear on the sales order.

The extensions and footings on each invoice in the sample should be proved to be arithmetically correct. In addition, the date of each invoice should be compared with two other dates: (1) the date on the related shipping document and (2) the date of entry in the accounts receivable subsidiary ledger.

Consistent pricing and sales discount policies are a necessary element of good internal control over sales transactions. After discussing the policies with management, the auditors can verify the prices and discounts on the invoices selected for testing by comparison with authorized price lists, catalogs, or contracts with customers. After proving the accuracy of selected individual invoices, the auditors next trace the invoices to the sales journal and to postings in the accounts receivable subsidiary ledger.

When performing tests of sales transactions, the auditors should be alert for indications of consigned shipments treated as sales. Some companies that dispose of only a small portion of their total output by consignment fail to make any distinction between consignment shipments and regular sales.

If the subsidiary records for receivables include some accounts with large debit entries and more numerous small credit entries, this should suggest to the auditors that goods have been shipped on consignment and that payments are being received only as the

**FIGURE 11.3**   **Overview of the Revenue and Cash Receipts Cycle—Documents and Accounts**

**Sales**

```
                                                    78644
              PURCHASE ORDER
                 Pilot Stores
                 1425 G St.
               Irvine, CA 92345

   To:  Wood Supply Co.        Date:  Nov. 10, 20X0
        21 Main St.
        Suisun, CA 95483       Ship via:  Jon Trucking

                               Terms:  2/10, n/40

   Enter our order for

   | Qty     | Description | Price    | Total    |
   | 20 doz. | Q Clamps    | $235.00  | $4700.00 |
   |         | #26537489   |          |          |
   | 10      | 120 hp      | 355.00   | 3550.00  |
   |         | Generators  |          |          |
   |         | #45983748   |          |          |

                       Wood Supply Co.
                       By:  Bill Jones
```

```
                                                    10026574
              BILL OF LADING

   Wood Supply Co.
   21 Main St.
   Suisun, CA 95483          Date:  Nov. 25, 20X0

   Shipped to:               Order No.:  476538
        Pilot Stores
        1425 G St.           Shipper:  Jon Trucking
        Irvine, CA 92345

   | Quantity | Description      | Weight |
   | 5 Boxes  | 20 doz. Q Clamps | 142    |
   |          | #26537489        |        |
   | 10 Crates| 10 hp Generators | 2560   |
   |          | #45983748        |        |
   |          |                  | 2702   |

              Shipper's Acceptance:  Bill Warren
```

```
                                                    476538
              SALES ORDER

            Wood Supply Co.
              21 Main St.
           Suisun City, CA 95483

   To:  Pilot Stores          Date:  Nov. 23, 20X0
        1425 G St.
        Irvine, CA 92345      Credit Approval:  MS

   Cust. No.:  12654

   | Description     | Part No. | Quantity |
   | Q Clamps        | 26537489 | 20 doz.  |
   | 120 hp Generators | 45983748 | 10     |
```

**Cash Receipts**

**Check**

```
   Pilot Stores
   1425 G St.
   Irvine, CA 92345            Date: Dec. 5, 20X0

   Pay to the
   order of     Wood Supply Co.            $8085.00
        Eight thousand eighty-five and no/100

   First National Bank         Pilot Stores
   California                  Jackie Cohen

                 Remittance Advice
   Wood Supply Co.

   Inv. #7462537                           $8085.00
```

consignee makes sales. Notations such as "Consignment shipment" or "On approval" are sometimes found in subsidiary ledgers or on the duplicate copies of sales invoices. Numerous large returns of merchandise are also suggestive of consignment shipments.

The auditors should also investigate the controls for sales to related parties. Effective control over intercompany or interbranch transfers of merchandise often requires the same kind of formal procedures for billing, shipping, and collection functions as for sales to outsiders; hence, these movements of merchandise are often invoiced and recorded as sales. When the operations of the several organizational units are combined or consolidated into one income statement, however, it is apparent that any transactions not representing sales to outsiders should be eliminated from consolidated sales. In the audit of a client that operates subsidiaries or branches, the auditors should investigate the procedures for recording movements of merchandise among the various units of the company.

### b. Compare a Sample of Shipping Documents to Related Sales Invoices.

The preceding step in the audit program called for an examination of selected sales transactions and a comparison of the invoices with sales records and shipping documents.

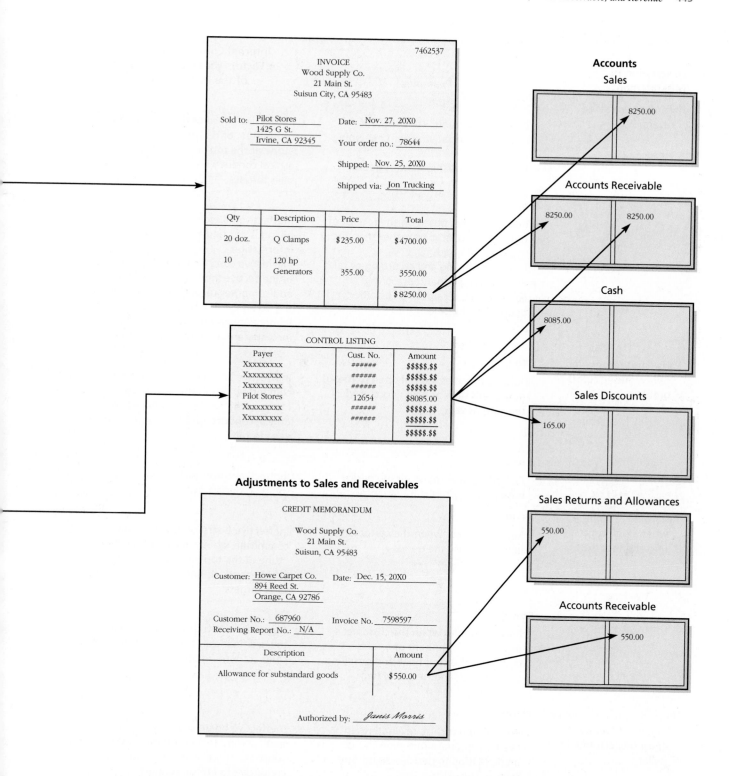

That procedure would not, however, disclose orders that had been shipped but not billed. To assure that all shipments are billed, the auditors may obtain a sample of shipping documents issued during the year and compare these to sales invoices. In making this test, particular emphasis should be placed upon accounting for all shipping documents by serial number. Any voided shipping documents should have been mutilated and retained in the files. The purposeful or accidental destruction of shipping documents before the creation of a sales invoice might go undetected if this type of test is not made.

FIGURE 11.4 **Potential Misstatements—Revenue**

| Description of Misstatement | Examples | Internal Control Weaknesses or Factors that Increase the Risk of the Misstatement |
|---|---|---|
| Recording unearned revenue | **Fraud:**<br>• Recording fictitious sales without receiving a customer order or shipping the goods<br>• Intentional overshipment of goods | • Ineffective board of directors, audit committee, or internal audit function; "tone at the top" not conducive to ethical conduct; undue pressure to meet sales targets |
| | **Errors:**<br>• Recording sales based on the receipt of orders from customers rather than the shipment of goods<br>• Inaccurate billing and recording of sales<br>• Recording cash that represents a liability (e.g., receipt of a customer's deposit) as revenue | • Ineffective billing process in which billing is not tied to shipping information<br>• Ineffective controls for testing invoices, or ineffective input validation checks and computer reconciliations to ensure the accuracy of databases<br>• Inadequate accounting manual; incompetent accounting personnel |
| Early (late) recognition of revenue—"cutoff problems" | **Fraud:**<br>• Holding the sales journal open to record next year's sales as having occurred in the current year | • Ineffective board of directors, audit committee, or internal audit function; "tone at the top" not conducive to ethical conduct; undue pressure to meet sales targets |
| | **Error:**<br>• Recording sales in the wrong period based on incorrect shipping information | • Ineffective cutoff procedures in the shipping department |
| Recording revenue when significant uncertainties exist | **Fraud:**<br>• Recording sales when the customer is likely to return the goods | • Ineffective board of directors, audit committee, or internal audit function; "tone at the top" not conducive to ethical conduct; undue pressure to meet sales targets |
| | **Error:**<br>• Recording sales when the customer's payment is contingent upon the customer receiving financing or selling the goods to another party (e.g., consignment sales) | • Aggressive attitude of management toward financial reporting; incompetent chief accounting officer |
| Recording revenue when significant services still must be performed by seller | **Fraud:**<br>• Recording franchise revenue when the franchises are sold even though an obligation to perform significant services still exists | • Ineffective board of directors, audit committee, or internal audit function; "tone at the top" not conducive to ethical conduct; undue pressure to meet sales targets |
| | **Error:**<br>• Amount of revenue earned on franchises is miscalculated | • Aggressive attitude of management toward financial reporting; incompetent chief accounting officer |

## FIGURE 11.4 Concluded

| Description of Misstatement | Examples | Internal Control Weaknesses or Factors that Increase the Risk of the Misstatement |
| --- | --- | --- |
| Overestimation of the amount of revenue earned | **Fraud:**<br><br>• Misstating the percentage of completion of several projects by a construction company using the percentage-of-completion method of revenue recognition<br><br>• Overestimating the percentage of completion on projects by a construction company using the percentage-of-completion method of revenue recognition | • Ineffective board of directors, audit committee, or internal audit function; "tone at the top" not conducive to ethical conduct; incompetent individuals involved in the estimation process<br>• Aggressive attitude of management toward financial reporting; incompetent personnel involved in the estimation/accounting process |

### c. Review the Use and Authorization of Credit Memoranda.

All allowances to customers for returned or defective merchandise should be supported by serially numbered credit memoranda signed by an officer or responsible employee having no duties relating to handling cash or to the maintenance of customers' ledgers. Good internal control over credits for returned merchandise usually includes a requirement that the returned goods be received and examined before credit is granted. The memoranda should then bear the date and serial number of the receiving report on the return shipment.

In addition to establishing that credit memoranda were properly authorized, the auditors should make tests of these documents similar to those suggested for sales invoices. Prices, extensions, and footings should be verified, and postings traced from the sales return journal or other accounting record to the customers' accounts in the subsidiary receivable ledgers.

### d. Reconcile Selected Cash Register Tapes and Sales Tickets with Sales Journals.

In the audit of clients that make a substantial amount of sales for cash, the auditors may compare selected daily totals in the sales journal with cash register readings or tapes. The serial numbers of all sales tickets used during the selected periods should be accounted for and the individual tickets examined for accuracy of calculations and traced to the sales summary or journal.

### e. Test IT Application Controls.

If the client has established effective IT application controls for sales transactions, the auditors might decide to test these controls directly instead of testing a sample of sales transactions. Tests of application controls might involve inspecting evidence of the operations control group's reconciliation of batch control totals for sales transactions, as well as the follow-up on any transactions that are listed on exception reports. The auditors might also observe the application of input validity tests as sales transactions are entered. They may even enter test data to obtain additional evidence about performance of application controls.

### f. Examine Evidence of Review and Approval of Revenue Estimates.

When a client uses accounting principles that require estimates of significant amounts of revenue, the auditors may examine evidence of review and approval of the estimates.

---

**Focus on the Airline Industry**

Electronic ticketing has become basic to the airline industry. Under these systems a passenger may book a flight over the telephone or by computer and be assigned a reservation number rather than being issued a physical ticket. Since no ticket is created until the passenger checks in for the flight, the auditor is limited in the extent to which he or she can examine "paper" support for transactions. Accordingly, audit procedures must be developed relating to the associated revenues and receivables. Auditors often choose to test the computer controls in such situations.

## 2. If Necessary, Revise the Risks of Material Misstatement Based on the Results of Tests of Controls.

When the auditors have completed the procedures described in the preceding sections, they should reassess the extent of the risk of material misstatement for each financial statement assertion regarding receivables and sales transactions. These assessments will determine whether the auditors should modify their planned substantive procedures for the financial statement assertions about receivables and sales. Figure 11.5 summarizes the relationships among these assertions, the controls, and typical tests of controls. This figure illustrates which controls affect the auditors' assessment of the risks of material misstatement for the various assertions.

**FIGURE 11.5**   Relating Controls to Assertions

| Control | Typical Tests of the Control | Existence & Occurrence | Completeness | Cutoff | Rights & Obligations | Valuation & Accuracy | Presentation & Disclosure |
|---|---|---|---|---|---|---|---|
| Segregate duties over sales and collections of receivables. | Observe and make inquiries about the performance of various functions. | X | X | | X | X | |
| Match sales invoices with shipping documents, purchase orders, and sales orders. | Select a sample of sales invoices and compare details to shipping documents, purchase orders, and sales orders. | X | | X | X | X | |
| Review of the clerical accuracy of sales invoices by a second person. | Select a sample of sales invoices and examine them for evidence of second-person review. | | | | | X | |
| Obtain credit approval of sales prior to shipment. | Make inquiries about credit policies; select a sample of sales transactions and examine evidence of credit approval. | X | | | | X | |
| Mail monthly statements to customers and follow up on errors reported. | Observe and make inquiries about the mailing of statements and review evidence of follow-up. | X | X | | X | X | |
| Reconcile bank (financial institution) accounts monthly. | Review a sample of bank reconciliations performed during the year. | X | | | X | X | |
| Use control listing to control cash collections. | Observe, make inquiries about the process, and reconcile selected listings to the bank and accounting records. | X | X | | X | X | |
| Use budgets and analyze variances from actual amounts. | Examine budgets and evidence of follow-up on variances. | X | X | | X | X | |
| Use prenumbered shipping and billing documents, and account for the sequence. | Observe and make inquiries about the use of prenumbered documents and inspect evidence of accounting for the sequence. | | X | X | | | |
| Use credit memoranda for authorization of adjustments to sales and receivables. | Select a sample of credits to customers' accounts and inspect credit memoranda and other supporting documents. | | | | X | | X |
| Use a chart of accounts and an independent review of account classifications. | Inspect the chart of accounts and evidence of the review of account classifications. | | | | | | X |

**FIGURE 11.6**   **Computerized Aging of Accounts Receivable**

The Fairview Corporation
Account No. 121
Accounts Receivable—Trade
December 31, 20X5

B-1

*V.M.H.*
*1/12/X6*

*Prepared by Client*

| Confirmation Number | Customer | Balance 12/31/X5 | Billed for December | Billed for November | Billed for October | Billed prior to October | Credit Balances | Collections Subsequent to 12/31/X5 | Estimated Uncollectible |
|---|---|---|---|---|---|---|---|---|---|
| 1 *cx* | Adams & Sons | $ 8,255.60 *uy* | $ 7,921.60 | | $ 334.00 *i* | | | $ 7,921.60 | |
| 2 *c* | Baker Company, Inc. | 205.00 *uy* | | $ 205.00 *i* | | | | 205.00 | |
| 3 *c* | Cross Mfg. Corp | 7,310.20 *uy* | 1,500.20 *i* | 1,210.00 *i* | 500.00 *i* | $4,100.00 *i* | | 4,100.00 | |
| | Douglas Supply Co. | 22.00 *uy* | | | | 22.00 *i* | | | 22.00 |
| 4 *c* | Electric Mfg. Co., Inc. | 1,250.00 *uy* | 1,250.00 *i* | | | | | 1,250.00 | |
| | J.R. Farmer | 3,000.00 *uy* | 3,000.00 *i* | | | | | | |

| | | | | | | | | | |
|---|---|---|---|---|---|---|---|---|---|
| 64 *cx* | Young Industries | 1,825.00 *uy* | 1,575.00 *i* | | 250.00 *i* | | | | |
| | Zappa M'fg. | 47.19 *uy* | 47.19 *i* | | | | | 47.19 | |
| | | *u* $78,624.62 ✓ | $48,801.67 | $21,245.60 | $2,278.20 | $6,302.15 | $(600.00) | $62,406.44 | $ 4,100.00 |
| | | (3,000.00) | (3,000.00) | | | | | | *ß* |
| | | 75,624.62 | 45,801.67 | | | | | | |
| | | *ß* | | | | | | | |

*u* = Footed and cross-footed.
✓ = Agreed to general ledger.
*y* = Traced to accounts receivable subsidiary ledger.
*i* = Verified aging.
*c* = Confirmed; no exception.
*cx* = Confirmed with exception. See B-1-1.

See audit program (B-2) for extent of confirmation and other auditing procedures.

**Conclusion:**

The results of the confirmation and other tests described in the audit program (B-2) provide sufficient appropriate evidence of existence of, and rights to, trade accounts receivable in the aggregate amount of $75,624.62.

*V.M.H.*
*Jan. 20, X6*

*A.J.E. 12*
Accounts Receivable—Officers   3,000.00
　　Accounts Receivable—Trade   3,000.00
Correct classification of account
receivable from J. R. Farmer,
President

## E. Perform Further Audit Procedures—Substantive Procedures for Receivables and Revenue.

### 1. Obtain an Aged Trial Balance of Trade Accounts Receivable and Analyses of Other Accounts Receivable and Reconcile to Ledgers.

Primary Audit Objective:

Valuation ☑

An **aged trial balance** of trade accounts receivable at the audit date is commonly prepared by employees of the client for the auditors, often in the form of a computer printout. The client-prepared schedule illustrated in Figure 11.6 has a multipurpose format designed to display the aging of customers' accounts, the estimate of probable credit losses, and the confirmation control information. The summary of so many phases of the examination of receivables in a single working paper is practicable only for small concerns with a limited number of customers. If the client has any accounts receivable other than trade accounts, the auditors also should obtain similar analyses of those accounts.

When trial balances or analyses of accounts receivable are furnished to the auditors by the client's employees, some independent verification of the listing is essential. Determination of the proper extent of testing should be made in relation to the adequacy of the controls over receivables. The auditors should test footings, cross-footings, and agings. In testing agings, it is important to test some accounts classified as current, as well as those shown as past due. These selected accounts should be traced to the subsidiary ledgers. The totals of schedules prepared by client personnel should also be compared with

**Illustrative Case**    *Equity Funding Fraud*

In the Equity Funding Corporation of America fraud, fictitious receivables selected for confirmation by the auditors bore addresses of employees who were conspirators in the fraud. The fictitious confirmation requests were thus signed and returned to the auditors by the recipients.

related controlling accounts. In addition, the balances of the subsidiary ledger records should be verified by footing the debit and credit columns on a test basis. Generalized computer audit programs may be used to perform these tests when the client's accounts receivable are processed by an IT system.

### 2. Obtain Analyses of Notes Receivable and Related Interest and Reconcile to the General Ledger.

An analysis of notes receivable supporting the general ledger control account may be prepared for the auditors by the client's staff. The information to be included in the analysis normally will include the name of the maker, date, maturity, amount, and interest rate. In addition to verifying the accuracy of the analysis prepared by the client, the auditors should trace selected items to the accounting records and to the notes themselves.

### 3. Inspect Notes on Hand and Confirm Those with Holders.

The inspection of notes receivable on hand should be performed concurrently with the count of cash and securities to prevent the concealment of a shortage by substitution of cash for misappropriated negotiable instruments, or vice versa. Any securities held by the client as collateral for notes receivable should be inspected and listed at the same time. The auditors should maintain complete control over all negotiable instruments until the count and inspection are completed.

Notes receivable owned by the client may be held by others at the time of the examination. Confirmation in writing from the *holder* of the note is considered an acceptable alternative to inspection; it does not, however, eliminate the need for securing confirmation from the *maker* of the note. The confirmation letter sent to a bank, collection agency, secured creditor, or other holder should contain a request for verification of the name of the maker, the balance of the note, the interest rate, and the due date.

Printed note forms are readily available at any bank and may be easily prepared using commercially available software; an unscrupulous officer or employee of the client company desiring to create a fictitious note could do so by obtaining a bank note form and filling in the amount, date, maturity, and signature. The relative ease of creating a forged or fictitious note suggests that physical inspection by the auditors represents a less significant and conclusive audit procedure for verification of notes receivable than for cash or securities.

### 4. Confirm Receivables with Debtors.

An **external confirmation** is audit evidence obtained by the auditors as a direct written response to the auditors' **confirmation request** sent to a third party (the **confirming party**). The external confirmation may be in paper form, electronic form, or other medium (e.g., the auditors' direct access to information held by a third party). Direct communication with debtors is the most essential and conclusive step in the verification of accounts and notes receivable. By obtaining written acknowledgment of the debt by the debtor, the auditors obtain audit evidence that helps (*a*) establish the existence and gross valuation of the asset, and *(b)* provides some assurance that no lapping or other manipulation affecting receivables is being carried on at the balance sheet date. However,

---

**Primary Audit Objectives:**

Valuation    ☑
Accuracy     ☑

---

**Primary Audit Objectives:**

Existence    ☑
Occurrence   ☑
Rights       ☑

---

**Primary Audit Objectives:**

Existence    ☑
Occurrence   ☑
Rights       ☑
Valuation    ☑
Accuracy     ☑

the confirmation of a receivable provides only limited evidence about the completeness and valuation assertions because only recorded amounts are confirmed, and debtors may acknowledge debts even though they are not able to pay them.

A better understanding of the emphasis placed on confirmation of receivables can be gained by a brief review of auditing history. Audit objectives and procedures were drastically revised in the late 1940s. Before that time the usual audit did not include procedures to assure that the receivables were genuine claims against existing companies or that inventories actually existed and had been accurately counted. Requiring the auditors to confirm receivables (or to observe the taking of physical inventory) was considered too expensive and not particularly important. Auditors generally relied in that early era upon a written statement by management concerning the validity of receivables and the existence of inventories. This approach was drastically revised after some spectacular fraud cases involving millions of dollars in fictitious receivables and inventories showed the need for stronger audit evidence.

AICPA AU 330 (PCAOB 330) indicates that there is a presumption that the auditors will confirm accounts receivable, unless *(a)* accounts receivable are immaterial, *(b)* the use of confirmations would be ineffective, or *(c)* the auditors' assessment of the risk of material misstatement is low and the auditors plan to obtain sufficient appropriate audit evidence by performing other substantive procedures. This requirement differs from the international auditing standards that accept confirmation as an audit procedure, but do not require the use of confirmation requests in any particular situations.

The confirmation process may be performed using a paper form or by electronic or other medium. Figure 11.7 shows the steps involved in the accounts receivable confirmation process, whether it be by hard copy or electronic. Sending confirmation requests in paper form and receiving confirmations in paper form is by far still the most frequent approach used by auditors. As discussed in Chapter 5, such externally generated evidence potentially offers very relevant and reliable evidence. However, in both hard-copy and electronic environments various risks are involved, including:

- The information may be delivered to an inappropriate address and signed by a nonauthentic source. For example, if CPAs are provided an incorrect address for ABC Company, the individual that controls that address may fraudulently reply to the confirmation.

**FIGURE 11.7** **Accounts Receivable Confirmation Process**

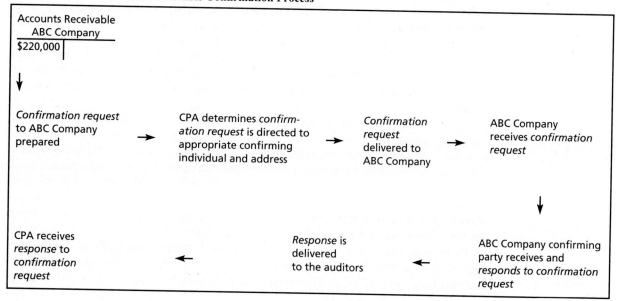

- Improper intervention into the delivery of a properly addressed confirmation request. For example, CPA placement of a confirmation in an unsecure mail bag (or electronic delivery through an insecure channel) may make it possible for a nonauthentic source to intervene and reply.
- The information may be delivered properly to a debtor company, but an inappropriate individual may reply. For example, an employee of ABC Company in purchasing, who has no knowledge of the balance due but an interest in maintaining a "no problem" relationship with the supplier may simply sign the confirmation with no exception noted.

To control risks such as the above, after confirmation requests are prepared, the auditors should determine that they are directed towards an appropriate confirming party at a proper address. Ordinarily, one would expect an individual within the customer's accounts payable function to be such a respondent. Concerning the address used, a sample of addresses may be verified through use of the Internet as well as through information available from the client (e.g., customer orders). Note, however, that simply using address information provided by the client alone may not disclose a fraud in which client personnel have created false receivables and related documentation. When using paper confirmations, the auditors should thoroughly investigate any suspicious circumstances, such as an excessive number of *individual* debtors with addresses that are post office boxes; the boxes may have been rented under fictitious debtors' names by employees of the client company who are engaged in accounts receivable fraud. Electronic confirmations sent via e-mail may offer similar challenges to the auditors in assuring that they have proper addresses. The auditors may wish to telephone prospective respondents to determine that correct e-mail addresses are being used.

When using the paper form, all requests for confirmation of notes and accounts receivable should be mailed in envelopes bearing the CPA firm's return address. A stamped or business reply envelope addressed to the office of the auditors also should be enclosed with the request. Confirmation requests should be mailed personally by the auditors at a post office or in a government mailbox. These procedures are designed to prevent the client's employees from having any opportunity to alter or intercept confirmation requests or the customers' replies. The entire process of confirming receivables is subject to manipulation if the confirmation requests or replies from customers pass through the hands of client personnel. Requests returned as undeliverable by the post office may be of prime significance to the auditors and hence should be returned directly to their office.

Various electronic approaches are used for confirming balances. For example, the auditors may transmit the confirmation request via e-mail using a scanned copy of the document that has been signed by a client. When e-mail is used, the auditors should maintain control over the electronic confirmation requests and replies. As indicated earlier, the auditors ordinarily will verify e-mail addresses supplied by management. When electronic replies are received, auditors will validate the source of the electronic information. For example, the use of *encryption,* and a *digital signature* may be used to validate the source.

As discussed in Chapter 10, the respondent to an electronic confirmation or a trusted third-party provider may also provide the auditors (with the client's authorization) access to a secure Web site that contains the requested information. Since the Web site location and access information are obtained directly from the confirming party or a trusted third-party service provider, the auditors can consider the information confirmed by the third party. However, if access codes are obtained only from the client personnel, the information should not be considered to be confirmed by the third party because of the risk that the Web site or account might be manipulated by client personnel.

To improve the rate of responses to confirmation requests, the auditors should carefully design the form to make sure that the person receiving the confirmation is likely to have easy access to the information requested. For example, customers that use a voucher system for cash disbursements may be better able to confirm individual unpaid transactions, rather than total receivable balances. The auditors should also try to include on the form the details of the transactions, such as customers' purchase order numbers.

In some cases, the confirmation process may involve obtaining oral responses, generally through a telephone call made by an auditor to the responding individual. Oral responses do not meet the definition of an external confirmation, which is defined as including a written response. When the auditors consider a written response to be necessary, they should request the individual making the oral response to also respond in writing directly to the auditors. If the written response is not received, alternative audit procedures will not provide sufficient and appropriate audit evidence; the auditors must determine the implications for the audit and the auditors' report (i.e., a scope limitation is involved that, if considered significant enough, may result in either a qualified opinion or a disclaimer of opinion as discussed in Chapter 17). If the auditors conclude that a written response is not required, they should properly document the oral response in the working papers (e.g., including details on the identity of the responding individual, and the date and time of the conversation). When relying on oral responses, the auditors may perform additional precautionary procedures such as initiating the call to the respondent using a telephone number independently obtained.

When fax replies are received, the auditors must take particular care because it is possible to program a fax machine with an incorrect transmitting number and name, thus leaving the recipient with misleading information about the source of the document. For example, a dishonest individual can send a falsified fax reply that appears to be from the debtor's offices. This risk may be controlled to a certain extent by using a fax machine that verifies the telephone number from which the reply is received (as opposed to simply printing the alleged telephone number) or by calling the purported sender to ensure the confirmation received is valid.

### Positive and Negative Confirmation Requests

There are two methods of confirming receivables by direct communication with the debtor. In each type of communication, the *client* makes the formal request for confirmation, although the auditors control the entire confirmation process.

The use of **positive confirmation requests,** as illustrated by Figure 11.8, consists of a request addressed to the debtor asking for a reply. Most positive forms ask the debtor to confirm directly to the auditors the accuracy of the dollar amount shown on the confirmation request. Other positive forms, referred to as *blank forms,* do not state the amount on the request, but ask the debtor company to fill in the balance.

The use of **negative confirmation requests** consists of a communication addressed to the debtor company asking it to advise the auditors *only* if the balance shown is incorrect. A negative confirmation request may be in the form of a letter or it may be made merely by applying a rubber stamp to the customer's regular monthly statement, or by attaching a gummed label bearing the words shown in Figure 11.9.

When the negative form of confirmation request is used, the lack of a reply from a given customer is interpreted as satisfactory evidence, when in fact the customer may simply have ignored the confirmation request. Since the auditors need not follow up on nonreplies, the expense of using negative confirmation requests is less than for the positive form; thus, more customers can be contacted for the same or less cost.

The positive form provides more assurance than the negative form because the auditors are alerted to the need for further investigation if a reply is not received. However, when positive confirmations ask recipients to confirm the accuracy of information provided on the request, there is a risk that the recipient may simply sign and return it without verifying the information. Blank forms control this risk by requiring the recipient to provide the information. But blank confirmations generally result in lower response rates and, therefore, require more follow-up procedures.

Although positive confirmation requests may be used in any circumstance, the use of solely negative requests should be reserved for situations in which at least one of the

**FIGURE 11.8**

**Positive Form of Accounts Receivable Confirmation Request (with Customer Reply)**

---

**SMITH & CO.** _____

*1416 Eighteenth Street • Los Angeles • California • 90035*

December 31, 20X1

Martin, Inc.
6700 Holmes Street
Kansas City, Missouri 64735

Dear Sirs:

Please confirm directly to our auditors

Adams, Barnes & Co.
Certified Public Accountants
1800 Avenue of the Stars
Los Angeles, California 90067

the correctness of the balance of your account payable to us as shown below and on the enclosed statement at December 31, 20X1. If the amount is not in agreement with your records at that date, please provide any information which will aid our auditors in reconciling the difference.

Your prompt return of this form in the enclosed stamped envelope is essential to the completion of the audit of our financial statements and will be appreciated.

Smith & Co.

By _M.J. Crowley_
(Controller)

THIS IS NOT A REQUEST FOR PAYMENT, BUT MERELY FOR
CONFIRMATION OF YOUR ACCOUNT.

- - - - - - - - - - - - - - - - - - - - - - - - - - - - - - - - - - - - - - - - -

The statement of our account showing a balance of $24,689.00 due Smith & Co. at December 31, 20X1, is correct except as noted below.

Martin, Inc.

Date: _January 16, 20X2_          By _Howard Martin_

Exceptions: _None_

---

following circumstances exists: *(a)* the assessed level of the risk of material misstatement is low and sufficient appropriate audit evidence has been obtained on operating effectiveness of controls, *(b)* a large number of small, homogeneous balances are involved, *(c)* a low exception rate is expected, or *(d)* the auditors are not aware of circumstances that would cause recipients of the request to disregard them. When the auditors use negative requests, they should consider supplementing the confirmation process with other substantive procedures. In many situations, a combination of positive and negative confirmation requests is used, with the positive form used for large balances and the negative form for small balances.

### Size of Sample

In the audit of most companies, the confirmation process for accounts receivable is limited to a sample. The sample should always be large enough to warrant the drawing of valid inferences about the entire population of receivables. Generally, auditors are able

**FIGURE 11.9**
**Negative Form of Accounts Receivable Confirmation Request**

Please examine this statement carefully. If it does not agree with your records, please report any differences to our auditors.

> Adams, Barnes & Co.
> Certified Public Accountants
> 1800 Avenue of the Stars
> Los Angeles, California 90067

A business reply envelope requiring no postage is enclosed for your convenience.

THIS IS NOT A REQUEST FOR PAYMENT

to stratify the population in a manner that allows confirmation of a majority of the dollar amount of receivables.

As discussed in Chapter 9, the size of the sample will vary with the levels of sampling risk accepted (the risk of incorrect rejection and acceptance), the tolerable misstatement, and certain characteristics of the population. The results of confirmation tests in prior years may serve as another factor in setting sample size; significant exceptions in prior years' confirmation results signal the need for extensive confirmation of the current year's receivables. Finally, the choice between the positive and negative forms of confirmation requests influences the size of the sample. The number of confirmations mailed is usually increased when the negative form is used.

In selecting the individual accounts to be confirmed, it is customary to include all customers with balances above a selected dollar amount and to select a sample of accounts from the remaining receivables. Generalized audit software is useful in stratifying computer-processed accounts receivable to facilitate the selection of a representative sample.

*Management's Refusal to Allow the Auditors to Perform External Confirmation Procedures*

If management refuses to allow the auditors to perform external confirmation procedures, the auditors should inquire and evaluate management's reasons, evaluate the implications of this refusal to the assessment of the risks of misstatement, and perform alternative audit procedures designed to obtain relevant and reliable audit evidence. If the auditors consider management's reasons to be unreasonable, or if the auditors are unable to obtain relevant and reliable audit evidence from alternative audit procedures, the auditors should communicate with those charged with governance about the matter. The auditors should also determine the implications for the auditors' opinion since this represents a scope limitation that may result in either a qualified opinion or a disclaimer of opinion (Chapter 17 discusses scope limitations in detail).

*Discrepancies in Customers' Replies*

The auditors should resolve differences reported by customers. The majority of such reported discrepancies arise because of normal lags in the recording of cash receipts or sales transactions, or because of a misunderstanding on the part of the customer company as to the date of the balance it is asked to confirm. Some replies may state that the balance listed is incorrect because it does not reflect recent cash payments; in such instances, the auditors normally trace the reported payments to the cash records.

*Alternative Audit Procedures for Nonrespondents*

The percentage of replies to positive confirmation requests that can be expected will vary greatly according to the type of debtor. When using positive confirmation requests, the auditors should generally follow up with a second and sometimes a third request to produce replies. When replies are still not received, the auditors should apply alternative procedures to the accounts, unless (1) the amount of the nonresponses is not significant when projected as a 100 percent misstatement to the total balance of receivables, and (2) there are no unusual characteristics related to the nonresponses. The best *alternative*

## Illustrative Case

### Importance of Follow-Up on Nonrespondents

During the first audit of a small manufacturing company, the auditors sent confirmation requests to all customers whose accounts showed balances in excess of $1,000. Satisfactory replies were received from all but one account, which had a balance of approximately $30,000. A second confirmation request sent to this customer produced no response; but before the auditors could investigate further, they were informed by the cashier-accountant that the account had been paid in full. The auditors asked to examine the customer's check and the accompanying remittance advice, but they were told that the check had been deposited and the remittance advice destroyed. Further questioning concerning transactions with this customer evoked such vague responses that the auditors decided to discuss the account with the officers of the company. At this point, the cashier-accountant confessed that the account in question was a fictitious one created to conceal a shortage and that to satisfy the auditors he had "collected" the account receivable by diverting current collections from other customers whose accounts had already been confirmed.

*auditing procedure* ordinarily is examination of subsequent cash receipts in payment of the receivable. However, in order to make certain that the payment is for a receivable that existed at year-end, the auditors also may need to examine shipping documents, customer purchase orders, or sales invoices for the sales transactions making up the receivable. Examination of these sales documents is also the alternative procedure used for receivables that are not paid during the subsequent period.

A summary should be prepared for the working papers outlining the extent and nature of the confirmations sent and the overall results obtained. Such a summary is a highly important part of audit documentation.

### The Confirmation Process in Perspective

The auditors face more than one type of risk in relying upon the confirmation process to form an opinion about the fairness of the accounts receivable as a whole. We have already recognized the risk that some accounts with erroneous balances may not be included in the confirmation sample, the risk of inappropriate intervention by client personnel, and the risk that replies may not be received from some customers with erroneous balances. Finally, there is also a risk that customers may routinely return confirmation requests without actually comparing the balance with their records. Such responses would give the auditors a false sense of security. Despite these risks, however, the confirming of accounts receivable provides valuable evidence and represents an important part of the auditors' work.

As indicated previously, the best proof available to the auditors as to the existence of an account receivable ordinarily is its collection before completion of the audit. However, this statement requires qualification, as indicated by the situation described in the above "Illustrative Case."

### Reviewing and Confirming Accounts and Notes Written Off as Uncollectible

If any accounts or notes receivable of significant amounts were written off as uncollectible during the year, the auditors should determine that these write-offs were properly authorized. In the absence of proper authorization procedures, a dishonest employee could conceal permanently a theft of cash merely by a charge to accounts or notes receivable followed by a write-off of that asset.

A systematic review of the notes and accounts written-off can conveniently be made by obtaining or preparing an analysis of the allowance for doubtful accounts and notes. Debits to the allowance may be traced to the authorizing documents and to the control record of accounts and notes written off; confirmation requests may be mailed to some of the debtors to determine that the account or note was genuine when it was first recorded in the accounts. Credit entries should be compared with the charges to uncollectible accounts and notes expense. Any write-off that appears unreasonable should be fully investigated. Charge-off of a note or account receivable from an officer, stockholder, or director is unreasonable on its face and warrants the most searching investigation by the auditors. Analytical procedures including the computation of the ratios of the year's write-offs to net credit sales, to uncollectible accounts expense, and to the allowance for doubtful accounts may be useful in bringing to light any abnormal write-offs.

### 5. Review the Year-End Cutoff of Sales Transactions.

| Primary Audit Objectives: | |
|---|---|
| Existence | ☑ |
| Occurrence | ☑ |
| Rights | ☑ |
| Completeness | ☑ |
| Cutoff | ☑ |

One of the more common methods of falsifying accounting records is to inflate the sales for the year by holding open the sales journal beyond the balance sheet date. Shipments made in the first part of January may be covered by sales invoices bearing a December date and included in December sales. The purpose of such misleading entries is to present a more favorable financial picture than actually exists. Since sales are frequently used as the base for computation of bonuses and commissions, an additional incentive for padding the Sales account is often present. A related abuse affecting accounts receivable is the practice of holding the cash journals open beyond the balance sheet date; auditing procedures designed to detect this practice were described in connection with the audit of cash transactions in Chapter 10.

To guard against misstatements due to inaccurate cutoff of sales records (whether accidental or intentional), the auditors should compare the sales recorded for several days before and after the balance sheet date with the duplicate sales invoices and shipping documents. The effectiveness of this step is largely dependent upon the degree of segregation of duties between the shipping, receiving, and billing functions. If warehousing, shipping, billing, and receiving are independently controlled, it is most unlikely that records in all these departments will be manipulated to disguise shipments of one period as sales of the preceding period. On the other hand, one individual with control over both shipping records and billing documents could manipulate both sets of records to overstate the year's sales.

Fictitious sales are occasionally recorded at year-end as a means of overstating financial results. Therefore, auditors should be aware of and investigate:

a. Unusually large increases in year-end sales to a single customer or a few. This might be indicative of **bill and hold transactions,** in which sales are billed but goods are not shipped. Bill and hold transactions must meet stringent requirements to qualify as a sale as set forth in SEC *Staff Accounting Bulletin No. 104.*

b. Large increases in revenue and receivables along with increases in gross profit margins that are inconsistent with the client's experience or industry averages.

c. Inappropriate changes in accounting principles that result in an increase in recorded revenue.

d. Substantial sales returns following the balance sheet date that might indicate merchandise shipped to customers without a customer order for those goods or **channel stuffing,** in which sales are boosted by inducing customers to buy substantially more inventory than they can promptly resell.

As discussed in Chapter 10, the term **window dressing** refers to actions taken around the balance sheet date to improve the financial picture presented in the financial statements. A number of window dressing practices represent proper and appropriate business practices, such as a special year-end promotion to boost sales and making diligent efforts to ship out all orders. However, window dressing practices such as those listed above result in fraudulent misstatements of the financial statements. To guard against such manipulations, the auditors should review carefully all substantial sales returns following the balance sheet date that may apply to receivables originating in the year under audit. Consideration should be given to reflecting these returns in the current year's business

## Illustrative Case

### What Do You Do with Stale Doughnuts?

Former company and franchise employees stated that by mid-2003 Krispie Kreme Doughnuts, Inc., was double-shipping wholesale orders to some grocers at the end of quarterly reporting periods in order to temporarily boost sales and earnings, even though executives knew many of the doughnuts would be returned for credit later. It was reported that it was commonplace for management to inappropriately channel stuff in order to meet analysts' expectations. This was inappropriate because Krispie Kreme's management did not take into consideration the additional amounts of sales returns involved.

by means of adjusting entries. Confirmation of accounts receivable, if performed at the balance sheet date, should also serve to bring any large unauthorized shipments to the attention of the auditors.

Primary Audit Objectives:

| | |
|---|---|
| Existence | ☑ |
| Occurrence | ☑ |
| Rights | ☑ |
| Completeness | ☑ |
| Cutoff | ☑ |
| Valuation | ☑ |
| Accuracy | ☑ |

### 6. Perform Analytical Procedures for Accounts Receivable, Notes Receivable, and Revenue.

In planning the audit, professional standards require the auditors to perform analytical procedures with the objective of identifying potential misstatements of revenue. Several ratios and relationships can be computed to indicate the overall reasonableness of the amounts shown for accounts receivable, revenue, and notes receivable. Examples include (*a*) the gross profit rate (by product line, store, or region), (*b*) the ratio of sales in the last month or week to total sales for the quarter or year, (*c*) revenue in relation to productive capacity, (*d*) units shipped in relation to revenues and production records, (*e*) accounts receivable turnover, (*f*) the ratio of accounts receivable to the year's net credit sales, (*g*) the ratio of accounts written off during the year to the ending balance of accounts receivable, (*h*) the ratio of returns and allowances to sales, (*i*) the ratio of interest revenue to notes receivable, and (*j*) the ratio of uncollectible account expense to credit sales. These ratios and relationships are compared with corresponding data for the preceding years, and with budgets, performance statistics, or comparable industry averages.

### Focus on the Casino Industry

Casinos have few documents to support their revenue transactions. This makes it difficult for auditors to apply tests of details to the revenues of these types of organizations. An AICPA *Audit Risk Alert* on the casino industry emphasizes the use of analytical procedures to audit revenues. In developing expectations about the amounts of revenues, the auditors should consider:

- Demographic data of casino clientele.
- Betting limits established by regulatory agencies.
- Effects of adverse weather conditions or special events, such as conventions, on casino attendance.
- Seasonality of casino operations.
- General economic conditions.
- Effects of intense competition.
- Impact of promotional programs.
- Probable win ratios.

Auditors are warned that while, in the long term, fluctuations may be likely to conform to expected patterns, the element of chance—a fundamental characteristic of casino operations—makes short-term fluctuations common.

### 7. Review Significant Year-End Sales Contracts for Unusual Terms.

To boost the level of sales for a period, management may be inclined to modify the terms of sales contracts near year-end. These modifications may affect the collectibility of the related accounts receivable, the customers' return rights, and even whether the sales meet the criteria to be recognized in the current period. Therefore, the auditors should carefully review any significant year-end sales contracts for unusual pricing, billing, delivery, return, exchange, or acceptance clauses.

### 8. Test the Valuation of Notes Receivable, Computations of Interest Income, Interest Receivable, and Amortization of Discount or Premium.

Unless a company elects the fair value option, notes receivable are valued at their outstanding face value plus or minus any unamortized premium or discount. When a company has not adopted the fair value option, the auditors may effectively audit valuation, interest income, interest receivable, and the amortization by performing an independent computation of the interest earned during the year on notes receivable. The working paper used to analyze notes receivable should show the interest rate and date of issuance of each note. The interest section of this working paper consists of four columns, which show for each note receivable owned during the year the following information:

*a.* Accrued interest receivable at the beginning of the year (taken from the preceding year's audit working papers).

*b.* Interest earned during the year (computed from the terms of the notes).

*c.* Interest collected during the year (traced to cash receipts records).

*d.* Accrued interest receivable at the end of the year (computed by the auditors).

These four columns compose a self-balancing set. The beginning balance of accrued interest receivable (first column) plus the interest earned during the year (second column) and minus the interest collected (third column) should equal the accrued interest receivable at the end of the year (fourth column). The totals of the four columns should be cross-footed to ensure that they are in balance; in addition, the individual column totals should be traced to the balances in the general ledger.

If the interest earned for the year as computed by the auditors does not agree with interest earned as shown in the accounting records, the next step is an analysis of the ledger account. Any unaccounted-for credits in the Interest Earned account deserve particular attention because these credits may represent interest received on notes that have never been recorded.

For financial institutions or other clients having numerous notes receivable, the auditors may verify interest computations on only a sample of the notes. In addition, they should test the reasonableness of total interest earned for the year by applying a weighted average rate of interest to the average balance of the Notes Receivable ledger account during the year.

The fair value option for valuation of notes receivable (as presented in Chapter 5) is available. When the fair value option has been elected, the auditors must evaluate the propriety of the valuation techniques and inputs (assumptions) used.

### 9. Evaluate the Propriety of the Client's Accounting Methods for Receivables and Revenue.

As indicated earlier in this chapter, many instances of misstatements in financial statements have involved the inappropriate recognition of revenue and related receivables—often through the premature recording of revenues or the recording of fictitious revenues. Previous steps in this audit program have addressed this risk through consideration of a proper year-end cutoff of sales transactions (step 5); performance of analytical procedures for accounts receivable, notes receivable, and revenue (step 6); and the review of significant year-end sales contracts for unusual terms (step 7). In step 9, we directly address the propriety of the accounting methods relating to receivables and revenue.

From a conceptual standpoint, "revenues are considered to have been earned when the entity has substantially accomplished what it must do to be entitled to the benefits represented by the revenues."[2] The SEC, in *Staff Accounting Bulletin No. 104,* provides the following criteria that ordinarily should exist for revenue to be recognized:

- Persuasive evidence of an arrangement exists.
- Delivery has occurred or services have been rendered.
- The seller's price to the buyer is fixed or determinable.
- Collectibility is reasonably assured.

The auditors must carefully evaluate the propriety of the client's treatment of certain transactions to determine that they meet these criteria, not only in form but also in substance. Problems that the auditors might discover include:

a. An allowance for sales returns may not be set up for goods shipped to customers with the right to return the goods under certain circumstances.

b. Management or client personnel may have established, formally or informally, **side agreements** that significantly alter the terms of sale.

c. Cash receipts from franchise fees may be inappropriately recognized when services have not been rendered to the franchisees.

d. Bill and hold transactions may be recorded when they do not meet the requirements for revenue recognition.

e. Notes receivable may not bear reasonable interest rates at the time they are accepted, resulting in a need to discount the notes to present values.

f. Management might use the percentage-of-completion method of revenue recognition in inappropriate circumstances or might overestimate the amount of revenue earned.

g. Management of a software company might recognize excessive amounts of revenue on a multiple element agreement that involves providing software and postcontract customer support.

The following illustration focusing on the construction industry makes it clear that auditors must have a thorough understanding of generally accepted accounting principles and the *substance,* as well as the form, of the client's revenue transactions. The auditors must carefully examine the various documents pertaining to the transactions to determine that proper accounting principles have been followed. If they believe that there is a risk that the terms of contracts may have been modified, they should consider confirming the terms with the customer.

---

### Focus on the Construction Industry

Construction contractors often use the percentage-of-completion method to recognize income on long-term contracts. Under this method, a contractor computes the extent of progress toward completion of each contract in progress. For example, if a contract is 70 percent complete at year-end and on target cost-wise, the contractor will recognize 70 percent of the contract's revenues, costs, and gross profit. Although the method is well established in the construction industry, auditors must carefully consider whether the contractor's estimate of costs to complete the contracts is reasonable, and whether it is probable that losses may be incurred on the contract. When making this determination, auditors should consider:

- The controls over the contractor's estimation process, including the competence of the personnel making the estimates.
- Explanations for apparent disparities between estimates and past performance on contracts.
- Information gained in other areas of the audit.
- Industry and economic conditions, and expected future trends.

When slow economic growth is expected and intense competition exists, there may be an increased risk that a construction contractor may be inclined to compensate for low revenue growth by underestimating the costs to complete projects. Overestimating the percentage of completion is another way of underestimating costs.

---

[2] Statement of Financial Accounting Concepts No. 5, para. 83b.

## 10. Evaluate Accounting Estimates Related to Revenue Recognition.

The auditors are responsible for evaluating the reasonableness of accounting estimates related to receivables and the recognition of revenue. Examples of these accounting estimates include sales returns, revenues accounted for by the percentage-of-completion method, and the allowance for uncollectible accounts. In accordance with AICPA AU 540 (PCAOB 342), the auditors audit accounting estimates by reviewing and testing management's method of developing the estimates, by developing their own estimates, or by reviewing subsequent transactions and other events that provide evidence about the accuracy of the estimates.

Because fraudulent financial reporting often is accomplished through the intentional misstatement of accounting estimates, the auditors are required to perform a retrospective review of the prior year's significant accounting estimates to determine whether they indicate bias on the part of management. As an example, the auditors of a construction contractor may compare prior-year estimates of cost to completed projects with the actual costs incurred. If these comparisons indicate a bias on the part of management, the auditors will use this information in auditing the current year accounting estimates.

## 11. Determine the Adequacy of the Client's Allowance for Uncollectible Accounts.

The allowance for uncollectible accounts represents a particularly significant accounting estimate for most organizations. Accordingly, we will provide a detailed explanation of the audit procedures applied to this account. As a starting point, the retrospective analysis of accounting estimates described in the preceding section provides overall information about the quality of management's prior estimates. This information will almost certainly influence the auditors' approach to auditing the allowance account, which may primarily involve evaluating management's process of developing the estimate, reviewing subsequent transactions, or developing the auditors' own estimate.

If the auditors elect to use the overall approach of evaluating management's process, they will consider both the reasonableness of the process and the competence of the personnel involved. If the process is well designed and controlled, the auditors may decide to focus on tests of controls to obtain much or all of the evidence about the reasonableness of the allowance.

Since the best evidence of the *collectibility* of accounts receivable is payment by the debtors subsequent to the balance sheet date, the approach of analyzing subsequent transactions is also an appropriate overall audit approach. In the audit working papers, the auditors should document the subsequent payments inspected; the illustrated trial balance of trade accounts receivable (Figure 11.6, page 447) includes a special column for this purpose.

The auditors also may decide to independently develop their own estimate of the amount of uncollectible receivables to compare to management's estimate. The following procedures may be used by the auditors both in developing an estimate and in evaluating the reasonableness of management's estimate:

a. Compare the details of the aging of accounts receivable to prior years' aging. Examine the past-due accounts receivable listed in the aging schedule that have not been paid subsequent to the balance sheet date, noting such factors as the size and recentness of payments, the settlement of old balances, and whether recent sales are on a cash or a credit basis. The client's customer correspondence file may contain much of this information.

b. Investigate the credit ratings for delinquent and unusually large accounts. This is particularly efficient when receivables from one or a few customers represent a major portion of the total. Financial statements and credit data should be available in the client's credit files.

c. Review confirmation exceptions for an indication of amounts in dispute or other clues as to possible uncollectible accounts.

d. Summarize in a working paper those accounts whose collectibility is doubtful based on the preceding procedures. List customer names, doubtful amounts, and reasons for considering these accounts doubtful.

e. Review with the credit manager the current status of significant doubtful accounts, determining the collection action taken and the opinion of the credit manager as to ultimate collectibility. Indicate in the working papers the credit manager's opinion as to the collectible portion of each account listed, and use this information to assist in evaluating the collectibility of specific accounts.

f. Compute relationships, such as the number-of-days' sales in accounts receivable and the relationship of the valuation allowance to (1) accounts receivable and (2) net credit sales. Compare the ratios to comparable ratios for prior years and industry averages, and investigate any unexpected results.

After completion of procedures such as the above, the auditors will determine the reasonableness of management's estimate of the allowance for uncollectible accounts.

### Receipt of a Note in Settlement of a Past-Due Receivable

A client may receive a note receivable from a customer in settlement of a past-due account receivable—thereby creating an interest-bearing asset. When this occurs, may the auditors conclude that the collectibility of the account does not need to be considered? The answer here is no, because collectibility issues may very well exist with respect to the note. First, the decision to accept a note in payment as opposed to a cash payment leads one to question the financial stability of the note maker. A provision for loss becomes more probable when notes have been repeatedly renewed, payments on installment notes have been late and/or irregular, notes have been defaulted upon, and the makers of the notes are companies known to be having financial difficulties. To appraise the collectibility of notes receivable, the auditors may investigate the credit standing of the makers. Reports from credit-rating agencies and financial statements from the makers of the notes should be available for this purpose in the client's credit department.

Evaluation of any collateral supplied by makers of notes is another step in determining the collectibility of notes receivable. The auditors should determine the current market value of securities held as collateral by the client, either by reference to market quotations or by inquiry of brokers.

## 12. Ascertain Whether Any Receivables Have Been Pledged.

The auditors should inquire directly as to whether any notes or accounts receivable have been pledged or assigned. Evidence of the **pledging of receivables** may also be disclosed through the medium of financial institution confirmation requests, which specifically call for a description of the collateral securing bank loans. Analysis of the interest expense accounts may reflect charges from the pledging of receivables to finance companies.

Accounts receivable that have been pledged should be plainly identified through coding in the accounts receivable records. Accounts labeled in this manner would be identified by the auditors in their initial review of receivables and confirmed by direct correspondence with the bank to which they were pledged. The auditors cannot, however, proceed on the assumption that all pledged receivables have been labeled to that effect, and they must be alert to detect any indications of an unrecorded pledging of accounts receivable.

## 13. Investigate Any Transactions with or Receivables from Related Parties.

Transactions between the corporation and its officers, directors, stockholders, or affiliates require particular attention from the auditors because these related party transactions are not the result of arm's-length bargaining by parties of opposing interests. Furthermore, such transactions may be prohibited by federal or state law or by the corporation's bylaws. The independent auditors have an obligation to stockholders, creditors, and others who rely upon audited statements to require adequate disclosure of any significant related party transactions.

To identify related party transactions, the auditors should review (1) proxy and other filings with the SEC or other regulatory agencies, (2) conflict-of-interest statements obtained by the company from its management, (3) transactions with customers or suppliers that have unusual terms, and (4) accounting records for unusual balances or transactions, particularly those occurring near year-end. If related party transactions are discovered, the auditors should obtain an understanding of the transactions, determine whether the transactions have been approved by the board of directors or other appropriate officials, confirm the terms of the transactions with the related parties, evaluate the collectibility of any receivables outstanding, and evaluate the adequacy of disclosure of the details of the transactions in the notes to the financial statements.

| Primary Audit Objectives: | |
|---|---|
| Valuation | ☑ |
| Accuracy | ☑ |
| Presentation | ☑ |

### 14. Evaluate the Business Purpose of Significant and Unusual Sales Transactions.

Auditors are required to evaluate the business purpose of any transaction that comes to their attention that is significant and unusual. Such transactions may be indicative of fraudulent financial reporting.

| Primary Audit Objective: | |
|---|---|
| Presentation | ☑ |

### 15. Evaluate Financial Statement Presentation and Disclosure of Receivables and Revenue.

The auditors must determine that the financial presentation of accounts and notes receivable and the related disclosures are in accordance with generally accepted accounting principles. Related party receivables should be shown separately with disclosure of the nature of the relationships and the amounts of the transactions. Any unusual terms of notes receivable should be disclosed in the notes. Also, the amounts of allowances for uncollectible receivables should be shown as deductions from the related receivables. Finally, significant concentrations of credit risk arising from trade accounts receivable should be disclosed in accordance with *FASB ASC* 310-10-50.

## Interim Audit Work on Receivables and Revenue

Much of the audit work on receivables and revenue can be performed one or two months before the balance sheet date. The **interim audit work** may consist of the consideration of controls and, in some cases, the confirmation of accounts receivable as well. A decision to carry out the confirmation of receivables at an interim date rather than at year-end is justified only if the risk of material misstatement for existence of accounts receivable is low.

If interim audit work has been done on receivables and revenue, the year-end audit work may be modified considerably. For example, if the confirmation of accounts receivable was performed at October 31, the year-end audit program would include preparation of a summary analysis of postings to the Accounts Receivable controlling account for the period from November 1 through December 31. This analysis would list the postings by month, showing the journal source of each. These postings would be traced to the respective journals, such as the sales journal and cash receipts journal. The amounts of the postings would be compared with the amounts in preceding months and with the corresponding months in prior years. The purpose of this work is to bring to light any significant variations in receivables during the months between the interim audit work and the balance sheet date.

In addition to this analysis of the entries to the receivable accounts for the intervening period, the audit work at year-end would include obtaining the aging of the accounts receivable at December 31, confirmation of any large accounts in the year-end trial balance that are new or delinquent, and the usual investigation of the year-end cutoff of sales and cash receipts.

# Chapter Summary

In this chapter, we described the details of controls over receivables and revenue, the auditors' consideration of these controls, and substantive procedures for the receivables and revenue accounts. To summarize:

1. The audit of receivables and revenue represents significant audit risk because (*a*) many incidences of financial statement fraud have involved the overstatement of receivables and revenue, (*b*) revenue recognition may be based on complex accounting rules, and (*c*) receivables and revenue are usually subject to valuation using significant accounting estimates. Companies should establish effective high-level controls over the financial reporting of these accounts, including (*a*) an audit committee to oversee the reliability of reporting of revenue, (*b*) an internal audit department to monitor compliance with other revenue cycle controls, (*c*) human resource policies and practices to ensure that competent personnel are involved in determining revenue and receivables estimates, and (*d*) effective monitoring policies and procedures. In addition, a sound accounting system and effective control activities should be established for the revenue cycle.

2. The revenue cycle includes the receiving of orders from customers, the delivery and billing of goods and services, and the recording and collection of accounts receivable. Effective internal control over sales transactions is best achieved by having separate departments responsible for preparing sales orders, approving credit, shipping merchandise, billing customers, maintaining the accounts receivable subsidiary ledger, and authorizing adjustments to sales and accounts receivable.

3. The auditors' assessment of the risks of material misstatement is used to determine the nature, timing, and extent of substantive procedures for the assertions related to receivables and revenue. If the audit plan includes an expectation of the operating effectiveness of controls, the auditors must design and perform tests of controls.

4. The primary objectives for the auditors' substantive procedures for receivables and revenue are to (*a*) substantiate the existence of receivables and the occurrence of revenue transactions, (*b*) establish the completeness of receivables and revenue, (*c*) verify the cutoff of revenue transactions, (*d*) determine that the client has rights to the recorded receivables, (*e*) establish the proper valuation of receivables and the accuracy of revenue transactions, and (*f*) establish that the presentation and disclosure of receivables and revenue are appropriate.

5. The most time-consuming and critical audit procedures for receivables and revenue are those designed to test the assertions of existence, occurrence, and valuation. Among the procedures designed to achieve these objectives is confirmation of accounts receivable, which is generally required in audits. Acknowledgment of the debt provides evidence of the existence of receivables and the occurrence of sales, as well as the gross valuation of the amounts. An important part of obtaining evidence about the proper valuation of accounts receivable is the auditors' evaluation of the adequacy of the allowance for uncollectible accounts. Since this account is a management estimate, it is typically audited by a combination of inquiry of management, analytical procedures, and inspection of various documents.

6. Other significant aspects of the audit include evaluation of the appropriateness of the client's methods of revenue recognition and procedures directed at identifying and evaluating the disclosure of related party transactions and receivables.

# Key Terms Introduced or Emphasized in Chapter 11

**Aged trial balance (447)**   A listing of individual customers' accounts classified by the number of days subsequent to billing, that is, by age. A preliminary step in estimating the collectibility of accounts receivable.

**Bill and hold transactions (455)**   Transactions in which sales of merchandise are billed to customers prior to delivery, with the goods being held by the seller. These transactions may overstate revenues and net income if they do not meet specific requirements for recognition as sales.

**Channel stuffing (455)** A marketing practice that suppliers sometimes use to boost sales by inducing customers to buy substantially more inventory than they can promptly resell. Channel stuffing without appropriate provision for sales returns is an example of booking tomorrow's revenue today in order to window dress the financial statements.

**Confirmation request (448)** A request sent to a *confirming party* requesting that the confirming party consider the accuracy of information included in that request. A confirmation request may take one of two forms: *positive confirmation request* and *negative confirmation request.*

**Confirming party (448)** The individual who responds to the confirmation request. Responses to confirmation requests provide more relevant and reliable audit evidence when the confirmation requests are sent to confirming parties who the auditors believe are knowledgeable about the information to be confirmed. For example, an individual in accounts payable may provide more relevant and reliable audit evidence with respect to a client's receivable balance than an individual who has no direct access to accounts payable records.

**External confirmation (448)** Audit evidence obtained by the auditors as a direct written response to the auditors from a third party (the *confirming party*) in paper form or by electronic or other medium (e.g., the auditors' direct access to information held by a third party).

**Interim audit work (461)** Those audit procedures that are performed before the balance sheet date. The purpose is to facilitate earlier issuance of the audit report and to spread the auditors' work more uniformly over the year.

**Negative confirmation request (451)** A request that the *confirming party* respond directly to the auditors indicating where the confirming party disagrees with the information in the request.

**Pledging of receivables (460)** To assign to a bank, factor, finance company, or other lender an exclusive claim against accounts receivable as security for a debt.

**Positive confirmation request (451)** A request that the *confirming party* respond directly to the auditor providing the requested information or indicating whether the confirming party agrees or disagrees with the information in the request.

**Side agreements (458)** Formal or informal modifications of normal terms and conditions of sales transactions to entice customers to accept delivery of goods or services.

**Window dressing (455)** Action taken by the client shortly before the balance sheet date to improve the financial picture presented in the financial statements.

## Review Questions

11–1. Explain the difference between a *customer's order* and a *sales order,* as these terms might be used by a manufacturing company making sales on credit.

11–2. Explain why the audit of revenue and receivables may present the auditors with significant audit risk.

11–3. An inexperienced clerk assigned to the preparation of sales invoices in a manufacturing company became confused as to the nature of certain articles being shipped, with the result that the prices used on the invoices were far less than called for in the company's price lists. What controls could be established to guard against such errors?

11–4. State briefly the objective of the billing process. What important document is created by the billing department?

11–5. Criticize the following quotation: "A credit memorandum should be issued only when an account receivable is determined to be uncollectible."

11–6. The controller of a new client operating a medium-size manufacturing business complains to you that he believes the company has sustained significant losses on several occasions because certain sales invoices were misplaced and never recorded as accounts receivable. What control can you suggest to guard against such problems?

11–7. Comment on the following: "Any voided prenumbered shipping documents should be properly canceled and disposed of to eliminate any possibility of improper shipment of goods."

11–8. The accounts receivable section of the accounting department in Wind Power, Inc., maintains subsidiary ledgers that are posted from copies of the sales invoices transmitted daily from the billing department. How may the accounts receivable section be sure that it receives promptly a copy of each sales invoice prepared?

11–9. Among specific procedures that contribute to good internal control over the business processes related to accounts receivable are (*a*) the approval of uncollectible account write-offs and credit memoranda by an executive and (b) the sending of monthly statements to all customers. State three other procedures conducive to strong internal control.

11–10. In the audit of an automobile agency, you find that installment notes received from the purchasers of automobiles are promptly discounted with a bank. Would you consider it necessary to confirm these notes by a communication with the bank? With the makers? Explain.

11–11. Your review of notes receivable from officers, directors, stockholders, and affiliated companies discloses that several notes of small amounts were written off to the allowance for uncollectible notes during the year. Have these transactions any special significance? Explain.

11–12. What auditing procedures, if any, are necessary for notes receivable but not required for accounts receivable?

11–13. The confirmation of accounts receivable is an important auditing procedure. Should the formal request for confirmation be made by the client or by the auditors? Should the return envelope be addressed to the client, to the auditors in care of the client, or to the auditors' office? Explain.

11–14. State briefly the *audit objectives* that are addressed by the following audit procedure: "Confirm accounts receivable and notes receivable by direct communication with debtors."

11–15. In selecting accounts receivable for confirmation, the auditors discover that the client company's records show the addresses of many individual customers to be post office boxes. What should be the auditors' reaction to this situation?

11–16. Several accounts receivable confirmations have been returned with the notation, "Verification of vendors' statements are no longer possible because of our data processing system." What alternative auditing procedures could be used to verify these accounts receivable?

11–17. What alternative auditing procedures may be undertaken in connection with the confirmation of accounts receivable where customers having substantial balances fail to reply after second request forms have been mailed directly to them?

11–18. A CPA firm wishes to test the client's sales cutoff at June 30, 20X0. Describe the steps that the auditors should include in this test.

11–19. In your first audit of Hydro Manufacturing Company, a manufacturer of outboard motors, you discover that an unusually large number of sales transactions were recorded just before the end of the fiscal year. What significance would you attach to this unusual volume?

11–20. In connection with an audit, what are the purposes of a review of sales returns and allowances subsequent to the balance sheet date?

11–21. In the examination of credit memoranda covering allowances to customers for goods returned, how can the auditors ascertain whether the customer actually did return merchandise in each case in which accounts receivable were reduced?

11–22. Cite various procedures auditors employ that might lead to the detection of an inadequate allowance for doubtful accounts receivable.

11–23. Give an example of a type of receivable originating without arm's-length bargaining. Comment on the presentation of such receivables in the balance sheet.

11–24. Describe a retrospective review of an accounting estimate. With respect to the audit of revenue, what is the purpose of performing this review?

## Questions Requiring Analysis
### LO 1, 4, 6

11–25. You have been assigned to the audit of Processing Solutions, Inc., a privately held corporation that develops and sells computer systems. The systems are sold under one- to five-year contracts that provide for a fixed price for licensing, delivery, and setup of the systems and maintenance and technical support for the life of the contract. Your review of the working papers reveals that premature revenue recognition is a risk that must be addressed in the audit.

*Required:*

a. Describe the criteria from SEC *Staff Accounting Bulletin No. 104* that must be met to recognize revenue under generally accepted accounting principles.

b. Describe two techniques that management of Processing Solutions might use to overstate revenue.

c. For the two techniques identified in (b), describe an auditing procedure that might be employed by the auditors to detect the overstatement of revenue.

**LO 4, 6** 11–26. Listed below are audit situations that may affect the audit of receivables and revenue.

    *a.* The audit of a machinery manufacturing company that engages in bill and hold transactions.

    *b.* The audit of a software company that engages in multiple element agreements that involve a fixed fee for software, updates, and customer support.

    *c.* The audit of a construction company that uses the percentage-of-completion method of accounting for contracts.

    *d.* The audit of a manufacturing company that uses complex sales agreements that allow product returns under certain circumstances.

    *e.* The audit of a software company whose salespeople often modify the terms of sales contracts with various side agreements.

*Required:* For each circumstance, provide an indication of its audit significance and any special audit procedures that would result.

**LO 3, 5** 11–27. If you were preparing a credit sales system flowchart, what document would you show as:

    *a.* The source for posting debits to a customer's account in the accounts receivable ledger?

    *b.* Authorization to the finished goods stores to release merchandise to the shipping department?

    *c.* The source for preparing a sales order?

    *d.* The source for preparing a bill of lading?

    *e.* The source for an entry in the sales journal?

(AICPA, adapted)

**LO 6** 11–28. In their work on accounts receivable and elsewhere in an audit, the independent auditors often make use of confirmation requests.

    *a.* What is an audit confirmation request?

    *b.* What characteristics should an audit confirmation response possess if a CPA firm is to consider it to be valid evidence?

    *c.* Distinguish between a positive confirmation request and a negative confirmation request in the auditors' examination of accounts receivable.

    *d.* In confirming a client's accounts receivable, what characteristics should be present in the accounts if the CPA firm is to use negative confirmations?

**LO 6** 11–29. During preliminary conversations with a new staff assistant, you instruct her to send out confirmation requests for both accounts receivable and notes receivable. She asks whether the confirmation requests should go to the makers of the notes or to the holders of the notes, in the case of notes that have been discounted. Provide an answer to her question and give reasons for your answer.

**LO 6** 11–30. Lakeside Company has retained you to conduct an audit so that it will be able to support its application for a bank loan with audited financial statements. The president of Lakeside states that you will have unlimited access to all records of the company and may carry out any audit procedures you consider necessary, except that you are not to communicate with customers. The president feels that contacts with customers might lead them to believe that Lakeside is in financial difficulty. Under these circumstances, will it be possible for you to issue the auditors' standard unqualified audit report? Explain.

**LO 2, 6** 11–31. During the audit of Solar Technologies, Inc., the auditors sent confirmation requests to customers whose accounts had been written off as uncollectible during the year under audit. An executive of Solar protested, saying, "You people should be verifying that the receivables on the books are collectible. We know the ones we wrote off are no good."

*Required:*     *a.* What purpose, if any, is served by this audit procedure?

    *b.* Does the Solar executive's statement suggest some misunderstanding of audit objectives? Explain.

**LO 6** 11–32. Walter Conn, CPA, is engaged to audit the financial statements of Matthews Wholesaling for the year ended December 31, 20X0. Conn obtained and documented an understanding of the client and its environment, including internal control over the business processes relating to accounts receivable. He assessed the risks of material misstatement for all of the assertions about accounts receivable at a moderate level. Conn requested and obtained from Matthews an aged accounts receivable schedule listing the total amount owed by each customer as of December 31, 20X0, and sent positive confirmation requests to a sample of the customers.

*Required:*    What additional substantive audit procedures should Conn consider applying in auditing the accounts receivable?

(AICPA, adapted)

**LO 2, 5, 6**    11–33.    An assistant auditor was instructed to "test the aging of accounts receivable as shown on the trial balance prepared by the client." In making this test, the assistant traced all past-due accounts shown on the trial balance to the ledger cards in the accounts receivable subsidiary ledger and computed the aging of these accounts. The assistant found no discrepancies and reported to the senior auditor that the aging work performed by the client was satisfactory.

Comment on the logic and adequacy of this test of the aging of accounts receivable.

**LO 1, 4**    11–34.    You have been assigned to the audit of Utopia Industries, Inc., for the year ended December 31, 20X1. The company makes components for communications and defense applications. To obtain an understanding of the methods of revenue recognition used by such businesses and the risks involved, you decide to review the SEC filings of other companies in the same industry.

*Required:*    a. Use the Internet to search the SEC's EDGAR (Electronic Data Gathering and Retrieval System) for the 10-Ks of two companies that are in Utopia's industry (Standard Industrial Classification Code—3812—Search, Detection, Navigational, Guidance, Aeronautical Systems). The URL for EDGAR is www.sec.gov/edgarhp.htm. You can obtain a list of these companies by searching for the number 3812.

b. Review the notes to the financial statements of the two companies and summarize their methods of revenue recognition.

c. Describe the audit risks that are inherent in the methods of revenue recognition used by the companies.

**LO 4, 6**    11–35.    Hale Nelson, CPA, is engaged to audit the financial statements of Hollis Manufacturing, Inc. Hollis engages in very complex sales agreements that create issues with respect to revenue recognition. As a result, Nelson has identified revenue recognition as an audit area of significant risk that requires special audit consideration.

*Required:*    a. Describe the implications of Nelson's identification of revenue recognition as an area of significant risk.

b. Describe how Nelson might decide to react to the significant risk related to revenue recognition.

## Objective Questions

All applicable questions are available with McGraw-Hill's *Connect*™ *Accounting*. ▦ connect|ACCOUNTING

**LO 4**    11–36.    **Multiple Choice Questions**

Select the best answer for each of the following and explain fully the reason for your selection.

a. Which of the following is *least* likely to be considered an inherent risk relating to receivables and revenues?

(1) Restrictions placed on sales by laws and regulations.

(2) Decline in sales due to economic declines.

(3) Decline in sales due to product obsolescence.

(4) Over-recorded sales due to a lack of control over the sales entry function.

**LO 3, 6**    b. Which of the following would provide the most assurance concerning the valuation of accounts receivable?

(1) Trace amounts in the accounts receivable subsidiary ledger to details on shipping documents.

(2) Compare receivable turnover ratios to industry statistics for reasonableness.

(3) Inquire about receivables pledged under loan agreements.

(4) Assess the allowance for uncollectible accounts for reasonableness.

**LO 1, 4, 5**

c. Which of the following is most likely to be an example of fraudulent financial reporting relating to sales?

(1) Inaccurate billing due to a lack of controls.

(2) Lapping of accounts receivable.

(3) Misbilling a client due to a data input error.

(4) Recording sales when the customer is likely to return the goods.

**LO 1, 4**

d. Which of the following is an example of misappropriation of assets relating to sales?

(1) Accidentally recording cash that represents a liability as revenue.

(2) Holding the sales journal open to record next year's sales as having occurred in the current year.

(3) Intentionally recording cash received from a new debt agreement as revenue.

(4) Theft of cash register sales.

**LO 6**

e. There is a presumption that auditors will confirm accounts receivable *unless* the auditors' assessment of the risk of material misstatement is low.

(1) And accounts receivable are immaterial, or the use of confirmations would be ineffective.

(2) And accounts receivable are composed of large accounts.

(3) And the effectiveness of confirmations is absolutely determined.

(4) Or accounts receivable are from extremely reputable customers.

**LO 1**

f. Which of the following is *not* among the criteria that ordinarily exist for revenue to be recognized?

(1) Collectibility is reasonably assured.

(2) Delivery has occurred or is scheduled to occur in the near future.

(3) Persuasive evidence of an arrangement exists.

(4) The seller's price to the buyer is fixed or determinable.

**LO 2, 5, 6**

g. To determine that all sales have been recorded, the auditors would select a sample of transactions *from* the:

(1) Shipping documents file.

(2) Sales journal.

(3) Accounts receivable subsidiary ledger.

(4) Remittance advices.

**LO 3, 4, 6**

h. Which of the following would most likely be detected by an auditor's review of the client's sales cutoff?

(1) Excessive goods returned for credit.

(2) Unrecorded sales discounts.

(3) Lapping of year-end accounts receivable.

(4) Inflated sales for the year.

**LO 2, 3, 6**

i. To test the existence assertion for recorded receivables, the auditors would select a sample *from* the:

(1) Sales orders file.

(2) Customer purchase orders.

(3) Accounts receivable subsidiary ledger.

(4) Shipping documents (bills of lading) file.

**LO 2, 3, 6**

j. Which assertion relating to sales is most directly addressed when the auditors compare a sample of shipping documents to related sales invoices?

(1) Existence or occurrence.

(2) Completeness.

(3) Rights and obligations.

(4) Presentation and disclosure.

**LO 2, 6**

k. Cooper, CPA, is auditing the financial statements of a small rural municipality. The receivable balances represent residents' delinquent real estate taxes. Internal control at the municipality is weak. To determine the existence of the accounts receivable balances at the balance sheet date, Cooper would most likely:

(1) Send positive confirmation requests.

(2) Send negative confirmation requests.

(3) Examine evidence of subsequent cash receipts.

(4) Inspect the internal records, such as copies of the tax invoices that were mailed to the residents.

**LO 2, 6**

*l.* Identify the control that is most likely to prevent the concealment of a cash shortage resulting from the improper write-off of a trade account receivable:

(1) Write-offs must be approved by a responsible official after review of credit department recommendations and supporting evidence.

(2) Write-offs must be approved by the accounts receivable department.

(3) Write-offs must be authorized by the shipping department.

(4) Write-offs must be supported by an aging schedule showing that only receivables overdue by several months have been written off.

**LO 4, 5** 11–37. **Simulation**

An auditor's working papers include the following narrative description of the cash receipts and billing portions of Southwest Medical Center's internal control. Evaluate each condition following the narrative as being either (1) a strength, (2) a deficiency, (3) not a strength or a deficiency.

Southwest is a health care provider that is owned by a partnership of five physicians. It employs 11 physicians, including the five owners, 20 nurses, five laboratory and X-ray technicians, and four clerical workers. The clerical workers perform such tasks as reception, correspondence, cash receipts, billing, accounts receivable, bank deposits, and appointment scheduling. These clerical workers are referred to as office manager, clerk #1, clerk #2, and clerk #3. Assume that the narrative is a complete description of the system.

About two-thirds of Southwest's patients receive medical services only after insurance coverage is verified by the office manager and communicated to the clerks. Most of the other patients pay for services by cash or check when services are rendered, although the office manager extends credit on a case-by-case basis to about 5 percent of the patients.

When services are rendered, the attending physician prepares a prenumbered service slip for each patient and gives the slip to clerk #1 for pricing. Clerk #1 completes the slip and gives the completed slip to clerk #2 and a copy to the patient.

Using the information on the completed slip, clerk #2 performs one of the following three procedures for each patient:

• Clerk #2 files an insurance claim and records a receivable from the insurance company if the office manager has verified the patient's coverage, or

• Clerk #2 posts a receivable from the patient on clerk #2's PC if the office manager has approved the patient's credit, or

• Clerk #2 receives cash or a check from the patient as the patient leaves the medical center, and clerk #2 records the cash receipt.

At the end of each day, clerk #2 prepares a revenue summary.

Clerk #1 performs correspondence functions and opens the incoming mail. Clerk #1 gives checks from insurance companies and patients to clerk #2 for deposit. Clerk #2 posts the receipt of patients' checks on clerk #2's PC patient receivable records and insurance companies' checks to the receivables from the applicable insurance companies. Clerk #1 gives mail requiring correspondence to clerk #3.

Clerk #2 stamps all checks "for deposit only" and each day prepares a list of checks and cash to be deposited in the bank. (This list also includes the cash and checks personally given to clerk #2 by patients.) Clerk #2 keeps a copy of the deposit list and gives the original to clerk #3.

Clerk #3 personally makes the daily bank deposit and maintains a file of the daily bank deposits. Clerk #3 also performs appointment scheduling for all of the doctors and various correspondence functions. Clerk #3 also maintains a list of patients whose insurance coverage the office manager has verified.

When insurance claims or patient receivables are not settled within 60 days, clerk #2 notifies the office manager. The office manager personally inspects the details of each instance of nonpayment. The office manager converts insurance claims that have been rejected by insurance companies into patient receivables. Clerk #2 records these patient receivables on clerk #2's PC and deletes these receivables from the applicable insurance companies. Clerk #2 deletes the patient receivables that appear to be uncollectible from clerk #2's PC when authorized by the office manager. Clerk #2 prepares a list of patients with uncollectible balances and gives a copy of the list to clerk #3, who will not allow these patients to make appointments for future services.

Once a month an outside accountant posts clerk #2's daily revenue summaries to the general ledger, prepares a monthly trial balance and monthly financial statements, accounts for prenumbered service slips, files payroll forms and tax returns, and reconciles the monthly bank statements to the general ledger. This accountant reports directly to the physician who is the managing partner.

All four clerical employees perform their tasks on PCs that are connected through a local area network. Each PC is accessible with a password that is known only to the individual employee and the managing partner. Southwest uses a standard software package that was acquired from a software company and that cannot be modified by Southwest's employees. None of the clerical employees are able to write checks on the company's account.

For each of the following conditions, indicate whether they represent an internal control "strength" or "deficiency." If the condition is not an internal strength or deficiency, respond that the condition is "neither."

### Conditions

*a.* Southwest is involved only in medical services and has not diversified its operations.

*b.* Insurance coverage for patients is verified and communicated to the clerks by the office manager before medical services are rendered.

*c.* The physician who renders the medical services documents the services on a prenumbered slip that is used for recording revenue and as a receipt for the patient.

*d.* Cash collection is centralized in that clerk #2 receives the cash (checks) from patients and records the cash receipt.

*e.* Southwest extends credit rather than requiring cash or insurance in all cases.

*f.* The office manager extends credit on a case-by-case basis rather than using a formal credit search and established credit limits.

*g.* The office manager approves the extension of credit to patients and also approves the write-offs of uncollectible patient receivables.

*h.* Clerk #2 receives cash and checks and prepares the daily bank deposit.

*i.* Clerk #2 maintains the accounts receivable records and can add or delete information on the PC.

*j.* Prenumbered service slips are accounted for on a monthly basis by the outside accountant who is independent of the revenue generating and revenue recording functions.

*k.* The bank reconciliation is prepared monthly by the outside accountant who is independent of the revenue generating and revenue recording functions.

*l.* Computer passwords are only known to the individual employees and the managing partner, who has no duties in the revenue recording functions.

*m.* Computer software cannot be modified by Southwest's employees.

*n.* None of the employees who perform duties in the revenue generating and revenue recording are able to write checks.

**LO 1, 2, 3, 4, 5**   **11–38.** **Simulation**

An assistant on the Carter Company audit has been working in the revenue cycle and has compiled a list of possible errors and fraud that may result in the misstatement of Carter Company's financial statements and a corresponding list of controls that, if properly designed and implemented, could assist in preventing or detecting the errors and fraud.

For each possible error and fraud numbered *a* through *o,* select one internal control from the following answer list that, if properly designed and implemented, most likely could assist management in preventing or detecting the errors and fraud. Each response in the list of controls may be selected once, more than once, or not at all.

## Controls

A. Shipping clerks compare goods received from the warehouse with the details on the shipping documents.

B. Approved sales orders are required for goods to be released from the warehouse.

C. Monthly statements are mailed to all customers with outstanding balances.

D. Shipping clerks compare goods received from the warehouse with approved sales orders.

E. Customer orders are compared with the inventory master file to determine whether items ordered are in stock.

F. Daily sales summaries are compared with control totals of invoices.

G. Shipping documents are compared with sales invoices when goods are shipped.

H. Sales invoices are compared with the master price file.

I. Customer orders are compared with an approved customer list.

J. Sales orders are prepared for each customer order.

K. Control amounts posted to the accounts receivable ledger are compared with control totals of invoices.

L. Sales invoices are compared with shipping documents and approved customer orders before invoices are mailed.

M. Prenumbered credit memos are used for granting credit for goods returned.

N. Goods returned for credit are approved by the supervisor of the sales department.

O. Remittance advices are separated from the checks in the mailroom and forwarded to the accounting department.

P. Total amounts posted to the accounts receivable ledger from remittance advices are compared with the validated bank deposit slip.

Q. The cashier examines each check for proper endorsement.

R. Validated deposit slips are compared with the cashier's daily cash summaries.

S. An employee, other than the bookkeeper, periodically prepares a bank reconciliation.

T. Sales returns are approved by the same employee who issues receiving reports evidencing actual return of goods.

### Possible Errors and Fraud

a. Invoices for goods sold are posted to incorrect customer accounts.

b. Goods ordered by customers are shipped, but are **not** billed to anyone.

c. Invoices are sent for shipped goods, but are **not** recorded in the sales journal.

d. Invoices are sent for shipped goods and are recorded in the sales journal, but are *not* posted to any customer account.

e. Credit sales are made to individuals with unsatisfactory credit ratings.

f. Goods are removed from inventory for unauthorized orders.

g. Goods shipped to customers do **not** agree with goods ordered by customers.

h. Invoices are sent to allies in a fraudulent scheme and sales are recorded for fictitious transactions.

i. Customers' checks are received for less than the customers' full account balances, but the customers' full account balances are credited.

j. Customers' checks are misappropriated before being forwarded to the cashier for deposit.

k. Customers' checks are credited to incorrect customer accounts.

l. Different customer accounts are each credited for the same cash receipt.

m. Customers' checks are properly credited to customer accounts and are properly deposited, but errors are made in recording receipts in the cash receipts journal.

n. Customers' checks are misappropriated after being forwarded to the cashier for deposit.

o. Invalid transactions granting credit for sales returns are recorded.

**LO 6**   11–39.   **Simulation**

An auditor may use confirmations of accounts receivable. Reply as to whether the following statements are correct or incorrect with respect to the confirmation process when applied to accounts receivable.

a. The confirmation requests should be mailed to respondents by the CPAs.

b. A combination of positive and negative request forms must be used if receivables are significant.

c. Second requests are ordinarily sent for positive form confirmations requests when the first request is not returned.

    *d.* Confirmations address existence more than they address completeness.

    *e.* Confirmation of accounts receivable is a generally accepted auditing standard.

    *f.* There ordinarily is a presumption that the auditor will confirm accounts receivable.

    *g.* Auditors should always confirm the total balances of accounts rather than individual portions (e.g., if the balance is made up of three sales, all three should be confirmed).

    *h.* Auditors may ignore individually immaterial accounts when confirming accounts receivable.

    *i.* The best way to evaluate the results of the confirmation process is to compare the total misstatements identified to the account's tolerable misstatements amounts.

    *j.* Accounts receivable are ordinarily confirmed on a standard form developed by the American Institute of Certified Public Accountants and the Financial Executives Institute.

**LO 1, 2, 4, 5**    11–40.    **Simulation**

The auditors have determined that each of the following objectives will be part of the audit of SSC Corporation. For each audit objective, select a substantive procedure (see the list below) that would help to achieve that objective. Each of the procedures may be used once, more than once, or not at all.

**Audit Objective:**

    *a.* Establish the completeness of receivables transactions.

    *b.* Determine that the valuation of receivables is at appropriate net realizable values.

    *c.* Verify the cutoff of sales transactions.

    *d.* Establish the accuracy of sales transactions.

    *e.* Determine that the presentation and disclosure of receivables is adequate.

    *f.* Establish that the client has rights to the recorded receivables.

**Substantive Procedures:**

    (1) Analyze the relationship of accounts receivable and purchases and compare it with relationships for preceding periods.

    (2) Vouch sales recorded in January of 20X9.

    (3) Vouch sales recorded in November of 20X8.

    (4) Review the aged trial balance for significant past due accounts.

    (5) Obtain an understanding of the business purpose of transactions that resulted in accounts receivable balances.

    (6) Review board of director minutes for approval of all customers' credit limits.

    (7) Review drafts of financial statements.

**Problems**     **All applicable problems are available with McGraw-Hill's *Connect*™ *Accounting*.** ▓ connect
|ACCOUNTING

**LO 4, 6**    11–41.    Halston Toy Manufacturing Co. introduced a number of new products in the last quarter of the year. The company has a liberal return policy allowing retail customers to return products within 120 days of purchase.

*Required:*    *a.* Describe the audit problem indicated by this scenario.

    *b.* List audit procedures that could be used to audit the allowance for sales returns.

**LO 3, 4, 5, 6**    11–42.    The following are typical questions that might appear on an internal control questionnaire for accounts receivable:

    1. Are sales invoices checked for proper pricing, terms, and clerical accuracy?

    2. Are shipping documents prenumbered and all numbers accounted for?

    3. Is customer credit approval obtained from the credit department prior to shipment of goods?

*Required:*    *a.* Describe the purpose of each of the above controls.

    *b.* Describe the manner in which the operating effectiveness of each of the above procedures might be tested.

    *c.* Assuming that the operating effectiveness of each of the above procedures is found to be inadequate, describe how the auditors might alter their substantive procedures to compensate for the increased level of control risk (risk of material misstatement).

**LO 1, 6**  11–43.  During your examination of the financial statements of Martin Mfg. Co., a new client, for the year ended March 31, 20X0, you note the following entry in the general journal dated March 31, 20X0:

| | | |
|---|---|---|
| Notes Receivable | 550,000 | |
| Land | | 500,000 |
| Gain on sale of land | | 50,000 |

To record sale of excess plant-site land to Ardmore Corp. for 8 percent note due five years from date. No interest payment required until maturity of note.

Your review of the contract for sale between Martin and Ardmore, your inquiries of Martin executives, and your study of the minutes of Martin's directors' meetings uncover the following facts:

(1) The land has been carried in your client's accounting records at its cost of $500,000.

(2) Ardmore Corp. is a land developer and plans to subdivide and resell the land acquired from Martin Mfg. Co.

(3) Martin had originally negotiated with Ardmore on the basis of a 12 percent interest rate on the note. This interest rate was established by Martin after a careful analysis of Ardmore's credit standing and current money market conditions.

(4) Ardmore had rejected the 12 percent interest rate because the total outlay on a 12 percent note for $550,000 would amount to $880,000 at the end of five years, and Ardmore thought a total outlay of this amount would leave it with an inadequate return on the subdivision. Ardmore held out for a total cash outlay of $770,000, and Martin Mfg. Co. finally agreed to this position. During the discussions, it was pointed out that the present value of $1 due five years hence at an annual interest rate of 12 percent is approximately $0.567.

*Required:*  Ignoring income tax considerations, is the journal entry recording Martin's sale of the land to Ardmore acceptable? Explain fully and draft an adjusting entry if you consider one to be necessary.

**LO 6**  11–44.  Lawrence Company maintains its accounts on the basis of a fiscal year ending October 31. Assume that you were retained by the company in August to perform an audit for the fiscal year ending October 31, 20X0. You decide to perform certain auditing procedures in advance of the balance sheet date. Among these interim procedures is the confirmation of accounts receivable, which you perform at September 30.

The accounts receivable at September 30 consisted of approximately 200 accounts with balances totaling $956,750. Seventy-five of these accounts with balances totaling $650,725 were selected for confirmation. All but 20 of the confirmation requests have been returned; 30 were signed without comments, 14 had minor differences that have been cleared satisfactorily, and 11 confirmations had the following comments:

1. We are sorry, but we cannot answer your request for confirmation of our account because Moss Company uses a computerized accounts payable voucher system.

2. The balance of $1,050 was paid on September 23, 20X0.

3. The above balance of $7,750 was paid on October 5, 20X0.

4. The above balance has been paid.

5. We do not owe you anything at September 30, 20X0, since the goods represented by your invoice dated September 30, 20X0, Number 25,050, in the amount of $11,550, were received on October 5, 20X0, on FOB destination terms.

6. An advance payment of $2,500 made by us in August 20X0 should cover the two invoices totaling $1,350 shown on the statement attached.

7. We never received these goods.

8. We are contesting the propriety of the $12,525 charge. We think the charge is excessive.

9. Amount okay. As the goods have been shipped to us on consignment, we will remit payment upon selling the goods.

10. The $10,000, representing a deposit under a lease, will be applied against the rent due to us during 20X0, the last year of the lease.

11. Your credit in the amount of $440, dated September 5, 20X0, cancels the above balance.

*Required:*  What steps would you take to clear satisfactorily each of the above 11 comments?

(AICPA, adapted)

**LO 1, 2, 6**  11–45.  As part of his audit of the financial statements of Marlborough Corporation for the year ended March 31, 20X0, Mark Wayne, CPA, is reviewing the balance sheet presentation of a $1,200,000 advance to Franklin Olds, Marlborough's president. The advance, which represents 50 percent of current assets and 10 percent of total assets, was made during the year ended March 31, 20X0. It has been described in the balance sheet as "miscellaneous accounts receivable" and classified as a current asset.

Olds informs the CPA that he has used the proceeds of the advance to purchase 35,000 shares of Marlborough's common stock, in order to forestall a takeover raid on the company. He is reluctant to have his association with the advance described in the financial statements because he does not have voting control and fears that this will "just give the raiders ammunition."

Olds offers the following four-point program as an alternative to further disclosure:

(1) Have the advance approved by the board of directors. (This can be done expeditiously because a majority of the board members are officers of the company.)

(2) Prepare a demand note payable to the company with interest of 12 percent (the average bank rate paid by the company).

(3) Furnish an endorsement of the stock to the company as collateral for the loan. (During the year under audit, despite the fact that earnings did not increase, the market price of Marlborough common rose from $20 to $40 per share. The stock has maintained its $40 per share market price subsequent to year-end.)

(4) Obtain a written opinion from the company attorney supporting the legality of the company's advance and the use of the proceeds.

*Required:*

a. Discuss the proper balance sheet classification of the advance to Olds and other appropriate disclosures in the financial statements and notes. (Ignore SEC regulations and requirements, tax effects, creditors' restrictions on stock repurchases, and the presentation of common stock dividends and interest revenue.)

b. Discuss each point of Olds's four-point program as to whether it is desirable and as to whether it is an alternative to further disclosure.

c. If Olds refuses to permit further disclosure, what action should the CPA take? Discuss.

d. In his discussion with the CPA, Olds warns that the raiders, if successful, probably will appoint new auditors. What consideration should the CPA give to this factor? Explain.

(AICPA, adapted)

**LO 1, 6**  11–46.  You are conducting an annual audit of Granite Corporation, which has total assets of approximately $1 million and operates a wholesale merchandising business. The corporation is in good financial condition and maintains an adequate accounting system. Granite Corporation owns about 25 percent of the capital stock of Desert Sun, Inc., which operates a dude ranch. This investment is regarded as a permanent one and is accounted for by the equity method.

During your audit of accounts and notes receivable, you uncover the information shown below concerning three short-term notes receivable due in the near future. All three of these notes receivable were discounted by Granite Corporation with its bank shortly before the balance sheet date.

1. A 13 percent 60-day note for $50,000 received from a customer of unquestioned financial standing.

2. A 15 percent six-month note for $60,000 received from the affiliated company, Desert Sun, Inc. The affiliated company is operating profitably, but it is presently in a weak cash position because of recent additions to buildings and equipment. The president of Granite Corporation intends to make an $80,000 advance with a five-year maturity to Desert Sun, Inc. The proposed advance will enable Desert Sun, Inc., to pay the existing 15 percent $60,000 note at maturity and to meet certain other obligations.

3. A 14 percent $20,000 note from a former key executive of Granite Corporation whose employment had been terminated because of chronic alcoholism and excessive gambling. The maker of the note is presently unemployed and without personal resources.

*Required:*  Describe the proper balance sheet presentation with respect to these discounted notes receivable. Use a separate paragraph for each of the three notes, and state any assumptions you consider necessary.

**LO 1** 11–47. The July 31, 20X0, general ledger trial balance of Aerospace Contractors, Inc., reflects the following accounts associated with receivables. Balances of the accounts are after all adjusting journal entries proposed by the auditors and accepted by the client.

| | |
|---|---:|
| Accounts receivable—commercial | $ 595,000 |
| Accounts receivable—U.S. government | 3,182,000 |
| Allowance for uncollectible accounts and notes | 75,000 cr. |
| Claims receivable—public carriers | 7,000 |
| Claims receivable—U.S. government terminated contracts | 320,000 |
| Due from Harwood Co., investee | 480,000 |
| Notes receivable—trade | 15,000 |

Remember that two or more ledger accounts are often combined into one amount in the financial statements in order to achieve a concise presentation. The need for brevity also often warrants the disclosure of some information parenthetically: for example, the amount of the allowance for doubtful accounts.

*Required:*

*a.* Draft a partial balance sheet for Aerospace Contractors at July 31, 20X0. In deciding which items deserve separate listing, consider materiality as well as the nature of the accounts.

*b.* Write an explanation of the reasoning employed in your balance sheet presentation of these accounts.

**In-Class Team Case**

**LO 6** 11–48.

Ming, CPA, is engaged to audit the financial statements of Wellington Sales, Inc., for the year ended December 31, 20X0. Ming obtained and documented an understanding of the client's business and environment, including internal control over business processes relating to accounts receivable. She assessed the risks of material misstatement for the assertions of existence, rights, and valuation of accounts receivable at a high level. Ming requested and obtained from Wellington an aged accounts receivable schedule listing the total amount owed by each customer as of December 31, 20X0, and sent positive confirmation requests (signed by Sam Blocker, the controller of Wellington). Ming has asked Zimber, the staff assistant assigned to the engagement, to follow up on the nine returned confirmations that appear on the following two pages. Assume that each confirmation is material if the potential misstatement is projected to the population. Also, assume that in all cases the debit balance is the result of a credit to "Sales." In several circumstances, a "Note to files" is included with additional information relating to the confirmation.

*Required:*

Describe the procedure or procedures, if any, that Zimber should perform to resolve each of the nine confirmations (below) with exceptions that were returned and, if possible, provide the audited value of the account. Assume that all amounts involved are considered material.

---

**Confirmation #5**

The statement of our account showing a balance of $20,000 due Wellington Sales, Inc., at December 31, 20X0, is correct except as noted below:

Abbington Co.
By *Alfred Martin*

Date: 1/16/X1

Exceptions: *Yes, we ordered $20,000 worth of merchandise from Wellington in November. However, we mailed Wellington a check for $20,000 on 12/18/X0.*

Note to files: *Blocker indicates that the check was received and deposited on 12/28/X0, but posted to the wrong customer's account.*

---

**Confirmation #22**

The statement of our account showing a balance of $12,222 due Wellington Sales, Inc., at December 31, 20X0, is correct except as noted below:

Wilson Dilco
By *Kent Parry*

Date: 2/2/X1

Exceptions: *No way. Forget it. Wellington said we'd have these goods in 10 days on December 2. When we didn't receive them, I canceled the order on December 12th. Wiggo Smiggo*

*Corporation shipped us similar goods overnite. We'll never deal with Wellington again as long as I am around.*

---

## Confirmation #47

The statement of our account showing a balance of $22,000 due Wellington Sales, Inc., at December 31, 20X0, is correct except as noted below:

*The Big Edge*
By *Bert Quinton*

Date: 1/22/X1

Exceptions: *We use a voucher system by individual invoice. We cannot verify the balance, but Wellington is one of our regular suppliers. We probably owe them something.*

---

## Confirmation #51

The statement of our account showing a balance of $75,000 due Wellington Sales, Inc., at December 31, 20X0, is correct except as noted below:

*Farkele Corporation of America and the World*
By *Robby Boertson*

Date: 1/9/X1

Exceptions: *Our records show that we sent them a check for the amount due on 12/29/X0.*

---

## Confirmation #62

The statement of our account showing a balance of $2,500 due Wellington Sales, Inc., at December 31, 20X0, is correct except as noted below:

*Pibson Gonker Corporation*
By *Sam Sheffield*

Date: 1/30/X1

Exceptions:
Note to files: *This confirmation was returned by the postal service as "return to sender, address unknown."*

---

## Confirmation #68

The statement of our account showing a balance of $66,000 due Wellington Sales, Inc., at December 31, 20X0, is correct except as noted below:

*Yanrarian Ruckus Company*
By *Tom Turken*

Date: 2/7/X1

Exceptions: *We mailed that check for the full amount on 1/3/X1. The merchandise was not received until 12/23/X0.*

---

## Confirmation #72

The statement of our account showing a balance of $22,000 due Wellington Sales, Inc., at December 31, 20X0, is correct except as noted below:

*Yeg Co.*
By *Alfred Martin*

Date: 1/30/X1

Exceptions: *Yes, I guess we owe this amount, but Wellington made clear to us that we could return any of the items we did not sell. But, so far, sales are good, and we've sold most of the items.*

---

## Confirmation #77

The statement of our account showing a balance of $32,000 due Wellington Sales, Inc., at December 31, 20X0, is correct except as noted below:

*Zell Incorporated*
By *John Nolan*

Date: 1/19/X1

Exceptions: *We received $24,000 worth of goods on consignment from Wellington on 2/10/X0, but they are not sold yet.*

**Confirmation #79**

The statement of our account showing a balance of $42,000 due Wellington Sales, Inc., at December 31, 20X0, is correct except as noted below:

*Zentigton Corporation*
*By Wallace Olson*

Date: 1/22/X1

Exceptions: ***Yes, we ordered $42,000 of merchandise on October 15, but Wellington was out of stock until recently. They seem to always be out of stock. We finally received the goods on January 4, 20X1.***

## Ethics Cases

**LO 1, 2, 6**

**11–49.** You are an assistant auditor with Zaird & Associates, CPAs. Universal Air (UA), your fifth audit client in your eight months with Zaird, is a national airline based in your hometown. UA has continued to grow while remaining healthy financially over the eight years of its existence. Indeed, as you start the audit, you notice that (unaudited) sales are up 30 percent this year (20X1), with earnings up 40 percent. Your firm, Zaird & Associates, has been UA's only auditor.

During the audit you noticed that UA records sales when tickets are sold—debit receivable (or cash), credit sales. In performing substantive procedures relating to receivables, you also found that some of the "sales" are for 20X2 flights—generally in January and early February. You brought up this matter to your in-charge senior and she indicated that she also wondered about this last year when she worked on the audit. She suggested that she concluded that this isn't likely to be a problem for at least three reasons (any one of which would be sufficient to allow the current method):

1. The company has been using this approach since its inception eight years ago. Thus, any overstatement of this year's sales at year-end is likely to be "averaged out" by an understatement at the beginning of the year, since the company followed the same policy last year (and the years before).

2. Valid reasons exist for including the sales when "booked." The small airline's earnings process is probably best considered about complete when the sale is made because this is the toughest part of the revenue generation process. The planes are scheduled to fly for the first six months of next year, and will fly, regardless of whether these relatively few passengers who paid before year-end for next year's flights are on them; there are virtually no variable costs incurred for these passengers, except for a few very small bags of peanuts and a few cans of soda.

3. Imagine what a nightmare it would be to have to record an entry when a passenger buys a ticket, and then another one when the flight occurs.

She says she is willing to discuss this with you if you disagree, but at this point she thinks it isn't a problem.

*Required:*

*a.* Discuss whether you agree or disagree with each of her reasons.

Now assume that you potentially agree with her first justification. You think that maybe a journal entry could be made at year-end to estimate the liability for next-year flights. Yet this wouldn't be necessary if everything does "average out" and any year-end liability is immaterial.

*b.* Given this situation, would you expect the procedure to "average out" over the year?

*c.* How might one determine whether it does "average out" over the year?

**LO 1, 5, 6    11–50.** You have worked with Zaird & Associates, CPAs, for a little more than a year and are beginning your second audit of Universal Air (UA). This year you even have an assistant reporting to you—Jane McClain.

Jane has come to you with a concern. She noticed that when sales are "booked" over the Internet an entry is made debiting a receivable account (from the credit card) and crediting sales. When a ticket is canceled, the only entry made is to a database that maintains specific flight information on seat availability. Jane has discovered that customers are e-mailed a "Canceled Reservation" form when this occurs. But no accounting journal entry is recorded, and no refund occurs until the customer requests (in writing) a refund. If the customer never requests the refund, the receivable is billed to the credit card and collected; when it is billed to the credit card, many customers complain and are given a refund, with an accompanying journal entry being made for the cancellation.

After analyzing the "Canceled Reservation" form, you note that it says nothing about requiring a written cancellation for a refund. UA's controller responded to your inquiry about the policy of requiring a written request for a refund by indicating that the policy is presented on the Web site's "business policies and procedures" section. Furthermore, the controller says that in total about two-thirds of the customers ask for and receive refunds, while one-third do not. She then states to you that "the other one-third must not be aware of the policy, or simply don't care. What the heck, *caveat emptor!*"

At this point, you discussed the situation with Bill Radman, partner-in-charge of the audit. Subsequently, he made an inquiry of Zaird's attorneys about the legality of the policy, and received a reply that while it is probably a questionable policy, they are unable to say it is illegal—in fact, it probably is not. Upon further investigation you find that this policy has been in existence for three years (since your first year on the audit) and neither you nor anyone else in your firm has identified it previously.

*Required:*

a. Is this a significant deficiency? Should it be reported to the audit committee?

b. Should it be reported elsewhere? Where? How?

c. What impact should this policy have on the audit?

## Appendix 11A

# Illustrative Audit Case: Keystone Computers & Networks, Inc.

## Part II: Consideration of Internal Control

This second part of the audit case of Keystone Computers & Networks, Inc. (KCN), illustrates the manner in which auditors obtain an understanding of internal control, perform tests of controls, and assess control risk. The process is illustrated with the revenue and cash receipts cycle and includes the following working papers:

- A questionnaire to document the control environment, risk assessment, and monitoring components of the company's internal control. Since this questionnaire is designed for nonpublic companies, it does not address factors that are generally found only in public companies, such as an audit committee of the board of directors.
- An organizational chart for the company. This working paper helps the auditors evaluate the overall segregation of functions within the company.
- A flowchart description of the revenue and cash receipts cycle of the company and the related controls prepared by the staff of Adams, Barnes & Co. (ABC), CPAs.
- ABC's working paper for assessment of control risk for accounts receivable and revenue as it would appear before any tests of controls are performed. This working paper identifies the controls and deficiencies for the revenue and cash receipts cycle. It also relates the controls and deficiencies to the various financial statement assertions about revenue and accounts receivable.
- The audit program for tests of controls for the revenue and cash receipts cycle. This working paper describes the various tests of controls that were performed by the staff of ABC to obtain evidence about the operating effectiveness of the controls. These tests provide the support for the auditors' assessed level of control risk.

- ABC's working paper documenting the results of tests of controls that were performed using audit sampling.
- ABC's working paper for assessment of control risk for accounts receivable and revenue as it would appear after all tests of controls are performed. Notice that the auditors have checked the boxes indicating that the controls are operating effectively. This allows ABC's staff to arrive at the final assessed level of control risk as indicated at the bottom of the working paper.

You should read through the information to obtain an understanding of the way in which auditors document their understanding of internal control and the assessment of control risk for a transaction cycle. You may also wish to review the planning documentation presented on pages 237–244 of Chapter 6 to refresh your knowledge about the nature of the company's business.

## OBTAINING AND DOCUMENTING AN UNDERSTANDING OF THE REVENUE AND CASH RECEIPTS CYCLE

ABC's consideration of the controls relating to the revenue cycle began by updating various working papers, including the following:

- Control Environment, Risk Assessment, and Monitoring Questionnaire—IC-3 and IC-4.
- Organizational Chart of KCN—IC-5.
- Revenue and Cash Receipts Cycle Flowchart—IC-8.
- Assessment of Control Risk Worksheet (before tests of controls are performed)—IC-20.[3]

The Control Environment, Risk Assessment, and Monitoring Questionnaire (IC-3 and IC-4), the Organizational Chart (IC-5), and the description of Internal Control—Sales and Collection Cycle (IC-8) required only limited updating because there were few changes in internal control during the year, and key personnel are the same as in the preceding year. After completing the description of internal control, the audit staff of ABC observed operation of the system and found that the controls had been placed in operation.

The staff of ABC then used the documentation of internal control to identify controls and deficiencies on Schedule IC-20. This schedule includes check boxes in the appropriate columns to designate the financial statement assertions that are addressed by the internal control policy or procedure. For the deficiencies, an "X" is included in the appropriate columns. Before tests of controls are performed, the check boxes are blank because the auditors do not know whether the controls are operating effectively.

---

[3] This schedule is included twice (incomplete and complete) for illustrative purposes. In an actual audit, only the completed schedule would be included.

| **Control Environment, Risk Assessment, and Monitoring Questionnaire—Nonpublic Companies** |
|---|

**Client:** *Keystone Computers & Networks, Inc.*

**Financial Statement Date:** *12/31/X5*

| Control Environment | Yes | No | N/A | Comments |
|---|---|---|---|---|
| **Management Philosophy and Operating Style** | | | | |
| 1. Does management adequately consider the potential effects of taking large or unusual business risks prior to doing so? | ✔ | | | |
| 2. Are business risks adequately monitored? | ✔ | | | |
| 3. Is management not overly aggressive with respect to financial reporting? | ✔ | | | |
| 4. Are financial statement estimates developed in a conscientious manner? | ✔ | | | |
| **Organizational Structure** | | | | |
| 5. Is the organization of the entity clearly defined in terms of lines of authority and responsibility? | ✔ | | | |
| 6. Does the entity have a current organizational chart and related materials such as job descriptions? | ✔ | | | |
| 7. Are policies and procedures for authorization of transactions established at an adequately high level? | ✔ | | | |
| 8. Are such policies and procedures adequately adhered to? | ✔ | | | |
| **Methods of Assigning Authority and Responsibility** | | | | |
| 9. Are authority and responsibility to deal with organizational goals and objectives, operating functions, and regulatory requirements adequately delegated? | ✔ | | | |
| 10. Has management established and communicated policies about appropriate business practices and conduct and conflicts of interest? | ✔ | | | |
| 11. Has the entity developed an IT systems documentation that indicates the procedures for authorizing transactions and approving systems changes? | ✔ | | | |
| **Board of Directors, Integrity and Ethical Values, Commitment to Competence** | | | | |
| 12. Is the level of experience, status, and independence of the members of the board of directors appropriate for the organization? | ✔ | | | |
| 13. Are there regular meetings of the board of directors to set policies and objectives, review the entity's performance, and take appropriate action; and are minutes of such meetings prepared and signed on a timely basis? | ✔ | | | |

*(continued)*

**Control Environment, Risk Assessment, and Monitoring Questionnaire—Nonpublic Companies**

IC-4
*WL*
*11/10/X5*

**Client:** *Keystone Computers & Networks, Inc.*

**Financial Statement Date:** *12/31/X5*

| Control Environment | Yes | No | N/A | Comments |
|---|---|---|---|---|

**Board of Directors, Integrity and Ethical Values, Commitment to Competence**

14. Has management taken adequate actions to reduce incentives and temptations that might prompt employees to engage in dishonest, illegal, and unethical acts? ✔

15. Does management exhibit an adequate commitment to competence in the performance of essential jobs within the organization? ✔

**Human Resource Policies and Procedures**

16. Does the entity employ sound hiring practices, including background investigations, where appropriate? ✔

17. Are employees adequately trained to meet their job responsibilities? ✔

18. Is employee performance evaluated at regular intervals? ✔

19. Are employees in positions of trust bonded? ✔

20. Are employees in positions of trust required to take vacations and are their duties rotated while they are on vacation? ✔

**Risk Assessment**

21. Is the chief executive officer attuned to external and internal factors that affect the risk of achieving the entity's objectives? ✔

**Monitoring**

22. Are key management personnel sufficiently involved with operations to monitor the effectiveness of internal controls? ✔

23. Does management have a formal process for considering reportable conditions from external auditors? ✔

Evidence used to complete this questionnaire was obtained from discussions with the following individuals:

| | |
|---|---|
| *Sam Best* | *11/8/X5* |
| *Linda Tyler* | *11/9/X5* |
| *James Edwards* | *11/9/X5* |
| *John Watson* | *11/9/X5* |
| *Loren Steele* | *11/10/X5* |

Conclusion: *The control environment, risk assessment process, and monitoring procedures appear to be adequate to provide an atmosphere conducive to the effective operation of other controls.*

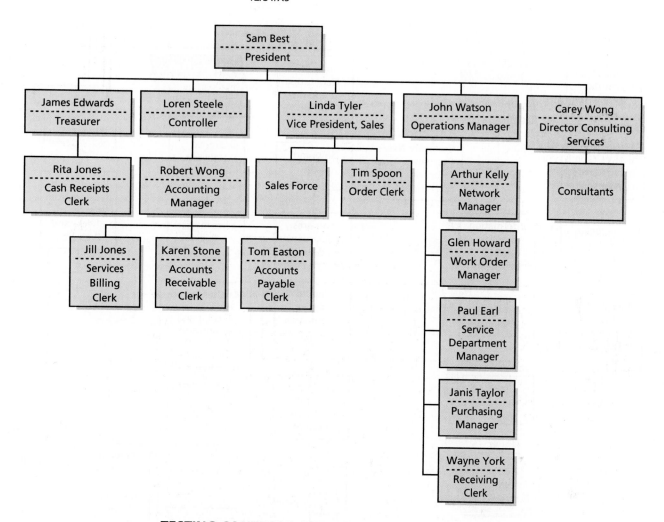

**KEYSTONE COMPUTERS & NETWORKS, INC.**
Organizational Chart
12/31/X5

## TESTING CONTROLS AND ASSESSING CONTROL RISK

When obtaining an understanding of the overall internal control, ABC's audit staff first considered the elements of control environment, risk assessment, and monitoring as documented with the questionnaire (IC-3 and IC-4). As indicated on the questionnaire, they found these components to be strong for a nonpublic company and to reflect an atmosphere conducive to the effective operation of the accounting information system and control activities.

Based on their understanding of internal control, ABC's staff planned assessed levels of control risk at a low level for completeness and at a moderate level for existence or occurrence, rights, and valuation. As with most small businesses, the auditors found that KCN had no effective controls to address the presentation and disclosure assertion. Based on the planned assessed levels, the audit staff of ABC designed a program (IC-12 and IC-13) to test the controls. Schedule IC-15 illustrates how they determined sample size and evaluated the results of tests of controls that involved audit sampling.

The completed Schedule IC-20 on pages 489–490 includes check marks to indicate that the tests of controls demonstrated that the related controls were operating effectively. Based on these results, the auditors' assessed levels of control risk—indicated in the last row of Schedule IC-20—were supported at their planned levels. These assessments will be used in conjunction with the inherent risk assessments to determine the nature, timing, and extent of substantive procedures for revenue and accounts receivable. These tests are illustrated in Part III of the case in Appendix 11B.

**KEYSTONE COMPUTERS & NETWORKS, INC.**
Internal Control—Sales and Collections Cycle
12/31/X5

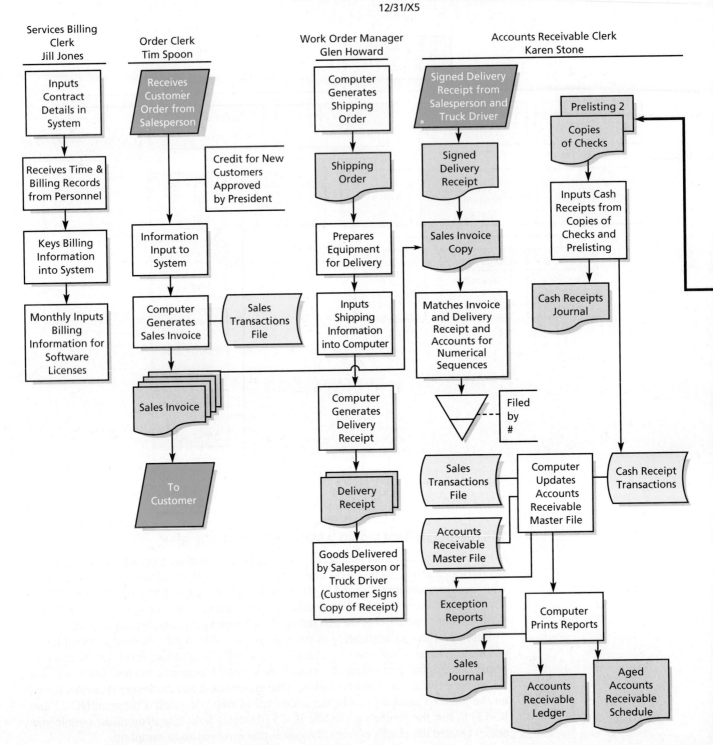

## Cash Receipts Clerk
## Rita Jones

**Notes:**

1. The company uses Microsoft Dynamics GP, a commercial accounting software package that has not been modified.
2. The company has a local area network, with computer terminals in the purchasing, work order, and accounting departments.
3. All consulting, license, and service contracts are reviewed by Loren Steele, controller.
4. Monthly service billings are reviewed for reasonableness by Loren Steele, controller.
5. Sales orders are entered on an online terminal that applies the following application controls:
   - The order clerk's password is verified before transactions are accepted.
   - Customer numbers are agreed to customer master file information.
   - Computer determines whether the customer has sufficient credit limit remaining to make the purchase. If rejected, the customer's credit limit must be increased by the president or the terms must be changed to cash on delivery.
   - Computer will require override of the transaction by the order clerk any time the sales price of an item is less than its cost.
   - Computer assigns number to sales invoice.
6. Shipping information is entered on an online terminal that applies the following controls:
   - The work order manager's password is verified before shipping data are accepted.
   - The shipping data are agreed to details of the sales transactions that were entered by the sales order clerk. If the name of the customer or the quantities shipped do not agree, the system will reject the data. Override will be accepted by the system only from the vice president of sales by password.
   - Computer assigns number to delivery receipt.
7. Cash receipts are entered to an online terminal that applies the following controls:
   - The accounts receivable clerk's password is verified before transactions are accepted.
   - When the customer number is entered, the company name is presented on screen for comparison by clerk.
8. As the computer updates the accounts receivable master file, it produces an exception report that contains any items with invalid customer numbers and any unusually large cash payments in relation to the customer's account balance. The accounting manager reviews and follows up on exceptions and any corrections are made the same day.
9. The accounting manager reconciles the master file of accounts receivable to the general ledger on a monthly basis.
10. Monthly statements are mailed to customers.
11. The receptionist endorses incoming checks "for deposit only" to the company's account.
12. Cash sales are minor in amount and the cash is accepted by the receptionist who maintains the company's cash fund.
13. Cash deposits are made daily.
14. Computer summaries of cash collections of accounts receivable and cash sales are reconciled to validated bank deposit slips and the prelisting of cash receipts by the accounting manager.
15. Sales returns and allowances are approved by the vice president of sales.
16. Write-offs of accounts receivable are approved by the president after initiation by the controller, but not on a regular basis.
17. Accounting manager reconciles bank account on a monthly basis.

**KEYSTONE COMPUTERS & NETWORKS, INC.**
Assessment of Control Risk—Revenue Cycle
12/31/X5

IC-20
*WL*
*11/13/X5*

| Controls | Existence or Occurrence | Completeness | Cutoff | Rights | Valuation and Accuracy | Presentation and Disclosure |
|---|---|---|---|---|---|---|
| **Sales** | | | | | | |
| 1. Separation of duties for authorization, credit approval, shipping, and accounting for sales transactions. | ☐ | ☐ | | ☐ | ☐ | |
| 2. Company uses an unmodified commercial software package. | ☐ | ☐ | | ☐ | ☐ | |
| 3. Credit lines are approved by the president. | | | | | ☐ | |
| 4. Service contracts and billings are reviewed by the controller. | ☐ | ☐ | ☐ | ☐ | ☐ | |
| 5. Computer verifies the clerk's password before sales data can be entered. | ☐ | | | ☐ | ☐ | |
| 6. Application controls (input validation checks) are applied to ensure the accuracy of the billing process. | | | | | ☐ | |
| 7. Computer assigns numbers to sales invoices. | | ☐ | ☐ | | | |
| 8. Computer verifies the work order manager's password before shipping data can be entered. | ☐ | | | ☐ | ☐ | |
| 9. Input validation checks are applied to shipping data as they are entered. | | | | | ☐ | |
| 10. Computer assigns numbers to delivery receipts. | | ☐ | ☐ | | | |
| 11. Accounts receivable clerk matches invoices with delivery receipts and accounts for numerical sequences. | | ☐ | ☐ | | | |
| 12. Accounting manager reconciles the accounts receivable master file to the general ledger monthly. | ☐ | ☐ | | ☐ | ☐ | |
| 13. Monthly statements are mailed to customers. | ☐ | ☐ | | ☐ | ☐ | |

KEYSTONE COMPUTERS & NETWORKS, INC.
Assessment of Control Risk—Revenue Cycle
12/31/X5

**IC-20**

*WL*
*11/13/X5*

| Controls | Existence or Occurrence | Completeness | Cutoff | Rights | Valuation and Accuracy | Presentation and Disclosure |
|---|---|---|---|---|---|---|
| **Sales** | | | | | | |
| 14. Sales returns and allowances are approved by the vice president of sales. | | | | | ☐ | |
| 15. Separation of duties of custody of cash from records of cash receipts and accounts receivable. | ☐ | | | ☐ | ☐ | |
| 16. Checks are prelisted and stamped with restrictive endorsement when received. | ☐ | | | ☐ | ☐ | |
| 17. Application controls (input validation checks) are applied to ensure the accuracy of the recording of cash receipts. | | | | | ☐ | |
| 18. Control totals are reconciled by the accounting manager. | ☐ | ☐ | | ☐ | ☐ | |
| 19. Exception reports are reviewed and followed up by the accounting manager. | | | | | ☐ | |
| 20. Computer summaries of cash collections and cash sales are reconciled to bank deposits and prelisting of cash receipts by accounting manager. | ☐ | ☐ | | ☐ | ☐ | |
| 21. Accounting manager reconciles bank account on a monthly basis. | ☐ | ☐ | | ☐ | ☐ | |
| **Internal Control Weaknesses** | | | | | | |
| 1. Sales invoices are prepared and mailed prior to delivery of goods. | X | | X | X | X | |
| 2. Accounts receivable are not written off on a regular basis. | | | | | X | |
| **Planned Assessed Level of Control Risk** | *Moderate* | *Low* | *Moderate* | *Moderate* | *Moderate* | *Maximum* |

## Audit Program—Tests of Controls—Revenue Cycle

**IC-12**
*WL*
*11/12/X5*

**Client:** *Keystone Computers & Networks, Inc.*

**Financial Statement Date:** *12/31/X5*

| Procedure | Performed by | |
|---|---|---|
| | Initials | Date |

**Sales Transactions**

| Procedure | Initials | Date |
|---|---|---|
| 1. Walk three product and three service transactions through sales processes to confirm our understanding as documented. | *WL* | *11/14/X5* |
| 2. Agree billings for a sample of 25 consulting contracts to contract terms. | *WL* | *11/14/X5* |
| 3. Observe and inquire about the segregation of duties for sales transactions. | *WL* | *11/15/X5* |
| 4. Inspect documentation of the Microsoft Dynamics GP software package. | *WL* | *11/15/X5* |
| 5. Inquire about the president's procedures for approving credit limits. | *WL* | *11/15/X5* |
| 6. Observe the order clerk when entering customer orders and enter several test transactions to determine that: | | |
|    *a.* Password must be entered to enter customer orders. | *MP* | *11/14/X5* |
|    *b.* The system performs a validity check for the customer's number. | *MP* | *11/14/X5* |
|    *c.* The system determines that the customer's credit limit is not exceeded. | *MP* | *11/14/X5* |
|    *d.* The system compares sales price to cost of product and requires override when cost exceeds sales price. | *MP* | *11/14/X5* |
| 7. Observe that the computer assigns numbers to sales invoices. | *MP* | *11/14/X5* |
| 8. Review the sales invoice file with delivery reports attached to obtain evidence that all numbers are accounted for and all invoices have an attached delivery report. | *MP* | *11/14/X5* |
| 9. Inquire about the accounting manager's procedures for reconciling the accounts receivable master file to the general ledger. | *WL* | *11/15/X5* |
| 10. Observe the mailing of monthly statements. | *MP* | *1/6/X6* |
| 11. Inquire about the procedures for approval of sales returns and allowances by the vice president of sales. | *WL* | *11/15/X5* |

| | | |
|---|---|---|
| **Audit Program—Tests of Controls—Revenue Cycle** | | |

**IC-13**
*WL*
*11/12/X5*

*(Concluded)*

**Client:** *Keystone Computers & Networks, Inc.*

**Financial Statement Date:** *12/31/X5*

| | Performed by | |
|---|---|---|
| **Procedure** | **Initials** | **Date** |

**Cash Receipts**

| Procedure | Initials | Date |
|---|---|---|
| 12. Walk three cash receipts through cash receipts processes to confirm our understanding as documented. | *WL* | *11/14/X5* |
| 13. Observe and inquire about the segregation of duties for cash receipts. | *WL* | *11/15/X5* |
| 14. Observe the prelisting and endorsement of checks by the receptionist. | *MP* | *11/13/X5* |
| 15. Observe the accounts receivable clerk entering cash receipts to determine that: | | |
|     *a.* Password must be entered to enter cash receipts. | *MP* | *11/14/X5* |
|     *b.* Customer's name is shown on screen when customer number is entered. | *MP* | *11/14/X5* |
| 16. Test the procedures for reconciling control totals from the accounts receivable program as follows: | | |
|     *a.* Inquire about the procedures. | *WL* | *11/14/X5* |
|     *b.* Select a sample of printouts of the control totals and inspect them for evidence of reconciliation. Use the following parameters: | | |
|         (1) Risk of assessing control risk too low—10%. | | |
|         (2) Tolerable deviation rate—7%. | | |
|         (3) Expected deviation rate—1%. | *WL* | *11/14/X5* |
| 17. Test the procedures for review and follow up on the exception reports from the accounts receivable program as follows: | | |
|     *a.* Inquire about the procedures. | *WL* | *11/14/X5* |
|     *b.* Select a sample of exceptions reports and inspect them for evidence of follow-up on the exceptions. Use the following parameters: | | |
|         (1) Risk of assessing control risk too low—10%. | | |
|         (2) Tolerable deviation rate—10%. | | |
|         (3) Expected deviation rate—0%. | *WL* | *11/14/X5* |
| 18. Test the procedures for reconciling the computer summary of cash collections and cash sales to the deposit slips and prelisting of cash receipts as follows: | | |
|     *a.* Inquire about the procedures. | *WL* | *11/14/X5* |
|     *b.* Select a sample of the computer summaries and inspect them for evidence of reconciliation. Use the following parameters: | | |
|         (1) Risk of assessing control risk too low—10%. | | |
|         (2) Tolerable deviation rate—10%. | | |
|         (3) Expected deviation rate—1%. | *WL* | *11/14/X5* |
| 19. Inquire about the procedures for reconciliation of bank accounts. | *WL* | *11/14/X5* |
| 20. Inspect four bank reconciliations performed during the year. | *WL* | *11/14/X5* |

KEYSTONE COMPUTERS & NETWORKS, INC.

Attributes Sampling Summary—Revenue Cycle

*December 31, 19X5*

IC-15

*WL*

*11/14/X5*

**Objectives of test:** *(1) To test the operating effectiveness of the procedures for reconciling control totals of computer run for updating accounts receivable; (2) to test the operating effectiveness of the procedures for review and follow-up on the exception reports from the computer run for updating accounts receivable; (3) to test the operating effectiveness of the procedures for reconciling the computer summary of cash collections and cash sales to the deposit slips and prelisting of cash receipts.*

| Test | Population | Size |
|------|-----------|------|
| 1 | Control total reports | 234 |
| 2 | Exception reports | 234 |
| 3 | Computer summaries of collections and cash sales | 234 |

**Sampling unit:** *Individual reports*

**Random selection procedure:** *Random number table*

**Risk of assessing control risk too low:** *10 percent*

| | Planning Parameters | | | Sample Results | |
|---|---|---|---|---|---|
| **Attributes Tested:** | **Tolerable Deviation Rate** | **Expected Deviation Rate** | **Sample Size** | **Number of Deviations** | **Achieved Maximum Rate** |
| 1. Existence of a reconciliation of control totals initialed by the accounting manager. | 7% | 1% | 55 | 1 | 7% |
| 2. Indication of disposition of exceptions initialed by the accounting manager. | 10% | 0% | 22 | 0 | 10% |
| 3. Existence of a reconciliation of cash collections and cash sales to prelisting and deposit slips initialed by the accounting clerk. | 10% | 1% | 38 | 0 | 6.4% |

**Conclusion:** *The results support the assessment of control risk for completeness at a low level, and for existence, occurrence, cutoff, rights, valuation, and accuracy at a moderate level.*

KEYSTONE COMPUTERS & NETWORKS, INC.                                    **IC-20**
Assessment of Control Risk—Revenue Cycle                               *WL*
*12/31/X5*                                                             *11/13/X5*

| Controls | Existence or Occurrence | Completeness | Cutoff | Rights | Valuation and Accuracy | Presentation and Disclosure |
|---|:---:|:---:|:---:|:---:|:---:|:---:|
| **Sales** | | | | | | |
| 1. Separation of duties for authorization, credit approval, shipping, and accounting for sales transactions. | ☑ | ☑ | | ☑ | ☑ | |
| 2. Company uses an unmodified commercial software package. | ☑ | ☑ | | ☑ | ☑ | |
| 3. Credit lines are approved by the president. | | | | | ☑ | |
| 4. Service contracts and billings are reviewed by the controller. | ☑ | ☑ | ☑ | ☑ | ☑ | |
| 5. Computer verifies the clerk's password before sales data can be entered. | ☑ | | | ☑ | ☑ | |
| 6. Application controls (input validation checks) are applied to ensure the accuracy of the billing process. | | | | | ☑ | |
| 7. Computer assigns numbers to sales invoices. | | ☑ | ☑ | | | |
| 8. Computer verifies the work order manager's password before shipping data can be entered. | ☑ | | | ☑ | ☑ | |
| 9. Input validation checks are applied to shipping data as they are entered. | | | | | ☑ | |
| 10. Computer assigns numbers to delivery receipts. | | ☑ | ☑ | | | |
| 11. Accounts receivable clerk matches invoices with delivery receipts and accounts for numerical sequences. | | ☑ | ☑ | | | |
| 12. Accounting manager reconciles the accounts receivable master file to the general ledger monthly. | ☑ | ☑ | | ☑ | ☑ | |
| 13. Monthly statements are mailed to customers. | ☑ | ☑ | | ☑ | ☑ | |
| 14. Sales returns and allowances are approved by the vice president of sales. | | | | | ☑ | |
| 15. Separation of duties of custody of cash from records of cash receipts and accounts receivable. | ☑ | | | ☑ | ☑ | |

*(continued)*

KEYSTONE COMPUTERS & NETWORKS, INC.                                    IC-20
Assessment of Control Risk—Revenue Cycle                                WL
12/31/X5                                                              11/13/X5

(Concluded)

| Controls | Existence or Occurrence | Completeness | Cutoff | Rights | Valuation and Accuracy | Presentation and Disclosure |
|---|---|---|---|---|---|---|
| **Sales** | | | | | | |
| 16. Checks are prelisted and stamped with restrictive endorsement when received. | ☑ | | | ☑ | ☑ | |
| 17. Application controls (input validation checks) are applied to ensure the accuracy of the recording of cash receipts. | | | | | ☑ | |
| 18. Control totals are reconciled by the accounting manager. | ☑ | ☑ | | ☑ | ☑ | |
| 19. Exception reports are reviewed and followed up by the accounting manager. | | | | | ☑ | |
| 20. Computer summaries of cash collections and cash sales are reconciled to bank deposits and prelisting of cash receipts by accounting manager. | ☑ | ☑ | | ☑ | ☑ | |
| 21. Accounting manager reconciles bank account on a monthly basis. | ☑ | ☑ | | ☑ | ☑ | |
| **Internal Control Deficiencies** | | | | | | |
| 1. Sales invoices are prepared and mailed prior to delivery of goods. | X | | X | X | X | |
| 2. Accounts receivable are not written off on a regular basis. | | | | | X | |
| **Assessed Level of Control Risk** | *Moderate* | *Low* | *Moderate* | *Moderate* | *Moderate* | *Maximum* |

## Appendix 11A Problems

**LO 2, 5, 6**

*Required:*

11A–1.  A summary of the controls for the revenue and cash receipts cycle of Keystone Computers & Networks, Inc., appears on pages 477–490.

a.  For the following three controls over sales, indicate one type of error or fraud that the control serves to prevent or detect. Organize your solution as follows:

| Control | Error or Fraud Controlled |
|---|---|
| 1. Application controls are applied when customer orders are entered by the sales order clerk. | |
| 2. The computer assigns numbers to sales invoices when they are prepared. | |
| 3. Monthly statements are mailed to customers. | |

*b.* For the following three controls over cash receipts, indicate one type of error or fraud that the control serves to prevent or detect. Organize your solution as follows:

| Control | Error or Fraud Controlled |
|---|---|
| 1. Cash receipts are prelisted by the receptionist. | |
| 2. The accounting manager reconciles control totals generated by the accounts receivable computer program. | |
| 3. The computer summaries of cash collections and cash sales are reconciled to prelistings of cash receipts and cash deposits by the accounting manager. | |

**LO 4, 5, 6**   11A–2.   As indicated on the control risk assessment working paper on page 490, the auditors identified two weaknesses in internal control over the revenue cycle of KCN. Describe the implications of each of the two weaknesses in terms of the type of errors or fraud that could result.

**LO 1, 5, 6**   11A–3.   As indicated on the working paper on page 488, the auditors decided to apply audit sampling to three controls for the revenue and cash receipts cycle.

*Required:*

*a.* Describe the characteristic that a control must possess in order to be tested with audit sampling.

*b.* Assume that the auditors decided to use audit sampling to test the operating effectiveness of the procedures for matching sales invoices with delivery receipts. Determine the required sample size, using the following parameters.

- Risk of assessing control risk too low—5 percent
- Tolerable deviation rate—15 percent
- Expected deviation rate—1 percent

*c.* Prepare a working paper similar to the one on page 488 documenting the planned audit procedure described in part (*b*).

---

## Appendix 11B

# Illustrative Audit Case: Keystone Computers & Networks, Inc.

## Part III: Substantive Tests—Accounts Receivable and Revenue

This part of the audit case illustrates the manner in which the auditors design substantive tests of balances. The substantive tests are illustrated for two accounts—receivables and revenue. This aspect of the audit is illustrated with the following audit documentation:

- ABC's risk assessment working paper that combines the auditors' assessments of inherent and control risks into an overall risk of material misstatement for the assertions.
- The substantive audit program of accounts receivable and revenue.
- The audit sampling plan for the confirmation of accounts receivable.

Adams, Barnes & Co.'s assessment of control risk is described in Part II of the audit case on pages 477–490. To refresh your knowledge of the case, review that part as well as Part I on pages 237–244 of Chapter 6.

KEYSTONE COMPUTERS & NETWORKS, INC.
Relating Risks to Further Audit Procedures
12/31/X5

| Ref / Item No. | Description of Risk | Significant Risk? | Relevant Assertion(s) | Assessed Risks of Material Misstatement — Inherent | Control | Combined Risk of Material Misstatement | Summary of Audit Approach | Ref / Audit Program Step |
|---|---|---|---|---|---|---|---|---|
| **Revenue—Overall Risks** | | | | | | | | |
| | Gross Receivables and Gross Revenue | No | Existence/ Occurrence/ Rights | High | Moderate | Moderate | • Confirm receivables by PPS sample at 12/31/X5. | B-6, Steps 1–7 |
| | | No | Completeness | Moderate | Low | Moderate/Low | • Use generalized audit software to test client records. | B-6, Step 3 |
| | | No | Cutoff | Moderate | Moderate | Moderate | • Perform extensive cutoff of sales. | B-6, Step 12 |
| | | No | Accuracy | Moderate | Moderate | Moderate | • Perform substantive analytical procedures. | B-6, Step 14 |
| **Revenue—Specifically Identified Risks** | | | | | | | | |
| 1 | **Inherent Risk Considerations** Audited financial statements are required by Western Financial Services as a part of the company's line of credit agreement. | No | Existence/ Occurrence | Moderate | Moderate | Moderate | During the brainstorming session, staff members were informed of the need to increase their professional skepticism regarding any matters that would increase the amount of net income. | |
| 2 | **Inherent Risk Considerations** KCN has engaged in a strategy to sell to customers with higher credit risk. | Yes | Valuation | High | Moderate | High | In Process | |
| 3 | **Inherent Risk Considerations** The officers of the company receive significant bonuses based on quarterly results. | Yes | Existence/ Occurrence | High | Moderate | Moderate/High | In Process | |

| Audit Program—Substantive Tests—Accounts Receivable and Revenues |
|---|

**Client:** *Keystone Computers & Networks, Inc.*

**Financial Statement Date:** *12/31/X5*

| Procedure | Performed by | |
|---|---|---|
| | Initials | Date |
| **Sales Transactions** | | |
| 1. Obtain an aged trial balance of accounts receivable as of 12/31/X5. | *MP* | *1/6/X6* |
| 2. Select a sample of customers' accounts at 12/31/X5 for positive confirmation using probability-proportional-to-size sampling based on the following parameters: | | |
|    *a.* Risk of incorrect acceptance of 5%. | | |
|    *b.* Tolerable misstatement of $150,000. | | |
|    *c.* Expected misstatement of $20,000. | *MP* | *1/7/X6* |
| 3. Use generalized audit software to: | | |
|    *a.* Foot the master file of accounts receivable at 12/31/X5. | *MP* | *2/12/X6* |
|    *b.* Test the client-prepared aging of accounts receivable. | *MP* | *1/7/X6* |
|    *c.* Select the specific accounts for confirmation. | *MP* | *1/7/X6* |
| 4. Mail accounts receivable confirmation requests. | *MP* | *1/8/X6* |
| 5. Send second requests for all unanswered confirmation requests. | *MP* | *1/25/X6* |
| 6. For confirmation requests to which no reply is received, perform the following alternative procedures: | | |
|    *a.* Test items subsequently paid to remittance advices which identify the specific invoices paid. If necessary, reconcile the amounts paid to sales invoices and delivery receipts. | *MP* | *2/16/X6* |
|    *b.* For items not paid, inspect the invoices and delivery receipts for the sales transactions making up the account balance. | *MP* | *2/16/X6* |
| 7. Resolve exceptions noted on confirmation requests. | *MP* | *2/16/X6* |
| 8. Review credit files for customers with accounts receivable above $150,000 at 12/31/X5. Investigate any indications of fictitious accounts. | *MP* | *2/16/X6* |
| 9. Summarize the results of the confirmation procedures. | *MP* | *2/16/X6* |

*(continued)*

<table>
<tr><td colspan="3">

**Audit Program—Substantive Tests—Accounts Receivable and Revenues**

B-6
*WL*
*11/13/X5*

*(Concluded)*

</td></tr>
</table>

**Client:** *Keystone Computers & Networks, Inc.*

**Financial Statement Date:** *12/31/X5*

| Procedure | Performed by Initials | Date |
|---|---|---|
| 10. Review the adequacy of the allowance for uncollectible accounts by performing the following procedures: | | |
|    a. Review the aged trial balance of accounts receivable with the president. | *WL* | *2/13/X6* |
|    b. Review confirmation exceptions for indications of disputed amounts. | *WL* | *2/13/X6* |
|    c. Analyze and review trends in the following relationships: | | |
|      (1) Accounts receivable to net sales. | *WL* | *2/15/X6* |
|      (2) Allowance for bad debts to accounts receivable. | *WL* | *2/15/X6* |
|      (3) Bad debt expense to net sales. | *WL* | *2/15/X6* |
| 11. At year-end, review the file of sales invoices that are waiting to be matched with delivery receipts for any sales transactions that were not executed and, therefore, should be recorded in the subsequent period. | *MP* | *12/31/X5* |
| 12. For all sales recorded in the last week of the year, inspect the related delivery receipt to determine that the sale occurred before 12/31/X5. | *MP* | *2/12/X6* |
| 13. Review credit memoranda for sales returns and allowances through the last day of fieldwork to determine if an adjustment is needed to record the items as of year-end. | *MP* | *2/16/X6* |
| 14. Perform analytical procedures for sales and accounts receivable including comparison of the following to prior years and/or industry data: | *WL* | *2/12/X6* |
|    a. Gross profit percentage by month. | *WL* | *2/12/X6* |
|    b. Sales by month by salesperson. | *WL* | *2/16/X6* |
|    c. Accounts receivable turnover. | *WL* | *2/16/X6* |
|    d. Advertising expense as a percentage of sales. | *WL* | *2/16/X6* |
|    e. Net receivables as a percentage of total current assets. | *WL* | *2/16/X6* |
| 15. Ascertain whether any accounts have been assigned, pledged, or discounted by review of agreements and confirmation with banks. | *WL* | *2/13/X6* |
| 16. Ascertain by inquiry whether any accounts are owed by employees or related parties such as officers, directors, or shareholders, and: | | |
|    a. Obtain an understanding of the business purpose for the transactions that resulted in the balances. | *WL* | *2/16/X6* |
|    b. Ascertain the amounts involved. | *WL* | *2/16/X6* |
|    c. Confirm the balances. | *WL* | *1/25/X6* |

KEYSTONE COMPUTERS & NETWORKS, INC.
Audit Sample Plan for Confirmation of Accounts Receivable
12/31/X5

**Objective:** *Establish the existence and gross valuation of accounts receivable and occurrence and accuracy of sales by confirmation.*

**Population:** *The trial balance of 933 accounts receivable at 12/31/X5, with a total book value of $10,235,457.*

**Definition of Misstatement:** *Any amount that is determined not to be a valid account receivable.*

**Sampling Technique:** *Probability-proportional-to-size.*

**Sampling Parameters:**

1. **Tolerable misstatement:**

   | | |
   |---|---:|
   | *Total materiality as indicated in the audit plan* | $300,000 |
   | *Less: Estimate of undetected misstatement (50% of overall materiality)* | 150,000 |
   | *Tolerable misstatement for this test* | $150,000 |

2. **Risk of incorrect acceptance:**

   *Because we have assessed the risk of material misstatement as high, the risk of incorrect acceptance will be set at 5 percent.*

3. **Expected misstatement:**

   *Based on prior-year audits, the expected misstatement for the account is $20,000.*

**Calculation of Sample Size and Sampling Interval:**

$$\text{Sample size} = \frac{\text{Book value of population} \times \text{Reliability factor}}{\text{Tolerable misstatement} - (\text{Expected misstatement} \times \text{Expansion factor})}$$

$$= \frac{\$10,235,457 \times 3.00}{\$150,000 - (\$20,000 \times 1.6)}$$

$$= 260$$

$$\text{Sampling interval} = \frac{\text{Book value of population}}{\text{Sample size}} = \frac{\$10,235,457}{260} = \$39,400 \text{ (rounded)}$$

*Actual sample size was only 142 because a number of accounts were more than twice the sampling interval.*

*WLD*
1/9/X6

## KEYSTONE COMPUTERS & NETWORKS, INC.
### Monthly Sales Report
### For the Three Years Ended 12/31/X5

| | Sales of Computers | | | Consulting Revenue | | | Service Revenue | | |
|---|---|---|---|---|---|---|---|---|---|
| | 20X3 | 20X4 | 20X5 | 20X3 | 20X4 | 20X5 | 20X3 | 20X4 | 20X5 |
| January | 3,348,340 | 3,479,482 | 3,268,584 | 3,626,893 | 3,521,682 | 3,180,808 | 342,440 | 341,981 | 307,519 |
| February | 3,365,453 | 3,692,918 | 3,593,775 | 4,145,019 | 3,519,281 | 3,328,754 | 369,309 | 390,835 | 348,522 |
| March | 3,667,774 | 3,782,262 | 3,781,385 | 3,857,171 | 3,849,059 | 3,772,588 | 369,310 | 366,410 | 378,522 |
| April | 3,741,928 | 3,638,318 | 3,176,864 | 3,799,601 | 3,802,120 | 3,402,726 | 372,440 | 390,835 | 359,525 |
| May | 3,810,378 | 3,628,391 | 3,360,305 | 3,914,740 | 3,708,240 | 3,513,685 | 376,180 | 366,408 | 348,522 |
| June | 3,747,632 | 3,797,153 | 3,727,187 | 3,799,601 | 3,942,939 | 4,105,463 | 399,610 | 415,263 | 389,174 |
| July | 3,884,532 | 3,484,446 | 3,318,613 | 4,202,589 | 3,708,240 | 3,550,671 | 396,180 | 390,835 | 348,874 |
| August | 3,873,124 | 3,742,554 | 3,568,760 | 3,972,310 | 4,083,758 | 3,772,588 | 368,810 | 366,408 | 348,522 |
| September | 3,850,307 | 3,980,806 | 3,885,613 | 3,914,740 | 3,942,939 | 4,290,394 | 389,510 | 390,535 | 409,525 |
| October | 3,998,615 | 3,792,190 | 3,160,187 | 4,317,728 | 4,083,758 | 3,883,546 | 421,750 | 391,335 | 369,274 |
| November | 4,186,852 | 3,841,826 | 3,539,576 | 4,202,589 | 4,271,517 | 4,179,435 | 385,780 | 390,635 | 348,874 |
| December | 4,203,965 | 4,030,442 | 3,964,826 | 4,145,019 | 4,318,457 | 4,697,241 | 376,580 | 366,408 | 368,924 |
| Total | 45,678,900 | 44,890,788 | 42,345,675 | 47,898,000 | 46,751,990 | 45,677,899 | 4,567,899 | 4,567,888 | 4,325,777 |

Note: Amounts were generated by ACL program from Keystone's general ledger.

## Appendix 11B Problems

**11B–1.** In Part III (Appendix 11B) of the audit case, the audit staff of Adams, Barnes & Co. identified specific revenue risks on working paper RA-12 (page 492). However, the "Summary of Audit Approach" section is incomplete (in process) for risks 2 and 3.

*Required:*
Review the audit program (working paper B-6) on pages 493–494 and identify the substantive audit procedures that were designed specifically to address these risks of material misstatement.

**LO 4, 6**  **11B–2.** Assume that you have been assigned to the audit of Keystone after audit planning has occurred. Review the planning information on pages 237–244 and the audit program for the accounts receivable and revenue (B-6 on pages 493–494). The manager on the engagement has given you the task of reviewing the monthly revenue report on page 496 (B-11).

a. Based on your review of the report, describe any unusual relationships that might indicate a risk of misstatement of revenues based on your knowledge of the company derived from a review of the information on pages 237–244.

b. Identify any procedures on the audit program for receivables and revenue that might address the risk(s) identified in (a).

c. Design two other procedures that would address the risk(s) identified in (a).

**11B–3.** Keystone Computers & Networks, Inc. (KCN), has 933 accounts receivable, with a total book value of $10,235,457. From that population, Adams, Barnes & Co. (ABC), CPAs, selected a sample of 260 accounts (142 unique accounts) for confirmation for the year ended December 31, 20X5, as illustrated by the working paper on page 495. First and second confirmation requests resulted in replies for all but 10 of those accounts. ABC performed alternative procedures on those 10 accounts and noted no exceptions. Of the replies, 5 had exceptions as described below (with ABC follow-up):

1. "The balance of $120,000 is incorrect because we paid that amount in full on December 31, 20X5." *Follow-up: An analysis of the cash receipts journal revealed that the check had been received in the mail on January 9, 20X6.*

2. "Of the balance of $30,000, $330 is incorrect because on December 19 we returned a printer to Keystone when we found that we didn't need it. We ordered it in the middle of November when we had anticipated a need for it. When we received the printer, we realized it was unnecessary and returned it unopened." *Follow-up: An analysis of the transaction revealed that it was received by Keystone on December 31, 20X5, and that the adjustment to the account had been processed on January 2, 20X6.*

3. "The balance of $214,000 is correct, and we paid it on January 5, 19X6." *Follow-up: An analysis of the cash receipts journal revealed that the check had been received on January 10, 20X6.*

4. "Of the balance of $130,000, $10,000 is incorrect because it represents goods that we didn't receive until January 5, 20X6." *Follow-up: Inspection of shipping records reveals that the item was shipped on January 3, 20X6.*

5. "Of the account's $18,000 balance, we paid $17,460 and the $540 (3 percent of the total) remains unpaid because the Keystone salesperson told us that she would be able to obtain a 'special' discount beyond the normal." *Follow-up: While inspection of the sales agreement indicated no such discount arrangement, discussions with Loren Steele (controller) and Sam Best (president) indicated that the salesperson had inappropriately granted such a discount to the client. On January 15 of 20X6, they processed the discount and credited the account for $540.*

*Required:*
a. For each of the five exceptions, determine the account's proper "audited value."

b. Use the probability-proportional-to-size method with your analysis from part (a) to evaluate your sample's results. The risk of incorrect acceptance is 5 percent.

# 12

# Inventories and Cost of Goods Sold

**LO1**

Describe the nature of inventories and cost of goods sold.

The interrelationship of inventories and cost of goods sold makes it logical for the two topics to be considered together. The controls that assure the fair valuation of inventories are found in the purchases (or acquisition) cycle. These controls include procedures for selecting vendors, ordering merchandise or materials, inspecting goods received, recording the liability to the vendor, and authorizing and making cash disbursements. In a manufacturing business, the valuation of inventories also is affected by the production (or conversion) cycle, in which various manufacturing costs are assigned to inventories, and the cost of inventories is then transferred to the cost of goods sold.

The selection of an accounting method and the consistency of its application also affect the valuation of both inventories and cost of goods sold. During periods of inflation, limitations of historical cost affect the relevance of cost of goods sold as much as they affect inventories. Thus, it is not surprising that the Financial Accounting Standards Board (FASB) experimented with requiring supplemental disclosure of current replacement cost of inventories.[1] Although companies are no longer required to disclose this information, many companies include a discussion of the effects of inflation in "Management's Discussion and Analysis of Financial Condition," which is a required section of a company's annual Form 10-K filed with the SEC.

## Inventories and Cost of Goods Sold

### Sources and Nature of Inventories and Cost of Goods Sold

The term *inventories* is used in this chapter to include (1) goods on hand ready for sale, whether the merchandise of a trading concern or the finished goods of a manufacturer; (2) goods in the process of production; and (3) goods to be consumed directly or indirectly in production, such as raw materials, purchased parts, and supplies.

### The Auditors' Objectives in Auditing Inventories and Cost of Goods Sold

**LO2**

Describe the auditors' objectives in the audit of inventories and cost of goods sold.

The auditors' *objectives* in the audit of inventories and cost of goods sold are to:

1. Use the understanding of the client and its environment to consider *inherent risks,* including fraud risks, related to inventories and cost of goods sold.
2. Obtain an understanding of *internal control* over inventories and cost of goods sold.
3. Assess the risks of material misstatement and design tests of controls and substantive procedures that:
   a. Substantiate the *existence* of inventories and the *occurrence* of transactions affecting cost of goods sold.
   b. Establish the *completeness* of recorded inventories.

---

[1] The requirement for mandatory disclosure of current cost information was rescinded by *FASB Statement No. 89,* "Financial Reporting and Changing Prices."

    *c.* Verify the *cutoff* of transactions affecting cost of goods sold.

    *d.* Determine that the client has *rights* to the recorded inventories.

    *e.* Establish the proper *valuation* of inventories and the *accuracy* of transactions affecting cost of goods sold.

    *f.* Determine that the *presentation* and *disclosure* of information about inventories and cost of goods sold are appropriate, including disclosure of the classification of inventories, accounting methods used, and inventories pledged as collateral for debt.

In conjunction with the audit of inventories and cost of goods sold, the auditors will also obtain evidence about the related purchases, sales, purchase returns, and sales returns accounts.

The responsibilities of independent auditors with respect to the validity of inventories can best be understood by considering the spectacular *McKesson & Robbins* fraud case. The hearings conducted by the SEC in 1939 disclosed that the audited financial statements of McKesson & Robbins, Inc., a drug company listed on the New York Stock Exchange, contained $19 million of fictitious assets, about one-fourth of the total assets shown on the balance sheet. The fictitious assets included $10 million of nonexistent inventories. How was it possible for the independent auditors to have conducted an audit and to have issued an unqualified report without discovering this gigantic fraud? The audit program followed for inventories in this case was in accordance with customary auditing practices of the 1930s. The significant point is that in that period it was customary to limit the audit work on inventories to an examination of records only; the standards of that era did not require any **observation,** physical count, or other actual contact with the inventories.

Up to the time of the *McKesson & Robbins* case, auditors had avoided taking responsibility for verifying the accuracy of inventory quantities and the physical existence of the goods. With questionable logic, many auditors had argued that they were experts in handling figures and analyzing accounting records but were not qualified to identify and measure the great variety of raw materials and manufactured goods found in the factories, warehouses, and store buildings of their clients.

The *McKesson & Robbins* case brought a quick end to such limited views of the auditors' responsibilities. In 1939, Statements on Auditing Procedures 1 and 2, the first formal auditing standards issued by the AICPA, affirmed the importance of the auditors' observation of physical inventories, but authorized the substitution of other auditing procedures under certain circumstances. Auditing standards continue to distinguish between companies that determine inventory quantities solely by an annual physical count (**periodic inventory system**) and companies with a well-kept **perpetual inventory system.** The latter companies often have strong internal control over inventories and may employ sampling techniques to verify the records by occasional test counts throughout the year rather than by a complete annual count of the entire inventory. For those clients, the auditors' observation of physical inventory may be limited to such counts as they consider appropriate, and these counts may occur during or after the end of the period being audited.

The auditors' approach to the verification of inventories and cost of goods sold should be one of awareness of the possibility of fraud, as well as of the prevalence of accidental error in the determination of inventory quantities and amounts. Fraudulent misstatement of inventories has often been employed to evade income taxes, to conceal shortages arising from various illegal schemes, and to mislead stockholders or other inactive owners as to a company's profits and financial position.

## Internal Control over Inventories and Cost of Goods Sold

The importance of adequate internal control over inventories and cost of goods sold from the viewpoint of both management and the auditors can scarcely be overemphasized. In some companies, management stresses controls over cash and securities but pays little attention to control over inventories. Since many types of inventories are composed of items not particularly susceptible to theft, management may consider controls to be unnecessary in this area. Such thinking ignores the fact that controls for inventories affect nearly all the functions involved in producing and disposing of the company's products.

## Illustrative Case · *Bid Rigging at Sheraton*

The need for proper control over the purchasing function is dramatically illustrated by a case in which two buyers for the Sheraton hotels allegedly rigged the bidding for produce products by providing one supplier with competitive bid information. With this information, the supplier obtained a number of contracts by placing the lowest bid. In exchange, the buyers allegedly received hundreds of thousands of dollars in kickback payments, received monthly from the supplier in the form of cash slid under the door of the buyers' offices.

The "off the books" nature of kickbacks makes them particularly difficult for auditors to detect. In this case, the two buyers were arrested as a part of a federal investigation of corruption at city produce markets. Factors that might indicate the existence of kickbacks include:

- A purchasing employee who appears to be living beyond his or her means.
- An improper or questionable basis for selecting suppliers.
- Selection of a supplier with high prices, or prices that have increased significantly since the supplier was first selected.
- Purchasing records that indicate that one company consistently "wins contracts" as the lowest bidder, often by a relatively small amount.
- Continued purchases from a supplier providing products of questionable quality.
- Tips from other employees.

## Control Environment

As described in Chapter 7, the control environment reflects the overall attitude, awareness, and actions of management and the board of directors concerning the importance of control and the way it is used in the entity. The aspects of the control environment that are particularly relevant to the auditors' consideration of the inventories and cost of goods sold include:

1. **Commitment to competence and human resource policies and practices.** These policies and practices help ensure that appropriately qualified and trained personnel are assigned the responsibilities for purchasing goods and services and receiving and storing the goods. A *commitment to competence* with respect to plant personnel is important to ensuring that the manufacturing process is efficient and effective and that prescribed control activities are being performed.

2. **Integrity and ethical values.** Purchasing and cash disbursement activities provide ample opportunity for fraud by employees, as well as by management. Communication of management's integrity and ethical values helps ensure that disbursements are for authorized and legitimate goods that were actually received and that the accounting for the purchases is appropriate. The importance of competence and integrity may be illustrated by considering the company's purchasing agents who negotiate the terms of purchases with the company's various suppliers. If these individuals are incompetent, they may commit the company to large purchases at unfavorable terms. If purchasing agents accept "kickbacks," the company not only will lose the amounts accepted, but may make purchases of substandard goods or pay excessive prices.

3. **Organizational structure and assignment of authority and responsibility.** Internal control is improved when the client's organizational structure is appropriate and when levels of authority and responsibility for purchasing and production activities are clearly communicated. It is especially important for personnel involved in purchasing, receiving, and production to understand their responsibilities for the application of controls.

## Risk Assessment

The risk of material misstatement of the financial statements is reduced when management evaluates and manages the risks related to purchasing and producing goods and services. Aspects of concern to the auditors include management's assessment of risks related to (1) the availability of a supply of goods, services, and skilled labor; (2) the stability of prices and labor rates; (3) the generation of sufficient cash flow to pay for purchases; (4) changes in technology that affect manufacturing processes; and (5) the obsolescence of inventory.

## Monitoring

Relevant monitoring controls for the purchases cycle include management review of reports of purchases from suppliers, inventory on hand, and accounts payable balances. Management also may establish a process of obtaining feedback from suppliers, including complaints about delays in payments. Monitoring controls for the production cycle include observations by production supervisors of the performance of various activities and functions and quality and performance reviews. Management should also have a formal process for considering recommendations by the internal auditors for improvements in the purchasing and production functions and the related control activities.

## Purchases and Production Cycles— Accounting Systems and Control Activities

**LO3**

Describe the documents, records, and accounts that are involved in the purchases and production (conversion) cycles and the fundamental controls over inventories, purchasing, and production.

Purchasing, receiving, storing, issuing, processing, and shipping are the physical functions directly connected with inventories; the cost accounting system and the perpetual inventory records compose the recording functions. Since the auditors are interested in the final products of the recording functions, it is necessary for them to understand and evaluate the cost accounting system and the perpetual inventory records, as well as the various control activities and original documents underlying the preparation of financial data.

### The Purchasing Function

Strong internal control over purchases ordinarily involves an organizational structure that delegates to a separate department of the company exclusive authority to make all purchases of materials and services. The purchasing, receiving, and recording functions should be clearly separated and lodged in separate departments. In small companies, this type of departmentalized operation may not be possible, but even in very small enterprises, it is usually feasible to make one properly supervised person responsible for all purchase transactions.

A purchase transaction begins with the issuance of a properly approved *purchase requisition* (bottom left) by the stores department or another department needing the goods or services. A copy of the requisition is sent to the purchasing department to provide a basis for preparing the serially numbered *purchase order* (bottom right). The requisition should include a precise description of the type and quantity of the goods or services desired.

| 67467500 |
| --- |
| **Perfect Manufacturing Co.** |
| Purchase Requisition |

| **Department:** | Date: <u>May 10, 20X1</u> |
| --- | --- |
| <u>Raw Materials Stores</u> | Date Required: <br> <u>June 5, 20X1</u> |

| Quantity | Description |
| --- | --- |
| 9,000 sheets | 2×8, 1/2″ steel sheets <br> #278473 |

| Approved By: <br> *Casey Rowe* |
| --- |

| AA09847 |
| --- |
| **PURCHASE ORDER** <br> Perfect Manufacturing Co. <br> 1212 Belaire Blvd. <br> Houston, TX  77062 |

To: <u>Carson Steel Co.</u>          Date: <u>May 12, 20X1</u>
<u>1671 21st St.</u>
<u>Houston, TX 77021</u>     Ship via: <u>SOS Delivery</u>

Terms: <u>2/10, n/30</u>

Enter our order for:

| Qty. | Description | Price | Total |
| --- | --- | --- | --- |
| 9,000 sheets | 2×8, 1/2″ steel <br> #278473 | $21.00 | $189,000 |

Perfect Manufacturing Co.
By: *Linda Jones*

| | 5874983 |
|---|---|
| **Perfect Manufacturing Co.**<br>Receiving Report | |

| **Received From:** | |
|---|---|
| Carson Steel Co.<br>1671 21st St.<br>Houston, TX  77021 | Date: <u>June 5, 20X1</u><br><br>Order No: <u>AA09847</u><br>Carrier: <u>SOS Delivery</u> |

| Quantity | Description |
|---|---|
| 9,000 sheets | 2×8, 1/2" steel #278473 |

| | Received By:<br><u>Don Warren</u> |
|---|---|

| | 4503945 |
|---|---|
| **Perfect Manufacturing Co.**<br>Materials Requisition | |
| | Production Order: 8576409 |

| **Department:** | |
|---|---|
| Milling #23 | Date: <u>June 10, 20X1</u><br><br>Date Required:<br><u>June 10, 20X1</u> |

| Quantity | Description | Unit Cost | Total Cost |
|---|---|---|---|
| 350 sheets | 2×8, 1/2" steel | $32.40 | $11,340.00 |

| | Approved By:<br><u>John West</u> |
|---|---|

Copies of the purchase order should be forwarded to the accounting and receiving departments. The copy sent to receiving should have the quantities blacked out to increase the likelihood that receiving personnel will make independent counts of the merchandise received. Even though the buyer may actually place an order by telephone, the formal purchase order should be prepared and forwarded. In many large organizations, purchase orders are issued only after compliance with extensive procedures for (1) determining the need for the item, (2) obtaining competitive bids, and (3) obtaining approval of the financial aspect of the commitment.

### The Receiving Function

All goods received by the company—without exception—should be cleared through a receiving department that is independent of the purchasing, storing, and shipping departments. The receiving department is responsible for (1) the determination of quantities of goods received, (2) the detection of damaged or defective merchandise, (3) the preparation of a *receiving report* (top left), and (4) the prompt transmittal of goods received to the stores department.

### The Storing Function

As goods are delivered to stores, they are counted, inspected, and receipted for. The stores department then notifies the accounting department of the amount received and placed in stock. In performing these functions, the stores department makes an important contribution to overall control of inventories. By signing for the goods, it fixes its own responsibility, and by notifying the accounting department of actual goods stored, it provides verification of the receiving department's work.

### The Issuing Function

The stores department, being responsible for all goods under its control, has reason to insist that a prenumbered requisition (top right) be issued for all items passing out of its hands to serve as a signed receipt from the department accepting the goods. Requisitions are usually prepared in triplicate. The department making the request retains one copy; another serves as the stores department's receipt; and the third is a notice to the accounting department for cost distribution. To prevent the indiscriminate writing of requisitions for questionable purposes, some organizations establish policies requiring that requisitions be drawn only upon the authority of a bill of materials, an engineering order, or a sales order. In wholesale and retail concerns, shipping orders, rather than factory requisitions, serve to authorize withdrawals from stores.

*The Production (Conversion) Function*

Overall production should be controlled with a **master production schedule** that presents the gross production needs for a particular period. Because the schedule is developed based on forecasts of demand for the company's products, it helps to ensure that the company will meet its customers' needs, while not overstocking particular products. The master production schedule also ensures that materials and labor are available, on a timely basis, to meet the production demands for the period. Once the required resources are determined to be available, **production orders** are prepared to authorize the production of specific products.

Responsibility for the goods in production must be fixed, usually on factory supervisors or superintendents. *Materials requisitions* and *move tickets* document the flow of the goods and related responsibility as they progress through the production process. Thus, from the time materials are delivered to the factory until they are completed and routed to a finished goods storeroom, a designated supervisor should be in control and be prepared to answer for their location and disposition.

**Job time tickets** (bottom left) are prepared to document the labor or machine hours devoted to a particular production job. Each job time ticket should be reviewed and approved by the department supervisor before it is entered into the cost accounting system.

The controls for goods in production usually include regular inspection procedures to reveal defective work. This aids in disclosing inefficiencies in the productive system and also tends to prevent inflation of the goods in process inventory by the accumulation of cost of goods that will eventually be scrapped. If scrapped materials have substantial salvage value, the materials should be segregated, controlled, and inventoried.

*The Shipping Function*

Shipments of goods should be made only after proper authorization has been received. This authorization will normally be a sales order approved by the credit department, although the shipping function also includes the returning of defective goods to suppliers. In this latter case, the authorization may take the form of a shipping authorization from a purchasing department executive.

---

**Perfect Manufacturing Co.**
Job Time Ticket
Production Order: 8576409

Date: 06/18/X1
Dept. No. 23
Dept. Milling

| Employee | | Hourly Rate | Operation |
|---|---|---|---|
| No. 2954 | Name Larry Cobb | $22.50 | Cut to shape |

| Start Time 6:00 A.M. | End Time 11:30 A.M. | Total Hours 5.5 | Total Labor Dollars $123.75 |
|---|---|---|---|

Quantity Completed:

350 Valve Bases

Approved By:
*Chee Chow*

---

54654566

SHIPPING DOCUMENT
Perfect Manufacturing Co.
1212 Belaire Blvd.
Houston, TX 77062

Consigned to:
Flour Valve Co.
5485 First St.
Kansas City, MO 66220

Date: Oct. 21, 20X1

Order No. 6779938

Shipper: Union Pacific

| Quantity | Description | Weight |
|---|---|---|
| 150 | 9' Outflow valves #2988388 | 7845 |
| Packed by: *Leon Jones* | | Received by: *John Carr* |

The shipping department will prepare, or the computer system will generate, a pre-numbered *shipping document* (previous page bottom right) indicating the goods shipped. One copy of the shipping document should be retained by the shipping department as evidence of shipment; a second copy should be sent to the billing department where it will be used—with the customer's purchase order and the sales order—as the basis for invoicing the customer; and a third copy should be enclosed as a packing slip with the goods when they are shipped. The control aspect of this procedure is strengthened by the fact that an outsider, the customer, will generally inspect the packing slip and notify the company of any discrepancy between this list, the goods ordered, and the goods actually received.

When the goods are shipped using a common carrier, a fourth copy of the shipping document, required in this case to be a **bill of lading,** is provided to the carrier. In addition, the copy forwarded to billing will include additional evidence of shipment in the form of trucking bills, carriers' receipts, or freight bills. Subsequent audit of the transactions is facilitated by grouping together the documents showing that shipments were properly authorized and carried out.

Established shipping routines should be followed for all types of shipments, including the sale of scrap, return of defective goods, and forwarding of materials and parts to subcontractors.

### The Cost Accounting System

An adequate cost accounting system is necessary to account for the usage of raw materials and supplies, to determine the content and value of goods in process inventories, and to compute the finished goods inventory. This system comprises all the records, orders, and requisitions needed for proper accounting for the disposition of materials as they enter the flow of production and as they continue through the factory in the process of becoming finished goods. The cost accounting system also serves to accumulate labor costs and indirect costs that contribute to the goods in process and the finished goods inventories. The cost accounting system thus forms an integral part of the internal control over inventories.

The figures produced by the cost accounting system should be controlled by general ledger accounts. The costs of direct materials and labor are recorded in individual goods (work) in process accounts for each job order or process. Periodically, manufacturing overhead is applied to the jobs or processes and recorded in the accounts.

Underlying this upper level of control between the factory records and the general ledger is a system of production orders, material requisitions, job tickets or other labor distributions, and factory overhead distributions. Control is affected by various procedures that verify the accuracy of production records. Allocations of direct materials and labor costs are recomputed and reconciled to material and payroll records. Manufacturing overhead costs that are applied using predetermined rates are adjusted to actual costs at the end of the period.

Many companies have established standard cost systems that help identify the causes of ineffectiveness and waste through a study of variances between actual and standard costs. These systems provide for the prompt pricing of inventories and for control over operations. All the various types of cost accounting systems are alike in that they are designed to contribute to effective internal control by tracing the execution of managerial directives in the factory, providing reliable inventory figures and safeguarding company assets.

### The Perpetual Inventory System

Perpetual inventory records constitute an extremely important part of internal control. These records, by showing at all times the quantity of goods on hand, provide information essential to intelligent purchasing, sales, and production-planning policies. With such a record it is possible to guide procurement by establishing points of minimum and maximum quantities for each standard item stocked.

The use of a perpetual inventory system allows companies to control the high costs of holding excessive inventory, while minimizing the risk of running out of stock. The company can control inventories through reorder points and economic order quantities, including *just-in-time* ordering systems in which inventory levels are kept to a minimum.

If perpetual inventory records are to produce the control implicit in their nature, it is desirable that the subsidiary records be maintained in both quantities and dollars for all stock, that the subsidiary records be controlled by the general ledger, and that trial balances be prepared at reasonable intervals. In addition, both the detailed records and the general ledger control accounts should be adjusted to agree with physical counts whenever they are taken.

Perpetual inventory records discourage inventory theft and waste, since storekeepers and other employees are aware of the accountability over goods established by this continuous record of goods received, issued, and on hand. The records, however, must be periodically verified through the physical counting of goods.

### IT Systems

An IT-based inventory system makes it much easier for the client to maintain control over inventories, purchasing, and the manufacturing process. The IT system can automatically generate purchase requisitions and orders when inventory levels reach predetermined reorder points. The client's purchasing system may even be linked to the system of its suppliers, allowing **electronic data interchange (EDI)** to completely coordinate production and purchasing. The IT system also maintains records of responsibility for goods as they are routed through the production process. Details of direct labor and materials usage are entered, and the computer allocates these direct costs to jobs or processes, applies manufacturing overhead costs based on predetermined rates, and maintains perpetual records of the costs of goods in process, finished, and sold. The system also generates various financial reports, including *responsibility accounting reports* that indicate actual costs, standard costs, and the related variances.

Good internal control in IT systems requires the normal segregation of the purchasing, receiving, storing, processing, and shipping functions. In addition, the client should establish appropriate IT controls that promote the accuracy of data as they are entered into the system and ensure that data maintain their integrity after they are entered.

**Audit Documentation for Inventories and Cost of Goods Sold**

The auditors may prepare a great variety of working papers in their verification of inventories and cost of goods sold. These papers will range in form from written comments on the manner in which the physical inventory was taken to elaborate analyses of production costs of finished goods and goods in process. Selected working papers will be illustrated in connection with the audit procedures to be described in later sections of this chapter.

## Audit of Inventories and Cost of Goods Sold

The following steps indicate the general pattern of work performed by the auditors in the verification of inventories and costs of goods sold. Selection of the most appropriate procedures for a particular audit will be guided by the nature of the internal controls that have been implemented and by the results of the auditors' risk assessments.

A. Use the understanding of the client and its environment to consider inherent risks, including fraud risks, related to inventories and cost of goods sold.

B. Obtain an understanding of internal control over inventories and cost of goods sold.

C. Assess the risks of material misstatement and design further audit procedures.

D. Perform further audit procedures—tests of controls.
   1. Examples of tests of controls:
      a. Examine significant aspects of a sample of purchase transactions.
      b. Perform tests of the cost accounting system.

FIGURE 12.1
**Objectives of Major Substantive Procedures for Inventories and Cost of Goods Sold**

| Substantive Procedures | Primary Audit Objectives |
|---|---|
| Obtain listings of inventory and reconcile to ledgers. | *Existence, occurrence,* and *rights* |
| Evaluate the client's planning of physical inventory. Observe the taking of the physical inventory. Review the year-end cutoff of purchase and sales transactions. Obtain a copy of the completed physical inventory and test its accuracy. | *Existence, occurrence,* and *rights* *Completeness* *Valuation* *Cutoff* |
| Evaluate the bases and methods of inventory pricing. | *Valuation* |
| Test the pricing of inventories. | *Valuation* *Accuracy* |
| Perform analytical procedures. | *Existence* and *rights* *Completeness* *Valuation* *Accuracy* |
| Determine whether any inventories have been pledged and review commitments. | *Valuation* *Presentation* and *disclosure* |
| Evaluate financial statement presentation and disclosure. | *Presentation* and *disclosure* |

2. If necessary, revise the risks of material misstatement based on the results of tests of controls.

E. Perform further audit procedures—substantive procedures for inventories and cost of goods sold.
   1. Obtain listings of inventory and reconcile to ledgers.
   2. Evaluate the client's planning of physical inventory.
   3. Observe the taking of physical inventory and make test counts.
   4. Review the year-end cutoff of purchases and sales transactions.
   5. Obtain a copy of the completed physical inventory, test its clerical accuracy, and trace test counts.
   6. Evaluate the bases and methods of inventory pricing.
   7. Test the pricing of inventories.
   8. Perform analytical procedures.
   9. Determine whether any inventories have been pledged and review purchase and sales commitments.
   10. Evaluate financial statement presentation of inventories and cost of goods sold, including the adequacy of disclosure.

Figure 12.1 relates the objectives of the major substantive procedures for inventories and cost of goods sold to the primary audit objectives.

LO4

Use the understanding of the client and its environment to consider inherent risks (including fraud risks) related to inventories, purchases, and cost of goods sold.

### A. Use the Understanding of the Client and Its Environment to Consider Inherent Risks, Including Fraud Risks.

Generally, inventories represent an asset with significant inherent risks. Some of these risks arise from business risks faced by management, such as the risk of losses due to poor product quality, obsolescence, or theft. Other factors that affect the risks of material misstatement of inventories include:

1. Inventories often constitute a large current asset of an enterprise and are very susceptible to major errors and fraud.

2. The accounting profession allows numerous alternative methods for valuation of inventories, and different methods may be used for various classes of inventories.

3. The determination of inventory value directly affects the cost of goods sold and has a major impact on net income for the year. Therefore, if management is inclined to engage in fraudulent financial reporting, the fraud will likely involve overstatement of inventory.

4. The determination of inventory quality, condition, and value is inherently a more complex and difficult task than is the case with most other elements of financial position. Many items, such as precious gems, sophisticated electronic parts, and construction in progress, present significant problems of identification and valuation.

If auditors identify a fraud risk with respect to inventories, they will make sure that they understand the programs and controls established by management to control the risk. They will also determine that the controls have been implemented. Finally, the auditors will design appropriate procedures to respond to that risk.

**LO5**

Obtain an understanding of internal control over inventories and cost of goods sold.

## B. Obtain an Understanding of Internal Control over Inventories and Cost of Goods Sold.

As previously indicated, the consideration of controls may involve the filling out of a questionnaire, the writing of descriptive memoranda, or the preparation of flowcharts depicting the organizational structure and the flow of materials and documents. In obtaining an understanding of internal control over inventory, the auditors should become thoroughly familiar with the procedures for purchasing, receiving, storing, and issuing goods and for controlling production, and they should obtain an understanding of the cost accounting system and the perpetual inventory records.

The auditors should also give consideration to the physical protection of inventories. Any deficiencies in storage facilities, in guard service, or in physical handling that may lead to losses from weather, fire, flood, or theft may appropriately be called to the attention of management.

The matters to be investigated in the auditors' consideration of controls over inventory and cost of sales are fairly well indicated by the following questions: Are perpetual inventory records maintained for each class of inventory? Are perpetual inventory records verified by physical inventories at least once each year? Do the procedures for physical inventories include the use of prenumbered tags, with all tag numbers accounted for? Are differences between physical inventory counts and perpetual inventory records investigated before the perpetual records are adjusted? Is a separate purchasing department responsible for purchasing all materials, supplies, and equipment? Does a separate receiving department process all incoming shipments? Are materials and supplies held in the custody of a stores department and issued only upon receipt of properly approved requisitions?

After the auditors have prepared a flowchart (or other description) of internal control, they should determine that the client is using those procedures; that is, they should determine whether the controls have been *implemented*. This information may be obtained through inquiries of entity personnel, inspection of documents, and observation of activities, which are often performed in conjunction with a walk-through of the accounting cycle. As the auditors obtain their understanding of the controls, they will observe whether there is an appropriate segregation of duties and inquire as to who performed various functions throughout the year. They will also inspect various documents, such as purchase requisitions, purchase orders, material requisitions, move tickets, time tickets, and shipping advices, and review document files to determine that the client is appropriately accounting for the sequence of prenumbered documents. Inventory, production, and responsibility accounting reports will be examined, and the auditors will review the evidence of follow-up on variances from standard costs.

---

**Focus on the Agribusiness Industry**

Accounting for the inventory of an agricultural producer provides a good example of the need for industry expertise when obtaining an understanding of a client's internal control over inventory. Auditors of agricultural producers that are involved in raising animals must pay special attention to the effectiveness of the agricultural producer's internal control, including whether:

- The controls provide accurate quantity and cost data for the raised animals.
- The payroll records are sophisticated enough to allow labor cost to be allocated to the appropriate animal component of inventory.
- Direct and indirect costs of developing animals raised for a productive function are accurately accumulated until the animals reach maturity, at which point the costs are depreciated over the animals' estimated productive life.
- Direct and indirect costs of developing animals raised for sale are accumulated to ensure the accuracy of inventory and the cost of animals sold.

---

**LO6**

Assess the risks of material misstatement of inventories and cost of goods sold and design further audit procedures, including tests of controls and substantive procedures, to address the risks.

### C. Assess the Risks of Material Misstatement and Design Further Audit Procedures.

After considering the information about the client and its environment, including internal control, the auditors assess the risks of material misstatement related to the assertions about inventories and cost of goods sold. To make these assessments, the auditors must consider the relationships between specific misstatements and controls. Figure 12.2 provides examples of potential misstatements of inventories and cost of goods sold and weaknesses in internal control that would make them more likely to occur. You should also refer back to Figure 11.4, on pages 444–445, which includes a number of misstatements of revenue that may also involve misstatements of inventory.

The auditors' assessments of the risks of material misstatement (inherent and control risks) are used to design further audit procedures, including tests of controls and substantive procedures. The further audit procedures must include tests of controls when the auditors' assessments of control risk assume that controls are operating effectively but, in regard to their understanding of the client's internal control, the auditors have not obtained sufficient evidence that controls are operating effectively.

Some of the risks identified by the auditors may be considered to be significant risks that require special audit consideration. As an example, a client may have inventories that have a very high risk of obsolescence. This significant risk may require the auditors to perform more procedures focused on identifying inventories that are overvalued, such as the performance of detailed analytical procedures. It is important to remember that for any significant risk, the auditors:

1. Must evaluate the design of the related controls and determine that they are implemented.
2. May not rely solely on analytical procedures to address the risk.
3. May not rely on evidence obtained in prior periods regarding the operating effectiveness of the related controls.

### D. Perform Further Audit Procedures—Tests of Controls.

Tests directed toward the effectiveness of controls help to evaluate the client's internal control and determine whether the auditors can support their planned assessed levels of control risk for the assertions about the inventory and cost of goods sold accounts. Certain tests of controls are performed as the auditors obtain an understanding of the client's internal control; these tests were described in our discussion of that process.

#### 1. Examples of Tests of Controls.

#### a. Examine Significant Aspects of a Sample of Purchase Transactions.

The proper recording of purchase transactions and cash disbursements is essential to reliable accounting records. Therefore, the auditors test the key control procedures in

**FIGURE 12.2    Potential Misstatements—Inventory***

| Description of Misstatement | Examples | Internal Control Weaknesses or Factors that Increase the Risk of the Misstatement |
|---|---|---|
| Misstatement of inventory costs | **Fraud:**<br>• Intentional misstatement of production costs assigned to inventory<br>• Intentional misstatement of inventory prices | • Ineffective board of directors, audit committee, or internal audit function; "tone at the top" not conducive to ethical conduct; undue pressure to meet earnings targets |
| | **Errors:**<br>• The assignment of direct labor costs, direct material costs, or factory overhead to inventory items is inaccurate<br>• Erroneous pricing of inventory | • Ineffective cost accounting system; failure to update standard costs on a timely basis<br>• Ineffective input validation controls on the database of inventory costs; ineffective supervision of the personnel that enter the costs on the final inventory schedule |
| Misstatement of inventory quantities | **Fraud:**<br>• Items are stolen with no journal entry reflecting the theft<br>• Inventory quantities in locations not visited by auditors are systematically overstated | • Ineffective physical controls over inventories<br>• Ineffective board of directors, audit committee, or internal audit function; "tone at the top" not conducive to ethical conduct; undue pressure to meet earnings targets |
| | **Error:**<br>• Miscounting of inventory by personnel involved in physical inventory | • Ineffective controls or supervision of physical inventory |
| Early (late) recognition of purchases—"cutoff problems" | **Fraud:**<br>• Intentional recording of purchases in the subsequent period | • Ineffective board of directors, audit committee, or internal audit function; "tone at the top" not conducive to ethical conduct; undue pressure to meet earnings targets |
| | **Error:**<br>• Recording purchases of the current period in the subsequent period | • Ineffective accounting procedures that do not tie recorded purchases to receiving data |

*See also Figure 11.4, Potential Misstatements—Revenue, since many types of revenue misstatements involve misstatement of inventory.

the client's purchasing transaction cycle. Tests of this cycle may include the following steps:

1. Select a sample of purchase transactions.
2. Examine the purchase requisition or other authorization for each purchase transaction in the sample.
3. Examine the related vendor's invoice, receiving report, and paid check for each purchase order in the sample. Trace transactions to the voucher register and check register.
4. Inspect vendors' invoices for approval of prices, freight and credit terms, and account distribution, and recompute extensions and footings.

5. Compare quantities and prices in the invoice, purchase order, and receiving report.

6. Trace postings from voucher register to general ledger and any applicable subsidiary ledgers.

### b.  Perform Tests of the Cost Accounting System.

For a client in the manufacturing field, the auditors must become familiar with the client's cost accounting system. A wide variety of practices will be encountered for the costing of finished units. The cost accounting records may be controlled by general ledger accounts or operated independently of the general accounting system. In the latter case, the cost of completed units may be difficult or impossible to verify and may represent nothing more than a well-reasoned guess. Because cost accounting methods vary so widely, even among manufacturing concerns in the same industry, audit procedures for a cost accounting system must be designed to fit the specific circumstances encountered in each case.

In any cost accounting system, the three elements of manufacturing cost are direct materials costs, direct labor costs, and manufacturing overhead. Cost accounting systems may accumulate either actual costs or standard costs according to *processes* or *jobs*. The auditors' tests of the client's cost accounting system are designed to determine that costs allocated to specific jobs or processes are appropriately compiled.

To achieve this objective, the auditors test the propriety of direct materials quantities and unit costs, direct labor-hours and hourly rates, and overhead rates and allocation bases. Quantities of direct materials charged to jobs or processes are vouched to materials requisitions, and unit materials costs are traced to the raw materials perpetual inventory records or purchase invoices. The auditors examine job time tickets or time summaries supporting direct labor-hour accumulations and trace direct labor hourly rates to union contracts or individual employee personnel files.

The auditors must recognize that a variety of methods are generally accepted for the application of manufacturing overhead to inventories. A predetermined rate of factory overhead applied on the basis of machine-hours, direct labor dollars, direct labor-hours, or some similar basis is used by many manufacturing companies. Accounting standards provide that variable manufacturing costs should be allocated to products on the basis of the actual level of activity. Fixed manufacturing overhead, on the other hand, should be allocated based on the normal capacity of the production facility.

A distinction between factory overhead, on the one hand, and overhead costs pertaining to selling or general administration of the business, on the other, must be made under generally accepted accounting principles because selling expenses and general and administrative expenses are expensed in the period incurred. The difference in the accounting treatment accorded to factory overhead and to nonmanufacturing overhead implies a fundamental difference between these two types of cost. Nevertheless, as a practical matter it is often impossible to say with finality what proportion of a particular expenditure, such as the salary of a vice president in charge of production, should be classified as factory overhead and as general and administrative expense. Despite this difficulty, a vital procedure in the audit of cost of goods sold for a manufacturing concern is determining that factory overhead costs are reasonably allocated in the accounts. Failure to distribute factory costs to the correct accounts can cause significant distortions in the client's predetermined overhead rate and in over- or underapplied factory overhead. The auditors may find it necessary to obtain or prepare analyses of a number of the factory overhead subsidiary ledger accounts and to verify the propriety of the charges thereto. Then, the auditors must determine the propriety of the total machine-hours, direct labor-hours, or other aggregate allocation base used by the client company to predetermine the factory overhead rate.

If standard costs are in use, it is desirable to compare them with actual costs for representative items and to determine whether the standards reflect current materials and labor usage and unit costs. The composition of factory overhead, the basis for its distribution by department and product, and the effect of any change in basis during the year should be reviewed. The standard costs of selected products should be verified by testing computations, extensions, and footings and by tracing charges for labor, materials, and overhead to original sources. Normal variances between standard costs and actual costs are allocated to cost of goods and inventories on a pro rata basis.

The auditors' study of a manufacturing company's cost accounting system should give special attention to any changes in cost methods made during the year and the effect of such changes on the cost of sales. Close attention should also be given to the methods of summarizing costs of completed products and to the procedures for recording the cost of partial shipments.

If the client company has supply contracts with U.S. government agencies, the auditors should determine whether standards issued by the **Cost Accounting Standards Board** were complied with. Cost accounting standards issued to date have dealt with such matters as consistency in estimating, accumulating, allocating, and reporting costs and depreciation of plant assets.

### 2. If Necessary, Revise the Risks of Material Misstatement Based on the Results of Tests of Controls.

The description and tests of controls of the client's internal control over inventories and cost of goods sold provide the auditors with evidence as to weaknesses and strengths of the system. If the tests of controls reveal problems, the auditors must reassess the risks of material misstatement for the financial statement assertions about inventories and cost of goods sold. Figure 12.3 illustrates the relationship between the assertions and the various controls. It also shows how these policies and procedures are typically tested. The auditors' assessments of the risks of material misstatement are then used to design the substantive tests for these accounts.

### E. Perform Further Audit Procedures—Substantive Procedures for Inventories and Cost of Goods Sold.

#### 1. Obtain Listings of Inventory and Reconcile to Ledgers.

| Primary Audit Objectives: | |
| --- | --- |
| Existence | ☑ |
| Occurrence | ☑ |
| Rights | ☑ |

The auditor will obtain a schedule of listings of inventories that will be reconciled to both the general ledger and appropriate subsidiary ledgers. The nature of the listings will vary depending upon whether the client engages in manufacturing or simply sells products at retail. The auditors' goal in performing this step is to make sure the inventory records agree with what is recorded in the financial statements.

#### 2. Evaluate the Client's Planning of Physical Inventory.

| Primary Audit Objectives: | |
| --- | --- |
| Existence | ☑ |
| Occurrence | ☑ |
| Completeness | ☑ |
| Rights | ☑ |
| Valuation | ☑ |
| Cutoff | ☑ |

Efficient and effective inventory taking requires careful advance planning. Cooperation between the auditors and client personnel in formulating the procedures to be followed will prevent unnecessary confusion and will aid in securing a complete and well-controlled count. A first step is the designation by the client management of an individual employee, often a representative of the controller, to assume responsibility for the physical inventory. This responsibility will begin with the drafting of procedures and will carry through to the final determination of the dollar value of all inventories.

In planning the physical inventory, the client should consider many factors, such as (*a*) selecting the best date or dates, (*b*) suspending production in certain departments of the plant, (*c*) segregating obsolete and defective goods, (*d*) establishing control over the counting process through the use of inventory tags or sheets, (*e*) achieving proper cutoff of sales and purchase transactions, and ( *f* ) arranging for the services of engineers or other specialists to determine the quantity or quality of certain goods or materials.

Once the plan has been developed, it must be documented and communicated in the form of written instructions to the personnel taking the physical inventory. These instructions normally will be drafted by the client and reviewed by the auditors, who will judge their adequacy. A set of instructions prepared by the controller of a large clothing store for use by supervisors is shown in Figure 12.4. In evaluating the adequacy of the instructions, the auditors should consider the nature and materiality of the inventories, as well as the

**FIGURE 12.3** Relating Controls to Assertions

| Internal Control Policy or Procedure | Typical Tests of the Control Policy or Procedure | Existence & Occurrence | Completeness | Cutoff | Rights & Obligations | Valuation & Accuracy | Presentation & Disclosure |
|---|---|---|---|---|---|---|---|
| Segregate duties over purchases and custody of inventories. | Observe and make inquiries about the performance of various functions. | X | X | | X | X | |
| Use prenumbered requisitions, purchase orders, and receiving reports and account for the sequence of documents. | Observe and make inquiries about the use of prenumbered documents and inspect evidence of accounting for the sequence. | | X | X | | | |
| Establish procedures for authorizing purchase transactions, reconciling purchase invoices to purchase orders and receiving reports, and verifying the clerical accuracy of purchase invoices. | Observe and make inquiries about purchase procedures, and test a sample of purchase transactions by inspecting evidence of authorizations and reconciliations, comparing the details to authorized purchase orders and receiving reports, and recomputing the invoice amounts. | X | | | X | X | |
| Establish general ledger control of inventories of raw materials, goods in process, and finished goods, and periodically reconcile to production records. | Inspect accounting and production records and selected reconciliations. | X | | | X | X | X |
| Establish controls for the cost accounting system that accumulate appropriate inventory costs on a job order or process cost basis, such as independent review of cost accumulations. | Inspect evidence of independent reviews of cost accumulations, recompute materials costs by reference to requisitions and purchase invoices, and recompute direct labor costs by reference to time and payroll records and overhead application rates. | | | | | X | |
| Analyze and follow up on variances from standard costs. | Inspect inventory reports and examine evidence of follow-up on variances. | X | X | | | X | |
| Use perpetual records to control inventories. | Inquire about the perpetual inventory procedures, and test the records by reference to purchase invoices, receiving reports, and production records. | X | X | X | | X | X |
| Use appropriate procedures for taking the physical inventory. | Review the inventory instructions and observe the inventory-taking process. | X | X | X | X | X | |
| Establish appropriate physical controls over inventories. | Observe and inquire about the physical control policies and procedures. | X | | | X | | |

existing internal control. Normally, the auditors will insist that the inventory be taken at or near the balance sheet date. However, if the client has effective internal control, including perpetual records, the auditors may be satisfied to observe inventory counts performed during the year. If the client plans to use a statistical sampling technique to estimate the quantities of inventories, the auditors will evaluate the statistical validity of the sampling method and the propriety of the sampling risk and the allowance for sampling risk.

## Illustrative Case    *Fraud at Phar-Mor*

Several years ago, it was reported that audits of Phar-Mor, Inc., a discount drugstore chain, did not detect a $50 million overstatement of inventory. The allegedly fraudulent overstatements occurred at stores at which the client knew in advance that the CPAs did not intend to observe inventory counts. The client refrained from making fraudulent adjustments at the stores where it knew that the CPAs would observe the inventories. In another case, auditors are reported to have permitted company officials to follow them and record where test counts of inventory were taken; the managers subsequently falsified counts for inventory items that weren't test counted by the auditors.

**FIGURE 12.4**

**Instructions for Physical Inventory**

---

### GLEN HAVEN DEPARTMENT STORES, INC.

Instructions for Physical Inventory,
August 5, 20X0

TO ALL SUPERVISORS:

A complete physical inventory of all departments in each store will be taken Sunday, August 5, 20X0, beginning at 8:30 a.m. and continuing until completed. Employees are to report at 8:15 a.m. to receive their final briefing on their instructions, which are appended hereto.

Within one week prior to August 5, supervisors should make sure that merchandise in departments is well organized. All merchandise with the same stock number should be located together. Merchandise that is damaged should be segregated for separate listing on inventory sheets.

Each count team should be formed and started by a supervisor and should be periodically observed by that supervisor to assure that instructions are being complied with in the counting and listing processes.

A block of sequential prenumbered inventory sheets will be issued to each supervisor at 8:00 a.m. August 5, for later issuance to count teams. Each supervisor is to account for all sheets—used, unused, or voided. In addition, each supervisor will be furnished at that time with a listing of count teams under his or her supervision.

When a count team reports completion of a department, that team's supervisor should accompany a representative of the independent auditors, McDonald & Company, in performing test counts. A space is provided on each inventory sheet for the supervisor's signature as reviewer. When the independent auditors have "cleared" a department, the supervisor responsible should take possession of the count sheets. All completed count sheets are to be placed in numerical sequence and turned over to me when the entire inventory has been completed.

Before supervisors and employees leave the stores Saturday evening, August 4, they are to make certain that "housekeeping" is in order in each department and that all merchandise bears a price ticket.

If you have any questions about these instructions or any other aspect of the physical inventory, please see me.

*J. R. Adams*

J. R. Adams
Controller
July 24, 20X0

Advance planning by the senior auditor-in-charge is also necessary to ensure efficient use of audit staff members during the inventory taking. The auditor-in-charge should determine the dates of the counts, the extent of the test counts, the need for client assistance, the number of auditors needed at each location, and the estimated time required. When multiple locations are involved, the auditors must determine whether the assessed levels of the risks of material misstatement justify omission of observation at certain locations. When only certain locations are to be observed, the auditors should consider not informing the client of the specific locations in advance. In addition, the observation should be planned in a manner that ensures that client employees are not aware of the exact nature of all items that are test-counted by the auditors.

Advance planning may also reveal to the auditors a need to rely upon the advice of a **specialist** for discharging their responsibility for testing inventory. For example, the auditors of a retail jeweler might engage an independent expert in gems to assist in identifying the precious stones and metals included in the client's inventory. Similarly, the auditors of a chemical producer might rely upon the expert opinion of an independent chemist as to the identity of components of the client's inventories. Guidelines for using the work of a specialist were presented in Chapter 5.

When written instructions are prepared by the auditing firm for the use of its staff in a particular engagement, these instructions are not made available to the client. Their purpose is to help ensure that all auditors understand their assignments and can therefore work efficiently during the physical inventory. Figure 12.5 provides an example of such instructions.

### 3. Observe the Taking of Physical Inventory and Make Test Counts.

Primary Audit
Objectives:

| | |
|---|---|
| Existence | ☑ |
| Occurrence | ☑ |
| Completeness | ☑ |
| Rights | ☑ |
| Valuation | ☑ |
| Cutoff | ☑ |

It is not the auditors' function to *take* the inventory or to control or supervise the taking; this is the responsibility of management. The auditors' responsibility is to *observe* the inventory taking. However, to observe the inventory taking implies a much more active role than that of a mere spectator.

The auditors' responsibility is to attend the physical inventory counting by the client and:

- Inspect the inventory to determine its existence and to evaluate its condition, and make test counts.
- Observe compliance with management's instructions for the count.
- Obtain audit evidence about the reliability of the count procedures.

Throughout this process, the auditors seek to determine that all usable inventory owned by the client is included in the count, as well as to be alert to the possibility of inclusion of any obsolete or damaged merchandise in inventory.

Excessive dust or rust on raw materials inventory items may be indicative of obsolescence or infrequent sale. Such merchandise should be segregated by the client and written down to its net realizable value.

The auditors will also *record the serial number of the final receiving and shipping documents issued before the taking of inventory* so that the accuracy of the cutoff can be determined at a later date. Shipments or receipts of goods taking place during the counting process should be closely observed and any necessary reconciliations made. Observation of the physical inventory by the auditors also stresses determining that the client is controlling the inventory tags or sheets properly. These should be prenumbered so that all tags or sheets can be accounted for.

During the inventory observation, the auditors will make test counts of selected inventory items. The extent of the test counts will vary widely, depending upon the levels of the risks of material misstatement and the materiality of the client's inventory. A representative number of test counts should be recorded in the audit working papers for subsequent comparison with the completed inventory listing.

Serially numbered (or computer-generated) inventory count tags are usually attached to each lot of goods during the taking of a physical inventory. The design of the tag and the procedures for using it are intended to guard against two common pitfalls: (*a*) accidental omission of goods from the count and (*b*) double counting of goods.

**FIGURE 12.5**
**Inventory Observation Instructions**

---

### MCDONALD & COMPANY
*Certified Public Accountants*

Glen Haven Department Stores, Inc.
Inventory Observation—Instructions for Audit Staff
August 1, 20X0

We will observe physical inventory taking at the following stores of Glen Haven Department Stores, Inc., on August 5, 20X0.

| Store | Store Manager | Our Staff |
|---|---|---|
| Wilshire | J. M. Baker | John Rodgers, Faye Arnold |
| Crenshaw | Roberta Bryan | Weldon Simpkins |
| Valley | Hugh Remington | Roger Dawson |

Report to assigned stores promptly at 8:00 a.m. Attached are copies of the company's detailed instructions to employees who are to take the physical inventories and to supervisors who are to be in charge. These instructions appear to be complete and adequate; we should satisfy ourselves by observation that the instructions are being followed.

All merchandise counted will be listed on prenumbered inventory sheets. We should make test counts of approximately 5 percent of the stock items to ascertain the accuracy of the physical counts. A majority of the counts should be performed on the high-value stock, as described on the enclosed listing. Test counts are to be recorded in working papers, with the following information included:

  Department number
  Inventory sheet number
  Stock number
  Description of item
  Quantity
  Selling price per price tag

We should ascertain that adequate control is maintained over the prenumbered inventory sheets issued. Also, we should prepare a listing of the last numbers used for transfers, markdowns, and markups in the various departments and stores. Inventory sheets are not to be removed from the departments until we have "cleared" them; we should not delay this operation.

Each staff member's working papers should include an opinion on the adequacy of the inventory taking. The papers should also include a summary of time incurred in the observation.

No cash or other cutoff procedures are to be performed as an adjunct to the inventory observation.

---

Many companies use two-employee teams to count the inventories. Each team is provided with a sequence of the serially numbered tags and is required to return to the physical inventory supervisor any voided or unused tags.

The actual counting, the filling in of inventory tags, and the pulling of these tags are done by the client's employees. While the inventory tags are still attached to the goods, the auditors may make such test counts as they deem appropriate in the circumstances. The auditors will list in their working papers the tag numbers for which test counts were made. The client employees will not ordinarily collect (pull) the inventory tags until the auditors indicate that they are satisfied with the accuracy of the count.

In comparing their test counts to the inventory tags, the auditors are alert for errors not only in quantities but also in part numbers, descriptions, units of measure, and all other aspects of the inventory item. For test counts of goods in process inventory, the auditors must determine that the percentage or stage of completion indicated on the inventory tag is appropriate.

## Illustrative Case

### Fraudulent Misstatement of Inventories

Unscrupulous management has used a variety of methods to misstate inventories. One method involved recording fictitious inventory, sometimes in such quantities that the resulting total recorded inventory was in excess of the company's storage capacity. Another method involved placing scrap materials in product boxes to be counted as inventory. Two other methods involved retaining items in inventory, even though they had been recorded as sales (**bill and hold** schemes), and recording inventory that had been shipped between the company's warehouses in the inventory totals of more than one warehouse.

The ways in which management has circumvented the auditors' tests have also varied. In one instance, fictitious count sheets were created. In another situation, client personnel obtained knowledge of the items tested by the auditors and increased the recorded quantities of items not tested. Finally, client personnel have actually gained access to the auditors' working papers and altered them to support the fictitious inventory.

These cases illustrate the need for extreme care by the auditors in planning and performing inventory procedures.

If the test counts made by the auditors indicate discrepancies, the goods are recounted at once by the client's employees and the error corrected. If an excessive number of errors are found, the inventories for the entire department or even for the entire company should be recounted.

The client often transfers the information listed on the inventory tags to serially numbered inventory sheets. These sheets are used in pricing the inventory and in summarizing the dollar amounts involved. After the inventory tags have been collected, the client employee supervising the inventory determines that all tags are accounted for by serial number. The auditors should ascertain that numerical control is maintained over both inventory tags and inventory sheets.

Clients using electronic equipment may facilitate inventory counting and summarizing through machine-readable inventory tags. Prior to the physical inventory, the tags may be encoded with tag numbers, part numbers, descriptions, and unit prices. After the physical inventory, the information from the tags is scanned into the computer, which extends quantity times unit price for each inventory item and prints out a complete inventory summary.

The test counts and tag numbers listed by the auditors in their working papers will be traced later to the client's inventory summary sheets. A discrepancy will be regarded not as an error in counting but as a mistake in copying data from the tags, a purposeful alteration of a tag, or the creation of a fictitious tag.

During the observation of physical inventories, the auditors should make inquiries to determine whether any of the materials or goods on hand are the property of others, such as goods held on **consignment** or customer-owned materials sent in for machine work or other processing.

Audit procedures applicable to goods held by the client on consignment may include a comparison of the physical inventory with the client's records of consigned goods on hand, review of contracts and correspondence with consignors, and direct written communication with the consignors to (1) confirm the quantity and value of goods held at the balance sheet date and to (2) disclose any client liability for unremitted sales proceeds or from inability to collect consignment accounts receivable.

Each auditor participating in the observation of the inventory will prepare working papers. These papers should indicate the extent of test counts, describe any deficiencies noted, and express a conclusion as to whether the physical inventory appeared to have been properly taken in accordance with the client's instructions. The auditor-in-charge should prepare a concise summary memorandum indicating the overall extent of observation and the percentage of inventory value covered by quantity tests. The memorandum may also include comments on the consideration given to the factors of quality and condition of stock, the treatment of consigned goods on hand, and the control of shipments and receipts during the counting process. Figure 12.6 illustrates this type of memorandum.

### Outside Inventory Taking Firms

Some clients may hire firms that specialize in taking physical inventories for other organizations. As an example, retail store chains often hire these firms to take physical inventories of the company's individual stores. The inventory-taking firm typically counts, lists, prices, and subsequently values the inventory on hand at the date of the physical count. Even though these firms may be independent of client personnel, the counts made by these firms are not, by themselves, sufficient appropriate audit evidence regarding the client's inventory. The auditors should evaluate the effectiveness of the procedures used by the outside firm and perform other procedures as outlined in the preceding sections as considered appropriate.

**FIGURE 12.6**
**Documentation of Physical Inventory Observation**

THE WILSHIRE CORPORATION
Comments on Observation of Physical Inventory                     D-9

December 31, 20X0

1.  Advance Planning of Physical Inventory.

    A physical inventory was taken by the client on December 31, 20X0. Two weeks in advance of this date we reviewed the written inventory instructions prepared by L. D. Frome, Controller. These instructions appeared entirely adequate and reflected the experience gained during the counts of previous years. The plan called for a complete closing down of the factory on December 31, since the preceding year's count had been handicapped by movements of productive material during the counting process. Training meetings were conducted by Frome for all employees assigned to participate in the inventory; at these meetings the written instructions were explained and discussed.

2.  Observation of Physical Inventory.

    We were present throughout the taking of physical inventory on December 31, 20X0. Prior to the count, all materials had been neatly arranged, labeled, and separated by type. Two-employee inventory teams were used: one employee counting and calling quantities and descriptions; the other employee filling in data on the serially numbered inventory tags. As the goods were counted, the counting team tore off the "first count" portion of the inventory tag. A second count was made later by another team working independently of the first; this second team recorded the quantity of its count on the "second count" portion of the tag.

    We made test counts of numerous items, covering approximately 60 percent of the total inventory value. These counts were recorded on our working papers and used as noted below. Our observation throughout the plant indicated that both the first and second counts required by the inventory instructions were being performed in a systematic and conscientious manner. The careful and alert attitude of employees indicated that the training meetings preceding the count had been quite effective in creating an understanding of the importance of an accurate count. Before the "second count" portions of the tags were removed, we visited all departments in the company with Frome and satisfied ourselves that all goods had been tagged and counted.

    No goods were shipped on December 31. We ascertained that receiving reports were prepared on all goods taken into the receiving department on this day. We recorded the serial numbers of the last receiving report and the last shipping advice for the year 20X0. (See D-9-1.) We compared the quantities per the count with perpetual inventory records and found no significant discrepancies.

3.  Quality and Condition of Materials.

    Certain obsolete parts had been removed from stock prior to the count and reduced to a scrap carrying value. On the basis of our personal observation and questions addressed to supervisors, we have no reason to believe that any obsolete or defective materials remained in inventory. During the course of inventory observation, we tested the reasonableness of the quantities of 10 items, representing 40 percent of the value of the inventory, by comparing the quantity on hand with the quantity used in recent months; in no case did we find that the quantity in inventory exceeded three months' normal usage.

*V.M.H.*
*Jan. 3, 20X1*

*Inventories in Public Warehouses and on Consignment*

Companies that store inventories in public warehouses ordinarily receive receipts for those goods. Examination of these receipts is not sufficient verification of goods stored in public warehouses. The AICPA has recommended direct confirmation in writing from outside custodians of inventories and supplementary procedures when the amounts involved represent a significant proportion of the current assets or of the total assets of a concern. These supplementary procedures include review of the client's procedures for investigating prospective warehouses and evaluating the performance of warehouses having custody of the client's goods. The auditors should also consider obtaining accountants' reports on the warehouses' controls relevant to custody of stored goods. If the amounts are material, or if any reason for doubt exists, the auditors may decide to visit the warehouses and observe a physical inventory of the client's merchandise stored at the warehouses.

A starting point for the verification of goods in the hands of consignees is to obtain from the client a list of all consignees and copies of the consignment contracts. Contract provisions concerning the payment of freight and other handling charges, the extension of credit, computation of commissions, and frequency of reports and remittances require close attention. After review of the contracts and the client's records of consignment shipments and collections, the auditors should communicate directly with the consignees and obtain full written information on consigned inventory, receivables, unremitted proceeds, and accrued expenses and commissions as of the balance sheet date.

Often, the client may own raw materials that are processed by a subcontractor before being used in the client's production process. The auditors should request the subcontractor to confirm quantities and descriptions of client-owned materials in the subcontractor's possession.

*Inventory Verification When Auditors Are Engaged after the End of the Year*

A company desiring an independent audit should engage the auditors well before the end of the year so they can participate in advance planning of the physical inventory and be prepared to observe the actual counting process. Occasionally, however, auditors are not engaged until after the end of the year and therefore find it impossible to observe the taking of inventory at the close of the year. For example, the illness or death of a company's individual practitioner CPA near the year-end might lead to the engagement of new auditors shortly after the balance sheet date.

Under these circumstances, the auditors may conclude that sufficient appropriate evidence cannot be obtained concerning inventories to permit them to express an opinion on the overall fairness of the financial statements. On the other hand, under other circumstances, the auditors may be able to obtain satisfaction concerning the inventories by alternative auditing procedures. These favorable circumstances might include the existence of strong internal control, perpetual inventory records, availability of instructions and other records showing that the client had carried out a well-planned physical inventory at or near the year-end, and the making of test counts by the newly appointed auditors. If the auditors are to express an unqualified opinion, their investigation of inventories must include some physical contact with items of inventory and must be thorough enough to compensate for the fact that they were not present when the physical inventory was taken. Whether such alternative auditing procedures will be feasible and will enable the auditors to satisfy themselves depends upon the circumstances of the particular engagement.

### 4. Review the Year-End Cutoff of Purchases and Sales Transactions.

Primary Audit Objectives:

Existence ☑
Occurrence ☑
Completeness ☑
Rights ☑
Valuation ☑
Cutoff ☑

An accurate cutoff of purchases is one of the most important factors in verifying the existence and completeness of the year-end inventory. It requires that items for which the company holds title as of year-end be included in inventory as well, and that related accounts be properly stated. Assume that a shipment of goods costing $10,000 is received from a supplier on December 31, but the purchase invoice does not arrive until January 2 and is entered as a January transaction. If the goods are included in the December 31 physical inventory but there is no December entry to record the purchase and the liability, the result will be an overstatement of both net income for the year and retained earnings and an understatement of accounts payable, each error being in the full amount of $10,000 (ignoring income taxes).

An opposite situation may arise if a purchase invoice is received and recorded on December 31, but the merchandise covered by the invoice is not received until several days later and is not included in the physical inventory taken at the year-end. The effect on the financial statements of recording a purchase without including the goods in the inventory is to understate net income, retained earnings, and inventory.

How can the auditors determine that the liability to suppliers has been recorded for all goods included in inventory? Their approach is to *examine on a test basis the purchase invoices and receiving reports for several days before and after the inventory date.* Each purchase invoice in the files should have a receiving report attached; if an invoice recorded in late December is accompanied by a receiving report dated December 31 or earlier, the goods must have been on hand and included in the year-end physical inventory. However, if the receiving report carried a January date, the goods were not included in the physical count made on December 31.

A supplementary approach to the matching of purchase invoices and receiving reports is to examine the records of the receiving department. For each shipment received near the year-end, the auditors should determine that the related purchase invoice was recorded in the same period.

The effect on the financial statements of failing to include a year-end in-transit purchase as part of physical inventory is often not a serious one, *provided* the related liability is not recorded until the following period. In other words, a primary point in effecting an accurate cutoff of purchases is that both sides of a purchase transaction must be reflected in the same accounting period. If a given shipment is included in the year-end physical inventory of the purchaser, the entry debiting Inventories and crediting Accounts Payable must be made. If the shipment is not included in the purchaser's year-end physical inventory, the purchase invoice must not be recorded until the following period.

Adjustments to achieve an accurate cutoff of purchases should, of course, be made by the client's staff; the function of the auditors should be to review the cutoff and determine that the necessary adjustments have been made.

Chapter 11 includes a discussion of the audit procedures for determining the accuracy of the sales cutoff. The sales cutoff is mentioned again at this point to emphasize its importance in determining the fairness of the client's inventory and cost of goods sold as well as accounts receivable and sales.

### 5. Obtain a Copy of the Completed Physical Inventory, Test Its Clerical Accuracy, and Trace Test Counts.

The testing of extensions and footings on the final inventory listing may disclose misstatements of physical inventories. Often this test consists of "sight-footing" to the nearest hundred dollars or thousand dollars of the inventory listings. Generalized audit software also may be used to test extensions and footings.

In testing extensions, the auditors should be alert for two sources of substantial errors—misplaced decimal points and the incorrect extension of *count* units by *price* units. For example, an inventory listing that extends 1,000 units times $1C (per hundred) as $1,000 will be overstated by $990. An inventory extension of 1,000 sheets of steel times $5 per pound will be substantially understated if each sheet of steel weighs more than one pound.

The auditors also should trace to the completed physical inventory their test counts made during the observation of physical inventory. During this tracing, the auditors should be alert for any indications that inventory tags have been altered or that fictitious inventory tags have been created. The auditors also reconcile inventory tag number sequences in the physical inventory listing to tag numbers noted in their audit working papers for the inventory observation. This procedure is designed to determine that the client has not omitted inventory items from the listing or included additional items that were not present during the physical inventory.

Another test of the clerical accuracy of the completed physical inventory is the reconciliation of the physical counts to inventory records. Both the quantities and the values of

## Illustrative Case

### Fraudulent Financial Reporting at U.S. Foodservices

An alleged fraud at U.S. Foodservices (USF) provides an illustration of the often complex nature of inventory valuation. In a typical promotional allowance arrangement, USF would pay the full wholesale price for a product and then receive rebates of a portion of the price from the supplier if certain purchase volume and other conditions were met.

To meet earnings targets, federal prosecutors charged that nine former USF employees overstated the promotional allowances (and earnings) by more than $800,000,000. To hide the fraud, USF convinced suppliers to return confirmations to auditors confirming the fraudulent amounts.

Participation by the suppliers makes this sort of fraud extremely difficult—and, perhaps, impossible—for auditors to detect. It is possible that industry knowledge would lead the auditors to question the large amount of allowances. Also, if details of the computation of allowances are included in sales agreements, the auditors could calculate the proper amounts and compare them with the recorded amounts. However, if the allowances are based on unwritten side agreements between the parties, examining agreements will not be effective in detecting the misstatements. Certainly, subsequent years' results will reveal the misstatements.

the items should be compared to the company's perpetual records. The totals of various sections of inventory also should be compared with the corresponding control accounts. All substantial discrepancies should be investigated fully. The number, type, and cause of the discrepancies revealed by such comparisons are highly significant in assessing control risk for inventories.

### 6. Evaluate the Bases and Methods of Inventory Pricing.

| Primary Audit Objectives: |   |
|---|---|
| Valuation | ☑ |

The auditors are responsible for determining that the bases and methods of pricing inventory are in accordance with generally accepted accounting principles. The investigation of inventory pricing often will emphasize the following three questions:

1. What method of pricing does the client use?
2. Is the method of pricing the same as that used in prior years?
3. Has the method selected by the client been applied consistently and accurately in practice?

For the first question—the method of pricing—a long list of alternatives is possible, including such methods as cost; cost or market, whichever is lower; the retail method; and quoted market price (as for metals and staple commodities traded on organized exchanges). The cost method, of course, includes many diverse systems, such as last-in, first-out (LIFO); first-in, first-out (FIFO); specific identification; weighted average; and standard cost. It is important to note that the international accounting standards do not allow the use of LIFO as a method for pricing inventory.

The second question raised in this section concerns a change in method of pricing inventory from one year to the next. For example, let us say that the client has changed from the FIFO method to the LIFO method. The nature and justification of the change in method of valuing inventory and its effect on income should be disclosed. In addition, the auditors must insert in the audit report an explanatory paragraph concerning the lack of consistency between the two years.

The third question posed deals with consistent accurate application in practice of the method of valuation adopted by the client. To answer this question, the auditors must test the pricing of a representative number of inventory items.

### 7. Test the Pricing of Inventories.

| Primary Audit Objectives: |   |
|---|---|
| Valuation | ☑ |
| Accuracy | ☑ |

The testing of prices applied to inventories of raw materials, purchased parts, and supplies by a manufacturing company is similar to the testing of prices of merchandise in a trading business. In both cases, the cost of inventory items, whether LIFO, FIFO, weighted average, or specific identification, is readily verified by reference to purchase invoices.

**FIGURE 12.7** **Test of Inventory Pricing**

The Wilshire Corporation
Test of Pricing—Raw Materials and Purchased Parts
December 31, 20X0                                                                    D-5

| Part No. | Description | Per Inventory Quantity/Price | Vendor | Date | No. | Quantity @ Price | |
|----------|-------------|------------------------------|--------|------|-----|------------------|---|
| 8Z 182 | Aluminum 48 x 144 x .025 | 910 sheets @ 10.10 | Hardy & Co. | Dec. 18, X0 | 5415 | 1000 @ 10.10 | 𝑦 |
| 8Z 195 | Aluminum 45/72 x .032 | 804 sheets @ 9.01 | Watson Mfg. Co. | Nov. 28, X0 | 3201 | 500 @ 9.01 | 𝑦 |
|  |  |  |  | Dec. 22, X0 | 3456 | 400 @ 9.01 | 𝑦 |
| K1125 | Stainless steel .025 x 23 | 80,625 lbs @ .80 | Ajax Steel Co. | Dec. 3, X0 | K182 | 100,000 @ .80 | 𝑦 |
| K1382 | Stainless steel .031 x 17 | 65,212 lbs @ .82 | Ajax Steel Co. | Dec. 3, X0 | K182 | 75,000 @ .82 | 𝑦 |
| XL3925 | 10 H.P. Electronic Motor | 50 units @ 400.00 | Cronyn Mfg. Co. | Nov. 18, X0 | D2532 | 100 @ 400.00 | 𝑦 |
| XJ3824 | 3/4 H.P. Electronic Motor | 645 units @ 30.50 | Long & Co. | Dec. 29, X0 | E9215 | 650 @ 30.50 | 𝑦 |

*Per Vendor's Invoice*

Inventory value of raw materials and purchased parts selected for price testing—$301,825.56.

Percent of total raw materials and purchased parts selected for price testing—$301,825.56/$503,615.10 = 60%.

See audit program B-4 for method of selecting raw materials and purchased parts for price testing.

𝑦 = Agreed to prices on the vendor's invoice.

*Conclusion:*

*Based on our tests, the pricing of raw materials and purchased parts appears to be materially correct.*

*CMB*
*1/4/X1*

An illustration of a computerized working paper prepared by an auditor in making price tests of an inventory of raw materials and purchased parts is presented in Figure 12.7.

Audit procedures for verification of the inventory values assigned to goods in process and finished goods are not so simple and conclusive as in the case of raw materials or merchandise for which purchase invoices are readily available. To determine whether the inventory valuation method used by the client has been properly applied, the auditors must make tests of the pricing of selected items of finished goods and goods in process. The pricing of these items must be tested by reference to the client's cost accounting records of accumulated direct material, direct labor, and manufacturing overhead costs. Items of large total value will be selected for testing so that the tests will encompass a significant portion of the dollar amount of inventories.

### Lower-of-Cost-or-Market Test

As a general rule, inventories should not be carried at an amount in excess of net realizable value. Under U.S. generally accepted accounting standards, the lower-of-cost-or-market rule is used to measure any loss of utility in the inventories. This test generally involves comparing recorded cost of inventory items with their replacement cost, within the ceiling (net realizable value) and the floor (net realizable value minus normal profit).

Under international accounting standards, the recorded cost of the items are compared to their net realizable values. Also, under international standards, the inventory items may be written back up if the value subsequently recovers.

### 8. Perform Analytical Procedures.

Material misstatements of inventory may be disclosed by analytical procedures designed to establish the general reasonableness of inventory figures. As an example, major

Primary Audit
Objectives:

| | |
|---|---|
| Existence | ☑ |
| Completeness | ☑ |
| Rights | ☑ |
| Valuation | ☑ |
| Accuracy | ☑ |

increases or decreases in the amounts of various types of inventory as compared to prior-year amounts may be identified and investigated.

In certain lines of business, particularly retail and wholesale companies, gross profit margins may be quite uniform from year to year. Any major difference between the ending inventory estimated by the gross profit percentage method and the count of inventory at year-end should be investigated fully. If the client has inventory in a number of stores, some of which were not visited by the auditors, comparing gross profit by store may reveal overstatements in those not visited.

Another useful test is the computation of rates of inventory turnover (preferably by individual product) based on the relationship between the cost of goods sold for the year and the average inventory as shown on the monthly financial statements. These turnover rates may be compared with rates prevailing in prior years. A decreasing rate of turnover suggests the possibility of obsolescence or of unnecessarily large amounts of inventories. Scanning perpetual inventory records may also reveal obsolete items.

### Focus on the Computer Hardware and Software Industry

Given the pace of technological advances and the highly competitive nature of the computer hardware and software industry, rapid inventory obsolescence is common. Product life cycles are typically short and competitive products with superior price and performance can quickly enter the marketplace. Analytical procedures may be used to determine whether inventory amounts and trends appear proper. However, simply making comparisons of the current year's amounts and ratios to those of prior years is not effective. The auditors must consider what is expected to happen in the industry. In developing expected amounts for analytical procedures, consideration must be given to expected future demand for the client's products and anticipated technological advances that render existing inventories obsolete. The auditors may find analyses of management's sales forecasts useful for this purpose.

The auditors' analytical procedures for inventory transactions will often include a comparison of the volume of purchase transactions from period to period. Comparisons of transactions, classified by vendor and type of product, may reveal unusual variations of quantities purchased or unusual concentrations of purchases with particular vendors, indicating possible conflicts of interest.

The auditors also should scan all general ledger accounts relating to cost of goods sold to make certain that they contain no apparent misstatements. For example, the auditors may discover that miscellaneous revenue and expenses were erroneously closed into cost of goods sold.

The auditors of a manufacturer should obtain from the client or prepare an analysis of costs of goods sold by month, broken down into raw materials, direct labor, and factory overhead elements. The analysis should also include a description of all unusual and non-recurring charges or credits to cost of goods sold.

*Using Nonfinancial Information*

Using nonfinancial information for developing expectations for analytical procedures can be especially effective for inventories. For example, when the client has inventory stored in a number of warehouses, the auditor may compare the amount of inventory stored in each warehouse with its size in square feet. Comparisons can also be made between inventory in dollars and in units, and, for a manufacturing firm, inventory and cost of goods sold amounts may be compared to various production statistics, such as direct labor-hours and machine-hours.

### 9. Determine Whether Any Inventories Have Been Pledged and Review Purchase and Sales Commitments.

Primary Audit
Objectives:

| | |
|---|---|
| Valuation | ☑ |
| Presentation | ☑ |

The verification of inventories includes a determination by the auditors as to whether any goods have been pledged or subjected to a lien of any kind. Pledging of inventories to secure bank loans may be brought to light when bank balances and indebtedness are confirmed.

A record of outstanding **purchase commitments** is usually readily available, since this information is essential to management in maintaining day-to-day control of the company's inventory position and cash flow.

In some lines of business, it is customary to enter into firm contracts for the purchase of merchandise or materials well in advance of the scheduled delivery dates. Comparison by the auditors of the prices quoted in such commitments with the vendors' prices prevailing at the balance sheet date may indicate substantial losses if firm purchase commitments are not protected by firm sales contracts. Such losses should be reflected in the financial statements.

The quantities of purchase commitments should be reviewed in the light of current and prospective demand, as indicated by past operations, the backlog of sales orders, and current conditions within the industry. If quantities on order appear excessive by these standards, the auditors should seek full information on this phase of operations. Purchase commitments may need to be disclosed in the financial statements.

**Sales commitments** are indicated by the client's *backlog* of unfilled sales orders. Losses inherent in firm sales commitments are generally recognized in the lower-of-cost-or-market valuation of inventories, with *market* being defined as the net realizable value of the goods in process or finished goods inventories applicable to the sales commitments. In addition, the backlog may include sales orders for which no production has been started as of the balance sheet date. The auditors must review the client's cost estimates for these sales orders. If estimated total costs to produce the goods ordered exceed fixed sales prices, the indicated loss and a related liability should be recorded in the client's financial statements for the current period.

### 10. Evaluate Financial Statement Presentation of Inventories and Cost of Goods Sold, Including the Adequacy of Disclosure.

Primary Audit Objectives:

Presentation ☑

One of the most important factors in proper presentation of inventories in the financial statements is disclosure of the inventory pricing method or methods in use. Other important disclosures include the following:

- Changes in methods of valuing inventory, with the dollar effect and justification for the change reported.
- The various classifications of inventory, such as finished goods, work in process, and raw materials.
- The details of any arrangements relating to any pledged inventory.
- Deduction of valuation allowance for inventory losses.
- Existence and terms of inventory purchase commitments.

The auditors will review the client's disclosures of such matters to determine whether they comply with generally accepted accounting principles.

## Problems Associated with Inventory of First-Year Audit Clients

The need for the auditors to be present to observe the taking of the ending inventory has been strongly emphasized in auditing literature. However, the figure for beginning inventory is equally significant in determining the cost of goods sold and the net income for the year. In the initial audit of a client, the auditors may not have been present to observe the taking of inventory at the beginning of the year. What procedures can they follow to obtain evidence that the beginning inventories are fairly stated?

The first factor to consider is whether another CPA firm audited the client for the preceding year. If a review of the predecessor firm's working papers indicates compliance with generally accepted auditing standards, the new auditors can accept the beginning inventories with a minimum of investigation. That minimum might include the following steps: (1) study of the inventory valuation methods used, (2) review of the inventory records, (3) review of the inventory sheets used in taking the preceding year's physical inventory, and (4) comparison of the beginning and ending inventories, broken down by product classification.

If there was no satisfactory audit for the preceding year, the investigation of the beginning inventories would include not only the procedures mentioned above but also the following steps: (1) discussion with the person in the client's organization who supervised the physical inventory at the preceding balance sheet date, (2) study of the written instructions used in planning the inventory, (3) tracing of numerous items from the inventory tags or count sheets to the final summary sheets, (4) tests of the perpetual inventory records for the preceding period by reference to supporting documents for receipts and withdrawals, and (5) tests of the overall reasonableness of the beginning inventories in relation to sales, gross profit, and rate of inventory turnover. An investigation along these lines will sometimes give the auditors assurance that the beginning inventory was carefully compiled and reasonable in amount; in other cases, these procedures may raise serious doubts about the validity of the beginning inventory figure. In these latter cases, the auditors will not be able to issue an unqualified opinion as to *statements of income and cash flows.* They may be able, however, to give an unqualified opinion on the *balance sheet,* since this financial statement does not reflect the beginning inventories.

## Chapter Summary

This chapter described details of the controls over inventories and cost of goods sold, the auditors' consideration of these controls, and substantive procedures for inventories and cost of goods sold. To summarize:

1. The audit of inventories presents the auditors with special risks because (*a*) they often represent a very substantial portion of current assets, (*b*) numerous valuation methods are used for inventories, (*c*) the valuation of inventories directly affects cost of goods sold, and (*d*) the determination of inventory quality, condition, and value is inherently complex.

2. Effective internal control over inventories requires appropriate controls over purchasing, receiving, and issuing supplies and materials, producing and shipping products, and cost accounting. A perpetual inventory system is also important.

3. The auditors' objectives for the substantive procedures for inventories and cost of goods sold are to (*a*) substantiate the existence of inventories and the occurrence of related transactions; (*b*) establish the completeness of recorded inventories; (*c*) verify the cutoff of inventory-related transactions; (*d*) determine that the client has rights to the recorded inventories; (*e*) establish the proper valuation of inventories and accuracy of related transactions; and (*f*) determine that presentation and disclosures of inventory accounts are appropriate.

4. The auditors' consideration of inherent risks and the controls over inventories, purchases, and production will allow them to design appropriate further audit procedures for inventory and cost of goods sold accounts.

5. In the audit of inventories, a primary concern of the auditors is existence assertion, that is, the possibility of overstatement of year-end balances. Therefore, a primary substantive procedure for inventory accounts is observation of the client's physical inventory. Other substantive procedures include price tests of the valuation of inventory items, cutoff tests, analytical procedures, and tests of the financial statement presentation and disclosure.

## Key Terms Introduced or Emphasized in Chapter 12

**Bill and hold transactions (516)**　Transactions in which sales of merchandise are billed to customers prior to delivery, with the goods being held by the seller. These transactions may overstate revenues and net income if they do not meet specific requirements for recognition as sales.

**Bill of lading (504)**　A document issued by a common carrier acknowledging the receipt of goods and setting forth the provisions of the transportation agreement.

**Consignment (516)**　A transfer of goods from the owner to another person who acts as the sales agent of the owner.

**Cost Accounting Standards Board (511)**   A five-member board established by Congress to narrow the options in cost accounting that are available under generally accepted accounting principles. Companies having significant supply contracts with certain U.S. government agencies are subject to the cost accounting standards established by the board.

**Electronic data interchange (EDI) (505)**   A system in which data are exchanged electronically between the computers of different companies. In an EDI system, source documents are replaced with electronic transactions created in a standard format.

**Job time tickets (503)**   A document designed to accumulate the labor and machine time devoted to a particular production order.

**Master production schedule (503)**   A schedule that is used to plan overall production for a period of time. The schedule illustrates the gross production of each of the company's products.

**Observation (499)**   The auditors' evidence-gathering technique of viewing a client activity to obtain physical evidence of performance.

**Periodic inventory system (499)**   A method of accounting in which inventories are determined solely by means of a physical inventory at the end of the accounting period.

**Perpetual inventory system (499)**   A method of accounting for inventories in which controlling accounts and subsidiary ledgers are maintained to record receipts and issuances of goods, both in quantities and in dollar amounts. The accuracy of perpetual inventory records is tested periodically by physical inventories.

**Production order (503)**   A document that authorizes the production of a specific quantity of a product.

**Purchase commitment (523)**   A contractual obligation to purchase goods at fixed prices, entered into well in advance of scheduled delivery dates.

**Sales commitment (523)**   A contractual obligation to sell goods at fixed prices, entered into well in advance of scheduled delivery dates.

**Specialist (514)**   A person possessing special skill or knowledge in a field other than accounting or auditing, such as a real estate appraiser.

## Review Questions

12–1.   Many auditors consider the substantiation of the figure for inventory to be a more difficult and challenging task than the verification of most other items on the balance sheet. List several specific factors that support this view.

12–2.   Explain the significance of the purchase order to adequate internal control over purchase transactions.

12–3.   What segregation of duties would you recommend to attain maximum internal control over purchasing activities in a manufacturing concern?

12–4.   Do you believe that the normal review of purchase transactions by the auditors should include examination of receiving reports? Explain.

12–5.   The client's cost accounting system is often an important part of the CPAs' audit of the financial statements of a manufacturing company. For what purposes do the auditors consider the cost accounting system?

12–6.   What part, if any, do the independent auditors play in the planning for a client's physical inventory?

12–7.   What are the purposes of the auditors' observation of the taking of the physical inventory? (Do not discuss the procedures or techniques involved in making the observation.)

12–8.   For what purposes do the auditors make and record test counts of inventory quantities during their observation of the taking of the physical inventory? Discuss.

12–9.   Once the auditors have completed their test counts of the physical inventory, will they have any reason to make later reference to the inventory tags used by the client's employees in the counting process? Explain.

12–10.   When perpetual inventory records are maintained, is it necessary for a physical inventory to be taken at the balance sheet date? Explain.

12–11.   What is meant by a "bill and hold" scheme?

12–12.   What charges and credits may be disclosed in the auditors' analysis of the Cost of Goods Sold account of a manufacturing concern?

12–13.   A client company wishes to conduct its physical inventory on a sampling basis. Many items will not be counted. Under what general conditions will this method of taking inventory be acceptable to the auditors?

12–14.    Hana Ranch Company, which has never been audited, is asked on October 1 by its bank to arrange for a year-end audit. The company retains you to make this audit and asks what measures, if any, it should take to ensure a satisfactory year-end physical inventory. Perpetual inventories are not maintained. How would you answer this inquiry?

12–15.    "A well-prepared balance sheet usually includes a statement that the inventories are valued at cost." Evaluate this quotation.

12–16.    Darnell Equipment Company uses the LIFO method of valuation for part of its inventories and weighted-average cost for another portion. Would you be willing to issue an unqualified opinion under these circumstances? Explain.

12–17.    "If the auditors can determine that all goods in the physical inventory have been accurately counted and properly priced, they will have discharged fully their responsibility with respect to inventory." Evaluate this statement.

12–18.    How do the independent auditors use the client's backlog of unfilled sales orders in the examination of inventories?

12–19.    The controller of a new client company informs you that most of the inventories are stored in bonded public warehouses. He presents warehouse receipts to account for the inventories. Will careful examination of these warehouse receipts constitute adequate verification of these inventories? Explain.

12–20.    Enumerate specific steps to be taken by the auditors to ascertain that a client's inventories have not been pledged or subjected to a lien of any kind.

## Questions Requiring Analysis

**LO 3, 5**    12–21.    Nolan Manufacturing Company retains you on April 1 to perform an audit for the fiscal year ending June 30. During the month of May, you make extensive studies of internal control over inventories.

All goods purchased pass through a receiving department under the direction of the chief purchasing agent. The duties of the receiving department are to unpack, count, and inspect the goods. The quantity received is compared with the quantity shown on the receiving department's copy of the purchase order. If there is no discrepancy, the purchase order is stamped "OK—Receiving Dept." and forwarded to the accounts payable section of the accounting department. Any discrepancies in quantity or variations from specifications are called to the attention of the buyer by returning the purchase order to him with an explanation of the circumstances. No records are maintained in the receiving department, and no reports originate there.

As soon as goods have been inspected and counted in the receiving department, they are sent to the factory production area and stored alongside the machines in which they are to be processed. Finished goods are moved from the assembly line to a storeroom in the custody of a stock clerk, who maintains a perpetual inventory record in terms of physical units, but not in dollars.

What weaknesses, if any, do you see in the internal control over inventories?

**LO 1, 2, 6**    12–22.    At the beginning of your annual audit of Crestview Manufacturing Company's financial statements for the year ended December 31, 200X, the company president confides in you that Henry Ward, an employee, is living on a scale in excess of that which his salary would support.

The employee has been a buyer in the purchasing department for six years and has charge of purchasing all general materials and supplies. He is authorized to sign purchase orders for amounts up to $500. Purchase orders in excess of $500 require the countersignature of the general purchasing agent.

The president understands that the usual audit of financial statements is not designed, and cannot be relied upon, to provide absolute assurance that fraud and conflicts of interest will be discovered, although their discovery may result. The president authorizes you, however, to expand your regular audit procedures and to apply additional audit procedures to determine whether there is any evidence that the buyer has been misappropriating company funds or has been engaged in activities that were conflicts of interest.

*Required:*    List the audit procedures you would apply to the company records and documents in an attempt to discover evidence within the purchasing department of defalcations being committed by the buyer. Give the purpose of each audit procedure.

(AICPA, adapted)

**LO 1, 2, 6**   12–23.   A number of companies employ outside service companies that specialize in counting, pricing, extending, and footing inventories. These service companies usually furnish a certificate attesting to the value of the physical inventory.

*Required:*   Assuming that the service company took the client company's inventory on the balance sheet date:

    *a.* How much reliance, if any, can the auditors place on the inventory certificate of outside specialists? Discuss.

    *b.* What effect, if any, would the inventory certificate of outside specialists have upon the type of report the auditors would render? Discuss.

    *c.* What reference, if any, would the auditors make to the certificate of outside specialists in their audit report?

(AICPA, adapted)

**LO 6**   12–24.   Ace Corporation does not conduct a complete annual physical count of purchased parts and supplies in its principal warehouse, but uses statistical sampling instead to estimate the year-end inventory. Ace maintains a perpetual inventory record of parts and supplies and believes that statistical sampling is highly effective in determining inventory values and is sufficiently reliable to make a physical count of each item of inventory unnecessary.

*Required:*       *a.* Identify the audit procedures that should be used by the independent auditor that change or are in addition to normal required audit procedures when a client utilizes statistical sampling to determine inventory value and does not conduct a 100 percent annual physical count of inventory items.

    *b.* List at least 10 normal audit procedures that should be performed to verify physical quantities whenever a client conducts a periodic physical count of all or part of its inventory.

(AICPA, adapted)

**LO 6**   12–25.   The observation of a client's physical inventory is a mandatory auditing procedure when possible for the auditors to carry out and when inventories are material.

*Required:*       *a.* Why is the observation of physical inventory a mandatory auditing procedure? Explain.

    *b.* Under what circumstances is observation of physical inventory impossible?

    *c.* Why is the auditors' review of the client's control of inventory tags important during the observation of physical inventory? Explain.

**LO 1, 6**   12–26.   During your observation of the November 30, 20X0, physical inventory of Jay Company, you note the following unusual items:

    *a.* Electric motors in finished goods storeroom not tagged. Upon inquiry, you are informed that the motors are on consignment to Jay Company.

    *b.* A cutting machine (one of Jay's principal products) in the receiving department, with a large "REWORK" tag attached.

    *c.* A crated cutting machine in the shipping department, addressed to a nearby U.S. naval base, with a Department of Defense "Material Inspection and Receiving Report" attached, dated November 30, 20X0, and signed by the Navy Source Inspector.

    *d.* A small, isolated storeroom with five types of dusty raw materials stored therein. Inventory tags are attached to all of the materials, and your test counts agree with the tags.

*Required:*   What additional procedures, if any, would you carry out for each of the above? Explain.

**LO 2, 6**   12–27.   One of the problems faced by the auditors in their verification of inventory is the risk that slow-moving and obsolete items may be included in the goods on hand at the balance sheet date. In the event that such items are identified in the physical inventory, their carrying value should be written down to an estimated scrap value or other recoverable amount.

Prepare a list of the auditing procedures that the auditors should employ to determine whether slow-moving or obsolete items are included in the physical inventory.

**LO 1, 6**   12–28.   You are engaged in the audit of Reed Company, a new client, at the end of its first fiscal year, June 30, 20X1. During your work on inventories, you discover that all of the merchandise remaining in stock on June 30, 20X1, had been acquired July 1, 20X0, from Andrew Reed, the sole shareholder and president of Reed Company, for an original selling price of $10,000 cash and a note payable due July 1, 20X3, with interest at 15 percent, in the amount of $90,000. The merchandise had been used by the president when he operated a similar business as a sole proprietor.

How can you verify the pricing of the June 30, 20X1, inventory of Reed Company? Explain.

**LO 2, 6**   12–29.   Many CPAs are sharing information over the Internet. Auditnet is an Internet site that contains audit programs donated by various CPAs. Auditnet's address is www.auditnet.org. You can get to the audit programs by registering for the free material.

*a.* Select the inventory program, and summarize the procedures for testing inventory cutoff.

*b.* Describe the inspection procedures done by the auditors when they arrive at an inventory location for their observation.

**LO 6**   12–30.   Grandview Manufacturing Company employs standard costs in its cost accounting system. List the audit procedures that you would apply to ascertain that Grandview's standard costs and related variance amounts are acceptable and have not distorted the financial statements. (Confine your audit procedures to those applicable to raw materials.)

## Objective Questions

**All applicable questions are available with McGraw-Hill's *Connect*™ *Accounting*.** ▦ connect |ACCOUNTING

12–31.   **Multiple Choice Questions**

Select the best answer for each of the following and explain fully the reason for your selection.

**LO 2**

*a.* Which of the following is *least* likely to be among the auditors' objectives in the audit of inventories and cost of goods sold?

(1) Determine that the valuation of inventories and cost of goods sold is arrived at by appropriate methods.

(2) Determine the existence of inventories and the occurrence of transactions affecting cost of goods sold.

(3) Establish that the client includes only inventory on hand at year-end in inventory totals.

(4) Establish the completeness of inventories.

**LO 3, 5**

*b.* The receiving department is *least* likely to be responsible for the:

(1) Determination of quantities of goods received.

(2) Detection of damaged or defective merchandise.

(3) Preparation of a shipping document.

(4) Transmittal of goods received to the store's department.

**LO 3, 5**

*c.* The document issued by a common carrier acknowledging the receipt of goods and setting forth the provisions of the transportation agreement is the:

(1) Bill of lading.

(2) Job time shipping.

(3) Production order.

(4) Production schedule.

**LO 3, 5**

*d.* Which of the following should be included as a part of inventory costs of a manufacturing company?

|     | Direct Labor | Raw Materials | Factory Overhead |
| --- | --- | --- | --- |
| (1) | Yes | Yes | Yes |
| (2) | Yes | No | No |
| (3) | No | Yes | No |
| (4) | No | No | No |

**LO 3, 5**

*e.* The organization established by Congress to narrow the options in cost accounting that are available under generally accepted accounting principles is the:

(1) Cost Accounting Standards Board.

(2) Financial Accounting Standards Board.

(3) Public Company Accounting Oversight Board.

(4) Securities and Exchange Commission.

**LO 2, 4**   *f.* When a primary risk related to an audit is possible overstated inventory, the assertion most directly related is:

   (1) Existence.

   (2) Completeness.

   (3) Clarity.

   (4) Presentation.

**LO 5**   *g.* Instead of taking a physical inventory count on the balance-sheet date, the client may take physical counts prior to the year-end if internal control is adequate and:

   (1) Well-kept records of perpetual inventory are maintained.

   (2) Inventory is slow-moving.

   (3) Computer error reports are generated for missing prenumbered inventory tickets.

   (4) Obsolete inventory items are segregated and excluded.

**LO 5, 6**   *h.* The auditor's analytical procedures will be facilitated if the client:

   (1) Uses a standard cost system that produces variance reports.

   (2) Segregates obsolete inventory before the physical inventory count.

   (3) Corrects material weaknesses in internal control before the beginning of the audit.

   (4) Reduces inventory balances to the lower of cost or market.

**LO 4, 5, 6**   *i.* When perpetual inventory records are maintained in quantities and in dollars, and internal control over inventory is weak, the auditor would probably:

   (1) Want the client to schedule the physical inventory count at the end of the year.

   (2) Insist that the client perform physical counts of inventory items several times during the year.

   (3) Increase the extent of tests for unrecorded liabilities at the end of the year.

   (4) Have to disclaim an opinion on the income statement for that year.

**LO 3, 6**   *j.* Which of the following is the best audit procedure for the discovery of damaged merchandise in a client's ending inventory?

   (1) Compare the physical quantities of slow-moving items with corresponding quantities in the prior year.

   (2) Observe merchandise and raw materials during the client's physical inventory taking.

   (3) Review the management's inventory representations letter for accuracy.

   (4) Test overall fairness of inventory values by comparing the company's turnover ratio with the industry average.

**LO 5, 6**   *k.* McPherson Corp. does not make an annual physical count of year-end inventories, but instead makes weekly test counts on the basis of a statistical plan. During the year, Sara Mullins, CPA, observes such counts as she deems necessary and is able to satisfy herself as to the reliability of the client's procedures. In reporting on the results of her examination, Mullins:

   (1) Can issue an unqualified opinion without disclosing that she did not observe year-end inventories.

   (2) Must comment in the scope paragraph as to her inability to observe year-end inventories, but can nevertheless issue an unqualified opinion.

   (3) Is required, if the inventories are material, to disclaim an opinion on the financial statements taken as a whole.

   (4) Must, if the inventories are material, qualify her opinion.

**LO 2, 6**   *l.* The primary objective of a CPA's observation of a client's physical inventory count is to:

   (1) Discover whether a client has counted a particular inventory item or group of items.

   (2) Obtain direct knowledge that the inventory exists and has been properly counted.

   (3) Provide an appraisal of the quality of the merchandise on hand on the day of the physical count.

   (4) Allow the auditor to supervise the conduct of the count in order to obtain assurance that inventory quantities are reasonably accurate.

(AICPA, adapted)

**LO 5, 6**　12–32.　**Simulation**

Andy Watson, CPA is a senior auditor on the audit of Carlson, Inc. Andy is reviewing the results of analytical procedures related to inventory. For results (*a*), (*b*), and (*c*), select the explanation that is most likely to be consistent with the change described. Explanations may be used once, more than once, or not at all.

*Explanation:*

(1) Inventory increased as of year-end.

(2) Debt outstanding increased.

(3) A larger percentage of sales occurred during the last month of 20X8, as compared to 20X7.

(4) Interest expense increased during 20X8 due to the acquisition of new debt.

(5) The percentage tax included in the provision for income taxes for 20X8 is less than the percentage used in 20X7.

(6) Increases in costs of purchases were not completely passed on to customers through higher selling prices.

(7) Owners' equity increased due to retention of profits.

(8) Interest expense increased during 20X8.

(9) A significant amount of long-term debt became current at the end of 20X8.

*a.*　Inventory turnover (as measured by cost of goods sold/ending inventory) went from 7.95 in 20X7 to 10.52 in 20X8. Which of the explanations is consistent with the change in inventory turnover at SSC?

*b.*　Net income increased in 20X8. Which of the explanations is most consistent with the changes in net income?

*c.*　The gross profit percentage (gross profit/revenue) changed from .166 in 20X7 to .154 in 20X8. Which of the explanations is consistent with the change in gross profit percentage at SSC?

*Note: Section (d) is possible to work in a meaningful way only if you have the AICPA professional standards available—preferably in electronic form.*

*d.*　Auditors ordinarily must observe the counting of inventories that are on hand. Use the professional standards to find this requirement and the related guidance. Provide the AICPA AU section that includes the guidance.

**LO 1, 3, 4, 5, 6**　12–33.　**Simulation**

Auditors often observe the counting of their clients' inventories. You are working in the area of inventory with a new assistant on the audit of Jilco Inc. The assistant has a number of questions concerning inventory and the observation of inventory. Please reply "yes" or "no" to answer the following questions. Provide your rationale.

**Statement**

*a.*　With strong internal control, may Jilco Inc.'s inventory count be performed during the year rather than at year end?

*b.*　Jilco Inc. has inventory at many locations. Do we need to be present for the count at all locations?

*c.*　Must I document all my test counts in the working papers?

*d.*　Am I correct that our observation of the counting of the inventory primarily addresses the existence of inventory, and not the completeness of the count?

*e.*　Is it correct that, since Jilco Inc. manufactures a product, direct labor and overhead ordinarily become a part of inventory costs?

*f.*　Should Jilco's inventory be valued at the lower of standard cost or market?

*g.*　Is it safe to assume that any inventory items present as "consigned in" should not be included in the clients' inventory?

*h.*　When I take test counts of items, does this eliminate the need for Jilco Inc. personnel to count those items?

*i.*　Do I need to count all items in the inventory?

*j.*　At the completion of the count, should I leave Jilco Inc. personnel with a copy of all my inventory test counts to help assure inventory accuracy?

**LO 2, 5, 6**  12–34.  **Multiple Choice Questions**

    *a.* An auditor most likely would make inquiries of production and sales personnel concerning possible obsolete inventory to address:

       (1) Valuation.

       (2) Rights.

       (3) Existence.

       (4) Presentation.

    *b.* An auditor selects items from the client's inventory listing and identifies the items in the warehouse. This procedure is most likely related to:

       (1) Rights.

       (2) Completeness.

       (3) Existence.

       (4) Valuation.

    *c.* An auditor concluded that no excessive costs for an idle plant were charged to inventory. This conclusion is most likely related to presentation and disclosure and:

       (1) Valuation.

       (2) Completeness.

       (3) Existence.

       (4) Rights.

    *d.* During the inventory count an auditor selects items and determines that the proper description and quantity were recorded by the client. This procedure is most closely related to:

       (1) Rights.

       (2) Completeness.

       (3) Existence.

       (4) Valuation.

    *e.* An auditor most likely would analyze inventory turnover rates to obtain evidence about:

       (1) Existence.

       (2) Rights.

       (3) Presentation.

       (4) Valuation.

## Problems

**All applicable problems are available with McGraw-Hill's *Connect*™ *Accounting*.** 🔳 connect
|ACCOUNTING

**LO 3, 4, 5, 6**  12–35.  Described below are potential financial statement misstatements that are encountered by auditors.

    *a.* Inventory is understated because warehouse personnel overlooked several racks of parts in taking the physical inventory.

    *b.* Inventory is overstated because warehouse personnel included inventory items received subsequent to year-end while recording the purchase in the subsequent year to hide inventory shortages.

    *c.* Inventory is overstated because management instructed computer personnel to make changes in the file used to price inventories.

*Required:* For each misstatement, identify whether the misstatement results from error or fraud, the type of controls that would serve to prevent or detect the misstatement, and the substantive procedures that might be used by the auditors to detect the misstatement. Organize your answer as follows:

| Misstatement | Error or Fraud | Control | Substantive Procedure |
|---|---|---|---|
| *a.* | | | |

**LO 1, 3, 4, 5, 6**  12–36.  Williams Pharmaceutical Company produces a number of drugs that are regulated by various agencies, including, in the United States, the federal Food and Drug Administration (FDA).

These agencies issue licenses that approve drugs for sale and establish specific regulations regarding production quality and inventory security, violations of which can result in fines or the suspension of product licenses. All the drugs are protected under patents filed in various jurisdictions, and Williams markets the drugs in the United States as well as in a number of other countries. The company faces significant competition from other pharmaceutical companies globally.

*Required:*

a. Identify three business risks that are faced by Williams with respect to production processes and inventories.

b. For each of the risks identified in part (*a*), state whether the business risk results in a current-period inherent risk of material misstatement of the financial statements (financial reporting risk). If the business risk results in a financial reporting risk, describe that risk in terms of the type of financial statement misstatement that could occur.

c. Provide examples of how Williams's management might mitigate the risks (e.g., specific controls) identified in part (*b*) as financial reporting risks.

d. For each risk identified in part (*b*) as a financial reporting risk, describe substantive auditing procedures that might be used by the auditors if management did not have controls to mitigate the risk.

**LO 1, 3, 5** 12–37. You have been engaged by the management of Alden, Inc., to review its controls over the purchase, receipt, storage, and issue of raw materials. You have prepared the following comments, which describe Alden's procedures.

(1) Raw materials, which consist mainly of high-cost electronic components, are kept in a locked storeroom. Storeroom personnel include a supervisor and four clerks. All are well trained, competent, and adequately bonded. Raw materials are removed from the storeroom only upon written or oral authorization of one of the production supervisors.

(2) There are no perpetual-inventory records; hence, the storeroom clerks do not keep records of goods received or issued. To compensate for the lack of perpetual records, a physical inventory count is taken monthly by the storeroom clerks, who are well supervised. Appropriate procedures are followed in making the inventory count.

(3) After the physical count, the storeroom supervisor matches quantities counted against a predetermined reorder level. If the count for a given part is below the reorder level, the supervisor enters the part number on a materials requisition list and sends this list to the accounts payable clerk. The accounts payable clerk prepares a purchase order for a predetermined reorder quantity for each part and mails the purchase order to the vendor from whom the part was last purchased.

(4) When ordered materials arrive at Alden, they are received by the storeroom clerks. The clerks count the merchandise and agree the counts to the carrier's bill of lading. All bills of lading are initialed, dated, and filed in the storeroom to serve as receiving reports.

*Required:*

Describe the weaknesses in internal control and recommend improvements in Alden's procedures for the purchase, receipt, storage, and issuance of raw materials. Organize your answer sheet as follows:

| Weakness | Recommended Improvements |
|----------|--------------------------|
|          |                          |

(AICPA, adapted)

**LO 4, 6** 12–38. Described below are potential financial statement misstatements that are encountered by auditors in the audit of inventory and cost of goods sold.

a. Management of a chain of discount department stores systematically overstates inventory quantities at selected locations.

b. Accounting personnel of a manufacturing company make computational errors that understate the production costs of certain inventory items.

c. Management of a computer reseller overstates inventory value by failing to recognize the loss in value of certain inventory items that are obsolete.

d. Production personnel for a high-tech manufacturing company include in inventory items that failed to meet essential quality standards.

*Required:*  For each misstatement, describe the substantive auditing procedures that may be used by auditors to detect the misstatement. Organize your answer as shown below:

| Misstatement | Audit Procedures |
|---|---|
| *a.* | |

**LO 3, 5, 6** 12–39. The following are typical questions that might appear on an internal control questionnaire for inventory:

1. Are written procedures prepared by the client for the taking of the physical inventory?
2. Do the client's inventory-taking procedures include a requirement to identify damaged inventory items?
3. Does the client maintain perpetual inventory records?

*Required:*
a. Describe the purpose of each of the above controls.
b. Describe the manner in which each of the above procedures might be tested.
c. Assuming that the operating effectiveness of each of the above procedures is found to be inadequate, describe how the auditors might alter their substantive procedures to compensate for the increased level of risk.

**LO 3, 5, 6** 12–40. Late in December, your CPA firm accepted an audit engagement at Nash Jewelers, Inc., a corporation that deals largely in diamonds. The corporation has retail jewelry stores in several eastern cities and a diamond wholesale store in New York City. The wholesale store also sets the diamonds in rings and other quality jewelry.

The retail stores place orders for diamond jewelry with the wholesale store in New York City. A buyer employed by the wholesale store purchases diamonds in the New York diamond market; the wholesale store then fills orders from the retail stores and from independent customers and maintains a substantial inventory of diamonds. The corporation values its inventory by the specific identification cost method.

*Required:*  Assume that at the inventory date you are satisfied that Nash Jewelers, Inc., has no items left by customers for repair or sale on consignment and that no inventory owned by the corporation is in the possession of outsiders.

a. Discuss the problems the auditors should anticipate in planning for the observation of the physical inventory on this engagement because of the:
   (1) Different locations of inventories.
   (2) Nature of the inventory.
b. Assume that a shipment of diamond rings was in transit by corporation messenger from the wholesale store to a retail store on the inventory date. What additional audit steps would you take to satisfy yourself as to the gems that were in transit from the wholesale store on the inventory date?

(AICPA, adapted)

**LO 3, 5, 6** 12–41. You are an audit manager of the rapidly growing CPA firm of Raye and Coye. You have been placed in charge of three new audit clients, which have the following inventory features:

1. Canyon Cattle Co., which maintains 15,000 head of cattle on a 1,000-square-mile ranch, mostly unfenced, near the south rim of the Grand Canyon in Arizona.
2. Rhoads Mfg. Co., which has raw materials inventories consisting principally of pig iron loaded on gondola freight cars on a siding at the company's plant.
3. Strawser Company, which is in production around the clock on three shifts, and which cannot shut down production during the physical inventory.

*Required:*  What problems do you anticipate in the observation of physical inventories of the three new clients, and how would you deal with the problems?

**LO 2, 6** 12–42. Smith is the partner in charge of the audit of Blue Distributing Corporation, a wholesaler that owns one warehouse containing 80 percent of its inventory. Smith is reviewing the working papers that were prepared to support the firm's opinion on Blue's financial statements, and Smith wants to be certain essential audit records are well documented.

*Required:*  What substantive procedures should Smith expect to find in the working papers to document management's assertion about completeness as it relates to the inventory quantities at the end of the year?

(AICPA, adapted)

**LO 1, 3, 6**  **12–43.**  David Anderson, CPA, is engaged in the audit of the financial statements of Redondo Manufacturing Corporation for the year ended June 30, 20X0. Redondo's inventories at year-end include finished merchandise on consignment with consignees and finished merchandise stored in public warehouses. The merchandise in public warehouses is pledged as collateral for outstanding debt.

*Required:*    Normal inventory and notes payable auditing procedures have been satisfactorily completed. Describe the specific additional auditing procedures that Anderson should undertake with respect to:

    *a.* Consignments out.

    *b.* Finished merchandise in public warehouses pledged as collateral for outstanding debt.

(AICPA, adapted)

**In-Class Team Case**    **LO 1, 2, 6**    **12–44.**  Hovington, CPA, knows that while audit objectives relating to inventories may be stated in terms of the assertions as presented in this chapter, they may also be subdivided and stated more specifically. He has chosen to do so and has prepared the second column of the following table.

| Financial Statement Assertion | Specific Audit Objective | Audit Procedure |
|---|---|---|
| | 1. The entity has legal title to inventories. | |
| | 2. Recorded inventory quantities include all products on hand. | |
| | 3. Inventories are reduced, when appropriate, to replacement cost or net realizable value. | |
| | 4. Cost of inventories is properly calculated. | |
| | 5. The major categories of inventories and their basis of valuation are adequately reported in the financial statements. | |

*Required:*    Assume that Hovington's client, a retail department store, does no production. For each specific inventory audit objective listed above, select the most closely related financial statement assertion and the most appropriate audit procedure from the following:

| Financial Statement Assertion | Audit Procedure |
|---|---|
| A. Completeness and cutoff | F. Examine current vendors' price lists. |
| B. Existence or occurrence | G. Review drafts of the financial statements. |
| C. Presentation and disclosure | H. Select a sample of items during the physical inventory count and determine that they have been included on count sheets. |
| D. Rights and obligations | I. Select a sample of recorded items and examine supporting vendors' invoices and contracts. |
| E. Valuation and accuracy | J. Select a sample of recorded items on count sheets during the physical inventory count and determine that items are on hand. |
| | K. Test reasonableness of direct labor rates. |

Financial statement assertions and audit procedures may be selected once, more than once, or not at all.

**Ethics Case**    **LO 1, 5, 6**    **12–45.**  You have been with Zaird & Associates for approximately three months and are completing your work on the BizCaz audit. BizCaz produces pullover knit shirts to address the business casual market for both men and women. Although your experience has been limited, an unexpected staff resignation has resulted in your working directly with the engagement's in-charge senior on inventory. This has been a learning experience for you, because you have helped perform various tests of controls which may be summarized as indicating that internal control over inventory (including the perpetual records) seems strong. It is your impression that those tests resulted in a decrease in substantive procedures, thereby allowing a particularly efficient audit.

At the beginning of the audit, Jan Wheeler, the in-charge senior, told you that the management team of BizCaz has always been helpful and friendly. Throughout the audit, you have found the situation to be as good as described. In fact, BizCaz allows each auditor to purchase up to three shirts at a particularly attractive price of $12 per shirt, the cost for which employees may purchase shirts. The shirts have a market value of around $50, although the direct labor and material costs of each shirt are only $10.

Near the conclusion of the audit, after you and the other three staff members paid the controller and told him your sizes, he walked to the warehouse, removed 12 shirts from the appropriate piles, and brought them out. That evening you gave the situation some thought. On the one hand, the company didn't lose any money on your purchase of the shirts—but on the other hand, you would never have been able to purchase such high-quality clothes for such a low price.

*Required:*

1.  Is it acceptable to purchase these shirts from the audit client in this manner?
2.  Discuss the effect of any information presented in the case on the adequacy of the audit.

**Research and Discussion Case**    **LO 1, 6**    12–46.

Western Trading Company is a sole proprietorship engaged in the grain brokerage business. On December 31, 20X0, the entire grain inventory of the company was stored in outside bonded warehouses. The company's procedure of pricing inventories in these warehouses includes comparing the actual cost of each commodity in inventory with the market price as reported for transactions on the commodity exchanges at December 31. A write-down is made on commodities in which cost is in excess of market. During the course of the 20X0 audit, the auditors verified the company's computations. In addition to this, they compared the book value of the inventory with market prices at February 15, 20X1, the last day of fieldwork. The auditors noted that the market prices of several of the commodities had declined sharply subsequent to year-end, until their market price was significantly below the commodities' book values.

The inventory was repriced by the auditors on the basis of the new market prices, and the book value of the inventory was found to be in excess of market value on February 15 by approximately $21,000. The auditors proposed that the inventories be written down by $17,000 to this new market value, net of gains on the subsequent sales. The management protested this suggestion, stating that in their opinion the market decline was only temporary and that prices would recover in the near future. They refused to allow the write-down to be made. Accordingly, the auditors qualified their audit opinion for a departure from generally accepted accounting principles.

*Required:*

*a.*  Were the auditors justified in issuing a qualified opinion in this situation? Discuss fully, including alternative courses of action.

*b.*  State your opinion as to the course of action that was appropriate in this situation.

# Property, Plant, and Equipment: Depreciation and Depletion

## Learning objectives

After studying this chapter, you should be able to:

LO1 Describe the nature of property, plant, and equipment and depreciation.

LO2 Identify the auditors' objectives in the audit of property, plant, and equipment.

LO3 Explain the fundamental controls over property, plant, and equipment.

LO4 Use the understanding of the client and its environment to consider inherent risks (including fraud risks) related to property, plant, and equipment.

LO5 Obtain an understanding of internal control over property, plant, and equipment.

LO6 Assess the risks of material misstatement of property, plant, and equipment and design further audit procedures, including tests of controls and substantive procedures, to address the risks.

LO7 Explain the auditors' approach to the audit of depreciation.

LO8 Describe how the auditors design audit procedures to audit intangible assets.

**LO1**

Describe the nature of property, plant, and equipment and depreciation.

The term *property, plant, and equipment* includes all tangible assets with a service life of more than one year that are used in the operation of the business and are not acquired for the purpose of resale. Three major subgroups of such assets are generally recognized:

1. *Land,* such as property used in the operation of the business, has the significant characteristic of not being subject to depreciation.
2. *Buildings, machinery, equipment, and land improvements,* such as fences and parking lots, have limited service lives and are subject to depreciation.
3. *Natural resources* (wasting assets), such as oil wells, coal mines, and tracts of timber, are subject to depletion as the natural resources are extracted or removed.

Acquisitions and disposals of property, plant, and equipment are usually large in dollar amount, but concentrated in only a few transactions. Individual items of plant and equipment may remain unchanged in the accounts for many years.

## Property, Plant, and Equipment

### The Auditors' Objectives in Auditing Property, Plant, and Equipment

**LO2**

Identify the auditors' objectives in the audit of property, plant, and equipment.

The auditors' *objectives* in the audit of property, plant, and equipment are to:

1. Use the understanding of the client and its environment to consider *inherent risks,* including fraud risks, related to property, plant, and equipment.
2. Obtain an understanding of *internal control* over property, plant, and equipment.
3. Assess the risks of material misstatement and design tests of controls and substantive procedures that:
   a. Substantiate the *existence* of property, plant, and equipment and the occurrence of the related transactions.
   b. Establish the *completeness* of recorded property, plant, and equipment.
   c. Verify the *cutoff* of transactions affecting property, plant, and equipment.
   d. Determine that the client has *rights* to the recorded property, plant, and equipment.
   e. Establish the proper *valuation* or *allocation* of property, plant, and equipment and the *accuracy* of transactions affecting property, plant, and equipment.
   f. Determine that the *presentation* and *disclosure* of information about property, plant, and equipment are appropriate, including disclosure of depreciation methods.

In conjunction with the audit of property, plant, and equipment, the auditors also obtain evidence about the related accounts of depreciation expense, accumulated depreciation, and repairs and maintenance expense.

## Contrast with Audit of Current Assets

In many companies, the investment in plant and equipment amounts to 50 percent or more of the total assets. However, the audit work required to verify these properties is usually a much smaller proportion of the total audit time spent on the engagement. The verification of plant and equipment is facilitated by several factors not applicable to audit work on current assets.

First, a typical unit of property or equipment has a high dollar value, and relatively few transactions may lie behind a large balance sheet amount. Second, there is usually little change in the property accounts from year to year. The Land account often remains unchanged for a long span of years. The durable nature of buildings and equipment also tends to hold accounting activity to a minimum for these accounts. By way of contrast, such current assets as accounts receivable and inventory may have a complete turnover several times a year.

A third point of contrast between the audit of plant assets and the audit of current assets is the significance of the year-end cutoff of transactions on net income. For current assets, the year-end cutoff is a critical issue; for plant assets, it is of lesser importance. For example, in our discussion of inventories in Chapter 12, we emphasized the importance of an accurate year-end cutoff of the transactions for purchases and sales of merchandise. An error in the cutoff of a $50,000 purchase or sales transaction may cause a $50,000 error in the year's pretax net income. The possibility of such errors is substantial because a large volume of merchandise transactions is normal at year-end. For plant assets, on the other hand, a year-end cutoff error in recording an acquisition or retirement ordinarily will not affect net income for the year. Moreover, for many companies, there may be no transactions in plant assets occurring at the year-end. Of course, a cutoff error relating to acquisition or retirement of plant assets could cause slight inaccuracies in depreciation or in the timing of gains or losses on disposals. The problem of year-end cutoff for plant assets, however, must be considered of less importance in contrast to the audit of current assets.

## Internal Control over Plant and Equipment

**LO3**

Explain the fundamental controls over property, plant, and equipment.

The amounts invested in plant and equipment represent a large portion of the total assets of many industrial concerns. Maintenance, rearrangement, and depreciation of these assets are major expenses in the income statement. The total expenditures for the assets and related expenses make strong internal control essential to the preparation of reliable financial statements. Errors in measurement of income may be material if assets are scrapped without their cost being removed from the accounts, or if the distinction between capital and revenue expenditures is not maintained consistently. The losses that inevitably arise from uncontrolled methods of acquiring, maintaining, and retiring plant and equipment are often greater than the losses from fraud in cash handling.

In large enterprises, the auditors may expect to find an annual plant budget used to forecast and control acquisitions and retirements of plant and equipment. Many small companies also forecast expenditures for plant assets. Successful utilization of a plant budget presupposes the existence of reliable and detailed accounting records for plant and equipment. A detailed knowledge of the kinds, quantities, and condition of existing equipment is an essential basis for intelligent forecasting of the need for replacements and additions to the plant.

Other key controls applicable to plant and equipment are as follows:

1. A subsidiary ledger consisting of a separate record for each unit of property. An adequate plant and equipment ledger facilitates the auditors' work in analyzing additions and retirements, in verifying the depreciation provision and maintenance expenses, and in comparing authorizations with actual expenditures.

2. A system of authorizations requiring advance executive approval of all plant and equipment acquisitions, whether by purchase, lease, or construction. Serially numbered capital **work orders** are a convenient means of recording authorizations.

3. A reporting procedure assuring prompt disclosure and analysis of variances between authorized expenditures and actual costs.

4. An authoritative written statement of company policy distinguishing between **capital expenditures** and **revenue expenditures.** A dollar minimum ordinarily will be established for capitalization; any expenditures of a lesser amount automatically are classified as charges against current revenue.

5. A policy requiring all purchases of plant and equipment to be handled through the purchasing department and subjected to standard routines for receiving, inspection, and payment.

6. Periodic physical inventories designed to verify the existence, location, and condition of all property listed in the accounts and to disclose the existence of any unrecorded units.

7. A system of retirement procedures, including serially numbered *retirement work orders* (bottom), stating reasons for retirement and bearing appropriate approvals.

## Audit Documentation

The key audit working paper for property, plant, and equipment is a summary analysis such as that illustrated in Figure 13.1. This working paper follows the approach we have previously described of *emphasizing changes during the year under audit.* The working paper shows the beginning balances for the various types of plant assets; these amounts are the ending balances shown in the prior year's working papers. Next, the working paper shows the additions and retirements during the year. These are the transactions upon which the auditors' attention will be focused. A final column shows the ending balances that must equal the beginning balances plus the additions and minus the retirements. A similar set of four columns is used to summarize the changes in the accounts for accumulated depreciation.

Among the other audit working papers for property, plant, and equipment are analyses of the year's additions and retirements, analyses of repairs and maintenance expense accounts, and tests of depreciation. The analyses of plant additions and retirements and the tests of depreciation are cross-indexed to the summary analysis, as illustrated in Figure 13.1. In the audit of larger companies, it is common practice for the client to prepare for the auditors both a listing of the year's additions and a schedule of the year's disposals. In addition, the auditors document internal controls and risk assessments for property, plant, and equipment.

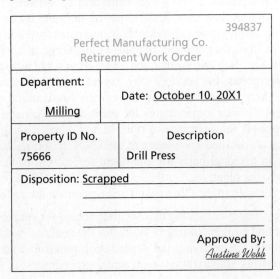

**FIGURE 13.1** **Analysis of Property, Plant, and Equipment**

K-1

THE MANDVILLE CORPORATION
Summary of Property, Plant, and Equipment and Accumulated Depreciation
December 31, 20X2

| Account Number | Description | Assets | | | | Method | Rate | Accumulated Depreciation | | | |
|---|---|---|---|---|---|---|---|---|---|---|---|
| | | Balance 12/31/X1 | Additions | Retirements | Balance 12/31/X2 | | | Balance 12/31/X1 | Provision | Retirements | Balance 12/31/X2 |
| 151 | Land | 500,000 ⅋ | 151,000 | | 651,000 | | | | | | |
| 152-3 | Land Improv. | 135,000 ⅋ | 10,000 | | 145,000 ✓ | S.L. | 5% | 13,500 ⅋ | 7,000 | | 20,500 ✓ |
| 154-5 | Buildings | 4,500,000 ⅋ | 495,000 | | 4,995,000 ✓ | S.L. | 3% | 292,000 ⅋ | 142,420 | | 434,420 ✓ |
| 156-7 | Equipment | 800,000 ⅋ | 110,000 | 60,000 | 850,000 ✓ | S.L. | 10% | 235,000 ⅋ | 70,600 | 50,600 | 255,000 ✓ |
| | TOTALS | 5,935,000 | 766,000 | 60,000 | 6,641,000 | | | 540,500 | 220,020 | 50,600 | 709,920 |
| | | | | K-1-1 | K | | | | K-1-2 | K-1-1 | K |

⅋ Agreed to prior year work papers.

✓ Footed plant and equipment subsidiary ledger cards. No exceptions.

Conclusion:

As a result of our audit procedures for property, plant, and equipment and related depreciation, it is our opinion that the 12/31/X2 balances are fairly stated.

EMH
1/17/X3

CMW
1/25/X3

**Initial Audits and Repeat Engagements**

The auditing procedures listed in subsequent pages are applicable to repeat engagements and therefore concern only transactions of the current year. In the auditors' first audit of a new client that has changed auditors, a review of the predecessor auditor's audit documentation may provide substantial audit evidence about opening balances and consistency of accounting principles. However, the nature, timing, and extent of audit work performed and conclusions reached are the responsibility of the successor auditor. Nonetheless, if previous audits were performed by a reputable CPA firm, that firm's work will be extremely helpful to the successor auditor.

In a first audit of a company that has *not* previously been audited, or one in which access to a predecessor's audit work is not available, the ideal approach is a complete historical analysis of the property accounts. By thorough review of all major charges and credits to the property accounts since their inception, the auditors can establish the validity of the beginning balances of property, plant, and equipment and accumulated depreciation.

If the client has been in business for many years, the review of transactions in earlier years necessarily must be performed on a test basis in order to stay within reasonable time limits. However, the importance of an analysis of transactions of prior years deserves emphasis. Only by this approach can the auditors be in a sound position to express an opinion as to the propriety of the current period's depreciation. If repair and maintenance expenses have been capitalized, or asset additions have been recorded as operating expenses, or retirements of property have gone unrecorded, the depreciation expense will be misstated regardless of the care taken in the selection of depreciation rates. The auditors should make clear to the client that the initial examination of plant and equipment requires procedures that need not be duplicated in subsequent engagements.

## Audit of Property, Plant, and Equipment

The following steps indicate the general pattern of work performed by the auditors in the verification of property, plant, and equipment. The procedures for depreciation are covered in a separate program on pages 549–550. Selection of the most appropriate procedures for a particular audit will be guided by the nature of the controls that have been implemented and by the results of the auditors' risk assessments.

A. Use the understanding of the client and its environment to consider inherent risks, including fraud risks, related to property, plant, and equipment.

B. Obtain an understanding of internal control over property, plant, and equipment.

C. Assess the risks of material misstatement and design further audit procedures.

D. Perform further audit procedures—tests of controls.
  1. Nature of tests of controls.
  2. If necessary, revise the risks of material misstatement based on the results of tests of controls.

E. Perform further audit procedures—substantive procedures for property, plant, and equipment.
  1. Obtain a summary analysis of changes in property owned and reconcile to ledgers.
  2. Vouch additions to property, plant, and equipment during the year.
  3. Make a physical inspection of major acquisitions of plant and equipment.
  4. Analyze repair and maintenance expense accounts.
  5. Investigate the status of property, plant, and equipment not in current use.
  6. Test the client's provision for depreciation.
  7. Investigate potential impairments of property, plant, and equipment.
  8. Investigate retirements of property, plant, and equipment during the year.
  9. Examine evidence of legal ownership of property, plant, and equipment.
  10. Review rental revenue from land, buildings, and equipment owned by the client but leased to others.
  11. Examine lease agreements on property, plant, and equipment leased to and from others.
  12. Perform analytical procedures for property, plant, and equipment.
  13. Evaluate financial statement presentation and disclosure for plant assets and for related revenue and expenses.

**FIGURE 13.2**

**Objectives of Major Substantive Procedures for Property, Plant, and Equipment and Depreciation**

| Substantive Procedures | Primary Audit Objectives |
|---|---|
| Obtain a summary analysis of changes in property owned and reconcile to ledgers. | *Valuation* |
| Vouch additions during year. Make physical inspection of major acquisitions. | *Existence, occurrence,* and *rights* <br> *Valuation* or *allocation* <br> *Accuracy* <br> *Cutoff* |
| Analyze repair and maintenance expense accounts. | *Valuation* or *allocation* |
| Investigate the status of property not in current use. | *Valuation* or *allocation* <br> *Presentation* and *disclosure* |
| Test the client's provision for depreciation. Investigate potential impairments. | *Valuation* and *allocation* |
| Investigate retirements of property during the year. Examine evidence of legal ownership. Review rental revenue. | *Existence, occurrence,* and *rights* |
| Examine lease agreements. Perform analytical procedures. | *Existence* and *rights* <br> *Completeness* <br> *Valuation* or *allocation* |
| Evaluate financial statement presentation and disclosure. | *Presentation* and *disclosure* |

These substantive audit procedures are summarized in Figure 13.2 along with the primary audit objectives.

**LO4**

Use the understanding of the client and its environment to consider inherent risks (including fraud risks) related to property, plant, and equipment.

### A. Use the Understanding of the Client and Its Environment to Consider Inherent Risks, Including Fraud Risks.

After they have obtained an understanding of the client and its environment, the auditors will identify and assess inherent risks related to property, plant, and equipment.

If any of the inherent risks identified by the auditors involve the possibility of fraud, they will make sure that they understand the programs and controls established by management to control the risk. They will also determine that the controls have been implemented. Finally, the auditors will design an appropriate response to the risk.

### B. Obtain an Understanding of Internal Control over Property, Plant, and Equipment.

In obtaining an understanding of internal control over property, plant, and equipment, the auditors may utilize a written description, flowcharts, or an internal control questionnaire. The following are typical of the questions included in a questionnaire: Are plant ledgers regularly reconciled with general ledger control accounts? Are periodic physical inventories of plant assets compared with the plant ledgers? Are variances between plant budgets and actual expenditures for plant assets subject to review and approval of executives? Does the sale, transfer, or dismantling of equipment require written executive approval on a serially numbered retirement work order? Is there a written policy for distinguishing between capital expenditures and revenue expenditures?

**LO5**

Obtain an understanding of internal control over property, plant, and equipment.

After preparing a description of internal control, the auditors will determine whether the controls as described to them have been *implemented*. To confirm their understanding of these policies and procedures, they will observe whether there is an appropriate segregation of duties over the acquisition of plant assets and inquire as to who performed various functions throughout the period. They will also inspect the subsidiary ledger of property, plant, and equipment; the serially numbered work orders; and the plant and equipment budget and examine evidence of the follow-up on variances from the budget. These procedures may provide the auditors with sufficient evidence to assess control risk for certain financial statement assertions about property, plant, and equipment as being at less than the maximum.

FIGURE 13.3    Potential Misstatements—Investments in Property, Plant, and Equipment

| Description of Misstatement | Examples | Internal Control Weaknesses or Factors that Increase the Risk of the Misstatement |
|---|---|---|
| Misstatement of acquisitions of property, plant, and equipment | **Fraud:**<br>• Expenditures for repairs and maintenance expenses recorded as property, plant, and equipment acquisitions to overstate income<br><br>**Error:**<br>• Purchases of equipment erroneously reported in maintenance and repairs expense account | • Undue pressure to meet earnings targets<br><br><br><br>• Inadequate accounting manual; incompetent accounting personnel |
| Failure to record retirements of property, plant, and equipment | **Error:**<br>• An asset that has been replaced is discarded due to its lack of value, without an accounting entry | • Inadequate accounting policies, e.g., failure to use retirement work orders |
| Improper reporting of unusual transactions | **Error:**<br>• A "gain" recorded on an exchange of nonmonetary assets that lacks commercial substance | • Inadequate accounting manual; incompetent accounting personnel |

### C. Assess the Risks of Material Misstatement and Design Further Audit Procedures.

**LO6**

Assess the risks of material misstatement of property, plant, and equipment and design further audit procedures, including tests of controls and substantive procedures, to address the risks.

After considering the information about the client and its environment, including internal control, the auditors assess the risks of material misstatement related to the assertions about property, plant, and equipment. To make these assessments, the auditors must consider the relationships between specific misstatements and controls. Figure 13.3 provides examples of potential misstatements of property, plant, and equipment and weaknesses in internal control that would make them more likely to occur.

The auditors' assessments of the risks of material misstatement (inherent and control risks) are used to design further audit procedures, including tests of controls and substantive procedures. The further audit procedures must include tests of controls when the auditors' assessments of control risk assume that controls are operating effectively but, in regard to their understanding of the client's internal control, the auditors have not obtained sufficient evidence that controls are operating effectively.

Some of the risks identified by the auditors may be considered to be significant risks that require special audit consideration. The auditors must design procedures that are focused on these significant risks. In addition, the auditors:

1. Must evaluate the design of the related controls and determine that they are being implemented.
2. May not rely solely on analytical procedures to address the risk.
3. May not rely on evidence obtained in prior periods regarding the operating effectiveness of the related controls.

### D. Perform Further Audit Procedures—Tests of Controls.

### 1. Nature of Tests of Controls.

Tests directed toward the effectiveness of controls are used to evaluate the client's internal control and determine whether the auditors can justify their planned assessed levels of control risk for the assertions about property, plant, and equipment accounts. Certain tests of controls are performed as the auditors obtain an understanding of the client's internal control; these tests were described in our discussion of that process. Additional tests of controls, for example, might include selecting a sample of purchases of plant and equipment to test the controls related to authorization, receipt, and proper recording of the transactions. A sample of recorded retirements also may be tested for proper authorization and supporting retirement work orders. These tests often will be combined with the substantive tests of additions and retirements described below.

### 2. If Necessary, Revise the Risks of Material Misstatement Based on the Results of Tests of Controls.

If the tests of controls reveal that the operating effectiveness of controls over property, plant, and equipment is not as anticipated, the auditors will have to reassess the risks of material misstatement. This will allow them to determine the substantive procedures that must be performed.

### E. Perform Further Audit Procedures—Substantive Procedures for Property, Plant, and Equipment.

### 1. Obtain a Summary Analysis of Changes in Property Owned and Reconcile to Ledgers.

The auditors may verify the beginning balances of plant and equipment assets by reference to the prior year's audit working papers. In addition to beginning balances, the summary analysis will show the additions and retirements of plant and equipment during the year under audit. As the audit progresses, the auditors will examine a sample of these additions and retirements. The detailed working papers showing this verification will support and be cross-indexed to the summary analysis worksheet.

Before making a detailed analysis of changes in property accounts during the year, the auditors will want to be sure that the amounts in the subsidiary ledgers agree in total with the balances in the controlling accounts. Reconciliation of the subsidiary ledgers with the controlling accounts can be performed very quickly with the use of generalized audit software.

### 2. Vouch Additions to Property, Plant, and Equipment during the Year.

The vouching of additions to the property, plant, and equipment accounts during the period under audit is one of the most important substantive tests. The extent of the vouching is dependent upon the auditors' assessment of control risk for the existence and valuation of plant and equipment. The vouching process utilizes a working paper analysis of the general ledger control accounts and includes the tracing of entries through the journals to original documents, such as contracts, deeds, construction work orders, invoices, canceled checks, and authorization by appropriate individuals.

The specific steps to be taken in investigating the year's additions usually will include the following:

a. On a test basis, vouch purchases of property, plant, and equipment to invoices, deeds, contracts, or other supporting documents. Recompute extensions, footings, and treatment of discounts. Make certain repairs and maintenance expenses (or other expenses) were not improperly capitalized.

b. Investigate all instances in which the actual cost of acquisitions substantially exceeded authorized amounts. Determine whether such excess expenditures were analyzed and approved by appropriate officials.

c. Investigate fully any debits to property, plant, and equipment accounts not arising from acquisition of physical assets.

d. Determine that the total cost of any plant and equipment assets purchased on the installment plan is reflected in the asset accounts and that the unpaid installments are set up as liabilities.

e. Review changes during the year in construction in progress and examine supporting work orders, both incomplete and closed.

f. Trace transfers from the Construction in Progress account to the property accounts, observing propriety of classification. Determine that all completed items have been transferred out of the account.

The accounting for plant assets acquired in a nonmonetary exchange is specified by *FASB ASC* 845-10-30. Generally, these assets are recorded at fair value, unless fair value is not determinable, the exchange is to facilitate sales to customers, or the exchange lacks commercial substance.

Assets constructed by a company for its own use should be recorded at the cost of direct materials, direct labor, and applicable overhead cost. However, auditors may apply the additional test of comparing the total cost of self-constructed equipment with bids or estimated purchase prices for similar equipment from outside suppliers; excess costs of self-constructed assets should be expensed in the period that construction is completed.

### Related Party Transactions

Assets acquired from affiliated corporations, from promoters or stockholders, or by any other type of related party transaction not involving arm's-length bargaining between buyer and seller have sometimes been recorded at inflated amounts. The auditors should inquire into the methods by which the sales price was determined, the cost of the property to the vendor, length of ownership by the vendor, and any other available evidence that might indicate an arbitrarily determined valuation. Material related party transactions must be disclosed in the notes to the financial statements.

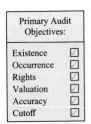

Primary Audit
Objectives:

| | |
|---|---|
| Existence | ☑ |
| Occurrence | ☑ |
| Rights | ☑ |
| Valuation | ☑ |
| Accuracy | ☑ |
| Cutoff | ☑ |

### 3.  Make a Physical Inspection of Major Acquisitions of Plant and Equipment.

The auditors usually make a physical inspection of major units of plant and equipment acquired during the year under audit. This step is helpful in maintaining a good working knowledge of the client's operations and also in interpreting the accounting entries for both additions and retirements.

The audit procedure of physical inspection may flow in either direction between the plant assets and the records of plant assets. By tracing items in the plant ledger to the physical assets, the auditors prove that the assets shown in the accounting records *actually* exist and are in current use. The alternative testing procedure is to inspect selected assets in the plant and trace these assets to the detailed records. This test provides evidence that existing assets are recorded (completeness).

The physical inspection of plant assets may be limited to major units acquired during the year or may be extended to include tests of older equipment as well. In a few situations (especially when the risk of material misstatement is very high), the auditors may conclude that the taking of a complete physical inventory is needed. Bear in mind, however, that a complete physical inventory of plant and equipment is a rare event. If such an inventory is required, the auditors' role is to *observe* the physical inventory.

Let us consider an example of a situation in which the auditors might conclude that a complete physical inventory of equipment is needed. Assume that a client is engaged in commercial construction work and that the client owns and operates a great many units of costly mobile equipment. Such equipment may often be scrapped or sold upon the authorization of a field supervisor. Under these circumstances, the auditors might regard a complete physical inventory of plant and equipment as essential. Similarly, in the audit of clients owning a large number of automobiles and trucks, the auditors may insist upon observing a physical count, as well as examining legal title.

Some large companies, as part of their internal control, perform occasional physical inventories of plant and equipment at certain locations or in selected departments. The *observation* of these limited counts is often carried out by the client's internal auditing staff rather than by the independent auditors.

Primary Audit
Objective:

| | |
|---|---|
| Valuation | ☑ |

### 4. Analyze Repair and Maintenance Expense Accounts.

The auditors' principal objective in analyzing repair and maintenance expense accounts is to discover items that should have been capitalized. Many companies have a written policy setting the minimum expenditure to be capitalized. For example, company policy may prescribe that no expenditure for less than $300 shall be capitalized regardless of the service life of the item purchased. In such cases, the auditors will analyze the repair and maintenance accounts with a view toward determining the consistency of application of this policy as well as compliance with generally accepted accounting principles. To determine that the accounts contain only proper repair and maintenance charges, the auditors will trace the larger expenditures to written authorizations for the transaction. The accuracy of the client's accounting for the expenditures may be verified by reference to vendors' invoices, material requisitions, and labor time records.

One useful means of identifying capital expenditures that have been included in the repair and maintenance accounts is to obtain or prepare an analysis of the monthly amounts of expense with corresponding amounts listed for the preceding year. Any significant variations from month to month or between corresponding months of the two years should be fully investigated. If maintenance expense is classified by the departments serviced, the variations are especially noticeable.

### 5. Investigate the Status of Property, Plant, and Equipment Not in Current Use.

Land, buildings, and equipment not in current use should be investigated thoroughly to determine the prospects for their future use in operations. Plant assets that are temporarily idle need not be reclassified, and depreciation may be continued at normal rates. On the other hand, idle equipment that has been dismantled, or that for any reason appears unsuitable for future operating use, should be written down to an estimated realizable value and excluded from the plant and equipment classification. In the case of standby equipment and other property not needed at present or prospective levels of operation, the auditors should consider whether the carrying value is recoverable through future use in operations.

### 6. Test the Client's Provision for Depreciation.

See the separate *depreciation* program following this audit program.

### 7. Investigate Potential Impairments of Property, Plant, and Equipment.

Accounting standards require that long-lived assets be reviewed for impairment whenever events or changes in circumstances indicate that the carrying amount of an asset may not be recoverable. In these circumstances, if the sum of the expected undiscounted future cash flows from the asset is less than its carrying amount, an impairment loss is recognized. The impairment loss is equal to the difference between the book value and the fair market value of the asset. International accounting standards have similar requirements, but these standards allow the asset to be written back up with a reversal of the loss if the value recovers. U.S. accounting standards do not allow the loss to be reversed in future periods.

Auditors must be alert for any changes in circumstances that may affect the recoverability of property, plant, and equipment as well as long-lived intangible assets. Examples of changes in circumstances that should result in a test of impairment include a significant decrease in the market value of the asset, a significant adverse change in the way the asset is used, or an adverse change in the physical condition of the asset. If specific assets appear to be impaired, the auditors should evaluate the reasonableness of management's determination of the impairment loss.

The determination of the amount of an impairment loss often involves subjective estimates as to the fair value of assets. Recall from the discussion in Chapter 5 that fair value is the price that would be received to sell an asset or paid to transfer a liability in an orderly transaction between market participants at the measurement date. The best evidence about fair value is obtained when there is an active market for the asset and the value of the asset may be determined by reference to sales of identical assets. However, in many cases, an active market does not exist for the specific asset, and fair value must be determined through the application of a valuation model, often involving discounted cash flows. The accuracy of these estimates of fair value depends on the reasonableness of the model's underlying assumptions.

The audit of estimates of fair values often involves substantial risks of material misstatement. For a particular estimate, the level of risk is influenced by a number of factors, such as the length of the cash flow forecast period, the number of significant and complex assumptions, the degree of subjectivity associated with those assumptions, and the availability of objective data. In auditing the values determined by valuation models, the auditors should evaluate:

- The appropriateness of the valuation model used.
- Whether the significant assumptions are reasonable and consistent with economic conditions, existing market information, management's plans and strategies, past experience, other financial statement assumptions, and the risk associated with the cash flows.
- The accuracy, completeness, and relevance of the important data on which the fair value measurements are based.

The auditors should consider the processes and controls used by management to develop the estimates and examine appropriate internal and external data in support of the significant assumptions. The auditors should also consider whether any other information or evidence gathered indicates that one or more significant assumptions are not reasonable. In some cases, the auditors may decide to develop their own estimate of fair value to evaluate the reasonableness of management's estimate.

As a part of their substantive procedures, the auditors may decide to use the work of a valuation specialist. Regardless of whether the specialist is engaged by management or by the auditors, the auditors should evaluate the professional qualifications and experience of the valuation specialist and obtain an understanding of the nature of the specialist's work and conclusions.

### 8. Investigate Retirements of Property, Plant, and Equipment during the Year.

Primary Audit Objectives:

Existence ☑
Occurrence ☑
Rights ☑

The principal purpose of this procedure is to determine whether any property has been replaced, sold, dismantled, or abandoned without such action being reflected in the accounting records. Nearly every thorough physical inventory of plant and equipment reveals missing units of property—units disposed of without a corresponding reduction of the accounts.

If a machine is sold for cash or traded in on a new machine, the transaction generally will involve the use of documents, such as a cash receipts form or a purchase order; the processing of these documents may bring the retirement to the attention of accounting personnel. However, plant assets may be scrapped rather than sold or traded in on new equipment; consequently, there may be no paperwork related to the disappearance of a machine. How is the accounting department expected to know when the asset has been retired?

As explained previously, one method of preventing unrecorded retirements is enforcement of a companywide policy that no plant asset shall be retired from use without prior approval on a special type of serially numbered retirement work order. A copy of the retirement work order is routed to the accounting department, thus providing some assurance that retirements will be reflected in the accounting records.

What specific steps should the auditors take to discover any unrecorded retirements? The following measures often are effective:

a. If major additions of plant and equipment have been made during the year, determine whether old equipment was traded in or replaced by the new units.

b. Analyze the Miscellaneous Revenue account to locate any cash proceeds from the sale of plant assets.

c. If any of the company's products have been discontinued during the year, investigate the disposition of plant facilities formerly used in manufacturing such products.

d. Inquire of executives and supervisors whether any plant assets have been retired during the year.

e. Examine retirement work orders or other source documents for authorization by the appropriate official or committee.

f. Investigate any reduction of insurance coverage to determine whether this was caused by retirement of plant assets.

### 9. Examine Evidence of Legal Ownership of Property, Plant, and Equipment.

To determine that plant assets are the property of the client, the auditors look for such evidence as a deed, a title insurance policy, property tax bills, receipts for payments to a mortgagee, and fire insurance policies. Additionally, the fact that rental payments are not being made is supporting evidence of ownership.

It is sometimes suggested that the auditors may verify ownership of real property and the absence of liens by examination of public records. This step is seldom taken. Inspection of the documentary evidence listed above usually provides adequate proof of ownership. If some doubt exists as to whether the client has clear title to property, the auditors should obtain the opinion of the client's legal counsel or request that a title search be performed by a title insurance company.

Possession of a deed is not proof of present ownership, because when real property is sold, a new deed is prepared and the seller retains the old one. This is true of title insurance policies as well. Better evidence of continuing ownership is found in property tax bills made out in the name of the client and in fire insurance policies, rent receipts from lessees, and regular payments of principal and interest to a mortgagee or trustee.

The disclosure of liens on property is considered during the examination of liabilities, but in the audit work on plant and equipment the auditors should be alert for evidence indicating the existence of liens. Purchase contracts examined in verifying the cost of property may reveal unpaid balances. Insurance policies may contain loss payable endorsements in favor of a secured party.

The auditors can readily ascertain the ownership of automobiles and trucks by reference to certificates of title and registration documents. The ease of transfer of title to automotive equipment, plus the fact that it is often used as collateral for loans, makes it important that the auditors examine the title to such property.

### 10. Review Rental Revenue from Land, Buildings, and Equipment Owned by the Client but Leased to Others.

In testing rental revenue from land and buildings, it is often desirable for the auditors to obtain or to sketch a map of the property and to make a physical inspection of each unit. This may disclose that premises reported as vacant are in fact occupied by lessees and are producing revenue not reflected in the accounting records. If the client's property includes an office or apartment building, the auditors should obtain a floor plan of the building as well as copies of all lease contracts. In this way, they can account for all available rental space as revenue-producing or vacant and can verify reported vacancies by physical inspection at the balance sheet date. If interim audit work is being performed, vacancies should also be verified by inspection and discussion with management during the year.

Examination of leases will indicate whether tenants are responsible for the cost of electricity, water, gas, and telephone service. These provisions should be reconciled with utility expense accounts. Rental revenue accounts should be analyzed in all cases and the amount compared with lease agreements and cash records.

### 11. Examine Lease Agreements on Property, Plant, and Equipment Leased to and from Others.

The preceding step addressed rental revenue from leases. The auditors also must be aware that generally accepted accounting principles require differing accounting treatments for operating and capital leases. The auditors should carefully examine lease agreements to determine whether the accounting for the assets involved is proper. For example, the auditors must be alert for the client's possible use of improper accounting techniques, such as the following.

- Assets under a lease that are being improperly accounted for (e.g., leases that meet the criteria for capital treatment are treated as operating leases).
- Leasehold improvements to buildings under operating leases that are being depreciated over the estimated useful life of the improvements rather than the shorter term of the lease, when renewal of the lease is not reasonably assured.
- A lease that provides a rent holiday that is not properly accounted for. For example, if a lease provides for six months of free rent, this benefit should be amortized over the life of the lease.

## 12. Perform Analytical Procedures for Property, Plant, and Equipment.

The specific trends and ratios used in judging the overall reasonableness of recorded amounts for plant and equipment will vary with the nature of the client's operations. Among the ratios and trends used by auditors for this purpose are the following:

*a.* Total cost of plant assets divided by annual output in dollars, pounds, or other units.

*b.* Total cost of plant assets divided by cost of goods sold.

*c.* Comparison of repairs and maintenance expense on a monthly basis and from year to year.

*d.* Comparison of acquisitions for the current year with prior years.

*e.* Comparison of retirements for the current year with prior years.

Acquisitions and retirements may vary widely from year to year; however, it is essential that the auditors be aware of these variations and judge their reasonableness in the light of trends in the client's past and present operations. Analytical procedures relating to depreciation are discussed later in this chapter as part of the audit program for depreciation.

## 13. Evaluate Financial Statement Presentation and Disclosure for Plant Assets and for Related Revenue and Expenses.

The balance sheet or accompanying notes should disclose balances of major classes of depreciable assets. Accumulated depreciation may be shown by major class or in total, and the method or methods of computing depreciation should be stated. The total amount of depreciation should be disclosed in the income statement or supporting notes.

In addition, adequate financial statement presentation and disclosure will ordinarily reflect the following principles:

*a.* The basis of valuation should be explicitly stated. At present, cost is the generally accepted basis of valuation for plant and equipment; property not in use should be valued at the lower of cost or estimated realizable value.

*b.* Property pledged to secure loans should be clearly identified.

*c.* Property not in current use should be segregated in the balance sheet.

# Depreciation

## The Auditors' Perspective toward Depreciation

**LO7**

Explain the auditors' approach to the audit of depreciation.

Determining the annual depreciation expense involves two decisions by the client company: first, an estimate of the useful economic lives of various groups of assets and, second, a choice among several depreciation methods, each of which would lead to a different answer. The wide range of possible amounts for annual depreciation expense because of these decisions made by the client suggests that the auditors should maintain a perspective of looking for assurance of overall reasonableness. Specifically, overall tests of the year's depreciation expense are of special importance.

Among the methods of computing depreciation expense most frequently encountered are the straight-line method and the declining-balance method. Far less common, although quite acceptable, are methods based on units of output or hours of service. The most widely adopted types of accelerated depreciation methods are fixed percentage of declining balance and sum-of-the-years' digits. The essential characteristic of these and other similar methods is that depreciation is greatest in the first year and becomes smaller in succeeding years.

CPAs often encounter clients maintaining their records using federal income tax rules, such as the modified accelerated cost recovery system (MACRS). Although such methods are considered a systematic method of depreciating the cost of an asset, the depreciable lives of the assets are often much shorter than their useful economic lives. If the recovery periods are not reasonable, depreciation expense may be materially misstated and the auditors will not be in a position to issue an unqualified opinion on the financial statements.

## The Auditors' Objectives in Auditing Depreciation

Depreciation is an accounting estimate. Recall from Chapter 5 that, in evaluating the reasonableness of accounting estimates, auditors first obtain an understanding of the client's processes and controls. Then, they use one or more of the following three basic approaches:

1. Review and test management's process of developing the estimate.
2. Review subsequent events or transactions bearing on the estimate.
3. Independently develop an estimate of the amount to compare to management's estimate.

For depreciation, while a combination of all of the above approaches may be used, the emphasis is ordinarily upon the first basic approach—reviewing and testing management's process for calculating depreciation.

As we discussed earlier, depreciation relates most directly to the *valuation* or *allocation* audit objective. To meet this objective, the auditors, in examining management's process for calculating depreciation, determine (1) that the methods in use are acceptable, (2) that the methods are being followed consistently, and (3) that the calculations required by the chosen methods are accurate. The audit program in the following section conveys a more detailed picture of the auditors' objectives.

## Audit Program— Depreciation Expense and Accumulated Depreciation

The following outline of substantive procedures to be performed by the auditors in reviewing depreciation is stated in sufficient detail to be largely self-explanatory. Consequently, no point-by-point discussion will be presented. Techniques for testing the client's provision for depreciation for the year are, however, discussed immediately following the audit program.

1. Review the depreciation policies set forth in company manuals or other management directives. Determine whether the methods in use are designed to allocate costs of plant and equipment assets systematically over their service lives.
   a. Inquire whether any extra working shifts or other conditions of accelerated production are present that might warrant adjustment of normal depreciation rates.
   b. Discuss with executives the possible need for recognition of obsolescence resulting from technological or economic developments. For example, assume that a new, improved model of computer has recently become available and that it would fit the company's needs more effectively. Should the remaining estimated useful life of an older computer presently owned by the company be reevaluated in the light of this technological advance?

2. Obtain or prepare a summary analysis (see Figure 13.1) of accumulated depreciation for the major property classifications as shown by the general ledger control accounts, listing beginning balances, provisions for depreciation during the year, retirements, and ending balances.
   a. Compare beginning balances with the audited amounts in last year's working papers.
   b. Determine that the totals of accumulated depreciation recorded in the plant and equipment subsidiary records agree with the applicable general ledger controlling accounts.

3. Test the provisions for depreciation.
   a. Compare rates used in the current year with those employed in prior years and investigate any variances.
   b. Test computations of depreciation provisions for a representative number of units and trace to individual records in the property ledger. Be alert for excessive depreciation on fully depreciated assets. Generalized audit software can be used to test the depreciation calculations in the client's records if the client maintains computer-based records.
   c. Compare credits to accumulated depreciation accounts for the year's depreciation provisions with debit entries in related depreciation expense accounts.

4. Test deductions from accumulated depreciation for assets retired.
   a. Trace deductions to the working paper analyzing retirements of assets during the year.
   b. Test the accuracy of accumulated depreciation to date of retirement.
5. Perform analytical procedures for depreciation.
   a. Compute the ratio of depreciation expense to total cost of plant and compare with prior years.
   b. Compare the percentage relationships between accumulated depreciation and related property accounts with those prevailing in prior years. Discuss significant variations from the normal depreciation program with appropriate members of management.

## Testing the Client's Provision for Depreciation

We have emphasized the importance of determining the overall reasonableness of the amount of depreciation expense, which is usually a material amount on the income statement. An *overall* test of the annual provision for depreciation requires the auditors to perform the following steps:

1. List the balances in the various asset accounts at the beginning of the year.
2. Deduct any fully depreciated assets, since these items should no longer be subject to depreciation.
3. Add one-half of the asset additions for the year.
4. Deduct one-half of the asset retirements for the year (exclusive of any fully depreciated assets).

These four steps produce average amounts subject to depreciation at the regular rates in each of the major asset categories. By applying the appropriate rates to these amounts, the auditors determine on an overall average basis the amount of the provision for depreciation. The computed amount is then compared with the client's figures. Precise agreement is not to be expected, but any material difference between the depreciation expense computed in this manner and the amount set up by the client should be investigated fully.

## Examination of Natural Resources

In the audit of companies operating properties subject to depletion (mines, oil and gas deposits, timberlands, and other natural resources), the auditors follow a pattern similar to that used in evaluating the provision for depreciation expense and accumulated depreciation. They determine whether depletion has been recorded consistently and in accordance with generally accepted accounting principles, and they test the mathematical accuracy of the client's computations.

The depletion of timberlands is usually based on physical quantities established by **cruising.** (The term *cruising* means the inspection of a tract of forestland for the purpose of estimating the total lumber yield.) The determination of physical quantities to use as a basis for depletion is more difficult in many mining ventures and for oil and gas deposits. The auditors often rely upon the opinions of such specialists as mining engineers and geologists about the reasonableness of the depletion rates being used for such resources. Under these circumstances, the auditors must comply with the provisions of AICPA AU 630 (PCAOB 336) "Using the Work of an Auditor's Specialist," as discussed in Chapter 5.

If the number of tons of ore in a mining property could be accurately determined in advance, an exact depletion cost per ton could be computed by dividing the cost of the mine by the number of tons available for extraction. In reality, the contents of the mine can only be estimated, and the estimates may require significant revision as mining operations progress.

The auditors investigate the ownership and the cost of mining properties by examining deeds, leases, tax bills, vouchers, paid checks, and other records in the same manner that they verify the plant and equipment of a manufacturing or trading concern. The costs of exploration and development work in a mine customarily are capitalized until such time as commercial production begins. After that date, additional development work generally is treated as an expense. The large oil companies capitalize the costs of drilling oil wells only if they are found to be productive. Under this "successful efforts" policy, the costs of drilling wells that prove not to be productive are immediately written off. However, some smaller companies follow an alternative "full-cost" policy, under which all drilling costs are capitalized and amortized over future years.

## Audit of Intangible Assets

**LO8**

Describe how the auditors design audit procedures to audit intangible assets.

The balance sheet caption "Intangible Assets" includes a variety of assets. All intangible assets are characterized by a lack of physical substance. Furthermore, they do not qualify as current assets, and they are nonmonetary—that is, they do not represent fixed claims to cash.

Among the more prominent intangible assets are goodwill, patents, trademarks, franchises, and leaseholds. Since intangible assets lack physical substance, their value lies in the rights or economic advantages afforded in their ownership. Because of their intangible nature, these assets may be more difficult to identify than units of plant and equipment. When a client treats an expenditure as creating an intangible asset, the auditors must look for objective evidence that a genuine asset has come into existence.

The auditors' substantiation of intangible assets may begin with an analysis of the ledger accounts for these assets. Debits to the accounts should be traced to evidence of payment having been made and to documentary evidence of the rights or benefits acquired. Credits to the accounts should be reconciled with the client's program of amortization or traced to appropriate authorization for the write-off of the asset.

One intangible asset that may be large in amount yet of questionable future economic benefit is *goodwill*. Goodwill arises in accounting for business combinations in which the price paid to acquire another company exceeds the fair value of the identifiable net assets acquired. When business combinations result in the recording of goodwill, the auditors should review the allocation of the lump-sum acquisition cost among tangible assets, identifiable intangible assets, and goodwill. They must also determine whether goodwill is properly allocated to all the various reporting units acquired in the acquisition. Often, the auditors will have to use the services of a business valuation specialist to assist them in evaluating the reasonableness of the valuation and allocation.

Once goodwill is acquired, it remains at its purchase price; it is not amortized. Instead, goodwill assigned to reporting units should be tested for impairment on an annual basis and between annual tests in certain circumstances. As explained previously, impairment tests involve determining the fair value of the reporting units for comparison to their carrying value. If the fair value of a reporting unit is less than its carrying value, an impairment loss is recognized for the difference.

As part of an analysis of intangible assets with definite useful lives, the auditors should review the reasonableness of the client's amortization program. Amortization is ordinarily computed by the straight-line method over the assets' estimated useful lives. As with property, plant, and equipment, long-lived intangible assets must be continually reviewed for impairment when circumstances indicate that the carrying value of the asset may not be recoverable.

The issues regarding the potential impairment of intangible assets are similar to those regarding property, plant, and equipment, as discussed on pages 548–550. If specific intangible assets appear to be impaired, the auditors should evaluate the reasonableness of management's estimate of the fair values of those assets.

## Audit of Plant, Equipment, and Intangibles in Advance of the Balance Sheet Date

Most of the audit work on plant, equipment, and intangibles can be done in advance of the balance sheet date. For the initial audit of a new client, the time-consuming task of reviewing the records of prior years and establishing the beginning balances in the accounts for the current period ordinarily will be completed before the year-end.

In repeat engagements, as well as in first audits, the consideration of internal control can be carried out at a convenient time during the year. Many auditing firms lighten their year-end workloads by performing interim work during October and November, including the analysis of the plant and equipment ledger accounts for the first 9 or 10 months of the year. After the balance sheet date, the work necessary on property accounts is then limited to examination of the transactions for the final two or three months.

## Chapter Summary

In this chapter, we presented the appropriate controls for property, plant, and equipment accounts, the auditors' consideration of these controls, and the substantive procedures for property, plant, and equipment. To summarize:

1. The financial statement caption "Property, Plant, and Equipment" includes tangible assets with a useful life of more than one year that are used in operations. In the audit of property, plant, and equipment, the auditors' primary substantive procedure objectives are to (a) substantiate the existence of property, plant, and equipment and the occurrence of related transactions; (b) establish the completeness of recorded property, plant, and equipment; (c) verify the cutoff of transactions affecting property, plant, and equipment; (d) determine that the client has rights to the recorded property, plant, and equipment; (e) establish the proper valuation or allocation of property, plant, and equipment and the accuracy of related transactions; and (f) evaluate the adequacy of presentation and disclosure for property, plant, and equipment.

2. Key controls over property, plant, and equipment should include proper authorization of acquisitions, adequate records for the various units of property, periodic physical inspection of property, and the use of serially numbered retirement work orders.

3. In the audit of property, plant, and equipment for a continuing client, the emphasis of the testing is on transactions that occurred during the year, as contrasted to an emphasis on ending balances. Depreciation expense is often tested by recomputation or through the use of analytical procedures.

4. The auditors' objectives for the audit of natural resources and intangible assets are similar to those for property, plant, and equipment. Often in auditing the depletion of natural resources, the auditors must rely upon specialists to estimate the quantity and quality of the resource. The audit of intangible assets typically involves vouching the cost of the assets and evaluating and testing the allocation methods used by the client.

5. In some audits, a substantial risk with respect to property, plant, and equipment and intangible assets is the risk of unrecognized impairment.

## Key Terms Introduced or Emphasized in Chapter 13

**Capital expenditure (538)**   An expenditure for property, plant, and equipment that is properly charged to an asset account.

**Cruising (550)**   The inspection of a tract of forestland for the purpose of estimating the total lumber yield.

**Revenue expenditure (538)**   An expenditure for property, plant, and equipment that is properly charged to an expense account.

**Work order (538)**   A serially numbered accounting document authorizing the acquisition of plant assets. A separate series of retirement work orders may be used to authorize the retirement or disposal of plant assets, and a third variety consists of documents authorizing repair or maintenance of plant assets.

## Review Questions

13–1.   The auditors' verification of plant and equipment is facilitated by several factors not applicable to audit work on current assets. What are these factors?

13–2.   K-J Corporation has current assets of $5 million and approximately the same amount of plant and equipment. Should the two groups of assets require about the same amount of audit time? Give reasons.

13–3.   What are the objectives of establishing internal control over plant and equipment?

13–4.   Identify at least three elements of strong internal control over property, plant, and equipment.

13–5.   Explain the use of a system of authorizations for additions to plant and equipment.

13–6.   Moultrie Company discovered recently that a number of its property and equipment assets had been retired from use several years ago without any entries being made in the accounting records. The company asks you to suggest procedures that will prevent unrecorded retirement of assets.

13–7.   Does a failure to record the retirement of machinery affect net income? Explain.

13–8.   The auditors' verification of current assets such as cash, securities, and inventories emphasizes observation, inspection, and confirmation to determine the physical existence of these assets. Should the auditors take a similar approach to establish the existence of the recorded plant assets? Explain fully.

13–9.   You are making your first audit of Clarke Manufacturing Company. The Plant and Equipment account represents a very substantial portion of the total assets. What verification, if any, will you make of the balances of the ledger accounts for Plant and Equipment as of the beginning of the period under audit?

13–10.  What documentary evidence is usually available to the auditors in the client's office to substantiate the legal ownership of property, plant, and equipment?

13–11.  Should the auditors examine public records to determine the legal title of property apparently owned by the client?

13–12.  In response to threats from a terrorist organization, Technology International installed protective measures consisting of chainlink fences, concrete road barriers, electronic gates, and underground parking at its manufacturing facilities. The costs of these installations were debited to the Land account. Indicate with reasons your approval or disapproval of this accounting treatment.

13–13.  Should the independent auditors observe a physical inventory of property and equipment in every audit engagement? Discuss.

13–14.  Hamlin Metals Company has sales representatives covering several states and provides automobiles for them and for its executives. Describe any substantive procedures you would consider appropriate for the company's fleet of more than 100 automobiles, other than the verification procedures generally applicable to all property and equipment.

13–15.  What is a principal objective of the auditors in analyzing a Maintenance and Repairs expense account?

13–16.  Gibson Manufacturing Company acquired new factory machinery this year and ceased using the old machinery. The old equipment was retained, however, and is capable of being used if the demand for the company's products warrants additional production. How should the old machinery be handled in the accounting records and on the financial statements?

13–17.  List three substantive procedures the auditors could use to detect unrecorded retirements of property, plant, and equipment.

13–18.  Do the auditors question the service lives adopted by the client for plant assets, or do they accept the service lives without investigation? Explain.

13–19.  Explain why the auditors may need to use the work of a specialist in the audit of goodwill.

13–20.  Explain how the existence of lease agreements may result in understated plant and equipment.

13–21.  Suggest several comparisons to be made as part of the auditors' analytical procedures for:

   *a.* Plant and Equipment.

   *b.* Depreciation.

## Questions Requiring Analysis

**LO 3, 5**

13–22.  Give the purposes of each of the following procedures that may be included in internal control, and explain how each procedure contributes to strong internal control:

   *a.* Forecasting of expenditures for property, plant, and equipment.

   *b.* Maintaining a plant ledger for property, plant, and equipment.

(AICPA, adapted)

**LO 1, 3, 5**

13–23.  An executive of a manufacturing company informs you that no formal procedures have been followed to control the retirement of machinery and equipment. A physical inventory of plant assets has just been completed. It revealed that 25 percent of the assets carried in the ledger were not on hand and had presumably been scrapped. The accounting records have been adjusted to agree with the physical inventory. Outline internal control practices to govern future retirements.

**LO 4, 6, 8**    13–24.    Gruen Corporation is a large diversified company with a large amount of property, plant, and equipment and intangible assets, including goodwill. In the past year the company has experienced a significant decline in a number of its lines of business.

*Required:*

    *a.*  What risk of material misstatement is indicated from the information provided?

    *b.*  Describe how the auditors would generally obtain evidence about the value of goodwill.

**LO 1, 3, 4, 6**    13–25.    Kadex Corporation, a small manufacturing company, did not use the services of independent auditors during the first two years of its existence. Near the end of the third year, Kadex retained Jones & Scranton, CPAs, to perform an audit for the year ended December 31. Officials of the company requested that the CPA firm perform only the audit work necessary to provide an audit report on the financial statements for the current year.

    During the first two years of its operation, Kadex had erroneously treated some material acquisitions of plant and equipment as revenue expenditures. No such errors occurred in the third year.

    *a.*  Under these circumstances, would Jones & Scranton, CPAs, be likely to learn of the transactions erroneously treated as revenue expenditures in years 1 and 2? Explain.

    *b.*  Would the income statement and balance sheet prepared at the end of year 3 be affected by the above accounting errors made in years 1 and 2? If so, identify the specific items. Explain fully.

**LO 1, 2, 4**    13–26.    Allen Fraser was president of three corporations: Missouri Metals Corporation, Kansas Metals Corporation, and Iowa Metals Corporation. Each of the three corporations owned land and buildings acquired for approximately $500,000. An appraiser retained by Fraser in 20X1 estimated the current value of the land and buildings in each corporation at approximately $3,000,000. The appraisals were recorded in the accounts. A new corporation, called Midwest Corporation, was then formed, and Fraser became its president. The new corporation purchased the assets of the three predecessor corporations, making payment in capital stock. The balance sheet of Midwest Corporation shows land and buildings "valued at cost" in the amount of $9,000,000, the carrying values to the vendor companies at the time of transfer to Midwest Corporation. Do you consider this treatment acceptable? Explain.

**LO 1, 3, 6**    13–27.    Your new client, Ross Products, Inc., completed its first fiscal year March 31, 20X4. During the course of your audit you discover the following entry in the general journal, dated April 1, 20X3.

| | | |
|---|---|---|
| Building | 2,400,000 | |
|     Mortgage Note Payable | | 1,400,000 |
|     Common Stock | | 1,000,000 |

To record (1) acquisition of building constructed by J. A. Ross Construction Co. (a sole proprietorship); (2) assumption of Ross Construction Co. mortgage loan for construction of the building; and (3) issuance of entire authorized common stock (10,000 shares, $100 par value) to J. A. Ross.

*Required:*

Under these circumstances, what steps should the auditors take to verify the $2,400,000 recorded cost of the building? Explain fully.

**LO 1, 3, 4, 6**    13–28.    Shortly after you were retained to audit the financial statements of Case Corporation, you learned from a preliminary discussion with management that the corporation had recently acquired a competing business, the Mall Company. In your study of the terms of the acquisition, you find that the total purchase price was paid in cash and that the transaction was authorized by the board of directors and fully described in the minutes of the directors' meetings. The only aspect of the acquisition of the Mall Company that raises any doubts in your mind is the allocation of the total purchase price among the several kinds of assets acquired. The allocation, which had been specifically approved by the board of directors of Case Corporation, placed very high values on the tangible assets acquired and allowed nothing for goodwill.

    You are inclined to believe that the allocation of the lump-sum price to the several types of assets was somewhat unreasonable because the total price for the business was as much as or more than the current replacement cost of the tangible assets acquired. However, as an auditor, you do not claim to be an expert in property values. Would you question the propriety of the directors' allocation of the lump-sum purchase price? Explain fully.

**LO 6**    13–29.    List and state the purpose of all audit procedures that might reasonably be applied by the auditors to determine that all property and equipment retirements have been recorded in the accounting records.

**LO 8** 13–30. Girard Corporation has just completed the acquisition of Williams, Inc., at a purchase price significantly higher than the fair values of the identifiable assets. Describe the audit issues caused by the acquisition and how the auditors would likely resolve the issues.

**LO 1, 4, 6** 13–31. You are part of the audit team that is auditing Happy Chicken, Inc., a company that franchises Happy Chicken family restaurants. During the current year, management of Happy Chicken purchased for $2 million one of its franchised locations, a store that was having financial difficulties. In performing its analysis for impairment of assets at year-end, management of Happy Chicken determined that the carrying value of the asset may not be recoverable. As a result, management developed an estimate of the fair value of the location using a discounted cash flow model. The estimated fair value of the location was determined to be $1.5 million, which resulted in an impairment loss of about $500,000. The undiscounted future cash flows are equal to $1.7 million.

*Required:*

a. State why the audit of fair values is often difficult.

b. Describe how you might approach the audit of the impairment loss in this situation.

c. If you decide to use the work of a valuation specialist to audit the estimate of fair value, describe your responsibilities with respect to using the specialist's work.

d. List two significant assumptions that you would expect to underlie Happy Chicken management's estimate of the fair value of its recently purchased franchise location.

e. For the significant assumptions that you identified in (*d*), describe the types of evidence that you would expect to examine in order to support those assumptions.

## Objective Questions

All applicable questions are available with McGraw-Hill's *Connect™ Accounting*. ■ connect
|ACCOUNTING

**LO 3, 5** 13–32. **Multiple Choice Questions**

Select the best answer for each of the questions below and explain fully the reason for your selection.

a. To assure accountability for fixed asset retirements, management should implement an internal control that includes:

(1) Continuous analysis of miscellaneous revenue to locate any cash proceeds from the sale of plant assets.

(2) Periodic inquiry of plant executives by internal auditors as to whether any plant assets have been retired.

(3) Utilization of serially numbered retirement work orders.

(4) Periodic observation of plant assets by the internal auditors.

**LO 6, 7** b. The auditors may conclude that depreciation charges are insufficient by noting:

(1) Insured values greatly in excess of book values.

(2) Large amounts of fully depreciated assets.

(3) Continuous trade-ins of relatively new assets.

(4) Excessive recurring losses on assets retired.

**LO 3, 5** c. Which of the following is an internal control weakness related to factory equipment?

(1) Checks issued in payment of purchases of equipment are not signed by the controller.

(2) All purchases of factory equipment are required to be made by the department in need of the equipment.

(3) Factory equipment replacements are generally made when estimated useful lives, as indicated in depreciation schedules, have expired.

(4) Proceeds from sales of fully depreciated equipment are credited to other income.

**LO 6** d. Which of the following accounts should be reviewed by the auditors to gain reasonable assurance that additions to property, plant, and equipment are *not* understated?

(1) Depreciation.

(2) Accounts Payable.

(3) Cash.

(4) Repairs.

**LO 5, 6** e. The auditors are most likely to seek information from the plant manager with respect to the

(1) Adequacy of the provision for uncollectible accounts.

(2) Appropriateness of physical inventory observation procedures.

(3) Existence of obsolete machinery.

(4) Deferral of procurement of certain necessary insurance coverage.

**LO 3, 5**

*f.* To strengthen internal control over the custody of heavy mobile equipment, the client would most likely institute a policy requiring a periodic:

(1) Increase in insurance coverage.

(2) Inspection of equipment and reconciliation with accounting records.

(3) Verification of liens, pledges, and collateralizations.

(4) Accounting for work orders.

**LO 1**

*g.* Which of the following statements is *not* typical of property, plant, and equipment as compared to most current asset accounts?

(1) A property, plant, and equipment cutoff error near year-end has a more significant effect on net income.

(2) Relatively few transactions occur in property, plant, and equipment during the year.

(3) The assets involved with property, plant, and equipment ordinarily have relatively longer lives.

(4) Property, plant, and equipment accounts typically have a higher dollar value.

**LO 1, 6**

*h.* For the audit of a continuing nonpublic client, the emphasis of the testing for property accounts is on:

(1) All transactions resulting in the ending balance.

(2) Tests of controls over disposals.

(3) Transactions that occurred during the year.

(4) Performing analytical procedures on beginning balances of the accounts.

**LO 2, 6**

*i.* Audit of which of the following accounts is most likely to reveal evidence relating to recorded retirements of equipment?

(1) Accumulated depreciation.

(2) Cost of goods sold.

(3) Purchase returns and allowances.

(4) Purchase discounts.

**LO 2, 6**

*j.* An effective procedure for identifying unrecorded retirements of equipment is to:

(1) Foot related property records.

(2) Recalculate depreciation on the related equipment.

(3) Select items of equipment in the accounting records and then locate them in the plant.

(4) Select items of equipment and then locate them in the accounting records.

**LO 7**

*k.* Which of the following is *not* an overall test of the annual provision for depreciation expense?

(1) Compare rates used in the current year with those used in prior years.

(2) Test computation of depreciation provisions for a representative number of units.

(3) Test deductions from accumulated depreciation for assets purchased during the year.

(4) Perform analytical procedures.

**LO 8**

*l.* The audit of intangible assets typically involves

| | Vouching the Cost of Assets | Testing Allocation Methods |
|---|---|---|
| (1) | Yes | Yes |
| (2) | Yes | No |
| (3) | No | Yes |
| (4) | No | No |

(AICPA, adapted)

**LO 3, 6, 7, 8**   13–33.   **Multiple Choice Questions**

*a.* Analysis of which account is *least* likely to reveal evidence relating to recorded retirement of equipment?

(1) Accumulated depreciation.

(2) Insurance expense.

(3) Property, plant, and equipment.

(4) Purchase returns and allowances.

b. Which of the following explanations most likely would satisfy an auditor who questions management about significant debits to the accumulated depreciation accounts?
   (1) The estimated remaining useful lives of plant assets were revised upward.
   (2) Plant assets were retired during the year.
   (3) The prior year's depreciation expense was erroneously understated.
   (4) Overhead allocations were revised at year-end.

c. Treetop Corporation acquired a building and arranged mortgage financing during the year. Verification of the related mortgage acquisition costs would be least likely to include an examination of the related:
   (1) Deed.
   (2) Canceled checks.
   (3) Closing statement.
   (4) Interest expense.

d. In testing plant and equipment balances, an auditor may select recorded additions in the analysis of plant and equipment and inspect the actual asset(s) involved. Which management assertion is this procedure most directly related to?
   (1) Existence.
   (2) Completeness.
   (3) Rights.
   (4) Valuation.

e. A search for overstated property, plant, and equipment purchases would most likely include:
   (1) Accounts receivable.
   (2) Property, plant, and equipment.
   (3) Purchase discounts.
   (4) Repairs and maintenance expense.

# Problems

**All applicable problems are available with McGraw-Hill's *Connect™ Accounting.*** ■ connect
|ACCOUNTING

**LO 3, 4, 5, 6**  13–34. The following are typical questions that might appear on an internal control questionnaire relating to plant and equipment:

1. Has a dollar minimum been established for expenditures to be capitalized?
2. Are subsidiary ledgers for plant and equipment regularly reconciled with general ledger controlling accounts?

*Required:*
a. State the purpose of each of the above controls.
b. Describe the manner in which each of the above procedures might be tested.
c. Assuming that the operating effectiveness of each of the above procedures is found to be inadequate, describe how the auditors might alter their substantive procedures to compensate for the increased level of risks of material misstatements.

**LO 1, 6**  13–35. J. Barnes, CPA, has been retained to audit a manufacturing company with a balance sheet that includes the caption Property, Plant, and Equipment. Barnes has been asked by the company's management if audit adjustments or reclassifications are required for the following material items that have been included or excluded from Property, Plant, and Equipment.

1. A tract of land was acquired during the year. The land is the future site of the client's new headquarters, which will be constructed in the following year. Commissions were paid to the real estate agent used to acquire the land, and expenditures were made to relocate the previous owner's equipment. These commissions and expenditures were expensed and are excluded from Property, Plant, and Equipment.

2. Clearing costs were incurred to make the land ready for construction. These costs were included in Property, Plant, and Equipment.

3. During the land-clearing process, timber and gravel were recovered and sold. The proceeds from the sale were recorded as other income and are excluded from Property, Plant, and Equipment.

4. A group of machines were purchased under a royalty agreement, which provides royalty payments based on units of production from the machines. The cost of the machines, freight costs, unloading charges, and royalty payments were capitalized and are included in Property, Plant, and Equipment.

5. A machine originally budgeted to be purchased at an amount was purchased for less than that amount. The asset was recorded in Property, Plant, and Equipment for the budgeted amount, with the difference being recorded in purchase discounts and allowances (an income statement account).

*Required:*

a. Describe the general characteristics of assets, such as land, buildings, improvements, machinery, equipment, and fixtures, that should normally be classified as Property, Plant, and Equipment, and identify audit objectives (i.e., how an auditor can obtain audit satisfaction) in connection with the examination of Property, Plant, and Equipment. Do not discuss specific audit procedures.

b. Indicate whether each of the preceding items 1–5 requires one or more audit adjustments or reclassifications, and explain why such adjustments or reclassifications are required or not required. Organize your answer as follows:

| Item Number | Is Audit Adjustment or Reclassification Required? | Reason(s) Audit Adjustment or Reclassification Is Required or Not Required |
|---|---|---|
| | Yes or No? | |

(AICPA, adapted)

**LO 1, 2, 4**  13–36.  Assume that you are auditing the financial statements of Agee Corporation. During the course of the audit, you discover the following circumstances.

1. Management of Agee has decided to discontinue the production of consumer electronics, which represents a moderately large line of business for the company.

2. In auditing facility rent expense, you note that the amount is significantly less than in the prior year. When you discuss the matter with management, you are informed that management entered into a new 10-year building lease agreement about nine months ago, which provided for no lease payments for the first year of the lease.

3. In vouching additions to plant assets, you find that management has capitalized the leasehold improvements made on the building acquired in (2), which are being depreciated over an estimated useful life of 12 years.

4. Management has provided you with the following information about a test of impairment of the company's clothing and apparel reporting unit and a large piece of equipment used in the consumer products division of the company. The Clothing and Apparel reporting unit has $1,200,000 in goodwill associated with it.

| **Clothing and Apparel Reporting Unit** | |
|---|---|
| Carrying value of the unit | $12,600,000 |
| Discounted value of estimated future cash flows | 12,200,000 |
| Market value of the unit | 11,500,000 |
| **Equipment** | |
| Carrying value of the equipment | $1,200,000 |
| Undiscounted estimated future cash flows | 1,250,000 |
| Discounted value of estimated future cash flows | 1,000,000 |
| Market value of the equipment | 975,000 |

*Required:*

Describe the implications of each of these circumstances, including any additional information or evidence that the auditors might require to resolve the issues identified.

**LO 1, 4, 6**  13–37.  Nova Land Development Corporation is a closely held corporation engaged in purchasing large tracts of land, subdividing the tracts, and installing paved streets and utilities. The corporation does not construct buildings for the buyers of the land and does not have any affiliated construction companies. Undeveloped land usually is leased for farming until the corporation is ready to begin developing it.

The corporation finances its land acquisitions by mortgages; the mortgagees require audited financial statements. This is your first audit of the company, and you have now begun the audit of the financial statements for the year ended December 31.

*Required:*   The corporation has three tracts of land in various stages of development. List the audit procedures to be employed in the verification of the physical existence and title of the corporation's three landholdings.

(AICPA, adapted)

**LO 1, 4, 6**   13–38.   You are engaged in the audit of the financial statements of Holman Corporation for the year ended December 31, 20X6. The accompanying analyses of the Property, Plant, and Equipment and related accumulated depreciation accounts have been prepared by the chief accountant of the client. You have traced the beginning balances to your prior year's audit working papers.

### HOLMAN CORPORATION
#### Analysis of Property, Plant, and Equipment and Related Accumulated Depreciation Accounts
#### Year Ended December 31, 20X6

| Description | Final 12/31/X5 | Assets | | Per Ledger 12/31/X6 |
|---|---|---|---|---|
| | | Additions | Retirements | |
| Land | $422,500 | $ 5,000 | | $427,500 |
| Buildings | 120,000 | 17,500 | | 137,500 |
| Machinery and equipment | 385,000 | 40,400 | $26,000 | 399,400 |
| | $927,500 | $62,900 | $26,000 | $964,400 |

| Description | Final 12/31/X5 | Accumulated Depreciation | | Per Ledger 12/31/X6 |
|---|---|---|---|---|
| | | Additions* | Retirements | |
| Buildings | $ 60,000 | $ 5,150 | | $ 65,150 |
| Machinery and equipment | 173,250 | 39,220 | | 212,470 |
| | $233,250 | $44,370 | | $277,620 |

*Depreciation expense for the year.

All plant assets are depreciated on the straight-line basis (no residual value taken into consideration) based on the following estimated service lives: building, 25 years; and all other items, 10 years. The company's policy is to take one half-year's depreciation on all asset additions and disposals during the year.

Your audit revealed the following information:

1. On April 1, the company entered into a 10-year lease contract for a die casting machine, with annual rentals of $5,000 payable in advance every April 1. The lease is cancelable by either party (60 days' written notice is required), and there is no option to renew the lease or buy the equipment at the end of the lease. The estimated service life of the machine is 10 years with no residual value. The company recorded the die casting machine in the Machinery and Equipment account at $40,400, the present value at the date of the lease, and $2,020 applicable to the machine has been included in depreciation expense for the year.

2. The company completed the construction of a wing on the plant building on June 30. The service life of the building was not extended by this addition. The lowest construction bid received was $17,500, the amount recorded in the Buildings account. Company personnel constructed the addition at a cost of $16,000 (materials, $7,500; labor, $5,500; and overhead, $3,000).

3. On August 18, $5,000 was paid for paving and fencing a portion of land owned by the company and used as a parking lot for employees. The expenditure was charged to the Land account.

4. The amount shown in the machinery and equipment asset retirement column represents cash received on September 5 upon disposal of a machine purchased in July 20X2 for $48,000. The chief accountant recorded depreciation expense of $3,500 on this machine in 20X6.

5. Harbor City donated land and a building appraised at $100,000 and $400,000, respectively, to Holman Corporation for a plant. On September 1, the company began operating the plant. Since no costs were involved, the chief accountant made no entry for the above transaction.

*Required:*   Prepare the adjusting journal entries that you would propose at December 31, 20X6, to adjust the accounts for the above transactions. Disregard income tax implications. The accounts have not been closed. Computations should be rounded off to the nearest dollar. Use a separate adjusting journal entry for each of the preceding five paragraphs.

(AICPA, adapted)

**LO 1, 4, 6**　13–39.　Chem-Lite, Inc., maintains its accounts on the basis of a fiscal year ending March 31. At March 31, 20X1, the Equipment account in the general ledger appeared as shown below. The company uses straight-line depreciation, a 10-year life, and 10 percent salvage value for all its equipment. It is the company's policy to take a full year's depreciation on all additions to equipment occurring during the fiscal year, and you may treat this policy as a satisfactory one for the purpose of this problem. The company has recorded depreciation for the fiscal year ended March 31, 20X1.

| Equipment | | |
|---|---:|---|
| 4/1/X0 Bal. forward | 100,000 | |
| 12/1/X0 | 10,500 | |
| 1/2/X1 | 1,015 | |
| 2/1/X1 | 1,015 | |
| 3/1/X1 | 1,015 | |

Upon further investigation, you find the following contract dated December 1, 20X0, covering the acquisition of equipment:

| | |
|---|---:|
| List price | $30,000 |
| 5% sales tax | 1,500 |
| Total | $31,500 |
| Down payment | 10,500 |
| Balance | 21,000 |
| 8% interest, 24 months | 3,360 |
| Contract amount | $24,360 |

*Required:*　Prepare in good form, including full explanations, the adjusting entry (entries) you would propose as auditor of Chem-Lite, Inc., with respect to the equipment and related depreciation accounts at March 31, 20X1. (Assume that all amounts given are material.)

(AICPA, adapted)

**LO 1, 4, 6**　13–40.　You are the senior accountant in the audit of Granger Grain Corporation, whose business primarily involves the purchase, storage, and sale of grain products. The corporation owns several elevators located along navigable water routes and transports its grain by barge and rail. Your staff assistant submitted the following working paper analysis for your review:

| GRANGER GRAIN CORPORATION | |
|---|---:|
| Advances Paid on Barges Under Construction—a/c 210 | |
| December 31, 20X1 | |
| Advances made: | |
| 1/15/X1—Ck. No. 3463—Jones Barge Construction Co. | $100,000* |
| 4/13/X1—Ck. No. 4129—Jones Barge Construction Co. | 25,000* |
| 6/19/X1—Ck. No. 5396—Jones Barge Construction Co. | 63,000* |
| Total payments | 188,000 |
| Deduct cash received 9/1/X1 from City Life Insurance Co. | 188,000† |
| Balance per general ledger—12/31/X1 | $　—0— |

*Examined approved check request and paid check and traced to cash disbursements journal.
†Traced to cash receipts journal and to duplicate deposit ticket.

*Required:*

a. In what respects is this brief analysis incomplete for audit purposes? (Do not include any discussion of specific auditing procedures.)

b. What two different types of contractual arrangements may be inferred from your assistant's analysis?

c. What additional auditing procedures would you suggest that your staff assistant perform before you accept the working paper as being complete?

(AICPA, adapted)

**In-Class Team Case**    **LO 1, 3, 6**    13–41.    You are reviewing the property, plant, and equipment working papers of Mandville Corporation, a company that publishes travel guides. The lead schedule for the account is included in the chapter as Figure 13.1. The following are among the findings relating to changes in the account:

1. *Land:* The addition represents the purchase of land adjacent to the company's existing plant and is financed as follows:

   | | |
   |---|---|
   | Contract sales price—2,000 shares of Mandville Corporation Common Stock | |
   | Liabilities assumed by Mandville | |
   |   Accrued county taxes at settlement date | (4,600) |
   |   Unpaid sewer installation assessment | (6,400) |

   On June 17, the date on which the buyer and seller discussed the transaction, shares of Mandville Corporation stock were selling for $77.50. On June 30, the settlement date (day of the sale), Mandville stock was selling for $70.00 per share. The journal entry for the purchase was recorded as:

   | | | |
   |---|---|---|
   | Land | $151,000 | |
   |   Common Stock | | $ 20,000 |
   |   Paid-in capital in excess of par | | 120,000 |
   |   Accrued taxes payable | | 4,600 |
   |   Accrued sewer assessment payable | | 6,400 |

   Examination of publicly available records has indicated that prices of comparable land in the area have been relatively constant, selling in a range from $140,000 to $160,000 during the past 18 months.

2. *Land improvements:* This account was increased by three journal entries (each recorded with a debit to land improvements and a credit to cash) during the year. Each of these improvements relates to the new land which was purchased in point (1) above.

   | | |
   |---|---|
   | Sidewalk to building | $2,500 |
   | Repaving of road to building | 3,500 |
   | Chain link fence (replaces rusted chain link fence surrounding property) | 4,000 |

3. *Building:* The building was constructed by an independent contractor; the contract was for $473,000. Progress payments were made during construction through use of proceeds of a bank loan, for which the building serves as collateral. The interest during construction was capitalized ($22,000) while the interest subsequent to construction but prior to year-end ($20,000) was expensed.

4. *Equipment:* The change in the equipment was a trade of old book "update printing equipment" for two new computer servers and associated software that will maintain electronic updates. Until recently, updates of outdated portions of guidebooks were printed and "shrinkwrapped" with the guidebook. Now the updates will be available on Mandville's Web site. The old equipment had a cost of $60,000 and accumulated depreciation of $50,600 and was worth approximately its book value of $9,400, although the salesperson suggested that he was providing the company a $19,400 trade-in value. Accordingly, the following entry was made to record the exchange:

   | | | |
   |---|---|---|
   | Equipment—computer servers | $110,000 | |
   | Accumulated Depr. (old equipment) | 50,600 | |
   |   Cash | | $90,600 |
   |   Equipment—printing equipment | | 60,000 |
   |   Gain on exchange of assets | | 10,000 |

5. *Depreciation provisions:* Mandville uses software to calculate depreciation to the exact day.

**Required:**    a. For additions (1) through (4) above, prepare any necessary adjusting entries. If in any case your adjusting entry relies upon an assumption, provide that assumption.

   b. For item (5), prepare a calculation of the depreciation provisions and determine whether they appear reasonable. For this calculation, assume that acquisitions, on average, occur at mid-year. If the provision does *not* appear reasonable, discuss follow-up procedures related to the provisions. Use the following table for your calculation:

| Acct. | Rate | Depr. on Beg. Balance | Add: Depr. on Additions | Less: Depr. on Retirements | Est. Depr. | Book Depr. | Difference |
|---|---|---|---|---|---|---|---|
| 152–3 | 5% | | | | | | |
| 154–5 | 3% | | | | | | |
| 156–7 | 10% | | | | | | |
| Totals | | | | | | | |

# Accounts Payable and Other Liabilities

In this chapter, we discuss accounts payable and other current liabilities. Chapter 15 includes material on long-term debt, equity capital, and loss contingencies.

## Accounts Payable

### Sources and Nature of Accounts Payable

Describe the nature of accounts payable and other liabilities.

The term *accounts payable* (often referred to as *vouchers payable* for a voucher system) is used to describe short-term obligations arising from the purchase of goods and services in the ordinary course of business. Typical transactions creating accounts payable include the acquisition on credit of merchandise, raw materials, plant assets, and office supplies. Other sources of accounts payable include the receipt of services, such as legal and accounting services, advertising, repairs, and utilities. Interest-bearing obligations should not be included in accounts payable but shown separately as bonds, notes, mortgages, or installment contracts.

Invoices and statements from suppliers usually support accounts payable arising from the purchase of goods or services and most *other liabilities*. However, **accrued liabilities** (sometimes called *accrued expenses*) generally accumulate over time, and management must make accounting estimates of the year-end liability. Such estimates are often necessary for salaries, pensions, interest, rent, taxes, and similar items.

### The Auditors' Objectives in Auditing Accounts Payable

Describe the auditors' objectives in the audit of accounts payable.

The auditors' *objectives* in the audit of accounts payable are to:

1. Use the understanding of the client and its environment to consider *inherent risks,* including fraud risks, related to accounts payable.
2. Obtain an understanding of *internal control* over accounts payable.
3. Assess the risks of material misstatement and design tests of controls and substantive procedures that:
   a. Substantiate the *existence* of accounts payable and the client's *obligation* to pay these liabilities, and establish the *occurrence* of purchase transactions.
   b. Establish the *completeness* of recorded accounts payable.
   c. Verify the *cutoff* of purchase transactions.
   d. Establish the proper *valuation* of accounts payable and the *accuracy* of purchase transactions.
   e. Determine that the *presentation* and *disclosure* of information about accounts payable are appropriate.

Lawsuits against CPA firms typically allege that the auditors failed to detect an overstatement of earnings. Management, especially of publicly held firms, is often under some pressure to report increased earnings. In previous chapters, we discussed the auditors' concern about exaggeration of earnings that results from the overstatement of assets. In the audit of liabilities, the auditors are primarily concerned with the possibility of understatement, or omission, of liabilities. An *understatement of liabilities* will exaggerate the financial strength of a company and conceal fraud just as effectively as an *overstatement of assets*. Furthermore, the understatement of liabilities is usually accompanied by the understatement of expenses and an overstatement of net income. For example, delaying the recording of bills for December operating expenses until January overstates income while understating accounts payable. Therefore, audit procedures for liabilities should have as a primary objective the determination of the *completeness* of recorded payables.

Audit procedures for detecting understated liabilities differ from those used to detect overstated assets. Overstating an asset account usually requires an improper entry in the accounting records, as by the recording of a fictitious transaction. Such an improper entry can be detected by the auditors through verification of the individual entries making up the balance of an asset account. By way of contrast, understating a liability account is generally possible merely by *failing to make an entry* for a transaction creating a liability. The omission of an entry is less susceptible to detection than is a fictitious entry. If the omission is detected, it is much easier to pass it off as an accidental error. Auditors have long recognized that the most difficult type of fraud to detect is one based on the *nonrecording* of transactions.

When accounts payable entries have been recorded, the existence of a definite financial commitment makes accomplishment of the valuation audit objective less difficult than for assets (other than cash). The situation with accrued liabilities is different. As we suggested earlier, in many circumstances exact measurement of these accounts will be difficult; the auditors must audit management's accounting estimates.

## Internal Control over Accounts Payable

**LO3**

Identify and explain the fundamental controls over payables.

In thinking about internal control over accounts payable, it is important to recognize that the accounts payable of one company are the accounts receivable of other companies. It follows that there is little danger of errors being overlooked permanently since the client's creditors will generally maintain complete records of their receivables and will inform the client if payment is not received. This feature also aids auditors in the discovery of fraud, since the perpetrator must be able to obtain and respond to the demands for payment. Some companies, therefore, may choose to minimize their record keeping of liabilities and to rely on creditors to call attention to any delay in making payment. This viewpoint is not an endorsement of inaccurate or incomplete records of accounts payable, but merely a recognition that the self-interest of creditors constitutes an effective control in accounting for payables that is not present in the case of accounts receivable.

Discussions of internal control applicable to accounts payable may logically be extended to the entire purchase or acquisition cycle. In an effective purchasing system, a stores or inventory control department will prepare and approve the issuance of a purchase requisition that will be sent to the purchasing department. A copy of the purchase requisition will be filed numerically and matched with the subsequently prepared purchase order and finally with a copy of the receiving report.

The purchasing department, upon receiving the purchase requisition, will (1) determine that the item should be ordered and (2) select the appropriate vendor, quality, and price. Then, a serially numbered purchase order is issued to order the goods. Copies of the purchase order should be sent to stores, receiving, and the accounts payable department. The copy sent to receiving is generally "blind" in that the quantities are not included in order to encourage counting of quantities by the receiving department. But the fact that a vendor's packing slip (with quantities) is almost always included when goods are received may decrease the effectiveness of this control.

The receiving department should be independent of the purchasing department. When goods are received, they should be counted and inspected. Receiving reports should be prepared for all goods received. These documents should be serially numbered and prepared in a sufficient number of copies to permit prompt notification of the receipt of goods to the stores department, the purchasing department, and the accounts payable department.

Within the accounts (vouchers) payable department, all forms should be stamped with the date received. **Vouchers** and other documents originating within the department can

## Illustrative Case

### The Importance of Controls over Accounts Payable

The need for good IT system controls has become increasingly important as in recent years companies have downsized their accounts payable department. For example, *The Wall Street Journal* reports that General Electric Co., which processes in excess of 10 million invoices annually, reduced its accounts payable staff from approximately 400 employees to 180. Part of this reduction was made possible by a decision not to compare invoices with support prior to payment of vendors; payables were analyzed only after the money had been disbursed. *The Journal* reports that GE reduced payroll costs, but duplicate payments and overpayments to vendors increased.

Other companies have encountered similar situations. One corporate official suggests that unscrupulous vendors have become skilled in fooling computerized payables checking systems. He suggests that some vendors send two invoices with different numbers for the same item, and others add a letter to the end of an invoice number.

be controlled through the use of serial numbers. Each step in the verification of an invoice should be evidenced by entering a date and signature on the voucher. Comparison of the quantities listed on the invoice with those shown on the receiving report and purchase order prevents the payment of charges for goods in excess of those ordered and received. Comparison of the prices, discounts, and terms of shipment as shown on the purchase order and on the vendor's invoice provides a safeguard against the payment of excessive prices.

The separation of the function of invoice verification and approval from the function of cash disbursement is another step that tends to prevent errors and fraud. Before invoices are approved for payment, written evidence must be presented to show that all aspects of the transaction have been verified. The official who signs checks should stamp or perforate the voucher and supporting documents so that they cannot be presented to support payment a second time.

In an IT-based purchasing system, vendor invoice information is entered by the accounting department and may be matched by the IT system with other information. When goods are received, information may be keyed into the IT system with subsequent automated preparation of a receiving report and updating of inventory records. The IT system can match the information from purchase orders, receiving reports, and vendors' invoices and approve appropriate payments of accounts payable. As indicated in Chapter 10, electronic processing of both cash receipts and disbursements can provide management with a continually up-to-date cash record. However, the information technology controls discussed in Chapter 8 must be implemented to ensure the accuracy of the IT system's input, processing, and output.

**STATEMENT**
Carson Supply Co.
1671 21st St.
Houston, TX 77021

Customer:  <u>Morris Construction Co.</u>                   <u>June 30, 20X1</u>
<u>1212 Belaire Blvd.</u>
<u>Houston, TX 77062</u>

| Date | | Amount | Balance |
|------|---|--------|---------|
| June 1 | Beginning balance | | $32,785.00 |
| June 5 | Invoice #3276485 | $ 5,250.00 | 38,035.00 |
| June 9 | Payment | −23,300.00 | 14,734.00 |
| June 12 | Credit #49944 | −235.00 | 14,500.00 |
| June 15 | Invoice #3276678 | 10,220.00 | 24,720.00 |
| June 26 | Payment | 14,500.00 | |
| June 30 | Ending balance | | $10,220.00 |

Another control that the auditors may expect to find in a well-managed accounts payable department is the monthly balancing of the detailed records of accounts payable (or vouchers) to the general ledger control account. These reconciliations should be preserved as evidence of the performance of this procedure and as an aid in locating any subsequent errors.

**Vendors' statements** (previous page bottom), received monthly, should be reconciled promptly with the accounts payable ledger or list of open vouchers, and any discrepancies fully investigated. In some industries, it is common practice to make advances to vendors, which are recovered by making percentage deductions from invoices. When such advances are in use, the auditors should ascertain that procedures are followed to assure that deductions from the invoices are made in accordance with the agreement.

The operation of a purchase or acquisition transaction cycle is illustrated in Figure 14.1.

**FIGURE 14.1   Flowchart of a Purchases System**

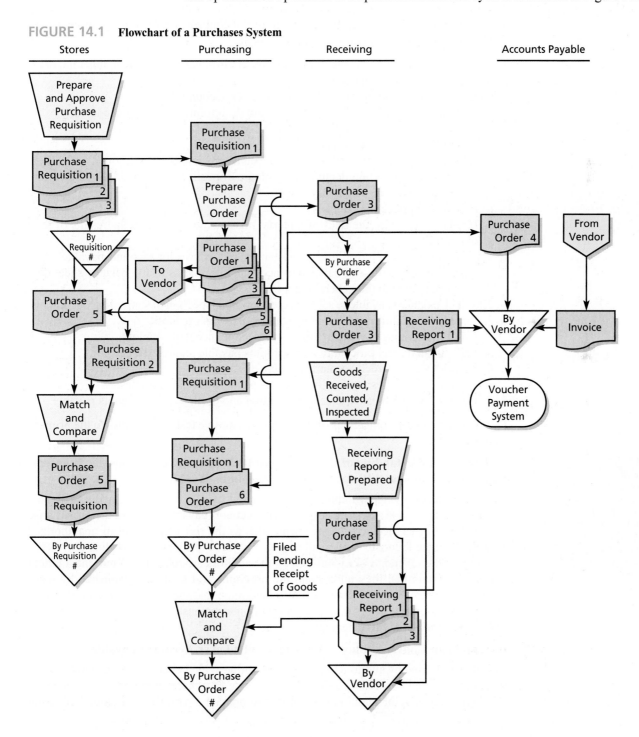

## Audit Documentation for Accounts Payable

The principal working papers are a lead schedule for accounts payable, trial balances of the various types of accounts payable at the balance sheet date, and confirmation requests for accounts payable. The trial balances are often in the form of computer printouts. In addition, the auditors may prepare a listing of *unrecorded* accounts payable discovered during the course of the audit, as illustrated later, in Figure 14.6 (page 575). The auditors also will document the controls and risk assessments for accounts payable.

# Audit of Accounts Payable

The following steps indicate the general pattern of work performed by the auditors in the verification of accounts payable. Selection of the most appropriate procedures for a particular audit will be guided by the nature of the controls that have been implemented and by the results of the auditors' risk assessments.

A. Use the understanding of the client and its environment to consider inherent risks, including fraud risks, related to accounts payable.
B. Obtain an understanding of internal control over accounts payable.
C. Assess the risks of material misstatement and design further audit procedures.
D. Perform further audit procedures—tests of controls.
   1. Examples of tests of controls.
      *a.* Verify a sample of postings to the accounts payable control account.
      *b.* Vouch to supporting documents a sample of postings in selected accounts of the accounts payable subsidiary ledger.
      *c.* Test IT application controls.
   2. If necessary, revise the risks of material misstatement based on the results of tests of controls.
E. Perform further audit procedures—substantive procedures for accounts payable.
   1. Obtain or prepare a trial balance of accounts payable as of the balance sheet date and reconcile with the general ledger.
   2. Vouch balances payable to selected creditors by inspection of supporting documents.
   3. Reconcile liabilities with monthly statements from creditors.
   4. Confirm accounts payable by direct correspondence with vendors.
   5. Perform analytical procedures for accounts payable and related accounts.
   6. Search for unrecorded accounts payable.
   7. Perform procedures to identify accounts payable to related parties.
   8. Evaluate proper balance sheet presentation and disclosure of accounts payable.

Figure 14.2 relates the objectives of the major substantive tests of payables to the primary audit objectives.

**LO4**

Use the understanding of the client and its environment to consider inherent risks (including fraud risks) related to accounts payable.

### A. Use the Understanding of the Client and Its Environment to Consider Inherent Risks, Including Fraud Risks, Related to Accounts Payable.

After they obtain an understanding of the client and its environment, the auditors are in a position to identify and assess inherent risks of accounts payable. Many of these risks arise from business risks faced by management, such as the risk of payment of unauthorized payables, and the failure to capture all accounts payable for financial reporting purposes.

If any of the inherent risks identified by the auditors are related to fraud, the auditors will make certain that they understand the programs and controls established by management to control the risk. They will also determine that the controls have been implemented. Finally, the auditors will design appropriate responses to these fraud risks and all other risks of material misstatement.

### B. Obtain an Understanding of Internal Control over Accounts Payable.

One approach used by auditors in becoming familiar with a client's internal control over accounts payable is to prepare a flowchart or to use flowcharts prepared by the client. In some engagements, the auditors may choose to prepare a narrative description covering

**FIGURE 14.2**

**Objectives of Major Substantive Procedures for Accounts Payable**

| Substantive Procedures | Primary Audit Objectives |
|---|---|
| Obtain trial balance of payables and reconcile with the ledgers. | *Valuation* and *accuracy* |
| Vouch balances payable to selected creditors by inspecting supporting documents. | *Existence, occurrence,* and *obligations*<br>*Valuation* and *accuracy*<br>*Cutoff* |
| Reconcile liabilities with creditor's monthly statements.<br>Confirm accounts payable.<br>Perform analytical procedures. | *Completeness*<br>*Existence, occurrence,* and *obligations*<br>*Valuation* and *accuracy*<br>*Cutoff* |
| Search for unrecorded accounts payable. | *Completeness*<br>*Cutoff* |
| Perform procedures to identify accounts payable to related parties.<br>Evaluate financial statement presentation and disclosure. | *Presentation* and *disclosure* |

such matters as the independence of the accounts payable department and the receiving department from the purchasing department. The auditors might also use a questionnaire to obtain a description of accounts payable controls. Typical of the questions are the following: Is an accounts payable trial balance prepared monthly and reconciled to the general ledger controlling account? Are monthly statements from vendors reconciled with accounts payable ledgers or unpaid vouchers? Are advance payments to vendors recorded as receivables and controlled in a manner that assures that they will be recovered by offset against vendors' invoices? Are debit memos issued to vendors for discrepancies in invoice prices, quantities, or computations? Are debit balances in vendors' accounts brought to the attention of the credit and purchasing departments?

After the auditors have prepared a flowchart (or other description) of internal control, they determine whether the client is actually using the controls described to them; that is, they determine whether the controls have been implemented. The auditors will typically perform a walk-through of several purchase transactions and observe the implementation of the various controls. Figure 14.3 (pages 568–569) illustrates the documents and accounts that the auditors typically encounter in their consideration of controls over purchase transactions.

As the auditors verify their understanding of internal control, they will observe and inquire about the segregation of duties for purchases and cash disbursements. They will also inspect the various documents and reconciliations that are important to the client's internal control over accounts payable. For example, the reconciliations of monthly statements from vendors to the payables ledger will be inspected. Budgets for cash disbursements will be inspected and the auditors will review the evidence of the follow-up on variances from budgeted amounts of disbursements. These procedures may serve as tests of controls that provide the auditors with sufficient evidence to assess control risk for certain financial statement assertions about accounts payable as being at less than the maximum.

**LO5**

Obtain an understanding of internal control over accounts payable.

### C. Assess the Risks of Material Misstatement and Design Further Audit Procedures.

Based on their understanding of the client and its environment, including internal control over accounts payable, the auditors develop their planned assessed levels of the risks of material misstatement for the assertions about accounts payable. To support these assessments, the auditors may need to obtain additional evidence of the operating effectiveness of various controls. This evidence is obtained by performing tests of controls. In designing these tests, the auditors must decide which ones will result in sufficient reductions in substantive procedures to justify the time spent performing them.

**FIGURE 14.3    Overview of the Purchases Cycle—Documents and Accounts**

**Purchases**

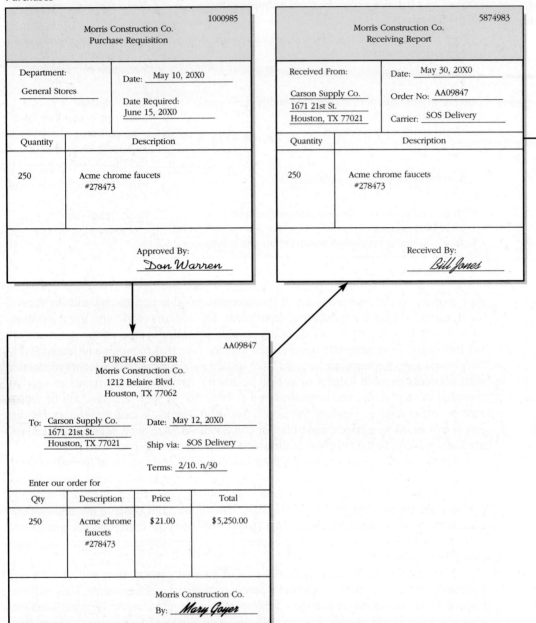

The auditors' assessment of control risk, along with their assessment of inherent risk, will be used to plan the nature, timing, and extent of substantive procedures for accounts payable. In designing planned substantive procedures, the auditors will consider potential misstatements that may occur and the weaknesses in control or other factors that make the misstatements more likely, as illustrated in Figure 14.4 (page 570).

## D. Perform Further Audit Procedures—Tests of Controls.

Tests directed toward the effectiveness of controls help to evaluate the client's internal control and determine whether the auditors can support their planned assessed levels of the risks of material misstatement for the assertions about accounts payable. A number of tests of controls relating to accounts payable have already been discussed in Chapters 10 and 12. In this chapter, we briefly recap several significant tests.

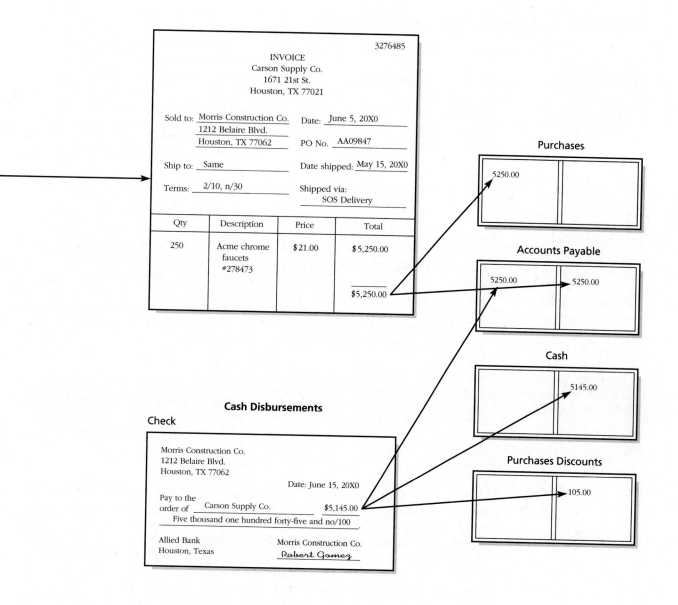

## 1. Examples of Tests of Controls.

### a. Verify a Sample of Postings to the Accounts Payable Control Account.

The validity of the amount in the general ledger control account for accounts payable is established by tracing postings to the **voucher register** and cash disbursements journal. This work is performed before the balance sheet date as part of a general test of postings to all records. At the same time, the auditors should scrutinize all entries to the control account for the entire period under audit and should investigate any unusual entries.

### b. Vouch to Supporting Documents a Sample of Postings in Selected Accounts of the Accounts Payable Subsidiary Ledger.

Testing the voucher register or the accounts payable ledgers by vouching specific items back through the cash payments journal, purchases journal, and other journals to original

**FIGURE 14.4** Potential Misstatements—Accounts Payable

| Description of Misstatement | Examples | Internal Control Weaknesses or Factors that Increase the Risk of the Misstatement |
|---|---|---|
| Inaccurate recording of a purchase or disbursement | **Fraud:**<br>• A bookkeeper prepares a check to himself and records it as having been issued to a major supplier.<br><br>**Error:**<br>• A disbursement is made to pay an invoice for goods that have not been received. | • Inadequate segregation of duties of record keeping and preparing cash disbursements, or check signer does not review and cancel supporting documents<br><br>• Ineffective controls for matching invoices with receiving documents before disbursements are authorized |
| Misappropriation of purchases | **Fraud:**<br>• Goods are ordered but delivered to an inappropriate address and stolen. | • Ineffective controls for matching invoices with receiving documents before disbursements are authorized |
| Duplicate recording of purchases | **Error:**<br>• A purchase is recorded when an invoice is received from a vendor and recorded again when a duplicate invoice is sent by the vendor. | • Ineffective controls for review and cancelation of supporting documents by the check signer |
| Late (early) recording of cost of purchases—"cutoff problems" | **Fraud:**<br>• Purchases journal "closed early" with this period's purchases recorded as having occurred in subsequent period. | • Ineffective board of directors, audit committee, or internal audit function; "tone at the top" not conducive to ethical conduct; undue pressure to meet earnings target |

documents (such as purchase orders, receiving reports, invoices, and paid checks) is necessary to determine the operating effectiveness of certain controls. If the functions of purchasing, receiving, invoice verification, and cash disbursement are delegated to separate departments and controls appear adequate, the vouching of individual items from the ledgers to the original records may provide the auditors with sufficient evidence to assess control risk for certain assertions (e.g., existence) related to accounts payable as being at a low level.

The auditors may also perform tests by following the audit trail in the opposite direction. By tracing a representative sample of entries from the source documents to the accounts payable ledger, the auditors can verify that accounts payable are completely and accurately recorded on a timely basis.

### c. Test IT Application Controls.

When the client has established effective IT application controls for purchase transactions, the auditors may find it more efficient to test these controls rather than to test a sample of purchase transactions. Batch processing controls might be tested by inspecting evidence of the reconciliations of batch control totals by the control group. In addition, a sample of the exception reports printed by the computer when the vendors' invoices do not match purchasing and receiving information might be inspected, as well as evidence of follow-up on these exceptions.

### 2. If Necessary, Revise the Risks of Material Misstatement Based on the Results of Tests of Controls.

Completion of the above audit procedures enables the auditors to perform a final assessment of the risk of material misstatement for each of the major financial statement assertions about accounts payable. The auditors use the reassessment of control risk to determine whether it is necessary to modify their planned program of substantive procedures.

LO6

Assess the risks of material misstatement of accounts payable and design further audit procedures, including tests of controls and substantive procedures, to address the risks.

An assessment of low control risk for accounts payable often means that the auditors have found that serially numbered receiving reports are prepared promptly by the client for all goods received, that serially numbered vouchers are prepared and recorded in the voucher register, and that payments are made promptly on the due dates and immediately recorded in the cash payments journal and accounts payable subsidiary ledger. Finally, at the end of each month, an employee who does not participate in processing accounts payable compares the individual accounts in the accounts payable subsidiary ledger with vendors' statements and also compares the total of the subsidiary record with the general ledger control account. This strong internal control would enable the auditors to minimize substantive procedures for accounts payable.

On the other hand, an assessment of high control risk for accounts payable often means that the auditors have found that the subsidiary record of accounts payable is not in agreement with the general ledger control account, that receiving reports and vouchers are used haphazardly, that purchase transactions often are not recorded until payment is made, and that many accounts payable are long past due. In this situation, the auditors must undertake extensive substantive work if they are to determine that the balance sheet amount for accounts payable includes all liabilities in existence at the balance sheet date.

### E. Perform Further Audit Procedures—Substantive Procedures.

#### 1. Obtain or Prepare a Trial Balance of Accounts Payable as of the Balance Sheet Date and Reconcile with the General Ledger.

One purpose of this procedure is to determine that the liability figure appearing in the balance sheet is in agreement with the individual items comprising the detailed records. A second purpose is to provide a starting point for substantive procedures. The auditors will use the list of vouchers or accounts payable to select a representative group of items for careful examination.

The client company usually furnishes the auditors with a year-end trial balance. The auditors should verify the footing and the accuracy of individual amounts in the trial balance. If the schedule of individual items does not agree in total with the control account, the cause of the discrepancy must be investigated. In most situations, the auditors will arrange for the client's staff to locate such errors and make the necessary adjustments. Agreement of the control account and the list of individual account balances is not absolute proof of the total indebtedness; invoices received near the close of the period may not be reflected in either the control account or the subsidiary records, and other similar errors may exist without causing the accounts to be out of balance.

#### 2. Vouch Balances Payable to Selected Creditors by Inspection of Supporting Documents.

The vouching of selected creditors' balances to supporting vouchers, invoices, purchase orders, and receiving reports is a substantive procedure that addresses the existence and valuation of accounts payable. For companies that use a voucher system, the verification of the individual vouchers is made most conveniently at the balance sheet date, when the vouchers will be together in the unpaid voucher file. The content of the unpaid voucher file changes daily; as vouchers are paid, they are removed from the file and filed alphabetically by vendor. Consequently, it is important that the client maintain a list of year-end unpaid vouchers. This listing should show the names of vendors, voucher numbers, dates, and amounts.

#### 3. Reconcile Liabilities with Monthly Statements from Creditors.

In some companies, it is a regular practice each month to reconcile vendors' statements with the detailed records of payables. If the auditors find that the client's staff regularly performs this reconciliation, they may limit their review of vendors' statements to determining that the reconciliation work has been satisfactory.

If the client's staff has not reconciled vendors' statements and accounts payable, the auditors may do so on a selected basis. When the risk of material misstatement for accounts payable is high, the auditors may control incoming mail to assure that all vendors' statements received by the client are made available to the auditors. Among the discrepancies often revealed by reconciliation of vendors' statements are charges by the vendor for shipments not yet received or recorded by the client. Although conceptually all goods on which title has passed should be included in inventory (thus items shipped FOB [free on board] shipping point as of year-end and not yet received should be included), normal accounting procedures often do not provide for recording invoices as liabilities until the merchandise has been received. In-transit shipments on which title has passed should be listed and a decision reached as to whether they are sufficiently material to warrant year-end adjustment.

### 4. Confirm Accounts Payable by Direct Correspondence with Vendors.

| Primary Audit Objectives: | |
|---|---|
| Completeness | ☑ |
| Existence | ☑ |
| Occurrence | ☑ |
| Obligations | ☑ |
| Valuation | ☑ |
| Accuracy | ☑ |
| Cutoff | ☑ |

Although **confirmation** of accounts payable is a widely used procedure, it is generally considered less necessary than is the confirmation of accounts receivable. One reason is that for accounts payable the auditors will find in the client's possession externally created evidence such as vendors' invoices and statements that substantiate the accounts payable. Generally only limited external evidence (e.g., the customer's purchase order) is on hand to support accounts receivable.

Another reason for the difference in significance attached to confirmation of accounts payable is that the greatest risk in the audit of liabilities is the possibility of unrecorded amounts. While confirmation can provide evidence about completeness, it is a more effective procedure for establishing existence and valuation of an item. To make the confirmation procedure more effective at addressing the completeness of accounts payable, the auditors will often use a *blank form,* as illustrated by Figure 14.5. This form asks the vendor to fill in the amount of the liability rather than to confirm a recorded amount.

Also, accounts payable confirmation requests should be mailed to vendors from whom substantial purchases have been made during the year, regardless of the size of their accounts at the balance sheet date (even to suppliers whose accounts show *zero balances*). These substantial suppliers may be identified by reference to cash disbursement records or computer printouts of purchase volume by individual supplier, inquiry of purchasing department personnel, and examination of the accounts payable subsidiary ledger. Other accounts that often are confirmed by the auditors include those for which monthly statements are not available, accounts reflecting unusual transactions, accounts with parent or subsidiary corporations, and accounts secured by pledged assets.

### 5. Perform Analytical Procedures for Accounts Payable and Related Accounts.

| Primary Audit Objectives: | |
|---|---|
| Completeness | ☑ |
| Existence | ☑ |
| Occurrence | ☑ |
| Obligations | ☑ |
| Valuation | ☑ |
| Accuracy | ☑ |
| Cutoff | ☑ |

To gain assurance as to the overall reasonableness of accounts payable, the auditor may compute ratios such as purchases divided by accounts payable and accounts payable divided by total current liabilities. These ratios are compared with ratios for prior years to disclose trends that warrant investigation.

The list of amounts payable to individual vendors should be reviewed to identify any companies from which the client does not ordinarily acquire goods or services. The amounts owed to individual creditors should also be compared with balances in prior years. By studying yearly variations in purchases and other accounts closely related to accounts payable, the auditors may become aware of errors in accounts payable. Finally, the portion of accounts payable that is past due at year-end should be compared with corresponding data for previous years.

The auditors may test purchase discounts by computing the ratio of cash discounts earned to total purchases during the period and comparing this ratio from period to period. Any significant decrease in the ratio might indicate a change in terms of purchases, failure to take discounts, or fraudulent manipulation.

### 6. Search for Unrecorded Accounts Payable.

| Primary Audit Objectives: | |
|---|---|
| Completeness | ☑ |
| Cutoff | ☑ |

Throughout the audit, the auditors must be alert for any unrecorded payables. For example, the preceding three steps of this program—reconciliation, confirmation, and analytical procedures—may disclose unrecorded liabilities. In addition to normal trade payables that may be unrecorded, other examples include unrecorded liabilities related to customers' deposits recorded as credits to accounts receivable, obligation for securities purchased but

**FIGURE 14.5**
**Accounts Payable Confirmation**

---

### PACKAGE SYSTEMS, INC.

9200 CHANNEL STREET
NEW ORLEANS, LOUISIANA 70128

January 2, 20X2

Grayline Container, Inc.
4800 Madison Street
Dallas, Texas 75221

Dear Sirs:

   Our independent auditors, Nelson & Gray, CPAs, are performing an audit of our financial statements. For this reason, please inform them in the space provided below the amount, if any, owed to you by this company at December 31, 20X1.

   Please attach an itemized statement supporting any balance owed, showing all unpaid items. Your reply should be sent directly to Nelson & Gray, CPAs, 6500 Lane Avenue, New Orleans, Louisiana 70128. A stamped, addressed envelope is enclosed for your reply. Thank you.

Sincerely,

*Robert W. James*

Robert W. James
Controller

- - - - - - - - - - - - - - - - - - - - - - - - - - - - - - - - - - - - - - - - - -

Nelson & Gray, CPAs

   Our records show that the amount of $_____26,800_____ was owed to us by Package Systems, Inc., at December 31, 20X1, as shown by the itemized statement attached.

Date: Jan. 6, 20X2

Signature *Sharon Steele*

Title *Controller*

---

not settled at the balance sheet date, unbilled contractor or architect fees for a building under construction at the audit date, and unpaid attorney or insurance broker fees.

   In addition to the prior audit steps, when searching for unrecorded accounts payable the auditors will examine transactions that were recorded following year-end. A comparison of cash payments occurring after the balance sheet date with the accounts payable trial balance is generally the most effective means of disclosing unrecorded accounts payable. All liabilities must eventually be paid and will, therefore, be reflected in the accounts at least by the time they are paid. Regular monthly expenses, such as rent and utilities, are often posted to the ledger accounts directly from the cash disbursements journal without any account payable or other liability having been set up. Therefore, the auditors will often examine all cash disbursements over specific dollar amounts that are made by the client during the **subsequent period.**

The auditors should also consider potential sources of unrecorded payables such as the following:

a. Unmatched invoices and unbilled receiving reports. These documents are called *work in process* in a voucher system. The auditors should review such unprocessed documents at the balance sheet date to ascertain that the client has recorded an account payable where appropriate.

b. Vouchers payable entered in the voucher register subsequent to the balance sheet date. Inspection of these records may uncover an item that should have been recorded as of the balance sheet date.

c. Invoices received by the client after the balance sheet date. Not all vendors send invoices promptly when goods are shipped or services are rendered. Accordingly, the auditors' review of invoices received by the client in the subsequent period may disclose unrecorded accounts payable as of the balance sheet date.

d. **Consignments** in which the client acts as a consignee. The consignee assumes liability for consigned merchandise when those goods have been sold to third parties. Those sales, especially shortly before the year-end, may not have been set up as a liability to the consignor. While the auditors' overall knowledge about the accounting for such consigned items will dictate the appropriate procedures, those related to the revenue cycle, such as tests of sales transactions around year-end, may reveal such sales.

A form of audit working paper used to summarize unrecorded accounts payable discovered by the auditors is illustrated in Figure 14.6.

When the auditors discover unrecorded liabilities, the next question is whether the omissions are sufficiently material to warrant proposing an adjusting entry. Will the adjustment cause a sufficient change in the financial statements to give a different impression of the company's current position or of its earning power? As previously indicated in the discussion of the reconciliation of vendors' statements with accounts payable, auditors may choose not to propose adjustments for the purpose of adding shipments in transit to the year-end inventory unless the shipments are unusually large.

As a further illustration of the factors to be considered in deciding upon the *materiality* of an unrecorded transaction, let us use as an example the December 31 annual audit of a small manufacturing company in good financial condition with total assets of $3 million and preadjustment net income of $100,000. The auditors' procedures bring to light the following unrecorded liabilities:

a. An invoice of $1,400, dated December 30 and bearing terms of FOB shipping point. The goods were shipped on December 30 but were not received until January 4. The invoice was also received and recorded on January 4.

In considering the materiality of this omission, the first point is that net income is not affected. The adjusting entry, if made, would add equal amounts to current assets (inventories) and to current liabilities; hence it would not change the amount of working capital. The omission does affect the current ratio very slightly. The auditor would probably consider this transaction as not sufficiently material to warrant adjustment.

b. Another invoice for $4,000, dated December 30 and bearing terms of FOB shipping point. The goods arrived on December 31 and were included in the physical inventory taken that day. The invoice was not received until January 8 and was entered as a January transaction.

This error should be corrected because the inclusion of the goods in the physical inventory without recognition of the liability has caused an error of $4,000 in pretax income for the year. Since the current liabilities are understated, both the amount of working capital and the current ratio are overstated. The owners' equity is also overstated. These facts point to the materiality of the omission and constitute strong arguments for an adjusting entry.

c. An invoice for $1,500, dated December 31, for a new office safe. The safe was installed on December 31, but the invoice was not recorded until paid on January 15.

FIGURE 14.6  **Search for Unrecorded Liabilities**

```
                          THE PALERNO COMPANY                      M-1-1
                        Unrecorded Accounts Payable
                           December 31, 20X3                        LK
                                                                  2/19/X4

           Invoice                                    Account
  Date     Number         Vendor and Description      Charged       Amount

12/31/X3    2581    Hayes Mfg. Co.—invoice and shipment in transit  Inventories   $10,650.00

12/31/X3    2428    Tax & Williams—unpaid legal fees—see M-4        Legal          1,000.00
                                                                    Expenses

12/31/X3     -      Allen Enterprises—12/19 account sales for       Sales         25,680.00
                    consigned goods

   -         -      Hart & Co.—machinery repairs (paid 1/1/X4)      Repairs       12,600.00
                                                                    Expense

   -         -      Grant Co.—shipment received 12/31/X3 per        Cost of Sales 15,820.00
                    receiving report no. 2907; invoice not yet
                    received

   -         -      Arthur & Baker—earned but unpaid architects' fee Construction
                    for building under construction—see K-5         in Progress   23,370.00

                                                                                 $89,120.00


A.J.E. #8   131 Inventories                            10,650.00
            501 Cost of Sales                          15,820.00
            156 Construction in Progress               23,370.00
            401 Sales                                  25,680.00
            518 Legal Expenses                          1,000.00
            527 Repairs Expense                        12,600.00
            203 Accounts Payable                                    89,120.00

       To record unrecorded accounts payable at 12/31/X3


       The above payables were identified principally in the audit of accounts payable.
       See audit program B-4 for procedures employed. In my opinion the $89,120
       adjustment includes all material unrecorded accounts payable.
                                                                    LK
                                                                  2/23/X4
```

Since the transaction involves only asset and liability accounts, the omission of an entry does not affect net income. However, working capital and the current ratio are affected by the error since the debit affects a noncurrent asset and the credit affects a current liability. Most auditors would probably not propose an adjusting entry for this item.

d. An invoice for $3,000, dated December 31, for advertising services rendered during October, November, and December. The invoice was not recorded until paid on January 15.

The argument for treating this item as sufficiently material to warrant adjustment is based on the fact that net income is affected, as well as the amount of working capital and the current ratio. The adjusting entry should probably be recommended in these circumstances.

The preceding examples suggest that a decision as to the materiality of an unrecorded transaction hinges to an important extent on whether the transaction affects net income. Assuming that an omitted transaction *does* affect net income and there is doubt as to whether the dollar amount is large enough to warrant adjustment, the auditors should bear in mind that about one-third of the effect of the error on net income may be eliminated by corporate income taxes. In other words, an adjusting entry to record an omitted expense item of $10,000 may reduce after-tax income by only $6,500. If the adjusting entry is not made, the only ultimate effect is a shift of $6,500 between the net incomes of two successive years. Unless the client requests all adjusting entries, the auditors should avoid proposing adjusting entries for clearly inconsequential errors in the year-end cut-off of transactions. However, it should be borne in mind that a number of insignificant individual misstatements may be material in their *cumulative* effect on the financial statements. Therefore, the auditors will accumulate the effects of the adjusting entries not proposed (passed) to consider them with misstatements detected in other accounts, as discussed in Chapter 16.

### 7. Perform Procedures to Identify Accounts Payable to Related Parties.

Payables to a corporation's officers, directors, stockholders, or affiliates require particular attention by the auditors since they are not the result of arm's-length bargaining by parties of opposing interests. Here the auditors should consider the possibility that these payables relate to purchases of inventory or other asset items for which there may be valuation questions.

The independent auditors must search for such payables. All material payables to related parties must be disclosed in the financial statements.

### 8. Evaluate Proper Balance Sheet Presentation and Disclosure of Accounts Payable.

Proper balance sheet presentation of accounts payable requires that any material amounts payable to related parties (directors, principal stockholders, officers, and employees) be listed separately from amounts payable to trade creditors.

Debit balances of substantial amount sometimes occur in accounts payable because of such events as duplicate payments made in error, return of merchandise to vendors after payment has been made, and advances to suppliers. If these debit balances are material, a reclassification entry should be made in the audit working papers so that the debit balances will appear as assets in the balance sheet rather than being offset against other accounts payable with credit balances.

If the client company acts as a consignee of merchandise, it is possible that sales of consigned goods shortly before the year-end may not have been set up as a liability to the consignor. An accurate determination of any amounts owing to consignors at the balance sheet date is one step in the proper balance sheet presentation of liabilities.

Accounts payable secured by pledged assets should be disclosed in the balance sheet (or a note thereto) and cross-referenced to the pledged assets.

## Other Liabilities

Notes payable are discussed in the next chapter. In addition to the accounts payable previously considered, other items classified as current liabilities include:

1. Amounts withheld from employees' pay.
2. Sales taxes payable.
3. Unclaimed wages.
4. Customers' deposits.
5. Accrued liabilities.

### Amounts Withheld from Employees' Pay

Payroll deductions are numerous; among the more important are Social Security taxes and individual income taxes. Although the federal and state governments do not specify the exact form of records to be maintained, they do require that records of amounts earned and withheld be adequate to permit a determination of compliance with tax laws.

Income taxes withheld from employees' pay and not remitted as of the balance sheet date constitute a liability to be verified by the auditors. Accrued employer payroll taxes may be audited at the same time. This verification usually consists of tracing the amounts withheld to the payroll summary sheets, testing computations of taxes withheld and

---

Primary Audit Objective:

Presentation    ☑

---

Primary Audit Objective:

Presentation    ☑

accrued, determining that taxes have been deposited or paid in accordance with federal and state laws and regulations, and reviewing quarterly tax returns.

Payroll deductions also are often made for union dues, charitable contributions, retirement plans, insurance, savings bonds, and other purposes. Besides verifying the liability for any such amounts withheld from employees and not remitted as of the balance sheet date, the auditors should review the adequacy of the withholding procedures and determine that payroll deductions have been properly authorized and accurately computed.

## Sales Taxes Payable

In most sections of the United States, business concerns involved in retail sales are required to collect sales taxes imposed by state and local governments. These taxes do not represent an expense to the business; the retailer merely acts as a collecting agent. Until the amounts collected from customers are remitted to the taxing authority, they constitute current liabilities of the business. The auditors' verification of this liability includes a review of the client's periodic tax returns. The reasonableness of the liability also is tested by a computation applying the tax rate to total taxable sales. In addition, the auditors should examine a number of sales invoices to ascertain that customers are being charged the correct amount of tax. Debits to the liability account for remittances to the taxing authority should be traced to copies of the tax returns and vouched to the paid checks.

## Unclaimed Wages

Unclaimed wages are, by their very nature, subject to misappropriation. The auditors, therefore, are concerned with the adequacy of internal control over this item. A list of unpaid wages should be prepared after each payroll distribution. The payroll checks should not be left for more than a few days in the payroll department. Prompt deposit in a special bank account provides much improved control. The auditors will analyze the Unclaimed Wages account for the purpose of determining that (1) the credits represent all unclaimed wages after each payroll distribution and (2) the debits represent only authorized payments to employees, remittances to the state under unclaimed property laws, or transfers back to general cash funds through approved procedures.

## Customers' Deposits

Many companies require that customers make deposits on returnable containers. Public utilities and common carriers also may require deposits to guarantee payment of bills or to cover equipment on loan to the customer. A review of the procedures followed in accepting and returning deposits should be made by the auditors with a view to disclosing any shortcomings in internal control. In some instances, deposits shown by the records as refunded to customers may in fact have been abstracted by employees.

The verification should include obtaining a list of the individual deposits and a comparison of the total with the general ledger control account. If deposits are interest-bearing, the amount of accrued interest should also be tested for reasonableness. As a general rule, the auditors do not attempt to confirm deposits by direct communication with customers; however, this procedure is desirable if the amounts involved are substantial or controls are considered to be deficient.

## Accrued Liabilities

Most accrued liabilities (expenses) represent obligations payable sometime during the succeeding period for services or privileges received before the balance sheet date. Examples include interest payable, accrued property taxes, accrued payrolls and payroll taxes, income taxes payable, and amounts accrued under service guarantees.

Accrued liabilities represent accounting estimates made by the client of amounts that will subsequently become payable. Recall from Chapter 5 that, in evaluating the reasonableness of accounting estimates, auditors use one or more of the following three basic approaches:

1. Review and test management's process of developing the estimate.
2. Review subsequent events or transactions bearing on the estimate.
3. Independently develop an estimate of the amount to compare to management's estimate.

For most accrued liabilities, the audit approach will emphasize a review and test of management's process of developing the estimates (see particularly audit program steps 1 through 5 below).

Subjective (as well as objective) factors may make it difficult to establish control over accrued liabilities. As a result, these estimates may be particularly susceptible to misstatement, especially in circumstances in which management is under pressure to show increased earnings.

The basic auditing steps for accrued liabilities are:

1. Examine any contracts or other documents on hand that provide the basis for the accrual.
2. Appraise the accuracy of the detailed accounting records maintained for this category of liability.
3. Identify and evaluate the reasonableness of the assumptions made that underlie the computation of the liability.
4. Test the computations made by the client in setting up the accrual.
5. Determine that accrued liabilities have been treated consistently at the beginning and end of the period.
6. Consider the need for accrual of other accrued liabilities not presently considered (that is, test completeness).
7. For significant estimates, perform a retrospective analysis of the prior year's estimates for evidence of management bias.

The following sections describe the nature of the audit of various accrued liabilities.

### Accrued Property Taxes

Property tax payments are usually few in number and substantial in amount. It is, therefore, feasible for the audit working papers to include an analysis showing all of the year's property tax transactions. Tax payments should be verified by inspection of the property tax bills issued by local government units and by reference to the related paid checks. If the tax accruals at the balance sheet date differ significantly from those of prior years, an explanation of the variation should be obtained. The auditors should verify that property tax bills have been received on all taxable property or that an estimated tax has been accrued.

### Accrued Payrolls

The audit of payrolls from the standpoint of appraising the adequacy of controls and substantiating the expenditures for the period under audit is considered in Chapter 16. The present consideration of payrolls is limited to the procedures required for testing accrued payrolls at the balance sheet date.

Accrued gross salaries and wages appear on the balance sheets of virtually all concerns. The accuracy of the amount accrued may be significant in the determination of total liabilities and also in the proper matching of costs and revenue. The verification procedure consists principally of comparing the amounts accrued to the actual payroll of the subsequent period and reviewing the method of allocation at the balance sheet date. Payments made at the first payroll dates of the subsequent period are reviewed to determine that no significant *unrecorded* payroll liability existed as of the balance sheet date.

### Pension Plan Accruals

Auditing procedures for the accrued liability for pension costs may begin with a review of the copy of the pension plan in the auditors' permanent file. Then consideration should be given to the provisions of the Employee Retirement Income Security Act (ERISA). The auditors must determine that the client's accrued pension liability is presented in accordance with *FASB ASC* 715, including consideration of service cost, interest cost, amortization of transition and service costs, and gains and losses on pension plan assets.

In auditing these amounts, the auditors will obtain representations from an actuary and confirm the activity in the plan with the trustee. In evaluating the evidence from the actuary, the auditors should comply with the requirements of AICPA AU 620 (PCAOB 336) for using the work of a specialist, as discussed in Chapter 5.

### Postemployment Benefits Other than Pensions

Under *FASB ASC* 715, companies must accrue, during the years that employees perform services, the expected cost of providing health and similar retirement benefits to the employees, their beneficiaries, and their dependents. Determining the amount of these liabilities is a very complex procedure, because assumptions must be made about matters such as employee work lives and increases in medical costs. Since actuaries and other specialists develop these assumptions, the auditors should evaluate the assumptions and the specialists' qualifications in accordance with AICPA AU 620 (PCAOB 336).

### Accrued Vacation Pay

Closely related to accrued salaries and wages is the liability that may exist for accrued vacation pay. This type of liability arises from two situations: (1) An employee entitled by contract to a vacation during the past year may have been prevented from taking it by an emergency work schedule, and (2) an employee may be entitled to a future vacation of which part of the cost must be accrued to achieve a proper matching of costs and revenue.

The auditors' verification of accrued vacation pay may begin with a review of the permanent file copy of the employment contract or agreement stipulating vacation terms. The computation of the accrual should then be verified both as to arithmetical accuracy and for agreement with the terms of the company's vacation policy.

### Product Warranty Liabilities

The products of many companies are sold with a guarantee of free service or replacement during a rather extended warranty period. The costs of rendering such services should be recognized as expenses in the year the product is sold rather than in a later year in which the replacement is made or the repair service is performed. If this policy is followed, the company will make an annual charge to expense and a credit to a liability account based on the amount of the year's sales and the estimated future service or replacement cost. As repairs and replacements take place, the costs will be charged to the liability account.

The auditors should review the client's annual provision for estimated future expenditures and compute the percentage relationship between the amount in the liability account and the amount of the year's sales. If this relationship varies sharply from year to year, the client should be asked for an explanation. The auditors should also review the charges to the liability account month by month and be alert for the improper recording of other expenses in this account. Sudden variations in the monthly charges to the liability account require investigation. In general, the auditors should determine that the balance in the liability account for service guarantees moves in reasonable relationship with the trend of sales. The auditors also should be alert for changes in the client's products or repair costs that might affect the amount of the warranty liability.

Current income tax laws prohibit the deduction of provisions for warranty liabilities; deductions are permitted only when actual expenditures are incurred. Accordingly, the auditors should ascertain that the client is properly allocating income taxes attributable to the nondeductible provisions.

### Accrued Commissions and Bonuses

Accrued commissions to sales representatives and bonuses payable to managerial personnel also require verification. The essential step in this case is reference to the authority for the commission or bonus. The basic contracts should be examined and traced to minutes of directors' meetings. If the bonus or commission is based on the total volume of sales or some other objective measure, the auditors should verify the computation of the accrual by applying the prescribed rate to the amount used as a base.

---

### Focus on the Airline Industry

The frequent flyer travel award programs in the airline industry are similar to product warranty liabilities in the sense that a free service is associated with the purchase of airline tickets. These programs provide an excellent example of the accounting and auditing difficulties involved with many accrued liabilities. In these programs, travelers earn frequent flier mileage for flying with the airline, which may be exchanged for flight awards.

In accounting for these programs, estimates must be made of the percentage of the mileage that will ultimately be redeemed as well as the expected cost of providing the travel. Currently, airlines account for the awards by the incremental cost method, which calculates the airline's liability as the incremental cost associated with transporting a passenger in an otherwise empty seat. While auditors may easily test computations and determine that the liability has been treated consistently at the beginning and end of the period, determining the reasonableness of the estimates of redemption rates and future costs is more difficult. Generally, they must use analytical procedures that focus on the prior experience of the client and other airline companies.

---

#### Income Taxes Payable

Federal, state, and foreign income taxes on corporations represent a material factor in determining both net income and financial position. The auditors cannot express an opinion on either the balance sheet or income statement of a corporation without first obtaining evidence that the provision for income taxes has been properly computed. In the audit of small and medium-size companies, it is customary for the audit engagement to include the preparation of the client's tax returns. If the client's staff or other persons have prepared the income tax returns, the auditors must nevertheless verify the reasonableness of the tax liability if they are to express an opinion on the fairness of the financial statements. In performing such a review of a tax return prepared by the client's staff or by others, the auditors may sometimes discover an opportunity for a tax saving that has been overlooked; obviously such a discovery tends to enhance the client's appreciation of the services rendered by the auditors.

The auditors should analyze the Income Taxes Payable account and vouch all amounts to income tax returns, paid checks, or other supporting documents. The final balance in the Income Taxes Payable account will ordinarily equal the computed federal, state, and foreign taxes on the current year's income tax returns, less any payments thereon.

The tax expected to be paid by a corporation often differs from the actual tax paid due to temporary differences between taxable income and pretax accounting income. These differences result in the need to establish deferred tax liabilities or assets. The auditors determine the amount of deferred tax liabilities using schedules referred to as "tax accrual" working papers, which usually are reviewed by one of the CPA firm's tax specialists.

Besides reviewing the computation of the income tax liability for the current year, the auditors should determine the date on which income tax returns for prior years were examined by IRS agents, as well as the particulars of any disputes or additional assessments. Review of the reports of revenue agents is also an essential step. In the first audit of a new client, the auditors should review any prior years' income tax returns not yet examined by revenue agents to make sure that there has been no substantial underpayment of taxes that would warrant presentation as a liability.

#### Accrued Professional Fees

Fees of professional firms include charges for the services of attorneys, public accountants, consulting engineers, and other specialists who often render services of a continuing nature but present bills only at infrequent intervals. By inquiry of officers and by review of corporate minutes, the auditors may learn of professional services received for which no liability has yet been reflected in the accounts. Review of the expense account for legal fees is always essential because it may reveal damage suits, tax disputes, or other litigation warranting disclosure in the financial statements.

## Balance Sheet Presentation

Accrued expenses—interest, taxes, rent, and wages—are included in the current liability section of the balance sheet and sometimes combined into one figure. Income taxes payable, however, may be sufficiently material to be listed as a separate item. Deferred federal income taxes resulting from tax allocations should be classified as current liabilities (or assets) if they relate to the next year. Otherwise, deferred federal income taxes are classified as noncurrent.

Deferred credits to revenue for such items as rent or interest collected in advance that will be included in earnings in the succeeding period are customarily included in current liabilities. Deposits on contracts and similar advances from customers also are accorded the status of current liabilities because the receipt of an advance increases the current assets total and because the goods to be used in liquidating the advance are generally included in current assets.

## Time of Examination

The nature and amount of **trade accounts payable** may change greatly within a few weeks' time; consequently, the auditors' verification of these rapidly changing liabilities is most effective when performed immediately after the balance sheet date. As emphasized at the beginning of this chapter, failure to record a liability will cause an overstatement of financial position. Audit work on accounts payable performed before the balance sheet date is of little value if the client fails to record important liabilities coming into existence during the remaining weeks of the year under audit. For this reason, many auditors believe that most of the audit work on accounts payable should be performed *after the balance sheet date.* Certainly, the auditors' search for unrecorded liabilities must be made after the balance sheet date because this search is concentrated on the transactions occurring during the first few weeks of the new year.

Some current liability accounts other than accounts payable are more suitable for preliminary audit work. The documents relating to accrued property taxes, for example, may be available in advance of the balance sheet date. Amounts withheld from employees' pay also can be reviewed before the end of the year. The propriety of amounts withheld and of amounts remitted to the tax authorities during the year can be verified before the pressure of year-end work begins. The working papers relating to such liability accounts then may be completed very quickly after the end of the accounting period.

## Chapter Summary

This chapter explained the fundamental controls over accounts payable and purchase transactions. It also discussed the auditors' consideration of these controls and the substantive procedures for accounts payable and purchases. To summarize:

1. Accounts payable are short-term obligations arising from the purchase of goods and services in the ordinary course of the business.
2. The purchases cycle includes initiating and authorizing purchases, ordering goods and services, and recording and paying accounts payable. Effective internal control over purchase transactions is best achieved by having separate departments responsible for purchasing, receiving, and accounting for the transactions. In this manner, payments are made only for those purchases that are properly authorized and received.
3. The auditors' principal objectives for the substantive procedures for accounts payable and purchases are to (*a*) substantiate the existence of recorded accounts payable and the occurrence of purchase transactions, (*b*) establish the completeness of accounts payable and purchase transactions, (*c*) determine that the client has obligations to pay the recorded accounts payable, (*d*) verify the cutoff of purchase transactions, (*e*) determine the appropriate valuation and accuracy of accounts payable, and (*f*) determine that the presentation and disclosure of accounts payable and purchases are appropriate.

4. In auditing accounts payable and other liabilities, it is important for the auditors to remember that an understatement of liabilities will exaggerate the financial strength of a company in the same way as an overstatement of assets. Therefore, the auditors' substantive procedures primarily focus on the objective of determining the completeness of recorded amounts. A number of these procedures involve inspecting documents related to transactions occurring during the subsequent period to determine whether these items should have been recorded as liabilities at year-end.

5. Accrued liabilities represent obligations payable for services received before the balance sheet date that will be paid in the subsequent period. Examples include accrued warranty liabilities, accrued payroll, and accrued pension liabilities. The substantive procedures to audit these liabilities generally include inspection of documents, recomputation, and analytical procedures.

## Key Terms Introduced or Emphasized in Chapter 14

**Accrued liabilities (accrued expenses) (562)**   Short-term obligations for services of a continuing nature that accumulate over time. Examples include interest, taxes, rent, salaries, and pensions. They generally are not evidenced by invoices or statements.

**Confirmation (572)**   Direct communication with vendors or suppliers to determine the amount of an account payable. Represents high-quality evidence because it is a document created outside the client organization and transmitted directly to the auditors.

**Consignment (574)**   A transfer of goods from the owner to another person who acts as the sales agent of the owner.

**Subsequent period (573)**   The time extending from the balance sheet date to the date of the auditors' report.

**Trade accounts payable (581)**   Current liabilities arising from the purchase of goods and services from trade creditors, generally evidenced by invoices or statements received from the creditors.

**Vendor's statement (565)**   A monthly statement prepared by a vendor (supplier) showing the beginning balance, charges during the month for goods or services, amounts collected, and ending balance. This externally created document should correspond (except for timing differences) with an account in the client's accounts payable subsidiary ledger.

**Voucher (563)**   A document authorizing a cash disbursement. A voucher usually provides space for the initials of employees performing various approval functions. The term *voucher* may also be applied to the group of supporting documents used as a basis for recording liabilities or for making cash disbursements.

**Voucher register (569)**   A journal used in a voucher system to record liabilities requiring cash payment in the near future. Every liability recorded in a voucher register corresponds to a voucher authorizing future payment.

## Review Questions

14–1.   If a corporation overstates its earnings, are its liabilities more likely to be overstated or understated? Explain.

14–2.   Lawsuits against CPA firms are most likely to allege that the auditors were negligent in not detecting which of the following? (*a*) overstatement of liabilities and earnings, (*b*) understatement of assets and earnings, or (*c*) overstatement of owners' equity. Explain the reasoning underlying your choice.

14–3.   Assume that a highly placed employee has stolen company assets and is now planning to conceal the fraud by failing to make an accounting entry for a large transaction. Would the omission probably be for a transaction creating an asset or a liability? Explain.

14–4.   Suggest two reasons why the adjustments proposed by independent auditors more often than not call for reducing recorded earnings.

14–5.   Compare the auditors' approach to the verification of liabilities with their approach to the verification of assets.

14–6. The auditors usually find in the client's possession documentary evidence, such as invoices, supporting both accounts receivable and accounts payable. Is there any difference in the quality of such evidence for accounts receivable and for accounts payable? Explain.

14–7. Describe briefly an internal control activity that would prevent a paid disbursement voucher from being presented for payment a second time.

14–8. The operating procedures of a well-managed accounts payable department will provide for the verification of several specific points before a vendor's invoice is recorded as an approved liability. What are the points requiring verification?

14–9. List the major responsibilities of an accounts payable department.

14–10. In achieving adequate internal control over operations of the accounts payable department, a company should establish procedures that will ensure that extensions and footings are proved on all invoices and that the propriety of prices is reviewed. What is the most effective means of assuring consistent performance of these duties?

14–11. Which do you consider the more significant step in establishing strong internal control over accounts payable transactions: the approval of an invoice for payment, or the issuance of a check in payment of an invoice? Explain.

14–12. For which documents relating to the accounts payable operation would you recommend the use of serial numbers as an internal control activity?

14–13. What internal control activity would you recommend to call attention to a failure to pay invoices within the discount period?

14–14. During the verification of the individual invoices composing the total of accounts payable at the balance sheet date, the auditors discovered some receiving reports indicating that the merchandise covered by several of these invoices was not received until after the balance sheet date. What action should the auditors take?

14–15. As part of the investigation of accounts payable, auditors sometimes vouch entries in selected creditors' accounts back through the journals to original documents, such as purchase orders, receiving reports, invoices, and paid checks. What is the principal purpose of this procedure?

14–16. Outline a method by which the auditors may test the propriety of cash discounts taken on accounts payable.

14–17. Is the confirmation of accounts payable by direct communication with vendors as useful and important an audit procedure as such confirmation of accounts receivable? Explain.

14–18. Whitehall Company records its liabilities in an accounts payable subsidiary ledger. The auditors have decided to select some of the accounts for confirmation by direct communication with vendors. The largest volume of purchases during the year has been made from Ranchero Company, but at the balance sheet date this account has a zero balance. Under these circumstances, should the auditors send a confirmation request to Ranchero Company, or would they accomplish more by limiting their confirmation program to accounts with larger year-end balances?

14–19. Vendors' statements and accounts payable confirmations are both forms of documentary evidence created outside the client organization and useful in audit work on accounts payable. Which of these two represents higher quality evidence? Why?

14–20. Explain how the auditors coordinate the year-end cutoff of accounts payable with their observation of the year-end physical inventory.

14–21. Identify three audit procedures (other than "Search for unrecorded accounts payable") that are concerned directly or indirectly with disclosing unrecorded accounts payable.

14–22. What do you consider to be the most important single procedure in the auditors' search for unrecorded accounts payable? Explain.

14–23. What is the purpose of the auditors' review of cash payments subsequent to the balance sheet date?

14–24. Most auditors are interested in performing as many phases of an audit as possible in advance of the balance sheet date. The verification of accounts payable, however, generally is regarded as something to be done after the balance sheet date. What specific factors can you suggest that make the verification of accounts payable less suitable than many other accounts for interim work?

14–25. What documentary evidence created outside the client's organization is particularly important to the auditors in verifying accrued property taxes?

14–26. What differences should auditors expect to find in supporting evidence for accrued liabilities as contrasted with accounts payable?

**Questions Requiring Analysis**

LO 1, 6    14–27.    Compare the confirmation of accounts receivable with the confirmation of accounts payable under the following headings:

a.  Generally accepted auditing procedures. (Justify the differences revealed by your comparison.)

b.  Selection of accounts to be confirmed.

(AICPA, adapted)

LO 4, 6    14–28.    In the course of your initial audit of the financial statements of Sylvan Company, you determine that of the substantial amount of accounts payable outstanding at the close of the period, approximately 75 percent is owed to six creditors. You have requested that you be permitted to confirm the balances due to these six creditors by communicating with the creditors, but the president of the company is unwilling to approve your request on the grounds that correspondence in regard to the balances—all of which contain some overdue items—might give rise to demands on the part of the creditors for immediate payment of the overdue items and thereby embarrass Sylvan Company.

Given these circumstances, what alternative procedure would you adopt in an effort to satisfy yourself that the accounting records show the correct amounts payable to these creditors?

(AICPA, adapted)

LO 6    14–29.    The subsequent period in an audit is the time extending from the balance sheet date to the date of the auditors' report.

*Required:*    Discuss the importance of the subsequent period in the audit of trade accounts payable.

LO 1, 3, 4, 6    14–30.    Early in your first audit of Star Corporation, you notice that sales and year-end inventory are almost unchanged from the prior year. However, cost of goods sold is less than in the preceding year, and accounts payable also are down substantially. Gross profit has increased, but this increase has not carried through to net income because of increased executive salaries. Management informs you that sales prices and purchase prices have not changed significantly during the past year, and there have been no changes in the product line. Star Corporation relies on the periodic inventory system. Your initial impression of internal control is that several weaknesses may exist.

Suggest a possible explanation for the trends described, especially the decrease in accounts payable while sales and inventory were constant and gross profit increased. Explain fully the relationships involved.

LO 1, 4, 6    14–31.    During the course of any audit, the auditors are always alert for unrecorded accounts payable or other unrecorded liabilities.

*Required:*    For each of the following audit areas, (1) describe an unrecorded liability that might be discovered and (2) state what auditing procedure or procedures might bring it to light.

a.  Construction in progress (property, plant, and equipment).

b.  Prepaid insurance.

c.  License authorizing the client to produce a product patented by another company.

d.  Minutes of directors' meetings.

LO 6    14–32.    In connection with their audit of the financial statements of Davis Company, the auditors reviewed the Federal Income Taxes Payable account.

*Required:*    a.  Discuss reasons why the auditors should review the federal income tax returns for prior years and the reports of internal revenue agents.

b.  What information will these reviews provide? (Do not discuss specific tax return items.)

(AICPA, adapted)

LO 1, 6    14–33.    Describe the audit steps that generally would be followed in establishing the propriety of the recorded liability for federal income taxes of a corporation you are auditing for the first time. Consideration should be given to the status of (*a*) the liability for prior years and (*b*) the liability arising from the current year's taxable income.

**Objective Questions**

All applicable questions are available with McGraw-Hill's *Connect*™ *Accounting*.  ▦ connect |ACCOUNTING

14–34.    **Multiple Choice Questions**

Select the best answer for each of the following and explain the reason for your selection.

LO 6    a.  Which of the following procedures is *least* likely to be completed before the balance sheet date?

(1)  Confirmation of receivables.

(2)  Search for unrecorded liabilities.

(3)  Observation of inventory.

(4)  Review of internal accounting control over cash disbursements.

**LO 2, 4, 6**      b.  An audit of the balance in the accounts payable account is ordinarily not designed to:

(1) Detect accounts payable that are substantially past due.

(2) Verify that accounts payable were properly authorized.

(3) Ascertain the reasonableness of recorded liabilities.

(4) Determine that all existing liabilities at the balance sheet date have been recorded.

**LO 4, 6**      c.  Which of the following is the best audit procedure for determining the existence of unrecorded liabilities?

(1) Examine confirmation requests returned by creditors whose accounts appear on a subsidiary trial balance of accounts payable.

(2) Examine unusual relationships between monthly accounts payable balances and recorded purchases.

(3) Examine a sample of invoices a few days prior to and subsequent to year-end to ascertain whether they have been properly recorded.

(4) Examine selected cash disbursements in the period subsequent to year-end.

**LO 1, 4, 6**      d.  Auditor confirmation of accounts payable balances at the balance sheet date may be unnecessary because:

(1) This is a duplication of cutoff tests.

(2) Accounts payable balances at the balance sheet date may *not* be paid before the audit is completed.

(3) Correspondence with the audit client's attorney will reveal all legal action by vendors for nonpayment.

(4) There is likely to be other reliable external evidence available to support the balances.

**LO 1, 3, 5**      e.  A client erroneously recorded a large purchase twice. Which of the following internal control measures would be most likely to detect this error in a timely and efficient manner?

(1) Footing the purchases journal.

(2) Reconciling vendors' monthly statements with subsidiary payable ledger accounts.

(3) Tracing totals from the purchases journal to the ledger accounts.

(4) Sending written quarterly confirmation to all vendors.

**LO 3, 5**      f.  For effective internal control, the accounts payable department should compare the information on each vendor's invoice with the:

(1) Receiving report and the purchase order.

(2) Receiving report and the voucher.

(3) Vendor's packing slip and the purchase order.

(4) Vendor's packing slip and the voucher.

**LO 3, 6**      g.  When confirming accounts payable, the approach is most likely to be one of:

(1) Selecting the accounts with the largest balances at year-end, plus a sample of other accounts.

(2) Selecting the accounts of companies with whom the client has previously done the most business, plus a sample of other accounts.

(3) Selecting a random sample of accounts payable at year-end.

(4) Confirming all accounts.

**LO 2, 6**      h.  In an audit, the valuation of year-end accounts payable is most likely addressed by:

(1) Confirmation.

(2) Examination of cash disbursements immediately prior to year-end.

(3) Examination of cash disbursements immediately subsequent to year-end.

(4) Analytical procedures applied to vouchers payable at year-end.

**LO 1, 2**      i.  Ordinarily, the most significant assertion relating to accounts payable is:

(1) Completeness.

(2) Existence.

(3) Presentation.

(4) Valuation.

**LO 1, 6**      j.  The *least* likely approach in auditing management's estimate relating to an accrued liability is to:

(1) Independently develop an estimate of the amount to compare to management's estimate.

(2) Review and test management's process of developing the estimate.

(3)  Review subsequent events or transactions bearing on the estimate.

(4)  Send confirmations relating to the estimate.

**LO 3, 5**

*k.*  To determine that each voucher is submitted and paid only once, when a payment is approved, supporting documents should be canceled by the:

(1)  Authorized members of the audit committee.

(2)  Accounting department.

(3)  Individual who signs the checks.

(4)  Chief executive officer.

**LO 2, 6**

*l.*  In performing a test of controls, the auditors vouch a sample of entries in the purchases journal to the supporting documents. Which assertion would this test of controls most likely test?

(1)  Completeness.

(2)  Existence.

(3)  Valuation.

(4)  Rights.

**LO 1, 2, 5**    14–35.    **Simulation**

The following flowchart depicts the activities relating to the purchasing, receiving, and accounts payable departments of Model Company, Inc. Assume that you are a supervising assistant assigned to the Model Company audit.

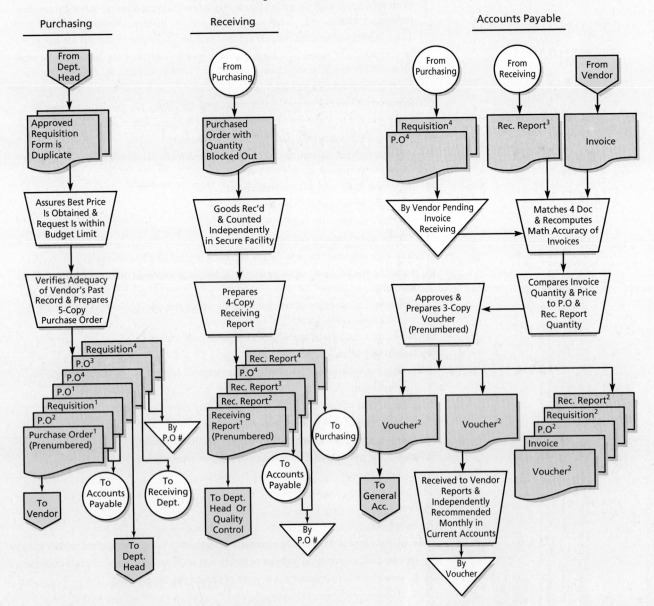

Joe Werell, a beginning assistant, analyzed the flowchart and has supplemented the flowchart by making certain inquiries of the controller. He has concluded that the internal control over purchasing, receiving, and accounts payable is strong and has provided the following list of what he refers to as internal control strengths. Review his list and for each internal control strength indicate whether you agree or disagree that each represents a strength. For those in which you disagree, briefly explain why.

### Internal Control Strengths Prepared by Joe Werell

*Purchasing*

a. The department head of the requisitioning department selects the appropriate supplier.

b. Proper authorization of requisitions by department head is required before purchase orders are prepared.

c. Purchasing department makes certain that a low-cost supplier is always chosen.

d. Purchasing department assures that requisitions are within budget limits before purchase orders are prepared.

e. The adequacy of each vendor's past record as a supplier is verified.

*Receiving*

f. Secure facilities limit access to the goods during the receiving activity.

g. Receiving department compares its count of the quantity of goods received with that listed on its copy of the purchase order.

h. A receiving report is required for all purchases, including purchases of services.

i. The requisitioning department head independently verifies the quantity and quality of the goods received.

j. Requisitions, purchase orders, and receiving reports are matched with vendor invoices as to quantity and price.

*Accounts Payable*

k. Accounts payable department personnel recompute the mathematical accuracy of each invoice.

l. The voucher register is independently reconciled to the control accounts monthly by the originators of the related vouchers.

m. All supporting documentation is marked "paid" by accounts payable immediately prior to making it available to the treasurer.

n. All supporting documentation is required for payment and is made available to the treasurer.

o. The purchasing, receiving, and accounts payable functions are segregated.

**LO 2, 6** 14–36. **Simulation**

The auditors of SSC Company are working on both audit objectives for the various accounts and documentation requirements. Parts (*a*) through (*d*) of this question relate to objectives, while part (*e*) addresses documentation.

The auditors have established the objectives listed below as a part of the audit. For each objective, select a substantive procedure (from the list of substantive procedures) that will help achieve that objective. Each of the procedures may be used once, more than once, or not at all.

*Audit Objectives*

a. Determine the existence of year-end recorded accounts payable and that the client has obligations to pay these liabilities.

b. Establish the completeness of recorded accounts payable.

c. Determine that the presentation and disclosure of accounts payable are appropriate.

d. Determine that the valuation of warranty loss reserves is measured in accordance with GAAP.

*Substantive Procedures*

1. Obtain a trial balance of payables and reconcile with the accounts payable subsidiary ledger.

2. Vouch sales from throughout the year.

3. Vouch purchases recorded after year-end.

4. Vouch sales recorded shortly before year-end.

5. Vouch major warranty expenses paid during 20X8.

6. Inquire of management concerning the existence of related party transactions.

7. Test the computations made by the client to set up the accrual.

8. Test the reasonableness of general and administrative labor rates.

9. Confirm outstanding year-end balances of payables.

10. Confirm warranty expenses payable as of year-end.

*Note: Part (e) is possible to work in a meaningful way only if you have the professional standards available—preferably in electronic form.*

e. The auditors believe that it will be necessary to depart from a requirement relating to accounts payable that is considered presumptively mandatory. Provide the AU section and paragraph(s) that address documentation requirements in this situation. You need only present the requirement, not the application and other explanatory material.

**LO 1, 4, 6**  14–37. In applying audit procedures and evaluating the results of those procedures, auditors may encounter specific information that may raise a question concerning the existence of noncompliance with laws and related party transactions. Indicate whether each of the following is more likely related to noncompliance with a law (NL) or a related party transaction (RP).

*Statement*

(a) Purchases have been made from a vendor at a price well above the market price for the goods involved.

(b) A purchasing agent's spouse has the same name as a major vendor of the company.

(c) Unexplained payments have been made to government officials.

(d) The company exchanged certain real estate property for similar real estate property.

(e) A purchasing agent of the company has received large cash payments from a major vendor of the company.

## Problems

**All applicable problems are available with McGraw-Hill's *Connect*™ *Accounting*.**  connect |ACCOUNTING

**LO 1, 3, 5**  14–38. The following are typical questions that might appear on an internal control questionnaire for accounts payable.

1. Are monthly statements from vendors reconciled with the accounts payable listing?

2. Are vendors' invoices matched with receiving reports before they are approved for payment?

*Required:*

a. Describe the purpose of each of the above internal control activities.

b. Describe the manner in which each of the above procedures might be tested.

c. Assuming that the operating effectiveness of each of the above procedures is found to be inadequate, describe how the auditors might alter their substantive procedures to compensate for the increased level of the risk of material misstatement.

**LO 1, 3, 6**  14–39. As part of your first audit of the financial statements of Marina del Rey, Inc., you have decided to confirm some of the accounts payable. You are now in the process of selecting the individual companies to whom you will send accounts payable confirmation requests. Among the accounts payable you are considering are the following:

| Company | Amount Payable at Year-End | Total Purchases from Vendor during Year |
|---|---|---|
| Dayco, Inc. | $ — | $1,980,000 |
| Gearbox, Inc. | 22,650 | 46,100 |
| Landon Co. | 65,000 | 75,000 |
| Western Supply | 190,000 | 2,123,000 |

*Required:*

a. Which two of the above four accounts payable would you select as the most important to confirm? Explain your choice in terms of the audit objectives in sending accounts payable confirmation requests.

b. Assume that you are selecting accounts receivable to be confirmed. Assume also that the four companies listed above are customers of your client rather than suppliers and that the dollar amounts are accounts receivable balances and total sales for the year. Which two companies would you select as the most important to confirm? Explain your choice.

**LO 1, 3, 6**  14–40. Taylor, CPA, is engaged in the audit of Rex Wholesaling for the year ended December 31. Taylor obtained an understanding of internal control relating to the purchasing, receiving, trade accounts payable, and cash disbursement cycles and has decided not to proceed with tests of controls. Based upon analytical procedures, Taylor believes that the trade accounts payable on the balance sheet as of December 31 may be understated.

Taylor requested and obtained a client-prepared trade accounts payable schedule listing the total amount owed to each vendor.

*Required:*

What additional substantive audit procedures should Taylor apply in examining the trade accounts payable?

**LO 1, 3, 6**  14–41.  Nancy Howe, your staff assistant on the April 30, 20X2, audit of Wilcox Company, was transferred to another audit engagement before she could complete the audit of unrecorded accounts payable. Her working paper, which you have reviewed and are satisfied is complete, appears below.

| Invoice Date | Wilcox Company<br>Unrecorded Accounts Payable<br>April 30, 20X2 | M-1-1 |
|---|---|---|
| | Vendor and Description | Amount |
| | Hill & Harper—unpaid legal fees at Apr. 30, X2 (see lawyer's letter at M-4) | 1000 *y* |
| Apr. 1, X2 | Drew Insurance Agency—unpaid premium on fire insurance for period Apr. 1, X2–Mar. 31, X5 (see insurance broker letter at J-1-1) | 1800 *y* |
| Apr. 30, X2 | Mays and Sage, Stockbrokers—advice for 100 shares of Madison Ltd. common stock (settlement date May 7, X2) | 2125 — *y* |
| | Lane Company—shipment received Apr. 30, X2 per receiver no. 3361 and included in Apr. 30, X2, physical inventory; invoice not yet received (amount is per purchase order) | 5863 — *y* |
| | | 10788 — |

*y-Examined document described.*

*In my opinion, the $10,788 adjustment includes all material unrecorded accounts payable.*

*N.A.H.*
*May 29, X2*

*Required:*  Prepare a proposed adjusting journal entry for the unrecorded accounts payable of Wilcox Company at April 30, 20X2. The amounts are material. (Do not deal with income taxes.)

**LO 1, 3, 6**  14–42.  You were in the final stages of your audit of the financial statements of Scott Corporation for the year ended December 31, 20X0, when you were consulted by the corporation's president, who believes there is no point to your examining the 20X1 voucher register and testing data in support of 20X0 entries. He stated that (1) bills pertaining to 20X0 that were received too late to be included in the December voucher register were recorded as of the year-end by the corporation by journal entry, (2) the internal auditors made tests after the year-end, and (3) he would furnish you with a letter representing that there were no unrecorded liabilities.

*Required:*

a. Should the independent auditors' test for unrecorded liabilities be affected by the fact that the client made a journal entry to record 20X0 bills that were received late? Explain.

b. Should the independent auditors' test for unrecorded liabilities be affected by the fact that a letter is obtained in which a responsible management official represents that to the best of his knowledge all liabilities have been recorded? Explain.

c. Should the independent auditors' test for unrecorded liabilities be eliminated or reduced because of the internal audit tests? Explain.

*d.* Assume that the client company, which handled some government contracts, had no internal auditors but that auditors for a federal agency spent three weeks auditing the records and were just completing their work at this time. How would the independent auditors' unrecorded liability test be affected by the work of the auditors for a federal agency?

*e.* What sources in addition to the 20X1 voucher register should the independent auditors consider to locate possible unrecorded liabilities?

(AICPA, adapted)

**LO 1, 3, 4, 6** 14–43. During the current year, your audit client, Video Corporation, was licensed to manufacture a patented type of television component. The licensing agreement called for royalty payments of 50 cents for each component manufactured by Video Corporation. What procedures would you follow in connection with your regular annual audit at December 31 to obtain evidence that the liability for royalties is correctly stated?

(AICPA, adapted)

**In-Class Team Case** **LO 1, 3, 4, 6** 14–44. You have just been assigned as a member of the audit team of Bozarkana Company (a new client) and are considering accounts payable. Bozarkana Company uses a computerized voucher system for payables. As a starting point, you asked Bill Bozarkana, the controller, for a summary of payables and received the following schedule of more than 1,000 unpaid vouchers at year-end:

| Voucher# | Vendor Number | Purchase Order# | Receiving Report# | Date Payment Due | Amount |
|----------|---------------|-----------------|-------------------|------------------|--------|
| 2334555 | 2133 | 654444 | 106500 | 1/2/0Y | $ 2,020.21 |
| 2334558 | 1098 | 654579 | 106820 | 1/2/0Y | 12,344.56 |
| 2334567 | 2133 | 654593 | 106920 | 1/2/0Y | 322.43 |
| ⋮ | | | | | |
| ⋮ | | | | | |
| ⋮ | | | | | |
| 2335643 | 2231 | 655456 | 107654 | 1/28/0Y | 2,346.62 |
| TOTAL PAYABLE | | | | | $2,225,980.83 |

| File Name | Information in Table | Comment |
|-----------|----------------------|---------|
| Purchase requisitions | Purchase requisition number<br>Date requisitioned<br>Item number<br>Item description<br>Quantity | The table includes one row for each purchase requisition—only one type of item per requisition may be requisitioned. |
| Purchase orders | Purchase order number<br>Date ordered<br>Purchase requisition number<br>Vendor number<br>Item number<br>Quantity<br>Cost | The table includes multiple rows for each purchase order—one for each item ordered. |
| Receiving reports | Receiving report number<br>Date shipped<br>Date received<br>Item number<br>Quantity | The table includes multiple rows for each receiving report—one for each item received. |
| Vendor master | Vendor number<br>Vendor name<br>Vendor address | The table includes one line for each vendor. |
| Cash disbursements | Disbursement number<br>Vendor number<br>Check number or electronic funds transfer number<br>Voucher number<br>Amount | The table includes one line for each check or funds transfer (electronic payment). |

Bill Bozarkana has indicated that the schedule is a listing of the vouchers payable file as of year-end and that the total is the result of a separate question (query) of that file asking for total payables. You have the schedule in electronic and hard-copy form. Vouchers are issued sequentially, and voucher number 2335643 was the last one issued prior to year-end. You also have obtained the information relating to the following other computer files, which are available to you in electronic form, as shown on the previous page.

The client has made copies of these files available so that you and the assistant can perform the necessary steps on the files. Furthermore, you have compared these copies to the client's copies and find that they are identical. Finally, you may assume that tests of controls have been performed on the controls related to the dates on the files. The controls were found to be effective.

*Required:*

a. Discuss how you would establish samples in the following situations:

   (1) Randomly select 30 vouchers as of year-end and obtain the necessary information to send confirmations.

   (2) Randomly select 30 accounts with balances payable (per vendor) as of December 31.

   (3) Select all accounts (per vendor) with which the company has disbursed more than $500,000 during the year, but whose balance at year-end is zero.

b. Provide detailed guidance on the following:

   (1) All purchases are sent to Bozarkana Company "FOB shipping point." Identify a procedure for testing whether any items shipped to the client prior to year-end have been omitted from vouchers payable as of year-end.

   (2) Select all disbursements over $300,000 in the first two weeks of January, and, for those not included as liabilities as of December 31, determine whether title to the goods had passed as of year-end, resulting in an unrecorded liability.

## Appendix 14A

# Illustrative Audit Case: Keystone Computers & Networks, Inc.

## Part IV: Consideration of Internal Control

This part of the audit case of Keystone Computers & Networks, Inc. (KCN), illustrates the nature of internal control over the acquisition cycle and the way in which auditors assess control risk for this cycle. The following working papers are included:

- A flowchart description of the acquisition cycle of the company and the related controls prepared by the staff of Adams, Barnes & Co. (ABC), CPAs. This flowchart focuses on the (accounting) information system and control activities.

- ABC's working paper for the assessment of control risk for accounts payable and purchases as it would appear before any tests of controls are performed. This working paper identifies the prescribed controls and weaknesses for the revenue cycle. It also relates the controls and weaknesses to the various financial statement assertions about accounts payable and purchases.

You should read through the information to obtain an understanding of typical controls for this cycle. You may also wish to review the planning documentation presented on pages 237–244 of Chapter 6 to refresh your knowledge about the nature of the company's business and its environment. The Control Environment, Risk Assessment, and Monitoring Questionnaire on pages 479–480 and the Organizational Chart of KCN on page 481 can be used to help refresh your memory about these components of internal control.

KEYSTONE COMPUTERS & NETWORKS, INC.
Assessment of Control Risk—Acquisition Cycle
12/31/X5

| Internal Controls | Existence or Occurrence | Completeness | Cutoff | Rights and Obligations | Valuation and Accuracy | Presentation and Disclosure |
|---|---|---|---|---|---|---|
| **Sales** | | | | | | |
| 1. Separation of duties for authorization of purchases, receiving merchandise, approving payment to vendors, and signing checks. | ☐ | ☐ | | ☐ | ☐ | |
| 2. Computer assigns number to purchase orders, receiving reports, and checks. | | ☐ | ☐ | | | |
| 3. Computer matches information from vendors' invoices with purchase orders and receiving data. | ☐ | | ☐ | ☐ | | |
| 4. Computer tests numerical accuracy of vendors' invoices. | | | | | ☐ | |
| 5. Approval of vendors' invoices prior to payment. | ☐ | | | ☐ | ☐ | |
| 6. Checks are mailed by the check signer. | | ☐ | | | ☐ | |
| 7. Monthly reconciliation of bank accounts by an employee who is independent of invoice processing, cash disbursements, cash receipts, petty cash, and general ledger functions. | ☐ | ☐ | | ☐ | ☐ | |
| 8. Comparison of actual disbursements to budgeted amounts and investigation of variances. | ☐ | ☐ | | | ☐ | ☐ |
| **Internal Control Weakness** | | | | | | |
| 1. Approved vendors are selected by purchasing manager who also purchases goods. | | | | | X | |
| 2. Vendors' statements are not reconciled to the accounting records. | X | X | | | X | |
| **Planned Assessed Level of Control Risk** | *Low* | *Moderate* | *Moderate* | *Low* | *Moderate* | *Maximum* |

# KEYSTONE COMPUTERS & NETWORKS, INC.
## Internal Control—Acquisition Cycle
### 12/31/X5

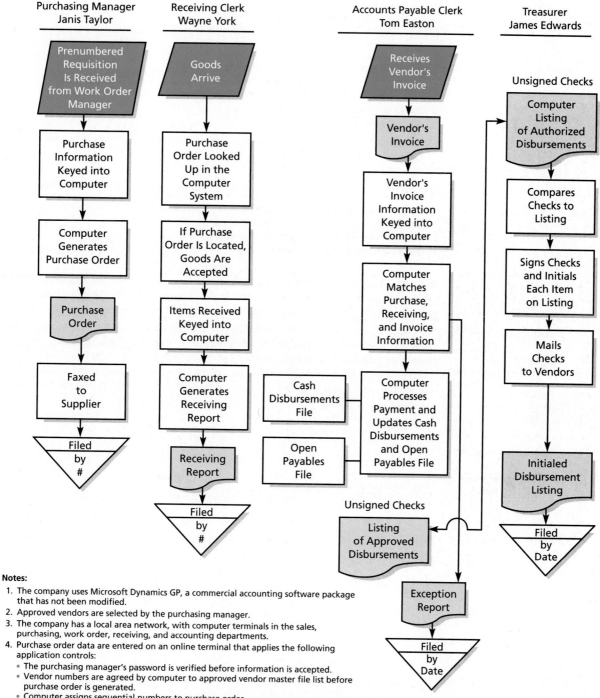

**Notes:**

1. The company uses Microsoft Dynamics GP, a commercial accounting software package that has not been modified.
2. Approved vendors are selected by the purchasing manager.
3. The company has a local area network, with computer terminals in the sales, purchasing, work order, receiving, and accounting departments.
4. Purchase order data are entered on an online terminal that applies the following application controls:
   - The purchasing manager's password is verified before information is accepted.
   - Vendor numbers are agreed by computer to approved vendor master file list before purchase order is generated.
   - Computer assigns sequential numbers to purchase order.
5. Receiving information is entered on an online terminal that applies the following controls:
   - The receiving clerk's password is verified before information is accepted.
   - Computer assigns sequential numbers to purchase order.
6. Vendors' invoice information is entered on an online terminal that applies the following controls:
   - The accounts payable clerk's password is verified before information is accepted.
   - The computer recomputes the individual items and the total amount of the invoice.
7. Computer agrees with purchase order, receiving, and invoice data and produces an exception report for any situation in which the documents do not match. Accounts payable clerk follows up on exceptions and describes resolution on report.
8. Computer updates cash disbursements and open payables files.
9. The accounting manager reconciles the cash and open payables accounts to the general ledger on a monthly basis.
10. The accounting manager reconciles the bank account on a monthly basis.
11. Cash disbursements are budgeted and the controller analyzes and explains variances.

## Appendix 14A Problems

*Required:*
**LO 1, 3, 5, 6**

14A–1. A summary of the controls for the acquisition cycle of Keystone Computers & Networks, Inc., appears on pages 592–593.

*a.* For the following three controls over the acquisition cycle, indicate one type of error or fraud that the control serves to prevent or detect. Organize your solution as follows:

| Control | Error or Fraud Controlled |
|---|---|
| 1. Computer matches information from vendors' invoice with purchase order and receiving data. | |
| 2. The computer assigns numbers to receiving reports. | |
| 3. Checks are mailed by check signer. | |

*b.* For each of the controls described above, indicate how the auditors could test the control. Organize your answer as follows:

| Control | Tests of Controls |
|---|---|
| 1. Computer matches information from vendors' invoice with purchase order and receiving data. | |
| 2. The computer assigns numbers to receiving reports. | |
| 3. Checks are mailed by check signer. | |

**LO 1, 4, 5** 14A–2. As indicated on the control risk assessment working paper on page 592, the auditors identified two weaknesses in internal control over the acquisition cycle of KCN. Describe the implications of each of the two weaknesses in terms of the type of errors or fraud that could result.

**LO 3, 5, 6** 14A–3. The auditors' working paper that relates control strengths and weaknesses to the assertions about purchases and accounts payable is presented on page 592. This working paper also presents the auditors' planned assessed level of control risk for each of the assertions.

Prepare an audit program for tests of the controls over the acquisition cycle. (Note: You may want to use the tests of controls program for the revenue cycle, which is on pages 486–487, as a guide.)

# Debt and Equity Capital

Business corporations obtain substantial amounts of their financial resources by incurring debt and issuing capital stock. The acquisition and repayment of capital is sometimes referred to as the *financing cycle.* This transaction cycle includes the sequence of procedures for authorizing, executing, and recording transactions that involve bank loans, mortgages, bonds payable, and capital stock as well as the payment of interest and dividends. In this chapter, we present material on the auditors' approach to both debt and equity capital accounts.

## Debt

### Source and Nature of Debt

Long-term debt usually is substantial in amount and often extends for periods of 20 years or more. Debentures, secured bonds, and notes payable (sometimes secured by mortgages or trust deeds) are the principal types of long-term debt. **Debenture bonds** are backed only by the general credit of the issuing corporation and not by liens on specific assets. Since in most respects debentures have the characteristics of other corporate bonds, we shall use the term *bonds* to include both debentures and secured bonds payable.

> **LO1**
>
> Describe the nature of debt.

The formal document creating bond indebtedness is called the *indenture* or **trust indenture.** When creditors supply capital on a long-term basis, they often insist upon placing certain restrictions on the borrowing company. For example, the indenture often includes a restrictive covenant that prohibits the company from declaring dividends unless the amount of working capital is maintained above a specified amount. The acquisition of plant and equipment, or the increasing of managerial salaries, may be permitted only if the current ratio is maintained at a specified level and if net income reaches a designated amount. Another device for protecting the long-term creditor is the requirement of a sinking fund or redemption fund to be held by a trustee. If these restrictions are violated, the indenture may provide that the entire debt is due on demand.

### The Auditors' Objectives in Auditing Debt

The auditors' *objectives* in the audit of debt are to:

1. Use the understanding of the client and its environment to consider *inherent risks,* including fraud risks, related to debt.
2. Obtain an understanding of *internal control* over debt.

> **LO2**
>
> Describe the auditors' objectives in auditing debt.

3. Assess the risks of material misstatement and design tests of controls and substantive procedures that:

  a. Substantiate the *existence* of debt and the *occurrence* of the related transactions.

  b. Establish the *completeness* of recorded debt.

  c. Verify the *cutoff* of transactions affecting debt.

  d. Determine that the client has *obligations* to pay the recorded debt.

  e. Establish the proper *valuation* of debt and the *accuracy* of transactions affecting debt.

  f. Determine that the *presentation* and *disclosure* of information about debt are appropriate, including disclosure of major provisions of loan agreements.

In conjunction with the audit of debt, the auditors will also obtain evidence about interest expense, interest payable, and bond discount and premium.

Many of the principles related to accounts payable also apply to the audit of other forms of debt. As is the case for accounts payable, the understatement of debt is considered to be a major potential audit problem. Related to disclosure of debt, the auditors must determine whether the company has met all requirements and restrictions imposed upon it by debt agreements.

## Assessment of the Inherent Risks Related to Debt

**LO3**

Use the understanding of the client and its environment to consider inherent risks (including fraud risks) related to debt.

A major business risk related to debt is ensuring that the client obtains capital in an effective and efficient manner. This risk is not indicative of a risk of material misstatement of the financial statements and, therefore, is not of primary concern to the auditors. However, other business risks do equate to risks of material misstatement. As an example, management must be concerned with the business risk of noncompliance with debt covenants. This is also a concern of the auditors because noncompliance may affect the classification of debt and related disclosures. Many of the principles related to accounts payable also apply to the audit of debt. As is the case for accounts payable, the understatement of debt, whether due to error or fraud, is considered to be a major potential inherent risk.

## Internal Control over Debt

**LO4**

Obtain an understanding of internal control over the financing cycle.

### Authorization by the Board of Directors

Effective internal control over debt begins with the authorization to incur the debt. The bylaws of a corporation usually require that the board of directors approve borrowing. The treasurer of the corporation will prepare a report on any proposed financing, explaining the need for funds, the estimated effect of borrowing upon future earnings, the estimated financial position of the company in comparison with others in the industry both before and after the borrowing, and alternative methods of raising the funds. Authorization by the board of directors will include review and approval of such matters as the choice of a bank or trustee, the type of security, registration with the SEC, agreements with investment bankers, compliance with requirements of the state of incorporation, and listing of bonds on a securities exchange. After the issuance of long-term debt, the board of directors should receive a report stating the net amount received and its disposition as, for example, acquisition of plant assets, addition to working capital, or other purposes.

### Use of an Independent Trustee

Bond issues are always for large amounts—usually many millions of dollars. Therefore, only relatively large companies issue bonds; small companies obtain long-term capital through mortgage loans or other sources. Any company large enough to issue bonds and able to find a ready market for the securities will almost always utilize the services of a large bank as an independent trustee.

The trustee is charged with the protection of the creditors' interests and with monitoring the issuing company's compliance with the provisions of the indenture. The trustee also maintains detailed records of the names and addresses of the registered owners of the bonds, cancels old bond certificates and issues new ones when bonds change ownership, follows procedures to prevent overissuance of bond certificates, distributes interest payments, and distributes principal payments when the bonds mature. Use of an independent trustee largely solves the problem of internal control over bonds payable. Internal control is strengthened by the fact that the trustee does not have access to the issuing company's assets or accounting records and the fact that the trustee is a large financial institution with legal responsibility for its actions.

### Interest Payments on Bonds and Notes Payable

Many corporations assign the entire task of paying interest to the trustee for either *bearer bonds* or *registered bonds*. Highly effective control is then achieved, since the company will issue a single check for the full amount of the semiannual interest payment on the entire bond issue. In the case of bearer bonds (coupon bonds), the trustee upon receipt of this check will make payment for coupons presented, cancel the coupons, and file them numerically. A second count of the coupons is made at a later date; the coupons then are destroyed and a cremation certificate is delivered to the issuing company. The trustee does not attempt to maintain a list of the holders of coupon bonds, since these securities are transferable by the mere act of delivery. If certain coupons are not presented for payment, the trustee will hold the funds corresponding to such coupons for the length of time prescribed by statute. In the case of registered bonds, the trustee will maintain a current list of holders and will remit interest checks to them in the same manner as dividend checks are distributed to stockholders.

For a note payable, there generally is only one recipient of interest. Companies control that disbursement in the same manner as other cash disbursements, without using a trustee.

## Audit Documentation

A copy of the loan agreement or the indenture relating to a bond issue should be placed in the auditors' permanent file. A listing of the restrictions placed on the company is extracted from these documents to facilitate the auditors' tests of compliance with the debt provisions. Analyses of ledger accounts for notes and bonds payable, and the related accounts for interest and discount or premium, should be obtained for the current working papers file or the permanent file. In addition, the auditors should include documentation of internal control and risk assessment for debt. A lead schedule is often not required for short-term notes payable or for long-term debt.

# Audit of Debt

**LO5**

Assess the risks of material misstatement of debt and design further audit procedures to address the risks.

After obtaining an understanding of the client and its environment, including internal control, the auditors will assess the risks of material misstatement and design further audit procedures for debt. This audit program does not provide for the usual distinction between tests of controls and substantive procedures. This is because individual transactions will generally be examined for all large debt agreements. To document internal control, the auditors will usually prepare a written description, as well as an internal control questionnaire. Questions included on a typical questionnaire are the following: (1) Are amounts of new debt authorized by appropriate management? (2) Is an independent trustee used for all bond issues? (3) Does a company official monitor compliance with debt provisions?

Because transactions are few in number but large in dollar amount, the auditors are generally able to substantiate the individual transactions. Therefore, testing of controls occurs through what actually amounts to dual-purpose transaction testing. As discussed further in Chapter 18, in an integrated audit, more controls will be tested.

Audit procedures appropriate for the verification of debt include the following:

1. Obtain or prepare analyses of debt accounts and related interest, premium, and discount accounts.
2. Examine copies of notes payable and supporting documents.
3. Confirm debt with payees or appropriate third parties.
4. Vouch borrowing and repayment transactions to supporting documents.
5. Perform analytical procedures to test the overall reasonableness of interest-bearing debt and interest expense.
6. Test the valuation of debt, computation of interest expense, interest payable, and amortization of discount or premium.
7. Evaluate whether debt provisions have been met.
8. Trace authority for issuance of debt to the corporate minutes.
9. Review notes payable paid or renewed after the balance sheet date.
10. Perform procedures to identify notes payable to related parties.

**FIGURE 15.1**
**Objectives of Major Substantive Procedures for Debt Transactions and Balances**

| Substantive Procedures | Primary Audit Objectives |
|---|---|
| Obtain analyses of debt and related accounts. | *Valuation* |
| Examine copies of notes payable and supporting documents.<br>Confirm debt.<br>Vouch borrowing and repayment transactions. | *Completeness*<br>*Existence* and *obligations*<br>*Accuracy*<br>*Cutoff* |
| Perform analytical procedures.<br>Test computations of interest expense, interest payable, and amortization of discount and premium. | *Completeness*<br>*Existence* and *obligations*<br>*Valuation* |
| Evaluate whether debt provisions have been met.<br>Trace authority for issuance of debt to corporate minutes.<br>Review notes payable paid or renewed after the balance sheet date.<br>Perform procedures to identify notes payable to related parties.<br>Send confirmation letters about financing arrangements.<br>Evaluate financial statement presentation and disclosure. | *Presentation* and *disclosure* |

11. Send confirmation letters to financial institutions to obtain information about financing arrangements.

12. Evaluate proper financial statement presentation and disclosure of debt and related transactions.

Figure 15.1 relates these substantive procedures to their primary audit objectives.

### 1. Obtain or Prepare Analyses of Debt Accounts and Related Interest, Premium, and Discount Accounts.

Primary Audit Objective:

Valuation ☑

A notes payable analysis shows the beginning balance of each individual note, additional notes issued and payments on notes during the year, and the ending balance of each note. In addition, the beginning balances of interest payable or prepaid interest, interest expense, and interest paid and the ending balances of interest payable or prepaid interest may be presented in the analysis working paper.

An analysis of the Notes Payable account will serve a number of purposes: (*a*) the payment or other disposition of notes listed as outstanding in the previous year's audit can be verified, (*b*) the propriety of individual debits and credits can be established, and (*c*) the amount of the year-end balance of the account is proved through the step-by-step examination of all changes in the account during the year.

In the first audit of a client, the auditors will analyze the ledger accounts for Bonds Payable, Bond Issue Costs, and Bond Discount (or Bond Premium) for the years since the bonds were issued. The working paper is placed in the auditors' permanent file; in later audits, any further entries in these accounts may be added to the analysis.

The accounts of the financing cycle are often relatively free of material misstatement. When misstatements occur, they may be due to improper reporting of debt (e.g., a loan is recorded with a debit to cash and a credit to a revenue account), incomplete recording of debt (e.g., a loan is not recorded and the proceeds are maintained "off the books"), or improper amortization of loan-related discount and premium accounts. In some situations, note disclosures related to debt are incomplete.

The auditors must also be aware of clients with complex organizational structures involving numerous or unusual legal entities or contractual arrangements and transactions involving related parties. In these cases, questions arise as to proper recording of the transactions. Also, the auditors should realize that a lack of compliance with the provisions of a debt agreement usually makes the debt involved entirely due and payable on demand.

**Primary Audit Objectives:**

Existence ☑
Completeness ☑
Obligations ☑
Accuracy ☑
Cutoff ☑

## 2. Examine Copies of Notes Payable and Supporting Documents.

The auditors should examine the client's copies of notes payable and supporting documents such as mortgages and trust deeds. The original documents will be in the possession of the payees, but the auditors should make certain that the client has retained copies of the debt instruments and that their details correspond to the analyses described in the first procedure of this audit program.

**Primary Audit Objectives:**

Existence ☑
Completeness ☑
Obligations ☑
Accuracy ☑
Cutoff ☑

## 3. Confirm Debt with Payees or Appropriate Third Parties.

Notes payable to financial institutions are confirmed as part of the confirmation of cash deposit balances. The standard confirmation form illustrated in Chapter 10 includes a request that the financial institution confirm all borrowings by the depositor.

Confirmation requests for notes payable to payees other than financial institutions should be drafted on the client's letterhead stationery, signed by the controller or other appropriate executive, and mailed by the auditors. Payees should be requested to confirm dates of origin, due dates, unpaid balances of notes, interest rates, dates to which interest has been paid, and collateral for the notes.

The auditors may also substantiate the existence and amount of a mortgage liability outstanding by direct confirmation with the mortgagee. The information received should be compared with the client's records and the audit working papers. When no change in the liability account has occurred in the period under audit, the only major procedure necessary will be this confirmation with the creditor. At the same time that the mortgagee is asked to confirm the debt, it may be asked for an indication of the company's compliance with the mortgage or trust deed agreement.

Bond transactions usually can be confirmed directly with the trustee. The trustee's reply should include an exact description of the bonds, including maturity dates and interest rates; bonds retired, purchased for the treasury, or converted into stock during the year; bonds outstanding at the balance sheet date; and **sinking fund** transactions and balances.

**Primary Audit Objectives:**

Existence ☑
Completeness ☑
Obligations ☑
Accuracy ☑
Cutoff ☑

## 4. Vouch Borrowing and Repayment Transactions to Supporting Documents.

The auditors must obtain evidence that transactions in debt accounts were valid. To accomplish this objective, the auditors vouch the cash recorded as received from the issuance of notes, bonds, or mortgages to the validated copy of the bank deposit slip and to the bank statement. Any remittance advices supporting these cash receipts are also examined. The auditors can find further support for the net proceeds of a public issue by referring to the underwriting contract and to the prospectus filed with the SEC.

Debits to a Notes Payable or a Mortgages Payable account generally represent payments in full or in installments. The auditors should examine these payments; in so doing, they also will account for payments of accrued interest. The propriety of installment payments should be verified by reference to the repayment schedule set forth in the note or mortgage copy in the client's possession.

A comparison of canceled notes payable with the debit entries in the Notes Payable account provides further assurance that notes indicated as paid during the year have, in fact, been retired. The auditors' inspection of these notes should include a comparison of the maturity date of the note with the date of cash disbursement. Failure to pay notes promptly at maturity is suggestive of financial weakness.

There is seldom any justification for a paid note to be missing from the files; a receipt for payment from the payee of the note is not a satisfactory substitute. If, for any reason, a paid note is not available for inspection, the auditors should review the request for a check or other vouchers supporting the disbursement and should discuss the transaction with an appropriate official.

In examining the canceled notes, the auditors should also trace the disposition of any collateral used to secure these notes. A convenient opportunity for diversion of pledged securities or other assets to an unauthorized user might be created at the time these assets are returned by a secured creditor.

Primary Audit
Objectives:

Existence          ☑
Completeness    ☑
Obligations       ☑
Valuation          ☑

### 5. Perform Analytical Procedures to Test the Overall Reasonableness of Interest-Bearing Debt and Interest Expense.

One of the most effective ways to determine the overall reasonableness of interest-bearing debt is to examine the relationship between recorded interest expense and the average principal amount of debt outstanding during the year. If the client is paying interest on debt that is not recorded, this relationship will not be in line with the interest rate at which the client company should be able to borrow. Therefore, the auditors can use these procedures as a test of the *completeness* of recorded interest-bearing debt.

The auditors also compare the year-end amount of interest-bearing debt with the amount in the prior year's balance sheet. A similar comparison is made of interest expense for the current year and the preceding year.

Primary Audit
Objectives:

Existence          ☑
Completeness    ☑
Obligations       ☑
Valuation          ☑

### 6. Test the Valuation of Debt, Computations of Interest Expense, Interest Payable, and Amortization of Discount or Premium.

Unless management elects the fair value option, debt is valued at its outstanding face value plus or minus any unamortized premium or discount. To test valuation, the auditors test the amounts of amortization of debt premiums or discounts. In addition, the auditors test the accuracy of the client's computations of interest expense and interest payable, including examining paid checks supporting interest payments. An analysis of interest payments is another means of bringing to light any unrecorded interest-bearing liabilities.

The fair value option, as presented in Chapter 5, is available for companies that wish to value these financial liabilities at market value. As indicated in Chapter 5, depending upon the circumstances involved, valuation may be with observable inputs (e.g., market prices) or unobservable inputs (discounted cash flows). When the fair value option has been selected, the auditors must evaluate the propriety of the valuation techniques and the inputs.

Primary Audit
Objective:

Presentation    ☑

### 7. Evaluate Whether Debt Provisions Have Been Met.

In the first audit of a client or upon the issuance of a new bond issue, the auditors will obtain a copy of the bond indenture for the permanent file. The indenture should be carefully studied, with particular attention to such points as the amount of bonds authorized, interest rates and dates, maturity dates, descriptions of property pledged as collateral, provisions for retirement or conversion, duties and responsibilities of the trustee, and any restrictions imposed on the borrowing company.

The indenture provisions may require maintenance of a sinking fund, maintenance of stipulated minimum levels of working capital, and insurance of pledged property. The indenture also may restrict dividends to a specified proportion of earnings, limit management compensation, and prohibit additional long-term borrowing, except under stipulated conditions. The auditors will perform tests to evaluate whether the company is in compliance with these provisions. For example, the auditors will examine evidence of insurance coverage, vouch payments to the sinking fund, and compare the amounts of management compensation and dividends paid to amounts allowed by the agreements.

If the company has not complied fully with the requirements, the auditors should inform both the client and the client's legal counsel of the violation. In some cases of violation, the entire bond issue may become due and payable on demand, and hence a current liability. When the client is in violation of an indenture provision and the penalty is to make the debt become payable upon demand, the client usually will be able to obtain a waiver of compliance with the provision. In other words, creditors often choose not to enforce contract terms fully. To enable the liability to be presented as long term, the waiver must waive compliance for a period of one year from the balance sheet date. Even if an appropriate waiver of compliance is obtained, the matter should be disclosed in the notes to the client's financial statements.

Auditors do not judge the legality of a bond issue; this is a problem for the client's attorneys. The auditors should be familiar, however, with the principal provisions of the federal Securities Act of 1933 and the corporate blue sky laws of the client's state of incorporation. They should determine that the client has obtained an attorney's opinion

## Illustrative Case

### Violations of Debt Covenants

In the audit of a large construction company, the auditors found the client's working capital to be far below the minimum level stipulated in the indenture of long-term secured bonds payable. In addition, the client had allowed the required insurance coverage of pledged assets to lapse. These violations of the indenture were sufficient to cause the bond issue to become payable on demand.

Although the client agreed to reclassify the bond issue as a current liability and disclose the problem in the financial statements, the auditors were unable to satisfy themselves that the client could meet the obligation if the bondholders demanded payment. Also, if the bondholders foreclosed on the pledged assets, the ability of the client to continue as a going concern would be questionable. Thus, even after the liability was reclassified as current, the auditors had to add an explanatory paragraph to their report referring to the uncertainty regarding the company's ability to meet its obligations and remain a going concern.

---

on the legality of the bond issuance. In doubtful cases, they should obtain representations from the client's legal counsel.

**Primary Audit Objective:**

Presentation ☑

### 8. Trace Authority for Issuance of Debt to the Corporate Minutes.

The authority to issue debt generally lies with the board of directors. To determine that the bonds outstanding were properly authorized, the auditors should read the passages in the minutes of directors' (and stockholders') meetings concerning the issuance of debt. The minutes usually will cite the applicable sections of the corporate bylaws permitting the issuance of debt instruments and may also contain reference to the opinion of the company's counsel concerning the legality of the issue.

**Primary Audit Objective:**

Presentation ☑

### 9. Review Notes Payable Paid or Renewed after the Balance Sheet Date.

If any of the notes payable outstanding at the balance sheet date are paid before completion of the audit engagement, such cash payments provide the auditors with additional evidence on the liability. Renewal of notes maturing shortly after the balance sheet date may alter the auditors' thinking as to the proper classification of these liabilities.

In the discussion of notes receivable in Chapter 11, emphasis was placed on the necessity of close scrutiny of loans to officers, directors, and affiliates because of the absence of arm's-length bargaining in these related party transactions. Similar emphasis should be placed on the examination of notes payable to insiders or affiliates, although the opportunities for self-dealing are more limited than with receivables. The auditors should scan the notes payable records for the period between the balance sheet date and the completion of the audit so that they may be aware of any unusual transactions, such as the reestablishment of an insider note that had been paid just prior to the balance sheet date.

**Primary Audit Objective:**

Presentation ☑

### 10. Perform Procedures to Identify Notes Payable to Related Parties.

As has been the case in other portions of the audit, the auditors must perform procedures to determine that any related party debt is properly disclosed. Note here that the lower number of transactions makes discovery of such transactions less difficult than in accounts with a large number of transactions such as accounts payable.

**Primary Audit Objective:**

Presentation ☑

### 11. Send Confirmation Letters to Financial Institutions to Obtain Information about Financing Arrangements.

Financing arrangements and transactions can be very complex, and the details of these arrangements and transactions must be adequately disclosed in the notes to the financial statements. If the auditors determine that additional evidence is needed to verify these details, they will send a *separate* confirmation letter to the financial institution. For example, confirmation letters may be used to obtain information about lines of credit, contingent

**FIGURE 15.2**

**Illustrative Letter for Confirmation of Lines of Credit**

---

**Wallace Manufacturing, Inc.**
**1400 Main St.**
**Los Angeles, CA 90015**

January 31, 20X5

Mr. Richard M. Smith
Senior Loan Officer
First United Bank
2330 Fourth Ave.
Los Angeles, CA 90010

Dear Mr. Smith:

In connection with an audit of the financial statements of Wallace Manufacturing, Inc., as of December 31, 20X4, and for the year then ended, we have advised our independent auditors of the information listed below, which we believe is a complete and accurate description of our line of credit from your financial institution as of the close of business on December 31, 20X4. Although we do not request or expect you to conduct a comprehensive, detailed search of your records, if during the process of completing this confirmation additional information about other lines of credit from your financial institution comes to your attention, please include such information below.

1. The company has available at your financial institution a line of credit totaling $47 million.
2. The current terms of the line of credit are contained in the letter dated May 11, 20X2.
3. The amount of unused line of credit, subject to the terms of the related letter, at December 31, 20X4, was $19 million.
4. The interest rate at the close of business on December 31, 20X4, was 9.2%.
5. There are no requirements for compensating balances in connection with this line of credit.

Please confirm whether the information about the line of credit presented above is correct by signing below and returning this letter directly to our independent auditors, Warren & Clark, CPAs, 2100 Century Blvd., Los Angeles, CA 90053.

Sincerely,
Wallace Manufacturing, Inc.

By: _*Robert Barr*_
     Robert Barr
     Controller

— — — — — — — — — — — — — — — — — — — — — — — — — — —

Dear Warren & Clark, CPAs:

The above information regarding the line of credit agrees with the records of this financial institution. Although we have not conducted a comprehensive, detailed search of our records, no information about other lines of credit came to our attention. [Note exceptions below or in an attached letter.]

_____
_____
_____
_____

First United Bank

By: _Richard Smith, Senior Loan Officer_      _2/20/X5_
     (Officer and Title)          (Date)

---

liabilities, compensating balance arrangements, letters of credit, or futures contracts. These letters are signed by the client and specifically addressed to the client's loan officer or another official at the financial institution that is knowledgeable about the information. This expedites a response to the confirmation and enhances the quality of the evidence received. Figure 15.2 provides an example of a letter to confirm information about lines of credit.

## 12. Evaluate Proper Financial Statement Presentation and Disclosure of Debt and Related Transactions.

Because of the interest of creditors in the current liability section of the balance sheet and the inferences that may be drawn from various uses of notes payable, adequate

| Primary Audit Objective: |
|---|
| Presentation ☑ |

informative disclosure is extremely important. Classification of notes by types of payees, as well as by current or long-term maturity, is necessary. Notes payable to banks, notes payable to trade creditors, and notes payable to officers, directors, stockholders, and affiliates should be listed separately.

Secured liabilities and pledged assets should be cross-referenced to one another with an explanation in the notes to the financial statements. In the event of financial difficulties and dissolution, creditors expect to share in the assets in proportion to their respective claims; if certain assets, such as current receivables, have been pledged to one creditor, the risk to unsecured creditors is increased. Current liabilities should include not only those notes maturing within a period of 12 months (or a longer operating cycle) but also any installments currently payable on long-term obligations such as mortgages.

The essential point in balance sheet presentation of long-term liabilities is that they be adequately described, including details about the types of debt, amounts authorized and issued, interest rates, maturity dates, and any conversion or subordination features.

### Long-Term Debt Payable in the Current Period

Long-term liabilities include all debts that will not be liquidated with the use of current assets. In other words, any bonds or notes falling due in the coming operating cycle that are to be paid from special funds or refinanced will be classified as long-term obligations regardless of maturity date. Before accepting a long-term classification for maturing obligations, auditors must satisfy themselves that the client has both the *intent* and the *ability* to refinance the obligation on a long-term basis. Intent and ability to refinance are demonstrated by the client through either (1) refinancing the obligation on a long-term basis before the issuance of the financial statements, or (2) entering into a financing agreement by that date, which clearly permits such refinancing. Any debt maturing currently and payable from current assets should be classified as a current liability.

### Restrictions Imposed by Long-Term Debt Agreements

The major restrictions imposed on the company by long-term loan agreements are significant to the company's investors and creditors. Consequently, the nature of the restrictions should be clearly set forth in a note to the financial statements.

### Unamortized Bond Premium or Discount

Unamortized premium should be added to the face amount of the bonds or debentures in the liability section of the balance sheet. Similarly, unamortized discount should be deducted from the face amount of the debt.

## Time of Examination— Debt

Analysis of the ledger accounts for debt and interest expense takes very little time in most audits because of the small number of entries. Consequently, most auditors prefer to wait until the end of the year before analyzing these accounts.

Audit procedures intended to reveal any unrecorded liabilities cannot ordinarily be performed in advance of the balance sheet date. Such steps as the evaluation of compliance with debt provisions, tests of interest expense, and the investigation of notes paid or renewed shortly after the balance sheet date must necessarily await the close of the period being audited. The opportunities for performing audit work in advance of the balance sheet date are thus much more limited in the case of debt than for most of the asset groups previously discussed.

# Equity Capital

## Sources and Nature of Owners' Equity

Most of this section is concerned with the audit of stockholders' equity accounts of corporate clients; the audit of owners' equity in partnerships and sole proprietorships is discussed briefly near the end of the chapter.

**LO6**

Describe the nature of equity accounts.

Owners' equity for corporate clients consists of capital stock accounts (preferred and common) and retained earnings. Balances in the capital stock accounts change when the corporation issues or repurchases stock. Transfer of ownership of shares from one shareholder to another does not affect the account balances. Retained earnings are normally increased by earnings and decreased by dividend payments. Additionally, a few journal entries (e.g., prior period adjustments) may directly affect retained earnings. Transactions in the owners' equity accounts are generally few in number, but material in amount. No change may occur during the year in the capital stock accounts, and perhaps only one or two entries will be made to the retained earnings account.

## The Auditors' Objectives in Auditing Owners' Equity

The auditors' *objectives* in the audit of owners' equity are to:

1. Use the understanding of the client and its environment to consider *inherent risks,* including fraud risks, related to owners' equity.
2. Obtain an understanding of *internal control* over owners' equity.
3. Assess the risks of material misstatement and design tests of controls and substantive procedures that:

    *a.* Substantiate the *existence* of owners' equity and the *occurrence* of the related transactions.
    *b.* Establish the *completeness* of recorded owners' equity.
    *c.* Verify the *cutoff* of transactions affecting owners' equity.
    *d.* Establish the proper *valuation* of owners' equity and the *accuracy* of transactions affecting owners' equity.
    *e.* Determine that the *presentation* and *disclosure* of information about owners' equity are appropriate.

**LO7**

Describe the auditors' objectives in the audit of equity accounts.

In conjunction with the audit of owners' equity accounts, the auditors will also obtain evidence about the related accounts of dividends payable and capital stock discounts and premiums.

## Internal Control over Owners' Equity

There are three principal elements of strong internal control over capital stock and dividends: (1) the proper authorization of transactions by the board of directors and corporate officers, (2) the segregation of duties in handling these transactions (preferably the use of independent agents for stock registration and transfer and for dividend payments), and (3) the maintenance of adequate records.

### Control of Capital Stock Transactions by the Board of Directors

**LO8**

Obtain an understanding of the fundamental controls over capital stock and other types of equity accounts.

All changes in capital stock accounts should receive formal advance approval by the board of directors. The board of directors must determine the number of shares to be issued and the price per share; if an installment plan of payment is to be used, the board must prescribe the terms. If plant and equipment, services, or any consideration other than cash is to be accepted in payment for shares, the board of directors must establish the valuation on the noncash assets received. Transfers from retained earnings to the Capital Stock and Paid-in Capital accounts, as in the case of stock dividends, are initiated by action of the board. In addition, stock splits and changes in par or stated value of shares require formal authorization by the board.

Authority for all dividend actions rests with the directors. The declaration of a dividend must specify not only the amount per share but also the date of record and the date of payment.

### Independent Registrar and Stock Transfer Agent

In appraising internal control over capital stock, the first question that the auditors consider is whether the corporation employs the services of an independent stock registrar and a stock transfer agent or handles its own capital stock transactions. Internal control is far stronger when the services of an independent stock registrar and a stock transfer agent are utilized because the banks or trust companies acting in these capacities will have the experience, the specialized facilities, and the trained personnel to perform the work in an expert manner. Moreover, by placing the responsibility for handling capital stock certificates in separate and independent organizations, the corporation achieves to the fullest extent the internal control concept of separation of duties. The New York Stock Exchange and most other exchanges require that listed corporations utilize the services of an independent registrar.

The primary responsibility of the **stock registrar** is to avoid any overissuance of stock. The danger of overissuance is illustrated by the old story of a promoter who sold a 25 percent interest in a new corporation to each of 10 investors. To prevent such frauds, the registrar must make certain that the issuance of stock is properly controlled. Historically, control was exerted over the issuance of paper stock certificates related to stock transactions. Currently, most frequently, paper stock certificates are not issued and the control involved relates to the associated electronic records.

Corporations with actively traded securities also employ independent **stock transfer agents.** Although the stock transfer agent maintains a record of the total shares outstanding, its primary responsibility is maintaining detailed stockholder records (name and address of each stockholder) and carrying out transfers of stock ownership.

### The Stock Certificate Book and Stockholders Ledger

If the corporation does not utilize the services of an independent registrar and stock transfer agent, the board of directors usually assigns these functions to the secretary of the company. The board of directors should designate officers who are authorized to (1) sign stock certificates, (2) maintain records of stockholders, (3) maintain custody of unissued certificates, and (4) sign dividend checks. The stock certificates should be serially numbered by the printer, and from the time of delivery to the company until issuance, they should be in the exclusive custody of the designated officer. The signatures of two officers are generally required on stock certificates.

The certificates often are prepared in and torn from bound books called **stock certificate books,** with attached stubs similar to those in a checkbook. Each stub shows the certificate number and contains blank spaces for entering the number of shares represented by the certificate, the name of the stockholder, and the serial number of any previously issued certificate surrendered in exchange for the new one. Certificates should be issued in numerical sequence and not signed or countersigned until the time of issuance. When outstanding shares are transferred from one holder to another, the old certificate is surrendered to the company. The designated officer cancels the old certificate by perforating and attaching it to the corresponding stub in the certificate book.

The stock certificate book is not in itself an adequate record of the capital stock outstanding. The certificates appear in the book in serial number order, and a single stockholder may own several certificates listed at various places in the certificate book. A transfer journal may be used to record transfers of shares between shareholders. A **stockholders ledger** provides a separate record for each stockholder, thus making it possible to determine at a glance the total number of shares owned by any one person. This record may be used in compiling the list of dividend checks or for any other communication with shareholders.

### Internal Control over Dividends

The nature of internal control over the payment of dividends, as in the case of stock issuance, depends primarily upon whether the company performs the function of dividend payment itself or utilizes the services of an independent dividend-paying agent. If an independent dividend-paying agent is used, the corporation will provide the agent with a certified copy of the dividend declaration and a check for the full amount of the dividend. The bank or trust company serving as stock transfer agent is usually appointed to distribute the dividend, since it maintains the detailed records of stockholders. The agent issues dividend checks to the individual stockholders and sends the corporation a list of the payments made. The use of an independent fiscal agent is to be recommended from the standpoint of internal control, for it materially reduces the possibility of fraud or error arising in connection with the distribution of dividends.

In a small corporation that does not use the services of a dividend-paying agent, the responsibility for payment of dividends is usually lodged with the treasurer and the secretary. After declaration of a dividend by the board of directors, the secretary prepares a list of stockholders as of the date of record, the number of shares held by each, and the amount of the dividend each is to receive. The total of these individual amounts is proved by multiplying the dividend per share by the total number of outstanding shares.

Dividend checks controlled by serial numbers are drawn payable to individual stockholders in the amounts shown on the list described above. If the stockholders ledger is maintained on a computer master file, the dividend checks may be prepared by the computer directly from this record. The stockholder list and dividend checks are submitted to the treasurer for approval and signature. The checks should be reconciled by the treasurer with the total of shares outstanding and mailed without again coming under control of the officer who prepared them.

Cash in the amount of the total dividend is then transferred from the general bank account to a separate dividend bank account. As the individual dividend checks are paid from this account and returned by the bank, they should be matched with the check stubs or marked *paid* in the dividend check register. A list of outstanding checks should be prepared monthly from the open stubs or open items in the check register. This list should agree in total with the balance remaining in the dividend bank account. Companies with numerous stockholders prepare dividend checks in machine-readable form, so that the computer may perform the reconciliation of outstanding checks.

## Audit Documentation for Owners' Equity

In addition to the lead schedule for owners' equity accounts, the auditors prepare an analysis of each equity account for the permanent file. A detailed analysis is essential for all aspects of a stock option plan: options authorized, issued, and outstanding. For a closely held corporation not served by a transfer agent, the auditors will often prepare for the permanent file a list of shareholders and the number of shares owned by each. In addition, documentation will include descriptions of internal control and the auditors risk assessment.

## Audit Program—Capital Stock

**LO9**

Describe further audit procedures for equity accounts.

The following procedures are typical of the procedures required in many engagements for the verification of capital stock:

1. Obtain an understanding of internal control over capital stock transactions.
2. Examine articles of incorporation, bylaws, and minutes for provisions relating to capital stock.
3. Obtain or prepare analyses of the capital stock accounts.
4. Account for all proceeds from stock issues.
5. Confirm shares outstanding with the independent registrar and stock transfer agent.
6. For a corporation acting as its own stock registrar and transfer agent, reconcile the stockholder records with the general ledger.
7. Determine that appropriate accounting is applied to employee stock compensation plans.
8. Determine that compliance with restrictions and preferences pertaining to capital stock and disclosures are appropriate.

Capital stock transactions are usually few in number; consequently, the auditors usually substantiate all transactions in audits of nonpublic companies. In public company integrated audits, the auditors will rely on controls because they must be tested to attest to internal control. In addition to the preceding steps, the auditors must determine the appropriate financial statement presentation of capital stock. This topic is discussed later in this chapter, along with the financial statement presentation of other elements of owners' equity.

### 1. Obtain an Understanding of Internal Control over Capital Stock Transactions.

Even though the examination of capital stock consists primarily of substantive procedures, the auditors, even in the audits of nonpublic companies, must acquire an understanding of the client's procedures for authorizing, executing, and recording capital stock transactions. This may be achieved by preparing a written description or flowchart of the system or by filling in an internal control questionnaire. If the questionnaire approach is employed, typical questions to be answered might include the following: Does the company utilize the services of an independent registrar and stock transfer agent? Are stockholders ledgers and transfer journals maintained? Are entries in owners' equity accounts reviewed periodically by an appropriate officer?

### 2. Examine Articles of Incorporation, Bylaws, and Minutes for Provisions Relating to Capital Stock.

In a first audit, copies of the articles of incorporation and bylaws obtained for the permanent file should be read carefully. The information required by the auditors for each issue of capital stock includes the number of shares authorized and issued; the par or stated value; dividend rates, if any; call and conversion provisions; stock splits; and stock options. The auditors will also review minutes of the meetings of directors and stockholders for authorizations of transactions related to the company's stock. By gathering evidence on these points, the auditors obtain assurance that capital stock transactions and dividend payments have been in accordance with legal requirements and specific authorizations by stockholders and directors. Also, they will be able to judge whether the balance sheet contains all necessary information to describe adequately the various stock issues and other elements of corporate capital.

### 3. Obtain or Prepare Analyses of the Capital Stock Accounts.

In an initial audit engagement, capital stock accounts should be analyzed from the beginning of the corporation to provide the auditors with a complete historical picture of corporate capital. Analysis of capital stock includes an appraisal of the nature of all changes and the vouching of these changes to the supporting documents and records. All changes in capital stock should bear the authorization of the board of directors.

The analyses of capital stock accounts may be prepared in a manner that permits additions during later audit engagements. After the initial audit, if the analyses are kept in the auditors' permanent file, all that will be necessary is to record the current period's increases and decreases and to vouch these transactions. The auditors then will have working papers showing all changes in capital stock from the inception of the corporation.

The auditors also should analyze the Treasury Stock account and prepare a list showing the number of shares of **treasury stock** on hand. Any certificates on hand then may be inspected. If certificates are not available, the transactions should be confirmed with the transfer agent.

In their review of treasury stock transactions, the auditors should refer to permanent file copies of the minutes of directors' meetings to determine (*a*) that the acquisition or reissuance of treasury stock was authorized by directors and (*b*) that the price paid or received was in accordance with prices specified by the board.

### 4. Account for All Proceeds from Stock Issues.

Closely related to the analyses of capital stock accounts is the audit procedure of accounting for the receipt and proper disposition of all funds derived from the issuance of capital stock. The proceeds should be traced to the cash records and bank statements.

SEC registration statements and contracts with underwriters may also be available as evidence of the amounts received from stock issues.

When assets other than cash are received as consideration for the issuance of capital stock, the entire transaction requires careful study. Generally, the value of assets and services received in exchange for capital shares is established by action of the board of directors. The auditors must determine that these accounting estimates made by the client result in a reasonable valuation.

| Primary Audit Objectives: | |
| --- | --- |
| Existence | ☑ |
| Occurrence | ☑ |
| Completeness | ☑ |
| Cutoff | ☑ |

### 5. Confirm Shares Outstanding with the Independent Registrar and Stock Transfer Agent.

The number of shares issued and outstanding on the balance sheet date may be confirmed by direct communication with the independent registrar and stock transfer agent. The confirmation request should be written by the client on the client's letterhead, but it should be mailed by the auditors. Confirmation replies should be sent directly to the auditors, not to the client. All information contained in these replies should be traced to the corporate records. It is essential that the general ledger controlling accounts agree with the amount of stock issued as reported by the independent registrar and stock transfer agent. Because of the strong controls usually maintained over stock transactions, it is not customary to communicate with individual stockholders in establishing the number of shares outstanding.

| Primary Audit Objectives: | |
| --- | --- |
| Existence | ☑ |
| Occurrence | ☑ |
| Completeness | ☑ |
| Cutoff | ☑ |

### 6. For a Corporation Acting as Its Own Stock Registrar and Transfer Agent, Reconcile the Stockholder Records with the General Ledger.

When a corporation acts as its own transfer agent and registrar, the auditors must adopt alternative procedures to obtain evidence that is not available by direct confirmation with outside parties. These procedures include (*a*) accounting for stock certificate numbers, (*b*) examining canceled certificates, and (*c*) reconciling the stockholders ledger and stock certificate book with the general ledger.

The audit working papers should include a record of the last certificate number issued during the year. Reference to the working papers for the preceding audit, combined with the verification of certificate numbers issued during the current period, will enable the auditors to account for all certificates by serial number.

A working paper prepared during the auditors' examination of the stock certificate book of a small closely held corporation is designed to be utilized during several audits; it may be retained in the permanent file or forwarded to successive current files. Additionally, it is desirable for the auditors to inspect the unissued certificates to determine that all certificates purported to be unissued are actually on hand and blank.

Adequate internal control for corporations not utilizing the services of an independent registrar and stock transfer agent requires that all canceled stock certificates be perforated or marked in a manner precluding the possibility of further use. Canceled certificates should be attached to the corresponding stubs in the stock certificate book and permanently preserved. If reacquired certificates are not canceled properly, the danger exists that they may be reissued fraudulently by officers or employees. Auditors, therefore, will examine all canceled stock certificates on hand, noting in particular that they have been voided. The general ledger account for capital stock shows the total par value or stated value of all shares outstanding, plus any treasury shares. The stockholders ledger includes an account for each stockholder. The stock certificate book contains all canceled certificates and also open stubs for outstanding certificates. The auditors must reconcile these three records (general ledger control account, stockholders ledger, and stock certificate book) to establish the amount of outstanding stock and to rule out the possibility of an overissuance of shares. If this verification were not made, it would be possible for a dishonest official to issue unlimited amounts of stock and withhold the proceeds from such sales.

A trial balance of the subsidiary stockholder records may be obtained from the client or prepared by the auditors and compared with the general ledger controlling account.

**Illustrative Case**   *Backdating of Stock Options*

Several years ago, financial headlines revealed that a number of companies have engaged in "backdating" of stock option grants to officers and employees. Some of these companies announced restatements of previously issued financial statements as a result of the practice. The PCAOB has indicated that auditors should be alert to the risk that a company may not have properly accounted for stock options and, as a result, may have materially misstated its financial statements. In cases where the risk of misstatement is significant, the auditors should react to the risk by considering assigning more experienced staff to the audit and evaluating the nature of the audit procedures to be performed for the options.

In conjunction with this procedure, the total shares outstanding, as shown by the stock certificate book stubs, should also be reconciled with the control account and with the subsidiary trial balance. These procedures assure the auditors of the accuracy of the ledger account balances for capital stock.

| Primary Audit Objectives: |
| --- |
| Valuation ☑ |
| Accuracy ☑ |
| Presentation ☑ |

### 7. Determine that Appropriate Accounting Is Applied to Employee Stock Compensation Plans.

Many corporations grant stock options or other similar instruments to officers and employees through incentive-type compensation plans. Accounting standards now require companies to recognize the compensation cost related to these awards. Specifically, the compensation cost is measured as the fair value of the options on the date they are granted to the employee. This cost is then recognized as compensation expense over the period in which the options vest.

The accounting for these instruments at fair value presents a particular challenge for the auditors. Because options are not traded on a market, the fair values of the options are determined by using option pricing models, such as the Black Scholes and the binomial models. Estimates of fair value or variability of stock prices are often determined by reference to the behavior of stock and option prices of comparable companies. The auditors must determine that the assumptions underlying the estimates of fair value are reasonable. In addition, they must obtain evidence that the computations are accurate. Chapter 5 describes the guidance for auditing financial statement items that are measured at fair value. In this area, the auditors may decide to use the work of a specialist.

| Primary Audit Objective: |
| --- |
| Presentation ☑ |

### 8. Determine that Compliance with Restrictions and Preferences Pertaining to Capital Stock and Disclosures Are Appropriate.

When *stock options* are granted, the corporation must hold a portion of the authorized but unissued stock in reserve so that it will be in a position to fulfill the option agreements. Similarly, corporations with convertible debentures or convertible preferred stock outstanding must hold in reserve a sufficient number of common shares to meet the demands of preferred stockholders and debenture holders who may elect to convert their securities into common stock.

The auditors must become thoroughly familiar with the terms of any stock options and stock purchase plans and with the conversion features of debenture bonds and preferred stock, so that they can determine appropriate measurement and adequate disclosure of these agreements. The auditors must also verify the shares issued during the year through conversion or exercise of stock options and must ascertain that the number of shares held in reserve at the balance sheet date does not exceed the corporation's authorized but unissued stock.

## Retained Earnings and Dividends

Audit work on retained earnings and dividends includes two major steps: (1) the analysis of retained earnings and any appropriations of retained earnings and (2) the review of dividend procedures for both cash and stock dividends.

On a first-year audit, the analysis of retained earnings and any appropriations of retained earnings should cover the entire history of these accounts. Such an analysis is prepared for the permanent file and is updated during each annual audit. Credits to the Retained Earnings account ordinarily represent amounts of net income transferred from the Income Summary account. Debits to the Retained Earnings account ordinarily include entries for net losses, cash and stock dividends, and the creation or enlargement of appropriated reserves. Appropriations of retained earnings require specific authorization by the board of directors. The only verification necessary for these entries is to ascertain that the dates and amounts correspond to the actions of the board.

In the verification of cash dividends, the auditors usually will perform the following steps:

1. Determine the dates and amounts of dividends authorized.
2. Verify the amounts paid.
3. Determine the amount of any preferred dividends in arrears.
4. Review the treatment of unclaimed dividend checks.

The auditors' analysis of dividend declarations may reveal the existence of cash dividends declared but not paid. These dividends must be shown as liabilities in the balance sheet. The auditors also may review the procedures for handling unclaimed dividends and ascertain that these items are recognized as liabilities. The amount of any accumulated dividends in arrears on preferred stock should be computed. If a closely held company has irregular dividend declarations or none at all, the auditors should consider whether the federal penalty surtax on reasonably accumulated retained earnings might be assessed. In the verification of stock dividends, there is an additional responsibility of determining that the proper amounts have been transferred from retained earnings to capital stock and paid-in capital accounts for both large and small stock dividends.

## Financial Statement Presentation of Stockholders' Equity

The presentation of capital stock in the balance sheet should include a complete description of each issue. Information to be disclosed includes the title of each issue; par or stated value; dividend rate, if any; dividend preference; conversion and call provisions; number of shares authorized, issued, and in treasury; dividends in arrears, if any; and shares reserved for stock options or for conversions.

Treasury stock preferably is shown in the stockholders' equity section, at cost, as a deduction from the combined total of paid-in capital and retained earnings. In many states, an amount of retained earnings equivalent to the cost of the treasury shares must be restricted. A note to the financial statements discloses this restriction.

Changes in retained earnings during the year may be shown in a separate statement or combined with the income statement. A combined statement of income and retained earnings often is presented. In this form of presentation, the amount of retained earnings at the beginning of the year is added to the net income figure, dividends paid are subtracted from the subtotal, and the final figure represents the new balance of retained earnings.

One of the most significant points to consider in determining the presentation of retained earnings in the balance sheet is the existence of any restriction on the use of this retained income. Agreements with banks, bondholders, and other creditors very commonly impose limitations on the payment of dividends. These restrictions must be fully disclosed in the notes to financial statements.

**Time of Examination—Stockholders' Equity**

The transactions involving stockholders' equity accounts generally are few in number, but material in amount. Because so few transactions occur, it usually is efficient to make the analysis after the close of the period. In the first audit of a new client, however, some preliminary work can be done in terms of obtaining and reviewing copies of the articles of incorporation and bylaws and analyzing the capital accounts.

For a continuing client, the auditors will often find that audit time required will be small in relation to the dollars in these accounts and much less than is required for assets, liabilities, revenue, or expense. Thus, while the capital stock account often has a larger balance than the cash account, the audit work required for capital stock is usually far less.

## Audit of Partnerships and Sole Proprietorships

Perhaps the most common reason for a small business to arrange for an independent audit is the need for audited financial statements in order to obtain a bank loan. Often, when approached by the owners of a small business applying for a loan, a banker will request audited financial statements as an aid to reaching a decision on the loan application.

*Procedures for the Audit of Partners' Accounts*

A most significant document underlying the partnership form of organization is the partnership contract. The auditors are particularly interested in determining that the distribution of net income has been carried out in accordance with the profit-sharing provisions of the partnership contract. Maintenance of partners' capital accounts at prescribed levels and restriction of drawings by partners to specified amounts are other points often covered in the contract; compliance with these clauses should be verified by the auditors in determining the propriety of the year's entries in the capital accounts. Partners' loan accounts also require reference to the partnership contract to determine the treatment intended by the partners.

Occasionally, the auditors may find that a partnership is operating without any written agreement of partnership. This situation raises a question of whether profits have been divided in accordance with the understanding existing between the partners. For their own protection, the auditors may wish to obtain from each partner a written statement confirming the balance in his or her capital account and approval of the method used in dividing the year's earnings. They may also suggest that the firm develop a written partnership agreement.

*Procedures for the Audit of Sole Proprietorships*

In general, the same principles described for the audit of corporate capital are applicable to the examination of the capital accounts and drawing accounts of a sole proprietorship or partnership. Analyses are made of all proprietorship accounts from the beginning of the business; the initial capital investment and any additions are traced to the cash and asset records; and the net income or loss for the period and any withdrawals are verified. In the case of a sole proprietorship, a common source of difficulty is the practice of intermingling business and personal transactions, making it necessary for the auditors to segregate personal net worth from business capital. Adjustments may also be required to transfer from expense accounts to the owner's drawing account any personal expenditures paid with company funds.

**Chapter Summary**

The details of the audit of long-term debt and equity accounts were discussed in this chapter. The chapter includes a description of the controls for these types of accounts and the audit procedures that auditors use to substantiate long-term debt and equity accounts. To summarize:

1. The financing cycle involves those activities of the company that are designed to obtain capital funds. It typically involves the issuance and repayment of debt and equity, as well as payment of interest and dividends. A primary concern for both of

these types of transactions is proper authorization by the appropriate official in the company or by the board of directors.

2. Control over the issuance of bonds by a company is enhanced when an independent trustee represents the interest of the bondholders. The responsibilities of the trustee include monitoring the company's compliance with the requirements of the bond agreement and processing the payments of interest and principal to individual bondholders.

3. Capital stock transactions are best controlled by employing a registrar/transfer agent who monitors the issuance of the company's stock and handles transfers of shares between investors. In smaller companies, capital stock is controlled through the maintenance of a stock certificate book and a stockholders ledger.

4. After the auditors obtain an understanding of the client and its environment, including internal control over the financing cycle, they will often perform only limited tests of controls because of the limited number of transactions typically involved. In audits of nonpublic companies, it is usually more efficient to assess control risk at a high level and perform detailed substantive procedures for transactions. Internal controls must be tested in an integrated audit of a public company.

5. In the audit of debt, the auditors' primary substantive procedures will include vouching selected transactions occurring during the period, examining debt agreements, confirming balances and terms, and evaluating compliance with restrictive covenants.

6. The auditors' primary substantive procedures for equity transactions will typically include vouching the major equity transactions occurring during the period, confirming the number of shares outstanding with the registrar, and evaluating the company's compliance with stock option plan requirements and other restricting agreements.

## Key Terms Introduced or Emphasized in Chapter 15

**Debenture bond (595)**   An unsecured bond, dependent upon the general credit of the issuer.

**Sinking fund (599)**   Cash or other assets set aside for the retirement of a debt.

**Stock certificate book (605)**   A book of serially numbered certificates with attached stubs. Each stub shows the corresponding certificate number and provides space for entering the number of shares represented by the certificate, the name of the shareholder, and the serial number of the certificate surrendered in exchange for the new one. Surrendered certificates are canceled and replaced in the certificate book.

**Stock registrar (605)**   An institution charged with responsibility for avoiding overissuance of a corporation's stock. Every new certificate must be presented to the registrar for examination and registration before it is issued to a stockholder.

**Stock transfer agent (605)**   An institution responsible for maintaining detailed records of shareholders and handling transfers of stock ownership.

**Stockholders ledger (605)**   A record showing the number of shares owned by each stockholder. This is the basic record used for preparing dividend payments and other communications with shareholders.

**Treasury stock (607)**   Shares of its own stock acquired by a corporation for the purpose of being reissued at a later date.

**Trust indenture (595)**   The formal agreement between bondholders and the issuer as to the terms of the debt.

## Review Questions

15–1.   What does the trust indenture used by a corporation in creating long-term bonded indebtedness have to do with the payment of dividends on common stock?

15–2.   Long-term creditors often insist upon placing certain restrictions upon the borrowing company for the term of the loan. Give three examples of such restrictions, and indicate how each restriction protects the long-term creditor.

15–3.   Most corporations with bonds payable outstanding utilize the services of a trustee. What relation, if any, does this practice have to the maintenance of adequate internal control?

15–4.   What information should be requested by the auditors from the trustee responsible for an issue of debentures payable?

15–5.  Palmer Company has issued a number of notes payable during the year, and several of these notes are outstanding at the balance sheet date. What sources of information should the auditors use in preparing a working paper analysis of the notes payable?

15–6.  Is the confirmation of notes payable usually correlated with any other specific phase of the audit? Explain.

15–7.  What is the principal reason for testing the reasonableness of the Interest Expense account in conjunction with the verification of notes payable?

15–8.  In addition to verifying the recorded liabilities of a company, the auditors must also give consideration to the possibility that other unrecorded liabilities exist. What specific steps may be taken by the auditors to determine that all their client's interest-bearing liabilities are recorded?

15–9.  Audit programs for examination of accounts receivable and notes receivable often include investigation of selected transactions occurring after the balance sheet date as well as transactions occurring during the year under audit. Are the auditors concerned with notes payable transactions subsequent to the balance sheet date? Explain.

15–10.  "Auditors are not qualified to pass on the legality of a bond issue; this is a question for the company's attorneys. It is therefore unnecessary for the auditors to inspect the bond indenture." Criticize the quotation.

15–11.  Mansfield Corporation has outstanding an issue of 30-year bonds payable. There is no sinking fund for these bonds. Under what circumstances, if any, should this bond issue be classified as a current liability?

15–12.  Two assistant auditors were assigned by the auditor-in-charge to the verification of long-term liabilities. Some time later, they reported to the auditor-in-charge that they had determined that all long-term liabilities were properly recorded and that all recorded long-term liabilities were genuine obligations. Does this determination constitute a sufficient examination of long-term liabilities? Explain.

15–13.  Compare the auditors' examination of owners' equity with their work on assets and current liabilities. Among other factors to be considered are the relative amounts of time involved and the character of the transactions to be inspected.

15–14.  What do you consider to be the most important control a corporation can adopt with respect to capital stock transactions?

15–15.  What is the primary responsibility of an independent registrar with respect to capital stock?

15–16.  In the audit of a small corporation not using the services of an independent stock registrar and stock transfer agent, what use is made of the stock certificate book by the auditors?

15–17.  Describe the significant features of a stock certificate book, its purpose, and the manner in which it is used.

15–18.  You have been retained to perform an audit of Valley Products, a small corporation which has not been audited during the previous 10 years of its existence. How will your work on the Capital Stock account in this initial audit differ from that required in a repeat engagement?

15–19.  Your new client, Black Angus Valley Ranch, is a small corporation with fewer than 100 stockholders. It does not utilize the services of an independent stock registrar or transfer agent. For your first audit, you want to obtain or prepare a year-end list of stockholders showing the number of shares owned by each. From what source or record should this information be obtained? Explain.

15–20.  Corporations sometimes issue their own capital stock in exchange for services and various assets other than cash. As an auditor, what evidence would you look for to determine the propriety of the values used in recording such transactions?

15–21.  In your second annual audit of a corporate client, you find a new account in the general ledger called Treasury Stock, which has a balance of $306,000. Describe the procedures you would follow to verify this item.

15–22.  In auditing the financial statements of Foster Company, you observe a debit entry for $200,000 labeled as Dividends in the Retained Earnings account. Explain in detail how you would verify this entry.

15–23.  Name three situations that might place a restriction on retained earnings, limiting or preventing dividend payments. Explain how the auditors might become aware of each such restricting factor.

15–24.  Comment on the desirability of audit work on the owners' equity accounts before the balance sheet date.

15–25. Delta Company has issued stock options to four of its officers, permitting them to purchase 5,000 shares each of common stock at a price of $25 per share at any time during the next five years. The president asks you what effect, if any, the granting of the options will have upon the balance sheet presentation of the stockholders' equity accounts.

15–26. What errors are commonly encountered by the auditors in their examination of the capital and drawing accounts of a sole proprietor?

## Questions Requiring Analysis

**LO 1, 5** 15–27. The only long-term liability of Range Corporation is a note payable for $1 million secured by a mortgage on the company's plant and equipment. You have audited the company annually for the three preceding years, during which time the principal amount of the note has remained unchanged. The maturity date is 10 years from the current balance sheet date. You are informed by the president of the company that all interest payments have been made promptly in accordance with the terms of the note. Under these circumstances, what audit work, if any, is necessary with respect to this long-term liability during your present year-end audit?

**LO 1, 4, 5** 15–28. During your annual audit of Walker Distributing Co., your assistant, Jane Williams, reports to you that, although a number of entries were made during the year in the general ledger account Notes Payable to Officers, she decided that it was not necessary to audit the account because it had a zero balance at year-end.

*Required:* Do you agree with your assistant's decision? Discuss.

**LO 1, 5** 15–29. You are engaged in the audit of the financial statements of Armada Corporation for the year ended August 31, 20X0. The balance sheet, reflecting all your audit adjustments accepted by the client to date, shows total current assets, $8,000,000; total current liabilities, $7,500,000; and stockholders' equity, $1,000,000. Included in current liabilities are two unsecured notes payable—one payable to United National Bank in the amount of $900,000 due October 31, 20X0; the other payable to First State Bank in the amount of $800,000 due September 30, 20X0. On September 30, the last scheduled date for your audit fieldwork, you learn that Armada Corporation is unable to pay the $832,000 maturity value of the First State Bank note, that Armada executives are negotiating with First State Bank for an extension of the due date of the note, and that nothing definite has been decided as to the extension.

*Required:*
a. Should this situation be disclosed in the notes to Armada Corporation's August 31 financial statements?

b. After the question of financial statement disclosure has been resolved to the auditors' satisfaction, might this situation have any effect upon the audit report?

**LO 1, 4, 5** 15–30. You are retained by Columbia Corporation to audit its financial statements for the fiscal year ended June 30. Your consideration of internal control indicates a fairly satisfactory condition, although there are not enough employees to permit an extensive separation of duties. The company is one of the smaller units in its industry, but it has realized net income of about $500,000 in each of the last three years.

Near the end of your fieldwork, you overhear a telephone call received by the president of the company while you are discussing the audit with him. The telephone conversation indicates that on May 15 of the current year the Columbia Corporation made an accommodation endorsement of a 60-day $430,000 note issued by a major customer, Brill Corporation, to its bank. The purpose of the telephone call from Brill was to inform your client that the note had been paid at the maturity date. You had not been aware of the existence of the note before overhearing the telephone call.

*Required:*

a. From an ethical standpoint, do you think the auditors would be justified in acting on information acquired in this manner?

b. Should the balance sheet as of June 30 disclose the contingent liability? Give reasons for your answer.

c. Prepare a list of auditing procedures that might have brought the contingency to light. Explain fully the likelihood of detection of the accommodation endorsement by each procedure listed.

**LO 6, 7, 8, 9** 15–31. Valley Corporation established a stock option plan for its officers and key employees this year. Because the options granted have a higher option price than the stock's current market price, the company has not recognized any cost for the options in the financial statements. However, a note to the financial statements includes all required disclosures.

*Required:*
    *a.* Do you believe that Valley's management has appropriately accounted for the stock option plan? Explain your answer.

    *b.* What responsibility do the auditors have for the information in the notes to the financial statements?

    *c.* List the audit procedures, if any, that you believe should be applied to the stock option plan.

## Objective Questions

**All applicable questions are available with McGraw-Hill's *Connect*™ *Accounting.*** ⬛connect |ACCOUNTING

15–32. **Multiple Choice Questions**

Select the best answer choice for each of the following, and justify your selection in a brief statement.

**LO 2**
    *a.* Which of the following is *least* likely to be an audit objective for debt?

       (1) Determine the existence of recorded debt.

       (2) Establish the completeness of recorded debt.

       (3) Determine that the client has rights to receive proceeds relating to the redemption of debt.

       (4) Determine that the valuation of debt is in accordance with generally accepted accounting principles.

**LO 5**
    *b.* The auditors would be most likely to find unrecorded long-term liabilities by analyzing:

       (1) Interest payments.

       (2) Discounts on long-term liabilities.

       (3) Premiums on long-term liabilities.

       (4) Recorded long-term liability accounts.

**LO 1, 5**
    *c.* A likely reason that consideration of client compliance with debt provisions is important to an audit is that violation of such debt provisions may affect the total recorded:

       (1) Number of debt restrictions.

       (2) Current liabilities.

       (3) Long-term assets.

       (4) Capital stock.

**LO 6, 8, 9**
    *d.* A transfer agent and a registrar are most likely to provide the auditor with evidence on:

       (1) Restrictions on the payment of accounts payable.

       (2) Shares issued and outstanding.

       (3) Preferred stock liquidation value.

       (4) Transfers occurring between management and related parties.

**LO 5, 9**
    *e.* The audit procedure of confirmation is least appropriate with respect to:

       (1) The trustee of an issue of bonds payable.

       (2) Holders of common stock.

       (3) Holders of notes receivable.

       (4) Holders of notes payable.

**LO 6, 9**
    *f.* An auditor is most likely to trace treasury stock purchase transactions to the:

       (1) Numbered stock certificates on hand.

       (2) Articles of incorporation.

       (3) Year's interest expense.

       (4) Minutes of the audit committee.

**LO 1, 6**
    *g.* In the continuing audit of a manufacturing company of medium size, which of the following areas would you expect to require the *least* amount of audit time?

       (1) Owners' equity.

       (2) Revenue.

       (3) Assets.

       (4) Liabilities.

**LO 1, 4, 5**

*h.* The auditors can best verify a client's bond sinking fund transactions and year-end balance by:

(1) Recomputation of interest expense, interest payable, and amortization of bond discount or premium.

(2) Confirmation with individual holders of retired bonds.

(3) Confirmation with the bond trustee.

(4) Examination and count of the bonds retired during the year.

**LO 2, 5**

*i.* The auditors' program for the examination of long-term debt should include steps that require the:

(1) Verification of the existence of the bondholders.

(2) Examination of copies of debt agreements.

(3) Inspection of the accounts payable subsidiary ledger.

(4) Investigation of credits to the bond interest income account.

**LO 1, 4**

*j.* All corporate capital stock transactions should ultimately be traced to the:

(1) Minutes of the board of directors.

(2) Cash receipts journal.

(3) Cash disbursements journal.

(4) Numbered stock certificates.

**LO 7, 9**

*k.* Which of the following is *most* likely to be an audit objective in the audit of owners' equity?

(1) Establish that recorded owners' equity includes all long-term debt and equity balances.

(2) Determine that common stock is valued at current market value.

(3) Determine that the presentation and disclosure of owners' equity is appropriate.

(4) Determine that the existence of recorded owner's equity is in conformity with equity accounting rule valuations.

**LO 9**

*l.* In an audit of a sole proprietorship, a common difficulty is lack of:

(1) Segregation of personal net worth and business capital.

(2) Availability of the owner.

(3) Agreement as to the distribution between retained earnings and owners' capital.

(4) Proper measures of dividends.

(AICPA, adapted)

**LO 4**

*m.* Which of the following questions would an auditor most likely include on an internal control questionnaire for notes payable?

(1) Are assets that collateralize notes payable critically needed for the entity's continued existence?

(2) Are two or more authorized signatures required on checks that repay notes payable?

(3) Are the proceeds from notes payable used for the purchase of noncurrent assets?

(4) Are direct borrowings on notes payable authorized by the board of directors?

**LO 8**

*n.* The primary responsibility of a bank acting as registrar of capital stock is to:

(1) Ascertain that dividends declared do *not* exceed the statutory amount allowable in the state of incorporation.

(2) Account for stock certificates by comparing the total shares outstanding to the total in the shareholders' subsidiary ledger.

(3) Act as an independent third party between the board of directors and outside investors concerning mergers, acquisitions, and the sale of treasury stock.

(4) Verify that stock is issued in accordance with the authorization of the board of directors and the articles of incorporation.

**LO 8**

*o.* Where an independent stock transfer agent is not employed and the corporation issues its own stocks and maintains stock records, canceled stock certificates should:

(1) Be defaced to prevent reissuance and attached to their corresponding stubs.

(2) Not be defaced but segregated from other stock certificates and retained in a canceled certificates file.

(3) Be destroyed to prevent fraudulent reissuance.

(4) Be defaced and sent to the secretary of state.

**LO 5**

*p.* An auditor most likely would inspect loan agreements under which an entity's inventories are pledged to support management's financial statement assertion of:

(1) Presentation and disclosure.

(2) Valuation or allocation.

(3) Existence or occurrence.

(4) Completeness.

**LO 8**

*q.* An auditor usually obtains evidence of stockholders' equity transactions by reviewing the entity's:

(1) Minutes of board of directors meetings.

(2) Transfer agent's records.

(3) Canceled stock certificates.

(4) Treasury stock certificate book.

**LO 1, 5, 6, 8**    15–33.    Match the following definitions (or partial definitions) to the appropriate term. Each term may be used once or not at all.

| Definition (or Partial Definition) | Term |
|---|---|
| a. An institution charged with responsibility for avoiding overissuance of a corporation's stock | 1. Common stock |
| b. An institution responsible for maintaining detailed records of shareholders and handling changes of ownership of stock ownership | 2. Debenture bond<br>3. Sinking fund<br>4. Stock certificate book |
| c. Cash or other assets set aside for the retirement of a debt | 5. Stock certificate holder |
| d. Shares of its own stock acquired by a corporation for the purpose of being reissued at a later date | 6. Stock registrar<br>7. Stock transfer agent |
| e. The formal agreement between bondholders and the issuer as to the terms of the debt | 8. Treasury stock<br>9. Trust indenture |

## Problems

**All applicable problems are available with McGraw-Hill's *Connect*™ *Accounting.***  connect |ACCOUNTING

**LO 1, 2, 5**    15–34.    The following covenants are extracted from the indenture of a bond issue of Case Company. The indenture provides that failure to comply with its terms in any respect automatically advances the due date of the loan to the date of noncompliance (the regular due date is 20 years hence). Give any audit procedures or reporting requirements you think should be taken or recognized in connection with each of the following:

1. "The debtor company shall endeavor to maintain a working capital ratio of 2-to-1 at all times; and in any fiscal year following a failure to maintain said ratio, the company shall restrict compensation of officers to a total of $2 million. Officers for this purpose shall include the chairman of the board of directors, the president, all vice presidents, the secretary, the controller, and the treasurer."

2. "The debtor company shall keep all property that is security for this debt insured against loss by fire to the extent of 100 percent of its actual value. Policies of insurance comprising this protection shall be filed with the trustee."

3. "The debtor company shall pay all taxes legally assessed against property that is security for this debt within the time provided by law for payment without penalty, and shall deposit receipted tax bills or equally acceptable evidence of payment of same with the trustee."

4. "A sinking fund shall be deposited with the trustee by semiannual payments of $900,000, from which the trustee shall, in its discretion, purchase bonds of this issue."

(AICPA, adapted)

**LO 1, 2, 5**    15–35.    You have been retained to audit the financial statements of Midwest Products, Inc., for the year ended December 31. During the current year, Midwest had obtained a long-term loan from its bank in accordance with a financing agreement which provided that:

1. The loan is secured by the company's inventory and accounts receivable.

2. The company must maintain a debt-to-equity ratio not to exceed 2-to-1.

3. The company may not pay dividends without permission from the bank.

4. Monthly installment payments will commence July 1 of the next year.

In addition, during the current year, Midwest Products, Inc., borrowed from its president on a short-term basis, including substantial amounts just prior to the year-end.

*Required:*

a. For the purpose of your audit of the financial statements of Midwest Products, Inc., what procedures would you employ in examining the earlier-described items? Do not discuss internal control.

b. What financial statement disclosures are appropriate with respect to the loans from the president?

(AICPA, adapted)

**LO 1, 2, 3, 4, 5**    15–36.

Robert Hopkins was the senior office employee at the Griffin Equipment Company. He enjoyed the complete confidence of the owner, William Barton, who devoted most of his attention to sales, engineering, and production problems. All financial and accounting matters were entrusted to Hopkins, whose title was office manager. Hopkins had two assistants, but their only experience in accounting and financial work had been gained under Hopkins's supervision. Barton had informed Hopkins that it was his responsibility to keep him (Barton) informed on the financial position and operating results of the company but not to bother him with details.

The company was short of working capital and would occasionally issue notes payable in settlement of past-due open accounts to suppliers. The situations warranting the issuance of notes were decided upon by Hopkins, and the notes were drawn by him for signature by Barton. Hopkins was aware of the weakness in internal control and finally devised a scheme for defrauding the company through understating the amount of notes payable outstanding. He prepared a note in the amount of $24,000 payable to a supplier to whom several invoices were past due. After securing Barton's signature on the note and mailing it to the creditor, Hopkins entered the note in the Notes Payable account of the general ledger as $4,000, with an offsetting debit of $4,000 to Accounts Payable. Subsequently, when funds became available to the company, he paid the $20,000 of accounts payable that remained on the books.

Several months later when the note matured, a check for $24,000 plus interest was issued and properly recorded, including a debit of $24,000 to the Notes Payable account. Hopkins then altered the original credit in the account by changing the figure from $4,000 to $24,000. He also changed the original debit to Accounts Payable from $4,000 to $24,000. This alteration caused the Notes Payable account to have a balance in agreement with the total of other notes outstanding. To complete the fraud, Hopkins called the supplier to whom the check had been sent and explained that the check should have been for only $4,000 plus interest.

Hopkins explained to the supplier that the note of $24,000 originally had been issued in settlement of a number of past-due invoices, but that while the note was outstanding, checks had been sent in payment of all the invoices. "In other words," said Hopkins over the telephone, "we made the mistake of giving you a note for those invoices and then going ahead and sending you checks for them as soon as our cash position had improved. Then we paid the note at maturity. So please excuse our mistakes and return the overpayment." After reviewing the record of invoices and checks received, the supplier agreed he had been overpaid by $20,000 plus interest and promptly sent a refund, which Hopkins abstracted without making any entry in the accounts.

*Required:*

a. Assuming that an audit by CPAs was made while the note was outstanding, do you think that the $20,000 understatement of the Notes Payable account would have been detected? Explain fully the reasoning underlying your answer.

b. If the fraud was not discovered while the note was outstanding, do you think that an audit subsequent to the payment of the note would have disclosed the fraud? Explain.

c. What controls would you recommend for Griffin Equipment Company to avoid fraud of this type?

**LO 6, 8, 9**    15–37.    You are engaged in the first audit of Microdent, Inc. The corporation has both a stock transfer agent and an independent registrar for its capital stock. The transfer agent maintains the record of stockholders, and the registrar determines that there is no overissue of stock. Signatures of both are required to validate stock certificates.

It has been proposed that confirmations be obtained from both the transfer agent and the registrar as to the stock outstanding at the balance sheet date. If such confirmations agree with the accounting records, no additional work is to be performed as to capital stock.

If you agree that obtaining the confirmations as suggested would be sufficient in this case, give the justification for your position. If you do not agree, state specifically all additional steps you would take and explain your reasons for taking them.

(AICPA, adapted)

**LO 6, 8, 9**  15–38.  You are engaged in the audit of Phoenix Corp., a new client, at the close of its first fiscal year, April 30, 20X1. The accounts had been closed before the time you began your year-end fieldwork.

You review the following stockholders' equity accounts in the general ledger:

| Capital Stock | | |
|---|---|---|
| | 5/1/X0 CR1 | 500,000 |
| | 4/28/X1 J12-5 | 50,000 |

| Paid-in Capital in Excess of Stated Value | | |
|---|---|---|
| | 5/1/X0 CR1 | 250,000 |
| | 2/2/X1 CR10 | 2,500 |

| Retained Earnings | | |
|---|---|---|
| 4/28/X1 J12-5 | 50,000 | |
| | 4/30/X1 J12-14 | 800,000 |

| Treasury Stock | | |
|---|---|---|
| 9/14/X0 CP5 | 80,000 | |
| | 2/2/X1 CR10 | 40,000 |

| Income Summary | | |
|---|---|---|
| 4/30/X1 J12-13 | 5,200,000 | 4/30/X1 J12-12 | 6,000,000 |
| 4/30/X1 J12-14 | 800,000 | | |

Other information in your working papers includes the following:

1. Phoenix's articles of incorporation filed April 17, 20X0, authorized 100,000 shares of no-par-value capital stock.

2. Directors' minutes include the following resolutions:

    4/18/X0   Established $50 per share stated value for capital stock.

    4/30/X0   Authorized issue of 10,000 shares to an underwriting syndicate for $75 per share.

    9/13/X0   Authorized acquisition of 1,000 shares from a dissident holder at $80 per share.

    2/1/X1    Authorized reissue of 500 treasury shares at $85 per share.

    4/28/X1   Declared 10 percent stock dividend, payable May 18, 20X1, to stockholders of record May 4, 20X1.

3. The following costs of the May 1, 20X0, and February 2, 20X1, stock issuances were charged to the named expense accounts: Printing Expense, $2,500; Legal Fees, $17,350; Accounting Fees, $12,000; and SEC Fees, $150.

4. Market values for Phoenix Corp. capital stock on various dates were:

    9/13/X0   $78.50        2/2/X1    $85.00

    9/14/X0   $79.00        4/28/X1   $90.00

5. Phoenix Corp.'s combined federal and state income tax rates total 55 percent.

*Required:*

a. Prepare the necessary adjusting journal entries at April 30, 20X1.

b. Prepare the stockholders' equity section of Phoenix Corp.'s April 30, 20X1, balance sheet.

# Chapter 16

# Auditing Operations and Completing the Audit

This chapter presents information about the manner in which auditors examine the client's income statement accounts and the procedures and considerations involved in completing the audit engagement. These procedures and judgments, completed at or near the last day of fieldwork, are important in determining the nature and content of the auditors' report.

## Auditing Operations

Today, with great emphasis being placed upon corporate earnings as an indicator of the health and well-being of corporations as well as of the overall economy, the income statement is of fundamental importance to management, stockholders, creditors, employees, and the government. The relative level of corporate earnings is often a key factor in the determination of such issues as wage negotiations, income tax rates, subsidies, and government fiscal policies. In fact, accountants generally agree that the measurement of income is the most important single function of accounting. While this text has emphasized the relationships of revenues and expenses to various balance sheet accounts, this section presents additional details on the auditing of operations.

### The Auditors' Approach to Auditing Operations

**LO1**

Identify the audit objectives for revenue and expense accounts.

The doctrine of **conservatism** is a powerful force influencing decisions on revenues and expenses. The concept remains important in large part due to the subjectivity involved with many accounting estimates (as for expected future credit losses on receivables, lives of assets, and the warranty liability for products sold). Conservatism in the valuation of assets means that when two (or more) reasonable alternative values are indicated, the accountant will choose the lower amount. For valuation of liabilities, the higher amount is chosen. Therefore, when applied to the income statement, the conservatism concept results in a low or "conservative" income figure.

Most auditors have considerable respect for the doctrine of conservatism. In part, this attitude springs from the concept of legal liability to third parties. Financial statements that *understate* financial position and operating results almost never lead to legal action against the auditors involved. Nevertheless, auditors must recognize that overemphasis on conservatism in financial reporting is a narrow and shortsighted approach to meeting the needs of our society. To be of greatest value, financial statements should present fairly, rather than understate, financial position and operating results.

Auditors obtain evidence about many income statement accounts concurrently with related balance sheet accounts. Depreciation expense, for example, is most conveniently verified along with the plant and equipment accounts. Once the existence and cost of depreciable assets are established, the verification of depreciation expense is merely an additional step. On the other hand, to verify depreciation expense without first establishing the nature and amount of assets owned and subject to depreciation would obviously be a cart-before-the-horse approach. The same line of reasoning suggests that the auditors' work on inventories, especially in determining that inventory transactions were accurately cut off at the end of the period, is a major step toward the verification of the income statement figures for sales and cost of goods sold.

The auditors' examination of operations should, however, be much more than an incidental by-product of the examination of assets and liabilities. They use a combination of cross-referencing, analytical procedures, and analysis of specific transactions to bring to light errors, omissions, and inconsistencies not disclosed in the audit of balance sheet accounts.

Specifically, the objectives for the audit of revenues and expenses are to:

1. Use the understanding of the client and its environment to consider *inherent risks,* including fraud risks, related to revenues and expenses.
2. Consider *internal control* over revenues and expenses.
3. Assess the *risks of material misstatement* of revenues and expenses and design further audit procedures that:
   a. Establish the *occurrence* of recorded revenue and expense transactions.
   b. Determine the *completeness* of recorded revenue and expense transactions.
   c. Establish the *accuracy* of revenue and expense transactions.
   d. Verify the *cutoff* of revenue and expense transactions.
   e. Determine that the *presentation* and *disclosure* of revenue and expense accounts are appropriate, including the proper classification of amounts and the proper presentation of earnings-per-share data.

## Revenue

LO2

Explain the relationships between revenue and expense accounts and balance sheet accounts.

The auditors' review of revenue was considered in connection with accounts receivable in Chapter 11. In this section, we consider (1) the relationship of revenue to various balance sheet accounts and (2) the miscellaneous revenue account.

### Relationship of Revenue to Balance Sheet Accounts

As pointed out previously, most revenue accounts are verified by the auditors in conjunction with the audit of a related asset or liability. The following list summarizes the revenue verified in this manner:

| Balance Sheet Item | Revenue |
| --- | --- |
| Accounts receivable | Sales |
| Notes receivable | Interest |
| Securities and other investments | Interest, dividends, gains on sales, share of investee's income |
| Property, plant, and equipment | Rent, gains on sale |
| Intangible assets | Royalties |

### Miscellaneous Revenue

Miscellaneous revenue, by its very nature, is a mixture of minor items, some nonrecurring and others likely to be received at irregular intervals. If the client's personnel receive a cash payment and are not sure of the source, it is likely that it will be recorded as miscellaneous revenue. Because of the nature of items often recorded in the Miscellaneous Revenue account, the auditors will obtain an analysis of the account. Among the items the auditors might find improperly included as miscellaneous revenue are the following:

1. Collections on previously written-off accounts or notes receivable, which should properly be recorded as a reduction of the allowance for uncollectible notes account.
2. Write-offs of old outstanding checks or unclaimed wages. In many states, unclaimed properties revert to the state after statutory periods; in such circumstances, these write-offs should be credited to a liability account rather than to miscellaneous revenue.

3. Proceeds from sales of scrap. Scrap sale proceeds generally should be applied to reduce cost of goods sold, under by-product cost accounting principles.

4. Rebates or refunds of insurance premiums. These refunds should be offset against the related expense or unexpired insurance.

5. Proceeds from sales of plant assets. These proceeds should be accounted for in the determination of the gain or loss on the assets sold.

The auditors should propose adjusting journal entries to classify correctly any material items of the types described in the preceding list that have been included in miscellaneous revenue by the client. Before concluding the work on revenue, the auditors should perform analytical procedures and investigate unusual fluctuations. Material amounts of unrecorded revenue, as well as significant misclassifications affecting revenue accounts, may be discovered by these procedures.

# Expenses

The auditors' work relating to purchases and cost of goods sold was covered in Chapter 12. We are now concerned with audit procedures for other types of expenses.

## Relationship of Expenses to Balance Sheet Accounts

Let us consider for a moment the expense accounts for which we have already outlined audit procedures in the chapters dealing with balance sheet topics:

| Balance Sheet Item | Expenses (and Costs) |
| --- | --- |
| Accounts and notes receivable | Uncollectible accounts and notes expense |
| Inventories | Purchases, cost of goods sold, and payroll |
| Property, plant, and equipment | Depreciation, repairs and maintenance, and depletion |
| Intangible assets | Amortization |
| Accrued liabilities | Commissions, fees, bonuses, product warranty expenses, and others |
| Interest-bearing debt | Interest |

In the following sections, we shall complete our review of expenses by considering additional audit objectives and procedures for selling, general, and administrative expenses other than those listed above.

## Substantive Procedures for Selling, General, and Administrative Expenses

**LO3**

Describe the nature of appropriate substantive audit procedures to accomplish the objectives for the audit of revenue and expense accounts.

For other expenses not verified in the audit of balance sheet accounts, the following substantive tests are appropriate:

1. Perform analytical procedures related to the accounts.
   a. Develop an expectation of the account balance.
   b. Determine the amount of difference from the expectation that can be accepted without investigation.
   c. Compare the company's account balance with the expected account balance.
   d. Investigate significant deviations from the expected account balance.
2. Obtain or prepare analyses of selected expense accounts.
3. Obtain or prepare analyses of critical expenses in income tax returns.

**1. Perform Analytical Procedures Related to the Accounts.**

**a. Develop an Expectation of the Account Balance.**

Auditors develop an expectation of the account balance by considering factors such as budgeted amounts, the prior-year audited balances, industry averages, relationships among financial data, and relevant nonfinancial data.

An effective budgeting program will reduce the risk of material misstatement, since budgets provide management with information as to expected amounts. The existence of these expected expense amounts increases the likelihood that errors will be detected by management, since any significant discrepancy between budgeted and actual amounts receives timely attention.

The existence of a good budgeting program also helps the auditors in their audit of expense accounts. When the control over budgeting has been found to be effective, the budgeted amounts often provide the auditors with very good expected amounts for their analytical procedures.

One of the previously described audit objectives was to determine whether expenses had been correctly classified. The classification of such costs may affect net income. For example, manufacturing overhead costs may properly be carried forward as part of inventory cost, whereas the expenses of selling, general, and administrative functions usually are deducted from revenue in the period incurred. The auditors' review of the propriety of classification of expenses can be linked conveniently with the comparison of amounts of the various expenses. Comparison of yearly totals is accomplished by inclusion of amounts for the preceding year on the auditors' lead schedules or working trial balance, but this procedure may be supplemented by comparison of expenses on a month-by-month basis.

Comparison of expense (as well as revenue) accounts with industry and nonfinancial data is another means of bringing to light circumstances that require investigation. The auditors may also examine relationships between financial and nonfinancial information, such as between production records stated in gallons or pounds and the dollar amounts of sales.

### b. Determine the Amount of Difference from the Expectation that Can Be Accepted without Investigation.

The auditors use their estimates of materiality to arrive at which differences are to be investigated and which might be expected to occur by chance. However, the extent of the assurance desired from the analytical procedure must also be considered.

### c. Compare the Company's Account Balance with the Expected Account Balance.

Comparisons of the revenue and expense accounts with expected amounts may reveal significant differences that warrant investigation. Figure 16.1 illustrates a working paper that compares major income statement categories for the year under audit with the prior year amounts and industry averages.

### d. Investigate Significant Deviations from the Expected Account Balance.

The starting point for investigating significant variations in expenses generally is inquiry of management. The auditors substantiate management's explanations for significant variations by various means, including analyses of accounts.

### 2. Obtain or Prepare Analyses of Selected Expense Accounts.

As a result of the above procedure, the auditors will have chosen certain expense accounts for further verification. The client should be requested to furnish analyses of the accounts selected, together with related vouchers and other supporting documents, for the auditors' review.

Which expense accounts are most important for the auditors to analyze? The American Institute of Certified Public Accountants (AICPA) has suggested investigation of (1) advertising, (2) research and development, (3) legal expenses and other professional fees, (4) maintenance and repairs, and (5) rents and royalties.[1]

---

[1] See AICPA, *Audit and Accounting Manual* (New York, 2010), paragraph AAM 5400.170.

**FIGURE 16.1    Comparative Income Statement**

```
                         CHEVIOT CORPORATION
                      Comparative Income Statement              R-1-4
                      Year Ended December 31, 20X3


                    20X2                      20X3             Industry

             Amount      Percentage    Amount      Percentage  Percentage
```

| | 20X2 Amount | 20X2 Percentage | 20X3 Amount | 20X3 Percentage | Industry Percentage |
|---|---|---|---|---|---|
| Sales | $5,487,842 ✔ | 100% | $6,107,401 ⊽ ▽ | 100% | 100% |
| Cost of goods sold | 3,746,583 ✔ | 68 | 4,030,701 ⊽ ⊘ | 66 | 65 |
| Gross profit | 1,741,259 | 32 | 2,076,700 ⊘ | 34 | 35 |
| Selling expenses | 554,841 ✔ | 10 | 856,540 ⊽ △ | 14 | 15 |
| General and administrative expenses | 796,347 | 15 | 875,570 ⊽ ⊘ | 14 | 12 |
| Income before taxes | 390,071 | 7 | 344,590 ⊘ | 6 | 8 |
| Taxes | 128,732 ✔ | 2 | 68,693 ⊽ ✗ | 1 | 3 |
| Net income | 261,339 | 5 | 275,897 ⊘ | 5 | 5 |

∧　*Footed.*

⊽　*Agreed to the general ledger.*

✔　*Agreed to the prior year working papers.*

⊘　*Amount is reasonable in relation to prior year results and industry statistics.*

▽　*See audit procedures performed on sales, R-1-2.*

△　*Large increase in selling expenses is due to the addition of a salesperson to the sales staff. Based on a review of the payroll records, the increase in the amount appears reasonable.*

✗　*Decrease in tax rate is due to the realization of several thousand dollars in tax credits. See tax accrual working paper, O-3.*

*Conclusion:*

*The comparative analysis revealed no unusual fluctuations that could not be adequately explained.*

*VMH*
*2/21/X4*

*Concur*
*C.M.*
*2/25/X4*

The analyses of legal and other professional fees may disclose legal and audit fees properly chargeable to costs of issuing stock of debt instruments, or to costs of business combinations. Also, the analysis of professional fees expense furnishes the names of attorneys to whom letters should be sent requesting information as to pending litigation and other loss contingencies. Figure 16.2 illustrates an analysis of the professional fees expense account.

### 3. Obtain or Prepare Analyses of Critical Expenses in Income Tax Returns.

Income tax returns generally require schedules for officers' salaries, directors' fees, taxes, travel and entertainment, contributions, and casualty losses. In addition to these, officers' expense account allowances are presented in the analysis of officers' salaries. Accordingly, the auditors should obtain or prepare analyses of any of these expenses that were not analyzed when performing other audit steps. The auditors should bear in mind that details of these expenses will probably be closely scrutinized when the state or federal revenue agents examine the client's tax returns.

**FIGURE 16.2** **Professional Fees Analysis**

```
                              CHEVIOT CORPORATION
Acct. No. 547                Professional Fees Expense              R-3-7
                           Year Ended December 31, 20X3

      Date        Reference     Payee          Description           Amount

Various          Various      Hale and    Monthly retainer for legal   $12,000
                              Hale        services—12 x $1,000

Mar. 5, X3       CD 411       Jay & Wall, Fee for the audit            22,000 √
                              CPAs

May 2, X3        CD 602       Hale and    Fee for legal services relating  6,000 √
                              Hale        to acquisition of real property
                                          adjoining Vancouver plant

Sept. 18, X3     DC 1018      Hale and    Fee for legal services relating   800 √
                              Hale        to modification of installment
                                          sales contract forms
                                                                      _____
Dec. 31, X3                               Balance per Ledger          $40,800
```

Dec. 31, X3    AJE 41      To capitalize May 2, X3, disbursement       6,000
                           as part of cost of land      K-1

Dec. 31, X3    Adjusted balance                                     $34,800 ∧

                                                                     to R-3
               AJE 41
               Land                          6,000
                    Professional Fees                  6,000
                    To capitalize legal fees
                    for acquiring land

∧ Footed and agreed to general ledger balance.
√ Examined billing and copy of client's check in payment thereof.
Conclusion:
    Professional fees expense is fairly presented in the adjusted amount of $34,800.

                           KGL              CMM
                           2/15/X4          2/20/X4

## The Audit of Payroll

The payroll in many companies is the largest operating cost and therefore deserves the close attention of management as well as the auditors. In the past, payroll frauds were common and often substantial. Today, however, such frauds may be more difficult to conceal for several reasons: (1) extensive segregation of duties relating to payroll; (2) the use of computers, with proper controls, for preparation of payrolls; and (3) the necessity of filing frequent reports to the government listing employees' earnings and tax withholdings.

### Internal Control over Payroll

**LO4**

Describe the fundamental controls over payroll.

The establishment of strong internal control over payroll remains important for several reasons. Although payroll frauds are less frequent today, the possibility of large-scale payroll fraud still exists. Such frauds may involve listing fictitious persons on the payroll, overpaying employees, and continuing employees on the payroll after their separation from the company. A second reason for emphasizing internal control over payroll is that a great mass of detailed information concerning hours worked and rates of pay must be processed quickly and accurately if workers are to be paid promptly and without error. Good employee relations demand that direct deposits to employee bank accounts or paychecks be processed on time and be free from error. As pointed out in previous chapters, internal control is a means of securing accuracy and dependability in accounting data as well as a means of preventing fraud.

Still another reason for emphasizing the importance of internal control over payroll is the existence of various payroll tax and income tax laws that require that certain payroll records be maintained and that payroll data be reported to the employee and to governmental agencies. Complete and accurate records of time worked are also necessary if a company is to protect itself against lawsuits under the Fair Labor Standards Act.

To control payroll costs means to avoid waste and to obtain efficient production from the dollars expended for services of employees. As a means of establishing control over payroll costs, many companies delegate to department heads and other supervisors responsibility for the control of costs in their respective units of the business. Budgets are prepared using estimates of departmental labor costs for the coming period. As the year progresses and actual labor costs are compiled, the controller submits monthly reports to top management comparing the budgeted labor costs and the actual labor costs for each department. The effectiveness of this control procedure will depend largely upon the extent to which top management utilizes these reports and takes action upon variances from the budget.

Most important of all controls over payroll is the division of payroll work among several departments of the company. Payroll activities include the functions of (1) employment (human resources), (2) timekeeping, (3) payroll preparation and record keeping, and (4) distribution of pay to employees. For effective internal control, a separate department of the company should handle each of these functions. These several phases of payroll activities will now be considered individually.

### Employment (Human Resources)

The first significant step in establishing strong internal control over payroll should be taken by the human resources department when a new employee is hired. At this point, the authorized rate of pay should be entered on a pay-rate record. The employee also should sign a payroll deduction authorization specifying any amounts to be withheld and a withholding tax exemption certificate. These records should be kept in the human resources department, but a notice of the hiring of the new employee, the rate of pay, and the payroll deductions should be sent to the payroll department. When a computer is used, this information will be keyed into an employee payroll master file. The human resources department, the payroll department, or data processing will enter the data into the computer system.

Under no circumstances should a name be added to the payroll without having received the formal authorization notice from the human resources department. When an employee's rate of pay is changed, the new rate should be entered on the pay-rate record (often computerized) that is maintained in the human resources department. An authorization for the new rate should be sent to the payroll department before the change can be made effective on the payroll. Upon termination of an employee, notice of termination should be sent from the human resources department to the payroll department. The work of the payroll department and the propriety of names and pay raises used in preparing the payroll, therefore, rest upon formal documents or computer input originating outside the payroll department.

Adequate internal control demands that the addition and removal of names from the company payroll, as well as rate changes and reclassification of employees, be evidenced by written approval of an executive in the human resources department and by the head of the operating department concerned. To permit the payroll department to initiate changes in pay rates or to add names to the payroll without formal authorization from the human resources department increases the likelihood of fraud.

### Timekeeping

The function of timekeeping consists of determining the number of hours (or units of production) for which each employee is to be paid. The use of electronic time-recording equipment is of considerable aid in establishing adequate internal control over the time-keeping function. In addition, supervisors should maintain contact with subordinates and prepare time reports summarizing the use of labor.

Internal control can be improved by the practice of regular comparison of the time reports prepared by timekeepers or supervisors with time clock records showing the arrival and departure times of employees. If pay is based on piecework, a comparison may be made between the reports of units produced and the quantities that are added to the perpetual inventory records.

Salaried employees receiving a fixed monthly or weekly salary may not be required to use time clocks. Some companies require salaried employees to fill out a weekly or semi-monthly report indicating the time devoted to various activities. If a salaried employee is absent, the department head usually has authority to decide whether a pay reduction should be made.

### Payroll Preparation and Record Keeping

In a manual system, the payroll department has the responsibility for computing the amounts to be paid to employees and for preparing all payroll records. It is important that the payroll department *not* perform the related functions of timekeeping, employment, or distribution of pay to employees. The output of the payroll department may be thought of as (1) the payroll checks or direct deposits (or pay envelopes, if wages are paid in cash); (2) individual employee statements of earnings and deductions; (3) a payroll journal; (4) an employees ledger, summarizing earnings and deductions for each employee; (5) a payroll distribution schedule, showing the allocation of payroll costs to direct labor, over-head, and various departmental expense accounts; and (6) quarterly and annual reports to the government showing employees' earnings and taxes withheld. If the client utilizes a centralized computer, many of these functions may be delegated to data processing.

In a computerized system, the payroll is calculated by the computer, using the work hours reported by the timekeeping department and the authorized pay rates and payroll deductions reported by the human resources department. In addition to preparing the payroll journal, the payroll department prepares the payroll checks or the pay envelopes, if wages are paid in cash. Checks are then forwarded to the treasurer for signature.

Regardless of the system used, the auditors should expect the client's system to include such basic records as time cards, payroll journals, labor distributions, and employee earnings records. In a computerized system, some or all of these documents may exist only in computer-readable form.

### Distributing Pay: Direct Deposit, Paychecks, or Cash

The distribution of pay through direct deposit, paychecks, or pay envelopes (with cash enclosed) should be performed by an individual who performs no other payroll activity. If pay is deposited directly into employee bank accounts, controls over that process are necessary, such as authorization of deposits by personnel in the treasurer's department. If pay is distributed as paychecks or pay envelopes, the task should be that of the paymaster.

Most companies that pay employees by check or direct deposit use a special payroll bank account. A voucher for the entire amount of the weekly payroll may be prepared in the general accounting department based on the payroll summary prepared in the payroll department. This voucher is sent to the treasurer, who issues a check on the general bank account for the amount of the payroll. The check is deposited in the special payroll bank account and checks or direct deposits to individual employees are drawn on the account. It also is the practice of some companies to require dual signatures on large checks and to have printed on the check a statement that this type of check is not valid if issued for an amount in excess of a specified dollar amount.

If employees are paid in cash, the paymaster will use a copy of the payroll journal and the information on the payroll envelopes (both prepared by the payroll department) to fill the payroll envelopes with cash. The paymaster will require proof of identity when distributing checks or cash to employees and require them to sign a receipt for any cash received. All checks or pay envelopes for an absent employee should be retained and neither returned to the payroll department nor turned over to another employee for delivery.

When wages are paid in cash, any unclaimed wages should be deposited in the bank and credited to a special liability account. Subsequent disbursement of these funds to employees then will be controlled by the necessity of drawing a check and preparing supporting documents. The dangers inherent in permitting unclaimed pay envelopes to be retained by the paymaster, returned to the payroll clerk, or intermingled with petty cash are apparent.

## Documentation of Internal Control for Payroll

Typical of the questions to be posed by the auditors prior to the completion of an internal control questionnaire, a systems flowchart, or other record of payroll controls are the following: Are employees paid by check or direct deposit? Is a payroll bank account maintained on an imprest basis? Are the activities of timekeeping, payroll compilation, payroll check signing, and paycheck distribution performed by separate departments or employees? Are all operations involved in the preparation of payrolls subjected to independent verification before the paychecks are distributed? Are employee time reports approved by supervisors? Is the payroll bank account reconciled monthly by an employee having no other payroll duties?

## Audit Program for Payroll

**LO5**

Complete an audit program for payroll.

After obtaining an understanding of the client and its environment, including internal control, the auditors will assess the risks of material misstatement and design further audit procedures, including:

1. Perform tests of controls over payroll transactions for selected pay periods, including the following specific procedures:
   a. Compare names and wage or salary rates to records maintained by the human resources department.
   b. Compare time shown on payroll to time cards and time reports approved by supervisors.
   c. If payroll is based on piecework rates rather than hourly rates, reconcile earnings with production records.
   d. Determine basis of deductions from payroll and compare with records of deductions authorized by employees.
   e. Test extensions and footings of payroll.
   f. Compare total of payroll with total of payroll checks issued.
   g. Compare total of payroll with total of labor cost summary prepared by cost accounting department.
   h. If wages are paid in cash, compare receipts obtained from employees with payroll records.
   i. If wages are paid by check, compare paid checks with payroll and compare endorsements to signatures on withholding tax exemption certificates.
   j. If wages are paid by direct deposit, compare listing of employee payments with payroll and direct deposit authorizations.
   k. Observe the use of time clocks by employees reporting for work and investigate time cards not used.
2. Perform analytical procedures to test the reasonableness of payroll expense; for example, develop an expectation about the amount of payroll expense by multiplying the amount of one pay period by the number of pay periods in the year.
3. Investigate any extraordinary fluctuations in salaries, wages, and commissions.
4. Obtain or prepare a summary of compensation of officers for the year and compare to contracts, minutes of directors' meetings, or other authorization.
5. Test the period end accrual of payroll expense.
6. Test computations of compensation earned under profit-sharing or bonus plans.

**FIGURE 16.3**
**Objectives of Major Substantive Procedures for Payroll**

| Substantive Procedures | Primary Audit Objectives |
|---|---|
| Perform analytical procedures. Investigate fluctuations in salaries, wages, and commissions. Obtain a summary of amounts of officers' compensation and trace to authorization. | *Existence* and *occurrence* *Completeness* *Accuracy* |
| Test the period end accrual of payroll expenses. | *Existence* and *occurrence* *Completeness* *Accuracy* *Cutoff* |
| Test computations of compensation under profit-sharing or bonus plans. Test commission earnings. Test pension obligations. | *Accuracy* |

7. Test commission earnings by examination of contracts and detailed supporting records.

8. Test pension obligations by reference to authorized pension plans and supporting records.

Figure 16.3 relates these procedures to their primary audit objectives.

In addition to the preceding procedures, the auditors may plan a surprise observation of a regular distribution of paychecks to employees. The auditors' objective in observing the distribution of checks or cash to employees on a regular payday is to determine that every name on the company payroll is that of a bona fide employee presently on the job. This audit procedure is especially desirable if the various phases of payroll work are not sufficiently segregated by departments to afford good internal control. The history of payroll frauds shows that permitting one person to have custody of employment records, time cards, paychecks, and employees' earnings records has often led to the entering of fictitious names on the payroll and to other forms of fraud, such as use of excessive pay rates and continuance of pay after the termination of an employee. When performing this procedure, the auditors first will determine that they have possession of all the checks or envelopes comprising the payroll. They will then accompany representatives of the client around the plant as all the checks or envelopes are distributed to employees. It is essential that the auditors establish the identity of each employee receiving payment.

## Audit of the Statement of Cash Flows

The statement of cash flows is prepared from other financial statements and from analyses of increases and decreases in selected account balances. The amounts included in the statement of cash flows are audited in conjunction with the audit of balance sheet and income statement accounts. Thus, limited substantive procedures are necessary. The auditors merely compare the amounts included in the statement of cash flows to other financial statement balances and amounts included in audit working papers.

Since receipts and payments must be classified in the statement of cash flows as to whether they are from operating, investing, or financing activities, the presentation and disclosure audit objective is especially important. The auditors must determine that the concept of cash or cash and cash equivalents analyzed in the statement agrees with an amount shown on the balance sheet. Finally, the auditors should ascertain that a statement of cash flows is presented for each year for which an income statement is presented.

## Completing the Audit

**LO6**

Explain the types of procedures that are necessary to complete the audit.

The auditors' report should not be dated prior to the date they have gathered sufficient, appropriate evidence. This date is often the last day of fieldwork but it may be a later date. Therefore, the auditors' opinion on the financial statements is based on all evidence gathered by the auditors up to the date of the audit report and any other information that comes to their attention between that date and the issuance of the financial statements. To be effective, certain audit procedures described in previous chapters cannot be completed before the end of the audit. Among those procedures are the following:

1. Search for unrecorded liabilities.
2. Review the minutes of meetings.
3. Perform final analytical procedures.
4. Perform procedures to identify loss contingencies.
5. Perform the review for subsequent events.
6. Obtain the representation letter.

## Search for Unrecorded Liabilities

As discussed in Chapter 14, auditors must be alert for unrecorded payables. The search for unrecorded liabilities includes procedures performed near the date of the auditors' report, such as examining subsequent cash disbursements. These procedures are designed to detect liabilities that existed at year-end but were omitted from the liabilities recorded in the client's financial statements.

## Review the Minutes of Meetings

The auditors should review the **minutes** of meetings of stockholders and directors, including important subcommittees of directors such as the audit committee and the investment committee. This review includes meetings held through the date of the audit report. In completing the audit, the auditors must determine that they have considered all minutes, including those for meetings subsequent to year-end. They will also obtain written representation from management that all minutes have been made available.

## Perform Final Analytical Procedures

The discussion of **analytical procedures** in Chapter 5 pointed out that they must be performed in planning as well as for overall review purposes at the completion of the audit. Analytical procedures performed as a part of the overall review assist the auditors in assessing the validity of the conclusions reached, including the opinion to be issued. This final review may identify areas that need to be examined further as well as provide a consideration of the adequacy of data gathered in response to unusual or unexpected relationships identified during the audit. AICPA AU 240 (PCAOB 316) specifically requires auditors to evaluate whether analytical procedures performed as substantive procedures or in the overall review stage indicate a previously unrecognized risk of material misstatement due to fraud.

## Perform Procedures to Identify Loss Contingencies

A **loss contingency** may be defined as a *possible* loss, stemming from past events that will be resolved as to existence and amount by some future event. Central to the concept of a contingent loss is the idea of uncertainty—uncertainty as to both the amount of loss and whether, in fact, any loss has been incurred. This uncertainty is resolved when some future event occurs or fails to occur.

Most loss contingencies may also appropriately be called **contingent liabilities.** Loss contingencies, however, is a broader term, encompassing the possible impairment of assets as well as the possible existence of liabilities. The audit problems with respect to loss contingencies are twofold. First, the auditors must determine the existence of the loss contingencies. Because of the uncertainty factor, most loss contingencies do not appear in the accounting records, and a systematic search is required if the auditors are to have reasonable assurance that no important loss contingencies have been overlooked. Second, the auditors must appraise the probability that a loss has been incurred and its amount. This is made difficult both by the uncertainty factor and also by the tendency of the client management to maintain at least an outward appearance of optimism.

In *FASB ASC* 450-20, "Loss Contingencies," the Financial Accounting Standards Board set forth the criteria for accounting for loss contingencies. Such losses should be reflected in the accounting records when both of the following conditions are met: (1) information available prior to the issuance of the financial statements indicates that it is *probable* that a loss has been sustained before the balance sheet date, and (2) the amount of the loss can be *reasonably estimated.* Recognition of the loss may involve either recognition of a liability or reduction of an asset. When a loss contingency has been accrued in the accounts, it is usually desirable to explain the nature of the contingency in a note to the financial statements and to disclose any exposure to loss in excess of the amount accrued.

Loss contingencies that do not meet both of the above criteria should still be disclosed in a note to the financial statements when there is at least a *reasonable possibility* that a loss has been incurred. This disclosure should describe the nature of the contingency and, if possible, provide an estimate of the possible loss. If the amount of possible loss cannot be reasonably estimated, the disclosure should include either a range of loss or a statement that an estimate cannot be made.

Certain contingent liabilities traditionally have been disclosed in financial statement notes even though the possibility that a loss has occurred is remote. Such items include notes receivable discounted and guarantee endorsements. With the exception of those items for which disclosure is traditional, disclosure need not be made of loss contingencies when the possibility of loss is remote.

The procedures undertaken by auditors to identify the existence of loss contingencies and to assess the probability of loss vary with the nature of the contingent item. Regardless of the procedures performed, it is important that they be extended to near the date of the auditors' report, so that the auditors have the latest available information to evaluate the financial statement presentation and disclosure of loss contingencies. To illustrate these types of procedures, we will discuss several of the more frequent types of contingencies warranting financial statement disclosure.

### Litigation

Perhaps the most common loss contingency appearing in the financial statements is that stemming from actual or potential litigation. AICPA AU 501 (PCAOB 337) provides guidance in this area and requires that auditors design and perform audit procedures to identify litigation, claims, and assessments that may give rise to a risk of material misstatement, including:

- Inquiring about these matters with management and others in the organization, including in-house legal counsel.
- Obtaining from management a description and evaluation of litigation, claims, and assessments, including identification of those matters referred to legal counsel.
- Reviewing (1) minutes of meetings of those charged with governance, (2) documents in management's possession regarding litigation, claims, and assessments, and (3) correspondence with legal counsel.
- Reviewing legal expense accounts and invoices from legal counsel.

When actual or potential litigation is identified, the auditors obtain evidence relevant to identifying the cause, degree of probability of an unfavorable outcome, and the amount of potential loss.

Unless the above audit procedures indicate no actual or potential litigation, claims, or assessments, the auditors should directly communicate with the client's external legal counsel through a **letter of inquiry** prepared by management and sent by the auditors. The letter should ask legal counsel to reply as of a date approximating the estimated date of the audit report to allow the auditors to receive the most current information possible.

The letter of inquiry asks legal counsel to corroborate the information provided by management and to comment on those areas where their views differ from those of management. Legal counsel is also requested to identify any pending claims, litigation, or assessments that have been omitted from management's list. If in-house legal counsel has primary responsibility for any particular litigation, claim, or assessment, similar information should be requested of them, although this is not a substitute for seeking the information from external counsel.

Auditors should also inquire of legal counsel regarding the possibility of **unasserted claims** on which individuals have not yet taken legal action. An unasserted claim should be disclosed if it is (1) *probable* that a claim will be asserted and (2) *reasonably possible* that a loss will result. Management's list of legal matters should include such unasserted claims, and legal counsel should provide any relevant additional information related to those listed unasserted claims. However, if management fails to list an unasserted claim, legal counsel is *not* required to describe the claim in the reply to the auditors; the lawyer is, however, generally required to inform the client of the omission and to consider resignation if the client fails to inform the auditors about the claim. For this reason, auditors should always consider carefully the reasons for any legal counsel's resignation.

What should the auditors do if the client's legal counsel refuses to respond appropriately to the letter of inquiry or management refuses to provide the auditors with permission to communicate with legal counsel? In these situations, the auditors should attempt to obtain evidence by performing alternative procedures. If the auditors are unable to obtain sufficient appropriate audit evidence by performing alternative audit procedures, they should modify their opinion due to the lack of sufficient appropriate audit evidence, as discussed in Chapter 17.

### Illustration of Disclosure

The following note to the financial statements of an aircraft manufacturer illustrates the disclosure of the contingent liability associated with pending litigation.

> A number of suits are pending against the Company as the result of accidents in prior years involving airplanes manufactured by the Company. It is believed that insurance carried by the Company is sufficient to protect it against loss by reason of suits involving the lives of passengers and damage to aircraft. Other litigation pending against the Company involves no substantial amount or is covered by insurance.

The note of another large corporation contained the following note concerning contingent liabilities:

> The Company is a party to a number of lawsuits and claims (some of which are for substantial amounts) arising out of the conduct of its business, including those relating to commercial transactions, product liability, and environmental, safety, and health matters. While the ultimate results of lawsuits or other proceedings against the Company cannot be predicted with certainty, management does not expect that these matters will have a material adverse effect on the consolidated financial position or results of operations of the Company.

### Income Tax Disputes

The necessity of estimating the income tax liability applicable to the year under audit was discussed in Chapter 14. In addition to the taxes relating to the current year's income, uncertainty often exists concerning the amount ultimately payable for prior years. A lag of two or three years often exists between the filing of income tax returns and the final settlement after review by the Internal Revenue Service (IRS). Disputes between the taxpayer and the IRS may create contingent liabilities not settled for several more years. The auditors should determine whether internal revenue agents have examined any returns of the client since the preceding audit and, if so, whether any additional taxes have been assessed. In addition, the auditors should review any correspondence with the IRS and any other regulatory agencies.

### Accommodation Endorsements and Other Guarantees of Indebtedness

The endorsement of notes of other concerns or individuals is very seldom recorded in the accounts, but may be reflected in the minutes of directors' meetings. The practice is more common among small concerns—particularly when one person has a proprietary interest in several companies. Officers, partners, and sole proprietors of small organizations should be questioned as to the existence of any contingent liability from this source. Inquiry should also be made as to whether any collateral has been received to protect the company. The auditors may also decide to confirm written or oral guarantees or other contingent liabilities with appropriate financial institutions, using a specially designed confirmation letter.

### Accounts Receivable Sold or Assigned with Recourse

When accounts receivable are sold or assigned *with recourse,* a guarantee of collectibility is given. Authorization of such a transaction should be revealed during the auditors' reading of the minutes, and evidence of such agreements also may be found during the examination of transactions and correspondence with financial institutions. Confirmation by direct communication with the purchaser or assignee is necessary for any receivables sold or assigned.

### Environmental Issues

Environmental remediation liability laws, written at all levels of government, are increasingly leading to both contingent and accrued liabilities. The Resource, Conservation, and Recovery Act, Superfund, and various clean air and water acts create potential liability for companies, as illustrated in the following example focusing on the electronics industry.

---

**Focus on the Electronics Industry**

The electronics industry and other high-technology enterprises may find themselves liable for remediation of environmental contamination. As described in an AICPA industry *Audit Risk Alert,* Superfund legally empowers the United States Environmental Protection Agency to seek recovery from both current and previous owners or operators of a contaminated site, or anyone who generated or transported hazardous substances to or from such a site. The use of toxic or hazardous materials in the electronics industry or the manufacturing of by-products that adversely affect the environment may create environmental cleanup issues. Various professional pronouncements released interpret *FASB No. 5* for environmental matters to help companies determine when it is appropriate to disclose or possibly accrue liabilities for such matters.

---

### Commitments

Closely related to contingent liabilities are obligations termed **commitments.** The auditors may discover during their audit any of the following commitments: inventory purchase commitments, commitments to sell merchandise at specified prices, contracts for the construction of plant and equipment, pension or profit-sharing plans, long-term operating leases of plant and equipment, employee stock option plans, and employment contracts with key officers. A common characteristic of these commitments is the contractual obligation to enter into transactions *in the future.*

To illustrate the relationship of a commitment to a loss contingency, assume that a manufacturer commits to sell a substantial part of its output at a fixed price over the next three years. At the time of forming the agreement, the manufacturer, of course, believes the arrangement to be advantageous. However, it is possible that rising price levels may transform the fixed price sales agreement into an unprofitable one, requiring sales to be made at prices below manufacturing cost. Such circumstances may warrant recognition of a loss in the financial statements.

All classes of material commitments may be described in a single note to financial statements, or they may be included in a "Contingencies and Commitments" note.

### General Risk Contingencies

In addition to loss contingencies and commitments, all businesses face the risk of loss from numerous factors called **general risk contingencies.** A general risk contingency represents a loss that *might occur in the future,* as opposed to a loss contingency that *might have occurred in the past.* Examples of general risk contingencies are threat of a strike or consumer boycott, risk of price increases in essential raw materials, and risk of a natural catastrophe.

Since the events that might produce a loss actually have not occurred and they are part of the general business environment, general risk contingencies ordinarily *need not be disclosed* in financial statements. The lack of insurance coverage is a general risk contingency. Neither the adequacy nor the lack of insurance coverage is required to be presented in financial statements.

### The Auditors' Procedures for Loss Contingencies

An overview of the auditors' procedures to detect and evaluate loss contingencies is described below.

1. Review the minutes of directors' meetings to the date of completion of fieldwork. Important contracts, lawsuits, and dealings with subsidiaries are typical of matters discussed in board meetings that may involve loss contingencies.
2. Send a letter of inquiry to the client's lawyer requesting:
    a. A description (or evaluation of management's description) of the nature of pending and threatened litigation and tax disputes.
    b. An evaluation of the likelihood of an unfavorable outcome in the matters described.
    c. An estimate of the probable loss or range of loss, or a statement that an estimate cannot be made.
    d. An evaluation of management's description of any unasserted claims that, if asserted, have a reasonable possibility of an adverse outcome.
    e. A statement of the amount of any unbilled legal fees.
3. Send confirmation letters to financial institutions to request information on contingent liabilities of the company.
4. Review correspondence with financial institutions for evidence of accommodation endorsements, guarantees of indebtedness, or sales or assignments of accounts receivable.
5. Review reports and correspondence from regulatory agencies to identify potential assessments or fines.
6. Obtain a representation letter from the client indicating that all liabilities known to officers are recorded or disclosed.

## Perform the Review for Subsequent Events

Evidence not available at the close of the period under audit often becomes available before the auditors finish their fieldwork and issue their audit report. The CPA's opinion on the fairness of the financial statements may be changed considerably by these subsequent events. The term **subsequent event** refers to an event occurring after the date of the balance sheet but prior to the date of the auditors' report (the date on which the auditors have obtained sufficient appropriate audit evidence to support their opinion). *FASB ASC* 855 divides subsequent events into two broad categories: (1) those providing additional evidence about facts existing on or before the balance sheet date ("recognized subsequent events"), and (2) those involving facts coming into existence subsequent to the balance sheet date ("nonrecognized subsequent events").

**LO7**

Describe the auditors' responsibilities for the detection and evaluation of various types of subsequent events.

### Type 1 Subsequent Events

The first type of subsequent event provides additional evidence as to *conditions that existed at the balance sheet date* and affects the estimates inherent in the process of preparing financial statements. This type of subsequent event requires that the financial statement amounts be adjusted to reflect the changes in estimates resulting from the additional evidence.

As an example, let us assume that a client's accounts receivable at December 31 included one large account and numerous small ones. While management regarded the large account's balance as fully collectible at year-end, during the course of the audit the customer entered bankruptcy. The auditors' procedures revealed that, although the bankruptcy occurred early in January, the financial strength of the customer had deteriorated before December 31, and the client was simply in error in believing the receivable to be fully collectible at that date. Accordingly, the auditors recommended an increase in the December 31 allowance for uncollectible accounts. Evidence becoming available after the balance sheet date through the date of issuance of the auditors' report should be used in making judgments about the valuation of receivables.

Other examples of this first type of subsequent event include the following:

1. Customers' checks included in the cash receipts of the last day of the year prove to be uncollectible and are charged back to the client's account by the bank. If the checks were material in amount, an adjustment of the December 31 cash balance may be necessary to exclude the checks now known to be uncollectible.

2. A new three-year union contract signed two weeks after the balance sheet date provides evidence that the client has materially underestimated the total cost to complete a long-term construction project on which revenue is recognized by the percentage-of-completion method. The amount of income (or loss) to be recognized on the project in the current year should be recomputed using revised cost estimates.

3. Litigation pending against the client is settled shortly after the balance sheet date, and the amount owed by the client is material. This litigation was to be disclosed in notes to the financial statements, but no liability had been accrued because at year-end no reasonable estimate could be made as to the amount of the client's loss. Now that appropriate evidence exists as to the dollar amount of the loss, this loss contingency meets the criteria for accrual in the financial statements, rather than mere note disclosure.

### Type 2 Subsequent Events

The second type of subsequent event involves conditions *coming into existence after the balance sheet date.* These events do not require adjustment to the dollar amounts shown in the financial statements, *but they should be disclosed in the financial statement notes if the statements otherwise would be misleading.* To illustrate, assume that shortly after the balance sheet date a client sustains an uninsured fire loss destroying most of its plant assets. The carrying value of plant assets should not be reduced in the balance sheet because these assets were intact at year-end. However, people analyzing the financial statements would be misled if they were not advised that most of the plant assets are no longer in a usable condition.

What types of events occurring after the balance sheet date warrant disclosure in the financial statements? To explore this question, assume that the following events occurred after the balance sheet date but prior to completion of the audit fieldwork:

1. Business combination with a competing company.
2. Early retirement of bonds payable.
3. Adoption of a new pension plan requiring large near-term cash outlays.
4. Death of the company treasurer in an airplane crash.
5. Introduction of a new line of products.
6. Plant closed by a labor strike.

Although these events may be significant in the future operations of the company and of interest to many who read the audited financial statements, none of these occurrences has any bearing on the results of the year under audit, and their bearing on future results is not easily determinable.

It is generally agreed that subsequent events involving business combinations, substantial casualty losses, and other significant changes in a company's financial position or financial structure should be disclosed in notes. Otherwise, the financial statements might be misleading rather than informative. Consequently, the first three of the preceding examples (combination with a competing company, early retirement of bonds payable, and adoption of a new pension plan) should be disclosed in notes to the financial statements. The last three subsequent events (personnel changes, product line changes, and strikes) are nonaccounting matters and are not disclosed in notes unless particular circumstances make such information essential to the proper interpretation of the financial statements.

### Pro Forma Statements as a Means of Disclosure

Occasionally subsequent events may be so material that supplementary *pro forma financial statements* should be prepared giving effect to the events as if they had occurred as of the balance sheet date. The pro forma statements (usually a balance sheet only) may be presented in columnar form next to the audited financial statements. This form of disclosure is used only when the subsequent event has a significant effect upon the asset structure or capital structure of the business. An example would be a business combination.

### Distinguishing between the Two Types of Subsequent Events

In deciding whether a particular subsequent event should result in an adjustment to the financial statements or a note disclosure, the auditor should carefully consider *when the underlying conditions came into existence.* For example, assume that shortly after the balance sheet date, a major customer of the audit client declares bankruptcy, with the result that a large receivable previously considered fully collectible now appears to be uncollectible. If the customer's bankruptcy resulted from a steady deterioration in financial position, the subsequent event provides evidence that the receivable actually was uncollectible at year-end, and the allowance for doubtful accounts should be increased. On the other hand, if the customer's bankruptcy stemmed from a casualty (such as a fire) occurring after year-end, the conditions making the receivable uncollectible came into existence after the balance sheet date. In this case, the subsequent event should be disclosed in a note to the financial statements.

### Audit Procedures Relating to Subsequent Events

For the period after year-end through the date of the auditors' report, the auditors should perform audit procedures to obtain sufficient appropriate audit evidence that all subsequent events that require adjustment or disclosures in the financial statements have been identified. During this period, the auditors should determine that proper cutoffs of cash receipts and disbursements and sales and purchases have been made, and they should examine data to aid in the evaluation of assets and liabilities as of the balance sheet date. In addition, the auditors should:

1. Obtain an understanding of management's procedures to ensure that subsequent events are identified.
2. Inquire of management (and those charged with governance) about whether subsequent events have occurred.
3. Read available minutes of directors, stockholders, and appropriate committee meetings that have been held after the date of the financial statements and inquire about matters discussed at any such meeting for which minutes are not yet available.
4. Read the company's latest subsequent interim financial statements, if any.

Generally, the auditors' responsibility for performing procedures to gather evidence as to subsequent events extends only through the date of the audit report. However, even after completing normal audit procedures, the auditors are responsible for evaluating subsequent events that come to their attention prior to the report release date. Suppose, for example, that the auditors completed their work for a December 31 audit on February 3 and thereafter began drafting their report. On February 11, before issuing their report, the client informed the auditors that the client had settled a lawsuit on that day by a substantial payment. In such a circumstance, generally accepted accounting principles require that the liability be established in the December 31 balance sheet. If the adjustment does not also require a note disclosure, the audit report ordinarily continues to be dated as of the date the auditor had sufficient audit evidence, February 3. If a related note disclosure is necessary, auditors have two methods available for dating the audit report. They may *dual-date* their report "February 3, except for Note X, as to which the date is February 11." Alternatively, they might decide to return to the client's facilities for further review of subsequent events through the date of the subsequent event, February 11; in this case, the audit report would bear that date only.

Dual-dating extends the auditors' responsibility for disclosure through the later date *only with respect to the specified item.* Using the later date for the date of the report extends the auditors' responsibility with respect to all areas of the financial statements. Finally, in the unusual circumstance in which the client does not agree to properly reflect the event, the departure from generally accepted accounting principles may result in either a qualified or adverse opinion.

**FIGURE 16.4**
**Subsequent Events**

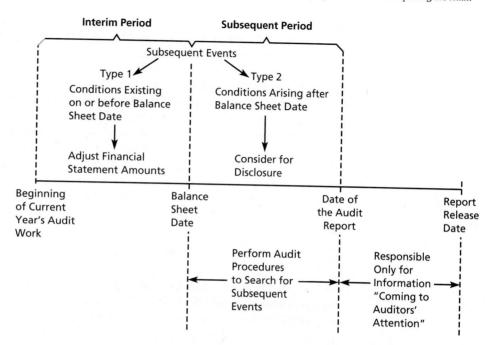

Figure 16.4 summarizes the auditors' responsibilities for subsequent events with respect to the balance sheet date, the date of the audit report, and date the auditors grant the client permission to use the audit report—the **report release date.**

*The Auditors' S-1 Review in an SEC Registration*

The Securities Act of 1933 (Section 11 [a]) extends the auditors' liability in connection with the registration of new securities with the Securities and Exchange Commission (SEC) to the *effective date* of the registration statement—the date on which the securities may be sold to the public. In many cases, the effective date of the registration statement may be several weeks or even months later than the date the auditors completed their fieldwork. Accordingly, on or as close as practicable to the effective date, the auditors return to the client's facilities to conduct an **S-1 review,** so-called because of the "Form S-1" title of the traditional SEC registration statement for new securities issues. In addition to completing the subsequent events review described in the preceding section, the auditors should read the entire prospectus and other pertinent portions of the registration statement. They should also inquire of officers and other key executives of the client whether any events not reported in the registration statement have occurred that require amendment of the registration statement to prevent the audited financial statements therein from being misleading.

## Obtain Representation Letter

Chapter 5 included a general description of the **representation letter** that the auditors must obtain from management. The primary purpose of the representation letter is to have the client's principal officers acknowledge that they are primarily responsible for the fairness of the financial statements. Since the financial statements must reflect all material subsequent events, the representation letter should be dated as of the date of the audit report. As indicated in Chapter 5, while representation letters are part of the audit evidence the auditors obtain, they are not a substitute for the application of other necessary audit procedures. Thus, for example, obtaining a management representation as to the reasonableness of the estimated allowance for doubtful accounts should not result in fewer other audit procedures relating to that account.

## Communicate Misstatements to Management

Throughout the course of the audit, the auditors accumulate and communicate to management all misstatements identified, other than those the auditors believe to be trivial. Because the financial statements are the representations of management, management makes the final decision as to whether to approve and record any adjustments and disclosures. In some circumstances, management may propose alternative amounts for the adjustments and disclosures. Since the auditors' responsibility is to express an opinion on the financial statements, unresolved differences between the auditors and management with respect to such adjustments may result in modification of the auditors' report. Also, if any adjusting entries are not recorded, management must represent to the auditors (in the representation letter) that management believes the adjustments to be immaterial. Of course the auditors must make their own conclusions about whether the amounts involved are material or immaterial.

Misstatements identified by the auditors may include amounts that are known to be misstated, likely to be misstated, or both. **Known misstatements** are specific misstatements identified during the course of the audit (e.g., the amount of misstatement in a particular account receivable that was confirmed). **Likely misstatements** may be due to either extrapolation from audit evidence or differences in accounting estimates:

- *Extrapolation differences* are generally projected misstatements determined through the use of sampling. As an example, if the book value of accounts receivable is $6,250,000 and the auditors, using audit sampling, estimate the audited value to be $6,100,000, the projected misstatement is $150,000 ($6,250,000 – $6,100,000). However, this amount should be decreased by the amount of the known misstatement (the actual misstatements identified in the sample).
- *Accounting estimate differences* are differences between management's and the auditors' judgment concerning the appropriate amounts of accounting estimates. For these items, the estimated (likely) misstatement is the difference between management's estimate and the closest amount that the auditors consider reasonable. An example would be a situation in which management estimates the company's warranty liability to be $90,000 and the auditors develop an estimate of between $120,000 and $140,000 for the liability. The likely misstatement is $30,000 ($120,000 – $90,000).

The auditors should request that management record the adjustment needed to correct all known misstatements other than those considered trivial. When the auditors identify a likely misstatement due to an extrapolation difference, they should request that management examine the accounts involved in order to identify and correct other misstatements. When accounting estimates include what the auditors believe to be likely misstatements, the auditors should request that management review the assumptions and methods used in developing their estimate (e.g., the allowance for doubtful accounts).

## Evaluate Audit Findings

LO8

Explain the steps involved in evaluating audit findings.

As indicated, the auditors will request that management record any adjustments required to correct misstatements. When management refuses to correct these misstatements, the auditors must evaluate their importance. Any known *material* misstatements must be corrected, or the auditors cannot issue an unqualified opinion on the financial statements. In evaluating whether an individual misstatement is material, the auditors consider both quantitative and qualitative factors. For example, a $10,000 related party transaction might be considered material for a particular audit, whereas a misstatement of trade accounts receivable of the same amount might not be considered material. Immaterial misstatements that are discovered by the auditors and not corrected by the client are accumulated in a working paper that is given a title such as "Adjusting Entries Passed."

*Evaluation Materiality—Considering Quantitative Factors*
To issue an unqualified opinion, the auditors must conclude that there is a low level of risk of material misstatement of the financial statements. Prior to evaluating the effect of uncorrected misstatements, the auditors should reassess materiality to confirm whether it remains appropriate in the context of the client's actual financial results. They will consider the quantitative and qualitative effects of uncorrected misstatements on relevant classes of transactions, accounts, and disclosures.

If the auditors estimate that the total of known and likely misstatements is material to the financial statements, they will conclude that the risk of material misstatement is too high to issue an unqualified opinion on the financial statements. As this total approaches the materiality level, the auditors should consider whether there is a greater than acceptably low level of risk that undetected misstatements could cause the total to exceed the materiality level. If so, the auditors should reconsider the nature and extent of further audit procedures.

The auditors will conclude that the risk of material misstatement is sufficiently low to issue an unqualified opinion only when the *aggregated misstatements (known and likely) are significantly less than a material amount.* The relationship between the aggregated misstatements and materiality is often documented in a working paper similar to that shown in Figure 16.5. As illustrated, the auditors must consider the effects of the aggregated misstatements on the various components of the financial statements, such as current assets and net income. As we have emphasized, whether a misstatement is material depends on its specific effect on the financial statements.

Notice that the misstatements in Figure 16.5 are adjusted for the effects of income taxes. To illustrate, consider the first misstatement, which represents an overstatement of prepaid expenses of $6,500. If that adjustment is not made, net income before taxes will be overstated by that amount. However, since taxable income is also overstated by $6,500, the company's income tax expense is overstated, in this case by $2,600 (40 percent of $6,500). Note that the 40 percent rate is used because it represents the company's marginal tax rate.

### Evaluation Materiality—Considering Qualitative Factors

While a schedule such as that presented in Figure 16.5 is helpful for assessing the quantitative effects of misstatement, auditors must also consider qualitative factors when evaluating the materiality of such misstatements. Both AICPA AU 320 (PCAOB 312) and SEC *Staff Accounting Bulletin No. 99,* "Materiality," provide examples of such qualitative factors. One or more misstatements are likely to be material from a qualitative perspective when they:

- Arise from an item capable of precise measurement (e.g., the amount of a sale) rather than from an estimate (e.g., the amount in the allowance for doubtful accounts).
- Mask a change in earnings or other trends.
- Hide a failure to meet analysts' consensus expectations for the company.
- Change a loss into income, or vice versa.
- Concern a particularly important segment or other portion of the registrant's business.
- Affect compliance with regulatory requirements, loan covenants, or other contractual requirements.
- Increase management's compensation.
- Involve concealment of an unlawful transaction.
- Are of an amount that management or the auditors believe would affect the stock's price.

In addition, the SEC requires that management and auditors apply a *reasonableness* standard when considering fairness of financial presentation. This somewhat ill-defined standard suggests that the need for proper presentation is not entirely a function of the above types of qualitative considerations. For example, the intentional misrecording of certain immaterial transactions might be considered unreasonable. Indeed, intentional misstatements may in some circumstances be unlawful; as such, they may require auditor consideration, as discussed in Chapter 2. Note that the situation being considered by the SEC in this case is one in which a client intentionally misrecords items to manage earnings (e.g., reporting sales in the wrong year), as opposed to a situation in which an accounting expediency is being applied to an immaterial area (e.g., the expensing of immaterial office supplies rather than listing them as an asset).

### Evaluation Materiality—Considering the Effects of Prior Year Uncorrected Misstatements

When uncorrected misstatements exist from prior years, should those misstatements be included in this year's materiality calculations? For example, assume that a client's previous year financial statements understated the estimated warranty payable by $60,000, an immaterial amount. Furthermore, the auditors estimate that this year's accrual is

## FIGURE 16.5 Aggregated Misstatements

SOUTHMADE PRODUCTS, INC.
Aggregated Misstatements
December 31, 20X4
Overstatement (Understatement)

| W/P ref. | Current Assets | Noncurrent Assets | Current Liabilities | Noncurrent Liabilities | Owners' Equity | Income before Taxes | Tax Expense |
|---|---|---|---|---|---|---|---|
| **Uncorrected Known Misstatements** | | | | | | | |
| D8 Overstatement of prepaid expenses | $ 6,500 | | $ 2,600 | | $ 6,500 (2,600) | $ 6,500 | $ 2,600 |
| F-6 Overstatement of prior year's depreciation | | ($10,000) | (4,000) | | (10,000) 4,000 | | |
| M-4 Unrecorded liabilities | | | (11,215) 4,486 | | 11,215 (4,486) | 11,215 | 4,486 |
| **Projected Misstatements** | | | | | | | |
| C-5 Overstatement of accounts receivable (confirmation results) | 30,000 | | 12,000 | | 30,000 (12,000) | 30,000 | 12,000 |
| **Other Estimated Misstatements** | | | | | | | |
| C-10 Understatement of allowance for uncollectible accounts | 5,000 | | 2,000 | | 5,000 (2,000) | 5,000 | 2,000 |
| Total Likely Misstatements | $ 41,500 | ($10,000) | $ 5,871 | — | $ 25,629 | $ 52,715 | $21,086 |
| Amount considered material | $100,000 | $125,000 | $100,000 | $125,000 | $200,000 | $150,000 | |

*Conclusion: Total likely misstatements are small enough in amount to result in a sufficiently low level of audit risk to justify our opinion.*  2/17/X5 JW

understated by an additional $70,000. In making materiality judgments, should the auditors consider only this year's $70,000? Or should they consider the total of $130,000 ($70,000 + $60,000)?

Historically, auditors have been allowed to use either of two approaches to make this decision: the **rollover approach** or the **iron curtain approach.** The *rollover approach* considers only the amount of the misstatement originating in the current year income statement—in this case, $70,000. In contrast, the *iron curtain approach* considers the balance sheet effect of correcting the total misstatement existing at the end of the year, regardless of when the misstatement originated—in this case, $130,000.

SEC *Staff Accounting Bulletin No. 108* decreased the auditor's flexibility in choosing between these methods by requiring that both the rollover and iron curtain approaches be considered. If either approach results in a material misstatement, an adjustment must be made. Thus, if the $130,000 misstatement is considered material to the financial statements, the client's financial statements should be adjusted. The adjustment may be disaggregated as:

- $70,000 current year effect.
- $60,000 balance sheet carryover misstatement that originated in the preceding year.

The current year financial statements should be adjusted for $70,000. If the $60,000 misstatement relating to the prior year (or years) is material to the current year, the prior year financial statements should be adjusted, even if the amounts remain immaterial to those prior years. If the $60,000 is immaterial to this year's financial statements, it may be included as an expense on this year's income statement rather than requiring restatement of the prior year's financial statements.

### Evaluating the Risks of Material Misstatement

At or near the completion of fieldwork, the auditors should evaluate whether the accumulated results of their procedures and observations affect the assessments of the risks of material misstatement made earlier in the engagement. In addition, the partner in charge of the engagement should determine that information or conditions indicative of risks of material misstatement due to fraud have been communicated to the audit team members.

### Review the Financial Statement Disclosures

Throughout the audit, the auditors must recognize the need to determine that financial statement note disclosures are adequate. These disclosure requirements arise in numerous pronouncements of the Financial Accounting Standards Board, such as *FASB ASC* 450-20 on "Loss Contingencies" and *FASB ASC* 280-50 on reporting on segment information. In addition, the auditors should be aware of the requirements of AICPA *Statement of Position 94-6,* "Disclosure of Certain Significant Risks and Uncertainties." That statement establishes disclosure requirements concerning (1) the nature of company operations, (2) the use of estimates in the preparation of financial statements, (3) certain significant estimates, and (4) current vulnerability due to concentrations (e.g., dependence upon a particular customer, supplier, or product).

It is not effective to rely on the auditors' memories to evaluate the adequacy of disclosures, and it is not efficient for them to research the required disclosures each time they review a set of financial statements. Thus, many CPA firms use **disclosure checklists** that list all specific disclosures required by the FASB, the GASB, the FASAC, and the SEC. The auditors complete the checklist as a part of their review of the completed financial statements.

### Client Approval of Adjusting Entries and Disclosures

During the course of the audit, the auditors may suggest various adjustments and disclosures concerning the financial statements. However, because they are the representations of management, the financial statements are not modified to reflect these items until management approves them. In some circumstances, management may propose differing adjustments and disclosures. Since the auditors' responsibility is to express an opinion on the financial statements, unresolved differences between auditor and client with respect to such differences may result in modification of the auditors' report. If any adjusting entries are not recorded, management must represent to the auditors (in the representation letter) that management believes the adjustments are not material.

## Review the Engagement

AICPA AU 300 (PCAOB 311) states that "the work performed by each assistant should be reviewed to determine whether it was adequately performed and documented and to evaluate the results, relative to the conclusions to be presented in the auditors' report." This review of the work of the audit staff is primarily accomplished through a review of the audit working papers. The seniors on audit engagements typically perform their review of the audit working papers as the papers are completed. While audit partners and managers will generally communicate with seniors and other staff members throughout the audit, their review of the working papers generally is not completed until near (or after) completion of fieldwork. The audit partner and manager will devote special attention to those accounts that have a higher risk of material misstatement, such as the significant accounting estimates of inventory obsolescence and warranty obligations. Also, a final consideration will be made of whether the results of procedures performed throughout the audit, including while completing the audit, identify conditions and events that indicate there could be substantial doubt about the company's ability to continue as a going concern. Finally, if a second partner review is required by the CPA firm's quality control policies, this review is usually performed just prior to issuance of the audit report.

# Responsibilities for Other Information

Audited financial statements generally are included with annual reports to shareholders and in reports to the SEC. These documents may include a considerable amount of information in addition to the audited financial statements. In completing the audit engagement, the auditors must fulfill certain responsibilities regarding the additional information.

## Other Information in Documents Containing Audited Financial Statements

**Other information** is financial and nonfinancial information that is included in a document that contains audited financial statements, except it does not include required supplementary information (see next section). Examples of other information include a report by management discussing the year's operating results, financial summaries, employment data, planned capital expenditures, financial ratios, and names of officers and directors. AICPA AU 720 (PCAOB 550) requires auditors to read this information for inconsistencies, if any, with the audited financial statements. If no inconsistencies are identified, the auditors are not required to reference the other information in the auditors' report on the financial statements. However, if they so choose, they may include an **other matter paragraph** disclaiming an opinion on the other information. Other matter paragraphs are discussed in Chapters 17 and 19.

If inconsistencies are identified, the auditors first request the client to revise any incorrect information. If the client refuses, and the other information is incorrect, this will lead to (1) an other matter paragraph being added to a report with an unmodified opinion, (2) withholding the auditors' report, or (3) withdrawing from the engagement. If it is the financial statements that are incorrect, it will be treated as a departure from GAAP, resulting in either a qualified or adverse opinion.

## Required Supplementary Information

Certain organizations are required by a designated accounting standards setter (i.e., FASB, GASB, FASAB, IASB) to present supplementary information. Such **required supplementary information,** while not considered a part of the general purpose financial statements, is required to be presented as unaudited supplementary schedules accompanying the financial statements. AICPA AU 725 (PCAOB 558) requires auditors to apply the following procedures to this information:

- *Inquire* of management about methods of preparing information, including whether (1) it was prepared following prescribed guidelines, (2) methods of measurement or presentation have changed from the prior period, and (3) there were any significant assumptions or interpretations underlying the measurement or presentation of the information.
- *Compare information* for consistency with (1) management's responses to the inquiries, (2) the basic financial statements, and (3) other knowledge obtained during the audit.
- *Obtain written representations* from management (1) acknowledging its responsibility for the information, (2) about whether the information is measured within guidelines, (3) about whether the methods have changed, and (4) about any significant assumptions or interpretations.

When no significant exceptions are identified, the reporting responsibilities differ between the AICPA and PCAOB standards. The AICPA standards require inclusion of an emphasis of matter paragraph in the financial statement audit report indicating that the procedures were performed; the paragraph provides no assurance. Under PCAOB standards, no mention of the information is required in the auditors' report.

When the supplementary information is omitted or improperly stated, under both AICPA and PCAOB standards, the situation is described in an emphasis of matter paragraph. The opinion paragraph of the report is not modified since the supplementary information is not considered a part of the audited information.

## Supplementary Information in Relation to the Financial Statements as a Whole

AICPA AU 725 (PCAOB 551) provides guidance on a non-required form of auditor association with **supplementary information** that goes beyond that described in the preceding two sections. With this service, auditors perform procedures to allow them to provide assurance on whether supplemental information is fairly stated, in all material respects, in relation to the financial statements as a whole. While the supplementary information may be presented in a document containing audited financial statements or separately from the financial statements, it must be derived from, and relate directly to, the underlying accounting and other records. Examples of information derived from the underlying accounting records include consolidating information, historical summaries of accounts, and statistical data. To provide this assurance, the auditors must perform the following procedures:

- Inquire of management about the purpose of the information and criteria used to prepare it.
- Determine the propriety of the form and content of the information.
- Obtain an understanding of how the information was prepared.
- Compare and reconcile information to underlying accounting and other records.
- Inquire of management concerning significant assumptions.
- Evaluate the appropriateness and completeness of the information.
- Obtain written representations.

When the information is found to be fairly stated in relation to the financial statements, an **emphasis of matter paragraph** is added describing the procedures followed and including an opinion that "the information is fairly stated in all material respects in relation to the financial statements as a whole." If the auditors conclude that the information is not fairly stated in all material respects, the paragraph so states. The opinion paragraph of the audit report is not modified since the supplementary information is not considered a part of the audited information.

Figure 16.6 summarizes the reporting standards for both other information and supplementary information.

**FIGURE 16.6**   **Summary of Other Information and Supplementary Information Reporting**

| Circumstance Giving Rise to Other Matter Paragraph | Effect on Audit Report If Properly Presented | Effect on Audit Report If Improperly Presented |
|---|---|---|
| Other information in documents containing audited financial statements | No change required (that is, other matter paragraph need *not* be added). However, the auditor may choose to include an other matter paragraph disclaiming an opinion on the other information. | The paragraph (other matter or emphasis of matter) indicates that information is incorrect or omitted, as appropriate. The audit opinion remains unmodified unless the audited information is misstated, in which case a qualified or adverse opinion is appropriate. |
| Required supplementary information | For audits performed under AICPA standards, an other matter paragraph is added; the paragraph provides no assurance on the required supplementary information. For audits performed under PCAOB standards, no paragraph is added. | |
| Supplementary information in relation to the financial statements as a whole | An emphasis of matter paragraph is added; the paragraph includes an opinion that the information is fairly stated in all material respects in relation to the financial statements as a whole. | |

Note: In all circumstances, the added paragraph follows the opinion paragraph.

## Opinion Formulation and Report Issuance

After the preceding procedures have been performed, the auditors will ordinarily be in a position to issue their audit report. When the auditors have obtained reasonable assurance that the financial statements follow generally accepted accounting principles and the audit has been performed in conformity with generally accepted auditing standards, including no significant scope limitations, an unqualified opinion will ordinarily be issued. As we will discuss in Chapter 17, when various circumstances have occurred (e.g., changes in accounting principles, substantial doubt about the entity's ability to continue as a going concern, and when other auditors are involved), explanatory language may be added to the audit report.

## Additional Communications

Auditors must communicate certain matters relating to fraud, illegal acts, reportable conditions, and certain other matters to the audit committee or the equivalent group with responsibility for oversight of the financial reporting process. All the communications may be communicated either orally or in writing.

### Fraud and Illegal Acts
AICPA AU 240 (PCAOB 316) and AICPA AU 250 (PCAOB 317) require that the audit committee be informed about fraudulent or illegal acts that the auditors become aware of, unless those acts are clearly inconsequential. Although these disclosures are also normally made to management, when management is believed to be involved with such an act, the communications should be made directly to the audit committee.

### Significant Deficiencies
Recall from our discussion in Chapter 7 that AICPA AU 265 (PCAOB 325) requires that the auditors communicate to the audit committee any significant deficiencies in internal control (previously known as reportable conditions).

### Other Communications
AICPA AU 260 requires an oral or written communication of certain information to those charged with governance of the company being audited. Those charged with governance means those with responsibility for overseeing the strategic direction of the entity and obligations related to the accountability of the entity—this ordinarily includes the board of directors or audit committee. The communication is aimed at providing information related to corporate governance matters related to the financial statement audit that are

significant and relevant for overseeing the financial reporting process. It includes information on:

- The auditors' responsibility under generally accepted auditing standards (i.e., to form and express an opinion) and management's responsibilities.
- An overview of the planned scope and timing of the audit.
- Significant findings from the audit.

The discussion of significant findings from the audit is particularly complex in that it involves communication of qualitative aspects of the company's significant accounting practices, audit difficulties encountered, uncorrected misstatements, disagreements with management, management consultations with other accountants, auditor independence issues, and other significant issues.

## Post-Audit Responsibilities

### The Auditors' Subsequent Discovery of Facts Existing at the Date of Their Report

**LO9**

Discuss the auditors' post-audit responsibilities.

After the issuance of its audit report, a CPA firm may encounter evidence indicating that the client's financial statements were materially misstated or lacked required disclosures. The auditors must immediately investigate such subsequently discovered facts. If the auditors determine that the facts are significant and existed at the date of the audit report, they should advise the client to make appropriate disclosure of the facts to anyone actually or likely to be relying upon the audit report and the related financial statements. If the client refuses to make appropriate disclosure, the CPAs should inform each member of the client's board of directors of such refusal. They should also notify regulatory agencies having jurisdiction over the client, and, if practicable, each person known to be relying upon the audited financial statements, that the CPAs' report can no longer be relied upon.

### Subsequent Discovery of Omitted Audit Procedures

What actions should the auditors take if, after issuing an audit report, they find that they failed to perform certain significant audit procedures? The omission of appropriate audit procedures in a particular engagement might be discovered during a peer review or other subsequent review of the auditors' working papers. Unlike the situation described in the previous section, the auditors do not have information indicating that the financial statements are in error. Instead, the subsequent review has revealed that they may have issued their audit report without having gathered sufficient evidential matter. In addressing this sensitive problem, AICPA AU 585 (PCAOB 390) states that the auditors should assess the importance of the omitted procedures to their previously issued opinion. If they believe that the omitted procedures impair their ability to support their previously issued opinion, and their report is still being relied upon by third parties, they should attempt to perform the omitted procedures or appropriate alternative procedures. Because of the legal implications of these situations, the auditors should consider consulting their legal counsel.

### Chapter Summary

This chapter explained auditing operations and the considerations and procedures involved in completing the audit. To summarize:

1. The analysis throughout the text has emphasized the need to consider revenue and expense accounts in conjunction with the audit of asset and liability accounts. However, vouching and other substantive procedures are generally necessary for revenue and expense accounts that are less directly associated with transaction cycles, such as miscellaneous revenue and selling, general, and administrative expenses.
2. Substantive procedures for payroll accounts address the overall reasonableness of payroll costs and the proper allocation of these costs to the functional areas of manufacturing, selling, and administration. In addition, tests must be performed on the allocation of manufacturing costs to work in process, finished goods, and cost of goods sold.

3. Because of their objectives, certain audit procedures cannot be completed before the end of the audit. These procedures include (*a*) search for unrecorded liabilities, (*b*) review the minutes of meetings, (*c*) perform final analytical procedures, (*d*) perform procedures to identify loss contingencies, (*e*) perform the review for subsequent events, and (*f*) obtain the representation letter.

4. The auditors must perform audit procedures to determine that loss contingencies have been properly presented and disclosed. To identify loss contingencies, auditors perform various procedures, such as reviewing minutes of directors' meetings, inquiring of the client's lawyer, reviewing correspondence with financial institutions and regulatory agencies, sending confirmations to financial institutions, and obtaining a representation letter from officers of the company.

5. Subsequent events may be classified into two broad categories: (*a*) those providing additional evidence about facts existing on or before the balance sheet date (which may require adjusting entries), and (*b*) those involving facts coming into existence after the balance sheet date (which may require note disclosures). Many of these subsequent events relate to loss contingencies, and the audit procedures involved are similar to the ones used to audit those items.

6. Also important to completing the audit are the procedures performed to evaluate audit findings and review the audit work. In evaluating audit findings, the auditors accumulate known misstatements, projected misstatements, and other estimated misstatements to determine if the aggregate results of their procedures support the fairness of the financial statements. In addition, the auditors should consider whether any audit results indicate a need to reassess the risks of material misstatement of the financial statements.

7. Auditors also have certain post-audit responsibilities. When auditors find, subsequent to the issuance of their audit report, that the financial statements are materially misleading, they should take steps to prevent continued reliance on their report. In some cases, this might involve notification of regulatory agencies.

## Key Terms Introduced or Emphasized in Chapter 16

**Analytical procedures (630)**  Evaluations of financial information made by a study of plausible relationships between financial and nonfinancial information.

**Commitment (633)**  A contractual obligation to carry out a transaction at specified terms in the future. Material commitments should be disclosed in the financial statements.

**Conservatism (620)**  An accounting doctrine for asset valuation in which the lower of two alternative acceptable asset valuations is chosen.

**Contingent liability (630)**  A possible liability, stemming from past events, that will be resolved as to existence and amount by some future event.

**Disclosure checklist (641)**  A list of specific disclosures required by the FASB, the GASB, the FASAC, and the SEC that is used to evaluate the adequacy of the disclosures in a set of financial statements.

**Emphasis of matter paragraph (643)**  A paragraph included in the auditors' report that is required by GAAS or is included at the auditors' discretion, and that refers to a matter appropriately presented or disclosed in the financial statements that, in the auditor's judgment, is of such importance that it is fundamental to users' understanding of the financial statements.

**General risk contingency (633)**  An element of the business environment that involves some risk of a future loss. Examples include the risk of accident, strike, price fluctuations, or natural catastrophe. General risk contingencies should not be disclosed in financial statements.

**Iron curtain approach (641)**  An approach to making materiality judgments that quantifies the total likely misstatement as of the current year-end based on the effects of reflecting all misstatements (including projecting misstatements where appropriate) existing in the balance sheet at the end of the current year, irrespective of whether the misstatements occurred in the current year or previous years. For example, if expenses were understated by $20,000 in the previous year and $45,000 during the current year, the iron curtain method would quantify the misstatement as $65,000. Also see *rollover approach*.

**Known misstatements (638)**  Specific misstatements identified by the auditors during the course of the audit.

**Letter of inquiry of the client's lawyer (631)**  A letter sent by auditors to a client's legal counsel requesting a description and evaluation of pending or threatened litigation, unasserted claims, and other loss contingencies. The returned letter from the lawyer is referred to as the lawyer's letter.

**Likely misstatements (638)**  Misstatements identified by the auditors during the course of the audit that are due to either extrapolation from audit evidence or differences in accounting estimates.

**Loss contingency (630)**  A possible loss, stemming from past events, that will be resolved as to existence and amount by some future event. Loss contingencies should be disclosed in notes to the financial statements if there is a reasonable possibility that a loss has been incurred. When loss contingencies are considered probable and can be reasonably estimated, they should be accrued in the accounts.

**Minutes (630)**  A formal record of the issues discussed and actions taken in meetings of stockholders and the board of directors.

**Other information (642)**  Financial and nonfinancial information (other than the financial statements and the auditors' report thereon) that is included in a document containing audited financial statements and the auditors' report thereon but is not required by a designated accounting standards setter.

**Other matter paragraph (642)**  A paragraph included in the auditors' report that refers to a matter other than those presented or disclosed in the financial statements that, in the auditors' judgment, is relevant to users' understanding of the audit, the auditors' responsibilities, or the auditors' report.

**Report release date (637)**  The date the auditors grant the client permission to use the audit report in connection with the financial statements. This is sometimes referred to as the date of issuance of the audit report.

**Representation letter (637)**  A single letter or separate letters prepared by officers of the client company at the auditors' request setting forth certain representations about the company's financial position or operations.

**Required supplementary information (642)**  Information that a designated accounting standards setter requires to accompany an entity's basic financial statements. Required supplementary information differs from other types of information outside the basic financial statements because a designated accounting standards setter considers the information an essential part of the financial reporting of certain entities and because authoritative guidelines for the measurement and presentation of the information have been established.

**Rollover approach (641)**  An approach to making materiality judgments that quantifies the total likely misstatement as of the current year-end based on the effects of reflecting misstatements (including projecting misstatements where appropriate) only during the current year. For example, if expenses were understated by $20,000 in the previous year, and $45,000 during the current year, the rollover method would quantify the misstatement as $45,000, ignoring the previous year misstatement. Also see *iron curtain approach*.

**S-1 review (637)**  Procedures carried out by auditors at the client company's facilities on or as close as practicable to the effective date of a registration statement filed under the Securities Act of 1933.

**Subsequent event (634)**  An event occurring after the date of the balance sheet but prior to completion of the audit and issuance of the audit report.

**Supplementary information (643)**  Information presented outside the basic financial statements, excluding required supplementary information, that is not considered necessary for the financial statements to be fairly presented in accordance with the applicable financial reporting framework. Such information may be presented in a document containing the audited financial statements or separate from the financial statements.

**Unasserted claim (632)**  A possible legal claim of which no potential claimant has exhibited an awareness.

## Review Questions

16–1.  Identify three revenue accounts that are verified during the audit of balance sheet accounts; also, identify the related balance sheet accounts.

16–2.  How are analytical procedures used in the verification of revenue?

16–3.  Identify three items often misclassified as miscellaneous revenue.

16–4.  Identify three expense accounts that are verified during the audit of balance sheet accounts; also, identify the related balance sheet accounts.

16–5.  For which expense accounts should the auditors obtain or prepare analyses to be used in preparation of the client's income tax returns?

16–6.  When you are first retained to audit the financial statements of Wabash Company, you inquire whether a budget is used to control costs and expenses. The controller, James Lowe, replies that he personally prepares such a budget each year, but that he regards it as a highly confidential document. He states that you may refer to it if necessary, but he wants you to make sure that no employee of the firm sees any of the budget data. Comment on this use of a budget.

16–7.　What auditing procedure can you suggest for determining the reasonableness of selling, general, and administrative expenses?

16–8.　Describe how the auditors use analytical procedures in the examination of selling, general, and administrative expenses.

16–9.　What division of duties among independent departments is desirable to achieve maximum internal control over payroll?

16–10.　What safeguards should be employed when the inaccessibility of banking facilities makes it desirable to pay employees in cash?

16–11.　You are asked by a client to outline the procedures you would recommend for handling of unclaimed wages. What procedures do you recommend?

16–12.　What specific procedures are suggested by the phrase "test of controls over payroll transactions"?

16–13.　Should the auditors make a complete review of all correspondence in the client's files? Explain.

16–14.　What is the purpose of analytical procedures performed as a part of the overall review?

16–15.　List the audit procedures that must be completed near the date of the audit report.

16–16.　What are *loss contingencies?* How are such items presented in the financial statements? Explain.

16–17.　What is the usual procedure followed by the CPA in obtaining evidence regarding pending and threatened litigation against the client?

16–18.　Explain how a loss contingency exists with respect to an *unasserted* claim. Should unasserted claims be disclosed in the financial statements?

16–19.　If the federal income tax returns for prior years have not as yet been reviewed by federal tax authorities, would you consider it necessary for the client to disclose this situation in a note to the financial statements? Explain.

16–20.　What is the meaning of the term *commitment?* Give examples. Do commitments appear in financial statements? Explain.

16–21.　What are *general risk contingencies?* Do such items require disclosure in the financial statements?

16–22.　What are *subsequent events?*

16–23.　Describe the manner in which the auditors evaluate their audit findings.

16–24.　Describe a disclosure checklist. What is its purpose?

16–25.　When the auditors have audited the financial statements, what is their responsibility with respect to other information (not including required supplemental information) included in an annual report to shareholders?

16–26.　Does incorrect required supplemental information included with audited financial statements result in a qualified or adverse audit opinion? Explain.

## Questions Requiring Analysis

**LO 7**　16–27.　In your audit of the financial statements of Wolfe Company for the year ended April 30, you find that a material account receivable is due from a company in reorganization under Chapter 11 of the Bankruptcy Act. You also learn that on May 28 several former members of the bankrupt company's management formed a new company and that the new company had issued a note to Wolfe Company that would pay off the bankrupt customer's account receivable over a four-year period. What presentation, if any, should be made of this situation in the financial statements of Wolfe Company for the year ended April 30? Explain.

**LO 6**　16–28.　During an audit engagement, Robert Wong, CPA, has satisfactorily completed an examination of accounts payable and other liabilities and now plans to determine whether there are any loss contingencies arising from litigation, claims, or assessments.

　　　　　What are the audit procedures Wong should follow with respect to the existence of loss contingencies arising from litigation, claims, or assessments? Do not discuss reporting requirements.

**LO 6, 7**　16–29.　You are the audit manager in the audit of the financial statements of Midwest Grain Storage, Inc., a new client. The company's records show that, as of the balance sheet date, approximately 15 million bushels of various grains are in storage for the Commodity Credit Corporation, an agency of the U.S. government.

In your review of the audit senior's working papers, you ascertain the following facts:

*a.* All grain is stored under a Uniform Grain Storage Agreement, which holds Midwest responsible for the quantity and quality of the grain.

*b.* Losses due to shrinkage, spoilage, and so forth are inherent in the storage of grain. Midwest's losses, however, have been negligible due to the excellence of its storage facilities.

*c.* Midwest carries a warehouseman's bond covering approximately 20 percent of the value of the stored grain.

In the loss contingencies section of the working papers, the senior auditor has made the following notation: "I propose recommending to Midwest's controller that the contingent liability for grain spoilage and shrinkage be disclosed in a note to the financial statements."

Do you concur with the senior's proposal? Explain.

**LO 1, 2, 3**  16–30.  Warren Cook, CPA, is auditing the State University Bookstore and has obtained the following summary of revenues and cost of sales from the client's computer.

|  | New Course Books | Used Course Books | Trade Books | Student Supplies | Insignia Items | Other |
|---|---|---|---|---|---|---|
| Sales | $543,400 | $234,100 | $45,500 | $63,400 | $45,300 | $34,200 |
| Cost of sales | 396,682 | 154,974 | 27,300 | 40,893 | 27,633 | 20,178 |

*a.* Calculate the gross margin for each of State University's product lines.

*b.* Compare State University's gross margins to those presented by the National Association of College Stores. Indicate any margins that appear out of line, in relation to the industry. The association statistics may be obtained at the following Internet address: www.nacs.org.

**LO 7**  16–31.  The auditor's opinion on the fairness of financial statements may be affected by subsequent events.

*Required:*

*a.* Define what is commonly referred to in auditing as a subsequent event, and describe the two general types of subsequent events.

*b.* Identify those auditing procedures that the auditor should apply at or near the completion of fieldwork to disclose significant subsequent events.

**LO 6, 7**  16–32.  Linda Reeves, CPA, receives a telephone call from her client, Lane Company. The company's controller states that the board of directors of Lane has entered into two contractual arrangements with Ted Forbes, the company's former president, who has recently retired. Under one agreement, Lane Company will pay the ex-president $7,000 per month for five years if he does not compete with the company during that time in a rival business. Under the other agreement, the company will pay the ex-president $5,000 per month for five years for such advisory services as the company may request from the ex-president.

Lane's controller asks Reeves whether the balance sheet as of the date the two agreements were signed should show $144,000 in current liabilities and $576,000 in long-term liabilities, or whether the two agreements should be disclosed in a contingencies note to the financial statements.

How should Linda Reeves reply to the controller's questions? Explain.

**LO 8**  16–33.  Justin Kealey, CPA, is auditing Tustin Companies, Inc. Kealey has accumulated known and likely misstatements for the current year to evaluate whether there is a sufficiently low risk of material misstatement of the financial statements to issue an opinion. However, Kealey notes that there are several misstatements that have been carried over from prior years.

*Required:*

*a.* Distinguish between the *iron curtain* and the *rollover* approaches to considering the misstatements from prior years.

*b.* Describe how SEC *Staff Accounting Bulletin No. 108* requires auditors to consider misstatements carried over from prior periods.

**LO 7, 9**  16–34.  On July 27, 20X0, Arthur Ward, CPA, issued an unqualified audit report on the financial statements of Dexter Company for the year ended June 30, 20X0. Two weeks later, Dexter Company mailed annual reports, including the June 30 financial statements and Ward's audit report, to 150 stockholders and to several creditors of Dexter Company. Dexter Company's stock is not actively traded on national exchanges or over the counter.

On September 5, the controller of Dexter Company informed Ward that an account payable for consulting services in the amount of $170,000 had inadvertently been omitted from Dexter's June 30 balance sheet. As a consequence, net income for the year ended June 30 was overstated by $90,500, net of applicable federal and state income taxes. Both Ward and

Dexter's controller agreed that the misstatement was material to Dexter's financial position at June 30, 20X0, and operating results for the year then ended.

What should Arthur Ward's course of action be in this matter? Discuss.

**LO 8** 16–35. Linda Tanner, CPA, is auditing the Carson Company. For the current year, Carson is presenting December 31, 20X5, financial statements with comparative financial statements for the year ended December 31, 20X4. In the prior year audit, Linda identified an understatement of prepaid expenses of $100,000 at December 31, 20X4, that was not corrected. In the current year, Linda found that prepaid expenses were understated by another $50,000 at December 31, 20X5.

*Required:*

a. Using the *iron curtain* approach, describe how Tanner would consider whether an adjustment is required.

b. Using the *rollover* approach, describe how Tanner would consider whether an adjustment is required.

c. Describe what SEC *Staff Accounting Bulletin No. 108* requires in this situation.

# Objective Questions

**All applicable questions are available with McGraw-Hill's *Connect*™ *Accounting*. ■connect** |ACCOUNTING

16–36. **Multiple Choice Questions**

Select the best answer for each of the following and give reasons for your choice:

**LO 5**
a. Which of the following is *least* likely to be considered a substantive procedure relating to payroll?

(1) Investigate fluctuations in salaries, wages, and commissions.

(2) Test computations of compensation under profit sharing for bonus plans.

(3) Test commission earnings.

(4) Test whether employee time reports are approved by supervisors.

**LO 5**
b. Which of the following is the *best* way for the auditors to determine that every name on a company's payroll is that of a bona fide employee presently on the job?

(1) Examine human resources records for accuracy and completeness.

(2) Examine employees' names listed on payroll tax returns for agreement with payroll accounting records.

(3) Make a surprise observation of the company's regular distribution of paychecks on a test basis.

(4) Visit the working areas and verify that employees exist by examining their badge or identification numbers.

**LO 6**
c. As a result of analytical procedures, the independent auditors determine that the gross profit percentage has declined from 30 percent in the preceding year to 20 percent in the current year. The auditors should:

(1) Express an opinion that is qualified due to the inability of the client company to continue as a going concern.

(2) Evaluate management's performance in causing this decline.

(3) Require note disclosure.

(4) Consider the possibility of a misstatement in the financial statements.

**LO 5**
d. When auditing the statement of cash flows, which of the following would an auditor *not* expect to be a source of receipts and payments?

(1) Capitalization.

(2) Financing.

(3) Investing.

(4) Operations.

**LO 6**
e. The search for unrecorded liabilities for a public company includes procedures usually performed through the:

(1) Day the audit report is issued.

(2) End of the client's year.

(3) Date of the auditors' report.

(4) Date the report is filed with the SEC.

**LO 8**　　*f.* The aggregated misstatement in the financial statements is made up of:

| | Known Misstatements | Projected Misstatements | Other Misstatements |
|---|---|---|---|
| (1) | Yes | Yes | Yes |
| (2) | Yes | Yes | No |
| (3) | No | Yes | No |
| (4) | No | Yes | Yes |

**LO 6**　　*g.* A possible loss, stemming from past events that will be resolved as to existence and amounts, is referred to as a(n):

(1) Analytical process.

(2) Loss contingency.

(3) Probable loss.

(4) Unasserted claim.

**LO 7**　　*h.* Which of the following is most likely to be considered a Type 1 subsequent event?

(1) A business combination completed after year-end, but for which negotiations began prior to year-end.

(2) A strike subsequent to year-end due to employee complaints about working conditions which originated two years ago.

(3) Customer checks deposited prior to year-end, but determined to be uncollectible after year-end.

(4) Introduction of a new line of products after year-end for which major research had been completed prior to year-end.

**LO 6**　　*i.* An auditor accepted an engagement to audit the 20X8 financial statements of EFG Corporation and began the fieldwork on September 30, 20X8. EFG gave the auditor the 20X8 financial statements on January 17, 20X9. The auditor completed the audit on February 10, 20X9, and delivered the report on February 16, 20X9. The client's representation letter normally would be dated:

(1) December 31, 20X8.

(2) January 17, 20X9.

(3) February 10, 20X9.

(4) February 16, 20X9.

**LO 8**　　*j.* Which of the following procedures is most likely to be included in the final review stage of an audit?

(1) Obtain an understanding of internal control.

(2) Confirmation of receivables.

(3) Observation of inventory.

(4) Perform analytical procedures.

**LO 9**　　*k.* Subsequent to the issuance of the auditor's report, the auditor became aware of facts existing at the report date that would have affected the report had the auditor then been aware of such facts. After determining that the information is reliable, the auditor should next:

(1) Notify the board of directors that the auditor's report must no longer be associated with the financial statements.

(2) Determine whether there are persons relying or likely to rely on the financial statements who would attach importance to the information.

(3) Request that management disclose the effects of the newly discovered information by adding a footnote to subsequently issued financial statements.

(4) Issue revised pro forma financial statements taking into consideration the newly discovered information.

**LO 7**

*l.* Which of the following events occurring on January 5, 20X2, is most likely to result in an adjusting entry to the 20X1 financial statements?

(1) A business combination.

(2) Early retirement of bonds payable.

(3) Settlement of litigation.

(4) Plant closure due to a strike.

**LO 7** 16–37. In connection with your audit of the financial statements of Hollis Mfg. Corporation for the year ended December 31, 20X3, your review of subsequent events disclosed the following items:

*a.* January 7, 20X4: The mineral content of a shipment of ore en route to Hollis Mfg. Corporation on December 31, 20X3, was determined to be 72 percent. The shipment was recorded at year-end at an estimated content of 50 percent by a debit to Raw Materials Inventory and a credit to Accounts Payable in the amount of $82,400. The final liability to the vendor is based on the actual mineral content of the shipment.

*b.* January 15, 20X4: Following a series of personal disagreements between Ray Hollis, the president, and his brother-in-law, the treasurer, the latter resigned, effective immediately, under an agreement whereby the corporation would purchase his 10 percent stock ownership at book value as of December 31, 20X3. Payment is to be made in two equal amounts in cash on April 1 and October 1, 20X4. In December, the treasurer had obtained a divorce from his wife, who is Ray Hollis's sister.

*c.* January 16, 20X4: As a result of reduced sales, production was curtailed in mid-January and some workers were laid off.

*d.* On January 18, 20X4, a major customer filed for bankruptcy. The customer's financial condition had been degenerating over recent years.

*e.* On January 28, 20X4, a famous analyst who followed the industry provided a negative report on his expectations concerning the short and intermediate term for the industry.

*Required:* For each of the subsequent events, indicate whether they should result in:

Adjustment—an adjusting entry as of 20X3.

Disclosure—note disclosure as of 20X3.

No Disclosure—no disclosure as of 20X3.

(AICPA, adapted)

**LO 7** 16–38. In connection with her audit of the financial statements of Flowmeter, Inc., for the year ended December 31, 20X3, Joan Hirsch, CPA, is aware that certain events and transactions that have taken place after December 31, 20X3, but before she has issued her report dated February 28, 20X4, may affect the company's financial statements.

The following material events or transactions have come to her attention:

*a.* On January 3, 20X4, Flowmeter, Inc., received a shipment of raw materials from Canada. The materials had been ordered in October 20X3 and shipped FOB shipping point in December 20X3.

*b.* On January 15, 20X4, the company settled and paid a personal injury claim of a former employee as the result of an accident that had occurred in March 20X3. The company had not previously recorded a liability for the claim.

*c.* On January 25, 20X4, the company agreed to purchase for cash the outstanding stock of Porter Electrical Co. The business combination is likely to double the sales volume of Flowmeter, Inc.

*d.* On February 1, 20X4, a plant owned by Flowmeter, Inc., was damaged by a flood, resulting in an uninsured loss of inventory.

*e.* On February 5, 20X4, Flowmeter, Inc., issued to an underwriting syndicate $2 million in convertible bonds.

*Required:* For each of the subsequent events, indicate whether they should result in:

Adjustment—an adjusting entry as of 20X3.

Disclosure—note disclosure as of 20X3.

No Disclosure—no disclosure as of 20X3.

(AICPA, adapted)

**LO 6, 7, 8, 9**    16–39.    Match the following terms to the appropriate definition (or partial definition). Each definition is used once.

| Term | Definition (or Partial Definition) |
|---|---|
| a. Commitment<br>b. Contingent liability<br>c. General risk contingency<br>d. Iron curtain approach<br>e. Known misstatements<br>f. Likely misstatements<br>g. Loss contingency<br>h. Rollover approach | 1. A contractual obligation to carry out a transaction at specified terms in the future. Material commitments should be disclosed in the financial statements.<br>2. A possible liability, stemming from past events, that will be resolved as to existence and amount by some future event.<br>3. A possible loss, stemming from past events, that will be resolved as to existence and amount by some future event.<br>4. An approach to making materiality judgments that quantifies the total likely misstatement as of the current year-end based on the effects of reflecting all misstatements (including projecting misstatements where appropriate) existing in the balance sheet at the end of the current year, irrespective of whether the misstatements occurred in the current year or previous years.<br>5. An approach to making materiality judgments that quantifies the total likely misstatement as of the current year-end based on the effects of reflecting misstatements (including projecting misstatements where appropriate) only during the current year.<br>6. An element of the business environment that involves some risk of a future loss. Examples include the risk of accident, strike, price fluctuations, or natural catastrophe. General risk contingencies should not be disclosed in financial statements.<br>7. Misstatements identified by the auditors during the course of the audit that are due to either extrapolation from audit evidence or differences in accounting estimates.<br>8. Specific misstatements identified by the auditors during the course of the audit. |

## Problems

All applicable problems are available with McGraw-Hill's *Connect*™ *Accounting.* **connect** |ACCOUNTING

**LO 1, 3**    16–40.    Rita King, your staff assistant on the April 30, 20X2, audit of Maxwell Company, was transferred to another assignment before she could prepare a proposed adjusting journal entry for Maxwell's Miscellaneous Revenue account, which she had analyzed per the working paper given on the next page. You have reviewed the working paper and are satisfied with King's procedures. You are convinced that all the miscellaneous revenue items should be transferred to other accounts. Maxwell Company's state of incorporation has an Unclaimed Properties Law.

Draft a proposed adjusting journal entry at April 30, 20X2, for Maxwell Company's Miscellaneous Revenue account.

**LO 1, 2, 3**    16–41.    Your client is a company that owns a shopping center with 30 store tenants. All leases with the store tenants provide for a fixed rent plus a percentage of sales, net of sales taxes, in excess of a fixed dollar amount computed on an annual basis. Each lease also provides that the lessor may engage CPAs to audit all records of the tenant for assurance that sales are being properly reported to the lessor.

You have been requested by your client to audit the records of Traders Restaurant to determine that the sales totaling $390,000 for the year ended December 31, 20X2, have been properly reported to the lessor. The restaurant and the shopping center entered into a five-year lease on January 1, 20X1. Traders Restaurant offers only table service; no liquor is served. During mealtimes, there are four or five waiters and waitresses in attendance who prepare handwritten prenumbered restaurant checks for the customers. Payment is made at a cash register, operated by the proprietor, as the customer leaves. All sales are for cash. The proprietor also is the accountant. Complete files are kept of restaurant checks and cash register tapes. A daily sales journal and general ledger are also maintained.

*Required:*    List the auditing procedures that you would employ to verify the total annual sales of Traders Restaurant.

(AICPA, adapted)

```
                              Maxwell Company
Acct. No. 430              Miscellaneous Revenue                    Q-2
                          Year Ended April 30, 20X2
                                                    C.M.
                                                    May 19, X2

Date              Description                   Reference      Amount

May 8, 20X1,      Proceeds of sale of scrap from    Various CR    $5,843 Y
through           manufacturing process (total of
April 7, 20X2     12 monthly sales)

July 18, 20X1     Write-off of old outstanding checks;   GJ 7-4     1,100 Y
                  nos. 118—$500; 214—$400; 407—$200

Sept. 22, 20X1    Recovery of previously written off     CR 9-1     4,381 Y
                  account receivable from Wilson
                  Company

Feb. 6, 20X2      Cash proceeds from sale of machine.     CR 2-1     3,500 Y
                  Cost of $10,000 and accumulated
                  depreciation of $8,000 as of Feb. 6,
                  X2, not removed from accounts

April 28, 20X2    Refund of premium overcharge on        CR 4-1       600 Y
                  fire insurance policy no. 1856,
                  for period April 1, 20X2—Mar. 31, 20X3

April 30, 20X2    Balance per ledger                              $15,424
```

*Y—Traced to cash receipts journal or general journal;
vouched to appropriate supporting documents.*

R.A.K.
May 18, X2

**LO 4, 5** 16–42. The following are typical questions that might appear on an internal control questionnaire for payroll activities:

1. Is there adequate separation of duties between employees who maintain human resources records and employees who approve payroll disbursements?

2. Is there adequate separation of duties between personnel who maintain timekeeping or attendance records for employees and employees who distribute payroll checks?

*Required:*

a. Describe the purpose of each of the above controls.

b. Describe the manner in which each of the above controls might be tested.

c. Assuming that the operating effectiveness of each of the above controls is found to be inadequate, describe how the auditors might alter their substantive procedures to compensate for the increased level of control risk.

**LO 4, 5** 16–43. In connection with an audit of the financial statements of Olympia Company, the auditors are reviewing procedures for accumulating direct labor-hours. They learn that all production is by job order and that all employees are paid hourly wages, with time and a half for overtime hours.

Olympia's direct labor-hour input process for payroll and job-cost determination is summarized in the flowchart that is illustrated next. Steps A and C are performed in timekeeping, step B in the factory operating departments, step D in payroll audit and control, step E in data input, and step F in computer operations.

*Required:*

For each input processing step A through F:

a. List the possible errors or discrepancies that may occur.

b. Cite the corresponding control that should be in effect for each error or discrepancy.

Note: Your discussion of Olympia's procedures should be limited to the input for direct labor-hours, as shown in steps A through F in the flowchart. Do not discuss human resources procedures for hiring, promotion, termination, and pay-rate authorization. In step F, do not discuss equipment, computer program, and general computer controls.

Organize your answer for each input-processing step as follows:

| Step | Possible Misstatements or Discrepancies | Control |
|------|------------------------------------------|---------|
| A |  |  |

(AICPA, adapted)

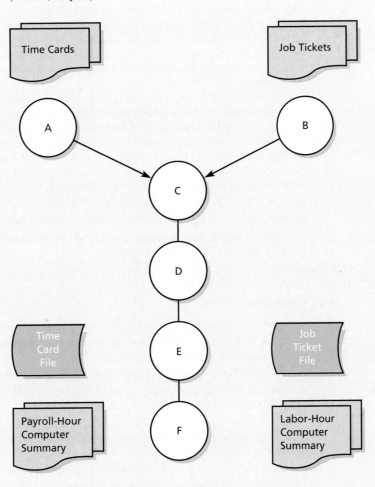

**LO 4** 16–44. Rowe Manufacturing Company has about 50 production employees and uses the following payroll procedures.

The factory supervisor interviews applicants and on the basis of the interview either hires or rejects the applicants. After being employed, the applicant prepares a W-4 form (Employee's Withholding Exemption Certificate) and gives it to the supervisor. The supervisor writes the hourly rate of pay for the new employee in the corner of the W-4 form and then gives the form to a payroll clerk as notice that the applicant has been employed. The supervisor verbally advises the payroll department of pay-rate adjustments.

A supply of blank time cards is kept in a box near the entrance to the factory. Each employee takes a time card on Monday morning, signs it, and notes in pencil on the time card the daily arrival and departure times. At the end of the week, the employees drop the time cards in a box near the door to the factory.

The completed time cards are taken from the box on Monday morning by a payroll clerk. Two payroll clerks divide the cards alphabetically between them, one taking the A–L section of the payroll and the other taking the M–Z section. Each clerk is fully responsible for one section of the payroll. The payroll clerks compute the gross pay, deductions, and net pay; post the details to the employees' earnings records; and prepare and number the payroll checks. Employees are automatically removed from the payroll when they fail to turn in time cards.

The payroll checks are manually signed by the chief accountant and given to the supervisor, who distributes the checks to the employees in the factory and arranges for the delivery of the checks to the employees who are absent. The payroll bank account is reconciled by the chief accountant, who also prepares the various quarterly and annual payroll tax reports.

*Required:*    List your suggestions for improving Rowe Manufacturing Company's internal control over factory hiring practices and payroll.

(AICPA, adapted)

**LO 4, 5**    16–45.    City Loan Company has 100 branch loan offices. Each office has a manager and four or five employees who are hired by the manager. Branch managers prepare the weekly payroll, including their own salaries, and pay employees from cash on hand. The employees sign the payroll sheet signifying receipt of their salary. Hours worked by hourly personnel are inserted in the payroll sheet from time reports prepared by the employees and approved by the manager.

The weekly payroll sheets are sent to the home office, along with other accounting statements and reports. The home office compiles employee earnings records and prepares all federal and state payroll tax returns from the weekly payroll sheets.

Salaries are established by home office job-evaluation schedules. Salary adjustments, promotions, and transfers of full-time employees are approved by a home office salary committee based upon the recommendations of branch managers and area supervisors. Branch managers advise the salary committee of new full-time employees and terminations. Part-time and temporary employees are hired without referral to the salary committee.

*Required:*    *a.*    How might funds for payroll be diverted in the above system?

*b.*    Prepare a payroll internal audit program to be used in the home office to audit the branch office payrolls of City Loan Company.

(AICPA, adapted)

**LO 4**    16–46.    The following "conditions" are excerpts from a report of an operational audit of a company's human resources department:

*Condition I:* The company's payroll is prepared by the human resources department.

*Condition II:* The firm's human resources manager is the proprietor's son, who has one year of experience in the human resources field.

*Condition III:* The distribution of payroll checks is made by the human resources department.

*Condition IV:* The human resources department makes a quarterly test of all personnel records to be assured that all required documentation is present.

*Condition V:* Personnel hiring is initiated by the human resources department only upon the receipt of a request from the user department. The request must be signed by the user department manager or assistant manager.

*Condition VI:* When documentation supporting a particular human resources action is received by the human resources department, a human resources clerk is assigned the task of making the appropriate changes on the file or files affected. No one, at any time, is assigned the task of verifying that the entries are correctly transcribed.

The internal auditor is preparing a "recommendations" section for the report. The following controls are to be used: (1) competence and integrity of personnel, (2) segregation of incompatible functions, (3) execution of activities, (4) proper recording of events, (5) appropriate limitation of access to assets, and (6) comparison of existing records with records required. The internal auditor notes that one of the controls is addressed by each of the six conditions identified.

*Required:*    *a.*    Identify the control most directly addressed, using one policy or procedure per condition with no repeats.

*b.*    State whether or not that control is violated by the condition.

*c.*    If the control is violated, describe the possible consequences of any such violation.

*d.*    If the control is violated, prescribe one corrective action for any such violation. Use the format shown next.

| Condition | a. Control (1)–(6) | b. Violated? | c. Possible Consequences | d. Corrective Action Needed |
|---|---|---|---|---|
| I. | | | | |
| II. | | | | |
| III. | | | | |
| IV. | | | | |
| V. | | | | |
| VI. | | | | |

(AICPA, adapted)

**LO 7**  16–47.  Robertson Company had accounts receivable of $200,000 at December 31, 20X0, and had provided an allowance for uncollectible accounts of $6,000. After performing all normal auditing procedures relating to the receivables and to the valuation allowance, the independent auditors were satisfied that this asset was fairly stated and that the allowance for uncollectible accounts was adequate. Just before completion of the audit fieldwork late in February, however, the auditors learned that the entire plant of Thompson Corporation, a major customer, had been destroyed by a flood early in February and that as a result Thompson Corporation was hopelessly insolvent.

The account receivable from Thompson Corporation in the amount of $44,000 originated on December 28; terms of payment were net 60 days. The receivable had been regarded as entirely collectible at December 31, and the auditors had so considered it in reaching their conclusion as to the adequacy of the allowance for uncollectible accounts. In discussing the news concerning the flood, the controller of Robertson Company emphasized to the auditors that the probable loss of $44,000 should be regarded as a loss of the following year, and not of 20X0, the year under audit.

What action, if any, should the auditors recommend with respect to the receivable from Thompson Corporation?

**In-Class Team Case**

**LO 8**  16–48.  The audit staff of Adams, Barnes & Co. (ABC), CPAs, reported the following audit findings in their audit of Keystone Computers & Networks (KCN), Inc.:

1. Unrecorded liabilities in the amount of $6,440 for purchases of inventory. These inventory items were counted and included in the year-end total.

2. Projected misstatement from confirmation of accounts receivable in the amount of $2,042 understatement.

3. Projected misstatement from price tests of inventory of $9,510 overstatement.

4. The staff of ABC believes that the amount of KCN's allowance for uncollectible accounts should be increased by $5,000.

In addition, the audit staff has decided that for evaluating a material misstatement of the financial statements, the following guidelines should be used:

Current assets—$50,000

Noncurrent assets—$75,000

Current liabilities—$50,000

Noncurrent liabilities—$75,000

Total owners' equity—$100,000

Net income before taxes—$65,000

*Required:*  *a.*  Prepare a schedule modeled after Figure 16.5 on page 640 to be used to evaluate the above audit findings, assuming that KCN's marginal tax rate is 25 percent.

*b.*  Decide whether the results indicate that there is a sufficiently low risk of material misstatement to justify ABC's audit opinion.

**Research and Discussion Case**

**LO 6, 8**  16–49.  Marshall and Wyatt, CPAs, has been the independent auditor of Interstate Land Development Corporation for several years. During these years, Interstate prepared and filed its own annual income tax returns.

During 20X4, Interstate requested Marshall and Wyatt to audit all the necessary financial statements of the corporation to be submitted to the Securities and Exchange Commission (SEC) in connection with a multistate public offering of 1 million shares of Interstate common stock.

This public offering came under the provisions of the Securities Act of 1933. The audit was performed carefully and the financial statements were fairly presented for the respective periods. These financial statements were included in the registration statement filed with the SEC.

While the registration statement was being processed by the SEC, but before the effective date, the Internal Revenue Service (IRS) obtained a federal court subpoena directing Marshall and Wyatt to turn over all its working papers relating to Interstate for the years 20X1–20X4. Marshall and Wyatt initially refused to comply for two reasons. First, Marshall and Wyatt did not prepare Interstate's tax returns. Second, Marshall and Wyatt claimed that the working papers were confidential matters subject to the privileged communications rule. Subsequently, however, Marshall and Wyatt did relinquish the subpoenaed working papers.

Upon receiving the subpoena, Wyatt called Dunkirk, the chairman of Interstate's board of directors, and asked him about the IRS investigation. Dunkirk responded, "I'm sure the IRS people are on a fishing expedition and that they will not find any material deficiencies."

A few days later Dunkirk received a written memorandum from the IRS stating that it was contending Interstate had underpaid its taxes during the period under review. The memorandum revealed that Interstate was being assessed $800,000, including penalties and interest for the three years. Dunkirk forwarded a copy of this memorandum to Marshall and Wyatt. This $800,000 assessment was material relative to the financial statements as of December 31, 20X4. The amount for each year individually, exclusive of penalty and interest, was not material relative to each respective year.

*Required:*

a. In general terms, discuss the extent to which a CPA firm's potential liability to third parties is increased in an SEC registration audit.

b. Discuss the implications of the IRS investigation, if any, relative to Marshall and Wyatt's examination of Interstate's 20X4 financial statements. Discuss any additional investigative procedures that the auditors should undertake or any audit judgments that should be made as a result of this investigation.

c. Can Marshall and Wyatt validly refuse to surrender the subpoenaed working papers to the IRS? Explain.

(AICPA, adapted)

## Suggested References

*Part a:*
This textbook, pp. 114–116.

*Part b:*
This textbook, pp. 634–637.
AICPA, Professional Standards, Statements on Auditing Standards, AU section 560.
*FASB Accounting Standard Codification* section 450-20, "Loss Contingencies."

*Part c:*
This textbook, pp. 87–88 and 159–161.

# Auditors' Reports

Expressing an independent and expert opinion on the fairness of financial statements is the most frequently performed attestation service rendered by the public accounting profession. This opinion, which is expressed in the auditors' report, provides users of financial statements with an opinion on whether the statements are in conformity with the appropriate financial reporting framework, most frequently generally accepted accounting principles.

In Chapter 2, we saw that the auditors' **standard report** states that the audit was performed in conformity with generally accepted auditing standards and expresses an opinion that the client's financial statements are presented fairly in conformity with generally accepted accounting principles. However, auditors *cannot* issue the standard report if:

- There are conditions, although not departures from GAAP, about which the readers of the financial statements should be informed (e.g., a lack of consistent application of GAAP).
- There are material departures from GAAP in the client's financial statements.
- The auditors are unable to obtain sufficient appropriate audit evidence (e.g., due to client not retaining certain important records).

Instead, they must alter their report to communicate those matters.

In this chapter, we describe the different types of audit reports that auditors issue in various circumstances. Their goal in reporting is to present clearly the nature of the audit and their opinion on the financial statements.

## Financial Statements and Standard Unmodified Audit Reports

Because we are discussing audit reports on financial statements, we first briefly provide an overview of financial statements, including disclosures. Next, we discuss in detail the standard unmodified audit reports included in AICPA Auditing Standards Board and Public Company Accounting Oversight Board professional standards.

**Financial Statements**

Auditors most frequently report upon a complete set of financial statements: that is, the balance sheet, the income statement, the statement of retained earnings, and the statement of cash flows and related notes.[1] In some cases, the statement of retained earnings is either expanded to a statement of stockholders' equity or combined with the income

[1] As is discussed in further detail in Chapter 19, an auditor may report on less than the complete set of financial statements. Thus, for example, an auditor could issue an audit report with an opinion on a balance sheet alone. One issue that complicates matters is a GAAP requirement that when a company presents a balance sheet and an income statement, it must also present a statement of cash flows; if a statement of cash flows is omitted in this situation, a departure from GAAP exists.

## Learning objectives

After studying this chapter, you should be able to:

LO1   Describe the standard audit report for non-public entity (nonissuer) audits.

LO2   Describe the standard audit report for public entity (issuer) audits.

LO3   Identify the circumstances that result in audit reports with emphasis of matter paragraphs and unmodified opinions.

LO4   Identify the circumstances that result in modified audit opinions.

LO5   Describe the auditors' responsibilities for reporting on comparative financial statements.

statement. Financial statements generally are presented in comparative form for the current year and one or more preceding years. The financial statements for a parent corporation usually are consolidated with those of the subsidiaries. In the United States, these financial statements are most frequently prepared following the **general-purpose framework** referred to as *accounting principles generally accepted in the United States of America.*[2]

## Financial Statement Disclosures

The purpose of notes to financial statements is to properly disclose information required by generally accepted accounting principles that cannot be adequately conveyed on the face of the financial statements. Adequate disclosure in the notes to the financial statements is necessary for the auditors to issue an unmodified opinion on the financial statements.

The Financial Accounting Standards Board (FASB), the Government Accounting Standards Board (GASB), the Federal Accounting Standards Advisory Board (FASAB), and the Securities and Exchange Commission (SEC) have issued numerous pronouncements that have added extensive disclosure requirements. Examples of these requirements include the disclosure of significant accounting policies, accounting changes, loss contingencies, and lease and post-retirement benefit information.

In evaluating financial reporting disclosures, the auditors should keep in mind that disclosures are meant to *supplement* the information on the face of the financial statements—not *correct* improper financial statement presentation. Thus, a note or supplementary schedule, no matter how skillfully drafted, does not compensate for the erroneous presentation of an item in the financial statements.

## Comparative Financial Statements

**Comparative financial statements** are financial statements for one or more prior periods, included for comparison with the financial statements of the current period. Comparative financial statements allow users to identify changes and trends in the financial position and operating results of a company over an extended period, and thus are more useful to investors and creditors than are financial statements for a single period. Publicly owned companies are required to include in their annual reports the balance sheets for each of the last two years and the related statements of income, retained earnings, and cash flows for each of the last three years. The auditors' report covers all financial statements that are presented. Later in this chapter, we will describe in detail the auditors' reporting responsibilities when management presents comparative financial statements.

## The Auditors' Standard Report— Nonpublic Clients

Chapter 2 includes a standard audit report on the audit of a nonpublic company's financial statements for two years. The following is a nonpublic company standard unmodified report on financial statements for one year (*AICPA* AU 700):

**LO1**

Describe the standard audit report for nonpublic entity (nonissuer) audits.

---

### Independent Auditors' Report

To the Board of Directors and Stockholders of ABC Company:

    We have audited the accompanying consolidated financial statements of ABC Company and its subsidiaries, which comprise the consolidated balance sheet as of December 31, 20X1, and the related consolidated statements of income, changes in stockholders' equity and cash flows for the year then ended, and the related notes to the financial statements.

*Management's Responsibility for the Financial Statement*

Management is responsible for the preparation and fair presentation of these consolidated financial statements in accordance with accounting principles generally accepted in the United

---

[2] While financial statements may be prepared using a number of financial reporting frameworks other than GAAP (e.g., *International Financial Reporting Standards, Cash Basis, Tax Basis*), throughout this chapter we will ordinarily just refer to GAAP unless a distinction relating to another framework is being made.

States of America; this includes the design, implementation, and maintenance of internal control relevant to the preparation and fair presentation of consolidated financial statements that are free from material misstatement, whether due to fraud or error.

*Auditors' Responsibility*

Our responsibility is to express an opinion on these consolidated financial statements based on our audit. We conducted our audit in accordance with auditing standards generally accepted in the United States of America. Those standards require that we plan and perform the audit to obtain reasonable assurance about whether the consolidated financial statements are free of material misstatement.

An audit involves performing procedures to obtain audit evidence about the amounts and disclosures in the consolidated financial statement. The procedures selected depend on the auditors' judgment, including the assessment of the risks of material misstatement of the consolidated financial statements, whether due to fraud or error. In making those risk assessments, the auditor considers internal control relevant to the entity's preparation and fair presentation of the consolidated financial statements in order to design audit procedures that are appropriate in the circumstances, but not for the purpose of expressing an opinion on the effectiveness of the entity's internal control. Accordingly, we express no such opinion. An audit also includes evaluating the appropriateness of accounting policies used and the reasonableness of significant accounting estimates made by management, as well as evaluating the overall presentation of the consolidated financial statements.

We believe that the audit evidence we have obtained is sufficient and appropriate to provide a basis for our audit opinion.

*Opinion*

In our opinion, the consolidated financial statements referred to above present fairly, in all material respects, the financial position of ABC Company and its subsidiaries as of December 31, 20X1, and the results of their operations and their cash flows for the year then ended in accordance with accounting principles generally accepted in the United States of America.

Phoenix, Arizona
February 5, 20X2

*Williams & Co., LLP*

---

Before continuing, notice several details about this report. It has a title that includes the word *independent.* It is addressed to those for whom it is prepared, generally the audited company itself or to those charged with governance. After the introductory paragraph, the report is divided into sections with headings.

The introductory paragraph of the auditors' report identifies the financial statements that have been audited. The section heading of *Management's Responsibility for the Financial Statement* indicates that management is responsible for the preparation and fair presentation of the financial statements, in accordance with generally accepted accounting principles (or another **financial reporting framework** such as cash basis, if appropriate) and its responsibility for internal control. The *Auditors' Responsibility* section includes three paragraphs that (1) indicate that it is the auditors' responsibility to express an opinion on the financial statements based on an audit conducted in accordance with generally accepted auditing standards, (2) outline the nature of an audit, and (3) conclude that the auditors believe that sufficient appropriate audit evidence has been obtained to provide a basis for the audit opinion. Finally, the *Opinion Section* presents the auditors' opinion on whether the financial statements are presented fairly in conformity with accounting principles generally accepted in the United States.[3]

---

[3] Auditors sometimes have reporting responsibilities related to other legal and regulatory requirements. For example, for audits performed under *Government Auditing Standards,* the auditors may be required to report on internal control over financial reporting and on compliance with laws, regulations, and other matters. It is when the relevant law or regulation requires or permits the auditors to report within the auditors' report on the financial statements that this becomes relevant. In such a situation, the overall report is divided as described below:

- *Report on Financial Statements.* This heading is added above the introductory paragraph.
- *Report on Other Legal and Regulatory Requirements.* This heading and the related report follow the opinion paragraph on the financial statements.

Note that this treatment is not applicable for emphasis of matter or other matter paragraphs added to an audit report and is not required by the PCAOB.

Historically, audit reports referred simply to generally accepted auditing standards and generally accepted accounting principles. Today, however, a number of nations have their own *generally accepted* standards (principles), and those standards generally differ from one another. To reduce confusion, audit reports issued in the United States now use terms such as "generally accepted auditing standards (United States of America)" or "auditing standards generally accepted in the United States of America." A similar modification is made relating to generally accepted accounting principles. For simplicity's sake, in our text discussion, we often will use the simpler historical terms or their abbreviations "GAAP" and "GAAS."

Notice that the audit report is signed with the name of the CPA firm, not the name of an individual partner in the firm. This signature stresses that it is the firm, not the individual, that takes responsibility for the audit report. If the CPA is practicing under his or her own name as a sole practitioner, the report is signed with the CPA's personal signature. In addition, a sole practitioner should use *I* instead of *we* in the audit report.[4]

Also notice the date under the signature. The auditors' report should not be dated earlier than the date on which the auditors have obtained sufficient appropriate audit evidence to support their opinion on the financial statements. Sufficient appropriate audit evidence has been obtained when all audit documentation has been reviewed, the financial statements (including notes) are prepared, and management has asserted that they have taken responsibility for these financial statements (ordinarily through a representation letter). The date of the audit report is quite significant because the auditors have a responsibility to perform procedures through that date to search for any subsequent events that may affect the fairness of the client's financial statements (see Chapter 16), and due to requirements relating to changes in documentation that arise after that date (see Chapter 5).

An auditors' report with an unmodified opinion may be issued only when the auditors have obtained sufficient appropriate audit evidence to conclude that the financial statements, as a whole, are not materially misstated.

## The Auditors' Standard Report— Public Clients

**LO2**

Describe the standard audit report for public entity (issuer) audits.

The following is an example of a standard audit report for audits of public companies.

---

**Report of Independent Registered Public Accounting Firm**

To the Board of Directors and Stockholders of Southwest Airlines Co.:

We have audited the accompanying consolidated balance sheets of Southwest Airlines Co. as of December 31, 2010 and 2009, and the related consolidated statement of income, stockholders' equity, and cash flows for each of the three years in the period ended December 31, 2010. These financial statements are the responsibility of the Company's management. Our responsibility is to express an opinion on these financial statements based on our audits.

We conducted our audits in accordance with the standards of the Public Company Accounting Oversight Board (United States). Those standards require that we plan and perform the audit to obtain reasonable assurance about whether the financial statements are free of material misstatement. An audit includes examining, on a test basis, evidence supporting the amounts and disclosures in the financial statements. An audit also includes assessing the accounting principles used and significant estimates made by management, as well as evaluating the overall financial statement presentation. We believe that our audits provide a reasonable basis for our opinion.

---

[4] Section ISA 700 of the *International Standards on Auditing* allows the signature to be that of the audit firm, the personal name of the auditor who directed the audit, or both, as appropriate for the particular jurisdiction.

In our opinion, the financial statements referred to herein present fairly, in all material respects, the consolidated financial position of Southwest Airlines Co. at December 31, 2010 and 2009, and the consolidated results of its operations and its cash flows for each of the three years in the period ended December 31, 2010, in conformity with U.S. generally accepted accounting principles.

We also have audited, in accordance with the standards of the Public Company Accounting Oversight Board (United States), Southwest Airlines Co.'s internal control over financial reporting as of December 31, 2010, based on criteria established in the Internal Control-Integrated Framework issued by the Committee of Sponsoring Organizations of the Treadway Commission, and our report dated January 29, 2011, expressed an unmodified opinion thereon.

*Ernst & Young, LLP*

Dallas, Texas
January 29, 2011

There are a number of differences between this PCAOB audit report and the report used for audits of nonpublic companies. The primary differences are that the PCAOB report:

- Includes the words "Registered" in the title.
- References standards of the PCAOB rather than generally accepted auditing standards.
- Includes less detailed discussions of management and auditor responsibilities.
- Includes an additional paragraph indicating that the auditors have also issued a report on the client's internal control over financial reporting. (For a description of audits of internal control over reporting, see Chapters 7 and 18.)
- Does not include section headings.

We will now turn our attention to modifications of auditors' standard reports. Although our illustrations are for audit reports of nonpublic companies, they require few or no changes to be used for the PCAOB audit report.

## Expression of an Opinion

The options when expressing an opinion on financial statements may be summarized as being either **unmodified** or **modified** as follows:

**Unmodified Opinions**

- *Unmodified opinion—standard report.* This report may be issued only when the auditors have obtained sufficient appropriate audit evidence to conclude that the financial statements, taken as a whole, are not materially misstated and there is no need to add an **emphasis of matter paragraph,** an **other matter paragraph** or to indicate a group audit situation.[5]
- *Unmodified opinion with an emphasis of matter paragraph.* An emphasis of matter paragraph in an audit report follows the opinion paragraph and is included to refer to a matter that is appropriately presented or disclosed in the financial statements but is being emphasized through the audit report. In certain circumstances, an emphasis of matter paragraph is required (e.g., when there is substantial doubt about a company's ability to continue as a going concern and when the company changes accounting principles). In others, it is included at the auditors' discretion (e.g., an uncertainty relating to future exceptional litigation, significant transactions with related parties, or unusually important subsequent events).

[5] PCAOB standards use the term "unqualified" rather than "unmodified." In 2010, the AICPA Auditing Standards Board switched from using "unqualified" to align its terminology with *International Standards on Auditing.*

- *Unmodified opinion with an other matter paragraph.* An other matter paragraph in an audit report follows the opinion paragraph (and any emphasis of matter paragraph) and refers to a matter *other than* those presented or disclosed in the audited financial statements. The matter is, in the auditors' judgment, relevant to users' understanding of the audit, the auditors' responsibilities, or the auditors' report. These may arise in a variety of circumstances, including those presented in Chapter 16, relating to other information in documents containing audited financial statements and required supplementary information. Also, as discussed in Chapter 19, an other matter paragraph is added when financial statements are prepared in accordance with special-purpose frameworks. In this chapter, we discuss other matter paragraphs used to (1) report on comparative statements when there are predecessor auditors and (2) alert readers about the intended use of an audit report when it is not for general use.

- *Unmodified opinion on group financial statements.* This circumstance involves a situation in which two or more CPA firms are involved in the audit of components of group financial statements (e.g., the component auditors may audit one subsidiary of an organization structured as a parent company with five subsidiaries). When the audit firm that does the remainder of the audit does not wish to take responsibility for the work of the component auditors, the audit report is modified to divide responsibility between the CPA firms. This situation is unique in that the report alterations do not involve inclusion of an emphasis of matter or an other matter paragraph.

### Modified Opinions

- *Qualified opinion.* A qualified opinion states that the financial statements are presented fairly in conformity with generally accepted accounting principles "except for" the effects of some matter. **Qualified opinions** are issued when the financial statements are materially misstated ("a departure from GAAP") *or* when the auditors are unable to obtain sufficient appropriate audit evidence on which to base the opinion ("a scope limitation"). In both cases, the likely effects, while **material,** are *not* considered **pervasive.** All significant reasons for the issuance of a qualified opinion should be set forth in a **basis for modification paragraph (expanatory paragraph** under PCAOB standards) that precedes the opinion paragraph.

- *Adverse opinion.* An adverse opinion states that the financial statements are *not* presented fairly in conformity with generally accepted accounting principles. Auditors issue an adverse opinion when the deficiencies in the financial statements are both material and pervasive. All significant reasons for the issuance of an adverse opinion should be set forth in a basis for modification paragraph that precedes the opinion paragraph.

- *Disclaimer of opinion.* A disclaimer of opinion most frequently is the result of a scope limitation that creates a situation in which the auditors are *unable to obtain sufficient appropriate audit evidence* on which to base the opinion, and they conclude that the possible effects on the financial statements of undetected misstatements, if any, could be both material and pervasive. A disclaimer is not an opinion; it simply states that the auditors do not express an opinion on the financial statements. All significant reasons for the issuance of a disclaimer of opinion should be set forth in a basis for modification paragraph that precedes the opinion paragraph. As we discuss later in this chapter, disclaimers may also result from substantial doubt about a client's ability to continue as a going concern or multiple uncertainties relating to the financial statements.

We structure our discussion of audit reports around the two basic types of opinions just outlined—unmodified and modified opinions. Since several circumstances may result in either an unmodified or a modified opinion (e.g., substantial doubt about going-concern status and uncertainties), we emphasize those circumstances that are encountered most frequently.

# Reports with an Unmodified Opinion and an Emphasis of Matter Paragraph

**LO3**

Identify the circumstances that result in audit reports with emphasis of matter paragraphs and unmodified opinions.

Auditors express an unmodified opinion when they are able to obtain sufficient appropriate audit evidence to conclude that the financial statements as a whole are free from material misstatement. As indicated in the preceding section, under certain circumstances auditors add an emphasis of matter paragraph that refers to a matter that is appropriately presented or disclosed in the financial statements. This paragraph always *follows* the opinion paragraph and states that the auditors' opinion is not modified with respect to the matter.[6]

## Substantial Doubt about a Company's Going-Concern Status

The professional standards require that auditors evaluate whether there is substantial doubt about the client's ability to continue as a going concern for a reasonable period of time, which is defined as not to exceed one year beyond the date of the financial statements being audited. Going-concern status is a significant issue for users of financial statements, because assets and liabilities are normally recorded and classified on the assumption that the company will continue to operate. Assets, for example, may be presented at amounts that are significantly greater than their liquidation values.

The professional standards state that although the auditors are *not required to perform procedures specifically designed to test the going-concern assumption,* they must evaluate the assumption in relation to the results of the normal audit procedures. When performing risk assessment procedures, the auditors should consider whether there are events or conditions that indicate that there could be substantial doubt about the entity's ability to continue as a going concern. Also, throughout the audit the auditors should remain alert for audit evidence indicating such substantial doubt.

Conditions that may cause the auditors to question the going-concern assumption include negative cash flows from operations, defaults on loan agreements, adverse financial ratios, work stoppages, and legal proceedings. When such conditions or events are identified, the auditors should gather additional information and consider whether management's plans for dealing with the conditions are likely to mitigate the problem. If, after evaluating the information and management's plans, the auditors conclude that the substantial doubt is resolved, they may issue a standard report. If, on the other hand, substantial doubt still exists about the company's ability to continue as a going concern for a period of one year from the balance sheet date, the auditors should add an emphasis of matter paragraph to their unmodified opinion or issue a disclaimer of opinion.[7] Including an emphasis of matter paragraph with an unmodified opinion is the most frequent resolution.

The following is an example of an emphasis of matter paragraph relating to substantial doubt about a company's ability to continue as a going concern (emphasis added):

---

*Emphasis of Matter*

The accompanying consolidated financial statements have been prepared assuming that the Company will continue as a going concern. As discussed in Note 1 to the consolidated financial statements, the Company has suffered negative cash flows from operations and has an accumulated deficit, conditions that raise *substantial doubt* about the Company's *ability to continue as a going concern.* Management's plans in regard to these matters are also described in Note 1. The consolidated financial statements do not include any adjustments that might result from the outcome of this uncertainty. Our opinion is not modified with respect to this matter.

---

[6] PCAOB standards require that consistency and going-concern emphasis of matter paragraphs follow the opinion paragraph of the audit report; other emphasis of matter paragraphs may either precede or follow the opinion paragraph. PCAOB standards also do not require a statement concerning the opinion not being modified. (*International Standards of Auditing [ISA]* are consistent with GAAS in this area.)

[7] *The International Standards on Auditing* (ISA 570) state that in rare cases involving multiple material uncertainties that are significant to the financial statements, the auditor may consider it appropriate to issue a disclaimer of opinion. This is consistent with GAAS and PCAOB standards.

Regardless of whether the auditors decide to add an emphasis of matter paragraph to a report with an unmodified opinion or to issue a disclaimer of opinion, the auditors should consider the adequacy of financial statement disclosures that relate to the firm's going-concern status. Financial statement disclosures include:

- Pertinent conditions and events giving rise to the substantial doubt and their possible effects.
- Management's evaluation of the significance of the conditions and effect and management's plans for dealing with them.
- Possible discontinuance of operations.
- Information about the recoverability or classification of recorded asset amounts and the amounts and classification of liabilities.

If such disclosures are materially inadequate, a departure from GAAP exists and a qualified or adverse opinion is appropriate.

When conditions and events indicate that there could be substantial doubt about the entity's ability to continue as a going concern, the auditors should document in the working papers the conditions and events and significant management plans. In addition, they should document the auditing procedures performed to evaluate management's plans, the conclusion about whether substantial doubt exists, and their consideration of the adequacy of financial statement disclosures.

Recall that this section applies when there is "substantial doubt" about the client's ability to continue as a going concern. What about the situation in which liquidation of the company is imminent (that is, the company definitely is not a going concern)? In such a case, the liquidation basis of accounting is considered the appropriate basis under generally accepted accounting principles. The auditors' report ordinarily should use an emphasis of matter paragraph that states that the company has changed the basis of accounting from the going-concern basis to a liquidation basis. On the other hand, when a client's financial statements follow the going concern basis of accounting when liquidation is imminent, a departure from GAAP exists.

## Generally Accepted Accounting Principles Not Consistently Applied

United States auditing standards for both public and nonpublic companies require that auditors evaluate the client's current period financial statements for consistency of application of accounting principles in relation to prior periods. Which periods should be considered in this evaluation? Both Auditing Standards Board and PCAOB standards base that decision on the periods covered by the auditors' report on the financial statements.

- When the auditors are reporting only on the current period, they should evaluate whether the current-period financial statements are consistent with those of the preceding period, regardless of whether the preceding period is presented.
- When the auditors are reporting on two or more periods, they should evaluate consistency between such periods and the consistency of such periods with the period prior thereto if that prior period is presented with the financial statements being reported upon.

When the client makes a **change in accounting principles,** the nature of, justification for, and effect of the change are reported in a note to the financial statements for the period in which the change is made. The auditors should evaluate the change by determining whether it meets the following four accounting requirements:

1. The newly adopted principle is generally accepted.
2. The method of accounting for the effect of the change is in conformity with GAAP.
3. The disclosures related to the change are adequate.
4. Management has justified that the new accounting principle is preferable.

When the auditors believe that the new principle meets the four requirements, an emphasis of matter paragraph is added to the audit report to highlight the lack of consistent application of acceptable accounting principles; but the opinion remains unmodified.[8] Following is an example of an emphasis of matter paragraph that would follow the opinion paragraph:

> *Emphasis of Matter*
> As discussed in Note 5 to the consolidated financial statements, the Company adopted Statement of Financial Accounting Standards Update No. XXX, *Provide Title*, as of December 31, 20X8. Our opinion is not modified with respect to this matter.

When the auditors believe that the new principle does not meet one or more of the four requirements, a departure from generally accepted accounting principles exists. In such a circumstance, the auditors should issue either a qualified or an adverse opinion.

A client's correction of a material misstatement in previously issued financial statements also results in addition of an emphasis of matter paragraph to the audit report. The paragraph is only included in the year of correction and includes a statement that the previously issued financial statements have been restated for correction of a material misstatement and a reference to the entity's disclosure of the correction in the notes to the financial statements.

Among situations that ordinarily *do not* result in an emphasis of matter paragraph on consistency are changes in accounting estimates (e.g., changing the life of a fixed asset) and changes in principles with an immaterial effect (even if the effects are expected to be material in the future); absent other circumstances, a standard report may be issued in the year of the change. Finally, because consistency is a between-periods concept, a consistency modification is not appropriate for a company in the first year of its existence.

## Auditor Discretionary Circumstances that Result in an Emphasis of Matter Paragraph

While the professional standards require auditors to include an emphasis of matter paragraph in the circumstances presented previously, in the following circumstances the auditors may elect to include an emphasis of matter paragraph.

### Uncertainties

Uncertainties are situations in which conclusive audit evidence concerning the ultimate outcome cannot be expected to exist at the time of the audit, since that outcome will occur in the future. While all financial statements are affected to some extent by uncertainties, it is only those whose outcome is unusually important that auditors consider adding an emphasis of matter paragraph; for example, unusually important ongoing litigation or regulatory action in process against the client. The following illustrates an emphasis of matter paragraph describing an uncertainty:

> *Emphasis of Matter*
> As discussed in Note X to the financial statements, the company is a defendant in a lawsuit [briefly describe the nature of the litigation consistently with the Company's description in the note to the financial statements]. Our opinion is not modified with respect to this matter.

Adding an emphasis of matter paragraph for matters such as the above is at the discretion of the auditors. A major assumption underlying the inclusion of an emphasis of matter paragraph is that the matter is adequately disclosed in the notes to the financial statements. The auditors simply choose to emphasize it. As is the case with other emphasis of matter paragraphs, a discretionary emphasis paragraph follows the opinion paragraph.

While a report with an unmodified opinion and an emphasis of matter paragraph is the most frequent resolution regarding a particularly important uncertainty, there are situations in which a disclaimer may be issued. When multiple uncertainties cause the

---

[8] *International Standards on Auditing* (ISA 706) allow, but do not require, an emphasis of matter paragraph relating to a properly accounted for change in accounting principles.

auditors to conclude that it is not possible to form an opinion on the financial statements as a whole due to the interaction and cumulative possible effects of the uncertainties, a disclaimer may be appropriate.

If a matter such as those just described is *not* adequately disclosed in the financial statements, a departure from GAAP exists; as described later in the chapter, either a qualified or an adverse opinion is then appropriate.

### Additional Circumstances that May Result in an Emphasis of Matter Paragraph

Auditors also may at their own discretion choose to add an emphasis of matter paragraph to a report with an unmodified opinion for other circumstances relating to the financial statements. Examples of such matters include:

- A major catastrophe that has had, or continues to have, a significant effect on the organization.
- Significant transactions with related parties.
- Unusually important subsequent events.

Note that the matter should relate to the financial statements, not to the audit itself (e.g., adding an emphasis of matter paragraph relating to an audit procedure performed would not be appropriate).

## Group Financial Statements

Group financial statements include financial information of a company that is composed of more than one component. For example, group financial statements may include financial information of a parent and one or more subsidiaries, or joint ventures. When one CPA firm audits the entire group, no particular audit reporting complications arise. It is when one or more components are audited by **component auditors** other than the **group auditors**[9] that issues arise about the component auditors' and group auditors' responsibility for planning and performing the audit and reporting. Note that this situation involves two or more CPA firms auditing one year—*not* two or more CPA firms auditing different years of comparative financial statements. The most common group audit is one in which auditors of one firm rely upon the work of auditors who audited a component of a consolidated entity; for example, the component auditors may audit one of the company's five subsidiaries while the group auditors audit the other four as well as the consolidated financial statements.

When component auditors are involved in an audit, the group auditors should determine whether sufficient appropriate audit evidence can reasonably be expected to be obtained regarding the overall group controls, the consolidation process, and the financial information of the components. In addition, the group engagement team should obtain an understanding of:

- Whether the component auditors are competent and understand and will comply with all ethical requirements, particularly independence.
- The extent to which the group engagement team will be involved with the component auditors.
- Whether the group engagement team will be able to obtain necessary information on the consolidation process from the component auditors.
- Whether the component auditors operate in a regulatory environment that actively oversees auditors.

---

[9] GAAS (ASB AU 600) and *International Standards of Auditing* (ISA 600) use the terms "group engagement partner" and "group engagement team"—for simplicity sake, in parts of the discussion, we will use the term "group auditors." Also, previously, the group auditors were referred to as the **"principal auditors"** and the component auditors as "other auditors." The terms "principal auditors" and "other auditors" are still used in PCAOB auditing standards (PCAOB 543).

The group auditors should communicate with the component auditors. Specifically, the group auditors should inform the component auditors of (1) how their work will be used, (2) ethical requirements, (3) known related parties, and (4) significant risks of misstatements of the group financial statements. Near the end of the audit, the component auditors should communicate matters relevant to the group auditors' conclusions on the group audit.

If the group auditors encounter problems in performing the above procedures, they should obtain sufficient appropriate audit evidence without using the work of the component auditors. In addition, the group auditors will not use work of the component auditors when that work is unlikely to be completed in time to meet group auditors' requirements, or when differences exist in auditing standards applied by the component auditors.

The group auditors should establish an overall group audit strategy and develop a group audit plan. In developing the group audit plan, the group auditors should determine whether the work of the component auditors will be referred to in the group audit report. Under GAAS and PCAOB standards, the group auditors have two basic reporting alternatives:[10]

1. *Make reference to the component auditors.* When the group auditors make reference to the work performed by the component auditors, they communicate that the source of their audit evidence on the component is obtained through the component auditors. In essence, it *divides* the responsibility for the engagement *among the participating CPA firms.* Historically, this type of report has often been called a **shared responsibility opinion,** even though it is signed only by the group auditors. When the group auditors decide to make reference to the component auditors, they should perform the procedures described previously relating to the availability of sufficient appropriate audit evidence and characteristics of the component auditors. In addition, the group auditors should read the component's financial statements and the component auditors' report on those statements to identify significant findings and issues. If considered necessary, the group auditors should obtain additional information directly from the component auditors. Also, the group auditors may only make reference to the component auditors when the component's financial statements are prepared using the same financial reporting framework (e.g., GAAP) as the group and the component auditors have performed an audit and issued an audit report that is not restricted as to use.

A shared responsibility report indicates the portion of the engagement performed by the component auditors in terms of dollars or percentages in the *Auditors' Responsibility* section and also refers to the component auditors in the *Opinion* section. The actual report modifications are italicized in the following excerpt from the audit report.

---

*Auditors' Responsibility*

Our responsibility is to express an opinion on these consolidated financial statements based on our audits. *We did not audit the financial statements of B Company, a wholly owned subsidiary, which statements reflect total assets and revenues constituting 20 percent and 22 percent, respectively, of the related consolidated totals. Those statements were audited by other auditors whose report has been furnished to us, and our opinion, insofar as it relates to the amounts included for B Company, is based solely on the report of the other auditors.* We conducted our audits in accordance with auditing standards generally accepted in the United States of America. Those standards require that we plan and perform the audit to obtain reasonable assurance about whether the consolidated financial statements are free of material misstatement.

An audit involves performing procedures to obtain audit evidence about the amounts and disclosures in the consolidated financial statements. The procedures selected depend on the auditors' judgment, including the assessment of the risks of material misstatement of the consolidated financial statements, whether due to fraud or error. In making those risk assessments, the auditors consider internal control relevant to the entity's preparation and fair presentation

---

[10] *International Standards on Auditing* (ISA 600) do not permit the audit report to make reference to component auditors unless required by law or regulation.

of the consolidated financial statements in order to design audit procedures that are appropriate in the circumstances, but not for the purpose of expressing an opinion on the effectiveness of the entity's internal control. An audit also includes evaluating the appropriateness of accounting policies used and the reasonableness of significant accounting estimates made by management, as well as evaluating the overall presentation of the consolidated financial statements.

We believe that the audit evidence we have obtained is sufficient and appropriate to provide a basis for our audit opinion.

*Opinion*

In our opinion, *based on our audit and the report of the other auditors,* the consolidated financial statements referred to herein present fairly, in all material respects, the financial position of ABC Company and its subsidiaries as of December 31, 20X1 and 20X0, and the results of their operations and their cash flows for the years then ended in accordance with accounting principles generally accepted in the United States of America.

The additional wording in the illustration is not a qualification, but rather an indication of the divided responsibility between the auditors who conducted the audits of the various portions of the overall financial statements.[11]

What if the component auditors modify the opinion of their report on the component? Are the group auditors required to qualify the report on the consolidated financial statements? The answer to this question depends on the *materiality* of the matter. The consolidated financial statements ordinarily will have much larger amounts and totals than those of the component. Matters that were material to the component's financial statements may be quite insignificant to the consolidated entity. To determine whether a qualification is in order, the group auditors must evaluate the materiality of the matter *in relation to the consolidated financial statements.*

2. *Make no reference to the component auditors.* If the group auditors make no reference in their report to the portions of the engagement performed by the component auditors, they assume responsibility for the entire audit. This approach is usually followed when the component auditors are well known or when the group auditors are responsible for hiring the component auditors. Also, when difficulties arise relating to the component auditors' competence or work, the group auditors may decide to audit the component and not refer to the component auditors. If the group auditors elect to make no reference, they will issue the standard auditors' report with no additional wording.

When the group auditors decide not to make reference to the work of the component auditors, they must perform certain additional audit procedures. First, they should evaluate the appropriateness of performance materiality at the component level. The additional required procedures relating to the component depend upon whether that component is considered to be a *significant component;* a significant component is one identified by the group engagement team as having financial significance to the group or, due to its nature, is likely to include significant risks of material misstatement of the group financial statements. Figure 17.1 summarizes the audit work that ordinarily must be performed for components when no reference is made to the component auditors.

Group auditors are never *forced* to rely on the work of component auditors. Instead, they may insist upon *personally* auditing any aspect of the client's operations. If the client refuses to permit them to do so, the auditors may regard this as a **scope limitation** and, depending upon materiality, issue a qualified report or a disclaimer of opinion. As a practical matter, opinions are seldom modified for this reason. Satisfactory arrangements about who will audit the various aspects of a client's business normally will be worked out before the audit begins.

---

[11] Another acceptable, although less frequently used, option allows the group auditor to obtain the permission of the component auditors to explicitly use that auditors' name in the audit report. In such circumstances, the component auditors' report must also be presented with the report of the group auditors.

**FIGURE 17.1**

**Additional Procedures When Not Making Reference to the Component Auditors**

| Component Nature | Audit Procedures |
|---|---|
| Not significant | The group engagement team should perform analytical procedures at the group level. Audit additional components *if* sufficient appropriate audit evidence has not been obtained. |
| Significant due to its individual financial significance to the group | 1. The group auditors or component auditors should perform an audit of the component, adapted as necessary to the needs of the group engagement team, using the materiality of the component.<br>2. The group engagement team should be involved in the risk assessment and should:<br>  • Discuss with the component auditors or component management the component's business activities of significance to the group.<br>  • Discuss with the component auditors the susceptibility of the component to material misstatement.<br>  • Review the component auditors' documentation of identified significant risks of material misstatement of the group financial statements. |
| Significant because it is likely to include significant risks of material misstatement of the group financial statements | 1. The group auditors or the component auditors:<br>  • Should perform an audit of the component, adapted as necessary to the needs of the group engagement team, using the materiality of the component.<br>  • Should audit one or more component account balances, classes of transactions, or disclosures that relate to the significant risks.<br>  • Should perform specified audit procedures relating to the likely significant risks of material misstatement of the group financial statements.<br>2. Requirement 2 above. |

Figure 17.2 summarizes important points related to emphasis of matter paragraphs and group audits.

**FIGURE 17.2**    **Summary of Emphasis of Matter Paragraphs and Group Audits**

| Matter Giving Risk to Emphasis of Matter Paragraph | Effect on Audit Report If the Matter Is Properly Presented | Effect on Audit Report If the Matter Is Improperly Presented in Financial Statements |
|---|---|---|
| *Going Concern*—Substantial doubt about ability to remain a going concern<br>*Consistency*—GAAP not consistently applied<br>*Auditor Discretionary*—Circumstances in which the auditors may add an emphasis of matter paragraph (e.g., an uncertainty, a major catastrophe, significant related party transactions, or unusually significant subsequent events) | *Emphasis of matter paragraph* added after the opinion paragraph. (Going concern and uncertainties may also lead to disclaimers of opinion.) | A departure from GAAP is involved and the auditors modify the opinion paragraph to either a qualified or adverse opinion and add a basis for modification paragraph preceding the opinion paragraph. |
| *Group Audits* | The component auditors are referred to when the group auditors do not take responsibility for the component auditors' work. If the group auditors take responsibility, no modification of the audit report is necessary. | Not applicable because it is an auditor reporting concern. |

# Modified Opinions

**LO4**

Identify the circumstances that result in modified audit report opinions.

Modified opinions are required in two circumstances:

- *Materially misstated financial statements (i.e., a "departure from GAAP")*—The auditors conclude that the financial statements as a whole are materially misstated.
- *Inability to obtain sufficient appropriate audit evidence (i.e., a "scope limitation")*— The auditors are unable to obtain sufficient appropriate audit evidence to conclude that the financial statements as a whole are free from material misstatements (AICPA AU 705; PCAOB 508).

Recall from earlier in the chapter the three types of modified opinions: qualified opinions, adverse opinions, and disclaimers of opinion. Figure 17.3 describes the situations in which each type of modified opinion is issued.

As indicated in Figure 17.3, materially misstated financial statements result in either a qualified opinion or an adverse opinion depending on the size and pervasiveness of the misstatement. Similarly, an inability to obtain sufficient appropriate audit evidence leads to either a qualified opinion or a disclaimer opinion based on the *possible effects* on the financial statements of undetected misstatements. In both situations, the decision is based on whether misstatements or possible misstatements are both *material and pervasive.*

In the context of misstatements, *pervasive* is the term used to describe the effects on the financial statements of misstatements (departures from GAAP) or the possible effects on the financial statements of misstatements (scope limitations). Effects of misstatements become pervasive when, in the auditors' judgment, they meet one or more of the following three criteria:

- They are not confined to specific elements, accounts, or items of the financial statements.
- If confined, they represent or could represent a substantial proportion of the financial statements.
- In relation to disclosures, they are fundamental to users' understanding of the financial statements.

When a modified opinion is issued, the report includes a basis for modification paragraph *prior to* the opinion paragraph. The following sections discuss modified opinions (1) for misstated financial statements and (2) for the inability to obtain sufficient appropriate audit evidence.

## Materially Misstated Financial Statements ("Departures from GAAP")

The auditors sometimes do not agree with the accounting principles used in preparing the financial statements—that is, they believe that the financial statements depart from GAAP. As indicated in Figure 17.3, they must consider the materiality of the effects of any departure from GAAP to determine the appropriate type of audit report to issue. When the effects of the departures are *immaterial,* an unmodified opinion may be issued: when the effects are *material,* the auditors must issue either a qualified opinion or an adverse opinion based on whether the misstatement is considered pervasive.

**FIGURE 17.3**
**Modified Audit Opinions**

| Nature of Matter Giving Rise to the Modification | Auditors' Judgment about the Pervasiveness of the Effects or Possible Effects on the Financial Statements | | |
|---|---|---|---|
| | **Not Material (Accordingly, also Not Pervasive)** | **Material but Not Pervasive** | **Material and Pervasive** |
| *Materially Misstated Financial Statements (Departure from GAAP)* | Unmodified | Qualified | Adverse |
| *Inability to Obtain Sufficient Appropriate Audit Evidence (Scope Limitation)* | Unmodified | Qualified | Disclaimer |

The distinction between the effects of departures from generally accepted accounting principles that are material but not pervasive and those that are material and pervasive is a matter of professional judgment. In the discussions that follow, it will not be practical to present sufficient detail for readers to make these judgments. Therefore, we will either (1) use the terms *material, but not pervasive* and *material and pervasive,* or (2) use terms from the criteria for when a misstatement is pervasive, such as "a substantial proportion of the financial statements" or "fundamental to users' understanding."

When the report is qualified for a departure from GAAP, the modification involves adding a basis for modification paragraph immediately above the opinion paragraph and qualifying the opinion paragraph. The opinion section should have a heading indicating the nature of the opinion and including the phrase *except for the effects of the matter(s) described in the Basis for Qualified Opinion paragraph.*[12] The following is an example of basis for modification and opinion paragraphs of an audit report qualified for a departure from generally accepted accounting principles. The report's other paragraphs would contain standard wording.

---

*Basis for Qualified Opinion*

The company has excluded from property and debt in the accompanying balance sheets certain lease obligations that, in our opinion, should be capitalized in order to conform with accounting principles generally accepted in the United States of America. If these lease obligations were capitalized, property would be increased by $15,000,000, long-term debt by $14,500,000, and retained earnings by $500,000 as of December 31, 20X8. Additionally, net income would be increased by $500,000 and earnings per share would be increased by $1.22 for the year then ended.

*Qualified Opinion*

In our opinion, *except for the effects of not capitalizing certain lease obligations as discussed in the Basis for Qualified Opinion paragraph,* the financial statements referred to above present fairly, in all material respects, the financial position of Wend Company as of December 31, 20X8, and the results of its operations and its cash flows for the year then ended in conformity with accounting principles generally accepted in the United States of America.

---

If the material misstatement is considered pervasive, an **adverse opinion** is appropriate. An adverse opinion is the opposite of an unmodified opinion; it states that the financial statements *do not* present fairly the financial position, results of operations, and cash flows. When the auditors express an adverse opinion, they should include a separate basis for modification paragraph—similar to that of a report with a qualified opinion, as illustrated above (although a pervasive misstatement may require a longer paragraph). An illustration of an adverse opinion paragraph follows:

---

*Adverse Opinion*

In our opinion, *because of the significance of the matter discussed in the Basis for Adverse Opinion paragraph,* the consolidated financial statements referred to above *do not express fairly* the financial position of Wend Company as of December 31, 20X8, and the results of its operations and its cash flows for the year then ended.

---

A material misstatement may exist due to the omission of information; that is, disclosures required by GAAP for a fair presentation may have been omitted. In such a circumstance, if, after communicating with those charged with governance, the

---

[12] *International Standards on Auditing* (ISA 705) follow the same approach. PCAOB standards are similar, but rather than "Basis for Modification Opinion paragraph" the phrase used is "preceding paragraph." The PCAOB also follows this approach for adverse opinions and disclaimers of opinion.

information is still considered necessary and omitted, the auditors will issue a qualified or adverse opinion based upon the pervasiveness of the resulting misstatement.[13]

The professional standards require the auditors to describe in the basis for modification paragraph the nature of the omitted information and include the omitted information if it is practicable to do so. Practicable, as used here, means that the information is reasonably obtainable from the accounts and records and that in providing the information in the report the auditors do not assume the position of a preparer of the financial statements. For example, the auditors would not be expected to prepare a basic financial statement or segment information and include it in the auditors' report when management omits such information. Also, disclosing the information in the basis of modification paragraph would not be practicable if the information, in the auditors' judgment, would be unduly voluminous in relation to the auditors' report.

Ordinarily, a client that is reluctant to make a particular disclosure would rather disclose the information in a note than have it highlighted in the auditors' report. Therefore, very few auditors' reports actually are qualified because of inadequate disclosure. Instead, the requirements of the professional standards usually convince the client to include the necessary disclosure among the notes to the financial statements.[14]

## Inability to Obtain Sufficient Appropriate Audit Evidence (Scope Limitation)

Limitations on the scope of an audit may create a situation in which the auditors are unable to obtain sufficient appropriate audit evidence. Such limitations may occur due to:

- Circumstances beyond the control of the client (e.g., important accounting records were destroyed).
- Circumstances relating to the nature and timing of the auditors' work (e.g., the auditors are hired too late to observe the client's beginning inventory[15]).
- The client (e.g., the client's refusal to allow the auditors to send confirmations to customers).

Client-imposed limitations are very significant since they may have other implications for the audit, such as for the auditors' assessment of fraud risks and consideration of whether to continue the engagement or to withdraw. If management imposes a limitation, the auditors should communicate the limitation to those charged with governance.

When a scope limitation is encountered, the auditors attempt to obtain sufficient appropriate audit evidence by performing alternative procedures. If those procedures provide the required evidence, no report modification is necessary. If they do not, a decision needs to be made about whether a qualified opinion is necessary or whether the possible effects on the financial statements are so pervasive as to require a disclaimer of opinion.

---

[13] As indicated in footnote 1, GAAP require that when a balance sheet and an income statement are presented, a statement of cash flows should also be presented and its omission is a departure from GAAP. Historically this has led to a qualified opinion, although the current GAAS standards are silent on whether a qualified opinion or an adverse opinion standard should be issued. PCAOB standards, in this case the superseded GAAS standards that were adopted by the PCAOB as interim standards, still recommend a qualified opinion. *International Auditing Standards* do not explicitly address omission of the statement of cash flows.

[14] Rule 203 of the AICPA *Code of Professional Conduct* recognizes that in unusual circumstances a departure from accounting principles may be justified. However, the FASB does not allow such a departure from authoritative body pronouncements and this type of report is not generally issued. Under a financial reporting framework that allows such a departure, when the auditors agree with such departure, the auditors may issue a report with an unmodified opinion, but must disclose the departure in an emphasis of matter paragraph after the opinion paragraph. When the auditors do not agree that the departure is justified, a qualified or an adverse opinion is appropriate. Note that it is very seldom that the auditors would consider such a departure as justified under any financial reporting framework.

[15] Note that, even though this may be the "fault" of the client, it is not considered a limitation imposed by management because the client is not refusing to allow the auditors to perform a procedure that is possible to perform.

If the auditors decide that the possible effects on the financial statements of undetected misstatements, if any, could be material but not pervasive, a qualified opinion is appropriate. The report will include a Basis for Modification Paragraph and a modification of the opinion paragraph as follows (the remainder of the report uses the standard wording):

---

*Basis for Qualified Opinion*

We were unable to obtain audited financial statements supporting the Company's investment in a foreign affiliate stated at $20,500,000, or its equity in earnings of that affiliate of $6,250,450, which is included in net income, as described in Note 8 to the financial statements; nor were we able to satisfy ourselves as to the carrying value of the investment in the foreign affiliate or the equity in earnings by other auditing procedures.

*Qualified Opinion*

In our opinion, *except for the possible effects of the matters described in the Basis for Qualified Opinion paragraph*, the financial statements referred to above present fairly, in all material respects, the financial position of XYZ Company as of December 31, 20XX, and the results of its operations and its cash flows for the year then ended in conformity with accounting principles generally accepted in the United States of America.

---

Notice in the opinion paragraph that the qualification is worded as being due to the possible effects of the matter(s) on the financial statements, and not to the scope limitation itself.

When the auditors conclude that the possible effects on the financial statements could be both material and pervasive, a disclaimer of opinion is appropriate. A **disclaimer of opinion** is *no opinion*. Auditors issue a disclaimer whenever they are unable to form an opinion or have not formed an opinion as to the fairness of presentation of the financial statements. The following is an example of the paragraphs modified when a disclaimer of opinion is issued:

---

*Auditors' Responsibility*

Our responsibility is to express an opinion on these financial statements based on conducting the audit in accordance with auditing standards generally accepted in the United States of America. Because of the matter described in the Basis for Disclaimer of Opinion paragraph, however, we were not able to obtain sufficient appropriate audit evidence to provide a basis for an audit opinion.

*Basis for Disclaimer of Opinion*

We were unable to obtain audited financial statements supporting the Company's investment in a foreign affiliate stated at $20,500,000, or its equity in earnings of that affiliate of $6,250,450, which is included in net income, as described in Note 8 to the financial statements; nor were we able to satisfy ourselves as to the carrying value of the investment in the foreign affiliate or the equity in earnings by other auditing procedures.

*Disclaimer of Opinion*

Because of the significance of the matter described in the Basis for Disclaimer of Opinion paragraph, we have not been able to obtain sufficient appropriate audit evidence to provide a basis for an audit opinion. Accordingly, we do not express on opinion on these financial statements.

---

### Scope Limitations versus Uncertainties

It is important to be able to distinguish between an inability to obtain sufficient appropriate audit evidence (a scope limitation) and an uncertainty. This is because a scope limitation may result in either a qualified opinion or disclaimer of opinion, while an uncertainty may result in a report with an unmodified opinion and an emphasis of matter paragraph (or, less frequently, a disclaimer of opinion).

An inability to obtain sufficient appropriate audit evidence (a scope limitation) occurs in situations in which audit evidence should be available and is not—due to circumstances beyond the control of the organization, circumstances dealing with the timing of the auditors' work, or limitations imposed by management. Alternatively, an uncertainty involves a situation that is expected to be resolved at a future date, at which time conclusive audit evidence concerning its outcome would be expected to become available.

Complicating the matter is the fact that a situation involving an uncertainty may also involve a scope limitation. As an example, assume that an uncertainty exists relating to the future outcome of a lawsuit against the company. Also assume that the lawyer engaged by the client who has devoted substantive attention to the matter refuses to provide appropriate information on the uncertainty. Here the lawyer's refusal to reply may result in a lack of sufficient appropriate audit evidence (a scope limitation) relating to the litigation (an uncertainty). The appropriate audit opinion would be either qualified or a disclaimer of opinion.

*A Disclaimer Is Not an Alternative to an Adverse Opinion*

A disclaimer cannot be issued when the auditors have formed an opinion on the financial statements. For example, if the auditors have already formed an opinion that the financial statements are materially and pervasively misstated, an adverse opinion is appropriate. A disclaimer of opinion *cannot* be used as a way to avoid expressing an adverse opinion. In fact, even when auditors issue a disclaimer of opinion, they should express in the basis for modification paragraph of their report *any and all material reservations* they have concerning the financial statements. These reservations would include any material departures from generally accepted accounting principles, including inadequate disclosure. In short, the issuance of a disclaimer can never be used to avoid warning financial statement users about problems that the auditors know to exist in the financial statements.

**Summary of Auditors' Reports**

Figure 17.4 summarizes the types of auditors' reports that should be issued under different conditions.

## Additional Reporting Issues

**Two or More Report Modifications**

An audit report may be qualified for two or more matters. For example, an audit report may include a modification for a scope limitation and for a departure from generally accepted accounting principles. The wording of such a report would include the appropriate qualifying language and basis for modification for both types of qualifications.

**FIGURE 17.4**   **Summary of Auditors' Reports**

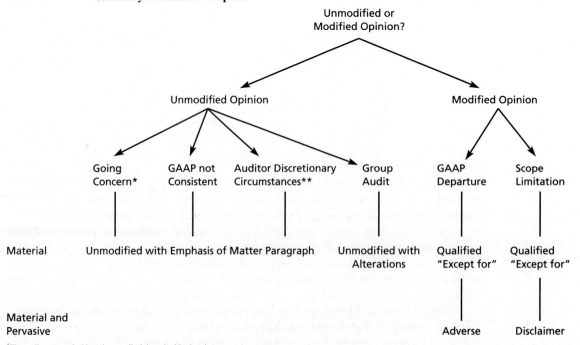

*The auditors may decide to issue a disclaimer in this situation.
**Examples include an uncertainty relating to the outcome of an unusually important event, a major catastrophe, related party transactions, unusually important subsequent events. Also, note that in circumstances involving multiple uncertainties, the auditors may issue a disclaimer of opinion.

When there are several matters requiring the qualification of an opinion, the auditors should consider the cumulative effects of those matters. If the effect involves material and pervasive known misstatements, an adverse opinion would be appropriate, not a qualified opinion.

When several matters requiring modification of the audit report exist, separate emphasis of matter and basis for modification paragraphs will ordinarily refer to each matter. As an example, consider the audit report for a company in extremely weak financial condition and with financial statements that include a material departure from generally accepted accounting principles. The audit report would likely include an emphasis of matter paragraph describing substantial doubt about the ability of the company to continue as a going concern, and a basis for modification paragraph and opinion modification relating to the departure from generally accepted accounting principles.

## Reporting on Comparative Financial Statements

**LO5**

Describe the auditors' responsibilities for reporting on comparative financial statements.

As indicated previously, many companies present with the current year's financial statements' comparative financial statements for one or more prior years. When comparative financial statements are presented by the client company, the auditors' report should cover the current year's financial statements as well as those for prior periods that were audited by the firm.

The auditors may express different opinions on the financial statements of different years. In addition, auditors should update their reports for all prior periods presented for comparative purposes. *Updating* the report means either reexpressing the opinion originally issued or, depending upon the circumstances, revising the opinion from that originally issued. A different opinion on the prior-period financial statements may be warranted because new information may have come to light that causes the auditors to alter their original opinion. For example, the client may revise previously issued financial statements to correct a departure from GAAP, resulting in a situation in which a qualified opinion is no longer warranted.

In some situations, the current auditors have not audited the prior period financial statements, because those financial statements are either unaudited or audited by predecessor auditors. If the financial statements of prior comparative periods are unaudited, this fact should be indicated on the applicable financial statements and the auditors' report should include a disclaimer of opinion on those statements. If the prior-period financial statements were audited by predecessor auditors, the current (successor) auditors' *opinion* will cover only the period or periods that they have audited. For the financial statements audited by the predecessor auditors, there are two reporting options. First, the report of the predecessor auditors may be *reissued* by them bearing its original date. Before reissuing the report, the predecessor auditors should read the subsequent period financial statements, compare them with the prior-period financial statements, and obtain representation letters from both management and the successor auditors in essence indicating that they are not aware of information that would indicate that the financial statements are incorrect or improper. The second reporting option is to have the successor auditors *refer to the report of the other auditors* by indicating in an other matter paragraph of the current auditors' report: (1) that the prior-period statements were audited by predecessor auditors, (2) the type of opinion expressed by the predecessor and, if the opinion was modified, the reasons therefore, (3) the nature of any emphasis of matter paragraph or other matter paragraph included in the predecessor auditors' report, and (4) the date of the predecessor auditors' report.

An example of an other matter paragraph of a report in which the predecessor auditors' report on the prior year was qualified but not presented in the current year is illustrated below, with the explanatory language emphasized.

---

*Other Matter*
*The financial statements of XYZ Company for the year ended December 31, 20X7, were audited by a predecessor auditing firm whose opinion, dated March 1, 20X8, on those statements was qualified as being presented fairly except for the effects on the 20X7 statements of the adjustments pertaining to the valuation of inventory, as discussed in Note X to the financial statements.*

---

## Different Opinions on Different Statements

The professional standards provide an illustration of a situation in which auditors may provide differing opinions on the respective financial statements. The situation involves auditors being retained *after* the client has taken its *beginning* inventory count and the auditors being unable to obtain sufficient appropriate audit evidence relating to that beginning inventory. Here the auditors satisfy themselves as to the amounts in the year-end balance sheet, but they are unable to satisfy themselves as to the statements of income, retained earnings, and cash flows due to the effects on these statements of the beginning inventory. In this situation, the auditors would normally issue an unmodified opinion on the balance sheet and a disclaimer of opinion on the other financial statements.

## Alerting Readers about the Intended Use of the Auditors' Report

Audit reports on a complete set of general-purpose financial statements (e.g., those prepared following GAAP) ordinarily are not restricted as to use or users. Indeed, for public companies the SEC requires this to be the case. However, nothing in GAAS precludes an auditor from "restricting use," that is indicating that the report is only for use by specified users. As an example, the auditors might indicate that an audit report of a nonpublic company is restricted to use by management, the board of directors, and shareholders. This, however, is seldom done, and when done, it must be a part of the understanding with the client. When a restriction on use is included in an audit report, it is included in an other matter paragraph that:

- Indicates that the report is intended solely for the information and use of the specified parties indicated in the audit report.
- Identifies the specified parties.
- Indicates that the report is not intended to be used by anyone other than the specified parties.[16]

## Reports to the SEC

Most publicly owned corporations are subject to the financial reporting requirements of the federal securities laws, administered by the Securities and Exchange Commission (SEC). Many of the reports, or *forms,* filed with the SEC include audited financial statements for one or more years. Among the most important of these forms are the following:

- *Forms S-l through S-11.* These are the "registration statements" for companies planning to issue securities to the public.
- *Forms SB-1 and SB-2.* These are more simplified registration forms for small businesses.
- *Form 8-K.* This is a "current report" filed for any time in which significant events occur for a company subject to the Securities Exchange Act of 1934. If the significant event is a business combination, audited financial statements of the acquired company often are required in the current report. An 8-K report is also used to notify the SEC of a change in auditors.
- *Form 10-Q.* This form is filed quarterly with the SEC by publicly owned companies. It contains unaudited financial information. The company's auditors perform reviews of this information, but their work is substantially less in scope than an audit.
- *Form 10-K.* This report is filed annually with the SEC by publicly owned companies. The report includes audited financial statements and other detailed financial information. It also includes management and the auditors' reports on internal controls over financial reporting.

---

[16] In some circumstances, restriction of particular reports issued by auditors is required. As we discussed in Chapter 7, two reports arising from an audit, communicating internal control related matters and the auditor's communication with those charged with governance, result in reports alerting readers as to intended use. Also, as discussed in Chapter 19, agreed-upon procedures engagements and audits of special-purpose financial statements prepared in accordance with a contractual or regulatory basis of accounting must be restricted.

Auditors dealing with these reports should be well versed on the requirements of each form, as well as in the provisions of the SEC's Regulation S-X, which governs the form and content of financial statements filed with the various forms.

The SEC, in conjunction with the Public Company Accounting Oversight Board (PCAOB), has the power to enforce a high-quality performance by auditors of issuers (public companies). The federal securities laws provide both civil and criminal penalties for any person, including auditors, responsible for misrepresentations of fact in audited statements filed with the SEC. The auditors' legal liability under the federal securities acts is discussed in Chapter 4.

## Chapter Summary

This chapter explained the different types of reports that auditors issue to indicate the character of their audit and the degree of responsibility they are taking. To summarize:

1. Audit reports in this chapter include those with unmodified opinions and those with modified opinions. A report with an unmodified opinion may be a "standard report" or include an emphasis of matter or other matter paragraph. The three types of modified opinions are qualified, adverse, and disclaimer of opinion.

2. A report with an unmodified opinion and standard in form includes an introductory paragraph, sections describing management and auditor responsibilities, and an opinion section. The report has a title that includes the word *independent,* is addressed to the company whose financial statements are being audited or to its board of directors or stockholders, and is signed with the name of the CPA firm. The public company audit report includes similar but less detailed information on management and auditor responsibilities.

3. An *emphasis of matter* paragraph is included following an unmodified opinion paragraph to emphasize matters described in the audited financial statements. Circumstances in which emphasis of matter paragraphs are *required* include substantial doubt about a client's ability to remain a going concern and inconsistency in the application of GAAP. Auditors *may choose to add* an emphasis of matter paragraph in a variety of circumstances involving matters properly described in the financial statements that they believe merit emphasis (e.g., uncertainties, related party transactions, and unusually important significant events).

4. An *other matter* paragraph is included following an unmodified opinion paragraph to emphasize something other than information described in the audited financial statements. Other matter paragraphs are included when required supplementary information is present and sometimes regarding information included in a document with audited financial statements; other matter paragraphs are also used when an audit report's use is restricted to certain parties. Group financial statements describe the situation when multiple audit firms are involved in an audit and the group auditors do not wish to take responsibility for a component auditors' work.

5. Modified opinions are issued when material departures from GAAP exist or when a scope limitation is involved. Figure 17.2 provides details on the appropriate modifications required for each of these types of reports.

6. When a client presents comparative financial statements for one or more prior periods with the current-period financial statements, the auditors should make certain that all periods are covered by an audit report. Audit reports on prior periods should be updated based on any new information that might affect the auditors' opinion. When predecessor auditors have audited the prior-period financial statements, the current (successor) auditors may summarize the predecessor auditors' opinion in the current-year audit report, or the client may arrange to have the predecessor auditors reissue their audit report.

7. Auditors of publicly held corporations must understand the various reporting requirements of the SEC. The reports filed with the SEC must be in accordance with Regulation S-X, which governs the form and content of the corporation's financial statements.

**Key Terms Introduced or Emphasized in Chapter 17**

**Adverse opinion (673)**   An opinion that the financial statements *do not* fairly present financial position, results of operations, and cash flows in conformity with generally accepted accounting principles. This situation occurs when the auditors believe that departures from GAAP are both material and pervasive.

**Basis for modification paragraph (664)**   A paragraph added to a report with a modified opinion (qualified, adverse, or disclaimer) that provides a description of the matter giving rise to the modification. The paragraph should be placed immediately before the opinion paragraph in the auditors' report and use the heading "Basis for Qualified Opinion," "Basis for Averse Opinion," or "Basis for Disclaimer of Opinion," as appropriate.

**Change in accounting principle (666)**   Changes in accounting principles and reporting entities result in an emphasis of matter paragraph being added to the auditors' report.

**Comparative financial statements (660)**   A complete set of financial statements for one or more prior periods included for comparison with the financial statements of the current period.

**Component auditors (668)**   Auditors that audit one or more components of a group of entities that provide consolidated financial statements. In the PCAOB standards, component auditors are referred to as other auditors.

**Disclaimer of opinion (675)**   A form of report in which the auditors state that they do not express an opinion on the financial statements.

**Emphasis of matter paragraph (663)**   A paragraph included in the auditors' report that is required by GAAS or is included at the auditors' discretion, and that refers to a matter appropriately presented or disclosed in the financial statements that, in the auditors' judgment, is of such importance that it is fundamental to users' understanding of the financial statements (e.g., a lack of consistent application of GAAP, substantial doubt about an entity's ability to continue as a going concern).

**Explanatory paragraph (664)**   A paragraph inserted in an auditors' report to explain a matter or to describe the reasons for giving an opinion that is other than unmodified. This term is still used in PCAOB standards, but has been replaced in AICPA standards by an emphasis of matter paragraph and an other matter paragraph.

**Financial reporting framework (661)**   A set of criteria used to determine measurement, recognition, presentation, and disclosure of all material items appearing in the financial statements: for example, accounting principles generally accepted in the United States of America, *International Financial Reporting Standards (IFRS)* issued by the International Accounting Standards Board (IASB), or a special-purpose framework (discussed in Chapter 19). An "applicable financial reporting framework" is the framework adopted by management of the company being audited in a particular situation.

**General-purpose framework (660)**   A financial reporting framework designed to meet the common financial information needs of a wide range of users (e.g., GAAP, *International Financial Reporting Standards*).

**Group auditors (668)**   Auditors that are responsible for issuing the audit report on a group of companies (e.g., a parent and its subsidiaries). In the PCAOB standards, group auditors are referred to as the principal auditors.

**Material (664)**   Being of substantial importance. Significant enough to affect evaluations or decisions by users of financial statements. Information that should be disclosed in order for the financial statements to constitute a fair presentation. Determining what is material involves both quantitative and qualitative criteria.

**Modified opinion (663)**   A qualified opinion, an adverse opinion, or a disclaimer of opinion.

**Other matter paragraph (663)**   A paragraph included in the auditors' report that is required by GAAS or is included at the auditors' discretion, and that refers to a matter other than those presented or disclosed in the financial statements that, in the auditors' judgment, is relevant to users' understanding of the audit, the auditors' responsibilities, or the auditors' report.

**Pervasive (664)**   A term used, in the context of misstatements, to describe the effects on the financial statements of misstatements or the possible effects on the financial statements of misstatements, if any, that are undetected due to an inability to obtain sufficient appropriate audit evidence. Pervasive effects on the financial statements are those that, in the auditors' judgment:

- Are not confined to specific elements, accounts, or items of the financial statements.

- If confined, represent or could represent a substantial proportion of the financial statements.

- In relation to disclosures, are fundamental to users' understanding of the financial statements.

**Principal auditors (668)**   The term previously used by the AICPA to describe the group auditors. This term is still used in PCAOB standards.

**Qualified opinion (664)** A modification of the auditors' standard report, employing a clause such as *except for* to limit the auditors' opinion on the financial statements. A qualified opinion indicates that, except for the effects of some limitation on the scope of the audit or some departure from generally accepted accounting principles, the financial statements are fairly presented.

**Scope limitation (670)** A restriction that prevents the auditors from being able to apply all of the audit procedures that they consider necessary in the circumstances. Scope limitations may be client imposed or may be imposed by other circumstances.

**Shared responsibility opinion (669)** An auditors' report in which the principal auditors decide to share responsibility with other auditors who have audited some segment of the client's business. The sharing of responsibility is done by making reference to the other auditors. Making reference is not, in itself, a qualification of the auditors' report.

**Standard report (659)** An audit report with (1) an unmodified (unqualified) opinion and (2) no additional matters emphasized (e.g., a change in according principles) beyond the information required in all audit reports. Note that while this term is frequently used in practice, the AICPA no longer formally uses it in its standards.

**Unmodified opinion (663)** The opinion expressed by the auditors when they conclude that the financial statements are prepared, in all material respects, in accordance with the applicable financial reporting framework (e.g., GAAP).

## Review Questions

17–1. Identify the sections of the standard audit report for a nonpublic company.

17–2. What is the function of notes to financial statements?

17–3. List three primary differences between the audit report for nonpublic entities and the one for public entities.

17–4. Comment on whether you agree with the following and why: GAAP and GAAS represent two frequently used financial reporting frameworks.

17–5. Provide a list of the types of unmodified and modified audit opinions.

17–6. Howard Green, a partner with Cary, Loeb, & Co., and his audit team have completed the audit of Baker Manufacturing. Determine the proper date of the audit report.

- December 31, 20X0: Baker's year-end.
- February 15, 20X1: Green completed audit procedures performed at Baker's location.
- February 19, 20X1: The financial statements were completed.
- February 20, 20X1: All audit procedures were completed, including the review of all audit documentation.
- February 25, 20X1: Green signed the audit report.
- February 26, 20X1: Green delivered the audit report to Baker.

17–7. When the current auditors make reference to the work of the component auditors, does this result in expression of a qualified opinion? Explain.

17–8. Explain three situations in which the wording of a report with an unmodified opinion might depart from the auditors' standard report.

17–9. Wade Corporation has been your audit client for several years. At the beginning of the current year, the company changed its method of inventory valuation from average cost to last in, first out (LIFO). The change, which had been under consideration for some time, was in your opinion a logical and proper step for the company to take. What effect, if any, will this situation have on your audit report for the current year?

17–10. What are the two circumstances that result in modified opinions?

17–11. Comment on the following: "If the financial statements contain an immaterial departure from generally accepted accounting principles, the auditors issue a qualified opinion; if the financial statements contain a material departure from GAAP, the auditors issue an adverse opinion."

17–12. What factors determine whether a misstatement is considered *pervasive?*

17–13. Can the client change a set of financial statements to receive an unmodified opinion instead of an opinion qualified as to the adequacy of disclosure? Explain.

17–14. Describe the alterations from the standard report when a scope limitation has occurred and the auditors have issued a qualified opinion.

17–15. The auditors know that the client's accounting for deferred income taxes is not in accordance with generally accepted accounting principles, but because of a very significant scope limitation they have not been able to determine the amount of the misstatement involved and have not been able to form an opinion on the financial statements taken as a whole. What type of report should they issue?

17–16. Why are adverse opinions rare?

17–17. Comment on whether you agree with the following: A basis for modified opinion paragraph is the same as a basis for qualified opinion paragraph.

17–18. Assume that CPAs are attesting to comparative financial statements. Can the CPAs express differing opinions on the sets of financial statements of two successive years?

17–19. Assume that CPAs are attesting to comparative financial statements. Can the CPAs change their report on the prior year's statements?

17–20. Describe the reports containing audited financial statements that are customarily filed by a company subject to the reporting requirements of the SEC.

## Questions Requiring Analysis

**LO 1, 2** 17–21. An accountant of an audit client made the following statement: It is important to read the notes to financial statements, even though they are presented in technical language and are incomprehensible. Auditors may reduce their exposure to third-party liability by stating something in the notes that contradicts completely what the client has presented in the balance sheet or income statement.

Evaluate the above statement and indicate:

a. Areas of agreement, if any.

b. Areas of misconception, incompleteness, or fallacious reasoning included in the statement.

**LO 3** 17–22. Rowe & Myers audits the financial statements of Dunbar Electronics. During the audit, Ross & Myers engaged Jones & Abbot, a Canadian public accounting firm, as a component auditor to audit Dunbar's wholly owned Canadian subsidiary.

*Required:* a. Must Rowe & Myers make reference to the component auditor in its audit report? Explain.

b. Assume that Jones & Abbott issued a qualified report on the Canadian subsidiary. Must Rowe & Myers include the same qualification in its report on Dunbar Electronics?

**LO 3** 17–23. Lando Corporation is a domestic company with two wholly owned domestic subsidiaries. Michaels, CPA, has been engaged to audit the financial statements of the parent company and one of the subsidiaries and to act as the group auditors. Thomas, CPA, has audited financial statements of the other subsidiary. Michaels has not yet decided whether to make reference to the audit of Thomas.

*Required:* a. What audit procedures should Michaels perform with respect to the component auditor, regardless of whether Michaels decides to make reference to Thomas in the report?

b. What modifications are made to the audit report if Michaels decides to make reference to the audit of Thomas?

**LO 3** 17–24. While performing your audit of Williams Paper Company, you discover evidence that indicates that Williams may not have the ability to continue as a going concern.

a. Discuss types of information that may indicate substantial doubt about a client's ability to remain a going concern.

b. Explain the auditors' obligation in such situations.

## Objective Questions

**All applicable questions are available with McGraw-Hill's *Connect™ Accounting*.** 📖 connect
|ACCOUNTING

17–25. **Multiple Choice Questions**

**LO 4** a. A material departure from generally accepted accounting principles will result in auditor consideration of:

(1) Whether to issue an adverse opinion rather than a disclaimer of opinion.

(2) Whether to issue a disclaimer of opinion rather than a qualified opinion.

(3) Whether to issue an adverse opinion rather than a qualified opinion.

(4) Nothing, because none of these opinions is applicable to this type of exception.

**LO 1, 2**  b. The auditors' report should be dated as of the date the:

(1) Report is delivered to the client.

(2) Auditors have accumulated sufficient evidence.

(3) Fiscal period under audit ends.

(4) Peer review of the working papers is completed.

**LO 3**  c. In an audit report on combined financial statements, reference to the fact that a portion of the audit was performed by a component auditor is:

(1) Not to be construed as a qualification, but rather as a division of responsibility between the two CPA firms.

(2) Not in accordance with generally accepted auditing standards.

(3) A qualification that lessens the collective responsibility of both CPA firms.

(4) An example of a dual opinion requiring the signatures of both auditors.

**LO 1, 2**  d. Assume that the opinion paragraph of an auditors' report begins as follows: "With the explanation given in Note 6, . . .the financial statements referred to above present fairly. . ." This is:

(1) An unmodified opinion.

(2) A disclaimer of opinion.

(3) An "except for" opinion.

(4) An improper type of reporting.

**LO 3**  e. The auditors who wish to draw reader attention to a financial statement note disclosure on significant transactions with related parties should disclose this fact in:

(1) An emphasis of matter paragraph to the auditors' report.

(2) A footnote to the financial statements.

(3) The body of the financial statements.

(4) The "summary of significant accounting policies" section of the financial statements.

**LO 4**  f. What type or types of audit opinion are appropriate when financial statements are materially and pervasively misstated?

|     | Qualified | Adverse |
| --- | --- | --- |
| (1) | Yes | Yes |
| (2) | Yes | No |
| (3) | No | Yes |
| (4) | No | No |

**LO 3**  g. Which of the following ordinarily involves the addition of an emphasis of matter paragraph to an audit report?

(1) A consistency modification.

(2) An adverse opinion.

(3) A qualified opinion.

(4) Part of the audit has been performed by component auditors.

**LO 2**  h. An audit report for a public client indicates that the audit was performed in accordance with:

(1) Generally accepted auditing standards (United States).

(2) Standards of the Public Company Accounting Oversight Board (United States).

(3) Generally accepted accounting principles (United States).

(4) Generally accepted accounting principles (Public Company Accounting Oversight Board).

**LO 2**  i. An audit report for a public client indicates that the financial statements were prepared in conformity with:

(1) Generally accepted auditing standards (United States).

(2) Standards of the Public Company Accounting Oversight Board (United States).

(3) Generally accepted accounting principles (United States).

(4) Generally accepted accounting principles (Public Company Accounting Oversight Board).

**LO 3**

*j.* When the matter is properly disclosed in the financial statements, the likely result of substantial doubt about the ability of the client to continue as a going concern is the issuance of which of the following audit opinions?

| | Qualified | Unmodified with Emphasis of Matter |
|---|---|---|
| (1) | Yes | Yes |
| (2) | Yes | No |
| (3) | No | Yes |
| (4) | No | No |

**LO 4**

*k.* A change in accounting principles that the auditors believe is not justified is likely to result in which of the following types of audit opinions?

| | Qualified | Unmodified with Emphasis of Matter |
|---|---|---|
| (1) | Yes | Yes |
| (2) | Yes | No |
| (3) | No | Yes |
| (4) | No | No |

**LO 3**

*l.* Which of the following is *least* likely to result in inclusion of an emphasis of matter paragraph in an audit report?

(1) The company is a component of a larger business enterprise.

(2) An unusually important significant event.

(3) A decision not to confirm accounts receivable.

(4) A risk or uncertainty.

**LO 3, 4**    17–26.    For each of the following brief scenarios, assume that you are reporting on a client's financial statements. Reply as to the type(s) of opinion possible for the scenario. In addition:

- Unless stated otherwise, assume the matter involved is material.

- If the problem does not state that a misstatement (or possible misstatement) is pervasive, assume that it may or may not be pervasive (thus, the appropriate reply may include two possible reports).

- Do not read more into the circumstance than what is presented.

Do not consider an auditor discretionary circumstance for modification of the audit report unless the situation explicitly suggests that the auditors wish to emphasize a particular matter. Report Types may be used once, more than once, or not at all.

| Situation | Report Types |
|---|---|
| a. Bowles Company is engaged in a hazardous trade and has obtained insurance coverage related to the hazard. Although the likelihood is remote, a material portion of the company's assets could be destroyed by a serious accident. | 1. Unmodified— standard report |
| b. Draves Company owns substantial properties that have appreciated significantly in value since the date of purchase. The properties were appraised and are reported in the balance sheet at the appraised values (which materially exceed costs) with related disclosures. The CPAs believe that the appraised values reported in the balance sheet reasonably estimate the assets' current values. | 2. Unmodified with an emphasis of matter paragraph |
| c. During the audit of Eagle Company, the CPA firm has encountered a significant scope limitation relating to inventory record availability and is unable to obtain sufficient appropriate audit evidence in that area. | 3. Qualified 4. Adverse |
| d. London Company has material investments in stocks of subsidiary companies. Stocks of the subsidiary companies are not actively traded in the market, and the CPA firm's engagement does not extend to any subsidiary company. The CPA firm is able to determine that all investments are carried at original cost, but has no real idea of market value. Although the difference between cost and market could be material, it could not have a pervasive effect on the overall financial statements. | 5. Disclaimer 6. Either qualified or adverse 7. Either qualified or disclaimer |
| e. Slade Company has material investments in stocks of subsidiary companies. Stocks of the subsidiary companies are actively traded in the market. Management insists that all investments be carried at original costs, and the CPA firm is satisfied that the original costs are accurate. The CPA firm believes that the client will never ultimately realize a substantial portion of the investments because the market value is much lower than the cost; the client has fully disclosed the facts in notes to the financial statements. | 8. Either adverse or disclaimer |

**LO 3, 4**   17–27.   Use the following to provide the type of audit report the auditors generally should issue in the situations presented below:

1. Unmodified—standard.
2. Unmodified—with an emphasis of matter paragraph.
3. Qualified.
4. Adverse.
5. Disclaimer

*Situation:*   a. Client-imposed restrictions significantly limit the scope of the auditors' procedures, and they are unable to obtain sufficient appropriate audit evidence. The possible effects on the financial statements of undetected misstatements, if any, could be both material and pervasive.

b. The auditors decide not to make reference to the report of a component auditor that audited a portion of group financial statements.

c. The auditors believe that the financial statements have been presented in conformity with generally accepted accounting principles in all respects, except that a loss contingency that should be disclosed through a note to the financial statements is not included. While they consider this a material omission, they do not believe that it pervasively affects the financial statements.

d. The client has changed from LIFO to FIFO for inventory valuation purposes; the auditors concur with this change. The effect is considered material to the financial statements, although inventory is not a large part of total assets.

e. The client has changed from LIFO to FIFO for inventory valuation purposes; the auditors do not concur with this change. The effect is considered material and pervasive.

**LO 3**   17–28.   Auditors report on the consistency of application of accounting principles. Assume that the following list describes changes that have a material effect on a client's financial statements for the current year.

(1) A change from the completed-contract method to the percentage-of-completion method of accounting for long-term construction contracts.

(2) A change in the estimated service lives of previously recorded plant assets based on newly acquired information.

(3) Correction of a mathematical error in inventory pricing made in a prior period.

(4) A change from direct costing to full absorption costing for inventory valuation.

(5) A change from deferring and amortizing preproduction costs to recording such costs as an expense when incurred because future benefits of the costs have become doubtful. The new accounting method was adopted in recognition of the change in estimated future benefits.

(6) A change to including the employer's share of FICA taxes as "Retirement benefits" on the income statement. This information was previously included with "Other taxes."

(7) A change from the FIFO method of inventory pricing to the LIFO method of inventory pricing.

*Required:*   For each of the above situations, state whether the audit report should include an emphasis of matter paragraph on consistency.

**LO 3, 4**   17–29.   **Simulation**

*Items 1 through 5* present various independent factual situations an auditor might encounter in conducting an audit. For each situation, assume:

• The auditor is independent.

• The auditor previously expressed an unmodified opinion on the prior year's financial statements.

• Only single-year (not comparative) statements are presented for the current year.

• The conditions for an unmodified opinion exist unless contradicted in the factual situations.

• The conditions stated in the factual situations are material.

• No report modifications are to be made except in response to the factual situation.

1. In auditing the long-term investments account, an auditor is unable to obtain audited financial statements for an investee located in a foreign country. The auditor concludes that sufficient appropriate audit evidence regarding this investment cannot be obtained.

2. Due to recurring operating losses and working capital deficiencies, an auditor has substantial doubt about an entity's ability to continue as a going concern for a reasonable period of time. However, the financial statement disclosures concerning these matters are adequate. The auditor has decided *not* to issue a disclaimer of opinion.

3. A group auditor decides to take responsibility for the work of a component CPA who audited a wholly owned subsidiary of the entity and issued an unmodified opinion. The total assets and revenues of the subsidiary represent 17 percent and 18 percent, respectively, of the total assets and revenues of the entity being audited.

4. An entity changes its depreciation method for production equipment from straight-line to a units-of-production method based on hours of utilization. The auditor concurs with the change, although it has a material effect on the comparability of the entity's financial statements.

5. An entity discloses certain lease obligations in the notes to the financial statements. The auditor believes that the failure to capitalize these leases is a departure from generally accepted accounting principles and, although the possible effects on the financial statements of the misstatements is material, they could not be pervasive.

*Required:*  List A represents the types of opinions the auditor ordinarily would issue and List B represents the report modifications (if any) that would be necessary. Select as the best answer for each situation (items 1 through 6) the type of opinion and alterations, if any, the auditor would normally select. Replies may be selected once, more than once, or not at all.

(AICPA, adapted)

| List A: Types of Opinions | List B: Report Alteration |
|---|---|
| A. Unmodified | H. Add an emphasis of matter paragraph—prior to opinion paragraph. |
| B. Qualified | |
| C. Adverse | I. Add an emphasis of matter paragraph—after opinion paragraph. |
| D. Disclaimer | J. Add a basis for modification paragraph—prior to opinion paragraph. |
| E. Qualified or adverse | |
| F. Qualified or disclaimer | K. Add a basis for modification paragraph—after opinion paragraph. |
| G. Disclaimer or adverse | L. Modifications other than addition of a paragraph. |
| | M. Issue standard report without alteration. |

**LO 3, 4, 5**   17–30.   **Simulation\***

For each of the following brief scenarios, assume that you are reporting on a client's financial statements. Reply as to the type(s) of opinion (per below) possible for the scenario. In addition:

• Unless stated otherwise, assume the matter involved is material. If the problem doesn't tell you whether a misstatement *pervasively* misstates the financial statements or doesn't list a characteristic that indicates pervasiveness, two reports may be possible (i.e., replies 6 to 9).

• Do not read more into the circumstances than what is presented.

• Do not consider an auditor discretionary circumstance for modification of the audit report unless the situation explicitly suggests that the auditor wishes to emphasize a particular matter.

**Types of Opinion**

1. Unmodified—standard.
2. Unmodified with an emphasis of matter paragraph.
3. Qualified.
4. Adverse.
5. Disclaimer.
6. Unmodified with an emphasis of matter paragraph or disclaimer.
7. Qualified or adverse.
8. Qualified or disclaimer.
9. Adverse or disclaimer.
10. Other.

\* Note that this simulation has more parts than one would expect in a particular CPA exam simulation. We present it to provide examples of many types of reporting situations in one problem.

| Situation | Report |
| --- | --- |

1. A company has not followed generally accepted accounting principles in the recording of its leases.

2. A company has not followed generally accepted accounting principles in the recording of its leases. The amounts involved are immaterial.

3. A company valued its inventory at current replacement cost. Although the auditor believes that the inventory costs do approximate replacement costs, these costs do not approximate any GAAP inventory valuation method.

4. A client changed its depreciation method for production equipment from the straight-line method to the units-of-production method based on hours of utilization. The auditor concurs with the change.

5. A client changed its depreciation method for production equipment from the straight-line to a units-of-production method based on hours of utilization. The auditor does not concur with the change.

6. A client changed the depreciable life of certain assets from 10 years to 12 years. The auditor concurs with the change.

7. A client changed the depreciable life of certain assets from 10 years to 12 years. The auditor does not concur with the change. Confined to fixed assets and accumulated depreciation, the misstatements involved are not considered pervasive.

8. A client changed from the method it uses to calculate postemployment benefits from one acceptable method to another. The effect of the change is immaterial this year, but is expected to be material in the future.

9. A client changed the salvage value of certain assets from 5 percent to 10 percent of original cost. The auditor concurs with the change.

10. A client uses the specific identification method of accounting for valuable items in inventory, and LIFO for less valuable items. The auditor concurs that this is a reasonable practice.

11. Due to recurring operating losses and working capital deficiencies, an auditor has substantial doubt about an entity's ability to continue as a going concern for a reasonable period of time. The notes to the financial statements adequately disclose the situation.

12. Due to recurring operating losses and working capital deficiencies, an auditor has substantial doubt about an entity's ability to continue as a going concern for a reasonable period of time. The notes to the financial statements do not adequately disclose the substantial doubt situation, and the auditor believes the omission fundamentally affects the users' understanding of the financial statements.

13. An auditor reporting on group financial statements decides to take responsibility for the work of a component auditor who audited a 70 percent owned subsidiary and issued an unmodified opinion. The total assets and revenues of the subsidiary are 5 percent and 8 percent, respectively, of the total assets and revenues of the entity being audited.

14. An auditor reporting on group financial statements decides not to take responsibility for the work of a component auditor who audited a 70 percent owned subsidiary and issued an unqualified opinion. The total assets and revenues of the subsidiary are 5 percent and 8 percent, respectively, of the total assets and revenues of the entity being audited.

15. An auditor was hired after year-end and was unable to observe the counting of the year-end inventory. She is unable to apply other procedures to determine whether ending inventory and related information are properly stated.

16. An auditor was hired after year-end and was unable to observe the counting of the year-end inventory. However, she was able to apply other procedures and determined that ending inventory and related information are properly stated.

17. An auditor discovered that a client made illegal political payoffs to a candidate for president of the United States. The auditor was unable to determine the amounts associated with the payoffs because of the client's inadequate record-retention policies. The client has added a note to the financial statements to describe the illegal payments and has stated that the amounts of the payments are not determinable.

18. An auditor discovered that a client made illegal political payoffs to a candidate for president of the United States. The auditor was unable to determine the amounts associated with the payoffs because of the client's inadequate record-retention policies. Although there is no likelihood that the financial statements are pervasively misstated, they may be materially misstated. The client refuses to disclose the payoffs in a note to the financial statements.

19. In auditing the long-term investments account of a new client, an auditor finds that a large contingent liability exists that is material to the consolidated company. It is probable that this contingent liability will be resolved with a material loss in the future, but the amount is not estimable. Although no adjusting entry has been made, the client has provided a note to the financial statements that describes the matter in detail.

20. In auditing the long-term investments account of a new client, an auditor finds that a large contingent liability exists that is material to the consolidated company. It is probable that this contingent liability will be resolved with a material loss in the future, and this amount is reasonably estimable as $2,000,000. Although no adjusting entry has been made, the client has provided a note to the financial statements that describes the matter in detail and includes the $2,000,000 estimate in that note.

| Situation | Report |
|---|---|

21. A client is issuing two years of comparative financial statements. The first year was audited by another auditor who is *not* being asked to reissue her audit report. (Reply as to the successor auditors' report.)

22. A client is issuing two years of comparative financial statements. The first year was audited by another auditor who is being asked to reissue her audit report. (Reply as to the successor auditors' report.)

23. A client's financial statements follow GAAP, but the auditor wishes to emphasize in his audit report a significant related party transaction that is adequately described in the notes to the financial statements.

24. A client's financial statements follow GAAP except that they do not include a note on a significant related party transaction.

**LO 3, 4**   17–31.   **Simulation**

Last year, Johnson & Barkley, CPAs, audited the consolidated financial statements of Jordan Company (a nonpublic company) for the year ended December 31, 20X0, and expressed a standard unmodified report.

Johnson & Barkley also audited Jordan's this year's financial statements—for the year ended December 31, 20X1. These consolidated financial statements are being presented on a comparative basis with those of the prior year, and an unmodified opinion is being expressed. Smith, the engagement supervisor, instructed Abler, an assistant on the engagement, to draft the auditors' report. In drafting the report below, Abler considered the following:

- Jordan changed its method of accounting for inventory from LIFO to FIFO in 20X1.

- Larkin & Lake, CPAs, audited the financial statements of BX, Inc., a consolidated subsidiary of Jordan, for the year ended December 31, 20X1. The subsidiary's financial statements reflected total assets and revenues of 2 percent and 3 percent, respectively, of the consolidated totals. Larkin & Lake expressed an unmodified opinion and furnished Johnson & Barkley with a copy of the auditors' report. Johnson & Barkley has decided to assume responsibility for the work of Larkin & Lake insofar as it relates to the expression of an opinion on the consolidated financial statements taken as a whole and has applied the necessary audit procedures.

- Jordan is a defendant in a lawsuit alleging patent infringement. This is adequately disclosed in the notes to Jordan's financial statements, but no provision for liability has been recorded because the ultimate outcome of the litigation cannot presently be determined.

Abler drafted the following audit report:

---

### Auditors' Report

We have audited the accompanying consolidated financial statements of Jordan Company and its subsidiaries, which comprise the consolidated balance sheets as of December 31, 20X1 and 20X0, and the related consolidated statements of income, changes in stockholders' equity, and cash flows for the years then ended, and the related notes to the financial statements.

*Auditors' Responsibility*

Our responsibility is to express an opinion on these consolidated financial statements based on our audits. We conducted our audits in accordance with auditing standards generally accepted in the United States of America. Those standards require that we plan and perform the audit to obtain reasonable assurance about whether the consolidated financial statements are free of material misstatement.

An audit involves performing procedures to obtain audit evidence about the amounts and disclosures in the consolidated financial statements. The procedures selected depend on the auditors' judgment, including the assessment of the risks of material misstatement of the consolidated financial statements, whether due to fraud or error. In making those risk assessments, the auditors consider internal control relevant to the entity's preparation and fair presentation of the consolidated financial statements in order to design audit procedures that are appropriate in the circumstances, but not for the purpose of expressing an opinion on the effectiveness of the entity's internal control. Accordingly, we express no such opinion. An audit also includes evaluating the appropriateness of accounting policies used and the reasonableness of significant accounting estimates made by management, as well as evaluating the overall presentation of the consolidated financial statements.

> We believe that the audit evidence we have obtained is sufficient and appropriate to provide a basis for our audit opinion.
>
> *Emphasis of Matter*
> As discussed in Note 2 to the consolidated financial statements, the Company adopted the first-in-first-out method of inventory valuation in 20X1. Our opinion is not modified with respect to this matter.
>
> *Opinion*
> In our opinion, the consolidated financial statements referred to here present fairly, in all material respects, the financial position of Jordan Company and its subsidiaries as of December 31, 20X1 and 20X0, and the results of their operations and their cash flows for the years then ended in accordance with accounting principles generally accepted in the United States of America.
>
> *Johnson & Barkley, CPAs*
>
> Phoenix, Arizona
> December 31, 20X1

**Required:**

Smith reviewed Abler's draft and stated in the *Supervisor's Review Notes* below that there were deficiencies in Abler's draft. Items 1 through 10 represent the deficiencies noted by Smith. For each deficiency, indicate whether Smith is correct or incorrect in the criticism of Abler's draft.

1. The report's title is incorrect as it should include the word "independent."

2. The report should have an addressee such as the board of directors.

3. There should be a section entitled *Management's Responsibility for the Financial Statements.*

4. The first sentence of the *Auditors' Responsibility* section should state that "Our responsibility is to provide assurance . . .," not "Our responsibility is to express an opinion . . ."

5. The *Auditors' Responsibility* and the *Opinion* sections should both refer to the component auditors.

6. The third paragraph under the *Auditors' Responsibility* section is not required—let's omit it.

7. The emphasis of matter paragraph should follow the opinion paragraph.

8. The *Opinion* section should indicate that the principles were consistently applied except for the change in method of inventory valuation.

9. The report should be dated as of the date sufficient appropriate audit evidence has been gathered, not as of year-end.

10. The names of the individual financial statements should be included in the *Opinion* section.

# Problems

**All applicable problems are available with McGraw-Hill's *Connect*™ *Accounting*.** 🔲 connect
|ACCOUNTING

**LO 1, 3**   17–32.   The auditors' report that follows was drafted by a staff accountant of Williams & Co., CPAs, at the completion of the audit of the financial statements of Lenz Corporation (nonpublic company) for the year ended December 31, 20X1. Assume that there is substantial doubt about the entity's ability to continue as a going concern, and that this doubt is properly disclosed in the financial statements.

> **Independent Auditors' Report**
>
> To the Board of Directors and Stockholders of Lenz Corporation:
>     We have audited the accompanying consolidated financial statements of Lenz Corporation and its subsidiaries, and the related notes to the financial statements.
>
> *Management's Responsibility for the Financial Statements*
> Management is responsible for the preparation and fair presentation of these consolidated financial statements in accordance with accounting principles generally accepted in the United States of America; this includes the design, implementation, and maintenance of internal control relevant to the preparation and fair presentation of consolidated financial statements that are free from material misstatement, whether due to fraud or error.

*Auditors' Responsibility*

Our responsibility is to express an opinion on these consolidated financial statements based on our audit. Those standards require that we plan and perform the audit to obtain reasonable assurance about whether the consolidated financial statements are in conformity with accounting principles generally accepted in the United States of America.

An audit involves performing procedures to obtain audit evidence about the amounts and disclosures in the consolidated financial statements. The procedures selected depend on the auditors' judgment, including the assessment of the risks of material misstatement of the consolidated financial statements, whether due to fraud or error. In making those risk assessments, the auditors consider internal control relevant to the entity's preparation and fair presentation of the consolidated financial statements in order to design audit procedures that are appropriate in the circumstances, but not for the purpose of expressing an opinion on the effectiveness of the entity's internal control. Accordingly, we express no such opinion. An audit also includes evaluating the appropriateness of accounting policies used and the reasonableness of significant accounting estimates made by management, as well as evaluating the overall presentation of the consolidated financial statements.

*Emphasis of Matter*

The accompanying consolidated financial statements have been prepared assuming that the Company will continue as a going concern. As discussed in Note 1 to the consolidated financial statements, the Company has suffered negative cash flows from operations and has an accumulated deficit that raises substantial doubt about the Company's ability to continue as a going concern beyond a reasonable time. Management's plans in regard to these matters are also described in Note 1. The consolidated financial statements do not include any adjustments that might result from the outcome of this uncertainty. Our opinion is modified with respect to this matter.

*Opinion*

In our opinion, except for the effects of the matter described in the preceding paragraph, the consolidated financial statements referred to above present fairly, in all material respects, the financial position of Lenz Corporation and its subsidiaries and the results of their operations and their cash flows for the year then ended in accordance with accounting principles generally accepted in the United States of America applied on a basis consistent with that of the preceding year.

*Williams & Co., LLP*

Phoenix Arizona
February 15, 20X2

---

*Required:* Identify deviations from the appropriate nonpublic company audit report.

**LO 2**  17–33. The auditors' report that follows was drafted by a staff accountant of Smith & Co., CPAs, at the completion of the audit of the financial statements of Lenses Co. (a public company) for the year ended December 31, 20X1.

---

### Report of Registered Public Accounting Firm

To the Management of Lenses Co.:

We have examined the accompanying consolidated balance sheet of Lenses Co. as of December 31, 20X1 and 20X0, and the related consolidated statement of income, stockholders' equity, and cash flows for each of the three years in the period ended December 31, 20X1. These financial statements are the responsibility of the Company's management. Our responsibility is to express an opinion on these financial statements based on our audits. All PCAOB requirements were met on this audit.

We conducted our audits in accordance with the standards of generally accepted auditing standards (United States). Those standards require that we plan and perform the audit to obtain positive assurance about whether the financial statements are free of all misstatements. An audit includes examining, on a test basis, evidence supporting the amounts and disclosures in the financial statements. An audit also includes assessing the accounting principles used and significant estimates made by management, as well as evaluating the overall financial statement presentation. We believe that our audits provide a reasonable basis for our opinion.

In our opinion, the financial statements referred to above present, in all material respects, the consolidated financial position of Lenses Co. at December 31, 20X1 and 20X0, and the consolidated results of its operations and its cash flows for each of the three years in the period ended

December 31, 20X1, in conformity with U.S. generally accepted accounting principles applied on a consistent basis.

We also have reviewed, in accordance with the standards of the Public Company Accounting Oversight Board (United States), Lenses Co.'s internal control over financial reporting as of December 31, 20X1, based on criteria established in the Internal Control-Integrated Framework issued by the Committee of Sponsoring Organizations of the Treadway Commission, and our report dated February 15, 20X2, expressed an unmodified opinion thereon.

*Smith & Co., CPAs*

Dallas, Texas
February 15, 20X2

*Required:* Identify deviations from the public company standard report.

**LO 4** 17–34. Sturdy Corporation (a nonpublic company) owns and operates a large office building in a desirable section of New York City's financial center. For many years, management of Sturdy Corporation has modified the presentation of its financial statement by:

1. Reflecting a write-up to appraisal values in the building accounts.
2. Accounting for depreciation expense on the basis of such valuations.

Wyley, CPA, was asked to audit the financial statements of Sturdy Corporation for the year ended December 31, 20X3. After completing the audit, Wyley concluded that, consistent with prior years, an adverse opinion would have to be expressed because the material misstatements were considered pervasive.

*Required:*
a. Describe in detail the appropriate content of the basis for modification section of the auditors' report on the financial statements of Sturdy Corporation for the year ended December 31, 20X3. Do not discuss deferred taxes.
b. Write a draft of the opinion paragraph of the auditors' report on the financial statements of Sturdy Corporation for the year ended December 31, 20X3.

**LO 1, 3, 4** 17–35. Roscoe & Jones, Ltd, a CPA firm in Silver Bell, Arizona, has completed the audit of the financial statements of Excelsior Corporation as of, and for, the year ended December 31, 20X1. Findings related to the financial statements and the audit include:

- Excelsior is a nonpublic company that presents only current-year financial statements.
- Roscoe was unable to perform normal accounts receivable confirmation procedures, but alternate procedures were used to satisfy Roscoe as to the validity of the receivables.
- Excelsior Corporation is the defendant in litigation, the outcome of which is highly uncertain. If the case is settled in favor of the plaintiff, Excelsior will be required to pay a substantial amount of cash that might require the sale of certain assets. The litigation and the possible effects have been properly disclosed in Note 11. Roscoe wishes to include discussion of this matter in the audit report.
- During 20X1 Excelsior changed its method of accounting for long-term construction contracts and properly reflected the effect of the change. Roscoe is satisfied with Excelsior's justification for making the change. The change is discussed in Note 12.
- Excelsior issued debentures on January 31, 20X1, in the amount of $10 million. The funds obtained from the issuance were used to finance the expansion of plant facilities. The debenture agreement restricts the payment of future cash dividends to earnings after December 31, 20X1. Excelsior declined to disclose these data in the notes to the financial statements. Roscoe considers this a material, but not pervasive omission.
- Roscoe gathered sufficient appropriate audit evidence as of February 10, 20X2, and planned a report release date of February 16, 20X2.

*Required:* Consider all facts given and prepare an auditors' report in an acceptable and complete format, incorporating any necessary departures from the standard report.

**LO 2, 3, 4** 17–36. Rotter & Co, Ltd, a CPA firm in Silver Bell, Arizona, has completed the audit of the financial statements of Exchecker Corporation as of, and for, the year ended December 31, 20X1. Findings related to the financial statements and the audit include:

- Exchecker is a public company that presents two years of balance sheets and three years of the other financial statements in accordance with SEC reporting requirements.

- During 20X1, Exchecker changed its method of accounting for long-term construction contracts and properly reflected the effect of the change. Rotter is satisfied with Exchecker's justification for making the change. The change is discussed in Note 12.
- Rotter was unable to perform normal accounts receivable confirmation procedures, but alternate procedures were used to satisfy Rotter as to the validity of the receivables.
- Exchecker Corporation is the defendant in litigation, the outcome of which is highly uncertain. If the case is settled in favor of the plaintiff, Exchecker will be required to pay a substantial amount of cash that might require the sale of certain assets. The litigation and the possible effects have been properly disclosed in Note 11. Rotter wishes to include discussion of this matter in the audit report.
- Rotter gathered sufficient appropriate audit evidence as of February 10, 20X2, and planned a report release date of February 16, 20X2.

*Required:*    Consider all facts given, and prepare an auditors' report in an acceptable and complete format incorporating any necessary departures from the standard report.

**In-Class Team Cases**

**LO 3, 4, 5    17–37.**    For each of the following brief scenarios, assume that you are the CPA reporting on the client's financial statements. Using the form included with this problem, describe the reporting circumstance involved, the type or types of opinion possible in the circumstance, and the appropriate report alterations. Since more than one report may be possible in several of the circumstances, a second "type of opinion" and "report alteration" row is added for each circumstance. For example, if the problem doesn't tell you whether a misstatement *pervasively* misstates the financial statements or doesn't list a characteristic that indicates pervasiveness, two reports may be possible.

In most cases, you will not need to use the second row. Do not read more into the circumstance than what is presented, and only reply "emphasis of matter" in auditor discretionary circumstances such as those suggested in the chapter. Unless stated otherwise, assume that the information presented is material to the financial statements.

| Circumstance | | Type of Opinion | | Report Alteration | |
|---|---|---|---|---|---|
| GC | Going concern | U | Unmodified | EOM | Emphasis of matter paragraph added |
| CON | Consistency | Q | Qualified | OM | Other matter paragraph added |
| EMPH | Auditor discretionary emphasis of matter | D | Disclaimer | BFM | Basis for modification paragraph added |
| GROUP | Group audit | A | Adverse | OTHER | Other alteration, but no paragraph added |
| GAAP | Departure from GAAP | | | NO | No alteration |
| SCOPE | Scope limitation | | | | |
| COMP | Comparative financial statements | | | | |
| NONE | No circumstance | | | | |

1. Your client has declined to depreciate its assets this year because the depreciation expense would reduce the year's small income to a loss.

2. A client's financial statements follow GAAP, but you wish to emphasize that the client is a subsidiary of Webster Corporation in the audit report.

3. In auditing the long-term investments account of a new client, you are unable to obtain audited financial statements for the investee located in a foreign country. You conclude that sufficient appropriate audit evidence regarding this investment cannot be obtained.

4. Due to a very major lawsuit, you have substantial doubt about a client's ability to continue as a going concern for a reasonable period of time. The financial statement disclosures related to this lawsuit are adequate.

5. You decide not to take responsibility for the work of the component auditors who audited a 70 percent owned subsidiary and issued an unmodified opinion. The total assets and revenues of the subsidiary are 5 percent and 8 percent, respectively, of the total assets and revenues of the entity being audited.

6. You decide to take responsibility for the work of the component auditors who audited a 70 percent owned subsidiary and issued an unmodified opinion. The total assets and revenues of the subsidiary are 5 percent and 8 percent, respectively, of the total assets and revenues of the entity being audited.

7. A company has changed the remaining life of a significant asset from 12 to 10 years. You believe that the change is reasonable.

8. A company changes from FIFO to LIFO for inventory valuation and you concur with the change. The change has an immaterial effect on the entity's financial statements this year, but it is expected to have a material effect in the future.

9. Your client is a defendant in a major lawsuit. It is probable that the company will experience a material loss due to the lawsuit, although it is impossible to calculate the likely amount. The financial statements include a note adequately describing the matter. You decide that a standard report is inappropriate.

10. Predecessor auditors audited last year's financial statements and you audited the current year. You have decided not to ask the predecessor to reissue that audit report. Comparative financial statements are being issued on the two years.

| | Circumstance | Type Opinion(s) | Report Alteration |
|---|---|---|---|
| 1 | | | |
| | | | |
| 2 | | | |
| | | | |
| 3 | | | |
| | | | |
| 4 | | | |
| | | | |
| 5 | | | |
| | | | |
| 6 | | | |
| | | | |
| 7 | | | |
| | | | |
| 8 | | | |
| | | | |
| 9 | | | |
| | | | |
| 10 | | | |
| | | | |

**LO 3, 4, 5**  **17–38.** For each of the following brief scenarios, assume that you are reporting on a client's current year financial statements. Reply as to the type or types of opinion possible in the circumstance.

S    Unmodified—standard

U    Unmodified with emphasis of matter or other matter paragraph

Q    Qualified

D    Disclaimer

A    Adverse

Since more than one report may be possible in several of the circumstances, a second "opinion" column is added for each circumstance. In certain cases, you will not need to use the second column. Do not read more into the circumstance than what is presented, and do not consider the possibility of an auditors' discretionary emphasis of matter paragraph being added to the audit report. Unless stated otherwise, assume that the information presented is material to the financial statements. If the situation doesn't tell you whether a misstatement *pervasively* misstates the financial statements or doesn't list a characteristic that indicates pervasiveness, two reports may be possible.

| Situation | Opinion | Opinion |
|---|---|---|
| 1. A company in its first year of existence values its inventory at current replacement cost. Although you believe that the inventory costs do approximate replacement costs, these costs do not approximate any GAAP inventory valuation method. The difference involved is material, but not pervasively material to the financial statements. | | |
| 2. Due to recurring operating losses and working capital deficiencies, you have substantial doubt about an entity's ability to continue as a going concern for a reasonable period of time. The notes to the financial statements adequately disclose the substantial doubt situation. | | |
| 3. You have discovered that a client made illegal payoffs to a candidate for president of the United States. You are unable to determine the amounts associated with the payoffs because of the client's inadequate record retention policies. The client has added a note to the financial statements to describe this information, and has stated that the amounts of the payments are not determinable. | | |
| 4. In auditing the long-term investments account of a new client, you find that a $2,000,000 contingent liability exists that is material to the consolidated company. It is probable that this contingent liability will be resolved with a material loss in the future. Although no adjusting entry has been made, the client has provided a note to the financial statements that describes the matter in detail and includes the $2 million estimate. | | |
| 5. A client is issuing two years of comparative financial statements. The first year was audited by other auditors who are not being asked to reissue their audit report. | | |
| 6. An entity changes its depreciation method for production equipment from the straight-line to the units-of-production method based on hours of utilization. You concur with the change. | | |
| 7. A client has changed the method it uses to calculate postemployment benefits from one acceptable method to another acceptable method. The effect of the change is immaterial this year, but is expected to be material in the future. | | |
| 8. Component auditors have audited a subsidiary of your client as a part of a group audit. You have decided to rely upon the component auditors' work. | | |
| 9. A client omits note disclosure related to significant accounting policies that the auditors believe to be fundamental to users' understanding of the financial statements. | | |
| 10. A client does not count its year-end inventory. The auditors are unable to obtain sufficient appropriate audit evidence related to the inventory, and they consider inventory to represent an extremely substantial proportion of the financial statements. | | |

## Research and Discussion Case

LO 3, 4

11–39. Your firm audits Metropolitan Power Supply (MPS). The issue under consideration is the treatment in the company's financial statements of $700 million in capitalized construction costs relating to Eagle Mountain, a partially completed nuclear power plant.

Seven years ago, MPS began construction of Eagle Mountain, with an original cost estimate of $400 million and completion expected within five years. Cost overruns were enormous, and construction has been repeatedly delayed by litigation initiated by the antinuclear lobby. At present, the project is little more than 50 percent complete, and construction has been halted because MPS does not have the funds to continue.

If Eagle Mountain is ultimately completed, the state utilities commission will determine the extent to which MPS may recover its construction costs through its rate structure. The commission's rulings are difficult to predict, but it is quite possible that the commission will not allow MPS to include all of the Eagle Mountain construction costs in its "rate base." If Eagle Mountain were abandoned today, none of the construction costs would be recoverable. The related write-off would amount to over 70 percent of MPS's stockholders' equity, but the company would survive.

MPS's management, however, remains committed to the completion of the Eagle Mountain facility. Management has obtained authorization from the company's stockholders to issue $500 million in bonds and additional shares of common stock to finance completion of the project. If MPS incurs this additional debt and is still not able to make Eagle Mountain fully operational, it is doubtful that the company can avoid bankruptcy. In short, management has elected to gamble—all its chips are riding on Eagle Mountain.

*Required:*

a. Discuss the arguments for and against the auditors insisting that MPS begin expensing some portion of the construction costs rather than continuing to accumulate an ever-increasing asset. Indicate the position you would take as the auditor.

b. Discuss whether the auditors should modify their report because of uncertainty about whether or not MPS can remain a going concern. Indicate the type of opinion that you would issue. (You need not limit yourself to a "going-concern" modification.)

*Part a:*

*FASB Accounting Standards Codification* sections 360-10 and 450-20-25-2.

*Part b:*

AICPA AU sections 570 and 700–706; PCAOB sections 341 and 508.

# 18

# Integrated Audits of Public Companies

**LO1**

Describe the nature of an integrated audit.

In this chapter, we provide information on **integrated audits** based on the provisions of Public Company Accounting Oversight Board (PCAOB) *Standard No. 5,* "An Audit of Internal Control Over Financial Reporting That Is Integrated with an Audit of Financial Statements." Throughout this chapter, our emphasis is on presenting (1) details on audits of internal control over financial reporting and (2) information on how financial statement audits are modified when the auditors perform an integrated audit. Although we have referred to integrated audits earlier in the text, in this chapter we emphasize in detail the nature of a public company audit. While an integrated audit involves an enhanced consideration of internal control, the financial statement audit's various planning, evidence gathering, and reporting procedures remain largely unchanged. Accordingly, the focus of this chapter is on audits of internal control over financial reporting (hereafter, internal control).

## Overview

The Sarbanes-Oxley Act of 2002 requires that, in addition to reporting upon financial statements, auditors of public companies should also report upon internal control over financial reporting (hereafter, internal control). Consistently, PCAOB *Standard No. 5* recognizes this relationship and states that the internal control and financial statement audits should be viewed as integrated.

Section 404 is composed of two distinct sections.[1] **Section 404(a),** which applies to all public companies, requires that each annual report filed with the Securities and Exchange Commission include an internal control report prepared by management in which management acknowledges its responsibility for establishing and maintaining adequate internal control and provides an assessment of internal control effectiveness as of the end of the most recent fiscal year. **Section 404(b),** which applies to public companies with a market capitalization in excess of $75,000,000, requires the CPA firm to audit internal control and express an opinion on the effectiveness of internal control. While the emphasis of this chapter is on the auditors' responsibility under Section 404(b), we will begin with an overview of management's responsibility.

---

[1] While we emphasize Section 404 in this chapter, we also incorporate information from Section 103, which requires auditor reporting on internal control. In addition, other sections of the Sarbanes-Oxley Act are also relevant to the overall area of audits of financial statements. Section 302 requires each of a company's principal executives and financial officers to certify the financial and other information contained in the company's quarterly and annual reports. These certifications must indicate that, based on the officer's knowledge, the financial statements and other financial information included in the report fairly present, in all material respects, the financial condition and results of operations of the company as of, and for, the period presented in the report. Section 906 includes a similar certification requirement but amends the Federal Criminal Code and explicitly sets forth possible criminal penalties for certifications that do not comply with the requirements.

# Management's Responsibility for Internal Control

**LO2**

Discuss management's responsibility for reporting on internal control as required by the Sarbanes-Oxley Act of 2002.

Management has always been responsible for maintaining effective internal control. However, the **Sarbanes-Oxley Act of 2002** increases management's responsibility for demonstrating that controls are effective. As operationalized by the Securities and Exchange Commission (SEC), management is required to:

- Accept responsibility for the effectiveness of internal control.
- Evaluate the effectiveness of internal control using suitable control criteria.
- Support the evaluation with sufficient evidence.
- Provide a report on internal control.

Management's report and the auditors' opinion must be included in Form 10-K, the annual report filed with the SEC. The Sarbanes-Oxley Act requires management to perform the above steps in a meaningful manner to support its report. While the exact wording of the report is left to management's discretion, Section 404(a) of the Sarbanes-Oxley Act requires the report to:

- State that it is management's responsibility to establish and maintain adequate internal control.
- Identify management's framework for evaluating internal control.
- Include management's assessment of the effectiveness of the company's internal control over financial reporting as of the end of the most recent fiscal period, including a statement as to whether internal control over financial reporting is effective.
- Include a statement that the company's auditors have issued an attestation report on management's assessment.

## Management's Evaluation Process and Assessment

For most SEC registrants, passage of Sarbanes-Oxley resulted in a one-time major project of evaluating and improving internal control to allow both management and the auditors to conclude that the company's internal control is effective. Then, for each subsequent year's reporting, the analysis is updated. The overall process is one of identifying the significant controls and testing their design and operating effectiveness.

The project is performed either by the company itself or by the company assisted by consultants—often personnel from a CPA firm that does not audit the company's financial statements. The company's external auditing firm may provide only limited assistance to management to avoid a situation in which its assessment is in essence part of management's assessment, as well as its own. That is, the CPA firm performing the audit should not create a situation in which management relies in any way on the CPA firm's assessment in making its own assessment.

As a starting point, the Securities and Exchange Commission, which provides operational guidance for implementing the Sarbanes-Oxley requirements, has adopted the following definition for internal control:

> Internal control over financial reporting is a process designed by, or under the supervision of, the company's principal executive and principal financial officers, or persons performing similar functions, and affected by the company's board of directors, management, and other personnel, to provide reasonable assurance regarding the reliability of financial reporting and the preparation of financial statements for external purposes in accordance with generally accepted accounting principles and includes those policies and procedures that:
>
> 1. Pertain to the maintenance of records that, in reasonable detail, accurately and fairly reflect the transactions and dispositions of the assets of the company;
> 2. Provide reasonable assurance that transactions are recorded as necessary to permit preparation of financial statements in accordance with generally accepted accounting principles, and that receipts and expenditures of the company are being made only in accordance with authorizations of management and directors of the company; and
> 3. Provide reasonable assurance regarding prevention or timely detection of unauthorized acquisition, use, or disposition of the company's assets that could have a material effect on the financial statements.

FIGURE 18.1
**Comparison of Control Deficiency, Significant Deficiency, and Material Weakness Definitions**

| Deficiency | Severity | Does Existence Result in Required Modification of Management's Assessment and Auditors' Report? |
|---|---|---|
| **Control Deficiency** | Not directly considered in definition | Only if it is a material weakness |
| **Significant Deficiency** | Less severe than a material weakness | No |
| **Material Weakness** | Reasonable possibility of a material misstatement | Yes |

**FIGURE 18.2**
**Levels of Severity of Control Deficiencies**

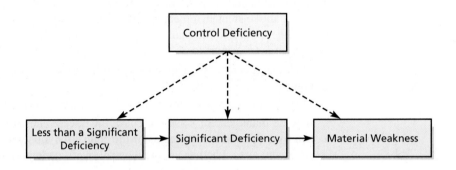

Management's report must be based on the preceding definition of internal control and must result from an evaluation using an accepted "control framework." Although not required, the control framework ordinarily used is the *Internal Control–Integrated Framework,* created by the Committee of Sponsoring Organizations of the Treadway Commission (COSO). The COSO framework, discussed in detail in Chapter 7, is the internal control framework commonly used in audits of financial statements.

To perform its evaluation and make its assessment,[2] management must understand the concepts of control deficiency, significant deficiency, and material weakness—concepts originally presented in Chapter 7 of this text, although the latter two terms are defined differently for purposes of an integrated audit. A **control deficiency** exists when the design or operation of a control does not allow management or employees, in the normal course of performing their functions, to prevent or detect misstatements on a timely basis.

A **material weakness** is a control deficiency, or combination of control deficiencies, in internal control over financial reporting, such that there is a reasonable possibility that a material misstatement of the company's annual or interim financial statements will not be prevented or detected on a timely basis. A reasonable possibility exists when the likelihood is either "reasonably possible" or "probable" as those terms are used in *FASB ASC* 450-20 "Loss Contingencies."

A **significant deficiency** is a control deficiency, or a combination of control deficiencies, in internal control over financial reporting that is less severe than a material weakness, yet important enough to merit attention by those responsible for oversight of the company's financial reporting.

Figures 18.1 and 18.2 illustrate relationships among deficiencies, significant deficiencies, and material weaknesses.

---

[2] The "evaluation" or "evaluation process" refers to the methods and procedures management implements to comply with the requirements. The "assessment" is the disclosure required in management's report on internal control discussing any material weaknesses and management's assessment of the effectiveness of internal control.

In evaluating the significance of identified deficiencies, both quantitative and qualitative factors are considered. Quantitative factors address the potential amount of loss. Qualitative factors include consideration of the nature of the accounts and assertions involved and the possible future consequences of the deficiency. Chapters 6 and 16 of this text include discussions of qualitative factors affecting materiality judgments.

Additionally, the consideration of a control deficiency should also include analysis of whether a **compensating control** exists to either prevent or detect the possible misstatement. For example, assume a company has a deficiency in control over cash disbursements. The compensating control of reconciliation of cash accounts by a competent individual who is otherwise independent of the cash function might make the likelihood of not detecting a significant misstatement less than reasonably possible. Therefore, while a deficiency might exist, it might not be a significant deficiency or a material weakness due to the existence of a compensating control.

Management must identify the significant financial statement accounts in order to evaluate the controls over major classes of transactions. **Major classes of transactions** are those that materially affect significant financial statement accounts—either directly through entries in the general ledger or indirectly through the creation of rights or obligations that may or may not be recorded in the general ledger.

The overall objective of management's evaluation of internal control is to provide it with a reasonable basis for its annual assessment as to whether there are any material weaknesses in internal control as of the end of the fiscal year. How does management go about achieving this objective? The SEC guidance is structured about two broad principles—(1) evaluating the design of controls to identify controls and risks and (2) evaluating the operation of the controls. This is consistent with the internal control coverage throughout the text—first consider the design, and then the operating effectiveness of controls.

### Evaluating Design Effectiveness of Controls

The evaluation process begins with identifying and assessing the risks to reliable financial reporting. Management then considers whether it has controls placed in operation (implemented) that are designed to adequately address those risks. Management ordinarily uses a top-down approach in which it begins with the identification of entity-level controls and works down to detailed controls only to the extent necessary. For example, if management determines that a control within the company's period-end financial reporting process (an entity-level control) is designed to adequately address the risk of a material misstatement of interest expense, management may not need to identify any additional controls related to interest expense. When additional assurance is needed, consideration of additional controls becomes necessary. Since the process auditors go through is similar, we discuss this in greater detail later in the chapter.

### Evaluating Operating Effectiveness of Internal Control

Management then evaluates operating effectiveness of controls in those areas that pose a high risk to reliable financial reporting. Evidence on operating effectiveness is obtained from tests of controls and from ongoing monitoring activities related to the controls. Tests of controls are similar to those performed by financial statement auditors as described in detail in Chapter 7. Ongoing monitoring includes activities that provide information about the operation of controls. This information is obtained, for example, through assessments made by employees, assessments made by management (referred to as *self-assessment* procedures), and the analysis of performance measures designed to track the operation of controls (e.g., budgets).

### Documentation

A required part of management's evaluation process is appropriate documentation of internal control. The documentation often occurs throughout the entire evaluation

## FIGURE 18.3
**Management Report on Internal Control**

Management is responsible for establishing and maintaining adequate internal control over financial reporting. Carver Company's internal control system was designed to provide reasonable assurance to the company's management and board of directors regarding the preparation and fair presentation of published financial statements.

All internal control systems, no matter how well designed, have inherent limitations. Therefore, even a system determined to be effective can provide only reasonable assurance with respect to financial statement preparation and presentation. [*Note: This paragraph is not required.*]

We assessed the effectiveness of the company's internal control over financial reporting as of December 31, 20X4. In making this assessment, we used the criteria set forth by the Committee of Sponsoring Organizations of the Treadway Commission (COSO) in *Internal Control–Integrated Framework*. Based on our assessment, we believe that, as of December 31, 20X4, the company's internal control over financial reporting is effective based on those criteria.

Carver Company's independent auditors have issued an audit report on our assessment of the company's internal control over financial reporting. This report appears on page XX.

*Sally Jones*
Chief Executive Officer
February 12, 20X5

*John Hankson*
Chief Financial Officer

process. Virtually all of the documentation tools included in Chapters 7 and 8 of this text are relevant for both management's evaluation and the external auditors' audit of internal control.

### Reporting

Management's evaluation process culminates with the issuance of management's report on internal control, which includes management's assessment. If management believes that no material weaknesses exist at year-end, it is able to issue a report concluding that the company maintained effective internal control over financial reporting. An illustration of such a report is included in Figure 18.3. In the next section, we will describe the auditors' process for evaluating and reporting on internal control.

# The Auditors' Responsibility for Reporting on Internal Control in PCAOB Audits

**LO3**

Describe the auditors' responsibility for reporting on internal control through integrated audits as required by the Public Company Accounting Oversight Board.

The auditors' objective in an audit of internal control is to express an opinion on the company's internal control over financial reporting. To meet this objective, the auditors must plan and perform the audit to obtain reasonable assurance about whether material weaknesses exist as of the date specified in management's assessment. Evidence is gathered on both the design and operating effectiveness of internal control as of the date specified in management's assessment—normally the last day of the company's fiscal year. The audit may be viewed as consisting of the following five stages.

1. Plan the engagement.
2. Use a top-down approach to identify controls to test.
3. Test and evaluate design effectiveness of internal control.
4. Test and evaluate operating effectiveness of internal control.
5. Form an opinion on the effectiveness of internal control.

## Plan the Engagement

**LO4**

Present the auditors' approach to analyzing internal control when performing an integrated audit.

As indicated in Figure 18.4, the auditors first plan the engagement. Efficient planning requires coordination with the financial statement audit. For purposes of both audits, the auditors consider matters related to the client's industry, regulatory matters, the client's business, and any recent changes in the client's operations. The auditors' knowledge of a client's internal control at the planning stage of the engagement will differ significantly depending upon the nature of the client and the auditors' experience with that client, and this in turn will affect the scope of the auditors' procedures. For example, when the auditors have previously performed audits of the client, the auditors begin the integrated audit with more information than in a circumstance in which the company is a new audit client. Accordingly, they only have to perform procedures to update their knowledge.

**FIGURE 18.4**

**An Audit of Internal Control over Financial Reporting**

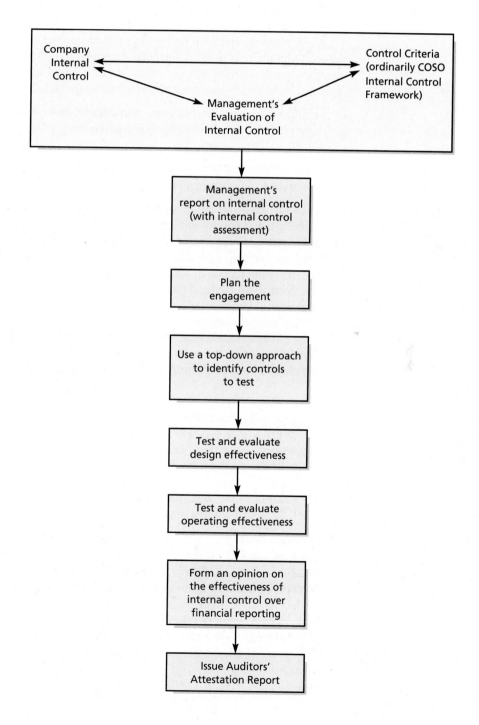

There is a subtle difference between the auditors' consideration of internal control for the audit of internal control as compared to their consideration of internal control in an audit of financial statements. In the audit of internal control, the focus is on whether internal control is effective at a point in time—the **as of date**—which is ordinarily the last day of the client's fiscal period. To express the internal control opinion, the auditors must obtain sufficient evidence on the effectiveness of controls at the as of date. By itself, this would involve performing tests of controls for a period that is usually significantly less than the entire year. On the other hand, in a financial statement audit the consideration of internal control is performed to help plan the audit and to assess control risk for the entire financial statement period. Therefore, the auditors must perform tests of controls of transactions occurring throughout the year to meet the objective of obtaining sufficient evidence to support the opinion on internal control and assess control risk. This distinction is discussed in more detail later in this chapter.

When planning and performing the audit of internal control, the auditors should take into account the results of the financial statement fraud risk assessment. Specifically, the auditors should identify and test controls that address the risk of fraud, including management override of other controls. These controls include those over:

- Significant unusual transactions, particularly those reported late in the period and those related to the period-end financial reporting process.
- Related party transactions.
- Significant management estimates.
- Incentives for management to falsify or inappropriately manage financial results.

When planning and performing the audit of internal control, the auditors should also recognize internal control differences between small and large clients. Often these differences are related to the degree of complexity of their operations. For example, when the auditors are auditing a small company, many control objectives may be accomplished through daily interaction of senior management and other company personnel rather than through formal policies and procedures. Because of the extensive involvement of senior management in performing controls and the period-end financial reporting process, the auditors of a small company should realize that controls to prevent management override are even more important than it is for a large company. Accordingly, for example, while detailed oversight by the audit committee may be an important control for most companies, it may be particularly important for a small company.

## Use a Top-Down Approach to Identify Controls to Test[3]

Figure 18.4 indicates that the auditors use a top-down approach to identify controls to test. What is a "top-down" approach? As indicated in Figure 18.5, the "top-down" approach starts at the top—the financial statements and entity-level controls—and links the financial statement elements and entity-level controls to significant accounts, relevant assertions, and to the major classes of transactions. The goal is to focus on testing those controls that are most important to the auditor's conclusion on internal control, while avoiding those that are less important.

### Entity-Level Controls

Entity-level controls often are those included in the control environment or monitoring components of internal control. For example, the portions of the control environment dealing with the tone at the top, assignment of authority and responsibility, and corporate codes of conduct have a pervasive effect on internal control. Also, information technology general controls over program development, program changes, and computer controls over processing have a pervasive effect in that they help ensure that specific controls over processing are operating effectively. The pervasiveness of entity-level controls distinguishes them

---

[3] This terminology is used in PCAOB *Standard No. 5*. This stage corresponds to obtaining an understanding of internal control in a financial statement audit.

**FIGURE 18.5**

**A Top-Down Approach to Testing Internal Control**

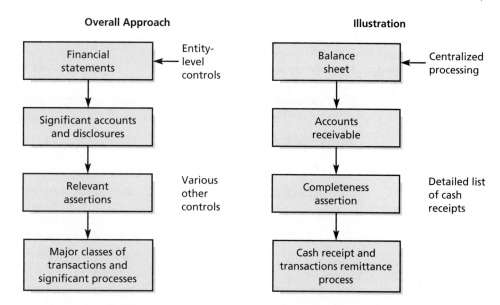

from other controls that are designed to achieve the specific objectives. As an example of a control that is not an entity-level control, consider control of requiring accounting for all shipping documents. This control activity is aimed primarily at assuring the completeness of recorded sales and does not have the pervasive effect of an entity-level control.

Entity-level controls relating to audit committee effectiveness, fraud, and the period-end financial reporting process are particularly emphasized in *Standard No. 5*. The audit committee is particularly important since an effective audit committee exercises oversight responsibility over both financial reporting and internal control. Indeed, ineffective audit committee oversight by itself is regarded as a strong indication that a material weakness in internal control exists.

PCAOB *Standard No. 5* also emphasizes the need for controls specifically intended to address the risk of fraud. These controls range from entity-level control environment controls, such as an appropriate tone at the top, corporate codes of conduct, and an effective antifraud program, to control activities, such as the reconciliation of cash accounts. Figure 18.6 provides examples of antifraud programs and elements.

The period-end financial reporting process (often referred to as "financial statement close") is also very significant. The period-end process involves the procedures used to enter transaction totals into the general ledger through the end of the financial statement reporting process. Auditors must thoroughly evaluate this process, including the manner in which financial statements are produced, the extent of information technology involved, who participates from management, the locations involved, and the types of adjusting entries and oversight by appropriate parties.

In considering entity-level controls, the auditors should be aware that controls may have either an indirect or a direct effect on the likelihood of misstatement. Controls with an indirect effect on the likelihood of misstatement might affect the auditors' decisions about the other controls that the auditors select for testing, as well as the nature, timing, and extent of procedures the auditors perform on other controls. For example, a positive tone at the top of the organization may lead to more effective lower level control performance, yet it does not have a direct effect on the likelihood of misstatement for any particular assertion. Such a control might allow the auditors to decrease the testing of other lower level controls.

Controls with a direct effect on the likelihood of misstatement operate at varying levels of precision. Some of these controls might be designed to identify possible breakdowns in lower level controls and operate at a level of precision that would allow auditors to reduce, but not eliminate, the testing of other controls. As an example, a monitoring control that detects only relatively large misstatements may fall into this category. When

**FIGURE 18.6**

**Entity-Level Antifraud Programs and Elements**

| Antifraud Program or Element | Strong Indicator of Significant Deficiency |
|---|---|
| Management accountability | Senior management conducts ineffective oversight of antifraud programs and controls. |
| Audit committee | Audit committee passively conducts oversight. It does not actively engage the topic of fraud. |
| Internal audit | Inadequate scope of activities. Inadequate communication, involvement, and interaction with the audit committee. |
| Code of conduct/ethics | Nonexistent code or code that fails to address conflicts of interest, related party transactions, illegal acts, and monitoring by management and the board. Ineffective communication to all covered persons. |
| "Whistleblower" program* | No program for anonymous submissions. Inadequate process for responding to allegations of suspicions of fraud. Whistleblower program significantly defective in design or operation. |
| Hiring and promotion procedures | Failure to perform substantive background investigations for individuals being considered for employment or promotion to a position of trust. |
| Remediation | Failure to take appropriate and consistent remedial actions with regard to identified significant deficiencies, material weaknesses, actual fraud, or suspected fraud. |

* A program for handling complaints and for accepting confidential submissions of concerns about questionable accounting, auditing, and other matters (e.g., hotlines).

such a control is operating effectively, it might allow the auditor to reduce, but not eliminate, the testing of other controls.

Other entity-level controls that have a direct effect on the likelihood of misstatement might be designed to operate at a level of precision that would adequately prevent or detect material misstatements to one or more relevant assertions. Such controls may allow the auditor to omit testing additional controls relating to that risk. Monitoring controls that identify relatively small misstatements may fall into this category. Note, however, that this area has been controversial as some have asked how frequently such controls actually exist, and thus allow the elimination of testing of controls beneath "the top."

### Significant Accounts and Disclosures

As shown in Figure 18.5, the auditors must obtain an understanding of **significant accounts** and disclosures. An account is significant if there is a reasonable possibility that it could contain a misstatement that, individually or when aggregated with others, has a material effect on the financial statements, considering both the risks of understatement and overstatement. The assessment should be made without giving any consideration to the effectiveness of internal control. Factors that the auditors consider in deciding whether an account is significant include:

- Size and composition.
- Susceptibility of loss due to errors or fraud.

- Volume of activity, complexity, and homogeneity of individual transactions.
- Nature of the account.
- Accounting and reporting complexity.
- Exposure to losses.
- Possibility of significant contingent liabilities.
- Existence of related party transactions.
- Changes from the prior period.

### Identifying Relevant Financial Statement Assertions

Once they have determined the significant accounts and disclosures, the auditors must determine which financial statement assertions are relevant to the significant accounts: (1) existence or occurrence; (2) completeness; (3) valuation or allocation; (4) rights and obligations; and/or (5) presentation and disclosure. Relevant assertions for an account are those that have a meaningful bearing on whether the account is presented fairly. For example, valuation may be very relevant to determining the amount of receivables, but it is not ordinarily relevant to cash unless currency translation is involved.

### Obtaining a Further Understanding of Likely Sources of Misstatement

To further understand the likely sources of potential misstatements, auditors should understand the flow of transactions related to the relevant assertions. This understanding allows the auditors to identify points within the company's processes where a material misstatement could arise and to identify the controls to prevent or detect these misstatements.

Throughout the text (e.g., Chapter 6, Chapters 11–16), we have discussed the concept of transaction cycles. Transaction cycles (also referred to as classes of transactions) are those transaction flows that have a meaningful bearing on the totals accumulated in the company's significant accounts and, therefore, have a meaningful bearing on relevant assertions. Consider a company whose sales may be initiated by customers either through the Internet or in a retail store. These two types of sales may be viewed as representing two major classes of transactions within the sales process.

Although not explicitly discussed in PCAOB *Standard No. 5,* it is helpful to classify transactions by *transaction type*—routine, nonroutine, or accounting estimates. **Routine transactions** are for recurring activities, such as sales, purchases, cash receipts and disbursements, and payroll. **Nonroutine transactions** occur only periodically; they generally are not part of the routine flow of transactions and include transactions such as counting and pricing inventory, calculating depreciation expense, or determining prepaid expenses. **Accounting estimates** are activities involving management's judgments or assumptions, such as determining the allowance for doubtful accounts, estimating warranty reserves, and assessing assets for impairment.

Throughout the audit of internal control, auditors must be concerned about all three transaction types. However, the auditors must be aware that the unique nature of non-routine transactions and the subjectivity involved with accounting estimate transactions make them particularly prone to misstatement unless they are properly controlled.

To understand the likely sources of potential misstatements and as a part of selecting the controls to test, the auditors should:

- Understand the flow of transactions;
- Verify points within the company's processes at which a misstatement could arise that could be material;
- Identify the controls management has implemented to address these potential misstatements; and
- Identify the controls management has implemented to prevent or detect on a timely basis unauthorized acquisition, use, or disposition of the company's assets that could result in a material misstatement.

## FIGURE 18.7    Relationships among Processes, Transaction Types, and Significant Accounts

| Example Processes | Transaction Types | Cash | Accounts Receivable | Allowance for Doubtful Accounts | Inventories | Inventory Reserves | Prepaid | Property, Plant, & Equipment | Other Accounts | Stockholders' Equity |
|---|---|---|---|---|---|---|---|---|---|---|
| Financial statement close | Nonroutine | X | X | X | X | X | X | X | X | X |
| Cash receipts | Routine | X | X | | | | | | X | |
| Cash disbursements | Routine | X | | | | | | | X | |
| Payroll | Routine | | | | | | | | | |
| Inventory costing (CGS) | Routine | X | | | X | | | | | |
| Estimate purchase commitments | Estimation | | | | | | | | X | |
| Estimate excess and obsolete inventory | Estimation | | | | | X | | | | |
| Lower-of-cost-or-market calculation | Estimation | | | | | X | | | | |
| LIFO calculation | Nonroutine | | | | | X | | | | |
| Physical inventory count | Nonroutine | | | | | X | | | | |
| Accounts receivable and sales | Routine | | X | | | | | | | |

Source: Adapted from Ernst & Young, *Evaluating Internal Control: Considerations for Documenting Controls at the Process, Transaction, or Application Level,* 2003.

Figure 18.7 provides an illustration of the relationships among significant accounts, processes, and transaction types emphasizing inventory processes; it presumes one major class of transactions for each process.

*Selecting Controls to Test*

The auditors should test those controls that are important to their conclusion about whether the company's controls sufficiently address the risk of misstatement for each relevant assertion. It is not necessary to design tests of all controls. For example, tests of **redundant controls** (those that duplicate other controls) need not be designed when tests of the related control are planned, unless redundancy itself is a control objective. The auditors may decide to design tests of preventive controls, detective controls, or a combination of both for the various assertions and significant accounts. Preventive controls have the objective of preventing errors or fraud from occurring; detective controls have the objective of detecting errors or fraud that have already occurred. Effective internal control generally involves "levels" of controls composed of a combination of both preventive and detective controls. Some controls are **complementary controls** in that they work together to achieve a particular control objective. When tests are being performed related to that control objective, the complementary controls must be tested.

A question that arises when a client has multiple locations is: Must the auditors design and perform tests at all locations? The answer is no. In determining the locations at which to perform tests of controls, the auditor should assess the risk of material misstatement to the financial statements of each location and base the amount of testing on the degree of risk.

*Performing Walk-throughs*

While not required, performing walk-throughs may frequently be the most effective way to obtain an understanding of the likely sources of misstatement. A **walk-through** involves literally tracing a transaction from its origination through the company's information system until it is reflected in the company's financial reports. Walk-throughs provide the auditors with evidence to:

- Verify that they have identified points at which a significant risk of misstatement to a relevant assertion exists.
- Verify their understanding of the design of controls, including those related to the prevention or detection of fraud.
- Evaluate the effectiveness of the design of controls.
- Confirm whether controls have been placed in operation (implemented).

Because much judgment is required in performing a walk-through, the auditors should either perform walk-throughs themselves or supervise the work of others who provide assistance to them (e.g., internal auditors).

While performing walk-throughs, the auditors ask those involved to describe their understanding of the processing involved and to demonstrate what they do. In addition, follow-up inquiries should be made to help identify abuse of controls or indicators of fraud. Examples of such follow-up inquiries include:

- What do you do when you find an error?
- What kind of errors have you found?
- What happened as a result of finding the errors, and how were the errors resolved?
- Have you ever been asked to override the process or controls? If yes, why did it occur and what happened?

## Test and Evaluate Design Effectiveness of Internal Control over Financial Reporting

The auditors test the design effectiveness of controls by determining whether the company's controls, if operating properly, satisfy the company's control objectives and can effectively prevent or detect errors or fraud that could result in material misstatements. The procedures performed here include a combination of inquiry of appropriate personnel, observation of the company's operations, and inspection of relevant documentation. Figure 18.8 provides an example of control objectives, risks, and controls using the COSO framework. The auditors specifically consider whether the controls, if functioning, would reduce the risks to an appropriately low level.

## Test and Evaluate Operating Effectiveness of Internal Control over Financial Reporting

Tests of the operating effectiveness of a control determine whether the control functions as designed and whether the person performing the control possesses the necessary authority and qualifications. In deciding how to design tests of operating effectiveness, the auditors must focus on the nature, timing, and extent of the tests.

*Nature of Tests of Operating Effectiveness*

Tests of controls, in the order of increasing persuasiveness, include a combination of inquiries of appropriate personnel, inspection of relevant documents, observation of the company's operations, and reperformance of the application of controls. For example, to evaluate whether the second control objective in Figure 18.8, the accurate and complete recording of invoices, is achieved, the auditors might use generalized audit software to inspect electronic documents to determine that no gaps exist in the sequence of shipping documents. Also, *Standard No. 5* states that the auditors should vary the exact tests performed when possible to introduce unpredictability into the audit process.

Evaluating responses to inquiries represents a particular challenge in that the responses may range from formal written inquiries (e.g., representation letters) to informal oral inquiries. Because of the possibility of misrepresentation or misunderstanding of the

FIGURE 18.8    **Process: Accounts Receivable**

| Control Objective | Risks | Controls |
|---|---|---|
| 1. Ensure that all goods shipped are accurately billed in the proper period. | Missing documents or incorrect information<br><br>Improper cutoff of shipment at the end of a period | • Use standard shipping or contract terms.<br>• Communicate nonstandard shipping or contract terms to accounts receivable department.<br>• Identify shipments as being before or after period end by means of a shipping log and prenumbered shipping documents. |
| 2. Accurately record invoices for all authorized shipments and only for such shipments. | Missing documents or incorrect information | • Prenumber and account for shipping documents and sales invoices.<br>• Match orders, shipping documents, invoices, and customer information, and follow through on missing or inconsistent information.<br>• Mail customer statements periodically and investigate and resolve disputes or inquiries by individuals independent of the invoicing function.<br>• Monitor number of customer complaints regarding improper invoices or statements. |
| 3. Accurately record all authorized sales returns and allowances and only such returns and allowances. | Missing documents or incorrect information<br><br><br><br><br>Inaccurate input of data | • Authorization of credit memos by individuals independent of accounts receivable function.<br>• Prenumber and account for credit memos and receiving documents.<br>• Match credit memos and receiving documents and resolve unmatched items by individuals independent of the accounts receivable function.<br>• Mail customer statements periodically and investigate and resolve disputes or inquiries by individuals independent of the invoicing function. |
| 4. Ensure continued completeness and accuracy of accounts receivable. | Unauthorized input for nonexistent returns, allowances, and write-offs | • Review correspondence authorizing returns and allowances.<br>• Reconcile accounts receivable subsidiary ledger with sales and cash receipts transactions.<br>• Resolve differences between the accounts receivable subsidiary ledger and the accounts receivable control account. |
| 5. Safeguard accounts receivable records. | Unauthorized access to accounts receivable records and stored data | • Restrict access to accounts receivable files and data used in processing receivables. |

Source: Adapted from *Internal Control–Integrated Framework, Evaluation Tools.*

responses, inquiry alone does not provide sufficient evidence to support the operating effectiveness of a control. Thus, auditors should substantiate the responses to inquiries by performing other procedures, such as inspecting reports or other documentation relating to the inquiries.

*Timing of Tests of Controls*

Tests of controls should be performed over a period of time sufficient to determine whether, as of the date specified in management's report, the controls were operating effectively. The auditors are aware that some controls operate continuously (e.g., controls over routine transactions, such as sales), while others operate only periodically (e.g., controls over nonroutine transactions or events, such as the preparation and analysis of monthly or quarterly financial statements). For controls that operate only periodically, it may be necessary to wait until after the date of management's report to test them; for example, controls over period-end financial reporting normally operate only after the date

**Illustrative Case** | *Frequency of Testing*

One CPA firm provided the following guidance to its auditors as to frequency of testing:

| Frequency of Control | Suggested Number of Items to Test |
| --- | --- |
| Annual | 1 |
| Quarterly | 2 |
| Monthly | 3–6 |
| Weekly | 10–20 |
| Daily | 20–40 |
| Multiple times per day | 30–60 |

of management's report. The auditors' tests can be performed only at the time the controls are operating.

### Extent of Tests of Controls

PCAOB *Standard No. 5* requires the auditors to obtain sufficient evidence about the effectiveness of controls for all relevant assertions related to all significant accounts. This means that the auditors must design procedures to provide a high level of assurance that the controls related to each relevant assertion are operating effectively. For manual controls, this generally involves more extensive testing than for automated controls. Generally, the more frequently controls operate, the more auditors should test them, and controls that are relatively more important should be tested more extensively. Also, the auditors cannot be satisfied with less-than-persuasive evidence because of a belief that management is honest.

When control exceptions are identified, the auditors should critically assess the nature and extent of testing and consider whether additional testing is appropriate. Also, a conclusion that an identified control exception does not represent a control deficiency is only appropriate if evidence beyond what the auditors had originally planned, and beyond inquiry, supports that conclusion. The issue of evaluating exceptions will be described in more detail later in this chapter.

Can auditors use the work of others—internal auditors, company personnel, and third parties—in the audit of internal control? For example, if client personnel have already performed certain procedures that the auditors had intended, may the auditors use that work? The answer is yes because PCAOB *Standard No. 5* allows auditors to use the work of others. It is expected that the work of others used by the auditors will often be related to relatively low-risk areas. In any event, the auditors must understand that when they use the work of others they remain responsible for their opinion and they cannot share responsibility with those others. In all cases in which the work of others is used, the auditors should evaluate the competence and objectivity of those individuals and test the work they have performed.

Another issue relates to the degree to which auditors must retest controls in detail each year. In audits subsequent to the first year, auditors should incorporate knowledge obtained during past audits of internal control. Using this "cumulative audit knowledge" (knowledge obtained from prior audits), the auditors often may be able to reduce the amount of work performed. In making decisions as to the necessary testing, the auditors should consider the various risk factors related to a control as well as:

- The nature, timing, and extent of procedures performed in previous audits,
- The results of the previous years' testing of the control, and
- Whether there have been changes in the control, or the significant process in which it operates, since the previous audit.

To illustrate, assume that a control presents a low risk overall in that there is a low inherent risk, a low degree of complexity, few changes in controls, and the previous year revealed no deficiencies. In such a case, the auditors may determine that sufficient evidence of operating effectiveness could be obtained by performing a walk-through. In addition, the auditors may use the work of others to a greater extent than in the past. But, on an overall basis, the auditors must test controls every year and cannot "rotate" analysis of various transaction types between various years (e.g., consider controls over sales this year, and purchases next year).

**LO5**

Explain how findings relating to the audits of internal control and the financial statements may affect one another.

### *Relationship between Tests of Controls Performed for the Internal Control Audit and Those Performed for the Financial Statement Audit*

Are the types of tests of controls performed for an internal control audit the same as those performed for a financial statement audit? May the evidence from tests performed for an internal control audit be used for the financial statement audit? While the answer to both of these questions is yes, the auditors must consider the differences in the objectives of the tests.

The objective of tests of controls in an audit of internal control is to obtain evidence about the effectiveness of controls to support the auditors' opinion on whether management's assessment of the effectiveness of internal control, taken as a whole, is fairly stated as of a point in time. Accordingly, to express this opinion the auditors must obtain evidence about the effectiveness of controls over all relevant assertions for all significant accounts and disclosures in the financial statements.

The objective of tests of controls for a financial statement audit is to assess control risk. If the auditors decide to assess control risk at less than the maximum, they are required to obtain evidence that the relevant controls operated effectively during the entire period upon which they plan to place reliance on those controls. However, the auditors are not required to assess control risk at less than the maximum for all assertions.

How may these two different approaches for tests of controls be reconciled in an integrated audit? PCAOB *Standard No. 5,* for purposes of the internal control audit, allows the auditors to obtain evidence about operating effectiveness at different times throughout the year—provided that the auditors update those tests or obtain other evidence that the controls still operated effectively at the end of the year. Thus, although the timing for issuing the internal control report will not ordinarily require tests from throughout the year, the integrated nature of the two audits suggests that testing should be spread throughout the year.

The requirements of *Standard No. 5* have had the effect of pushing auditors to perform financial statement audits using the systems approach—an approach with heavy reliance on internal control evidence. In essence, since extensive tests of controls are required for each significant account for the internal control audit, the auditors should have significant evidence about the effectiveness of internal control for the financial statement audit. The auditors generally must merely extend the tests to cover the financial statement period in order to assess control risk at a low level for purposes of the financial statement audit.

### *Effect of Tests of Controls on Financial Statement Audit Substantive Procedures*

Historically, to enhance audit efficiency and effectiveness, auditors often have used a substantive audit approach that is not acceptable for integrated audits. Auditors have traditionally relied primarily (or completely) on evidence from substantive procedures rather than testing controls in audit areas when a substantive approach was considered the most cost-effective approach. To illustrate, when only a financial statement audit is being performed, auditors often rely heavily upon substantive procedures to audit areas such as property, plant, and equipment; investments; and long-term debt. Since auditors must now report on the effectiveness of internal control, approaches limiting the testing of controls are not acceptable.

Historically, another efficiency that has developed in financial statement audits is minimizing the testing of controls aimed at **preventive controls** (e.g., transaction level controls), and emphasizing the testing of **detective controls** (e.g., various types of reconciliations and exception reports). When auditors express an opinion on internal

## Illustrative Case

### *Using Attributes Sampling to Consider Control Deficiencies*

It is possible to use statistical attribute sampling (presented in Chapter 9) to consider control deficiency seriousness. Consider a control over authorization of sales transactions:

    1% = Deviation rate in the auditors' sample
    6% = Achieved upper deviation rate
    5% = Risk of assessing control risk too low

If one further assumes that $3,000,000 of the transaction type occurred, the auditor may estimate that $180,000

(6% × $3,000,000) worth of transactions may not have been properly approved. That is, there is less than a reasonable possibility that $180,000 in transactions were not properly approved.

If one assumes that $180,000 is material, the deficiency represents a material weakness. Alternatively, if it is not considered quantitatively material, an auditor must judgmentally determine whether it represents a significant deficiency that should be communicated to the audit committee. Note, however, that the auditors must also take into account qualitative considerations.

control, the auditors are more likely to use an approach that includes testing of both preventive and detective controls.

Since an integrated audit requires tests of controls for all major accounts and relevant assertions, circumstances in which controls are found to be effective will lead to a decreased scope of substantive procedures as compared to a situation in which tests of controls have revealed an ineffective system or a situation in which tests of controls have not been performed. However, when significant deficiencies or material weaknesses have been identified, the auditors must obtain assurance that such deficiencies have not resulted in undetected material misstatements. As an example, if controls over the recording of revenues are considered ineffective, the auditors must determine whether the audit procedures designed into their audit program must be modified to obtain more evidence about the fairness of revenue.

The extensive level of controls testing performed during an integrated audit leads to the question of whether substantive tests may be omitted completely in areas in which controls have been found to operate effectively. This is not acceptable. Regardless of the assessed level of control risk, the auditors must perform substantive procedures for all relevant assertions related to all significant accounts and disclosures.

### *Effect of Financial Statement Substantive Procedures on the Audit of Internal Control*

We have shown that the audit of internal control may affect the scope of substantive procedures performed for the financial statement audit. Alternatively, the results of substantive procedures may affect the audit of internal control. The findings obtained while performing substantive procedures in the financial statement audit may provide evidence of the effectiveness or ineffectiveness of internal control over financial reporting. For example, identification of a material misstatement in the financial statements is considered indicative of at least a significant deficiency in internal control. Additional examples of substantive procedures findings that might affect the internal control audit are those relating to illegal acts, related party transactions, the reasonableness of accounting estimates, and the client's overall selection of accounting principles.

**Form an Opinion on the Effectiveness of Internal Control over Financial Reporting**

In forming an opinion on internal control over financial reporting, the auditors evaluate all evidence, including:

1. The results of their evaluation of the design,
2. The results of tests of the operating effectiveness of controls,
3. Negative results of substantive procedures performed during the financial statement audit, and
4. Any identified control deficiencies.

**LO6**

Discuss circumstances that require auditors to modify their report on internal control.

An unqualified audit opinion may be issued when no material weaknesses in internal control have been identified as existing at the as of date (year-end) and when there have been no restrictions on the scope of the auditors' work. The auditors may issue separate reports on the financial statements and internal control or a combined report. Figure 18.9 is an example of a separate report on internal control.

One or more material weaknesses in internal control result in an adverse opinion.[4] Scope limitations may result in either a disclaimer or withdrawal from the engagement depending on the extent of the limitation.

Determining whether deficiencies have been identified and, if so, the likelihood and potential amount of misstatement is key to identifying the proper opinion to issue. If no deficiencies have been identified and no scope limitations are involved, an unqualified opinion is appropriate.

### Evaluating Deficiencies

The auditors must evaluate whether identified control deficiencies, individually or in combination, are significant deficiencies or material weaknesses. This involves a consideration of both quantitative and qualitative factors.

When a deficiency has been identified, the auditors will consider whether any other controls effectively mitigate the risk of potential misstatement and create a situation in which the deficiency is not significant or, at least, does not constitute a material weakness. Earlier in this chapter, we used the example of a weakness in cash disbursements that was mitigated by the compensating control of reconciliation of the bank account by an individual otherwise independent of the cash function. Such a compensating control might cause the auditors to alter their assessment of a deficiency—reducing it from one that otherwise would be considered significant (or a material weakness) to one that is simply a control deficiency.

In evaluating the potential amount of misstatement related to a control deficiency, the auditors should consider not only the misstatements identified, but also the amount that could occur with a reasonable possibility. Although there are various possible approaches to this evaluation, one is to directly consider whether a reasonable possibility exists that a material amount of misstatement could occur. If that is the case, the deficiency is a material weakness. Alternatively, if the deficiency is less severe than a material weakness, yet important enough to merit the attention by those responsible for oversight of the company's financial reporting (ordinarily the audit committee), the deficiency represents a significant deficiency.

The auditors must also consider qualitative factors when evaluating materiality, as is the case with financial statement audits. Examples of qualitative factors include whether the weakness relates to related party transactions and whether there are changes in account characteristics in relation to the prior year. Chapter 6 presents additional information on qualitative factors that are used by the auditors. In essence, the auditors should attempt to determine what a prudent official in the conduct of his or her own affairs would consider a significant deficiency and a material weakness.

While a material weakness in internal control can arise in a wide variety of situations, PCAOB *Standard No.* 5 provides the following indicators of material weaknesses:

- Identification of fraud, whether or not material, on the part of senior management.
- Restatement of previously issued financial statements to reflect the correction of a material misstatement.
- Identification by the auditors of a material misstatement in circumstances that indicate that the misstatement would not have been detected by the company's internal control.
- Ineffective oversight of the company's external financial reporting and internal control by the company's audit committee.

---

[4] Notice that this is different from reports on audits of financial statements. In an audit of financial statements, a departure from generally accepted accounting principles results in either a qualified opinion or an adverse opinion based on materiality.

**FIGURE 18.9** **Report with Standard Unqualified Opinion on Internal Control over Financial Reporting**

### Report of Independent Registered Public Accounting Firm

To the Audit Committee and Stockholders of Carver Company:

[*Introductory paragraph*]

We have audited Carver Company's internal control over financial reporting as of December 31, 20X8, based on criteria established in *Internal Control–Integrated Framework issued by the Committee of Sponsoring Organizations of the Treadway Commission (COSO)*. Carver Company's management is responsible for maintaining effective internal control over financial reporting, and for its assessment of the effectiveness of internal control over financial reporting, included in the accompanying [title of management's report]. Our responsibility is to express an opinion on the company's internal control over financial reporting based on our audits.

[*Scope paragraph*]

We conducted our audit in accordance with the standards of the Public Company Accounting Oversight Board (United States). Those standards require that we plan and perform the audit to obtain reasonable assurance about whether effective internal control over financial reporting was maintained in all material respects. Our audit included obtaining an understanding of internal control over financial reporting, assessing the risk that a material weakness exists, and testing and evaluating the design and operating effectiveness of internal control based on the assessed risk. Our audit also included performing such other procedures as we considered necessary in the circumstances. We believe that our audit provides a reasonable basis for our opinion.

[*Definition paragraph*]

A company's internal control over financial reporting is a process designed to provide reasonable assurance regarding the reliability of financial reporting and the preparation of financial statements for external purposes in accordance with generally accepted accounting principles. A company's internal control over financial reporting includes those policies and procedures that (1) pertain to the maintenance of records that, in reasonable detail, accurately and fairly reflect the transactions and dispositions of the assets of the company; (2) provide reasonable assurance that transactions are recorded as necessary to permit preparation of financial statements in accordance with generally accepted accounting principles, and that receipts and expenditures of the company are being made only in accordance with authorizations of management and directors of the company; and (3) provide reasonable assurance regarding prevention or timely detection of unauthorized acquisition, use, or disposition of the company's assets that could have a material effect on the financial statements.

[*Inherent limitations paragraph*]

Because of its inherent limitations, internal control over financial reporting may not prevent or detect misstatements. Also, projections of any evaluation of effectiveness to future periods are subject to the risk that controls may become inadequate because of changes in conditions, or that the degree of compliance with the policies or procedures may deteriorate.

[*Opinion paragraph*]

In our opinion, Carver Company maintained, in all material respects, effective internal control over financial reporting as of December 31, 20X8, based on criteria established in *Internal Control–Integrated Framework issued by the Committee of Sponsoring Organizations of the Treadway Commission (COSO)*.

[*Explanatory paragraph*]

We have also audited, in accordance with the standards of the Public Company Accounting Oversight Board (United States), the balance sheets of Carver Company as of December 31, 20X8 and 20X7, and the related statements of income, shareholders' equity and comprehensive income, and cash flows for each of the three years for the period ended December 31, 20X8, of Carver Company. Our report, dated February 12, 20X9, expressed an unqualified opinion.

*Willington & Co., CPAs*

Bisbee, Arizona, United States of America
February 20X9

FIGURE 18.10 **Abstract of Report with Adverse Opinion on Internal Control over Financial Reporting**

(Paragraphs 1–4 and the final paragraph are identical to Figure 18.9 standard unqualified report)

[*Explanatory paragraph*]

A material weakness is a control deficiency, or a combination of control deficiencies, in internal control over financial reporting, such that there is a reasonable possibility that a material misstatement of the company's annual or interim financial statements will not be prevented or detected on a timely basis. A material weakness was identified and is described in management's assessment of internal control. That material weakness relates to [describe the material weakness, including its actual and potential effect on the financial statements].

[*Opinion paragraph*]

In our opinion, because of the effect of the material weakness described above on the achievement of the objectives of the control criteria, Carver Company has not maintained effective internal control over financial reporting as of December 31, 20X8, based on criteria established in *Internal Control–Integrated Framework issued by the Committee of Sponsoring Organizations of the Treadway Commission (COSO).*

*Correcting a Material Weakness*

Recall that the audit report is modified for material weaknesses that exist at the as of date (year-end). Consider a situation in which four months prior to year-end management identifies a material weakness. If management corrects this weakness prior to year-end, can the auditors issue an unqualified opinion on internal control? Yes, but only if the auditors have sufficient evidence to provide reasonable assurance that the new control is operating effectively. Obtaining such evidence is much easier for controls that operate frequently, in contrast to those that operate only monthly or quarterly (e.g., financial statement close). All in all, the timing of the identification of the material weakness is very important. For example, if the material weakness is not identified until after year-end, an adverse opinion must be issued even if the weakness is corrected: The control did not operate effectively on the date of management's report.

## Audit Report Modifications

*Existence of a Material Weakness*

A material weakness in internal control that exists at year-end results in the issuance of an adverse opinion. When expressing an adverse opinion, the auditors' report must define a material weakness, indicate that one has been identified, and refer to the description of it in management's report. Figure 18.10 provides an example of an adverse opinion.

*Scope Limitations*

If a restriction on the scope of the audit is imposed by the circumstances, the auditors should withdraw from the engagement or disclaim an opinion. Earlier we discussed the situation in which the auditors identify a material weakness and management takes steps to correct that material weakness prior to year-end. If the auditors are unable to obtain sufficient evidence that the new controls are effective for a sufficient period of time, they will issue a disclaimer of opinion on internal control.

*Management's Report on Internal Control Is Incomplete or Improperly Presented*

When management's report on internal control (including its assessment) is found to be inadequate, the auditors should modify their report to include an explanatory paragraph describing the reasons for this determination. If management does not disclose a material weakness properly, the auditors should state that the material weakness is not included in management's assessment and describe it in the audit report. Note that the auditors' report is already adverse due to the existence of a material weakness. In this situation, the auditors also are required to communicate in writing to the audit committee that the material weakness was not disclosed or identified as a material weakness in management's report. Figure 18.11 summarizes reporting for this and the preceding circumstances described in this section.

FIGURE 18.11   **Circumstances Affecting Auditors' Opinion on Internal Control**

| Circumstance | Auditors' Opinion |
| --- | --- |
| **Material Weakness Exists** | Adverse |
| **Material Weakness Existed during Year, System Changed Prior to the As of Date** | |
| Auditors test new system and material weakness eliminated | Unqualified |
| Auditors do not have sufficient time to test new system | Treat as scope restriction |
| **Scope Restriction\*** | **Disclaimer or Withdraw from Engagement** |
| **Management's Report on Internal Control Is Incomplete or Improperly Presented** | |
| Report does not acknowledge a material weakness identified by the auditor | Adverse |
| **Other Issues** | Unqualified (but with an explanatory paragraph) |

\* If the auditors intend to issue a disclaimer of opinion, yet know of a material weakness, the material weakness should be described in the report.

### Reliance on Other Auditors

When other auditors have performed a portion of the audit, the auditors must decide whether they are able to serve as the principal auditors. The considerations and reporting requirements are essentially the same as when other auditors are involved in the financial statement audit. The auditors who are able to serve as the principal auditors of the financial statements ordinarily also serve as principal auditors of internal control. When the principal auditors decide to refer in their report to the work of the other auditors, this reference is included both in describing the scope of the audit and in expressing the opinion.

### Subsequent Events

Subsequent events relevant to the internal control audit are changes in internal control subsequent to year-end but before the date of the auditors' report. The auditors have a responsibility to make inquiries of management about whether there have been any such changes. If the auditors obtain knowledge of subsequent events that materially and adversely affect the effectiveness of internal control, they should issue an adverse opinion. If the auditors are unable to determine the effect of the subsequent event, they should disclaim an opinion.

### Issuing a Combined Report on the Financial Statements and Internal Control

PCAOB *Standard No. 5* allows auditors to either issue separate reports on their audits of the financial statements and internal control or issue one combined report. The illustrations in this chapter have been based on separate reports. Figure 18.12 provides an illustration of a combined unqualified report on both the financial statements and internal control.

## Other Communication Requirements

PCAOB *Standard No. 5* requires that auditors communicate in writing to management all control deficiencies, regardless of their severity—this includes material weaknesses, significant deficiencies, and other deficiencies. In addition, a written communication to the audit committee must be issued that includes material weaknesses, significant deficiencies, and an indication that all deficiencies have been communicated to management. The written communications on weaknesses to both management and the audit committee should be made prior to issuance of the audit report on internal control.

In addition, when the auditors conclude that the oversight of the company's external financial reporting and internal control over financial reporting is ineffective, they must communicate that conclusion in writing to the board of directors.

FIGURE 18.12    **Combined Report with Standard Unqualified Opinion on Financial Statements and Internal Control over Financial Reporting**

## Report of Independent Registered Public Accounting Firm

To the Audit Committee and Stockholders of Carver Company

*[Introductory paragraph]*

We have audited the accompanying balance sheets of Carver Company as of December 31, 20X8 and 20X7, and the related statements of income, stockholders' equity and comprehensive income, and cash flows for each of the years in the three-year period ended December 31, 20X8. We also have audited Carver Company's internal control over financial reporting as of December 31, 20X8, based on [Identify control criteria: for example, "criteria established in *Internal Control–Integrated Framework issued by the Committee of Sponsoring Organizations of the Treadway Commission (COSO)*"]. Carver Company's management is responsible for these financial statements, for maintaining effective internal control over financial reporting, and for its assessment of the effectiveness of internal control over financial reporting included in the accompanying [title of management's report]. Our responsibility is to express an opinion on these financial statements and an opinion on the company's internal control over financial reporting based on our audits.

*[Scope paragraph]*

We conducted our audits in accordance with the standards of the Public Company Accounting Oversight Board (United States). Those standards require that we plan and perform the audits to obtain reasonable assurance about whether the financial statements are free of material misstatement and whether effective internal control over financial reporting was maintained in all material respects. Our audits of the financial statements included examining, on a test basis, evidence supporting the amounts and disclosures in the financial statements, assessing the accounting principles used and significant estimates made by management, and evaluating the overall financial statement presentation. Our audit of internal control over financial reporting included obtaining an understanding of internal control over financial reporting, assessing the risk that a material weakness exists, and testing and evaluating the design and operating effectiveness of internal control based on the assessed risk. Our audits also included performing such other procedures as we considered necessary in the circumstances. We believe that our audits provide a reasonable basis for our opinions.

*[Definition paragraph]*

A company's internal control over financial reporting is a process designed to provide reasonable assurance regarding the reliability of financial reporting and the preparation of financial statements for external purposes in accordance with generally accepted accounting principles. A company's internal control over financial reporting includes those policies and procedures that (1) pertain to the maintenance of records that, in reasonable detail, accurately and fairly reflect the transactions and dispositions of the assets of the company; (2) provide reasonable assurance that transactions are recorded as necessary to permit preparation of financial statements in accordance with generally accepted accounting principles, and that receipts and expenditures of the company are being made only in accordance with authorizations of management and directors of the company; and (3) provide reasonable assurance regarding prevention or timely detection of unauthorized acquisition, use, or disposition of the company's assets that could have a material effect on the financial statements.

*[Inherent limitations paragraph]*

Because of its inherent limitations, internal control over financial reporting may not prevent or detect misstatements. Also, projections of any evaluation of effectiveness to future periods are subject to the risk that controls may become inadequate because of changes in conditions, or that the degree of compliance with the policies or procedures may deteriorate.

*[Opinion paragraph]*

In our opinion, the financial statements referred to above present fairly, in all material respects, the financial position of Carver Company as of December 31, 20X8 and 20X7, and the results of its operations and its cash flows for each of the years in the three-year period ended December 31, 20X8, in conformity with accounting principles generally accepted in the United States of America. Also in our opinion, Carver Company maintained, in all material respects, effective internal control over financial reporting as of December 31, 20X8, based on [identify control criteria: for example, "criteria established in *Internal Control–Integrated Framework issued by the Committee of Sponsoring Organizations of the Treadway Commission (COSO)*"].

*Willington & Co., CPAs*

Bisbee, Arizona, United States of America
February 20X9

## Reporting on Whether a Previously Reported Material Weakness Continues to Exist

After the existence of a material weakness has led to an adverse opinion in an internal control audit report, the company is ordinarily motivated to eliminate the weakness as quickly as is reasonably possible. When management believes that the material weakness has been eliminated, the auditors may be engaged to report on whether the material weakness continues to exist. PCAOB *Standard No. 4,* "Reporting on Whether a Previously Reported Material Weakness Continues to Exist," provides the guidance for such engagements.

To engage the auditors to perform this service, management must first gather sufficient evidence to demonstrate that the material weakness has been eliminated, document this evidence, and provide a written assertion stating that the material weakness no longer exists. The auditors then plan and perform an engagement that focuses on controls that are relevant to the particular weakness. If they determine that the controls are now effective, the auditors may issue an unqualified report indicating that the material weakness no longer exists. PCAOB *Standard No. 4* provides other reporting guidance, including:

- A significant scope limitation on the auditors' procedures should result in either a disclaimer of opinion or the resignation of the auditors (qualified opinions are not allowed).
- When the auditors' original report includes other material weaknesses that are not being considered in this engagement, the report should be modified to disclose that the other weaknesses are not addressed by the opinion.
- After a change in auditors, the successor auditors may issue such a report, but they first must obtain a sufficient understanding of the entity and the related material weakness.
- If, while performing the engagement, the auditors discover an additional material weakness, the auditors should inform the audit committee about the matter, but they are not required to modify their report.

## Integrated Audits for Nonpublic Companies

While nonpublic companies are not required to undergo integrated audits, the option is available. As an example, management may be considering taking the company public in the relatively near future and might choose to undergo such an audit. Attestation standard *AT 501* provides guidance for performing the internal control portion of an integrated audit for a *nonpublic* company.

The procedures for a nonpublic integrated audit are very similar to those for a public company that we have emphasized throughout this chapter. Accordingly, we will not provide extensive detail, but will simply summarize significant differences as shown below.

| Issue | PCAOB *Standard 5* | AT 501 |
|---|---|---|
| Title of the engagement? | Audit | Examination |
| Report on subject matter and/or assertion? | Only on subject matter | Subject matter or assertion when no material weakness exists; when a material weakness exists, subject matter |
| May the report issued indicate that no material weaknesses were identified? | Yes | No |
| Which standards are followed by the CPA as indicated in the report? | PCAOB Standards | Attestation standards established by the AICPA |

# Chapter Summary

This chapter explained the nature of integrated audits of public companies performed in response to the Sarbanes-Oxley Act of 2002 and in accordance with Public Company Accounting Oversight Board *Standard No. 5*. To summarize:

1. Section 404(a) of the Sarbanes-Oxley Act requires management to acknowledge its responsibility for establishing and maintaining adequate internal control and provide an assessment of internal control effectiveness as of the end of the most recent fiscal year.

2. Section 404(b) of the Sarbanes-Oxley Act requires the auditors to provide an opinion on the effectiveness of internal control.

3. Material weaknesses involve a reasonable possibility that a material misstatement of the financial statements will not be prevented or detected on a timely basis. Significant deficiencies are less severe than maternal weaknesses, yet important enough to merit attention by those responsible for oversight of the company's financial reporting.

4. An integrated audit includes an audit report on both the financial statements and internal control. To issue such a report, the auditors perform procedures to test controls over all significant accounts, as well as substantive tests to support their opinion on the fairness of the financial statements.

5. Internal control audit reports are modified for a material weakness that exists at year-end. The report issued includes an adverse opinion indicating that effective internal control does not exist. If the scope of the auditors' work is limited, they should issue a disclaimer of opinion, or withdraw from the engagement.

6. After a client has remediated a material weakness that led to an adverse report, auditors may be engaged to attest to the elimination of the material weakness.

# Key Terms Introduced or Emphasized in Chapter 18

**Accounting estimate (705)**   A transaction involving management's judgments or assumptions, such as determining the allowance for doubtful accounts, establishing warranty reserves, and assessing assets for impairment.

**As of date (702)**   An audit of internal control over financial reporting assesses internal control as of a particular point in time, the "as of" date, as opposed to the entire period under audit. This date is ordinarily the last day of the client's fiscal period.

**Compensating control (699)**   A control that reduces the risk that an existing or potential control weakness will result in a failure to meet a control objective (e.g., avoiding misstatements). Compensating controls are ordinarily controls performed to detect, rather than prevent, the misstatement from occurring. For example, a reconciliation of the bank account performed by an individual otherwise independent of the cash function serves to detect a variety of possible misstatements (both errors and fraud) that may have occurred in the processing of cash receipts and disbursements.

**Complementary controls (706)**   Controls that function together to achieve the same control objective (e.g., avoiding misstatements).

**Control deficiency (698)**   A weakness in the design or operation of a control that does not allow management or employees, in the normal course of performing their functions, to prevent or detect misstatements on a timely basis.

**Detective controls (710)**   Policies and procedures that are designed to identify errors or fraud after they have occurred. Detective controls can be applied to groups of transactions (e.g., bank reconciliations).

**Integrated audit (under PCAOB *Standard No. 5*) (696)**   An audit that includes audit reports on both a company's internal control over financial reporting and the financial statements.

**Major classes of transactions (699)**   Those transaction flows that have a meaningful bearing on the totals accumulated in the company's significant accounts and, therefore, have a meaningful bearing on relevant assertions.

**Material weakness (698)**   A control deficiency, or a combination of control deficiencies, in internal control over financial reporting, such that there is a **reasonable possibility** that a material misstatement of the company's annual or interim financial statements will not be prevented or detected on a timely basis.

**Nonroutine transaction (705)** A transaction that occurs only periodically, such as counting and pricing inventory, calculating depreciation expense, or determining prepaid expenses.

**Preventive controls (710)** Procedures designed to prevent an error or fraud. Preventive controls are normally applied at the individual transaction level.

**Redundant controls (706)** Duplicate controls that both achieve a control objective.

**Routine transaction (705)** A transaction for a recurring financial activity recorded in the accounting records in the normal course of business, such as sales, purchases, cash receipts, cash disbursements, and payroll.

**Sarbanes-Oxley Act of 2002 (697)** An act passed by the U.S. Congress to protect investors from the possibility of fraudulent accounting activities by corporations by improving the accuracy and reliability of corporate disclosures.

**Section 404 (696)** The primary section of the Sarbanes-Oxley Act dealing with management and auditor reporting on internal control over financial reporting. Section 404(a) requires that each annual report filed with the Securities and Exchange Commission include an internal control report prepared by management in which management acknowledges its responsibility for establishing and maintaining adequate internal control and an assessment of internal control effective *as of the end of the most recent fiscal year*. Section 404(b) requires that the CPA firm attest to and report internal control.

**Significant account (704)** An account for which there is a reasonable possibility that it could contain misstatements that individually, or when aggregated with others, could have a material effect on the financial statements.

**Significant deficiency (698)** A deficiency, or a combination of deficiencies, in internal control over financial reporting that is less severe than a material weakness, yet important enough to merit attention by those responsible for oversight of the company's financial reporting.

**Walk-through (707)** A procedure in which an auditor follows a transaction from origination through the company's processes, including information systems, until it is reflected in the company's financial records, using the same documents and information technology that company personnel use. Walk-through procedures usually include a combination of inquiry, observation, inspection of relevant documentation, and reperformance of controls.

## Review Questions

18–1. Section 404 of the Sarbanes-Oxley Act of 2002 includes two sections. Describe those sections.

18–2. Identify management's four overall responsibilities with respect to internal control over financial reporting that arise due to the Securities and Exchange Commission's implementation of the Sarbanes-Oxley Act of 2002.

18–3. What information must be included in management's report on internal control over financial reporting in the annual report filed with the Securities and Exchange Commission?

18–4. Describe the difference between a significant deficiency and a material weakness in internal control.

18–5. Comment on the accuracy of the following statement: "Since both significant deficiencies and material weaknesses must be reported to the audit committee, for practical purposes, there is no distinction between the two."

18–6. What is meant by the "as of" date when reporting on internal control over financial reporting?

18–7. What is a compensating control?

18–8. Provide examples of antifraud programs that the auditors might expect the client to have.

18–9. Describe what is meant by a "walk-through." Must walk-throughs be performed during audits of internal control over financial reporting? May the client perform a walk-through and the auditors then review the client's work?

18–10. While performing a walk-through, auditors ordinarily make certain inquiries of employees. Provide three examples of such inquiries.

18–11. Auditors often perform walk-throughs in integrated audits. Describe the evidence that is typically provided by a walk-through.

18–12. When performing an audit of internal control over financial reporting, auditors may distinguish among the following types of transactions: routine, nonroutine, and accounting estimates. Distinguish between these three types of transactions and give an example of each.

18–13. When performing an integrated audit, auditors must identify significant accounts and disclosures. What makes an account significant? What factors should be considered in deciding whether an account is significant?

18–14. A client operates out of 25 locations. Must the CPA perform tests related to internal control at each of these locations?

18–15. Comment on the following: "Auditors must decide, based on cost considerations, whether to test the design effectiveness or operating effectiveness of controls."

18–16. Provide an example of a situation in which the design of controls may be effective but those controls do not operate effectively.

18–17. Comment on the following: "Inquiry alone does not provide sufficient evidence to support the operating effectiveness of a control."

18–18. Comment on the following: "All controls should be tested either prior to or on the 'as of' date."

18–19. What requirements exist when the auditors use the work of client personnel as a part of the evidence obtained for an audit of internal control? In which areas of the audit would one expect this to be most likely to occur?

18–20. Provide an example of a situation in which the performance of substantive procedures for the financial statement audit might affect the internal control audit.

18–21. Provide an example of a situation in which the performance of tests of controls for the internal control audit might affect the performance of substantive procedures in a financial statement audit.

18–22. Distinguish between entity-level controls and controls designed to achieve specific control objectives.

18–23. Provide three examples of findings by the auditors that are at least significant deficiencies and strong indicators of the existence of a material weakness in internal control.

18–24. The auditors have completed an examination of internal control and are preparing to issue a report. Does the opinion paragraph on the client's internal control conclude on internal control or management's assessment of internal control?

18–25. What type of report on internal control is likely to be issued when management imposes a scope limitation?

18–26. If an adverse internal control report is issued by the auditors, may an unqualified report be issued on the financial statements?

18–27. Which types of deficiencies must be communicated to the audit committee?

18–28. Describe the requirements involved when auditors are engaged to report on whether a previously reported material weakness continues to exist.

## Questions Requiring Analysis

**LO 3** 18–29. The CPA firm of Carson & Boggs LLP is performing an internal control audit in accordance with PCAOB *Standard No. 5*. The partner in charge of the engagement has asked you to explain the process of determining which controls to test. Describe the process, presenting each of the links in this process and a short summary of how the auditors approach each of them.

**LO 1, 5** 18–30. Tests of controls are ordinarily performed for both financial statement audits and internal control audits.

a. What is the objective of tests of controls when performed for internal control audits?

b. What is the objective of tests of controls when performed for financial statement audits?

c. How are these different objectives reconciled in an integrated audit?

**LO 6** 18–31. The CPA firm of Webster, Warren, & Webb LLP issued an adverse opinion on the internal control of Alexandria Financial, a public company, due to a material weakness. The weakness involved the lack of sufficient accounting expertise to evaluate and adopt appropriate accounting principles. Subsequent to issuance of the report, management of Alexandria hired a new controller to eliminate the weakness.

a. Describe what steps Alexandria must perform to engage Webster, Warren, & Webb to issue a report indicating that the weakness no longer exists.

b. Describe how Webster, Warren, & Webb should approach the engagement.

c. Describe what Webster, Warren, & Webb must do if, during the course of the engagement, a member of the audit team discovers another material weakness in internal control over financial reporting. Will the new weakness affect the auditors' report?

## Objective Questions

All applicable questions are available with McGraw-Hill's *Connect*<sup>TM</sup> *Accounting.* ■ connect |ACCOUNTING

18–32.   **Multiple Choice Questions**

Select the best answer for each of the following questions. Explain the reasons for your selection:

**LO 3**   *a.* In an integrated audit, which of the following must the auditors communicate to the audit committee?

|  | Known Material Weaknesses | Known Significant Deficiencies |
|---|---|---|
| (1) | Yes | Yes |
| (2) | Yes | No |
| (3) | No | Yes |
| (4) | No | No |

**LO 6**   *b.* In an integrated audit, which of the following lead(s) to an adverse opinion on internal control?

|  | Known Material Weaknesses | Known Significant Deficiencies |
|---|---|---|
| (1) | Yes | Yes |
| (2) | Yes | No |
| (3) | No | Yes |
| (4) | No | No |

**LO 2**   *c.* In an integrated audit, which of the following must be communicated by management to the audit committee?

|  | Known Material Weaknesses | Known Significant Deficiencies |
|---|---|---|
| (1) | Yes | Yes |
| (2) | Yes | No |
| (3) | No | Yes |
| (4) | No | No |

**LO 6**   *d.* Which of the following is most likely to be considered a material weakness in internal control?

(1) Ineffective oversight of financial reporting by the audit committee.

(2) Restatement of previously issued financial statements due to a change in accounting principles.

(3) Inadequate controls over nonroutine transactions.

(4) Weaknesses in risk assessment.

**LO 3**   *e.* Which of the following is defined as a weakness in internal control that allows a reasonable possibility of a misstatement that is material?

(1) Control deficiency.

(2) Material weakness.

(3) Reportable condition.

(4) Significant deficiency.

**LO 6**   *f.* The auditors identified a material weakness in internal control in August. The client was informed and the client corrected the material weakness prior to year-end (December 31); the auditors concluded that management eliminated the material weakness prior to year-end. The appropriate audit report on internal control is:

(1) Adverse.

(2) Qualified.

(3) Unqualified.

(4) Unqualified with explanatory language relating to the material weakness.

**LO 2**

g. Which of the following need *not* be included in management's report on internal control under Section 404(a) of the Sarbanes-Oxley Act of 2002?

(1) A statement that the company's auditors have issued an attestation report on management's assertion.

(2) An identification of the framework used for evaluating internal control.

(3) Management's assessment of the effectiveness of internal control.

(4) Management's acknowledgment of its responsibility to establish and maintain internal control that detects all significant deficiencies.

**LO 2**

h. Management's documentation of internal control ordinarily should include information on:

| | Controls Designed to Prevent Fraud | Controls Designed to Ensure Employee Personal Integrity |
|---|---|---|
| (1) | Yes | Yes |
| (2) | Yes | No |
| (3) | No | Yes |
| (4) | No | No |

**LO 3**

i. A material weakness is a control deficiency (or combination of control deficiencies) that results in a reasonable possibility that a misstatement of at least what amount will not be prevented or detected?

(1) Any amount greater than zero.

(2) A greater amount than zero, but an amount that is at least inconsequential.

(3) A greater amount than inconsequential.

(4) A material amount.

**LO 4**

j. A procedure that involves tracing a transaction from origination through the company's information systems until it is reflected in the company's financial report is referred to as a(n):

(1) Analytical analysis.

(2) Substantive test.

(3) Test of a control.

(4) Walk-through.

**LO 4**

k. Which of the following is *not* a typical question asked during a walk-through?

(1) Have you ever been asked to override the process or controls?

(2) What do you do when you find an error?

(3) What is the largest fraudulent transaction you ever processed?

(4) What kind of errors have you found?

**LO 4**

l. An audit of internal control over financial reporting ordinarily assesses internal control:

(1) As of the last day of the fiscal period.

(2) As of the last day of the auditor's fieldwork.

(3) For the entire fiscal period.

(4) For the entire period plus the period of the auditor's fieldwork.

**LO 4** 18–33. While performing an internal control audit in conformity with PCAOB *Standard No. 5,* the auditors must be able to identify both control strengths and control weaknesses. Items (1) through (11) present various control strengths and deficiencies. For each item, select from the following list the appropriate response.

A. Control strength for the revenue cycle (including cash receipts).

B. Control deficiency for the revenue cycle (including cash receipts).

C. Control strength unrelated to the revenue cycle.

*Items to be answered:*

1. Credit is granted by a credit department.

2. Sales returns are presented to a sales department clerk who prepares a written prenumbered shipping report.

3. Statements are sent monthly to customers.

4. Write-offs of accounts receivable are approved by the controller.

5. Cash disbursements over $10,000 require two signatures on the check.

6. Cash receipts received in the mail are received by a secretary with no record keeping responsibility.

7. Cash receipts received in the mail are forwarded unopened, with remittance advices, to accounting.

8. The cash receipts journal is prepared by the treasurer's department.

9. Cash is deposited weekly.

10. Support for disbursement checks is canceled after payment by the treasurer.

11. Bank reconciliation is prepared by individuals independent of cash receipts record keeping.

**LO 4**   18–34.   **Simulation**

Bill Jensen, a staff member of Zhan & Co., CPAs, has given you the following list of what he refers to as "internal control deficiencies" for the Zabling Co. audit and has asked you to review each point and make certain that you agree that each is an internal control deficiency. For each of the following items, reply A (Agree) or D (Disagree) indicating whether the item represents an internal control deficiency.

*a.* Voided checks are torn up and destroyed.

*b.* Separate sequences of prenumbered checks are used for each bank account.

*c.* The purchasing department manager and assistant manager are the authorized check signers.

*d.* No checks are made payable to cash.

*e.* The authorized check signers reconcile bank accounts.

*f.* All cash receipts (checks) received through the mail are prelisted by the two individuals who open the mail.

*g.* All cash receipts received through the mail are restrictively endorsed when received.

*h.* When a disbursement is made based on paper supporting documents, those supporting documents are canceled by the individual who signs the check.

**LO 2, 3, 4, 6**   18–35.   Match the following definitions (or partial definitions) to the appropriate term. Each term may be used once or not at all.

| Definition (or Partial Definition) | Term |
|---|---|
| a. A control deficiency, or a combination of control deficiencies, in internal control over financial reporting, such that there is a reasonable possibility that a material misstatement of the company's annual or interim financial statements will not be prevented or detected on a timely basis | 1. Control deficiency<br>2. Detective controls<br>3. Major classes of transactions<br>4. Material weakness<br>5. Nonroutine transaction<br>6. Routine transaction<br>7. Section 243<br>8. Section 404<br>9. Significant account<br>10. Significant deficiency<br>11. Substantive procedure<br>12. Walk-through |
| b. A weakness in the design or operation of a control that does not allow management or employees, in the normal course of performing their functions, to prevent or detect misstatements on a timely basis | |
| c. An account for which there is a reasonable possibility that it could contain misstatements that individually, or when aggregated with others, could have a material effect on the financial statements | |
| d. The primary section of the Sarbanes-Oxley Act dealing with management and auditor reporting on internal control over financial reporting | |
| e. Those transaction flows that have a meaningful bearing on the totals accumulated in the company's significant accounts and, therefore, have a meaningful bearing on relevant assertions | |
| f. Tracing a transaction from origination through the company's information systems until it is reflected in the company's financial reports | |

## Problems

**All applicable problems are available with McGraw-Hill's *Connect*<sup>TM</sup> *Accounting.*** ▦ connect
[ACCOUNTING]

**LO 4**  18–36.  Your working papers for an integrated audit being performed under PCAOB *Standard No. 5* include the narrative description below of the cash receipts and billing portions of internal control of Slingsdale Building Supplies, Inc. Slingsdale is a single-store retailer that sells a variety of tools, garden supplies, lumber, small appliances, and electrical fixtures to the public, although about half of Slingsdale's sales are to construction contractors on account. Slingsdale employs 12 salaried sales associates, a credit manager, three full-time clerical workers, and several part-time cash register clerks and assistant bookkeepers. The full-time clerical workers perform such tasks as cash receipts, billing, and accounting and are adequately bonded. They are referred to in the narrative as "accounts receivable supervisor," "cashier," and "bookkeeper."

*Narrative:*  Retail customers pay for merchandise by cash or credit card at cash registers when merchandise is purchased. A contractor may purchase merchandise on account if approved by the credit manager, based only on the manager's familiarity with the contractor's reputation. After credit is approved, the sales associate files a prenumbered charge form with the accounts receivable (AR) supervisor to set up the receivable.

The AR supervisor independently verifies the pricing and other details on the charge form by reference to a management-authorized price list, corrects any errors, prepares the invoice, and supervises a part-time employee who mails the invoice to the contractor. The AR supervisor electronically posts the details of the invoice in the AR subsidiary ledger; simultaneously, the transaction's details are transmitted to the bookkeeper. The AR supervisor also prepares a monthly computer-generated AR subsidiary ledger (without a reconciliation with the AR control account) and a monthly report of overdue accounts.

The cash receipts functions are performed by the cashier, who also supervises the cash register clerks. The cashier opens the mail, compares each check with the enclosed remittance advice, stamps each check "for deposit only," and lists checks for deposit. The cashier then gives the remittance advices to the bookkeeper for recording. The cashier deposits the checks daily, separate from the daily deposit of cash register receipts. The cashier retains the verified deposit slips, to assist in reconciling the monthly bank statements, but forwards to the bookkeeper a copy of the daily cash register summary. The cashier does not have access to the journals or ledgers.

The bookkeeper receives the details of transactions from the AR supervisor and the cashier for journalizing and posting to the general ledger. After recording the remittance advices received from the cashier, the bookkeeper electronically transmits the remittance information to the AR supervisor for subsidiary ledger updating. The bookkeeper sends monthly statements to contractors with unpaid balances upon receipt of the monthly report of overdue balances from the AR supervisor. The bookkeeper authorizes the AR supervisor to write off accounts as uncollectible when six months have passed since the initial overdue notice was sent. At this time, the credit manager is notified by the bookkeeper not to grant additional credit to that contractor.

*Required:*  *a.* Based only on the information in the narrative, describe the internal control deficiencies in Slingsdale's internal control over the cash receipts and billing functions. Organize the weaknesses by employee job function: Credit manager, AR supervisor, Cashier, and Bookkeeper.

*b.* Assume that you have performed your audit of internal control in conformity with PCAOB standards. Based on your results for part (a), you believe that several of the deficiencies represent material weaknesses. What effect will this have on your report on Slingsdale's internal control? Which types of opinions may be appropriate?

*c.* What communication responsibilities do you have for any weaknesses that represent significant deficiencies?

## In-Class Team Cases

**LO 6**  18–37.  For each of the following independent cases, state the highest level of deficiency that you believe the circumstances represent—a control deficiency, a significant deficiency, or a material weakness. Explain your decision in each case.

*Case 1:*  The company processes a significant number of routine intercompany transactions. Individual intercompany transactions are not material and primarily relate to balance sheet activity—for example, cash transfers between business units to finance normal operations. A formal management policy requires monthly reconciliation of intercompany accounts and confirmation of balances between business units. However, there is not a process in place to ensure performance of these procedures. As a result, detailed reconciliations of intercompany accounts are not performed on a timely basis. Management does perform monthly procedures to investigate selected large-dollar intercompany account differences. In addition, management prepares a detailed monthly variance analysis of operating expenses to assess their reasonableness.

*Case 2:*      During its assessment of internal control over financial reporting, management identified the following deficiencies. Based on the context in which the deficiencies occur, management and the auditors agree that these deficiencies individually represent significant deficiencies:

- Inadequate segregation of duties over certain information system access controls.
- Several instances of transactions that were not properly recorded in the subsidiary ledgers; the transactions involved were not material, either individually or in the aggregate.
- No timely reconciliation of the account balances affected by the improperly recorded transactions.

*Case 3:*      The company uses a standard sales contract for most transactions, although sales personnel are allowed to modify sales contract terms as necessary to make a profitable sale. Individual sales transactions are not material to the entity. The company's accounting personnel review significant or unusual modifications to the sales contract terms, but they do not review changes in the standard shipping terms. The changes in the standard shipping terms could require a delay in the timing of revenue recognition. Management reviews gross margins on a monthly basis and investigates any significant or unusual relationships. In addition, management reviews the reasonableness of inventory levels at the end of each accounting period. The company has experienced limited situations in which revenue has been inappropriately recorded in advance of shipment, but amounts have not been material.

*Case 4:*      The company has a standard sales contract, but sales personnel frequently modify the terms of the contract. Sales personnel frequently grant unauthorized and unrecorded sales discounts to customers without the knowledge of the accounting department. These amounts are deducted by customers in paying their invoices and are recorded as outstanding balances on the accounts receivable aging. Although these amounts are individually insignificant, they are material in the aggregate and have occurred consistently over the past few years.

*Case 5:*      The company has found it necessary to restate its financial statements for the past two years due to a material overstatement of revenues two years ago (and an equal understatement last year). The errors are due to sales of certain software that allowed the purchasers extremely lenient rights of return. The errors were discovered shortly following the end of the current accounting year. Members of management indicated that the misstatements occurred because they simply didn't know the accounting rules. Now they know the rules and they won't let it happen again.

*Case 6:*      Assume the same facts exist as in Case (5) except that you, the auditor, have identified the misstatements at the end of June of the year currently under audit. Members of management acknowledged that the misstatements occurred because they simply didn't know the rules at the time, and now they know the rules. Management, within the last six months of the year under audit, hired a new financial accounting expert and believes that the control weakness has been corrected as of year-end. Management believes that it is extremely unlikely that such a misstatement could occur again with the new expert reviewing these matters.

*Case 7:*      Assume the same facts exist as in Case (6), except that management has informed the chief financial officer that she must watch over these matters much more carefully. She has attended several CPE courses on accounting and seems to be caught up in the area in which the misstatements occurred.

*Case 8:*      Subsequent to year-end, the auditors have determined that they believe that management has understated its warranty obligations. The auditors know that, according to the Professional Standards, they should consider the difference between management's estimate and the closest reasonable estimate as "likely misstatement." The chief financial officer (CFO) has argued that this amount is reasonable. Yet, in fact, neither the auditors nor the CFO knows which amount is right. The CFO is under no particular pressure to meet an earnings forecast; he just thinks that the warranty obligations for many of the products will expire and will not be exercised. Still, the CFO can't convince the auditors. Likewise, the auditors can't convince the CFO of their position. The CFO finally agrees to a material adjustment to get to the auditors' amount and "keep the peace."

(Adapted from PCAOB *Standard No. 5*)

# Additional Assurance Services: Historical Financial Information

## Learning objectives

After studying this chapter, you should be able to:

LO1    Discuss additional audit-based services, including reporting on compliance with contractual agreements, letters for underwriters, and summary financial statements.

LO2    Identify the types of special-purpose financial reporting frameworks and the nature of the audit reports issued.

LO3    Describe the auditors' responsibilities when auditing financial statements that use a generally accepted financial reporting framework of another country.

LO4    Discuss audits of single financial statements and specific accounts or items of a financial statement.

LO5    Explain the special considerations involved in auditing personal financial statements.

LO6    Describe the nature of financial statement reviews conducted under *Statements on Standards for Accounting and Review Services.*

LO7    Discuss how reviews performed under *Statements on Standards for Accounting and Review Services* differ from those performed under the *Statements on Auditing Standards.*

LO8    Explain the accountant's responsibilities when performing a compilation of financial statements.

In the preceding chapters, we emphasized the audit of financial statements prepared in accordance with accounting principles generally accepted in the United States, including resulting auditor communications through audit reports, and communications to those charged with corporate governance. In addition, in Chapters 7 and 18 we discussed the audit of internal control. These services represent the CPAs' principal type of attestation engagement. However, CPAs provide additional communications related to these audits and perform a variety of other types of assurance, attestation, and accounting services.

Chapter 19 begins with a discussion of services that use the financial statement audit as a starting point but result in providing assurance on additional information. Next we describe engagements that involve audits of information prepared using a financial reporting framework other than GAAP. Then we provide a summary of several assurance services not discussed previously in the text. Finally, we present a discussion of compilation services in which no assurance is provided by CPAs.

## Audit-Based Services: Assurance on Additional Information

**LO1**

Discuss additional audit-based services, including reporting on compliance with contractual agreements, letters for underwriters, and summary financial statements.

Auditors who have audited the financial statements of an organization are sometimes asked to use the audit results as a starting point for providing assurance on additional subject matter. Here we discuss reporting situations in which an audit has been performed and the auditors are engaged to (1) report on compliance with contractual or regulatory requirements, (2) issue letters for underwriters, or (3) report on summary financial information.

### Reporting on Compliance with Aspects of Contractual Agreements or Regulatory Requirements in Connection with Audited Financial Statements

Regulatory requirements and debt agreements often require companies to provide compliance reports prepared by their independent auditors. A common example of such reports is one prepared for a bond trustee as evidence of the company's compliance with restrictions contained in the bond indenture. The auditors typically provide negative assurance with respect to the client's compliance with indenture provisions relating to the maintenance of certain financial ratios and restrictions on the payment of dividends.

Professional standards indicate that to provide this service, the auditors *must first have performed an audit* of the related financial statements and must have subjected the applicable restrictions to audit procedures applied in the financial statement audit (AICPA AU 806; PCAOB 623). The auditors may provide such assurance either in the audit report accompanying the financial statements or in a separate report. When a separate report is issued, it includes an introductory paragraph summarizing the audit report on the financial statements, a paragraph providing negative assurance with respect to compliance, and a paragraph indicating that the report is solely for the use of the client and the specified third party. The paragraph providing negative assurance about compliance is illustrated below.[1]

> In connection with our audit, nothing came to our attention that caused us to believe that the Company was not in compliance with any of the terms, covenants, provisions, or conditions of Sections 8 to 15, inclusive, of the Indenture dated July 21, 20X1, with First National Bank. However, our audit was not directed primarily toward obtaining knowledge of such noncompliance.

When the auditors have identified one or more incidences of noncompliance that they believe should be reported, the items should be identified in the report. When they believe that noncompliance is pervasive, they should consider whether a negative assurance statement is appropriate. Also, issuance of this type of report is not appropriate if the auditors have expressed an adverse opinion or disclaimed an opinion on the financial statements to which the covenants relate.

## Letters for Underwriters

Investment banking firms that underwrite securities issues often request independent auditors who have audited the financial statements and schedules in the registration statement to issue a letter for the underwriters. This letter is commonly called a **comfort letter,** and the professional standards provide guidance on its content (AICPA AU 920; PCAOB 634). The standards indicate that a comfort letter may include assurance about the following matters:

1. A statement that the auditors are independent.
2. Whether the audited financial statements and financial statement schedules included in the registration statement comply with the accounting requirements of the Securities Act of 1933 and related regulations.
3. Unaudited financial statements, condensed interim financial information, capsule financial information, pro forma financial information, financial forecasts, and management's discussion and analysis.
4. Changes in selected financial statement items during a period subsequent to the date and period of the latest financial statements included in the registration statement.
5. Tables, statistics, and other financial information included in the registration statement.
6. Certain nonfinancial statement information included in the registration statement complies with SEC regulations.

Auditors may provide positive assurance on items 1 and 2 of the preceding list. For items 3 through 6, depending upon the situation (e.g., in some circumstances an interim review must have been performed on interim information), auditors are often able to provide negative assurance. This negative assurance indicates that, based on the procedures performed, nothing has come to their attention to cause them to believe that any material modifications need to be made to the information (or that the information does not comply with SEC requirements).

Comfort letters aid the underwriters in fulfilling their obligation to perform a reasonable investigation of the securities registration statement. No definitive criteria exist for the underwriters' "reasonable investigation." Therefore, the underwriters should approve the adequacy of the CPAs' procedures serving as a basis for the comfort letter.

---

[1] The auditing reporting standards are in a period of change in that, historically, reports do not include section headings and many reports still do not (e.g., compilation and review reports). In this chapter, with the exception of our illustration of an audit report on a special-purpose financial framework, we do not include section headings.

| Illustrative Case | *Summary Annual Reports* |

A number of corporations have experimented with issuing summary annual reports to shareholders. These reports generally include condensed financial statements and refer shareholders desiring more detailed information to the annual report filed with the SEC (Form 10-K). The auditors of these companies issue a report on the summary financial statements that refers to their report included with the Form 10-K.

**Summary Financial Statements**

Occasionally, a client-prepared document will include **summary financial statements (condensed financial statements)** developed from audited financial statements. These statements typically include considerably less detail than the audited financial statements. The auditors who issued the report on the audited financial statements may be asked to report on the summary statements. Unless they have issued an adverse opinion or a disclaimer of opinion on the audited financial statements, the auditors may accept an engagement related to the summary financial statements (AICPA AU 810; PCAOB 552). In these circumstances, the auditors determine whether the criteria applied by management in the preparation of the summary financial statements is acceptable and whether those criteria have been properly applied. Although they need not accompany the summary financial statements, the audited financial statements should be readily available to any user who wishes to obtain them (e.g., available on the company's Web site). When the CPAs have concluded that the summary financial information is properly presented, they may issue an opinion stating that the summary financial statements are consistent, in all material respects, with the financial statements from which they have been derived, in accordance with the applied criteria.

## Auditing Financial Statements that Use a Financial Reporting Framework Other than GAAP

Recall that in Chapter 2 we briefly discussed **financial reporting frameworks,** which are sets of criteria for preparing financial statements (e.g., generally accepted accounting principles are referred to as a **general-purpose financial reporting framework**). Auditors are sometimes engaged to audit financial statements that are prepared using a financial reporting framework *other than* generally accepted accounting principles. In this section, we describe special-purpose frameworks and frameworks used in a foreign country.

**Audits of Financial Statements Prepared in Accordance with Special-Purpose Financial Reporting Frameworks**

LO2

Identify the types of special-purpose financial reporting frameworks and the nature of the audit reports issued.

The professional standards (AICPA AU 800) define five **special-purpose financial reporting frameworks:** (a) cash basis, (b) tax basis, (c) contractual basis, and (d) regulatory basis.[2]

When considering accepting an engagement in which a special-purpose financial reporting framework is used, the auditors should obtain an understanding of the purpose of the financial statements, the intended users, and steps taken by management to determine that the framework is acceptable in the circumstances. In addition, management must acknowledge that it understands its responsibilities with respect to the framework. When planning and performing the audit, the auditors adapt AU sections that are relevant in the circumstances.

An audit report on financial statements prepared using a special-purpose financial reporting framework departs from the standard form in several ways. Most importantly, the report must include an emphasis of matter paragraph that states that the financial

---

[2] Under the current PCAOB standard (623), the cash basis, tax basis, and regulatory basis financial reporting frameworks are referred to as "other comprehensive bases of accounting." The AICPA eliminated the term from its standards in 2010.

statements are prepared using a special-purpose framework that is a basis of accounting other than GAAP. The paragraph should also describe the basis of accounting being used or refer to a financial statement note that provides such a description. The essence of the report is the expression of an opinion about whether the financial statements fairly present what they purport to present.

The auditors should be cautious about the titles given to the financial statements. Titles such as "balance sheet," "income statement," and "statement of cash flows" are generally associated with financial statements presented in accordance with GAAP. Consequently, the professional standards require more descriptive titles for statements that are presented on some other basis. For example, a cash-basis "balance sheet" is more appropriately titled "statement of assets and liabilities arising from cash transactions." Perhaps the most common financial statements prepared on a basis other than GAAP are cash-basis statements. The body of an unmodified report on cash-basis statements is shown below with the distinctive wording emphasized.

---

We have audited the accompanying financial statements of ABC Partnership, which comprise the *statement of assets and liabilities arising from cash transactions* as of December 31, 20X1, and the *related statement of revenue collected and expenses* paid for the year then ended.

*Management's Responsibility for the Financial Statements*
Management is responsible for the preparation and fair presentation of these financial statements in *accordance with the cash receipts and disbursements basis of accounting described in Note X;* this includes determining that the cash receipts and disbursements basis of accounting is an acceptable basis for the preparation of the financial statements in the circumstances. Management is also responsible for the design, implementation, and maintenance of internal control relevant to the preparation and fair presentation of financial statements that are free from material misstatement, whether due to fraud or error.

*Auditors' Responsibility*
Our responsibility is to express an opinion on these financial statements based on our audit. We conducted our audit in accordance with auditing standards generally accepted in the United States of America. Those standards require that we plan and perform the audit to obtain reasonable assurance about whether the financial statements are free from material misstatement.

An audit involves performing procedures to obtain audit evidence about the amounts and disclosures in the financial statements. The procedures selected depend on the auditor's judgment, including the assessment of the risks of material misstatement of the financial statements, whether due to fraud or error. In making those risk assessments, the auditor considers internal control relevant to the partnership's preparation and fair presentation of the financial statements in order to design audit procedures that are appropriate in the circumstances, but not for the purpose of expressing an opinion on the effectiveness of the partnership's internal control. An audit also includes evaluating the appropriateness of accounting policies used and the reasonableness of significant accounting estimates made by management, as well as evaluating the overall presentation of the financial statements.

We believe that the audit evidence we have obtained is sufficient and appropriate to provide a basis for our audit opinion.

*Opinion*
In our opinion, the financial statements referred to above present fairly, in all material respects, the *assets and liabilities arising from cash transactions* of ABC Partnership as of December 31, 20X1, and its revenue collected and expenses paid during the year then ended in accordance with *the cash receipts and disbursements basis of accounting* described in Note X.

*Basis of Accounting*
Without modifying our opinion, we draw attention to Note X to the financial statements, which describes the basis of accounting. The financial statements are prepared on the cash receipts and disbursements basis of accounting, which is a basis of accounting other than generally accepted accounting principles.

---

If the special-purpose financial statements are prepared in accordance with a contractual or regulatory basis of accounting, the auditors' report should also include an other matter paragraph alerting users about the intended use of the auditors' report (e.g., for those within the entity, the parties to the contract or agreement, or the regulatory agencies to whose jurisdiction the entity is subject). The following is an illustration of this paragraph:

> Intended use
> Our report is intended solely for the information and use of ABC Company and Regulator DEF and is not intended to be and should not be used by parties other than these specified parties.

Figure 19.1 provides overall reporting requirements relating to the various special-purpose frameworks.

*Auditors' Report Prescribed by Law or Regulation*

When the auditors are involved with financial information prepared on a regulatory basis, they may be requested to use a specific layout, form, or wording (hereafter, layout) for the auditors' report. If the layout includes the basic reporting requirements (e.g., title,

FIGURE 19.1    **Overview of Reporting Requirements**

| | **Cash Basis** | **Tax Basis** | **Contractual Basis** | **Regulatory Basis** | **Regulatory Basis (General Use Statements)** |
|---|---|---|---|---|---|
| **Opinion(s)** | Single opinion on special-purpose framework | Single opinion on special-purpose framework | Single opinion on special-purpose framework | Single opinion on special-purpose framework | Dual opinion on special-purpose framework and on GAAP |
| **Description of purpose for which special-purpose financial statements are prepared** | No | No | Yes | Yes | Yes |
| **Alert users in an emphasis of matter paragraph that the special-purpose framework is a basis other than GAAP** | Yes | Yes | Yes | Yes | No |
| **Alert users in an other matter paragraph about intended use of auditors' report** | No | No | Yes | Yes | No |
| **Additional requirements unique to category** | | | The auditors must obtain an understanding of significant management interpretations of the contract. | If a specific layout, form, or wording is required that the auditors have no basis to make, then the auditors should reword the form or attach an appropriately worded separate report. | |

addresses, management and auditor responsibilities, opinion paragraph), they may use it. If the layout is not acceptable, or would cause the auditors to make a statement they have no basis to make, they should reword it or attach an appropriately worded separate report. If this is not allowable, the auditors should not accept the audit engagement unless required by law or regulation to do so. If so required, the auditors should not include any reference within the auditors' report to the audit having been conducted in accordance with GAAS.

## Financial Statements Prepared Using a Financial Reporting Framework Generally Accepted in Another Country

### LO3

Describe the auditors' responsibilities when auditing financial statements that use a generally accepted financial reporting framework of another country.

A U.S.-based company may prepare financial statements for use in other countries. For example, the company may have a subsidiary in Germany and may prepare financial statements for that subsidiary as part of an effort to raise capital in Germany. The professional standards (AICPA AU 910; PCAOB 534) address the auditors' responsibility in this situation. When auditing the information, the auditors should comply with standards to the extent the standards are appropriate. In addition, the auditors should obtain an understanding of the other country's financial reporting framework. Also, if the terms of the engagement require the auditors to apply either the auditing standards of that country or the international standards, the auditors should obtain an understanding of them and apply those standards.

When the financial statements are *intended for use only outside* the United States, the auditors should issue one report, using either:

- A United States form of report that indicates that the financial statements have been prepared in accordance with a financial reporting framework generally accepted in another country, or
- The other country audit report.

When the financial statements are also intended for use in the United States, a second report is also issued. In that report, the auditors use a U.S. form of opinion. For nonpublic companies, this report includes an emphasis of matter paragraph stating the financial reporting framework used and that it differs from GAAP; an unmodified opinion may be issued relating to the financial reporting framework used. For public companies, the PCAOB requires that an opinion also be added on whether the financial statements follow GAAP.

## Additional GAAS Audits

In this section, we describe CPA association with:

- Single financial statements (e.g., an income statement, and not the other financial statements), and specific elements, accounts, or items of financial statement (e.g., a schedule of accounts receivable).
- Personal financial statements.

## Single Financial Statements and Specific Elements, Accounts, or Items of Financial Statements

Auditors may be engaged to audit a single financial statement or a specific element, account, or item (hereafter, element) of a financial statement. A company may request the audit because it has entered into an agreement such as:

- A loan agreement that includes a requirement that the balance sheet (but not other financial statements) be audited annually.
- A lease agreement with a requirement that annual company revenues be audited because lease payments are based in part on the lessee's revenue.

When auditing a single financial statement or a specific element of a financial statement, the auditors should adapt GAAS to the extent necessary in the circumstances and

**LO4**

Discuss audits of single financial statements and specific accounts or items of a financial statement.

then apply it. The auditors should perform procedures on interrelated items as necessary to meet the objectives of the audit. Examples of interrelated items include sales and receivables; inventory and payables; and building and equipment and depreciation. Thus, when auditing the sales account, the auditors will normally need to perform procedures on accounts receivable.

When the CPAs are engaged to audit a particular account or element, they modify the standard audit report to indicate the information audited, the basis of accounting used, and whether the information is presented fairly on that basis. For example, the following represents the opinion paragraph of a report on the audit of accounts receivable.

In our opinion, the schedule of accounts receivable referred to above presents fairly, in all material respects, the accounts receivable of ABC Company as of December 31, 20X1, in accordance with accounting principles generally accepted in the United States of America relevant to preparing such a statement.

In some situations the auditors may be engaged to report on a schedule of accounts that, other than not being a balance sheet, income statement, or statement of cash flows, is otherwise prepared in accordance with GAAP. Examples of such schedules include:

- A governmental agency may require a schedule of gross income and certain expenses of a company's real estate operation in which income and expenses are measured in accordance with GAAP, but expenses are defined to exclude certain items such as interest, depreciation, and income taxes.
- An agreement in which one company is considering acquiring another company may specify a schedule of gross assets and liabilities of the company measured in accordance with GAAP, but limited to the assets to be sold and liabilities to be transferred according to the agreement.

In these situations, the auditors' report should include an emphasis of matter paragraph stating the purpose of the presentation, referring to a note that describes the basis of presentation and stating that the presentation is not intended to be a complete presentation of the organization's assets, liabilities, revenues or expenses.

To this point we have discussed situations in which auditors are asked to audit information that is less than a complete set of financial statements. In some circumstances, when they have performed an audit of the complete set of financial statements, they may also be asked to audit and report on a single financial statement or element. In such circumstances:

- A separate opinion should be issued on each engagement.
- Different materiality measures will ordinarily be used for the two engagements (e.g., materiality for a particular element generally will be less than for the overall financial statements).
- When both the complete set of financial statements and the single financial statement (or element) are being published together, the auditors must be satisfied that there is a clear differentiation between them.
- When the auditors' report on the complete set of financial statements is modified, the auditors should consider its effect on the single financial statement (or element) report. When the matter relates to the specific element, the report on the element is also likely to be modified. When it does not relate to the specific element, it may be possible to issue an unmodified report on the element if the two reports are not published together and the specific element does not constitute a major portion of the complete set of financial statements.

### Reviews and Agreed-Upon Procedures Engagements

On occasion, the client may request the CPAs *not to perform an audit, but to* perform either *review* or *agreed-upon procedures* on a financial statement or specified elements of financial statements. A review ordinarily consists of analytical procedures and inquiries. Again using the shopping center example, the landlord of a shopping center may request that the CPAs perform review procedures (analytical procedures and inquiry procedures) related to the revenue account. Typical review procedures are presented later in this chapter.

Finally, a CPA may be engaged to perform agreed-upon procedures on specified elements. The attestation standards provide guidance for these engagements that result in a summary of findings that is intended only for specified parties (AICPA and PCAOB AT 201). Agreed-upon procedures engagements are "customer driven" services in that the "specified parties" agree with the CPAs on the procedures to be performed and take responsibility for their *sufficiency.* In our example, these might include procedures such as substantiating the revenue reported by tenants by agreeing the figures with the tenants' internal financial statements and state sales tax returns. In this situation, the CPAs will meet with representatives of the landlord (the specified party) to agree upon the procedures to be performed. The accountants' report indicates that it is intended for the specified party and lists the procedures performed and related findings. The report *should* include a disclaimer of opinion and *should not include negative assurance,* that indicates that nothing came to the CPAs' attention to indicate that the financial statement element is not fairly presented.

Another common example of an agreed-upon procedures engagement is one in which a bankruptcy trustee (the specified party) engages the CPA to help establish claims of creditors. In this situation, a CPA may be engaged to perform agreed-upon procedures relating to accounts payable and issue a report such as the following (emphasis added):

---

### Independent Accountants' Report on Applying Agreed-Upon Procedures

To the Trustee of Mardem Company:

*We have performed the procedures described below, which were agreed to by the Trustee of Mardem Company,* with respect to the claims of creditors to determine the validity of claims of Mardem Company as of May 31, 20X1, as set forth in accompanying Schedule A. This engagement to apply agreed-upon procedures was performed in accordance with standards established by the American Institute of Certified Public Accountants. The sufficiency of these procedures is solely the responsibility of the Trustee of Mardem Company. Consequently, we *make no representation regarding the sufficiency of the procedures* described below either for the purpose for which this report has been requested or for any other purpose. The procedures and associated findings are as follows:

1. Compare the total of the trial balance of accounts payable at May 31, 20X1, prepared by Mardem Company, to the balance in the related general ledger account.

    The total of the accounts payable trial balance agrees with the balance in the related general ledger account.

2. Compare the amounts for claims received from creditors (as shown in claim documents provided by Mardem Company) to the respective amounts shown in the trial balance of accounts payable. Using the data included in the claims documents and in Mardem Company's accounts payable detail records, reconcile any differences found to the accounts payable trial balance.

    All differences noted are presented in column 3 of Schedule A. Except for those amounts shown in column 4 of Schedule A, all such differences were reconciled.

3. Examine the documentation submitted by creditors in support of the amounts claimed and compare it to the following documentation in Mardem Company's files: invoices, receiving reports, and other evidence of receipt of goods or services.

    Invoices, receiving reports, and other evidence existed for all documents submitted by creditors.

We were not engaged to, and did not perform an audit, the objective of which would be the expression of an opinion on the specified elements, accounts, or items. Accordingly, *we do not express such an opinion.* Had we performed additional procedures, other matters might have come to our attention that would have been reported to you.

*This report is intended solely for the use of the Trustee of Mardem Company and should not be used by those who have not agreed to the procedures and taken responsibility for the sufficiency of the procedures for their purpose.*

---

## Audits of Personal Financial Statements

**LO5**

Explain the special considerations involved in auditing personal financial statements.

Audited personal financial statements may be required in a variety of circumstances, including when an individual seeks a large loan or wishes to purchase a business using his or her personal credit. Generally accepted accounting principles applied to personal financial statements are quite different from those applicable to business entities. In personal financial statements, assets are shown at their *estimated current values* and liabilities are presented at their *estimated current amounts*. Thus, auditors must apply audit procedures that will substantiate these estimates. On occasion, the auditors may need to rely upon appraisers, following the guidelines set forth for using the work of a specialist (AICPA AU 620; PCAOB 336).

The "balance sheet" for an individual is termed a *statement of financial condition*. This statement shows the individual's *net worth* in lieu of "owners' equity" and includes a liability for income taxes on the differences between the estimated current values of assets and liabilities and their income tax bases. The "income statement" for an individual is called the *statement of changes in net worth*. In addition to showing revenue and expenses, this statement includes the increases and decreases in both the estimated current values of assets and the estimated amounts of liabilities during the period.

Accounting principles and auditing guidance for personal financial statements are presented in the AICPA's audit and accounting guide titled "Personal Financial Statements,"[3] The reports issued on personal financial statements are standard in form, modified only for the change in financial statement names.

### Completeness—A Special Problem in Personal Financial Statements

One of the assertions that a client makes regarding its financial statements is that the statements are complete—that is, they reflect all of the client's assets, liabilities, and transactions for the period. Determining the completeness of financial statements may be especially difficult in the audit of personal financial statements for several reasons. First, there is generally poor internal control because all aspects of each transaction usually are under the control of the individual. Second, some individuals may seek to omit assets and income from their personal financial statements. The motivation to conceal earnings or assets may stem from income tax or estate tax considerations, anticipation of a divorce, or illegal sources of income.

The omission of assets from financial statements is far more difficult for auditors to detect than is the overstatement of assets or omission of liabilities. Thus, in deciding whether to accept a personal financial statements audit engagement, auditors should assess the risk that an individual may be concealing assets. If auditors conclude during an engagement that the individual is concealing assets, it is doubtful that they can ever develop confidence that their audit procedures have located all the concealed assets. Therefore, they should withdraw from the engagement.

Most engagements involving personal financial statements are *not* audits, because individuals seldom need audited financial statements. The approaches described for reviews and compilations later in this chapter are more commonly applied to personal financial statements.

## Reviews of Historical Financial Statements

Auditors perform reviews of the financial statements of nonpublic companies, as well as reviews of the interim information of public companies.

### SSARS Reviews of Nonpublic Companies (Nonissuers)

Serving the needs of small business represents a sizable part of the practice of many public accounting firms. For a smaller public accounting firm, especially one with only a single office, nonpublic clients may represent the firm's entire practice. To provide CPAs with guidance in meeting the accounting needs of these nonpublic (**nonissuer**) clients, the AICPA established the Accounting and Review Services Committee. This committee

---

[3] AICPA, "Personal Financial Statements," AICPA *Audit and Accounting Guide* (New York, 2010).

**LO6**

Describe the nature of financial statement reviews conducted under *Statements on Standards for Accounting and Review Services.*

sets professional standards for CPAs associated with the *unaudited* financial statements, or other unaudited financial information of nonpublic companies. These standards are published in a sequentially numbered series called *Statements on Standards for Accounting and Review Services (SSARS)*. The *SSARS* include guidance for two types of engagements involving unaudited financial statements of nonpublic companies: **compilations** (AR 80) and **reviews** (AR 90). Compilation services are described in detail in the final section of this chapter.

We will refer to reviews performed under these standards as "*SSARS* reviews," to distinguish them from reviews of interim information performed under the requirements of the PCAOB or the Auditing Standards Board. *SSARS* reviews apply in the situation in which there is no annual audit performed. The objective of such a review is to obtain limited assurance that there are no material modifications that should be made to the financial statements in order for the statements to be in conformity with GAAP, or other applicable financial reporting framework.

Rule 202 of the AICPA *Code of Professional Conduct* requires members to comply with the standards set forth in the *SSARS.* Thus, the Accounting and Review Services Committee has authority comparable to that of the Auditing Standards Board (ASB). The *SSARS* pronouncements apply to nonpublic companies that *do not have an annual audit*. Although this ordinarily involves annual financial statements, the standard also applies to reviews of interim financial statements.

A review is an attest service in which the accountants (1) perform analytical procedures, (2) make inquiries of management and others within the organization, (3) perform other procedures considered necessary, and (4) obtain representations from management relating to the financial statements. The review report provides **limited (negative) assurance.** *SSARS* reviews of nonpublic companies are ordinarily performed on annual information.

### Screening the Client

One of the basic elements of quality control in a public accounting firm relates to the acceptance and continuance of clients. The purpose of policies and procedures in this area is to minimize the risk of association with a client whose management lacks integrity. One means of acquiring information about a prospective client is to contact the client's predecessor CPAs.

*SSARS 19* provides guidelines for accountants who decide to make inquiries of the predecessor accountants before accepting a review (or compilation) engagement. These inquiries include questions regarding the integrity of management, disagreements over accounting principles, the willingness of management to provide or to revise information, and the reasons for the change in accountants. The decision of whether to contact the predecessor accountants is left to the judgment of the successor CPAs. However, if inquiries are made with the client's consent, the predecessor accountants are generally required to respond.

### Engagement Letters

Reviews and compilations are quite different from audits. The need to establish a clear understanding with the client concerning the nature of such services was dramatically illustrated in the *1136 Tenants' Corporation* case discussed in Chapter 4. CPAs must avoid the implication that they are performing audits when they are engaged to perform other services. Accordingly, the professional standards require that CPAs prepare an *engagement letter* clearly specifying the objectives of the engagement, management's responsibilities, the accountant's responsibilities, and limitations of the engagement.

### Understanding the Client and Its Industry

After a client has been accepted, the auditors obtain further understanding of both the client and its industry. This information is used to help design review procedures as well as to evaluate the responses to their inquiries and the results of the review procedures. The CPAs' understanding of the client's business should include a general understanding of the company's organization, its methods of operation, and the nature of its financial statement accounts.

*Review Procedures*

As we have indicated, during a review engagement the accountants (1) perform analytical procedures, (2) make inquiries of management and others within the organization, (3) perform other procedures considered necessary, and (4) obtain representations from management relating to the financial statements.

Analytical procedures (generally comparisons of accounts and ratios) are applied to the financial data by reference to prior financial statements, budgets, and other operating data. The approach used when the accountants perform analytical procedures[4] is to compare recorded amounts and ratios to expected values, identify significant differences that might indicate a misstatement, and then to investigate the unexpected values. For example, revenue reported by month, product line, or business segment may be compared to amounts from comparable prior periods. When unexpected differences are noted, they are investigated further by making inquiries of management or performing other procedures.

The CPAs' *inquiries* should focus on whether the financial statements are in accordance with generally accepted accounting principles, changes in business activities, significant subsequent events, and knowledge of material fraud or suspected fraud.

Other procedures performed in a review include inquiries concerning actions taken at stockholder and director meetings, reading the interim financial information, and obtaining reports from other accountants who have reviewed significant components of the company.

Although a review ordinarily does not require accountants to corroborate management's responses, they should consider the consistency of management responses in light of the results of other review procedures. Additional procedures should be performed if the accountants become aware that information may be incorrect, incomplete, or otherwise unsatisfactory. The accountants should perform these procedures to the extent considered necessary to obtain limited assurance that there are no material modifications that should be made to the statements. For example, if review procedures lead an accountant to question whether a significant sales transaction is recorded in conformity with generally accepted accounting principles, it may become necessary to discuss the terms of the transaction with both senior marketing and accounting personnel and to read the sales contract. Figure 19.2 summarizes analytical procedures, inquiries, and other review procedures.

**FIGURE 19.2**
**Nonpublic Company Analytical Procedures, Inquiries, and Other Review Procedures**

| **Analytical Procedures** | **Inquiries of Management Members with Responsibility for Financial and Accounting Matters About:** |
| --- | --- |
| • Develop *expectations* by identifying and using plausible relationships that are reasonably expected to exist.<br>• Compare recorded amounts or ratios developed from recorded amounts to expectations.<br>• Compare the consistency of management's responses in light of results of other review procedures and knowledge of business and industry.<br><br>**Other Review Procedures**<br><br>• Inquire as to actions taken at shareholder, board of director, and other committees of board of directors.<br>• Read financial statements.<br>• Obtain reports from other accountants, if any, that have reviewed significant components. | • Whether financial statements **are** prepared in conformity with GAAP<br>• The accounting principles, practices, and methods applied<br>• Any unusual or complex situations that might affect the financial statements<br>• Significant transactions taking place near the end of the period<br>• Status of uncorrected misstatements identified in a previous engagement<br>• Questions that have arisen in applying review procedures<br>• Subsequent events<br>• Knowledge of potentially material fraud or suspected fraud<br>• Significant journal entries and other adjustments<br>• Communications from regulatory agencies |

[4] Chapter 5 presents general guidance on analytical procedures.

Finally, the auditors must obtain a representation letter that is tailored to the circumstances of the particular engagement. However, all representation letters should be dated as of the date of the review report and include management's acknowledgment of its:

- Responsibility for the financial statements' conformity with generally accepted accounting principles and its belief that it has met this responsibility.
- Responsibility to prevent and detect fraud, as well as to divulge any knowledge that it has of any actual or suspected fraud that is material.
- Responsibility to respond fully and truthfully to all inquiries and to provide complete information, including that on subsequent events.

### Review Reports

The assurance provided by a review report is necessarily limited because of the limited scope of the accountants' procedures. Although these procedures may bring to the CPAs' attention significant departures from GAAP, they do not guarantee that the CPAs will become aware of all of the significant matters that would be discovered in an audit. A review is not sufficient to enable the accountants to express an opinion on the fairness of the financial statements. Therefore, the accountants' report concludes with a statement that the accountants do not express such an opinion. The body of an accountants' standard report on a review of a nonpublic company's financial statements[5] reads as follows:

> We have reviewed the accompanying balance sheet of XYZ Company as of December 31, 20XX, and the related statements of income, retained earnings, and cash flows for the year then ended. A review includes primarily applying analytical procedures to management's financial data and making inquiries of company management. A review is substantially less in scope than an audit, the objective of which is the expression of an opinion regarding the financial statements as a whole. Accordingly, we do not express such an opinion.
>
> Management is responsible for the preparation and fair presentation of the financial statements in accordance with accounting principles generally accepted in the United States of America and for designing, implementing, and maintaining internal control relevant to the preparation and fair presentation of the financial statements.
>
> Our responsibility is to conduct the review in accordance with *Statements on Standards for Accounting and Review Services* issued by the American Institute of Certified Public Accountants. Those standards require us to perform procedures to obtain limited assurance that there are no material modifications that should be made to the financial statements. We believe that the results of our procedures provide a reasonable basis for our report.
>
> Based on our review, we are not aware of any material modifications that should be made to the accompanying financial statements in order for them to be in conformity with accounting principles generally accepted in the United States of America.

The date of an accountant's review report should not be earlier than the date on which the accountant has accumulated review evidence sufficient to provide a reasonable basis for providing limited assurance on the financial statements. Also, each page of the financial statements should include a caption such as "See Accountants' Review Report."

To provide any degree of assurance about the fairness of information, the CPAs must be independent. Thus, professional standards require the accountants to be independent of the client.

### Departures from Generally Accepted Accounting Principles

A modification of the report is required when the accountants become aware of a material departure from generally accepted accounting principles (or some other comprehensive basis of accounting). The departure is referred to in the report's fourth paragraph, as illustrated below:

> With the exception of the matter described in the following paragraph, we are not aware of any material modifications. . . .

---

[5] Review reports do not include section headings as do audit reports for nonpublic companies.

Notice that the report is neither "qualified" nor "adverse" in form as would be the case with an audit report in which a departure from GAAP exists. Audit reports, not review reports, result in an opinion, whether it is unmodified, qualified, or adverse.

In a separate paragraph of the review report, the departure will be described. The following is an example of a report paragraph that discusses a departure from generally accepted accounting principles:

> As disclosed in Note 6 to the financial statements, generally accepted accounting principles require that land be stated at cost. Management has informed us that the Company has stated its land at appraised value and that, if generally accepted accounting principles had been followed, the land account and stockholders' equity would have been decreased by $500,000.

Review reports are not required to be altered in situations involving a lack of consistent application of generally accepted accounting principles or the existence of major uncertainties (including going-concern uncertainties) that have been properly reported in the financial statements. However, when that information is not properly presented or disclosed in the financial statements, the financial statements contain a departure from generally accepted accounting principles, and the review report should be appropriately modified. Finally, in all circumstances in which an accountant is unable to perform the necessary review procedures due to a scope limitation, the review is considered incomplete and no review report should be issued.

*Review Reports on Comparative Statements*

As with audited financial statements, accountants who have reviewed prior-period financial statements presented with those of the current period should report on both years. *AR 200* provides guidance on the format of the accountants' reports on comparative financial statements. If the accountants have reviewed both sets of financial statements, they will merely update their review report on the prior year by issuing one review report covering both years. The report will be dated as of the completion of the current year's review procedures.

In certain situations, the accountants may be engaged to perform a lower level of service on the current year's financial statements than they performed on the prior year's financial statements (e.g., a review this year and an audit last year or a compilation this year and a review last year). In these situations, the CPAs should not update the prior year's report. This would imply that they have performed those types of services to the date of the current year's report. Instead, the CPAs should either reissue the prior year's report bearing its original date and present it with the current year's report, or include a reference to the prior year's report in the current year's report. For example, the following paragraph could be added to a compilation report on the current year's financial statements to refer to a review of the comparative financial statements for the prior year.

> The accompanying 20X1 financial statements of XYZ Company were previously reviewed by us, and our report dated March 1, 20X2, stated that we were not aware of any material modifications that should be made to those statements in order for them to be in conformity with generally accepted accounting principles. We have not performed any procedures in connection with that review engagement after the date of our report on the 20X1 financial statements.

A reference similar to the one above should also be included in the current report when another public accounting firm, whose report is not presented, reviewed the comparative financial statements.

*Other Communications*

As with annual financial statement audits, the CPAs should communicate to the audit committee the information about significant adjustments found during the review and the

| Illustrative Case | *Difference between CPAs' Responsibilities* |

The difference between CPAs' responsibilities when performing audits and reviews of financial statements was dramatically illustrated by the ZZZZ Best case. ZZZZ Best, Inc. was a company engaged in the business of carpet cleaning and restoring fire- and flood-damaged buildings. The company, which was founded by 16-year-old Barry Minkow, reported operating results that were almost wholly fictitious.

In the review of the financial statements of ZZZZ Best, the partner-in-charge of the engagement insisted upon observing two major restoration jobs, a finished job, and a carpet warehouse. However, Minkow and other officers of the company cleverly faked these locations. As a result, the observations did not result in detection of the fraud, and the public accounting firm also agreed not to make follow-up contacts with the insurance companies and building owners involved. The court ruled that the accounting firm was not liable for failing to detect the misstatements of the financial statements. The court noted that the accountants' review report specifically disclaimed an opinion on ZZZZ Best's financial statements.

---

acceptability and quality of significant accounting policies and estimates. The audit committee should also be informed about any disagreements with management over accounting principles or review procedures, or any other difficulties encountered in performing the review. These communication responsibilities with respect to an audit were described in detail in Chapter 16. Finally, the CPAs should make sure that the audit committee is informed about any instances of fraud or illegal acts that come to their attention, as well as any significant deficiencies and material weaknesses related to the preparation of financial statements.

## PCAOB and Auditing Standards Board Reviews of Interim Information

**LO7**

Discuss how reviews performed under *Statements on Standards for Accounting and Review Services* differ from those performed under the *Statements on Auditing Standards.*

**Public companies (issuers)** are required to have annual audits and *interim reviews* of the first three quarters of the year prior to public release of that information. The guidance for public companies interim reviews is included in PCAOB 722. **Nonpublic companies** that have their annual financial statements audited also may choose to undergo interim reviews in accordance with Auditing Standards Board (ASB) standards (AICPA AU 930). Interim reviews under standards of the PCAOB and the Auditing Standards Board are both very similar to reviews performed under the *SSARS*.

As is the case with a *SSARS* review, a starting point for a PCAOB or ASB interim review is to establish an understanding with the client regarding the nature of the engagement. The understanding, which preferably should be in writing, includes information on management's responsibilities, the accountants' responsibilities, and the nature of reviews. An engagement letter is often used to document the understanding. A review includes obtaining an understanding of the client's business and internal control, performing review procedures, and communicating results.

Since PCAOB and ASB interim reviews are very similar in scope to those of *SSARS* reviews, we will not go through these engagements in detail. We simply highlight the following major differences:

- PCAOB and Auditing Standards Board reviews are conducted on interim information of public and nonpublic companies that have had annual audits, while *SSARS* reviews are conducted on nonpublic companies that have not had an annual audit. Public companies must undergo interim reviews; it is an option for nonpublic companies.
- The most significant procedural difference between a *SAARS* and an ASB or PCAOB interim review is that the latter two require that the accountant obtain a more detailed understanding of the company's business and particularly its internal control. The understanding that is necessary for an ASB or PCAOB interim review is one that allows the accountants to identify types of potential material misstatements and their

likelihood of occurrence. This understanding allows them to select appropriate procedures that serve as the basis for the review.

- The accountants ordinarily are not required to issue a review report on interim financial statements.[6] The decision on report issuance is made by the accountant and the client.
- Although the ASB interim review report is very similar to the *SSARS* report, the PCAOB report differs somewhat and is presented below.

---

### Report of Independent Registered Public Accounting Firm

We have reviewed the balance sheet and related statements of income, retained earnings, and cash flows of ABC Company and consolidated subsidiaries as of September 30, 20X2 and 20X1, and for the three-month and nine-month periods then ended. These financial statements are the responsibility of the company's management.

We conducted our review in accordance with the *standards of the Public Company Accounting Oversight Board.* A review of interim financial information consists principally of applying *analytical procedures* to financial data and making *inquiries of* persons responsible for financial and accounting matters. It is *substantially less in scope than an audit* conducted in accordance with generally accepted auditing standards, the objective of which is the expression of an opinion regarding the financial statements taken as a whole. Accordingly, we *do not express such an opinion.*

Based on our review, we *are not aware of any material modifications* that should be made to the accompanying financial statements for them to be in conformity with generally accepted accounting principles.

*Warren & Warren LLP*
Houston, TX
April 12, 20X2

---

## Compilations of Historical Financial Statements

Many clients request CPAs to perform a compilation rather than a review or an audit. Reports resulting from compilations provide no explicit assurance that the information constitutes a fair presentation. Because no explicit assurance is provided, accountants performing such services need *not* be independent of their client.[7]

### Nature of a Financial Statement Compilation

LO8

Explain the accountant's responsibilities when performing a compilation of financial statements.

A compilation involves assisting management in presenting financial information in the form of financial statements. To perform a compilation, *SSARS* require the accountants to have knowledge of the accounting principles and practices used within the client's industry and a general understanding of the client's business transactions and accounting records. The accountants must evaluate the client's representations in light of this knowledge.

At a minimum, the accountants must read the compiled statements for appropriate format and obvious material misstatement. When performing a compilation, the accountants must not accept patently unreasonable information. If the client's information appears to be incorrect, incomplete, or otherwise unsatisfactory, the accountants should insist upon revised information. If the client refuses to provide revised information, the accountants should withdraw from the engagement. Beyond these basic requirements, accountants have no responsibility to perform any investigative procedures to substantiate the client's representations.

Proper reporting on compiled statements depends on whether the financial statements are expected to be used by a third party (i.e., a party other than management). If no such third-party use is expected, an accountant may either (1) issue a compilation report or

---

[6] An exception is that a document containing the reviewed interim financial information makes reference to the accountant's review—in such a situation, a review report must be issued.

[7] AR 60 describes compilations as being attest engagements, but not assurance engagements. As is discussed in Chapters 1 and 20, the AICPA and PCAOB *Attestation Standards* define attestation engagements as those in which an auditor issues an examination, review, or agreed-upon procedures report on subject matter. The AICPA *Code of Professional Conduct* provides a different definition when it defines attest engagements as those engagements that require independence, as defined in *AICPA Professional Standards.* Compilations may be performed by independent or not independent accountants, yet are considered attestation engagements.

(2) not issue a compilation report, and document the understanding with the client through use of an engagement letter. The engagement letter, signed by management, must make clear the services performed and the limitations on the use of the financial statements. A phrase such as "Restricted for Management's Use Only" should be included on each page of the financial statements when no compilation report is issued.

If the financial statements are to be used by a third party (or reasonably might be expected to be used by a third party), a compilation report must be issued by the accountants. This report disclaims an opinion or any other form of assurance on the financial statements.

The body of a standard financial statement compilation report is shown below:

> We have compiled the accompanying balance sheet of XYZ Company as of December 31, 20XX, and the related statements of income, retained earnings, and cash flows for the year then ended. We have not audited or reviewed the accompanying financial statements and, accordingly, do not express an opinion or any assurance about whether the financial statements are in accordance with accounting principles generally accepted in the United States of America.
>
> Management is responsible for the preparation and fair presentation of the financial statements in accordance with accounting principles generally accepted in the United States of America and for designing, implementing, and maintaining internal control relevant to the preparation and fair presentation of the financial statements.
>
> Our responsibility is to conduct the compilation in accordance with *Statements on Standards for Accounting and Review Services* issued by the American Institute of Certified Public Accountants. The objective of a compilation is to assist management in presenting financial information in the form of financial statements without undertaking to obtain any assurance that there are no material modifications that should be made to the financial statements.

Each page of the unaudited financial statements should be marked "See Accountants' Compilation Report," and the accountants' report should be dated as of the completion of the compilation.

Accountants may issue a compilation report on one or more individual financial statements, without compiling a complete set of statements. Also, financial statements may be compiled on a framework of accounting *other than* generally accepted accounting principles. In this case, the basis of accounting used must be disclosed either in the statements or in the accountants' report.

### Departures from Generally Accepted Accounting Principles

Treatment of departures from generally accepted accounting principles parallels that for reviews of financial statements. A departure from generally accepted accounting principles requires the accountants to discuss the departure in a separate paragraph in the compilation report. If the accountant believes that modification of the standard report is not adequate to indicate the deficiencies in the financial statements, the accountant should withdraw from the engagement. As is the situation with review reports, compilation reports are not required to be altered in situations involving a lack of consistent application of generally accepted accounting principles or the existence of major uncertainties (including going-concern uncertainties) that have been properly reported in the financial statements. When that information is not properly reported in the financial statements, the accountants should modify the compilation report for a departure from generally accepted accounting principles.

### Compilations that Omit Substantially All Disclosures

The numerous disclosures required by generally accepted accounting principles may not be particularly useful in the financial statements of a nonpublic business, especially when the statements are intended for internal use by management. Therefore, a nonpublic client may request CPAs to compile financial statements that omit substantially all of the disclosures required by GAAP. CPAs may compile such statements, provided that the omission is clearly indicated in the accountants' report. In such situations, the accountants should add the following last paragraph to their report:

> Management has elected to omit substantially all of the disclosures (and the statement of cash flows) required by generally accepted accounting principles. If the omitted disclosures were included in the financial statements, they might influence the user's conclusions about the company's financial position, results of operations, and cash flows. Accordingly, these financial statements are not designed for those who are not informed about such matters.

If the client wishes to include only some of the disclosures required by GAAP, these disclosures should be labeled "Selected Information—Substantially All Disclosures Required by Generally Accepted Accounting Principles Are Not Included."

### Compilations of Information in Prescribed Forms

Prescribed forms refer to standard preprinted forms designed or adopted by the institution or agency to which the form is to be submitted. An example is a bank loan application. Since these prescribed forms often require financial statement items to be presented on a basis other than generally accepted accounting principles, accountants compiling the forms indicate that the financial statements are presented in accordance with the requirements of the regulatory body rather than GAAP. The accountants should modify the report to point out material departures from the requirements of the prescribed form.

### Compilations When the CPAs Are Not Independent

CPAs may perform compilations even when they are not independent of the client. However, they should indicate their lack of independence by adding the following last paragraph to their compilation report:

> We are not independent with respect to XYZ Company.

The CPAs may also provide reason(s) for the lack of independence (e.g., a member of the audit team had a direct financial interest in XYZ Company).

---

## Chapter Summary

This chapter described CPA services on historical financial information other than audits of corporation financial statements in accordance with U.S. generally accepted accounting principles. To summarize:

1. Auditors sometimes are asked to provide additional assurance services after having conducted an audit. Regulatory requirements and debt agreements often require companies to provide compliance reports prepared by their auditors, including limited assurance about whether the company has complied with the particular requirements. In letters for underwriters (comfort letters), the auditors provide limited assurance about various information contained in registration statements used for the sale of securities. Also, clients may issue summary financial statements developed from audited financial statements, and CPAs may attest as to whether they are consistent, in all material respects, with the audited financial statements.

2. The professional standards define *special-purpose financial reporting frameworks* as: (a) cash basis, (b) tax basis, (c) regulatory basis, and (d) contractual basis. CPAs may audit financial statements following these bases and issue an audit report that alerts users to the basis being followed. Financial statements following a regulatory or contractual basis are ordinarily restricted to the use of those in the company, the parties to the contract or agreement, or regulatory agencies.

3. The nature of auditors' reporting responsibilities on financial statements prepared using a financial framework generally accepted in another country depends upon whether there will be use of those financial statements in the United States. When the

intended use is only outside the Untied States, the auditors may issue a U.S. form of report modified as appropriate, or the standard report of the other country. When use is also intended in the Untied States, a second report is issued using a U.S. form, with alterations that depend upon whether a nonpublic or public company is involved.

4. Auditors may audit and issue an opinion on single financial statements and specific elements, accounts, or items of a financial statement. However, they must design the engagement to provide appropriate sufficient audit evidence about the subject matter of the audit.

5. There are several major differences between personal financial statements and those of other types of organizations. For example, assets and liabilities on personal financial statements are presented at their estimated current values and amounts. Accountants may audit, review, or compile personal financial statements.

6. Nonpublic companies that do not have annual audits may engage CPAs to review their annual or interim financial statements under *SSARS*. The procedures performed in a review engagement consist primarily of (1) performing analytical procedures, (2) making inquiries of management and others within the organization, (3) performing other procedures considered necessary, and (4) obtaining representations from management relating to the financial statements. A review report provides limited (negative) assurance that the financial statements contain no material departures from GAAP. The accountants will adjust the specific procedures based on their knowledge of the client's internal control and business.

7. Public companies must engage CPAs to review the company's interim financial statements while nonpublic companies that have annual audits may choose to do so; these reviews are under ASB or PCAOB standards. These interim reviews are similar in nature to those performed under *SSARS*. However, under ASB and PCAOB standards, the auditors must obtain an understanding of client internal control.

8. In a compilation, the accountants provide no assurance with respect to the propriety of the financial statements. When compiled financial statements are not expected to be used by a third party, either a compilation report may be issued or an understanding with the client regarding use of the statements may be documented in an engagement letter. When third-party reliance is anticipated, the accountants must issue a report that provides no explicit assurance. CPAs who are not independent may perform compilations.

| | |
|---|---|
| **Key Terms Introduced or Emphasized in Chapter 19** | **Comfort letter (727)**  A letter issued by the independent auditors to the underwriters of securities registered with the SEC under the Securities Act of 1933. Comfort letters deal with such matters as the auditors' independence and the compliance of unaudited data with requirements of the SEC. |

**Compilation (735)**  An accounting service that involves the preparation of information from client records. No assurance is provided in a compilation.

**Financial reporting framework (728)**  A set of criteria used to determine measurement, recognition, presentation, and disclosure of all material items appearing in the financial statements. Financial reporting frameworks may be general-purpose financial reporting frameworks or special-purpose financial reporting frameworks.

**General-purpose financial reporting frameworks (728)**  Financial reporting frameworks designed to meet the common financial information needs of a wide range of users. Examples of general-purpose financial reporting frameworks are accounting principles generally accepted in the United States of America and *International Financial Reporting Standards* issued by the International Accounting Standards Board.

**Limited assurance (negative assurance) (735)**  The level of assurance provided by CPAs who review historical financial statements.

**Negative assurance (735)**  An assertion by CPAs that after applying limited investigative techniques to certain information, they are not aware of the need to modify the presentation of the information. Negative assurance is equivalent to limited assurance.

**Nonissuer (734)**　A company whose securities are *not* registered under requirements of the Securities and Exchange Commission; ordinarily, a "nonissuer" is a nonpublic company. This is in contrast to an issuer, a company whose securities are registered under the requirements of the Securities and Exchange Commission.

**Nonpublic company (739)**　A company other than one whose securities are traded on a public market or one that makes a filing with a regulatory agency in preparation for the sale of securities on a public market.

**Public company (issuers) (739)**　A company whose stock is traded on a public market or a company in the process of registering its stock for public sale.

**Review of financial statements (735)**　A form of attestation based on inquiry and analytical procedures applied for the purpose of expressing limited assurance that historical financial statements are presented in accordance with generally accepted accounting principles or some other appropriate basis.

**Special-purpose financial reporting frameworks (728)**　Financial reporting frameworks other than GAAP, which are one of the following bases of accounting: cash basis, tax basis, regulatory basis, and contractual basis. Common special-purpose financial reporting frameworks include:

*Cash basis.*　The cash receipts and disbursements basis of accounting, and modifications of the cash basis having substantial support, such as recording depreciation on fixed assets or accruing income taxes.

*Tax basis.*　The basis of accounting that the entity uses or expects to use to file its income tax return for the period covered by the financial statements.

*Regulatory basis.*　A basis of accounting in accordance with the requirements or financial reporting provisions of a regulatory agency to whose jurisdiction the entity is subject. An example is a basis of accounting that insurance companies use pursuant to the rules of a state insurance commission.

*Contractual basis.*　A basis of accounting in accordance with an agreement between the entity and one or more third parties other than the auditors.

**Summary financial statements (condensed financial statements) (728)**　Historical financial information that is derived from the financial statements but contains less detail, while still providing a structured representation consistent with the financial statements.

## Review Questions

19–1.　Evaluate this statement: "All companies should be audited annually."

19–2.　Evaluate this statement: "Auditors perform attestation services and accountants perform accounting services."

19–3.　In communications with clients, should CPAs refer to themselves as auditors or as accountants? Explain.

19–4.　Can auditors express an unmodified opinion on financial statements that are not presented on the basis of generally accepted accounting principles? Explain.

19–5.　Provide four types of special-purpose financial reporting frameworks.

19–6.　Comment on the following: "Because of the nature of the frameworks the clients use, audits of *special-purpose* financial reporting frameworks result in an audit report that is restricted for use by those within the entity."

19–7.　A client has prepared financial statements using a financial reporting framework generally accepted in another country. The statements are intended only to be used in that country. Describe the auditor's reporting options.

19–8.　Jane Wilson has prepared personal financial statements in which her assets are valued at her historical cost, less appropriate depreciation. Is this presentation in conformity with generally accepted accounting principles? Can a public accounting firm audit these statements and issue a standard unmodified opinion?

19–9.　What are the general types of procedures performed during a review of the quarterly financial statements of a company that has audits of its annual financial statement?

19–10.　Describe a unique reporting aspect about the CPAs' required review of the quarterly financial statements of public companies.

19–11.　How do CPAs of public companies assist audit committees in performing their oversight function with respect to quarterly financial statements?

19–12.　What types of services may be performed by CPAs with respect to the financial statements of nonpublic companies?

19–13. How does a review of the financial statements of a nonpublic company differ from an audit?

19–14. What are the types of procedures performed during the review of the financial statements of a nonpublic company?

19–15. Are engagement letters needed for accounting and review services? Explain.

19–16. What is the purpose of a comfort letter? Discuss.

19–17. What form of opinion will the auditors normally issue with respect to *summary financial statements* that the client has developed from the audited financial statements?

19–18. What procedures are required when a CPA performs a compilation of financial statements?

19–19. Can the CPAs report on a nonpublic client's financial statements that omit substantially all disclosures required by generally accepted accounting principles? Explain.

19–20. What should the accountants do if they discover that the financial statements they are compiling contain a material departure from generally accepted accounting principles?

19–21. Describe a CPA's reporting responsibility when compiling financial statements that are not expected to be used by a third party.

19–22. Assume that a public accounting firm is reviewing the financial statements of a nonpublic company and discovers that the firm is not independent. What alternatives are available to the firm?

## Questions Requiring Analysis

**LO 6, 8**   19–23. You have been asked by Ambassador Hardware Co., a small nonpublic company, to submit a proposal for the audit of the company. After performing an investigation of the company, including its management and accounting system, you advise the president of Ambassador that the audit fee will be approximately $20,000. Ambassador's president was somewhat surprised at the fee, and after discussions with members of the board of directors, he concluded that the company could not afford an audit at this time.

*Required:*

   *a.* Discuss management's alternatives to having their company's financial statements audited in accordance with generally accepted auditing standards.

   *b.* What should Ambassador's management consider when selecting the type of service that you should provide? Explain.

**LO 2**   19–24. Rose & Co., CPAs in Kansas City, MO, have satisfactorily completed the audit of the financial statements of Dale, Booster & Co., a partnership, for the year ended December 31, 20X1. The financial statements that were prepared on the entity's income tax (cash) basis include notes that indicate that the partnership was involved in continuing litigation of material amounts relating to alleged infringement of a competitor's patent. The amount of damages, if any, resulting from this litigation could not be determined at the time of completion of the engagement. The prior years' financial statements were not presented.

*Required:*

   Prepare an auditors' unmodified report on the financial statements of Dale, Booster & Co. Your report should include two emphasis of matter paragraphs: one referring to the basis of accounting and another regarding the pending litigation. Address your report to Dale, Booster & Co.

(AICPA, adapted)

**LO 4**   19–25. Occasionally, public accounting firms are engaged to report on specified elements, accounts, and items of financial statements.

*Required:*

   *a.* Discuss three types of reports that may be provided for specified elements, accounts, and items of financial statements.

   *b.* Why should reports on the application of agreed-upon procedures to information be restricted to specified users?

**LO 6**   19–26. You have been engaged by the management of Pippin, Inc., a nonpublic company, to review the company's financial statements for the year ended December 31, 20XX. To prepare for the engagement, you consult the *Statements on Standards for Accounting and Review Services*.

*Required:*

   *a.* Discuss the procedures required for the performance of a review of financial statements.

   *b.* Explain the content of the report on a review of financial statements.

   *c.* Discuss your responsibilities if you find that the financial statements contain a material departure from generally accepted accounting principles.

**LO 1**   19–27. In connection with a public offering of first-mortgage bonds by Guizzetti Corporation, the bond underwriter has asked Guizzetti's CPAs to furnish it with a comfort letter giving as much assurance as possible on Guizzetti's unaudited financial statements for the three months ended March 31. The CPAs had expressed an unqualified opinion on Guizzetti's financial statements for the year ended December 31, the preceding year; they also performed a review of Guizzetti's financial statements for the three months ended March 31. Nothing has come to their attention that would indicate that the March 31 statements are not properly presented.

*Required:*

a. Explain what can be stated about the unaudited financial statements in the letter.

b. Discuss other matters that are typically included in comfort letters.

**LO 8**    19–28.    Andrew Wilson, CPA, has assembled the financial statements of Texas Mirror Co., a small nonpublic company. He has not performed an audit of the financial statements in accordance with generally accepted auditing standards. Wilson is confused about the standards applicable to this type of engagement.

*Required:*

a. Explain where Wilson should look for guidance concerning this engagement.

b. Explain Wilson's responsibilities with respect to a preparation of these financial statements.

## Objective Questions

**All applicable questions are available with McGraw-Hill's *Connect*™ *Accounting*.** connect
|ACCOUNTING

19–29.    **Multiple Choice Questions**

Select the best answer for each of the following and explain fully the reason for your selection.

**LO 6**    a. Which of the following is *not* typically performed when the auditors are performing a review of client financial statements?

(1) Analytical procedures applied to financial data.

(2) Inquiries about significant subsequent events.

(3) Confirmation of accounts receivable.

(4) Obtaining an understanding of accounting principles followed in the client's industry.

**LO 6**    b. Which of the following must be obtained in a review of a nonpublic company?

|     | Engagement Letter | Representation Letter |
|-----|-------------------|----------------------|
| (1) | Yes | Yes |
| (2) | Yes | No |
| (3) | No | Yes |
| (4) | No | No |

**LO 6, 8**    c. A CPA who is *not* independent may perform which of the following services for a nonpublic company?

|     | Compilation | Review |
|-----|-------------|--------|
| (1) | Yes | Yes |
| (2) | Yes | No |
| (3) | No | Yes |
| (4) | No | No |

**LO 6**    d. When performing a review of a nonpublic company, which is *least* likely to be included in auditor inquiries of management members with responsibility for financial and accounting matters?

(1) Subsequent events.

(2) Significant journal entries and other adjustments.

(3) Communications with related parties.

(4) Unusual or complex situations affecting the financial statements.

**LO 4**    e. The proper report by an auditor relating to summarized financial statements includes:

(1) A statement about the type of opinion expressed in the prior year.

(2) An adverse opinion.

(3) An opinion on whether the summarized information is fairly stated in all material respects in relation to the basic financial statements.

(4) No assurance on the information.

**LO 7**    *f.* Concerning interim quarterly financial statements, management of public companies:

(1) Must engage CPAs to audit the statements.

(2) Must engage CPAs to review the statements.

(3) May choose to engage CPAs to review the statements.

(4) May not engage CPAs to become associated with the statements.

**LO 8**    *g.* A proper compilation report on financial statements that omit note disclosures:

(1) Includes an adverse opinion.

(2) Includes a disclaimer of opinion on the accuracy of such note disclosures.

(3) Indicates that management has omitted such information.

(4) Indicates that note disclosures are not necessary for those not informed about such matters.

**LO 1, 6, 8**    *h.* Which of the following forms of accountant association always leads to a report intended solely for certain specified parties?

(1) Compilation.

(2) Review.

(3) Examination.

(4) Agreed-upon procedures.

**LO 5**    *i.* Which assertion is generally most difficult to attest to with respect to personal financial statements?

(1) Existence and occurrence.

(2) Rights and obligations.

(3) Completeness.

(4) Valuation.

**LO 2**    *j.* Financial statements prepared following which of the following are most likely to be considered a special-purpose financial reporting framework?

(1) Generally accepted accounting principles.

(2) *International Financial Reporting Standards.*

(3) Financial reporting standards of a foreign nation.

(4) The cash basis of accounting.

**LO 6, 8**    *k.* In which of the following reports should a CPA *not* express negative (limited) assurance?

(1) A standard compilation report on financial statements of a nonpublic entity.

(2) A standard review report on interim financial statements of a public entity.

(3) A standard review report on financial statements of a nonpublic entity.

(4) A comfort letter on financial information included in a registration statement filed with the Securities and Exchange Commission.

**LO 1**    *l.* Comfort letters to underwriters are normally signed by the:

(1) Independent auditor.

(2) Underwriter.

(3) Client's lawyer.

(4) Chief executive officer.

**LO 2**    19–30.    The following statements relate to auditor reporting on financial statements prepared using special-purpose financial reporting frameworks. For each, indicate whether the statement is correct or incorrect.

| Statement | Correct | Incorrect |
|---|---|---|
| 1. A special-purpose financial reporting framework is any framework other than GAAP. | | |
| 2. An audit report on financial statements that are prepared using a special-purpose framework must, in some, but not all circumstances indicate that the financial statements are intended solely for certain specified users. | | |
| 3. An audit report on financial statements that are prepared using a special-purpose framework must include an emphasis of matter paragraph alerting users that the financial statements were prepared in accordance with the framework. | | |
| 4. An audit report on financial statements that are prepared using a special-purpose framework must in all circumstances include a description of the purposes for which the statements are prepared. | | |
| 5. An audit opinion on financial statements that use a special-purpose framework may be unmodified. | | |
| 6. The *Statements on Standards for Attestation Engagements,* not the *Statements on Auditing Standards,* apply to engagements involving special-purpose frameworks. | | |
| 7. If a regulatory agency requires a particular layout for the audit report, the auditor may be able to use that layout rather than the suggested report included in the *Professional Standards.* | | |
| 8. An audit report on financial statements that are prepared using a special-purpose framework will indicate that the audit was conducted in accordance with the special-purpose financial reporting framework auditing standards. | | |

**LO 3**   19–31.   Bill Jones, the president of AMTO, a nonpublic audit client of your firm, has come to you and indicated that his company established a subsidiary in the country of Laos this year and that he wants your firm to issue an audit report on that subsidiary for use in Laos for various purposes. The financial statements should follow Laotian generally accepted principles. Answer the following questions relating to this situation.

| Question | Yes | No |
|---|---|---|
| 1. Is this considered an audit of financial statements using a special-purpose financial reporting framework? | | |
| 2. In performing the audit, must your firm consider GAAS to the extent the standards are appropriate? | | |
| 3. If the resulting audit report will not be used in the United States, must it include an opinion on whether U.S. GAAP are followed? | | |
| 4. If the resulting audit report will be used extensively both in the United States and in Laos, must the report include an opinion on whether U.S. GAAP are followed? | | |
| 5. If Laotian generally accepted auditing standards do not require the Laotian form of audit report, may your firm use the U.S. report form and modify it as necessary? | | |
| 6. If Laotian generally accepted auditing standards do not require the Laotian form of audit report, may your firm use the Laotian report form? | | |
| 7. Must a paragraph be added to the report indicating that the financial statements are intended solely for certain specified users? | | |

**LO 2**   19–32.   State whether you agree or disagree with each of the following relating to the topic of special-purpose financial reporting frameworks.

    *a.* *International Financial Reporting Standards* are considered a special-purpose financial reporting framework.

    *b.* Cash basis financial statements are considered as having been prepared following a special-purpose financial reporting framework, and their use should be restricted to specified users.

c. Financial statements prepared following a contractual basis are considered as having been prepared following a special-purpose financial reporting framework, and their use should be restricted to specified users.

d. An emphasis of a matter paragraph should be added to a cash basis set of financial statements indicating that the framework is other than GAAP.

e. When financial statements are prepared following a contractual basis, the auditors must obtain an understanding of significant management interpretations of the contract.

**LO 2, 4, 8**　　19–33.　**Simulation**

Indicate whether a CPA may provide each of the following services, and whether independence is required, by placing a check in the appropriate box.

| Service | May Provide; Independence Is Required | May Provide; Independence Is Not Required | May Not Provide |
|---|---|---|---|
| a. Provide an opinion on whether financial statements are prepared following the cash basis of accounting. | | | |
| b. Compile the financial statements for the past year and issue a publicly available report. | | | |
| c. Apply certain agreed-upon procedures to accounts receivable for purposes of obtaining a loan, and express a summary of findings relating to those procedures. | | | |
| d. Review quarterly information and issue a report that includes limited assurance. | | | |
| e. Provide an opinion on whether financial statements are prepared following generally accepted accounting principles. | | | |
| f. Compile the financial statements for the past year, but do not issue a report since the financial statements are only for the company's use. | | | |

**LO 1, 4, 6, 7, 8**　　19–34.　**Simulation**

Auditors who audit public and nonpublic companies must be familiar with professional standards developed by a variety of sources. For each of the types of services below, indicate the proper source of professional requirements. Each source may be used once, more than once, or not at all.

| Service | Source of Standards |
|---|---|
| a. An annual review of the financial statements of a nonpublic company.<br>b. A quarterly review of the financial statements of a nonpublic company that has an annual audit.<br>c. A quarterly review of the financial statements of a public company that has an annual audit.<br>d. An audit of the financial statements of a nonpublic company.<br>e. A compilation of the financial statements of a nonpublic company.<br>f. A quarterly review of the financial statements of a nonpublic company that annually has a review of its financial statements. (Note: The question is on the quarterly review.)<br>g. A letter to an underwriter of a public company.<br>h. A report on summary financial statements of a nonpublic company.<br>i. An audit of a public company. | 1. Accounting and Review Services Committee *Statements on Standards for Accounting and Review Services*<br>2. Auditing Standards Board *Statements on Auditing Standards*<br>3. PCAOB *Auditing Standards* |

## Problems

**LO 2**    19–35.    Jiffy Clerical Services is a company that furnishes temporary office help to its customers. The company maintains its accounting records on a basis of cash receipts and cash disbursements. You have audited the company for the year ended December 31, 20X4, and have concluded that the company's financial statements represent a fair presentation on that basis.

*Required:*

    *a.* Draft the unqualified auditors' report you would issue covering the financial statements (a statement of assets and liabilities and the related statement of revenue collected and expenses paid) for the year ended December 31, 20X4.

    *b.* Briefly discuss and justify your modifications of the conventional standard auditors' report on GAAP financial statements.

**LO 6**    19–36.    Loman, CPA, who has audited the financial statements of the Broadwall Corporation, a publicly held company, for the year ended December 31, 20X6, was asked to perform a review of the financial statements of Broadwall Corporation for the period ending March 31, 20X7. The engagement letter stated that a review does not provide a basis for the expression of an opinion.

*Required:*

    *a.* Explain why Loman's review will *not* provide a basis for the expression of an opinion.

    *b.* What are the review procedures Loman should perform, and what is the purpose of each procedure? Structure your response as follows:

| Procedure | Purpose of Procedure |
| --- | --- |
|  |  |

(AICPA, adapted)

**LO 8**    19–37.    Norman Lewis, an inexperienced member of your staff, has compiled the financial statements of Williams Grocery. He has submitted the following report for your review:

> The accompanying financial statements have been compiled by us. A compilation is an accounting service, but we also applied certain analytical procedures to the financial data.
>
> As explained in Note 3, the Company changed accounting principles for accounting for its inventories. We have not audited or reviewed the accompanying financial statements, but nothing came to our attention to indicate that they are in error.

*Required:*

Describe the deficiencies in the report, give reasons why they are deficiencies, and briefly discuss how the report should be corrected. Do not discuss the addressee, signature, and date. Organize your answer sheet as follows:

| Deficiency | Reason | Correction |
| --- | --- | --- |
|  |  |  |

**LO 7**    19–38.    The limitations on the CPAs' professional responsibilities when they are associated with unaudited financial statements are often misunderstood. These misunderstandings can be substantially reduced if the CPAs follow professional pronouncements in the course of their work and take other appropriate measures.

*Required:*

The following list describes seven situations CPAs may encounter, or contentions they may have to deal with, in their association with and preparation of *unaudited* financial statements. Briefly discuss the extent of the CPAs' responsibilities and, if appropriate, the actions they should take to minimize any misunderstandings. Mark your answers to correspond to the letters in the following list.

    *a.* The CPAs were engaged by telephone to perform write-up work, including the compilation of financial statements. The client believes that the CPAs have been engaged to audit the financial statements and examine the records accordingly.

    *b.* A group of investors who own a farm that is managed by an independent agent engage CPAs to compile quarterly unaudited financial statements for them. The CPAs prepare the financial statements from information given to them by the independent agent. Subsequently, the investors find the statements were inaccurate because their independent agent was embezzling funds. They refuse to pay the CPAs' fee and blame them for allowing the situation to go undetected, contending that the CPAs should not have relied on representations from the independent agent.

c. In comparing the trial balance with the general ledger, the CPAs find an account labeled Audit Fees in which the client has accumulated the CPAs' quarterly billings for accounting services, including the compilation of quarterly unaudited financial statements.

d. To determine appropriate account classification, the CPAs examined a number of the client's invoices. They noted in their working papers that some invoices were missing, but did nothing further because it was felt that the invoices did not affect the unaudited financial statements they were compiling. When the client subsequently discovered that invoices were missing, he contended that the CPAs should not have ignored the missing invoices when compiling the financial statements and had a responsibility to at least inform him that they were missing.

e. The CPAs are engaged to compile the financial statements of a nonpublic company. During the engagement, the CPAs learn of several items for which generally accepted accounting principles would require adjustments of the statements and note disclosure. The controller agrees to make the recommended adjustments to the statements, but says that she is not going to add the notes because the statements are unaudited.

(AICPA, adapted)

**LO 8**  19–39.  Brown, CPA, received a telephone call from Calhoun, the sole owner and manager of a small corporation. Calhoun asked Brown to compile the financial statements for the corporation and emphasized that the statements were needed in two weeks for external financing purposes. Calhoun was vague when Brown inquired about the intended use of the statements. Brown was convinced that Calhoun thought Brown's work would constitute an audit. To avoid confusion, Brown decided not to explain to Calhoun that the engagement would be to compile the financial statements only. Brown, with the understanding that a substantial fee would be paid if the work was completed in two weeks, accepted the engagement and started the work at once.

During the course of the work, Brown discovered an accrued expense account labeled Professional Fees and learned that the balance in the account represented an accrual for the cost of Brown's services. Brown suggested to Calhoun's bookkeeper that the account name be changed to Fees for Limited Audit Engagement. Brown also reviewed several invoices to determine whether accounts were being properly classified. Some of the invoices were missing. Brown listed the missing invoice numbers in the working papers with a note indicating that there should be a follow-up on the next engagement. Brown also discovered that the available records included the fixed asset values at estimated current replacement costs. Based on the records available, Brown compiled a balance sheet, income statement, and statement of stockholders' equity. In addition, Brown drafted the notes, but he decided that any mention of the replacement costs would only confuse the readers. Brown suggested to Calhoun that readers of the financial statements would be better informed if they received a separate letter from Calhoun explaining the meaning and effect of the estimated replacement costs of the fixed assets. Brown mailed the financial statements and notes to Calhoun with the following note included on each page:

> The accompanying financial statements are submitted to you without complete audit verification.

*Required:*   Identify the inappropriate actions of Brown, and indicate what Brown should have done to avoid each inappropriate action. Organize your answer sheet as follows:

| Inappropriate Action | What Brown Should Have Done to Avoid Inappropriate Action |
| --- | --- |
|  |  |

(AICPA, adapted)

19–40.  Webstar, a nonpublic company, is owned by Ben Williams and three of his friends. Previously the company's financing has been internally generated, with limited equity contributions by the owners. The company has not been audited in the past, and Williams has said to you that while he generally understands the nature of an audit, he would like to discuss services other than an audit. Specifically, he read a brief article in a management journal which described reviews, compilations, financial statements prepared following another comprehensive basis of accounting (other than generally accepted accounting principles), and auditing specified elements of financial statements. Among his questions are the following:

a.  *Review of financial statements:*

(1)  Is the review form of association available for Webstar's financial statements?

(2)  What procedures are typically included in a review?

(3)  What type of assurance is included in a review report?

(4)  What will result in modification of a review report?

(5)  Williams says that he heard something about there being a requirement that every company obtain a review of its financial statements. He has been concerned, since he never has had this done. What's the story with this?

b.  *Compilation of financial statements:*

(1)  Is the compilation form of association available?

(2)  What procedures are typically included in a compilation?

(3)  If a compilation is performed, must a compilation report be issued?

(4)  What type of assurance would be provided in a compilation report?

(5)  What will result in modification of a compilation report?

c.  *Financial statements:* Williams says he isn't sure he wants to prepare financial statements following GAAP. He says he needs only statements based on the income tax method he uses to file his income taxes.

(1)  Are you able to issue an audit report based on the income tax basis?

(2)  What type of report is this?

(3)  How will the report issued differ from that of a GAAP audit?

d.  *Auditing a small portion of financial statements:* Williams has given some thought to having an audit of just his company's revenues for the year and receivables at year-end.

(1)  May you perform an audit of only these two accounts?

(2)  What types of engagements are possible here?

(3)  What type of assurance will be provided in these reports?

*Required:*  Draft brief answers to each of the above questions.

19–41.  You are a young CPA just starting your own practice in Hollywood, California, after five years' experience with a "Big 4" firm. You have several connections in the entertainment industry and hope to develop a practice rendering income tax, auditing, and accounting services to celebrities and other wealthy clients.

One of your first engagements is arranged by John Forbes, a long-established business manager for a number of celebrities and a personal friend of yours. You are engaged to audit the personal statement of financial condition (balance sheet) of Dallas McBain, one of Forbes's clients. McBain is a popular rock star, with a net worth of approximately $100 million. However, the star also has a reputation as an extreme recluse who is never seen in public except at performances.

Forbes handles all of McBain's business affairs, and all your communications with McBain are through Forbes. You have never met McBain personally and have no means of contacting the star directly. All of McBain's business records are maintained at Forbes's office. Forbes also issues checks for many of McBain's personal expenses, using a check-signing machine and a facsimile plate of McBain's signature.

During the audit, you notice that during the year numerous checks totaling approximately $500,000 have been issued payable to Cash. In addition, the proceeds of a $250,000 sale of marketable securities were never deposited in any of McBain's bank accounts. In the accounting records, all of these amounts have been charged to the account entitled "Personal Living Expenses." There is no further documentation of these disbursements.

When you bring these items to Forbes's attention, he explains that celebrities such as McBain often spend a lot of cash supporting various "hangers-on," whom they don't want identified by name. He also states, "Off the record, some of these people also have some very expensive habits." He points out, however, that you are auditing only the statement of assets and liabilities, not McBain's revenue or expenses. Furthermore, the amount of these transactions is not material in relation to McBain's net worth.

*Required:*

a. Discuss whether the undocumented disbursements and the missing securities' proceeds should be of concern to you in a balance sheet–only audit.

b. Identify the various courses of action that you might at least consider under these circumstances. Explain briefly the arguments supporting each course of action.

c. Explain what you would do and justify your decision.

d. Assume that you are a long-established CPA, independently wealthy, and that the McBain account represents less than 5 percent of the annual revenue of your practice. Would this change in circumstances affect your conclusion in part (c)? Discuss.

**Suggested References**

This textbook, discussion of *1136 Tenants Corporation* case, pp. 121–122; "Audit of Partnerships and Sole Proprietorships," p. 611; and "Audits of Personal Financial Statements," p. 734.

AICPA, *Personal Financial Statements Guide* (New York, 2009). AICPA AU 265, "Communicating Internal Control Related Matters Identified in an Audit."

# Additional Assurance Services: Other Information

To this point, we have focused primarily on services involving historical financial information, but CPAs are often asked to provide a wide range of other assurance services. In this chapter, we first focus on the broad concept of assurance services. Next, we address the attestation standards, which apply to a majority of the new assurance services. Finally, we provide a detailed description of a number of existing and developing services.

## Assurance Services

| LO1 |
| --- |
| Describe the differences among assurance services, attestation services, and audits. |

**Assurance services** provided by CPAs are professional services that are meant to improve the quality of information, or its context for decision makers and other users.[1] The AICPA's Assurance Standards Executive Committee seeks to (1) identify and prioritize emerging trends and market needs for assurance in areas not covered by other authoritative standards, and (2) develop related assurance methodology guidance and tools as needed. As such the Committee is involved with developing assurance services that are meant to assure the quality, relevance, and usefulness of information or its context for decision makers and other users.

As discussed in Chapter 1, assurance services go beyond attestation services. Figure 20.1 illustrates that while assurance services encompass audits of financial statements and all other attestation services, the concept also includes additional services. Assurance services may involve analyzing data or putting them in a form to facilitate decision making. For example, CPAs may collect information that is generally considered to be relevant to a particular decision and synthesize it for the user. CPAs may also provide assurance that the user has a complete set of information with which to make a decision. In an assurance engagement, a report may or may not be issued and, if one is issued, it could be in oral, symbolic, or any other appropriate form.

Attestation services are defined in the attestation standards (AT 101.01) as being engagements to issue an examination, review, or agreed-upon procedures report on the subject matter or an assertion about the subject matter that is the responsibility of another party.[2] In an attest engagement, the practitioner must evaluate the subject matter of the

---

[1] CPAs are not alone in the role of providing assurance. Although a wide variety of examples are possible, consider information available on a wide variety of products from Consumers Union (www.consumerreports.org), automobile reliability provided by organizations such as Edmunds, Inc. (e.g., www.edmunds.com), and restaurant quality from Zagat Survey (www.zagat.com). Also, because of the wide variety of assurance services provided that are discussed in this chapter, we use either *CPA* or *practitioner* rather than *auditor* throughout this chapter.

[2] The AICPA Code of Professional Conduct (ET 92.01) defines attestation services more generally as "engagements that require independence as defined in the AICPA *Professional Standards.*"

## Illustrative Case · *Types of Assurance Services*

A wide variety of assurance services are currently being performed by accounting firms. In a survey of 21 large- and medium-sized CPA firms, the Special Committee on Assurance Services identified over 275 types of assurance services. A few examples will provide an identification of the breadth of the subject matter of these engagements: (a) customer satisfaction, (b) investment performance, (c) software functionality, (d) effectiveness of risk management, (e) clinical results of in-vitro fertilization, and (f) the distance that golf balls travel.

FIGURE 20.1   **The Relationship between Assurance Services and Attestation Services**

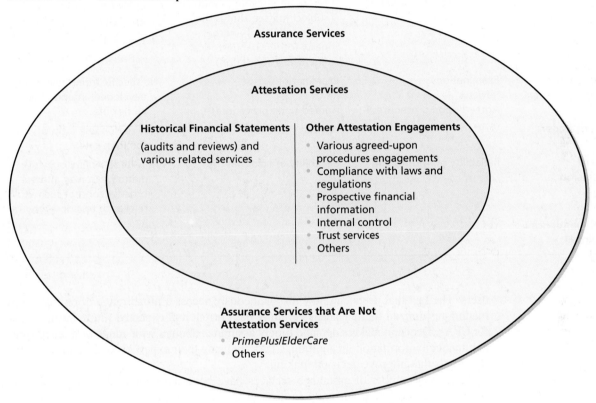

engagement against **suitable criteria.**[3] Figure 20.2 summarizes selected characteristics of the various types of assurance engagements.

## The Demand for Assurance Services

The demand for new types of assurance services developed as a natural extension of the audit function. Management realized that contracting costs could be reduced in many situations by providing investors, creditors, customers, and others transacting with the company access to information that is *certified* as to its reliability. As with an audit, these new assurance services reduce information risk for the outside parties and thus enable the company to contract at more favorable terms.

Much of the demand for other assurance services arises from developments in information technology, which have significantly changed the expectations of information

[3] Recall that financial statements are prepared following an appropriate *financial reporting framework.* "Suitable criteria" is the generalization of that term to include information other than financial statements.

**FIGURE 20.2    Selected Characteristics of Assurance Services**

| | Assurance Services | | |
|---|---|---|---|
| | **Assurance Services that Are Attestation Services** | | |
| | **Historical Financial Statement–Related Information** | **Other Attestation Engagements** | **Other Assurance Services** |
| **Primary Source of Standards** | Auditing standards Review standards (SSARS) | Attestation standards | General performance standards of AICPA *Code of Professional Conduct* (Rule 201) |
| **Nature** | Providing assurance on the reliability of historical financial statement information | Providing assurance on the reliability of subject matter, or an assertion about subject matter, that is the responsibility of another party (other than historical financial information) | Independent professional services that assure the quality, relevance, and usefulness of information or its context |
| **Primary Forms of Engagements** | Examinations Reviews Agreed-upon procedures | Examinations Reviews Agreed-upon procedures | No specific forms have been developed; intended to be flexible |
| **Form of Report** | Written | Written | Any reasonable form of communication |
| **Type of Conclusion** | Reliability of information | Reliability of information | May be reliability of information, but may address broader concept such as relevance to a decision |
| **Is Independence Required?** | Yes | Yes | Yes |

users. The fact that users can now instantaneously access a broad range of online information customized to their needs certainly has current and expected future implications for CPAs. Decision makers demand timely assurance about a wide range of financial and nonfinancial information. In addition, CPAs are using their expertise to place information in formats that improve decision making.

To date, a number of assurance services have been developed. Many of these new services are performed currently in accordance with the *Statements on Standards for Attestation Services;* an example, discussed later in this chapter, is Trust Services. Other products are being developed involving services that, at least portions of which, are not encompassed by those statements, including **PrimePlus/ElderCare** and XBRL.

## Attestation Standards

Explain the applicability of the attestation standards.

Attestation standards, presented in *Codification of the Statements on Standards for Attestation Engagements,* apply to engagements in which practitioners are engaged to issue or do issue an examination, a review, or an agreed-upon procedures report on subject matter, or an assertion about subject matter, that is the responsibility of another party. It is important to distinguish between the subject matter and the assertion about the subject matter. The **subject matter** of an **attestation engagement** may take many forms, including:

• Historical or prospective performance or condition (e.g., historical prospective financial information, performance measurements, and backlog data).

• Physical characteristics (e.g., narrative descriptions, square footage of facilities).

- Historical events (e.g., price of a market basket of goods on a certain date).
- Analyses (e.g., break-even analyses).
- Systems or processes (e.g., internal control).
- Behavior (e.g., corporate governance, compliance with laws and regulations, and human resource practices).

Generally, practitioners may attest to this subject matter at a point in time or for a period of time.

An **assertion** is a declaration about whether the subject matter is presented in accordance with certain criteria. To perform an attestation engagement, the practitioners generally must obtain an appropriate assertion from the party responsible for the subject matter. For example, in an engagement on a company's internal control over financial reporting, management (the responsible party) might assert that the company has maintained effective internal control.

While the practitioners generally must obtain an appropriate assertion about the subject matter, they ordinarily may report on either the *assertion about the subject matter* or on the *subject matter* itself. Continuing with our internal control engagement example, if reporting on the assertion, the practitioner's opinion would provide assurance on whether management's assertion about internal control is properly stated. Alternatively, when reporting on the subject matter, the practitioner's opinion would include assurance directly on the effectiveness of internal control. The following exhibit presents the two methods of reporting.[4]

| Reporting on Subject Matter | Reporting on Assertion |
| --- | --- |
| In our opinion, Welsing Corporation maintained effective internal control over financial reporting . . . based on [identify the criteria]. | In our opinion, *management's assertion that* Welsing Corporation maintained effective internal control over financial reporting . . . based on [identify the criteria]. |

If the practitioners are reporting on an assertion about the subject matter, the assertion is presented with the subject matter or in the practitioners' report. If the practitioners are reporting *directly* on the subject matter, the assertion normally is included only in a representation letter that the practitioners obtain from the responsible party.

There is an exception to the option of reporting directly upon the subject matter *or* on management's assertion. When the examination reveals material departures from the suitable criteria, to most effectively communicate with the reader of the report, the practitioner should report directly upon the subject matter, and not on the assertion.

The 11 attestation standards provide a general framework for all such engagements. These standards, which were originally presented in Chapter 2, are shown again in Figure 20.3 for convenience.

## The Criteria

Criteria are standards or benchmarks that are used to evaluate the subject matter of the engagement. Criteria are important in reporting the practitioners' conclusion to the users because they convey the basis on which the conclusion was formed. Without this frame of reference, the practitioners' report is subject to misinterpretation. For example, generally accepted accounting principles are ordinarily used as the frame of reference—the criteria—to evaluate financial statements.

In most areas, however, the criteria are not as well established as are generally accepted accounting principles. Accordingly, a practitioner must evaluate the criteria being followed. As indicated in the third general standard, the criteria used in an attestation engagement must be *suitable* and *available* to the users.

[4] These options are only available for reporting on a nonpublic (nonissuer) client. As indicated in Chapter 18, public company internal control reports are on the subject matter.

FIGURE 20.3
**AICPA Attestation Standards**

## General Standards

1. The practitioner must have adequate technical training and proficiency to perform the attestation engagement.
2. The practitioner must have adequate knowledge of the subject matter.
3. The practitioner must have reason to believe that the subject matter is capable of evaluation against criteria that are suitable and available to users.
4. The practitioner must maintain independence in mental attitude in all matters relating to the engagement.
5. The practitioner must exercise due professional care in the planning and performance of the engagement and the preparation of the report.

## Standards of Fieldwork

1. The practitioner must adequately plan the work and must properly supervise any assistants.
2. The practitioner must obtain sufficient evidence to provide a reasonable basis for the conclusion that is expressed in the report.

## Standards of Reporting

1. The practitioner must identify the subject matter or the assertion being reported on and state the character of the engagement in the report.
2. The practitioner must state the practitioner's conclusion about the subject matter or the assertion in relation to the criteria against which the subject matter was evaluated in the report.
3. The practitioner must state all of the practitioner's significant reservations about the engagement, the subject matter, and, if applicable, the assertion related thereto in the report.
4. The practitioner must state in the report that the report is intended solely for the information and use of the specified parties under the following circumstances:
   - When the criteria used to evaluate the subject matter are determined by the practitioner to be appropriate only for a limited number of parties who either participated in their establishment or can be presumed to have an adequate understanding of the criteria.
   - When the criteria used to evaluate the subject matter are available only to specified parties.
   - When reporting on subject matter and a written assertion has not been provided by the responsible party.
   - When the report is on an attestation engagement to apply agreed-upon procedures to the subject matter.

*Suitable Criteria*

Suitable criteria are those that are *objective* and permit reasonably *consistent measurements*. In addition, the criteria must be sufficiently *complete* such that no relevant factors are omitted that would affect a conclusion about the subject matter. Finally, the criteria must measure some characteristic of the subject matter that is *relevant* to a user's decision.

Criteria are ordinarily suitable if they are developed by regulatory agencies or other bodies composed of experts that use due process, including exposing the proposed criteria for public comment. For example, the Committee of Sponsoring Organizations (COSO), discussed in Chapter 7, is an organization that followed due process in the development of its control criteria pertaining to internal control. Figure 20.4 illustrates the relationships among the responsible party, suitable criteria, subject matter, the written assertion, and the CPA's report.

Criteria developed by management or industry groups without due process may be suitable, but the practitioner should carefully evaluate them in relation to the characteristics described in the previous two paragraphs. Criteria that are overly subjective should not be used in an attestation engagement. For example, an assertion that a particular

FIGURE 20.4

**Illustration of
Relationships among
Terms Used in
Attestation Engagements**

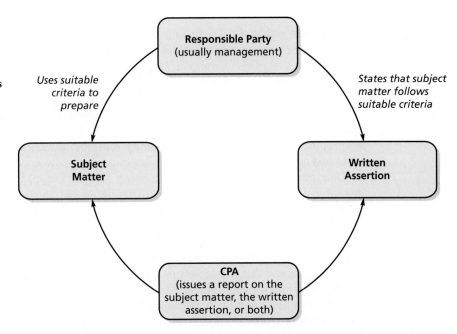

software product is the *best on the market* is too subjective for an attestation engagement. There are no generally accepted criteria for what constitutes the *best* software product.

Some criteria for evaluating subject matter may be suitable only for those who established them (referred to as *specified parties*). As such, they are not suitable for *general use.* For example, criteria developed based on a lengthy, involved contract between two parties might result in a report whose use is restricted to the two parties. In such situations, the attestation report should be *restricted* to the use of the specified parties.

*Available Criteria*

In addition to meeting the requirement that they be *suitable,* the criteria also must be *available* to users. This requirement of availability has two parts in that, not only must the criteria be available, but they also must be understandable to users. The criteria may be made *available and understandable* to the users in a variety of ways. If the criteria were developed by a regulatory agency or an expert body using due process, it is likely that they are publicly available to users; it ordinarily is presumed that such criteria are understandable.

Alternatively, the criteria may be made available to the users in the presentation of the subject matter, in the assertion, or in the practitioners' report. Making the criteria available in one of these manners is particularly important when there is no "generally accepted" way of evaluating the related subject matter. Take for example the subject matter of customer satisfaction. There are a number of possible measures of customer satisfaction, including customer opinion, rate of customer referral, rate of return customer sales, and increase in dollar amount of sales to existing customers. Particular criteria might employ one or more of these or other customer satisfaction measures. If the practitioner found the criteria being followed to be suitable, the presentation of the subject matter on customer satisfaction would most likely include the criteria describing the way in which customer satisfaction was defined and measured.

When criteria are available only to certain users, the practitioners' report should be restricted to those *specified parties.* Here again a contract between two parties provides a good illustration. In the preceding section on suitable criteria, we suggested that the provisions of a contract may not be suitable for those who are not a party to the contract. Therefore, we find that the report on the provisions is generally restricted. These situations often have in common the fact that they have been developed by and agreed to by the parties to the engagement and are not generally understandable to, or usable for, those not involved.

## Attestation Risk and Materiality

**Attestation risk** is the risk that the practitioners will unknowingly fail to appropriately modify their report on subject matter that is materially misstated. Like audit risk, attestation risk consists of three components—inherent risk, control risk, and detection risk. In this context, *inherent risk* is the risk that the subject matter is materially misstated before considering any internal control. *Control risk* is the risk that internal control will fail to prevent or detect a material misstatement of the subject matter, and *detection risk* is the risk that the practitioners' procedures will fail to detect a material misstatement of the subject matter. In an attestation engagement, the practitioners assess inherent and control risks and design procedures to restrict detection risk to the appropriate level.

Determining materiality for an attestation engagement may be very difficult because the subject matter may not be financial in nature. In fact, the subject matter may not even be presented in quantitative terms. As an example, the practitioners may be attesting to material compliance with specific provisions of a regulation. To determine what is material for planning and reporting purposes, the practitioners must attempt to determine the likely needs of the intended users and consider the extent and nature of misstatements of the subject matter that would be significant to their decisions.

Materiality for the engagement may be considered in the context of quantitative or qualitative factors. If the subject matter is quantitative, materiality should generally be a relative rather than an absolute amount. That is, as the quantitative amounts of the presentation increase, the amount considered to be material should also increase. For qualitative subject matter, the practitioners must use professional judgment to consider what omission or misstatement would have a significant effect on the presentation of the subject matter.

## The Character of the Engagement

LO3

Describe the nature of attestation engagements, including examinations, reviews, and agreed-upon procedures engagements.

The practitioners should issue an attestation report that clearly describes the nature of the assurance being provided as an *examination,* a *review,* or the performance of *agreed-upon procedures.*

### Examinations

An **examination** is designed to provide the highest level of assurance that CPAs provide—the same level of assurance about other types of subject matter as an audit provides for financial statements. When performing an examination, practitioners select from all available procedures to gather sufficient evidence to allow the issuance of a report that includes positive assurance about whether the subject matter being examined follows some established or stated criteria. Sufficient evidence exists when it is enough to drive attestation risk to an appropriate *low level.*

At the completion of the examination, the practitioners issue an appropriate report. Figure 20.5 illustrates an annotated standard unqualified examination report *directly on the subject matter.*[5] This standard report, however, is not appropriate in all cases. The following table illustrates circumstances that result in modification of the standard unqualified report.

| Situation | Report Modification |
|---|---|
| 1. Criteria are agreed-upon or only available to specified parties | A statement of limitations on the use of the report |
| 2. Departure of subject matter from criteria | Qualified or adverse opinion, depending on materiality of the departure |
| 3. Limitation on scope of engagement | Qualified opinion or disclaimer |
| 4. When reporting on subject matter and a written assertion is not obtained from the responsible party | A statement of limitations on the use of the report |

[5] In its Clarity Project, the AICPA has not addressed the attestation standards. Accordingly, the term "unqualified" rather than "unmodified" report is used. Also, reports issued by the practitioners do not include section titles (see Chapter 17).

**FIGURE 20.5**

**Standard Unqualified Examination Report on Subject Matter**

| Title | Independent Accountants' Report |
|---|---|
| Introductory paragraph | We have examined the accompanying schedule of investment performance statistics of Terrill Investment Fund for the year ended December 31, 20X2. Terrill Investment Fund's management is responsible for the schedule of investment performance statistics. Our responsibility is to express an opinion on this schedule based on our examination. |
| Scope paragraph | Our examination was conducted in accordance with attestation standards established by the American Institute of Certified Public Accountants and, accordingly, included examining, on a test basis, evidence supporting the schedule and performing such other procedures as we considered necessary in the circumstances. We believe that our examination provides a reasonable basis for our opinion. |
| Opinion paragraph | In our opinion, the schedule of investment performance statistics referred to above presents, in all material respects, the performance of Terrill Investment Fund for the year ended December 31, 20X2, in conformity with the measurement and disclosure criteria set forth by the Association of Investment Management Research, Inc., as described in Note 1. *Wesley & Ward, LLP* January 22, 20X3 |

### Reviews

A **review** engagement involves performing limited procedures, such as inquiries and analytical procedures. In performing a review, the practitioners endeavor to gather sufficient evidence to drive attestation risk to a *moderate level.* Accordingly, the resulting report provides only limited assurance that the information is fairly presented. **Limited assurance** is also referred to as **negative assurance** because the practitioners' report disclaims an opinion on the reviewed information but includes a statement such as, "We are not aware of any material modifications that should be made in order for the information to be in conformity with the criteria." An example of an annotated unmodified review report *directly on the subject matter* is presented in Figure 20.6. Of course, when an uncorrected material departure from the criteria is noted, the report must be modified to describe the departure. The following table lists circumstances that result in modification of the practitioners' review report.

| Situation | Report Modification |
|---|---|
| 1. Criteria are agreed-upon or only available to specified parties | A statement of limitations on the use of the report |
| 2. Departure of subject matter from criteria | Modified report describing the departure |
| 3. Limitation on scope of the engagement | Report cannot be issued |
| 4. When reporting on subject matter and a written assertion is not obtained from the responsible party | A statement of limitations on the use of the report |

### Agreed-Upon Procedures

Practitioners may also be engaged to perform procedures that were agreed upon by specified parties of the report. **Agreed-upon procedures** reports include a list of procedures performed (or reference thereto) and the related findings. Because specified parties have agreed upon the nature of the procedures, the reports for such engagements are intended for those parties only. Consequently, reports on agreed-upon procedures are referred to

**FIGURE 20.6**
**Standard Unmodified Review Report on Subject Matter**

| Title | Independent Accountants' Report |
|---|---|
| Introductory paragraph | We have reviewed the accompanying schedule of investment performance statistics of Keller Investment Fund for the year ended December 31, 20X2. Keller Investment Fund's management is responsible for the schedule of investment performance statistics. |
| Nature of review and disclaimer paragraph | Our review was conducted in accordance with attestation standards established by the American Institute of Certified Public Accountants. A review is substantially less in scope than an examination, the objective of which is the expression of an opinion on the schedule. Accordingly, we do not express such an opinion. |
| Negative assurance paragraph | Based on our review, nothing came to our attention that caused us to believe that the accompanying schedule of investment performance statistics of Keller Investment Fund for the year ended December 31, 20X2, is not presented, in all material respects, in accordance with the measurement and disclosure criteria set forth by the Association of Investment Management Research, Inc., as described in Note 1. |

*George Little & Associates, LLP*
January 15, 20X3

as *restricted-use* reports, in contrast with *general-use* reports, such as those on examinations and reviews. As previously indicated, examination and review reports ordinarily may be used by all third parties. Only when the criteria have been agreed upon by the parties involved and such criteria are not generally understandable to those not involved with the information must an examination or review report be restricted.

# Assurance Service Examples

## Assurance on Internal Control over Financial Reporting

Chapters 7 and 18 presented information on auditors' reports on internal control over financial reporting. This is a primary assurance service, particularly as performed for public companies which are required to have their internal control audited as a part of the integrated audit required by the Sarbanes-Oxley Act of 2002 and implemented by the PCAOB. As we indicated in Chapter 18, nonpublic companies are also able to engage their auditors in such a service. Also, the Federal Deposit Insurance Corporation Improvement Act of 1991, which applies to financial institutions with total assets of $500 million or more, requires an internal control report similar to that described in detail in Chapter 18.

We will not repeat detailed coverage of internal control reporting in this chapter. Yet, reporting on internal control provides a good example of an assurance service that differs broadly from reporting on financial statements because with internal control the subject matter of the engagement is a process rather than historical results.

## Assurance on Prospective Financial Statements

**LO4**

Describe the fundamental attributes of attestation services for prospective financial statements.

Securities analysts and loan officers give considerable attention to prospective financial statements. Although such statements may be presented in various forms, CPAs most frequently are involved *with financial forecasts and financial projections.* A **financial forecast** presents information about the entity's *expected* financial position, results of operations, and cash flows. On the other hand, a **financial projection** presents expected results, *given one or more hypothetical assumptions.* For example, a projection might present expected results assuming the company expanded its plant. While a forecast may be issued for general use, a projection's use should be restricted to the party with whom the company is negotiating, for example, a bank that is considering loaning funds to the company to expand the plant. Both forecasts and projections must include certain minimum *prospective financial statement* items, background information, and a list of the major assumptions and accounting policies.

Users of forecasts and projections may request assurance that this forward-looking information is properly presented and based upon reasonable assumptions. To provide such assurance, CPAs may be engaged to examine prospective statements, or they may be asked to perform certain agreed-upon procedures or perform a compilation, but the attestation standards *prohibit* the review of prospective financial statements. Criteria for evaluation of the fairness of a forecast or projection are presented in AT Section 301 and include a set of presentation guidelines.[6]

### Examinations of Prospective Financial Statements

In an examination of prospective financial statements, the practitioners gather evidence relating to the client's procedures for preparation of the statements, evaluate the underlying assumptions, obtain a written representation letter from the client, and evaluate whether the statements are presented in conformity with AICPA guidelines. The report issued is ordinarily on the subject matter and states whether, in the practitioners' opinion, the statements are presented in conformity with AICPA guidelines and whether the underlying assumptions provide a reasonable basis for the statements. In no circumstance is the practitioners' report to vouch for the achievability of the forecast or projection.

The following is an example of an unqualified forecast examination report (emphasis added).

---

### Independent Accountants' Report

We have *examined* the accompanying forecasted balance sheet, statements of income, retained earnings, and cash flows of Tyler Company as of December 31, 20X2, and for the year then ending. Tyler Company's management is responsible for the preparation of the forecast. Our responsibility is to express an opinion on the forecast based on our examination.

*Our examination was conducted in accordance with attestation standards for an examination of a forecast established by the American Institute of Certified Public Accountants* and, accordingly, included such procedures as we considered necessary to evaluate both the assumptions used and the preparation and presentation of the forecast. We believe our examination provides a reasonable basis for our opinion.

In our opinion, the accompanying forecast is *presented in conformity with guidelines for presentation of a forecast established by the American Institute of Certified Public Accountants,* and *the underlying assumptions provide a reasonable basis for management's forecast.* However, there will usually be differences between the forecasted and actual results, because events and circumstances frequently do not occur as expected, and those differences may be material. We have no responsibility to update this report for events and circumstances occurring after the date of this report.

*Owen & Co., CPAs*
February 20, 20X3

---

As with other attestation reports, the standard report is not appropriate in all circumstances. The report should be modified in the following situations:

| Situation | Report Modification |
|---|---|
| 1. Material departure from presentation criteria | Qualified or adverse opinion (if underlying assumptions are omitted, an adverse opinion should be issued) |
| 2. One or more significant assumptions do not provide a reasonable basis for the prospective financial statements | Adverse opinion |
| 3. Limitation on scope of engagement | Disclaimer of opinion |

---

[6] Further details of required disclosures are presented in the AICPA's "Guide for Prospective Financial Information" (New York, 2009).

The report on a financial projection is similar to the one illustrated for a forecast, but a paragraph is added prior to the opinion paragraph indicating that the use of the report should be restricted to the specified party. In addition, the opinion paragraph explicitly states the hypothetical assumptions.

*Agreed-Upon Procedures on Prospective Financial Statements*

Specific users may request the practitioners to perform certain agreed-upon procedures on prospective financial statements. In such circumstances, the practitioners may perform the procedures and provide a summary of findings. As is the case with all engagements involving agreed-upon procedures, the report should indicate that its use is restricted to the specified parties.

## Assurance on Compliance

AT Section 601, "Compliance Attestation," provides guidance for two types of compliance attestation engagements:

1. Attesting to an entity's compliance with specified requirements of laws, regulations, rules, contracts, or grants.
2. Attesting to the effectiveness of an entity's internal control over compliance with specified requirements.

Practitioners are permitted to perform an examination or agreed-upon procedures on such matters, but they are *prohibited* from performing reviews of compliance or internal control over compliance. These types of engagements and reports are described in detail in Chapter 21.

## Assurance on Management's Discussion and Analysis

**LO5**

Describe the fundamental attributes of attestation services for management discussion and analysis.

Management of a public company is required to provide a narrative explanation of financial results as reported in the financial statements filed with the SEC. This narrative explanation, referred to as **Management's Discussion and Analysis (MD&A),** is a required part of Form 10-K (for annual financial statements) and Form 10-Q (for interim financial statements) filed with the SEC. Practitioners may examine or review MD&A under the guidance of AT Section 701.

To accept an engagement to examine MD&A, the practitioners must have audited the most recent financial statement period to which the MD&A applies, and the other financial statement periods also must have been audited by them or other auditors. The practitioners' objective in such an engagement is to provide assurance on whether (1) the presentation includes, in all material respects, the required elements of the rules and regulations adopted by the SEC; (2) the historical financial amounts included in the presentation have been accurately derived, in all material respects, from the entity's financial statements; and (3) the underlying information, determinations, estimates, and assumptions of the entity provide a reasonable basis for the disclosures contained in the presentation. Practitioners also may be engaged to perform a review of MD&A for an annual or interim period. However, if a review is performed and the report is not intended to be filed with the SEC, it should be restricted as to use.

## Trust Services

Describe the nature of Trust Services.

Information technology has a profound effect on the way in which companies do business. Increasingly, companies have developed technology-enabled systems that not only maintain historical information but also produce products and services, directly interact with customers and suppliers, and run portions of the business. As a result, system reliability is of major concern not only to management, but also to stockholders, creditors, business partners, and other stakeholders in the company. The public accounting profession has developed a set of **Trust Services** that are defined as a set of professional attestation and advisory services based on a core set of principles and criteria that addresses the risks and opportunities of IT-enabled systems and privacy programs.

Trust Services are intended to help entities differentiate themselves by demonstrating that they are attuned to the risks posed by their environment and that they are equipped with controls that address those risks. There are potentially a wide range of beneficiaries of Trust Services assurance reports, including consumers, business partners, bankers, creditors, regulators, and outsourcers. Trust Services, jointly developed by the AICPA and the Canadian Institute of Chartered Accountants (CICA), are services in which a practitioner examines a system's controls and attests to the system's reliability. This is a part of a broader future vision of the accounting profession to supply real-time assurance on information databases and systems and is viewed as a natural extension of the CPA's audit and information technology consulting functions.

In a Trust Services engagement, management prepares and communicates a description of the aspects of the system that are to be encompassed by the practitioner's engagement. Management's description can be included on the company's Web site, attached to the practitioners' report, or communicated to users in some other manner. It must clearly articulate the boundaries of the system to allow individuals to understand both the scope of management's assertions related to it and the practitioners' report.

*Performing a Trust Services Engagement*

In performing a Trust Services engagement, the practitioner (1) performs procedures to determine that management's description of the system is fairly stated, and (2) obtains evidence that the controls over the system are designed and operating effectively to meet the Trust Services Principles and Criteria—the suitable criteria required for an attest engagement. The evidence obtained should bear on whether the system meets one or more of the following principles over a particular reporting period:

1. *Security.* The system is protected against unauthorized access (both physical and logical).
2. *Availability.* The system is available for operation and use as committed or agreed-upon.
3. *Processing integrity.* System processing is complete, accurate, timely, and authorized.
4. *Confidentiality.* Information designated as confidential is protected as committed or agreed upon.
5. *Privacy.* Personal information is collected, used, retained, disclosed, and destroyed in conformity with the commitments in the entity's privacy notice and with criteria set forth in generally accepted privacy principles issued by the AICPA and CICA.

Each of the principles has four criteria associated with it that fit into the following four broad areas:

1. *Policies.* The entity has defined and documented its policies relevant to the particular principle.
2. *Communications.* The entity has communicated its defined policies to responsible parties and authorized users of the system.
3. *Procedures.* The entity placed in operation procedures to achieve the objectives in accordance with its defined policies.
4. *Monitoring.* The entity monitors the system and takes action to maintain compliance with its defined policies.

*Types of Trust Services Engagements*

At present, CPAs offer two types of Trust Services, both providing either agreed-upon procedures or examination-level assurance. **WebTrust** provides assurance on electronic commerce systems, while *SysTrust* provides assurance on any system. To this point, **SysTrust** has gained wider market acceptance.

*Reporting*

The reports issued for *SysTrust* and *WebTrust* are similar. The box on the next page provides the body of a *SysTrust* report on all five *SysTrust* principles for Capital Confirmation, Inc., the company referred to in Chapter 10, which is a leader in the electronic confirmation process. Both *WebTrust* and *SysTrust* are designed to incorporate a seal management process by which a seal (logo) may be included on a client's Web site as an electronic representation of the practitioners unqualified *WebTrust* report. If the client wishes to continue to use the seal (logo), the engagement must be updated at least annually. Also, the initial reporting period must include at least two months.

---

We have examined management's assertion that during the period June 1, 2009, through November 30, 2009, Capital Confirmation, Inc. (Capital Confirmation), maintained effective controls over the Confirmation.com™ system based on the AICPA and CICA trust services availability, security, processing integrity, confidentiality, and privacy criteria to provide reasonable assurance that:

- the system was available for operation and use, as committed or agreed;
- the system was protected against unauthorized access (both physical and logical);
- the system processing was complete, accurate, timely, and authorized;
- information designated as confidential was protected by the system as committed or agreed; and
- personal information was collected, used, retained, disclosed, and disposed of in conformity with the commitments in the entity's privacy notice and with criteria set forth in *Generally Accepted Privacy Principles* issued by the AICPA and CICA,

based on the AICPA and CICA trust services security, availability, processing integrity, confidentiality, and privacy criteria.

Capital Confirmation's management is responsible for this assertion. Our responsibility is to express an opinion based on our examination. Management's description of the aspects of the Confirmation.com system covered by its assertion is attached. We did not examine this description, and accordingly, we do not express an opinion on it.

Our examination was conducted in accordance with attestation standards established by the American Institute of Certified Public Accountants and, accordingly, included (1) obtaining an understanding of Capital Confirmation's relevant controls over the availability, security, processing integrity, confidentiality, and privacy of the Confirmation.com system; (2) testing and evaluating the operating effectiveness of the controls; and (3) performing such other procedures as we considered necessary in the circumstances. We believe that our examination provides a reasonable basis for our opinion.

Because of the nature and inherent limitations of controls, Capital Confirmation's ability to meet the aforementioned criteria may be affected. For example, controls may not prevent or detect and correct error or fraud, unauthorized access to systems and information, or failure to comply with internal and external policies or requirements. Also, the projection of any conclusions based on our findings to future periods is subject to the risk that changes may alter the validity of such conclusions.

In our opinion, management's assertion referred to above is fairly stated, in all material respects, based on the AICPA and CICA trust services security, availability, processing integrity, confidentiality, and privacy criteria.

The *SysTrust*® Seal on Capital Confirmation, Inc.'s Web site constitutes a symbolic representation of the contents of this report and is not intended, nor should it be construed, to update this report or provide any additional assurance.

---

### Service Organization Reports versus SysTrust

In the last section of Chapter 8, we discussed service auditor reports. A **service auditor report** is issued by CPAs in situations in which a service organization performs similar processing services for numerous clients. For example, a bank trust department may invest and service assets of numerous employee benefit plans. If the auditors of each employee benefit plan were to visit the bank trust department to review controls, they would ask similar questions and perform similar tests of controls over and over. Service organizations engage their auditors to study their internal control and issue a service auditors' report on them. These reports may be on either (1) management's description and design of its controls (Type 1 reports) or (2) management's description and design of its controls and control operating effectiveness (Type 2 reports). Auditors of companies that employ the service organization are often able to use the service auditors' report as a portion of their consideration of the user's internal control (here the employee benefit plan being audited). Thus, both service organization reports and *SysTrust* reports address system reliability. Yet the reports and purposes of the engagements differ.

Service auditor reports are restricted-use reports. They are technical reports, ordinarily meant to communicate from one auditor to another, or from the service auditor to the company that uses the services of the company. *SysTrust* reports are ordinarily general-use reports meant to provide an easy-to-understand report that may be shared with customers, business partners, and any other interested party. The earlier presented *SysTrust* report on Capital Confirmation, Inc., provides a good example. A number of companies (including Capital Confirmation, Inc.) receive both service auditor reports and *SysTrust* reports.

*Competition*

Several other organizations provide services that compete with the AICPA/CICA's Trust services. The Better Business Bureau's *BBBOnLine* program grants two different logos— a privacy seal and a reliability seal. The privacy seal is granted to companies that adopt appropriate standards regarding the safeguarding of customer information. Companies that employ appropriate business practices (e.g., follow Better Business Bureau truth-in-advertising and dispute resolution standards) can obtain the reliability seal. However, attestation is not part of the Better Business Bureau's program.

Another program offered by *TRUSTe* provides assurance that customer information will be protected. A company participating in *TRUSTe* must openly indicate what personal information is being gathered, how it will be used, with whom it will be shared, and whether the user has an option to control its dissemination. Based on such disclosure, users can make informed decisions about whether or not to release their personally identifiable information (e.g., credit card numbers) to the Web site. Finally, the International Computer Security Association (ICSA) certifies Web sites using technology that protects customer data. ICSA's process includes a combination of self-reporting, on-site evaluation, remote testing, and spot-testing.

## PrimePlus/ElderCare Services

**LO7**

Describe the nature of *PrimePlus/ElderCare* services.

The population of the United States is aging, with the greatest increase in adults over 65 years of age expected to occur between now and 2030. In response to these demographics, the AICPA and the Canadian Institute of Chartered Accountants have developed *PrimePlus/ElderCare* services. These services focus on the specific needs and goals of older adults. In providing these services, you draw upon your strengths and competencies in a variety of areas, including accounting, cash flow planning and budgeting, pre- and postretirement planning, insurance reviews, estate planning, and tax planning. The intent is to help older Americans maintain for as long as possible their lifestyle and financial independence. The profession sees three primary markets for these services:

- Older clients of the CPA who have the financial resources to avail themselves of the services.
- The children of older adults who have the resources and interest to see that their loved ones are cared for.
- Other professionals who deal with older adults (e.g., lawyers and health care professionals).

The services involved are of two types—financial and nonfinancial. Financial services include goal-setting, funding analysis, cost management, and needs assessment. Nonfinancial services may involve interpersonal and relationship management, as well as management of the interaction between service providers and the client. Figure 20.7 provides more detailed examples of each of these services.

## Future Assurance Services

**LO8**

List several developing assurance services.

The AICPA, through its various committees, continues to consider and develop a number of other services to be provided by CPAs, including XBRL, health care performance measurement, and continuous auditing.

*XBRL*

**XBRL,** eXtensible Business Reporting Language, is an international information format designed specifically for business information. It assigns all individual disclosure items

**FIGURE 20.7**

*Examples of PrimePlus/ ElderCare* **Services**

| Financial Services | Nonfinancial Services |
|---|---|
| • Planning for fiduciary needs<br>• Evaluating financing options<br>• Receiving, depositing, and accounting for client receipts<br>• Ensuring that expected revenues are received<br>• Submitting claims to insurance companies<br>• Protecting the elderly from predators<br>• Estate planning<br>• Income tax planning and preparation<br>• Gift tax return preparation<br>• Evaluating investments and trust activity<br>• Portfolio management<br>• Risk management and insurance planning | • Lifestyle planning<br>• Lifestyle management services<br>• Coordinating support and health care services<br>• Functioning as the "quarterback" or as a member of the *PrimePlus/ElderCare* team—which consists of health care, legal, and other professionals<br>• Helping family members monitor the elder's care<br>• Communicating family expectations to care providers<br>• Establishing, in concert with the family, appropriate standards of care<br>• Establishing performance monitoring systems |

within business reports unique electronically readable tags that are mapped to taxonomies. XBRL offers major benefits in the preparation, analysis, and communication of business information through its cost-effectiveness and improved reliability as compared to other existing systems.

The AICPA's XBRL Assurance Task Force is in the process of developing guidance that will assist CPAs in public practice who are requested to provide assurance on XBRL-related documents. The task force is currently focusing on:

- Developing practice guidance that will assist CPAs in applying existing standards to information reported in XBRL format.
- Recommending, where deemed necessary and appropriate, to the appropriate standard setting bodies changes to existing standards and/or the development of new standards.
- Collaborating with key stakeholders, including the SEC, PCAOB, various AICPA groups, and others.

*Health Care Performance Measurement*

Health care recipients and their employers are increasingly concerned about the quality and availability of health care services. This service provides assurance about the effectiveness of health care services provided by health maintenance organizations, hospitals, doctors, and other providers.

*Continuous Auditing*

A demand exists for assurance beyond that provided on quarterly and annual financial statements. As indicated earlier in this chapter, **continuous auditing** provides assurance using a series of reports provided simultaneously or shortly after the related information is released. The area of continuous auditing is in its infancy but is expected to grow dramatically as companies provide more and more up-to-date financial information on their Web sites.

# Chapter Summary

This chapter described assurance services, focusing on those that are governed by *Statements on Standards for Attestation Engagements*. To summarize:

1. Assurance services are defined as professional services that improve the quality of information, or its context, for decision makers. Assurance services go beyond attestation services in that they may involve analyzing data or putting data in a form to facilitate decision making, or they may address relevance to a decision.

2. The vast majority of currently provided assurance services are attestation services that are performed in accordance with *Statements on Standards for Attestation Engagements*. The attestation standards apply to a variety of types of information (e.g., prospective financial statements, compliance with laws and regulations, and management's discussion and analysis). They do not apply to professional services specifically covered by the following other standards: *Statements on Auditing Standards, Statements on Standards for Accounting and Review Services,* and *Statements on Standards for Consulting Services.* They also do not cover various types of tax services.

3. Attestation engagements include examinations, reviews, and agreed-upon procedures engagements. Examinations and reviews involve providing assurance about the correspondence of subject matter with suitable criteria. An agreed-upon procedures engagement involves performing procedures and issuing a report on the findings.

4. CPAs may perform examinations, compilations, or agreed-upon procedures on prospective financial statements. Reviews of prospective financial statements are prohibited. Prospective financial statements include forecasts that reflect expected financial results and projections that reflect expected financial results given one or more hypothetical assumptions.

5. Practitioners may examine or review Management's Discussion and Analysis (MD&A). MD&A consists of a narrative explanation of financial results that must be included in annual and quarterly filings with the SEC. The practitioners' objective in an examination is to provide assurance on whether (a) the presentation includes all required elements, (b) any historical amounts have been accurately derived from the entity's financial statements, and (c) the underlying information, determinations, estimates, and assumptions provide a reasonable basis for the disclosures included.

6. Trust Services provide assurance on one or more of the following Trust Principles: *(a)* security, *(b)* availability, *(c)* processing integrity, *(d)* confidentiality, and *(e)* privacy. Currently, two services have been developed—*WebTrust,* which provides assurance on electronic commerce systems, and *SysTrust,* which provides assurance on other systems.

7. *PrimePlus/ElderCare* services focus on the specific needs and goals of older adults. In providing these services, CPAs draw upon their strengths and competencies in a variety of areas, including accounting, cash flow planning and budgeting, pre- and postretirement planning, insurance reviews, estate planning, and tax planning.

8. The AICPA's XBRL Assurance Task Force is in the process of developing guidance that will assist CPAs in public practice who are requested to provide assurance on XBRL-related documents. Other assurance services being developed by the profession include health care performance measurement and continuous auditing.

## Key Terms Introduced or Emphasized in Chapter 20

**Agreed-upon procedures (761)** An attestation engagement in which the CPAs agree to perform specific procedures for a specified party or parties and issue a report that expresses the CPAs' findings. The report is restricted to use by the specified party or parties.

**Assertion (757)** An assertion is a declaration about whether subject matter is presented in accordance with certain criteria.

**Assurance services (754)** Professional services that improve the quality of information, or its context, for decision makers. Many assurance services involve some form of attestation.

**Attestation engagement (756)** Providing assurance about whether some subject matter, or an assertion about the subject matter, is in accordance with suitable criteria.

**Attestation risk (760)** The risk that the practitioners will issue an unmodified report on subject matter that is materially misstated.

**Continuous auditing (768)** To provide assurance using a series of reports provided simultaneously or shortly after the related information is released.

**Examination (760)** An attestation engagement designed to provide the highest level of assurance that CPAs provide on subject matter or an assertion about the subject matter. An examination of financial statements is referred to as an audit.

**Financial forecast (762)** Prospective financial statements that present an entity's expected financial position, results of operations, and cash flows for one or more future periods.

**Financial projection (762)** Prospective financial statements that present expected results, given one or more hypothetical assumptions.

**Limited assurance (negative assurance) (761)** The level of assurance provided by CPAs who have performed a review of subject matter. Provides substantially less assurance than the reasonable assurance provided by an examination.

**Management's Discussion and Analysis (MD&A) (764)** Management's discussion of the company's operating results, liquidity, and financial position that is required in the regular form filings with the SEC. CPAs may examine or review this information. However, if the information is reviewed, the report must be restricted as to its use.

**Negative assurance (761)** See *limited assurance.*

*PrimePlus/ElderCare* **(756)** Services to help older individuals maintain, for as long as possible, their lifestyle and financial independence.

**Review (761)** An engagement designed to provide only a limited (moderate) degree of assurance about the conformance of subject matter, or an assertion about subject matter, with suitable criteria.

**Service auditor report (766)** A report issued by the auditor of a service organization to provide information about the internal control of the organization. User auditors make use of these reports in considering the internal control over data processing performed for their clients by the service organization.

**Subject matter (756)** The underlying topic of the engagement. For example, subject matter may be prospective financial information or internal control.

**Suitable criteria (755)** Criteria that are objective and permit reasonably consistent measurement.

*SysTrust* **(765)** A Trust Service developed by the AICPA and CICA to provide assurance about the reliability of systems other than electronic commerce systems.

**Trust Services (764)** Engagements that provide assurance on systems. Trust Services provide assurance on one or more of the following Trust Principles: (a) security, (b) availability, (c) processing integrity, (d) online privacy, and (e) confidentiality. Currently, two services have been developed. *WebTrust* provides assurance on electronic commerce systems, and *SysTrust* provides assurance on other systems.

*WebTrust* **(765)** A Trust Service developed by the AICPA and CICA to provide assurance on electronic commerce systems.

**XBRL (eXtensible Business Reporting Language) (767)** An international information format designed specifically for business information. It assigns all individual disclosure items within business reports unique electronically readable tags that are mapped to taxonomies. The AICPA is in the process of developing guidance that will assist CPAs in public practice who are requested to provide assurance on XBRL-related documents.

## Review Questions

20–1. Explain the relationship between assurance services and attestation services.

20–2. Comment on the correctness of the following statement: Since all attest services are assurance services, all assurance services are also attest services.

20–3. Describe the forces that have fueled the demand for assurance services.

20–4. Is a written report from the accountant involved for all attestation and other assurance services? Explain.

20–5. List and describe the three types of attestation engagements.

20–6. Distinguish between forms of attestation engagements that result in reports that are designed for "general use" and those that result in reports that are designed for "restricted use."

20–7. Distinguish between an attestation engagement in which the practitioners report directly on the subject matter and one in which the practitioners report on an assertion about the subject matter.

20–8. What are "suitable criteria" and how do they relate to an attestation engagement?

20–9. Explain what is meant by *attestation risk.* What are its components?

20–10. Comment on the accuracy of the following: A client's uncorrected material departure from the suitable criteria identified during an examination conducted under the attest standards is treated as a departure from GAAP in a financial statement audit—either a qualified or adverse opinion is appropriate.

20–11. What is XBRL? How do assurance services relate to it?

20–12. "A company would normally include a financial projection in its annual report rather than a financial forecast." Comment on the validity of this statement.

20–13. Describe the major elements of a report on the examination of a financial forecast.

20–14. Describe the two types of compliance services that may be performed under AT section 601.

20–15. Identify the circumstances under which CPAs may examine Management's Discussion and Analysis.

20–16. Describe the objectives of the practitioners' examination of Management's Discussion and Analysis.

20–17. List the principles that may be included in the criteria for a Trust Services engagement.

20–18. Contrast the types of systems on which assurance is provided in a *WebTrust* engagement as compared to a *SysTrust* engagement.

20–19. Discuss CPAs' competition for *WebTrust* in the market for consumer-to-business electronic commerce.

20–20. The attestation standards provide guidance on agreed-upon procedures, review, and examination engagements. Which of these types of engagements are available for *WebTrust* and *SysTrust?*

20–21. What types of *PrimePlus/ElderCare* services do CPAs typically perform?

20–22. Identify three types of assurance services that are currently under development by the AICPA.

## Questions Requiring Analysis

**LO 1** 20–23. Other types of assurance services provided by CPAs have developed as a natural extension of the audit function.

Required:

   *a.* Explain what is meant by the term *assurance services.*

   *b.* Describe the forces that have caused a demand for other types of assurance services.

   *c.* Describe the subset of assurance services governed by the *Statements of Standards for Attestation Engagements.*

**LO 3** 20–24. The attestation standards provide guidance for three basic types of engagements.

Required:

   *a.* Describe these three types of engagements.

   *b.* Describe the types of procedures performed for each of these three types of engagements.

   *c.* Discuss the degree of assurance provided by each type of engagement.

   *d.* Identify when each of the three types of engagements results in reports that are appropriate for *general use.*

**LO 4** 20–25. The management of Williams Co. is considering issuing corporate debentures. To enhance the marketability of the bond issue, management has decided to include a financial forecast in the prospectus. Management has requested that your CPA firm examine the financial forecast to add credibility to the prospective information.

Required:

   *a.* Explain what is involved in an examination of a financial forecast.

   *b.* Discuss the elements of a report on the examination of a financial forecast. (Do not write a report.)

**LO 6** 20–26. The accounting profession has developed *Trust Services* to help entities differentiate themselves by demonstrating that they are attuned to the risks posed by their environment and that they are equipped with controls that address those risks.

Required:

   *a.* Present the principles on which a *Trust Services* engagement may be based.

   *b.* Contrast the *Trust Services* with competing services provided by other organizations.

**LO 2** 20–27. The third general attestation standard indicates that the subject matter of the engagement must be capable of reasonably consistent evaluation against criteria that are suitable and available to the user.

Required:

   *a.* Explain why criteria are needed for an attestation engagement.

   *b.* Describe what makes a particular set of criteria *suitable* for an attestation engagement.

   *c.* Explain how criteria are made *available* to users of the information.

## Objective Questions

20–28.   **Multiple Choice Questions**

Select the best answer for each of the following and explain fully the reason for your selection.

**LO 2**    *a.*  A report on an attestation engagement should:

(1)  State the nature of the client's control system.

(2)  State the practitioner's conclusion about the subject matter or assertion.

(3)  Include a reasonable limitations section pertaining to data inputs.

(4)  Refer to the auditor's assertion concerning the subject matter.

**LO 4**    *b.*  When an accountant examines a financial forecast that fails to disclose several significant assumptions used to prepare the forecast, the accountant should describe the assumptions in the accountant's report and issue a(n):

(1)  Qualified opinion.

(2)  Unqualified opinion with a separate explanatory paragraph.

(3)  Disclaimer of opinion.

(4)  Adverse opinion.

**LO 5**    *c.*  Which of the following is *not* an objective of a CPA's examination of a client's MD&A?

(1)  The presentation includes, in all material respects, the required elements of the rules and regulations adopted by the Securities and Exchange Commission.

(2)  The presentation is in conformity with rules and regulations adopted by the SEC.

(3)  The historical amounts included in the presentation have been accurately derived, in all material respects, from the entity's financial statements.

(4)  The underlying information, determinations, estimates, and assumptions provide a reasonable basis for the disclosures contained in the presentation.

**LO 6**    *d.*  A CPA's report relating to a *SysTrust* engagement is most likely to include:

(1)  An opinion on whether the system is electronically secure.

(2)  An opinion on management's assertion that the system meets one or more of the *SysTrust* principles.

(3)  Negative assurance on whether the system is secure.

(4)  No opinion or other assurance, but a summary of findings relating to the system.

**LO 5**    *e.*  When performing an examination, if a CPA finds one or more significant assumptions are not reasonable for a forecast, the most appropriate report is:

(1)  Adverse.

(2)  Disclaimer.

(3)  Qualified.

(4)  Unqualified with emphasis of matter paragraph.

**LO 8**    *f.*  The accounting profession is currently developing assurance services related to which of the following international information formats?

(1)  C++.

(2)  Webmat.

(3)  Object language.

(4)  XBRL.

**LO 7**    *g.*  CPA services performed under *PrimePlus/ElderCare* services may be:

|       | Financial | Nonfinancial |
|-------|-----------|--------------|
| (1)   | Yes       | Yes          |
| (2)   | Yes       | No           |
| (3)   | No        | Yes          |
| (4)   | No        | No           |

**LO 8**    *h.*  When reporting on a company's compliance with a law, the CPAs may report on:

|       | Compliance with the Law Itself | Effectiveness of Internal Control over Compliance |
|-------|--------------------------------|---------------------------------------------------|
| (1)   | Yes                            | Yes                                               |
| (2)   | Yes                            | No                                                |
| (3)   | No                             | Yes                                               |
| (4)   | No                             | No                                                |

**LO 1**    *i.* Which is *least* likely?

    (1) An assurance service that is also an attest service.

    (2) A service that is not an assurance service, but is an attest service.

    (3) A historical financial statement–related assurance service.

    (4) A nonhistorical financial information–related assurance service.

**LO 2**    *j.* Which of the following is *least* likely to be the subject matter of an attestation engagement?

    (1) Behavior.

    (2) Historical events.

    (3) Suitable criteria.

    (4) Systems or processes.

**LO 2**    *k.* Which of the following is *not* a basic type of attestation engagement?

    (1) Agreed-upon procedures.

    (2) Compilation.

    (3) Examination.

    (4) Review.

**LO 6**    *l.* The assurance services being developed that address user and preparer needs regarding issues of security, availability, processing integrity, confidentiality, and privacy within e-commerce and other systems are referred to as:

    (1) *PrimePlus* Services.

    (2) XBRL Services.

    (3) Risk Advisory Services.

    (4) Trust Services.

**LO 4, 5, 6, 7, 8**    20–29. Following are descriptions of potential needs of clients for assurance services. For each need, identify (1) the type of service that would best meet the client's need (i.e., attestation to prospective information, attestation to internal control, attestation to compliance, attestation to MD&A, *WebTrust, SysTrust, PrimePlus/ElderCare,* or other assurance service), (2) whether or not the service is an attestation service, and (3) the level of service that would be most appropriate (i.e., examination, review, agreed-upon procedures, or other).

| Client Need | Type of Service | Attestation Service? | Level of Service |
|---|---|---|---|
| *a.* A computer manufacturing company wants to provide assurance about estimated future results to be included in the company's annual report. | | | |
| *b.* A company wants to provide positive assurance on its pension processing services for its retired employees. | | | |
| *c.* A financial institution wants to provide assurance to banking regulators that its internal control over financial reporting is adequate. | | | |
| *d.* A company that maintains a business-to-business electronic commerce portal wants to provide positive assurance about the reliability of its system to potential customers. | | | |
| *e.* The relative of an institutionalized uncle wants a CPA firm to oversee the uncle's financial affairs. | | | |
| *f.* A public company wants to provide assurance to its shareholders about the narrative analysis of financial results provided in the company's Form 10-K. | | | |
| *g.* A grocery store wants to provide the highest level of assurance that its prices are less than the prices of its competitors. | | | |
| *h.* A bank wants a CPA firm to confirm the account receivables of a company that has pledged the receivables as collateral for a loan. | | | |
| *i.* A golf ball manufacturer wants to provide moderate assurance that its golf balls travel farther than those of its competitors. | | | |
| *j.* Management of a technology company wants a CPA firm to provide assurance that its risk assessment process has identified all major business risks. | | | |

**LO 2, 3, 5, 6, 7**  20–30.  Indicate whether a CPA may provide each of the following services, and whether independence is required, by placing a check in the appropriate box.

| Service | May Provide; Independence Is Required | May Provide; Independence Is Not Required | May Not Provide |
|---|---|---|---|
| a. Compile a forecast for the coming year. | | | |
| b. Perform a review of a forecast the company has prepared for the coming year. | | | |
| c. Perform an examination of Management's Discussion and Analysis when they have not audited the year's financial statements. | | | |
| d. Issue a *SysTrust* examination report on the security against unauthorized access of a service organization's electronic processing system. | | | |
| e. Assist an elderly client with his estate planning. | | | |

**LO 5, 6, 7, 8**  20–31.  For each of the situations (a) through (f), select the CPA engagement that is most likely to be appropriate from the lists of services below:

1. Compliance.
2. Continuous auditing.
3. Forecast.
4. Internal control over financial reporting.
5. MD&A.
6. *PrimePlus/ElderCare*.
7. Service organization audit.
8. *SysTrust*.
9. *WebTrust*.

Each reply may be used a maximum of one time, with two replies not being used at all.

| Situation | CPA Engagement |
|---|---|
| a. Williams is worried about the welfare of his father who lives in a distant state. | |
| b. ABC Company is involved in a very vibrant industry. It would like all of its press releases to include audited results, regardless of when they are issued. | |
| c. DEF Mortgage Banking Co. services mortgages for others, and the auditors of those other organizations are constantly inquiring of DEF concerning its internal control as a part of their audits of the other organizations. | |
| d. GHI Company would like to assure its Web site users of the reliability of its Web site and its operations. | |
| e. JKL would like all of its customers and potential customers to have assurance about the effectiveness of its internal controls related to processing information. | |
| f. MNO Company believes that it has effective internal control to assure itself that it complies with various legal requirements, but would like assurance from its CPA on compliance with the legal requirements. | |

**LO 6, 7, 8**  20–32.  Match the following definitions (or partial definitions) to the appropriate term. Each term may be used once or not at all.

| Definition (or Partial Definition) | Term |
|---|---|
| a. A service developed by the AICPA and CICA to provide assurance about the reliability of systems other than electronic commerce systems. | 1. CBIZ |
| | 2. Financial forecast |
| | 3. Financial projection |
| b. A service developed by the AICPA and CICA to provide assurance on electronic commerce systems. | 4. Limited assurance |
| | 5. *PrimePlus/ElderCare* |
| c. An international information format designed specifically for business information. | 6. Reasonable assurance |
| | 7. Review |
| d. Engagements that provide assurance on systems' (1) security, (2) availability, (3) processing integrity, (4) online privacy, and (5) confidentiality. | 8. Social Security services |
| | 9. Service auditor report |
| | 10. *SysTrust* |
| e. Prospective financial statements that present an entity's expected financial position, results of operations, and cash flows for one or more future periods. | 11. Trust Services |
| | 12. *WebTrust* |
| | 13. XBRL |
| f. Prospective financial statements that present expected results, given one or more hypothetical assumptions. | |
| g. Services to help older individuals maintain, for as long as possible, their lifestyle and financial independence. | |
| h. The level of assurance provided by CPAs who have performed a review of subject matter. | |

## Problems

All applicable problems are available with McGraw-Hill's *Connect*™ *Accounting.* 

**LO 7**

**20–33.** *SysTrust* and *WebTrust* are Trust Services developed by the AICPA and the CICA.

*Required:*
- a. Present and describe the Trust Services principles.
- b. Present and describe the "criteria" related to Trust Services.
- c. What is the relationship between the principles and the criteria?
- d. Must a *WebTrust* or *SysTrust* report provide assurance on all of the principles?

**LO 2, 3, 9**

**20–34.** Assume that you are a partner with the firm of Slater & Lowe LLP. You have been asked by Grayson, Inc., an industrial supply company, to provide assurance about the change in existing customer satisfaction over the last three years. Grayson's management has indicated that the criteria it intends to use to evaluate customer satisfaction are a combination of customer retention rate and increase in dollar sales. Grayson's management will provide a schedule of the customer satisfaction measures and a note that describes the criteria used.

*Required:*
- a. If Grayson wants to provide the presentation and the CPA's report for general use by prospective customers, identify any available standards that provide guidance for such a service and the type or types of services that your firm could provide.
- b. Describe the factors that you should consider in determining whether the criteria are suitable.
- c. Assuming that you conclude that the criteria are suitable, draft your firm's report assuming that you perform an examination of the subject matter.

**In-Class Team Case**

**LO 3, 8**

**20–35.** Katherine Whipple of Food Queen Grocery, Inc., has asked you and your team to meet with her concerning a possible attest engagement relating to the assertion that Food Queen has the lowest overall prices of all grocery stores in the Salt Lake City area. Food Queen has just recently moved into the Salt Lake City area and is trying to establish a high-volume, profitable position. Whipple has suggested to you that she believes that while Food Queen certainly doesn't have the lowest prices on all of the 25,000 types of items it sells, on most any rational basis she believes that its prices are "on the whole" lower than the competition—Albros, Kruegers, and Safest. In thinking about this, you realize that to perform such an attestation engagement, suitable criteria must be used to evaluate the subject matter.

*Required:*
- a. For this engagement, what would you consider to be the subject matter?
- b. Provide an approach on how one might derive suitable criteria for such an engagement, given that costs are considered lowest on an overall basis, but not necessarily for every item.
- c. Discuss the nature of the required assertion from management for an engagement such as this.

Now consider the following: Whipple has suggested to you that when the engagement is complete she will use the results as part of an advertising campaign in which the ads suggest that Food Queen has the "certified lowest overall costs." When you asked her what would happen if the engagement revealed that Food Queen didn't have the lowest prices, she suggested that she would simply not use the report and wait a month or two and have you perform another engagement when she had had time to bring her prices down even lower.

*d.* Are attestation engagements acceptable when the resulting report is to be used for advertising purposes?

*e.* Assume that your examination revealed that, based on the criteria developed, Whipple's assertion that Food Queen did have the lowest prices was fairly stated and that a general use report was proper. Outline the nature of the allowable presentation in the advertising materials.

**Research and Discussion Case**

**LO 6**  20–36.  Assume that you are a CPA interested in expanding your services to provide *SysTrust* Services. Access the AICPA Web site and find guidance that will help you achieve your goal. Provide both the document (or other item) name and a brief summary of the guidance it provides.

# Internal, Operational, and Compliance Auditing

To this point in the text, we have focused primarily on audits and other types of assurance services provided by independent public accountants. This chapter describes several additional types of auditing: internal, operational, and compliance auditing.

## Internal Auditing

**LO1**

Describe the functions performed by internal auditors.

Virtually every large corporation in the United States today maintains an internal auditing staff. This staff function has developed extremely rapidly as prior to 1940 few organizations had internal auditing departments. In 1941, **The Institute of Internal Auditors (IIA)** was founded with only 25 members. Now the IIA is a worldwide organization with over 170,000 members and with local chapters in principal cities throughout much of the world. The growth of the IIA has paralleled the recognition of internal auditing as an essential control function in all types of organizations.

### What Is the Purpose of Internal Auditing?

The Institute of Internal Auditors (IIA) defines **internal auditing** as:

An independent, objective assurance and consulting activity designed to add value and improve an organization's operations. It helps an organization accomplish its objectives by bringing a systematic, disciplined approach to evaluate and improve the effectiveness of risk management, control, and governance processes.

Internal auditors assist members of an organization in performing their responsibilities by furnishing them analyses, appraisals, recommendations, and counsel. In performing these functions, internal auditors can be thought of as a part of the organization's internal control. They represent a high-level control that functions by measuring and evaluating the effectiveness of other controls. As discussed in Chapter 7, generally accepted auditing standards include the internal auditing function as part of the "monitoring component" of an organization's internal control.

Internal auditors are not merely concerned with the organization's financial controls. Their work encompasses all of the organization's internal control. They evaluate and test the effectiveness of controls designed to help the organization meet all its objectives. Also, many progressive internal auditing departments provide a wide range of other assurance and consulting services to the management of their organizations.

### Evolution of Internal Auditing

Internal auditing has evolved to meet the needs of business and governmental and nonprofit organizations. Originally, a demand for internal auditing arose when managers of early large corporations recognized that annual audits of financial statements by CPAs were not sufficient. A need existed for timely employee involvement beyond that of the certified public accountants to ensure accurate and timely financial records and to prevent fraud. These original internal auditors focused their efforts on financial and accounting matters.

Subsequently, the role of internal auditors expanded as a result of demands by the major stock exchanges and the Securities and Exchange Commission (SEC) that management accept more responsibility for the reliability of published financial statements. These demands resulted in expanded internal auditor responsibilities, including more detailed analysis of internal control, as well as testing of interim and other accounting information not considered in annual audits performed by certified public accountants.

Gradually, the role of internal auditors expanded to encompass overall operational policies and procedures. Companies in the defense industry were among the first to demand such services. These companies recognized the need for reliable operating reports because they were used extensively by management to make decisions. The reports often were expressed not in dollars but in terms of operating factors, such as quantities of parts in short supply, adherence to schedules, and quality of the product. Work by the internal auditors devoted to ensuring the dependability of these operating reports was better spent than additional audit effort devoted to financial and accounting matters.

As organizations became larger and more complex, they encountered additional operational problems that could be addressed by internal auditing. The internal auditors' role of determining whether operating units in the organization follow authorized accounting and financial policies was readily extended to include the determination of whether they follow all the organization's operating policies, and whether the established policies provide sound and effective control over all operations. The extension of internal auditing into these operational activities required internal auditors with specialized knowledge in other disciplines such as economics, law, finance, statistics, computer processing, engineering, and taxation.

Several relatively recent events have been important to the evolution of the internal auditing profession. The first was the enactment of the Foreign Corrupt Practices Act of 1977. The accounting provisions of that act require public companies to establish and maintain effective internal accounting control. To ensure compliance with these provisions, many companies established or augmented their internal auditing departments.

Another event that affected the internal auditing profession was the issuance in 1987 of the *Report of the National Commission on Fraudulent Financial Reporting.* This report contains the commission's findings and recommendations about preventing fraudulent financial reporting by public companies. Among its recommendations was a suggestion that public companies establish an internal auditing function staffed with appropriately qualified personnel and fully supported by top management. The commission also recommended that the companies help ensure the internal auditing function's objectivity by positioning it suitably within the organization, maintaining a director of the internal auditing function with appropriate stature, and establishing effective reporting relationships between the director of internal auditing and the audit committee of the board of directors. Consistently, in 1998 the Blue Ribbon Committee Report on Audit Committee Effectiveness concluded that appropriate responsibility for the oversight of financial integrity and accountability of public companies may be viewed as a three-legged stool consisting of (1) management and internal audit, (2) the board of directors and its audit committee, and (3) the external auditors.

The reengineering of companies in the mid-1990s led companies to *outsource* many of their noncore functions, including, in some cases, internal auditing. When these functions are outsourced, a specialized service provider other than company employees performs a portion or all of the internal auditing function. In some cases, CPA firms that also performed the audit of the financial statements provided major portions of the internal auditing function for companies. Providing both internal and external auditing services for SEC reporting clients has since been prohibited by the Sarbanes-Oxley Act of 2002.

> **Focus on Outsourcing the Internal Auditing Function**
>
> Prior to its elimination, CPA firm performance of all or a portion of the internal audit function for an audit client was extremely controversial. CPA firms argued that they could provide internal auditing services effectively and promised such benefits as lower costs and improved specialization, while allowing management to focus on core business issues. The AICPA positioned such services as "extended audit services" that were acceptable if the client understood its responsibility for establishing and maintaining internal control and directing the internal auditing function. Representatives of the Institute of Internal Auditors questioned the propriety of CPAs' assuming responsibilities that are part of a corporation's internal control when they also audit that company.

## The Internal Auditors' Role in Sarbanes-Oxley Compliance

Describe the internal auditors' role with respect to the Sarbanes-Oxley Act.

Internal auditors possess skills and experience that make them particularly valuable to a company's compliance efforts related to the Sarbanes-Oxley Act. As a result, many companies have involved their internal audit departments in documenting and testing controls to support management's assertion about the effectiveness of internal control over financial reporting. However, it is important to remember that it is management's responsibility to ensure the organization is in compliance with the requirements of the Sarbanes-Oxley Act. The internal auditors' role in documenting and testing controls can be significant, but it must be compatible with the overall mission and **charter** of the internal audit function, and it should not be seen as impairing the internal auditors' objectivity.

The work of the internal auditors may also be used by the external auditors in fulfilling the external audit function. PCAOB *Standards* allow the external auditors to use certain work of the internal auditors in fulfilling their responsibilities to provide an opinion on internal control over financial reporting.

## Professional Standards of Internal Auditing

To maintain consistently high-quality services across the internal auditing profession, the IIA has issued *International Standards for the Professional Practice of Internal Auditing*. These standards, as presented in Figure 21.1, set forth the criteria by which the operations of an internal auditing department should be evaluated and measured.

**FIGURE 21.1**   **IIA** *International Standards for the Professional Practice of Internal Auditing*

**ATTRIBUTE STANDARDS**

**1000—Purpose, Authority, and Responsibility**
The purpose, authority, and responsibility of the internal audit activity must be formally defined in an internal audit charter, consistent with the Definition of Internal Auditing, the Code of Ethics, and the *Standards.* The chief audit executive must periodically review the internal audit charter and present it to senior management and the board for approval.
>    **Interpretation:**
>    The internal audit charter is a formal document that defines the internal audit activity's purpose, authority, and responsibility. The internal audit charter establishes the internal audit activity's position within the organization, including the nature of the chief audit executive's functional reporting relationship with the board; authorizes access to records, personnel, and physical properties relevant to the performance of engagements; and defines the scope of internal audit activities. Final approval of the internal audit charter resides with the board.
>    **1000.A1**—The nature of assurance services provided to the organization must be defined in the internal audit charter. If assurances are to be provided to parties outside the organization, the nature of these assurances must also be defined in the internal audit charter.
>    **1000.C1**—The nature of consulting services must be defined in the internal audit charter.

**1010—Recognition of the Definition of Internal Auditing, the Code of Ethics, and the *Standards* in the Internal Audit Charter**
The mandatory nature of the Definition of Internal Auditing, the Code of Ethics, and the *Standards* must be recognized in the internal audit charter. The chief audit executive should discuss the Definition of Internal Auditing, the Code of Ethics, and the *Standards* with senior management and the board.

*(continued)*

**FIGURE 21.1    (*Continued*)**

## ATTRIBUTE STANDARDS

### 1100—Independence and Objectivity

The internal audit activity must be independent, and internal auditors must be objective in performing their work.

> **Interpretation:**
>
> *Independence is the freedom from conditions that threaten the ability of the internal audit activity to carry out internal audit responsibilities in an unbiased manner. To achieve the degree of independence necessary to effectively carry out the responsibilities of the internal audit activity, the chief audit executive has direct and unrestricted access to senior management and the board. This can be achieved through a dual-reporting relationship. Threats to independence must be managed at the individual auditor, engagement, functional, and organizational levels.*
>
> *Objectivity is an unbiased mental attitude that allows internal auditors to perform engagements in such a manner that they believe in their work product and that no quality compromises are made. Objectivity requires that internal auditors do not subordinate their judgment on audit matters to others. Threats to objectivity must be managed at the individual auditor, engagement, functional, and organizational levels.*

### 1110—Organizational Independence

The chief audit executive must report to a level within the organization that allows the internal audit activity to fulfill its responsibilities. The chief audit executive must confirm to the board, at least annually, the organizational independence of the internal audit activity.

> **Interpretation:**
>
> Organizational independence is effectively achieved when the chief audit executive reports functionally to the board. Examples of functional reporting to the board involve the board:
>
> - Approving the internal audit charter;
> - Approving the risk-based internal audit plan;
> - Receiving communications from the chief audit executive on the internal audit activity's performance relative to its plan and other matters;
> - Approving decisions regarding the appointment and removal of the chief audit executive; and
> - Making appropriate inquiries of management and the chief audit executive to determine whether there are inappropriate scope or resource limitations.

**1110.A1**—The internal audit activity must be free from interference in determining the scope of internal auditing, performing work, and communicating results.

### 1111—Direct Interaction with the Board

The chief audit executive must communicate and interact directly with the board.

### 1120—Individual Objectivity

Internal auditors must have an impartial, unbiased attitude and avoid any conflict of interest.

> **Interpretation:**
>
> *Conflict of interest is a situation in which an internal auditor, who is in a position of trust, has a competing professional or personal interest. Such competing interests can make it difficult to fulfill his or her duties impartially. A conflict of interest exists even if no unethical or improper act results. A conflict of interest can create an appearance of impropriety that can undermine confidence in the internal auditor, the internal audit activity, and the profession. A conflict of interest could impair an individual's ability to perform his or her duties and responsibilities objectively.*

### 1130—Impairment to Independence or Objectivity

If independence or objectivity is impaired in fact or appearance, the details of the impairment must be disclosed to appropriate parties. The nature of the disclosure will depend upon the impairment.

> **Interpretation:**
>
> *Impairment to organizational independence and individual objectivity may include, but is not limited to, personal conflict of interest, scope limitations, restrictions on access to records, personnel, and properties, and resource limitations, such as funding.*
>
> *The determination of appropriate parties to which the details of an impairment to independence or objectivity must be disclosed is dependent upon the expectations of the internal audit activities and the chief audit executive's responsibilities to senior management and the board as described in the internal audit charter, as well as the nature of the impairment.*

**1130.A1**—Internal auditors must refrain from assessing specific operations for which they were previously responsible. Objectivity is presumed to be impaired if an internal auditor provides assurance services for an activity for which the internal auditor had responsibility within the previous year.

**1130.A2**—Assurance engagements for functions over which the chief audit executive has responsibility must be overseen by a party outside the internal audit activity.

**FIGURE 21.1** (*Continued*)

## ATTRIBUTE STANDARDS

**1130.C1**—Internal auditors may provide consulting services relating to operations for which they had previous responsibilities.

**1130.C2**—If internal auditors have potential impairments to independence or objectivity relating to proposed consulting services, disclosure must be made to the engagement client prior to accepting the engagement.

### 1200—Proficiency and Due Professional Care
Engagements must be performed with proficiency and due professional care.

#### 1210—Proficiency
Internal auditors must possess the knowledge, skills, and other competencies needed to perform their individual responsibilities. The internal audit activity collectively must possess or obtain the knowledge, skills, and other competencies needed to perform its responsibilities.

**Interpretation:**

*Knowledge, skills, and other competencies is a collective term that refers to the professional proficiency required of internal auditors to effectively carry out their professional responsibilities. Internal auditors are encouraged to demonstrate their proficiency by obtaining appropriate professional certifications and qualifications, such as the Certified Internal Auditor designation and other designations offered by The Institute of Internal Auditors and other appropriate professional organizations.*

**1210.A1**—The chief audit executive must obtain competent advice and assistance if the internal auditors lack the knowledge, skills, or other competencies needed to perform all or part of the engagement.

**1210.A2**—Internal auditors must have sufficient knowledge to evaluate the risk of fraud and the manner in which it is managed by the organization, but are not expected to have the expertise of a person whose primary responsibility is detecting and investigating fraud.

**1210.A3**—Internal auditors must have sufficient knowledge of key information technology risks and controls and available technology-based audit techniques to perform their assigned work. However, not all internal auditors are expected to have the expertise of an internal auditor whose primary responsibility is information technology auditing.

**1210.C1**—The chief audit executive must decline the consulting engagement or obtain competent advice and assistance if the internal auditors lack the knowledge, skills, or other competencies needed to perform all or part of the engagement.

#### 1220—Due Professional Care
Internal auditors must apply the care and skill expected of a reasonably prudent and competent internal auditor. Due professional care does not imply infallibility.

**1220.A1**—Internal auditors must exercise due professional care by considering the:

- Extent of work needed to achieve the engagement's objectives;
- Relative complexity, materiality, or significance of matters to which assurance procedures are applied;
- Adequacy and effectiveness of governance, risk management, and control processes;
- Probability of significant errors, fraud, or noncompliance; and
- Cost of assurance in relation to potential benefits.

**1220.A2**—In exercising due professional care, internal auditors must consider the use of technology-based audit and other data analysis techniques.

**1220.A3**—Internal auditors must be alert to the significant risks that might affect objectives, operations, or resources. However, assurance procedures alone, even when performed with due professional care, do not guarantee that all significant risks will be identified.

**1220.C1**—Internal auditors must exercise due professional care during a consulting engagement by considering the:

- Needs and expectations of clients, including the nature, timing, and communication of engagement results;
- Relative complexity and extent of work needed to achieve the engagement's objectives; and
- Cost of the consulting engagement in relation to potential benefits.

#### 1230—Continuing Professional Development
Internal auditors must enhance their knowledge, skills, and other competencies through continuing professional development.

### 1300—Quality Assurance and Improvement Program
The chief audit executive must develop and maintain a quality assurance and improvement program that covers all aspects of the internal audit activity.

(*continued*)

**FIGURE 21.1**   (*Continued*)

---

## ATTRIBUTE STANDARDS

**Interpretation:**

*A quality assurance and improvement program is designed to enable an evaluation of the internal audit activity's conformance with the "Definition of Internal Auditing" and the Standards and an evaluation of whether internal auditors apply the Code of Ethics. The program also assesses the efficiency and effectiveness of the internal audit activity and identifies opportunities for improvement.*

**1310—Requirements of the Quality Assurance and Improvement Program**

The quality assurance and improvement program must include both internal and external assessments.

**1311—Internal Assessments**

Internal assessments must include:

Ongoing monitoring of the performance of the internal audit activity; and periodic reviews performed through self-assessment or by other persons within the organization with sufficient knowledge of internal audit practices.

**Interpretation:**

*Ongoing monitoring is an integral part of the day-to-day supervision, review, and measurement of the internal audit activity. Ongoing monitoring is incorporated into the routine policies and practices used to manage the internal audit activity and uses processes, tools, and information considered necessary to evaluate conformance with the Definition of Internal Auditing, the Code of Ethics, and the Standards.*

*Periodic reviews are assessments conducted to evaluate conformance with the Definition of Internal Auditing, the Code of Ethics, and the Standards.*

*Sufficient knowledge of internal audit practices requires at least an understanding of all elements of the International Professional Practices Framework.*

**1312—External Assessments**

External assessments must be conducted at least once every five years by a qualified, independent reviewer or review team from outside the organization. The chief audit executive must discuss with the board:

- The need for more frequent external assessments; and
- The qualifications and independence of the external reviewer or review team, including any potential conflict of interest.

**Interpretation:**

*A qualified reviewer or review team demonstrates competence in two areas: the professional practice of internal auditing and the external assessment process. Competence can be demonstrated through a mixture of experience and theoretical learning. Experience gained in organizations of similar size, complexity, sector, or industry, and technical issues is more valuable than less relevant experience. In the case of a review team, not all members of the team need to have all the competencies; it is the team as a whole that is qualified. The chief audit executive uses professional judgment when assessing whether a reviewer or review team demonstrates sufficient competence to be qualified.*

*An independent reviewer or review team means not having either a real or an apparent conflict of interest and not being a part of, or under the control of, the organization to which the internal audit activity belongs.*

**1320—Reporting on the Quality Assurance and Improvement Program**

The chief audit executive must communicate the results of the quality assurance and improvement program to senior management and the board.

**Interpretation:**

*The form, content, and frequency of communicating the results of the quality assurance and improvement program is established through discussions with senior management and the board and considers the responsibilities of the internal audit activity and chief audit executive as contained in the internal audit charter. To demonstrate conformance with the Definition of Internal Auditing, the Code of Ethics, and the Standards, the results of external and periodic internal assessments are communicated upon completion of such assessments and the results of ongoing monitoring are communicated at least annually. The results include the reviewer's or review team's assessment with respect to the degree of conformance.*

**1321—Use of "Conforms with the International Standards for the Professional Practice of Internal Auditing"**

The chief audit executive may state that the internal audit activity conforms with the *International Standards for the Professional Practice of Internal Auditing* only if the results of the quality assurance and improvement program support this statement.

**Interpretation:**

The internal audit activity conforms with the *Standards* when it achieves the outcomes described in the Definition of Internal Auditing, Code of Ethics, and *Standards*. The results of the quality assurance and improvement program include the results of both internal and external assessments. All internal audit activities will have the results of internal assessments. Internal audit activities in existence for at least five years will also have the results of external assessments.

**FIGURE 21.1** (*Continued*)

## ATTRIBUTE STANDARDS

### 1322—Disclosure of Nonconformance
When nonconformance with the Definition of Internal Auditing, the Code of Ethics, or the *Standards* impacts the overall scope or operation of the internal audit activity, the chief audit executive must disclose the nonconformance and the impact to senior management and the board.

## PERFORMANCE STANDARDS

### 2000—Managing the Internal Audit Activity
The chief audit executive must effectively manage the internal audit activity to ensure it adds value to the organization.
> **Interpretation:**
> *The internal audit activity is effectively managed when:*
> * *The results of the internal audit activity's work achieve the purpose and responsibility included in the internal audit charter;*
> * *The internal audit activity conforms with the Definition of Internal Auditing and the Standards; and*
> * *The individuals who are part of the internal audit activity demonstrate conformance with the Code of Ethics and the Standards.*
> *The internal audit activity adds value to the organization (and its stakeholders) when it provides objective and relevant assurance, and contributes to the effectiveness and efficiency of governance, risk management, and control processes.*

### 2010—Planning
The chief audit executive must establish risk-based plans to determine the priorities of the internal audit activity, consistent with the organization's goals.
> **Interpretation:**
> *The chief audit executive is responsible for developing a risk-based plan. The chief audit executive takes into account the organization's risk management framework, including using risk appetite levels set by management for the different activities or parts of the organization. If a framework does not exist, the chief audit executive uses his/her own judgment of risks after consultation with senior management and the board.*

**2010.A1**—The internal audit activity's plan of engagements must be based on a documented risk assessment, undertaken at least annually. The input of senior management and the board must be considered in this process.

**2010.A2**—The chief audit executive must identify and consider the expectations of senior management, the board, and other stakeholders for internal audit opinions and other conclusions.

**2010.C1**—The chief audit executive should consider accepting proposed consulting engagements based on the engagement's potential to improve management of risks, add value, and improve the organization's operations. Accepted engagements must be included in the plan.

### 2020—Communication and Approval
The chief audit executive must communicate the internal audit activity's plans and resource requirements, including significant interim changes, to senior management and the board for review and approval. The chief audit executive must also communicate the impact of resource limitations.

### 2030—Resource Management
The chief audit executive must ensure that internal audit resources are appropriate, sufficient, and effectively deployed to achieve the approved plan.
> **Interpretation:**
> *Appropriate refers to the mix of knowledge, skills, and other competencies needed to perform the plan. "Sufficient" refers to the quantity of resources needed to accomplish the plan. Resources are effectively deployed when they are used in a way that optimizes the achievement of the approved plan.*

### 2040—Policies and Procedures
The chief audit executive must establish policies and procedures to guide the internal audit activity.
> **Interpretation:**
> *The form and content of policies and procedures are dependent upon the size and structure of the internal audit activity and the complexity of its work.*

### 2050—Coordination
The chief audit executive should share information and coordinate activities with other internal and external providers of assurance and consulting services to ensure proper coverage and minimize duplication of efforts.

### 2060—Reporting to Senior Management and the Board
The chief audit executive must report periodically to senior management and the board on the internal audit activity's purpose, authority, responsibility, and performance relative to its plan. Reporting must also include

(*continued*)

**FIGURE 21.1** (*Continued*)

## PERFORMANCE STANDARDS

significant risk exposures and control issues, including fraud risks, governance issues, and other matters needed or requested by senior management and the board.

> **Interpretation:**
>
> *The frequency and content of reporting are determined in discussion with senior management and the board and depend on the importance of the information to be communicated and the urgency of the related actions to be taken by senior management or the board.*

### 2070—External Service Provider and Organizational Responsibility for Internal Auditing

When an external service provider serves as the internal audit activity, the provider must make the organization aware that the organization has the responsibility for maintaining an effective internal audit activity.

> **Interpretation**
>
> *This responsibility is demonstrated through the quality assurance and improvement program which assesses conformance with the Definition of Internal Auditing, the Code of Ethics, and the* Standards.

## 2100—Nature of Work

The internal audit activity must evaluate and contribute to the improvement of governance, risk management, and control processes using a systematic and disciplined approach.

### 2110—Governance

The internal audit activity must assess and make appropriate recommendations for improving the governance process in its accomplishment of the following objectives:

- Promoting appropriate ethics and values within the organization;
- Ensuring effective organizational performance management and accountability;
- Communicating risk and control information to appropriate areas of the organization; and
- Coordinating the activities of and communicating information among the board, external and internal auditors, and management.

**2110.A1**—The internal audit activity must evaluate the design, implementation, and effectiveness of the organization's ethics-related objectives, programs, and activities.

**2110.A2**—The internal audit activity must assess whether the information technology governance of the organization supports the organization's strategies and objectives.

### 2120—Risk Management

The internal audit activity must evaluate the effectiveness and contribute to the improvement of risk management processes.

> **Interpretation:**
>
> *Determining whether risk management processes are effective is a judgment resulting from the internal auditor's assessment that:*
>
> - *Organizational objectives support and align with the organization's mission;*
> - *Significant risks are identified and assessed;*
> - *Appropriate risk responses are selected that align risks with the organization's risk appetite; and*
> - *Relevant risk information is captured and communicated in a timely manner across the organization, enabling staff, management, and the board to carry out their responsibilities.*
>
> *The internal audit activity may gather the information to support this assessment during multiple engagements. The results of these engagements, when viewed together, provide an understanding of the organization's risk management processes and their effectiveness.*
>
> *Risk management processes are monitored through ongoing management activities, separate evaluations, or both.*

**2120.A1**—The internal audit activity must evaluate risk exposures relating to the organization's governance, operations, and information systems regarding the:

- Reliability and integrity of financial and operational information.
- Effectiveness and efficiency of operations and programs;
- Safeguarding of assets; and
- Compliance with laws, regulations, policies, procedures, and contracts.

**2120.A2**—The internal audit activity must evaluate the potential for the occurrence of fraud and how the organization manages fraud risk.

**2120.C1**—During consulting engagements, internal auditors must address risk consistent with the engagement's objectives and be alert to the existence of other significant risks.

**2120.C2**—Internal auditors must incorporate knowledge of risks gained from consulting engagements into their evaluation of the organization's risk management processes.

**2120.C3**—When assisting management in establishing or improving risk management processes, internal auditors must refrain from assuming any management responsibility by actually managing risks.

**FIGURE 21.1** (*Continued*)

## PERFORMANCE STANDARDS

### 2130—Control
The internal audit activity must assist the organization in maintaining effective controls by evaluating their effectiveness and efficiency and by promoting continuous improvement.

**2130.A1**—The internal audit activity must evaluate the adequacy and effectiveness of controls in responding to risks within the organization's governance, operations, and information systems regarding the:
- Reliability and integrity of financial and operational information;
- Effectiveness and efficiency of operations and programs;
- Safeguarding of assets; and
- Compliance with laws, regulations, policies, procedures, and contracts.

**2130.C1**—Internal auditors must incorporate knowledge of controls gained from consulting engagements into evaluation of the organization's control processes.

### 2200—Engagement Planning
Internal auditors must develop and document a plan for each engagement, including the engagement's objectives, scope, timing, and resource allocations.

#### 2201—Planning Considerations
In planning the engagement, internal auditors must consider:
- The objectives of the activity being reviewed and the means by which the activity controls its performance;
- The significant risks to the activity, its objectives, resources, and operations and the means by which the potential impact of risk is kept to an acceptable level;
- The adequacy and effectiveness of the activity's risk management and control processes compared to a relevant control framework or model; and
- The opportunities for making significant improvements to the activity's risk management and control processes.

**2201.A1**—When planning an engagement for parties outside the organization, internal auditors must establish a written understanding with them about objectives, scope, respective responsibilities, and other expectations, including restrictions on distribution of the results of the engagement and access to engagement records.

**2201.C1**—Internal auditors must establish an understanding with consulting engagement clients about objectives, scope, respective responsibilities, and other client expectations. For significant engagements, this understanding must be documented.

### 2210—Engagement Objectives
Objectives must be established for each engagement.

**2210.A1**—Internal auditors must conduct a preliminary assessment of the risks relevant to the activity under review. Engagement objectives must reflect the results of this assessment.

**2210.A2**—Internal auditors must consider the probability of significant errors, fraud, noncompliance, and other exposures when developing the engagement objectives.

**2210.A3**—Adequate criteria are needed to evaluate controls. Internal auditors must ascertain the extent to which management has established adequate criteria to determine whether objectives and goals have been accomplished. If adequate, internal auditors must use such criteria in their evaluation. If inadequate, internal auditors must work with management to develop appropriate evaluation criteria.

**2210.C1**—Consulting engagement objectives must address governance, risk management, and control processes to the extent agreed upon with the client.

**2210.C2**—Consulting engagement objectives must be consistent with the organization's values, strategies, and objectives.

### 2220—Engagement Scope
The established scope must be sufficient to satisfy the objectives of the engagement.

**2220.A1**—The scope of the engagement must include consideration of relevant systems, records, personnel, and physical properties, including those under the control of third parties.

**2220.A2**—If significant consulting opportunities arise during an assurance engagement, a specific written understanding as to the objectives, scope, respective responsibilities, and other expectations should be reached and the results of the consulting engagement communicated in accordance with consulting standards.

**2220.C1**—In performing consulting engagements, internal auditors must ensure that the scope of the engagement is sufficient to address the agreed-upon objectives. If internal auditors develop reservations about the scope during the engagement, these reservations must be discussed with the client to determine whether to continue with the engagement.

**2220.C2**—During consulting engagements, internal auditors must address controls consistent with the engagement's objectives and be alert to significant control issues.

(*continued*)

**FIGURE 21.1** (*Continued*)

## PERFORMANCE STANDARDS

### 2230—Engagement Resource Allocation
Internal auditors must determine appropriate and sufficient resources to achieve engagement objectives based on an evaluation of the nature and complexity of each engagement, time constraints, and available resources.

### 2240—Engagement Work Program
Internal auditors must develop and document work programs that achieve the engagement objectives.

**2240.A1**—Work programs must include the procedures for identifying, analyzing, evaluating, and documenting information during the engagement. The work program must be approved prior to its implementation, and any adjustments approved promptly.

**2240.C1**—Work programs for consulting engagements may vary in form and content depending upon the nature of the engagement.

### 2300—Performing the Engagement
Internal auditors must identify, analyze, evaluate, and document sufficient information to achieve the engagement's objectives.

#### 2310—Identifying Information
Internal auditors must identify sufficient, reliable, relevant, and useful information to achieve the engagement's objectives.

**Interpretation:**
*Sufficient information is factual, adequate, and convincing so that a prudent, informed person would reach the same conclusions as the auditor. Reliable information is the best attainable information through the use of appropriate engagement techniques. Relevant information supports engagement observations and recommendations and is consistent with the objectives for the engagement. Useful information helps the organization meet its goals.*

#### 2320—Analysis and Evaluation
Internal auditors must base conclusions and engagement results on appropriate analyses and evaluations.

#### 2330—Documenting Information
Internal auditors must document relevant information to support the conclusions and engagement results.

**2330.A1**—The chief audit executive must control access to engagement records. The chief audit executive must obtain the approval of senior management and/or legal counsel prior to releasing such records to external parties, as appropriate.

**2330.A2**—The chief audit executive must develop retention requirements for engagement records, regardless of the medium in which each record is stored. These retention requirements must be consistent with the organization's guidelines and any pertinent regulatory or other requirements.

**2330.C1**—The chief audit executive must develop policies governing the custody and retention of consulting engagement records, as well as their release to internal and external parties. These policies must be consistent with the organization's guidelines and any pertinent regulatory or other requirements.

#### 2340—Engagement Supervision
Engagements must be properly supervised to ensure objectives are achieved, quality is assured, and staff is developed.

**Interpretation:**
*The extent of supervision required will depend on the proficiency and experience of internal auditors and the complexity of the engagement. The chief audit executive has overall responsibility for supervising the engagement, whether performed by or for the internal audit activity, but may designate appropriately experienced members of the internal audit activity to perform the review. Appropriate evidence of supervision is documented and retained.*

### 2400—Communicating Results
Internal auditors must communicate the results of engagements.

#### 2410—Criteria for Communicating
Communications must include the engagement's objectives and scope as well as applicable conclusions, recommendations, and action plans.

**2410.A1**—Final communication of engagement results must, where appropriate, contain the internal auditors' opinion and/or conclusions. When issued, an opinion or conclusion must take account of the expectations of senior managment, the board, and other stakeholders and must be supported by sufficient, reliable, relevant, and useful information.

**FIGURE 21.1** (*Continued*)

## PERFORMANCE STANDARDS

**Interpretation:**

*Opinions at the engagement level may be ratings, conclusions, or other descriptions of the results. Such an engagement may be in relation to controls around a specific process, risk, or business unit. The formulation of such opinions requires consideration of the engagement results and their significance.*

**2410.A2**—Internal auditors are encouraged to acknowledge satisfactory performance in engagement communications.

**2410.A3**—When releasing engagement results to parties outside the organization, the communication must include limitations on distribution and use of the results.

**2410.C1**—Communication of the progress and results of consulting engagements will vary in form and content depending upon the nature of the engagement and the needs of the client.

### 2420—Quality of Communications

Communications must be accurate, objective, clear, concise, constructive, complete, and timely.

**Interpretation:**

*Accurate communications are free from errors and distortions and are faithful to the underlying facts. Objective communications are fair, impartial, and unbiased and are the result of a fair-minded and balanced assessment of all relevant facts and circumstances. Clear communications are easily understood and logical, avoiding unnecessary technical language and providing all significant and relevant information. Concise communications are to the point and avoid unnecessary elaboration, superfluous detail, redundancy, and wordiness. Constructive communications are helpful to the engagement client and the organization and lead to improvements where needed. Complete communications lack nothing that is essential to the target audience and include all significant and relevant information and observations to support recommendations and conclusions. Timely communications are opportune and expedient, depending on the significance of the issue, allowing management to take appropriate corrective action.*

### 2421—Errors and Omissions

If a final communication contains a significant error or omission, the chief audit executive must communicate corrected information to all parties who received the original communication.

### 2430—Use of "Conducted in Conformance with the *International Standards for the Professional Practice of Internal Auditing*"

Internal auditors may report that their engagements are "conducted in conformance with the *International Standards for the Professional Practice of Internal Auditing*," only if the results of the quality assurance and improvement program support the statement.

### 2431—Engagement Disclosure of Nonconformance

When nonconformance with the Definition of Internal Auditing, the Code of Ethics, or the *Standards* impacts a specific engagement, communication of the results must disclose the:

- Principle or rule of conduct of the Code of Ethics or *Standard(s)* with which full conformance was not achieved;
- Reason(s) for nonconformance; and
- Impact of nonconformance on the engagement and the communicated engagement results.

### 2440—Disseminating Results

The chief audit executive must communicate results to the appropriate parties.

**Interpretation:**

*The chief audit executive or designee reviews and approves the final engagement communication before issuance and decides to whom and how it will be disseminated.*

**2440.A1**—The chief audit executive is responsible for communicating the final results to parties who can ensure that the results are given due consideration.

**2440.A2**—If not otherwise mandated by legal, statutory, or regulatory requirements, prior to releasing results to parties outside the organization, the chief audit executive must:

- Assess the potential risk to the organization;
- Consult with senior management and/or legal counsel as appropriate; and
- Control dissemination by restricting the use of the results.

**2440.C1**—The chief audit executive is responsible for communicating the final results of consulting engagements to clients.

**2440.C2**—During consulting engagements, governance, risk management, and control issues may be identified. Whenever these issues are significant to the organization, they must be communicated to senior management and the board.

(*continued*)

**FIGURE 21.1** *(Continued)*

---

**PERFORMANCE STANDARDS**

---

### 2450—Overall Opinions

When an overall opinion is issued, it must take into account the expectations of senior management, the board, and other stakeholders and must be supported by sufficient, reliable, relevant, and useful information.

**Interpretation:**

The communication will identify:

- The scope, including the time period to which the opinion pertains;
- Scope limitations;
- Consideration of all related projects including the reliance on other assurance providers;
- The risk or control framework or other criteria used as a basis for the overall opinion; and
- The overall opinion, judgment, or conclusion reached.

The reasons for an unfavorable overall opinion must be stated.

### 2500—Monitoring Progress

The chief audit executive must establish and maintain a system to monitor the disposition of results communicated to management.

**2500.A1**—The chief audit executive must establish a follow-up process to monitor and ensure that management actions have been effectively implemented or that senior management has accepted the risk of not taking action.

**2500.C1**—The internal audit activity must monitor the disposition of results of consulting engagements to the extent agreed upon with the client.

### 2600—Resolution of Senior Management's Acceptance of Risks

When the chief audit executive believes that senior management has accepted a level of residual risk that may be unacceptable to the organization, the chief audit executive must discuss the matter with senior management. If the decision regarding residual risk is not resolved, the chief audit executive must report the matter to the board for resolution.

---

**LO3**

Identify the standards for the professional practice of internal auditing.

### Purpose, Authority, and Responsibility

The purpose, authority, and responsibility of the internal auditing department should be set forth in the department's charter, as approved by the organization's board of directors. Its purpose should be consistent with the IIA's definition of internal auditing, the Code of Ethics, and *Standards*.

### Independence and Objectivity

Since internal auditors are employees of the organization, they cannot have the perceived independence of external auditors. However, independence is still very important to internal auditors. They should maintain an impartial, objective attitude and avoid conditions that threaten the ability to carry out work in an unbiased manner. Independence of the internal auditing department is enhanced when the **chief audit executive**[1] reports to a level within the organization that allows the internal audit activity to fulfill its responsibilities. Ideally, the chief audit executive should report directly to the audit committee of the board of directors. Independence is also enhanced when potential conflicts of interest are considered in assigning staff to audit assignments. For example, it would be a conflict of interest for an internal auditor to audit an area in which that individual was recently employed. It is difficult, if not impossible, to remain objective in evaluating one's own operating decisions.

### Proficiency and Due Professional Care

An internal auditing department should establish policies and procedures that ensure that staff members are competent to fulfill their assignments with professional proficiency. Ideally, the internal auditing department collectively should possess the skills and knowledge necessary to fulfill all the audit requirements of the organization. These skills and knowledge may be acquired through a combination of effective employment practices and continuing education programs.

---

[1] This title, used by the IIA, is equivalent to the director of internal auditing.

Internal auditors must apply due care in performing their work by considering factors that are critical to performing an engagement, including complexity, controls, materiality, and the probability of misstatements. Due care involves considering the use of technology-based and other data analysis techniques, and being alert to significant risks. In performing consulting engagements, internal auditors should consider the needs of the clients, complexity of the engagement, and the costs and benefits of the engagement.

### Quality Assurance and Improvement Program

The chief audit executive should establish a quality assurance and improvement program that covers all aspects of the internal audit activity and continuously monitors its effectiveness. The quality assurance and improvement program must include both internal and external assessments of effectiveness. In addition, the results of the quality assurance and improvement program should be communicated to senior management and the board of directors along with any instances where noncompliance affects the overall scope or operation of the internal audit activity.

### Managing the Internal Audit Activity

This group of standards provides guidance for the chief audit executive in managing the internal auditing function. The chief audit executive is responsible for properly administering the department to help assure that (1) audit activity is planned based on a risk assessment, (2) plans are approved by senior management and the board, (3) audit work is planned, controlled, and coordinated to ensure that maximum value is provided to the organization, and (4) the resources of the internal auditing department are efficiently and effectively employed.

### Nature of Work

The nature of the internal auditors' work should primarily involve improving risk management, control, and governance processes.

### Engagement Planning

The IIA's standards in this category recognize that if audit work is to be effective it must be adequately planned. Effective planning includes developing appropriate objectives, scope, timing, and resource allocations.

### Performing the Engagement

In performing every engagement, the internal auditors should identify relevant information, perform appropriate analysis and evaluation of the information, prepare work papers that support their conclusions, and adequately supervise staff members assigned to the engagement.

### Communicating Results

For audit work to have its intended effect, the results must be communicated to appropriate individuals accurately, objectively, completely, constructively, clearly, concisely, and on a timely basis. Communications should include the engagement's objectives as well as applicable conclusions and recommendations. When applicable, reports should indicate that the engagement was conducted in accordance with the IIA standards.

### Monitoring Progress

This aspect of auditing standards involves monitoring the progress of the organization with respect to the internal auditors' recommendations. The chief audit executive should follow up to determine that management has taken appropriate action on recommendations, or that management has decided to accept the risk of not taking any action.

### Resolution of Senior Management's Acceptance of Risks

When the chief audit executive believes that an unacceptable level of risk exists, the matter should be discussed with senior management. If the matter remains unresolved, both the chief audit executive and senior management should report the matter to the board of directors.

## Certification of Internal Auditors

Since 1974, The IIA has administered the **Certified Internal Auditor (CIA)** program. To become certified, a candidate must hold a bachelor's degree from an accredited college and successfully complete a four-part examination that is offered throughout the world. The four parts of the examination include: The Internal Audit Activity's Role in Governance, Risk and Control; Conducting the Internal Audit Engagement; Business Analysis and Information Technology; and Business Management Skills. Another requirement of certification is at least two years of work experience in internal auditing or its equivalent, although an advanced academic degree may be substituted for one year of work experience in meeting this requirement. When internal auditors become certified, they must meet requirements for continuing professional education. More information on internal auditing and the CIA examination is available from The Institute of Internal Auditors, 247 Maitland Avenue, Altamonte Springs, Florida 32701 or at www.theiia.org.

# Operational Auditing

**LO4**

Explain the nature and the purpose of an operational audit.

The term **operational auditing** refers to comprehensive examination of an operating unit or a complete organization to evaluate its systems, controls, and performance, as measured by management's objectives. Whereas a *financial audit* focuses on the measurement of financial position, results of operations, and cash flows of an entity, an operational audit focuses on the *efficiency, effectiveness,* and *economy* of operations. The operational auditor appraises management's operating controls and systems over such varied activities as purchasing, data processing, receiving, shipping, office services, advertising, and engineering.

## Objectives of Operational Audits

Operational audits are often performed by internal auditors for their organizations. The major users of operational audit reports are managers at various levels, including the board of directors. Top management needs assurance that every component of an organization is working to attain the organization's goals. For example, management needs the following:

1. Assessments of the unit's performance in relation to management's objectives or other appropriate criteria.
2. Assurance that its plans (as set forth in statements of objectives, programs, budgets, and directives) are comprehensive, consistent, and understood at the operating levels.
3. Objective information on how well its plans and policies are being carried out in all areas of operations, as well as information on opportunities for improvement in effectiveness, efficiency, and economy.
4. Information on weaknesses in operating controls, particularly as to possible sources of waste.
5. Reassurance that all operating reports can be relied on as a basis for action.

Governmental auditors, such as those employed by the Government Accountability Office (GAO), perform operational audits of governmental programs that are administered by both governmental and nongovernmental organizations. Operational auditing is especially applicable to governmental programs where the effectiveness of the programs cannot be evaluated in terms of profits; they must be evaluated by measuring such elements as the number of families relocated, the number of individuals rehabilitated, and the extent of the improvement in environmental conditions. In addition to internal and governmental auditors, CPA firms perform operational audits for clients through their consulting services departments.

## General Approach to Operational Audits

In many respects, the auditor's work in performing an operational audit is similar to that of a financial statement audit, but there are some significant differences. The steps may be set forth as (1) definition of purpose, (2) familiarization, (3) preliminary survey, (4) program

**FIGURE 21.2**
**The Operational Audit**

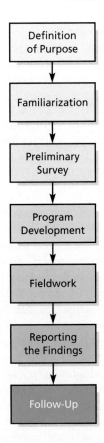

development, (5) fieldwork, (6) reporting the findings, and (7) follow-up. The operational audit process is illustrated in Figure 21.2.

*Definition of Purpose*

The broad statement of purpose of an operational audit usually includes the intention to appraise the performance of a particular organization, function, or group of activities. However, this broad statement must be expanded to specify precisely the scope of the audit and the nature of the report. The auditors must determine specifically which policies and procedures are to be appraised and how they relate to the specific objectives of the organization.

*Familiarization*

Before starting an operational audit, the auditors must obtain a comprehensive knowledge of the objectives, organizational structure, and operating characteristics of the unit being audited. This familiarization process might begin with a study of organizational charts, statements of the functions and responsibilities assigned, management policies and directives, and operating policies and procedures. At this stage, the auditors may read some of the published material available on the subject to acquaint themselves as fully as possible with the functions performed. This background information equips the auditor to visit the organization's facilities and interview supervisory personnel to determine their specific objectives, the standards used to measure accomplishment of those objectives, and the principal problems encountered in achieving those objectives. During these visits, the auditors will also observe the operations and inspect the available records and reports.

In summary, the auditors attempt to familiarize themselves as thoroughly as possible with the function being performed, particularly from the standpoint of administrative responsibility and control. The auditors' understanding of the organization is documented with questionnaires, flowcharts, and written narratives.

*Preliminary Survey*

The auditors' preliminary conclusions about the critical aspects of the operations and potential problem areas are summarized as the auditors' preliminary survey. This survey serves as a guide for the development of the audit program.

*Program Development*

The operational audit program is tailor-made to the particular engagement. It contains all the tests and analyses the auditors believe are necessary to evaluate the organization's operations. Based on the nature and difficulty of the audit work, appropriate personnel will be assigned to the engagement, and the work will be scheduled.

*Fieldwork*

The fieldwork phase involves executing the operational audit program. The auditors select the items to be reviewed to determine the adequacy of the procedures and how well they are followed. Just as in financial statement audits, the auditors will frequently select representative samples of the transactions from the records and inspect them to determine whether proper procedures have been followed and to discover the nature and extent of the problems encountered. In other cases, they may resort to inquiry or direct observation to satisfy themselves that the employees understand their instructions and are carrying out their work as intended.

Analysis is another important part of fieldwork. Actual performance by the organization is compared with various criteria, such as budgets, productivity goals, or performance by similar units. This analysis provides a basis for auditors' recommendations for improvements in effectiveness, efficiency, and economy.

As each phase of the fieldwork is completed, the auditors summarize the results and evaluate the material gathered. Deficiencies that appear to be significant are discussed with the supervisor involved. Frequently, corrective action may be taken at this time, although the primary purpose of this on-the-spot discussion is to make sure that all the relevant facts have been obtained.

During fieldwork, the auditors will document the planning, evidence gathered, analysis, interpretation, and findings in their *working papers.* The audit working papers should stand alone and support the auditors' report.

*Reporting the Findings*

On final completion of the fieldwork, the auditors should summarize their findings related to the basic purposes of the audit. The report will include suggested improvements in the operational policies and procedures of the unit and a list of situations in which compliance with existing policies and procedures is less than adequate. After

---

## Illustrative Cases | *Compliance Auditing: Two Examples*

### COMPLIANCE WITH THE CLEAN AIR ACT

The Environmental Protection Agency has issued guidelines for Oxygenated Gasoline Credit Programs under the Clean Air Act, which requires CPAs (or internal auditors) to perform agreed-upon procedures regarding a company's compliance with an EPA regulation that requires gasoline to contain at least 2 percent oxygen. Management's assertion indicates the company's compliance with the relevant requirements (which are specifically listed) of the Clean Air Act.

### COMPLIANCE WITH THE FDIC IMPROVEMENT ACT OF 1991

The Federal Depository Insurance Corporation (FDIC) Improvement Act of 1991 requires that CPAs be engaged to perform agreed-upon procedures engagements to test large financial institutions' compliance with certain provisions related to the "safety and soundness" of the institutions. The assertion in this case states management's belief that the institution has complied with the listed provisions of the act.

they have completed the draft report, they should arrange an *exit conference* to review the findings with all persons directly concerned with the operations audited. The conference ensures that the auditors have an accurate and complete story; if there is a question about the facts, further investigation will be made until any doubt is resolved. If a serious disagreement on the interpretation of the facts remains, it is usually best to disclose both interpretations in the report. The conference also provides an opportunity for the affected management to consider and take timely action on the problems disclosed.

A formal report, such as the one illustrated by Figure 21.3, is then issued to top management. For each finding, a complete report will describe (1) the *criteria* used to evaluate the activity, (2) the *condition* (e.g., problem) that exists, (3) the *cause,* (4) the *effect,* and (5) *recommendations* for improvement.

### Follow-Up

The final stage in the operational auditors' work is the follow-up action to ensure that any deficiencies disclosed in the audit report are satisfactorily handled. This follow-up responsibility may be given to a line organization or staff group, but most frequently it is held to be a responsibility of the audit staff. In some instances, the auditors find it

**FIGURE 21.3**
**Introductory Language for an Operational Audit Report**

---

Neal McGregor
Vice President—Operations
Baxter Corporation
Kansas City, Missouri

Dear Mr. McGregor:

In September 20X1, we concluded an operational audit of the data processing operations.

**Objectives, Scope, and Approach**
The general objectives of this engagement, which were more specifically outlined in our letter dated June 30, 20X1, were as follows:

- To document, analyze, and report on the status of current operations.
- To identify areas that require attention.
- To make recommendations for corrective action or improvements.

Our operational audit encompassed the centralized data processing facilities and the on-site computer operations of the company's retailing division. Our evaluations included both the financial and operational conditions of the units. Financial data consulted in the course of our analyses were not audited or reviewed by us, and, accordingly, we do not express an opinion or any other form of assurance on them.

The operational audit involved interviews with management personnel and selected operations personnel in each of the units studied. We also evaluated selected documents, files, reports, systems, procedures, and policies as we considered appropriate. After analyzing the data, we developed recommendations for improvements. We then discussed our findings and recommendations with appropriate unit management personnel, and with you, prior to submitting this written report.

**Findings and Recommendations**
All significant findings are included in this report for your consideration. The recommendations in this report represent, in our judgment, those most likely to bring about improvements in the operations of the organization. The recommendations differ in such aspects as difficulty of implementation, urgency, visibility of benefits, and required investment in facilities and equipment or additional personnel. The varying nature of the recommendations, their implementation costs, and their potential impact on operations should be considered in reaching your decision on courses of action.

(Specific Findings and Recommendations)

---

desirable to make brief reexaminations after a reasonable lapse of time to ensure that all significant recommendations have been implemented.

## Compliance Auditing

**LO5**

Distinguish among the various types of compliance audits.

Society has always been concerned about compliance with laws and regulations by all types of organizations. As a result, compliance auditing has evolved to become an important part of the work of both external and internal auditors. **Compliance auditing** involves testing and reporting on whether an organization has complied with the requirements of various laws, regulations, and agreements. Congress and various regulators have adopted compliance auditing requirements for a wide variety of business, governmental, and nonprofit organizations. The Auditing Standards Board has developed general guidelines for all types of engagements that involve attesting to compliance with laws and regulations, and more specific guidelines for compliance auditing of federal financial assistance programs.

### Attesting to Compliance with Laws and Regulations

Section 601 of *Statement on Standards for Attestation Engagements (SSAE) No. 10,* "Attestation Standards: Revision and Recodification,"[2] provides guidance for CPAs when they are engaged either to apply agreed-upon procedures or perform an examination on an organization's compliance with laws and regulations. *SSAE No. 10* prohibits CPAs from performing *reviews* of compliance with laws and regulations.

In compliance attestation engagements, CPAs address an organization's **compliance with specified requirements,** or its internal control over compliance with specific laws and regulations. Management[3] provides an assertion about compliance in writing in a representation letter to the CPAs. That assertion also may be presented in a formal report that accompanies the CPAs' report or be included in the CPAs' report. The CPAs' report provides assurance on either **management's assertion** or directly on compliance.

*Applying Agreed-Upon Procedures to Test Compliance with Specified Requirements*
Engagements to apply agreed-upon procedures to test compliance with specified requirements are common compliance engagements. The objective of an agreed-upon procedures engagement is to assist users in evaluating an entity's compliance with specified requirements based on procedures agreed upon by the users of the report. A major advantage of agreed-upon procedures engagements results from the fact that since the users participate in designing the procedures to be performed by the CPAs, it is likely that the work performed will meet their needs.

Agreed-upon procedures reports are restricted-use reports, intended for the audit committee, management, and other parties for whom the procedures were designed (e.g., the Environmental Protection Agency). The reports provide a summary of procedures performed and the CPAs' findings. The findings section of the report should set forth any instances of **noncompliance** with relevant laws and regulations noted by the CPAs, regardless of whether they became aware of them as a result of the procedures performed or in some other way, such as through an informal discussion with an internal auditor. The format of a report on the application of agreed-upon procedures to compliance is illustrated in the accompanying box.

---

[2] *SSAE No. 10* revises and recodifies the first nine SSAEs. Guidance on compliance attestation was originally presented in *SSAE No. 3,* "Compliance Attestation."

[3] Section 101 of *SSAE No. 10* provides that the report should identify the party responsible for the assertion or the subject matter of the assertion. The responsible party is defined as the person or persons, as either individuals or representatives of the entity, responsible for the subject matter. Management is deemed to be the "responsible party" throughout this chapter.

---

**Independent Accountant's Report**

TO LENOS COMPANY:

We have performed the procedures enumerated below, which were agreed to by the Illinois Department of Education, solely to assist the users in evaluating Lenos Company's compliance with Section F.2 of Illinois Department of Education Regulation 74A of *Employment Health Requirements* during the period ended December 31, 20X1, included in the accompanying Management Report. Management is responsible for Lenos Company's compliance with these requirements. This agreed-upon procedures engagement was conducted in accordance with attestation standards established by the American Institute of Certified Public Accountants. The sufficiency of these procedures is solely the responsibility of those parties specified in this report. Consequently, we make no representation regarding the sufficiency of the procedures described below either for the purpose for which this report has been requested or for any other purpose.

[Include paragraphs to enumerate procedures and findings.]

We were not engaged to and did not conduct an examination, the objective of which would be the expression of an opinion on compliance. Accordingly, we do not express such an opinion. Had we performed additional procedures, other matters might have come to our attention that would have been reported to you.

This report is intended solely for the information and use of the Illinois Department of Education and is not intended to be and should not be used by anyone other than these specified parties.

---

*Applying Agreed-Upon Procedures to Test the Effectiveness of Controls over Compliance*

As indicated previously, CPAs also may be engaged to test the effectiveness of the organization's internal control over compliance. An organization's **internal control over compliance** is the process by which management obtains reasonable assurance that the organization has complied with specific requirements. The CPAs' report on the application of agreed-upon procedures to test the effectiveness of controls over compliance is similar to the report on compliance that is presented above. It describes the tests of controls performed and the related findings and includes the appropriate limitations on the distribution of the report and other caveats.

*Performing Examinations*

CPAs are sometimes engaged to perform an examination of a client's compliance with specified requirements (the subject matter) or of management's assertion related thereto. In performing an examination engagement, the CPAs begin by obtaining a thorough understanding of the requirements. Then they plan the engagement, consider the organization's internal control over compliance, perform sufficient procedures to form an opinion on compliance (or on management's assertion about compliance), and issue an opinion on compliance with specified requirements. An unqualified opinion on compliance with laws and regulations is shown in the accompanying box.

---

**Independent Accountant's Report**

TO LENOS COMPANY:

We have examined Lenos Company's compliance with Section F.2 of Illinois Department of Education Regulation 74A of *Employment Health Requirements* during the period ended December 31, 20X1. Management is responsible for Lenos Company's compliance with those requirements. Our responsibility is to express an opinion on the Company's compliance based on our examination.

Our examination was conducted in accordance with standards established by the American Institute of Certified Public Accountants, and, accordingly, included examining, on a test basis, evidence about Lenos Company's compliance with those requirements and performing such other procedures as we considered necessary in the circumstances. We believe that our examination provides a reasonable basis for our opinion. Our examination does not provide a legal determination on Lenos Company's compliance with specified requirements.

In our opinion, Lenos Company complied, in all material respects, with the aforementioned requirements for the year ended December 31, 20X1.

The CPAs' examination report should be modified in the following circumstances:

- *Material noncompliance with specified requirements.* A qualified or adverse opinion should be issued when the auditors' procedures indicate that the organization did not comply with the requirements (reporting directly on the subject matter) or that management's report is not fairly stated.
- *Scope restriction.* A qualified opinion or disclaimer of opinion should be issued when the CPAs' procedures are restricted.
- *Involvement of another CPA firm in the examination.* In these circumstances, the principal CPA firm generally issues a report that indicates a division of responsibility.

Although the CPAs' examination report may generally be either on the subject matter or on management's assertion, when it is other than unqualified the CPAs must report directly on the subject matter.

## Compliance Auditing of Government Entities and Organizations Receiving Federal Financial Assistance

### LO6

Describe the auditing and reporting requirements of *Government Auditing Standards* and the Single Audit Act.

AICPA AU 935 provides guidance on performing tests of compliance in the following types of audits:

- Audits of the financial statements of entities receiving federal financial assistance in accordance with generally accepted auditing standards.
- Audits conducted in accordance with *Government Auditing Standards.*
- Audits conducted in accordance with the federal Single Audit Act.[4]

### Audits in Accordance with Generally Accepted Auditing Standards

As discussed in Chapter 2, auditors have a responsibility to design all audits to obtain reasonable assurance of detecting material misstatements resulting from violations of laws and regulations that have a *direct and material effect* on line-item amounts in the financial statements. Governmental organizations are subject to a variety of laws and regulations that affect their financial statements—many more than typical business enterprises. An important aspect of generally accepted accounting principles for governmental organizations is the recognition of various legal and contractual requirements. These requirements pertain to bases of accounting, fund structure, and other accounting principles. Therefore, in performing an audit of a governmental organization's financial statements, auditors are more likely to encounter laws and regulations that have a direct and material effect on the amounts in the organization's financial statements.

Governmental organizations receive funds from various sources, including taxes, special assessments, and bond issues. Laws and regulations often dictate the way the funds may be spent. While certain funds may be used for general government purposes, others are restricted to specific purposes, such as schools, libraries, or highways.

A governmental organization also may receive financial assistance from other governmental organizations in the form of grants, loans, loan guarantees, interest subsidies, insurance, and food commodities. This financial assistance often is provided subject to specified compliance requirements. For example, a federal agency may provide financial assistance to a governmental organization but require the organization to match the federal funding. In the event a governmental organization does not comply with the matching requirement, it may have to refund the federal financial assistance.

Auditors perform a number of procedures to identify the laws and regulations that have a direct effect on an organization's financial statements, including (1) discussing laws and regulations with management, program and grant administrators, and government auditors; (2) reviewing state and federal compliance requirement documents; (3) reviewing relevant grant and loan agreements; and (4) reviewing minutes of the legislative body of the governmental organization. Auditors also obtain written representations

---

[4] AICPA AU 935 refers to the Single Audit Act of 1984. This act was amended in its entirety by the Single Audit Act Amendments of 1996.

from management about the completeness of the laws and regulations identified and an acknowledgment of management's responsibility for compliance with them.

When auditors have an understanding of the important laws and regulations, they assess the risks that financial statement amounts might be materially affected by violations.[5] In making these assessments, they consider the controls designed to prevent violations, such as policies regarding acceptable operating practices, codes of conduct, and assignment of responsibility for complying and assessing compliance with legal and regulatory requirements. These risk assessments are then used to design the nature, timing, and extent of the auditors' substantive tests of compliance.

### Audits in Accordance with Government Auditing Standards

The Government Accountability Office issues *Generally Accepted Government Auditing Standards (GAGAS)* for use in auditing federal entities and organizations that receive federal financial assistance. They include standards for financial audits and performance audits. These standards are included in a publication entitled **Government Auditing Standards,** which is commonly referred to as the "Yellow Book." The standards apply (updated in 2007) only when required by law, regulation, or agreement. These standards impose additional requirements related to (1) ethics, (2) audit communication, (3) considering the results of previous audits, (4) noncompliance with provisions of contracts and grant agreements, (5) audit documentation, and (6) reporting.

*Ethical Principles*    GAGAS place additional emphasis on ethical principles as the basis for the implementation of the standards, including a description of the following five key principles that should guide government audits:

1. The public interest—Observing integrity, objectivity, and independence in performing professional services assists the auditors in serving the public interest.
2. Integrity—Public confidence in government is maintained by auditors' performing professional services with integrity.
3. Objectivity—Objectivity includes being independent in fact and appearance when providing audit and attest services, maintaining an attitude of impartiality, being intellectually honest, and being free from conflicts of interest.
4. Proper use of government information, resources, and position—These items should be used for official purposes and not for the auditors' personal gain or otherwise inappropriately.
5. Professional behavior—Auditors should comply with laws and regulations and avoid any conduct that might bring discredit to the auditors' work.

In addition, *GAGAS* contain additional descriptions of situations that impair auditor independence in performing audit and attest services.

*Audit Communication*    GAGAS require auditors to communicate information about the nature of the audit and the level of assurance provided not only to client management and those charged with governance, but also to appropriate oversight bodies requiring the audits, those responsible for acting on audit findings, and others authorized to receive such reports. In making these communications, the auditors should specifically address the planned work related to testing compliance with laws and regulations and internal control over financial reporting.

*Considering the Results of Previous Audits*    GAGAS require the auditors to consider the results of previous audits and follow up on known significant findings and recommendations in prior-year audit reports. The auditors' objective is to determine that client officers have taken appropriate corrective actions.

---

[5] Generally, laws and regulations concerning compliance with financial assistance programs do not discuss compliance in terms of whether or not noncompliance might materially misstate the financial statements. These laws and regulations discuss the effect of noncompliance in terms of whether it has a direct and material effect on financial assistance programs.

*Noncompliance with Provisions of Contracts and Grants*    As discussed in Chapter 2, generally accepted auditing standards require the auditors to plan an audit to provide reasonable assurance of detecting violations of laws and regulations that have a direct and material effect on the financial statements. *Generally Accepted Government Auditing Standards* make it clear that this responsibility extends to provisions of contracts and grants that have a direct and material effect on the financial statements.

*Audit Documentation*    *Generally Accepted Government Auditing Standards* have additional documentation requirements beyond those required by generally accepted auditing standards. These documentation requirements include:

- Before the report is issued, evidence of supervisory review of the work performed that supports findings, conclusions, and recommendations contained in the audit report.
- Any departures from *Generally Accepted Government Auditing Standards* and the impact on the audit or the auditors' conclusions.

*Reporting on Compliance with Laws and Regulations and Internal Control*    In performing an audit of financial statements in accordance with *Government Auditing Standards,* in addition to issuing an independent auditor's report on the financial statements, the auditor must also issue written reports on compliance with laws and regulations and on internal control.[6]

The report on compliance is based on the auditors' tests of compliance with laws, regulations, grants, and contracts that have a direct and material effect on the amounts in the financial statements—tests that are required by generally accepted auditing standards. The report describes the scope of the auditors' tests of compliance with laws and regulations and presents the auditors' findings.

Auditors may discover violations of provisions of laws, regulations, contracts, or grants that result in what they estimate to be a material misstatement of the organization's financial statements. In these circumstances, they must consider the effect on their opinion on the financial statements. The resulting misstatement, if left uncorrected, would normally require them to issue a qualified or adverse opinion. Of course, management will usually decide to correct the financial statements, allowing the auditors to issue an unqualified opinion. Even though the financial statements are corrected, the auditors must still modify their report on compliance with laws and regulations to include a description of the material instances of noncompliance. If the noncompliance resulted from a weakness in internal control considered by the auditors to be a significant deficiency, they would also modify their report on internal control to describe the condition. The auditors should also report a description of any fraudulent or other illegal acts that they become aware of, unless they are inconsequential.

Auditors also may be required to report fraudulent or illegal acts directly to a government agency or another third party. For example, when the client is required by law or regulation to notify specific external parties about a fraudulent or illegal act and fails to do so, the auditors are required to communicate the problem directly to the appropriate party. When the client fails to take appropriate steps to address fraudulent or illegal acts, auditors may also be required to notify a government agency.

When performing an audit in accordance with *GAGAS,* the auditors should include all significant deficiencies in internal control in the audit report and identify those considered to be material weaknesses. If the auditors have sufficient appropriate audit evidence that a significant deficiency has been remediated (eliminated) before their report is issued, the report still includes the significant deficiency, but indicates that it has been remediated. The report also includes a description of the scope of the auditors' testing of internal control.[7]

---

[6] *Government Auditing Standards* allow these reports on financial statements, internal control, and compliance to be presented separately or combined. The reporting options include (*a*) one report, all three combined; (*b*) two reports, with internal control and compliance combined; and (*c*) three separate reports.

[7] Auditors of SEC registrants also issue reports on internal control as a part of the audit. Chapter 18 presents details.

*Reference to Separate Reports*   *GAGAS* also require that if an auditor issues separate reports on the financial statements, compliance, and internal control, the report on the financial statements must include a final paragraph that refers to the reports on compliance and internal control, as shown below:

> In accordance with *Government Auditing Standards,* we have also issued our reports dated July 15, 20X0, on our consideration of the City of Springfield's internal control over financial reporting and on our tests of its compliance with certain provisions of laws, regulations, contracts, and grants. Those reports are an integral part of an audit performed in accordance with *Government Auditing Standards* and should be read in conjunction with this report in considering the results of our audit.

### Audits in Accordance with the Single Audit Act

A major impetus for the demands for increased *compliance auditing* comes from the federal government, which provides more than $500 billion in financial assistance annually through various federal financial assistance programs. This federal financial assistance must be spent in accordance with the respective programs' requirements. Federal financial assistance is provided primarily to states and local governmental units, such as cities, counties, and school districts, and to nonprofit organizations, such as private colleges and universities and research institutes. Business organizations may also receive federal financial assistance.

Congress passed the **Single Audit Act** to provide a mechanism for improving the management of federal financial assistance programs by providing a statutory requirement to test compliance with laws and regulations and internal controls over program compliance requirements. The Single Audit Act applies to states, local governments, and nonprofit organizations that expend $500,000 or more within a fiscal year in federal financial assistance. Audits in accordance with the Single Audit Act[8] are specifically designed to assess whether the billions of dollars in federal financial assistance are being managed and spent in accordance with applicable laws and regulations. Consequently, audits under the Single Audit Act are more extensive than audits of an organization's financial statements in accordance with generally accepted auditing standards and *Government Auditing Standards.*

The requirements of a single audit include determining and reporting on whether (1) the financial statements are presented fairly in all material respects in accordance with generally accepted accounting principles, (2) the schedule of expenditures of federal awards (illustrated in Figure 21.4) is fairly presented in all material respects in relation to the financial statements taken as a whole, and (3) the entity complied with the provisions of laws, regulations, and contracts or grants that may have a direct and material effect on each major federal financial assistance program. The requirements also include obtaining an understanding of internal control pertaining to compliance with the provisions of laws, regulations, contracts, or grants that may have a material effect on each major federal financial assistance program; assessing control risk; and performing tests of controls. With respect to internal control, auditors must report on the procedures performed, including any significant deficiencies identified, with specific identification of significant deficiencies that constitute material weaknesses.

*Identification of Major Programs*   An important aspect of performing an audit in accordance with the Single Audit Act is auditor identification of the **major federal financial assistance programs.** Major federal financial assistance programs are those programs to which the auditor must apply procedures to test for compliance and to test the effectiveness of controls. A major program is determined using a risk-based approach that considers both the amount of the program's expenditures and the risk of material non-compliance. However, the auditor must test compliance and controls of programs with

[8] The Single Audit Act requires the Director of the Office of Management (OMB) to issue guidance for implementing the act. OMB Circular A-133, *Audits of States, Local Governments, and Non-Profit Organizations,* provides that guidance.

**FIGURE 21.4   Schedule of Federal Financial Assistance**

|  | | | | |
|---|---|---|---|---|
| CITY OF ROSEBUD, NEW JERSEY<br>Schedule of Federal Financial Assistance<br>For the Year Ended June 30, 20X1 | | | | |
| **Federal Grantor** | **Federal CFDA Number** | **Program or Award Amount** | **Receipts** | **Disbursements** |
| Department of Housing and Urban Development, Community Development Block Grants/Entitlement Grants | 14.218 | $ 808,432 | $ 562,453 | $ 641,941 |
| Passed through the New Jersey Department of Transportation: Federal Transit—Capital Investment Grants | 20.500 | 483,993 | 483,993 | 483,993 |
| Department of Education, Title I Grants to Local Education Agencies | 84.010 | 158,700 | — | 30,910 |
|  | | $1,451,125 | $1,046,446 | $1,156,844 |

expenditures that, in the aggregate, equal 50 percent of total federal financial assistance program expenditures.[9] The Illustrative Case on page 801 provides an example of how the auditors identify major programs.

*Designing Compliance Procedures for Major Programs*   Auditors approach a single audit in much the same way they approach an audit in accordance with generally accepted auditing standards, but they must consider the additional auditing requirements for individual major federal financial assistance programs. In performing an audit in accordance with generally accepted auditing standards, auditors are concerned with compliance with laws and regulations that could have a *direct* and *material* effect on the organization's financial statements. Under the Single Audit Act, auditors are also concerned with compliance with laws and regulations that could have a direct and material effect on each major federal financial assistance program. Because materiality must be considered on a program-by-program basis, materiality for planning the compliance procedures will typically be much less than that for the financial statements. Further, an amount that is material to one major federal financial assistance program may not be material to another major program because of differences in program size and the differing significance of particular compliance requirements to each program. This lower level of planning materiality results in an increase in the extent of tests of compliance.

In designing the tests of compliance procedures, auditors first assess the inherent risk of material noncompliance with laws and regulations applicable to each major program by considering various factors, such as the amount of the program expenditures and any changes made in the program. Auditors then assess the *control risk* related to the organization's administration of the programs. When controls are considered likely to be effective, the Single Audit Act requires auditors to obtain an understanding of controls over compliance for major programs, assess control risk, and perform tests of controls sufficient to support an assessment of low control risk. But, when such controls are considered unlikely to be effective, auditors do not have to perform tests of controls.

Based on the auditors' assessments of the risks of material noncompliance and the related levels of control risk, they design sufficient substantive procedures to support an opinion on major program compliance with applicable laws and regulations. To provide assistance in designing these procedures, the Office of Management and Budget (OMB) issued the *OMB Circular A-133 Compliance Supplement (Compliance Supplement)*, which specifies the compliance requirements and provides suggested audit procedures for a large number of federal financial assistance programs. For those major programs not included in the **Compliance Supplement,** auditors may determine the significant specific requirements to be tested by (1) following the *Compliance Supplement*'s guidance

[9] For low risk organizations, this percentage is reduced to 25 percent.

**Illustrative Case** | *Identification of Major Programs*

The City of Woodruff receives funds through four federal financial assistance programs. The following are the total amount of expenditures for the programs for the year and the auditors' assessments of the risk of material noncompliance of each program.

| | Expenditures | Risk |
|---|---|---|
| Department of Education | | |
| Title I—Grants to Local Education Agencies | | |
| CFDA Number 84.010 | $1,350,422 | Moderate |
| Department of Transportation | | |
| Highway Planning and Construction | | |
| CFDA Number 20.205 | 787,900 | Low |
| Department of Housing and Urban Development | | |
| Community Development | | |
| Block Grants/Entitlement Grants | | |
| CFDA Number 14.218 | 340,000 | High |
| Department of Health and Human Services | | |
| Community Services Block Grant | | |
| CFDA Number 93.569 | 95,200 | Moderate |
| Total expenditures | $2,573,522 | |

Based on the amount of the expenditures and the risk of material noncompliance, the auditors have identified the first and third programs as major programs. Expenditures from these two programs total $1,690,422 ($1,350,422 + $340,000), which exceeds the required percentage of coverage of 50 percent of total federal financial assistance program expenditures. The second and fourth programs were not identified as major programs due to the auditors' assessments of the risk of material noncompliance and total amount, respectively.

for such programs; (2) considering knowledge obtained from prior years' audits; (3) discussing laws and regulations with management, lawyers, program administrators, or federal, state, and local auditors; and (4) reviewing grant and loan agreements.

*Compliance Requirements*   Under the Single Audit Act, auditors must test for compliance with the specific requirements of all major programs. The **specific requirements** that must be audited are those that, if not complied with, could have a direct and material effect on a major program. These requirements and the related audit objectives are described below:

1. *Activities allowed or not allowed.* Determine that the organization complies with the specific requirements regarding the activities allowed or not allowed by the program.

2. *Allowable costs/cost principles.* Determine that the organization complies with federal cost accounting policies applicable to the program.

3. *Cash management.* Determine that the recipient/subrecipient followed procedures to minimize the time elapsing between the transfer of funds from the U.S. Treasury, or pass-through entity, and their disbursement.

4. *Davis-Bacon Act.* Determine that wages paid are not less than those established for the locality of the project (prevailing wage rates) by the Department of Labor.

5. *Eligibility.* Determine that individuals or groups of individuals that are being provided goods or services under a program are eligible for participation in and for the levels of assistance received under that program.

6. *Equipment and real property management.* Determine that the organization safeguards and maintains equipment purchased with federal assistance and uses the equipment for appropriate purposes.

7. *Matching, level of effort, earmarking.* Determine that the organization contributes the appropriate amount of its own resources to the program.

8. *Period of availability of federal funds.* Determine that federal funds were spent or obligated within the period of availability.

9. *Procurement and suspension and debarment.* Determine that the organization uses appropriate policies for purchases with federal funds, and that the organization does not contract with vendors that are suspended or debarred.

10. *Program income.* Determine whether program income is correctly recorded and used in accordance with the program requirements.

11. *Real property acquisition and relocation assistance.* Determine that the organization complied with property acquisition, appraisal, negotiation, and residential relocation requirements.

12. *Reporting.* Determine that the organization has complied with prescribed reporting requirements.

13. *Subrecipient monitoring.* Determine whether **recipients** monitor the compliance of **subrecipients.**

14. *Special tests and provisions.* Determine that the organization complies with other significant specific requirements that apply to the program.

*Evaluating the Results of Compliance Procedures of Major Programs*    In evaluating whether an entity's noncompliance is material to a major program, auditors should consider the frequency of noncompliance, and whether it results in a material amount of questioned costs. A **questioned cost** is an expenditure that the auditor questions on the grounds that it does not meet the criteria for allowability, program eligibility, or other requirements or is not adequately supported with documentation. An example of a questioned cost is a payment of financial assistance to an individual who does not meet the eligibility requirements of a program. In evaluating the effect of the questioned cost on their reports, auditors not only consider the actual amount, but also develop an estimate of the total amount of the questioned costs. Thus, when auditors use audit sampling to select expenditures for testing, they consider the *projected amount* of questioned costs from the sample, as discussed in Chapter 9. Even if the estimated total questioned cost is not material enough to affect the auditors' opinion on compliance, they may be required to report the instances of noncompliance found and the resulting amounts of questioned costs. Auditors must report all questioned costs and likely questioned costs that exceed $10,000 in the Schedule of Findings and Questioned Costs, such as the example in Figure 21.5.

**FIGURE 21.5**
**Schedule of Findings and Questioned Costs**

CITY OF WAXVILLE, WASHINGTON
Schedule of Findings and Questioned Costs
April 30, 20X1

| Program | Finding/Noncompliance | Questioned Cost |
|---|---|---|
| Department of Housing and Urban Development, Community Development Block Grants/Entitlement Grants Program | | |
| 1. Grant No. 85-C-7061 Project No. C-1 CFDA No. 14.218 | Approximately $11,800 was expended for the payment of individual homeowners' property taxes and fire insurance. These are not allowable costs. The City intends to repay HUD for these costs. | $11,800 |
| 2. Grant No. 85-C-7071 Project No. C-1 CFDA No. 14.218 | A request for reimbursement of funds was in excess of the actual documented expenditures. The City intends to repay HUD for these costs. | 41,060 $52,860 |

*Reporting for a Single Audit* In addition to the reports required for an audit in accordance with *Generally Accepted Government Auditing Standards,* auditors must report on:

- Whether the schedule of expenditures of federal awards is fairly presented in all material respects in relation to the financial statements taken as a whole.
- Whether the entity complied with the provisions of laws, regulations, and contracts or grants that may have a direct and material effect on each major federal financial assistance program.
- The work performed on internal control relating to major federal financial assistance programs.

In addition, an auditor must prepare a *summary report* that summarizes the results of the audit as described in the auditor's opinion on the financial statements, reports on internal control, reports on compliance, and the schedule of findings and questioned costs that accompanies these reports.

**Compliance Auditing— A Summary**

The auditors' compliance auditing and reporting requirements are summarized in Figure 21.6. Notice that the requirements build on each other. An audit in accordance with *Generally Accepted Government Auditing Standards* includes the requirements of generally accepted auditing standards and a Single Audit includes the requirements of both standards.

**FIGURE 21.6** **Auditing and Reporting on Organizations Receiving Federal Financial Assistance—A Summary**

**Audit in Accordance with Generally Accepted Auditing Standards (GAAS)**

**Procedures Performed**
- Audit procedures required by GAAS, including tests of compliance with laws and regulations having a direct and material effect on line-item amounts in the financial statements.

**Report Issued**
- Opinion on financial statements.

**Audit in Accordance with Generally Accepted Government Auditing Standards (GAGAS)**

**Procedures Performed**
- Some additional requirements, primarily related to communication and documentation.

**Reports Issued**
- Opinion on financial statements.
- Report(s) on compliance with applicable laws and regulations and internal control.

**Audit in Accordance with the Single Audit Act**

**Procedures Performed**
- Same as GAAS, plus:
  - Tests of compliance with the requirements applicable to major federal assistance programs.
  - Tests of the internal control over major federal assistance programs.

**Reports Issued**
- Same as *Government Auditing Standards,* plus:
  - Report on the schedule of expenditures of federal awards.
  - Summary report of audit results relating to financial statements, internal control, and compliance.
  - Report of findings and questioned costs.

## Chapter Summary

This chapter described internal, operational, and compliance auditing. To summarize:

1. The Institute of Internal Auditors (IIA) defines *internal auditing* as an independent, objective assurance and consulting activity designed to add value and improve an organization's operations. It helps an organization accomplish its objectives by bringing a systematic, disciplined approach to evaluating and improving the effectiveness of risk management, control, and governance processes. The IIA's professional standards encompass attributes of internal auditors and performance of the internal audit function.

2. An *operational audit* is the examination of an operating unit or a complete organization to evaluate its performance, as measured by management's objectives. The stages of an operational audit might be summarized as definition of purpose, familiarization, preliminary survey, program development, fieldwork, reporting the findings, and follow-up.

3. *Compliance auditing* involves testing and reporting on whether an organization has complied with the requirements of various laws, regulations, and agreements.

4. The objective of a compliance audit engagement is the issuance of a report on the subject matter or an assertion by management regarding (*a*) the organization's compliance with specified requirements or (*b*) the organization's internal control over compliance with laws or regulations.

5. The objectives of compliance auditing of federal financial assistance programs are (*a*) to determine whether there have been violations of laws and regulations that may have a material effect on the organization's financial statements and major federal financial assistance programs and (*b*) to provide a basis for additional reports on compliance and internal controls. Compliance auditing is involved in audits of financial statements in accordance with generally accepted auditing standards, audits conducted in accordance with *Generally Accepted Government Auditing Standards,* and audits conducted in accordance with the federal Single Audit Act of 1984.

6. Audits of governmental organizations in accordance with generally accepted auditing standards must reflect the fact that such organizations are subject to a variety of laws and regulations that may have a direct and material effect on the amounts in the organization's financial statements.

7. In audits in accordance with *Generally Accepted Government Auditing Standards,* the auditors issue a report on the financial statements and also report on compliance with laws and regulations and on internal control.

8. Audits in conformity with the Single Audit Act of 1984 are specifically designed to help ensure that the billions of dollars in federal financial assistance are appropriately spent. The focus of these audits is on organizations receiving significant amounts of federal assistance in a year. The auditors are required to report on requirements of major programs for which federal assistance has been received.

## Key Terms Introduced or Emphasized in Chapter 21

**Certified Internal Auditor (CIA) (790)**   An individual who has passed an examination administered by The Institute of Internal Auditors and has met the experience requirements necessary to become certified.

**Charter (779)**   The charter of the internal audit activity is a formal written document that defines the activity's purpose, authority, and responsibility. The charter should (*a*) establish the internal audit activity's position within the organization; (*b*) authorize access to records, personnel, and physical properties relevant to the performance of engagements; and (*c*) define the scope of internal audit activities.

**Chief audit executive (788)**   Top position within the organization responsible for internal audit activities. Normally, this would be the internal audit director.

**Compliance auditing (794)**   Performing procedures to test compliance with laws and regulations.

**Compliance Supplement (800)**   A publication of the U.S. Office of Management and Budget that specifies audit procedures for federal financial assistance programs.

**Compliance with specified requirements (794)**   An entity's compliance with specified requirements of laws, regulations, rules, contracts, or grants.

*Government Auditing Standards* **(797)**   A document that contains standards for audits of government organizations, programs, activities, and functions and of government assistance received by contractors and other nonprofit organizations. These standards, often referred to as generally accepted government auditing standards (*GAGAS*), are to be followed by auditors when required by law or other requirement.

**The Institute of Internal Auditors (IIA) (777)**   The international professional organization of internal auditors.

**Internal auditing (777)**   An independent, objective assurance and consulting activity designed to add value and improve an organization's operations. It helps an organization accomplish its objectives by bringing a systematic, disciplined approach to evaluate and improve the effectiveness of risk management, control, and governance processes.

**Internal control over compliance (795)**   The process by which management obtains reasonable assurance of compliance with specified laws and regulations.

**Major federal financial assistance program (award) (799)**   A significant federal assistance program as determined by the auditors based on a risk-based approach. In a single audit, the auditors must provide an opinion on compliance related to major programs.

**Management's assertion (794)**   Any declaration, or set of related declarations taken as a whole, made by management. In the context of compliance attestation, management's assertion deals with the entity's compliance with specified requirements, the effectiveness of the entity's internal control over compliance, or both.

**Noncompliance (794)**   The failure to act in accordance with laws, regulations, agreements, or grants.

**Operational auditing (790)**   The process of reviewing a department or other unit of a business, governmental, or nonprofit organization to measure the effectiveness, efficiency, and economy of operations.

**Questioned costs (802)**   Those costs paid with federal assistance that appear to be in violation of a law or regulation, inadequately documented, unnecessary, or unreasonable in amount.

**Recipient (802)**   An organization receiving federal financial assistance directly from the federal agency administering the program.

**Single Audit Act (799)**   Legislation passed by the U.S. Congress that establishes uniform requirements for audits of federal financial assistance provided to state and local governments. The act was significantly amended in 1996.

**Specific requirements (of laws, regulations, rules, contracts, or grants) (801)**   In compliance attestation engagements, management asserts that the organization is in compliance with specified requirements, and the CPAs attest to this assertion.

**Subrecipient (802)**   An organization receiving federal financial assistance passed through from a recipient.

## Review Questions

21–1.   Define internal auditing.

21–2.   Describe the scope of activities of an internal auditing function.

21–3.   Nearly every large corporation now maintains an internal auditing department, but 50 years ago relatively few companies carried on a formal program of internal auditing. What have been the principal factors responsible for this rapid expansion?

21–4.   Identify the knowledge and skills that are necessary to the performance of modern internal auditing.

21–5.   "The principal distinction between public accounting and internal auditing is that the latter activity is carried on by an organization's own salaried employees rather than by independent professional auditors." Criticize this quotation.

21–6.   Compare the objectives of internal auditors with those of external auditors.

21–7.   Identify the 11 categories of the IIA's *International Standards for the Professional Practice of Internal Auditing.*

21–8.   Evaluate this statement: "Internal auditors cannot be independent of the activities that they audit."

21–9.   Describe how the organizational status of the internal audit department affects its independence.

21–10.   Briefly describe the factors that are important to the management of an internal auditing department.

21–11.   Describe the requirements for becoming a Certified Internal Auditor.

21–12.   Differentiate between financial statement audits and operational audits.

21–13.   Describe the purpose of an operational audit.

21–14.   Should the internal auditors generally disclose their findings to operating personnel of the department involved before transmitting the report to top management? Explain.

21–15.   Describe the two types of agreed-upon procedures engagements that CPAs may perform relating to compliance with laws and regulations.

21–16.   Evaluate this statement: "An agreed-upon procedures engagement on compliance with a law is designed to provide users with negative assurance on whether an entity has complied with that law."

21–17.   Explain why tests of compliance with laws and regulations are considered to be substantive tests.

21–18.   Explain the auditors' responsibility for testing compliance with laws and regulations in an audit in accordance with generally accepted auditing standards.

21–19.   Identify the three types of audits that a governmental organization might obtain.

21–20.   Describe the additional documentation requirements of *Generally Accepted Government Auditing Standards.*

21–21.   Describe the ethical principles set forth in *Generally Accepted Government Auditing Standards.*

21–22.   "In an audit in accordance with *Generally Accepted Government Auditing Standards* the auditors must perform tests of compliance with all laws and regulations." Criticize this quotation.

21–23.   Describe the additional audit report required by *Government Auditing Standards.*

21–24.   The auditors' responsibility for reporting violations of laws and regulations under *Generally Accepted Government Auditing Standards* differs from their responsibility under generally accepted auditing standards. Compare these responsibilities.

21–25.   Contrast the requirements of an audit in accordance with *Generally Accepted Government Auditing Standards* with the requirements of an audit in accordance with generally accepted auditing standards.

21–26.   Explain why compliance with laws and regulations is so important in the audit of governmental organizations.

21–27.   What is the purpose of the Single Audit Act?

21–28.   When is an organization required to have an audit in accordance with the Single Audit Act?

21–29.   Explain how major federal assistance programs are identified.

21–30.   Describe what is meant by a questioned cost.

21–31.   Distinguish between a subrecipient and a primary recipient. Provide an example of each.

21–32.   Identify the 14 requirements that may be applicable to federal financial assistance programs.

## Questions Requiring Analysis

**LO 1**

21–33.   In order to function effectively, the internal auditor must often educate auditees and other parties about the nature and purpose of internal auditing.

*Required:*

   *a.*  Define internal auditing.

   *b.*  Briefly describe three possible benefits of an internal audit department's program to educate auditees and other parties about the nature and purpose of internal auditing.

(CIA, adapted)

**LO 1, 4, 5**

21–34.   Steve Ankenbrandt, president of Beeb Corp., has been discussing the company's internal operations with the presidents of several other multidivision companies. Ankenbrandt discovered that most of them have an internal audit staff. The activities of the staffs at other companies include financial audits, operational audits, and sometimes compliance audits.

*Required:*

Describe the meaning of the following terms as they relate to the internal auditing function:

   *a.*  Financial auditing.

   *b.*  Operational auditing.

   *c.*  Compliance auditing.

(CIA, adapted)

**LO 3**

21–35.   Throughout this book, emphasis has been placed on the concept of independence as the most significant single element underlying the development of the public accounting profession. The term "independent auditor" is sometimes used to distinguish the public accountant from an internal auditor. Nevertheless, The Institute of Internal Auditors points to the factor of independence as essential to an effective program of internal auditing. Distinguish between the meaning of *independence* as used by the American Institute of Certified Public Accountants in describing the function of the certified public accountant and the meaning of *independence* as used by The Institute of Internal Auditors to describe the work of the internal auditor.

**LO 1, 3**   21–36.   You are conducting the first audit of the marketing activities of your organization. Your preliminary survey has disclosed indications of deficient conditions of a serious nature. You expect your audit work to document the need for substantial corrective action. You feel certain that your audit report will contain descriptions of a number of serious defects.

Your preliminary meeting with the director of the marketing division and the principal subordinates gave you reason to believe that they will be defensive, that your audit report will receive a chilly reception, that your stated facts are likely to be challenged, and that any deficient conditions reported will be denied or minimized.

*Required:*

a. Identify the aspect of the *International Standards for the Professional Practice of Internal Auditing* that applies to the problems described above.

b. Describe four techniques that you might use to improve the chances that your report will be well received and that appropriate corrective action will be taken.

(CIA, adapted)

**LO 5**   21–37.   Matt Gunlock, CPA, is performing an audit of the City of Ryan in accordance with generally accepted auditing standards.

*Required:*

a. Must Matt be concerned with the city's compliance with laws and regulations? Explain.

b. How should Matt decide on the nature and extent of the tests of compliance that should be performed in the audit?

**LO 6**   21–38.   Wixon & Co., CPAs, is performing an audit of the City of Brummet for the year ended June 30, 200X, in accordance with *Generally Accepted Government Auditing Standards.* During the course of the audit, Gerald Yarnell, a senior auditor, discovers violations of laws and regulations that constitute material instances of noncompliance.

*Required:*

a. Explain how these violations may affect the auditors' reports.

b. How would your answer to (*a*) change if management elected to correct the financial statements for the violations?

**LO 6**   21–39.   North County School District expended $1,450,000 in federal financial assistance this year.

*Required:*

a. Is North County School District required to have an audit in accordance with the Single Audit Act? Explain.

b. What are the requirements of an audit in accordance with the Single Audit Act?

**LO 6**   21–40.   The City of Westmore is confused about the type of audit that it should obtain: an audit in accordance with generally accepted auditing standards, an audit in accordance with *Generally Accepted Government Auditing Standards,* or an audit in accordance with the Single Audit Act.

*Required:*

a. Explain the differences between the three types of audits.

b. How should the City of Westmore decide which type of audit it is required to obtain?

## Objective Questions

**All applicable questions are available with McGraw-Hill's *Connect*™ *Accounting*.** ▓ connect |ACCOUNTING

**LO 1**   21–41.   **Multiple Choice Questions**

Select the best answer for each of the following questions. Explain the reasons for your selection.

a. Internal auditing can best be described as:

(1) An accounting function.

(2) A compliance function.

(3) An activity primarily to detect fraud.

(4) A control function.

(CIA, adapted)

**LO 1**

b. The independence of the internal auditing department will most likely be assured if it reports to the:

(1) Audit committee of the board of directors.

(2) President.

(3) Controller.

(4) Treasurer.

(CIA, adapted)

**LO 1**   c. When performing an operational audit, the purpose of a preliminary survey is to:

(1) Determine the objective of the activity to be audited.

(2) Determine the scope of the audit.

(3) Identify areas that should be included in the audit program.

(4) All of the above.

(CIA, adapted)

**LO 4**   d. Operational auditing is primarily oriented toward:

(1) Future improvements to accomplish the goals of management.

(2) Ensuring the accuracy of the data in management's financial reports.

(3) Determination of the fairness of the entity's financial statements.

(4) Compliance with laws and regulations.

**LO 6**   e. Which of the following bodies promulgates standards for audits of federal financial assistance programs?

(1) Governmental Accounting Standards Board.

(2) Financial Accounting Standards Board.

(3) Government Accountability Office.

(4) Governmental Auditing Standards Board.

(AICPA, adapted)

**LO 6**   f. As compared to an audit in accordance with GAAS, an audit in accordance with *Generally Accepted Government Auditing Standards* requires the auditors to:

(1) Use a lower level of materiality.

(2) Perform additional tests of internal control.

(3) Issue an additional report on compliance with laws and regulations and internal control.

(4) Fulfill all of the above requirements.

**LO 5**   g. In a compliance attestation engagement, CPAs may address an organization's:

|     | Compliance with Specified Requirements | Internal Control over Compliance with Specific Laws and Regulations |
| --- | --- | --- |
| (1) | Yes | Yes |
| (2) | Yes | No |
| (3) | No | Yes |
| (4) | No | No |

**LO 5**   h. The portion of internal control most directly related to a CPA's engagement to attest to compliance with laws and regulations is:

(1) Internal control over compliance.

(2) Internal control over financial reporting.

(3) Internal control over laws and regulations.

(4) Internal control over operations.

**LO 5**   i. When issuing an unqualified audit report in a compliance attestation engagement, the CPA may report on:

|     | Management's Assertion | Subject Matter |
| --- | --- | --- |
| (1) | Yes | Yes |
| (2) | Yes | No |
| (3) | No | Yes |
| (4) | No | No |

**LO 5**    *j.* When issuing a qualified audit report in a compliance attestation engagement, the CPA may report on:

|     | Management's Assertion | Subject Matter |
| --- | --- | --- |
| (1) | Yes | Yes |
| (2) | Yes | No |
| (3) | No | Yes |
| (4) | No | No |

**LO 6**    *k.* An important aspect of performing an audit in accordance with the Single Audit Act is to identify:

    (1) Major federal financial assistance programs.

    (2) Government generally accepted assertions.

    (3) Federal supplemental requirements.

    (4) Title determination sub-acts.

**LO 1**    *l.* The organization that administers the Certified Internal Auditor program is the:

    (1) American Institute of Certified Public Accountants—Certified Internal Auditor Division.

    (2) The Institute of Internal Auditors.

    (3) American Accounting Association

    (4) Securities and Exchange Commission.

**LO 6**  21–42.  **Simulation**

Under the Single Audit Act, auditors must test for compliance with the specific requirements of all major programs. State whether each of the following is required under that act:

| Statement | Is it required? |
| --- | --- |
| *a.* Determine that the organization complies with generally accepted accounting principles applicable to the program. | |
| *b.* Determine that the organization complies with specific requirements regarding the activities allowed or not allowed by the program. | |
| *c.* Determine that wages paid are not more than those established for the locality of the project by the Department of Labor. | |
| *d.* Determine that the organization contributes the appropriate amount of its own resources to the program. | |
| *e.* Determine that federal funds were spent or obligated within the period of availability. | |
| *f.* Determine whether program income is correctly recorded and used in accordance with the program requirements. | |
| *g.* Determine whether subrecipients monitor the compliance of recipients. | |
| *h.* Determine that only registered U.S. citizens work on the program. | |
| *i.* Determine that the organization does not contract with vendors that are suspended or disbarred. | |
| *j.* Determine that the organization followed procedures to minimize the time elapsing between the transfer of funds from the U.S. Treasury and their disbursement. | |

**LO 5, 6**   21–43.   Match the following terms with the appropriate definition (or partial definitions). Each definition may be used once or not at all.

| Term | Definition (or Partial Definition) |
|---|---|
| a. Compliance auditing<br>b. *Compliance Supplement*<br>c. *Government Auditing Standards*<br>d. Major federal financial assistance program<br>e. *Single Audit Act* | 1. A document that contains standards for audits of government organizations, programs, activities, and functions and of government assistance received by contractors and other nonprofit organizations.<br>2. A document that presents the major and minor program requirements for all federal contracts.<br>3. A publication of the U.S. Office of Management and Budget that specifies audit procedures for federal financial assistance programs.<br>4. A supplement to the U.S. Business Code, published by the General Accountability Office, dealing with overall compliance issues.<br>5. An act requiring that every single municipality undergo an annual audit of its financial statements.<br>6. Legislation passed by the U.S. Congress that establishes uniform requirements for audits of federal financial assistance provided to state and local governments.<br>7. Performing procedures to test compliance with laws and regulations.<br>8. A significant federal assistance program as determined by the auditors based on a risk-based approach. In a single audit, the auditors must provide an opinion on compliance related to major programs.<br>9. The process of reviewing a department or other unit of a business, governmental, or nonprofit organization to measure the effectiveness, efficiency, and economy of operations. |

## Problems

**All applicable problems are available with McGraw-Hill's *Connect™ Accounting*.** ▦ connect |ACCOUNTING

**LO 1, 3**   21–44.   You are the chief audit executive for the internal auditing function of a large municipal hospital. You receive monthly financial reports prepared by the accounting department, and your review of them has shown that total accounts receivable from patients have steadily and rapidly increased over the past eight months.

Other information in the reports shows the following conditions:

1. The number of available hospital beds has not changed.
2. The bed occupancy rate has not changed.
3. Hospital billing rates have not changed significantly.
4. The hospitalization insurance contracts have not changed since the last modification 12 months ago.

Your internal audit department performed a financial and operational audit of the accounts receivable accounting function 10 months ago. The working papers file for that assignment contains financial information, a record of the preliminary survey, documentation of the study, evaluation of controls, documentation of the procedures used to produce evidence about the validity and collectibility of the accounts, and a copy of your report that commented favorably on the controls and collectibility of the receivables.

However, the current increase in receivables has alerted you to the need for another audit. You remember news stories last year about the manager of the city water system who lost his job because his accounting department double-billed all the residential customers for three months. You plan to perform a preliminary survey of the problem, if indeed a problem exists.

*Required:*   a.   Write a memo to your senior auditor listing at least eight questions that should be used to guide and direct the preliminary survey. (*Hint:* The categories of questions used in the last preliminary survey were these: Who does the accounts receivable accounting? What data processing procedures and policies are in effect? and How is the accounts receivable accounting done? This time, you will use these categories and add a fourth category of questions: What financial or economic events have occurred in the past 10 months?)

b.   Describe the phases of the audit that would be performed after the preliminary survey is completed.

(CIA, adapted)

**LO 3**   21–45.   Devry Corporation has established an independent foundation for the purposes of community improvement. The foundation employs an executive director and eight staff people. The internal auditors of the company were requested to do an audit of the foundation in 20X1 to determine problems with the recording of transactions, the handling of cash, and documentation of transactions. The following items were found:

1. The foundation used the cash basis of reporting rather than the accrual basis.
2. The foundation lacked a copy of the plane ticket for airfare reimbursed for a trip taken by one of the volunteers.
3. Excess funds were invested in instruments other than those specified by the organization's policy manual.
4. The purchase of a desktop publishing system was expensed.
5. The foundation does not employ anyone with formal accounting training.
6. Many errors were made in recording transactions, which necessitated many year-end adjusting entries.
7. Numerous certificates of deposit were found in many different locations (e.g., filing cabinets, desk drawers, and a safe deposit box).
8. The checking account was reconciled by the individual who wrote the checks.

*Required:*   Write an internal audit report (in proper form) to the executive committee of the foundation indicating findings and recommendations.

(CIA, adapted)

**LO 6**   21–46.   In performing an audit in accordance with *Generally Accepted Government Auditing Standards,* the auditors are required to issue an additional combined report on compliance with laws and regulations and on internal control.

*Required:*   
a. Describe the nature of the procedures that the auditors must perform beyond those required by generally accepted auditing standards to provide a basis for this report.

b. Describe the specific contents of the auditors' combined report on compliance and internal control.

**LO 6**   21–47.   In performing an audit in accordance with both generally accepted auditing standards and *Generally Accepted Government Auditing Standards,* the auditors are required to communicate information about weaknesses in the organization's internal control. However, the requirements are different.

*Required:*   
a. Describe the differences between these requirements.

b. Describe the major aspects of the report on internal control required by *Government Auditing Standards.*

**In-Class Team Case**

**LO 6**   21–48.   Robert Myers, CPA, has been engaged to audit the City of Mystic in accordance with the Single Audit Act. Robert is aware that the Single Audit Act requires additional tests of major federal financial assistance programs, and he is trying to identify those programs for this audit. The City of Mystic participates in four federal financial assistance programs with the following amounts of expenditures and assessed risk of material noncompliance.

| Grant Program | Expenditures | Risk |
|---|---|---|
| Department of Education, Title I Grants to Local Education Agencies | $ 2,370,000 | High |
| Environmental Protection Agency, Ford Creek Modification | 6,780,000 | Moderate |
| Department of Housing and Urban Development | | |
| Project # C94-MC-08-0009 | 5,500,000 | Low |
| Project # C94-MC-08-0010 | 350,000 | Moderate |
| Total grant awards | $15,000,000 | |

*Required:*   
a. Identify the major federal assistance programs.

b. Describe the compliance testing requirements for major federal financial assistance programs under the Single Audit Act.

# Index

Page numbers followed by n indicate footnotes.

*Although both codifications present the same general topic, some section titles differ between the AICPA and those of the IFAC. Section titles presented here are those of the AICPA. Also, the international standards include a section 710, which differs from AICPA section 708. Those sections designated with[AICPA only] do not have an international corresponding section (including all parts of the 900 section).

*(continued)*

## Public Company Accounting Oversight Board (PCAOB) Auditing Standards

### Auditing Standards Issued by PCAOB

### Interim U.S. Standards (AICPA Standards Adopted by PCAOB in April 2003)

#### AU 100 Statements on Auditing Standards—Introduction

#### AU 200 The General Standards

#### AU 300 The Standards of Field Work

*(continued)*

*(continued from previous page)*